DICTIONARY
OF
UNCOMMON
WORDS

A WYNWOOD LEXICON

DICTIONARY OF UNCOMMON WORDS

LAURENCE URDANG, EDITOR IN CHIEF
ANNE RYLE AND TANYA H. LEE, EDITORS

WYNWOOD® Press
New York, New York

WYNWOOD PRESS EDITION 1991

This edition published by special arrangement with Gale Research Inc.

Library of Congress Cataloging-in-Publication Data

—ologies & —isms.
  Dictionary of uncommon words : over 17,000 entries often omitted
from standard dictionaries / Laurence Urdang, editor-in-chief ; Anne
Ryle and Tanya H. Lee, editors ; Frank R. Abate, associate editor.
      p.   cm.
  Reprint. Originally published: —ologies & —isms. 3rd ed. Detroit,
Mich. : Gale Research Co., c1986.
  Includes index.
  ISBN 0-922066-63-9
  1. English language—Reverse indexes. 2. English language—Terms
and phrases. 3. Learning and scholarship—Dictionaries. 4. English
language—Dictionaries. I. Urdang, Laurence. II. Ryle, Anne.
III. Lee, Tanya H. IV. Abate, Frank R. V. Title.
[PE1680.04 1991]
423'.1—dc20   90-2052
                                                                   CI

Copyright © 1986 by Gale Research Company
Published by WYNWOOD® Press
New York, New York
Printed in the United States of America

Contents

How
To
Use
This
Book

How to Use This Book

Dictionary of Uncommon Words is a thematic dictionary, with its entries organized under 430 thematic categories, each of which has two or (sometimes many) more appropriate entries listed beneath it. The 430 categories are presented in the text in alphabetic order by the name of the category heading (e.g., BIOLOGY, LITERATURE, PHOBIAS, WEATHER); a complete list, with ample cross references, is given in the **Table of Thematic Categories**, pages 13–48.

The organization by thematic categories allows *Dictionary of Uncommon Words* to be used like a thesaurus; that is, words can be found according to subject or concept. Having determined a desired category by consulting the **Table of Thematic Categories**, one has ready access to terms and their definitions without needing to know in advance the terms or their spelling. Thus, words like **syllogism** (under ARGUMENTATION and LOGIC), **biosphere** (under EARTH and LIFE), and **thalassography** (under SEA), whose form is not clearly suggestive of their subject, or which may simply be unfamiliar, are defined under appropriate categories, and can easily be consulted by this means.

Alphabetic access is also made possible through the **Index**, pages 589–795, which lists all entries—headwords, variants, and derivative forms. Thus, *Uncommon Words* can be used as a standard dictionary, by reference from the **Index** to the category or (as required) to the category *and* headword under which a term may be found.

To enhance accuracy and ease of use, certain terms, as appropriate, are defined under more than one category. For example, **empleomania**, defined as "an obsession with public employment," appears under categories BUREAUCRACY and WORK. In some cases, the same headword appears under two or more categories, but with a different definition at each, in accord with the category. An example is **sensationalism**, which appears as follows under four different categories:

237. LANGUAGE STYLE

sensationalism yellow journalism.

yellow journalism the practice of seeking out sensational news for the purpose of boosting a newspaper's circulation, or, if such stories are hard to find, of trying to make comparatively innocuous news appear sensational. Also called **sensationalism.—yellow journalist,** *n.*

248. LITERARY STYLE
sensationalism 1. the use of subject matter, language, or style designed to amaze or thrill. See also 265. MEDIA; 312. PHILOSOPHY.
2. such subject matter, language, or style itself. —**sensationalist,** *n.*—**sensationalistic,** *adj.*
265. MEDIA
sensationalism the act of shocking or intent to shock, especially through the media; the practice of using startling but superficial effects, in art, literature, etc., to gain attention. See also 248. LITERARY STYLE; 312. PHILOSOPHY. —**sensationalist,** *n.*
312. PHILOSOPHY
sensationalism 1. the doctrine that all ideas are derived from and essentially reducible to sense perceptions. Also called **sensuism.**
2. *Ethics.* the doctrine that the good is to be judged only by or through the gratification of the senses. Also called **sensualism.** See also 145. ETHICS; 248. LITERARY STYLE; 265. MEDIA. —**sensationalist,** *n.* — **sensationalistic,** *adj.*

Focusing as it does on nouns with certain specific suffixes and semantic content, *Dictionary of Uncommon Words* defines, in a convenient format, thousands of terms that can otherwise be found only in specialized and technical sources, and so can serve as a complement to any collection of dictionaries.

Table
of
Thematic
Categories

Table of
Thematic Categories

N.B.: *In the following table, both actual categories used in the text and synonyms that are references to categories are listed in one alphabetic order. Categories are numbered and set in all capital letters, while synonyms are not numbered and have only their initial letter capitalized.*

DICTIONARY OF UNCOMMON WORDS

A

1. ABORTION

See also 46. BIRTH; 327. PREGNANCY.

aborticide 1. destruction of a fetus. Also called feticide.
2. that which produces an abortion; an abortifacient.

abortifacient Cf. aborticide, 2.

feticide, foeticide the killing of a fetus; especially illegal abortion. Also called aborticide. —feticidal, foeticidal, adj.

2. ACROBATICS

See also 26. ATHLETICS; 395. TIGHTROPE WALKING.

acrobatics the acrobat's art; hence, other kinds of stunts, as aircraft acrobatics. Also spelled acrobatism.

acrobatism acrobatics.

equilibrist one who performs feats that require an unusual sense of balance, as a tightrope walker.

funambulism the art of walking a tightrope. —funambulist, n.

3. AGE

See also 77. CHILDREN; 299. OLD AGE.

ageism, agism discrimination on the basis of age, especially against older people.

antiquation the process of making antiquated or the condition of being antiquated.

coetaneity coevalneity. —coetaneous, adj.

coevalneity the state or quality of being alike in age or duration; contemporaneity. Also called coetaneity. —coeval, adj.

juniority the condition of being junior, as in age, rank, or position.

quadragenarianism the state of being in one's forties. —quadragenarian, n., adj. —quadragenary, adj.

quinquagenarianism the state of being in one's fifties. —quinquagenarian, n., adj. —quinquagenary, adj.

sexagenarianism the state of being in one's sixties. —**sexagenarian,** *n.*, *adj.* —**sexagenary,** *adj.*

4. AGREEMENT

analogy an agreement or correspondence in particular features between things otherwise dissimilar; in literature, the basis for metaphor and simile. —**analogic, analogical,** *adj.*

arbiter one chosen to settle a controversy; an umpire or arbitrator.

arbitratrix, arbitress a female arbiter.

armistice a temporary cessation of hostilities, by agreement between the belligerents, prior to the negotiation or signing of a peace treaty.

comity amity.

conciliation the process of conciliating or bringing to agreement. —**conciliator,** *n.*

congruence a correspondence in physical structure or thought; harmony. Also **congruity.** —**congruent,** *adj.*

consilience the process of concurring or agreeing. See also 73. CHANCE.

consonance, consonancy agreement, consistency.

dialogue a frank exchange of ideas, spoken or written, for the purpose of meeting in harmony.

equipollence, equipollency equalness of force, validity, etc. See also 250. LOGIC. —**equipollent,** *adj.*

indentureship 1. the state or period of being indentured or apprenticed; apprenticeship.
2. the state or period of being a servant bound to service for a specified time in return for passage to a colony.

negotiation the act or process of conferring or discussing to reach agreement in matters of business or state. See also 398. TRADE. —**negotiant, negotiator, negotriatrix,** *n.*

similarity a point, feature, or detail in which two items are alike.

5. AGRICULTURE
See also 319. PLANTS; 377. SOIL.

agriculture the art and science of farming. Also called **tillage.** —**agriculturist, agriculturalist,** *n.* —**agricultural,** *adj.*

agrogeology the branch of geology concerned with the adaptability of land to agriculture, soil quality, etc. —**agrogeologist,** *n.*

agronomics agronomy.

agronomy the science of management in farming. Also spelled **agronomics.** —**agronomist,** *n.*

chreotechnics *Rare*. useful arts, as agriculture, commerce, and manufacturing.

citriculture the cultivation of citrus fruits, as lemons, oranges, etc. —citriculturist, *n.*

culturist a cultivator or a person who grows things.

emblements *Law*. the growing of crops and the profits reaped therefrom.

fallowist *Rare*. a proponent of the practice of leaving fields fallow.

grangerism the principles and adherence to the principles of the Grange. —granger, *n.*

horticulture the practice and science of cultivating gardens, for the growth of flowers, fruits, or vegetables. —horticulturist, *n.* —horticultural, *adj.*

husbandry 1. *Obsolete*. domestic management, thrift, or frugality.
2. farming, especially the care of farm animals.

monoculture the use of land for the cultivation of only one type of crop. —monocultural, *adj.*

orchardist a person who tends or cultivates an orchard.

pastoralism the herding or tending of cattle as a primary economic activity or occupation. Also called pasturage. —pastoralist, *n.* —pastoral, *adj.*

pasturage pastoralism.

pomiculture the cultivation of fruit and fruit-trees.

tillage agriculture.

transhumance the seasonal migration of livestock and those who tend livestock between mountain and valley, as practiced in Switzerland. —transhumant, *adj.*

6. AID
See also 75. CHARITY.

abetment, abettal the act of abetting or inciting another to commit a crime. —abettor, abetter, *n.*

adjutancy the condition of holding the rank of adjutant.

almoner, almner an official, as of a monastery, whose duty is to distribute charity or alms. —almonership, *n.*

amanuensis *Formal*. 1. a secretary.
2. a scribe or copyist.

coadjuvancy joint aid or assistance; joint cooperation.

connivance passive assistance, especially in wrongdoing.

connivancy *Rare*. connivance.

eleemosynary 1. pertaining to alms.
2. *Obsolete*. an almsman; a person who lives on the charity of others.

orphanotrophy *Rare.* 1. a hospital or hostel for orphans.
2. the care and support of orphans.

pensionary a person paid to perform tasks or services, especially as a hireling.

7. ALCHEMY
See also 252. MAGIC.

arcanum the secret of life; a great elixir or remedy sought by the alchemists. See also 233. KNOWLEDGE.

elixir 1. the hypothetical substance sought by alchemists that was believed to transform base metals into gold and give eternal life. Also called **philosopher's stone, elixir of life.**
2. *Rare.* the quintessence or underlying principle. See also 350. REMEDIES.

Hermeticism[1] 1. the occult concepts, ideas, or philosophy set forth in the writings of the hermeticists of the late Middle Ages and the early Renaissance.
2. adherence to, belief in, or propagation of these concepts and ideas.
3. *Literature.* a symbolic and arcane style similar to that of the hermeticists, especially in the poetry of certain French symbolist poets. Cf. hermetics. —hermeticist, hermetist, *n.* —hermetic, hermetical, *adj.*

Hermeticism[2], hermeticism 1. the ideas or beliefs set forth in the writings of Hermes Trismegistus.
2. adherence to these ideas and beliefs.

hermetics the occult sciences, especially alchemy. Cf. Hermeticism[1]. —hermetist, *n.* —hermetic, hermetical, *adj.*

iatrochemistry 1. originally, alchemy devoted to medicinal purposes, especially the alchemy of the period 1525–1660, influenced by the theories of Paracelsus.
2. currently, chemistry for healing purposes. —iatrochemist, *n.*

spagyrist an alchemist.

transmutation the process or act of change, especially from one thing to another, as the change from base metal to gold, pursued by the alchemists. —transmutationist, *n.* —transmutative, *adj.*

transmutationist an alchemist who believed that, in one of several ways, it was possible to change less valuable elements into silver or gold.

8. ALCOHOL
See also 39. BEER; 158. FERMENTATION; 421. WINE.

absinthism an addiction to absinthe, a liqueur flavored with the narcotic wormwood, *Artemisia absinthium.* —absinthial, absinthian, *adj.*

abstinence a voluntary and habitual self-deprivation, especially from alcoholic beverages. —abstinent, *adj.*

alcoholism 1. an addiction to alcohol, especially involving compulsive, excessive consumption.
2. the pathological effects of such overindulgence. —**alcoholic, n.**

alcoholomania an obsession with alcohol.

alcoholphilia an excessive liking for alcoholic beverages. —**alcoholphile, n.**

antialcoholism the state or doctrine of opposition to the excessive consumption of liquor. —**antialcoholic, n., adj.**

bacchanalianism 1. a devotion to drunken revelry and carousal in honor of Bacchus.
2. a dedication to such behavior on other occasions. —**bacchanalian, n., adj.**

bibacity the state of being given to excessive drinking of alcohol. —**bibacious, adj.**

bibulosity excessive drinking of alcoholic beverages. —**bibulous, adj.**

compotation drinking together, usually to excess.

compotator a drinking companion.

crapulency, crapulence excessive indulgence in food or drink.

dipsomania an insatiable craving for alcohol; chronic drunkenness. —**dipsomaniac, n.** —**dipsomaniacal, adj.**

dipsophobia an abnormal fear of drinking. —**dipsophobe, n.**

drunkometer a device for measuring the amount of alcohol in the bloodstream, usually from the breath. Also called **breathalyzer.**

ebriety intoxication or inebriation, whether regarded as the condition, the process, or the habit.

ebriosity drunkenness or intoxication from alcohol, especially as a habitual state.

fermentology a science that deals with ferments and fermentation, especially those concerned with the production of alcoholic beverages. —**fermentologist, n.**

inebriety drunkenness.

insobriety the opposite of sobriety; inebriation.

libation *Jocular.* an alcoholic beverage.

mixology skill in the mixing of alcoholic drinks. —**mixologist, n.**

nephalism an adherence to the tenets of teetotalism. —**nephalist, n., adj.** —**nephalistic, adj.**

orgy 1. *In ancient Greece or Rome.* a wild celebration in honor of certain gods.
2. riotous merrymaking, especially with excessive indulgence in sex, alcohol, and drugs. —**orgiast, n.** —**orgiastic, adj.**

polydipsia extreme thirst; an abnormal and continuous craving for drink.

potation 1. excessive drinking of alcohol.
2. an alcoholic drink. See also 168. FOOD and NUTRITION.

potomania 1. an excessive tendency to drink alcoholic beverages.
2. Also called **tromomania.** delirium tremens.

prohibitionism 1. the principles governing the forbidding by law of the manufacture or sale of alcoholic beverages.
2. the interdiction itself. —**prohibitionist,** *n.* —**Prohibition,** *n.*

Rechabite a member of the Independent Order of Rechabites, a secret society devoted to total abstention from intoxicating liquors, founded in England in 1835.

teetotalism the principle or conscious practice of complete abstinence from alcoholic beverages. Also called **total abstinence.** —**teetotaler,** *n.*

tromomania delirium tremens. Also called **potomania.**

Volsteadism the theory or practice of prohibitionism; after the Volstead Act, which implemented U.S. prohibition, introduced by Andrew J. Volstead.

Washingtonian a member of the Washingtonian Society, a temperance society founded in the United States in 1843.

9. ALERTNESS

alacrity a cheerful readiness, promptitude, or willingness; briskness. —**alacritous,** *adj.*

pantaraxia any actions aimed at keeping people on their toes. (Coined by Nubar Gulbenkian, 1964.)

10. ALLEGIANCE
See also 289. NATIONALISM.

abjuration the act of renouncing upon oath, as by an alien applying for citizenship who renounces allegiance to a former country of nationality.

defection the act of abandoning a person or cause to which one has an obligation or allegiance, especially accompanied by flight from one's country. —**defector, defectionist,** *n.*

fealty 1. *In the Feudal System.* allegiance of a vassal to his lord.
2. allegiance.

genuflection, genuflexion kneeling or bending the knee, especially in worship or reverence.

myrmidon a follower who obeys orders without question. —**myrmidonian,** *adj.*

obeisance 1. a gesture of respect, as a bow.
2. homage or an act of homage. —**obeisant,** *adj.*

11. ALMANACS
See also 25. ASTRONOMY; 65. CALENDAR.

almanagist a person who compiles almanacs.

ephemeris an astronomical almanac giving, as an aid to the astronomer and navigator, the locations of celestial bodies for each day of the year.

12. ALPHABET
See also 236. LANGUAGE; 383. SPELLING; 428. WRITING.

abecedarian, abecedary a teacher or learner of an alphabet.

abecedarium an alphabet.

alphabetarian a person who is learning the alphabet.

alphabetics the science of alphabets.

alphabetism the representation of the sounds of speech in consistent graphic form.

alphabetology the study or science of alphabets. —alphabetologist, *n.*

analphabetic 1. unable to read or write.
2. descriptive of a language written without an alphabet; that is, with a syllabary (Cherokee), in hieroglyphics (ancient Egyptian), in ideograms (Chinese), or in pictograms (American Indian).

charactery 1. a system of symbols used to represent ideas.
2. expression by means of such symbols.

graphemics the study of written symbols or combinations of symbols representing letters of the alphabet or single phonems.

literalism the practice or theory of following the letter or literal sense of something written. —literalist, *n.*

metagraphy the art of transliteration. —metagraphic, *adj.*

transliteration the spelling of a word in one language with the alphabet of another language.

13. AMERICA
Americamania an obsession with America and things American.

un-Americanism the state or condition of being out of sympathy with or against an ideal of American behavior, attitudes, beliefs, etc. —un-American, *n., adj.*

14. ANATOMY

anatomy the study of the body and its parts. —anatomist, *n.* —anatomical, *adj.*

androtomy *Obsolete.* human anatomy.

anthropometry the study concerned with the measurements of the proportions, size, and weight of the human body. —anthropometrist, *n.* —anthropometric, anthropometrical, *adj.*

anthroposcopy *Physiology, Rare.* the labeling of the type of body structure by nonanthropometric means.

anthropotomy the anatomy of the human body. —anthropotomist, *n.* —anthropotomical, *adj.*

aponeurology *Physiology.* the study of aponeuroses, membranes that can serve as muscle sheaths or as connectors between muscles and tendons.

arteriography the scientific description of the arterial system. —arteriographic, arteriographical, *adj.*

desmography a written work on the ligaments of the human body. —desmographic, desmographical, *adj.*

eccrinology the branch of anatomy and physiology that studies secretions and the secretory glands.

gargoylism an abnormal physical condition characterized by extensive structural defects of the skeleton and by gross mental deficiency.

hepatography the description of the structure and function of the liver. —hepatographic, hepatographical, *adj.*

heprography the description of the structure and function of kidneys. —heprographic, heprographical, *adj.*

histology a branch of anatomy that deals with the microscopic features of animal and plant tissues. Also called microscopical anatomy. —histologist, *n.* —histological, *adj.*

laryngography the scientific description of the larynx. —laryngographic, laryngographical, *adj.*

microscopical anatomy histology.

myography the measurement of muscular phenomena, such as the velocity and intensity of muscular contractions. —myographic, *adj.*

myology 1. the branch of anatomy that studies muscles and musculature. 2. the muscular makeup of an animal or anatomical unit. —myologic, *adj.*

organography the scientific description of the organs of plants and animals. —organographist, *n.* —organographic, organographical, *adj.*

osteology the branch of anatomy that studies the skeleton and bones. —osteologist, *n.* —osteologic, osteological, *adj.*

pelycology the study of pelvic structure. —pelycologic, pelycological, *adj.*

pharyngography the scientific description of the pharynx. —pharyngographic, pharyngographical, *adj.*

pneumography 1. an account of the structure and function of the lungs.
2. the recording of the activity of the lungs during respiration. —pneumograph, *n.* —pneumographic, pneumographical, *adj.*

prosector 1. a person who dissects cadavers for the purpose of anatomical demonstration.
2. a person who performs autopsies. —prosectorial, *adj.*

splanchnology the branch of anatomy that studies the viscera.

syndesmography an anatomical treatise on or description of the joints and ligaments of the body.

syndesmology 1. the anatomy of the ligaments of the body.
2. the science or study of ligaments.

syntropy the condition of having a series of similar parts with the same spatial orientation, e.g. the ribs. —syntropic, *adj.*

syssarcosis the joining of two or more bones by muscle.

zootomy 1. the dissection of animals other than man.
2. the anatomy of animals. —zootomist, *n.* —zootomic, zootomical, *adj.*

15. ANCESTORS

See also 153. FATHER; 204. HEREDITY; 281. MOTHER; 304. ORIGINS; 307. PARENTS; 341. RACE.

archaism an inclination toward old-fashioned things, speech, or actions, especially those of one's ancestors. Also archaicism. —archaist, *n.* —archaistic, *adj.*

atavism the reappearance in the present of a characteristic belonging to a remote ancestor. —atavist, *n.* —atavistic, *adj.*

lemures *Ancient Rome.* the malevolent ghosts or spirits of a family's dead ancestors.

matriliny descent through the female line, as in ancestry, inheritance, etc. —matrilineal, matrilinear, *adj.*

patriliny relationship or descent by the male line, as in ancestry, inheritance, etc. —patrilineal, patrilinear, *adj.*

propositus the person from whom a line of descent originates.

16. ANIMALS

See also 45. BIRDS; 61. BULLS and BULLFIGHTING; 70. CATS; 88. COCKS; 125. DOGS; 164. FISH; 211. HORSES; 225. INSECTS; 353. REPTILES; 374. SNAKES; 423. WOLVES; 427. WORMS; 430. ZOOLOGY

acrodontism the condition of having teeth without roots attached to the alveolar ridge of the jaws, as in certain animals. —**acrodont,** *adj.*

amensalism a parasitic relationship between animals that has a destructive effect on one and no effect on the other. See also 44. BIOLOGY; 319. PLANTS.

Animalia the realm of animals; the animal kingdom.

animality 1. the state of being an animal.
2. animal existence or nature in human activity; the animal in man as opposed to the spiritual.

anthropoglot an animal with a tongue like that of man, as the parrot.

anthropoid a creature resembling man, as an ape. —**anthropoid, anthropoidal,** *adj.*

anthropopathism, anthropopathy the assignment of human feelings or passions to something not human, as a deity or an animal. —**anthropopathic,** *adj.*

artiodactyl a hoofed animal having an even number of toes or digits on each foot, as pigs, sheep, deer, etc. —**artiodactylous,** *adj.*

bestiarian 1. an advocate of kindness to animals.
2. *British.* an antivivisectionist.

bestiarist a compiler or writer of bestiaries.

bestiary an allegorical or moralizing commentary based upon real or fabled animals, usually medieval and sometimes illustrated.

biodynamics the study of the physiological processes of plants and animals. —**biodynamic, biodynamical,** *adj.*

bioecology the branch of ecology that studies the interrelationship of plant and animal life in their common environment. —**bioecologist,** *n.* —**bioecologic, bioecological,** *adj.*

biostatics the study of the relationship between structure and function in plants and animals. —**biostatical,** *adj.*

biota the animal or plant life of a particular region.

brachiation a method of movement, characteristic of certain animals, by swinging with the arms from one hold to another.

carcinology the branch of zoology that studies crustaceans. —**carcinologist,** *n.* —**carcinologic, carcinological,** *adj.*

carnivore a meat-eating animal. Cf. herbivore. —**carnivorous,** *adj.*

commensalism a relationship between animals or plants in which one lives with or on the other without damage to either. Cf. **parasitism.**

conatus a vital force in plants or animals, similar to human effort. See also 319. PLANTS.

doraphobia an intense fear of contact with animal fur or skin. —doraphobe, *n*.

echinology the study of sea urchins. —echinologist, *n*.

epizoism a nonparasitic relationship between animals in which one animal lives on the surface of the other.

epizootic, epizooty a disease affecting many animals at the same time; an epidemic amongst animals. —epizootic, *adj*.

epizootiology, epizootology the science concerned with the factors involved in the occurrence and spread of animal diseases. —epizootiologic, epizootiological, *adj*.

estrus, oestrus the condition of being in rut or sexual arousal, applied particularly to the female. Also spelled estrum, oestrum. —estrous, oestrous, *adj*.

ethology the study of animal behavior in relation to habitat. —ethologist, *n*. —ethological, *adj*.

extispicy haruspicy. —extispex, *n*. —extispicious, *Obsolete. adj*.

fauna 1. the animal life of a particular time or region.
2. a study of or treatise on the animal life of a particular time or region. —faunal, *adj*.

faunist a person who studies or writes on animal life; a naturalist.

faunology zoogeography.

haruspication haruspicy.

haruspicy a form of divination by natural phenomena, especially from inspection of the entrails of animal sacrifices. Also called extispicy, haruspication. —haruspex, aruspex, *n*. —haruspical, *adj*.

helminthology the study of worms, especially internal worms.

herbivore a plant-eating animal. Cf. carnivore. —herbivorous, *adj*.

heterosis abnormal development, especially increased size, in plants or animals, usually as a result of cross-breeding.

inquiline an animal that inhabits the burrow, nest, or other habitation of another animal. —inquiline, *adj*.

lipotype a particular type of animal life whose absence is a characteristic of a region. —lipotypic, *adj*.

locoism a disease, chiefly of farm animals, characterized by paralysis and impaired vision and caused by eating locoweed.

manticore a mythical or fabulous beast with the head of a man, the body of a lion or tiger, and the feet and tail of a dragon or scorpion. Also spelled mantichora.

morphology the branch of biology that studies the structure and form of animals and plants. —morphologist, *n.* —morphologic, morphological, *adj.*

musomania an abnormal love for mice.

musophobia an abnormal fear of mice.

nealogy the science of the early or youthful stage of animal development. —nealogic, *adj.*

oestrus estrus.

organism any animal or plant.

organography the scientific description of the organs of plants and animals and of their structure and function. —organographist, *n.* —organographic, organographical, *adj.*

organology the study of the organs of plants and animals. —organologist, *n.* —organologic, organological, *adj.*

ovipara *pl.* animals that lay eggs. Cf. ovovivipara, vivipara. —oviparity, *n.* —oviparous, *adj.*

ovovivipara *pl.* animals that lay eggs that are hatched in their bodies, so that young are born alive, without connection to a placenta.

parasitism a relationship between animals in which one gains sustenance from the other. Cf. commensalism. See also 44. BIOLOGY; 319. PLANTS.

phylon a group with genetic relationship. Cf. phylum.

phylum any of the major subdivisions of the plant or animal kingdom. Cf. phylon. See also 247. LINGUISTICS.

piggery a place where pigs are kept; pigpen; pigsty.

predacean a carnivorous animal. —predaceous, predacious, *adj.*

predation a relation between organisms or animals in which one feeds on the other. —predatory, *adj.*

quadrat a plot of land, square or rectangular, marked off or set out for the study of plant or animal life.

rabbitry 1. rabbits collectively.
2. a place where rabbits live or are kept.

relict an animal or plant surviving in one area after becoming extinct elsewhere; a survival of an earlier period. —relict, *adj.*

rookery a breeding or nesting place of rooks or of any gregarious bird or animal.

stirpiculture selective breeding to develop strains with particular characteristics. —stirpicultural, *adj.*

sybotism *Rare.* the business and art of raising swine.

taxidermy the art of preparing, stuffing, and mounting the skins of animals so that they appear lifelike. —**taxidermist**, *n.*

terrarium a container for keeping small animals.

theriomancy a form of divination based upon observation of the movements of animals. Also called **zoomancy.**

theriomorphism the worship of deities that are partly animal and partly human in form. Also called **therianthropism, theriolatry.** —**theriomorphic, theriomorphous,** *adj.*

thremmatology the branch of biology that studies the breeding of domestic plants and animals.

ungulate a mammal having hoofs, as the cow, horse, etc. —**ungulate,** *adj.*

vaccary *Obsolete.* a cow house, shed, pasture, or other place where cows are kept. Also **vachery.**

virilescence a condition of some animals, and especially of some fowls, in which the female, when old, assumes some of the characteristics of the male of the species. —**virilescent,** *adj.*

vivarium an enclosed environment, as a glass container, in which plants or animals are raised under conditions that approximate their natural habitat. Also **vivary.** ·

vivary a vivarium.

vivipara *pl.* animals that bear living young. Cf. **ovipara, ovovivipara.** —**viviparity,** *n.* —**viviparous,** *adj.*

vulpicide 1. the killing of a fox by methods other than by hunting it with hounds.
2. the killer of a fox.

zoanthropy a derangement in which a person believes himself to be an animal and acts accordingly. —**zoanthropic,** *adj.*

zoiatria the science of veterinary surgery.

zoobiology zoology.

zoogeography the distribution of animal life by geographical location. —**zoogeographer,** *n.* —**zoogeographic, zoogeographical,** *adj.*

zoogony, zoogeny 1. the generation of animals.
2. a study of animal generation. —**zoogonic, zoogenic,** *adj.*

zoography 1. the branch of zoology concerned with animal description.
2. pictorial art in general, but especially that which shows animals. —**zoographer,** *n.* —**zoographic, zoographical,** *adj.*

zoolatry the worship of animal gods. Cf. **theriomorphism.** Also called **zootheism.** —**zoolater,** *n.*

zoology the branch of biology that studies and classifies all living creatures. —zoologist, *n.* —zoological, *adj.*

zoomancy a form of divination based upon the observation of animals or their movements under certain circumstances. Also called **theriomancy.**

zoomania an abnormal love of animals.

zoometry the measurement and comparison of the sizes of animals and their parts.

zoomorphism the attribution of animal form or nature, especially to a deity. —zoomorphic, *adj.*

zoonomia zoonomy.

zoonomy, zoonomia the laws of animal life or the animal kingdom. —zoonomist, *n.* —zoonomic, *adj.*

zoopathology the study or science of the diseases of animals; animal pathology. Also **zoopathy.**

zoopathy zoopathology.

zoopery the performing of experiments on animals, especially the lower animals. —zooperal, *adj.*

zoophilia a love of animals. —zoophile, *n.*

zoophilism, zoophily love of animals. —zoophilist, *n.* —zoophilous, *adj.*

zoophobia an abnormal dread of animals. —zoophobe, *n.*

zoophysics the study of animal physiology and form. —zoophysical, *adj.*

zoophysiology the physiology of animals, as distinct from that of humans.

zoophyte an animal, as a sponge, coral, etc., that resembles a plant more than an animal; any of the *Zoophyta.* —zoophytic, zoophytical, zoophytoid, *adj.*

zoophytology the branch of zoology concerned with the zoophytes. —zoophytological, *adj.*

zooplasty the process of surgically grafting tissue from a lower animal onto the human body. —zooplastic, *adj.*

zoopsia a form of hallucination in which the sufferer imagines he sees animals. Also **zooscopy.**

zoopsychology a branch of psychology that studies animal behavior.

zooscopy zoopsia.

zootaxy zoological classification; the scientific classification of animals.

zootechny the principles of animal husbandry. Also spelled **zootechnics.** —zootechnician, *n.* —zootechnical, *adj.*

zootheism the worship of animal gods; zoolatry. —zootheist, *n.*

zootomy 1. the dissection of animals other than man.
2. the anatomy of animals. —zootomist, *n.* —zootomic, zootomical, *adj.*

17. ANTHROPOLOGY
See also 255. MANKIND; 341. RACE.

cultural anthropology a specialty that studies the creative achievements of societies, especially those passed on through later generations. Also called culturology.

dendranthropology the theory and work based on the theory that trees were involved in the origin of man. —dendranthropologic, dendranthropological, *adj.*

ethnocentricity ethnocentrism. —ethnocentric, *adj.*

ethnocentrism the belief in the superiority of one's own group or culture. Also ethnocentricity. —ethnocentric, *adj.*

ethnodicy *Rare.* the branch of ethnology that studies comparative legal systems.

ethnogeny the study of the origin of distinctive groups or tribes. —ethnogenist, *n.* —ethnogenic, *adj.*

ethnography the branch of anthropology that studies and describes the individual cultures of mankind. —ethnographer, *n.* —ethnographic, ethnographical, *adj.*

ethnology the study, often comparative, of the origins and development of the races of mankind. —ethnologist, *n.* —ethnologic, ethnological, *adj.*

ethography the description of moral and ethical systems. —ethnographer, *n.* —ethnographic, ethnographical, *adj.*

hybridism, hybridity the blending of diverse cultures or traditions.

isthmian a person who is a native or inhabitant of an isthmus. —isthmian, *adj.*

lacustrian a lake-dweller.

Leiotrichi people with smooth hair; a division of mankind characterized by people with such hair. Cf. Ulotrichi. —Leiotrichan, *adj.*

matrilocality the state or custom of residing with the family or tribe of the wife, as in certain primitive societies. Cf. patrilocality. —matrilocal, *adj.*

patrilocality the state or custom of residing with the family or tribe of the husband, as in certain primitive societies. Cf. matrilocality. —patrilocal, *adj.*

phratry 1. a subdivision of an ancient Greek tribe or phyle.
2. a clan or other unit of a primitive tribe.

physical anthropology the branch of anthropology that studies, describes, and interprets the evolutionary changes in man's bodily structure and the classification of modern races. Cf. cultural anthropology. Also called somatology.

social anthropology the branch of anthropology that studies human societies, emphasizing interpersonal and intergroup relations.

somatology physical anthropology.

synecdochism the belief that a part of a person or object can act in place of the whole and thus that anything done to the part will equally affect the whole.

Ulotrichi people with woolly, tightly curled, or crisp hair; a division of mankind characterized by people with such hair. —Ulotrichous, adj.

18. ANTIQUITY
See also 190. GREECE and GREEKS; 207. HISTORY.

antediluvian a person who lived before the Flood. —antediluvian, adj.

antiquarianism an interest in the customs, art, and social structure of earlier peoples and civilizations. —antiquarian, n., adj.

archaeography the field of description of antiquities. —archaeographical, adj. —archaeographer, n.

archaeology, archeology the scientific study of human remains and artifacts. —archaeologist, archeologist, n. —archeologic, archaeologic, archeological, archaeological, adj.

Assyriology the study of the language and culture of ancient Assyria. —Assyriologist, n. —Assyriological, adj.

classicism the principles or style of classic art or literature. —classicist, n.

Egyptology the study of ancient Egyptian language, history, and culture. —Egyptologist, n. —Egyptological, adj.

epigraphy the deciphering and interpreting of ancient inscriptions. —epigraphist, epigrapher, n. —epigraphic, epigraphical, adj.

Etruscology the study of Etruscan civilization, especially its artifacts and language. —Etruscologist, n.

Hellenism Ancient Greek culture and ideals. —Hellenist, n.

lipsanography Rare. the research and composition of treatises about relics. —lipsanographer, n.

momiology the study of mummies.

paleography, palaeography the study of ancient writings, including inscriptions. —paleographer, palaeographer, n. —paleographic, palaeographic, adj.

papyrology the study of ancient writings on papyrus. —papyrologist, n.

post-diluvian a person who lived after the Flood. —post-diluvian, *adj.*

romanism the policies and actions distinctive of ancient Rome.

19. ANTS
See also 225. INSECTS.

formicary, formicarium the dwelling of a colony of ants, as an anthill or nest.

formication a body sensation that feels as if ants are crawling over the skin.

myrmecology the branch of entomology that studies ants. —myrmecologist, *n.* —myrmecologic, myrmecological, *adj.*

myrmecophilism, myrmecophily the dependence upon or attraction to ants exhibited by certain plants and insects. —myrmecophile, *n.* —myrmecophilous, *adj.*

myrmecophobia 1. an abnormal fear of ants.
2. the repelling of ants by some plants through hairs or glands. —myrmecophobic, *adj.*

xenobiosis communal life, such as that of ants, in which colonies of different species live together but do not share the raising of the young.

20. ARCHITECTURE
See also 60. BUILDINGS; 212. HOUSES.

acropolis a citadel or elevated fortification of a settlement.

architectonics the science of architecture. See also 23. ART; 312. PHILOSOPHY. —architectonic, architectonical, *adj.*

Asiaticism a style of architecture distinguished by excessive ornamentation or floridity. —Asiatical, *adj.*

baroque a highly decorated form of art or ornamentation. —baroque, *adj.*

Brutalism an aggressive 20th-century style, usually in rough-textured and unfinished materials, that frankly exhibits both structural and mechanical systems.

bungaloid a 20th-century style dwelling, usually of one story, imitative of the true bungalow form characterized by low, sweeping roof gables and a large verandah in the front.

classicism 1. the employment of compositional formulas and decorative techniques based upon the architecture of ancient Greece or Rome, but often including new ideas.
2. the employment of formulas and decorative techniques with an emphasis upon the subordination of utility in order to stress perfection of form.

columniation 1. the use of columns in architectural design.
2. the pattern of columns used.

cuspidation a form of ornamentation composed of cusps or curves meeting in pairs at a tangent to the area being decorated. —cuspidate, cuspidal, *adj.*

eclecticism an international movement, most in vogue from 1820 until about 1930, characterized by almost total freedom of choice among historical styles of both overall composition and decoration in the design of public buildings, the freedom tempered by the intended use or location of the building.

Egyptian Revivalism a style imitative of antique Egyptian temple architecture, most influential after Napoleon's campaign in Egypt and lasting in the U.S. into the early 20th century.

entasis the slight convexity or outward curve given to a tower or other tall, narrow structure.

eurhythmy harmonious proportions in a building.

Federalism an American style based upon the classical theories and decorations of the English architect Robert Adams and his contemporaries, with lightness and delicacy as its outstanding qualities; practiced from 1775 until overwhelmed by Greek Revivalism, its most typical external features are doorways with fanlights and sidelights (often with attenuated pilasters) and the play of other curved elements against a basically boxlike structure. Also called **Early Federal Style, Early Republican.**

functionalism a philosophy of architectural design rather than a separate style, expressed in Louis Sullivan's "form follows function" and Le Corbusier's concept of a house as a machine for living in, under the premise that buildings ought to express construction, materials, and accommodation of purpose, usually with the assumption that the result would be aesthetically significant. Also called **structuralism.** —**functionalist,** *n., adj.*

Georgianism 1. in England, the modes of architecture, furniture, decoration, and silver produced from about 1714 to 1830; architecturally, it embraced several styles: Palladian, Early Gothic Revival, Chinese, and various other classical and romantic manners.
2. in America, the architectural style of the English colonies during the 18th century, based first upon the ideas of Christopher Wren and James Gibbs and later upon the Palladian style. It is typically characterized by construction in red brick with white or colored trim and double-hung windows, central halls, elaborately turned stair balusters, paneled and warmly colored walls, fine woodwork, and white plastered ceilings.

Gothicism, Gothic the general term employed to denote the several phases of European architecture in the period 1100–1530 that employ the pointed arch, or their imitations.

Gothic Revivalism a universal style current since its inception in Britain in the late 18th century, passing from a period of superficial decoration to one in which true Gothic massing yielded such masterpieces as the British Houses of Parliament and Pittsburgh's Cathedral of Learning.

Greek Revivalism   an austere American style of the period 1798–1850, embracing in either form or decoration such Greek features as bilateral symmetry, low-pitched roofs, frontal porticos with pediments, and horizontal doorheads; often executed in wood and painted white, the structures usually featured modifications of the classical orders and occasional imaginative use of interior vaulting.

intercolumniation   the space between columns; the pattern of spacing between columns.

Internationalism, International Style   a style, current since the 1920s, that makes use of modern constructional advances to create buildings reflecting characteristic industrial forms and emphasizing both volume and horizontality through ribbon windows, smooth and undecorated wall surfaces, and flat roofs, with contrasts introduced by curved or cylindrical forms and cantilevered projecting features.

Neo-Expressionism   a current style emphasizing dynamism achieved by employment of sweeping curves, acute angles, and pointed arches.

New Formalism   a current American manner, characterized by buildings that are freestanding blocks with symmetrical elevation, level rooflines (often with heavy, projecting roof slabs), many modeled columnar supports, and frequent use of the arch as a ruling motif to produce a kind of classicism without classical forms.

Palladianism   the classical style evolved by the 16th-century architect Andrea Palladio, featuring harmonic proportion based upon mathematics, extensive use of porticos, a neat contrast between openness and solidity, and features of Roman decoration; partially influential today in the so-called "Palladian motif," a window or other opening consisting of a central high arch flanked by lower rectangular areas, the whole supported by four columns (a feature actually invented before Palladio's time and used only sparingly by him).

Renaissance Revivalism   a style originating in England c.1830 and influential in the U.S. from 1850 through 1930, derived from the Renaissance palace architecture of Rome, Florence, and Venice; in the U.S., the structures were executed in masonry, wood, or cast iron.

structuralism   functionalism.

tectonics   a general term for the theory and techniques of construction. —tectonist, *n.* —tectonic, *adj.*

21. ARGUMENTATION
See also 250. LOGIC; 312. PHILOSOPHY; 354. RHETORIC and RHETORICAL DEVICES.

alogism   *Obsolete.* a statement that is nonsensical or illogical.

amphilogy *Obsolete.* a statement open to more than one interpretation; an ambiguity.

analogy an agreement or correspondence in particular features between things otherwise dissimilar; the inference that if two things agree with each other in one or more respects, they will probably agree in yet other respects. —analogous, *adj.*

antilogy a contradiction.

apagoge a method of argument in which the proposition to be established is emphasized through the disproving of its contradiction; *reductio ad absurdum.* —apagogic, *adj.*

apologist a person who defends, in speech or writing, a faith, doctrine, idea, or action.

circularism, circularity reasoning or arguing in a circle.

conciliationism the belief in and use of conciliation in an argument. —conhciliationist, *n.* —conciliatory, *adj.*

disceptation *Obsolete.* controversy or argument. —disceptator, *n.*

disputation a controversial debate or discussion; a dispute. See also 382. SPEECH. —disputant, *n.*

dissentation *Obsolete.* the act of dissenting or disagreeing. —dissenter, *n.*

divarication a difference of opinion.

doctrinarianism a stubborn attachment to a theory or doctrine without regard to its practicability. Also spelled doctrinairism. —doctrinaire, *n., adj.*

dogmatism 1. a statement of a point of view as if it were an established fact. 2. the use of a system of ideas based upon insufficiently examined premises. —dogmatist, *n.* —dogmatic, *adj.*

epagogue a method of induction in which enumeration of particulars leads to the inferred generalization. —epagogic, *adj.*

episyllogism a syllogism whose premises are the conclusion of a preceding syllogism.

ergotism the practice or habit of quibbling and wrangling; sophistical reasoning. —ergotize, *v.*

eristic 1. a participant in an argument or controversy. 2. the art of disputation. —eristic, eristical, *adj.*

forensics the art and study of argumentation and formal debate. —forensic, *adj.*

heuristics a method of argument in which postulates or assumptions are made that remain to be proven or that lead the arguers to discover the proofs themselves. —heuristic, *adj.*

hypothesis 1. a principle or proposition that is assumed for the sake of argument or that is taken for granted to proceed to the proof of the point in question.
2. a system or theory created to account for something that is not understood. —hypothesist, hypothetist, *n.* —hypothetic, hypothetical, *adj.*

logicaster 1. a person who is pedantic in argument.
2. a person whose logic is less valid than he thinks.

Megarianism Euclid of Megara's Socratic school of philosophy, known for the use of logical paradox and near-specious subtleties.

misology a hatred of argument, debate, or reasoning. —misologist, *n.*

noetics the laws of logic; the science of the intellect. —noetic, *adj.*

obscurantism the use of argument intended to prevent enlightenment or to hinder the process of knowledge and wisdom. Also spelled obscuranticism. —obscurantist, *n.* —obscurant, obscurantic, *adj.*

obstructionism deliberate interference with the progress of an argument. —obstructionist, *n.* —obstructionistic, *adj.*

paradoxology the proposing of paradoxical opinions; speaking in paradoxes. —paradoxer, *n.*

paralogism, paralogy, paralogia a method or process of reasoning which contradicts logical rules or formulas, especially the use of a faulty syllogism (the formal fallacy). —paralogist, *n.* —paralogistic, *adj.*

philopolemic *Rare.* related to a love of controversy and argument. —philopolemist, *n.*

pilpulist one who uses Talmudic dialectic; a subtle reasoner. —pilpulistic, *adj.*

polemicist, polemist a skilled debater in speech or writing. —polemical, *adj.*

polemics the art of dispute or argument. —polemic, *n.*, *adj.* —polemically, *n.*, *adv.*

polysyllogism a series of syllogisms set up systematically.

prolepsis anticipating an opponent's argument and answering it before it can be made. See also 174. FUTURE. —proleptic, *adj.*

pseudosyllogism a false syllogism whose conclusion does not follow from its premises.

quodlibet a nice or fine point, as in argument; a subtlety. —quodlibetal, *adj.*

quodlibetarian a person who likes to talk about or dispute fine points or quodlibets.

redargution *Obsolete.* the act or process of refuting or disproving. —redargutory, *adj.*

referee a person who decides a matter when the parties to it are in conflict; an umpire or judge.

simplism the tendency to concentrate on a single part of an argument and to ignore or exclude all complicating factors. —simplistic, *adj*.

sophism 1. a specious argument for displaying ingenuity in reasoning or for deceiving someone.
2. any false argument or fallacy. —sophister, *n*. —sophistic, *adj*.

sophist 1. *Ancient Greece.* a teacher of rhetoric, philosophy, etc.; hence, a learned person.
2. one who is given to the specious arguments often used by the sophists.

sophistry 1. the teachings and ways of teaching of the Greek sophists.
2. specious or fallacious reasoning, as was sometimes used by the sophists.

syllogism a form of reasoning in which two statements are made and a logical conclusion is drawn from them. See also 250. LOGIC. —syllogistic, *adj*.

trenchancy the state or quality of being forceful, incisive, or penetrating, as in words or an argument. —trenchant, *adj*.

trichoschisticism hair-splitting, as in argument; the making of overly fine points.

22. ARROWS
See also 416. WEAPONRY.

arbalist, arbalest a crossbowman. Also arcubalist.

belomancy A form of divination in which marks or words are placed on arrows which are then drawn from a quiver at random.

sagittary 1. pertaining to archery.
2. resembling an arrow; sagittate.

sagittate shaped like an arrowhead, especially plant leaves shaped like elongated triangles.

23. ART
See also 20. ARCHITECTURE; 128. DRAWING; 141. ENGRAVING;
218. IMAGES; 305. ORNAMENTATION; 369. SKILL and CRAFT.

Abstract Expressionism a spontaneous, intuitive painting technique producing nonformal work characterized by sinuous lines. Also called **Action Painting**.

abstractionism the creation of abstract art. —abstractionist, *n*., *adj*.

Abstractism a nonrepresentational style in painting or sculpture.

acrography etching in relief; the opposite of engraving.

Action Painting Abstract Expressionism.

aestheticism 1. the doctrine that aesthetic standards are autonomous and not subject to political, moral, or religious criteria.
2. used pejoratively to describe those who believe only in "art for art's sake," to the exclusion of all other human activities.

allegory an art form, as a story, painting, or sculpture, in which the components have a symbolic, figurative meaning. —allegorist, allegorizer, *n.* —allegorical, *adj.*

anaglyphy 1. the art of carving works in low relief.
2. a low-relief sculpture. Also spelled anaglyph. —anaglyphic, anaglyptic, *adj.*

anaglyptography the technique of making drawings and etchings that appear to be carved in low relief. —anaglyptographic, *adj.*

anamorphism a distorted image of an object, as in anamorphic art. Also spelled anamorphosis, anamorphosy. —anamorphic, *adj.*

anamorphoscope a cylindrical mirror for correcting the distorted image created by anamorphism.

anamorphosis anamorphism.

anamorphosy *Obsolete.* anamorphism.

aquarellist an artist who paints in water colors. Also called water-colorist.

archaism a taste for and imitation of earlier styles, a recurrent phenomenon since ancient times based on the premise that earlier works were somehow purer and simpler. Cf. primitivism.

architectonics structural design, especially of a work of art, as a painting or piece of music. See also 312. PHILOSOPHY.

artistry artistic achievement, quality, or workmanship.

autotelism a nonutilitarian theory of art holding that a work of art is an end in itself. —autotelic, *adj.*

baroque a highly decorated form of art or ornamentation. —baroque, *adj.*

charcoalist an artist who specializes in charcoal drawings or sketches.

chinoiserie anything typically Chinese or made in a Chinese manner.

cinquecentism the revival in arts and letters in the sixteenth century in Italy. —cinquecentist, *n.*, *adj.*

classicism 1. formerly, an imitation of Greek and Roman art.
2. currently, a dedication to the principles of that art: clarity of execution, balance, adherence to recognized standards of form, and conscious craftsmanship. —classicist, *n.* —classicistic, *adj.*

colorist an artist who uses color or who is distinguished by the way in which he uses color.

Cubism a movement in 20th-century painting in which several planes of an object in the form of cubes or other solids are presented in an arbitrary arrangement using a narrow range of colors or monochrome. —Cubist, *n.* —Cubistic, *adj.*

culturist a person who is well acquainted with culture, as literature, the arts, etc., and who advocates their worth to society.

Dadaism a revolt by certain 20th-century painters and writers in France, Germany, and Switzerland against smugness in traditional art and Western society; their works, illustrating absurdity through paintings of purposeless machines and collages of discarded materials, expressed their cynicism about conventional ideas of form and their rejection of traditional concepts of beauty. —Dadaist, *n.*

daubery, daubry a painting or other work executed in a messy or unskilled way. —dauber, daubster, *n.*

diptych a work of art composed of two attached panels.

divisionism the use of small juxtaposed dots of color on a canvas. Cf. Pointillism. —divisionist, *n., adj.*

duecentism the art and literature of thirteenth-century Italy. —duecentist, *n., adj.*

eclecticism a style that intermixes features borrowed from other artists or differing schools; applied especially when the result is unsuccessful. —eclecticist, *n.*

esthetology the study of the origin, development, and nature of the fine arts.

exoticism the condition of being foreign, striking, or unusual in color and design. —exoticist, *n.* —exotic, exotical, *adj.*

Expressionism a movement in the 20th century that attempted to express feeling and emotion directly by distorting forms, choosing violent subject matter and harsh colors, and keeping the overall design out of balance. —Expressionist, *n.* —Expressionistic, *adj.*

fantasticism the literary or artistic use of fantasy. —fantastic, *adj.* —fantasticality, fantasticalness, *n.*

Fauvism an early movement in 20th-century painting characterized by an emphasis on the use of unmixed bright colors for emotional and decorative effect. —Fauvist, *n.* —Fauve, *n., adj.*

Futurism a movement of the 20th century attempting to capture in painting the movement, force, and speed of modern industrial life by the simultaneous representation of successive aspects of forms in motion. —Futurist, *n.* —Futuristic, *adj.*

glyptotheca a room, building, or other place specifically used for the preservation of works of sculpture.

Gothicism the principles of the paintings, sculptures, stained glass, mosaics, and book illustrations of the period 1200–1450, embracing several disparate styles and emphases. —Gothicist, *n.*

Hellenism the forms and ideals of ancient Greek art. See also 18. ANTIQUITY.

iconology the description, history, and analysis of symbolic art or artistic symbolism, especially that of the late medieval and Renaissance periods. Also called iconography. —iconologist, *n.* —iconological, *adj.*

Impressionism a movement in the late 19th century in French painting, characterized by the goal of reproducing an impression of a subject by use of reflected light and color and the blurring of outlines. —Impressionist, *n.*, *adj.* —Impressionistic, *adj.*

Japonism, Japonisme a style of art, idiom, custom, mannerism, etc., typical of the Japanese.

landscapist a painter of landscapes.

luminarism a movement in painting concerned with precision in representing light and shade. —luminarist, *n.*

luminism 1. a movement in painting concerned with effects of light, especially the use of broken color in its full intensity with a minimum of shadow effects, applied especially to many Impressionist and Pointillist artists.
2. a technique of painting employing minute modulations of tone, developed in America (1825-65) by John Singer Sargent, Mary Cassatt, William Merritt Chase, and others. —luminist, *n.*

mannerism 1. an overemphasis on any distinctive technique of expression, occurring when the manner of expression obscures the feeling or idea expressed in the work of art; considered by many art critics to be a sign of decadence. —mannerist, *n.* —manneristic, *adj.*
2. *(usu. cap.)* a style, developed between c.1530 and c.1590, marked by deliberate violations of earlier standards of painting in depicting the artist's idea rather than nature by means of asymmetrical and crowded compositions, elongated and twisted figures, and emphasis upon devices like foreshortening. The style also affected both architecture and sculpture. —Mannerist, *n.*

miniaturist 1. *Obsolete.* an artist whose task it was to draw in red certain words or letters in manuscripts.
2. a painter of miniature pictures or portraits, as on china or ivory, characterized by fineness of detail.

modernism a mode of expression or practice characteristic of modern times. —modernist, *n.* —modernistic, *adj.*

monochromist one who paints or draws in shades or tints of a single color.

monolith a sculpture or monument made from a single large block of stone, as an Egyptian obelisk. —monolithic, *adj.*

Moresque decoration or ornamentation in the Moorish style, distinguished by intricate tracery and bright colors. —Moresque, *adj*.

Naturalism the goal of artists who attempt to represent a subject without stylization or interpretation, and to create a mirror for natural beauty. Cf. Verism. Also called **Realism**. —Naturalist, *n*. —Naturalistic, *adj*.

Neo-Classicism a European movement of the late 18th century differing from earlier classical revivals in that it deliberately and consciously imitated antique models such as those found between 1738–56 in Herculaneum, Paestum, and Pompeii. —Neo-Classicist, *n*. —Neo-Classic, Neo-Classical, *adj*.

Neo-Hellenism the practice of reviving Hellenism in modern art or life. —Neo-Hellenist, *n*. —Neo-Hellenistic, *adj*.

Neo-Impressionism Pointillism.

Neo-Plasticism the art principle of de Stijl which represented form as horizontal and vertical lines and which excluded all colors except the primaries, black, and white.

New Realism a term used to describe a trend away from abstract expressionism toward a subjective expressionism focusing on true-to-life forms, the factual, and easily evident forms.

nocturne a painting of a night scene, a genre particularly favored by Whistler. See also 284. MUSIC.

nuditarian a person who advocates the study of the nude body or figure.

origami the Japanese art of paper folding. —origamist, *n*.

ornamentalism 1. a use of ornament for decorative purposes, especially its overuse.
2. the employment of several traditional architectural and decorative features into the design of interiors, buildings, furniture, etc., influenced by Art Deco and Art Nouveau.

ornamentist, ornamentalist 1. an artist who specializes in ornamentation.
2. a person whose work is considered to be ornament rather than art.

Orphism a short-lived development of Cubism c.1912 that attempted to enliven the original approach by subordinating the geometrical forms and using unmixed bright colors. —Orphist, *n*.

pastelist, pastellist an artist who specializes in the use of pastels.

paysagist a painter of landscapes.

phelloplastics the art of carving or sculpting in cork.

pinacotheca a picture gallery or place where paintings are kept.

plasticism the theory or creation of plastic art.

plein-airism the practice of painting in the open air to obtain effects of light and atmosphere not possible in a studio. —plein-air, *adj*.

Pointillism a style of the late 19th century based upon some Impressionist techniques and the application of scientific theories of the process of vision; begun by Seurat, who gave it the name Divisionism, it consists of using dots of unmixed color side by side so that the viewer's eye may mix them into the appropriate intermediate color. Also called **Neo-Impressionism.** —**Pointillist,** *n.* —**Pointillistic,** *adj.*

polychromy the art of using many or various colors in painting, architecture, etc. —**polychromic, polychromatic,** *adj.* —**polychromatist,** *n.*

polyptych a work of art, as a painting, composed of several panels.

Pop Art British and American art movement of the 1960s which explored antitraditional and often antiesthetic means to present everyday objects and events.

portraitist an artist who paints portraits.

portraiture 1. the process or art of painting portraits.
2. the portrait itself.
3. portraits collectively.

Post-Impressionism a late 19th-century reaction to Impressionism, emphasizing on one hand the emotional aspect of painting and on the other a return to formal structure; the first led to Expressionism; the second, to Cubism. —**Post-Impressionist,** *n.*

Pre-Raphaelitism the principles of the 19th-century artists and writers who sought to restore the principles and practices thought to be characteristic of Italian art before Raphael. —**Pre-Raphaelite,** *n., adj.*

prettyism a deliberate affection or triviality of expression in art or literature.

primitivism 1. the self-conscious return, for inspiration, to the archaic forms produced by non-Western cultures.
2. the practice of painting in a way alien to academic or traditional techniques, often displaying a highly individual naiveté in interpretation and treatment of subjects. Cf. **archaism.** —**primitivist,** *n.* —**primitivistic,** *adj.*

pseudo-classicism the imitative use of classicism in art and literature, especially shown during the 18th century. —**pseudo-classic,** *adj.* —**pseudo-classical,** *adj.*

purism strict adherence to particular concepts, rules, or ideals of form, style, etc., either as formulated by the artist or as dictated by a school with which the artist is allied. See also 104. CRITICISM; 236. LANGUAGE. —**purist,** *n., adj.*

pyrography the art or process of burning designs on wood or leather, using heated tools. Also called **pyrogravure.** —**pyrographer,** *n.* —**pyrographic,** *adj.*

quattrocentism the art of fifteenth-century Italy. —**quattrocentist,** *n., adj.*

Realism 1. Naturalism.
2. a movement in the late 19th century stressing common rather than individual characteristics as the basis of reality. Cf. Verism. —**Realist,** *n.*

representationalism the practice of creating recognizable figures, objects, and natural forms in art. Cf. **Abstractism.**

rhypography, rhyparography still-life or genre painting, especially of trivial or sordid and unsuitable subjects.

rococo *Often Derogatory.* an artistic and literary style, developed from the baroque, characterized by complex and elaborate ornamentation. —**rococo,** *adj.*

Romanticism the reflection, in art, of a late 18th-century literary and philosophical movement in reaction against the intellectuality and rationality of Neo-Classicism. It produced no single artistic style or characteristic but strongly influenced the ideals of imagination, emotion, and the freedom of expression in other media. —**Romanticist,** *n.*

Russianism something characteristic of or influenced by Russia, its people, customs, language, etc.

sensationalism the act of shocking or intent to shock, especially through the media; the practice of using startling but superficial effects, in art, literature, etc., to gain attention. See also 249. LITERATURE; 265. MEDIA. —**sensationalist,** *n.*

serigraphy the procedure of making prints through the silk-screen process. —**serigrapher,** *n.*

socialist realism a Marxist-inspired artistic and literary theory or doctrine that calls on art and literature to promote the socialist cause and sees the artist, writer, etc. as a servant of the state or, in the words of Stalin, "the engineer of human souls."

statuary 1. statues collectively or a group of statues.
2. the art of making statues. —**statuary,** *adj.*

stereochromy the process of making stereochromes, pictures produced with water glass as a vehicle or preservative coating. Also called **waterglass painting.** —**stereochromic, stereochromatic** *adj.*

stylistics the study of particular styles, as in art, literature, etc.

Surrealism, Superrealism a controversial movement in art and literature between the two World Wars in which the artist attempted to portray, express, or interpret the workings of the subconscious mind; in painting it found expression in two techniques, the naturalistic (Dali) and the abstract (Miró). —**Surrealist,** *n.* —**Surrealistic,** *adj.*

synchronism an American movement, founded in 1913, based upon Abstractism in unmixed color, usually involving disklike forms. —**synchronist,** *n.* —**synchronistic,** *adj.*

Tachism, Tachisme a movement of the early 1950s which claimed to be in revolt against both Abstractism and naturalism, taking its name from patches of color (Fr. *taches*) placed on canvas spontaneously and by chance, the result being considered an emotional projection rather than an expression or a symbol. Cf. Abstract Expressionism. —Tachist, Tachiste, *n*.

tonalist a painter who pays special attention to qualities of tone or tint in his work. See also 284. MUSIC.

toreumatology *Rare*. the study of the art of toreutics.

toreutics the art of ivory- and metalworking, especially relief work, embossing, and chasing. —toreutic, *adj*.

ultramodernism the condition of being beyond the norm of modern. —ultramodernist, *n*. —ultramodernistic, *adj*.

Verism a naturalistic approach, especially in portraiture, in which every wrinkle and flaw of the subject is faithfully reproduced; extreme realism. Cf. Naturalism, Realism. —Verist, *n*. —Veristic, *adj*.

Vorticism an art movement in England in 1914–15 stimulated by Futurism and by the idea that all artistic creation must begin in a state of strong emotion; its products, intended to establish a form characteristic of the industrial age, tend to use angular, machinelike shapes. —Vorticist, *n*.

water-colorist aquarellist.

24. ASTROLOGY
See also 124. DIVINATION; 174. FUTURE.

apotelesm *Archaic*. the casting of horoscopes. —apotelesmatic, *adj*.

astroalchemy astrology. —astroalchemist, *n*.

astrodiagnosis astrology.

astrology 1. the study that assumes, and professes to interpret the influence of the stars and planets upon human existence.
2. *Obsolete*. astronomy. —astrologer, astrologist, *n*. —astrological, *adj*.

genethliac *Obsolete*. a person who is skilled in genethlialogy.

genethliacism the art or practice of casting genethliacs, or astrological nativities.

genethliacs genethlialogy.

genethlialogy the lore that underlies the art of casting genethliacs, or astrological nativities. Also genethliacs. —genethlialogic, genethlialogical, *adj*.

horoscopy 1. the art of casting horoscopes.
2. the position of the sun and stars at the time of a person's birth. —horoscoper, horoscopist, *n*.

Magianism the teaching and studies of the priestly caste in ancient Media and Persia whose belief in the advent of a savior involved them in intensive astrological research, including the following of a star to Bethlehem (See Matthew 2:1–12).

nativity 1. the time, place, and circumstances of a person's birth.
2. the configuration of the planets at the time of a person's birth and a representation, as a chart, of that configuration.

synastry coincidence in stellar or astrological influence; the condition of two or more persons having been born under the same stellar configuration.

25. ASTRONOMY
See also 100. COSMOLOGY; 259. MARS; 271. METEORITES; 280. MOON; 318. PLANETS; 387. SUN.

aerolithology the branch of astronomy that studies meteors.

aerolitics the branch of astronomy that studies aerolites, or stony meteors.

albedo the ratio between the light reflected from a surface and the total light falling upon that surface, as the albedo of the moon.

aphelion the point in the orbit of a heavenly body where it is farthest from the sun. Cf. perihelion.

apolune in an orbit around a moon, the point furthest from the moon. Cf. perilune.

areology the astronomical studies of the planet Mars. —areologist, *n*. —areologic, areological, *adj*.

asterism *Rare*. a constellation or small group of unrelated stars. —asterismal, *adj*.

astrogation the art of navigating in space. Cf. astronavigation. —astrogator, *n*.

astrogeny, astrogony the theory of the evolution of heavenly bodies.

astrogeology a geological specialty that studies celestial bodies.

astrognosy the branch of astronomy that studies the fixed stars.

astrography a scientific analysis and mapping of the stars and planets. —astrographic, *adj*.

astrolatry the worship of the heavenly bodies. Also called Sabaism. —astrolater, *n*.

astromancy 1. a form of divination involving studying the stars.
2. *Rare*. astrology. Also called sideromancy. —astromancer, *n*. —astromantic, *adj*.

astrometry the branch of astronomy that studies the dimensions of heavenly bodies, especially the measurements made to determine the positions and orbits of various stars. —astrometric, astrometrical, *adj*.

astronautics the science of space travel, concerned with both the construction and the operation of vehicles that travel through interplanetary or interstellar space. Also called **cosmonautics**. —astronautic, astronautical, *adj.* —astronaut, *n.*

astronavigation a type of navigation involving observations of the apparent positions of heavenly bodies. Also called **celestial navigation, celo-navigation**. —astronavigator, *n.*

astronomy the science that studies the stars and other features of the material universe beyond the earth's atmosphere. —astronomer, *n.* —astronomical, *adj.*

astrophile a person strongly attracted to knowledge about the stars. —astrophilic, *adj.*

astrophotography a form of photography used to record astronomical phenomena.

astrophysics the branch of astronomy concerned with the origin, and the chemical and physical nature of heavenly bodies. —astrophysicist, *n.*

celestial navigation astronavigation. Also called **celo-navigation**.

chromatoscopy the study of stars through a telescope in which the star appears as a ring of light, in order to observe the star's scintillation. —chromatoscope, *n.*

Copernicanism the fundamental theoretical basis of modern astronomy, first demonstrated in the early 16th century by Copernicus, who showed that the earth and the other planets orbit around the sun. Cf. **Ptolemaism**.

cosmolabe *Obsolete*. an instrument, like an astrolabe, used for astronomical observations.

cosmonautics astronautics. —cosmonaut, *n.* —cosmonautical, *adj.*

heliodon an instrument used in astronomy to show the apparent movement of the sun.

heliometer an instrument originally designed for measuring the sun's diameter, now used for measuring the angular distance between stars.

heliometry the practice of measuring the angular distance between stars by means of a heliometer. —heliometric, heliometrical, *adj.*

interlunation the period between the old moon and the new when the moon is invisible each month. —interlunar, *adj.*

meridian an imaginary great circle in the sphere of the heavens, passing through the poles and the zenith and nadir of any point and intersecting the equator at right angles. See also 178. GEOGRAPHY. —meridian, meridional, *adj.*

metagalaxy the entire system of galaxies, including the Milky Way. —metagalactic, *adj.*

nutation the periodic oscillation that can be observed in the precession of the earth's axis and the precession of the equinoxes. See also 133. EARTH. —**nutational,** *adj.*

obliquity the inclination of the earth's equator or the angle between the plane of the earth's orbit and the plane of the equator (23°27'). Also called **obliquity of the ecliptic.** See also 133. EARTH. —**obliquitous,** *adj.*

occultation the process of one heavenly body disappearing behind another as viewed by an observer.

paraselene a false moon, in reality a bright spot or a luminous ring surrounding the moon.

perihelion the point in the orbit of a heavenly body where it is nearest the sun. Also spelled **perihelium.** Cf. **aphelion.**

perihelium perihelion.

perilune in orbit around a moon, the point nearest the moon. Cf. **apolune.**

phantasmatography *Rare.* a work or treatise on astronomy or celestial bodies.

planetarium 1. a representation of the planetary system, particularly one in which the movements of the planets are simulated by projectors.
2. a room or building housing such an apparatus.

planetology the branch of astronomy that studies the planets. —**planetologist,** *n.* —**planetologic, planetological,** *adj.*

planisphere a map showing half or more of the sphere of the heavens, indicating which part is visible at what hour from a given location. —**planispheric, planispherical,** *adj.*

Ptolemaism the complicated demonstration of Ptolemy, 2nd-century geographer and astronomer, that the earth is the fixed center of the universe around which the sun and the other planets revolve; now discredited. Cf. **Copernicanism.**

Ptolemaist a supporter of the Ptolemaic explanation of planetary motions.

radioastronomy the branch of astronomy that studies radio frequencies emitted by the sun, planets, and other celestial bodies.

Sabaism astrolatry.

Sabianism, Sabaeanism, Sabeanism the religion of the Sabians, a group sometimes associated with worship of the sun, moon, and stars. See also 349. RELIGION.

schematism the combination or configuration of the aspects of the planets and other heavenly bodies.

selenography the scientific analysis and mapping of the moon's physical features. —**selenographer, selenographist,** *n.* —**selenographic, selenographical,** *adj.*

selenology the branch of astronomy that studies the moon. —selenologist, *n.* —selenologic, selenological, *adj.*

sideromancy a form of divination involving observations of the stars. Also called astromancy. —sideromancer, *n.* —sideromantic, *adj.*

siderophobia an abnormal fear of the stars.

uranianism *Obsolete.* astronomy.

uranography the branch of astronomy that deals with the description of the heavens by constructing maps and charts, especially of the fixed stars. Also called uranology. —uranographer, uranographist, *n.* —uranographic, uranographical, *adj.*

uranology 1. a written description of the heavens and celestial bodies.
2. another term for astronomy.

uranometry, uranometria 1. a treatise recording the positions and magnitudes of heavenly bodies.
2. the science of measuring the real or apparent distances of heavenly bodies from Earth. —uranometrical, *adj.*

26. ATHLETICS
See also 2. ACROBATICS; 55. BOXING; 176. GAMES; 347. RECREATION.

aerobics a form of physical activity characterized by strenuous exercise of many muscle groups and intended to increase muscle tone and cardiovascular fitness. —aerobic, *adj.*

agonist one who contends for a prize in public games. —agonistic, agonistical, *adj.*

agonistics the art of athletic combat or contests in public games.

aquatics the art and exercise of water sports.

athleticism 1. an active interest in sports.
2. an obsessive participation in physical activity. —athletic, *adj.*

calisthenics the science, art, or practice of bodily exercises intended to promote strength, health, and grace of movement. —calisthenic, calisthenical, *adj.*

contortionist a person who performs gymnastic feats involving distorted postures. —contortionistic, *adj.*

decathlon an athletic contest in which the contestants compete for points awarded for performances in ten different track and field events, the winner being the one with the highest aggregate score. The events include 100-meter, 400-meter, and 1500-meter runs, 110-meter high hurdles, long jump, high jump, pole vault, shot-put, javelin throw, and discus throw. Cf. heptathlon, pentathlon, triathlon.

discobolus 1. a discus thrower.
2. *cap., italics.* the famous 5th-century B.C. statue by Myron of a discus thrower.

gymnasiast a gymnast. See also 240. LEARNING.

gymnast a person who is involved in or skilled in the art of gymnastics.

gymnastics 1. regimented exercises performed on floor mats and on certain specialized equipment that entail the skills of tumbling and balancing and that are intended to display flexibility, grace, and strength.
2. physical or athletic exercises; calisthenics. —**gymnastic,** *adj.*

heptathlon an athletic competition in which contestants compete for points awarded for performances in seven different track and field events, the winner being the one with the highest aggregate score. The competition, usually for women, consists of 100-meter and 800-meter runs, 100-meter hurdles, high jump, long jump, javelin throw, and shot-put. Cf. **decathlon, pentathlon, triathlon.**

isometrics a form of physical exercise in which a set of muscles is tensed briefly, either in opposition to another set or against a solid surface. Cf. **isotonics.** —**isometric,** *adj.*

isotonics muscular exercise using free weights or fixed devices to simulate resistance of weight. Cf. **isometrics.** —**isotonic,** *adj.*

lampadedromy *Ancient Greece.* a race in honor of Prometheus in which the contestants ran bearing lit torches, the winner being the first to finish with his torch still lit. Also called **lampadrome, lampadephoria.**

lampadist a contestant in a lampadedromy. Also called **lampadephore, lampadophoros.**

natation the act or art of swimming or floating on water. —**natatory,** —**natatorial,** *adj.*

natator a swimmer.

natatorium a swimming pool, particularly an indoor facility.

palaestra, palestra *Ancient Greece.* a public place for athletics or wrestling. —**palaestric, palestric,** *adj.*

pancratiast a person skilled in the art of boxing or wrestling. —**pancratiastic,** *adj.*

pentathlon 1. *Track and Field.* an athletic contest in which the contestants compete for points awarded for performances in five different track and field contests, the winner being the one with the highest aggregate score. The events include, for women, an 800-meter run, 100-meter hurdles, high jump, long jump, and shot-put; for men, 200-meter and 1500-meter runs, long jump, javelin throw, and discus throw.
2. *Olympic Games. Usually,* **modern pentathlon** an athletic contest in which

the contestants compete for points awarded for performances in five events: fencing, horseback riding, pistol shooting, cross-country running, and swimming.

quinquennalia *Ancient Rome.* public games that took place every five years.

titlist a champion or one who holds a title.

trampolinist a person who performs feats of tumbling using a trampoline as a springboard. Also trampoliner. —trampoline, *n.*

triathlon an intense aerobic endurance competition, typically, in its longest form, consisting of a 2.4-mile ocean swim, a 112-mile bicycle ride, and a 26.2-mile marathon run, the winner being the one to finish all three events in the least time.

27. ATMOSPHERE
See also 85. CLIMATE; 87. CLOUDS; 142. ENVIRONMENT; 417. WEATHER; 420. WIND.

advection the horizontal movement of elements of the atmosphere. Cf. convection. —advective, *adj.*

aerodynamics the branch of dynamics that studies the motions of air and other gases, especially with regard to bodies in motion in these substances. See also 31. AVIATION. —aerodynamic, aerodynamical, *adj.*

aerographics, aerography the branch of meteorology that studies and describes atmospheric conditions. —aerographer, *n.* —aerographic, aerographical, *adj.*

aerology 1. *Obsolete.* the branch of meteorology that observed the atmosphere by using balloons, airplanes, etc.
2. meteorology. —aerologist, *n.* —aerologic, aerological, *adj.*

aeromancy 1. divination from the state of the air or atmospheric conditions, sometimes limited to weather.
2. *Humorous.* weather forecasting. See also 124. DIVINATION.

aerometry the science of measuring properties of air; pneumatics. —aerometric, *adj.*

aeropause the region in the upper part of the earth's atmosphere where the air is too thin for aircraft to operate properly.

aerophobia an abnormal dread of fresh air. —aerophobe, *n.*

aeroscepsy, aeroscepsis perception by means of the air, said to be a function of the antennae of insects.

aerosphere *Aeronautics.* the area outside the atmosphere of the earth where manned flight is possible.

atmolysis the separation of gases which are equally diffusible. —atmolyzer, *n.*

atmospherics 1. the sound, usually a crackling noise, heard over a radio receiver and caused by electromagnetic disturbances in the atmosphere; static.
2. the natural phenomena that create this disturbance.

barograph a barometer which automatically records, on a rotating cylinder, any variation in atmospheric pressure; a self-recording aneroid.

barometrography the branch of science that deals with the barometer.

barometry the art or science of barometric observation.

bioclimatology a branch of biology that studies the relationship between living creatures and atmospheric conditions. Also called **biometeorology**. —**bioclimatologist, bioclimatician,** *n.* —**bioclimatological,** *adj.*

chaomancy a form of divination involving aerial visions.

convection the vertical movement of elements of the atmosphere. Cf. **advection.**

eudiometer an instrument for measuring the amount of oxygen in the air and for analyzing gases.

exosphere the highest portion of the earth's atmosphere, from which air molecules can escape into space. Cf. **ionosphere.**

ionosphere the outermost part of the earth's permanent atmosphere, beyond the stratosphere, composed of heavily ionized molecules. It extends from about 50 to 250 miles above the surface of the earth. Cf. **exosphere.**

konimeter an instrument for measuring impurities in the air. —**konimetric,** *adj.*

konimetry the measurement of impurities in the air by means of a konimeter. —**konimetric,** *adj.*

koniology, coniology the study of atmospheric dust and other impurities in the air, as germs, pollen, etc., especially regarding their effect on plant and animal life.

miasmology the study of fogs and smogs, especially those affecting air pollution levels.

microbarograph a barograph for recording small fluctuations of atmospheric pressure.

ozonometry the determination of the proportion of ozone in the atmosphere. —**ozonometer,** *n.* —**ozonometric,** *adj.*

pneumatics a specialty in physics that studies the mechanical properties of air and other gases. Also called **pneumodynamics.**

stratosphere the upper part of the earth's atmosphere, characterized by an almost constant temperature throughout its altitude, which begins at about seven miles and continues to the ionosphere, at about 50 miles.

sympiesometer, sympiezometer an instrument for measuring the weight of the atmosphere by the compression of a column of gas. See also 226. INSTRU-MENTS.

tropopause the zone between the troposphere and the stratosphere where the temperature remains relatively constant above a given point on earth.

troposphere the region of the earth's atmosphere between the surface of the earth and the stratosphere.

vacuometer an instrument used for comparing barometers at varying pressures against a standard barometer.

28. ATTITUDES
See also 41. BEHAVIOR; 279. MOODS; 334. PSYCHOLOGY.

altruism a concern or regard for the needs of others, entirely without ulterior motive. —altruist, n. —altruistic, adj.

amateurism the views and principles of a person who engages in an activity for pleasure rather than profit. Cf. professionalism. —amateur, n.

animosity an active dislike or energetic hostility that leads to strong opposition.

antagonism a contentiousness toward or opposition to others or their ideas; hostility or antipathy. —antagonistic, adj.

anti-Gallicanism dislike of or opposition to anything French. —anti-Gallican, anti-Gallic, adj.

anti-Klanism opposition to the ideas and activities of the Ku Klux Klan.

authoritarianism 1. the habit of conduct, thought, and speech expressing total submission to rigid principles and rules.
2. the principles and views of the rule maker. —authoritarian, n., adj.

autotheism a person's elevation of himself into being his own god.

Babbittism adherence to a rigidly conventional set of mores and aspirations. The salient characteristics are the drive for business success and the lack of culture. The model for the characterization is George Babbitt, chief protagonist of Sinclair Lewis's novel, *Babbitt*. Also Babbittry.

beatnikism attitudes or behavior typical of a beatnik or one who has rejected conventions of society.

beauism the tendency to give excessive attention to matters of dress and etiquette. —beauish, adj.

bellicosity a warlike or hostile attitude. —bellicose, adj.

bigotry obtuse or narrow-minded intolerance, especially of other races or religions. —bigot, n. —bigoted, adj.

bucolicism the conduct and views suitable for a rural, rustic, or pastoral existence. —bucolic, bucolical, adj.

centrism adherence to a middle-of-the-road position, neither left nor right, as in politics. —centrist, *adj.*, *n.*

complaisance the quality or state of being agreeable, gracious, considerate, etc. —complaisant, *adj.*

conformism the act or practice of conforming, as to social convention, religious orthodoxy, or established political belief. —conformist, *n.*, *adj.*

constructionism the use of or reliance on construction or constructive methods. —constructionist, *n.*

controversialism the relation to controversy or to a subject of controversy. —controversialist, *n.*

conventionalism a variety of conduct and thought based solely upon the usages, opinions, and practices of one's own society. —conventionalist, *n.*

cosmopolitanism the opinions and behavior emerging from the theory that cultural and artistic activities should have neither national nor parochial boundaries. —cosmopolitan, *n.*, *adj.*

cynicism the holding or expressing of opinions that reveal disbelief and sometimes disdain for commonly held human values and virtues. Also called cynism. See also 312. PHILOSOPHY. —cynic, *n.* —cynical, *adj.*

dandyism excessive concern with matters of dress; foppishness. —dandy, *n.*

defeatism 1. the acceptance of defeat as a foregone conclusion and the resultant failure to make an effort to succeed.
2. the views underlying acceptance of the frustration or thwarting of a goal, especially by the failure to prevent them. Cf. futilitarianism. —defeatist, *n.*, *adj.*

didacticism the views and conduct of one who intends to teach, often in a pedantic or contemptuous manner, both factual and moral material. —didact, *n.* —didactic, *adj.*

die-hardism the attitudes or behavior of one who stubbornly holds on to something, as an outdated view, untenable position, etc. —die-hard, *n.*, *adj.*

egoism an extreme individualism; thought and behavior based upon the premise that one's individual self is the highest product, if not the totality, of existence. Cf. individualism. —egoist, *n.* —egoistic, *adj.*

egotism the practice of thought, speech, and conduct expressing high self-regard or self-exaltation, usually without skepticism or humility. —egotist, *n.* —egotistical, *adj.*

elitism the attitude that government should be by those who consider themselves superior to others by virtue of intelligence, social status, or greater accomplishment.

emotionalism an undue influence of feelings upon thought and behavior. —emotionalist, *n.* —emotionalistic, *adj.*

equanimity calmness of temperament; even-temperedness. —equanimous, *adj.*

eremitism 1. the state of being a hermit.
2. an attitude favoring solitude and seclusion. —eremite, *n.* —eremitic, *adj.*

ethicism a conscious tendency to moralize.

externalism attention paid to outward or outside matters, especially in religious affairs. —externalist, *n.*

extremism 1. the condition or act of taking an extreme view.
2. the taking of extreme action. —extremist, *n., adj.*

fanaticism an extreme and uncritical zeal or enthusiasm, as in religion or politics. —fanatic, *n., adj.* —fanatical, *adj.*

fatalism the viewpoints of believers in the doctrine that all things are determined by the nature of existence and beyond human influence. —fatalist, *n.* —fatalistic, *adj.*

faustianism spiritual or intellectual dissatisfaction combined with a desire for power or material advantage. After Johann Faust (c. 1480–c. 1538), German scholar portrayed by Marlowe and Goethe. —faustian, *adj.*

feminism an attitude favoring the movement to eliminate political, social, and professional discrimination against women. —feminist, *n., adj.* —feministic, *adj.*

finalism the belief in final causes. —finalist, *n.*

finicalism *Rare.* a conscious and sometimes affected fastidiousness and undue concern with trifles, especially those affecting elegance.

finicalness an undue fastidiousness or overniceness. Also called finicality, finicism. —finical, *adj.*

finicism *Rare.* finicalness.

fogyism, fogeyism an adherence to old-fashioned or conservative ideas and intolerance of change, often coupled with dullness or slowness of personality. —fogyish, fogeyish, *adj.*

formulism the basing of behavior and thinking upon existent categories, formulas, or systems of formulas; traditionalism. —formulist, *n.* —formulistic, *adj.*

fossilism behavior typical of an earlier time; old-fashioned or stuffy attitudes.

futilitarianism a belief in the uselessness of human endeavor and aspiration. Cf. defeatism. —futilitarian, *n., adj.*

gigmanism *Rare.* the habit of narrowmindedness, or philistinism.

girouettism the practice of frequently altering one's opinions or principles to follow popular trends.

gourmetism the theories and standards of connoisseurs in eating and drinking. Also called **gourmandism.**

Grundyism the censorship of personal conduct based upon narrow and unintelligent conventionalism. —**Grundyist, Grundyite,** *n.*

hidalgoism the characteristics of a member of the Spanish lower nobility.

hypersensitivity extreme or abnormal sensitivity, as to criticism. —**hypersensitive,** *adj.*

imaginationalism an attitude of mind in which the imagination dominates. —**imaginational,** *adj.*

impossibilism a defeatist attitude; the belief that all things are impossible.

impudicity lack of shame or modesty.

indeterminism the quality of not being clearly established or fixed. —**indeterminist,** *n.* —**indeterministic,** *adj.*

indifferentism the condition of being indifferent or of having no preference. See also 312. PHILOSOPHY; 349. RELIGION. —**indifferentist,** *n.*

individualism the practice of independence in thought and action on the premise that the development and expression of an individual character and personality are of the utmost importance. Cf. egoism. —**individualist,** *n.* —**individualistic,** *adj.*

insouciance lack of care or concern; a lighthearted attitude. —**insouciant,** *adj.*

jocundity the quality or condition of being merry or cheerful. —**jocund,** *adj.*

jovialist *Obsolete.* a person who leads a merry life.

Klanism the beliefs and practices of members of the Ku Klux Klan. Also called **Ku Kluxism, Ku Kluxery.**

Laodiceanism the quality of being indifferent in politics or religion.

latitudinarianism tolerance or broadmindedness, especially in matters of religion; the liberal interpretation of beliefs or doctrines. —**latitudinarian,** *n.,* *adj.*

lenity the quality or condition of being gentle or merciful. —**lenient,** *adj.*

levity frivolous or lighthearted behavior or attitude; an unserious approach to life. See also 213. HUMOR.

maidism 1. the state or quality of being a maid, a young or unmarried woman.
2. behavior or attitude typical of maidism.

malism the conviction that the world is evil.

mansuetude the state or quality of being gentle or mild.

masculinism 1. masculinity.
2. an attempt to protect masculine traits and qualities against the assaults of militant feminism. Cf. feminism.

megalopsychy *Obsolete.* generosity of spirit or magnanimity.

mercuriality 1. the state or quality of having a lively, fickle, volatile, or erratic attitude or character.
2. an instance of such behavior. —mercurial, *adj.*

militancy 1. the state or condition of being combative or disposed to fight.
2. the active championing of a cause or belief. —militant, *n., adj.*

misandry, misandria an extreme dislike of males, frequently based upon unhappy experience or upbringing. Cf. misogynism.

misanthropy a hatred of mankind; pessimistic distrust of human nature expressed in thought and behavior. Cf. philanthropy. —misanthrope, misanthropist, *n.* —misanthropic, *adj.*

misogynism, misogyny an extreme dislike of females, frequently based upon unhappy experience or upbringing. Cf. misandry.

misosophy *Rare.* a hatred of wisdom. —misosophist, *n.*

morbidity the state or quality of being excessively gloomy. —morbid, *adj.*

mordancy the quality or state of being sarcastic or caustic. —mordant, *adj.*

morosity the quality or state of being excessively sullen or gloomy. —morose, *adj.*

munichism an attitude that favors appeasement.

munificence the quality of being exceedingly generous; lavish generosity. —munificent, *adj.*

namby-pambyism weak or insipid behavior or attitude. —namby-pamby, *n.*

neanderthalism adherence to or advocacy of crude outmoded views, practices, etc. —neanderthal, *adj.*

negativism 1. an attitude characterized by an unwillingness to follow suggestions or orders, as in children.
2. a pessimistic approach to life. See also 312. PHILOSOPHY. —negativist, *n., adj.,* —negativistic, *adj.*

neoconservatism a new movement in conservatism, usually seen as a move further to the right of the position currently occupied by conservatives in politics or in attitudes. —neoconservative, *n., adj.*

nice-nellyism, nice-Nellyism an inordinate degree of modesty or prudishness, or the appearance of such characteristics. See also 237. LANGUAGE STYLES. —nice-nelly, —nice-Nelly, *n.*

nihilism total rejection of established attitudes, practices, and institutions. —nihilist, *n.* —nihilistic, *adj.*

nonconformism a deliberate and conscious refusal to conform to conventional practices or patterns of behavior. —**nonconformist,** *n.* —**nonconformity,** *n.*

obduracy the state or condition of being obstinate or hardhearted. —**obdurate,** *adj.*

objectivism views and behavior that are not moved by the emotional content of an event, argument, or problem. Also **objectivity.**

obsequence the desire, willingness, or eagerness to oblige, serve, please, etc.; obsequiousness. —**obsequent,** *adj.*

odium 1. hatred.
2. the infamy or opprobrium brought on by being hated or by hateful behavior. —**odious,** *adj.*

overoptimism an excessive and usually groundless optimism. —**overoptimist,** *n.* —**overoptimistic,** *adj.*

parochialism narrowness or pettiness of interests, opinions, or information. —**parochialist,** *n.*

parvanimity smallness or pettiness of mind.

passivism 1. the state or quality of being inactive, of not participating.
2. the doctrine or advocacy of a passive policy, as passive resistance. —**passivist,** *n.*

perfectibilism the attitude that anything short of perfection is unacceptable. —**perfectibilist,** *n.*

perfectionism 1. the religious or philosophical aspiration to be perfect in moral character.
2. a personality trait manifested by the rejection of personal achievements falling short of perfection, often leading to distress and self-condemnation. —**perfectionist,** *n.* —**perfectionistic,** *adj.*

pessimism a depressed and melancholy viewpoint manifested as a disposition to hold the least hopeful opinion of conditions or behavior. See also 312. PHILOSOPHY. —**pessimist,** *n.* —**pessimistic,** *adj.*

petulance 1. the condition or quality of being irritable, peevish, or impatient.
2. an irritable or peevish statement or action. Also **petulancy.** —**petulant,** *adj.*

philanthropy a deliberate affection for mankind, shown in contributions of money, property, or work for the benefit of others. Cf. **misanthropy.** —**philanthropist,** *n.* —**philanthropic,** *adj.*

philistinism the opinions, goals, and conduct of persons deficient in liberal culture. —**philistine,** *n., adj.*

philopater *Obsolete.* 1. one who loves his father.
2. one who loves his country.

plerophory a state or quality of full confidence or absolute certainty.

pococurantism indifference; nonchalance.

Pollyannaism blind or excessive optimism, after the character Pollyanna, created by American writer Eleanor Porter (1868-1920).

precisionism an insistence upon perfection in language, morals, or ritual. —**precisionist**, *n*. —**precisionistic**, *adj*.

professionalism the standards, views, and behavior of one who engages in an activity, especially sports or the arts, to make his livelihood. Cf. **amateurism**. —**professional**, *n*., *adj*.

protervity peevishness.

pudency modesty or shyness; embarrassment.

pudicity modesty, especially chastity or chastefulness.

racism 1. a belief that human races have distinctive characteristics that determine their respective cultures, usually involving the idea that one's race is superior and has the right to control others.
2. a belief in a policy of enforcing the asserted right of control. —**racist**, *n*., *adj*.

ritualism ceremonialism. —**ritualist**, *n*. —**ritualistic**, *adj*.

rubricism a tenacious adherence to rules of behavior or thought; formulism. —**rubrician**, *n*.

ruralism the motivations for exalting country above city living. —**ruralist**, *n*.

sanguinity the quality or condition of being ardent, confident, or optimistic. —**sanguine**, *adj*.

scientism 1. *Often Disparaging*. the style, assumptions, techniques, practices, etc., typifying or regarded as typifying scientists.
2. the belief that the assumptions and methods of the natural sciences are appropriate and essential to all other disciplines, including the humanities and the social sciences.
3. scientific or pseudoscientific language. —**scientistic**, *adj*.

sexism the practice of discriminating against women in the offering of job opportunities, increases in salary, and other matters now generally considered to belong to women by right.

skepticism, scepticism a personal disposition toward doubt or incredulity of facts, persons, or institutions. See also 312. PHILOSOPHY. —**skeptic**, *n*., *adj*. —**skeptical**, *adj*.

snobbism the double inclination to ape one's superiors, often through vulgar ostentation, and to be proud and insolent with one's inferiors. Also called **snobbery**. —**snob**, *n*. —**snobby, snobbish**, *adj*.

spartanism a devotion to the habits and qualities of the ancient Spartans, especially to an indomitable spirit, undaunted hardihood, and stark simplicity. —**spartan**, *n*., *adj*.

spectacularism the state of being spectacular.

standpattism an attitude of resistance to change; extreme conservatism.

subjectivism the views and behavior of one who tends to be affected by the emotional qualities of an event, argument, or problem. Also called **subjectivity.**

suburbanism the doctrines and conduct of those who regard life in suburbia superior to life in cities or country.

tokenism formal or superficial compliance with a law, requirement, convention, etc., especially in the hiring of members of a minority group.

traditionalism the tendency to submerge individual opinions or creativity in ideas or methods inherited from the past, distinguished from conventionalism in having reference more to the past than to the present. Also called **traditionism.** See also 69. CATHOLICISM. —**traditionalist,** *n.*

trivialism concern over things that are common or unimportant. —**triviality,** *n.* —**trivial,** *adj.*

troglodytism 1. an outlook or activity suitable to a cave dweller, especially among primitive tribes.
2. the motivation or condition of a modern cave-dwelling recluse, especially one who has rejected normal society.
3. coarse, brutal behavior, thought to resemble that of a primitive cave dweller. —**troglodyte,** *n.* —**troglodytic,** *adj.*

ultraism 1. an extremist point of view or act.
2. extremism. —**ultraist,** *n., adj.* —**ultraistic,** *adj.*

un-Americanism the state or condition of being out of sympathy with or against an ideal of American behavior, attitudes, beliefs, etc. —**un-American,** *n., adj.*

urbanism the views and behavior of those who champion urban living as superior to life elsewhere. Cf. **ruralism, suburbanism.** —**urbanistic,** *adj.*

vestryism selfishness and parochialism said to be characteristic of rural parishioners. Also called **vestrydom.** —**vestryish,** *adj.*

vulturism behavior or character typical of a vulture, especially in the sense of being rapacious. —**vulturous,** *adj.*

yokelism 1. the state or quality of being a yokel or country bumpkin.
2. behavior, language, etc., typical of a yokel.

29. AUTHORS

See also 53. BOOKS; 104. CRITICISM; 236. LANGUAGE; 237. LANGUAGE STYLE; 248. LITERARY STYLE; 249. LITERATURE; 346. READING; 354. RHETORIC and RHETORICAL DEVICES; 409. VERSE.

allonymity 1. an author's use of a name belonging to another, especially to a well-known person.
2. the state or quality, in a name, of being an allonym.

allonymy a name of one person used by another, such as a writer using the name of someone other than himself for concealment of identity or other purpose. Cf. pseudonym. —allonymous, *adj.*

pseudandry the use by a female writer of a male pseudonym. —pseudandrous, *adj.*

pseudogyny the use by a male writer of a female pseudonym. —pseudogynous, *adj.*

pseudonym a nom de plume or fictitious name, especially one used by an author to conceal his identity. Cf. allonymy. —pseudonymous, *adj.*

pseudonymity 1. use of a pseudonym by an author to conceal his identity.
2. the state or quality of being pseudonymous.

typomania an obsession with the expectation of publication.

30. AUTOMATION

automobilism the use or care of automobiles. —automobilist, *n.* —automobility, *n.*

bionics 1. the science or study of how man and animals perform tasks and solve certain types of problems involving use of the body.
2. the application of this study to the design of computer-driven and other automated equipment.
3. the application of this study to the design of artificial limbs, organs, and other prosthetic devices. —bionic, *adj.*

computerese the jargon or language typical of those involved with computers.

cybernetics the comparative study of complex electronic devices and the nervous system in an attempt to understand better the nature of the human brain. —cyberneticist, *n.* —cybernetic, *adj.*

robotics the application of automated machinery to tasks traditionally done by hand, as in manufacturing.

robotism the use of automated machinery or manlike mechanical devices to perform tasks. —robotistic, *adj.*

servomechanism a closed-circuit feedback system used in the automatic control of machines, involving an error-sensor using a small amount of energy, an amplifier, and a servomotor dispensing large amounts of power. Also called servo. —servomechanical, *adj.*

31. AVIATION

accelerometer an instrument for measuring and recording the rate of acceleration of an aircraft.

aerialist a person who performs aerial acrobatics, as a trapeze artist, tightrope walker, stunt flier, etc.

aeroballistics the science of ballistics combined with or from the special viewpoint of aerodynamics, particularly with regard to rockets, guided missiles, etc. —aeroballistic, *adj.*

aerobatics stunts performed with aircraft. See also 2. ACROBATICS.

aerocartography the process of mapmaking by means of aerial survey.

aerodonetics *Rare.* the science or art of gliding. —aerodonetic, *adj.*

aerodrome, airdrome an airport or airbase, not including the personnel.

aerodromics the art or science of flying airplanes.

aeroembolism *Medicine.* a condition caused by the formation of nitrogen bubbles in the blood as a result of a sudden lowering of atmospheric pressure, as when flying at high altitude or rising too rapidly from a deep underwater dive.

aeromedicine the medical specialty concerned with the health of those engaged in flying within the earth's atmosphere.

aeronautics 1. *Archaic.* the science or art of ascending and traveling in the air in lighter-than-air vehicles.
2. the technology or art of flying airplanes. —aeronaut, *n.* —aeronautic, aeronautical, *adj.*

aeronautism the technique of ballooning. —aeronautics, *n.*

aeropause the region in the upper part of the earth's atmosphere where the air is too thin for aircraft to operate properly.

aerophone an instrument for detecting the approach of aircraft by intensifying the sound waves it creates in the air.

aerophysics the branch of physics that studies the earth's atmosphere, especially the effects upon the atmosphere of objects flying at high speeds or at high altitudes. —aerophysicist, *n.*

aeroplanist an aviator or aircraft pilot.

aerostatics the study of the construction and operation of aerostats, lighter-than-air craft, as balloons or dirigibles. —aerostatic, aerostatical, *adj.*

avigation the science of aerial navigation.

avinosis airsickness.

avionics the science and technology of electrical and electronic devices or equipment used in aviation.

ballooning the art and science of operating balloons for sport or air travel. Also **balloonry.**

bioastronautics the science that studies the effects of space travel on life, especially human life and the human body.

ornithopter, orthopter da Vinci's exploratory design for a flying machine moved by flapping wings.

perastadics the science and art of space flying. —**perastadic,** *adj.*

photoreconnaisance reconnaissance for purposes of aerial photography; reconnaissance or surveillance by means of aerial photography.

radar an acronym for *R*Adio *D*etecting *A*nd *R*anging: a method and the equipment used for the detection and determination of the velocity of a moving object by reflecting radio waves off it.

rocketry the science and technology of rocket design and manufacture.

supersonic applied to aircraft moving at speeds beyond the speed of sound, about 750 mph (1207.5 kph) at sea level.

volitation flight, the act of flying, or the ability to fly.

B

32. BACTERIA

bacteriology the branch of biology that studies and classifies bacteria. —**bacteriologist,** *n.* —**bacteriologic, bacteriological,** *adj.*

chromatophobia a strong resistance by bacteria to absorbing stains. —**chromatophobic,** *adj.*

hemophile, haemophile a bacterium that grows well in the presence of hemoglobin. —**hemophilic,** *adj.*

microbiology the branch of biology that studies microorganisms, including bacteria, viruses, fungi, and pathogenic protozoa. —**microbiologist,** *n.*

microphobia, microbiophobia an abnormal fear of microorganisms. —**microphobic,** *adj.*

33. BALDNESS
See also 193. HAIR; 196. HEAD.

acomia baldness. Also called **alopecia, phalacrosis.** —**acomous,** *adj.*

alopecist *Medicine.* medical specialist who treats baldness.

atrichia *Medicine.* congenital or acquired baldness. Also **atrichosis.**

calvities, calvity baldness, especially at the top or back of the head. —**calvous,** *adj.*

peladophobia a dread of baldness.

phalacrosis baldness.

34. BANISHMENT

expatriation the process of abandoning one's native land or of being exiled. —**expatriate,** *n., adj., vb.*

ostracism 1. a casting out from social or political society.
2. the ancient Athenian process of temporary banishment by popular vote, using potsherds or tiles for ballots.

petalism the banishing of a citizen for five years if judged guilty of dangerous influence or ambition, as practiced in ancient Syracuse; olive leaves were used for ballots.

35. BAPTISM
See also 80. CHRISTIANITY; 349. RELIGION.

Abecedarian a member of a 16th-century Anabaptist sect who refused to learn to read, arguing that the guidance of the Holy Spirit was sufficient for the understanding of the Bible.

Anabaptism 1. a belief in adult, as opposed to infant baptism. **2.** membership in various Protestant sects advocating adult baptism. —Anabaptist, *n., adj.*

antipedobaptism, antipaedobaptism the denial, on scriptural grounds, of the validity of infant baptism. —antipedobaptist, antipaedobaptist, *n.*

baptisaphily an interest in collecting Christian baptismal names.

catabaptist an opponent of baptism.

conditional baptism Christian baptism administered when there is doubt whether a person has already been baptized or whether a former baptism is valid.

hemerobaptism the practice of ancient Jewish and early Christian sects involving daily ceremonial baptisms or ablutions. —hemerobaptist, *n.*

holobaptism a belief in baptism by immersion. Also called **immersionism.** —holobaptist, *n.*

palingenesis a belief that baptism effects a new birth or regeneration. Also palingenesy. —palingenesist, *n.* —palingenesian, *adj.*

parabaptism a baptism that is in some way irregular or unauthorized. —parabaptist, *n.*

pedobaptism, paedobaptism the historic Christian practice of infant baptism. —pedobaptist, paedobaptist, *n.*

ubbenite a member of a sect of Anabaptists founded in Germany in 1534 by Ubbe Phillips.

36. BATHING
See also 84. CLEANLINESS.

balneography a treatise on baths.

balneology the study of the therapeutic uses of various types of bathing; hydrotherapy. —balneologist, *n.* —balneologic, balneological, *adj.*

bathophobia an intense dislike of bathing.

caldarium *Ancient Rome.* a room where hot baths were taken.

hydrotherapy the treatment of diseases through the use of water, whether internal or external, as whirlpool baths, compresses, or drinking mineral waters. Also hydrotherapeutics. —hydrotherapist, *n.* —hydrotherapeutic, hydrotherapeutical, *adj.*

Kneippism a 19th-century treatment of diseases by types of hydrotherapy, as warm or cold baths and walking barefoot in dewy grass.

37. BEARDS
See also 149. FACIAL FEATURES; 193. HAIR.

pogoniasis *Medicine.* 1. an excessive growth of beard.
2. the development of a beard by a woman.

pogonology a treatise on beards. —**pogonologist,** *n.*

pogonophile an admirer of beards; a student of beards.

pogonophobia an abnormal fear or dislike of beards.

pogonotomy the cutting of beards.

pogonotrophy the cultivation of beards, beard-growing.

38. BEAUTY

adonism the beautification of a person, usually a male.

aesthetician, esthetician 1. a specialist in aesthetics.
2. a proponent of aestheticism.

aestheticism, estheticism the doctrine that the principles of beauty are basic and that other principles (the good, the right) are derived from them, applied especially to a late 19th-century movement to bring art into daily life. See also 23. ART.

aesthetics, esthetics a branch of philosophy dealing with beauty and the beautiful. —**aesthetic,** *n., adj.* —**aesthetical,** *adj.*

cosmetology the art or practice of the beautification of the skin, hair, or nails. —**cosmetologist,** *n.* —**cosmetological,** *adj.*

philocalist a lover of beauty. —**philocaly,** *n.*

pulchritude physical beauty, especially that of women. —**pulchritudinous,** *adj.*

39. BEER
See also 8. ALCOHOL; 158. FERMENTATION; 421. WINE.

beerocracy *England.* the aristocracy that gained its wealth and social position from the ownership of breweries.

cooperage the barrel or container used to store and ship draft beer.

labeorphily the collecting of beer bottle labels. —**labeorphile,** *n.*

meadophily the study of beer bottle labels. —**meadophile,** *n.*

tegetology the collecting of cardboard beer coasters. —**tegetologist,** *n.*

40. BEES

See also 225. INSECTS.

apiarist a person who tends bees.

apiary a beehive or collection of beehives. —**apiarian,** *adj.*

apiculture the art and science of beekeeping. —**apiculturist,** *n.*

apimania an abnormal love of bees.

apiology a specialty within entomology that studies honeybees. —**apiologist,** *n.*

apiphobia, apiophobia an intense fear of bees. Also called **melissophobia.**

melittology *Rare.* apiology. —**melittologist,** *n.*

41. BEHAVIOR

See also 28. ATTITUDES; 279. MOODS; 334. PSYCHOLOGY.

aberrance, aberrancy the condition or state of being deviant or aberrant.

abnormalism 1. having a tendency towards, or being in a state of abnormality.
2. something that is abnormal.

abnormalist a person who is characterized as being in some way abnormal.

adventurism impulsive, rash, or irresponsible actions or attitudes, especially in the sphere of public life. —**adventurist,** *n.* —**adventuristic,** *adj.*

alarmism the attitudes and behavior of one who exaggerates dangers or always expects disaster. —**alarmist,** *n.*

alogy *Obsolete.* illogicality, unreasonableness. —**alogic, alogical,** *adj.*

amazonism the taking on of masculine habits and occupations by women.

Arcadianism the dress and conduct suitable to a pastoral existence, usually with reference to the idealized description of pastoral life in literature. —**Arcadian,** *n., adj.*

arrivism 1. the state of having recently achieved wealth or position, especially by unscrupulous or unethical means.
2. behavior typical of arrivism. —**arriviste,** *n., adj.*

asceticism a severe self-deprivation for ethical, religious, or intellectual ends. —**ascetic,** *n., adj.*

atrabilarian 1. a sad and gloomy individual.
2. an irritable and bad-tempered person. —**atrabilious,** *adj.*

attitudinarianism the practice of striking poses, either to mask or to express personal feelings. —**attitudinarian,** *n.*

attorneyism the characteristics attributed to attorneys; slyness; unscrupulousness.

automatism an automatic or involuntary action. —**automatist,** *n.*

autophoby *Rare.* an abnormal fear of being egotistical, of referring to oneself.

babuism, babooism *Derogatory.* the practices of Hindus who had only a slight English education. From *bābū,* a Hindi title equivalent to *Sir* or *Mr.*

Barnumism showmanship or any activity taking advantage of people's credulity or desire for sensational entertainment, as practiced by P.T. Barnum (1810–91).

bashawism the characteristics of a bashaw, especially tyranny and imperiousness.

beatnikism attitudes or behavior typical of a beatnik or one who has rejected conventions of society.

bestiality a debased brutality, the opposite of humane activity: "I have lost the immortal part of myself, and what remains is bestial." *(Othello).* See also 364. SEX.

bizarrerie strangeness or grotesqueness, especially strange or unconventional behavior.

blackguardism behavior typical of a blackguard, characterized by use of obscene language and by roguish actions. —**blackguardery,** *n.* —**blackguardly,** *adj.*

bohemianism the practice of individualistic, unconventional, and relaxed conduct, often in an artistic context, expressing disregard for or opposition to ordinary conventions. —**bohemian,** *n., adj.*

boobyism conduct characteristic of a stupid person or clown. —**boobyish,** *adj.*

braggartism a braggart's usual activity; bragging. —**braggartist, braggart,** *n.*

brutalitarianism the practice of advocating or engaging in brutality. —**brutalitarian,** *adj.*

brutism the set of attributes that characterize a brute. —**brutish,** *adj.*

bullyism the actions of a bully.

careerism the characteristics associated with one who advances his career even at the expense of his pride and dignity. —**careerist,** *n.*

ceremonialism an addiction to ceremonies or ritualism, especially in social and other nonreligious contexts. —**ceremonialist,** *n.*

characterology the study of character, especially its development and its variations. —**characterologist,** *n.* —**characterologic, characterological,** *adj.*

charlatanism the quality of having characteristics of a fraud. —**charlatanic,** *adj.*

consuetude a habit or custom; usual behavior.

coxcombry foolish conceit or vanity; behavior typical of a coxcomb.

daredevilism reckless or foolhardy behavior. Also called **daredeviltry.** —**daredevil,** *n.*

debacchation *Obsolete.* raving or maniacal behavior, as that of a bacchanal.

decorum proper behavior; action that is seemly and in good taste. —**decorous,** *adj.*

die-hardism the attitudes or behavior of one who stubbornly holds on to something, as an outdated view, untenable position, etc. —**die-hard,** *n.*, *adj.*

dilettantism an admiration of or interest in the arts, often used pejoratively to designate a shallow, undisciplined, or frivolous attraction. —**dilettante,** *n.*, *adj.* —**dilettantish,** *adj.*

donkeyism 1. an action characterized as being donkeylike; foolishness.
2. the characteristic of being like a donkey. —**donkeyish,** *adj.*

do-nothingism idleness or indolence as a habit or regular practice.

dowdyism the habit of being shabbily dressed. —**dowdyish,** *adj.*

dramaticism the habit of performing actions in a histrionic manner.

ergoism a pedantic adherence to logically constructed rules.

erraticism an action or behavior that deviates from the norm; unpredictability in behavior.

exhibitionism 1. a deliberately conspicuous or exaggerated mode of behavior, intended to gain attention.
2. the abnormal practice of indecent exposure. —**exhibitionist,** *n.* —**exhibitionistic,** *adj.*

fainéance, faineancy laziness; the state of being idle. —**fainéant,** *adj.*

fairyism the quality of being a fairy or having fairylike characteristics.

fanfaronade swaggering boastfulness; vainglorious speech or behavior. —**fanfaron,** *n.*

faustianism spiritual or intellectual dissatisfaction combined with a desire for power or material advantage. After Johann Faust (c.1480–c.1538), German scholar portrayed by Marlowe and Goethe. —**faustian,** *adj.*

fiendism *Rare.* evil attitudes and actions.

flunkyism, flunkeyism 1. the quality or state of being a servant or toady.
2. behavior typical of flunkyism. —**flunky, flunkey,** *n.*

formularism the condition of adhering solely to set formulas. —**formularistic,** *adj.*

fossilism behavior typical of an earlier time; old-fashioned or stuffy attitudes; fogyism.

fraternalism the condition of having brotherly qualities. —**fraternalist,** *n.* —**fraternalistic,** *adj.*

functionarism the administrative duties of officials. —**functionary, *n.*, *adj.***

gangsterism the habit of using organized violence to achieve one's ends. —**gangster, *n.***

gasconism boastful or bragging behavior. Also **gasconade.**

gelastic 1. inclined to laughter.
2. laugh-provoking in conduct or speech.

gnathonism the extremely obsequious behavior of a sycophant. —**gnathonic, *adj.***

gourmandism, gormandism 1. a strong penchant for good food; gourmetism; epicurism.
2. gluttony. —**gourmand, gormand, *n.*, *adj.***

grandeeism attitudes and actions modeled on the grandees, Iberian nobles of the highest rank.

gypsyism, gipsyism the activities and style of living attributed to gypsies. —**gypsy, gipsy, *n.* —gypsyish, gipsyish, *adj.***

harlequinade a performance involving Harlequin or other characters of the *Commedia dell'Arte*; hence, buffoonery or clownish behavior. Also **harlequinery.**

hermitism the practice of retiring from society and living in solitude, based upon a variety of motives, including religious. Also called **hermitry, hermitship. —hermitic, hermitical, *adj.***

histriconism histrionicism.

histrionicism a tendency to theatrical or exaggerated action. Also **histriconism.** —**histrionics, *n.* —histrionic, *adj.***

hoboism the state of being a hobo or vagrant.

holidayism a dedication to taking holidays.

hooliganism lawless behavior or conduct typical of a hooligan.

horsyism, horseyism looking or acting in some way like a horse. —**horsy, horsey, *adj.* —horsily, *adv.***

Hottentotism any behavior attributed to the Hottentots, in particular, a kind of stammering or stuttering.

hoydenism ill-bred, boisterous, or tomboyish behavior in a woman. —**hoyden, *n.*, —hoydenish, *adj.***

humbuggery 1. pretentious behavior or attitudes.
2. imposing or deceptive behavior. —**humbug, humbugger, *n.***

humoralism, humouralism an obsolete physiological explanation of health, disease, and behavior, asserting that the relative proportions of four elemental bodily fluids or humors (blood–sanguinity, phlegm–sluggishness, black bile–melancholy, and yellow bile–choler) determined a person's physical and mental constitution. —humoral, humoural, *adj.*

hyphenism division of patriotic loyalties, ascribed by some to foreign-born citizens in the United States.

idiocrasy an idiosyncrasy or personal mannerism or peculiarity.

idiosyncrasy a mannerism, action, or form of behavior peculiar to one person or group. —idiosyncratic, idiosyncratical, *adj.*

impudicity lack of shame or modesty.

indecorum 1. indecorous, improper, or unseemly behavior.
2. an indecorous thing or action.

Indianism the customs or traditions of Indians, especially American Indians. —Indianist, *n.*

insurrectionism the quality of revolting against established authority. —insurrectionist, *n.*, *adj.* —insurrectionary, *adj.*

irascibility a tendency to irritability and sudden fits of anger. Also called irascibleness. —irascible, *adj.*

Johnsonianism the quality of having traits or characteristics like those of Samuel Johnson. —Johnsonian, *n.*, *adj.*

juvenilism, juvenility *Often pejorative.* a mode of action or thought characterized by apparent youthfulness. —juvenile, *n.*, *adj.*

landlordism the actions and characteristics of a landlord. —landlordly, *adj.*

larkinism frolicsomeness.

larrikinism the state of being noisy, rowdy, or disorderly. —larrikin, *adj.*, *n.*

libertinism a tendency to unrestrained, often licentious or dissolute conduct. Also libertinage. —libertine, *n.*, *adj.*

lionism the pursuit or adulation of celebrities. —lionize, *v.*

litigiousness 1. an inclination to dispute or disagree with others, esp. through civil suits.
2. argumentativeness. —litigious, *adj.*

Londonism the customs and characteristics of London and of those who reside there. —Londonish, *adj.*

macaronism, maccaronism a tendency to foppishness. —macaroni, maccaroni, *n.*

maenadism behavior characteristic of a maenad or bacchante; raging or wild behavior in a woman. —maenadic, *adj.*

maidism 1. the state or quality of being a maid, a young or unmarried woman.
2. behavior or attitude typical of maidism.

mannerism a style of action, bearing, thought, or speech peculiar to an individual or a special group. See also 23. ART. —**mannerist,** *n.* —**manneristic,** *adj.*

martinetism an emphasis on scrupulous attention to the details of methods and procedures in all areas of life. —**martinet,** *n.* —**martinetish,** *adj.*

maudlinism *Rare.* 1. a tendency in temperament to be mawkishly sentimental and tearfully emotional.
2. a degree of drunkenness characterized by mawkish emotionalism. —**maudlin,** *adj.*

melodramatics behavior typical of that portrayed in a melodrama, i.e., characterized by extremes of emotion.

mercuriality 1. the state or quality of having a lively, fickle, volatile, or erratic attitude or character.
2. an instance of such behavior. —**mercurial,** *adj.*

milksopism 1. the state or quality of being a weak and ineffectual person.
2. behavior or attitudes typical of a such a person.

mimicism an intense (and sometimes injurious) tendency to mimicry.

mountebankism boastful and pretentious behavior; quackery or any actions typical of a mountebank. Also **mountebankery.**

muckerism behavior characteristic of a boorish person.

mutualism the principle or practice of mutual dependence as the condition of individual and social welfare. —**mutualist,** *n.*

namby-pambyism weak or insipid behavior or attitude. —**namby-pamby,** *n.*, *adj.*

Negroism a quality or trait distinctive of Negroes.

ninnyism conduct characteristic of a ninny, or silly fool. —**ninnyish,** *adj.*

nomadism a rootless, nondomestic, and roving lifestyle. —**nomadic,** *adj.*

nudism the practice of going nude. —**nudist,** *n.*, *adj.*

Occidentalism the characteristics and customs of people situated in western regions, especially the Western Hemisphere, as western European countries and the United States. —**Occidentalist,** *n.*

ogreism the condition of resembling an ogre in actions and characteristics. —**ogreish,** *adj.*

opportunism the conscious policy and practice of taking selfish advantage of circumstances, with little regard for principles. —**opportunist,** *n.* —**opportunistic,** *adj.*

Orientalism the habits, qualities, and customs of Oriental peoples. —Orientalist, Orientality, *n.*

parrotism mindless imitation. Also called **parrotry.**

particularism the adherence to an exclusive subject, interest, or topic. —particularist, *n.* —particularistic, *adj.*

parvenuism 1. behavior or attitudes typical of one who has recently acquired wealth or social position.
2. the state or quality of being a parvenu or upstart. —parvenu, *n., adj.*

patricianism 1. the state of being a member of one of the original citizen families of ancient Rome.
2. the state of being noble or high born. —patriciate, *n.*

plebeianism the quality of having common manners, character, or style. —plebeian, *n., adj.*

pococurantism a tendency to conduct expressing indifference, nonchalance, or lack of concern. —pococurante, pococurantist, *n.* —pococurante, *adj.*

poltroonism the characteristics associated with being a coward or wretch. Also called **poltroonery.** —poltroonish, *adj.*

polypragmatism a penchant for meddlesomeness and officiousness. Also polypragmacy, polypragmaty. —polypragmatist, *n.* —polypragmatic, *adj.*

pornerast one whose conduct is unchaste, licentious, or lewd.

praxeology, praxiology the study of human behavior and conduct. —praxeological, *adj.*

preciosity excessive fastidiousness or over-refinement in language or behavior.

precipitancy hasty or rash action, behavior, etc.; undue or ill-considered haste. —precipitant, *adj.*

priggism the strict adherence to correctness of behavior. —prigger, *n.* —priggish, *adj.*

profligacy 1. dissolute or immoral behavior.
2. reckless and extravagant spending or behavior. —profligate, *adj.*

protagonism the actions and qualities of a protagonist. —protagonist, *n.*

protervity a tendency to peevish, petulant, or insolent conduct.

psychagogics, psychagogy a method of affecting behavior by assisting in the choice of desirable life goals. —psychagogue, *n.*

puppyism affected or impertinent behavior; conceit.

quixotism a tendency to absurdly chivalric, visionary, or romantically impractical conduct. —quixotic, quixotical, *adj.*

rabulism *Rare.* a tendency to railing and quibbling. —rabulistic, rabulous, *adj.*

reactionism the condition of being reactionary or resistant to change. —reactionist, *n.*, *adj.*

reporterism the characteristics of a reporter.

reunionism the qualities of a reunion or social gathering. —reunionist, *n.*

revolutionism the state of being revolutionary. —revolutionary, revolutionist, *n.* —revolutional, revolutionary, *adj.*

routinism the excessive adherence to a routine. —routinist, *n.*

rowdyism noisy, quarrelsome, or disorderly conduct or behavior. —rowdy, *n.*, *adj.*

ruffianism behavior typical or characteristic of a brutal and violent person. —ruffian, *n.*

Satanism diabolical behavior. —Satanist, *n.*

savagism the condition of having uncivilized or primitive qualities. —savagedom, *n.*

schoolboyism the practices characteristic of a schoolboy. —schoolboyish, *adj.*

scoundrelism the characteristics and behavior of a scoundrel. —scoundrelly, *adj.*

seclusionist a person who seeks solitude or removes himself from the society of others; a recluse.

sensorialism the quality of having sensation. —sensorial, *adj.*

seraphism *Archaic.* an ecstatic devotion, especially religious.

sermonist 1. a person who delivers sermons.
2. a person who adopts a preaching attitude.

Shandyism a tendency to whimsical conduct in accord with absurd theories from past ages. [Allusion to the actions of Walter, father of the hero in Sterne's *Tristram Shandy*.]

spasmodism a tendency to conduct marked by outbursts of strong emotion. —spasmodist, *n.* —spasmodic, spasmodical, *adj.*

Sundayism activity characteristic of the observance of Sunday as a holy day.

supermanism the condition of having qualities or traits like those of a superman. —supermanly, *adj.*

sybaritism a love of luxury. [Allusion to Sybaris, a Greek colony in Italy noted for its luxury.] —sybarite, *n.* —sybaritic, *adj.*

sycophantism the practice of self-serving or servile flattery. Also called sycophancy. —sycophant, *n.* —sycophantic, *adj.*

sympathism the condition of having coinciding emotions in two or more people.

tantalism *Obsolete.* a form of teasing or harassment in which a hope of some good or benefit is instilled in the victim, only to be repeatedly dashed and the reward shown to be unattainable.

tartuffism hypocrisy. [Allusion to Molière's hypocritical hero, Tartuffe.] Also called **tartuffery.**

theatricalism a tendency to actions marked by exaggerations in speech or behavior. Also called **theatricism.**

tidyism the habit of extreme neatness.

Timonism a personal despair leading to misanthropy. [Allusion to Shakespeare's *Timon of Athens.*]

toadyism a fawning flattery, obsequiousness, or sycophancy. —**toady,** *n.* —**toadyish,** *adj.*

tokenism formal or superficial compliance with a law, requirement, convention, etc.

tomboyism the conduct characteristic of a tomboy, a boyish girl. —**tomboyish,** *adj.*

Turcism, Turkism *Obsolete.* the attitudes and actions of the Turks.

ultracrepidarianism the habit of giving opinions and advice on matters outside of one's knowledge or competence. —**ultracrepidarian,** *n., adj.*

vagabondism 1. the tendency to wander from place to place without a settled home; nomadism.
2. the life of a tramp; vagrancy. Also called **vagabondage.** —**vagabond,** *n., adj.*

vandalism the malicious destruction or defamation of public or private property. —**vandal, vandalization,** *n.* —**vandalish,** *adj.*

vanguardism the actions or thoughts of members of a vanguard, those at the forefront of a movement, fad, etc. —**vanguardist,** *n.*

Victorianism the affection for or emulation of Victorian tastes or thoughts.

Vikingism the actions characteristic of a Viking, i.e., savagery, rapaciousness, etc.

voyeurism the compulsion to seek sexual gratification by secretively looking at sexual objects or acts; the actions of a Peeping Tom. —**voyeur,** *n.* —**voyeuristic,** *adj.*

vulpinism *Rare.* the state or quality of being foxlike, especially crafty or cunning. —**vulpine,** *adj.*

vulturism behavior or character typical of a vulture, especially in the figurative sense of being rapacious. —**vulturous,** *adj.*

werewolfism the quality of having the traits of a werewolf.

Yahooism   a penchant for rowdyism. [Allusion to Swift's characters in *Gulliver's Travels.*]

yokelism 1. the state or quality of being a yokel or country bumpkin.
2. behavior, language, etc., typical of a yokel.

zanyism the style of a zany or buffoon.

zealotism, zealotry a tendency to undue or excessive zeal; fanaticism.

zelotypia *Obsolete.* 1. abnormal zeal.
2. morbid jealousy. —zelotypic, *adj.*

42. BELLS

campanarian *Rare.* concerned with bells or the manufacture of bells.

campanile a tower for peals of bells or a carillon, usually freestanding. Also called campanario.

campanist one who plays a campanile or carillon; a carilloneur.

campanology the science or art of bell ringing. See also change ringing. —campanologist, campanologer, *n.* —campanological, *adj.*

change ringing the art of sounding a ring or set of from 3 to 12 tuned bells according to intricate patterns of sequences.

tintinnabulation 1. the sound made by ringing bells.
2. a tinkling, bell-like sound. —tintinnabular, *adj.*

43. BIBLE
See also 53. BOOKS; 69. CATHOLICISM; 80. CHRISTIANITY; 183. GOD and GODS; 203. HELL; 205. HERESY; 231. JUDAISM; 332. PROTESTANTISM; 349. RELIGION; 392. THEOLOGY.

apocrypha 1. religious writings of disputed origin, regarded by many authorities as uncanonical.
2. *(capitalized)* a group of 15 books, not part of the canonical Hebrew Bible, but present in the Septuagint and Vulgate and hence accepted by some as biblical. —apocryphal, *adj.*

biblicism a strict following of the teachings of the Bible.

biblicist 1. an expert in biblical text and exegesis.
2. a person who strictly follows the teachings of the Bible.

biblioclasm the destruction of books, especially the Bible. —biblioclast, *n.*

bibliolater, bibliolatrist a person who respects the Bible excessively and interprets it literally.

bibliomancy a form of divination using books, especially the Bible, in which passages are chosen at random and the future foretold from them.

dittology a double reading or interpretation, especially of a Bible passage.

eisegesis the introduction by an interpreter of his own ideas into a text under explication.

Elohist the author of part of the first six books in the Old Testament, so named because of references to God as *Elohim*. Cf. Yahwist.

exegesis critical explication or interpretation of Scripture.

exegetics the branch of theology that specializes in interpretation, or exegesis, of Biblical literature. Historically, exegetes have recognized four levels of meaning in the Bible: the historical or literal, the allegorical, the moral, and the anagogical or mystical, putting emphasis on the necessity of a foundation for the latter three in the literal sense. —exegete, *n.*

exegetist, exegist an exegete; one skilled in exegesis.

fundamentalism the rationale of conservative American Protestants who regard the Bible as free of errors or contradictions and emphasize its literal interpretation, usually without reference to modern scholarship. Also called literalism. —fundamentalist, *n., adj.*

hermeneutics the science of interpretation and explanation, especially the branch of theology that deals with the general principles of Biblical interpretation. —hermeneut, hermeneutist, *n.*

Higher Criticism the analysis of Biblical materials that aims to ascertain, from internal evidence, authorship, date, and intent. Cf. Lower Criticism.

Hutchinsonianism 1. the theories of John Hutchinson, an 18th-century Yorkshireman, who disputed Newton's theory of gravitation and maintained that a system of natural science was to be found in the Old Testament.
2. the tenets of the followers of Mrs. Anne Hutchinson, an antinomian who lived in the early days of the Massachusetts Colony. —Hutchinsonian, *adj.*

inspirationism the belief in inspiration arising from the Scriptures. —inspirationist, *n.* —inspirative, *adj.*

isagogics a branch of theology that is introductory to actual exegesis, emphasizing the literary and cultural history of Biblical writings. —isagogic, *adj.*

lection a reading from a text, especially a reading from the Bible as part of a church service.

lectionary a list of the lections, or texts, to be read in church services throughout the canonical year.

literalism 1. fundamentalism.
2. Scripturalism. —literalist, *n., adj.*

Lower Criticism the study of Biblical materials that intends to reconstruct their original texts in preparation for the tasks of Higher Criticism. Cf. Higher Criticism.

pseudepigrapha the spurious writings (other than the canonical books and the Apocrypha) professing to be biblical in character, as the Books of Enoch. —**pseudepigraphic, pseudepigraphical, pseudepigraphous,** *adj.*

Scripturalism a strict compliance with the literal interpretation of the Bible. Also called **literalism.**

synoptist a Biblical scholar who arranges side-by-side excerpts from the first three Gospels to show their resemblances in event, chronology, and language. —**synoptic,** *adj.*

Targumist 1. the writer of a Targum, a translation or paraphrase into Aramaic of a portion of the Old Testament.
2. an authority on Targumic literature. —**Targumic, Targumistic,** *adj.*

textualism the practice of adhering strictly to the Scriptures. —**textualist, textuary,** *n.*

textuary a textualist. -

tropist a person who explains the Scriptures in terms of tropes, or figures of speech.

tropology a method of interpreting biblical literature emphasizing the moral implications of the tropes, or figures of speech, used in its composition. —**tropological,** *adj.*

typology the analysis of symbolism, especially of the meaning of Scripture types. —**typologist,** *n.* —**typological,** *adj.*

Yahwist the author of part of the first six books in the Old Testament, so named because of numerous references therein to God as *Yahweh* (Jehovah). Cf. **Elohist.**

44. BIOLOGY
See also 16. ANIMALS; 54. BOTANY; 72. CELLS; 244. LIFE;
302. ORGANISMS; 319. PLANTS; 430. ZOOLOGY.

abiogenesis the process of generation of living organisms from inanimate matter; spontaneous generation. —**abiogenetic,** *adj.* —**abiogenetically,** *adv.*

agamogenesis asexual reproduction. —**agamogenetic,** *adj.*

agrobiology the branch of biology that studies the relation of soil management to the nutrition, growth, and crop yield of plants. —**agrobiologist,** *n.* —**agrobiologic, agrobiological,** *adj.*

amensalism the living together of two organisms in a relationship that is destructive to one and has no effect on the other.

anamorphism gradual change in type, usually from a lower to a higher type. Also **anamorphosis,** *(Obsolete)* **anamorphosy.** —**anamorphic.,** *adj.*

anastomosis connection between parts that have branched off from each other at some earlier point. —**anastomotic,** *adj.*

anisogamy a form of reproduction in which dissimilar gametes, often differing in size, unite. —**anisogamous, anisogamic,** *adj.*

apomixis any of several processes of asexual reproduction. Cf. **parthenogenesis.**

astrosphere 1. the central part of an aster, containing the centrosome.
2. the whole aster excluding the centrosome.

autecology the branch of ecology that studies the relation of an organism to its environment. Cf. **synecology.**

auxanography the branch of microbiology that studies the rate of growth or inhibition exhibited by individual organisms in various plate-culture media. —**auxanographic,** *adj.*

auxesis growth, especially owing to an increase in cell size. Cf. **merisis.** —**auxetic,** *adj.*

biodegradability the capacity of some substances to decompose readily by biological process. —**biodegradable,** *adj.*

biogenesis, biogeny 1. the process by which living organisms develop from other living organisms.
2. the belief that living organisms can only develop from other living organisms. —**biogenic, biogenetic,** *adj.* —**biogenetically, biogenically,** *adv.*

biogeography the branch of biology that studies the geographical distribution of animals and plants.

biologism a theory or doctrine based on a biological viewpoint. —**biologistic,** *adj.*

bioluminescence the property of some organisms, as fireflies, of producing light. —**bioluminescent,** *adj.*

biometrics, biometry 1. the calculation of the probable extent of human lifespans.
2. the application to biology of mathematical and statistical theory and methods. —**biometric, biometrical,** *adj.*

bionomics, bionomy ecology. —**bionomist,** *n.* —**bionomic, bionomical,** *adj.*

biophysiology the branch of biology that studies the growth, morphology, and physiology of organs. —**biophysiologist,** *n.*

bioscience any of the sciences that deal with living organisms.

biosphere that part of the earth where most forms of life exist, specifically, where there is water or atmosphere.

biosynthesis the formation of chemical compounds by living organisms, either by synthesis or degradation. —**biosynthetic,** *adj.*

biosystematics biosystematy.

biosystematy, biosystematics the science of the classification of living things. —**biosystematic, biosystematical,** *adj.*

biotypology the science or study of biotypes, or organisms sharing the same hereditary characteristics. —**biotypologic, biotypological,** *adj.*

cataplasia degeneration of cells or tissues. —**cataplastic,** *adj.*

cetology the study of whales. —**cetologist,** *n.* —**cetological,** *adj.*

chemotropism growth or motion in response to a chemical stimulus. —**chemotropic,** *adj.*

chiasmatypy the formation of chiasma, the basis for crossing over or the interchange of corresponding chromatid segments of homologous chromosomes with their linked genes. —**chiasmatypic,** *adj.*

chorology *Biogeography.* the study of organisms, especially their migrations and distribution. —**chorologic, chorological,** *adj.*

commensalism the living together of two organisms in a relationship that is beneficial to one and has no effect on the other. —**commensal,** *adj.*

consortism a relationship of mutual dependency between two living organisms.

crustaceology the study of crustaceans. —**crustaceologist,** *n.* —**crustaceological,** *adj.*

cryptobiosis *Medicine.* a state in which the signs of life of an organism have weakened to the point where they are barely measurable or no longer measurable. —**cryptobiotic,** *adj.*

ctetology the branch of biology that studies the origin and development of acquired characteristics. —**ctetologic, ctetological,** *adj.*

cytogenetics the branch of biology that studies the structural basis of heredity and variation in living organisms from the points of view of cytology and genetics. —**cytogeneticist,** *n.* —**cytogenetic, cytogenetical,** *adj.*

cytology the branch of biology that studies the structure, growth, and pathology of cells. —**cytologist,** *n.* —**cytologic, cytological,** *adj.*

diakinesis the final stage of prophase prior to the dissolution of the nuclear membrane. —**diakinetic,** *adj.*

dialysis the process whereby colloids and crystalloids separate in solution by diffusion through a membrane. —**dialytic,** *adj.*

diapause a period of rest or quiescence between phases of growth or reproduction.

digenesis successive reproduction by two different processes, sexual in one generation and asexual in the following generation. —**digenetic,** *adj.*

digitigradism *Zoology.* the condition of walking on the toes. —**digitigrade,** *adj.*

dysmerogenesis a form of generation characterized by irregularity of constituent parts, which differ in function, time of budding, etc. Cf. **eumerogenesis.** —dysmerogenetic, *adj.*

ecdysis the process of shedding skin or other covering, typical of snakes and some insects. Cf. **endysis.** —ecdysial, *adj.*

ecology, oecology 1. the branch of biology that studies the relations between plants and animals and their environment. Also called **bionomics, bionomy.**
2. the branch of sociology that studies the environmental spacing and interdependence of people and institutions, as in rural or in urban settings. —ecologist, oecologist, *n.* —ecological, oecological, *adj.* —ecologically, oecologically, *adv.*

electrobiology the study of electrical activity in organisms and of the effect of electricity on them. —electrobiologist, *n.* —electrobiological, *adj.*

embryogeny the formation and growth of an embryo. —embryogenic, embryogenetic, *adj.*

endogenesis, endogeny the formation of cells from within. —endogenous, *adj.* —endogenicity, *n.*

endysis the growth of new scales, hair, plumage, etc. Cf. **ecdysis.** —endysial, *adj.*

enzymology the branch of biology that studies fermentation and enzymes. Also called **zymology.** —enzymologist, *n.* —enzymologic, enzymological, *adj.*

epicenism the state or quality of combining characteristics of both sexes. —epicenity, *n.* —epicene, *adj.*

epigenesis the biological theory that germ cells are structureless and the embryo develops through the action of environment on the protoplasm. Cf. **preformation.** See also 46. BIRTH; 122. DISEASE and ILLNESS; 179. GEOLOGY. —epigenetic, *adj.*

epigenesist a supporter of the theory of epigenesis.

eumerogenesis generation by unit parts, as in the tape worm, in which each part repeats the one before. Cf. **dysmerogenesis.** —eumerogenetic, *adj.*

galactosis the process of producing milk.

galvanotropism growth or movement of an organism in response to an electric current. —galvanotropic, *adj.*

gamogenesis the process of reproduction by the joining of gametes, a form of sexual reproduction. Also called **zoogamy.** —gamogenetic, *adj.*

genetics the branch of biology that studies heredity and variation in plants and animals. —geneticist, *n.* —genetic, *adj.*

gnotobiotics a branch of biology that studies animals under germ-free conditions.

Haeckelism theories and doctrines of Ernst Haeckel (1834–1919), German biologist and philosopher, especially the notion "ontogeny recapitulates phylogeny." —**Haeckelian,** *adj.*

heterogamete a gamete differing from the gamete with which it unites in sex, structure, size, or form. Cf. **isogamete.**

heterogamy 1. the condition of being heterogamous, or reproducing sexually and asexually in alternating generations.
2. the process of indirect pollination. Cf. **heterogenesis.** —**heterogamous,** *adj.*

heterogenesis 1. reproduction by a sexual and asexual process alternately. Cf. **heterogamy.**
2. reproduction in which the parent bears offspring different from itself. Cf. **xenogenesis.** —**heterogenetic,** *adj.*
3. abiogenesis.

heterolysis the destruction of the cells of one species by the enzymes or lysins of another species. —**heterolytic,** *adj.*

heterotopism heterotopy.

heterotopy, heterotopia deviation from the normal ontogenetic sequence with regard to the placing of organs or other parts. Also **heterotopism.** See also 56. BRAIN. —**heterotopous,** *adj.*

hexiology, hexicology the study of the effects of environment on an organism's growth and behavior. —**hexiological, hexicological,** *adj.*

histogenesis, histogeny the growth of organic tissues. —**histogenic, histogenetic,** *adj.*

histography a treatise or other work on organic tissues, or histogenesis. —**histographer,** *n.* —**histographic, histographical,** *adj.*

histolysis the disintegration or dissolution of organic tissues. —**histolytic,** *adj.*

homodynamy the homology of serial segments. Cf. **parhomology.**

homogenesis the normal course of generation in which the offspring resembles the parent from generation to generation. Cf. **heterogenesis.** —**homogenetic,** *adj.*

homology 1. similarity of form or structure in two or more organisms owing to common descent.
2. similarity in form or structure between different parts of an organism owing to common origin. Cf. **homodynamy.** —**homologous,** *adj.*

isogamete a gamete that is not sexually differentiated from the other gamete with which it unites. Cf. **heterogamete.**

isogamy reproduction by means of the union of isogametes. —**isogamous,** *adj.*

isogenesis the state or process of deriving from the same source or origins, as different parts deriving from the same embryo tissues. Also **isogeny.**

isogonism production of similar reproductive parts from stocks that are dissimilar, as with certain hydroids. —isogonic, *adj.*

isomorphism similarity in the form or structure of organisms that belong to a different species or genus. —isomorph, *n.* —isomorphic, *adj.*

karyology a specialty within cytology that studies the anatomy of cell nuclei with emphasis upon the nature and structure of chromosomes. —karyologist, *n.* —karyologic, karyological, *adj.*

kinetogenesis 1. the genesis of organic structure by kinetic processes.
2. the belief that the structure of animals is determined and produced by their movements. —kinetogenetic, *adj.*

Lysenkoism the theories of the 20th-century Russian geneticist Trofim Lysenko, who argued that somatic and environmental factors have a greater influence on heredity than orthodox genetics has found demonstrable; now generally discredited.

macrobiotics the branch of biology that studies longevity. —macrobiosis, *n.* —macrobiotist, *n.*

malacology the study of molluscs. —malacologist, *n.*

Mendelianism the principles or use of Mendel's law. —Mendelian, *n.*, *adj.*

merisis any form of growth, especially as a product of cell division. Cf. auxesis. —meristic, *adj.*

merogenesis the process of segmentation in which similar parts unite and form a complex individual entity from the aggregate of the parts. —merogenetic, *adj.*

metagenesis alternation of generations across reproductive cycles. Cf. xenogenesis. —metagenetic, metagenic, *adj.*

Michurinism the biological theory of Ivan Michurin who asserted the fundamental influence of environmental factors on heredity in contradiction of orthodox genetics. —Michurinist, *n.* —Michurinite, *adj.*

microtomy the science or practice of preparing extremely thin slices of tissue, etc., cut by a microtome, for study under the microscope. —microtomist, *n.* —microtomic, *adj.*

mimicry the ability of some creatures to imitate others, either by sound or appearance, or to merge with their environment for protective purposes. See also 310. PERFORMING. —mimic, mimical, *adj.*

mitosis the normal process of cell division. —mitotic, *adj.*

monogenesis 1. asexual processes of reproduction, as budding.
2. development of an ovum directly into a form like that of the parent, without metamorphosis. —monogenetic, *adj.*

monosymmetry the state of being zygomorphic, or bilaterally symmetric, or divisible into symmetrical halves by one plane only. Cf. zygomorphism. See also 316. PHYSICS. —monosymmetric, monosymmetrical, *adj.*

morphology the study of the form and structure of plants and animals. —morphologist, *n.* —morphologic, morphological, *adj.*

mutualism the living together of two organisms in a mutually beneficial relationship.

neontology the scientific study of recently living plants and animals. —neontologist, *n.* —neontologic, neontological, *adj.*

ontogenesis ontogeny. —ontogenetic, ontogenetical, *adj.*

ontogeny the life cycle, development, or developmental history of an organism. Also ontogenesis. —ontogenic, *adj.* —ontogenic, *adj.*

oogamy the union of sexually differentiated reproductive cells. —oogamous, *adj.*

oogenesis the formative process of the ovum in preparation for fertilization and subsequent development. —oogenetic, *adj.*

ooscopy observation of the development of an embryo inside an egg by means of an ooscope.

organogenesis, organogeny the origin and growth of organs. —organogenetic, organogenic, *adj.*

organography the scientific description of the organs of plants and animals. —organographist, *n.* —organographic, organographical, *adj.*

organology the study of the structure and organs of plants and animals. —organologist, *n.* —organologic, organological, *adj.*

organonomy 1. the laws of organic life.
2. the doctrine upon which these laws are based. —organonomic, *adj.*

organonymy the nomenclature of organs. —organonymal, —organonymic, *adj.*

orthogamy the property or process of self-fertilization, as in certain plants and animals. —orthogamous, *adj.*

orthogenesis progressive evolution, leading to the development of a new form, as can be seen through successive generations. See also 376. SOCIETY. —orthogenetic, *adj.*

ovism the theory that the female reproductive cell contains the entire organism and that the male cell does not contribute anything, merely initiating the growth of the female cell.

ovology the study of the formation and structure of animal ova. —ovologist, *n.* —ovological, *adj.*

palynology the science that studies live and fossil spores, pollen grains, and other microscopic plant structures. —polynologist, *n.* —polynological, *adj.*

parabiosis the uniting of two individual organisms or animals anatomically and physiologically, under either experimental or natural conditions. —parabiotic, *adj.*

parasitism the living together of two organisms in a relationship that is beneficial to one and destructive to the other. —parasitic, parasitical, *adj.*

parasitology the branch of biology that studies parasites and parasitism. —parasitologist, *n.*

parhomology the biological process of imitative homodynamy. —parhomologous, *adj.*

parthenogenesis, parthogeny reproduction without fertilization, as certain ova, seeds and spores, insects, algae, etc. Also called unigenesis. —parthenogenetic, parthenogenic, *adj.*

photoperiodism, photoperiodicity the effect on the growth and reproduction of plants or animals of varying exposures to light and darkness. Cf. thermoperiodism. —photoperiod, *n.* —photoperiodic, *adj.*

photosynthesis the synthesis of complex organic substances from carbon dioxide, water, and inorganic salts, with sunlight as the energy source and a catalyst such as chlorophyll. —photosynthetic, *adj.*

phototropism growth or motion in response to light. —phototropic, *adj.*

physiogeny the history or science of the development or evolution of vital activities in the individual and the genesis of organic functions; a division of ontogeny. Also called physiogenesis. —physiogenetic, physiogenic, *adj.*

phytobiology plant biology. —phytobiologist, *n.* —phytobiological, *adj.*

pleomorphism, pleomorphy the existence of a plant or animal in two or more distinct forms during a life cycle. Also called polymorphism. —pleomorphic, pleomorphous, *adj.*

polygenesis 1. derivation from more than one kind of cell in the generative process.
2. Also called polygenism. the theory that different species have descended from different original ancestors. Cf. monogenesis. —polygenic, polygenetic, *adj.*

polyphagia, polyphagy the tendency to eat a wide variety of food. —polyphagist, *n.* —polyphagic, *adj.*

polyzoism the character of being made up of a number of smaller organisms that are acting as a colony. —polyzoic, *adj.*

preformation the theory that germ cells contain every part of the future organism in miniature form, future development being only a matter of increase in size. Cf. epigenesis.

preformationism the theory that an organism is fully formed at conception and that reproduction is thereafter simply a process of growth. —preformationist, *n.*

protozoology the study of protozoa, especially of those that cause disease. —protozoological, *adj.* —protozoologist, *n.*

psychobiology 1. the branch of biology that studies the interactions of body and mind, especially as exhibited in the nervous system.
2. psychology as studied in terms of biology. —psychobiologist, *n.* —psychobiologic, psychobiological, *adj.*

speciation the formation of new species.

spermism an obsolete biological theory that stated that sperm contained the preformed germ or the embryo. —spermist, *n.*

spongology the science and study of the sponges. —spongologist, *n.*

sporogenesis 1. the process of reproduction by means of spores.
2. the formation and growth of spores. —sporogenetic, sporogenous, *adj.*

stereotaxis orientation or movement of an organism in response to the stimulus of a solid object. Cf. stereotropism. —stereotactic, *adj.*

stereotropism growth or movement determined by contact with a solid. Cf. stereotaxis. Also thigmotropism. —stereotropic, *adj.*

stirpiculture selective breeding to develop strains with particular characteristics. —stirpicultural, *adj.*

superfetation a conception occurring during a pregnancy from an earlier conception.

symbiosis the living together of two dissimilar organisms; the relationship may be beneficial to both (mutualism and symbiosis), beneficial to one without effect on the other (commensalism), beneficial to one and detrimental to the other (parasitism), detrimental to the first without any effect on the other (amensalism), or detrimental to both (synnecrosis). —symbiotic, *adj.*

symphytism *Rare.* the tendency of two separate elements to grow together. —symphytic, *adj.*

synecology the branch of ecology that studies the relation of various groups of organisms to their common environment. Cf. autecology.

synnecrosis the living together of two organisms in a mutually destructive relationship.

teratology the branch of biology that studies abnormal formations in animals or plants. —teratologist, *n.* —teratologic, teratological, *adj.*

testaceology the study of the shell-bearing animals. —testaceological, *adj.*

thermoperiodism, thermoperiodicity the effect on the growth and reproduction of plants or animals of timed exposures to varied temperatures. —thermoperiod, *n.* —thermoperiodic, *adj.*

therology the study of animals. —**therologist,** *n.* —**therologic, therological,** *adj.*

thigmotaxis involuntary response or reaction to the touch of outside objects or bodies, as in motile cells. —**thigmotactic,** *adj.*

thigmotropism stereotropism. —**thigmotropic,** *adj.*

ultrastructure the submicroscopic, elemental structure of protoplasm. —**ultrastructural,** *adj.*

unigenesis parthenogenesis. —**unigenetic,** *adj.*

uterogestation the process of gestation taking place in the womb from conception to birth.

xenogenesis, xenogeny 1. abiogenesis; spontaneous generation.
2. metagenesis, or alternation of generations.
3. production of an offspring entirely different from either of the parents. —**xenogenetic, xenogenic,** *adj.*

zoogamy gamogenesis. —**zoogamous,** *adj.*

zygomorphism the state or quality of being bilaterally symmetrical, as certain organisms. Cf. **monosymmetry.** —**zygomorphic, zygomorphous,** *adj.*

zygosis the biological process of conjugation; the union of cells or gametes. —**zygose,** *adj.*

zymogenesis the process in which a zymogen becomes an enzyme, as in the fermentation process. —**zymogenic, zymogenous,** *adj.*

zymology enzymology. —**zymologist,** *n.* —**zymologic,** *adj.*

45. BIRDS
See also 16. ANIMALS; 88. COCKS.

anthropoglot an animal with a tongue like that of man, as the parrot.

avicide the killing of birds.

aviculture the raising or keeping of birds. —**aviculturist,** *n.*

caliology *Rare.* the study of birds' nests.

columbary a structure for keeping doves or pigeons; a dovecote or pigeon loft. Also **columbarium.**

falconry the practice of training and hunting with falcons or hawks.

heronry the breeding place of a colony of herons.

neossology the study of young birds.

nidification the process or instinct of nest-building.

nidology the study of birds' nests. —**nidologist,** *n.*

oograph a device for reproducing the outline of a bird's egg.

oology the branch of ornithology that collects and studies birds' eggs. —**oologist,** *n.* —**oologic, oological,** *adj.*

oometer a device for measuring eggs.

ooscopy observation of the development of an embryo inside an egg by means of an ooscope.

ornithology the branch of zoology that studies birds. —ornithologist, *n.* —ornithologic, ornithological, *adj.*

ornithomancy, ornithoscopy the observation of birds, especially in flight, for the purpose of divination.

ornithomania an abnormal love of birds.

ornithophobia an abnormal fear of birds.

ornithosis psittacosis, particularly in birds other than those of the parrot family.

ornithotomy the anatomy of birds. —ornithotomist, *n.* —ornithotomical, *adj.*

penisterophily *Rare.* the raising and training of pigeons.

poultry domestic fowl, particularly those raised for food or laying eggs.

psittacosis a disease of parrots and other birds communicable to human beings. —psittacotic, *adj.*

pteronophobia an abnormal fear of feathers.

pterylology the branch of ornithology that studies the areas upon which birds grow feathers. Also pterylography.

rookery a breeding or nesting place of rooks or of any gregarious bird or animal.

totipalmation the state of having all four toes fully webbed, as water birds. —totipalmate, *adj.*

virilescence a condition of some animals, and especially of some fowls, in which the female, when old, assumes some of the characteristics of the male of the species. —virilescent, *adj.*

volitation flight, the act of flying, or the ability to fly.

46. BIRTH
See also 281. MOTHER; 327. PREGNANCY.

amniomancy a form of divination by examining the embryonic sac or amniotic fluid.

autogeny, autogony the spontaneous generation of an organism in an inorganic fluid medium. —autogenous, autogenic, autogonic, autogonous, *adj.* —autogenously, autogonously, *adv.*

digoneutism the ability to produce two broods in a year. —digoneutic, *adj.*

epigenesis the theory that embryonic development is totally controlled by the cell's environment. Cf. syngenesis. —epigenesist, *n.* —epigenetic, *adj.*

epimorphosis development of an organism or form of animal life in which body segmentation is complete before hatching. —epimorphic, *adj.*

fetation, foetation the development of a fetus; gestation.

geniture *Obsolete.* birth; the process of generation.

gestation 1. the process of carrying in the womb.
2. fetation; the process of development of the fetus in the womb.

gravidity pregnancy. —gravid, *adj.*

hysterology scientific study of the uterus.

Lamaze technique psychoprophylaxis.

maieusiophobia tocophobia.

midwifery the principles and practice of a midwife. Cf. tocology.

multiparity the condition or process of producing more than one offspring at one birth. —multiparous, *adj.*

nativity 1. the time, place, and circumstances of a person's birth.
2. the configuration of the planets at the time of a person's birth and a representation, as a chart, of that configuration.

nulliparity the condition in a woman of never having given birth. —nullipara, *n.* —nulliparous, *adj.*

obstetrics the branch of medicine that deals with prenatal and postnatal care and with the delivery of a child. —obstetrician, *n.* —obstetric, obstetrical, *adj.*

omphalomancy a form of divination in which the number of knots in a newborn's umbilical cord are counted to foretell the number of children the mother will have later.

omphalotomy the surgical process of dividing the umbilical cord.

oviparism the bearing of offspring by laying eggs that mature outside of the body. —oviparity, *n.* —oviparous, *adj.*

ovoviviparism the bearing of offspring by producing eggs that mature within the body, with the young born alive. —ovoviviparity, *n.* —ovoviviparous, *adj.*

oxytocic a substance or drug that induces or stimulates childbirth. —oxytocic, *adj.*

palingenesis 1. partial or complete regeneration.
2. the doctrine that a soul passes through several bodies in a series of rebirths. Also palingenesia, palingenesy. —palingenetic, *adj.*

parity the state, quality, or fact of having given birth to or having borne offspring.

parturiency the state or condition of bringing forth young or being about to begin parturition. —parturient, *adj.*

parturition childbirth; the act or process of giving birth. —**parturient,** *adj.*

primigravida a woman who is pregnant for the first time.

primipara a woman who has given birth to one child or who is giving birth for the first time. —**primiparity,** *n.* —**primiparous,** *adj.*

psychoprophylaxis a method of preparing women for childbirth without anesthetic, by means of education, psychological and physical conditioning, and breathing exercises. Also called **Lamaze technique.** —**psychoprophylactic,** *adj.*

puerperium the state or condition of a woman during and immediately following childbirth. —**puerperal,** *adj.*

recrudescence the process of renewal or rebirth. —**recrudescent,** *adj.*

regeneracy the act or quality of being renewed, reformed, or reborn, especially in a spiritual rebirth. —**regenerate,** *adj.*

regenesis the act or process of renewal or rebirth.

secundigravida a woman who is pregnant for the second time.

spermicide a substance or preparation used for killing sperm, used in contraception. —**spermicidal,** *adj.*

superfetation a conception occurring after the onset of a pregnancy from an earlier conception.

syngenesis the theory that the form and development of the embryo are the result of the combined influence of sperm and egg. Cf. **epigenesis.** —**syngenetic,** *adj.*

thoracopagus a fetal abnormality, consisting of twins joined at the thorax.

tocology, tokology the science of obstetrics or midwifery. —**tocologist, tokologist,** *n.* —**tocological, tokological,** *adj.*

tocophobia, tokophobia an abnormal fear of childbirth. Also called **maieusiophobia.**

unigravida primigravida.

uterogestation the process of gestation taking place in the womb from conception to birth.

vasectomy surgical excision of part of the vas deferens, the duct which carries sperm from the testes, performed as a form of male contraception.

viviparism the bearing of living offspring, characteristic of almost all mammals, many reptiles, and some fishes. —**viviparity,** *n.* —**viviparous,** *adj.*

47. BLACKENING and BLACKNESS
See also 110. DARKNESS.

denigration literally, blackening; commonly, the sullying or defaming of a person, organization, or institution. —**denigrator,** *n.*

melanism a darkening caused by an unusually high amount of pigmentation in the skin, hair, and eyes.

melanosis abnormal production and presence of melanin, a black pigment, in the body tissues. —melanotic, *adj*.

melanosity darkness or blackness of eyes, hair, or complexion.

nigrescence the process of becoming black; blackness, as of the skin. —nigrescent, *adj*.

nigritude the condition of being black; blackness.

phaeism an intermediate darkening of the skin, hair, and eyes, of insufficient degree to be called melanism.

48. BLINDNESS
See also 148. EYES.

ablepsia, ablepsy a lack or loss of sight. —ableptical, *adj*.

amaurosis a condition of partial or total blindness, caused by a disease of the optic nerve. —amaurotic, *adj*.

amblyopia, amblyopy obscurity of vision, occurring without any organic change in the eyes; the first stage of amaurosis. —amblyopic, *adj*.

anopsy, anopsia, anoöpsia blindness.

cecity blindness.

chionablepsia *Medicine*. the condition of snow blindness.

eluscation *Obsolete*. the state of having defective eyesight; purblindness.

excecation *Obsolete*. the process of blinding.

glaucoma a disease of the eyes, in which the eyeball hardens and becomes tense, often resulting in blindness. —glaucomatous, *adj*.

hemeralopia the loss of sight in daylight. —hemeralopic, *adj*.

noctograph a writing frame designed for use by blind people.

nyctalopia the loss of sight in darkness. —nyctalopic, *adj*.

optophone a device combining a selenium cell and telephone apparatus that converts light energy into sound energy, used to enable blind people to sense light through the hearing and thus read printed matter.

scotograph an instrument for writing when unable to see.

scotoma, scotomy a blind spot or blind area in the field of vision.

typhlology the totality of medical knowledge concerning the causes, treatment, and prevention of blindness.

typhlophile a person who devotes himself to helping the blind.

typhlosis blindness. —typhlotic, *adj*.

49. BLOOD and BLOOD VESSELS

acidosis *Medicine.* a condition of the blood in which the alkali reserve is lower than normal. Also called **acid intoxication, autointoxication.** —**acidotic,** *adj.*

aneurism, aneurysm a disease of the artery wall that causes a localized dilatation of the artery and a pulsating tumor.

angiography the scientific description of blood vessels. —**angiographic, angiographical,** *adj.*

angiology the branch of anatomy that studies the blood vessels and the lymphatics.

angiopathology the pathology of, or changes seen in, diseased blood vessels.

anoxemia a lowering of the normal level of oxygen in the blood, often experienced at high altitudes.

diapedesis the process in which blood corpuscles soak into surrounding tissue through the natural pores of the blood vessels.

ecchymosis 1. the secretion of blood from a blood vessel into the surrounding tissue as a result of a bruise.
2. the bruise or discoloration thus caused.

embolism the sudden obstruction of a blood vessel by a foreign object, as an air bubble or a blood clot.

enriositatis drunkenness or intoxication from alcohol, especially as a habitual state.

enterotoxemia a condition in which the blood contains toxin from the intestines.

epistaxis bleeding from the nose; nosebleed.

erythrocytometer a device for measuring the count of red blood cells in the blood.

erythrocytometry measurement of the red blood cells in the blood by use of an erythrocytometer.

hemadynamometry the measurement of blood pressure.

hemaphobia, haemaphobia, hemophobia an abnormal fear of the sight of blood. Also **hematophobia.**

hematidrosis, haematidrosis the excretion of bloody sweat.

hematocrit, haematocrit a centrifuge used for separating blood cells from the plasma.

hematology, haematology the branch of medical science that studies the morphology of the blood and blood-forming tissues. —**hematologist, haematologist,** *n.* —**hematologic, haematologic, hematological, haematological,** *adj.*

hematomancy, haematomancy divination by means of blood.

hematophobia, haematophobia hemaphobia.

hematopoiesis, haematopoiesis the formation of blood. —hematopoietic, haematopoietic, *adj.*

hematosis, haematosis 1. hematopoiesis.
2. the conversion of venous blood into arterial blood by oxygenation in the lungs.

hemautography a method of tracing variations in blood pressure by having an arterial jet mark a special tracing paper. —hemautograph, *n.* —hemautographic, *adj.*

hemolysis, haemolysis the breaking down of erythrocytes with liberation of hemoglobin in the blood. —hemolytic, haemolytic, *adj.*

hemopathology, haemopathology, hemapathology, haematopathology the branch of medical science that studies the diseases of the blood.

hemophilia, haemophilia a tendency to uncontrolled bleeding. Also hemorrhaphilia, haemorrhaphilia. —hemophiliac, haemophiliac, *n.*, *adj.*

hemostasis, haemostasis the stoppage of bleeding or cessation of the circulation of the blood; stagnation of the blood in a part of the body. Also hemostasia, haemostasia.

hemostatic, haemostatic a styptic agent or substance. —hemostatic, haemostatic, *adj.*

homoiothermy, homoiothermism the state or condition of being warmblooded, as mammals and other animals. Cf. poikilothermy. —homoiothermal, homoiothermic, homoiothermous, homeothermal, homiothermal, *adj.*

hyperemia, hyperaemia a congestion of the blood, occurring in any part of the body. —hyperemic, hyperaemic, *adj.*

hypostasis a deposit or sediment, particularly a settling of blood in lower parts of the body as a result of a slowing down in the circulation. —hypostatic, hypostatical, *adj.*

manometer 1. an instrument for measuring the pressure of gases or vapors.
2. an instrument for measuring blood pressure. Also called sphygmanometer. —manometric, *adj.*

melanemia, melanaemia a disease of the blood, distinguished by the presence in the blood of black pigment.

pachyemia, pachyaemia thickening of the blood.

phagocyte a blood cell that ingests and destroys bacteria, foreign particles and other cells in the bloodstream. —phagocytic, *adj.*

phagocytosis the action of phagocytes in ingesting and destroying cells.

phlebography the scientific description of vein structure. —phlebographical, *adj.*

phlebology the study of the veins. —phlebological, *adj.*

phlebotomy a medical treatment involving incision of a vein; bloodletting. Also called venesection. —phlebotomist, *n.* —phlebotomize, *v.* —phlebotomic, phlebotomical, *adj.*

poikilothermy, poikilothermism the state or condition of being cold-blooded, as reptiles and other animals. Cf. homoiothermy. —poikilothermal, poikilothermic, poikilothermous, *adj.*

sapremia, sapraemia blood poisoning caused by putrefactive microorganisms in the bloodstream.

sepsis blood poisoning caused by absorption into the blood of pathogenic microorganisms. —septic, *adj.*

septicemia, septicaemia blood poisoning caused by pathogenic microorganisms and their toxic products in the bloodstream. —septicemic, —septicaemic, *adj.*

sphygmography the scientific description or recording of the pulse. —sphygmograph, *n.* —sphygmographic, sphygmographical, *adj.*

sphygmology *Medicine.* the sum of what is known about the pulse.

sphygmomanometer manometer, def. 2.

stypticity the property of being astringent or tending to halt bleeding by contraction of the tissues. —styptic, *adj.*

toxemia, toxaemia 1. a condition of illness due to the presence in the bloodstream of toxins.
2. blood poisoning. —toxemic, toxaemic, *adj.*

uremia, uraemia a toxic condition resulting from the presence of urinary constituents in the blood, caused by deficiencies in the secretion of urine. —uremic, uraemic, *adj.*

50. BODILY FUNCTIONS
See also 51. BODY, HUMAN.

deglutition the process or act of swallowing.

desquamation the shedding of the superficial epithelium, as of skin, the mucous membranes, etc.

diaphoresis sweating, especially when artificially induced. —diaphoretic, *adj.*

diastalsis the contraction of the alimentary canal in a downward direction as part of peristalsis.

diuresis an abnormally heavy or increased discharge or flow of urine. —diuretic, *n.*, *adj.*

egestion 1. the process of discharging waste matter from the body.
2. the matter discharged.

eructation 1. the process of belching.
2. that which is regurgitated in belching.

excretion the natural process of eliminating bodily wastes in the feces and urine.

galactosis the bodily process of producing milk.

gustation 1. the act of tasting.
2. the sense of taste.

introsusception intussusception.

intussusception the process by which food or other matter is taken into the body and converted into tissue. Also **introsusception**. —intussusceptive, *adj.*

lachrymation, lacrimation the act or process of shedding tears; weeping.

lactation 1. the secretion of milk by a mammary gland.
2. the period during which secretion takes place.

manducation the act or process of chewing or eating. —manducatory, *adj.*

micturition urination. —micturate, *v.*

olfaction 1. the sense of smell.
2. the act of smelling. —olfactory, olfactive, *adj.*

oscitation the act of yawning, as from fatigue or sleepiness.

osteoclasis the process by which bone tissue is broken down and absorbed by the body. See also 52. BONES.

pandiculation the process of yawning and stretching.

parhidrosis abnormally excessive perspiration.

peristalsis the process of contraction and relaxation by which products are moved through the alimentary canal. Cf. **diastalsis**. —peristaltic, *adj.*

polyuria the passing of an abornomally large amount of urine. —polyuric, *adj.*

proteolysis the breaking down or hydrolysis of proteins into simpler compounds, as in digestion. —proteolytic, *adj.*

protopepsia the primary system or process of digestion.

purulence, purulency 1. the state or condition of containing or secreting pus.
2. the production or generation of pus or similar matter. —purulent, *adj.*

pyrosis a burning feeling in the stomach and esophagus, sometimes accompanied by the belching of acid fluid; heartburn.

secernment *Rare.* the process of secretion. —secernent, *n.*, *adj.*

sialagogue a medicine or substance that stimulates the flow of saliva. —sialagogic, *n.*, *adj.*

sialorrhea, sialorrhoea the act or process of salivation.

stasis cessation in the flow of any of the bodily fluids, as the blood.

sternutation 1. the act of sneezing.
2. a sneeze. —sternutative, sternutatory, *adj.*

transudation the act or process of oozing or exuding or being exuded, as the process by which sweat passes through pores. —transudatory, *adj.*

urination the process of expelling fluids from the body in the urine.

vomition the act or process of vomiting.

vomiturition repeated but unsuccessful attempts to vomit; retching or slight vomiting.

51. BODY, HUMAN
See also 14. ANATOMY; 50. BODILY FUNCTIONS.

acrocephaly *Medicine.* having a high, pointed skull. Also called oxycephaly. —acrocephalic, acrocephalous, *adj.*

acromegaly *Medicine.* a disease resulting from abnormal activity of the pituitary gland in which bones of the extremities are enlarged. —acromegalic, *adj., n.*

adiposity the state of being obese. —adipose, *adj.*

anatomy the study of the body and its parts. —anatomist, *n.* —anatomical, *adj.*

androgynism, androgyny the possession of the characteristics of both sexes; hermaphroditism. Also androgyneity. —androgynous, *adj.*

ankylophobia a dread of stiff or immobile joints.

atonicity, atony lack of tone or tonus in the body; poor muscular condition. Cf. tonicity. —atonic, *adj.*

bioastronautics the science that studies the effects of space travel on life, especially human life and the human body.

bionics 1. the science or study of how man and animals perform tasks and solve certain types of problems involving use of the body.
2. the application of this study to the design of computer-driven and other automated equipment.
3. the application of this study to the design of artificial limbs, organs, and other prosthetic devices. —bionic, *adj.*

biophysiology the branch of biology that studies the growth, morphology, and physiology of organs. —biophysiologist, *n.*

biopsy the removal of a fragment of living tissue from the body for medical study. —bioptic, *adj.*

bisexualism, bisexuality the condition of combining male and female sexual characteristics in one body. See also 364. SEX. —bisexual, *adj.*

callipygia, callipygy the state of having well-shaped buttocks. Cf. steatopygia. —callipygian, callipygous, *adj.*

carnosity *Obsolete.* fleshiness; obesity.

caseation the change in consistency of tissue to a soft, cheeselike form, as in tuberculosis.

claudication a limp or limping movement.

clonism a state or condition in which the muscles undergo clonus, or rapid flexion and extension. —**clonic,** *adj.*

coenesthesia, coenesthesis, cenesthesia, cenesthesis the combination of organic sensations that comprise an individual's awareness of bodily existence. —**coenesthetic, cenesthetic,** *adj.*

deuteropathy an affection of the body that is secondary to and resulting from another affection.

diarthrosis a joint or articulation, as that at the knee, which allows maximum movement.

ectomorphy the condition or state of being an ectomorph, i.e., having a light, slender body structure. —**ectomorphic,** *adj.*

emaceration *Obsolete.* the act of making or becoming lean; emaciation.

endomorphy the condition or state of being an endomorph, i.e., having a rounded, stocky body structure with a tendency to obesity. Also called **pyknic.** —**endomorphic,** *adj.*

epicenism the state or quality of combining characteristics of both sexes. —**epicenity,** *n.* —**epicene,** *adj.*

excrescence 1. a normal outgrowth of the body, as hair, fingernails.
2. an abnormal outgrowth, as a corn, wart, etc. —**excrescent,** *adj.*

formication a body sensation that feels as if ants are crawling over the skin.

gynandrism, gynandry hermaphroditism. Also **gynandry.** —**gynandroid,** *n.,* *adj.*

gynecomastism an excessive development of mammary glands in males. Also **gynecomastia, gynecomasty.**

hermaphroditism the presence on an individual body of both male and female sex organs. Also called **androgynism, gynandrism, gynandry.** —**hermaphrodite,** *n.* —**hermaphroditic,** *adj.*

hyperkinesia, hyperkinesis a condition of the body in which muscular movement is abnormally agitated. —**hyperkinetic,** *adj.*

hypertrophy excessive growth of tissue or of an organ, independent of and out of proportion to the rest of the body. Cf. **hypoplasia.** —**hypertrophic, hypertrophical, hypertrophous,** *adj.*

hypoplasia a condition in which tissue or an organ of the body fails to grow to normal size. Cf. **hypertrophy.** —**hypoplastic,** *adj.*

hypothermia a condition in which the body temperature is abnormally low. —hypothermal, *adj.*

ichor a thin watery substance discharged from wounds or ulcers. See also 183. GOD and GODS. —ichorous, *adj.*

ictus *Medicine.* 1. a stroke or beat, as the beat of the pulse. See also 409. VERSE.
2. a paralytic stroke.

jactitation *Medicine.* twitching of the muscles or of other parts of the body. Also called **jactation.**

kinesiology *Medicine.* the study of the motions of the human body, especially as they apply to therapy through corrective exercise. Also called kinestherapy. —kinesiologic, kinesiological, *adj.*

kyphosis an abnormal condition of the spine in which it has a hump, kyphos, or curvature. —kyphotic, *adj.*

leptosomy ectomorphy. —leptosome, *n.* —leptosomic, leptosomatic, *adj.*

lordosis any abnormal curvature of the bones, especially forward curvature of the spine, resulting in a hollow in the back. —lordotic, *adj.*

macrosomatia the condition of having an abnormally large body. —macrosomatous, *adj.*

marasmus 1. a wasting away or atrophying of the body in the absence of disease.
2. the progressive emaciation that results from malnutrition. —marasmic, *adj.*

mesomorphy the condition or state of being a mesomorph, i.e., having an athletic body structure. —mesomorphic, *adj.*

microcephalism the condition of having an abnormally small head. Also microcephaly. —microcephalous, microcephalic, *adj.*

myoatrophy atrophy or wasting away of the muscles.

myotonia a condition of tonic muscle spasm or rigidity of the muscles. —myotonic, *adj.*

necrosis the death or decay of body tissue, the result of loss of blood supply or trauma. —necrotic, *adj.*

neoplasia the growth or formation of a neoplasm. —neoplastic, *adj.*

neoplasm any abnormal formation or growth of tissue, as a tumor. —neoplastic, *adj.*

orthopraxy, orthopraxis the use of mechanical apparatus or devices to correct bodily deformities.

orthosis the process of correcting bodily or mental distortion. —orthotic, *adj.*

osmidrosis an abnormal condition in which the sweat has a very strong odor.

osteoporosis the rarefaction of bone, resulting in abnormally porous and weak bony tissue.

oxycephaly acrocephaly. —oxycephalic, oxycephalous, *adj.*

oxygeusia extreme acuteness or sensitivity of the sense of taste.

paralysis abnormal loss of muscle function or of sensation. —paralytic, *n.*, *adj.*

paresis a state or process of partial paralysis. —paretic, *adj.*

paresthesia, paraesthesia any abnormal physical sensation, as itching, a tickling feeling, etc. —paresthetic, paraesthetic, *adj.*

pectoriloquism, pectoriloquy the transmission of the voice through the chest wall, so that it can be picked up by direct listening against the chest or with a stethoscope. It frequently indicates an abnormality in the lungs. —pectoriloquial, pectoriloquous, *adj.*

phocomelia, phocomely a deformity, usually congenital, in which the extremities of the limbs are abnormally short.

pinguidity the state or quality of being fat or unctuous. —pinguid, *adj.*

pneumology the scientific study of the human respiratory system. —pneumological, *adj.*

polymastism the condition of having more than two breasts. Also polymastia. —polymastic, *adj.*

psychroesthesia an abnormal condition in which part of the body, though actually warm, is felt as cold.

pulsimeter, pulsometer an instrument for measuring the rate of the pulse.

radiosensibility sensitivity to the effects of radiation, as of parts of the body. Also radiosensitivity. —radiosensible, *adj.*

rhigosis the feeling or sensation of coldness.

rictus the opening of the mouth, especially in a grimace or expression of pain.

rotundity the state or quality of being round or plump. —rotund, *adj.*

schematomancy divination of a person's future from observation of physical appearance.

sclerosis a hardening of body tissues or other parts, as by an excessive growth of fibrous connective tissue. See also 319. PLANTS. —sclerotic, *adj.*

scoliosis lateral curvature of the spine. —scoliotic, *adj.*

somatology the branch of anthropology that studies man's physical characteristics. Also physical anthropology, somatics. —somatologic, somatological, *adj.*

somatotype a particular type of human physique. Cf. ectomorphy, endomorphy, mesomorphy.

steatopygia, steatopygy excessive fatness of the hips and buttocks. Cf. callipygia. —steatopygic, *adj.*

syntexis the wasting of the body, as in consumption. —syntectic, syntectical, *adj.*

tabes any disease that wastes the body; atrophy. —tabetic, *n.*, *adj.*

tabescence 1. the process of emaciation or wasting of the body.
2. the condition of being wasted or in decay, especially as a gradual process. —tabescent, *adj.*

tabitude the state of being affected by tabes or by gradual wasting or decay.

tonicity the state or quality of muscular tone or tension. —tonic, *adj.*

torticollis a condition characterized by involuntary contraction of the cervical muscles, causing a twisting of the neck; wryneck.

tricrotism the condition of having three arterial beats for every one heartbeat, as in certain pulses. —tricrotic, *adj.*

turgescence, turgescency 1. the process of swelling.
2. the state of being swollen. —turgescent, *adj.*

valgus 1. an abnormally turned condition of a bone in part of the human body, especially the leg.
2. the condition of being bow-legged.

vellication a twitching, as of a part of the body; convulsive movement of a muscle.

ventripotence obesity, particularly in the region of the stomach. —ventripotent, *adj.*

ventrosity *Rare.* largeness of the belly; corpulence, especially in the abdominal region.

xeransis a dried or desiccated condition of the body. Also xerosis. —xerantic, *adj.*

xerotes a dry condition or tendency to dryness of the body. —xerotic, *adj.*

zonesthesia a feeling or sensation of constriction in the body, as from wearing a tight belt.

zooplasty the process of surgically grafting tissue from a lower animal onto the human body. —zooplastic, *adj.*

52. BONES
See also 14. ANATOMY; 51. BODY, HUMAN.

acromegaly *Medicine.* a disease resulting from abnormal activity of the pituitary gland in which bones of the extremities are enlarged. —acromegalic, *adj.*

agmatology 1. a branch of medical science that studies fractures.
2. a treatise on fractures.

atomy *Obsolete.* a skeleton.

comminution the breaking of a bone into small pieces.

cornification organic change into a hornlike form.

craniography the science of skull description. —**craniographer,** *n.* —**craniographic, craniographical,** *adj.*

diaphysis the shaft section of a long bone. —**diaphytical,** *adj.*

diarthrosis a joint or articulation, as that at the knee, which allows maximum movement.

exostosis an abnormal calcareous growth on a bone or tooth. See also 319. PLANTS.

gargoylism an abnormal physical condition characterized by extensive structural defects of the skeleton and by gross mental deficiency.

gomphosis an immovable joint, the bone being fixed in its socket in such a way that it does not move.

lordosis any abnormal curvature of the bones, especially forward curvature of the spine, resulting in a hollow in the back. —**lordotic,** *adj.*

luxation 1. the act of dislocating a bone or putting a joint out of position.
2. the condition of dislocation or being out of joint.

ossuarium, ossuary a place or receptacle for the bones of the dead. See also 112. DEATH.

osteoclasis the breaking of a bone either to correct a deformity or to reset a bone that has healed badly after a fracture. See also 50. BODILY FUNCTIONS.

osteography the study of bones for descriptive purposes. —**osteographer,** *n.* —**osteographic, osteographical,** *adj.*

osteology the branch of anatomy that studies the skeleton. Also called skeletology. —**osteologist, osteologer,** *n.* —**osteologic, osteological,** *adj.*

osteomalacia softening of the bones resulting from malnutrition and the consequent loss of essential salts from the bones.

osteomancy, osteomanty divination by the examination of bones. —**osteomantic,** *adj.*

osteometry the measurement of bones.

osteopathology 1. study of diseases of the bones.
2. any disease of the bone. —**osteopathologist,** *n.* —**osteopathologic, osteopathological,** *adj.*

osteopathy 1. a disease of the bone.
2. a therapeutic system based upon the premise that restoring or maintaining health requires manipulation of the skeleton and muscles to preserve normal structure. —**osteopath, osteopathist,** *n.* —**osteopathic,** *adj.*

osteoplasty the surgical practice of bone-grafting.

osteoporosis the rarefaction of bone, resulting in abnormally porous and weak bony tissue.

osteotomy 1. the dissection or anatomy of bones.
2. the cutting of bones as part of a surgical operation. —osteotomist, *n.*

ostosis ossification or the process of bone formation.

scapulomancy a form of divination in which a shoulder blade is heated in a fire and the resulting cracks in the bone are consulted for omens. —scapulomantic, *adj.*

siagonology the study of jawbones. —siagonologic, siagonological, *adj.*

skeletology osteology.

spatulamancy a form of divination by means of an animal's shoulder blade. —spatulamantic, *adj.*

symphysis the growing together or the fixed or almost fixed union of two bones, as the two halves of the lower jaw. —symphyseal, symphysial, symphystic, *adj.*

syssarcosis the joining of two or more bones by muscle.

valgus 1. an abnormally turned condition of a bone in part of the human body, especially the leg.
2. the condition of being bow-legged.

53. BOOKS
See also 29. AUTHORS; 43. BIBLE; 256. MANUSCRIPTS; 328. PRINTING; 346. READING.

abridgment, abridgement a shortened or condensed form of a book, article, etc.

addendum a supplement or appendix added to a book or other written work.

adversaria 1. a commonplace book.
2. a miscellany, in published or other collected form.

bibliogenesis bibliogony. —bibliogenetic, *adj.*

bibliognost a person who possesses an encyclopedic knowledge of books and bibliography. —bibliognostic, *adj.*

bibliogony the making of books; book production. Also bibliogenesis.

bibliography 1. the science that studies the history of books, noting their physical description, publication, and editions.
2. a list of books on a particular subject or by a particular author.
3. a list of source materials used or consulted in the preparation of a work or referred to in the text. —bibliographer, *n.* —bibliographic, bibliographical, *adj.*

bibliokleptomania an abnormal compulsion to steal books. Cf. bibliomania. —biblioklept, *n.*

bibliolater, bibliolatrist a person who is excessively fond of books. See also 43. BIBLE.

bibliolatry the worship of books, especially the Bible.

bibliology 1. the history of books; bibliography.
2. the study of the doctrines of the Bible. —**bibliologist,** *n.*

bibliomancy a form of divination using books, especially the Bible, in which passages are chosen at random and the future foretold from them.

bibliomania an excessive fondness for acquiring and possessing books. —**bibliomaniac,** *n.* —**bibliomaniacal,** *adj.*

bibliopegy the art of binding books. —**bibliopegist,** *n.* —**bibliopegic,** *adj.*

bibliophage a bookworm (literally, 'bookeater'). —**bibliophagy,** *n.* —**bibliophagous,** *adj.*

bibliophilism, bibliophily a love for books, especially for first or fine editions. —**bibliophile, bibliophilist,** *n.* —**bibliophilic,** *adj.*

bibliophobe a person who fears and distrusts books.

bibliophobia an abnormal dislike for books.

bibliopolism, bibliopoly the selling of books, especially rare or secondhand volumes. —**bibliopole, bibliopolist,** *n.* —**bibliopolic,** *adj.*

bibliotaphy the hoarding or hiding of books, often under lock and key. —**bibliotaph,** *n.* —**bibliotaphic,** *adj.*

bibliothecary a librarian.

bibliotherapy the therapeutic use of reading material in the treatment of nervous diseases. —**bibliotherapist,** *n.* —**bibliotherapeutic,** *adj.*

breviary *Catholicism.* a book containing the prayers, lessons, etc., needed by a priest for the reading of his daily office.

chartulary, cartulary 1. a book containing charters.
2. the official in charge of such a book.

collectanea a miscellany of passages from an author or authors, sometimes assembled for teaching purposes.

colophon 1. an inscription, formerly at the end of a book but now usually on the title page, with information about the book's publication and production.
2. an ornamental device or printer's or publisher's trademark.

cyclopedia, cyclopaedia encyclopedia. —**cyclopedist, cyclopaedist,** *n.* —**cyclopedic, cyclopaedic,** *adj.*

delectus a book of passages from Greek and Latin authors, used for study.

desiderata a list of books sought by a collector or library.

diaskeuasis the process of revision or editing books or other written material. —**diaskeuast,** *n.*

doublure the lining of the covers of a book, often decorated, as with marbled papers, gold tooling at the edges, etc.

emargination the state of being notched at the edge or the process of notching at the edge, as some leaves or the page of a book, particularly a reference work with thumb-indexing.

enchiridion a handbook or manual.

encyclopedia, encyclopaedia a book or set of books containing detailed knowledge and information about a variety of fields or sub-fields; an exhaustive work of learning or knowledge. Also called cyclopedia, cyclopaedia. —encyclopedist, encyclopaedist, *n.* —encyclopedic, encyclopaedic, encyclopedical, encyclopaedical, *adj.*

etymologicon a book of etymologies; any treatise on the derivation of words.

exordium the beginning or introductory part of a book or other printed work, or of a discourse.

fascicle an installment of a book or journal that is published in parts.

foliation the numbering of leaves in a book, rather than pages.

formulary any book of prescribed forms, as prayers, oaths, etc. See also 130. DRUGS.

grangerism 1. the augmentation of the illustrative material in a book by prints, sketches, and engravings not found in the original edition.
2. the mutilation of books to acquire extra illustrative materials. —grangerize, *v.*

incunabulum any of the rare, early examples of movable-type editions printed in the last part of the 15th century, as Caxton's editions of Chaucer and Malory. —incunabula, *n. pl.* —incunabulist, *n.* —incunabular, *adj.*

limner *Archaic.* a book illustrator or one who illuminates manuscripts.

marginalia notes written in the margins of a book, as by a student.

miscellanea, miscellany a varied collection, particularly a collection of literary works, extracts, fragments, etc., in book form. —miscellaneous, *adj.*

monograph a book, treatise, or other written work of a scholarly nature dealing with one specific subject. Also, *Rare.* monography. —monographer, *n.* —monographic, monographical, *adj.*

nomenclator *Obsolete.* a list or glossary, arranged alphabetically, of the terms or words particular to any art or science or other special field or subject. Also nomenclature. See also 83. CLASSIFICATION; 288. NAMES.

pagination 1. the process of numbering the pages of a book.
2. the number and arrangement of pages, as might be noted in a bookseller's catalogue.

palimpsest a piece of parchment or vellum from which earlier writing has been erased or scraped off to allow for reuse. —palimpsestic, *adj.*

paralipomena a supplement to a book or other work containing material previously omitted.

peerage a list or directory of peers, usually with genealogies, as *Burke's Peerage*.

philobiblist a lover of books; bibliophile.

photobibliography the use of photography as an aid to book description.

polyglot a book written in several languages. See also 236. LANGUAGE. —polyglot, polyglottic, polyglottous, *adj*.

proem, proemium a preface, preamble, or brief introduction, as to a book or other work.

prolegomenon a preliminary remark or introduction, as to a speech; the foreword to a book or treatise. —prolegomenary, prolegomenous, *adj*.

redaction 1. the preparation of a work for publication, as by editing or revising.
2. a work so treated, an edited version. —redactor, *n*. —redactorial, *adj*.

rubric in the early days of printing, a capital letter, group of words, etc., printed in red or in decorative lettering; hence, a heading, title, or subtitle in a book or other printed work. —rubric, *adj*. —rubricator, *n*.

scholium a marginal note or comment, especially in an appendix, providing explanation of a Greek or Latin text. Also scholy. —scholiast, *n*.

variorum a work containing all available versions and variants of a text to enable scholars to compare them and study the development of the work. —variorum, *adj*.

54. BOTANY
See also 44. BIOLOGY; 167. FLOWERS; 188. GRASSES; 241. LEAVES; 319. PLANTS; 401. TREES.

agrostology the branch of systematic botany that studies grasses. Also called graminology. —agrostologist, *n*. —agrostologic, agrostological, *adj*.

algology the branch of botany that studies seaweeds and algae. Also called phycology. —algologist, *n*. —algological, *adj*.

ampelography the branch of botany that studies the cultivation of grapes. —ampelographer, *n*.

anamorphosis an abnormal change in the form of a plant that falsely gives it the appearance of a different species. —anamorphic, *adj*.

anisotropy the state or condition of certain flowers or plants of having different dimensions along different axes. See also 316. PHYSICS. —anisotropic, *adj*.

batology the branch of botany that studies brambles. —batologist, *n*.

bisymmetry in botany, the condition of having two planes of symmetry at right angles to one another. —bisymmetric, bisymmetrical, *adj*.

botany a major division of biology that studies all plant life. Also called phytology. —botanist, *n.* —botanical, *adj.*

bryology the branch of botany that studies mosses and liverworts. —bryologist, *n.*

caprification the pollination process of figs, in which fig wasps, attracted by the caprifigs, or inedible fig-fruit, pollinate the figs. —caprificator, *n.*

caricologist a person who specializes in the study of sedges.

carpology the branch of botany that studies the structure of fruits and seeds. —carpologist, *n.* —carpological, *adj.*

chromatism abnormal coloration in parts of a plant that are usually green. See also 92. COLOR.

cryptogamist one proficient in cryptogamic botany, i.e., the study of plants, as ferns and mosses, that have no true flowers or seeds.

dendrology the branch of botany that studies trees. —dendrologist, *n.* —dendrologic, dendrological, *adj.*

epiphytology the study of the character, ecology, and causes of plant diseases, as blight, which destroy a large number of susceptible plants in a large area simultaneously. —epiphytologist, *n.*

ethnobotany a specialty in botany that studies the lore and uses of plants as illustrative of the customs of a (usually primitive) society. —ethnobotanist, *n.* —ethnobotanic, ethnobotanical, *adj.*

filicology the study of ferns. Cf. pteridology. —filicologist, *n.*

fungology the scientific study of fungi. —fungologist, *n.* —fungological, *adj.*

graminology agrostology. —graminologist, *n.* —graminologic, graminological, *adj.*

herbalist *Obsolete.* a descriptive botanist. See also 319. PLANTS.

herbarian, herbarist *Obsolete.* a herbalist.

herbarism *Obsolete.* botany.

herbarium a collection of dried plants, assembled and arranged for botanical study.

lichenology the study of lichens. —lichenologist, *n.* —lichenologic, lichenological, *adj.*

Linneanism a system of botanical nomenclature following the binomial procedures established by Swedish botanist Carl von Linné. —Linnaean, Linnean, *adj.*

muscology the study of mosses. —muscologist, *n.*

mycology 1. the branch of botany that studies fungi.
2. a catalogue of the fungi found in a specific area. —mycologist, *n.* —mycologic, mycological, *adj.*

orchidology   the branch of botany or horticulture that studies orchids. —orchidologist, *n.*

phycography a scientific description of seaweed. —phycographic, *adj.*

phycology algology. —phycologist, *n.*

phylum any of the basic divisions of the plant or animal kingdom. Cf. phylon.

phytogenesis   the science and history of the development of plants. Also phytogeny. —phytogenetic, phytogenetical, *adj.*

phytogeography   the study of plants according to their geographical distribution.   —phytogeographer, *n.*   —phytogeographic, phytogeographical, *adj.*

phytography the branch of botany that studies plant measurement and plant taxonomy.   —phytographer, phytographist, *n.*   —phytographic, phytographical, *adj.*

phytology botany.

phytosociology the branch of ecology that studies the interrelations of plants and plant communities. —phytosociologist, *n.* —phytosociologic, phytosociological, *adj.*

pomology 1. the branch of botany that studies the cultivation of fruit. 2. the science of growing, storing, and processing fruit. —pomologist, *n.*

pteridography the systematic description of ferns.

pteridology the branch of botany that studies ferns. Cf. filicology. —pteridologist, *n.*

Schwendenerism   the theory that lichens are parasitic fungi growing upon algae, first advanced by the German botanist S. Schwendener.

sphagnology the study of the sphagnum mosses. —sphagnologist, *n.*

stirpiculture selective breeding to develop strains with particular characteristics. —stirpicultural, *adj.*

symphyogenesis   production by union of elements that were formerly separate. —symphyogenetic, *adj.*

tautonym a botanical or zoological name in which two terms are combined, the generic name and the specific, with both being the same. (a practice no longer approved by the International Code of Botanical Nomenclature.)

uredinology a branch of mycology that studies rusts. —uredinologist, *n.*

55. BOXING
See also 26. ATHLETICS.

pancratiast a person skilled in the art of boxing or wrestling. —pancratiastic, *adj.*

pugilism the art or practice of fighting with fists; boxing. —pugilistic, *adj.*

pugilist a person who fights with his fists; prizefighter.

56. BRAIN
See also 14. ANATOMY; 51. BODY, HUMAN; 196. HEAD.

biofeedback the process of providing a person with visual or auditory evidence of the quality of an autonomic physiological function so that he may attempt to exercise conscious control over it.

cerebrology 1. *Obsolete.* the branch of psychology that studies the brain.
2. *Medicine.* the total knowledge concerning the brain.

craniotomy the surgical operation of opening the skull, as for an operation on the brain.

cybernetics the comparative study of complex electronic devices and the nervous system in an attempt to understand better the nature of the human brain. —cyberneticist, *n.* —cybernetic, *adj.*

encephalitis an inflamed condition of the brain.

heterotopy, heterotopia, heterotopism a condition in which normal tissue is misplaced, especially in the brain, so that masses of gray matter are found in the white matter. See also 44. BIOLOGY. —heterotopous, *adj.*

lobotomy surgical severing of certain nerve fibers in the frontal lobe of the brain, once commonly performed to treat intractable depression. Also called **prefrontal lobotomy**.

menticide the process of systematically altering beliefs and attitudes, especially through the use of drugs, torture, or psychological stress techniques; brainwashing.

phrenomagnetism brain stimulation by hypnosis or magnetism.

prosencephalon the forebrain. —prosencephalic, *adj.*

psychokinesis a form of extreme or violent cerebral activity caused by defective inhibition. —psychokinetic, *adj.*

psychosurgery the use of brain surgery to treat mental disorders. —psychosurgeon, *n.*

sensorium the sensory apparatus of the body as a whole; the seat of physical sensation, imagined to be in the gray matter of the brain.

synectics a procedure for the stating and solving of problems based upon creative thinking in figurative terms by a small, carefully chosen, and diversely specialized group.

telencephalon the anterior section of the forebrain, containing the cerebrum and related structures. —telencephalic, *adj.*

telergy the influence one brain is thought to exercise over another, from a distance, by means of some hypothetical mental energy.

topectomy surgical excision of part of the cerebral cortex, as to provide relief for pain or treat certain mental disorders.

57. BRASS
See also 23. ART; 270. METALS; 305. ORNAMENTATION.

chalcologue a student of brasses.

chalcomancy a technique of divination by examining vessels of brass.

chalcotript one who copies monumental brasses by taking rubbings.

58. BREVITY
brachylogy the practice of conciseness in speech or writing.

laconism, laconicism 1. the practice of using few words to say much. 2. a laconic utterance. —laconic, *n., adj.* —laconical, *adj.*

pauciloquy *Rare.* the speaking of few words; taciturnity or brevity. —pauciloquent, *adj.*

syntomy, syntomia *Rare.* brevity; conciseness.

telegraphese the brief, sometimes cryptic language used in telegrams.

59. BUDDHISM
See also 183. GOD and GODS; 267. MEDITATION; 285. MYSTICISM; 349. RELIGION; 392. THEOLOGY.

Buddhism the religion of the followers of Gautama Buddha, whose 6th-century B.C. doctrines strongly opposed the formalized, mechanical rituals of the Brahman sect in Hinduism; Buddha's teachings offered escape from endless reincarnation, a method of spiritual attainment through correct views and actions (The Eight-Fold Path), and a spiritual goal (Nirvana): a soul free from craving, suffering, and sorrow. See also Eight-Fold Path, The. —Buddhist, *n.* —Buddhistic, Buddhistical, *adj.*

Eight-Fold Path, The the method of spiritual attainment outlined in Buddha's sermons on the Four Noble Truths: pain, the cause of pain. the cessation of pain, and the path that leads to this cessation, emphasizing, in the last, right view, thought, speech, action, livelihood, effort, mindfulness, and concentration.

Fohism, Foism the predominant Chinese form of Buddhism, Foh being the Chinese name for Buddha. —Fohist, *n.*

Gelup-Ka Lamaism.

Hinayanism the earliest development of Buddhism after Buddha's death, emphasizing doctrines and practices originally formulated by Buddha and reflected in the "School of the Elders" (*Theravada*) of the Pali tradition; called the "lesser vehicle," it found followers in southern India and Ceylon. —Hinayana, *n., adj.*

Lamaism a reformation of Buddhism in Tibet intended to bring about stricter discipline in the monasteries; the dominant sect is Ge-lup-Ka (The Virtuous Way), with the patron deity Chen-re-zi (the Bodhisattva of Great Mercy), who is reincarnated as the successive Dalai Lamas. Also called **Ge-lup-Ka.** —**Lamaist,** *n.* —**Lamaistic,** *adj.*

Lamanism a form of Mahayana Buddhism marked by its complex organization and elaborate rituals. —**Lamanist,** *n.*

Mahayanism the "greater vehicle" or second development of Buddhism after the death of its founder as a reaction against the orthodox and conservative ideas of the Hinayana, asserting that Gautama is one of many manifestations of one primordial Buddha and emphasizing good works illustrating the six virtues of generosity, morality, patience, vigor, concentration, and wisdom necessary to ideal Buddhism; its tenets are preserved in Sanskrit texts, later translated into Chinese and Japanese. —**Mahayana,** *n., adj.*

Pan-Buddhism the principles, doctrines, and tenets that concern or are believed by all Buddhists. —**Pan-Buddhist,** *n.*

Tantrayana the mixed form of Buddhism practiced in Tibet, adding to ideas from both major Buddhist developments doctrines and practices from Hindu Tantric sects and the native Tibetan religion of nature worship and magic called Bönism; it combines the Hinayana concept of emancipation through self-discipline and the Mahayana concept of philosophical insight into reality for the sake of others with uniquely Tibetan magical rites and mystical meditation. —**Tantrayanic,** *adj.*

Zen Buddhism, Zenism an outgrowth of Mahayana, the "meditation" sect, developed in Japan from its earlier Chinese counterpart and divided into two branches: Rinzai, an austere and aristocratic monasticism emphasizing meditation on paradoxes; and Sōtō, a benevolent monasticism with great popular following, emphasizing ethical actions and charity, tenderness, benevolence, and sympathy as well as meditation on whatever occurs as illumination. —**Zen,** *n.* —**Zenic,** *adj.*

60. BUILDINGS
See also 20. ARCHITECTURE; 212. HOUSES; 317. PLACES.

batophobia 1. an abnormal fear of being too close to buildings.
2. an abnormal fear of tall buildings.

jerryism *British.* the use of shoddy techniques and materials in construction. Also called jerrybuilding. —**jerrybuilder,** *n.* —**jerrybuilt,** *adj.*

knacker *British.* a person who purchases old structures and disassembles them for salvageable materials and scrap.

naology the study of sacred buildings. —**naological,** *adj.*

61. BULLS and BULLFIGHTING
See also 16. ANIMALS.

aficionado an avid and informed devotee of bullfighting; now used of devotees of any sport, activity, or art.

bulldogging *Western U.S.* the seizing of a calf or steer by the horns and throwing it off its feet by twisting the head. —**bulldogger,** *n.*

picador a mounted bullfighter who jabs the bull between the shoulders with a lance to enrage it.

tauricide 1. the killing of a bull.
2. the killer of a bull.

taurobolium a part of an ancient religious rite involving baptism in the blood of a sacrificed bull. Also **tauroboly.**

taurokathapsia an ancient Cretan sport for both sexes involving grasping the horns of a bull and tumbling over him; bull-leaping.

tauromachy, tauromaquia 1. the art or technique of bullfighting.
2. a bullfight. —**tauromachian, tauromachic,** *adj.*

taurophobia an abnormal fear of bulls.

Taurus 1. the bull, second of the zodiacal constellations.
2. the bull, second of the astrological signs.

62. BUREAUCRACY
See also 185. GOVERNMENT.

beadledom the world of petty and officious bureaucrats. Cf. **bumbledom.**

bumbledom the world of petty and incompetent officials.

bureaucracy 1. a government typified by a rigid hierarchy of bureaus, administrators, and minor officials.
2. a body of administrators; officialdom.
3. administration characterized by excessive red tape and routine.
—**bureaucratic,** *adj.*

bureaucratese turgid, misleading language, as typical of bureaucracies. Cf. **federalese, officialese.**

empleomania an obsession with public employment.

federalese language typical of the U.S. federal government, especially bureaucratic jargon. Cf. **bureaucratese, officialese.**

officialdom 1. the realm or position of officials.
2. excessively close adherence to bureaucratic procedure.

officialese language characteristic of officialdom, typified by polysyllabism and much periphrasis. Cf. **bureaucratese, federalese.**

officialism 1. any official regulations or procedures.
2. an excessive emphasis on official regulations or procedures.
3. officials in general or collectively.

panjandrum designation for a pompous official, taken from a story by Samuel Foote (1755).

red-tapeism, red-tapism the practice of requiring excessive paperwork and tedious procedures before official action can be considered or completed. Also called red-tapery. —red-tapist *n*.

63. BURIAL
See also 99. CORPSES; 112. DEATH.

cerement, cerements the cloth or clothing in which the dead are wrapped for burial or other form of funeral.

columbarium a vault where the remains of cremated bodies are kept, usually in one of a number of recesses in a wall.

exequy 1. a funeral procession or cortege.
2. funeral rites or ceremony.

hydriotaphia a burial in an urn.

necropolis a cemetery, especially one attached to an ancient city.

obsequies a funeral or funeral ceremony. Sometimes obsequy.

sepelition *Obsolete*. burial or interment.

sindology the study of funeral shrouds.

taphephobia, taphiphobia, taphophobia an abnormal fear of being buried alive.

taphophilia a love for funerals.

64. BUTTERFLIES
See also 225. INSECTS.

Lepidoptera an order of insects comprising the butterflies, moths, and skippers, that as adults have four membranous wings more or less covered with scales. —lepidopterous, lepidopteral, *adj*.

lepidopterology a branch of zoology that studies butterflies and moths. —lepidopterist, *n*.

C

65. CALENDAR
See also 11. ALMANACS; 396. TIME.

analemma a figure-of-eight-shaped scale, for showing the declination of the sun and the equation of time for every day of the year. —**analemmatic,** *adj.*

bissextus the twenty-ninth day of February, added to the calendar every four years, except in centenary years evenly divisible by 400, to compensate for the discrepancy between the arbitrary 365-day calendar year and the actual time of the solar year. —**bissextile,** *adj.*

calendographer *Rare.* a person who makes calendars.

embolism 1. an intercalation of a day or days in the calendar to correct error. 2. the day or days intercalated. —**embolic, embolismic, embolismical,** *adj.*

heortology the study of the origin, growth, meaning, and history of Christian religious feasts. —**heortological,** *adj.*

indiction in the Roman Empire, the cyclical, fifteen-year fiscal period, used for dating ordinary events. Also called **cycle of indiction.** —**indictional,** *adj.*

intercalary inserted into the calendar, as the twenty-ninth day of February in a leap year. —**intercalation,** *n.* —**intercalative,** *adj.*

lunation the period of the moon's synodic revolution, from the time of the new moon to the next new moon; one lunar month or approximately 29 1/2 days.

lustrum, luster, lustre a period of five years.

menology 1. a list or calendar of months.
2. *Eastern Orthodoxy.* a calendar of all festivals for martyrs and saints, with brief accounts of their lives. Also **Menologion.**
3. a church calendar, listing festivals for saints.

metemptosis the practice of eliminating the bissextile day every 134 years to adjust the date of the new moon. Cf. **proemptosis.**

neomenia 1. the time of the new moon or the beginning of the month.
2. a heathen festival at the time of the new moon.

proemptosis the adding of a day every 300 and again every 2400 years to adjust the date of the new moon. Cf. **metemptosis.**

147

66. CANCER
See also 122. DISEASE and ILLNESS.

adenocele a cystic tumor that may develop in the glands.

adenosarcoma a malignant glandular tumor of the soft tissues of the body.

astroblastoma a malignant tumor that may invade the brain and spinal cord, especially investing blood vessels.

astrocytoma a brain tumor composed of large, star-shaped cells called astrocytes.

blastoma a neoplasm arising in the blastema, i.e., tissue from which an organ or part is formed. Also **blastocytoma**.

cancericidal of or pertaining to a chemical or process than can destroy malignant cells.

cancerophobia carcinomophobia.

cancroid 1. of or pertaining to a lesion that resembles cancer.
2. a malignant skin cancer.

carcinectomy the surgical removal of a cancer.

carcinogen any natural or artificial substance that can produce or trigger cancer, as arsenic, asbestos, ionizing radiation, ultraviolet rays, x rays, and many derivatives of coal tar. —**carcinogenic,** *adj.*

carcinoid a small, yellow tumor that may develop from argentaffin cells in the gastrointestinal mucosa and spread widely throughout the body.

carcinolysis the destruction of malignant cells, as by an antineoplastic drug.

carcinoma 1. a malignant tumor that may spread to surrounding tissue and distant areas of the body.
2. any kind of epithelial cancer. —**carcinomatous,** *adj.*

carcinomatosis carcinosis.

carcinomophobia, carcinomatophobia, carcinophobia an abnormal fear of cancer. Also called **cancerophobia**.

carcinophilia an affinity for cancerous tissue, a property of certain chemical agents. —**carcinophilic,** *adj.*

carcinosis 1. an abnormal condition characterized by the growth of numerous carcinomas throughout the body. Also **carcinomatosis**.
2. the process of development of carcinoma.

carcinostatic of or pertaining to the slowing or stopping of the growth of a carcinoma.

celiothelioma mesothelioma.

cerebroma any abnormal mass of brain tissue, malignant or benign.

chemosurgery a therapeutic procedure that uses chemicals to destroy pathogenic tissue, especially skin cancers.

chemotherapy a procedure that uses radioisotopes of various elements, as iodine, phosphorus, and gold, to treat cancers of the thyroid gland, lungs, and other organs.

chloroma a malignant, greenish tumor that invades myeloid tissue and fluoresces red under ultraviolet light.

chondrocarcinoma a malignant cartilageous tumor of the epithelium.

chondrosarcoma a malignant cartilageous tumor that most frequently invades the long bones, pelvis, and the scapula.

chordoma a rare congenital tumor of the brain.

chorioblastoma choriocarcinoma.

choriocarcinoma a uterine malignancy that may develop shortly after conception, during pregnancy, or after an abortion. Also called **chorioblastoma, chorionic epithelioma.**

comedocarcinoma a malignant tumor of the mammary ducts.

cystoma any neoplasm or tumor that contains cysts, especially any such tumor that invades the ovaries.

cytotechnology the study of human cells, especially to detect signs of cancer. —**cytotechnologist,** *n.* —**cytotechnologic,** *adj.*

erythroleukemia a malignancy of the blood characterized by abnormally productive bone marrow and the development of oddly-shaped blood cells.

glioma any of the predominant category of brain tumors composed of cancerous glial cells (a type of nerve cell).

hepatoma a malignant tumor of the liver that most commonly occurs in association with hepatitis or cirrhosis.

leukemia a malignancy of blood-producing tissues, characterized by proliferating immature white blood cells and infiltration of the spleen, liver, and other organs. Also **leukocythemia.** —**leukemic, leukemoid,** *adj.*

leukocythemia leukemia.

liposarcoma a cancerous growth of primitive fat cells. Also called **lipoma sarcomatode.**

lymphoma a growth of lymphoid tissue that is commonly cancerous and typically enlarges the lymph nodes.

medulloblastoma a malignant tumor that commonly originates in the cerebellum.

melanoma any malignant growth, especially in the skin, that is composed of melanin-producing cells.

mesothelioma a rare malignant tumor that may invade the linings of the lungs and the abdomen. Also called **celiothelioma.**

metastasis the spread of malignancies, characterized by the cancerous invasion of the lymphatic system, the blood, and body organs. —metastatic, *adj*. —metastasize, *v*.

neoplasia the abnormal proliferation of benign or malignant cells. —neoplastic, *adj*.

neoplasm the abnormal development of benign or cancerous tissue. —neoplastic, *adj*.

neurinoma a tumor that develops in a neural sheath and that may become malignant.

neuroblastoma a highly malignant tumor that may develop from the neural plate in an embryo and spread to the bones, liver, and other organs.

neurosarcoma a malignant growth composed of neural, connective, and vascular tissues. Also called **malignant neuroma**.

oncogenesis the process by which a tumor develops. —oncogenic, *adj*.

oncology the field of medicine that specializes in the study of tumors.

osteoclastoma a giant cell bone tumor that most commonly develops at the end of a long bone.

osteosarcoma a malignant bone tumor. Also called **osteogenic sarcoma**.

retinoblastoma a common childhood malignancy of the eye that develops from retinal cells.

sarcoma a rare malignant tumor of the soft tissues that commonly develops in the lower extremities.

ulocarcinoma a malignancy of the gums.

67. CANNIBALISM

androphagy the consumption of human flesh; cannibalism. —androphagous, *adj*.

anthropophagism, anthropophagy the consumption of human flesh; cannibalism. —anthropophagous, *adj*.

68. CAPTIVITY
See also 335. PUNISHMENT; 371. SLAVERY.

coarctation 1. *Obsolete*. the act of confining, as in a narrow space. 2. restriction of liberty.

infibulation the process of confining with a buckle or padlock. See also 364. SEX.

oubliette a secret place of imprisonment, usually with only one opening in the top, as found in some old castles.

69. CATHOLICISM

See also 79. CHRIST; 80. CHRISTIANITY; 260. MARY; 323. POPE; 349. RELIGION; 359. SAINTS; 392. THEOLOGY.

Americanism Heckerism.

Anglo-Catholicism the practices in the Anglican communion that hold that Catholicism is inherent in a church whose episcopate is able to trace its line of descent from the apostles and whose faith Catholics agree to be revealed truth. —Anglo-Catholic, *n., adj.*

anticlericalism an opposition to the influence and activities of the clergy in public affairs. —anticlericalist, *n.*

breviary a book containing the prayers, lessons, etc., needed by a priest for the reading of his daily office.

Cahenslyism a 19th-century plan of the German parliamentarian Cahensly, successfully opposed by American interests, to have the pope divide the foreign-born population of the U.S. into ethnic groups and to appoint bishops and priests of the same ethnic and linguistic background as each group.

catechumenism the condition of a person who is receiving basic instruction in the doctrines of Christianity in preparation for the sacrament of confirmation. Also **catechumenate.** —catechumen, *n.* —catechumenal, catechumenical, *adj.*

celibacy the state of being single or unmarried, especially in the case of one bound by vows not to marry. —celibate, *n., adj.*

chrism 1. a sacramental oil.
2. a sacramental anointing; unction.
3. *Eastern Christianity.* the rite of confirmation.

clericalism 1. an undue influence of the hierarchy and clergy in public affairs and government.
2. the principles and interests of the clergy.
3. the system, spirit, or methods of the priesthood; sacerdotalism. Cf. laicism. —clericalist, *n.*

Curialism 1. the philosophy and methods of the ultramontane party in the Roman Church.
2. the methods and processes of the Curia Romana, the bureaucracy of congregations and offices which assist the pope in the government of the Roman Church.

decretist 1. a canon lawyer versed in papal decrees on points in ecclesiastical law.
2. a person versed in the decretals. Also **decretalist.**

dulia the devotion, veneration, or respect accorded saints.

ecclesiarchy the control of government by clerics. Also called **hierocracy.** —ecclesiarch. *n.*

encyclical, encyclic a letter from the Pope to the Roman Catholic clergy on matters of doctrine or other concerns of the Church, often meant to be read from the pulpit.

extrascripturalism the view that the faith and practice of the Church are based in both tradition and the Scriptures. See also 43. BIBLE.

Gallicanism the body of doctrines, chiefly associated with French dioceses, advocating the restriction of papal authority, especially in administrative matters. Cf. ultramontanism. —**Gallican**, *n.*, *adj.*

Heckerism the teaching of a 19th-century Paulist priest, Isaac T. Hecker, who regarded Catholicism as the religion best suited to promoting human aspirations after liberty and truth and to the character and institutions of the American people. Also called **Americanism.**

hierocracy ecclesiarchy.

Hildebrandism the views of Hildebrand, Pope Gregory VII (1073–85), especially those underlying his drastic reforms within the Roman Church and his assertion of papal supremacy. Usually called **ultramontanism.** —**Hildebrandic, Hildebrandine,** *adj.*

imprimatur permission, particularly that given by the Roman Catholic Church, to publish or print; hence, any sanction or approval. (Latin: 'let it be printed.')

infallibilism 1. the belief in or adherence to the dogma of papal infallibility. **2.** the dogma itself.

Jesuitism 1. the doctrines, practices, etc., of the Jesuit order of priests. **2.** *Disparaging, lower case.* casuistry or equivocation. Also **Jesuitry.** —**Jesuitic, Jesuitical,** *adj.*

laicism 1. the nonclerical, or secular, control of political and social institutions in a society. **2.** lay participation in church matters. Cf. clericalism. —**laity,** *n.*

Liguorist, Liguorian a believer in the theological doctrines of St. Alfonso Maria da Liguori (1696-1787), founder of the Redemptorist Order.

Marianism *Rare.* a religious cult based on the veneration of the Virgin Mary.

Mariolatry, Maryology, Maryolatry the cult of the Blessed Virgin Mary. —**Mariolater,** *n.* —**Mariolatrous,** *adj.*

Maronism an Arabic-speaking Uniat sect in Lebanon, under the authority of the papacy since the 12th century but maintaining its Syriac liturgy, married clergy, and practice of communion in both bread and wine. —**Maronite,** *n., adj.*

marranism, marranoism the forced conversion of Jews or Moors in medieval Spain. —**marrano,** *n.*

martyrology 1. a history or registry of martyrs.
2. the branch of ecclesiastical history that studies the lives and deaths of martyrs.
3. an official catalog of martyrs and saints, arranged according to the dates of their feast days. —martyrologist, *n.* —martyrologic, martyrological, *adj.*

Molinism the doctrine of the 16th-century Jesuit Luis Molina, who taught that the work of grace depends on the accord of man's free will. —Molinist, *n.*

Norbertine a Premonstrant.

Novationism a 3rd-century controversy in the Roman diocese in which Novation, elected bishop of a schismatic group, declared that lapsed Christians could not be received again into the Church. —Novationist, *n.*

oblate a person resident and serving in a monastery but not under vows; a lay religious worker.

ostiary 1. a member of the lowest-ranking of the four minor orders in Roman Catholicism.
2. a doorkeeper of a church.

papalism 1. the institution and procedures of papal government.
2. the advocacy of papal supremacy. —papalist, *n.*, *adj.*

papism *Usually disparaging.* authoritarian government under the direction of the pope. Also papistry. —papist, *n.* —papistic, papistical, *adj.*

Petrinism the theological concepts taught by or ascribed to St. Peter. —Petrinist, *n.*

popeism, popery *Pejorative.* papal authority or actions.

portiforium a breviary.

postulator a priest who submits a plea for beatification or canonization.

Premonstrant one of the order of Roman Catholic monks founded at Premontre, France, by St. Norbert in 1119. Also called **Premonstratensian, Norbertine.**

recusancy resistance to authority or refusal to conform, especially in religious matters, used of English Catholics who refuse to attend the services of the Church of England. Also recusance. —recusant, *n.*, *adj.*

reunionism advocacy of the reunion of the Anglican and Catholic churches. —reunionist, *n.* —reunionistic, *adj.*

Ribbonism, Ribandism the principles of the Ribbon Society, a Roman Catholic secret society of the mid 19th century. —Ribbonist, Ribandist, *n.*

romanism the practices and doctrines of Roman Catholicism. —romanist, *n.* —romanistic, *adj.*

sacerdotalism the system, practices, or principles underlying the priesthood. —sacerdotal, *n.*, *adj.*

simonism, simony the practice or defense of the selling of church relics, preferments, etc. —simoniac, simonist, *n.*

sodality a fellowship, brotherhood, or other association of a benevolent nature, especially in the Roman Catholic Church. —sodalist, *n., adj.*

stigmatism the state of one who has received supernatural stigmata, i.e., marks on hands, feet, and side similar to the wounds of Christ. —stigmata, *n.* —stigmatic, *adj.*

synodist a member of a council, meeting to consult and decide on church matters. —synodical, synodal, *adj.*

traditionalism adherence to tradition, rather than to revelation, independent Bible study, or individual reasoning, as the authority controlling religious knowledge and practice. —traditionalist, *n.* —traditionalistic, *adj.*

Trappist a member of a Roman Catholic monastic order, a branch of the Cistercians, observing an austere, reformed rule, including a vow of silence; named after the monastery at La Trappe, France, where the reformed rule was introduced in 1664. —Trappist, *adj.*

ultramontanism the advocacy of the supremacy of the papacy and the papal system, in opposition to those favoring national churches and the authority of church councils. Cf. Gallicanism. —ultramontane, ultramontanist, *n.* —ultramontanistic, *adj.*

Uniatism the union of an Eastern Rite church with the Roman Church in which the authority of the papacy is accepted without loss of separate liturgies or government by local patriarchs. —Uniat, Uniate, *n.*

Vaticanism the doctrine or advocacy of papal supremacy. —Vaticanist, *n.*

70. CATS
See also 16. ANIMALS.

ailuromania an abnormal love of cats.

ailurophile, aelurophile a lover of cats. Also called felinophile, philofelist, philogalist.

ailurophobia, aelurophobia, elurophobia an abnormal fear of cats. Also called felinophobia.

felinophile ailurophile.

galeophilia an excessive fondness for cats.

gatophobia an abnormal fear of cats.

grimalkin 1. a cat, particularly an old female cat.
2. a bad-tempered old woman.

kitling *British dialect.* the young of an animal, especially a kitten or young cat.

malkin *British dialect.* a cat or hare. Also spelled mawkin.

philofelist ailurophile.

philogalist ailurophile.

71. CAVES

caving the term for speleology used by professionals.

speleology, spelaeology the branch of geology that explores, studies, and describes caves. —speleologist, spelaeologist, *n.* —speleological, spelaeological, *adj.*

spelunker a person who explores caves as a hobby. —spelunk, *v.*

72. CELLS
See also 44. BIOLOGY.

auxesis growth, especially owing to an increase in cell size. Cf. merisis. —auxetic, *adj.*

basophile a cell or tissue that stains easily. —basophilic, basophilous, *adj.*

chromatolysis the breakdown of the protoplasm that contains the genes in the cell nucleus.

cytochemistry the branch of cytology that deals with the chemistry of living cells. —cytochemical, *adj.*

cytology the branch of biology that studies the structure, function, multiplication, and life history of cells. —cytologist, *n.* —cytologic, cytological, *adj.*

cytolysis the degeneration of cells. —cytolytic, *adj.*

cytoplasm the protoplasm of a cell, not including the nucleus. —cytoplasmic, *adj.*

cytotechnology the study of human cells, especially to detect signs of cancer. —cytotechnologist, *n.* —cytotechnologic, *adj.*

ectoplasm the outer part of the cytoplasm of a cell. Cf. endoplasm. —ectoplasmic, *adj.*

embryogeny the formation and growth of an embryo. —embryogenic, —embryogenetic, *adj.*

endoplasm the inner part of the cytoplasm of a cell. Cf. ectoplasm. —endoplasmic, *adj.*

epigenesis the formation of a cell as a new product and not as the result of development from some existing cell. —epigenetic, *adj.*

karyology a branch of cytology dealing with the structure of cell nuclei, especially chromosomes. —karyologic, karyological, *adj.*

karyoplasm the substance forming the nucleus of a cell. —karyoplasmic, karyoplasmatic, *adj.*

karyotype the aggregate of morphological characteristics of the chromosomes in a cell. —karyotypic, karyotypical, *adj.*

lysis the destruction of cells by the action of certain lysins. See also 197. HEALTH. —lytic, *adj.*

merisis any form of growth, especially as a product of cell division. Cf. auxesis.

mitosis the normal process of cell division. —mitotic, *adj.*

monad any simple, single-cell organism. —monadic, monadical, monadal, *adj.*

neutrophile a cell or tissue that accepts a stain from a neutral solution. —neutrophilous, *adj.*

osmosis the process by which fluids pass through a semipermeable membrane into a solution of lower concentration to equalize the concentration on both sides of the membrane. —osmotic, *adj.*

phagocytosis the action of phagocytes in ingesting and destroying cells.

trophoplasm the form of protoplasm that constitutes the nutritive element of a cell. —trophoplasmic, trophoplasmatic, *adj.*

trophotropism the movement of cells in relation to food or nutritive matter. —trophotropic, *adj.*

73. CHANCE
See also 175. GAMBLING.

casualism the doctrine that events are ruled by chance.

casualty a chance happening. See also 223. INJURY.

consilience a chance happening or coincidence. See also 4. AGREEMENT.

fortuitism the doctrine that chance is involved in natural events rather than absolute determinism. See also 147. EVOLUTION. —fortuist, *n.*

fortuity a chance event, discovery, or occurrence. —fortuitousness, *n.* —fortuitous, *adj.*

lubricity the condition of being uncertain or unstable. —lubricious, *adj.*

serendipity a talent for making fortunate discoveries while searching for other things. —serendipitous, *adj.*

74. CHANGE

anabolism constructive metabolism.

cainotophobia, cainophobia misoneism.

catabolism 1. the metabolic process in which energy is liberated for use in work.
2. destructive metabolism.

catalysis the process of an agent that affects a chemical or other reaction without being itself changed or affected. See also 113. DECAYING. —catalyst, *n.*

metabolism the chemical and physical processes in an organism by which protoplasm is produced, sustained, and then decomposed to make energy available. Also, *Rare.* metaboly. —**metabolize,** *v.*

metamorphism change in form, structure, shape, appearance, etc. See also 179. GEOLOGY. —**metamorphic,** *adj.*

metamorphosis 1. change in form, structure, appearance, etc.
2. magical transformation. —**metamorphic, metamorphous,** *adj.*

metaphysis a change of form or type.

misoneism an abnormal dislike of novelty or innovation. Also called **neophobia, cainotophobia, cainophobia.**

neophobia misoneism.

physis 1. the principle or concept of growth and change in nature.
2. nature considered as the source of growth and change.
3. something that grows or develops.

transmogrification the process of complete and usually extreme or grotesque change from one state or form to another.

transmutation the process or act of change, especially from one thing to another, as the change from base metal to gold, pursued by the alchemists. —**transmutationist,** *n.* —**transmutative,** *adj.*

75. CHARITY
See also 251. LOVE; 325. POVERTY.

eleemosynary pertaining to charity or alms-giving.

philanthropy voluntary activity of or disposition towards donating money, property, or services to the needy or for general social betterment. —**philanthropic,** *adj.*

76. CHEESE
See also 168. FOOD and NUTRITION; 272. MILK.

caseation the formation of cheese from casein during the coagulation of milk.

fromology a knowledge of cheeses.

laclabphily the collecting of cheese labels.

tyromancy *Obsolete.* a form of divination involving observation of cheese, especially as it coagulates.

tyrosemiophily the collecting of Camembert cheese labels.

77. CHILDREN
See also 153. FATHER; 281. MOTHER; 307. PARENTS.

bastardism, bastardy the condition of being a bastard.

filicide 1. a parent who kills a son or daughter.
2. the killing of a son or daughter by a parent. —**filicidal,** *adj.*

hyperactivity abnormal or excessive activity or constant excitability, especially in children. —hyperactive, *adj*.

misopedia, misopaedia an abnormal dislike of children. —misopedist, misopaedist, *n*.

pedagogics, paedagogics the science or art of teaching or education. Also called pedagogy. —pedagogue, paedagogue, pedagog, *n*.

pederasty, paederasty a sexual act between two males, especially when one is a minor. —pederast, paederast, *n*.

pediatrics, paediatrics the branch of medicine that studies the diseases of children and their treatment. —pediatrician, paediatrician, *n*.

pedodontics, pedodontia a branch of dentistry specializing in children's dental care. —pedodontist, *n*.

pedology the branch of medical science that studies the physical and psychological events of childhood. —pedologist, *n*. —pedological, *adj*.

pedophilia a sexual attraction to children. —pedophiliac, pedophilic, *adj*.

pedophobia an abnormal fear of children. —pedophobiac, *n*.

postremogeniture the quality or condition of being the youngest child. See also 239. LAW.

primogeniture the quality or condition of being a firstborn child. See also 239. LAW.

prolicide 1. the crime of killing one's own children.
2. a parent who kills his own children. —prolicidal, *adj*.

tecnology pedology.

ultimogeniture postremogeniture.

unigeniture the quality or condition of being an only child.

78. CHINA

Chinamania an obsession with China and things Chinese.

chinoiserie anything typically Chinese or made in a Chinese manner.

Confucianism the philosophy and doctrines espoused by Confucius, 5th century B.C. Chinese philosopher and moral teacher.

Fohism, Foism the predominant Chinese form of Buddhism, Foh being the Chinese name for Buddha. —Fohist, *n*.

Maoism 1. the political and social theories and policies of Mao Zedong (1893-1976), Chinese communist leader, especially with regard to revolution and agrarian reform.
2. adherence to or belief in Mao's doctrines. —Maoist, *n*., *adj*.

Mohism the doctrines of Mo-Tze, Chinese sage of the 5th century, B.C., who advocated government by an absolute monarch and universal love. —Mohist, *n.*, *adj.*

Sinicism 1. a trait or custom peculiar to the Chinese.
2. the use in another language of a Chinese word, idiom, or expression.

Sinology the branch of anthropology that studies Chinese culture. —Sinologist, Sinologue, *n.* —Sinological, *adj.*

79. CHRIST

See also 80. CHRISTIANITY; 205. HERESY; 349. RELIGION; 392. THEOLOGY.

adoptionism the 8th-century heretical doctrine that Christ in His human nature was the son of God only by adoption; that in His spiritual nature, however, He was truly God's son. Also **adoptianism.** —adoptionist, *n.*, *adj.*

Arianism a 4th-century doctrine, considered heretical by orthodox Christianity, that Christ was merely the noblest of men and, being of a different substance, was not the son of God. Cf. **heteroousianism, psilanthropism.** —Arian, *n.*, *adj.* —Arianistic, Arianistical, *adj.*

Athanasianism the teachings of Athanasius, 4th-century bishop of Alexandria, asserting that Christ is of the same substance as God; adopted by the Council of Nicea as orthodox doctrine. Also called **homoousianism, homoiousianism.** —Athanasian, *n.*, *adj.*

autotheism the Calvinist doctrine of the separate existence of God the Son, derived from Calvin's assertion that Christ took His person from God, but not His substance. —autotheist, *n.* —autotheistic, *adj.*

chiliasm the doctrine that Christ will return to the world in a visible form and set up a kingdom to last 1000 years, after which the world will come to an end. —chiliast, *n.* —chiliastic, *adj.*

Christology the branch of theology that studies the personality, attitudes, and life of Christ. —Christological, *adj.*

Christophany one or all of Christ's appearances to men after the resurrection, as recorded in the Gospels.

Docetism the teaching of an early heretical sect asserting that Christ's body was not human or material, but celestial in substance. —Docetic, *adj.*

Dyophysitism a 5th-century doctrine that Christ had a dual nature, the divine and the human, united perfectly in Him, but not inextricably blended. Cf. **Monophysitism.** —Dyophysite, *n.* —Dyophysitic, *adj.*

Dyothelitism, Dyotheletism the doctrine that Christ had two wills, the human and the divine. Cf. **Monothelitism.** Also **Dyothetism.** —Dyothelite, Dyothelete, *n.*

Eutychianism Monophysitism. —Eutychian, *n.*

heteroousianism a position in the 4th-century controversy over Christ's nature, asserting that He and God were of different natures; Arianism. Also spelled heterousianism. —heteroousian, *n., adj.*

homoiousianism a position in the 4th-century controversy over Christ's nature, asserting that He and God were of similar, but not the same, natures; semi-Arianism. Also homoeanism. —homoiousian, *n., adj.*

homoousianism a position in the 4th-century controversy over Christ's nature, asserting that He and God are of the same nature; Athanasianism. —homoousian, *n., adj.*

impanation the theological doctrine that the body and blood of Christ are present in the bread and wine after they are consecrated.

Julianism the heretical theory of Julian, 6th-century bishop of Halicarnassus, who took the extreme Monophysite position that Christ's human nature had been subsumed in and altered by the divine. —Julianist, *n.*

kenoticism the theological concept that, through His incarnation, Christ humbled or emptied Himself and became a servant for man's sake. —kenosis, kenoticist, *n.* —kenotic, *adj.*

logia sayings or maxims attributed to Christ but of which there is no written record or mention in the Gospels. See also 422. WISDOM.

millenarianism 1. the doctrine of Christ's 1000-year kingdom. 2. a belief in the millennium; chiliasm. —millenarian, *n., adj.* —millenarist, *n.*

millennialism a doctrine that Christ will make a second Advent and that the prophecy in the book of Revelation will be fulfilled with an earthly millennium of peace and righteousness. Also called millenarianism, chiliasm. —millennialist, *n.*

Monophysitism a 5th-century heresy concerning the nature of Christ, asserting that He had only a divine nature or that the human and divine made one composite nature. Cf. Dyophysitism. —Monophysite, *n., adj.* —Monophysitic, Monophysitical, *adj.*

Monothelitism, Monotheletism a heretical position of the 7th century that Christ's human will had been superseded by the divine. Also Monothelism. —Monothelite, Monothelete, *n.* —Monothelitic, Monotheletic, *adj.*

Nestorianism a 5th-century heresy concerning Christ's nature, asserting that the human and divine were in harmony but separate and that Mary should be considered the Mother of Christ, not of God. —Nestorian, *n., adj.*

Patripassianism a heretical, monophysitic concept of the 2nd and 3rd centuries that held that, in the Crucifixion, the Father suffered equally with the Son. —Patripassian, Patripassianist, *n.*

Paulianism a 3rd-century heresy concerning the nature of Christ, denying the divine by asserting that Christ was inspired by God and was not a person in the Trinity. —Paulian, Paulianist, *n.*

Phantasiast a member of an early Christian sect that denied the reality of Christ's body.

psilanthropism the doctrine that Christ was merely a human being. Cf. Arianism. —psilanthropist, *n.* —psilanthropic, *adj.*

sindonology the study of fabric artifacts, especially the supposed burial shroud of Christ. —sindonologist, *n.*

soteriology the doctrine of salvation through Jesus Christ. —soteriologic, soteriological, *adj.*

theanthropism the condition of being, simultaneously, both god and man. Also theanthropology. —theanthropist, *n.* —theanthropic, *adj.*

trinitarianism the orthodox Christian belief that God exists as the Trinity of the Father, the Son, and the Holy Spirit. Cf. unitarianism. —trinitarian, *n.*, *adj.*

unitarianism the doctrines of those, including the Unitarian denomination, who hold that God exists only in one person. Cf. trinitarianism. —unitarian, *n.*, *adj.*

80. CHRISTIANITY
See also 69. CATHOLICISM; 79. CHRIST; 135. EASTERN ORTHODOXY;
151. FAITH; 183. GOD and GODS; 205. HERESY; 260. MARY;
332. PROTESTANTISM; 349. RELIGION; 392. THEOLOGY.

anathematism 1. *Obsolete.* the pronouncing of a curse or ban with religious solemnity by ecclesiastical authority; anathematization.
2. a curse or malediction. —anathema, *n.*

anthology a collection of prayers used for solemn feasts in the Orthodox Eastern Church. See also 53. BOOKS.

antichristianism 1. a belief in, or adherence to the system of, the Antichrist.
2. the state of opposing Christianity in thought or action. Also antichristianity.

apologetics the study of the methods and contents of defenses or proofs of Christianity. —apologetical, *adj.*

apostolicism the condition of adhering to the evangelical doctrine of sanctification and to practicing such rites as healing and foot washing; following the teachings of the twelve apostles. —apostolic, *n.* —apostolical, *adj.*

Azymite one of a sect of early Christians who used unleavened bread for the Eucharist.

Byzantinism Eastern Orthodoxy.

catechism 1. a manual of instruction in the principles of the Christian religion, usually in question and answer form.
2. catechetical instruction. —catechist, *n.* —catechetical, *adj.*

Catholicism the doctrines, system, and practice of the Catholic Church, especially the Roman Catholic Church. —Catholic, *n., adj.*

Christendom Christians collectively or the Christian world.

Christianism the religious tenets held by all Christians.

didachist 1. a writer of the anonymous 2nd-century Christian manual of morals and church practices called the *Didache*.
2. an expert on or student of the *Didache*.

Eastern Orthodoxy the doctrines, systems, and practices of local and national independent churches (including the Greek and Russian Orthodox Churches) in communion with the ecumenical patriarch of Constantinople and adhering to the Nicene Creed and to a common rite celebrated in various languages. Also called **Byzantinism.** —Eastern Orthodox, *n., adj.*

Ecumenism, Oecumenism a movement within Christianity toward the recovery of unity among all Christians. —Ecumenicist, *n.*

election the theological doctrine of God's predestination of individuals as objects of divine mercy and salvation.

Encratism the practices of a 2nd-century sect that abstained from marriage, wine, and meat. —Encratite, *n.*

ethnicism the state of not being a Christian. —ethnic, *n.* —ethnical, *adj.*

evangelism, evangelicalism the missionary, reforming, or redeeming spirit evident throughout the history of Christianity in various guises or emphases. —evangelical, evangelistic, *adj.*

flagellantism 1. the practice of ascetic individuals or groups who indulge in scourging for the sake of discipline or punishment.
2. (*cap.*) the practice of a 13th- and 14th-century fanatical European sect that indulged in scourging to avoid the punishment of God. —flagellant, *n., adj.*

impenitence, impenitency lack of repentance or contrition for sins committed. —impenitent, *n., adj.*

infralapsarianism the theological doctrine that man's fall was foreseen and permitted by God, who then decreed election as a method for the salvation of some of mankind. Cf. supralapsarianism. —infralapsarian, *n., adj.*

kerygma, kerugma 1. the original, oral gospel preached by the apostles.
2. the preaching of the Christian gospel, especially the activity of the earliest Christian missionaries. —kerygmatic, *adj.*

latria worship of the highest order that can be offered only to God.

Marcionism the beliefs of an anti-Semitic Gnostic sect in the early Christian church. —Marcionite, *n.*, *adj.*

monarchianism a 2nd- and 3rd-century Christian doctrine that maintained that God is a single person as well as a single being. —monarchian, *adj.*

monasticism 1. the rule or system of life in a monastery.
2. the life or condition of a monk. —monastic, *n.*, *adj.* —monastical, *adj.*

oblation 1. a religious offering, either as charity or to God or a god.
2. the Eucharist, especially the offering of bread and wine to God.

Oecumenism Ecumenism.

Paraclete the Holy Spirit, considered as comforter, intercessor, or advocate.

Parousia the coming of Christ on Judgement Day. Also called **Second Advent, Second Coming.**

Paulinism the teachings of the apostle Paul, who believed that people should be emancipated from Jewish law and allowed to follow the faith and spirit of Christ. —Paulist, *n.* —Paulinian, *adj.*

penitence, penitency the state or condition of regretting sins or offenses and being willing to atone for them. —penitent, *n.*, *adj.*

pneuma the Holy Spirit in Christian theology. See also 379. SOUL.

pneumatology *Theology.* 1. the doctrines concerning the Holy Spirit.
2. the belief in spiritual beings, as angels, between men and God. —pneumatologist, *n.* —pneumatologic, pneumatological, *adj.*

preterism the belief that the prophecies of the book of Revelation have already come to pass. —preterist, *n.*, *adj.*

Protestantism the doctrines and practices of those Western Christian churches not in communion with the Roman or Eastern churches. —Protestant, *n.*, *adj.*

psychopannychism *Theology.* the doctrine that death causes the soul to sleep until the day of resurrection. —psychopannychist, *n.* —psychopannychian, psychopannychistic, *adj.*

Quadragesima 1. the first Sunday of Lent. Also called **Quadragesima Sunday.**
2. *Obsolete.* the forty days of Lent. —Quadragesimal, quadragesimal, *adj.*

Quinquagesima the Sunday before Lent. Also called **Quinquagesima Sunday.**
—Quinquagesimal, quinquegesimal, *adj.*

sabbatarianism 1. the practice in Judaism and some Christian groups of keeping the seventh day holy.
2. the practice of keeping Sunday holy and free of work and pleasureful activity. —sabbatarian, *n.*, *adj.*

sacramentalism 1. the theological doctrines concerning the sacraments.
2. the doctrines asserting that the sacraments are necessary to salvation as a conveyor of grace to a human soul. —sacramentalist, *n.*

subordinationism   the theological tenet of progressively declining essence within the Trinity. —subordinationist, *n.*

supralapsarianism   the theological doctrine asserting that God's plan for the salvation of man decreed election before the fall of man and permitted the fall as an instrumentality for fulfilling the divine purposes. Cf. infralapsarianism. —supralapsarian, *n.*, *adj.*

synusiast, synousiast *Obsolete.* one who believes that Christ was a mixture of divine and human substance.

theopneusty   the force or process of divine inspiration; the power by which the Holy Spirit reveals truth to men. —theopneustic, theopneusted, *adj.*

tritheism 1. the heretical belief that the Trinity consists of three distinct gods. 2. any polytheistic religion having three gods. —tritheist, *n.* —tritheistic, tritheistical, *adj.*

viaticum   the Eucharist given to one about to die; last rites or extreme unction. —viatic, viatical, *adj.*

Zwinglianism   the doctrine that in the Lord's supper there is an influence of Christ upon the soul but that the true body of Christ is present only through faith and not reality. —Zwinglianist, *n.* —Zwinglian, *adj.*

81. CHURCH
See also 80. CHRISTIANITY; 349. RELIGION.

collegialism   the belief that the church as an organization is independent of and equal to the state, with its highest authority lying in its collective membership.

diaconate   the rank or office of a deacon.

ecclesiarch *Eastern Church.* sacristan.

ecclesiasticism   an excessive adherence to the doctrines and practices of the church. —ecclesiastic, *n.*, *adj.* —ecclesiastical, *adj.*

ecclesioclasticism *Rare.* an opposition to the church.

ecclesiography   a descriptive study of the church.   —ecclesiographer, *n.* —ecclesiographic, ecclesiographical, *adj.*

ecclesiolatry   an intense devotion to church forms, authority, and traditions.

ecclesiology 1. the study of church building and decoration. 2. *Theology.* the doctrine of the church. 3. the policy and operations of the church. —ecclesiologist, *n.* —ecclesiologic, ecclesiological, *adj.*

ecclesiophobia   an abnormal fear or dislike of the church.

festilogy   a dissertation on church festivals.

hieromania   a mania for priests.

lectionary a list of the lections, or texts, to be read in church services throughout the canonical year.

nonage formerly, a ninth part of a parishioner's movable property, which was claimed upon his death by the clergy in England. See also 239. LAW.

precentor a person who leads a church choir or congregation in singing.

sacrist, sacristan an official or cleric appointed curator of the vestments, sacred vessels, and relics of a religious body, church, or cathedral.

simonism, simony the sin or offense of selling or granting for personal advantage church appointments, benefices, preferments, etc. —simoniac, simonist, *n.*

spoliation *Church Law.* the taking of property by an incumbent upon resignation or any other departure. See also 366. SHIPS; 391. THEFT; 413. WAR.

82. CITIES

citycism urban attitudes and actions.

conurbation a densely populated urban area, usually a large city surrounded closely by smaller ones.

cosmopolis a city inhabited by people of many different nations; a city of international importance. —cosmopolite, *n.* —cosmopolitan, *n.*, *adj.*

megalopolis a densely populated area of continuous extent containing many cities and towns that are separate administrative units.

megalopolitanism the state or quality of being a megalopolis or like a megalopolis; the phenomenon of the formation of a megalopolis. —megalopolitan, *adj.*

slumism the development and growth of slums or substandard dwelling conditions in urban areas.

suburbanism the views of those who prefer to live in suburbs. —suburbanist, *n.*, *adj.*

synoecism a joining together of several towns to form a single community, as in ancient Greece. —synoecy, *n.* —synoecious, *adj.*

urbanism the views of those who prefer to live in cities. —urbanist, *n.*, *adj.*

urbanology the study of urban affairs and problems. —urbanologist, *n.*

urbiculture the study of and concern with the special practices and problems of city life.

83. CLASSIFICATION

See also 288. NAMES; 301. ORDER and DISORDER.

binomial a name composed of two terms, a generic and a specific. —binomial, *adj.*

biosystematics biosystematy. —biosystematic, biosystematical, *adj.*

biosystematy the science of the classification of living things. Also called biosystematics. —biosystematic, —biosystematical, *adj.*

cytotaxonomy the area of taxonomy that uses cytological structures, as chromosomes, in classifying organisms.

dichotomy division of material into two parts for the purpose of classification. —dichotomist, *n.*

methodology 1. the science of method or orderly arrangement and classification.
2. any system created to impose order. See also 250. LOGIC. —methodological, *adj.*

micrology the investigation and classification of trivial matters. —micrologist, *n.* —micrologic, micrological, *adj.*

museography the enumeration and description of a museum's collection. —museographer, museographist, *n.*

nomenclator a person who invents or assigns names, as in nomenclature. See also 53. BOOKS.

nomenclature 1. a system of names used in the classification of an art or science or other field or subject.
2. a naming system peculiar to a social group. See also 53. BOOKS.

onym *Biology.* a technical name, as one that forms part of a system of nomenclature or classification.

onymy the application of onyms; classification or systematic nomenclature.

organonymy the nomenclature of organs. —organonymal, organonymic, *adj.*

phylum any of the basic divisions of the plant or animal kingdom.

physiography the systematic classification and description of nature. See also 178. GEOGRAPHY; 179. GEOLOGY. —physiographer, *n.* —physiographic, physiographical, *adj.*

quinarian an advocate of the quinary system of animal classification, which regarded all animal groups as being naturally divisible by five. —quinarian, quinary, *adj.*

syntypicism the condition or quality of being of the same type. —syntypic, *adj.*

systematics the study of classification and methods of classification. —systematician, systematist, *n.*

systematism the practice or act of systematizing.

systematology the study or science of systematizing.

tautonym a botanical or zoological name in which the two terms, the generic name and the specific, are the same (a practice no longer approved by the International Code of Botanical Nomenclature). —tautonymic, tautonymous, *adj.*

taxonomy, taxology 1. the technique or science of classification.
2. the scientific identification, naming, and classification of living things. Also called systematics. —taxonomist, *n.* —taxonomic, taxonomical, *adj.*

terminology 1. the terms of any branch of knowledge, field of activity, etc.
2. the classification of terms associated with a particular field; nomenclature.
3. *Rare.* the science of classification. —terminologic, terminological, *adj.*

trichotomy division into three parts, especially the theological division of man's nature into the body, the soul, and the spirit. —trichotomic, trichtomous, *adj.*

trinomialism the use of three terms or names in the classification of a species, genus, variety, etc. —trinomial, *adj.*

trionym a trinomial or name composed of three terms.

typocosmy *Rare.* a universal system of nomenclature or classification.

zootaxy zoological classification; the scientific classification of animals.

84. CLEANLINESS
See also 36. BATHING.

ablutomania an abnormal desire to wash, especially the hands.

asepsis 1. absence of bacteria of a harmful nature.
2. the techniques of achieving this condition. —aseptic, *adj.*

automysophobia an abnormal fear of being dirty.

blennophobia an abnormal fear or dislike of slime. Also called myxophobia.

bromidrosiphobia an abnormal fear of having an unpleasant body odor.

coprophobia an abnormal fear of feces.

elutriation the process of elutriating, or purification by washing and straining.

immaculacy freedom from stain or blemish. —immaculate, *adj.*

mysophobia an abnormal fear or dislike of dirt.

myxophobia blennophobia.

sudarium 1. a cloth or handkerchief for wiping sweat from the face.
2. a sudatorium.

sudatorium a room where a sweat bath is taken. Also called sudarium.

85. CLIMATE

See also 142. ENVIRONMENT; 417. WEATHER.

climatography the science of the description of climate. —climatographer, *n.* —climatographical, *adj.*

climatology the science that studies climate or climatic conditions. —climatologist, *n.* —climatologic, climatological, *adj.*

cryptoclimate the climate of the inside of a building, airliner, or space ship, as distinguished from that on the outside.

hyetography the study of the geographical distribution of rainfall by annual totals. —hyetographic, hyetographical, *adj.*

meteorology the science that studies climate and weather variations. —meteorologic, meteorological, *adj.* —meteorologist, *n.*

microclimatology 1. the study of minute gradations in climate that are due to the nature of the terrain.
2. the study of microclimates or climates of limited areas, as houses or communities. —microclimatologist, *n.* —microclimatologic, microclimatological, *adj.*

phenology the branch of biology that studies the relation between variations in climate and periodic biological phenomena, as the migration of birds or the flowering of plants. —phenologist, *n.* —phenologic, phenological, *adj.*

86. CLOTHING

cerement, cerements the cloth or clothing in which the dead are wrapped for burial or other form of funeral.

couture the art and practice of dressmaking and designing. —couturier, couturière, *n.*

falalery, fallalery showy articles of clothing; finery. —fallal, *n.*

garmenture clothes or garments, considered collectively.

gaudery finery or showy adornment, as in clothing.

habiliments clothing, especially for professional, ceremonial, or other special purposes.

millinery the art and trade of designing and making women's hats. —milliner, *n.*

toggery 1. clothes, collectively.
2. a particular outfit of clothes.

87. CLOUDS

See also 27. ATMOSPHERE; 345. RAIN; 375. SNOW; 417. WEATHER.

ceilometer an instrument for measuring by triangulation and recording the distance between the earth and the cloud ceiling.

nephelognosy divination by the observation of clouds.

nepheloscope an apparatus for expanding moist air to demonstrate the process of cloud formation.

nephogram a photograph of clouds, taken with a nephograph.

nephograph an instrument for photographing clouds and producing nephograms.

nephology the branch of meteorology that studies clouds. —nephologic, nephological, *adj.* —nephologist, *n.*

nephophobia an abnormal fear of clouds.

noctilucence the condition of being visible during the short summer nights, especially high-altitude clouds. —noctilucent *adj.*

nubilation 1. the formation or arrangement of clouds.
2. the obscuration caused by clouds.

88. COCKS
See also 16. ANIMALS; 45. BIRDS.

alectoromachy, alectryomachy a contest between two cocks; cockfighting.

alectoromancy, alectryomancy a form of divination by recording the letters revealed as a cock eats kernels of corn that cover them.

89. CODE

cryptanalysis 1. the procedures and methods used in translating or interpreting codes and ciphers.
2. the science or study of such procedures. Also cryptanalytics. —cryptanalyst, *n.* —cryptanalytic, cryptanalytical, *adj.*

cryptogram a message or writing in code or cipher. Also cryptograph. —cryptogrammic, *adj.*

cryptography, cryptology 1. the science or study of secret writing, especially codes and ciphers.
2. the procedures and methods of making and using codes and ciphers. —cryptographer, cryptographist, *n.* —cryptographic, *adj.*

90. COLD
See also 85. CLIMATE; 200. HEAT.

algidity coldness. —algid, *adj.*

cheimaphobia, cheimatophobia an abnormal fear or dislike of cold.

cryogenics the branch of physics that studies the production and effects of very low temperatures. —cryogenic, *adj.*

cryology 1. the study of snow and ice.
2. the science of refrigeration.

cryometer a thermometer for measuring very low temperatures.

cryometry the measurement of extremely low temperatures, by means of a cryometer. —cryometric, *adj.*

cryophilia *Biology.* a preference for low temperatures. —cryophile, *n.* —cryophilic, *adj.*

cryophobia an abnormal fear of ice or frost.

cryoscopy the study of the freezing points of fluids.

cryosurgery a surgical technique using freezing to destroy tissue.

gelidity the state or condition of being extremely cold. —gelid, *adj.*

horripilation the raising of the hairs on the skin as a response to cold or fear; goose bumps or goose pimples.

lyophilization a process for preserving substances such as blood or serum by freeze-drying in a high vacuum.

psychroesthesia an abnormal condition in which part of the body, though warm, feels cold.

psychrophobia an abnormal fear of the cold.

rhigosis a feeling or sensation of coldness.

91. COLLECTIONS and COLLECTING

aerophilately the collecting of airmail stamps.

ana a collection of memoirs, anecdotes, etc.; a miscellany.

anthology a collection of writings by various authors. —anthologist, *n.*

arctophilist a collector of teddy bears.

argyrothecology the collecting of money boxes, as those found in churches or on dispensing machines.

bestiary a collection of fables, intended to teach a moral lesson, in which the characters are real or imaginary animals.

bibliophilism, bibliophily zeal for collecting books.

brandophily the collecting of cigar bands. Also called cigrinophily.

cagophily the collecting of keys.

cartophily the collecting of cigarette or chewing gum cards depicting famous people, baseball players, etc.

chrestomathy 1. a collection of literary selections, especially in a foreign language, as an aid to learning.
2. a collection of literary selections from one author. —chrestomathic, *adj.*

cigrinophily brandophily.

conchology 1. the collecting of shells.
2. the branch of zoology that studies shells. —conchologist, *n.*

copoclephily the collecting of key rings containing advertising. —**copoc-lephile,** *n.*

cumyxaphily the collecting of matchboxes.

curiosa a collection of oddities and rarities, especially books, often pornographic.

deltiology the collecting of picture postcards.

discophily the collecting of phonograph records.

doxography the collection and compiling of extracts from ancient Greek philosophers, to which editorial comments are added.   —**doxographer,** *n.* —**doxographic,** *adj.*

errinophily the collecting of stamps other than postage stamps, as revenue or tax stamps.

esoterica a collection of items of special, rare, or unusual interest, often pornographic.

florilegium 1. an anthology or collection of brief extracts or writings.
2. an anthology of good writing from the best writers for imitation.

Hebraica a collection of Hebrew materials, usually literary or historical.

herbalism 1. the science or art of collecting and dispensing herbs, chiefly medicinal.
2. *Obsolete.* botany. —**herbalist,** *n.*

homologumena, homologoumena the collection of books from the New Testament recognized from the earlier period of the Christian church as authoritative and canonical.

hostelaphily *Brit.* the collecting of outdoor signs from inns.

iconophilist a person who collects pictures, as prints, engravings, lithographs, etc.

Judaica a collection of literary or historical materials relating to Judaism or the Jews.

labeorphily the collecting of beer-bottle labels.   —**labeorphilist,** *n.* —**labeorphile,** *n.*

laclabphily the collecting of cheese labels.

legenda *Obsolete.* a collection of materials that may be or are to be read, usually for spiritual or moral edification.

legendary 1. a compilation of legends.
2. a collection of the lives of the saints.

Lincolniana objects, books, letters, sayings, etc. connected with Abraham Lincoln.

memorabilia a formal collection of written accounts about matters or events worthy to be remembered.

memoranda an informal collection of data to be remembered or preserved.

militaria a collection of objects or materials illustrating military history.

miscellany a varied collection, particularly a collection of literary works, extracts, fragments, etc., in book form. —**miscellaneous,** *adj.*

museology the science of collecting and arranging objects for museums. —**museologist,** *n.*

notaphily the collecting of bank notes.

numismatics the collecting and study of coins or medals. Also called **numismatology.** —**numismatist,** *n.*

numismatography the part of numismatics concerned with the description of coins. —**numismatographer,** *n.* —**numismatographic,** *adj.*

omnium-gatherum a miscellany or medley.

philately the collecting of postage stamps. —**philatelist,** *n.*

phillumeny the collecting of matchbox labels and matchbook covers. —**phillumenist,** *n.*

philometry a specialty within philately involving the collecting of first-day covers.

phonophily the collecting of phonograph records. —**phonophile,** *n.*

planganology the collecting of dolls. —**planganologist,** *n.*

tegestology the collecting of cardboard beer coasters. —**tegestologist,** *n.*

timbrology *Archaic.* philately.

timbromania a mania for collecting postage stamps.

tyrosemiophily the collecting of Camembert cheese labels.

vecturist a collector of tokens used in buses and subways.

vexillology the collecting of flags or banners. —**vexillologist,** *n.*

92. COLOR

achromaticity 1. the total absence of color.
2. the ability to emit, reflect, or transmit light without breaking down into separate colors. Also **achromatism.**

achromatopsy, achromatopsia color blindness. Also called **acritochromacy.**

acyanoblepsia a variety of color blindness characterized by an inability to distinguish blue.

albescence the condition of being or becoming white or whitish. —**albescent,** *adj.*

albication the process of turning white or whitish.

chatoyancy the condition or quality of changing in color or luster depending on the angle of light, exhibited especially by a gemstone that reflects a single shaft of light when cut in cabochon form. —chatoyant, *adj*.

chromatics the branch of optics that studies the properties of colors.

chromatism 1. *Optics*. dispersion or distortion of color.
2. abnormal coloration. See also 54. BOTANY.

chromatology the study of colors. Also called **chromatography**.

chromatrope an instrument consisting of an arrangement of colored discs which, when rotated rapidly, give the impression of colors flowing to or from the center.

chromophobia an abnormal fear of colors.

chromoptometer a device for measuring the degree of a person's sense of color.

chromotypography, chromotypy the process of color printing.

colorimetry the measurement of the physical intensity of colors, as opposed to their subjective brightness. —colorimeter, *n*. —colorimetric, colorimetrical, *adj*.

cyanometry the measurement of the intensity of the sky's blue color. —cyanometer, *n*. —cyanometric, *adj*.

Daltonism red-green color blindness.

deuteranopia a defect of the eyesight in which the retina does not respond to green. —deuteranope, *n*. —deuteranopic, *adj*.

dichroism a property, peculiar to certain crystals, of reflecting light in two different colors when viewed from two different directions. —dichroic, *adj*.

dichromatism 1. the quality of being dichromatic, or having two colors.
2. a form of color blindness in which the sufferer can perceive only two of the three primary colors and their variants. —dichromatic, *adj*.

dyschromatopsia difficulty in telling colors apart; color blindness.

erythrophobia an abnormal fear of the color red.

floridity the condition of being florid or highly colored, especially reddish, used especially of the complexion. —florid, *adj*.

glaucescence 1. the state or quality of being a silvery or bluish green in color.
2. the process of turning this color. —glaucescent, *adj*.

hyperchromatism the occurrence of unusually intense coloration. —hyperchromatic, *adj*.

indigometer an instrument used for determining the strength of an indigo solution.

indigometry the practice and art of determining the strength and coloring power of an indigo solution.

iridescence the state or condition of being colored like a rainbow or like the light shining through a prism. —iridescent, *adj.*

irisation the process of making or becoming iridescent.

iriscope a polished black glass, the surface of which becomes iridescent when it is breathed upon through a tube.

melanoscope an optical device composed of red and violet glass that transmits red light only, used for distinguishing red in varicolored flames.

metachromatism change in color, especially as a result of change in temperature.

monochromatism 1. the quality of being of only one color or in only one color, as a work of art.
2. a defect of eyesight in which the retina cannot perceive color. —monochromatic, *adj.*

mordancy, mordacity the property of acting as a fixative in dyeing. —mordant, *n.*, *adj.*

opalescence the quality of being opallike, or milkily iridescent. —opalescent, *adj.*

pallidity a faintness or deficiency in color. —pallid, *adj.*

panchromatism the quality or condition of being 1sensitive to all colors, as certain types of photographic film. —panchromatic, *adj.*

polychromatism the state or quality of being multicolored. —polychromatic, polychromic, *adj.*

protanopia a defect of the eyesight in which the retina does not respond to red. —protanope, *n.* —protanopic, *adj.*

rubescence 1. the state, condition, quality, or process of becoming or being red.
2. a blush.
3. the act of blushing. —rubescent, *adj.*

rufescence 1. the tendency to turn red or reddish.
2. reddishness. —rufescent, *adj.*

spectrogram a photograph of a spectrum. Also called spectrograph.

spectrograph 1. an optical device for breaking light down into a spectrum and recording the results photographically.
2. a spectrogram. —spectrographic, *adj.*

spectrography the technique of using a spectrograph and producing spectrograms.

trichroism a property, peculiar to certain crystals, of transmitting light of three different colors when viewed from three different directions. Also trichromatism. —trichroic, *adj.*

trichromatism 1. the condition of having, using, or combining three colors. 2. trichroism. —**trichromatic,** *adj.*

tritanopia a defect of the eyesight in which the retina does not respond to blue and yellow. —**tritanope,** *n.* —**tritanopic,** *adj.*

verdancy the quality or condition of being green, as the condition of being covered with green plants or grass or inexperience attributable to youth. —**verdant,** *adj.*

viridescence 1. the state or quality of being green or greenish. 2. greenishness. —**viridescent,** *adj.*

xanthocyanopsy, xanthocyanopy a form of color blindness in which only yellow and blue can be perceived.

93. COMMUNALISM
See also 376. SOCIETY.

collectivization the process of forming collectives or collective communities where property and resources are owned by the community and not individuals.

communalization the process of communalizing, or forming communes, where property and resources belong to the community and not the individual.

communitarianism a communal system based on cooperative groups that practice some of the principles of communism. —**communitarian,** *n., adj.*

Fourierism a utopian social reform, planned by the French social scientist F.M. Charles Fourier, that organized groups into cooperative units called phalansteries, as Brook Farm. Also called **phalansterianism.** —**Fourierist, Fourierite,** *n.*

Hutterites in the U.S. and Canada, descendants of Swiss Protestants exiled from their homeland in 1528 for communal living, pacifism, and Anabaptist views, still persecuted for their economic self-sufficiency and their refusal to allow their communities to be assimilated. Also called **Hutterian Brethren.**

kibbutz a communal farm in Israel, cooperatively owned, with members who receive no pay but who gain housing, clothing, medical care, and education from the cooperative. Also called **kvutzah.** —**kibbutzim,** *n. pl.*

Oneida Perfectionists a native American communal society active in the middle 19th century in Putney, Vermont, and Oneida, New York, practicing a pooling of all property and communal marriage for eugenic reasons.

Owenism the social and political theories of Robert Owen, an early 19th-century British reformer whose emphasis upon cooperative education and living led to the founding of communal experiments, including the ill-fated community of New Harmony, Indiana, purchased from the Rappites. —Owenite, *n.*

phalansterianism Fourierism.

Rappist, Rappite a follower of George Rapp, an early 19th-century German Pietistic preacher, whose experiments in a religion-based cooperative system involved the founding of Economy, Pennsylvania, and Harmonie, Indiana. Also called Harmonist, Harmonite.

xenobiosis communal life, such as that of ants, in which colonies of different species live together but do not share the raising of the young.

Zionite a believer in the doctrines of John Alexander Dowie who founded Zion City, Illinois, in 1901, as an industrial community for his followers.

94. COMMUNISM
See also 185. GOVERNMENT; 322. POLITICS; 357. RUSSIA.

autonomism Bakuninism.

Bakuninism a 19th-century theory of revolution in opposition to that of Karl Marx, advocating atheism, destruction of central government, and extreme individualism. Also called autonomism.

Bolshevism a radical wing of the Russian Social Democratic Labor party, favoring revolutionary tactics to achieve full socialization and, under the leadership of Ulyanov (Lenin), setting up from 1917–20 the present Soviet regime. —Bolshevik, Bolshevist, *n.*, *adj.*

Castroism the doctrines and policies of Fidel Castro, communist premier of Cuba.

collectivization the process of forming collectives or collective communities where property and resources are owned by the community and not individuals.

communism 1. a political and economic theory proposing the replacement of private ownership of goods or capital with common ownership and distribution upon need.
2. (*cap.*) the social and political system based upon revolutionary Marxist socialism and currently practiced in the U.S.S.R. —communist, *n.*, *adj.* —communistic, *adj.*

communization the process of communizing or being communized.

cosmopolitanism the tolerance of or sympathy for noncommunist ideas and institutions, used as a charge against Soviet intellectuals.

deviationism a position or rationale which departs from the established dogma of a political party, especially the Communist party. Also **deviationalism**. —**deviationist**, *n.*, *adj.*

dialectical materialism the combination of traditional materialism and Hegelian dialectic as espoused in the economic and political philosophies of Karl Marx and Friedrich Engels. —**dialectical materialist**.

Eurocommunism the form of communism found in some countries of Western Europe, independent of the Communist Party of the Soviet Union.

Fichteanism theories and beliefs of J. G. Fichte (1762–1814), German philosopher and social thinker, a precursor of socialism. —**Fichtean**, *n.*, *adj.*

Guevarism 1. the political doctrines, policies, and revolutionary program of Ernesto "Che" Guevara (1928–1967), Cuban communist revolutionary.
2. adherence to or belief in Guevarism. —**Guevarist**, *n.*, *adj.*

Kremlinology study of the policies, doctrines, programs, etc., of the government of the Soviet Union. —**Kremlinologist**, *n.*

Leninism the political doctrines of Vladimir Ilich Ulyanov (Lenin), founder of Bolshevism, architect of the current Soviet government, originator of the Comintern, and author of the imperative that the Soviets lead the proletariat of other nations to revolution and communism. —**Leninist, Leninite**, *n.*, *adj.*

Maoism 1. the political and social theories and policies of Mao Zedong (1893–1976), Chinese communist leader, especially with regard to revolution and agrarian reform.
2. adherence to or belief in Mao's doctrines. —**Maoist**, *n.*, *adj.*

Marxism 1. the doctrines developed from the political, economic, and social theories of Karl Marx, Friedrich Engels, and their followers: dialectical materialism, a labor-based theory of wealth, an economic class struggle leading to revolution, the dictatorship of the proletariat, and the eventual development of a classless society.
2. the contributions to these doctrines in the interpretations of Lenin; Leninism. —**Marxist**, *n.*, *adj.* —**Marxian**, *adj.*

Menshevism the minority wing of the Russian Social Democratic Labor party that in a 1903 convention split from the majority or Bolshevik wing, enabling the latter to direct and win power in the revolution of 1917–20. —**Menshevik**, *n.*, *adj.*

polycentrism the existence of a number of basic guiding principles in the political system of a Communist government. —**polycentrist**, *n.*, *adj.*

revisionism *Marxism.* any deviation from Marxist theory, doctrines, or practice, especially to modify revolution to evolution. —**revisionist**, *n.*, *adj.*

socialist realism a Marxist-inspired artistic and literary theory or doctrine that calls on art and literature to promote the socialist cause and sees the artist, writer, etc. as a servant of the state or, in the words of Stalin, "the engineer of human souls."

socialization the establishment of socialist government; the nationalization of industry and other national resources.

Stakhanovism a system of piecework incentives, speedup, and competition for bonuses and honors introduced into Russia in 1935 and named after A. G. Stakhanov, whose prodigious mining output is constantly emulated. —Stakhanovite, *n.*, *adj.*

Stalinism the communistic theories and practices developed by Joseph Stalin from Marxism and Leninism, especially his development of the cult of the individual with himself at its center, his advocacy of national revolution, and his extensive use of secret police and slave-labor camps to reduce opposition. —Stalinist, *n.*, *adj.* —Stalinistic, *adj.*

syndicalism a theory of revolutionary politics that, through the actions of labor unions, seeks to establish a society controlled by workers' cooperatives and trade unions. —syndicalist, *n.*, *adj.* —syndicalistic, *adj.*

Titoism 1. the social, political, and economic theories of Tito (Josip Broz), former premier of Yugoslavia.
2. the nationalistic practices of a communist country which deviate from or oppose the directives of the U.S.S.R. —Titoist, *n.*, *adj.*

Trotskyism the theories of Leon Trotsky on the social, political, and economic implications of communism, especially his opposition to Stalin in advocating international revolution. —Trotskyite, *n.*, *adj.*

95. COMPLEXION
See also 370. SKIN.

achromasia absence of pigmentation in the skin.

chlorosis greensickness; a disease of girls in puberty, characterized by, among other symptoms, greenishness of the complexion.

erythrism a redness of beard and hair and ruddiness of complexion. —erythristic, erythrismal, *adj.*

erythromania a mania for blushing.

etiolation paleness of color as a result of illness or exclusion from light. See also 319. PLANTS.

floridity the condition of being florid or highly colored, especially reddish, used especially of the complexion. —florid, *adj.*

greensickness chlorosis.

icterus jaundice.

jaundice a disease of the liver, characterized by, among other symptoms, yellowness of the skin. Also called **icterus**.

melanism darkness or blackness of eyes, hair, or complexion.

rubescence 1. the state, condition, quality, or process of becoming or being red.
2. a blush.
3. the act of blushing. —**rubescent**, *adj*.

rubicundity reddishness or ruddiness, especially of the complexion. —**rubicund**, *adj*.

telangiectasis a chronic condition of dilatation of the capillaries and other blood vessels, as seen in the reddish faces of heavy drinkers and people whose faces are continually exposed to cold climates. —**telangiectic**, *adj*.

xanthochroid a person with light-colored hair and fair complexion. —**xanthochroid, xanthochroous**, *adj*.

96. CONFLICT
See also 413. WAR.

antagonist an opponent in any kind of contest or conflict. Also called **antipathist**.

antipathist *Rare.* an antagonist.

antipathy an attitude of antagonism or aversion.

commination the act of threatening, especially revenge or punishment.

contumacy a refusal to obey; defiance.

duelist, duellist 1. a person engaged in a duel.
2. a person skilled at dueling.

feudist a person who participates in a feud or other conflict.

insurgentism the state of being an insurgent or rebel; the activities of insurgents or rebels.

jacquerie a revolt of peasants against the social classes above them.

monomachy, monomachia single combat; a duel. —**monomachist**, *n*.

neutrality the state or position of being impartial or not allied with or committed to any party or viewpoint in a conflict, especially a war or armed conflict. —**neutral**, *n.*, *adj*.

opponency 1. the state or quality of being an opponent.
2. an act or instance of opposing.

oppugnancy 1. the state or quality of being an antagonist.
2. an act or instance of antagonism. —**oppugnant**, *adj*.

pacation *Rare.* the act or process of appeasing.

rebeldom 1. rebels collectively or as a group.
2. an area or region held by rebels.

sciamachy, sciomachy battle with shadows or imaginary enemies.

velitation a skirmish or other minor conflict.

97. CONVERT
See also 349. RELIGION.

neophytism 1. the condition of a new convert to a religious belief.
2. the condition of a newly baptized convert to the early Christian church.
—neophyte, *n.* —neophytic, *adj.*

proselytism 1. the act of becoming or the condition of being a convert to an opinion, political party, or religious group.
2. an active policy of inviting or persuading converts, especially to a religious position. —proselyte, *n.* —proselyter, proselytist, *n.* —proselytize, *v.* —proselytistic, *adj.*

98. COPYING
See also 328. PRINTING.

chromograph hectograph.

copyism 1. the practice of imitation, especially in art or literature.
2. an instance of such imitation. —copyist, *n.*

cyclostyle an instrument for cutting stencils from which multiple copies of an original can be made. —cyclostylar, *adj.*

diagraph a device used for the mechanical reproduction of plans, outlines, etc., on any scale.

ectype an exact copy. —ectypal, *adj.*

hectograph, hektograph a copy produced by hectography. Also called **chromograph.**

hectography, hektography a reproductive process involving a prepared gelatin surface to which the original writing has been transferred. —hectographic, hektographic, *adj.*

mechanography the art or practice of producing multiple copies of an original by means of a machine. —mechanographist, *n.* —mechanographic, *adj.*

pantograph a mechanical device for making copies of plans or drawings on a scale different from that of the original. —pantographic, *adj.*

phototelegraphy the transmission of pictures, print, etc., by means of radio or telegraphy. —phototelegraphic, *adj.*

polygraphy a device for producing copies of a drawing or of writing. —polygrapher, —polygraphist, *n.* —polygraphic, *adj.*

reprography a collective term, introduced by UNESCO, for all processes of producing facsimiles of documents.

voltagraphy *Rare.* a process for copying a pattern by means of electrolysis.

xerography a process for copying graphic matter by electrostatically charging a surface in areas corresponding to the printed areas of the original so that powdered resin carrying an opposite charge adheres to them and can be fused to the surface by pressure, heat, or both. —**xerographic,** *adj.*

99. CORPSES
See also 63. BURIAL; 112. DEATH.

autopsy an inspection and dissection of a body after death, usually to determine the cause of death. Also called **necropsy, post-mortem examination.**

necromania an obsession with death or the dead. —**necromaniac,** *n.*

necrophagy the practice of feeding on carrion. —**necrophage,** *n.* —**necrophagous,** *adj.*

necrophilia, necrophily, necrophilism an abnormal attraction, especially erotic, to corpses. —**necrophile, necrophiliac,** *n.*

necrophobia 1. an abnormal fear of death. Also called **thanatophobia.**
2. an abnormal fear of corpses. —**necrophobe,** *n.* —**necrophobic,** *adj.*

necropsy autopsy.

necrotomy 1. the dissection of corpses.
2. the surgical excision of a piece of dead bone. —**necrotomist,** *n.* —**necrotomic,** *adj.*

resurrectionism the exhuming and stealing of bodies from graves, especially for dissection; body snatching. —**resurrection man,** *n.*

thanatophobia necrophobia, def. 1.

100. COSMOLOGY
See also 25. ASTRONOMY; 318. PLANETS; 387. SUN.

cosmism a 19th-century theory about cosmic evolution, developed from contemporary science, that regards the cosmos as self-existent and self-acting. —**cosmist,** *n.*

cosmogony 1. a theory about the origin and the evolution of the universe.
2. the branch of astrophysics that studies the origin and evolution of specific astronomical systems and the universe as a whole.
3. cosmology. —**cosmogonist,** *n.* —**cosmogonic,** *adj.*

cosmography 1. the branch of astronomy that maps and describes the main features of the universe.
2. a description or representation of the main features of the universe. —**cosmographer,** *n.* —**cosmographic, cosmographical,** *adj.*

cosmology 1. the branch of astronomy that studies the overall structure of the physical universe.
2. the branch of philosophy that studies the origin, structure, and evolution of the universe, especially such characteristics as space, time, causality, and freedom. —cosmologic, cosmological. *adj.* —cosmologist, *n.*

cosmotheism the concept that the universe and God are identical; pantheism. —cosmotheist, *n.*

cosmozoism the concept of the cosmos as alive.

creationism the belief concerning the creation by a transcendant God of the universe, matter, and living organisms out of nothing. —creationist, *n.*

geocentricism 1. the concept that the earth is the center of the universe.
2. *Astronomy.* the measurements or observations that are relative to the center of the earth. —geocentric, *adj.*

heliocentricism 1. the concept that the sun is the center of the universe.
2. *Astronomy.* the measurements or observations that are relative to the center of the sun. Also heliocentricity. —heliocentric, *adj.*

pancosmism the theory that the totality of existence comprises only the physical universe in time and space. —pancosmic, *adj.*

Pansatanism a Gnostic theory that considered Satan's to be the controlling will of the universe.

Spencerianism the philosophical theory of Herbert Spencer that cosmic evolution is cyclic, controlled by mechanical forces which tend toward equilibrium and relative complexity until a peak is reached, after which dissolution occurs, the universe reverts to a simple state, and the cycle begins again. —Spencerian, *n., adj.*

teleologism the belief that purpose and design control the development of the universe and are apparent through natural phenomena. —teleologist, *n.* —teleology, *n.*

universology the science of the universe. —universologist, *n.*

101. COURAGE

heroism 1. the state or condition of being a hero.
2. behavior typical of a hero. —heroic, *adj.*

potvaliancy, potvalor, potvalency courage or bravery occasioned by drunkenness; Dutch courage. —potvaliant, *adj.*

valiancy bravery or courage. Also valience.

102. COWARDICE
See also 41. BEHAVIOR; 156. FEAR.

invertebracy the state or quality of being without a backbone, hence, metaphorically, spinelessness; lack of strength of character.

poltroonery cowardice; cowardly behavior. —**poltroon,** *n.* —**poltroonish,** *adj.*

pusillanimity a cowardly, irresolute, or fainthearted condition. —**pusillanimous,** *adj.*

recreancy cowardice, treason, or disloyalty. —**recreant,** *n.,* *adj.*

103. CRIME
See also 239. LAW; 335. PUNISHMENT; 391. THEFT.

abetment, abettal the act of abetting or inciting another to commit a crime. —**abettor, abetter,** *n.*

bigamy the condition of having two spouses simultaneously. —**bigamist,** *n.* —**bigamous,** *adj.*

contrabandism the practice of smuggling. —**contrabandist,** *n.*

corruptionist a person who practices or advocates corruption, especially in politics or public life.

criminology the scientific study of crime and criminals. —**criminologist,** *n.* —**criminologic, criminological,** *adj.*

defalcation 1. unauthorized appropriation of money; embezzlement.
2. the sum embezzled.

depeculation *Obsolete.* the act of stealing or embezzling.

disseizin, disseisin the process of wrongfully or unlawfully dispossessing a person of his rightful real property.

embracery the crime of attempting to influence or suborn a judge or jury by bribery, threats, etc.

extortionist a person who practices the crime of extortion or the obtaining of money by threat of violence. Also **extortioner.**

fugitation fleeing from justice, as by a criminal.

gangdom the world of gangs or organized crime.

knavery petty dishonesty or fraud. —**knave,** *n.* —**knavish,** *adj.*

malfeasance wrongdoing or improper or dishonest conduct, especially by a person who holds public office or a position of trust. Cf. **misfeasance.** —**malfeasant,** *adj.*

malversation fraudulent behavior, extortion, or corruption by a person who holds public office or a position of trust.

mayhem *Law.* an intentional crippling, disfigurement, or mutilation of another.

miscreancy criminal action or behavior; wrong- or evil-doing. —**miscreant,** *n., adj.*

misfeasance a form of wrongdoing, especially the doing of something lawful in an unlawful way so that the rights of others are infringed. Cf. malfeasance. —misfeasor, *n.*

misprision improper conduct or neglectful behavior, especially by a person who holds public office.

mouchardism the practice of being a police spy. —mouchard, *n.*

peculation embezzlement.

penitence, penitency the state or condition of regretting crimes or offenses and being willing to atone for them. —penitent, *n., adj.*

penology 1. the science of the punishment of crime.
2. the science of the management of prisons. —penologist, *n.*

polygamy the condition of having more than two spouses simultaneously. —polygamist, *n.* —polygamous, *adj.*

recidivism a repeated relapsing into criminal or delinquent behavior. —recidivist, *n.* —recidivistic, recidivous, *adj.*

ropery *Archaic.* roguish or criminal behavior or action; conduct deserving of hanging.

signalment a detailed description of a person for purposes of identification by police.

skulduggery underhanded, dishonest, or deceptive behavior or actions.

trigamy the condition of having three spouses simultaneously. —trigamous, *adj.*

Whitefootism the actions of an Irish secret society (circa 1832) whose members committed murders and other crimes. —Whitefoot, *n.*

104. CRITICISM
See also 249. LITERATURE; 312. PHILOSOPHY.

anagraph a review or critique.

Aristotelian criticism a critical theory, doctrine, or approach based upon the method used by Aristotle in the *Poetics,* implying a formal, logical approach to literary analysis that is centered on the work itself. Cf. Platonic criticism.

chorizontist *Rare.* a critic of Homeric literature who claims the *Iliad* and the *Odyssey* had different authors.

contextualism a school of literary criticism that focuses on the work as an autonomous entity, whose meaning should be derived solely from an examination of the work itself. Cf. New Criticism. —contextualist, *n., adj.*

empirio-criticism the type of criticism whose aim is the reduction of knowledge to descriptions of pure experience and the elimination of such aspects as metaphysics. —empiriocritical, *adj.*

epicrisis a detailed criticism of a book, dissertation, or other writing.

exegesis a critical interpretation or explication, especially of biblical and other religious texts. —exegetic, exegetical, *adj.*

formal criticism a critical approach, doctrine, or technique that places heavy emphasis on style, form, or technique in art or literature, seeing these as more important than or even determining content.

formalism a critical emphasis upon style, arrangement, and artistic means with limited attention to content. —formalist, *n.* —formalistic, *adj.*

Freudianism the application of the theories of the personality developed by Freud to the development of characters and other aspects of artistic creation. Cf. psychoanalytical criticism. —Freudian, *n., adj.*

genre criticism a critical approach, doctrine, or technique that emphasizes, in evaluating a work, the genre or medium in which it can be placed rather than seeing it entirely as an autonomous entity.

hypercriticism the practice of unreasonable or unjustly severe criticism; faultfinding. —hypercritic, *n., adj.* —hypercritical, *adj.*

Jungian criticism a critical approach, doctrine, or practice that applies the theories of Jungian psychology to works of art and literature, especially with regard to Jungian theories of myth, archetype, and symbol. Cf. mythic criticism.

mimesis an imitation, used in literary criticism to designate Aristotle's theory of imitation. —mimetic, *adj.*

mythic criticism a critical approach or technique that seeks mythic meaning or imagery in literature, looking beyond the immediate context of the work in time and place. Cf. Jungian criticism.

New Criticism a critical approach to literature that concentrates upon analysis and explication of individual texts and considers historical and biographical information less important than an awareness of the work's formal structure. —New Critic, *n.*

new humanism an American antirealist, antinaturalist, and anti-Romantic literary and critical movement of circa 1915–1933, whose principal exponents were Babbitt, More, and Foerster, influenced by Matthew Arnold, and whose aims were to show the importance of reason and will in a context of rectitude and dignity. —new humanist, *n., adj.*

Platonic criticism a critical approach or doctrine based upon and applying the ideas and values of Plato and Platonism, implying a literary analysis which finds the value of a work in its extrinsic qualities and historical context, as well as in its non-artistic usefulness. Cf. Aristotelian criticism.

practical criticism a practical approach to literary criticism, in which the text is approached in universal terms with little recourse to an elaborate apparatus of reference outside the text. Cf. theoretical criticism.

psychoanalytical criticism an approach to criticism or a critical technique that applies the principles, theories and practices of psychoanalysis to literature, both in the analysis of the work and of the author. See also **Freudianism.**

purism in criticism, rigid or strict evaluation of a work of art or literature in terms of a code of standards of the critic or of a school of style or criticism related to or distinct from the critic, artist, or writer. See also 23. ART; 236. LANGUAGE; 249. LITERATURE. —**purist,** *n.*, *adj.*

self-criticism the action of finding one's own faults and shortcomings. —**self-critical,** *adj.*

textual criticism the close study of a particular literary work in order to establish its original text. —**textual critic,** *n.*

theoretical criticism a critical approach or doctrine that examines a literary work in the light of certain theories of literature or uses the text as a support for the development of literary theory. Cf. **practical criticism.**

Zoilism the practice of making bitter, carping, and belittling critical judgments. —**Zoilus, Zoili,** *n.*

105. CROWDS
See also 275. MOB.

demomania a mania for crowds. Also called **ochlomania.**

demophilia a fondness for crowds. —**demophil, demophile,** *n.*

demophobia an abnormal fear of crowds. Also called **ochlophobia.**

mobocracy government by the mob; the mob as ruler or dominant force in society. —**mobocrat,** *n.* —**mobocratic,** *adj.*

ochlomania demomania.

ochlophobia demophobia.

phalanx an ancient military formation of serried ranks surrounded by shields; hence, any crowded mass of people or group united for a common purpose.

106. CUNNING
callidity *Rare.* skill or craftiness. —**callid,** *adj.*

jesuitism crafty or deceitful practice. —**jesuitic, jesuitical,** *adj.*

jiggery-pokery subterfuge or devious and underhanded behavior; low cunning.

oneupmanship the art or process of gaining the advantage in situations by means of crafty or ingenious ploys.

tergiversation 1. the act or process of subterfuge or evasion.
2. the abandoning of a cause or belief; apostasy. —**tergiversator,** *n.*

vulpinism *Rare.* the state or quality of being foxlike, especially crafty or cunning. —vulpine, *adj.*

D

107. DAMPNESS
See also 414. WATER.

hygrophobia an abnormal fear of water, moisture, or dampness.

psychrometry the measurement of the humidity content of the air by use of a psychrometer. —psychrometric, psychrometrical, *adj.*

108. DANCING
See also 310. PERFORMING.

choreodrama a drama expressed in dance or with dance as an integral part of its content and form.

choreography 1. the art of composing dances for the stage, especially in conceiving and realizing the movements of the dancers.
2. the technique of representing dance movements through a notational scheme.
3. the art of dancing. Also called choregraphy, orchesography. —choreographer, *n.* —choreographic, *adj.*

choreomania a mania for dancing.

ecdysiast a striptease performer or exotic dancer.

orchesography choreography. Also orchesis, orchestics.

tripudiation *Rare.* the act of dancing. —tripudiary, *adj.*

109. DANTE
See also 29. AUTHORS; 249. LITERATURE.

Dantesque from or resembling the characters, scenes, or events in Dante's works.

Dantophily love of Dante or his writings. —Dantophile, *adj.*, *n.*

110. DARKNESS
See also 47. BLACKENING and BLACKNESS; 292. NIGHT.

achluphobia an abnormal fear of darkness. Also called scotophobia.

fuliginosity 1. the state or condition of being sooty or smoky.
2. soot or smoke. —fuliginous, *adj.*

noctiluca any thing or creature that shines or glows in the dark, especially a phosphorescent or bioluminescent marine or other organism. —**noctilucine,** *adj.*

noctimania an abnormal love of the night.

nyctophobia an abnormal fear of darkness or night.

obumbration *Rare.* the act or process of darkening or obscuring.

sciophobia an abnormal fear of shadows.

scotophobia achluophobia.

scotopia vision in dim light or darkness. See also photopia. —**scotopic,** *adj.*

111. DEAFNESS
See also 132. EAR; 198. HEARING.

aerophone a type of ear trumpet used by the deaf.

Ameslan an acronym for the American Sign Language for the Deaf, a system of communication through gestures and hand signals.

anaudia loss or absence of the power of hearing.

autophony a form of deafness in which the sufferer hears only his own voice, and that very loudly. See also 266. MEDICAL SPECIALTIES.

dactylology, dactyliology the technique of communicating through signs made with the fingers, as in the manual alphabet for the deaf.

deafmutism the condition of lacking both hearing and speech. Also called surdomutism. —**deafmute,** *n.*

manualism the teaching of communication through the use of hand signals to the deaf. —**manualist,** *n.*

oralism 1. the principles of the oral method of training the deaf, as lip reading.
2. the support or practice of these principles. Cf. **manualism.** —**oralist,** *n.*

osteophone a hearing device for the deaf that is placed against the upper teeth so it can transmit vibrations to the auditory nerve through the bones of the skull.

paracusis defective sense of hearing. Also **paracousia.**

phonautography a procedure for producing visible records of sound waves or speech sounds, especially to assist the deaf in using the telephone. Also called **visible speech.** —**phonautographic,** *adj.*

surdism *Pathology.* the degree of deafness that is sufficient to block the acquisition of speech by normal means.

surdomutism deafmutism. —**surdomute,** *n.*

112. DEATH
See also 63. BURIAL; 99. CORPSES; 232. KILLING.

autophonomania an obsession with suicide.

cerement, cerements the cloth or clothing in which the dead are wrapped for burial or other form of funeral.

cinerarium a place where the cremated remains of the dead are stored. —**cinerary**, *adj.*

columbarium a vault where the remains of cremated bodies are kept, usually in one of a number of recesses in a wall.

crematorium, crematory a place where cremations are done.

epitaph 1. an inscription on a monument, as on a gravestone.
2. a short piece of prose or verse written in honor of a dead person. —**epitaphial, epitaphian, epitaphic,** *adj.*

euthanasia the deliberate killing of painfully ill or terminally ill people to put them out of their misery. Also called **mercy killing.**

ktenology the science of putting people to death.

moribundity 1. the state or quality of being on the verge of death.
2. close to extinction or stagnant. —**moribund,** *adj.*

myriologue an improvised funeral song, composed for the dead and sung by women in modern Greece. —**myriologist,** *n.* —**myriologic, myriological,** *adj.*

necrolatry the worship of the dead.

necrology 1. an announcement of death; obituary.
2. a list of persons who have died within a certain time. Also **necrologue.** —**necrologist,** *n.*

necromancy 1. the magic practiced by a witch or sorcerer.
2. a form of divination through communication with the dead; the black art. Also **nigromancy.** —**necromancer, necromant, nigromancien,** *n.* —**necromantic,** *adj.*

necromania an obsession with death or the dead.

necromimesis an abnormal condition in which a person believes himself dead.

necrophilia, necrophilism an abnormal, often sexual attraction toward the dead or a dead body. —**necrophile,** *n.*

necrophobia an abnormal fear of death. Also called **thanatophobia.**

necrosis the death or decay of body tissue, the result of loss of blood supply or trauma. —**necrotic,** *adj.*

nerterology *Rare.* any learning that pertains to the dead.

ossuarium a place or receptacle for the bones of the dead. Also called **ossuary.**

taphophilia, taphephilia an excessive interest in graves and cemeteries.

thanatoid resembling death; deathly.

thanatology the study of death or the dead. Also **thanatism**. —**thanatological,** *adj.*

thanatomania an obsession with death. See also **necromania.**

thanatophobia necrophobia.

thanatopsis a survey of or meditation upon death.

viaticum the Eucharist given to one about to die; last rites or extreme unction. —**viatic, viatical,** *adj.*

113. DECAYING

atrophy degeneration as the result of disuse, malnutrition, etc.

biodegradability disposition to disintegrate as the result of natural processes. —**biodegradable,** *adj.*

caducity the condition of being perishable. —**caducous,** *adj.*

cariosity the condition of being decayed or carious, especially with regard to teeth.

catabolism the destructive process of metabolism in which living matter is turned into waste. —**catabolic,** *adj.*

cataclasm a breaking down; disruption. —**cataclasmic,** *n.*

catalysis *Rare.* the process of decay or deterioration. See also 74. CHANGE.

cataplasia degeneration of cells or tissues. —**cataplastic,** *adj.*

cataplasis the stage of decline in organic development.

cytolysis the degeneration of cells. —**cytolytic,** *adj.*

degradability the state or quality of being susceptible to breakdown or decomposition. —**degradable,** *adj.*

deteriorism the belief that the universe is gradually breaking down. See also **meliorism.**

fugacity the condition of being fugacious or transitory; evanescence. —**fugacious,** *adj.*

geratology the branch of biology that studies aging and its phenomena. Also **gereology.** —**geratologic, geratologous,** *adj.*

histolysis the disintegration or dissolution of organic tissues. —**histolytic,** *adj.*

labefaction, labefactation the process of coming apart, especially falling into ruin or decay.

lysis the decomposition of cells by antibodies called lysins.

myoatrophy atrophy or wasting away of the muscles.

necrosis the death or decay of body tissue, the result of loss of blood supply or trauma. —**necrotic,** *adj.*

pejoration depreciation, loss, or diminution in value, quality, etc.

photolysis the breakdown of matter or materials under the influence of light. —photolytic, *adj.*

putrescence 1. the state or process of rotting or putrefying.
2. rotting or putrefying matter. —putrescent, *adj.*

symptosis a gradual wasting away of the body or of any organ or part of the body.

syntexis the wasting of the body, as in consumption. —syntectic, syntectical, *adj.*

tabescence 1. the process of emaciation or wasting of the body.
2. the condition of being wasted or in decay, especially as a gradual process. —tabescent, *adj.*

tabitude the state of being affected by tabes, i.e., gradual wasting or decay.

114. DEMONS
See also 117. DEVIL; 146. EVIL; 182. GHOSTS; 203. HELL; 384. SPIRITS and SPIRITUALISM.

ademonist one who denies the existence of the devil or demons.

bogyism, bogeyism recognition of the existence of demons and goblins.

cacodemonia a mania that causes a person to believe himself possessed and controlled by an evil spirit. Also cacodemonomania. —cacodemonic, cacodemoniac, *adj.*

demonianism 1. a belief in the possibility of possession by a demon.
2. demoniac possession. Also demoniacism. —demonian, *adj.* —demoniac, *n.*, *adj.*

demonism 1. the belief in demons.
2. the worship of demons. Also demonolatry. —demonist, *n.*

demonocracy 1. the power of demons.
2. government or rule by demons. —demonocratic, *adj.*

demonography demonology. —demonographer, *n.*

demonolatry the worship, through propitiation, of ghosts, demons, and spirits. Also demonism.

demonology 1. the study of demons or superstitions about demons.
2. the doctrine of demons. Also demonography. —demonologist, *n.* —demonologic, demonological, *adj.*

demonomagy *Obsolete.* forms of magic that require the invocation or assistance of demons.

demonomancy a form of divination involving a demon or demons.

demonomist *Obsolete.* a person who is possessed by demons.

demonomy *Obsolete.* the sway or dominion of demons.

demonophobia an abnormal fear of spirits and demons.

demonurgy the working of magic with the aid of demons. —demonurgist, *n.*

devilism qualities and doctrines that are diabolical. —devilish, *adj.*

energumen a demoniac; a person possessed by an evil spirit. See also 150. FADS.

exorcism 1. the ceremony that seeks to expel an evil spirit from a person or place.
2. the act or process of exorcising. —exorcist, *n.* —exorcismal, exorcisory, exorcistic, exorcistical, *adj.*

incubus a demon alleged to lie upon people in their sleep and especially to tempt women to sexual relations. —incubi, *n. pl.*

nympholepsy 1. an ecstatic variety of demonic possession believed by the ancients to be inspired by nymphs.
2. a frenzy of emotion, as for something unattainable. —nympholeptic, *adj.*

pandemonism *Rare.* the worship of spirits dwelling in all forms of nature.

Pandemonium 1. the abode of all demons; Hell.
2. any scene of wild confusion or disorder.

polydemonism, polydaemonism a devotion to a multitude of demonic powers or spirits. —polydemonistic, polydaemonistic, *adj.*

succubus, succuba a demon that assumes a female form to tempt men to intercourse, especially appearing in their dreams. —succubi, succubae, *n. pl.*

115. DEPTH
See also 202. HEIGHTS.

bathometer, bathymeter *Oceanography.* a device for ascertaining the depth of water.

bathyclinograph a device for ascertaining vertical currents in the deeper parts of the sea.

bathymetry the measurement of the depths of oceans, seas, or other large bodies of water. —bathymetric, bathymetrical, *adj.*

bathyscaphe, bathyscape, bathyscaph *Oceanography.* a small, modified submarine for deep-sea exploration, usually having a spherical observation chamber fixed under a buoyancy chamber.

bathysphere *Oceanography.* a spherical diving apparatus from which to study deep-sea life.

bathythermograph a device that records the temperature of water as a reflex of depth.

benthos 1. the depths or bottom of the sea.
2. organic life that inhabits the bottom of the sea.

benthoscope an apparatus for surveying the depths or bottom of the sea.

116. DESERTS
See also 142. ENVIRONMENT.

eremite a religious hermit living alone, often in the desert. —**eremitic**, *adj.*

eremology the systematic study of desert features and phenomena.

xerophobia an abnormal fear of dryness and dry places, as deserts.

117. DEVIL
See also 114. DEMONS; 146. EVIL; 183. GOD and GODS; 203. HELL; 349. RELIGION; 367. SIN; 392. THEOLOGY.

adiabolist a person who denies the existence of the devil.

diabolism 1. belief in or worship of the devil.
2. *Theology.* an action aided or prompted by the devil; sorcery; witchcraft. —**diabolist**, *n.*

diabology, diabolology 1. the study of the devil.
2. devil lore.

Izedism the beliefs of the Izedis, a Mesopotamian sect said to worship the devil. Also **Yezdism, Yezidism.** —**Izedi, Yezdi, Yezidi**, *n.*

monodiabolism belief in the existence of only one devil. Cf. **polydiabolism.**

Pan-Satanism a Gnostic doctrine that the material world expresses the personality of Satan.

polydiabolism the belief that many devils exist. Cf. **monodiabolism.**

Satanism 1. the worship of Satan or evil powers.
2. a parody of Christian ceremonies in which the devil is worshiped. —**Satanist**, *n.*

Satanophany the appearance of Satan on earth.

Yezdism, Yezidism Izedism.

118. DINING
aristology *Rare.* the art or science of dining. —**aristologist**, *n.*

deipnophobia an abnormal fear of dining and dinner conversation.

deipnosophism the art of dinner conversation. —**deipnosophist**, *n.*

napery household linen collectively, especially tablecloths and napkins.

119. DIRT
See also 84. CLEANLINESS; 377. SOIL.

aischrolatreia a devotion to or worship of filth and obscenity.

automysophobia *Rare.* an abnormal fear of being dirty.

feculence, feculency 1. the condition of being befouled or besmirched.
2. the material causing this condition. —**feculent**, *adj.*

fuliginosity 1. the state or condition of being sooty or smoky.
2. soot or smoke. —fuliginous, *adj.*

maculacy the state or quality of being blemished, stained, or spotted, as with dirt. Also maculation. —maculate, *adj.*

misophobia, musophobia, mysophobia an abnormal fear of dirt, especially of being contaminated by dirt.

mysophilia an abnormal attraction to filth.

rhypophobia an abnormal fear of filth.

120. DISCONTENT

gravamen a grievance, especially one that is the cause of a legal action.

paramania an abnormal pleasure in complaints.

121. DISCRIMINATION
See also 155. FAVORITISM.

ageism, agism discrimination on the basis of age, especially against older people.

chauvinism ardent, unreasoned favoritism for a particular group. See also 289. NATIONALISM. —chauvinist, *n.*

racism discrimination on the basis of race, especially against blacks and other non-whites.

sexism discrimination on the basis of sex, especially against women.

122. DISEASE and ILLNESS
See also 32. BACTERIA; 66. CANCER; 130. DRUGS; 197. HEALTH; 224. INSANITY; 266. MEDICAL SPECIALTIES; 306. PAIN; 340. RABIES; 350. REMEDIES.

acetonemia, acetonaemia a condition caused by elevated levels of acetone in the blood.

achromatosis a disease characterized by an absence of pigmentation, as albinism.

acidosis a condition of the blood in which the alkali reserve is lower than normal. Also called acid intoxication, autointoxication. —acidotic, *adj.*

acromegaly a disease resulting from abnormal activity of the pituitary gland, causing bones of the extremities to become enlarged. —acromegalic, *adj.*

adynamia, adynamy loss of strength occasioned by a disease or illness; weakness. —adynamic, *adj.*

aeroembolism a condition caused by the formation of nitrogen bubbles in the blood as a result of a sudden lowering of atmospheric pressure, as when flying at high altitude or rising too rapidly from a deep underwater dive.

aeroneurosis a stress condition of aviators, manifested in such physical symptoms as stomach pains, digestive problems, etc.

aerophagy erratic gulping of air.

aetiology etiology.

ageusia the partial or complete loss of the sense of taste. Also **ageustia.**

alkalosis a condition in which the alkali content or reserve of the body is above normal.

aluminosis a respiratory disease caused by prolonged inhalation of aluminum particles.

amygdalitis inflammation of one or both tonsils; tonsillitis.

anabasis the progress of a disease, from onset to finish.

analepsis, analepsy *Obsolete.* a form of epileptic attack.

anaphylaxis extreme sensitivity to an antigen, causing secretion of histamine and attendant adverse reactions, sometimes fatal. —**anaphylactic,** *adj.*

anemia, anaemia 1. a lack of blood in the body.
2. a low proportion of red cells in the blood. —**anemic, anaemic,** *adj.*

anemotrophy insufficient nutrients in the blood.

anergy 1. a lack of strength.
2. the failure of the body to respond to an allergen or antigen.

anesis the remission of disease symptoms.

ankylosis the stiffening of the joints of the body, a result of the formation of a fibrous or bony union.

anorexia a complete lack of appetite. —**anorectic, anorexic,** *adj.*

anorexia nervosa a neurotic disorder characterized by refusal to eat and abnormal fear of obesity, seen especially in adolescent girls. —**anorectic, anorexic,** *adj.*

anoxia a condition characterized by insufficient oxygen in the tissues.

anthracosis a disease of coal miners caused by the inhalation of coal dust.

antipyretic any substance or medication effective in reducing fever. Also called **febrifuge.**

apnea, apnoea a temporary interruption in breathing. —**apneal, apneic, apnoeal, apnoeic,** *adj.*

argyrism, argyria a poisoning by silver or salts of silver, causing the skin to become ashy gray.

arthritism 1. a predisposition to gout.
2. a predisposition to joint diseases. —**arthritic, arthritical,** *adj.*

arthropathology the study of functional and structural changes made by diseases of the joints.

asepticism the prevention of infection by such means as sterilization.

ataxia, ataxy inability to coordinate bodily movements, especially movements of the muscles. See also 301. ORDER and DISORDER.

avitaminosis any disease or illness caused by an insufficiency of one or more vitamins. —**avitaminotic,** *adj.*

blennorrhea, blennorrhoea an abnormal discharge of mucous matter. —**blennorheal, blennorheic, blennorhoeal, blennorhoeic,** *adj.*

bromism a poisoning produced by excessive use of bromine or bromine compounds. Also **brominism, bromidism.**

bulimia, boulimia a raging hunger or voracious appetite. —**bulimic, boulimic, bulimiac, boulimiac,** *adj.*

bulimorexia, boulimorexia a psychological condition in which the person alternately gorges himself with food and fasts, often resorting to self-induced vomiting after gorging. —**bulimorexic, boulimorexic,** *adj.*

cacesthesia a morbid sensation or disordered sensibility.

cacoethes a chronic and overwhelming desire; mania. —**cacoethic,** *adj.*

calciphilia a tendency to calcification.

calenture a tropical fever accompanied by delirium.

carphology the motions of delirious or senile patients, especially motions of searching for and grasping at imaginary objects, plucking at bedclothes, etc. Also called **floccilation.**

caseation the change in consistency of tissue to a soft, cheeselike form, as in tuberculosis.

catabasis the tapering-off of a disease. —**catabatic,** *adj.*

catalepsy *Pathology, Psychiatry.* a physical condition characterized by a loss of sensation, muscular rigidity, fixity of posture, and often by a loss of contact with surroundings. Also **catalepsis.** —**cataleptic,** *adj.*

chalicosis a lung disease caused by the breathing in of dust, especially stone dust.

chloralism a sickness caused by excessive use of chloral hydrate.

chlorosis green sickness; a disease of girls in puberty, characterized by, among other symptoms, greenishness of the skin.

chorea a disease of the nervous system characterized by jerky, involuntary movement; St. Vitus's Dance.

choromania the dancing sickness (epidemic chorea).

cirrhosis a degenerative disease of the liver, marked by an excessive formation of tissue and contraction of the organ, usually brought on by chronic alcohol abuse. —**cirrhotic,** *adj.*

clonism a state or condition in which the muscles undergo clonus, or rapid flexion and extension. —clonic, *adj.*

coryza a condition of catarrh in the nose; a head cold.

cyanopathy cyanosis.

cyanosis bluish discoloration of the skin caused by lack of oxygen in the bloodstream. Also **cyanopathy.** —cyanotic, *adj.*

cypridophobia an abnormal fear of venereal disease. Also called **venereophobia.**

cytopathology *Medicine.* the branch of pathology that studies the effects of disease on the cellular level. —cytopathologist, *n.* —cytopathologic, cytopathological, *adj.*

delitescence the sudden disappearance of symptoms or of objective signs of a lesion or disease. —delitescent, *adj.*

diathesis a susceptibility to a certain disease. —diathetic, *adj.*

digitalism an abnormal condition caused by excessive consumption of digitalis.

diplegia a form of paralysis in which similar parts on both sides of the body are affected. —diplegic, *adj.*

Down's syndrome mongolism.

dysidrosis a condition of abnormally excessive secretion of sweat.

dysmenorrhea a condition of painful menstruation.

dyspepsia an impairment of the ability to digest food, usually a discomfort after meals. —dyspeptic, *n.*, *adj.* —dyspeptical, *adj.*

dysphagia, dysphagy a condition in which there is difficulty in swallowing. —dysphagic, *adj.*

dyspnea, dyspnoea a condition of painful or difficult breathing. —dyspneic, dyspnoeic, *adj.*

dystrophy, dystrophia any of various diseases characterized by weakening or defective function of the process of nutrition, resulting in degeneration of the muscles. See also 168. FOOD and NUTRITION. —dystrophic, *adj.*

dysuria difficulty or pain in urinating.

eclamptism a toxemia sometimes occurring in late pregnancy marked by visual impairment, headache, and, occasionally, convulsions. Also **eclampsia.**

ectasia the swelling of a hollow organ of the body, as a vein.

edema abnormal collecting of fluids in the cells, tissues, and other parts of the body, causing swelling. —edematous, edematose, *adj.*

emesis an act of vomiting. —emetic, *adj.*

emmeniopathy disorder in the process of menstruation.

empyema the collecting of pus in one of the cavities of the body, especially in the cavity containing the lungs.

epidemic a disease that is widely prevalent in a particular area. —**epidemical,** *adj.* —**epidemicity,** *n.*

epidemiography a work on epidemic diseases. —**epidemiographer, epidemiographist,** *n.* —**epidemiographic, epidemiographical,** *adj.*

epigenesis 1. the appearance of a secondary symptom in a disease or illness. 2. the secondary symptom itself. See also 44. BIOLOGY; 179. GEOLOGY. —**epigenetic,** *adj.*

epilepsy a disease of the nervous system characterized by convulsions, often leading to unconsciousness. —**epileptic,** *n.*, *adj.*

epitasis a period of violence in the course of a disease, especially a fever.

epithelioma a malignant tumor, found especially on the skin, mouth, larynx, and bladder. —**epitheliomatous,** *adj.*

erethism 1. an excessive irritability or sensibility to stimulation in any part of the body, especially the sexual organs. 2. a psychic disturbance characterized by irritability, emotional instability, depression, shyness, and fatigue, often caused by toxicity. —**erethistic, erethitic,** *adj.*

erysipelas an infectious disease of the skin marked by inflammation and accompanied by fever.

erythema an abnormal red condition of the skin, the result of capillary congestion. —**erythematous,** *adj.*

erythromelalgia a disease of the hands and feet characterized by a purplish discoloration and a sensation of burning pain. —**erythromelalgic,** *adj.*

erythrosis a pathological condition characterized by a reddish color of the skin and mucous membrane.

etiolation paleness of color as a result of illness or exclusion from light. See also 319. PLANTS.

etiology, aetiology 1. the branch of medical science that studies the causes of diseases and the factors underlying their spread. 2. the accumulated knowledge of disease causes. —**etiologist,** *n.* —**etiologic, etiological,** *adj.*

exanthematology a treatise on or study of diseases characterized by eruptions or rashes, as smallpox or measles. —**exanthematologic, exanthematological,** *adj.*

fabism, favism an acute anemia caused by the consumption of fava beans or the ingestion of fava pollen.

febrifacient any substance that produces a fever.

febrifuge antipyretic.

floccilation carphology.

fluidism a theory that accounts for all diseases as related to the state of the fluids in the body. —fluidist, *n.*

frambesia, framboesia a contagious tropical disease. Also called yaws.

gargoylism an abnormal physical condition characterized by extensive structural defects of the skeleton and by gross mental deficiency.

gastricism diseases and disorders of the stomach.

glossitis an inflamed condition of the tongue. —glossitic, *adj.*

glycophilia a condition in which a small amount of glucose produces hyperglycemia.

glycosuria presence of glucose in the urine, as in diabetics. —glycosuric, *adj.*

hemiplegia a condition of paralysis in which one side of the body is affected. —hemiplegic, *n., adj.*

hemophilia, haemophilia an hereditary tendency, in males, toward a deficiency in coagulation factors in the blood. —hemophiliac, haemophiliac, *n., adj.*

hepatitis an inflamed condition of the liver.

herpetography a description of any of the skin diseases collectively referred to as herpes. —herpetographical, *adj.*

hospitalism influences that adversely affect the mental and physical health of those being hospitalized.

hyperdynamia a state of excessive energy; abnormal nervous or muscular activity.

hyperesthesia, hyperaesthesia 1. an excessive sensitivity of skin in a particular area.
2. an excessive sensitivity of a particular sense, especially smell.
3. a heightened sensitivity to the environment. —hyperesthetic, hyperaesthetic, *adj.*

hyperglycemia a condition in which the level of glucose in the blood is abnormally high. —hyperglycemic, *adj.*

hyperkinesia, hyperkinesis a condition of the body in which muscular movement is abnormally agitated. —hyperkinetic, *adj.*

hyperpituitarism an abnormal condition of the pituitary gland that speeds up secretory activity and the growth of the endocrine organs. —hyperpituitary, *adj.*

hyperpnea rapid breathing; abnormally rapid respiration.

hyperpyrexia a condition of abnormally high fever. —hyperpyretic, *adj.*

hyperthermia, hyperthermy an abnormally high fever, sometimes induced as treatment for disease.

hyperthyroidism an abnormal thyroid condition distinguished by high metabolic rate and blood pressure and the enlargement of the thyroid. —hyperthyroid, *adj*.

hypoglycemia a condition in which the level of glucose in the blood is abnormally low. —hypoglycemic, *adj*.

hypopituitarism an abnormal condition of the pituitary gland that slows down the growth of and secretory activity of the endocrine organs. —hypopituitary, *adj*.

hypothermia, hypothermy an abnormally low body temperature, sometimes induced as treatment for disease.

hypothyroidism an abnormal thyroid condition marked by a low metabolic rate and loss of stamina. —hypothyroid, *adj*.

hysterocatalepsy hysteria accompanied by catalepsy.

hysteroepilepsy hysteria accompanied by epilepsy. —hysteroepileptic, *adj*.

hysteropathy any disease, illness, or disorder of the uterus.

hystricism an extreme form of a skin disease in which the skin is covered with horny prominences. Sometimes called the "porcupine disease."

idiopathy a disease or illness that is not occasioned or preceded by another. —idiopathic, *adj*.

invalidism a condition of prolonged ill health.

iodism a disease resulting from excessive intake of iodine or its compounds; iodine poisoning.

ischialgia sciatica.

isopathy 1. the theory that the product of a disease can be used to cure that same disease, as in the treatment of smallpox with substance taken from the varioles.
2. the belief that a diseased organ can be cured by eating the corresponding organ from a healthy animal.

laryngitis an inflamed condition of the larynx, producing a sore throat and sometimes loss of voice. —laryngitic, *adj*.

leontiasis a form of leprosy in which the face comes to resemble that of a lion.

leucodermia, leucoderma a congenital deficiency of skin pigmentation that results in white patches over the surface of the skin.

leucorrhea a white, mucous, vaginal discharge, usually the result of an infection of the vagina. Also called the whites.

lientery a variety of diarrhea in which food is excreted either partially or wholly undigested. —lienteric, *adj*.

lionism *Rare*. a lionlike appearance of the face caused by leprosy; leontiasis.

lipoma a tumor consisting of fatty tissue. —lipomatous, *adj*.

lipothymia, lipothymy fainting or a feeling of faintness; swooning; syncope. —lipothymic, lipothymous, *adj*.

lithiasis a condition causing concretions of mineral salts, or calculi, in the pancreas, tear ducts, appendix, or kidneys.

loimography the branch of medicine dealing with the description of plagues. —loimographer, *n*. —loimographic, loimographical, *adj*.

loimology *Rare*. the study of pestilential diseases and plagues.

luetism the venereal disease syphilis in any of three stages; lues. —luetic, *adj*.

malariology *Rare*. the study of malaria. —malariologist, *n*.

marasmus 1. a wasting away or atrophying of the body in the absence of disease.
2. the progressive emaciation that results from malnutrition. —marasmic, *adj*.

maturation suppuration, or the formation and discharge of pus. —maturative, *adj*.

melanopathia, melanopathy 1. an abnormal increase in the amount of pigment deposited in the skin or tissues.
2. any disease characterized by this condition.

melanuria 1. abnormal darkness of the urine.
2. discharge of abnormally dark urine. —melanuric, *adj*.

mercurialism chronic poisoning with mercury from either excessive medication or industrial exposure.

merycism *Pathology*. a rare disease in which food is chewed, swallowed, and then returned to the mouth and chewed again.

mescalism addiction to mescal, a narcotic derived from the cactus *Lophophora williamsii*.

metabasis an alteration in the nature of a disease or in its treatment. Also metabola, metabole. —metabatic, *adj*.

meteorism *Medicine*. a tendency to uncontrollable flatulence. Also called tympanites.

molysomophobia an abnormal fear of infection.

mongolism *Medicine*. the abnormal condition of a child born mentally deficient, with a flattened skull, narrow slanting eyes, and a short, flat-bridged nose. Now usually called Down's syndrome. —mongolic, *adj*.

monopathy a disease that affects only one part of the body.

myiasis any disease resulting from infestation of the body tissues or cavities by flies.

myxedema, myxoedema a disease resulting from the decreased function of the thyroid, characterized by a slowing down of mental and physical activity and thickening and drying of the skin. —**myxedematous, myxedoematous,** *adj.*

myxochondroma myxoma together with chondroma. —**myxochondromatous,** *adj.*

myxodermia an acute disease characterized by ecchymoses, softening of the skin, and the contraction of certain muscles.

myxolipoma myxoma together with lipoma.

myxoma a soft tumor formed of gelatinous tissue. —**myxomatous,** *adj.*

myxomatosis an infectious, highly fatal, virus disease of rabbits, transmitted by mosquitoes.

narcolepsy a condition characterized by an uncontrollable desire for sleep or sudden onsets of sleep. —**narcoleptic,** *adj.*

nephritis any of various acute and chronic diseases of the kidneys involving inflammation, degeneration, etc. —**nephritic, nephritical,** *adj.*

nicotinism the condition produced by an excessive use of tobacco. Also called **tabacism, tabagism, tobaccoism.**

nosography the description of the symptoms and etiology of diseases. —**nosographer,** *n.* —**nosographic, nosographical,** *adj.*

nosology the branch of medical science that classifies diseases. Also **nosonomy.** —**nosologist,** *n.* —**nosologic, nosological,** *adj.*

nosomania an obsession with imagined disease. Also **hypochondriacism.**

nosonomy nosology.

nosophilia an excessive, abnormal desire to be sick. Also called **pathophilia.**

nosophobia an abnormal fear of contracting disease.

oligidria a condition in which the body is deficient in the secretion of sweat.

orthopnea, orthopny a respiratory ailment in which the sufferer can breathe only when standing upright. —**orthopneic,** *adj.*

oxyesthesia a condition in which the senses are abnormally sharp.

palatoplegia paralysis of the palate.

paludism the state of having symptoms of malaria characterized by high fever and chills.

pandemia, pandemy an epidemic of unusually large proportions, affecting most of the inhabitants of a certain area at the same time. —**pandemic,** *adj., n.*

pangermism the theory that all disease is caused by germs.

paragraphia *Pathology*. a form of aphasia in which the subject writes one word in place of another. —**paragraphic,** *adj.*

paralysis loss of the ability to move or feel in part or all of the body, usually a result of nerve or muscle injury or dysfunction. —**paralytic, paralytical,** *adj.*

paresis a state or process of partial paralysis. —**paretic,** *adj.*

Parkinsonism a chronic condition of the nervous system marked especially by muscle tremors.

parotitis a swollen or inflamed condition of the parotid. Also called **mumps.** —**parotitic,** *adj.*

pathogenicity the capacity of a microorganism to produce disease. —**pathogenic,** *adj.*

pathology 1. the branch of medical science that studies the origin, nature, and course of diseases.
2. the conditions and processes of a disease. —**pathologist,** *n.* —**pathologic, pathological,** *adj.*

pathophilia nosophilia.

pathophobia an abnormal fear of disease.

pertussis whooping cough. —**pertussal,** *adj.*

pharmacomania a mania for medicines.

pharyngism a spasm in the throat.

phorology the branch of medical science that studies disease carriers and epidemic or endemic diseases. —**phorologist,** *n.*

phthisiology the body of knowledge accumulated about tuberculosis.

phthisiomania an abnormal interest in tuberculosis.

phthisis any disease causing a wasting away of part or all of the body, especially tuberculosis; consumption. —**phthisic, phthisical,** *adj.*

physiogenic somatogenic.

pneumoconiosis any of various chronic lung diseases caused by the inhalation of dust particles.

pneumonoultramicroscopicsilicovolcanoconiosis a disease caused by the prolonged inhalation of fine siliceous dust. Also spelled **pneumonoultramicroscopicsilicovolcanokoniosis.**

pollinosis hay fever.

polyphagia, polyphagy *Pathology*. excessive appetite or excessive eating.

poriomania an unconscious tendency to walk away from home; ambulatory automatism.

prodromata (*pl.*) the symptoms that appear before the outbreak of a disease. Also called **prodrome.** —**prodromatic,** *adj.*

psychogenesis the appearance of physical symptoms as a result of emotional problems. —psychogenic, psychogenetic, *adj.*

psychogenicity a medical theory that the cause of some illnesses is psychological and emotional and not organic. —psychogenic, *adj.*

psychopathy a disorder of the mind. —psychopathic, *adj.*

pyretography a treatise describing fevers. —pyretographer, *n.* —pyretographic, *adj.*

pyretology a branch of medical science that studies fevers and their treatment.

pyrosis a burning feeling in the stomach and esophagus, sometimes accompanied by the belching of acid fluid; heartburn.

recrudescence the return of an illness after a period of remission. —recrudescent, *adj.*

rheumatism any disorder of the connective tissue structures of the body, especially those in the back or the extremities, characterized by pain or stiffness. —rheumatic, *adj.*

rheumatology the branch of medical science that studies rheumatism. —rheumatologist, *n.*

sanies a thin fluid, sometimes greenish, discharged from wounds or sores. —sanious, *adj.*

sarcoma any of various malignant tumors formed in connective tissue. See also 66. CANCER. —sarcomatous, sarcomatoid, *adj.*

sarcomatosis a condition in which sarcomas spread throughout the body.

sciatica a painful condition in the region of the thighs and hips caused by neuritis of the sciatic nerve in the back of the thigh.

sclerosis a hardening of body tissues or other parts, as by an excessive growth of fibrous connective tissue. See also 319. PLANTS. —sclerotic, *adj.*

scorbuticism the condition of having scurvy. —scorbutic, *adj.*

semeiography *Pathology.* the science of description of symptoms. —semeiographer, *n.* —semeiographic, semeiographical, *adj.*

semeiology symptomatology.

sialism, sialismus excessive salivation, often a sign of poisoning.

siderosis 1. a disease caused by the inhalation of iron particles.
2. an abnormal amount of iron deposits in the body.

silicosis a disease of the lungs caused by prolonged inhalation of silica dust, an occupational disease of quarry-workers.

sinapism the use of mustard plaster for medical purposes.

solidism a doctrine that relates all diseases to the state of the solid parts of the body. —solidist, *n.* —solidistic, *adj.*

somatism the belief that emotional and mental disorders are of physical origin and caused by bodily lesions. —**somatist,** *n.*

somatogenic originating in the body or the cells of the body, as a disease. Also called **physiogenic.**

spasmatomancy a form of divination used to foretell disease by observing spasms or twitching of the potential sufferer's body.

spasmophilia an extreme tendency to convulsions. —**spasmophile,** *n.*

suppuration the formation and discharge of pus. Also called **maturation.**

symptomatology 1. the branch of medical science that studies the symptoms of diseases.
2. the combined symptoms of a particular disease. Also called **semeiology.**
—**symptomatologic, symptomatological,** *adj.*

symptosis a gradual wasting away of the body or of any organ or part of the body.

syntexis the wasting of the body, as in consumption. —**syntectic, syntectical,** *adj.*

tabacism nicotinism. Also spelled **tabagism.**

tabacosis poisoning or respiratory disease caused by tobacco smoking.

tabescence 1. the process of emaciation or wasting of the body.
2. the condition of being wasted or in decay, especially as a gradual process.
—**tabescent,** *adj.*

tabitude the state of being affected by tabes or by gradual wasting or decay.

tachypnea, tachypnoea abnormally rapid breathing or respiration.

tarantism a variety of dancing mania, popularly thought to be caused by the bite of a tarantula and to be cured by dancing.

thrombophilia a tendency to the occurrence of thrombosis or abnormal blood clotting.

thyroidism a condition caused by overactivity of the thyroid gland or excessive doses of thyroid.

tobaccoism nicotinism. Also **tabacism, tabagism.**

tomomania an obsession with surgery.

tomophobia an abnormal fear of surgical operations.

traumatophilia a condition in which a patient takes a subconscious delight in injuries or surgical operations.

trypanophobia an abnormal fear of vaccines and vaccination. Also called **vaccinophobia.**

tympanism an accumulation of gas in the abdominal tract that causes a distension of the abdomen. —**tympanitic,** *adj.*

typhomania the delirium that accompanies typhus or typhoid fever.

uridrosis a condition in which urine or its constituents appear in the perspiration.

vaccinophobia trypanophobia.

valetudinarianism the condition of being overly concerned with one's health. —valetudinarian, *n.*, *adj.*

vanillism an itching condition caused by excessive handling of vanilla.

venereophobia cypridophobia.

virilism 1. the early development of secondary masculine characteristics in a male.
2. the appearance of secondary masculine characteristics in a female. —virility, *n.*

xanthoma a skin disease characterized by the formation of yellow neoplastic growths, affecting especially the eyelids. Also called **xanthelasma**. —**xanthomatous**, *adj.*

xerostomia an abnormal dryness of the mouth, caused by lack of normal secretion of saliva.

zoonosis any disease of lower animals that may be transmitted to man. —**zoonotic**, *adj.*

zymosis *Rare*. 1. a process, similar to fermentation, thought to be the cause of infectious disease.
2. a disease so caused. See also 158. FERMENTATION. —**zymotic**, *adj.*

123. DISTANCE
See also 264. MEASUREMENT.

echolocation the fixing of the position of an object by transmitting a signal and measuring the time required for it to bounce back, typically done by radar or sonar.

hodometer odometer.

nauscopy the ability, sometimes pretended, to sight ships or land at great distances.

odograph a device that records the distance traveled; a recording odometer or pedometer.

odometer a device for measuring the distance passed over, as by an automobile. Also spelled **hodometer**.

pedometer a device that measures the distance walked by counting the number of steps taken.

tachymeter a surveying instrument for measuring distance, height, elevation, etc.

tachymetry the measurement of distance, height, elevation, etc., with a tachymeter.

telemeter 1. an instrument for measuring the distance of objects from the observer, as the range finder in artillery.
2. an electronic device for taking readings from other distant instruments.

telemetry the science or use of the telemeter; long-distance measurement.

telepheme *Rare*. a communication or conversation by telephone.

viameter an early form of odometer, for measuring the distance traveled by a carriage. Also viatometer.

124. DIVINATION
See also 24. ASTROLOGY; 174. FUTURE; 252. MAGIC.

aeromancy 1. the art or science of divination by means of the air or winds.
2. *Humorous*. weather forecasting. Cf. austromancy.

alectoromancy, alectryomancy a form of divination by recording the letters revealed as a cock eats kernels of corn that cover them.

aleuromancy an old form of divination using meal or flour. —aleuromantic, *adj*.

alomancy halomancy.

alphitomancy a form of divination involving the examination of barley.

ambulomancy a form of divination involving walking, usually in circles. Cf. gyromancy.

amniomancy a form of divination by examining the embryonic sac or amniotic fluid.

anthracomancy the art of divination through the study of burning coals. —anthracomantic, *adj*.

anthropomancy a form of divination using the entrails of dead men. —anthropomantist, *n*. —anthropomantic, *adj*.

arithmancy numerology.

armomancy a form of divination involving the shoulders of animals. Cf. spatulamancy.

aspidomancy a form of divination involving examination of a shield.

astragalomancy a form of divination involving dice or knuckle-bones, in which letters are marked on the faces of the dice and the future is foretold from the words formed as the dice fall. Also called cleromancy.

astrology a form of divination involving the relative positions of heavenly bodies. Also called genethlialogy, genethliacs.

astromancy divination by observation of the stars. Also called sideromancy.

augury 1. the art of foretelling the future by means of signs, originally by the flight of birds; divination.
2. an omen or portent from which the future is foretold. —**augur,** *n.* —**augurial,** *adj.* —**augurous,** *adj.*

austromancy divination by observing the winds, especially the south wind. Cf. **aeromancy.**

axinomancy a form of divination involving the use of an axhead. —**axinomantic,** *adj.*

belomancy divination in which marks or words are placed on arrows which are then drawn from a quiver at random.

bibliomancy a form of divination using books or the Bible in which passages are chosen at random and the future foretold from them.

botanomancy a form of divination involving the examination of plants.

capnomancy a form of divination involving smoke.

cartomancy a form of divination involving playing cards.

catoptromancy a form of divination involving a crystal ball or mirrors.

cephalomancy a form of divination involving the head.

ceraunomancy a form of divination involving thunder or thunderbolts.

ceromancy a form of divination involving dropping melted wax into water.

chalcomancy a form of divination involving brass vessels.

chaomancy a form of divination involving aerial visions.

chiromancy, cheiromancy palmistry.

chronomancy a divination to determine the precise time for action.

cleidomancy, clidomancy a form of divination involving a key or keys.

cleromancy astragalomancy.

coscinomancy a form of divination involving a sieve and shears. —**coscinomantic,** *adj.*

crithomancy a form of divination involving the strewing of grain over the bodies of sacrificed animals. —**crithomantic,** *adj.*

crystallomancy a form of divination involving crystal-gazing.

cubomancy *Rare.* a form of divination involving thrown dice. —**cubomantic,** *adj.*

dactyliomancy a form of divination involving finger rings.

demonomancy a form of divination involving a demon or demons.

empyromancy a form of divination involving a fire and smoke.

enoptromancy a form of divination involving a mirror and its reflections.

extispicy haruspicy. —**extispex,** *n.* —**extispicious,** *adj.*

gastromancy 1. a form of divination involving listening to stomach sounds.
2. a form of divination by gazing into a crystal ball or a glass full of water. Cf. **crystallomancy**. Also called **crystal-gazing**. —**gastromantic**, *adj.*

geloscopy, gelotoscopy a form of divination that determines a person's character or future from the way he laughs.

genethlialogy, genethliacs astrology.

geomancy a form of divination that analyzes the pattern of a handful of earth thrown down at random or of dots made at random on paper. —**geomancer**, *n.*

graphology 1. a form of divination involving analysis of handwriting. Also **graptomancy**.
2. a technique of personality analysis involving the examination of handwriting.

graptomancy graphology def. 1.

gyromancy a form of divination involving walking in a circle. Cf. **ambulomancy**.

halomancy a form of divination involving the use of salt. Also called **alomancy**.

hariolation the act or art of prognostication or divination; soothsaying.

haruspicy, haruspication a form of divination from lightning and other natural phenomena, but especially from inspection of the entrails of animal sacrifices. Also called **extispicy**. —**haruspex**, *n.* —**haruspical**, *adj.*

hematomancy, haematomancy divination by means of blood.

hieromancy a form of divination involving sacrificial remains or sacred objects. Also called **hieroscopy**.

hippomancy a form of divination involving the observation of horses, especially by listening to their neighing.

horoscopy 1. the art of casting horoscopes or divinations based upon the relative positions of heavenly bodies.
2. the position of the sun and stars at the time of a person's birth. —**horoscoper, horoscopist**, *n.*

hydromancy a form of divination involving observations of water or of other liquids.

ichnomancy the analysis of the personality and appearance of people by studying their footprints. —**ichnomantic**, *adj.*

ichthyomancy a form of divination involving the head or entrails of fishes.

idolomancy a form of divination involving idols.

lampadomancy a form of divination involving observation of the flame of a torch or lamp. Cf. **lychnomancy**.

lecanomancy a form of divination involving the examination of water in a basin.

lithomancy a form of divination involving rocks or stones.

logarithmomancy a form of divination involving logarithms.

logomancy a form of divination involving the observation of words and discourse.

lychnomancy a form of divination involving lamps. Cf. **lampadomancy**.

manticism the art of divination and prophecy. —**mantic**, *adj.*

mantology *Obsolete.* the art of fortune-telling. —**mantologist**, *n.*

margaritomancy a form of divination involving the examination of pearls.

meteoromancy a form of divination involving the observation of meteors.

metopomancy *Rare.* a form of divination involving examination of facial features.

molybdomancy *Rare.* a form of divination by studying the motion of molten lead.

moromancy a form of divination that is flawed or foolish.

myomancy a form of divination through observation of the movements of mice.

necromancy 1. the magic practiced by a witch or sorcerer.
2. a form of divination through communication with the dead. Also called **nigromancy**. —**necromancer, necromant, nigromancien**, *n.* —**necromantic**, *adj.*

nephelognosy divination by the observation of clouds.

nomancy a form of divination involving the examination of letters, possibly from a graphological point of view. Cf. **onomancy**.

numerology a form of divination involving numbers. Also called **arithmancy**.

oenomancy, oinomancy a form of divination involving observation of the colors and other features of wine.

omoplatoscopy a form of divination involving the examination of shoulder blades. Cf. **armomancy, scapulomancy, spatulamancy**.

omphalomancy a form of divination in which the number of knots in a newborn's umbilical cord are counted to foretell the number of children the mother will have later.

oneiromancy a form of divination involving dreams. —**oneiromancer**, *n.*

onomancy, onomomancy a form of divination involving the letters of a name. Cf. **nomancy**.

onychomancy a form of divination involving examination of the fingernails.

oomancy a form of divination involving eggs.

ophiomancy a form of divination involving snakes.

ornithomancy, ornithoscopy a form of divination involving the observation of birds, especially in flight.

osteomancy, osteomanty divination by the examination of bones. —**osteomantic,** *adj.*

palmistry a form of divination involving analysis of the appearance of the hand, especially of its various lines. Also called **chiromancy, cheiromancy.**

pedomancy a form of divination involving the study of the soles of the feet. Also called **podomancy.**

pegomancy a form of divination by studying springs or fountains. —**pegomantic,** *adj.*

pessomancy a form of divination involving pebbles. Also called **psephology, psephomancy.**

phyllomancy a form of divination involving the examination of leaves.

podomancy pedomancy.

psephology pessomancy.

psephomancy 1. pessomancy.
2. a form of divination involving the study of marks made on pebbles which are drawn at random from a container.

pseudomancy a form of divination that is deliberately false or misleading.

psychomancy a form of divination involving communication with the spirits of the dead.

pyromancy a form of divination involving fire or flames.

pythonism a form of divination in the manner of Pythia, the Delphic priestess.

rhabdomancy a form of divination involving a rod or wand, especially to locate objects or materials beneath the ground, as water or precious metals; dowsing.

rhapsodomancy a form of divination involving verses.

scapulomancy a form of divination in which a shoulder blade is heated in a fire and the resulting cracks in the bone are consulted for omens. Cf. **armomancy, omoplatoscopy, spatulamancy.** —**scapulomantic,** *adj.*

scatomancy a form of divination by examination of excrement.

schematomancy divination of a person's future from observation of physical appearance.

sciomancy a form of divination through communication with the spirits of the dead. —**sciomantic,** *adj.*

scyphomancy a form of divination involving the use of a cup.

selenomancy a form of divination involving observation of the moon.

sibyl *Ancient Greece and Rome.* a woman with oracular or prophetic powers, the most celebrated being that of Cumae. —sibyllic, —sibylic, sibylline, *adj.*

sibyllist 1. a believer in or follower of the sibyls.
2. a believer in their prophecies.

sideromancy 1. astromancy.
2. a form of divination involving observation of the sparks, shapes formed, etc., when straws are burnt against a red-hot iron.

sortilege a form of divination involving drawing lots.

spasmatomancy a form of divination used to foretell disease by observing spasms or twitching of the potential sufferer's body.

spatilomancy, spatalamancy a form of divination involving the examination of animal feces.

spatulamancy a form of divination by means of an animal's shoulder blade. Cf. armomancy, omoplatoscopy, scapulomancy. —spatulamantic, *adj.*

spodomancy a form of divination through the uses of ashes. —spodomantic, *adj.*

sternomancy a form of divination involving examination of the breastbone.

stichomancy a form of divination involving lines of poetry or passages from books.

stignomancy a form of divination involving the examination of writing on or carving in the bark of a tree.

sycomancy a form of divination involving figs or fig leaves.

telegnosis clairvoyance or other occult or supernatural knowledge.

tephramancy, tephromancy a form of divination involving the examination of the ashes remaining after a sacrifice.

theomancy a form of divination involving the responses of oracles or other soothsayers.

theriomancy 1. a form of divination involving wild beasts.
2. a form of divination based upon observation of the movements of animals. Cf. zoomancy.

tyromancy a form of divination involving observation of cheese, especially as it coagulates.

uromancy *Rare.* a form of divination by studying urine. —uromantic, *adj.*

xylomancy a form of divination involving pieces of wood.

zoomancy a form of divination based upon the observation of animals or their movements under certain circumstances. Cf. theriomancy.

125. DOGS
See also 16. ANIMALS.

cynanthropy *Psychiatry.* a delusion in which a person believes himself to be a dog.

cynologist a specialist in the care and breeding of dogs.

cynology the branch of zoology that studies the dog, especially its natural history.

cynomania an abnormal love of dogs.

cynophobia an intense dread of dogs.

mongrelism the state or quality of being a mixed breed. —**mongrelization,** *n.* —mongrely, *adj.*

philocynism the love of dogs. Also called philocyny. —**philocynic,** *n.*, *adj.* —philocynical, *adj.*

126. DOLLS
pedophobia, paedophobia an abnormal fear of dolls.

planganologist a collector of dolls.

127. DRAMA
See also 249. LITERATURE; 310. PERFORMING.

anagnorisis *Classical Drama.* recognition or discovery, as of a disguised character, one thought to be lost, or a critical fact.

antistrophe (in ancient Greek choral odes) 1. the response made to a preceding strophe, while the chorus is moving from left to right.
2. the movement of the chorus. Cf. **strophe.** See also 409. VERSE. —**antistrophic, antistrophal,** *adj.*

catastasis the climax of a play or other dramatic representation; that part preceding the catastrophe, where the action is at its height.

catharsis (in the Aristotelian concept of art, especially with reference to tragic drama) the purging of the emotions, traditionally said to be those of pity and fear. See also 334. PSYCHOLOGY.

choreodrama a drama expressed in dance or with dance as an integral part of its content and form.

constructivism the theories, attitudes, and techniques of a group of Soviet writers of the 1920s who attempted to reconcile ideological beliefs with technical achievement, especially in stage design, where effects produced were geometrical and nonrepresentational. —**constructivist,** *n.*, *adj.*

denouement the final resolution of the plot, following the climax.

deus ex machina the device of resolving dramatic action by the introduction of an unexpected, improbable, or forced character or incident.

deuteragonist *Greek Drama.* the role that is second in importance to that of the protagonist, or main character.

dramalogue a dramatic monologue.

dramaturgy the art of writing or producing plays. —dramaturge, dramaturgist, *n.*

duodrama a play or drama for two characters or actors.

duologue a dialogue for two people, especially as a complete dramatic performance or as part of one.

epilogue 1. the final section of a literary work, often added by way of explanation, comment, etc.
2. a closing speech in a play, often delivered after the completion of the main action. —epilogistic, *adj.*

epitasis the main action of a drama, leading up to the catastrophe. Cf. protasis.

exode 1. *Greek Drama.* the catastrophe or conclusion of a play.
2. *Roman Drama.* a comical or satirical piece added at the end of a play.

histrionics, histrionism the occupation of actors; playacting.

melodrama 1. a sensational drama with events and emotions extravagantly expressed.
2. an opera or a stage play with songs and music, often of a romantic nature. —melodramatic, *adj.*

monodrama a drama written for one actor or character. —monodramatic, *adj.*

peripeteia, peripetia, peripety *Literature.* a sudden change in the course of events, especially in dramatic works.

photodrama a photoplay or dramatic narrative illustrated with or related through photographs.

protagonist the principal character in the drama.

protasis *Classical Drama.* the first part of a play, when the characters are introduced. Cf. epitasis. See also 186. GRAMMAR; 422. WISDOM. —protatic, *adj.*

soliloquy a speech in which a character reveals his thoughts to the audience but not to other characters in the play. —soliloquist, *n.*

stagecraft the art or skill of producing or staging plays.

stichomythia dialogue in single alternating lines, as found in ancient Greek drama. —stichomythic, *adj.*

strophe that part of the ancient Greek choral odes sung by the chorus while moving from right to left. Cf. antistrophe. —strophic, *adj.*

tetralogy *Greek Drama.* a series of four dramas, three of them tragedies and one a satyr-play; hence, any series of four related works, literary, dramatic, operatic, etc.

theatrics the art of the theater or of acting. —**theatrical,** *n.*, *adj.*

theatromania a mania for the theater.

128. DRAWING
See also 23. ART; 141. ENGRAVING; 428. WRITING.

anaglyptography the technique of making drawings and etchings that appear to be carved in low relief. —**anaglyptographic,** *adj.*

arcograph cyclograph.

chalcography 1. *Archaic.* the art of engraving on copper plates, especially for printing.
2. the art of drawing with chalks or pastels.

charcoalist an artist who specializes in charcoal drawings or sketches.

chiaroscuro, chiarooscuro a technique of painting or drawing using light and shade to achieve a three-dimensional quality. —**chiaroscurist,** *n.*

cyclograph an instrument for drawing arcs with a flexible arc-shaped part connected at the sides to an extensible straight bar. Also called **arcograph.**

diagraph a device used for the mechanical reproduction of plans, outlines, etc., on a scale other than that of the original.

diagraphics the art of graphic representation or drawing. —**diagraphic, diagraphical,** *adj.*

graphiology the art or craft of writing or delineating. —**graphiologist,** *n.*

ichnography 1. the rendering of a horizontal section of an object in scale.
2. the rendering of a floor plan of a building in a specific scale. —**ichnographic, ichnographical,** *adj.*

isometric projection the rendering of an object or floor plan in scale as viewed from a stated angle. Cf. **orthographic projection.**

micrograph an apparatus used for miniature writing or drawing. —**micrography,** *n.*

monogram, monography *Obsolete.* a sketch or drawing in outline without color.

orthographic projection a rendering of an object or floor plan of a building in scale as viewed perpendicularly from above. Cf. **isometric projection.**

pastelist, pastellist an artist who specializes in the use of pastels.

perigraph a poorly executed or inaccurate delineation.

planography *Rare.* the art of drawing maps or plans. —**planographist,** *n.* —**planographic, planographical,** *adj.*

scenography the rendering of an object on a perspective plane. —**scenographer**, *n.* —**scenographic, scenographical**, *adj.*

skiagraphy 1. the technique of filling in the outline of the shadow made by an object to create a pictorial work or shadowgraph.
2. the creation of skiagrams on film with x rays. —**skiagram**, *n.* —**skiagrapher**, *n.*

stereography the art of representing the forms of solid bodies on a plane surface. —**stereographer**, *n.* —**stereographic, stereographical**, *adj.*

stylography the art of drawing, writing, or engraving with a style or similar instrument. —**stylographic, stylographical**, *adj.*

xylopyrography the art or technique of producing a picture or design on a piece of wood by burning it with a heated, pointed instrument. Also called **poker painting**.

129. DREAMS
See also 372. SLEEP.

autism 1. a tendency to daydream.
2. *Psychiatry.* an extreme withdrawal into fantasy in thought or behavior, not correctible by external information. —**autistic**, *adj.*

oneirocriticism the interpretation of dreams. —**oneirocritic**, *n.* —**oneirocritical**, *adj.*

oneirodynia *Medicine.* a disturbed sleep, involving nightmare and sometimes sleepwalking.

oneirology the science and interpretation of dreams. Also **oneiroscopy**.

oneiromancy a form of divination involving dreams. —**oneiromancer**, *n.*

phantasmagoria a type of magic-lantern show in which rapidly moving images blend, change size, etc.; hence, any series of images that move and change rapidly, as a dream. —**phantasmagorial, phantasmagoric**, *adj.*

pnigalion a nightmare.

reverist a person much inclined to dream, especially to day-dream; a dreamy person.

130. DRUGS
See also 122. DISEASE and ILLNESS; 350. REMEDIES.

adjuvant *Medicine.* a substance added to a medicinal preparation to assist the action of the principal ingredient.

alcoholomania an obsession with alcohol.

apothecary 1. a pharmacy.
2. a pharmacist.

barbiturism a condition of chronic poisoning caused by excessive use of barbiturates.

cannabism 1. addiction to marijuana.
2. a toxic condition caused by excessive use of marijuana.

cataphoresis the introduction of drugs into the body by means of an electric current.

chloroformism a condition caused by the habitual use of chloroform.

cinchonism a toxic condition owing to excessive use of cinchona and marked by headache, dizziness, and ringing in the ears. Also called **quininism, quinism.**

cinchonology a branch of pharmacology that studies cinchona and its derivatives, as quinine and quinidine. Also called **quinology.**

cocainism the condition of being addicted to cocaine.

cubebism a toxic condition caused by smoking cubeb or Java pepper, formerly dried and crushed for medicinal purposes.

diatesseron *Obsolete Pharmacy.* a mixture of four medicines in syrup or honey.

dosimetry dosiology. See also 264. MEASUREMENT; 342. RADIATION. —**dosimetrist,** *n.* —**dosimetric, dosimetrical,** *adj.*

dosiology, dosology the study and determination of the doses in which medicines should be administered. Also called **dosimetry.**

electuary a preparation consisting of pulverized medication mixed with honey.

etheromania a mania for ether.

formulary a book or list of medicines, with formulas and instructions for their preparation.

galactopoietic any substance that stimulates the production and flow of milk. —**galactopoietic,** *adj.*

hallucinogen a substance that induces hallucinations. —**hallucinogenic,** *adj.*

laudanum tincture of opium or any preparation, especially in liquid form, in which opium is the main ingredient.

lethomania a mania for narcotics.

magma a pharmaceutical preparation in which precipitated matter is suspended in a watery substance. See also 179. GEOLOGY. —**magmatic,** *adj.*

meconism an addiction to opium; opium eating. Also called **meconophagism.**

meconology *Rare.* a treatise on the opium poppy.

morphinism the condition produced by the excessive use of morphine. —**morphinist,** *n.*

morphiomania an addiction to and intense craving for morphine. Also **morphinmania.**

narcohypnosis hypnosis with the aid of drugs.

narcomania an abnormal desire for drugs.

narcosis, narcoma a condition of stupor or unconsciousness induced by drugs.

narcosynthesis a form of treatment for mental illness that involves placing the patient under the influence of a narcotic.

narcoticism, narcotism 1. the narcosis or narcoma induced by drugs.
2. an addiction to drugs.

opiomania an addiction to opium.

opiophagism, opiophagy the habitual use of opium.

opiumism the excessive and habitual use of opium.

pharmaceutics the science of pharmacy or pharmacology.

pharmacodynamics the division of pharmacology concerned with the action and breakdown of drugs in the body. —**pharmacodynamic, pharmacodynamical,** *adj.*

pharmacognosy, pharmacognosia, pharmacognosis, pharmacognostics the branch of pharmacology that studies the composition, use, and history of drugs. —**pharmacognosist,** *n.* —**pharmacognostic,** *adj.*

pharmacography the description of drugs and their effects.

pharmacology, pharmacologia the branch of medical science that studies the preparation, uses, and effects of drugs. —**pharmacologist,** *n.* —**pharmacologic, pharmacological,** *adj.*

pharmacopedics, pharmacopedia the branch of medical science that studies drugs and medicinal preparations. —**parmacopedic,** *adj.*

pharmacophobia an abnormal fear of drugs.

pharmacopoeia a book, usually of an official nature, containing a list of approved drugs and medicines, with information regarding their properties, preparation, and use. Also called **antidotary.**
2. a pharmacist's stock of drugs.

pharmacopolist an apothecary or pharmacist.

pharmacy 1. the art of preparing drugs and medicines, especially the discovery of new varieties.
2. the place where drugs are prepared, dispensed, or sold. Also called **apothecary.**
3. a drug therapy. —**pharmacist,** *n.*

potomania 1. an excessive tendency to drink alcoholic beverages.
2. delirium tremens. Also called **tromomania.**

quininism, quinism cinchonism.

sudorific a medicine or other substance that causes or stimulates sweating. Also called **diaphoretic, hidrotic.** —**sudorific,** *adj.*

synergism, synergy the joint action of agents, as drugs, that, taken together, produce a greater effect than the sum of their individual effects. —**synergistic,** *adj.*

tabacism, tabagism addiction to tobacco; poisoning from excessive use of tobacco. Also **tobaccoism.**

teaism the habitual use of tea.

theriac, theriaca a compound of sixty-four drugs made into an electuary, formerly used as an antidote for poison. Also called **Venice Treacle.** —**theriac, theriacal, therial,** *adj.*

tincture *Pharmacy.* a medicinal substance in soluble form, especially in a solution of alcohol.

toxicomania an addiction to drugs, especially opium or cocaine.

131. DUES and PAYMENT
See also 160. FINANCE; 276. MONEY.

anchorage a toll charged for anchoring in a harbor.

brassage a fee or charge levied for the coining of money.

brokerage a broker's fee or commission.

carriage a fee charged for transportation.

cartage a fee charged for carting of goods.

cellarage a fee charged for storage in a cellar.

corkage a fee charged in restaurants for opening a bottle of wine brought in by a patron.

demurrage the charge levied for the delay of a ship at mooring beyond the time stipulated for unloading or other purposes.

dockage a fee charged for the use of a dock.

drayage the fee charged for the use of a dray.

expressage a fee charged for transporting goods by any form of express.

freightage a fee charged for the transportation of goods, merchandise, etc.

hallage *Obsolete.* 1. a fee charged for sale of goods in a hall.
2. a commission or consignment fee.

haulage a fee charged for hauling goods, as on a railroad or truck.

honorarium a fee for professional services.

lighterage a fee charged for transportation by lighter.

metage the fee charged for the official measurement of weight or volume, as applied to certain commodities.

meterage a fee charged for measurement.

pedage a fee paid for passing on foot, as through a toll-gate.

perquisite a payment in addition to fee or salary, usually customary to the particular occupation; a fringe benefit. Also **perk**.

piccage *British.* a fee or tax charged for breaking ground at a fair.

pilotage a fee charged for piloting a vessel into or out of a harbor.

poundage a fee or fine charged for releasing animals from a pound.

quarterage a payment that is due quarterly or four times a year.

retainer the fee paid to a professional person, as a lawyer, to engage his services.

salvage compensation paid to those who recover a ship or its contents or cargo after sinking, damage, or abandonment.

scutage (in the feudal system) a payment, made to a lord in lieu of military service, by the holder of a property in fee.

solatium 1. payment or other recompense for mental suffering or financial or other loss.
2. *Scots Law.* a provision for a sum of money to be paid to an injured party by the party responsible for the injury, over and above compensation paid for damages for injury to feelings.

tallage (in the feudal system) a compulsory tax paid to a lord by a tenant.

wardage a fee charged for keeping guard or watch. Also called **ward penny**.

weregild, wergild (in Anglo-Saxon society) a payment made to the family of a slain man by his killer or the killer's family as compensation, atonement, and to avoid reprisals.

wharfage a fee charged for the use of a wharf and its facilities.

E

132. EAR
See also 14. ANATOMY; 51. BODY, HUMAN; 111. DEAFNESS; 198. HEARING.

audialgesia *Medicine.* a pain in the ear; earache.

auriscope an instrument for examining the ear.

auriscopy the art of using the auriscope.

otalgia an earache.

otiatrics, otiatry *Medicine.* the therapeutics of ear diseases. —otiatric, *adj.*

oticodinia a vertigo resulting from ear disease. Also oticodinosis.

otitis *Medicine.* any variety of inflammation in the ear. —otitic, *adj.*

otography 1. the science of the ear.
2. a scientific description of the ear.

otology 1. the branch of medicine that studies the ear and its diseases.
2. the treatment of ear disorders. —otologist, *n.* —otologic, otological, *adj.*

otopathy an abnormal condition or disease of the ear.

otoplasty plastic surgery of the ear.

otopyorrhea the discharge or flowing of pus from the ear.

otorrhea any flowing or discharge from the ear.

otoscopy a visual inspection of the ear drum and the auditory canal. —otoscopic, *adj.*

pachyotia abnormal thickness of the ears.

tinnitus a ringing or whistling sound in the ears, not caused by any outside stimulus.

133. EARTH
See also 85. CLIMATE; 134. EARTHQUAKES; 142. ENVIRONMENT; 143. EQUATOR; 178. GEOGRAPHY; 179. GEOLOGY; 235. LAND; 318. PLANETS; 377. SOIL.

biosphere that part of the earth's surface where most forms of life exist, specifically those parts where there is water or atmosphere.

chthonic, chthonian having to do with the underworld.

cosmosphere a hollow glass globe for depicting the position of the earth in relation to the fixed stars at a given time.

diastrophism the process of movement that causes the earth's crust to form continents, mountains, oceans, etc. —diastrophe, *n.* —diastrophic, *adj.*

epeirogeny, epeirogenesis the vertical movement or tilting of the earth's crust, affecting broad expanses of continents. —epeirogenic, epeirogenetic, *adj.*

geochronology the branch of geology that describes the past in terms of geologic rather than human time. —geochronologist, *n.* —geochronologic, geochronological, *adj.*

geodynamics the science of the forces at work within the earth. —geodynamic, *adj.*

geogony a theory or science about the formation of the earth. —geogonic, *adj.*

geolatry *Rare.* worship of the things of the earth or of the earth itself.

geology the science that studies the physical history of the earth, the rocks of which it is composed, and the changes the earth has undergone and is undergoing. —geologist, *n.* —geologic, geological, *adj.*

geomalism the tendency of organisms, under the influence of gravity, to be symmetrical. —geomalic, *adj.*

geomancy a form of divination that analyzes the pattern of a handful of earth thrown down at random or dots made at random on paper. —geomancer, *n.*

geomorphology the branch of geology that studies the form of the earth's surface. —geomorphologist, *n.* —geomorphologic, geomorphological, *adj.*

geophagism, geophagy, geophagia the eating of earthy matter, especially clay or chalk. —geophagist, *n.* —geophagous, *adj.*

georama a large globe or sphere in which a spectator can stand and view a representation of the earth's surface.

inclinometer an instrument for measuring the inclination or dip of the earth's magnetic force.

lithogenesy the science of explaining the minerals of which the earth is composed, their origins, and the cause of their form and arrangement.

lithosphere the solid part of the earth, as contrasted with the atmosphere and hydrosphere.

nutation the periodic oscillation that can be observed in the precession of the earth's axis and the precession of the equinoxes. See also 196. HEAD. —nutational, *adj.*

obliquity the inclination of the earth's equator or the angle between the plane of the earth's orbit and the plane of the equator (23°27′). See also 25. ASTRONOMY. Also called obliquity of the ecliptic. —obliquitous, *adj.*

planation the formation of a flat or level surface by the process of erosion.

sphericist *Rare.* a person who believes that the earth is round.

tellurist a dweller on the earth. Also **tellurian.**

134. EARTHQUAKES
See also 179. GEOLOGY.

bathyseism an earthquake occurring at very deep levels of the earth.

bradyseism the slow upward and downward motion of the earth's crust. —bradyseismic, *adj.*

cataclysm any major disaster, as an earthquake, flood, etc. See also 414. WATER. —cataclysmal, *adj.*

coseism a line drawn about an epicenter through all points affected by the same seismic shock. —coseismic, *adj.*

epicenter a point on the earth's surface directly above the true center of the seismic disturbance from which the shock waves of an earthquake seem to radiate.

macroseism a major earthquake. —macroseismic, *adj.*

megaseism a violent earthquake. —megaseismic, *adj.*

microseism an almost imperceptible earth tremor caused by a violent sea storm or an earthquake and detected only by a microseismometer. —microseismic, *adj.*

seismicity the intensity, frequency, and distribution of earthquakes in a specific area.

seismism, seism an earthquake. —seismic, *adj.*

seismogram the record of an earthquake's vibrations and intensity made by a seismograph.

seismograph any of various devices for measuring and recording the vibrations and intensities of earthquakes. —seismographer, *n.* —seismographic, seismographical, *adj.*

seismography 1. the scientific measuring and recording of the shock and vibrations of earthquakes.
2. seismology.

seismology the branch of geology that studies earthquakes and their effects. Also seismography. —seismologist, *n.* —seismologic, seismological, *adj.*

seismometer a special seismograph equipped to measure the actual movement of the ground. —seismometry, *n.* —seismometric, *adj.*

teleseism an earthquake that occurs in a part of the world far away from a recording station. —teleseismic, *adj.*

tromometer an instrument for detecting or measuring very slight earth tremors.

135. EASTERN ORTHODOXY
See also 80. CHRISTIANITY; 349. RELIGION; 392. THEOLOGY.

Achephali 1. any of various Middle Eastern Christian sects in the early church that lacked or rejected theological leaders.
2. a Flagellant. —Achephalist, n.

charisticary an official in the medieval Greek church who collected the money from a monastery or benefice.

chrismation a sacrament corresponding to confirmation in the Western church in which a baptized person is anointed with chrism.

eparchy a diocese. See also 190. GREECE and GREEKS.

Euchologion the principal service book of Eastern Orthodoxy. Also Euchology.

euchology 1. the study of Eastern Orthodox ritual.
2. (cap.) Euchologion.

exarch 1. in the early church, the head of a major diocese or province.
2. a bishop inferior to a patriarch but superior to a metropolitan.
3. a deputy of a patriarch, either a priest or a bishop.
4. the head of an autonomous church. —exarchal, adj.

hegumen the head of a monastery.

Hesychasm the quietistic practices of a 14th-century ascetic sect of mystics drawn from the monks of Mt. Athos. Also called Palamitism. —hesychast, n. —hesychastic, adj.

iconoclasticism 1. the practice of opposing the veneration of icons.
2. the practice of destroying icons.
3. (cap.) the principles of the religious party in the 8th-century Eastern church that opposed the use of icons. —iconoclast, n. —iconoclastic, adj.

idoloclast an iconoclast.

metropolitan the head of an ecclesiastic province.

Palamitism Hesychasm.

parathesis a bishop's prayer on behalf of catechumens. —parathetic, adj.

patriarch the head of any of the ancient sees or the see of another principal city or national church.

Sophianism a theological system centering on the Holy Wisdom developed by the 20th-century Russian priest Sergei Bulgakov. Also called Sophiology. —Sophianist, n.

synaxarist one who reads the synaxarion, or brief narrative of a saint's life, in Eastern Orthodox liturgies.

136. ECHOES
See also 380. SOUND.

catacoustics *Rare.* the branch of acoustics that studies echoes. Also called **cataphonics.**

phonocamptics *Obsolete.* the branch of physics that studies reflected sounds.

137. ECONOMICS
See also 160. FINANCE; 276. MONEY.

aphnology *Rare.* the science of wealth; plutology.

autarky a national policy of economic self-sufficiency or independence. —**autarkist,** *n.* —**autarkic, autarkical,** *adj.*

bilateralism the practice of promoting trade between two countries through agreements concerning quantity and price of commodities. Cf. **multilateralism.** —**bilateralistic,** *adj.*

boycottism the principles behind, and means of carrying out, a boycott. —**boycotter,** *n.*

cameralism the theories and adherence to the theories of the cameralists. —**cameralist,** *n.* —**cameralistic,** *adj.*

cameralist a mercantilist economist of the seventeenth and eighteenth centuries who believed in the doctrine that a nation's wealth could be made greater by increasing its supply of money. —**cameralistic,** *adj.*

capitalism a system of economics under which ownership of and investment in the means of production and distribution depends chiefly upon corporations and private individuals. —**capitalist,** *n.* —**capitalistic,** *adj.*

cartelism the practice of controlling production and prices by agreements between or among international companies. —**cartel,** *n.*

chrysology the study of the production of wealth, especially as attained from precious metals.

Cobdenism the economic doctrines of Richard Cobden (1804–65), who believed in peace and the withdrawal from European competition for balance of power.

Colbertism the mercantilist theories of Jean Colbert in the 17th century, especially his advocacy of high protective tariffs.

commercialism 1. the principles, practice, and spirit of commerce.
2. an excessive emphasis on high profit, commercial success, or immediate results.
3. a commercial custom, practice, or expression. —**commercialist,** *n.* —**commercialistic,** *adj.*

consumerism the principles and practices associated with the utilization of economic goods.

disintermediation an economic phenomenon of the late 1970s and early 1980s in which investors, finding that conventional savings and thrift methods did not pay sufficient interest to keep pace with inflation, transferred their funds to the money market and related savings and investment instruments, leading to a rapid growth in those resources and a loss of funds from institutions like savings banks.

economese language and jargon typical of economists and the field of economics.

econometrics mathematical methods used in the science of economics to prove and develop economic theories.

economics the study of the production, use, and consumption of goods and services in society. —economic, economical, *adj.* —economist, *n.*

economism a theory or doctrine that attaches principal importance to economic goals. —economist, *n.*

Fabianism a late 19th-century English movement that favored the gradual development of socialism by peaceful means. —Fabian, *n.*, *adj.*

Fordism the theory of Henry Ford stating that production efficiency is dependent on successful assembly-line methods.

industrialism a system of social and economic organization based upon highly mechanized industry. —industrialist, *n.*, *adj.*

inflationism the quality of advocating economic inflation. —inflationist, *n.*

joint stockism the principle of contribution and division of capital or stock by a number of persons.

Keynesianism the economic theories of John Maynard Keynes (1883–1946), English economist, and his advocates, especially his emphasis upon deficit spending by government to stimulate business investment. —Keynesian, *n.*, *adj.*

laissez-faireism the economic doctrine that the government should intervene as little as possible in economic affairs. —laissez-faireist, *n.*, *adj.*

macroeconomics the division of economics dealing with broad, general aspects of an economy, as the import-export balance of a nation as a whole. Cf. microeconomics. —macroeconomist, *n.* —macroeconomic, *adj.*

Malthusianism the theories of Thomas Malthus (1766–1834), English economist, stating that population growth tends to increase faster than production and that food and necessities will be in short supply unless population growth is restricted or war, disease, and famine intervene. —Malthusian, *n.*, *adj.*

Manchesterism the policies and principles of an English school of economists based in Manchester. —Manchesterist, *n.*

mercantilism a political and economic policy seeking to advance a state above others by accumulating large quantities of precious metals and by exporting in large quantity while importing in small. —**mercantilist,** *n.* —**mercantilistic,** *adj.*

microeconomics the division of economics dealing with particular aspects of an economy, as the price-cost relationship of a business. Cf. **macroeconomics.** —**microeconomist,** *n.* —**microeconomic,** *adj.*

monetarism 1. an economic theory maintaining that stability and growth in the economy are dependent on a steady growth rate in the supply of money. 2. the principle put forward by American economist Milton Friedman that control of the money supply and, thereby, of rate in the supply of credit serves to control inflation and recession while fostering prosperity. —**monetarist,** *n.*, *adj.*

multilateralism the practice of promoting trade among several countries through agreements concerning quantity and price of commodities, as the Common Market, and, sometimes, restrictive tariffs on goods from outsiders.

nationalization the act or process of the taking over of private industry by government. See also 185. GOVERNMENT.

Neo-Malthusianism the belief that the use of contraceptives as a means of lowering the population will eliminate such adverse elements as vice and elevate the standard of living. —**Neo-Malthusian,** *n.*, *adj.*

Owenism the principles of social and labor reform along communistic lines developed by Robert Owen (1771–1858). —**Owenite,** *n.*

pastoralism the herding or tending of cattle as a primary economic activity or occupation. Also **pasturage.** —**pastoralist,** *n.* —**pastoral,** *adj.*

plutology the branch of economics that studies wealth; theoretical economics. Also called **plutonomy.**

privatization the act or process of transferring to private ownership industry operated by a government, often industry that has been nationalized. See also 185. GOVERNMENT.

protectionism the theory or practice of a method of fostering or developing industry through restrictive tariffs on foreign imports. —**protectionist,** *n.*, *adj.*

Reaganomics the economic theories and policies of the administration of President Ronald Reagan (1981–), basically a policy of supply-side economics with emphasis on defense spending, encouragement of private and corporate development and investment, and reduction in government spending on social services.

Ricardian a believer in the economic theories of David Ricardo, English economist, especially that rental income is an economic surplus. —**Ricardian**, *adj*.

Saint-Simonism the theory of the Comte de Saint-Simon (1760–1825), who proposed a socialism in which all property and production be state-controlled with distribution on the basis of an individual's job and ability. —**Saint-Simonist**, *n*.

138. END OF THE WORLD

chiliasm the belief that Christ will return to earth in visible form and establish a kingdom to last 1000 years, after which the world will come to an end. Also called **millenarianism**. —**chiliast**, *n*. —**chiliastic**, *adj*.

eschatology *Theology*. any set of doctrines concerning final matters, as death, the judgment, afterlife, etc. —**eschatological**, *adj*. —**eschatologist**, *n*.

millenarianism chiliasm.

Millerism the preachings of the American William Miller (1782–1849), founder of the Adventist church, who believed that the end of the world and the return of Christ would occur in 1843. —**Millerite**, *n*.

139. ENGLAND

Anglist an authority on England, its language, or its literature.

Anglomania an extreme devotion to English manners, customs, or institutions.

Anglophilia great admiration for England and things English. —**Anglophile**, *n.*, *adj*.

Anglophobia a hatred or fear of England and things English. —**Anglophobe**, *n.*, *adj*.

Englishry 1. the state or condition of being English, especially by birth.
2. a population outside of England that is English or of English descent.

heptarchy *English History*. the seven principal concurrent early English kingdoms. —**heptarch**, *n*. —**heptarchic, heptarchical, heptarchal**, *adj*.

squirearchy the squires or landed gentry as a class.

140. ENGLISH
See also 236. LANGUAGE.

Anglicism 1. a word, idiom, or feature of the English language occurring in or borrowed by another language.
2. *U.S.* a Briticism.
3. any manner, idea, or custom typical of the English people. Also called **Englishism**.

Anglicist an authority on the English language or English literature.

Briticism, Britishism a word or phrase characteristic of speakers of English in Britain and not usually used by English speakers elsewhere.

141. ENGRAVING
See also 23. ART; 305. ORNAMENTATION.

acrography the art or technique of carving a wood block in relief. —acrographer, *n.* —acrographic, acrographical, *adj.*

burinist an engraver, usually in metal. Also called graver.

cameography the art or technique of engraving cameos.

dactylioglyph 1. the name of the engraver inscribed on a gemstone or finger ring.
2. an artist who engraves precious stones and metals. Also dactylioglyphist.

dactylioglyphy the art of engraving gemstones and finger rings.

dactyliography the art of engraving gemstones. —dactyliographer, *n.* —dactyliographic, *adj.*

ectypography a form of engraving in which the design is in relief instead of being sunk.

galvanography the use of chemically induced electric current rather than chemicals to produce plates for copperplate engraving. —galvanograph, *n.* —galvanographic, *adj.*

glyptograph 1. an engraving on a gemstone or other small object.
2. the stone or object engraved.

glyptology 1. the art of engraving, especially on gems.
2. the study of this art.

lithoglyph 1. an engraving or carving on a gem stone.
2. the stone thus engraved. —lithoglyphic, lithoglyptic, *adj.*

lithoglypher *Obsolete.* an engraver of precious stones.

lithoglyptics the art of engraving or carving precious stones. —lithoglyptic, *adj.*

medalist an engraver, designer, or maker of medals. See also 210. HONORS and REGALIA.

photoglyphy photogravure or the process of engraving by means of photography. —photoglyphic, *adj.*

photogravure 1. a form of photoengraving in which the photograph is reproduced on an intaglio surface and then transferred to paper.
2. the photograph produced by this process.

photolithography the process of making lithographs produced by photoengraving. Cf. photogravure. —photolithographer, *n.* —photolithographic, *adj.*

siderography a technique of engraving on steel plates, often used in the printing of banknotes. —siderograph, siderographist, *n.* —siderographic, siderographical, *adj.*

stylography the art of drawing, writing, or engraving with a style or similar instrument. —stylographic, stylographical, *adj.*

xylography the art of engraving on wood for printing. —xylographer, *n.* —xylographic, xylographical, *adj.*

zincography the process of engraving on zinc or of printing from a zinc plate. —zincographer, *n.* —zincographic, zincographical, *adj.*

142. ENVIRONMENT
See also 27. ATMOSPHERE; 44. BIOLOGY; 85. CLIMATE; 133. EARTH.

anthoecology the study of the relationship of flowers to their environment. —anthoecologic, anthoecological, *adj.*

anthroposociology the study of the effects upon each other of environment and race. —anthroposociologic, anthroposociological, *adj.*

autecology the study of an individual organism, or the species regarded collectively, in relation to environment. —autecologic, autecological, *adj.*

bioecology the study of the interrelation of plants and animals in their common environment. —bioecologist, *n.*

bionomics ecology. Also bionomy. —bionomist, *n.* —bionomic, bionomical, *adj.*

biotechnology ergonomics.

ecesis the transplanting of a plant to a new environment.

ecocide destruction of the environment.

ecology, oecology 1. the branch of biology that studies the relationship of organisms and environments. Also called bionomics, bionomy.
2. the branch of sociology that studies the environmental spacing and interdependence of people and their institutions, as in rural or urban settings. —ecologist, oecologist, *n.* —ecologic, oecologic, ecological, oecological, *adj.*

ecosystem any area or region regarded as a unit for ecological observation and study of the interrelationships between organisms and their environment.

ecotone a transitional area or zone between two different forms of vegetation, as between forest and plain. —ecotonal, *adj.*

ecotype a type or subspecies of life that is especially well adapted to a certain environment. —ecotypic, *adj.*

environmentalism concern for and action on behalf of the environment and its preservation. —environmentalist, *n.*

ergonomics the study of the relation of man to the environment in which he works and the application of anatomical, physiological, psychological, and engineering knowledge to the problems involved. Also called **biotechnology**. —ergonomic, *adj.*

euthenics a science concerned with improving the well-being of mankind through improvement of the environment. —euthenist, *n.*

genecology a combination of genetics and ecology that studies animal species and their environment. —genecologist, *n.* —genecologic, genecological, *adj.*

konimeter an instrument for measuring impurities in the air. —konimetric, *adj.*

konimetry the measurement of impurities in the air by means of a konimeter. —konimetric, *adj.*

koniology, coniology the study of atmospheric dust and other impurities in the air, as germs, pollen, etc., especially regarding their effect on plant and animal life.

miasmology the study of fogs and smogs, especially those affecting air pollution levels.

oligotrophy (of lakes) the quality of containing a low accumulation of dissolved nutrient salts, thus supporting little plant or animal life and having a high oxygen content owing to the low organic content. —oligotrophic, *adj.*

paleoecology, palaeoecology the branch of ecology that studies the relationship of ancient plants and animals to their environments. —paleoecologic, palaeoecologic, paleoecological, palaeoecological, *adj.*

preservationist a person who is concerned with or active in the preservation of wildlife, historical sites, natural habitats, and other features of the environment.

synecology the branch of ecology that studies the relationship between plant and animal communities and their environments. —synecologic, synecological, *adj.*

143. EQUATOR
See also 133. EARTH; 178. GEOGRAPHY.

antipodes two points on the surface of the earth diametrically opposite each other. —antipodean, *n., adj.*

Antiscians, Antiscii persons living on opposite sides of the equator but in the same longitude whose shadows at noon fall in opposite directions.

144. ESCAPE
drapetomania a mania for running away.

enatation *Obsolete.* swimming away, especially escaping by swimming.

escapism   the art or technique of escaping from chains, locked trunks, etc., especially when exhibited as a form of entertainment. —escapist, *n.*, *adj.*

fugitation   fleeing from justice, as by a criminal.

hegira   a flight or escape to safety.

145. ETHICS
See also 312. PHILOSOPHY; 407. VALUES.

amoralism   the state or quality of being without morality or of being indifferent to moral standards. —amoralist, *n.* —amoral, *adj.*

axiology   the branch of philosophy dealing with values, as those of ethics, aesthetics, or religion. —axiologist, *n.* —axiological, *adj.*

casuist   1. a person who studies and resolves questions of right and wrong in conduct.
2. an oversubtle or specious reasoner. —casuistic, *adj.*

casuistry   1. the branch of ethics or theology that studies the relation of general ethical principles to particular cases of conduct or conscience.
2. a dishonest or oversubtle application of such principles.

deontology   the branch of philosophy concerned with ethics, especially that branch dealing with duty, moral obligation, and right action. —deontologist, *n.* —deontological, *adj.*

eudemonism, eudaemonism, eudemonics, eudaemonics   the ethical doctrine that the basis of morality lies in the tendency of right actions to produce happiness, especially in a life governed by reason rather than pleasure. —eudemonist, eudaemonist, *n.*

metaethics   a branch of philosophy concerned with the foundations of ethics and especially with the definition of ethical terms and the nature of moral discourse.

moralism   the practice of morality, as distinct from religion. —moralist, *n.* —moralistic, *adj.*

sensationalism   sensualism. —sensationalist, *n.*

sensualism   the doctrine that the good is to be judged only by or through the gratification of the senses. Also called sensationalism.

synteresis   the belief or doctrine that the conscience is the repository of the laws of right and wrong. See also 197. HEALTH.

utilitarianism   the ethical doctrine that virtue is based upon utility and that behavior should have as its goal the procurement of the greatest happiness for the greatest number of persons. —utilitarian, *n.*, *adj.*

146. EVIL
See also 103. CRIME; 117. DEVIL; 367. SIN.

invultuation a form of witchcraft involving melting a wax image of the intended victim or, in voodoo, sticking it with pins.

malism the belief that the world is essentially bad or evil.

ponerology the branch of theology that studies sin and evil.

147. EVOLUTION
See also 44. BIOLOGY; 74. CHANGE; 191. GROWTH;
219. IMPROVEMENT.

Darwinism the theory of evolution by natural selection of those species best adapted to survive the struggle for existence. —**Darwinian,** *n., adj.*

evolutionism a principle or theory of evolution. —**evolutionist,** *n., adj.*

Lamarckism the theory of organic evolution advanced by the French naturalist Lamarck that characteristics acquired by habit, diseases, or adaptations to change in environment may be inherited. —**Lamarckian,** *n., adj.*

Neo-Darwinism the theory that maintains natural selection to be the major factor in plant and animal evolution and denies the possibility of inheriting acquired characteristics. —**Neo-Darwinist,** *n., adj.* —**Neo-Darwinian,** *n., adj.*

Neo-Lamarckism a modern theory based on Lamarckism that states that acquired characteristics are inherited. —**Neo-Lamarckian,** *n., adj.*

orthogenesis progressive evolution, leading to the development of a new form, as can be seen through successive generations. See also 376. SOCIETY. —**orthogenetic,** *adj.*

pangenesis the theory advanced by Darwin, now rejected, that each part of the body is represented in each cell by gemmules, which are the basic units of hereditary transmission. —**pangenetic,** *adj.*

phylogeny the history of the development of a plant, animal, or racial type. —**phylogenist,** *n.* —**phylogenetic,** *adj.*

primordialism a devotion to the conditions which existed at the beginning of creation.

transformism the ability of one species to change into another. —**transformist,** *n.*

tychism 1. the theory that chance is involved in evolution and that variation within a species is accidental.
2. the belief that chance rather than mere determinism operates in the cosmos. Cf. **uniformitarianism.**

uniformitarianism 1. *Philosophy.* a doctrine that the universe is governed only by rigid, unexceptionable law.
2. *Geology.* the concept that current geological processes explain all past geological occurrences. —**uniformitarian,** *n., adj.*

148. EYES

See also 14. ANATOMY; 48. BLINDNESS; 51. BODY, HUMAN; 149. FACIAL FEATURES.

achromatopsy, achromatopsia color blindness. Also called **acritochromacy.**

acyanoblepsia a form of color blindness characterized by the inability to see blue.

aniseikonia, anisoconia a defect of the eyesight in which the images on the retinas are different in size. —**aniseikonic,** *adj.*

anisometropia a defect of the eyesight in which each eye has a different power to refract light. Cf. isometropia. —**anisometropic,** *adj.*

astigmatism a defect in a lens, eye, or mirror that causes rays from one direction not to focus at one point. —**astigmatic,** *adj.*

blepharism twitching of the eyelids.

blepharitis soreness or inflammation of the eyelids.

blepharoptosis *Pathology.* a drooping of the upper eyelid.

collyrium an eyewash or other liquid preparation for the eyes. See also 350. REMEDIES.

conjunctivitis inflammation of the conjunctiva.

Daltonism red-green color blindness.

deuteranopia a defect of the eyesight in which the retina does not respond to green. —**deuteranope,** *n.* —**deuteranopic,** *adj.*

dichromation a form of color blindness in which the sufferer can perceive only two of the three primary colors.

dioptometer an instrument for measuring the refractive index of the lens of the eye.

dyschromatopsia color blindness.

emmetropia, emmetropy the normal refractive function of the eye in which light is focused exactly on the retina with the eye relaxed. —**emmetropic,** *adj.*

esotropia a condition of the eyes in which while one eye focuses on the object viewed the other eye turns inward; cross-eye.

glaucoma a disease of the eyes, in which the pressure inside the eyeball increases, often resulting in blindness. —**glaucomatous,** *adj.*

hemeralopia a condition of the eyes in which the sufferer can see clearly at night but has impaired vision during the day; day blindness.

hypermetropia the condition of farsightedness. Also called **hyperopia.** —**hypermetropic,** *adj.*

hyperopia hypermetropia. —**hyperopic,** *adj.*

iridotomy *Surgery*. the making of an artificial pupil in the eye by transverse division of iris fibers.

isometropia the state or quality of the eyes being equal in refraction. Cf. **anisometropia**.

keratitis an inflamed condition of the cornea.

keratoplasty the surgical process of corneal grafting.

keratotomy the process of surgical incision of the cornea.

lacrymatory, lachrimatory a lacrymal vase or small vessel for storing shed tears.

lagophthalmia, lagophthalmus a persistent, abnormal retraction of the eyelid so that the eyeball is not covered during sleep. —**lagophthalmic,** *adj.*

leucoscope an instrument for testing the eyes to determine the ability to distinguish variations in color or intensity of light.

leucosis the development of leucoma, a whitish clouding of the cornea caused by ulceration.

lippitude soreness of the eyes; a bleary-eyed condition.

macrography study or examination of an object with the naked eye as contrasted with examination under the microscope.

megalopsia a defect of the eyesight in which what is viewed is greatly magnified.

melanosity darkness or blackness of eyes, hair, or complexion.

miosis, myosis abnormal constriction of the pupil of the eye, caused by drugs or illness. Cf. **mydriasis.** —**miotic, myotic,** *adj.*

monoblepsia, monoblepsis a defect of the eyesight in which vision is best when only one eye is open.

monochromation a defect in which the retina cannot perceive color.

mydriasis abnormal dilatation of the pupil, the result of disease or the use of certain drugs. Cf. **miosis.** —**mydriatic,** *adj.*

myopia the condition of nearsightedness. —**myopic,** *adj.*

myosis miosis. —**myotic,** *adj.*

nauscopy the ability, sometimes pretended, to sight ships or land at great distances.

nictitation, nictation the process of winking or blinking rapidly, as in certain birds or animals or as the result of a tic in humans.

nyctalopia a condition of the eyes in which the sufferer can see clearly during the day or in bright light but has impaired vision at night or in poor light; night blindness.

nystagmus uncontrollable and rapid movement of the eyeball in any direction. —nystagmic, *adj.*

oculist a physician who specializes in ophthalmology.

ommatophobia an abnormal fear of eyes.

ophthalmology the branch of medical science that studies the eyes, their diseases and defects. —ophthalmologist, *n.* —ophthalmologic, ophthalmological, *adj.*

optician a person who makes and sells glasses according to prescriptions prepared by an oculist or optometrist.

optogram an image on the retina caused by bleaching of the pupils.

optography the act or practice of reproducing optograms.

optology *Archaic.* the testing of the eyes for lenses.

optometry the practice or profession of testing eyes for defects in vision and the prescribing of corrective glasses. —optometrist, *n.* —optometrical, *adj.*

optotype type used in the testing of eyesight.

orthoptics the art of treating visual defects by exercise and retraining in visual habits. —orthoptist, *n.* —orthoptic, *adj.*

oxyopia, oxyopy an extremely heightened acuteness of the eyesight, resulting from increased sensibility of the retina.

phantasmascope, phantascope an optical device that enables the viewer to converge the optical axes of the eyes and experience some of the phenomena of binocular vision.

photalgia pain in the eyes caused by light.

photangiophobia an abnormal fear of photalgia.

photopia vision, or the ability to see in bright light. Cf. scotopia. —photopic, *adj.*

polyopia, polyopsia, polyopsy, polyopy multiple vision; the seeing of one object as more than one.

presbytism a form of farsightedness that occurs in old age. Also called presbyopia, presbytia. Cf. hypermetropia. —presbytic, *adj.*

protanopia a defect of the eyesight in which the retina does not respond to red. —protanope, *n.* —protanopic, *adj.*

retinoscopy a method of determining the refractive error of an eye using an ophthalmoscope to illuminate the retina through the lens of the eye. Also called skiascopy. —retinoscopist, *n.*

scotopia vision in dim light or darkness. Cf. photopia. —scotopic, *adj.*

strabism the inability of both eyes to focus on one object thereby producing the effect of squinting or cross-eyes. Also called strabismus. —strabismal, strabismic, *adj.*

synechia a diseased condition characterized by adhesion, especially the adhesion of the iris to the cornea.

trachoma a contagious form of conjunctivitis, with the formation of inflammatory granules on the inner surface of the eyelid. —**trachomatous,** *adj.*

trichiasis a condition in which the hair, especially of the eyelashes, grows inward.

tritanopia a defect of the eyesight in which the retina does not respond to blue and yellow. —**tritanope,** *n.* —**tritanopic,** *adj.*

uveitis an inflamed condition of the uvea. —**uveitic,** *adj.*

xanthocyanopsy, xanthocyanopy a form of color blindness in which only yellows and blue can be perceived.

xerophthalmia, xerophthalmy a form of conjunctivitis, the result of a deficiency of vitamin A, marked by a dry and dull condition of the eyeball. Also called **xeroma.**

xerosis abnormal dryness, as of the eyes or skin. Also called **xeransis.** —**xerotic,** *adj.*

F

149. FACIAL FEATURES
See also 14. ANATOMY; 37. BEARDS; 51. BODY, HUMAN; 148. EYES.

gnathism the condition of having an upper jaw that protrudes beyond the plane of the face. —gnathic, *adj.*

hiation *Obsolete.* the act of gaping or letting the mouth hang open wide.

lineament a feature or detail in relation to outline or contour, as a feature of a face. —lineamental, *adj.*

mesognathism the condition of having medium-sized jaws that project only slightly from the plane of the face. —mesognathic, mesognathous, *adj.*

metopomancy *Rare.* a form of divination involving examination of facial features. —metopomantic, *adj.*

metoposcopy the art or science of physiognomy; the attempt to discern a person's character from the study of the facial features. —metoposcopist, *n.*, —metoposcopic, metoposcopical, *adj.*

opisthognathism the condition of having retracted jaws. —opisthognathic, opisthognathous, *adj.*

orthognathism the condition of having straight jaws. —orthognathic, orthognathous, *adj.*

pathognomy the study of the signs that reveal human passions. —pathognomonic, *adj.*

physiognomy, physiognomics 1. the art of determining character or personal qualities from the features or form of the body, especially the face.
2. divination by examining the features of a face. —physiognomist, *n.* —physiognomic, physiognomical, *adj.*

prognathism the condition of having jaws that project beyond the upper part of the face. —prognathic, prognathous, *adj.*

prosopalgia neuralgia affecting the face.

prosopography 1. *Obsolete.* a description of the face. See also 207. HISTORY.

150. FADS
See also 254. MANIAS.

dandyism excessive concern with matters of dress; foppishness. —dandy, *n.*

239

energumen a wild enthusiast; a faddist. See also 114. DEMONS.

faddism an inclination for adopting fads. —**faddishness, faddist,** *n.* —**faddish,** *adj.*

mania a manifestation of intense enthusiasm for something; craze or fad, as *musicomania.*

151. FAITH
See also 285. MYSTICISM; 349. RELIGION; 392. THEOLOGY.

fideism a reliance, in a search for religious truth, on faith alone. —**fideist,** *n.* —**fideistic,** *adj.*

pistic referring to or having a pure and genuine faith.

pistology the branch of theology that studies the characteristics of faith.

152. FASCISM
See also 94. COMMUNISM; 185. GOVERNMENT; 289. NATIONALISM; 322. POLITICS.

anti-Hitlerism the principles and practices of people who worked to dissolve Hitler's dictatorship and fascism.

Bundist a member of the German-American Volksbund, a U.S. pro-Nazi organization of the 1930s and 1940s. —**Bund,** *n.*

Falangism the doctrines of the Falange, the fascist party of Spain. —**Falangist,** *n.*

fascism 1. the tenets of a centralized totalitarian and nationalistic government that strictly controls finance, industry, and commerce, practices rigid censorship and racism, and eliminates opposition through secret police. 2. such a form of government, as that of Italy under Mussolini. —**fascist,** *n.* —**fascistic,** *adj.*

Hitlerism the tenets of German fascism as developed by Adolf Hitler; Nazism. —**Hitlerite,** *n., adj.*

Nazism the German form of fascism, especially that of the National Socialist (German: *Nazionalsozialist*) Workers' party under Adolf Hitler. —**Nazi,** *n., adj.*

Neo-Fascism the post-World War II rise of a movement whose principal aim is to incorporate the doctrines of fascism into existing political systems. —**Neo-Facist,** *n.*

putschism a method of revolution or overthrow involving secret planning, suddenness, and speed, as Hitler's 1938 invasion of Austria. —**putschist,** *n.*

Rexist a member of the Belgian pro-fascist party of the 1930s.

153. FATHER
See also 281. MOTHER; 307. PARENTS.

misopaterism the hatred of one's father. —misopaterist, *n.*

patriarchy 1. a community in which the father or oldest male is the supreme authority in the family, clan, or tribe, and descent is traced through the male line.
2. government by males, with one as supreme. —patriarchist, *n.* —patriarchic, patriarchical, *adj.*

patricentric tending to move toward or centering upon the father. See also matricentric.

154. FATIGUE
See also 372. SLEEP.

hebetude the state, condition, or quality of being dull, enervated, or lethargic. —hebetudinous, *adj.*

kopophobia an abnormal fear of mental or physical exhaustion.

ponophobia an abnormal fear of fatigue, especially through overworking.

155. FAVORITISM
See also 121. DISCRIMINATION.

favoritism the practice of giving preferential treatment to a person or persons.

nepotism favoritism shown to nephews or other relatives, as in politics or business. —nepotist, *n.* —nepotic, *adj.*

partisanism 1. favoritism shown to members of one's own party, faction, sect, or cause.
2. strong adherence to the tenets of one's party, faction, sect, or cause. —partisan, *n., adj.*

156. FEAR
See also 313. PHOBIAS.

horripilation the raising of the hairs on the skin as a response to cold or fear; goose bumps or goose pimples.

panophobia 1. a nonspecific fear, a state of general anxiety.
2. an abnormal fear of everything. Also panphobia, pantaphobia, pantophobia. —panophobe, *n.* —panophobic, *adj.*

phobophobia 1. an abnormal fear of being afraid; a fear of fear itself.
2. a fear of phobias.

polyphobia an abnormal fear of many things.

157. FEET and LEGS
See also 14. ANATOMY; 51. BODY, HUMAN; 412. WALKING.

arthropod any invertebrate of the phylum that includes insects, arachnids, crustaceans, and myriapods with jointed legs. —arthropod, arthropodal, arthropodan, arthropodous, *adj.*

artiodactyl a hooved animal having an even number of toes or digits on each foot, as pigs, sheep, deer, etc. —artiodactylous, *adj.*

biped an animal, as man, having two feet. —bipedal, *adj.*

chiropody an earlier and still frequent term for podiatry. —chiropodist, *n.* —chiropodial, *adj.*

monopus a person with only one leg or foot, usually as the result of a birth defect.

pedicure care of the feet, either in a cosmetic or medical sense. —pedicurist, *n.*

pentadactylism the quality of having five digits on each hand and foot. —pentadactylate, pentadactylic, pentadactylous, *adj.*

perissodactylism the condition of having more than the usual number of digits on a hand or foot which are also excessively large and uneven. —perissodactylate, perissodactylic, perissodactylous, *adj.*

podagra gout affecting the foot. —podagral, podagric, podagrical, podagrous, *adj.*

podiatry a medical specialty concerned with the care and treatment of the foot. Also called podology. —podiatrist, *n.* —podiatric, *adj.*

podology podiatry.

polydactylism the condition of having more than the normal number of toes or fingers. —polydactylous, *adj.*

sexdigitist a person who has six fingers or six toes.

talipes clubfoot; the state or condition of having a clubfoot. —taliped, *adj.*

158. FERMENTATION
See also 8. ALCOHOL; 39. BEER; 421. WINE.

enzymology the branch of biochemistry that studies enzymes. Also called zymology. —enzymologist, *n.*

zymetology zymology.

zymogenesis the process in which a zymogen becomes an enzyme, as in the fermentation process. —zymogenic, zymogenous, *adj.*

zymology the branch of biochemistry that studies fermentation. Also called zymetology.

zymolysis 1. the fermentative action of enzymes.
2. fermentation and its resulting changes. —zymolytic, *adj.*

zymometer a device for determining degrees of fermentation.

zymosis fermentation. See also 122. DISEASE and ILLNESS. —**zymotic** *adj.*

zymotechnics the application of the principles of fermentation. Also **zymotechny.** —**zymotechnic,** *adj.*

zymotic 1. caused by or causing fermentation.
2. causing or referring to infectious diseases.

zymurgy a branch of applied chemistry that studies fermentation processes, as in brewing.

159. FILMS
See also 315. PHOTOGRAPHY.

atmospherics special effects, extras, and the like used in order to establish an intended background or mood for a film.

bioscope 1. a film projector of the early 20th century.
2. *British.* a motion-picture theater.

cinematics the art or principles of making motion pictures.

cinematography the art or technique of motion-picture photography. —**cinematographer, cinematographist,** *n.* —**cinematographic,** *adj.*

cinemese language typical of the cinema, as that used in film dialogue or in film criticism.

cinephilia avid moviegoing. —**cinephile,** *n., adj.*

kinematograph, kinetograph a motion-picture camera.

nickelodeon an early name for a cinema, so called because of the five-cent admission charge. See also 284. MUSIC.

praxinoscope an instrument that represents the effect of moving images on a screen.

scenarist the writer of scenarios, story lines for motion pictures.

tachyscope a type of kinescope that presents the effect of moving pictures by use of a rotating glass plate with images attached to it.

vitascope an early form of motion-picture projector.

zoopraxiscope an early form of motion-picture projector.

160. FINANCE
See also 131. DUES and PAYMENT; 137. ECONOMICS; 276. MONEY.

acceptance 1. the acknowledgment of a bill of exchange, in writing across the back, binding the acceptor to make payment.
2. the bill so endorsed.

actuary a statistician of an insurance company who calculates risks and premiums.

agio 1. the exchange rate between the currencies of different nations.
2. the fee paid to effect an exchange of currency. See also **agiotage.**

agiotage the business of trading or speculating in foreign exchange. Also called **agio.**

amortization, amortizement the paying off of a debt in equal installments composed of gradually changing amounts of principal and interest.

annuity an investment that bears a fixed return yearly, for a fixed period or for the life of the recipient.

bursary the treasury, especially of a college. See also 240. LEARNING.

cambism cambistry. —**cambist,** *n.*

cambist 1. a dealer in bills of exchange.
2. a handbook listing the exchange values of moneys and the weights and measures of many countries.

cambistry the branch of economics that studies commercial exchange, especially international money values. Also **cambism.**

debenture an interest-bearing bond, often issued by corporations, usually unsecured but sometimes with a preferred status over other obligations of the issuer.

delinquency 1. the condition of being in arrears in payment of a debt.
2. the condition of a debt when overdue. See also 239. LAW.

entrepreneurship 1. the state, quality, or condition of being an entrepreneur, an organizer or promoter of business ventures.
2. the duration of a person's function as an entrepreneur.

fiduciary one who holds in trust; a trustee or depositary. See also 392. THEOLOGY.

hypothecation 1. the process of pledging property as security for a debt.
2. a claim made against property so pledged. —**hypothecator,** *n.* —**hypothecary,** *adj.*

mortgage 1. the giving of property, usually real property, as security to a creditor for payment of a debt.
2. the deed pledging the security.

tontine 1. an annuity, or loan, based on a group of annuities that are shared among several people with the provision that as each person dies his share is spread among those remaining, and the entire amount accrues to the survivor of them all.
2. the members of the group collectively.
3. each member's total share or annuity. —**tontine,** *adj.*

usury 1. the lending of money at excessive interest rates, especially rates above legal limits.
2. the excessive interest rate charged. —**usurer,** *n.* —**usurious,** *adj.*

Wall Streetese language typical of that used on Wall Street and in the financial markets, characterized by use of technical financial terms and arcane stock-market jargon.

161. FINGERS and TOES
See also 14. ANATOMY; 51. BODY, HUMAN; 194. HANDS.

adactyly a birth defect in which one or more fingers or toes are missing.

dactyl a digit; a finger or toe. See also 264. MEASUREMENT.

dactyliography the study of finger rings for purposes of description. —dactyliographer, *n.* —dactyliographic, *adj.*

dactyliology the study and making of finger rings. —dactyliologist, *n.* —dactyliologic, *adj.*

dactyliomancy a form of divination involving finger rings.

dactylitis an inflammation of a finger or toe.

dactylography the study of fingerprints. —dactylographer, *n.* —dactylogram, *n.* —dactylographic, *adj.*

dactylology the science of communicating by sign language using the hands and fingers.

dactylomegaly a condition in which one or more of the fingers is enlarged abnormally. —dactylomegalic, *adj.*

dactylonomy *Rare.* the practice of counting on the fingers.

dactyloscopy the comparison of fingerprints for identification. —dactyloscopist, *n.* —dactyloscopic, *adj.*

monodactyly *Zoology.* the condition of having only a single finger, toe, or claw on each limb. —monodactylous, monodactylic, *adj.*

onychia inflammation and ulceration at the base of a fingernail; a felon or whitlow.

onychomancy the art of divination through inspection of the fingernails. —onychomantic, *adj.*

onychophagia, onychophagy the habit of biting the fingernails.

onychoptosis the loosening and falling off of the fingernails.

onychosis disease of the fingernails or toenails.

paronychia a pus-producing inflammation at the base of a fingernail or toenail; a felon or whitlow. Also called **panaris.**

pentadactylism the condition of having five digits on each hand and foot. —pentadactylous, *adj.*

polydactylism the condition of having more than the normal number of fingers or toes. —polydactylous, *adj.*

sexdigitist a person who has six fingers or six toes.

162. FIRE
See also 200. HEAT; 373. SMOKE.

arsonist a person who destroys property by fire, for revenge, insurance, etc.

empyrosis *Obsolete.* a large-scale fire or conflagration.

incendiarism the deliberate destruction of property by fire; arson. —**incendiary**, *n., adj.*

phlogiston *Obsolete Chemistry.* a hypothetical ingredient thought to be released during combustion. —**phlogistic**, *adj.*

pyrogenous *Geology.* produced by the action of heat, hot solutions, etc. —**pyrogenic**, *adj.*

pyrography the process of burning designs on wood or leather with a heated tool. —**pyrograph, pyrographer**, *n.* —**pyrographic**, *adj.*

pyrolater, pyrolator a fire-worshiper.

pyrolatry the worship of fire.

pyromancy a form of divination involving fire or flames.

pyromania a persistent compulsion to start fires.

pyrophilia a love of fire.

pyrophobia an abnormal fear of fire.

tephramancy, tephromancy a form of divination involving the examination of the ashes remaining after a sacrifice.

ustulation *Rare.* the act or process of burning or searing. —**ustorious, ustulate**, *adj.*

vesuvian an early type of match that was difficult to extinguish.

163. FIREWORKS

pyrotechnics, pyrotechny 1. the art of making and using fireworks.
2. a brilliant and dazzling display, as of eloquence, wit, virtuosity, etc. —**pyrotechnic, pyrotechnical**, *adj.*

pyrotechnician a person skilled in the use and handling of fireworks. Also **pyrotechnist**.

164. FISH
See also 44. BIOLOGY; 430. ZOOLOGY.

anadromous a term describing fish that migrate upriver to spawn.

catadromous a term describing fish that migrate downriver to spawn.

halieutics 1. the activity of fishing.
2. a work on fishing. —**halieutic**, *adj.*

ichthyism, ichthyismus a toxic condition caused by toxic fish roe.

ichthyolatry the worship of fish or of fish-shaped idols.

ichthyology 1. the branch of zoology that studies fishes.
2. a zoological treatise on fish. —ichthyologist, n. —ichthyological, adj.

ichthyomancy a form of divination involving the heads or entrails of fish.

ichthyomania an abnormal love of fish.

ichthyophagy the practice of eating or subsisting on fish. —ichthyophagist, n.
—ichthyophagous, adj.

ichthyophobia 1. a ritual avoidance of fish, especially under the pressure of
taboo.
2. an abnormal fear of fish.

ichthyosis a dermatologic condition in which the skin resembles fish scales.
—ichthyotic, adj.

ichthyotomy the anatomical structure of fishes and its study. —ichthyotomist,
n. —ichthyotomic, adj.

piscary the right of one person to fish in waters belonging to another. See also
239. LAW.

piscatology Rare. the art or science of fishing.

piscatorian, piscatorialist an angler or fisherman.

pisciculture the breeding of fish, as a hobby or for scientific or commercial
purposes. —pisciculturist, n. —piscicultural, adj.

planktology, planktonology the branch of biology that studies plankton, especially as the sustenance of planktivorous fish.

Waltonian 1. a keen angler or fisherman, after Izaak Walton (1593-1683),
English author of The Compleat Angler.
2. an admirer of the works of Izaak Walton. —Waltonian, adj.

165. FLAGS

semaphore any of various types of signaling systems using flags, mechanical
arms, etc. —semaphorist, n. —semaphoric, semaphorical, adj.

telelograph a modified version of the semaphore, introduced at the end of the
eighteenth century.

vexillary a standard bearer.

vexillology the study of flags and flag design. —vexillologist, n. —vexillological, adj.

vexillum 1. a military standard or banner carried by ancient Roman troops.
2. the men serving under such a banner.

166. FLESH
See also 67. CANNIBALISM.

cannibalism the eating of human flesh generally not for nutritional purposes
but for primitive sacramental rites. —cannibalic, cannibalistic, adj.

creophagism, creophagy the use of flesh meat for sustenance. —creophagous, adj.

omophagia Rare. the eating of raw meat, especially as part of an initiation ritual. —omophagic, adj.

sarcophagy Rare. the act, practice, or custom of eating flesh. —sarcophagous, adj.

167. FLOWERS
See also 54. BOTANY; 319. PLANTS.

anthesis full bloom of a flower.

anthoecology the branch of ecology that studies the relationship of flowers to their environment.

anthography Botany. the description of flowers.

anthomania Rare. an extreme love for flowers.

anthophagy the habit, as of larvae, of feeding on flowers. —anthophagous, adj.

anthophobia an abnormal fear of flowers.

cleistogamy the state of bearing small flowers as well as fully developed ones, as in the pansy, in which the small ones do not open but are pollinated by their own anthers. —cleistogamous, adj.

conservatory a greenhouse, especially one used to grow delicate, rare, and exotic flowers and plants for decorative purposes. See also 284. MUSIC.

dichogamy the condition, in some flowering plants, in which the pistils and stamens mature at different times, thus preventing self-pollination. —dichogamous, adj.

diclinism the condition of having the stamens and pistils in separate flowers. —diclonous, adj.

efflorescence the process of flowering or blooming. —efflorescent, adj.

epanody peloria.

estivation, aestivation the arrangement of petals in a flower before it opens; prefloration. Also aestivation.

florescence 1. the state or condition of being in flower or blooming.
2. the period during which this occurs.
3. a period of great development. —florescent, adj.

floretum a garden specifically used for the growth and scientific study of flowers.

floribunda one of several varieties of rose characterized by their long blooming period and their large flowers, often in clusters.

floriculture the cultivation of flowers, especially of decorative flowering plants, usually on a commercial scale. —floriculturist, *n.* —floricultural, *adj.*

florimania a mania for plants and flowers.

homogony the condition of similarity in length and location of all the pistils and stamens in flowers of the same species. —homogonous, *adj.*

ikebana the Japanese art of flower arrangement, especially for the home.

peloria the phenomenon of a regular structure appearing as an abnormality in flowers which are usually irregular. Also called **epanody.** —peloric, pelorian, *adj.*

perigyny the state of having the pistils, stamens, petals, etc., arranged around a cuplike receptacle. —perigynous, *adj.*

phyllody the process by which floral organs turn into foliage. Also **phyllomorphy.**

rosarium a rose garden.

staminody the metamorphosis of various flower organs, as petals or sepals, into stamens.

synanthy whole or partial union of several flowers that are usually separate and distinct. —synanthous *adj.*

tulipomania a mania for planting and growing tulips, especially such a mania in Holland in the 1630s, when a sum equivalent to $5200 was paid for a single bulb. —tulipomaniac, *n.*

168. FOOD and NUTRITION
See also 76. CHEESE; 118. DINING; 272. MILK.

accubation *Rare.* the act or habit of reclining at meals.

alimentology *Medicine.* the science of nutrition.

allotriophagy *Pathology.* a desire for unusual or abnormal foods.

analepsis, analepsy *Obsolete.* the nutrition of an emaciated body.

anorexia lack of appetite, usually because of psychological reasons.

anthropophagism, anthropophagy the use of human flesh for food. —anthropophagous, *adj.*

autophagy, autophagia *Medicine.* 1. the eating of one's own body.
2. the nutrition of the body by its own tissues, as in dieting. —autophagous, *adj.*

Bantingism, bantingism a diet of high protein and low fat and carbohydrate, followed in a program to lose weight, named for its developer W. Banting, 19th-century English cabinet-maker.

biophagism the use of living organisms for food. —biophagery, *n.* —biophagous, *adj.*

botulism a toxic condition caused by a neurotoxin in improperly canned or preserved food.

bromatology *Rare.* the science of food.

bromography a treatise on food.

bulimia, boulimia a raging hunger or voracious appetite. Cf. **hyperorexia.** —**bulimic, boulimic, bulimiac, boulimiac,** *adj.*

bulimorexia, boulimorexia alternating gorging of food and vomiting, usually as a result of a psychological disturbance. —**bulimorexic, boulimorexic,** *n.*, *adj.*

cibophobia an abnormal fear of food. Also called **sitophobia, sitiophobia.**

commensalism the practice of eating together at the same table. Also **commensality.** —**commensal,** *n.*, *adj.*

coprophagy, coprophagia feeding on excrement, as certain beetles. —**coprophagous,** *adj.*

crapulency, crapulence excessive indulgence in food or drink.

culinarian a person skilled in the preparation of food.

cynorexia a doglike appetite; insatiable desire for food.

dystrophy, dystrophia poor or inadequate nutrition or growth. See also 122. DISEASE and ILLNESS.

epicureanism the habit of refined, often luxurious, enjoyment of sensuous pleasures, especially of food. —**epicurean,** *n.*, *adj.*

Fletcherism, fletcherism the practice of eating only when hungry and in small amounts, and especially chewing one's food thoroughly, recommended as an aid to digestion by Horace Fletcher (1849–1919), American dietitian. —**Fletcherite,** *n.* —**Fletcherize,** *v.*

fruitarianism the practice of subsisting chiefly on fruit. Cf. **vegetarianism.** —**fruitarian,** *n.*, *adj.*

gastronomy the art or science of good eating. —**gastronome, gastronomist,** *n.* —**gastronomic,** *adj.*

gavage forced feeding, either of animals or humans, by inserting a tube in the throat and using a force pump.

hippophagism, hippophagy the eating of horsemeat. —**hippophagous,** *adj.*

hyperorexia an abnormal craving for food; a voracious and insatiable appetite. Cf. **bulimia.**

magirics *Rare.* the science or art of cooking. Also called **magirology.** —**magirist,** *n.*

monophagism, monophagy the tendency to feed on a single type of food. —**monophagous,** *adj.*

opsomania a mania for special kinds of food. See also **phagomania, sitomania.**

pantophagy the ability to eat any type of food. —**pantophagist,** *n.* —**pantopha-gous,** *adj.*

phagology the study of eating or feeding habits.

phagomania a mania for food and eating. See also **opsomania, sitomania.**

phagophobia an abnormal fear of eating.

polyphagia, polyphagy 1. a desire for all kinds of food.
2. *Med.* excessive or gluttonous consumption of food. —**polyphagian,** *n.* —**polyphagic, polyphagous,** *adj.*

proteinphobia a strong aversion to protein foods.

sarcophagy *Rare.* the act, practice, or custom of eating flesh. —**sarcophagous,** *adj.*

sitomania an obsession with food. See also **phagomania, opsomania.**

sitophobia, sitiophobia cibophobia.

symposiarch *Ancient Greece.* the master of a feast or symposium; hence, a person presiding over a banquet or formal discussion.

syssitia the practice or custom, as among the ancient Spartans and Cretans, of eating the main meal of the day together in public to strengthen social and political bonds.

trichinosis a form of food-poisoning, caused by infestation by *Trichinella spiralis.* —**trichinous,** *adj.*

trophism the nourishment of the tissues. —**trophic,** *adj.*

trophology *Medicine.* the science of nutrition; alimentology.

trophoplasm the form of protoplasm that constitutes the nutritive element of a cell. —**trophoplasmic,** —**trophoplasmatic,** *adj.*

tsiology a treatise on tea.

vegetarianism the practice of subsisting chiefly or strictly on vegetables. —**vegetarian,** *n., adj.*

xerophagia, xerophagy 1. fasting for religious or other purposes.
2. the act or custom of eating only dry food or a very light diet.

zeism, zeismus a skin disease, thought to be the result of excessive consumption of corn.

zomotherapy a treatment for disease or illness consisting of a diet of raw meat.

169. FOREIGNERS

alienage the condition of being an alien.

androlepsy *Law.* the seizure of foreign subjects to enforce a claim for justice or other right against their nation.

gypsyologist, gipsyologist *Rare.* one who studies gypsies. Also **gypsologist, gipsologist.**

nativism the custom or policy of favoring native-born citizens over immigrants, as in the awarding of government jobs. See also 312. PHILOSOPHY. —**nativist,** *n.* —**nativistic,** *adj.*

naturalization the process of assuming or being granted citizenship of a country, usually a country other than that of the person's origin.

peregrinism 1. the state or quality of being foreign or of having come from abroad.
2. something typical or characteristic of a foreigner. —**peregrine,** *adj.*

tramontane 1. a person who lives beyond the mountains.
2. a foreigner or stranger. —**tramontane,** *adj.*

un-Americanism the state or condition of being out of sympathy with or against American behavior, attitudes, beliefs, etc. —**un-American,** *n., adj.*

xenelasia *Ancient Sparta.* a custom prohibiting strangers or foreigners from residing at Sparta and empowering magistrates to expel them.

xenia *Ancient Greece.* a custom of hospitality, specifically the giving of presents to guests or strangers, especially foreign ambassadors. —**xenial,** *adj.*

xenodocheum, xenodochium a building or special place for the reception of strangers. Also called **xenodochy.**

xenodochy 1. the reception of or extending of hospitality to strangers or foreigners.
2. xenodocheum.

xenomania a mania for foreigners.

xenophobia an abnormal fear or hatred of foreigners and strange things.

170. FORM

allomerism variability of a chemical compound in which there is no variation in crystalline form. —**allomeric,** *adj.*

amorphism the quality of being shapeless. Also, *Rare.* amorphy. —**amorphic,** *adj.*

anamorphism a distorted image of an object, as in anamorphic art. Also **anamorphosis.** —**anamorphic,** *adj.*

anamorphoscope a cylindrical mirror for correcting the distorted image created by anamorphism.

anamorphosis, anamorphosy anamorphism.

decussation the state of being in the form of an X. See also 230. JOINING.

geomorphology *Physical Geography.* the study of the characteristics, origins, and development of land forms. —**geomorphologist,** *n.* —**geomorphologic, geomorphological,** *adj.*

gibbosity the state or condition of being curved, especially convexly. —**gibbous,** *adj.*

hemitery any minor malformation.

heteromorphism, heteromorphy 1. the quality of differing in form from the standard or norm.
2. the condition of existing in different forms at different stages of development, as certain insects. —**heteromorphic,** *adj.*

idiomorphism the state or quality of having a peculiar or characteristic form; uniqueness or individuality in form. —**idiomorphic,** *adj.*

incorporealism the state of having no material body or form. —**incorporeity,** *n.*

morphogenesis the origin(s) of the various aspects of the form of an organism. Also called **morphogeny.** —**morphogenetic,** *adj.*

morphography the scientific description of form. —**morphographer,** *n.* —**morphographic,** *adj.*

morphology 1. the study of the form or structure of anything.
2. the branch of biology that studies the form and structure of plants and animals. See also **geomorphology.** —**morphologist,** *n.* —**morphologic, morphological,** *adj.*

morphometry the process or technique of measuring the external form of an object. —**morphometrical,** *adj.*

morphonomy the study of the laws governing form in nature. —**morphonomic,** *adj.*

morphophyly the study of the phylogeny of forms.

omniformity the state or quality of having every form. —**omniform,** *adj.*

orthogonality the state or quality of being right-angled or perpendicular. —**orthogonal,** *adj.*

palingenesis 1. the phase in the development of an organism in which its form and structure pass through the changes undergone in the evolution of the species.
2. the morphological and structural changes that occur during insect development. Also **palingenesia, palingenesy.** —**palingenetic,** *adj.*

promorphology the branch of morphology that studies the forms of organisms from a mathematical point of view. —**promorphologist,** *n.* —**promorphological** *adj.*

schematism the form, disposition, or outline of a thing or concept. —**schematist,** *n.*

tectology a branch of morphology that regards an organism as made up of other organisms. —**tectological,** *adj.*

tetramorphism the property of displaying four different forms. —tetramorph, *n.* —tetramorphic, *adj.*

trimorphism the state or quality of occurring in three distinct forms, usually at different stages of development, as certain plants, organisms, etc. —trimorphic, trimorphous, *adj.*

171. FOSSILS
See also 18. ANTIQUITY; 147. EVOLUTION.

fossilism the study of fossils. —fossilist, *n.*

ichnology the branch of paleontology that studies fossil footprints. Also called ichnolithology. —ichnological, *adj.*

paleichthyology, palaeichthyology, paleoichthyology, palaeoichthyology the study of fossil fish. —paleichthyologist, palaeichthyologist, paleoichthyologist, palaeoichthyologist, *n.* —paleichthyological, palaeichthyological, paleoichthyological, palaeoichthyological, *adj.*

paleobiology, palaeobiology the branch of paleontology that studies fossil plants and animals. —paleobiologist, palaeobiologist, *n.* —paleobiologic, palaeobiologic, paleobiological, palaeobiological, *adj.*

paleobotany, palaeobotany the branch of paleology that studies fossil plants, especially their origin, structure, and growth. —paleobotanist, palaeobotanist, *n.* —paleobotanic, palaeobotanic, paleobotanical, palaeobotanical, *adj.*

paleontology, palaeontology 1. the science of the forms of life existing in prior geologic periods from their fossilized remains.
2. an article on paleontology. —paleontologist, palaeontologist, *n.* —paleontologic, palaeontologic, paleontological, palaeontological, *adj.*

paleornithology, palaeornithology the study of fossil birds. —paleornithologic, palaeornithologic, paleornithological, palaeornithological, *adj.*

paleozoology, palaeozoology the study of fossil animals. —paleozoologic, palaeozoologic, paleozoological, palaeozoological, *adj.*

phytolithology *Obsolete.* the study of fossil plants.

pyrochromatography a process for detecting traces of organic elements in fossils by using heat or fire.

scatology the branch of paleontology that studies fossil excrement.

172. FRANCE

Francomania an obsession with France and things French.

Francophile Gallophil.

Francophobia a hatred of France or things French. Also called Gallophobia.

Frenchism a French expression used in English, as *outré*.

Gallomania a fondness or prejudice for French life, manners, etc.

Gallophil, Gallophile a person, not French, who loves France. Also called Francophile.

Gallophobia Francophobia.

Girondism a form of mild republicanism in France, 1791–1793, led by natives of the Gironde. —Girondist, *n.*, *adj.*

Normanism the traits, customs, and culture of the Normans. —Normanist, *n.* —Normanic, *adj.*

173. FREEDOM

autonomy independent self-rule free from outside influence.

democratism a doctrine of or belief in social equality or the right of all people to participate equally in politics.

eleutheromania *Rare.* a strong desire for freedom.

eleutherophobia an abnormal fear of freedom.

franchise 1. a condition of freedom.
2. a right or privilege, especially the right to vote.

libertarianism 1. the advocacy of freedom, especially in thought or conduct.
2. *Theology.* the advocacy of the doctrine of free will. See also necessitarianism. —libertarian, *n.*, *adj.*

liberticide 1. the destruction of freedom.
2. the destroyer of freedom. —liberticidal, *adj.*

manumission the act of setting free or being set free from slavery; emancipation.

174. FUTURE
See also 124. DIVINATION; 308. PAST; 396. TIME.

augury 1. the art of foretelling the future by means of signs; divination.
2. an omen or portent from which the future is foretold. —augur, *n.* —augurial, *adj.* —augurous, *Obsolete, adj.*

fatiloquence foretelling of the future; soothsaying.

futurism the seeking of life's meaning and fulfillment in the future. —futurist, *n.* —futuristic, *adj.*

futurition *Rare.* the state or condition of being about to exist.

futurology the art or practice of forecasting trends or developments in politics, science, society, etc.

hariolation the act or art of prognostication or divination; soothsaying.

oracularity the skill, condition, or an instance of being oracular.

prognostication 1. the act of forecasting or prophesying.
2. a forecast or prediction. —prognosticator, *n.* —prognosticative, *adj.*

prolepsis anticipation, as in anticipating or describing a future event. See also 21. ARGUMENTATION. —**proleptic,** *adj.*

telegnosis clairvoyance or other occult or supernatural knowledge.

vaticination 1. the act of prophesying.
    2. the thing foretold. —**vaticinator,** *n.*

G

175. GAMBLING
See also 73. CHANCE; 176. GAMES.

pari-mutuel a system of betting used at horseracing tracks under which holders of winning tickets divide the total amount wagered in proportion to their wagers.

philocubist a devotee of games involving dice.

sortition the casting of lots, as in a gambling game.

totalizator, totalizer a machine used in pari-mutuel betting for posting odds and results.

176. GAMES
See also 26. ATHLETICS; 175. GAMBLING; 337. PUZZLES;
347. RECREATION.

anagram 1. a word or phrase composed by rearranging the letters in another word or phrase.
2. a game based upon this activity.

anagrammatism the art or practice of making anagrams. Also called meta-grammatism.

conundrum a riddle the answer to which requires a pun or other word play.

gamesmanship *Facetious.* the use of methods that, while not dishonest or contrary to the rules, are dubious and give the user unfair advantage in a game or sport.

metagrammatism anagrammatism.

oneupmanship *Facetious.* the art or technique of keeping another person slightly off balance in order to gain an advantage.

wordsmanship *Facetious.* the art or technique of employing a vocabulary of arcane, recondite words in order to gain an advantage over another person.

177. GEMS
See also 385. STONES.

cameography the art or technique of engraving cameos.

chatoyancy the condition or quality of changing in color or luster depending on the angle of light, especially of a gemstone that reflects a single shaft of light when cut in cabochon form. —chatoyant, *adj.*

dactyliography the art of engraving on rings.

gemmary the scientific knowledge of gems.

gemmology the science of gemstones. Also spelled gemology. —gemmologist, *n.* —gemmological, *adj.*

glyptic glyptology.

glyptograph 1. an engraving on a gemstone or other small object.
2. the stone or object engraved.

glyptography the art of carving or engraving upon gemstones. —glyptographer, *n.* —glyptographic, *adj.*

glyptology the science or study of carved or engraved gemstones. Also called glyptic.

lapidary 1. one who cuts, polishes, or engraves precious stones.
2. a cutter of gemstones, especially diamonds.
3. the art of cutting gemstones.
4. a connoisseur of cut gemstones and the art of their cutting. —lapidarist, *n.* —lapidarian, *adj.*

lapidist a lapidary.

lithoglyph 1. an engraving or carving on a gem stone.
2. the stone thus engraved. —lithoglyphic, lithoglyptic, *adj.*

lithoglypher *Obsolete.* an engraver of precious stones.

lithoglyptics the art of engraving or carving precious stones. —lithoglyptic, *adj.*

sigillography the art of engraving on or designing signet rings.

178. GEOGRAPHY
See also 133. EARTH; 143. EQUATOR; 235. LAND; 257. MAPS.

anthropogeography the scientific study of man's geographical distribution and his relationship with his environment.

colatitude the complement of latitude; the difference between any given latitude and 90°.

gazetteer 1. a book of place names, sometimes with additional information, arranged alphabetically.
2. an index to an atlas.

geography 1. the science that studies and describes the surface of the earth and its physical, biological, political, economic, and demographic characteristics and the complex interrelations among them.
2. the topographical features of a specific area.
3. a book on this subject. —geographer, *n*. —geographic, geographical, *adj*.

geomorphology the study of the characteristics, origins, and development of land forms. —geomorphologist, *n*. —geomorphologic, geomorphological, *adj*.

geopolitics 1. the study or application of the effect of political or economic geography on the political structure, programs, or philosophy of a state.
2. a policy or policies based on such factors.
3. the complex of geographical and political factors affecting or determining the nature of a state or region.
4. the study of the relationship between geography and politics, applied especially to the study of the doctrines and actions of Nazi Germany in the context of world domination. —geopolitician, *n*. —geopolitical, *adj*.

hypsography the branch of geography that studies land areas above sea level to measure and map them. —hypsographic, hypsographical, *adj*.

islandology the science or study of islands. —islandologist, *n*.

loxodrome a rhumb line or curve on the surface of a sphere intersecting all meridians at the same angle; hence, the course of a ship or aircraft following a constant compass direction. —loxodromic, *adj*.

megameter an instrument for determining longitude by observation of the stars.

meridian 1. a great circle that passes through the earth's poles and any other given point on the earth's surface.
2. half of such a circle.
3. any line of longitude running north and south on a map. See also 25. ASTRONOMY. —meridian, meridional, *adj*.

orography the branch of physical geography that studies mountains and mountain systems. —orographic, orographical, *adj*.

paleogeography, palaeogeography the branch of geography that studies the features of the earth of past geologic times. —paleogeographer, palaeogeographer, *n*. —paleogeographic, palaeogeographic, paleogeographical, palaeogeographical, *adj*.

physiography 1. physical geography.
2. geomorphology. See also 83. CLASSIFICATION. —physiographer, *n*. —physiographic, physiographical, *adj*.

telmatology a branch of physical geography that studies wet lands, as marshes or swamps.

thermogeography the study of geographical variation and distribution of temperature. —thermogeographical, *adj*.

topography 1. the art or technique of preparing charts or maps of a specified area.

2. the physical features of an area. —**topographic, topographical,** *adj.*

topology the study of the physical features of a specific place or area, usually accompanied by maps or charts showing relationships and elevations. —**topologist,** *n.* —**topologic, topological,** *adj.*

179. GEOLOGY
See also 133. EARTH; 283. MOUNTAINS; 385. STONES; 411. VOLCANOES.

aerogeology the use of aerial observation and photography in the study of geological features. —**aerogeologist,** *n.* —**aerogeologic, aerogeological,** *adj.*

agrogeology the branch of geology concerned with the adaptability of land to agriculture, soil quality, etc.

anamorphism metamorphism from simple to more complex minerals, usually occurring deep beneath the earth's surface. See also **katamorphism, metamorphism.** —**anamorphic, anamorphotic,** *adj.*

aphanitism a minuteness of rock texture so fine that individual grains are invisible to the naked eye. —**aphanite,** *n.*

archeogeology, archaeogeology the branch of geology that studies the geological formations of the remote past. —**archeogeologic, archaeogeologic, archeogeological, archaeogeological,** *adj.*

brecciation the formation of breccia, or masses of rock composed of fragments of older rock fused together.

brontolith, brontolite a thunderstone or meteoric rock.

catastrophism the theory that geological changes have been caused by sudden upheaval rather than by gradual and continuing processes. Cf. **uniformitarianism.** —**catastrophist,** *n.*

clinometry the measurement of the elevations and slopes of mineral strata or of cuttings into rock formations. —**clinometer,** *n.* —**clinometric, clinometrical,** *adj.*

coprolite a small mass of rock composed of the petrified fecal remains of animals.

crustalogy the study of surface of the earth or the moon.

diastrophism the process of movement that causes the earth's crust to form continents, mountains, etc. —**diastrophic,** *adj.*

diluvianism a geological theory that maintains that some geological phenomena can be explained by extensive flooding of large areas of the earth's surface or by an equally strong condition of the weather.

epeirogeny, epeirogenesis the vertical movement or tilting of the earth's crust, affecting broad expanses of continents. —**epeirogenic, epeirogenetic,** *adj.*

epigenesis the process of metamorphism. See also 44. BIOLOGY; 122. DISEASE and ILLNESS. —epigenetic, *adj*.

fluvialist one who considers geological phenomena to be the result of the action of streams.

geognosy a branch of geology that studies the constituent parts of the earth, its atmosphere and water, its crust, and its interior condition. —geognosist, geognost, *n*. —geognostic, *adj*.

geotectology the branch of geology that studies the structure of the earth's crust; structural geology. Also called geotectonics. —geotectonic, *adj*.

geothermometry the branch of geology that measures temperatures deep below the surface of the earth; geologic thermometry.

glaciology the branch of geology that studies the nature, distribution, and movement of glaciers and their effects upon the earth's topography. —glaciologist, *n*. —glaciological, *adj*.

homotaxis, homotaxy the condition of being arranged in the same way, especially stratified layers that are similar in arrangement and place but not contemporaneous. —homotaxic, *adj*.

hydrogeology the study of water both on and beneath the earth's surface. —hydrogeological, *adj*.

isostasy the general equality of pressure in the crust of the earth. —isostatic, *adj*.

katamorphism metamorphism from complex to simpler minerals, usually occurring at or near the earth's surface. See also anamorphism, metamorphism. —katamorphic, *adj*.

lapillus a small stone ejected by a volcano.

limnology the branch of geology that studies ponds and lakes. —limnologist, *n*.

lithification the process by which loose mineral fragments or particles of sand are solidified into stone.

lithogenesy the science of explaining the minerals of which the earth is composed, their origins, and the cause of their form and arrangement.

lithoidology *Rare*. the study of rocks.

lithology the branch of geology that studies the mineral composition and structure of rocks, usu. macroscopically. Cf. petrography. —lithologic, lithological, *adj*.

lithotome a rock or stone formed by natural processes in such a way that it appears to have been artificially fashioned.

metamorphism 1. the process of change in the form and structure of rocks by the agency of heat, water, and pressure.
2. the change of particular types of rock, as limestone into marble. Also called epigenesis. See also 74. CHANGE. —metamorphic, *adj*.

metasomatism the process of chemical change in rocks or other mineral masses that results in the formation of new rocks or minerals. Also metasomatosis.

microlith 1. a very small isotropic needlelike crystal, found usually in volcanic rocks.
2. a very small stone tool or part of a tool, as a tooth of a primitive saw. —microlithic, *adj*.

mineralogy the branch of geology that studies the physical and chemical structures of minerals. —mineralogist, *n*. —mineralogic, mineralogical, *adj*.

neptunism the now obsolete theory that all rock surfaces were formed by the agency of water. Cf. plutonism. —neptunist, *n*.

orogeny the process by which mountains are created. —orogenic, orogenetic, *adj*.

oryctology mineralogy. Also called oryctognosy.

paleopedology, palaeopaedology a branch of soil science that studies the soils of past geologic times. —paleopedologist, palaeopaedologist, *n*. —paleopedologic, palaeopaedologic, paleopedological, palaeopaedological, *adj*.

perimorphism a phenomenon in which one mineral encloses another. —perimorphic, perimorphous, *adj*.

petrogensis, petrogeny the branch of petrology that studies the formation of rocks.

petrography the branch of geology that describes and classifies rocks, usually after microscopic study. Cf. lithology. —petrographer, *n*. —petrographic, petrographical, *adj*.

petrology the branch of geology that studies the origin, structure, composition, changing, and classification of rocks. —petrologist, *n*. —petrologic, petrological, *adj*.

plutonism the theory that all rock surfaces have solidified from magmas, some at great depths below the surface of the earth. Cf. neptunism. —plutonist, *n*.

pneumatolysis the process by which ores and minerals are formed from the action of vapors produced by igneous magmas. —pneumatolytic, *adj*.

pyritology the study of iron or copper sulfides, called pyrites.

regolith the layer of disintegrated and decomposed rock fragments, including soil, lying above the solid rock of the earth's crust. Also called mantle rock.

stratigraphy the branch of geology that studies the classification, correlation, and interpretation of stratified rocks. —stratigrapher, *n.* —stratigraphic, stratigraphical, *adj.*

tectonics the study of the structure and behavior of the earth's crust. —tectonic, *adj.*

uniformitarianism the thesis that early geological processes were not unlike those observed today, i.e., gradually occurring. Cf. catastrophism. —uniformitarian, *n.*

xenolith a fragment of rock embedded in another kind of rock.

180. GERMANY

geopolitics the study of the relationship between geography and politics, applied especially to the study of the doctrines and actions of Nazi Germany in the context of world domination.

Germanism a feature of the German language that is present in another language.

Germanomania an obsession with Germany and things German. Also called Teutonomania.

Germanophile a person who is especially attracted to or interested in Germany, its people, culture, etc.

Germanophobia intense fear or hatred of Germany, its people, language, etc.

Teutonicism 1. anything typical or characteristic of the Teutons or Germans, as customs, attitudes, actions, etc.
2. Germanism.

Teutonomania Germanomania.

181. GESTURE

chironomy, cheironomy 1. the science of gesture.
2. the art of conducting singers of Gregorian chant through hand gestures to mark the rise or fall of the melody. —chironomic, cheironomic, *adj.*

dactylology the science of manual sign language, as for use in communicating with the deaf. —dactylotogist, *n.* —dactylologic, dactylological, *adj.*

kinemics *Linguistics.* the study of units of gestural expression.

kinesics *Linguistics.* a systematic study of nonverbal body gestures, as smiles, hand motions, or other movements, in their relation to human communication; body language. Also called pasimology. —kinesic, *adj.*

pasimology kinesics.

pathognomy the study of the signs that reveal human passions. —pathognomonic, *adj.*

182. GHOSTS

See also 114. DEMONS; 384. SPIRITS and SPIRITUALISM.

Doppelgänger, doubleganger a supposedly ghostly counterpart or double of a living person.

eidolism a belief in ghosts.

eidolon a phantom or apparition.

phantasm a vision or other perception of something that has no physical or objective reality, especially in the sense of a ghost or other supernatural apparition. Also **phantasma**. See also 218. IMAGES; 312. PHILOSOPHY.

phantasmology spectrology.

phasmophobia an abnormal fear of ghosts.

sciomancy fortune-telling through communication with the spirits of the dead. —**sciomantic,** *adj.*

sciotheism a religion in which ghosts are worshiped instead of gods.

spectrology the study of ghosts, phantoms, or apparitions. Also called **phantasmology, spookology.** —**spectrological,** *adj.*

spectrophobia an abnormal fear of speeters or phantoms.

spookology spectrology.

supernaturalism 1. the condition or quality of existing outside the known experience of man or caused by forces beyond those of nature.
2. belief in supernatural events or forces. Also **supranaturalism.** —**supernaturalist,** *n.,* *adj.* —**supernatural, supernaturalistic,** *adj.*

supranaturalism supernaturalism. —**supranaturalist,** *n.,* *adj.* —**supranatural, supranaturalistic,** *adj.*

183. GOD and GODS

See also 59. BUDDHISM; 69. CATHOLICISM; 79. CHRIST;
80. CHRISTIANITY; 135. EASTERN ORTHODOXY; 151. FAITH; 206.
HINDUISM; 227. ISLAM; 231. JUDAISM; 286. MYTHOLOGY;
332. PROTESTANTISM; 349. RELIGION; 358. SACREDNESS;
392. THEOLOGY.

acosmism, akosmism a denial of, or disbelief in, the existence of an external world or of a world distinct from God. —**acosmist,** *n.* —**acosmic,** *adj.*

adevism the denial of legendary gods. —**adevist,** *n.*

agnosticism the tenet that neither the existence nor the nature of God is known or knowable. —**agnostic,** *n., adj.*

allotheism the worship of strange or foreign gods.

aniconism 1. the worship of an object symbolizing, but not representing God.
2. an opposition to icons or idols. —**aniconic,** *adj.*

animism 1. the belief that natural objects and phenomena and the universe itself possess souls and consciousness.
2. the belief in spiritual beings or agencies. —animist, *n.* —animistic, *adj.*

anthropolatry the deification and worship of a human being.

anthropomorphism the assignment of human shape and attributes to gods, animals, etc. —anthropomorphist, *n.* —anthropomorphic, anthropomorphical, anthropomorphistic, *adj.*

anthropopathism, anthropopathy the assignment of human feelings to a god or inanimate object. —anthropopathite, *n.* —anthropopathic, *adj.*

anthropophuism the assignment of human nature and emotions to God. —anthropophuistic, *adj.*

anthropotheism the belief that the gods have human nature, or are only deified men.

apotheosis deification; the elevation of a person to godhood. See also 210. HONORS and REGALIA.

Atenism the monotheistic religious system of the Egyptian pharaoh Ikhnaton, emphasizing the worship of the sun god Aten (Aton).

atheism the absolute denial of the existence of God or any other gods. —atheist, *n.* —atheistic, *adj.*

Baalism the worship, in ancient Canaan or Phoenicia, of any of a variety of chief deities referred to as *Baal*, 'lord.' —Baalite, *n.* —Baalistic, *adj.*

bitheism a belief in two gods. —bitheist, *n.* —bitheistic, *adj.*

chrematheism *Obsolete.* the worship of inanimate objects as usefully divine.

deicide 1. the killing of a god.
2. the killer of a god. —deicidal, *adj.*

deism the acknowledgment of the existence of a god upon the testimony of reason and of nature and its laws, and the rejection of the possibility of supernatural intervention in human affairs and of special revelation. —deist, *n.* —deistic, *adj.*

demiurgism the belief, in Platonism and some Gnostic sects, that the material and sensible world was created by a subordinate god under the direction of the Supreme Being. —demiurge, *n.* —demiurgic, *adj.*

ditheism 1. the belief or doctrine that there are two gods of equal power.
2. *Zoroastrianism.* the belief in two antagonistic deities, one a force for good, one for evil. —ditheist, *n.* —ditheistic, ditheistical *adj.*

euhemerism the belief that the mythological gods were merely early kings and heroes deified. —euhemerist, *n.* —euhemeristic, *adj.*

henotheism a belief in one supreme or specially venerated god who is not the only god. —henotheist, *n.*

heroogony the birth of heroes as a result of a union between gods and mortal women.

herotheism the worship of mortals who have been deified.

hylotheism the identification of God with matter or the universe. —hylotheist, *n.*

Isiac relating to the religious practices and objects involving the goddess Isis.

Mammonism the pursuit of material wealth and possessions, especially a dedication to riches that is tantamount to devotion. —Mammonist, Mammonite, *n.*

Mazdaism the worship of Ahura Mazda in Zoroastrianism as the source of all light and good. —Mazdaist, *n.*

mechanomorphism the concept that God is a mechanical force and that the universe is governed by natural laws. Cf. deism. —mechanomorphic, *adj.*

misotheism *Rare.* a hatred of gods or God.

Mithraism an oriental mystery cult, admitting only men, whose deity was Mithras, the savior hero of Persian myth. —Mithraist, *n.* —Mithraic, *adj.*

monolatry the worship of one god without excluding belief in others.

monotheism the doctrine of or belief in only one God. —monotheist, *n.*

myriotheism the worship of an unlimited number of gods.

Neptunianism the state of relating to the god or planet Neptune or to the ocean. —Neptunian, *adj.*

noumenalism the doctrine of the existence of noumena, whose existence is understood only by intellectual intuition, without the aid of the senses. —noumenalist, *n.*

panentheism the belief that the world is part, though not all of God. —panentheist, *n.*

pantheism the identification of God with the universe as His manifestation. —pantheist, *n.*

Parsiism, Parseeism the Zoroastrianism of southwest India, with religious literature in the Parsi dialect. —Parsi, *n.*

phallicism the worship of the phallus as symbolic of the generative power of nature. —phallicist, phallist, *n.*

philotheism a love for God. —philotheist, *n.* —philotheistic, *adj.*

physitheism 1. the assignment to God of a physical shape.
2. deification of the powers or phenomena of nature.

polytheism a belief in, or worship of, many gods. —polytheist, *n.*

pseudolatry devotion to false gods.

psychotheism the doctrine that God is pure spirit.

Sethite, Sethian a member of a Gnostic sect that regarded Seth, son of Adam, as the father of a pure race and considered the serpent as its deity.

supernaturalism 1. the condition or quality of existing outside the known experience of man or caused by forces beyond those of nature.
2. belief in supernatural events or forces. Also **supranaturalism.** —**supernaturalist,** *n., adj.* —**supernatural, supernaturalistic,** *adj.*

supranaturalism supernaturalism. —**supranaturalist,** *n., adj.* —**supranatural, supranaturalistic,** *adj.*

theanthropism 1. the attributing of human characteristics to God; anthropomorphism.
2. a belief in the divinity of a human being.
3. a belief in God's becoming man. Also called **theanthroposophy.** —**theanthropist,** *n.*

theism 1. a belief in the existence of God or gods.
2. a belief in one god as creator and ruler of the universe, without rejection of special revelation. Cf. **deism.** —**theism,** *n.*

theocentrism, theocentricity the belief that God is the center of all truth in the universe. —**theocentric,** *adj.*

theocrasy, theocrasia 1. a mingling of the attributes of several deities into one.
2. a union of an individual soul with God, especially through contemplation.

theodicy the vindication of the goodness of God in the face of the existence of evil. —**theodicean,** *adj.*

theogony 1. the origin of the gods.
2. a genealogical account of the origin of the gods. —**theogonist,** *n.*

theolepsy *Archaic.* a seizure or possession by a deity. —**theoleptic,** *n.*

theology the study of God and His relationship to the universe. —**theologist,** *n.* —**theological,** *adj.*

theomachist a person or a god who resists the divine will of God or the gods. —**theomachy,** *n.*

theomancy a form of divination involving divinely inspired oracles or others inspired by God.

theomania a religious madness in which a person believes he is God or is inspired by God.

theopathy religious emotion or excitement caused by contemplation of God. —**theopathetic,**- —**theopathic,** *adj.*

theophagy the act of eating one's god, either literally or symbolically. —**theophagite,** *n.* —**theophagous,** *adj.*

theophobia an abnormal fear of God.

theurgy 1. the working of some divine or supernatural agency in human affairs.
2. the art of invoking deities or spirits for aid or information or knowledge unachievable through human reason.
3. a divine act; miracle.
4. a system of supernatural knowledge or powers believed bequeathed to the Egyptian Platonists by beneficent deities. —theurgist, *n.* —theurgic, theurgical, *adj.*

titanism the condition of having qualities distinctive of the Titans, a family of giants in Greek mythology. —titanic, *adj.*

trieteric 1. a festival that occurs every third year, especially one honoring Bacchus.
2. occurring every third year, particularly in reference to festivals for divinities. —trieterical, *adj.*

tripersonality the quality of existing in three persons, as God in the Trinity. —tripersonal, *adj.*

tritheism 1. a belief in three gods.
2. a Christian heresy holding that the Trinity consists of three distinct gods. —tritheist, *n.*

ubiquitary a person or entity existing everywhere. —ubiquitary, *adj.*

Zemiism the religion of the Taino tribes of the West Indies, involving the invocation of Zemis, spirits or supernatural beings often dwelling in objects.

zoomorphism the attribution of animal form or nature to a deity.

184. GOODNESS

agathism the belief that all things incline toward the good. —agathist, *n.*

agathology the doctrine or science of the good. —agathologic, agathological, *adj.*

do-goodism attitudes or actions of well-intentioned but sometimes ineffectual people, especially in the area of social reform.

theodicy the vindication of the goodness of God in the face of the existence of evil. —theodicean, *adj.*

185. GOVERNMENT
See also 62. BUREAUCRACY; 94. COMMUNISM; 152. FASCISM;
322. POLITICS; 376. SOCIETY.

absolutism the theory and exercise of complete and unrestricted power in government. See also autarchy, autocracy, despotism, dictatorship, monarchy, oligarchy. —absolutist, *n.*, *adj.* —absolutistic. *adj.*

anarchism 1. a political theory advocating the elimination of governments and governmental restraint and the substitution of voluntary cooperation among individuals.
2. the methods and practices of anarchists. Cf. Nihilism. —anarchist, *n.* —anarchic, *adj.*

anarchy an absence of government and law; political disorder, often accompanied by violence. See also 301. ORDER and DISORDER.

angelocracy rule by angels.

antarchism *Rare.* the principle of opposition to all forms of government, or to all restraint of individuals by laws. —antarchist, *n.* —antarchistic, *adj.*

apartheid the policy of strict racial segregation and political and economic discrimination against non-whites practiced in the Republic of South Africa.

archology 1. the science of government.
2. the science of origins.

arithmocracy rule by that group which holds the numerical majority in a state. —arithmocratic, *adj.*

autarchy 1. an absolute sovereignty.
2. an autocratic government.
3. autarky. —autarch, *n.* —autarchic, autarchical, *adj.*

autocracy 1. a government in which one person has unrestricted control over others.
2. a country with an autocratic system. —autocrat, *n.* —autocratic, *adj.*

autonomy 1. the power or right of self-government.
2. a self-governing community. Cf. heteronymy. —autonomous, *adj.*

biarchy the rule of a nation, state, or community by two persons.

bicameralism 1. a legislative body having two branches, houses, or chambers.
2. advocacy of bicameral structure. Cf. unicameralism. —bicameralist, *n.* —bicameral, *adj.*

bipartisanism the state of being composed of members of two parties or of two parties cooperating, as in government. —bipartisan, *adj.*

caciquism the domination of areas in Spanish and Latin America by local political bosses. Also caciquismo.

carpetbaggism the practices of the carpetbaggers, Northerners who, after the Civil War, sought private gain in the South from the Reconstruction government. —carpetbaggery, *n.*

Castroism the doctrines and policies of Fidel Castro, communist premier of Cuba.

centralism a system, especially in government, in which power and administration are concentrated in a central group or institution. —centralist, *n.*, *adj.* —centralistic, *adj.*

chiliarchy a system with one thousand rulers.

chromatocracy rule by a single race.

colonialism the implementation of various political, economic, and social policies to enable a state to maintain or extend its authority and control over other territories. —colonialist, *n.*, *adj.* —colonialistic, *adj.*

condominium *International Law.* a joint sovereignty over a colony or dependent territory by several states. —condominate, *v.*

constitutional monarchy a system in which the powers of a monarch are defined and limited by law.

cosmocracy control of the whole world.

decarchy, dekarchy the control of a governmental system by ten persons. Also called **decadarchy.**

democracy a form of government in which sovereign power resides in the people and is exercised by them or by officers they elect to represent them. Cf. republicanism. —democrat, *n.* —democratic, *adj.*

demonocracy 1. the power of demons.
2. government or rule by demons. —demonocratic, *adj.*

despotism 1. a form of government with a ruler having absolute authority; autocracy.
2. a system ruled by a tyrant or dictator having absolute, usually oppressive power. —despot, *n.* —despotic, *adj.*

diarchy, dyarchy a government controlled by two rulers; biarchy. —diarch, dyarch, *n.*

dictatorship 1. a despotic system ruled by a dictator possessing absolute power and absolute authority.
2. the office of a dictator. —dictatorial, *adj.*

doulocracy, dulocracy *Rare.* a government controlled by slaves.

duarchy government by two persons.

duumvirate 1. a position in government held jointly by two men.
2. the two people holding such a position.

dynasticism 1. a system of government in which a sequence of rulers is derived from the same family, group, or stock.
2. the reign of such a sequence. —dynast, dynasty, *n.*

elitism the belief or practice that government should be by a self-appointed group who consider themselves superior to those governed by virtue of their higher birth. —elitist, *n.*, *adj.*

endarchy a centralized government.

ergatocracy a government controlled by workers.

ethnarchy the rank and position of a governor of a province or people. —ethnarch, *n*.

factionism the quality of being a clique or combination, as within a larger organization. Also called factionalism. —factionist, *n*. —factionary, *adj*.

fascism 1. the tenets of a centralized, totalitarian, and nationalistic government that strictly controls finance, industry, and commerce, practices rigid censorship and racism, and eliminates opposition through secret police.
2. such a government, as that of Italy under Mussolini. —fascist, *n*. —fascistic, *adj*.

federalese language typical of the federal government, especially bureaucratic jargon.

federalism 1. a union of states under a central government distinct from that of the separate states, who retain certain individual powers under the central government.
2. (*cap.*) the principles of the American Federalist party, especially its emphasis during the early years of the U.S. on a strong central government. —federalist, *n., adj*. —federalistic, *adj*.

feudalism a European system flourishing between 800–1400 based upon fixed relations of lord to vassal and all lands held in fee (as from the king), and requiring of vassal-tenants homage and service. Also feudality. —feudal, feudalistic, *adj*.

foolocracy government or domination of society by fools.

gerontocracy the system in which the rulers are old men.

governmentalism a theory that advocates the extension of governmental activity. —governmentalist, *n*.

hagiarchy 1. a system of government by priests.
2. a state so governed.

hagiocracy 1. a system of rule by persons considered holy.
2. a state so governed.

hecatonarchy a system of rule by 100 persons.

heptarchy 1. government by seven persons.
2. a group or confederacy of seven political units.
3. *English History.* the seven principal concurrent early English kingdoms. —heptarch, heptarchist, *n*. —heptarchal, heptarchic, heptarchical, *adj*.

heteronomy 1. the state or condition of being ruled, governed, or under the sway of another, as in a military occupation.
2. the state or condition of being under the influence or domination, in a moral, spiritual, or similar sense, of another person, entity, force, etc. Cf. autonomy. —heteronomous, *adj*.

hexarchy a group or confederacy of six political units.

hierarchism the system of government or authority of a hierarchy. —hierarchization, *n*. —hierarchial, *adj*.

isocracy a government in which there is equality of power among all the people. —isocrat, *n*. —isocratic, *adj*.

Jesuitocracy government by Jesuits.

justicialism a fascistic theory of government in Argentina under the Peron administration involving government intervention and economic control to ensure social justice and public welfare; Peronism.

kakistocracy a system of rule by the worst men.

kakotopia a state in which the worst possible conditions exist in government, society, law, etc. See also 406. UTOPIA.

kritarchy *Rare.* the rule, over ancient Israel, of the judges.

legitimist a supporter of legitimate authority, especially of claims to a throne based on the rights of heredity. —legitimism, *n.*

manorialism 1. the system of manorial social and political organization, as in the Middle Ages.
2. *Sometimes Pejorative.* any small, strong unit of local political and social organization.

matriarchate 1. a matriarchal form of government.
2. a family, tribe, or other social group ruled by a matriarch or matriarchs. —matriarchic, *adj*.

matriarchy a society organized with the mother or oldest female as head of the tribe or clan, with descent being traced through the female line. —matriarch, *n*. —matriarchal, *adj*.

mediocracy government or dominance of society by the mediocre.

mobocracy government by the mob; the mob as ruler or dominant force in society. —mobocratic, *adj*.

mobocrat 1. a person who advocates government by the mob.
2. a member of a mobocracy.

monarchism the doctrines and principles of a monarchical government. —monarchist, *n*. —monarchical, *adj*.

monarchy 1. a governmental system in which supreme power is actually or nominally held by a monarch.
2. supreme power and authority held by one person; autocracy. —**monarchic, monarchical,** adj.

moneyocracy government or domination of society by the rich.

monocracy a system ruled by one person; autocracy.

municipalism 1. the process of self-government by cities, towns, or municipalities.
2. a doctrine advocating such government. —**municipalist,** n.

myriarchy a system controlled by ten thousand rulers.

Napoleonism the adherence to the doctrines of Napoleon and his dynasty. —**Napoleonist,** n. —**Napoleonic,** adj.

neocracy a government by amateurs.

Nihilism the principles of a Russian revolutionary movement in the late 19th century, advocating the destruction of government as a means to anarchy and often employing terrorism and assassination to assist its program. —**nihilist,** n., adj. —**nihilistic,** adj.

nomarchy a provincial system of government, as in modern Greece, under officials called nomarchs.
2. the office or jurisdiction of a nomarch. Also called **nome.**

noninterventionism a policy under which government regulation of private industry is reduced or nonexistent. —**noninterventionist,** n., adj.

oligarchy 1. a system of rule by a few persons.
2. the people who form such a government. —**oligarch,** n. —**oligarchic, oligarchical,** adj.

palatinate the office of or territory governed by a nobleman with royal privileges.

panarchy Rare. a realm or dominion that includes the universe.

pantisocracy a utopian community where all are equal and all rule. —**pantisocratist,** n. —**pantisocratic, pantisocratical,** adj.

papyrocracy a system in which power is held by the printed media.

parliamentarianism advocacy of the parliamentary system of government. —**parliamentarian,** n., adj.

paternalism fatherlike control over subordinates in government. —**paternalist,** n. —**paternalistic,** adj.

patriarchism a patriarchal government in a society or a church. —**patriarchist,** n.

patriarchy a society organized to give supremacy to the father or the oldest male in governing a family, tribe, or clan. —**patriarch,** n.

pedantocracy rule or government by pedants; domination of society by pedants.

Peronism justicialism.

plutocracy 1. the rule of the rich or wealthy.
2. the rich or wealthy who govern under such a system. Also called plousiocracy. —plutocrat, *n.*

polyarchy 1. government by many rulers.
2. the condition of being polyarch. —polyarchist, *n.* —polyarchical, *adj.*

Pretorianism the state of relating to the administration or lifestyle of Pretoria, South Africa.

Prussianism the theories, actions, and principles of the Prussians. —Prussian, *n.*, *adj.*

ptochocracy a system of rule by the poor.

Quirinal the civil government of Italy, as contrasted with the papal government of the Vatican. —Quirinal, *adj.*

regalism the tenets of royal supremacy, especially in church affairs.

republicanism the principles of a theory of government in which the supreme power rests in the body of citizens entitled to vote and exercised by representatives they elect directly or indirectly and by an elected or nominated president.

revanchism the action taken and the policies followed by a government determined to recover a lost territory. —revanche, *n.* —revanchist, *n.*, *adj.*

Sabaeanism the customs of Saba, an ancient Arabic kingdom that flourished from 950 to 115 B.C. —Sabaean, *adj.*

satrapy *Persian Empire.* the system of provincial governments ruled by satraps, each of whom answered to the Persian emperor.

sectionalism an excessive devotion to the interests of one particular section of a country or community. —sectionalist, *n.*

serfism a feudal social and economic system in which persons of the lower class are bound to the soil, subject to the will of and service for their lord, and transferable to the new owner if the land is sold or otherwise deeded. Also serfdom.

socialism a theory of government based upon the ownership and control of capital, land, and means of production by the community as a whole.

sociocracy collective government or government by society as a whole.

Sovietism, sovietism 1. the soviet system of government and the principles and practices of such a government.
2. a policy, action, etc., typical of the Soviet Union. —Sovietist, sovietist, *n.*, *adj.*

statism, stateism 1. the principle of concentrating major political and economic controls in the state.
2. the support of the sovereignty of the state. —statist, *n.*, *adj.*

stratocracy a system of rule by the military.

tanistry an early Irish rule of succession in which the successor to a Celtic chief was chosen from among eligible males during the chief's lifetime. —tanist, *n.*

technocracy 1. a theory and movement of the 1930s advocating the control of production and distribution by technicians and engineers.
2. a system of government based on this theory. —technocrat, *n.* —technocratic, *adj.*

tetrarchy 1. the Roman practice of dividing authority over provinces among four governors.
2. a system of rule by four authorities. —tetrarch, tetrarchate, *n.* —tetrarchic, tetrarchical, *adj.*

thearchy 1. a system of government by God or a god.
2. an order or system of deities. —thearchic, *adj.*

theocracy 1. a system of government in which God or a deity is held to be the civil ruler; thearchy.
2. a system of government by priests; hagiarchy.
3. a state under such a form of rule. —theocrat, *n.* —theocratic, *adj.*

timocracy 1. *Platonism.* a state in which a love of honor and glory is the guiding principle of the rulers.
2. *Aristotelianism.* a state in which the ownership of property is a qualification for office. —timocratic, timocratical, *adj.*

toparchy *Ancient History.* a small state or division of a larger state, as Judea.

totalitarianism 1. a system of highly centralized government in which one political party or group takes control and grants neither recognition nor tolerance to other political groups.
2. autocracy in one of its several varieties.
3. the character or traits of an autocratic or authoritarian individual, party, government, or state. —totalitarian, *n.*, *adj.*

triarchy 1. the rule of a nation, state, or community by three persons.
2. a set of three joint rulers. Usually called **triumvirate**.
3. a country divided into three governments.
4. a group of three districts or three countries, each under its own ruler.

tribalism 1. the customs, life, and organization of a tribal society.
2. a strong loyalty to one's tribe, party, or group.

tuchungism the former Chinese practice of governing provinces through warlords, or *tuchuns.*

unicameralism 1. a representative form of government with a single legislative chamber.
2. an advocacy of unicameral structure. —**unicameralist,** *n.* —**unicameral,** *adj.*

unilateralism the state of being one-sided. —**unilaterality,** *n.* —**unilateralist,** *adj.*

vassalism 1. the feudal system of lands held in fee and of mandatory vassal-tenant homage, fealty, and service.
2. the condition of a person owing homage and fealty to a superior; vassalage.

vestryism local government by assemblies of parishioners, usually meeting in the vestry of the church. Also **vestrydom.** —**vestryish,** *adj.*

186. GRAMMAR
See also 236. LANGUAGE; 247. LINGUISTICS.

accidence the aspect of grammar that deals with inflections and word order.

agrammatism *Medicine.* a neurological defect resulting in an inability to use words in grammatical sequence.

amphibology 1. an ambiguity of language.
2. a word, phrase, or sentence that can be interpreted variously because of uncertainty of grammatical construction rather than ambiguity of the words used, as "John met his father when he was sick." Also **amphibologism, amphiboly.** —**amphibological, amphibolous,** *adj.*

anacoluthon a lack of grammatical sequence or coherence, as "He ate cereal, fruit, and went to the store." Also **anacoluthia.** —**anacoluthic,** *adj.*

antanaclasis a repetition of words to resume the sense after a long parenthetical digression. See also 354. RHETORIC and RHETORICAL DEVICES.

antiptosis the substitution of one grammatical case for another, e.g., use of the nominative where the vocative would normally occur. —**antiptotic,** *adj.*

apodosis the clause that expresses the consequence in a conditional sentence. Cf. **protasis.**

grammar 1. the study of the principles by which a language or languages function in producing meaningful units of expression.
2. knowledge of the preferred forms of expression and usage in language. See also 247. LINGUISTICS. —**grammarian,** *n.* —**grammatical,** *adj.*

grammarianism 1. *Rare.* the principles of the study of grammar followed by a grammarian.
2. excessive emphasis upon the fine points of grammar and usage, especially as a shibboleth; dedication to the doctrine of correctness; grammatism.

grammaticism a principle or a point of grammar.

grammatism excessively pedantic behavior about grammatical standards and principles. —grammatist, *n*.

hypotaxis arrangement of thoughts by subordination in grammatical construction. Cf. parataxis. —hypotactic, *adj*.

ingrammaticism *Rare*. a word or phrase that violates the rules of grammar. —ingrammatically, *adj*.

paradigm 1. a declension, conjugation, etc. that provides all the inflectional forms and serves as a model or example for all others.
2. any model or example. —paradigmatic, paradigmatical, *adj*.

parataxis arrangement of thoughts as coordinate units in grammatical construction. Cf. hypotaxis. —paratactic, *adj*.

periphrastic referring to the ability in some languages to use function words instead of inflections, as "the hair of the dog" for "dog's hair." —periphrasis, *n*.

protasis a clause containing the condition in a conditional sentence. Cf. apodosis. See also 127. DRAMA; 422. WISDOM AND FOOLISHNESS. —protatic, *adj*.

solecism a violation of conventional usage and grammar, as "I are sixty year old." —solecist, *n*. —solecistic, solecistical, *adj*.

syllepsis the use of a word or expression to perform two syntactic functions, especially to apply to two or more words of which at least one does not agree in logic, number, case, or gender, as in Pope's line "See Pan with flocks, with fruits Pomona crowned." —sylleptic, sylleptical, *adj*.

synesis the practice of using a grammatical construction that conforms with meaning rather than with strict regard for syntax, such as a plural form of a verb following a singular subject that has a plural meaning.

syntax the grammatical principles by which words are used in phrases and sentences to construct meaningful combinations. —syntactic, syntactical, *adj*.

187. GRANDEUR
See also 368. SIZE.

megalomania 1. *Psychiatry*. a form of mental illness marked by delusions of greatness, wealth, or power.
2. an obsession with doing extravagant or grand things. —megalomaniac, *n*. —megalomaniacal, *adj*.

paranoia *Psychiatry*. a slowly progressive personality disorder marked by delusions, especially of persecution and grandeur. —paranoid, paranoiac, *adj*.

188. GRASSES
See also 54. BOTANY; 319. PLANTS.

agrostography a description of grasses. —agrostographer, *n*.

agrostology the branch of systematic botany that studies grasses. Also called graminology. —agrostologist, *n.*

graminology agrostology.

189. GRAVITY
See also 316. PHYSICS.

baragnosis *Medicine.* the absence of the power to recognize weight through the senses; the absence of barognosis.

barognosis *Medicine.* the conscious perception of weight, especially through cutaneous and muscular nerves.

barology *Archaic.* a branch of physics that studied weight and its relationship to gravity.

barophobia an abnormal fear of gravity.

geotaxis the movement of an organism in response to the force of gravity.

geotropism *Botany.* the response of a plant to the force of gravity. —geotropic, *adj.*

Hutchinsonianism the theories of the 18th-century Yorkshireman John Hutchinson, which included a rejection of Newton's theory of gravitation. See also 43. BIBLE; 392. THEOLOGY. —Hutchinsonian, *adj.*

levity a hypothetical force, opposed to gravity, once believed to be a property inherent in certain bodies or materials.

telekinesis the production of motion in a body, apparently without the use of material force, a power long claimed by mediums and magicians. Also called teleportation. —telekinetic, *adj.*

tidology the science or theory of tides.

190. GREECE and GREEKS
See also 18. ANTIQUITY.

Alexandrianism the style and theories of the Greek writers of Alexandria, 325–30 B.C., whose style was highly ornamented and obscure and favored such forms as the elegy, epigram, epyllion, and lyric and also ventured into the drama. —Alexandrianist, *n.*, *adj.*

archon one of the nine magistrates in ancient Athens, chosen from the leading families to oversee the civil and religious life of the city.

Atticism the language and style typical of Athens and Attica, particularly in reference to a polished, elegant, and concise rhetorical style. —Atticist, *n.*

dithyramb *Ancient Greece.* a choral chant of a wild and abandoned nature; hence, any poem or similar composition of this nature, especially one of irregular form. —dithyrambic, *adj.*

docimasy *Ancient Greece.* the process whereby candidates for office or citizenship were judicially reviewed. See also 270. METALS.

eparchy *Ancient Greece.* the territory governed by an eparch or governor. See also 135. EASTERN ORTHODOXY.

etacism the pronunciation of the Greek letter η *(eta)*, like the *a* in *late.*

Grecism, Graecism 1. the spirit of Greek thought, art, etc., and the adoption or imitation of this spirit.
2. anything typical of Greek language, art, thought, etc.

Grecomania, Graecomania an obsession with Ancient Greece and Greeks.

Hellenism 1. the culture and ideals of the ancient Greeks.
2. the use of a Greek idiom in writing in another language.
3. the adoption or imitation of ancient Greek language, thought, art, or customs. —Hellenist, *n.*

Hellenist a classicist whose specialization or preference is for Greek language and culture.

hetaera a female companion or paramour of ancient Greece, a sort of professional prostitute.

himation a garment composed of a rectangular piece of cloth, thrown over the left shoulder and draped around the body, as worn in ancient Greece.

Homerology 1. the study of the poet Homer.
2. the study of the Homeric poems, especially of their authorship and dates.

Ionicism 1. *Architecture.* use or imitation of the Ionic order in construction or decoration.
2. the culture and ideals of ancient Ionia and the Ionians.
3. an Ionian idiom appearing in the midst of material in another language or in the dialect of Athens (Attic). Also **Ionism.**

isotely in ancient Athens, the granting of some of the rights of Athenian citizenship to noncitizens.

lampadedromy *Ancient Greece.* a race in honor of Prometheus in which the contestants ran bearing lit torches, the winner being the first to finish with his torch still lit. Also called **lampadrome, lampadephoria.**

lampadist a contestant in a lampadedromy. Also called **lampadephore, lampadophoros.**

metic *Ancient Greece.* a foreigner or a resident alien.

myriarch *Ancient Greece.* the commander of ten thousand men or soldiers.

Panhellenism 1. the idea of a union of all Greeks in a single political body.
2. advocacy of the idea of such a union. —Panhellenist, *n.* —Panhellenic, *adj.*

Philhellenism a habit of friendship or support for the Greeks. —Philhellenist, *n.* —Philhellenic, *adj.*

phratry 1. a subdivision of an ancient Greek tribe or phyle.
2. a clan or other unit of a primitive tribe.

psephism a decree made by an ancient assembly such as the ecclesia of Athens.

symposiarch *Ancient Greece.* the master of a feast or symposium; hence, a person presiding over a banquet or formal discussion.

synomosy *Ancient Greece.* fellowship or brotherhood bound by solemn oath.

syntrierarchy 1. the ancient Greek system in which a number of citizens were given the responsibility of equipping a trireme.
2. the position of one of the appointed citizens, or syntrierarchs. —**syntrierarch,** *n.*

syssitia the practice or custom, as among the ancient Spartans and Cretans, of eating the main meal of the day together in public to strengthen social and political bonds.

taxiarch *Ancient Greece.* a military commander of a taxis, or division of troops.

theatrocracy the absolute rule of the Athenian democracy, exercised in the course of mass meetings in the theater.

xenia *Ancient Greece.* a custom of hospitality, specifically the giving of presents to guests or strangers, especially foreign ambassadors. —**xenial,** *adj.*

191. GROWTH
See also 74. CHANGE; 147. EVOLUTION.

auxesis growth, especially owing to an increase in cell size. Cf. merisis. —**auxetic,** *adj.*

auxology *Obsolete. Medicine.* the science of growth, especially applied to micro-organisms. Also called **auxanology.**

bathmism a hypothetical vital force, thought to control growth and the function of nutrition.

chemotropism growth or motion in response to a chemical stimulus. —**chemotropic,** *adj.*

culturist a cultivator or a person who grows things.

embryogeny the formation and growth of an embryo. —**embryogenic, embryogenetic,** *adj.*

endogeny development or growth from within. —**endogenicity,** *n.* —**endogenous,** *adj.*

epiboly the growth of part of an organism in such a way that it overlays or surrounds another. —**epibolic,** *adj.*

galvanotropism growth or movement of an organism in response to an electric current. —**galvanotropic,** *adj.*

histogenesis, histogeny the growth of organic tissues. —**histogenic, histogenetic,** *adj.*

merisis any form of growth, especially as a product of cell division. Cf. **auxesis.**

neoplasia the growth or formation of a neoplasm. —neoplastic, *adj.*

neoplasm any abnormal formation or growth of tissue such as a tumor. —neoplastic, *adj.*

physis 1. the principle or concept of growth and change in nature.
2. nature considered as the source of growth and change.
3. something that grows or develops.

plagiotropism the tendency of some plants to diverge from the vertical in their growth. —plagiotropic, *adj.*

polyeidism the passing of an organism through several different forms in the growth process.

stereotaxis orientation or movement of an organism in response to the stimulus of a solid object. Cf. stereotropism. —stereotactic, *adj.*

stereotropism growth or movement determined by contact with a solid. Cf. stereotaxis. —stereotropic, *adj.*

teratology *Biology.* the study of malformations or abnormal growth in animals or vegetables. —teratologist, *n.* —teratological, *adj.*

thigmotropism stereotropism. —thigmotropic, *adj.*

192. GUIDES and GUIDING

cicerone a person who acts as a guide, especially to the historical sites and antiquities of a place.

courier *British.* a person hired by travelers to make arrangements for a tour and to act as guide.

cynosure anything that guides or leads; hence, a center of attention.

pharology the technique or practice of guiding ships by means of signal lights, as in lighthouses.

valet-de-place a man who acts as guide to strangers and travelers.

xenagogy *Obsolete.* the guiding of strangers. —xenagogue, *n.*

H

193. HAIR

See also 33. BALDNESS; 37. BEARDS.

alopecia 1. a loss of hair, feathers, or wool.
2. baldness. —alopecic, *adj.*

chaetophobia an abnormal fear of hair.

crinosity the state of being hairy. —crinous, *adj.*

electrology the use of electrolysis for removing moles, warts, or excess hair. —electrologist, *n.*

hirsutism 1. a condition of shaggy hairiness.
2. *Biology.* the state of being covered with long, stiff hairs. —hirsute, *adj.*

hispidity the state or quality of being covered with small spines or bristles. —hispid, *adj.*

hypertrichosis a condition of excessive hairiness either all over the body or covering a particular part.

Leiotrichi people with smooth hair; a division of mankind characterized by people with such hair. Cf. Ulotrichi. —Leiotrichan, *adj.*

madarosis the loss of hair, especially of the eyelashes, as a result of disease.

madisterium a surgical instrument for pulling out hairs.

melanosity darkness or blackness of eyes, hair, or complexion.

pilosism, pilosity an excessive hairiness; furriness. —pilose, *adj.*

psilosis falling out of the hair.

schizotrichia a condition of splitting of the hair.

tonsure 1. the act or process of cutting the hair, especially as a religious rite or custom.
2. the shaved part of the head, usually the crown, of a member of a religious order. —tonsorial, *adj.*

trichiasis a condition in which the hair grows inward, especially the eyelashes.

trichoanesthesia *Medicine.* a loss of hair sensibility.

trichobezoar a hairball.

trichoclasia a condition of extreme brittleness of the hair, often following an illness.

trichology *Medicine.* the scientific study of hair and its diseases. —trichologist, *n.*

trichoma a condition of the hair in which it is matted or crusted.

trichomania an obsession with hair.

trichomycosis any disease of the hair caused by a fungus.

trichopathy *Medicine.* any disease of the hair. —trichopathic, *adj.*

trichophagy the practice of eating hair.

trichorrhexomania a mania for pinching off one's hair.

trichosis 1. *Medicine.* any disease or abnormal growth of the hair.
2. a heavy growth of hair.

trichotillomania *Medicine.* an abnormal desire to pull out one's own hair, especially by delirious patients. Also called **trichologia**.

Ulotrichi people with woolly, tightly curled, or crisp hair; a division of mankind characterized by people with such hair. Cf. **Leiotrichi**. —ulotrichous, *adj.*

villosity the condition or quality of being covered with long, soft hairs, as certain plants, or hairlike appendages, as certain of the membranes of the body. —villous, *adj.*

xanthochroid a person with light-colored hair and fair complexion. —xanthochroid, xanthochroous, *adj.*

194. HANDS
See also 14. ANATOMY; 51. BODY, HUMAN; 161. FINGERS and TOES.

ambidextrianism 1. the ability to use both hands equally well.
2. an unusual cleverness.
3. deceitfulness. Also **ambidexterity**. —ambidextrous, *adj.*

chiragra a pain in the hand.

chirapsia a friction caused by rubbing skin with the hand; massage.

chirocosmetics a beautifying of the hands. —chirocosmetic, *adj.*

chirognomy, cheirognomy the theories and activity of palmistry. —chirognomist, cheirognomist, *n.*

chirology, cheirology *Rare.* the study of the hands.

chiromancy, cheiromancy palmistry.

chiroplasty plastic surgery of the hand.

chirothesia the imposition of hands, usually on the head, in certain rituals, as confirmation and ordination.

chirotony 1. *Ecclesiastic.* the extending of the hands in blessing during certain rituals.
2. an election by show of hands.

mancinism the state of left-handedness.

palmistry the art of telling a person's character, past, or future by the lines, marks, and mounts on his palms. Also called **chiromancy.** —palmist, *n.*

pendactylism the condition of having five digits on each hand and foot. —pendactylate, pendactylic, pendactylous, *adj.*

perissodactylism the condition of having more than the usual number of digits on a hand or foot which are also excessively large and uneven. —perissodactylate, perissodactylic, perissodactylous, *adj.*

polydactylism the condition of having more than a normal number of fingers or toes. —polydactylous, *adj.*

prestidigitation the performance of tricks and illusions by the quick and skillful use of the hands; conjuring; sleight of hand. Also called **prestigiation.** —prestidigitator, *n.* —prestidigitatorial, prestidigitatory, *adj.*

quadrumane an animal, as a monkey, having four hands. —quadrumanous, *adj.*

sexdigitism the condition of having six fingers on each hand.

sexdigitist a person who has six fingers or six toes.

sinistrality the condition of being left-handed. —sinistral, *adj.*

syndactylism the union of two or more digits, common in many birds such as kingfishers and hornbills. —syndactylic, *adj.* —syndactyly, *n.*

195. HAPPINESS
See also 28. ATTITUDES; 279. MOODS.

ataraxia a state of tranquility free from anxiety and emotional disturbance. —ataractic, ataraxic, *adj.*

athedonia an inability to be happy. —athedonic, *adj.*

cheromania an extreme love for gaiety.

cherophobia an abnormal fear of gaiety.

eudemonics, eudaemonics 1. an art or means of acquiring happiness; eudemonism.
2. the theory of happiness. —eudemonia, *n.* —eudemonic, eudemonical, *adj.*

eudemonism, eudaemonism *Ethics.* a moral system based upon the performance of right actions to achieve happiness. —eudemonist, eudaemonist, *n.*

euphoria, euphory 1. a state of happiness and well-being.
2. *Psychiatry.* an exaggerated state of happiness, with no foundation in truth or reality. —euphoric, *adj.*

jocundity the quality or condition of being merry or cheerful. —jocund, *adj.*

jovialist *Obsolete.* a person who leads a merry life.

joviality 1. the quality or state of being merry or jovial.
2. festivity.

jucundity *Obsolete.* the condition or act of being pleasant.

macarism the practice of making others happy through praise and felicitation. —macarize, *v.*

196. HEAD
See also 14. ANATOMY; 51. BODY, HUMAN.

brachycephalism, brachycephaly the condition of having a wide or broad head. —brachycephalic, brachycephalous, *adj.*

bumpology a sarcastic term for phrenology. —bumpologist, *n.*

cephalomancy a form of divination involving measurement of the head.

cephalometry the science of measuring the dimensions of the human head. —cephalometer, *n.* —cephalometric, cephalometrical, *adj.*

craniology the science that studies the size, shape, and other features of human skulls. —craniologist, *n.* —craniologic, craniological, *adj.*

craniometry the science of measuring skulls. —craniometrist, *n.* —craniometric, craniometrical, *adj.*

cranioscopy the observation, examination, and description of the human skull. —cranioscopist, *n.* —cranioscopic, cranioscopical, *adj.*

craniotomy the surgical operation of opening the skull, as for an operation on the brain.

dicephalism, dicephaly the state or condition of having two heads. —dicephalic, dicephalous, *adj.*

dolichocephalism, dolicocephaly the condition of having a long or narrow head. —dolicephalic, dolicocephalous, *adj.*

hypsicephaly the condition of very high vertical cranial development. —hypsicephalic, *adj.*

isocephalism, isocephaly the characteristic of depicting heads of figures at the same level, as in a painting. —isocephalic, isocephalous, *adj.*

macrocephalism, macrocephaly a condition in which the head or cranial capacity is unusually large. —macrocephalic, macrocephalous, *adj.*

orthocephalism, orthocephaly the condition of having an intermediate or medium relation between the height of the skull and its breadth or length. —orthocephalic, —orthocephalous, *adj.*

phrenology a system by which an analysis of character and of the development of faculties is attempted by studying the shape and protuberances of the skull. —phrenologist, *n.* —phrenologic, phrenological, *adj.*

plagiocephalism, plagiocephaly a deformity of the skull in which one side is more developed in the front, and the other more developed in the rear. —plagiocephalic, plagiocephalous, *adj.*

197. HEALTH
See also 122. DISEASE and ILLNESS.

analgesia, analgesy the absence of pain. —analgesic, analgetic, *adj.*

analogism *Medicine.* diagnosis of a condition on the basis of its resemblance to other conditions.

anatripsology the use of friction, especially rubbing, in therapy or as a remedy.

anesthesia, anaesthesia, anesthesis, anaesthesis the absence of physical sensation. —anesthesiologist, anaesthesiologist, anaesthetist, *n.* —anesthetic, anaesthetic, *n., adj.*

antisepsis the destruction of microorganisms that cause infection. —antiseptic, *adj.*

bacteriostasis the process of preventing the growth or spread of bacteria. —bacteriostat, *n.* —bacteriostatic, *adj.*

cachexia, cachexy general physical or mental poor health; weakness or malnutrition.

dyscrasia *Medicine.* an unhealthy condition, especially an imbalance of physiologic or constitutional elements, often of the blood. Cf. **eucrasia.** —dyscrasic, dyscratic, *adj.*

epulosis the formation of scar tissue as part of the healing process. —epulotic, *adj.*

eucrasia 1. *Medicine.* a normal state of health; good health.
2. physical well-being. Cf. **dyscrasia.** —eucrasic, eucratic, *adj.*

eupepsia, eupepsy a condition of good digestion. —eupeptic, *adj.*

evectics, euectics the theory of the achievement and maintenance of good health. —evectic, euectic, *adj.*

germicide any substance for killing germs, especially bacteria. —germicidal, *adj.*

hygeist, hygieist a hygienist.

hygiastics *Rare.* hygienics. Also called **hygiantics.**

hygienics 1. the branch of medical science that studies health and its preservation; hygiene.
2. a system of principles for promoting health. —hygienist, *n*. —hygienic, *adj*.

hygieology, hygiology *Rare*. the science of hygiene; hygienics.

hypochondriacism, hypochondriasis 1. *Psychiatry*. an abnormal state characterized by emotional depression and imagined ill health, often accompanied by symptoms untraceable to any organic disease.
2. excessive concern and conversation about one's health. Also called hypochondria, nosomania. —hypochondriac, *n*. —hypochondriacal, *adj*.

invalescence *Obsolete*. a state of good health; strength.

lysis the gradual process of a disease, ending in the recovery of the patient. See also 72. CELLS. —lyterian, lytic, *adj*.

prophylaxis protection from or prevention of disease. —prophylactic, *adj*.

sanability *Rare*. the state or condition of being curable; susceptibility to remedy. —sanable, *adj*.

soteriology *Rare*. 1. a treatise on health.
2. the science of attaining and maintaining good health. —soteriological, *adj*.

synteresis preventive or preservative treatment or measures; prophylaxis. See also 145. ETHICS.

tonicity the state or quality of having good muscular tone or tension. —tonic, *adj*.

trypanophobia an abnormal fear of vaccines and vaccination. Also called vaccinophobia.

valetudinarianism 1. a condition of poor health.
2. a state of being concerned with health, often excessively.
3. invalidism. —valetudinarian, *n., adj*.

198. HEARING
See also 111. DEAFNESS; 132. EAR; 309. PERCEPTION; 380. SOUND.

acoumetry the measurement of acuteness of hearing. —acoumeter, *n*. —acoumetric, *adj*.

anaudia loss or absence of the power of hearing.

audiclave an instrument that aids hearing.

audiology 1. the branch of medical science that studies hearing, especially impaired hearing.
2. the treatment of persons with impaired hearing. —audiologist, *n*.

audiometer an instrument for testing hearing. Also called sonometer. —audiometry, *n*. —audiometric, *adj*.

audiometry a testing of hearing ability by frequencies and various levels of loudness. —audiometrist, audiometrician, *n*. —audiometric, audiometrical, *adj*.

auditognosis *Medicine*. the sense by which sounds are understood and interpreted.

otocleisis a closure of the hearing passages.

otomyasthenia *Medicine*. a weakness of the ear muscles causing poor selection and amplification of sounds. —otomyasthenic, *adj*.

otophone 1. an external appliance used to aid hearing; a hearing aid.
2. *Medicine*. a tube used in the auscultation of the ear.

otosis a defect in hearing causing a false impression of sounds made by others.

paracusis defective sense of hearing. Also **paracousia**.

phonism a sound or a sensation of hearing produced by stimulus of another sense, as taste, smell, etc.

sonometer audiometer. —sonometry, *n*. —sonometric, *adj*.

199. HEART
See also 14. ANATOMY; 51. BODY, HUMAN.

anginophobia an abnormal fear of angina pectoris.

arrhythmia, arhythmia, arythmia, arrythmia any abnormality in the rhythm of the heartbeat. —arrhythmic, arhythmic, arythmic, arrythmic, *adj*.

cardialgia, cardialgy a burning or other painful feeling in the stomach or esophagus; heartburn.

cardioangiology *Medicine*. the specialty that treats the heart and the blood vessels.

cardiocentesis *Medicine*. the surgical puncture or incision of the heart. Also called **cardiopuncture**.

cardiodynamics the branch of medical science that studies the forces and motions involved in the heart's actions.

cardiodynia *Medicine*. a pain in the heart.

cardiogenesis *Medical Science*. the study of the development of the heart in the embryo.

cardiograph an instrument to record the action of the heart. —cardiographer, *n*. —cardiographic, *adj*.

cardiography *Medicine*. the technique of graphically recording some physical or functional features of heart action.

cardiokinetic an agent that stimulates action of the heart.

cardiology *Medicine*. the study of the heart and its functions. —cardiologist, *n*. —cardiologic, cardiological, *adj*.

cardiomalacia *Medicine.* a disease causing a softening of the muscle of the heart.

cardiomegaly *Medicine.* an abnormal enlargement of the heart.

cardiomyopathy *Medicine.* a general term designating the early stages of diseases of heart muscles.

cardiopaludism *Medicine.* a heart disease caused by malaria and marked by increases in heart rhythm and doubled beating.

cardiopathy any disease or disorder of the heart. —**cardiopath,** *n.* —**cardiopathic,** *adj.*

cardiophobia an abnormal fear of heart disease.

cardiopuncture cardiocentesis.

cardioversion *Medicine.* the restoration of proper heart rhythm by electrical shock.

carditis an inflamed condition of the heart.

crotism the condition of having a single (monocrotism), double (dicrotism), etc., heartbeat.

diastole the rhythmic dilatation of the heart during which the muscle relaxes and the chambers fill with blood. Cf. systole. —**diastolic,** *adj.*

dicrotism the condition of having a double heartbeat. —**dicrotic,** *adj.*

endocarditis an inflamed condition of the endocardium, the membrane that lines heart chambers.

eurhythmy an even pulsebeat. —**eurhythmic,** *adj.*

fibrillation the uncontrolled twitching of the muscular fibrils, especially of the cardiac muscles.

infarction a condition in which a localized area of muscular tissue is dying or dead owing to insufficient supply of blood, as occurs in a heart attack.

monocrotism the condition of having a single heartbeat. —**monocrotic,** *adj.*

myocarditis an inflamed condition of the muscular walls of the heart.

palpitation 1. rapid and irregular beating of the heart.
2. a trembling of the body, as from fear or anxiety.

pericarditis an inflamed condition of the pericardium, the membrane that surrounds the heart.

systole the rhythmic contraction of the heart, and especially of the ventricles, following each dilatation. Cf. diastole. —**systolic,** *adj.*

tachycardia abnormally rapid beating of the heart.

tricrotism the condition of having three arterial beats for every one heartbeat, as in certain pulses. —**tricrotic,** *adj.*

valvulitis inflammation of a cardiac valve, usually caused by syphilis or rheumatic fever.

200. HEAT
See also 90. COLD; 162. FIRE.

actinism the ability of light and heat and other forms of radiant energy to cause chemical changes, as hormonal changes in birds causing them to migrate or brood. —actinic, *adj.*

adiathermancy imperviousness to radiant heat or infrared radiation. Also called athermancy.

athermancy adiathermancy.

calorimetry the science of measuring heat. —calorimeter, *n.* —calorimetric, *adj.*

calorist *Rare.* one who believed the caloric theory, that heat is a material substance. —caloristic, *adj.*

galvanothermy the process of generating heat by means of an electric current.

geothermometry the branch of geology that measures temperatures deep below the surface of the earth; geologic thermometry.

pyrogenesis the production or generation of heat. —pyrogenetic, *adj.*

pyrolysis the chemical process of decomposition under the effect of heat. —pyrolitic, *adj.*

pyrophotometer a type of pyrometer that measures temperature optically or photometrically.

tepidity a moderate warmth; lukewarmness. —tepid, *adj.*

thermatology *Medicine.* the study of heat as a medical remedy or therapy. Also called thermotherapy.

thermionics the science or study of the emission of electrons from substances at high temperatures. —thermionic, *adj.*

thermochemistry the branch of chemistry that studies the relationship of heat to chemical changes, including the production of energy. —thermochemist, *n.* —thermochemical, *adj.*

thermodynamics the branch of physics that studies the relationship of heat and mechanical energy and the conversion, in various materials, of one into the other. —thermodynamicist, *n.* —thermodynamic, thermodynamical, *adj.*

thermogenesis, thermogeny the production of heat, especially in an animal body by physiological processes. —thermogenic, thermogenous, *adj.*

thermography 1. *Engineering.* a method of measuring surface temperatures by using luminescent materials.
2. a printing or photocopying process using infrared rays and heat.
3. a process of photography using far-infrared radiation; thermal photography. —thermographer, *n.* —thermographic, *adj.*

thermokinematics the study of the movement of heat. —thermokinematic, *adj.*

thermology *Archaic.* the science and study of heat. Also called **thermotics.**

thermoluminescence *Atomic Physics.* any luminescence appearing in materials upon application of heat, caused by electron movement which increases as the temperature rises. —thermoluminescent, *adj.*

thermolysis *Physiology.* the dispersion of heat from the body. —thermolytic, *adj.*

thermometry the branch of physics that deals with the measurement of temperature. —thermometric, *adj.*

thermophobia an abnormal fear of heat.

thermoscope a device for giving an approximation of the temperature change of a substance by noting the accompanying change in its volume. —thermoscopic, *adj.*

thermostatics the science or study of the equilibrium of heat.

thermotaxis 1. *Biology.* the movement of an organism toward or away from a source of heat.
2. *Physiology.* the regulation of body temperature by various physiological processes. —thermotactic, thermotaxic, *adj.*

thermotherapy thermatology.

thermotics thermology.

transcalency the property or quality by which matter permits the passage of heat. —transcalent, *adj.*

201. HEAVEN
See also 25. ASTRONOMY.

uranography the astronomical study and mapping of the heavens, especially the fixed stars. —uranographer, uranographist, *n.* —uranographic, uranographical, *adj.*

uranology uranography.

uranometry 1. measurement of the positions of astronomical bodies.
2. a chart showing such measurements and positions. —uranometrical, *adj.*

uranophobia, ouranophobia an abnormal fear of the heavens.

202. HEIGHTS
See also 283. MOUNTAINS.

acrophobia an abnormal fear of being at great heights Also called **altophobia, batophobia, hypsiphobia.**

altimetry the science of measuring heights, as with an altimeter. —**altimetrical,** *adj.*

altophobia acrophobia.

batophobia 1. acrophobia.
2. an abnormal fear of passing high buildings.

cremnomania an abnormal interest in cliffs.

cremnophobia an abnormal fear of precipices.

hypsiphobia, hypsophobia acrophobia.

hypsography a branch of geography that deals with the measurement and mapping of the varying elevations of the earth's surface above sea level. —**hypsographic, hypsographical,** *adj.*

hypsometer an instrument for measuring altitude by the relationship between atmospheric pressure and the boiling point of a liquid.

hypsometry the measurement of altitude and heights, especially with reference to sea level. —**hypsometric, hypsometrical,** *adj.*

tachymeter a surveying instrument for measuring distance, height, elevation, etc.

tachymetry the measurement of distance, height, elevation, etc., with a tachymeter.

203. HELL
See also 114. DEMONS; 117. DEVIL.

hadephobia an abnormal fear of hell. Also called **stygiophobia.**

stygiophobia hadephobia.

204. HEREDITY
See also 15. ANCESTORS; 44. BIOLOGY; 147. EVOLUTION; 307. PARENTS; 341. RACE.

abiogenesis generation of living organisms from inanimate matter. Also called **spontaneous generation.**

anencephaly the congenital absence of the brain and spinal cord in a developing fetus.

biotypology the science or study of biotypes, or organisms sharing the same hereditary characteristics —**biotypologic, biotypological,** *adj.*

blastogenesis the theory that hereditary characteristics are transmitted by germ plasm. Cf. **pangenesis.** —**blastogenetic,** *adj.*

cytoplasm the entire substance of a cell excluding the nucleus.

deoxyribonucleic acid (DNA) the complex substance that is the main carrier of genetic information for all organisms and a major component of chromosomes.

DNA deoxyribonucleic acid.

dysgenesis lack of or partial fertility, as found in hybrids like the mule, which cannot breed amongst themselves but only with the parent stock. —**dysgenetic**, *adj.*

geneagenesis alternation of generations. —**geneagenetic**, *adj.*

genetics 1. *Biology.* the science of heredity, studying resemblances and differences in related organisms and the mechanisms which explain these phenomena.
2. the genetic properties and phenomena of an organism. —**geneticist**, *n.* —**genetic**, *adj.*

hereditist a believer in the theory that heredity, more than environment, determines nature, characteristics, etc.

homogenesis the normal course of generation in which the offspring resembles the parent from generation to generation. —**homogenetic**, *adj.*

Mendelism the laws of inheritance through genes, discovered by Gregor J. Mendel. —**Mendelian**, *n.*, *adj.*

pangenesis the theory advanced by Darwin, now rejected, that transmission of traits is caused by every cell's throwing off particles called gemmules, which are the basic units of hereditary transmission. The gemmules were said to have collected in the reproductive cells, thus ensuring that each cell is represented in the germ cells. Cf. **blastogenesis**. —**pangenetic**, *adj.*

perigenesis Haeckel's theory of generation and reproduction, which assumes that a dynamic growth force is passed on from one generation to the next. —**perigenetic**, *adj.*

prepotency the capacity of one parent to impose its hereditary characteristics on offspring by virtue of its possessing a larger number of homozygous, dominant genes than the other parent. —**prepotent**, *adj.*

radiogenetics a division of radiobiology that studies the effects of radioactivity upon factors of inheritance in genetics. —**radiogenic**, *adj.*

recombinant DNA a DNA molecule in which the genetic material has been artificially broken down so that genes from another organism can be introduced and the molecule then recombined, the result being alterations in the genetic characteristics of the original molecule.

ribonucleic acid (RNA) a nucleic acid found in cells that transmits genetic instructions from the nucleus to the cytoplasm.

RNA ribonucleic acid.

telegony the supposed transmission of hereditary characteristics from one sire to offspring subsequently born to other sires by the same female. —telegonic, *adj.*

Weismannism the theories of development and heredity asserted by August Weismann (1834–1914), esp. that inheritable characteristics are carried in the germ cells, and that acquired characteristics are not hereditary. —Weismannian, *n.*, *adj.*

xenogenesis 1. abiogenesis; spontaneous generation.
2. metagenesis, or alternation of generations.
3. production of an offspring entirely different from either of the parents. Also xenogeny. —xenogenic, xenogenetic, *adj.*

xenogeny xenogenesis.

205. HERESY
See also 80. CHRISTIANITY; 349. RELIGION; 392. THEOLOGY.

Agnoetism 1. the tenet of a 4th-century Arian sect that God's omniscience was restricted to contemporary time.
2. the tenet of a 6th-century Monophysite sect that Christ possessed no omniscience. —Agnoete, Agnoite, *n.*

Albigensianism the beliefs and principles of an 11th-century Catharist sect of southern France, exterminated in the 13th century by order of Pope Innocent III. See Catharism. —Albigenses, *n. pl.* —Albigensian, *n.*, *adj.*

Apollinarianism a late 4th-century heretical doctrine asserting that Christ had a perfect divine nature, an imperfect human nature, and a mind replaced by the Logos. —Apollinarian, *n.*, *adj.*

Arianism the heretical doctrine of Arius (d. 336) that Christ the Son was not the substance or nature as God the Father. —Arian, *n.*

Berengarianism the beliefs of Berengar de Tours, 11th-century French churchman, especially his denial of transubstantiation. —Berengarian, *n.*, *adj.*

Cainism, Cainitism the beliefs of a 4th-century Gnostic sect, especially that the Old Testament concerns a demiurge and not God and that Cain, whom they revered, had been maligned. Cf. Gnosticism. —Cainite, *n.*

Catharism the beliefs of several sects in medieval Europe, especially the denial of infant baptism, purgatory, the communion of saints, images, and the doctrine of the Trinity; the abrogation of the institution of marriage; and the practice of rigorous asceticism. —Cathar, Cathari, Catharist, *n.* —Catharistic, *adj.*

Cyrillianism the Monophysitic tenet of Cyril, 5th-century archbishop of Alexandria, that Christ had only one nature, a composite of the human and the divine. —Cyrillian, *n.*, *adj.*

Docetism a very early heretical belief that held that Christ's body was not material or real, but only the appearance of a body. —**Docetae,** *n. pl.*

Donatism a heretical cult in N. Africa during the 4th through 7th centuries that emphasized high morality and rebaptism as necessary for church membership and considered invalid a sacrament celebrated by an immoral priest. —**Donatist,** *n.* —**Donatistic,** *adj.*

Ebionism, Ebionitism the beliefs of a Judaistic Christian Gnostic sect of the 2nd century, especially partial observation of Jewish law, rejection of St. Paul and gentile Christianity, acceptance of only one gospel (Matthew), and an early adoptionist Christology. —**Ebionite,** *n.* —**Ebionitic,** *adj.*

Encratism beliefs and practices of the Encratites, a 2nd-century Gnostic sect that renounced marriage and abstained from flesh and wine. —**Encratist,** *n.*

Eudoxian a member of a heretical sect, followers of Bishop Eudoxius, of Constantinople, who held extreme Arian views.

Gnosticism the beliefs and practices of pre-Christian and early Christian sects, condemned by the church, especially the conviction that matter is evil and that knowledge is more important than faith, and the practice of esoteric mysticism. Cf. **Cainism, Manichaeism, Valentinianism.** —**Gnostic,** *n., adj.*

heresiarch 1. the originator of a heresy.
2. the leader of a group of heretics.

heresimach a fighter of heresy and heretics.

heresiography a systematic exposition on heresy.

heresiology 1. *Theology.* the study of heresies.
2. a reference work on heresies. —**heresiologist,** *n.*

heresy 1. a religious opinion or doctrine at variance with accepted doctrine.
2. a willful and persistent rejection of any article of the faith by a baptized member of the Roman Catholic Church.
3. any belief or theory strongly at variance with established opinion. —**heretic,** *n.* —**heretical,** *adj.*

heretocide *Rare.* 1. the killing of a heretic.
2. the killer of a heretic. —**heretocidal,** *adj.*

idolomania a mania for idols.

Jansenism a heretical doctrine of the 17th and 18th centuries denying freedom of the will, accepting absolute predestination for part of mankind and condemnation to hell for the others, and emphasizing puritanical moral attitudes. —**Jansenist,** *n., adj.*

Jovinianist an adherent of Jovinian, a 4th-century monk who opposed asceticism and denied the virginity of Mary.

Macedonianism the doctrines of Macedonius, 4th-century bishop of Constantinople, who denied the divinity of the Holy Ghost. —**Macedonian,** *n.*

Manichaeism, Manicheism, Manicheanism 1. the doctrines and practices of the dualistic religious system of Manes, a blending of Gnostic Christianity, Buddhism, Zoroastrianism, and other elements, especially doctrines of a cosmic conflict between forces of light and darkness, the darkness and evilness of matter, and the necessity for a sexual, vegetarian asceticism.
2. any similar dualistic system, considered heretical by orthodox Christian standards. Cf. Gnosticism. —**Manichean,** *n., adj.* —**Manicheistic,** *adj.*

modalism the theological doctrine that the members of the Trinity are not three separate persons but modes or forms of God's self-expression. —**modalist,** *n.* —**modalistic,** *adj.*

Modalistic Monarchianism Sabellianism.

monergism the doctrine advanced by some Lutheran theologians that spiritual renewal is exclusively the activity of the Holy Spirit. Cf. **synergism.** —**monergist,** *n.* —**monergistic,** *adj.*

Montanism the 2nd-century doctrines of Montanus of Phrygia, who believed that the Holy Spirit, or Paraclete, dwelt within him and made him its instrument for guiding men in the Christian way. Cf. **Tertullianism.** —**Montanist,** *n.*

Patarinism 1. the beliefs and practices of 11th-century Bulgarian Manicheans who migrated to the Pataria section of Milan. Also called **Pataria.**
2. the beliefs and practices of various Cathari sects in France and Bulgaria. —**Patarine, Patarene,** *n.*

Patripassianism a heretical doctrine denying the distinct personhood of the Trinity and asserting that God the Father became incarnate and suffered for man's redemption. —**Patripassian,** *n.*

Pelagianism the heretical doctrines of Pelagius, 4th-century British monk, especially a denial of original sin and man's fallen spiritual nature, and an assertion that man's goodness was sufficient for him to work out his salvation without the assistance of the Holy Spirit. Cf. **Semi-Pelagianism.** —**Pelagian,** *n., adj.*

Phantasiast a member of an early Christian sect that denied the reality of Christ's body.

Photinianism the heresy of Photinus, 4th-century bishop of Sirmium, deposed because he denied the divinity of Christ.

Priscillianism the concepts of Priscillian, 4th-century bishop of Avila, executed for heresies influenced by Manichaeism, Docetism, and modalism. —**Priscillianist,** *n., adj.*

quietism a 17th-century Christian mystical theory, originated in Spain by Molinos and promulgated in France by Fénelon, involving passive contemplation and surrender of the will to God and indifference to the demands of the self or the outside world, declared heretical through efforts of the Inquisition. —quietist, *n.*, *adj.*

Racovianism Socinianism, so called because the sect was headquartered in Racow, Poland. Cf. Socinianism.

Sabellianism the modalistic doctrines of Sabellius, 3rd-century prelate, especially that the Trinity has but one divine essence and that the persons are only varying manifestations of God. Also called Modalistic Monarchianism. —Sabellian, *n.*, *adj.*

Semi-Pelagianism a heretical doctrine, of the 5th century that accepted the doctrine of original sin but asserted that man's turning to God of his own free will, not after the provocation of the Holy Ghost, begins the process of spiritual rebirth. Cf. Pelagianism.

Socinianism the heretical tenets of Faustus Socinius, a 16th-century Italian theologian, denying the divinity of Christ, the existence of Satan, original sin, the atonement, and eternal punishment, and explaining sin and salvation in rationalistic terms. Cf. Racovianism. —Socinian, *n.*, *adj.*

synergism an ancient heretical doctrine, extant since the 3rd century, which holds that spiritual renewal is a cooperative endeavor between a person and the Holy Ghost. Cf. Pelagianism, Semi-Pelagianism. —synergist, *n.* —synergistic, *adj.*

tergiversation 1. the act or process of subterfuge or evasion.
2. the abandoning of a cause or belief; apostasy. —tergiversator, *n.*

Tertullianism a form of Montanism, as modified by Tertullian in about 203, which opposed second marriages and absolution for penitents. Cf. Montanism. —Tertullianist, *n.*

Theopaschitism a 6th-century heretical doctrine maintaining that Christ had only one nature, the divine, and that this nature suffered at the Crucifixion. —Theopaschite, *n.*

Valentinianism a 2nd-century blending of Egyptian Gnosticism and Christianity into a system of heretical doctrines, especially the denial that Christ took his human nature from the Virgin Mary. Cf. Gnosticism. —Valentinian, *n.*, *adj.*

206. HINDUISM
See also 151. FAITH; 183. GOD and GODS; 349. RELIGION; 392. THEOLOGY.

Ayurvedism, Ayurveda the conventional Hindu system of medicine, founded chiefly on naturopathy and homeopathy. —Ayurvedic, *adj.*

Brahmanism, Brahminism the doctrines and practices of Brahmans and orthodox Hindus, characterized by the caste system, a diverse pantheism, and primary devotion to Brahma, the creator-god of the Hindu trinity.

Brahmoism the practices and doctrines of the Brahmos, members of a Hindu theistic society noted for its belief in social reform and monotheism.

Krishnaism the worship of Krishna as the eighth incarnation of the god Vishnu, the preserver-god of the Hindu trinity.

Ramaism the worship of Rama, a hero of Hindu epic, as an incarnation of the god Vishnu. —Ramaite, *n.*

Shaktism, Saktism 1. a Hindu sect worshipping Shakti as a mother goddess under such names as Kali and Durga through contemplation and humility; right-hand Shaktism.
2. a Hindu Tantric sect worshiping Shakti as the feminine principle of generation through rites involving ritual eating and orgy; left-hand Shaktism. See also **Tantrism.** —Shakta, Shakti, *n., adj.*

Sikhism the doctrines of a reformed Hindu sect opposed to the caste system, supremacy of Brahman priests, magic, idolatry, and pilgrimages. —Sikh, *n., adj.*

Sivaism, Shivaism, Saivism a cult made up of the worshipers of Siva, the destroyer-god of the Hindu trinity. —Sivaite, *n.*

sutteeism the Hindu practice or custom, now forbidden, of a widow's self-immolation upon her husband's funeral pyre. —suttee, sati, *n.*

Tantrism 1. the teachings of the Tantras, Sanskrit religious writings concerned with mysticism and magic rituals.
2. the beliefs and practices of Hindu adherents to the Tantras in place of the Vedas, especially magic rituals for healing, averting evil, and union with the female creative principle. —Tantrist, *n.* —Tantric, *adj.*

thuggeeism, thuggee a semi-religious Hindu cult with a highly organized system of murder and robbery, suppressed in India in the 19th century. Also **thuggery.** —thug, *n.*

Vaishnavism the worship of Vishnu in any of his forms or incarnations. —Vaishnava, Vaishnavite, *n.*

Vedaism, Vedism 1. the teachings of the Vedas, the four most sacred writings of Hinduism.
2. an adherence to these teachings; orthodox Hinduism. —Vedaic, Vedic, *adj.*

Vedantism the beliefs and practices of Vedanta, an orthodox Hindu philosophy emphasizing the teachings on contemplation found in the Vedas. —Vedantist, *n.* —Vedantic, *adj.*

Yogism, Yoga 1. an orthodox Hindu philosophical system concerned with the liberation of the self from its noneternal elements or states.
2. any system of exercises and disciplines for achieving such liberation of self. —**Yogi, Yogin,** *n.*

207. HISTORY
See also 18. ANTIQUITY; 308. PAST.

annalist one who chronicles yearly events; a writer of annals.

chronography *Obsolete.* the recording or study of past events.

cliometrics the application of mathematics, especially statistics, to the study of history. —**cliometrician,** *n.*

cyclicism the belief that history repeats itself, as suggested in the writings of Arnold Toynbee. Also **cyclicity.** —**cyclic,** *adj.*

genealogy 1. a record or account of the ancestry and descent of a person, family, or group.
2. the study of family ancestries or histories.
3. descent from an original form or progenitor; lineage. —**genealogist,** *n.* —**genealogic, genealogical,** *adj.*

heroology a work on heroes and their history. —**heroologist,** *n.* —**heroological,** *adj.*

historicism 1. a theory that history is determined by immutable laws.
2. a theory that all cultural phenomena are historically determined and that all historians should study a period on its own merits.
3. a search for the laws of historical evolution.
4. a profound or an excessive respect for historical institutions, as traditions or laws. Also **historism.** —**historicist,** *n., adj.*

historiography 1. the body of literature concerned with historical matters.
2. the methods of historical research and presentation.
3. an official history. —**historiographer,** *n.* —**historiographic, historiographical,** *adj.*

historiology the study or knowledge of history.

historism historicism.

medievalist 1. an expert in medieval history, literature, art, architecture, etc.
2. a person devoted to the art, culture, or spirit of the Middle Ages.

monism the theory that there is only one causal factor in history, as intellect or nature. —**monist,** *n.* —**monistic,** *adj.*

Orientalist a specialist in Oriental history, art, literature, etc.

prosopography 1. a biographical sketch containing a description of a person's appearance, qualities, and history.
2. a collection of such sketches. —**prosopographer,** *n.* See also 149. FACIAL FEATURES.

protohistory the earliest period of history, before the time when records were kept. —protohistorical, *adj.*

revisionism a movement to reexamine historical information in the light of current knowledge. —revisionist, *n., adj.*

208. HOMESICKNESS

nostomania an abnormal homesickness or nostalgia.

oikomania an abnormal attachment to home.

philopatridomania homesickness.

209. HOMOSEXUALITY
See also 364. SEX.

homoeroticism, homoerotism 1. the tendency to obtain sexual gratification from a member of the same sex.
2. homosexual activity. —homoerotic, *adj.*

homophobia fear of or apprension about homosexuality.

lesbianism the practice of homosexual relations between women. Also called Sapphism. —lesbian, *n., adj.*

tribadism, tribady a sexual activity between women that imitates heterosexual intercourse. —tribade, *n.* —tribadic, *adj.*

uranianism *Obsolete.* homosexuality.

uranism the practice of homosexuality between males. —uranist, *n.*

uranophobia an abnormal fear of homosexuals and homosexuality.

urningism male homosexuality. Also urnism. —urning, *n.*

210. HONORS and REGALIA
See also 326. PRAISE.

apotheosis any kind of honoring or glorification of a person. See also 183. GOD and GODS.

blazonry 1. the art of depicting or describing heraldic regalia.
2. coats of arms or other heraldic emblems. See also 305. ORNAMENTATION.

emblazonry heraldic display or decoration; emblazoning. See also 305. ORNAMENTATION.

emblematist a person who makes or designs emblems, as for heraldic display or other purposes.

emblematology the study of the meaning of emblems. —emblematologist, *n.*

heraldry 1. the art of pictorial representation of genealogy, as through coats of arms, crests, etc.
2. the science of genealogy with special reference to aristocratic lineage. —herald, *n.* —heraldic, *adj.*

laureate a person who has been crowned with a laurel as a mark of distinction, as a poet or scholar. —laureate, *adj*.

medalist a person who wins a medal in a sport, game, performance, etc. See also 141. ENGRAVING.

211. HORSES
See also 16. ANIMALS.

dressage the training of horses in obedience and the execution of precise movements.

equestrianism 1. the art of horsemanship.
2. the practice of this art. —equestrian, equestrienne, *n*. —equestrian, *adj*.

equitation the art or act of riding on horseback; horsemanship.

hippiatrics 1. the study and treatment of diseases of horses.
2. a work on the diseases of horses. Also hippiatry. —hippiatrist, *n*. —hippiatric, *adj*.

hippodrome *Ancient Greece and Rome*. an arena for horse races.

hippology the study of horses.

hippomancy a form of divination involving the observation of horses, especially by listening to their neighing.

hippomania a mania for horses.

hippopathology the study and treatment of the diseases of the horse.

hippophile a lover of horses.

hippophobia an abnormal fear of horses.

leucippotomy the sculpting of white horses on hillsides by cutting away grass and earth to reveal underlying stone or chalk deposits, thought to be a symbol of Odin, as near Uffington, England.

manège, manege 1. the art and practice of horsemanship.
2. the special paces taught to a horse in training.
3. the school or academy where they are taught.

212. HOUSES
See also 20. ARCHITECTURE; 60. BUILDINGS; 317. PLACES.

domatophobia the abnormal fear of being in a house.

ecophobia, oecophobia, oikophobia 1. an abnormal fear of home surroundings.
2. an aver:ion to home life.

213. HUMOR
See also 238. LAUGHTER; 336. PUNNING.

Atticism a concise witticism or well-turned phrase. —Atticist, *n*.

buffoonism 1. a tendency to amuse others by tricks, jokes, unusual gestures, and strange gestures.
2. a tendency toward coarse joking. Also **buffoonery.** —**buffoon,** *n.* —**buffoonish,** *adj.*

facetiae 1. amusing or witty writings and remarks.
2. coarsely witty stories or books. —**facetious,** *adj.*

jocosity 1. the habit of joking or jesting.
2. a joke or a jest.
3. the state or quality of humorousness or playfulness. —**jocose,** *adj.*

mordancy, mordacity the condition or quality of being biting or caustic, as humor, speech, etc. See also 382. SPEECH. —**mordant,** *adj.*

nugae trifles or trivia, especially light verses or sayings.

Pantagruelism the habit of dealing with serious matters in a spirit of good and sometimes cynical good humor. [Allusion to Rabelais' satirical novels *Gargantua* (1534) and *Pantagruel* (1532), especially to the behavior of Pantagruel, Gargantua's huge son.] —**Pantagruelian,** *adj.*

pianologue a humorous performance at the piano, sometimes with a verbal accompaniment by the performer.

Rabelaisian 1. a person who imitates or is an enthusiast for the works of François Rabelais.
2. a person given to coarse, satirical humor, like that of Rabelais. —**Rabelaisian,** *adj.*

Rabelaism the personality or character of Rabelais, as in the use of coarse, satirical humor. Also **Rabelaisianism.**

reparteeist a person skilled in the exchange of witticisms.

ribaldry coarse, vulgar, or obscene language or joking. —**ribald,** *adj.*

satirist 1. a writer of satire.
2. a person who uses satire or makes satirical comments.

214. HUNTING

cynegetics the sport of hunting. —**cynegetic,** *adj.*

falconry 1. the sport of hunting with falcons or other trained birds of prey.
2. the training of birds of prey.

venation *Archaic.* the sport or occupation of hunting. —**venatic, venatical, venational,** *adj.*

venery 1. *Archaic.* the sport, practice, or art of hunting or the chase.
2. the animals that are hunted.

215. HYPNOSIS
See also 334. PSYCHOLOGY.

autohypnotism, autohypnosis 1. the process of hypnotizing oneself.
2. the resulting state.

biomagnetism 1. animal magnetism, or the power that enables some people to induce a hypnotic state in others.
2. physical attraction between members of opposite sexes. —**biomagnetic,** *adj.*

hypnoanalysis psychoanalysis of a patient while he is under hypnosis. —**hypnoanalytic, hypnoanalytical,** *adj.*

hypnogenesis the process of inducing a state of hypnosis. —**hypnogenetic,** *adj.*

hypnotherapy psychotherapy employing hypnosis. —**hypnotherapeutic,** *adj.*

hypnotism the science that studies hypnosis and the process of inducing a hypnotic state. —**hypnotist,** *n.*

Mesmerism 1. hypnosis as induced by Dr. F. A. Mesmer through "animal magnetism," a 19th-century therapy.
2. hypnotism.
3. a compelling attraction; fascination. —**mesmerization,** *n.* —**mesmerist, mesmerizer,** *n.*

mesmeromania an obsession with hypnosis.

monoideism the focusing of the attention on a single thing, especially as a result of hypnosis.

narcohypnosis hypnosis with the aid of drugs.

odylism the theory of od, a hypothetical force formerly held to pervade all nature and to reveal itself in magnetism, mesmerism, chemical action, etc. —**odylic,** *adj.*

psycheism *Rare.* the state of being in a hypnotic trance.

somnipathy a state of sleep induced by hypnosis or mesmerism. —**somnipathist,** *n.*

I

216. IDEAS

See also 233. KNOWLEDGE; 312. PHILOSOPHY.

counteridea *Rare.* in logic, a contrary.

ideology the body of doctrines, philosophical bases, symbols, etc., associated with a particular social or political movement, large group, or individual. —ideological, *adj.* —ideologist, *n.*

instrumentalism the concept that ideas and thoughts are instruments of action and that their usefulness determines their truth. —instrumentalist, *adj.*

intellection 1. the exercise or use of the intellect.
2. a particular act or process of the intellect.

misocainea an abnormal dislike for new ideas.

neoteric a modern person; one accepting new ideas and practices.

schematist a person who forms schemes; a projector or promoter.

sophiology the science of ideas.

technology 1. the methods and tools that a society has developed in order to facilitate the solution of its practical problems.
2. any specific application of such. —technological, *adj.* —technologist, *n.*

theoretics the branch or part of any field of learning or knowledge that is concerned with theories or hypotheses, as contrasted with practical application.

theorist a person who forms theories or who specializes in the theory of a particular subject.

217. IDIOCY

See also 422. WISDOM.

bovinity the state or quality of being like a cow or ox, especially in the sense of being dull, stolid, and slow-witted. —bovine, *adj.*

cretinism *Medicine.* a congenital deficiency of thyroid secretion causing deformity and idiocy. —cretinoid, cretinous, *adj.*

idiotism 1. the condition of an idiot, especially an extreme degree of mental deficiency, usually a mental age of less than three or four years; idiocy.
2. idiotic conduct or action, especially in a normal person. —idiotic, *adj*.

moronism the condition of being slow or mentally deficient. —moronic, *adj*.

stultiloquence *Rare.* foolish talk or babble.

218. IMAGES
See also 23. ART; 170. FORM; 315. PHOTOGRAPHY; 352. REPRESENTATION.

diptych 1. a two-leafed waxed tablet for writing with a stylus.
2. a pair of paintings or other images on two hinged leaves.

hologram a three-dimensional representation in photographic form, recorded on film by a reflected laser beam of a subject illuminated by part of the same laser beam. —holograph, holography, *n*.

iconism *Obsolete.* imagery.

iconoclasm 1. the practice of destroying images, especially those created for religious veneration.
2. the practice of opposing cherished beliefs or traditional institutions as being founded on error or superstition.
3. the doctrines underlying these practices. —iconoclast, *n*. —iconoclastic, *adj*.

iconodule, iconodulist a person who worships images.

iconolatry the worship or adoration of images. Also called **idolatry.** —iconolater, *n*.

iconology 1. the study of images.
2. iconography. —iconologist, *n*. —iconological, *adj*.

iconomachy opposition to icons or other forms of sacred imagery.

iconomania a mania for icons.

phantasm the mental image or representation of a real person or thing. See also 182. GHOSTS; 309. PERCEPTION.

phantasmagoria a type of magic-lantern show in which rapidly moving images blend, change size, etc.; hence, any series of images that move and change rapidly, as a dream. —phantasmagorial, phantasmagoric, *adj*.

sciamachy, sciomachy battle with shadows or imaginary enemies.

simulacrum 1. an image or likeness.
2. a mere image or one that does not represent the reality of the original.

speciosity the state or quality of appearing to be greater or more than is to be found on a close examination, as an argument that has the appearance of merit but does not stand up to a close look. —specious, *adj*.

symbolism symbology, defs. 1 and 2.

symbology 1. the study and interpretation of symbols. Also called symbolism.
2. representation by means of symbols. Also called symbolism.
3. any system of symbols. —symbologist, *n.* —symbological, *adj.*

teliconograph an apparatus combining a telescope and the camera lucida, used for producing images of distant objects on a screen.

triptych a set of three paintings or images, each on a separate leaf, but hinged together.

whoredom *Bible.* the worship of idols instead of God; idolatry.

219. IMPROVEMENT

Couéism a method of self-help stressing autosuggestion, introduced into America about 1920 by the French psychotherapist Emile Coué and featuring the slogan "Every day in every way I am getting better and better."

eugenics the science of improving a breed or species through the careful selection of parents. —eugenicist, *n.* —eugenic, *adj.*

euthenics the art or science of improving a race or breed, especially the human race, by control of external influences, as environment. Cf. eugenics. —euthenist, *n.*

meliorism the doctrine that the world tends to get better or may be made better by human effort. —meliorist, *n., adj.* —melioristic, *adj.*

telesia, telesis the harnessing of natural and social forces for a beneficial goal.

220. INANIMATE OBJECTS

abiology the study of inanimate things.

animatism the assignment to inanimate objects, forces, and plants of personalities and wills, but not souls. —animatistic, *adj.*

resistentialism the apparently perverse or spiteful behavior of inanimate objects.

221. INDUSTRY

chemurgy the branch of chemistry that deals with the industrial use and application of organic substances. —chemurgic, chemurgical, *adj.*

chreotechnics *Rare.* useful arts, as agriculture, commerce, and manufacturing.

radiotechnology the science and technology of applying radiation and x rays to industrial use. See also 343. RADIO.

robotics the application of automated machinery to tasks traditionally done by hand, as in the manufacturing industry.

Zionite a believer in the doctrines of John Alexander Dowie who founded Zion City, Illinois, in 1901, as an industrial community for his followers.

222. INFESTATION

acariasis the condition of being infested by acarids or mites.

acaricide a substance or preparation for killing mites or ticks.

miticide a substance for killing mites. —miticidal, *adj*.

taeniacide, teniacide an agent or preparation for killing tapeworms. —taeni-acidal, teniacidal, *adj*.

taeniasis, teniasis infestation by tapeworms.

vermination the state or process of being infested with worms or vermin.

223. INJURY
See also 306. PAIN.

lapidation the process or act of pelting with stones, sometimes as a form of execution.

octogild *Anglo-Saxon Law*. payment for an injury, calculated at eight times its real or estimated value.

traumatism 1. any abnormal condition, either pathological or psychological, caused by wound or injury, either physical or psychological.
2. the trauma, wound, or injury itself. —traumatic, *adj*.

224. INSANITY
See also 122. DISEASE and ILLNESS; 254. MANIAS; 313. PHOBIAS; 334. PSYCHOLOGY.

abalienation *Obsolete*. insanity.

acromania a violent form of mania; incurable insanity.

amentia 1. a congenital condition of low intelligence.
2. a form of temporary insanity. Cf. dementia.

amenty *Obsolete*. amentia.

bedlamism behavior characteristic of insanity. See also 301. ORDER and DISOR-DER.

bedlamite a mental patient.

catatonia one of various forms of schizophrenia characterized by stupor, sometimes alternating with excited behavior and mechanical, repetitive behavior, accompanied by muscular rigidity. —catatonic, *n.*, *adj*.

delirium a state of maniacal excitement characterized by restless behavior, confused speech, and sometimes hallucinations.

dementia madness or insanity. Cf. amentia.

dementia praecox schizophrenia.

demonianism 1. *Obsolete*. the doctrine of demoniac possession.
2. *Archaic*. demonomania. —demonian, *n.*, *adj*.

demonomania *Medicine.* a monomania in which a person believes he is possessed of devils. Also called **demonopathy.**

diabolepsy *Medicine, Obsolete.* a state in which a person believes he is possessed by a devil or has been endowed with supernatural powers.

hallucinosis a disordered mental condition in which the sufferer is prone to hallucinations.

hebephrenia a form of insanity or dementia praecox that can appear at puberty, characterized by foolish behavior and deterioration of the mental faculties.

hypermania an acute mania.

lunacy 1. periodic insanity, once thought to be caused by the phases of the moon.
2. any form of insanity. —**lunatic,** *adj.*

lypemania an abnormal tendency toward deep melancholy.

lyssophobia an abnormal fear of becoming insane.

maniaphobia an abnormal fear of madness.

megalomania 1. *Medicine.* a form of mental illness characterized by the unreasonable conviction in the patient of his own greatness, goodness, power, or wealth.
2. an obsession with extravagant or grand actions. —**megalomaniac,** *n.,* *adj.*
—**megalomaniacal,** *adj.*

melancholia a condition of abnormal gloom or depression, often of an intensity to become a form of insanity. —**melancholiac,** *n.,* *adj.* —**melancholic,** *n.,* *adj.*

melancholian *Obsolete.* a person suffering from melancholia; a melancholiac.

narcosynthesis a form of treatment for mental illness that involves placing the patient under the influence of a narcotic.

orthosis the process of correcting bodily or mental distortion.

paranoia a mental disorder characterized by behavior that stems from an elaborately constructed system of delusions of persecution and grandeur. —**paranoiac,** *n.* —**paranoid,** *adj.*

paranoidism a state resembling paranoia.

pathomania moral insanity.

psychosis any severe mental disorder or disease. —**psychotic,** *n.,* *adj.*

schizophrenia a psychotic condition marked by erratic behavior, withdrawal from reality, and intellectual and emotional deterioration. Also called **dementia praecox.** —**schizophrenic,** *n.,* *adj.*

schizothymia a mild form of schizophrenia, characterized by withdrawal, inversion, etc. —schizothyme, *n.* —schizothymic, *adj.*

submania a mild mania.

zoanthropy a form of insanity or mental disorder in which the sufferer imagines that he is an animal. —zoanthropic, *adj.*

zoopsia a form of hallucination in which the sufferer imagines he sees animals. Also called zooscopy.

zooscopy zoopsia.

225. INSECTS
See also 19. ANTS; 40. BEES; 44. BIOLOGY; 64. BUTTERFLIES; 430. ZOOLOGY.

acarophobia a fear of itching or of the mites or ticks that cause it.

aeroscepsy, aeroscepsis perception by means of the air, said to be a function of the antennae of insects.

bugology *Informal.* entomology. —bugologist, *n.*

coleopterology the branch of entomology that studies beetles and weevils. —coleopterological, *adj.* —coleopterist, *n.*

dipterology the branch of entomology that studies the order of insects *Diptera*, including houseflies, mosquitoes, and gnats.

entomology the branch of zoology that studies insects. Also called **insectology**. —entomologist, *n.* —entomologic, entomological, *adj.*

entomomania an abnormal love of insects.

entomophobia an abnormal fear of insects.

ephemeron anything shortlived, or of brief duration, especially certain types of insects such as the mayfly.

gynandromorphism the condition of having one half of the body male and the other half female, as certain insects. —gynandromorph, *n.* —gynandromorphous, *adj.*

hemipterology the branch of entomology that studies the order *Hemiptera*, including bedbugs, squashbugs, and aphids.

heteromorphism 1. the quality of differing in form from the standard or norm.
2. the condition of existing in different forms at different stages of development, as certain insects. —heteromorphic, *adj.*

hymenopterology the branch of entomology that studies the order *Hymenoptera*, including bees, wasps, and ants.

hypermetamorphosis a process by which an insect goes through more than the usual number of transformations, as the larva being metamorphosed more than once.

ichneumonology the study of the life of the ichneumon fly.

insecticide a substance used for killing insects. —**insecticidal,** *adj.*

insectology entomology.

myrmecology the study of ants.

neoteny the capacity or state of becoming sexually mature in the larval stage. —**neotenous,** *adj.*

neuropterology the branch of entomology that studies the order *Neuroptera,* including lacewings and ant lions.

orthopterology the branch of entomology that studies the order *Orthoptera,* including cockroaches, grasshoppers, and mantises.

pediculophobia an abnormal fear of lice. Also called **phthiriophobia.**

pediculosis an infestation with lice; lousiness. —**pediculous,** *adj.*

pesticide any chemical substance used for killing pests, as insects, weeds, etc.

phthiriophobia pediculophobia.

polymorphism the occurrence of several forms or colors in one species of insect. —**polymorphous,** *adj.*

stridulation 1. an action characteristic of some insects of producing a shrill, grating noise by chafing a serrated part of the body against a hard part. 2. the noise so produced. —**stridulator,** *n.* —**stridulant, stridulatory,** *adj.*

vespiary 1. a wasps' nest. 2. a community or colony of wasps.

xenobiosis communal life, such as that of ants, in which colonies of different species live together but do not share the raising of the young. —**xenobiotic,** *adj.*

226. INSTRUMENTS
See also 264. MEASUREMENT.

accelerometer an instrument for measuring and recording the rate of acceleration of an aircraft.

algometer an instrument for measuring a person's sensitivity to pain produced by pressure. —**algometric, algometrical,** *adj.*

altimeter an instrument for determining altitude above a fixed level by comparison of air pressure readings.

ammeter an instrument for measuring the amperage of an electrical current.

anemoscope an instrument for recording the direction of the wind.

astrolabe a navigational instrument formerly used for taking bearings of the sun and stars. See also 352. REPRESENTATION.

auriscope an instrument for examining the ear. —**auriscopy,** *n.*

ballistic galvanometer fluxmeter.

barometer an instrument for measuring atmospheric pressure.

bioinstrumentation the use of instruments to measure, record, and transmit data on bodily functions.

breathalyzer drunkometer.

chromoptometer a device for measuring the degree of a person's sense of color.

chronometer a timing device of extreme accuracy, frequently with a device for checking and adjusting its accuracy. —**chronometric, chronometrical,** *adj.*

chronoscope an instrument for accurate measurement of very short periods of time, as the time of trajectory of missiles.

clepsydra an instrument for measuring time by the controlled flow of water or mercury through a small opening.

cosmolabe *Obsolete.* an instrument, like an astrolabe, used for astronomical observations.

cryometer a thermometer for measuring very low temperatures.

cyclometer an instrument for counting the revolutions of a wheel that is rolled along a surface and thus the distance traveled.

densimeter an instrument for measuring the density or specific gravity of a solid or liquid substance.

dioptometer an instrument for measuring the refractive index of the lens of the eye.

dosimeter a device, carried or worn by people working near radiation for measuring the amount of radiation to which they are exposed.

drunkometer a device for measuring the amount of alcohol in the bloodstream, usually from the breath. Also called **breathalyzer.**

erythrocytometer a device for measuring the count of red blood cells in the blood.

eudiometer an instrument for measuring the amount of oxygen in the air and for analyzing gases.

extensometer an instrument for measuring minute degrees of contraction, expansion, or deformation, as of metals.

fluorometer an instrument for measuring the emission of radiation in the form of visible light and identifying the substance that is its source. —**fluorometric,** *adj.*

fluoroscope a device fitted with a screen that fluoresces when exposed to radiation.

fluxmeter an instrument for measuring magnetic flux; a ballistic galvanometer.

galactometer lactometer.

galvanometer an instrument for measuring the strength and direction of an electric current. —galvanometric, galvanometrical, *adj.*

galvanoscope an instrument for detecting the presence of an electric current and determining its direction.

glossograph an instrument for recording the movements of the tongue during speech.

goniometer an instrument for measuring angles, especially those of solid bodies.

gramophone an instrument for reproducing sound from records; phonograph.

graphophone an instrument for reproducing sound from wax records.

graphoscope an optical device for magnifying pictures, as engravings, photographs, etc.

heliometer an instrument originally designed for measuring the sun's diameter, now used for measuring the angular distance between stars.

horometer an instrument for measuring time.

hydrometer an instrument for measuring the specific gravity of a liquid.

hygrometer an instrument for measuring the amount of moisture in the air.

hypsometer an instrument for measuring altitude by the relationship between atmospheric pressure and the boiling point of a liquid.

indigometer an instrument used for determining the strength of an indigo solution.

instrumentation 1. the technology of designing and constructing instruments, especially for use in science and industry.
2. a particular system of instruments in a special context.
3. instruments collectively.

interferometer an instrument that measures wavelengths, minute distances, or the refractivity of lenses by comparison of interference patterns generated by the splitting and reuniting of a beam of light passed through a lens. —interferometry, *n.*

jovilabe an instrument used for determining the positions of the satellites that surround the planet Jupiter.

kaleidophon, kaleidophone an instrument for the visual representation of sound waves.

kaleidoscope an optical device composed of bits of colored glass and several reflecting surfaces that presents to the viewer symmetrical patterns when shaken or rotated. —kaleidoscopic, *adj.*

kinetoscope an instrument for illustrating different combinations of kinematic curves. See also 265. MEDIA.

konimeter an instrument for measuring impurities in the air. —**konimetric,** *adj.*

lactometer an instrument for measuring the richness of milk from its specific gravity. Also called **galactometer.**

lactoscope an instrument for measuring the opacity of milk so that its cream content can be determined.

laryngoscope an apparatus for examining the larynx. —**laryngoscopist,** *n.* —**laryngoscopic,** *adj.*

leucoscope an instrument for testing the eyes to determine the ability to distinguish variations in color or intensity of light.

madisterium a surgical instrument for pulling out hairs.

manometer 1. an instrument for measuring the pressure of gases or vapors. 2. an instrument for measuring blood pressure. Also called **sphygmomanometer.** —**manometric.** *adj.*

megameter 1. an instrument for determining longitude by observation of the stars. 2. *Rare.* an instrument for measuring large objects.

melanoscope an optical device composed of red and violet glass that transmits red light only, used for distinguishing red in varicolored flames.

metrograph a device for recording the speed of locomotives and the time, place, and length of all their stops.

metronome an instrument for marking time in music that produces regular ticking sounds for a variety of rhythmic settings. —**metronomic, metronomical,** *adj.*

mutoscope an instrument for recording and reproducing the illusion of motion by means of a series of photographs.

myrioscope a form of kaleidoscope, especially one that is used when exhibiting carpets.

nauropometer *Rare.* an apparatus for measuring the inclination of a heeling or listing ship.

Nilometer an instrument used for measuring the increase in the level of the River Nile during its flood period, consisting of a water chamber containing a graduated pillar. Also called **Niloscope.**

noctograph an apparatus or register for recording timely and proper observance by watchmen of their patrols.

odometer an instrument for recording elapsed distance.

ohmmeter an instrument for measuring electrical resistance in ohms.

ondograph an instrument for recording oscillatory variations, as those in alternating currents. —**ondogram,** *n.*

ondometer an instrument for measuring the wavelengths of radio waves.

oometer a device for measuring eggs.

optotechnics the technology of optical instruments and apparatus.

osmometer an instrument for measuring osmotic pressure. —**osmometric,** *adj.*

pachymeter an instrument for measuring the thickness of things.

paralellometer an instrument for ascertaining the accuracy of parallel surfaces, as of a sheet of plate glass.

pedometer a device for measuring distance traversed on foot.

penetrometer an instrument for measuring the degree of penetrability of a solid.

phantasmascope, phantascope an optical device that enables the viewer to converge the optical axes of the eyes and experience some of the phenomena of binocular vision.

photodrome 1. an apparatus that regulates light flashes so that a rotating object appears to be stationary or moving in a direction opposite to its actual motion.
2. an apparatus for producing unusual optical effects by flashing light upon disks bearing various figures, patterns, etc.

photometer an instrument for measuring various characteristics of light, as intensity, distribution, flux, color, etc.

piezometer one of various devices for measuring the pressure of a fluid or the degree of compressibility of a substance when subjected to such pressure. —**piezometric,** *adj.*

planometer a device for measuring the flatness of a machined surface. Also called **surface plate.**

plastometer an instrument for measuring the plasticity of a material. —**plastometric,** *adj.*

pneumatograph an instrument for recording the movements of the chest during respiration.

praxinoscope an instrument that represents the effect of moving images on a screen.

pulsimeter, pulsometer an instrument for measuring the rate of the pulse.

pycnometer a container for measuring the density of liquids or solids.

pyrheliometer an instrument for measuring the intensity of the sun's radiation. —**pyrheliometric,** *adj.*

pyrometer an instrument for detecting and measuring high temperatures. —**pyrometric, pyrometry,** *adj.*

pyrophotometer a type of pyrometer that measures temperature optically or photometrically.

quadrant an instrument for measuring angular elevation, used in astronomy, navigation, surveying, etc., similar in principle to the sextant. —**quadrantal,** *adj.*

radiometer an instrument for measuring the intensity of radiant energy, composed of vanes which rotate at speeds proportionate to the intensity of the energy source. —**radiometric,** *adj.*

seismograph an instrument for measuring and recording the intensity of earth tremors.

sextant a navigational instrument for determining latitude and longitude by measuring the angles of heavenly bodies in relation to the horizon or other heavenly bodies.

snooperscope a device using infrared radiation and a fluoroscope to enable an observer to identify objects in the dark.

spectrobolometer an instrument combining a bolometer and a spectroscope, used for determining the distribution of energy in a spectrum. —**spectrobolometric,** *adj.*

spectroscope a device for producing and observing a spectrum of light or other radiation. —**spectroscopy,** *n.*

speedometer an instrument that records the speed of a vehicle in motion for the driver of the vehicle.

sphygmograph an instrument for measuring and recording various characteristics of the arterial pulse.

sphygmomanometer manometer, def. 2.

stadiometer 1. an instrument with a toothed wheel for measuring curves, broken lines, etc.
2. an obsolete form of tachymeter.

sympalmograph an apparatus for illustrating in graphic form the composition of two simple harmonic motions at right angles.

sympiesometer, sympiezometer 1. an instrument for measuring the pressure exerted by currents of water. See also 414. WATER.
2. an instrument for measuring the weight of the atmosphere by the compression of a column of gas. See also ATMOSPHERE.

tachistoscope an instrument for exposing pictures and other visual stimuli for very brief periods, used in psychological testing and various teaching methods.

tachometer an instrument for measuring revolutions per minute, especially of an internal combustion engine.

tachymeter a surveying instrument for measuring distance, height, elevation, etc.

tachyscope a type of kinescope that presents the effect of moving pictures by use of a rotating glass plate with images attached to it.

telemeter 1. an instrument for measuring the distance of objects from the observer, as the range finder in artillery.
2. an electronic device for taking readings from other distant instruments.

theodolite a surveying instrument for measuring vertical and horizontal angles. —theodolitic, *adj.*

thermometer an instrument for measuring temperature.

turbidimeter an instrument for measuring the turbidity of water or other fluids. —turbidimetric, *adj.*

udomograph a self-registering rain gauge.

urinometer an instrument for determining the specific gravity of urine.

vacuometer an instrument used for comparing barometers at varying pressures against a standard barometer.

velocimeter a device for measuring speed or velocity, especially that of projectiles.

viameter an early form of odometer, for measuring the distance traveled by a carriage. Also called viatometer.

viatometer viameter.

vibroscope an apparatus for the observation and recording of vibrations.

videophone an apparatus combining a telephone with a television transmitter and receiver so that the parties speaking to one another can also see one another.

voltammeter an instrument for measuring the voltage and amperage of an electrical current.

voltmeter an instrument for measuring the voltage of an electrical current.

volumenometer an instrument for measuring the volume of a solid body and its specific gravity by the quantity of a gas or liquid it displaces.

volumescope a graduated glass tube for showing the changes in volume in certain compounds as a result of chemical action.

volumeter an instrument for measuring the volumes of gases and liquids and of solids by the amount of gas or liquid they displace. —volumetric, volumetrical, *adj.*

227. ISLAM
See also 151. FAITH; 183. GOD and GODS; 349. RELIGION;
392. THEOLOGY.

Alcoranist a strict follower of the Koran.

Babism, Babiism the doctrines and practices of a 19th-century Persian sect that formed the basis for the current Baha'i organization, regarded as heretical by orthodox Muslims because its leader proclaimed himself to be the Imam Mahdi, the expected twelfth Imam of the Shiite sect, who would establish justice on earth. —**Babist,** *n.*

Ghazism the activities of the Ghazis, fanatics sworn to destroy all infidels.

Imamite a member of the Shi'a sect of Muslims, who believe in a succession of twelve divinely inspired imams, from Ali to Muhamad al Muntazar.

Islam, Islamism the religion of Islam; Muhammadanism. —**Islamist,** *n.* —**Islamitic,** *adj.*

Kaabism the tradition in Islam of venerating a shrine in Mecca through pilgrimage and prayers made after turning in its direction. —**Kaaba,** *n., adj.*

Karmathian an adherent of a heretical 9th-century Muslim sect that considers the Koran as mere allegory and is opposed to prayer, fasting, and revelation.

Mahdism the belief in Mahdi, the Muslim spiritual guide who, on Judgment Day, will lead the faithful to salvation. —**Mahdist,** *n.*

Muhammadanism, Mohammedanism the doctrines and practices of the religion founded by the prophet Muhammad and set forth in the Koran. Also called **Islam, Islamism.** —**Muhammadan, Mohammedan,** *n.*

Pan-Islamism the doctrines of Sultan Abdul-Hamid's 19th-century political movement that was against the westernization and unification of Islam. —**Pan-Islamist,** *n.* —**Pan-Islamic,** *adj.*

Senusism, Sanusism a 19th-century Islamic brotherhood observing a strict and ascetic religious orthodoxy and practicing militant political activity. Also **Senusiya, Sanusiya.** —**Senusi, Sanusi,** *n.*

Shiism the doctrines and practices of Shi'a, one of the two major branches of Islam, regarding Ali, the son-in-law of Muhammad, as the Prophet's legitimate successor. See also **Sunnism.** —**Shiite,** *n., adj.*

Sufiism, Sufism the beliefs and practices of an ascetic, retiring, and mystical sect in Islam. —**Sufi,** *n., adj.*

Sunnism the doctrines and practices of the larger of the two major branches of Islam, regarding as legitimate the first four caliphs after Muhammad's death and stressing the importance of the traditional portion of Muslim law (the Sunna). See also **Shiism.** —**Sunnite,** *n., adj.*

talismanist *Obsolete.* a Muslim holy man.

228. ITALY

cinquecentism the revival in arts and letters in the sixteenth century in Italy. —**cinquecentist,** *n., adj.*

duecentism the art and literature of thirteenth-century Italy. —**duecentist,** *n.,* *adj.*

Italomania an obsession with Italy and things Italian.

quattrocentism the art of fifteenth-century Italy. —**quattrocentist,** *n., adj.*

Quirinal the civil government of Italy, as contrasted with the papal government of the Vatican. —**Quirinal,** *adj.*

J

229. JAPAN

Japanism 1. devotion to or preference for the customs, policies, language, or culture of Japan.
2. anything peculiar to or characteristic of Japan or its people.

Japonism, Japonisme a style of art, idiom, custom, mannerism, etc., typical of the Japanese.

230. JOINING

parabiosis the uniting of two individual organisms or animals anatomically and physiologically, either under experimental or natural conditions. —parabiotic, *adj*.

symphytism *Rare*. coalescence; union or fusion.

synartesis 1. a close joining together.
2. the state of being fastened or knitted together.

synthesis 1. the process of putting two or more things, concepts, elements, etc., together to form a whole.
2. the whole formed of such combined parts. See also 393. THINKING. —synthesist, *n*., —synthetic, synthetical, *adj*.

syntheticism the principles or practice of synthesis or synthetic methods or techniques.

synthetist a person who practices or believes in synthetic methods or principles.

systasis *Obsolete*. a union, especially a political union as a federation or alliance.

231. JUDAISM
See also 151. FAITH; 183. GOD and GODS; 349. RELIGION; 392. THEOLOGY.

anti-Semitism an attitude or policy of hatred and hostility toward Jewish people. —anti-Semite, *n*.

Assideanism Hasidism, def. 2.

cabalism 1. the principles or doctrines of the cabala, a system of theosophy, theurgy, and mystical Scriptural interpretive methods originated by rabbis about the 8th century and affecting later Christian thinkers.
2. an interpretation made according to these doctrines.
3. an extreme traditionalism in theological concepts or Biblical interpretation.
4. obscurantism, especially that resulting from the use of obscure vocabulary. —cabalist, *n.* —cabalistic, *adj.*

Diaspora the scattering of the Jews after the period of Babylonian exile.

Gemarist a student of or expert on the Gemara, or second book of the Talmud. —Gemaric, *adj.*

gentilism the state or quality of being non-Jewish. —gentile, *n., adj.*

Haggada, Haggadah, Aggada, Aggadah 1. the explanatory matter in rabbinic and Talmudic literature, interpreting or illustrating the Scriptures.
2. a book in which is printed the liturgy for the Seder service. —haggadic, haggadical, *adj.*

Haggadist 1. a student of the Haggada.
2. a writer of the Haggada.

Halaka, Halakah, Halachah the entire body of Jewish law, comprising Biblical laws, oral laws transcribed in the Talmud, and subsequent codes altering traditional teachings. —Halakist, Halachist, *n.* —Halakic, *adj.*

Hasidism, Chasidism 1. the beliefs and practices of a mystical Jewish sect, founded in Poland about 1750, characterized by an emphasis on prayer, religious zeal, and joy.
2. the beliefs and practices of a pious sect founded in the 3rd century B.C. to resist Hellenizing tendencies and to promote strict observance of Jewish laws and rituals. Also Assideanism. —Hasidic, *adj.* —Hasidim, *n. pl.*

Hebraism the thought, spirit, and practice characteristic of the Hebrews. —Hebraist, *n.* —Hebraistic, Hebraistical, *adj.*

Jewry 1. the Jewish people collectively.
2. an area inhabited solely or mostly by Jews.

Judaism 1. the Jewish religion, rites, customs, etc.
2. adherence to the Jewish religion, rites, etc. —Judaist, *n.* —Judaic, Judaistic, *adj.*

Judophobism, Judophobia a hatred of Jews and of Jewish culture. Also called Judaeophobia.

Karaism a Jewish theology based on literal interpretation of the Old Testament and rejection of rabbinical commentary. —Karaite, *n.*

levirate the custom under the Mosaic code (Deut. xxv: 5–10) that required a widow to marry her dead husband's brother if she had no sons. —levirate, leviratical, *adj.*

Masorete, Masorite any of the Jewish scribes of the 10th century who compiled the Masora. —Masoretic, —Masoretical, *adj.*

Messianism 1. a belief in a Messiah coming to deliver the Jews, restore Israel, and rule righteously, first mentioned by the Prophet Isaiah.
2. the Christian belief that Jesus Christ was the Messiah prophesied.
3. the vocation of a Messiah. —Messianic, *adj.*

Mosaicity the condition of being rooted in Mosaic tradition.

Mosaism 1. the system of laws and rituals established by Moses.
2. devotion to the Mosaic laws. —Mosaist, *n.* —Mosaic, *adj.*

Phariseeism, Pharisaism 1. the beliefs and practices of an ancient Jewish sect, especially strictness of religious observance, close adherence to oral laws and traditions, and belief in an afterlife and a coming Messiah. Cf. **Sadduceeism.**
2. (*l.c.*) the behavior of a sanctimonious and self-righteous person. —Pharisee, pharisee *n.* —Pharisaic, pharisaic, *adj.*

Philonism the philosophy of Philo Judaeus, 1st-century B.C. Alexandrian, combining Judaism and Platonism and acting as a precursor of Neoplatonism. —Philonian, *adj.* —Philonic, *adj.*

rabbinism the beliefs, practices, and precepts of the rabbis of the Talmudic period. —rabbinic, rabbinical, *adj.*

Sabbatarianism the beliefs and principles underlying a strict observance of the Sabbath. —Sabbatarian, *n., adj.*

Sadduceeism, Sadducism the beliefs and practices of an ancient Jewish sect made up largely of the priestly aristocracy and opposing the Pharisees in both political and doctrinal matters, especially literal and less legalistic interpretation of the Jewish law, rejection of the rabbinical and prophetic traditions, and denying immortality, retribution in a future life, and the existence of angels. Cf. **Phariseeism.** —Sadducee, *n.* —Sadducean, *adj.*

scribism the beliefs and actions of Jewish scribes during the life of Christ.

Semitics the study of Semitic languages and culture. —Semitist, Semiticist, *n.*

Semitism 1. the state or quality of being Jewish.
2. anything typical or characteristic of Judaism, as customs, beliefs, influence, etc.

Sepher Torah Torah, def. 2.

Talmudism 1. the teachings of the collection of Jewish law and tradition called the Talmud.
2. the observance of and adherence to these teachings. —Talmudist, *n.* —Talmudic, *adj.*

Torah 1. the first five books of the Old Testament; the Pentateuch.
2. a scroll of these scriptures in Hebrew used for liturgical purposes. Also called **Sepher Torah**.
3. the entire body of Jewish law and tradition as found in the Old Testament and the Talmud.

tosaphist a writer of tosaphoth.

tosaphoth the explanatory and critical glosses made usually in the margins of Talmudic literature.

Yahwism 1. the worship of Yahweh (Jehovah).
2. the act or custom of naming Jehovah *Yahweh*.

Zealotism the beliefs, activities, and spirit of an ancient radical group in Judea that advocated overthrowing Roman rule.

Zionism a worldwide Jewish movement for the establishment in Palestine of a national homeland for Jews. —**Zionist, Zionite**, *n*. —**Zionist, Zionistic**, *adj*.

K

232. KILLING
See also 112. DEATH.

acaricide a substance or preparation for killing mites or ticks.

Aceldama a place of bloodshed, so called after the field purchased by Judas with the bribe he received for betraying Christ.

amicicide *Rare.* 1. the murder of one friend by another.
2. the killer of a friend.

androphonomania a homicidal mania.

avicide the killing of birds.

bactericide a substance for killing bacteria.

decollation the act of decapitation; beheading or being beheaded. —**decollator**, *n.*

defenestration the act of hurling from a window, especially people.

euthanasia 1. the act of putting to death without pain a person incurably ill or suffering great pain; mercy killing.
2. an easy, painless death. —**euthanasic**, *adj.*

felo-de-se 1. the act of suicide.
2. a person who commits suicide.

fratricide 1. the killing of one's brother.
2. a person who has killed his brother. —**fratricidal**, *adj.*

fungicide a substance that kills fungi or retards the growth of spores.

genocide the killing of an entire people or of a very large number of a people. —**genocidal**, *adj.*

germicide any substance for killing germs, especially bacteria. —**germicidal**, *adj.*

giganticide 1. the killing of a giant.
2. a person who kills giants.

hecatomb 1. a sacrifice of one hundred oxen at one time, as in ancient Greece.
2. any slaughter on a large scale; a massacre.

herbicide a substance for killing unwanted plant growth.

323

holocaust 1. a burnt offering or sacrifice.
   2. large-scale destruction by fire or other violent means.

homicide 1. a general term for murder; the killing of another human being.
   2. the murderer of another. —**homicidal,** *adj.*

homicidomania a mania for murder.

immolation the process of sacrificing, especially by fire. —**immolator,** *n.*

infanticide 1. the murder of infants.
   2. a person who kills infants. —**infanticidal,** *adj.*

insecticide a substance used for killing insects. —**insecticidal,** *adj.*

jugulation the act of cutting a person's throat. See also 350. REMEDIES.

lapidation the process or act of pelting with stones, sometimes as a form of execution.

macropicide the killing of kangaroos.

mactation the act of killing something for the purpose of sacrifice.

mariticide 1. the killing of one's husband.
   2. a person who has killed her husband. —**mariticidal,** *adj.*

matricide 1. the killing of one's mother.
   2. a person who has killed his mother. —**matricidal,** *adj.*

microbicide a substance that kills microbes.

miticide a substance for killing mites. —**miticidal,** *adj.*

occision *Obsolete.* a killing or an act of killing.

parricidism 1. the murder of a parent or close relative.
   2. one who has killed a parent or close relative. —**parricidal,** *adj.*

patricide 1. the killing of one's father.
   2. a person who has killed his father. —**patricidal,** *adj.*

pesticide any chemical substance used for killing pests, as insects, weeds, etc.

regicidism the murder of a king. —**regicide,** *n.* —**regicidal,** *adj.*

rodenticide a substance that kills rodents.

scaphism a punishment in old Persia, in which criminals were imprisoned in a log or hollow tree. The head, arms, and legs of a victim were left exposed and smeared with honey to attract insects.

sororicide 1. the killing of one's sister.
   2. a person who has killed his sister. —**sororicidal,** *adj.*

spermicide a substance or preparation used for killing sperm, used in contraception. —**spermicidal,** *adj.*

suicide 1. the killing of oneself.
   2. one who has killed himself. —**suicidal,** *adj.*

suttee 1. the suicide of a Hindu widow by immolation on the funeral pyre of her husband.
2. a Hindu widow who died by suttee.

taeniacide, teniacide an agent or preparation for killing tapeworms. —**taeniacidal, teniacidal,** *adj.*

tyrannicide 1. the killing of a tyrant.
2. the killer of a tyrant. —**tyrannicidal,** *adj.*

uxoricide 1. the killing of one's wife.
2. a person who has killed his wife. —**uxoricidal,** *adj.*

vaticide the killing of a prophet. —**vaticidal,** *adj.*

233. KNOWLEDGE
See also 240. LEARNING; 393. THINKING; 405. UNDERSTANDING.

acatalepsy the Skeptic doctrine that knowledge cannot be certain. —**acataleptic,** *n.*

agnoiology, agnoeology *Archaic.* the study of human ignorance.

anti-intellectualism antagonism to learning, education, and the educated, expressed in literature in a conscious display of simplicity, earthiness, even colorful semi-literacy. —**anti-intellectual,** *n.*, *adj.*

arcanum a secret or mystery; carefully hidden knowledge. See also 7. ALCHEMY. —**arcana,** *n. pl.*

chrestomathics the teaching of useful knowledge. —**chrestomathic,** *adj.*

clerisy men of learning as a class or collectively; the intelligentsia or literati.

determinacy the state of being determinate; the quality of being certain or precise.

empiricism a system of acquiring knowledge that rejects all *a priori* knowledge and relies solely upon observation, experimentation, and induction. Also **empirism.** —**empiricist,** *n.*, *adj.* —**empiric, empirical,** *adj.*

encyclopedism 1. the command of a wide range of knowledge.
2. the writings and thoughts of the 18th-century French Encyclopedists, especially an emphasis on scientific rationalism. —**encyclopedist,** *n.*

epistemology the branch of philosophy that studies the origin, nature, methods, validity, and limits of human knowledge. —**epistemologist,** *n.* —**epistemic, epistemological,** *adj.*

epistemophilia an excessive love or reverence for knowledge. —**epistemophiliac,** *n.*, *adj.*

experimentalism a reliance on principles of empiricism in philosophy or science. —**experimentalist,** *n.*

expertism the characteristic of being an expert.

factualism 1. excessive concern for facts.
2. a theory or belief relying heavily on fact. —**factualist**, *n.* —**factualistic**, *adj.*

gnosiology, gnoseology the philosophy of knowledge and the human faculties for learning. Also called **gnostology**. —**gnosiological, gnoseological**, *adj.*

Illuminism 1. (*l.c.*) the claim to possess superior knowledge.
2. the beliefs or claims of certain religious groups or sects that they possess special religious enlightenment. —**Illuminati, illuminati, Illuminist, illuminist**, *n.*

inconsequentia trifling or inconsequential facts or trivia.

inscience *Obsolete.* ignorance or the absence of knowledge. —**inscient**, *adj.*

intellectualism 1. the exercise of the intellect.
2. a devotion to intellectual activities.
3. an excessive emphasis on intellect and a resulting neglect of emotion. —**intellectualistic**, *adj.*

intuitionalism, intuitionism. 1. *Metaphysics.* the doctrine that the reality of perceived external objects is known intuitively, without the intervention of a representative idea.
2. *Metaphysics.* the doctrine that knowledge rests upon axiomatic truths discerned intuitively.
3. *Ethics.* the doctrine that moral values and duties can be perceived directly. Also called **intuitivism.** —**intuitionalist, intuitionist**, *n.*

maieutics the method used by Socrates in bringing forth knowledge through questions and insistence upon close and logical reasoning. —**maieutic**, *adj.*

mentalism the doctrine that objects of knowledge have no existence except in the mind of the perceiver. —**mentalist**, *n.* —**mentalistic**, *adj.*

misology a hatred of reason, reasoning, and knowledge. —**misologist**, *n.*

monism *Epistemology.* a theory that the object and datum of cognition are identical.

omniscience 1. universal or infinite knowledge.
2. the state of being all-knowing. Also *Obsolete,* **omniscious.** —**omniscient**, *adj.*

organon a method or means for communicating knowledge or for philosophical inquiry.

pansophism 1. the possession of universal knowledge. Cf. **pansophy.**
2. the claim to such enlightenment. —**pansophist**, *n.* —**pansophistical**, *adj.*

pansophy 1. a universal wisdom or encyclopedic learning.
2. a system of universal knowledge; pantology. —**pansophic**, *adj.*

pantology a systematic survey of all branches of knowledge. —**pantologist**, *n.* —**pantologic, pantological**, *adj.*

perceptionism the doctrine that asserts knowledge as relative to sensory perception. —**perceptionist,** *n.*

philonoist 1. *Rare.* a lover of learning.
2. (*cap.*) an advocate of Philonism. Also spelled **Philonist.**

plerophory a state or quality of full confidence or absolute certainty.

polyhistor a person of exceptionally wide knowledge; polymath. —**polyhistoric,** *adj.*

polymathy the possession of learning in many fields. —**polymath,** *n., adj.*

presentationism the theory that perception gives the mind an immediate cognition of an object. —**presentationalist, presentationist,** *n.*

quadrivium in the Middle Ages, one of the two divisions of the seven liberal arts, comprising arithmetic, geometry, astronomy, and music. See also **trivium.**

savant a scholar or person of great learning.

sciolism a superficial knowledge, especially when pretentiously revealed. —**sciolist,** *n.* —**sciolistic, sciolous,** *adj.*

sciosophy a supposed knowledge of natural and supernatural forces, usually based upon tradition rather than ascertained fact, as astrology and phrenology. —**sciosophist,** *n.*

sematology the theory of the use of signs, especially words, in their relation to knowledge and cognition.

semiotics a theory of symbology that embraces pragmatics and linguistics. —**semiotic,** *adj.*

specialism 1. a devotion or restriction to a particular pursuit, branch of study, etc.
2. a field of specialization within a science or area of knowledge, as otology within medicine. —**specialist,** *n.* —**specialistic,** *adj.*

technography the study and description of arts and sciences from the point of view of their historical development, geographical, and ethnic distribution.

telegnosis clairvoyance or other occult or supernatural knowledge.

trivia unimportant, trifling things or details, especially obscure and useless knowledge. —**trivial,** *adj.*

trivium in the Middle Ages, one of the two divisions of the seven liberal arts, comprising logic, grammar, and rhetoric. See also **quadrivium.**

L

234. LAKES

See also 356. RIVERS; 360. SEA; 414. WATER.

lacustrine of or pertaining to lakes.

limnophobia an abnormal fear of lakes.

235. LAND

See also 133. EARTH; 377. SOIL.

absenteeism the practice of extensive or permanent absence from their property by owners. —**absentee**, *n*.

alodialism, allodialism the 11th-century Anglo-Saxon estate system in which absolute possession was invested in the holder. —**alodialist, allodialist, alodiary, allodiary**, *n*.

burgage *British, Obsolete*. a form of land tenure under which land was held in return for payment of a fixed sum of money in rent or for rendering of service. Also called **socage**.

cadastration surveying for the purpose of showing boundary and property lines.

chorometry the science of land surveying.

dummyism the practice of purchasing land for another person who is not legally entitled to do so.

easement the right one landowner has been granted over the land of another, as the right of access to water, right of way, etc., at no charge.

embadometry *Obsolete*. the science of surveying.

feudalism a European system flourishing between 800–1400 based upon fixed relations of lord to vassal and all lands held in fee (as from the king), and requiring of vassal-tenants homage and service. Also **feudality**. —**feudal, feudalistic**, *adj*.

fiefdom *Medieval History*. the land over which a person exercises control after vows of vassalage and service to an overlord. See **feudalism**.

gromatics the science of surveying. —**gromatic**, *adj*.

photogrammetry the use of photography for surveying or map-making.

328

phototopography surveying or map-making by means of photography. —phototopographic, phototopographical, *adj.*

socage burgage.

stadia a system of surveying in which distances are measured by reading intervals on a graduated rod intercepted by two parallel cross hairs in the telescope of a surveying instrument. —stadia, *adj.*

theodolite a surveying instrument for measuring vertical and horizontal angles. —theodolitic, *adj.*

236. LANGUAGE
See also 12. ALPHABET; 53. BOOKS; 140. ENGLISH; 186. GRAMMAR; 237. LANGUAGE STYLE; 247. LINGUISTICS; 249. LITERATURE; 330. PRONUNCIATION; 346. READING; 354. RHETORIC and RHETORICAL DEVICES; 382. SPEECH; 383. SPELLING; 428. WRITING.

academese language typical of academics or the world of learning; pedantic language.

Americanism a word, phrase, or idiom peculiar to American English. Cf. Briticism, Canadianism.

anagrammatism the art or practice of making anagrams. Also called meta-grammatism.

Anglo-Saxonism anything characteristic of the Anglo-Saxon race, especially any linguistic peculiarity that stems from Old English and has not been affected by another language.

aphetism *Linguistics.* the loss of an initial unstressed vowel in a word, as *squire* for *esquire*. Also called apharesis, aphesis. —aphetic, *adj.*

aptotic of or relating to languages that have no grammatical inflections.

Aramaism a word, phrase, idiom, or other characteristic of Aramaic occurring in a corpus written in another language.

aulicism *Obsolete.* a courtly phrase or expression. —aulic, *adj.*

Bascology the study of the Basque language and culture.

bilingualism 1. the ability to speak two languages.
2. the use of two languages, as in a community. Also bilinguality, diglottism. —bilingual, bilinguist, *n.* —bilingual, *adj.*

biliteralism the state or quality of being composed of two letters, as a word. —biliteral, *adj.*

billingsgate coarse, vulgar, violent, or abusive language. [Allusion to the scurrilous language used in Billingsgate market, London.]

Briticism a word, idiom, or phrase characteristic of or restricted to British English. Also called Britishism. Cf. Americanism, Canadianism.

Canadianism 1. a word or phrase commonly used in Canadian rather than British or American English. Cf. **Americanism, Briticism.**
2. a word or phrase typical of Canadian French or English that is present in another language.
3. an instance of speech, behavior, customs, etc., typical of Canada.

Celticism 1. a word, phrase, or idiom characteristic of Celtic languages in material written in another language.
2. a Celtic custom or usage.

Chaldaism an idiom or other linguistic feature peculiar to Chaldean, especially in material written in another language. —**Chaldaic,** *n.*, *adj.*

Cilicism a word or phrase characteristic of Cilicia.

cledonism *Rare.* the use of euphemisms in order to avoid the use of plain words and any misfortune associated with them.

colloquialism a word, phrase, or expression characteristic of ordinary or familiar conversation rather than formal speech or writing, as "She's out" for "She is not at home." —**colloquial,** *adj.*

conversationalism a colloquial word or expression or one used in conversation more than in writing. Also **conversationism.**

coprolalomania a mania for foul speech.

cryptography 1. the science or study of secret writing, especially code and cipher systems.
2. the procedures and methods of making and using secret languages, as codes or ciphers. —**cryptographer, cryptographist,** *n.* —**cryptographic, crypto-graphical, cryptographal,** *adj.*

cryptology 1. the study of, or the use of, methods and procedures for translating and interpreting codes and ciphers; cryptanalysis.
2. cryptography. —**cryptologist,** *n.*

Danicism a word or expression characteristic of the Danish language.

demotic 1. of or relating to the common people; popular.
2. of, pertaining to, or noting the simplified form of hieratic writing used in ancient Egypt.
3. (*cap.*) of, belonging to, or connected with modern colloquial Greek. Also called **Romaic.**

demotist a student of demotic language and writings.

derism an expression of scorn. —**deristic,** *adj.*

dialecticism 1. a dialect word or expression.
2. dialectal speech or influence.

diglot a bilingual book or other work. —**diglottic,** *adj.*

disyllabism the condition of having two syllables. —**disyllable,** *n.* —**disyllabic, disyllabical,** *adj.*

Dorism the use of language that is characteristic of the Dorian Greeks.

dysphemism 1. a deliberate substitution of a disagreeable, offensive, or disparaging word for an otherwise inoffensive term, as *pig* for *policeman*.
2. an instance of such substitution. Cf. euphemism.

epigram a pithy statement, often containing a paradox.

epithesis paragoge.

equivocality, equivocacy the state or quality of being ambiguous in meaning or capable of double interpretation. —equivocal, *adj*.

etymologicon a book of etymologies; any treatise on the derivation of words.

etymology the branch of linguistics that studies the origin and history of words. —etymologist, *n*. —etymologic, etymological, *adj*.

euphemism 1. the deliberate or polite use of a pleasant or neutral word or expression to avoid the emotional implications of a plain term, as *passed over* for *died*.
2. an instance of such use. Cf. dysphemism, genteelism. —euphemist, *n*. —euphemistic, euphemistical, euphemious, *adj*.

Europeanism the customs, languages, and traditions distinctive of Europeans.

foreignism a custom or language characteristic peculiar to foreigners.

Franglais French characterized by an interlarding of English loan words.

Frenchism a French loanword in English, as *tête-à-tête*. Also called **Gallicism**.

Gallicism 1. a French linguistic peculiarity.
2. a French idiom or expression used in another language. Also called **Frenchism**.

genteelism 1. the deliberate use of a word or phrase as a substitute for one thought to be less proper, if not coarse, as *male cow* for *bull* or *limb* for *leg*.
2. an instance of such substitution.

Germanism, Germanicism a German loanword in English, as *gemütlich*. Also called **Teutonism, Teutonicism**.

glottogony the study of the origin of language. —glottogonic, *adj*.

grammatolatry 1. the worship of letters or words.
2. a devotion to the letter, as in law or Scripture; literalism.

Hebraism, Hebraicism 1. an expression or construction peculiar to Hebrew.
2. the character, spirit, principles, or customs of the Hebrew people.
3. a Hebrew loanword in English, as *shekel*. —Hebraist, *n*. —Hebraistic, Hebraic, *adj*.

heteronymy the state or quality of a given word's having the same spelling as another word, but with a different sound or pronunciation and a different meaning, as *lead* 'guide' and *lead* 'metal.' Cf. homonymy. —heteronym, *n.* —heteronymous, *adj.*

heterophemism, heterophemy an unconscious tendency to use words other than those intended. Cf. malapropism.

Hibernianism 1. an Irish characteristic.
2. an idiom peculiar to Irish English. Also called Hibernicism. —Hibernian, *adj.*

Hispanicism a Spanish word or expression that often appears in another language, as *bodega.*

holophrasis, holophrase the ability, in certain languages, to express a complex idea or entire sentence in a single word, as the imperative "Stop!" —holophrasm, *n.* —holophrastic, *adj.*

homonymy the state or quality of a given word's having the same spelling and the same sound or pronunciation as another word, but with a different meaning, as *race* 'tribe' and *race* 'running contest.' Cf. heteronymy. —homonym, *n.* —homonymous, *adj.*

hybridism 1. a word formed from elements drawn from different languages.
2. the practice of coining such words.

idiomatology a compilation of idiomatic words and phrases.

Idoism the advocacy of using the artificial language Ido, based upon Esperanto. —Ido, Idoist, *n.* —Idoistic, *adj.*

illeism the tendency in some individuals to refer to themselves in the third person. —illeist, *n.*

Interlingua an artificial international language, based upon the Romance languages, designed for use by the scientific community.

iotacism excessive use of the sound *i* and the substituting of this sound for other vowels. —iotacist, *n.*

Iricism *Rare.* an Irishism.

Irishism 1. a word or phrase commonly used in Ireland rather than England or America, as *begorra.*
2. a mode of speech, idiom, or custom characteristic of the Irish. Also Iricism.

isopsephism the numerical equality between words or lines of verse according to the ancient Greek notation, in which each letter receives a corresponding number. —isopsephic, *adj.*

Italianism an Italian loanword in English, as *chiaroscuro.* Also Italicism.

Italicism 1. an Italian loanword in English, as *chiaroscuro.*
2. Italianism. See also 328. PRINTING.

Japonism a style of art, idiom, custom, mannerism, etc., typical of the Japanese.

jargonist *Rare.* a person who makes use of a jargon in his speech.

Kenticism a word or expression whose root is the Kentish dialect.

Latinism 1. a mode of expression imitative of Latin.
2. a Latin word, phrase, or expression that often appears in another language. —**Latinize,** *v.*

Latinity 1. a particular way of speaking or writing Latin.
2. the use or knowledge of Latin.

lexicography the writing or compiling of dictionaries. —**lexicographer,** *n.* —**lexicographic, lexicographical,** *adj.*

linguist 1. a person skilled in the science of language. Also **linguistician.**
2. a person skilled in many languages; a polyglot.

localism a custom or manner of speaking peculiar to one locality. Also called provincialism. —**localist,** *n.* —**localistic,** *adj.*

logocracy a system in which ruling power is vested in words.

logodaedaly *Rare.* a cunning with words; verbal legerdemain. Also **logodaedalus.**

logolatry veneration or excessive regard for words. —**logolatrous,** *adj.*

logomachy 1. a dispute about or concerning words.
2. a contention marked by the careless or incorrect use of words; a meaningless battle of words. —**logomach, logomacher, logomachist,** *n.* —**logomachic, logomachical,** *adj.*

logomancy a form of divination involving the observation of words and discourse.

logomania a mania for words or talking.

logophile a lover of words. Also called **philologue, philologer.**

logophobia an abnormal fear or dislike of words.

logorrhea 1. an excessive or abnormal, sometimes incoherent talkativeness. —**logorrheic,** *adj.*

malapropism 1. the unconscious use of an inappropriate word, especially in a cliché, as *fender* for *feather* in "You could have knocked me over with a fender." [Named after Mrs. Malaprop, a character prone to such uses, in *The Rivals*, by Richard Brinsley Sheridan]
2. an instance of such misuse. Cf. **heterophemism.**

Medism a word or expression that comes from the language of the Medes.

Mekhitarist a member of an order of Armenian monks, founded in 1715 by Mekhitar da Pietro, dedicated to literary work, especially the perfecting of the Armenian language and the translation into it of the major works of other languages.

metagrammatism anagrammatism.

metaphrasis, metaphrase the practice of making a literal translation from one language into another. Cf. **paraphrasis.** —metaphrast, *n.* —metaphrastic, metaphrastical, *adj.*

monoglot a person capable of speaking only one language.

monosyllabism the condition of having only one syllable. —monosyllable, *n.* —monosyllabic, *adj.*

morology *Obsolete.* speaking foolishly. —morologist, *n.*

mutacism mytacism.

mytacism excessive use of or fondness for, or incorrect use of the letter *m* and the sound it represents. Also **mutacism.**

neologism, neology 1. a new word, usage, or phrase.
2. the coining or introduction of new words or new senses for established words. See also 392. THEOLOGY. —neologian, neologist, *n.* —neologistic, neological, *adj.*

neophrasis *Rare.* neologism. —neophrastic, *adj.*

neoterism 1. a neologism.
2. the use of neologisms. —neoterist, *n.*

New Yorkerism a word or phrase characteristic of those who reside in New York City.

nice-nellyism, nice-Nellyism a euphemism. See also 28. ATTITUDES.

norlandism a word or expression characteristic of a northern dialect.

orismology the science of defining technical terms. —orismologic, orismological, *adj.*

orthology the art of correct grammar and correct use of words. —orthologer, orthologian, *n.* —orthological, *adj.*

pantoglottism the ability to speak any language. —pantoglot, *n.*

paragoge the addition of a sound or group of sounds at the end of a word, as in the nonstandard *idear* for *idea.* Also called **epithesis.** —paragogic, paragogical, *adj.*

paraphrasis, paraphrase the recasting of an idea in words different from that originally used, whether in the same language or in a translation. Cf. metaphrasis, periphrasis. —paraphrastic, paraphrastical, *adj.*

parasynthesis 1. word formation by the addition of both a prefix and a suffix to a stem or word, as *international.*
2. word formation by the addition of a suffix to a phrase or compound word, as *nickel-and-diming.* —parasynthetic, *adj.*

parisology the use of equivocal or ambiguous terms. —parisological, *adj.*

paroemiology the collecting and study of proverbs. Cf. proverbialism. —paroemiologist, *n.* —paroemiologic, paroemiological, *adj.*

pasigraphy 1. an artificial international language using signs and figures instead of words.
2. any artificial language, as Esperanto. —pasigraphic, *adj.*

pejoratism *Linguistics.* a semantic change in a word to a lower, less respectable meaning, as in *hussy.* Also pejoration.

pentaglot a book or other work written in five languages. —pentaglot, *adj.*

periphrasis 1. a roundabout way of speaking or writing; circumlocution.
2. an expression in such fashion. Cf. paraphrasis. —periphrastic, *adj.*

perissology *Archaic.* a pleonasm.

phraseology 1. an idiom or the idiomatic aspect of a language.
2. a mode of expression.
3. *Obsolete.* a phrasebook. —phraseologist, *n.* —phraseologic, phraseological, *adj.*

platitudinarianism 1. an addiction to spoken or written expression in platitudes.
2. a staleness or dullness of both language and ideas. Also called platitudinism. —platitudinarian, *n.*

pleonasm 1. the use of unnecessary words to express an idea; redundancy.
2. an instance of this, as *true fact.*
3. a redundant word or expression. —pleonastic, *adj.*

Polonist a specialist in Polish language, literature, and culture.

polyglot 1. a person who speaks several languages.
2. a mixture of languages. See also 53. BOOKS. —polyglot, *n.*, *adj.* —polyglottic, polyglottous, *adj.*

polyglottism the ability to use or to speak several languages. —polyglot, *n.*, *adj.*

polyology *Rare.* verbosity.

polysemy a diversity of meanings for a given word.

polysyllabism the condition of having three or more syllables. —polysyllable, *n.* —polysyllabic, polysyllabical, *adj.*

portmantologism the creation or use of portmanteau words, or words that are a blend of two other words, as *smog* (from *smoke* and *fog*).

preciosity excessive fastidiousness or over-refinement in language or behavior.

prescriptivism purism.

prolixity excessive wordiness in speech or writing; longwindedness. —**prolix**, *adj.*

propheticism a phrase typical of the Biblical prophets.

proverbialism the composing, collecting, or customary use of proverbs. Cf. paroemiology. —**proverbialist**, *n.*

provincialism localism.

psilology a love of vacuous or trivial talk.

psychobabble obfuscating language and jargon as used by psychologists, psychoanalysts, and psychiatrists, characterized by recondite phrases and arcane names for common conditions.

purism the policy or attempt to purify language and to make it conform to the rigors of pronunciation, usage, grammar, etc. that have been arbitrarily set forth by a certain group. Also called **prescriptivism**. See also 23. ART; 104. CRITICISM; 249. LITERATURE; 352. REPRESENTATION. —**purist**, *n.*, *adj.*

ribaldry coarse, vulgar, or obscene language or joking. —**ribald**, *adj.*

Romaic demotic.

Russianism something characteristic of or influenced by Russia, its people, customs, language, etc.

rusticism a rustic habit or mode of expression. —**rustic**, *adj.* —**rusticity**, *n.*

Saxonism a word, idiom, phrase, etc., of Anglo-Saxon or supposed Anglo-Saxon origin.

Scotticism, Scoticism, Scottishism a feature characteristic of Scottish English or a word or phrase commonly used in Scotland rather than in England or America, as *bonny*.

semantics 1. the study of meaning.
2. the study of linguistic development by classifying and examining changes in meaning and form. —**semanticist, semantician**, *n.* —**semantic**, *adj.*

Semiticism a word, phrase, or idiom from a Semitic language, especially in the context of another language.

Semitics the study of Semitic languages and culture. —**Semitist, Semiticist**, *n.*

sesquipedalianism the practice of using very long words. Also **sesquipedalism, sesquipedality**. —**sesquipedal, sesquipedalian**, *adj.*

slangism a slangy expression or word.

Slavicism a Slavic loanword in English, as *blini*.

Slavicist one who specializes in the study of Slavic languages, literatures, or other aspects of Slavic culture. Also **Slavist**.

Spoonerism the transposition of initial or other sounds of words, usually by accident, as "queer dean" for "dear Queen." [After the Rev. W. A. Spooner, 1844–1930, noted for such slips.] —**spoonerize**, *v.*

steganography *Archaic.* the use of a secret language or code; cryptography. —**steganographer**, *n.*

Sumerology the study of the language, history, and archaeology of the Sumerians. —**Sumerologist**, *n.*

syllabarium a syllabary.

syllabary 1. a table of syllables, as might be used for teaching a language.
2. a system of characters or symbols representing syllables instead of individual sounds. Also **syllabarium.**

syncategorematic a word that cannot be used as a term in its own right in logic, as an adverb or preposition. —**syncategorematic**, *adj.*

Syriacism an expression whose origin is Syriac, a language based on the eastern Aramaic dialect.

tautologism *Rare.* tautology.

tautology needless repetition of a concept in word or phrase; redundancy or pleonasm. Also **tautologism.** —**tautologist**, *n.* —**tautological, tautologous**, *adj.*

terminology 1. the classification of terms associated with a particular field; nomenclature.
2. the terms of any branch of knowledge, field of activity, etc. —**terminologic, terminological**, *adj.*

Teutonicism 1. anything typical or characteristic of the Teutons or Germans, as customs, attitudes, actions, etc.
2. Germanism. —**Teutonic**, *adj.*

transatlanticism a word, phrase, or idiom in English that is common to both Great Britain and the United States.

triticism a trite, commonplace or hackneyed saying, expression, etc.; a platitude.

tuism 1. the use of the second person, as in apostrophe.
2. in certain languages, the use of the familiar second person in cases where the formal third person is usually found and expected.
3. an instance of such use.

univocacy *Rare.* the state or quality of having only one meaning or of being unmistakable in meaning, as a word or statement. —**univocal**, *adj.*

verbalism 1. a verbal expression, as a word or phrase.
2. the way in which something is worded.
3. a phrase or sentence devoid or almost devoid of meaning.
4. a use of words regarded as obscuring ideas or reality; verbiage.

verbiage wordiness or prolixity; an excess of words.

verbicide *Facetious.* misuse or overuse of a word or any use of a word which is damaging to it.

verbigeration meaningless repetition of words and phrases.

verbomania an excessive use of or attraction to words.

verbosity the quality or condition of wordiness; excessive use of words, especially unnecessary prolixity. —**verbose,** *adj.*

vernacularism 1. a word, phrase, or idiom from the native and popular language, contrasted with literary or learned language.
2. the use of the vernacular. —**vernacular,** *n., adj.*

villagism a word or phrase characteristic of a village or rural community.

Volapükist a speaker or advocate of Volapük, a language proposed for use as an international language.

vulgarism a word or phrase used chiefly in coarse, colloquial speech. —**vulgarian, vulgarist,** *n.*

wegotism the habit of referring to oneself by the pronoun "we."

westernism a word or form of pronunciation distinctive of the western United States.

witticism a remark or expression characterized by cleverness in perception and choice of words.

wordsmanship *Facetious.* the art or technique of employing a vocabulary of arcane, recondite words in order to gain an advantage over another person.

Yankeeism 1. a Yankee characteristic or character.
2. *British.* a linguistic or cultural trait peculiar to the United States.
3. *Southern U.S.* a linguistic or cultural trait peculiar to the states siding with the Union during the Civil War.
4. *Northern U.S.* a linguistic or cultural trait peculiar to the New England states.

Yiddishism a Yiddish loanword in English, as *chutzpa.*

Yorkshireism the language and customs of people living in the county of Yorkshire, England.

237. LANGUAGE STYLE
See also 236. LANGUAGE; 248. LITERARY STYLE; 249. LITERATURE;
354. RHETORIC and RHETORICAL DEVICES.

academese language typical of academics or the world of learning; pedantic language.

aeolism a tendency to longwindedness. —**aeolistic,** *adj.*

anecdotalism 1. the writing or telling of short narratives concerning an interesting, amusing, or curious incident or event.
2. an excessive use of anecdotes, as sometimes in the conversation of the aged. —anecdotalist, *n*.

archaism the deliberate use, for effect, of old-fashioned terminology in literature.

Asiaticism a manner of speech, writing, or architecture distinguished by excessive ornamentation or floridity. —Asiatical, *adj*.

barbarism the use of terms or constructions felt by some to be undesirably foreign to the established customs of the language. —barbarian, *n.*, *adj*.

battology futile repetition in speech or writing.

bureaucratese language characteristic of government bureaucracy, characterized by excessive use of jargon, convoluted construction, and periphrasis.

businessese language typical of that used by business people or the world of business, characterized by use of jargon and abbreviation.

causticism, causticity a sharp, tart wittiness. Also **causticness.** —caustic. *adj*.

cinemese language typical of the cinema, as that used in film dialogue or in film criticism.

collegese language typical of that used by college students, characterized by use of slang and neologisms.

computerese language used by those in the business of manufacturing, selling, servicing, or using electronic computers, characterized by many abbreviations and acronyms, excessive use of technical jargon, and, frequently, lack of concern for traditional spelling and grammar.

concettism 1. any writing characterized by conceits, i.e., elaborate and fanciful figures of speech, as in the opening lines of T.S. Eliot's "Prufrock."
2. the use of conceits in writing.

economese language and jargon typical of economists and the field of economics.

epigrammatism 1. the composition of brief witty, ingenious, or sententious statements.
2. the composition of short, concise poems, often satirical, displaying a witty or ingenious thought. —epigrammatist, *n*. —epigrammatic, *adj*.

federalese language typical of the federal government, especially bureaucratic jargon.

fustian a high-flown, bombastic style of writing or speaking. —fustianist, *n*.

journalese language typical of journalists and newspapers or magazines, characterized by use of neologism and unusual syntax. Also called **newspaperese.**

laconicism, laconism a tendency to use few words to express a great deal; conciseness. —**laconic,** *adj.*

legalese language typical of lawyers, laws, legal forms, etc., characterized by archaic usage, prolixity, and extreme thoroughness.

lexiphanicism *Archaic.* 1. the use of excessively learned and bombastic terminology.
2. an instance of this language style. —**lexiphanic,** *adj.*

literaryism 1. the habitual use of literary forms.
2. an expression belonging to a literary language.

lucidity the quality, state, or art of clarity in thought and style. —**lucidness,** *n.* —**lucid,** *adj.*

macaronicism a style of language in which Latin forms and words are mixed with vernacular words, as *skato, slippere, falli, bumptum.* —**macaronic,** *n.,* *adj.*

macrology an excessive wordiness.

newspaperese journalese.

officialese language characteristic of officialdom, typified by polysyllabism and much periphrasis.

paragraphism the system of writing paragraphs in newspaper-journalism style. —**paragraphist,** *n.* —**paragraphically,** *adv.*

parrhesia a tendency to boldness and frankness of speech; freedom of expression, as in much modern literature.

pedagese the language of pedagogues or language typical of pedagogues, characterized by pedanticism. Also called **academese.**

pedestrianism the use of a style lacking in vitality, imagination, or distinction; prosiness. —**pedestrian,** *adj.*

pellucidity the quality, state, or art of writing or speaking in a fashion that is easy to understand. —**pellucidness,** *n.* —**pellucid,** *adj.*

Pentagonese language typical of the Pentagon or the U.S. defense establishment, characterized by use of acronyms, neologisms and the use of nouns as verbs and adjectives.

postclassicism a written or spoken expression characteristic of the period following the classical period of a language. —**postclassical,** *adj.*

sardonicism a style of speaking or writing characterized by bitter, contemptuous, or scornful derision.

sensationalism yellow journalism.

societyese language typical of high society, characterized by affectation.

sociologese language or jargon typical of sociology or sociologists.

stagese language typical of the stage and stage people, characterized by affectation, hyperbole, and melodramatic effects.

stichometry the practice of expressing the successive ideas in a prose composition in single lines corresponding to natural cadences or sense divisions. —stichometric, stichometrical, *adj.*

telegraphese the brief, sometimes cryptic language used in telegrams.

Varietyese language typical of the entertainment journal *Variety*, characterized by a staccato, idiomatic, and neologistic style, with much use of abbreviation.

Wall Streetese language typical of that used on Wall Street and in the financial markets, characterized by use of technical financial terms and arcane stock-market jargon.

Washingtonese federalese.

yellow journalism the practice of seeking out sensational news for the purpose of boosting a newspaper's circulation, or, if such stories are hard to find, of trying to make comparatively innocuous news appear sensational. Also called **sensationalism**. —yellow journalist, *n.*

238. LAUGHTER
See also 213. HUMOR.

Abderian relating to foolish or excessive laughter. [Allusion to Democritus, the laughing philosopher, born in Abdero.]

cachinnation raucous laughter; loud whinnying.

geloscopy, gelotoscopy a form of divination that determines a person's character or future from the way he laughs.

jocundity the quality or condition of being merry or cheerful. —jocund, *adj.*

katagelophobia an abnormal fear or dislike of ridicule.

risibility 1. the ability or disposition to laugh.
2. a humorous awareness of the ridiculous and absurd.
3. laughter.

239. LAW
See also 103. CRIME; 185. GOVERNMENT.

allograph a signature of a proxy, one who is not party to the transaction at hand. —allographic, *adj.*

angary the right of a nation at war to destroy the property of a neutral, subject to indemnification.

anomie, anomy, anomia a state or condition of individuals or society characterized by an absence or breakdown of social and legal norms and values, as in the case of an uprooted people. —anomic, *adj.*

antinomia, antinomy a real or apparent contradiction in a statute. —anti-nomic, antinomian, *adj.*

antinomianism the theological doctrine maintaining that Christians are freed from both moral and civil law by God's gift of grace. —antinomian, antinomist, *n.*

asseveration the solemn affirmation of the truth of a statement. —asseverator, *n.* —asseverative, *adj.*

avowtry the crime of adultery.

barratry the offense of frequently exciting or stirring up suits and quarrels between others. —barrator, *n.* —barratrous, *adj.*

battery an intentional act that, directly or indirectly, causes harmful contact with another's person.

caveat a legal notice to beware; a notice placed on file until the caveator can be heard. —caveator, *n.* —caveatee, *n.*

civilist a person who studies civil law.

compurgation formerly, in common law, acquittal on the basis of endorsement by the friends or neighbors of the accused. Also called **trial by wager of law.** —compurgator, *n.* —compurgatory, *adj.*

compurgator one who testifies to the innocence of an accused person.

constructionist a person who puts a particular interpretation on provisions of the U.S. Constitution, especially those provisions dealing with the rights of individuals and states.

coverture the status of a married woman.

criminalism an act or action having the character of a crime. Also **criminality.** —criminal, *n., adj.*

culpability 1. the condition of blameworthiness, criminality, censurability. 2. *Obsolete.* guilt. —culpable, *adj.*

delinquency a condition of guilt; failure to do that which the law or other obligation requires. See also 160. FINANCE. —delinquent, *adj.*

dicealolgy *Obsolete.* a delineation of jurisdiction.

dikephobia an abnormal fear or dislike of justice.

disherison *Archaic.* 1. the act of disinheriting. 2. the condition of being disinherited.

Draconianism any unreasonable harshness or severity in laws. —Draconian, Draconic, *adj.*

easement the right one landowner has been granted over the land of another, as the right of access to water, right of way, etc., at no charge.

feudist 1. a specialist in law relating to the feudal system. 2. a person who holds or lets land under the provisions of the feudal system.

fiduciary a person to whom property or power is entrusted for the benefit of another. —fiducial, fiduciary, *adj.*

jurisprudence 1. law as a science or philosophy.
2. a system of laws or a particular branch of law. —jurisprudent, *adj.*

Justinianist an expert on the codification and revision of Roman laws ordered by the 6th-century Byzantine emperor Justinian. —Justinian code, *n.*

legalese language typical of lawyers, laws, legal forms, etc., characterized by archaic usage, prolixity, redundancy and extreme thoroughness.

legalism a strict and usually literal adherence to the law. —legalistic, *adj.*

legist a person who is skilled or well versed in law.

litigiomania a compulsion for involving oneself in legal disputes.

nomism the practice of religious legalism, especially the basing of standards of good actions upon the moral law.

nomocracy a system of government based on a legal code.

nomography 1. the art of drafting laws.
2. a treatise on the drawing up of laws. —nomographer, *n.* —nomographic, *adj.*

nomology the science of law. —nomologist, *n.* —nomological, *adj.*

nonage the state of being under the age required by law to enter into certain responsibilities or obligations, as marrying, entering into contracts, etc. See also 81. CHURCH; 331. PROPERTY and OWNERSHIP.

pandect, pandects a legal code or complete body or system of laws.

pandectist 1. the writer of a complete code of the laws of a country.
2. the writer of a complete digest of materials on a subject.

pettifogger 1. a lawyer whose practice is of a small or petty character; a lawyer of little importance.
2. a shyster lawyer. —pettifoggery, *n.*

postremogeniture the rights or legal status of the last child born in a family. Also called ultimogeniture. Cf. primogeniture.

primogeniture the rights or legal status of the first born in a family. Cf. postremogeniture.

publicist an expert in public or international law.

revisionism the advocacy of revision, especially in relation to court decisions. —revisionist, *n.* —revisionary, *adj.*

squatterism 1. the state or practice of being a squatter, or one who settles on government land, thereby establishing ownership.
2. the state or practice of settling in vacant or abandoned property, either for shelter or in an attempt to establish ownership. —squatter, *n.*

symbolaeography the drawing up of legal documents. —symbolaeographer, *n.*

ultimogeniture postremogeniture.

vassalage 1. the condition of land tenure of a vassal.
2. the fief or lands held.

240. LEARNING
See also 233. KNOWLEDGE; 338. QUESTIONING; 405. UNDERSTANDING.

academicism, academism 1. the mode of teaching or of procedure in a private school, college, or university.
2. a tendency toward traditionalism or conventionalism in art, literature, music, etc.
3. any attitudes or ideas that are learned or scholarly but lacking in worldliness, common sense, or practicality. —academic, *n., adj.* —academist, *n.*

academism 1. the philosophy of the school founded by Plato.
2. academicism. —academist, *n.* —academic, academical, *adj.*

anti-intellectualism antagonism to learning, education, and the educated, expressed in literature in a conscious display of simplicity, earthiness, even colorful semi-literacy. —anti-intellectual, *n., adj.*

autodidactics the process of teaching oneself. —autodidact, *n.*

bluestockingism 1. the state of being a pedantic or literal-minded woman.
2. behavior characteristic of such a woman.

clerisy men of learning as a class or collectively; the intelligentsia or literati.

didacticism 1. the practice of valuing literature, etc., primarily for its instructional content.
2. an inclination to teach or lecture others too much, especially by preaching and moralizing.
3. a pedantic, dull method of teaching. —didact, *n.* —didactic, *adj.*

didactics the art or science of teaching.

doctrinism the state of being devoted to something that is taught. —doctrinist, *n.*

educationist 1. *British.* an educator.
2. a specialist in the theory and methods of education. Also called educationalist.

Froebelist a person who supports or uses the system of kindergarten education developed by Friedrich Froebel, German educational reformer. Also Froebelian.

gymnasiast a student in a gymnasium, a form of high school in Europe. See also 26. ATHLETICS.

Gymnasium (in Europe) a name given to a high school at which students prepare for university entrance.

literati men of letters or learning; scholars as a group.

literator a scholarly or literary person; one of the literati.

lucubration 1. the practice of reading, writing, or studying at night, especially by artificial light; "burning the midnight oil."
2. the art or practice of writing learnedly. —lucubrator, n. —lucubrate, v.

opsimathy *Rare*. 1. a late education.
2. the process of acquiring education late in life.

paideutics, paedeutics the science of learning.

pedagogics, paedogogics the science or art of teaching or education. —pedagogue, paedagogue, pedagog, n. —pedagogic, paedagogic, pedagogical, paedagogical, *adj*.

pedagogism 1. the art of teaching.
2. teaching that is pedantic, dogmatic, and formal.

pedagogy, paedagogy 1. the function or work of a teacher; teaching.
2. the art or method of teaching; pedagogics.

pedanticism 1. the character or practices of a pedant, as excessive display of learning.
2. a slavish attention to rules, details, etc.; pedantry. —pedant, n. —pedantic, *adj*.

pedantocracy rule or government by pedants; domination of society by pedants.

pedantry pedanticism, def. 2.

polytechnic a school of higher education offering instruction in a variety of vocational, technical, and scientific subjects. —polytechnic, *adj*.

professorialism the qualities, actions, and thoughts characteristic of a professor. —professorial, *adj*.

propaedeutics the basic principles and rules preliminary to the study of an art or science. —propaedeutic, propaedeutical, *adj*.

quadrivium in the Middle Ages, one of the two divisions of the seven liberal arts, comprising arithmetic, geometry, astronomy, and music. See also **trivium**.

realia objects, as real money, utensils, etc., used by a teacher in the classroom to illustrate aspects of daily life.

savant a scholar or person of great learning.

scholarch a head of a school, especially the head of one of the ancient Athenian schools of philosophy.

sophist 1. *Ancient Greece*. a teacher of rhetoric, philosophy, etc.; hence, a learned person.
2. one who is given to the specious arguments often used by the sophists. —sophistic, sophistical, *adj*.

sophistry 1. the teachings and ways of teaching of the Greek sophists.
2. specious or fallacious reasoning, as was sometimes used by the sophists.

Sorbonist a doctor of the Sorbonne, of the University of Paris.

symposiarch *Ancient Greece.* the master of a feast or symposium; hence, a person presiding over a banquet or formal discussion.

symposiast *Rare.* a person participating in a symposium.

symposium learned discussion of a particular topic. Also spelled **symposion.**

technography the study and description of arts and sciences from the point of view of their historical development, geographical, and ethnic distribution.

theorist a person who forms theories or who specializes in the theory of a particular subject.

trivium in the Middle Ages, one of the two divisions of the seven liberal arts, comprising logic, grammar, and rhetoric. See also **quadrivium.**

tyrology *Rare.* a set of instructions for beginners.

241. LEAVES
See also **54. BOTANY; 167. FLOWERS; 188. GRASSES; 319. PLANTS; 401. TREES.**

frondescence 1. the process of growing leaves, as plants, trees, etc.
2. the period during which leaves are put out. —**frondescent,** *adj.*

phyllody the process by which floral organs turn into foliage. Also called **phyllomorphy.**

phyllomancy a form of divination involving the examination of leaves.

phyllomania abnormal development of leaf tissue; the growth of leaves in abnormal quantity or unusual locations.

phyllomorphosis the study of the transformations of leaves during different seasons.

phyllomorphy phyllody.

phyllotaxy, phyllotaxis 1. the arrangement of the leaves on the stem of a plant.
2. the science or study of the arrangement and distribution of leaves. —**phyllotactic,** *adj.*

242. LEFT
See also **355. RIGHT.**

levoduction motion or a tendency to move to the left, as the motion of the eye.

levorotation rotation toward the left; counterclockwise rotation, a characteristic of the plane of polarization of light. —**levorotatory,** *adj.*

levoversion the state or process of turning to the left.

sinistrality the state or quality of being left-handed or oriented towards the left in other ways, as a shell with counterclockwise spirals. Also **sinistration.** —**sinistral,** *adj.*

sinistrogyration levorotation. Also called **levogyration.** —**sinistrogyric,** *adj.*

243. LIES and LYING
See also 402. TRUTH and ERROR.

accismus *Rhetoric.* an affected or false refusal.

autothaumaturgist one who pretends to be notable or mysterious.

fabulist a person who tells lies.

falsism anything that is patently false or untrue.

hypocrisy the condition of a person pretending to be something he is not, especially in the area of morals or religion; a false presentation of belief or feeling. —**hypocrite,** *n.* —**hypocritic, hypocritical,** *adj.*

mendacity 1. untruthfulness; the act or process of lying.
2. a lie or untruth. —**mendacious,** *adj.*

mountebankism boastful and pretentious behavior; quackery or any actions typical of a mountebank. Also **mountebankery.**

mythomania *Psychiatry.* an abnormal propensity to lie, exaggerate, or twist the truth.

mythophobia an abnormal fear of making false statements.

perjury deliberate or willful uttering of untruths when under oath in a court or similar tribunal. —**perjurer,** *n.* —**perjurious,** *adj.*

polygraph a lie detecting device. —**polygrapher, polygraphist,** *n.* —**polygraphic,** *adj.*

pseudism a lie.

pseudology 1. the act of lying, especially when humorously proposed as an art or system.
2. a pretended field of study. —**pseudologer, pseudologist,** *n.* —**pseudological,** *adj.*

pseudomancy a form of divination that is deliberately false or misleading.

pseudomania *Psychiatry.* 1. pathological lying.
2. a false or pretended mental disorder.

quackery 1. false pretense to medical skill, knowledge, or qualification; medical charlatanry.
2. the actions or practice of a medical charlatan. —**quack,** *n., adj.*

quackism 1. the practice of quackery.
2. the behavior or actions of a quack.

Sinonism an act of perfidy. [Allusion to Sinon, whose false tale persuaded the Trojans to allow the wooden horse within the walls of Troy.]

244. LIFE
See also 44. BIOLOGY; 430. ZOOLOGY.

abiogenesis *Biology.* the production of living organisms from inanimate matter. Also called spontaneous generation. —abiogenetic, *adj.*

abiosis a state or condition in which life is absent. —abiotic, abiotical, *adj.*

anabiosis a revival or return to a living state after apparent death. —anabiotic, *adj.*

athanasia immortality.

biochemistry the study of the chemical processes that take place in living organisms. —biochemist, *n.* —biochemical, *adj.*

biogenesis, biogeny 1. the process by which living organisms develop from other living organisms.
2. the belief that this process is the only way in which living organisms can develop. —biogenetic, biogenic, *adj.*

biology the science or study of all manner of life and living organisms. —biologist, *n.* —biological, *adj.*

biolysis the destruction of life, as by bacteria. —biolytic, *adj.*

biometrics, biometry. 1. the calculation of the probable extent of human lifespans.
2. the application to biology of mathematical and statistical theory and methods. —biometric, biometrical, *adj.*

biosphere that part of the earth's surface where most forms of life exist, specifically those parts where there is water or atmosphere.

mechanism *Philosophy.* the theory or doctrine that all the phenomena of the universe, especially life, can ultimately be explained in terms of physics and chemistry and that the difference between organic and inorganic lies only in degree. Cf. vitalism. —mechanist, *n.* —mechanistic, *adj.*

ontogenesis ontogeny. —ontogenetic, ontogenetical, *adj.*

ontogeny the life cycle, development, or developmental history of an organism. Also called ontogenesis. —ontogenic, *adj.*

parthenogenesis *Biology.* the development of an egg or seed without fertilization. Also called unigenesis. —parthenogenetic, *adj.*

physiology the branch of biology that studies the functions and vital processes of living organisms. —physiologist, *n.* —physiologic, physiological, *adj.*

spontaneous generation abiogenesis.

unigenesis asexual reproduction; parthenogenesis. —unigenetic, *adj.*

vitalism 1. *Philosophy.* the doctrine that phenomena are only partly controlled by mechanistic forces and are in some measure self-determining.
2. *Biology.* the doctrine that the life in living organisms is caused and sustained by a vital principle that is distinct from all physical and chemical forces. Cf. mechanism. —vitalist, *n.* —vitalistic, *adj.*

vitativeness *Phrenology.* 1. the love of life and fear of death.
2. the organ serving as the seat of instincts of self-preservation.

zoism 1. *Philosophy.* a doctrine that the phenomena of life are controlled by a vital principle, as Bergson's *élan vital.*
2. a high regard for animal life.
3. a belief in animal magnetism. —zoist, *n.* —zoistic, *adj.*

245. LIGHT
See also 110. DARKNESS; 387. SUN.

actinology the study of the chemical effects of light in the violet and ultraviolet wavelengths. —actinologic, actinological, *adj.*

actinometry the measurement of the heating power of light in the violet and ultraviolet range. —actinometrist, *n.* —actinometric, actinometrical, *adj.*

albedo the ratio between the light reflected from a surface and the total light falling upon that surface, as the albedo of the moon.

birefringence double refraction; the separation of light into two unequally refracted, polarized rays, as by some crystals. —birefringent, *adj.*

catadioptrics the study of the reflection and refraction of light. —catadioptric, catadioptrical, *adj.*

catoptrics the study of light reflection. —catoptric, catoptrical, *adj.* —catoptrically, *adv.*

chatoyancy the condition or quality of changing in color or luster depending on the angle of light, especially of a gemstone that reflects a single shaft of light when cut in cabochon form. —chatoyant, *adj.*

dichroism a property, peculiar to certain crystals, of reflecting light in two different colors when viewed from two different directions. —dichroic, *adj.*

dioptrics the study of light refraction. —dioptric, *adj.*

iridescence the state or condition of being colored like a rainbow or like the light shining through a prism. —iridescent, *adj.*

iriscope a polished black glass, the surface of which becomes iridescent when it is breathed upon through a tube.

levorotation rotation toward the left; counterclockwise rotation, a characteristic of the plane of polarization of light. —levorotatory, *adj.*

lithophany the process of impressing porcelain objects, as lamp bases, with figures that become translucent when light is placed within or behind them. —lithophanic, *adj.*

noctiluca any thing or creature that shines or glows in the dark, especially a phosphorescent or bioluminescent marine or other organism. —noctilucine, *adj.*

optics the study of the properties of light. Also called **photology.** —optic, optical, *adj.*

pharology the study of signal lights, especially lighthouses.

phengophobia an abnormal fear of daylight.

photalgia pain in the eyes caused by light.

photangiophobia an abnormal fear of photalgia.

photics the study of light.

photodrome 1. an apparatus that regulates light flashes so that a rotating object appears to be stationary or moving in a direction opposite to its actual motion.
2. an apparatus for producing unusual optical effects by flashing light upon disks bearing various figures, patterns, etc.

photodynamics the science or study of light in relation to the movement of plants. —photodynamic, photodynamical, *adj.*

photography the process or art of creating and recording images of people, objects, and phenomena, essentially by means of reflected light or emanating radiation. —photographer, *n.* —photographic, photographical, *adj.*

photokinesis movement of bodies, organisms, etc., in response to the stimulus of light. —photokinetic, *adj.*

photology optics.

photolysis the breakdown of matter or materials under the influence of light. —photolytic, *adj.*

photomania an abnormal love of light.

photometry the measurement of the intensity of light. —photometrician, photometrist, *n.* —photometric, *adj.*

photopathy a pathologic effect produced by light. —photopathic, *adj.*

photophily the tendency to thrive in strong light, as plants. —photophilic, *adj.*

photophobia 1. an abnormal fear of light.
2. Also called **photodysphoria.** a painful sensitivity to light, especially visually.
3. a tendency to thrive in reduced light, as certain plants.

photosynthesis the synthesis of complex organic substances from carbon dioxide, water, and inorganic salts, with sunlight as the energy source and a catalyst such as chlorophyll. —photosynthetic, *adj.*

phototaxis, phototaxy the movement of an organism away from or toward a source of light. —phototactic, *adj.*

phototherapy, phototherapeutics the treatment of disease, especially diseases of the skin, with light rays. —phototherapeutic, *adj.*

phototropism motion in a particular direction under the stimulus of light, as manifested by certain plants, organisms, etc. —phototropic, *adj.*

polarimetry the measurement of the polarization of light, as with a polarimeter.

selaphobia an abnormal fear or dislike of flashes of light.

spectrogram a photograph of a spectrum. Also called spectrograph.

spectrograph 1. an optical device for breaking light down into a spectrum and recording the results photographically.
2. spectrogram. —spectrographic, *adj.*

spectrography the technique of using a spectrograph and producing spectrograms.

triboluminescence a form of luminescence created by friction. —triboluminescent, *adj.*

246. LIGHTNING
See also 27. ATMOSPHERE; 87. CLOUDS; 345. RAIN; 394. THUNDER; 417. WEATHER.

astraphobia, astrapophobia an abnormal fear of lightning.

ceraunography keraunography. —ceraunograph, *n.* —ceraunographic, *adj.*

ceraunophobia keraunophobia.

ceraunoscopia keraunoscopia.

keraunography, ceraunography the recording of occurrences of lightning and thunder on a time scale attached to a revolving drum. —keraunograph, *n.* —keraunographic, *adj.*

keraunophobia, ceraunophobia an abnormal fear of thunder and lightning.

keraunoscopia, ceraunoscopia, keraunoscopy a form of divination involving thunder and lightning.

247. LINGUISTICS
See also 186. GRAMMAR; 236. LANGUAGE; 330. PRONUNCIATION; 382. SPEECH.

betacism 1. excessive use of the sound *b.*
2. improper articulation of this sound. —betacist, *n.*

biolinguistics the study of the relations between physiology and speech. —biolinguist, *n.*

cherology the description and analysis of the distinctive units used in the sign language of the deaf. —**cherologist,** *n.* —**cherologic, cherological,** *adj.*

diachronism, diachrony the study and description of the change or development in the structural systems of a language over a stated period of time. Also called **historical linguistics.** Cf. **synchronic linguistics.** —**diachronic,** *adj.*

dialect a variety of a language peculiar to a particular region or group within a larger community, usually but not always existing in the spoken form only. —**dialectal,** *adj.*

dialect geography the study of dialects with regard to their geographic distribution, as well as how their distribution may be affected by geography, e.g., the spread of a particular dialect being halted at a mountain range, forest belt, body of water, etc.

dialectology 1. the study of dialects and dialect features.
2. the linguistic features of a dialect. —**dialectician, dialectologist,** *n.* —**dialectologic, dialectological,** *adj.*

echoism 1. the formation of sounds like those in nature; onomatopoesis.
2. the tendency of paired sounds to become more similar phonetically, as the *d* sound in *iced tea* which has become a *t;* assimilation. —**echoic,** *adj.*

etymology the study of the origin and history of individual words. —**etymologist,** *n.* —**etymological,** *adj.*

folk etymology the reanalysis of a word by native speakers into a new element or elements, e.g. *hamburger* (properly 'from Hamburg') being split into *ham-* and *-burger;* and the subsequent combination of *-burger* with a number of words in which it is used to mean 'ground patty.'

gammacism, gammacismus the inability to pronounce the soft palatal consonants such as *g* and *k.*

geolinguistics the study or science of linguistics in relation to geography. —**geolinguist,** *n.* —**geolinguistic,** *adj.*

glossematics the science or study of glossemes, the smallest unit of linguistic communication. —**glossematic,** *adj.*

glossologist *Archaic.* 1. a linguist; a philologist.
2. one who compiles glossaries.

glossology *Archaic.* linguistics.

glottochronology a statistical and lexical study of two languages deriving from a common source to determine the time of their divergence, as English and German. Cf. **lexicostatistics.** —**glottochronologist,** *n.* —**glottochronological,** *adj.*

glottology the science of linguistics.

grammar 1. the study of the formal system of a language, especially the aspects of sound, forms, and syntax.
2. a work detailing such an analysis. —grammarian, *n.* —grammatic, grammatical, *adj.*

graphemics the study of systems of writing and their relationship to the systems of the languages they represent. Also called graphonomy. —graphemic, *adj.*

hybridism 1. a word formed from elements drawn from different languages.
2. the practice of coining such words. —hybrid, *n., adj.*

idiolect a person's individual speech habits.

lallation *Phonetics.* 1. the replacement of *l* for *r* in speech.
2. the mispronunciation of *l.* Cf. lambdacism.

lambdacism *Phonetics.* the mispronunciation of double *l,* giving it the sound of *y* or *ly.*
2. Cf. rhotacism. substitution of the sound *l* for another sound, as that of *r.* Also labdacism. Cf. lallation.

lexicography the writing, editing, or compiling of dictionaries. —lexicographer, *n.* —lexicographic, lexicographical, *adj.*

lexicology the study of the meanings of words and of idiomatic combinations. —lexicologist, *n.* —lexicologic, lexicological, *adj.*

lexicostatistics the study of languages and their vocabularies by statistical methods for historical purposes. Cf. **glottochronology.** —lexicostatistic, lexicostatistical, *adj.*

lexigraphy *Rare.* the art of defining words or compiling lexicons. —lexigraphic, *adj.*

linguistic typology the classification of languages by structural similarity, e.g., similarity of syntactic or phonemic features, as opposed to classification on the basis of shared linguistic ancestry.

metalinguistics the science or study of language in relation to its cultural context. —metalinguist, *n.* —metalinguistic, metalinguistical, *adj.*

morphemics the study and description of the morphemes of a language, i.e., its minimum grammatical units, as *wait* and *-ed* in *waited.* —morphemicist, *n.*

morphology 1. a branch of linguistics that studies and describes patterns of word formation, including inflection, derivation, and compounding of a language.
2. such patterns of a particular language. —morphologist, *n.* —morphological, *adj.*

morphophonemics 1. the study of the relations between morphemes and their phonetic realizations, components, or distribution contexts.
2. the body of data concerning these relations in a specific language. —morphophonemicist, *n.* —morphophonemic, *adj.*

nasalism a tendency toward nasality in pronouncing words. Also **nasality.**

onomasiology onomastics. —onomasiologist, *n.* —onomasiologic, onomasiological, *adj.*

onomastics the study of names and their origins. —onomastic, *adj.* —onomastician, *n.*

orthoepy the study of correct pronunciation. —orthoepist, *n.* —orthoepic, orthoepical, orthoepistic, *adj.*

paronymy the state or condition of containing the same root or stem, as *perilous* and *parlous.* —paronym, *n.*

philology 1. the study of written records to determine their authenticity, original form, and meaning.
2. linguistics, especially historical linguistics. —philologist, philologer, *n.* —philologic, philological, *adj.*

phonematics phonemics.

phonemics 1. the study and description of phonemes, i.e., the set of basic units of sound used in a language and phonemic systems.
2. the phonemic system of a given language. Also **phonematics.** —phonemicist, *n.*

phonetics 1. the science or study of speech sounds and their production, transmission, and perception, and their analysis, classification, and transcription.
2. the science or study of speech sounds with respect to their role in distinguishing meanings among words.
3. the phonetic system of a particular language. Cf. **phonology.** —phonetician, *n.* —phonetic, phonetical, *adj.*

phonology 1. the study of the history and theory of sound changes in a language or in two or more languages comparatively.
2. the phonetics and phonemics of a language at a stated time; synchronic phonology. —phonologist, *n.* —phonological, *adj.*

psycholinguistics the study of the relationships between language and the behavioral mechanisms of its users, especially in language learning by children. —psycholinguist, *n.* —psycholinguistic, *adj.*

rhotacism *Phonetics.* 1. a misarticulation of the sound *r* or the substitution of another sound for it.
2. Cf. **lambdacism.** substitution of the sound sound *r* for another sound, as that of *l.*

2. the excessive use of the sound *r*.

3. *Phonology.* replacement of the sound *z* or *s* by *r* in Indo-European languages, as German *wesen*, English *were*. —rhotacize, *v.* —rhotacistic, *adj.*

semantics 1. the study of the meaning of words.
2. the study of linguistic development by examining and classifying changes in meaning. Also called semasiology, sematology, semology. —semanticist, *n.* —semantic, *adj.*

semasiology, sematology semantics.

semeiology, semiology, semology the study or science of signs; semantics. —semeiologist, semiologist, *n.* —semeiologic, semiologic, semeiological, semiological, *adj.*

semiotics, semiotic the study of the relationship between symbology and language. —semiotician, semioticist, *n.*

sigmatism a faulty pronunciation of sibilant sounds.

structuralism an emphasis in research and description upon the systematic relations of formal distinctions in a given language. Also called structural linguistics. —structuralist, *n.*

synchronic linguistics the study of the phonological, morphological, and syntactic features of a language at a stated time. Also called descriptive linguistics. Cf. diachronism.

syntax the study of the principles by which words are used in phrases and sentences to construct meaningful combinations. —syntactic, syntactical, *adj.*

tagmemics the study of the tagmemes of a language, i.e., the minimal units of grammatical construction, embodying such phenomena as distinctive word order and grammatical agreement. —tagmemic, *adj.*

tonetics the phonetic study and science of the tonal aspects of language. —tonetician, *n.* —tonetic, *adj.*

transformationalist an advocate or student of the theory of transformational grammar, a system of grammatical analysis that uses transformations of base sentences to explain the relations between thought and its syntactic manifestation and to express the relations between elements in a sentence, clause, or phrase, or between different forms of a word or phrase, as active or passive forms of a verb.

vocalism *Phonetics.* the system of vowels in a given language. —vocalic, *adj.*

248. LITERARY STYLE
See also 29. AUTHORS; 237. LANGUAGE STYLE; 249. LITERATURE.

Acmeism the work and theories of the Acmeists, an anti-symbolist movement of early twentieth-century Russian poets, including Mandelstam and Akhmatova, who strove for lucidity of style, definiteness, and texture in their poetry. —acmeist, *n., adj.*

Byronism the characteristics of the poetry and writings of George Gordon, Lord Byron (1788–1824).

centonism the practice, especially in verse, of writing by arranging quotations from other authors. Also **centonization.** —**cento,** *n.* —**centonical,** *adj.*

Ciceronianism the imitation of Cicero's literary and oratorical style. —**Ciceronist,** *n.* —**Ciceronian,** *adj.*

classicalism 1. an imitation of Greek or Roman literature. 2. classicism. —**classicalize,** *v.* —**classicalist,** *n.*

classicism a literary style characterized by formal adherence to traditions of structure, content, and genre. —**classicist,** *n.* —**classicize,** *v.*

conceptism *Rare.* the use of a particular form of literary conceit in Spanish prose.

concinnity harmony or fitness, especially of literary style. —**concinnous,** *adj.*

constructivism the theories, attitudes, and techniques of a group of Soviet writers of the 1920s who attempted to reconcile ideological beliefs with technical achievement, especially in stage design, where the effects produced were geometrical and nonrepresentational. —**constructivist,** *n.*, *adj.*

dialogism, dialoguism the representation of an author's thoughts through his use of a dialogue between two or more of his characters. —**dialogist,** *n.* —**dialogic,** *adj.*

eulogism an expression of praise or blessing as used in a eulogy. —**eulogization,** *n.* —**eulogistic,** *adj.*

Euphuism 1. an elaborate prose style invented by John Lyly c. 1580, characterized by bountiful figures of speech, Latinisms, extended similes, frequent antitheses, and highly involved syntax. 2. any similar ornate style of writing or speaking. Cf. **Gongorism.** —**euphuist,** *n.* —**euphuistic,** *adj.*

floridity a florid style; flowery and highly ornamented writing. See also 95. COMPLEXION. —**florid,** *adj.*

genteelism a polished style and graceful form in literary works.

Gongorism a Spanish verse style invented by the 17th-century poet Luis de Góngora y Argote, characterized by a studied obscurity, an emphasis on Latin terms and syntax, allusions to classical myths, and lavish use of metaphors, hyperbole, paradoxes, neologisms, and antitheses. Also called **cultismo, culteranismo.** Cf. **Euphuism.** —**Gongoristic, Gongoresque,** *adj.*

gothicism a style in fictional literature characterized by gloomy settings, violent or grotesque action, and a mood of decay, degeneration, and decadence. —**gothicist,** *n.* —**gothic,** *adj.*

Hermeticism 1. the occult concepts, ideas, or philosophy set forth in the writings of the hermeticists of the late Middle Ages and the early Renaissance.
2. adherence to, belief in, or propagation of these concepts and ideas.
3. a symbolic and arcane style similar to that of the hermeticists, especially in the poetry of certain French symbolist poets. —**hermeticist, hermetist,** *n.* —**hermetic, hermetical,** *adj.*

Ibsenism a dramatic invention characteristic of Henrik Ibsen, used in attacking conventional hypocrisies.

Johnsonese the literary style of Samuel Johnson or a style similar to or in emulation of his, especially one that is turgid and orotund.

juvenilia 1. the literary compositions produced in an author's youth.
2. literary productions intended for the young.

Kiplingism 1. a style resembling or having the features of the literary style of Rudyard Kipling.
2. an attitude of superiority over and sympathy for nonwhite peoples, as found in "Gunga Din." —**Kiplingesque,** *adj.*

Marinism a 17th-century Italian literary style marked by forced antitheses and elaborate metaphors. —**Marinist,** *n.*

Marlowism the style and topics characteristic of Christopher Marlowe. —**Marlovian, Marlowish, Marlowesque,** *adj.*

Ossianism writing in the style of Ossian and particularly writing in the epic or legendary vein which is of a recent period but which claims to belong to antiquity. [After Ossian or Oisin, an apocryphal Gaelic poet of the third century, whose supposed style was imitated in works created by James Macpherson (1736–1796).] —**Ossianic,** *adj.*

pastoralism a writing style that focuses on the life of shepherds or herdsman. —**pastoralist,** *n.*

Petrarchism a style of writing that is modeled after that of Petrarch. —**Petrarchist,** *n.* —**Petrarchan,** *adj.*

poetasterism the writing of a poetaster, an inferior and worthless poetry.

prosaicism a phrase written in the style of prose. Also **prosaism.** —**prosaist,** *n.* —**prosaic, prosaical,** *adj.*

quattrocentism the art and literature of 15th-century Italy. —**quattrocentist,** *n., adj.*

Ronsardism the composition of verse after the manner of French poet Pierre de Ronsard (1524–1585), characterized by neologisms and dialectal forms.

sensationalism 1. the use of subject matter, language, or style designed to amaze or thrill. See also 265. MEDIA; 312. PHILOSOPHY,
2. such subject matter, language, or style itself. —**sensationalist,** *n.* —**sensationalistic,** *adj.*

sentimentalism an excessive indulgence in sentiment or emotionalism, predominance of feeling over reason and intellect, as the death scene of Little Nell in Dickens's *Old Curiosity Shop.* —sentimentalist, *n.*

Shakespearianism the condition of having the qualities of or relating to the literary works of William Shakespeare. —Shakespearian, *n.*, *adj.*

Shavianism a comment, statement, etc., typical or reminiscent of or a quotation from the works of George Bernard Shaw. —Shavian, *adj.*

stylistics the study of particular styles, as in literature, art, etc.

Tolstoyism doctrines espoused in the works of Tolstoy, Russian novelist and social critic. —Tolstoyist, *n.*

Voltairianism, Voltairism the doctrines of Voltaire, marked mainly by religious skepticism, frequently seen in his literary works, such as *Candide.* —Voltairian, *n.*, *adj.*

Zolaism 1. an overemphasis on the coarser sides of life.
2. the objective types of naturalism and determinism underlying Zola's novelistic methods. —Zolaist, *n.*

249. LITERATURE

See also 29. AUTHORS; 53. BOOKS; 104. CRITICISM; 109. DANTE;
127. DRAMA; 236. LANGUAGE; 237. LANGUAGE STYLE; 248. LITERARY
STYLE; 256. MANUSCRIPTS; 328. PRINTING; 346. READING;
354. RHETORIC and RHETORICAL DEVICES; 409. VERSE; 428. WRITING.

Alexandrianism the style and theories of the Greek writers of Alexandria, 325–30 B.C., whose style was highly ornamented and obscure and favored such forms as the elegy, epigram, epyllion, and lyric and also ventured into the drama. —Alexandrianist, *n.*, *adj.*

allegory an art form, as a story, painting, or sculpture, in which the components have a symbolic, figurative meaning. —allegorist, allegorizer, *n.* —allegorical, *adj.*

anachorism the placing of a scene, character, event, etc., where it clearly does not belong, either for special effect or as an oversight. See also anachronism. —anachoristic, *adj.*

anachronism an error in chronology, as the placing of an event or figure in a period or scene in which it did not or could not belong. —anachronistic, *adj.*

anthology a collection of stories, poems, or other literary material. See also 80. CHRISTIANITY. —anthologist, *n.*

antiphrasis the satirical or humorous use of a word or phrase to convey an idea exactly opposite to its real significance, as Shakespeare's "honorable men" for Caesar's murderers. —antiphrastic, *adj.*

autoplagiarism the act or process of plagiarizing one's own work.

belletrism, belles-lettrism the view that literature is a fine art, especially as having a purely aesthetic function. —**belletrist,** *n.* —**belles lettres,** *n.* —**belletristic,** *adj.*

bestiary an allegorical or moralizing commentary, usually medieval and sometimes illustrated, based upon real or fabled animals.

bestsellerism the condition of having a book on the bestseller list.

bowdlerism the expurgation of a literary work in a highly prudish manner. Also **bowdlerization.** —**bowdlerize,** *v.*

cinquecentism the revival in arts and letters in the 16th century in Italy. —**cinquecentist,** *n., adj.*

criticism 1. the act or art of analyzing the quality of something, especially a literary or artistic work, a musical or dramatic performance, etc.
2. a critical comment, article, or essay; critique. —**critic,** *n.*

culturist a person who is well acquainted with culture, as literature, the arts, etc., and who advocates their worth to society.

diplomatology the analysis of original texts or documents.

duecentism the art and literature of 13th-century Italy. —**duecentist,** *n., adj.*

epistolography the art or practice of writing letters. —**epistolographic,** *adj.*

erotographomania an abnormal interest in erotic literature.

essayism 1. the habit of writing essays.
2. the quality that allows a composition to be called an essay. —**essayist,** *n.*

florilegium an anthology or select collection of literary pieces.

glossography the writing or compilation of marginal or interlinear notes in a manuscript text. —**glossographer,** *n.*

harmonist a scholar of literature who shows parallels or harmony between passages from different authors. See also 284. MUSIC.

Imagism a theory or practice of a group of English and American poets between 1909 and 1917, especially emphasis upon the use of common speech, new rhythms, unrestricted subject matter, and clear and precise images. —**Imagist,** *n.* —**Imagistic,** *adj.*

Mekhitarist a member of an order of Armenian monks, founded in 1715 by Mekhitar da Pietro, dedicated to literary work, especially the perfecting of the Armenian language and the translation into it of the major works of other languages.

melodramaticism an emphasis in narrative or dramatic literary works on the sensational in situation or action. —**melodramatist,** *n.* —**melodramatic,** *adj.*

memoirism the art or practice of writing memoirs. —**memoirist,** *n.*

Micawberism the excessively optimistic outlook of Wilkins Micawber, a character from Dickens's novel *David Copperfield.* —**Micawberish,** *adj.*

paleography, palaeography 1. ancient forms of writing, as in inscriptions, documents, and manuscripts.
2. the study of ancient writings, including decipherment, translation, and determination of age and date. —**paleographer, palaeographer,** *n.* —**paleographic, palaeographic,** *adj.*

Parnassianism the theories and practice of a school of French poets in the 19th century, especially an emphasis upon art for art's sake, careful metrics, and the repression of emotive elements. —**Parnassian,** *n., adj.*

Pecksniffianism the quality of being hypocritical or selfish like Dickens's character Seth Pecksniff in the novel *Martin Chuzzlewit.* —**Pecksniffery,** *n.* —**Pecksniffian,** *adj.*

pornographomania an abnormal interest in pornography.

purism strict adherence to particular concepts, rules, or ideals of form, style, etc., either as formulated by the artist or as dictated by a school with which the artist is allied. See also 23. ART; 104. CRITICISM; 236. LANGUAGE. —**purist,** *n., adj.*

regionalism a quality in literature that is the product of fidelity to the habits, speech, manners, history, folklore, and beliefs of a particular geographical section, as Thomas Hardy and Wessex. —**regionalist,** *n.* —**regionalistic,** *adj.*

scholiast an ancient commentator on the classics, especially the writing of marginalia (*scholia*) on grammatical and interpretive cruxes. —**scholiastic,** *adj.*

sillography the writing of satires. —**sillographer,** *n.*

storiology the systematic study of folklore and folk literature, especially concerning origin and transmission. —**storiologist,** *n.*

Struldbrugism the actions or characteristics of the imaginary inhabitants of Luggnagg, a country created by Swift in *Gulliver's Travels.*

Symbolism the principles of a literary movement originated during the latter part of the 19th century in France and highly influential in literature written in English, characterized especially by an emphasis upon the associative character of verbal, often private, symbols and the use of synesthetic devices to suggest color and music. —**Symbolist,** *n., adj.*

teratology 1. a type of mythmaking or storytelling in which monsters and marvels are featured.
2. a collection of such stories. —**teratologist,** *n.* —**teratological,** *adj.*

tetralogy a series of four related works. —**tetralogist,** *n.* —**tetralogical,** *adj.*

theotechny the introduction of gods or supernatural entities into a dramatic or literary work, especially to resolve situations. —**theotechnic,** *adj.*

trilogy a series of three related works. —**trilogist,** *n.* —**trilogical,** *adj.*

Wertherism the condition of having romantic qualities like Werther, a character from Goethe's *The Sorrows of Werther*. —Wertherian, *adj*.

Xanaduism a variety of academic or literary research attempting to find the sources behind works of the imagination, named after a noted study of this kind, John Livingston Lowes' *Road to Xanadu* (1927), an inquiry into Coleridge's poem, "Xanadu." —Xanaduist, *n., adj*.

250. LOGIC
See also 21. ARGUMENTATION; 262. MATHEMATICS; 312. PHILOSOPHY; 393. THINKING; 402. TRUTH and ERROR.

a posteriori the process of reasoning from effect to cause, based upon observation.

apriorism 1. the method of *a priori* reasoning, i.e., deductive reasoning, from cause to effect or from the general to the particular.
2. an *a priori* principle.

Barbara a mnemonic word to represent a syllogistic argument in the first figure, in which there are two universal affirmative premises and a universal affirmative conclusion.

Barmalip, Bramantip a mnemonic word to represent a syllogistic argument in the fourth figure, in which there are two universal affirmative premises and a particular affirmative conclusion.

Baroco a mnemonic word to represent a syllogistic argument in the second figure, in which there is one universal affirmative and one particular negative premise and a particular negative conclusion.

Bocardo a mnemonic word to represent a syllogistic argument in the third figure, in which there is one particular negative and one universal affirmative premise and a particular negative conclusion.

Camestres a mnemonic word to represent a syllogistic argument in the second figure, in which there is one universal affirmative and one universal negative premise and a universal negative conclusion.

Celarent a mnemonic word to represent a syllogistic argument in the first figure, in which there is one universal negative and one universal affirmative premise and a universal negative conclusion.

Cesare a mnemonic word to represent a syllogistic argument in the second figure, in which there is one universal negative and one universal affirmative premise and a universal negative conclusion.

Darapti a mnemonic word to represent a syllogistic argument in the third figure, in which there are two universal affirmative premises and a particular affirmative conclusion.

Darii a mnemonic word to represent a syllogistic argument in the first figure, in which there is one universal affirmative and one particular affirmative premise and a particular affirmative conclusion.

Datisi a mnemonic word to represent a syllogistic argument in the third figure, in which there is one universal affirmative and one particular affirmative premise and a particular affirmative conclusion.

definiendum 1. an expression that has to be defined in terms of a previously defined expression.
2. anything that has to be defined. —**definienda**, *n.*, *pl.*

Dimaris Dimatis.

Dimatis a mnemonic word to represent a syllogistic argument in the fourth figure, in which there is one universal affirmative and one affirmative premise and a particular affirmative conclusion. Also called **Dimaris**.

Disamis a mnemonic word to represent a syllogistic argument in the third figure, in which there is one particular affirmative and one universal affirmative premise and a particular affirmative conclusion.

elenchus a syllogistic argument that refutes a proposition by proving the direct opposite of its conclusion. —**elenchic, elenctic,** *adj.*

epicheirema a syllogism in which the truth of one of the premises is confirmed by an annexed proposition (*prosyllogism*), thus resulting in the formation of a compound argument. See also **prosyllogism**.

equipollence, equipollency equality between two or more propositions, as when two propositions have the same meaning but are expressed differently. See also 4. AGREEMENT.

Felapton a mnemonic word to represent a syllogistic argument in the third figure, in which there is one universal negative and one universal affirmative premise and a particular negative conclusion.

Ferio a mnemonic word to represent a syllogistic argument in the first figure, in which there is one universal negative and one particular affirmative premise and a particular negative conclusion.

Feriso a mnemonic word to represent a syllogistic argument in the third figure, in which there is one universal negative and one particular affirmative premise and a particular negative conclusion. Also **Ferison**.

Ferison Feriso.

Fesapo a mnemonic word to represent a syllogistic argument in the fourth figure, in which there is one universal negative and one universal affirmative premise and a particular negative conclusion.

Festino a mnemonic word to represent a syllogistic argument in the second figure, in which there is one universal negative and one particular affirmative premise and a particular negative conclusion.

Fresison a mnemonic word to represent a syllogistic argument in the fourth figure, in which there is one universal negative and one particular affirmative premise and a particular negative conclusion.

metalogic the metaphysics or metaphysical aspects of logic. —**metalogical,** *adj.*

methodology a division of logic devoted to the application of reasoning to science and philosophy. See also 83. CLASSIFICATION; 301. ORDER and DISORDER. —**methodological,** *adj.*

polylemma a multiple dilemma or one with many equally unacceptable alternatives; a difficult predicament.

prosyllogism a syllogism connected with another in such a way that the conclusion of the first is the premise of the one following.

schematism the form or character of a syllogism.

sorites an elliptical series of syllogism, in which the premises are so arranged that the predicate of the first is the subject of the next, continuing thus until the subject of the first is united with the predicate of the last. —**soritical, soritic,** *adj.*

syllogism a form of reasoning in which two propositions or premises are stated and a logical conclusion is drawn from them. Each premise has the subject-predicate form, and each shares a common element called the *middle term*.

syntheticism the principles or practice of synthesis or synthetic methods or techniques, i.e., the process of deductive reasoning, as from cause to effect, from the simple elements to the complex whole, etc.

251. LOVE

free-lovism the doctrine or practice of having sexual relations without marriage or any other commitment to an obligation.

inamorata a female lover or a woman who is loved.

inamorato a male lover or a man who is loved.

philauty *Obsolete.* self love; an excessive regard for oneself.

philostorgy *Obsolete.* natural love or affection.

M

252. MAGIC

See also 7. ALCHEMY; 124. DIVINATION; 285. MYSTICISM; 384. SPIRITS and SPIRITUALISM.

abracadabrism a reliance upon incantations or charms, often inscribed upon amulets, to ward off calamity. —**abracadabra**, *n*.

apotropaism the acting out of magic rites or the recital of incantatory formulas to ward off evil. —**apotropaic**, *adj*.

demonomagy *Obsolete*. forms of magic that require the invocation or assistance of demons.

illusionist a conjurer or magician who creates illusions, as by sleight of hand.

jujuism an African variety of magical fetishism characterized by the wearing of an exotic amulet called a *juju*. —**jujuist**, *n*.

legerdemain skill in or practice of feats of dexterity that create a magical illusion. —**legerdemainist**, *n*.

metamorphosis 1. change in form, structure, appearance, etc.
2. magical transformation. —**metamorphic, metamorphous**, *adj*.

obeahism 1. a kind of sorcery practiced by the black people of Africa, the West Indies, and elsewhere. Also called **obi, obism**.
2. the wearing of an obeah, a fetish or charm. Also called **obi**.

powwowism the belief among American Indians that a ceremony characterized by magic, feasting, and dancing can cure disease, ensure the success of a hunt or battle, etc. —**powwow**, *n*.

prestidigitation the art of legerdemain; sleight of hand. —**prestidigitator**, *n*. —**prestidigitatorial, prestidigitatory**, *adj*.

preternaturalism a condition of being exceptional or bizarre, beyond the realm of the ordinary course of nature. —**preternatural**, *adj*.

sorcery the art, practices, or spells of a person who is supposed to exercise supernatural powers through the aid of evil spirits; black magic; witchery. —**sorcerer**, *n*. —**sorcerous**, *adj*.

sortilege a form of divination involving drawing lots.

supernaturalism 1. the condition or quality of existing outside the known experience of man or caused by forces beyond those of nature.
2. belief in supernatural events or forces. Also **supranaturalism.** —supernaturalist, *n.*, *adj.* —supernatural, supernaturalistic, *adj.*

supranaturalism supernaturalism. —supranaturalist, *n.*, *adj.* —supranatural, supranaturalistic, *adj.*

synecdochism the belief that a part of a person or object can act in place of the whole and thus that anything done to the part will equally affect the whole.

thaumaturgism the quality of being able to perform magic. —thaumaturgist, *n.* —thaumaturgic, *adj.* —thaumaturgy, *n.*

theurgist a magician who persuades or compels a supernatural being to do or refrain from doing something. —theurgy, *n.* —theurgic, theurgical, *adj.*

voodooism, voudouism 1. the religious rites or practices, including magic or sorcery, of certain West Indian black people.
2. the practice of sorcery. —voodooist, *n.*

warlockry *Archaic.* sorcery; the craft or practice of a warlock.

witchery witchcraft or sorcery.

wizardry the art or practice of a wizard; sorcery; magic. —wizard, *n.*, *adj.*

Zendicism *Middle East.* 1. the practice of atheism.
2. the practice of heretical magic, especially with fire. —Zendic, Zendik, *n.* —Zendaic, *adj.*

253. MALE

See also 153. FATHER; 255. MANKIND; 364. SEX; 424. WOMEN.

androcracy the domination of society and politics by males. —androcratic, *adj.*

androgenesis *Biology.* the condition of an embryo that contains only paternal chromosomes; male parthenogenesis. —androgenetic, *adj.*

andromania in women, an obsession with men; nymphomania.

androphilia a preference for males. —androphilic, *adj.*

androphobia 1. an abnormal fear of men.
2. a hatred of males.

bachelorism 1. dedication to the state of being a bachelor.
2. behavior typical of a bachelor.

misandry, misandria in women, an abnormal aversion to males.

patriarchy 1. a community in which the father or oldest male is the supreme authority, and descent is traced through the male line.
2. government by males, with one as supreme. —patriarchist, *n.* —patriarchic, patriarchical, *adj.*

virilescence a condition of some animals, and especially of some fowls, in which the female, when old, assumes some of the characteristics of the male of the species. —virilescent, *adj.*

254. MANIAS
See also 150. FADS; 224. INSANITY; 311. -PHILE, -PHILIA, -PHILY; 313. PHOBIAS.

N.B.: Noun forms end in -mania and adjective forms end in -maniac or -maniacal.

acromania a violent form of mania; incurable insanity.

agoramania a mania for open spaces.

agyiomania a mania for streets.

ailuromania an abnormal love of cats.

alcoholomania an obsession with alcohol.

amaxomania a mania for being in vehicles.

amenomania a mania for pleasing delusions.

Americamania an obsession with America and things American.

andromania an obsession with men; nymphomania.

aphrodisiomania a mania for sexual pleasure.

apimania an abnormal love of bees.

automania an excessive liking for solitude.

autophonomania an obsession with suicide.

ballistomania an extreme interest in bullets.

bibliomania an excessive fondness for acquiring and possessing books.

cheromania an extreme love for gaiety.

Chinamania an obsession with China and things Chinese.

chionomania a mania for snow.

choreomania a mania for dancing.

chrematomania a mania for money.

clinomania an obsession with bed rest.

coprolalomania a mania for foul speech.

cremnomania an abnormal interest in cliffs.

cresomania a mania for great wealth.

cynomania an abnormal love of dogs.

Dantomania an obsession with Dante and his works.

demomania ochlomania.

doramania a mania for fur.

drapetomania a mania for running away.

dromomania a mania for travel.

ecdemiomania a mania for wandering.

edeomania an obsession with genitals.

empleomania an obsession with public employment.

enomania a mania for wine. Also called **oinomania.**

entheomania a mania for religion.

entomomania an abnormal love of insects.

eremiomania a mania for stillness.

ergasiomania a mania for activity.

ergomania a mania for work.

eroticomania an abnormal interest in erotica.

erotographomania an abnormal interest in erotic literature.

erotomania an excessive propensity for sexual desire.

erythromania a mania for blushing.

etheromania a mania for ether.

florimania a mania for plants and flowers.

Francomania an obsession with France and things French.

gamomania 1. *Obsolete.* a form of mania characterized by strange and extravagant proposals of marriage.
2. an excessive longing for the married state.

gephyromania a mania for crossing bridges.

Germanomania an obsession with Germany and things German. Also called **Teutonomania.**

graphomania an obsession with writing.

Grecomania an obsession with Ancient Greece and Greeks.

gymnomania a mania for nakedness.

gynecomania abnormal sexual desire for women.

hamartomania an obsession with sin.

hedonomania a mania for pleasure.

heliomania an abnormal love of the sun.

hieromania a mania for priests.

hippomania a mania for horses.

hodomania an abnormal love of travel.

homicidomania a mania for murder.

hydrodipsomania an abnormal love of drinking water.

hydromania an excessive love of water.

hylomania a mania for wood.

hypermania an acute mania.

hypnomania a mania for sleep.

hypomania a mild mania; submania.

hysteromania nymphomania.

ichthyomania an abnormal love of fish.

iconomania a mania for icons.

idolomania a mania for idols.

Italomania an obsession with Italy and things Italian.

kainomania a mania for novelty.

kathisomania a mania for sitting.

kinesomania a mania for movement.

lalomania an abnormal love of speech or talking.

lethomania a mania for narcotics.

logomania a mania for words or talking.

lycomania lycanthropy, a form of insanity in which a person imagines himself to be a wolf.

lypemania an abnormal tendency toward deep melancholy.

macromania a mania for becoming larger.

mania 1. a type of manic-depressive psychosis, exemplified by rapidly changing ideas, extremes of emotion, and physical overactivity.
2. any violent or abnormal behavior. —**maniac**, *n.* —**maniacal**, *adj.*

mentulomania an obsession with the penis.

mesmeromania an obsession with hypnosis.

micromania a mania for becoming smaller.

monomania 1. a partial insanity in which psychotic thinking is confined to one subject or group of subjects.
2. an excessive interest in or enthusiasm for a single thing, idea, or the like; obsession.

musicomania a mania for music.

musomania an abnormal love for mice.

necromania an obsession with death or the dead. Cf. **thanatomania**.

noctimania an abnormal love of the night.

nosomania an obsession with imagined disease. See also **hypochondriacism**.

nudomania a mania for nudity.

nymphomania in a woman, a mania for frequent, continued sexual intercourse. Also called **oestromania**. Cf. **satyromania**.

ochlomania a mania for crowds. Also called **demomania**.

oestromania nymphomania.

oikomania an abnormal attachment to home.

oinomania a mania for wine. Also called **enomania**.

oligomania a mania confined to several subjects. Cf. **monomania**, def. 1.

oniomania an excessive desire to buy articles of all kinds.

ophidiomania an abnormal love of reptiles.

opsomania a mania for special kinds of food. Cf. **phagomania**, **sitomania**.

orchidomania an obsession with testicles.

ornithomania an abnormal love of birds.

paramania an abnormal pleasure in complaints.

parousiamania an abnormal anticipation of the second coming of Christ.

pathomania moral insanity.

phagomania a mania for food and eating. Cf. **opsomania**, **sitomania**.

phaneromania a mania for picking at growths.

pharmacomania a mania for medicines.

philopatridomania homesickness.

phonomania an abnormal love of noise.

photomania an abnormal love of light.

phronemomania a mania for thinking.

phthisiomania an abnormal interest in tuberculosis.

politicomania a mania for politics.

pornographomania an abnormal interest in pornography.

potomania 1. an excessive tendency to drink alcoholic beverages.
2. delirium tremens. Also called **tromomania**.

Russomania an obsession with Russia and things Russian.

satyromania in a man, a mania for frequent, continued sexual intercourse. Cf. **nymphomania**.

scribomania a mania for writing.

sideromania an obsession with railroad travel.

sitomania an obsession with food. Cf. **phagomania**, **opsomania**.

sophomania an excessive respect for one's own wisdom.

squandermania a mania for spending money.

submania a mild mania; hypomania.

symmetromania a mania for symmetry.

Teutonomania Germanomania.

thalassomania an abnormal love of the sea.

thanatomania an obsession with death. Cf. necromania.

theatromania a mania for the theater.

timbromania a mania for postage stamps.

tomomania an obsession with surgery.

trichomania an obsession with hair.

trichorrhexomania a mania for pinching off one's hair.

tristimania melancholy.

tromomania delirium tremens. Also called potomania.

Turkomania an obsession with Turkey and things Turkish.

typomania an obsession with the expectation of publication.

xenomania a mania for foreigners.

zoomania an abnormal love of animals.

255. MANKIND
See also 17. ANTHROPOLOGY; 341. RACE; 424. WOMEN.

agriology the study of the customs of uncivilized people, usually on the comparative level. —agriologist, *n*. —agriological, *adj*.

animalism the theory that human beings lack a spiritual nature; animality. —animalist, *n*. —animalistic, *adj*.

anthropoglot an animal with a tongue like that of man, as the parrot.

anthropography the branch of anthropology that describes the varieties of mankind and their geographical distribution. —anthropographer, *n*. —anthropographic, *adj*.

anthropoid a creature resembling man, as an ape. —anthropoid, —anthropoidal, *adj*.

anthropology the study of the origins, development, racial and social character, and beliefs of mankind. —anthropologist, *n*. —anthropological, *adj*.

anthroponomy *Rare*. the branch of anthropology that studies the interrelation of the laws regulating human behavior and environment. Also anthroponomics. —anthroponomist, *n*. —anthroponomical, *adj*.

anthropophilic of insects, attracted to human beings.

anthropophobia an abnormal fear of people.

anthroposophy a movement developed from theosophy by Rudolf Steiner, Austrian social philosopher, to develop the faculty of cognition and the awareness of spiritual reality. —anthroposophist, *n*. —anthroposophical, *adj*.

biotechnology ergonomics. —biotechnologist, *n*. —biotechnologic, biotechnological, *adj*.

demography the science of vital and social statistics, as of the deaths, births, marriages, etc., of populations. —demographer, *n*. —demographic, *adj*.

demology the study of human activities and social conditions. —demological, *adj*.

demophobia a hatred of people.

ergonomics the study of the various factors affecting man in his working environment. Also called biotechnology. —ergonomic, *adj*.

ethnography a branch of anthropology that studies and describes individual human cultures. —ethnographer, *n*. —ethnographic, ethnographical, *adj*.

ethology the science proposed by John Stuart Mill for the study of the character formation in humans. —ethologic, ethological, *adj*.

folklore the study of the traditions of a particular people in custom, song, story, belief, etc. —folklorist, *n*.

hominid any of the two-legged primates, extinct or living, including man. —hominid, *adj*.

homunculus 1. a small man or midget.
2. the microcosmic human form formerly believed to be present in spermatozoon.

humanism 1. any system or mode of thought or action in which human interests, values, and dignity are taken to be of primary importance, as in moral judgments.
2. a devotion to or study of the humanities.
3. a theory of the life of man as a responsible being behaving independently of a revelation or deity. Also called naturalistic, scientific, or philosophical humanism. —humanist, *n*. —humanistic, *adj*.

humanoid 1. a creature resembling man, as one of man's early ancestors.
2. *Science Fiction*. any manlike creature from another planet. —humanoid, *adj*.

microcosmography the figurative description of man as a miniature universe.

misanthropism, misanthropy a hatred or distrust of all people. —misanthrope, *n*. —misanthropic, *adj*.

monogenism the theory that the entire human race is descended from a single ancestral pair. Also monogenesis, monogeny. —monogenist, *n*. —monogenistic, *adj*.

paleethnology, paleoethnology the study of the races of early man. —**paleeth-nologic, paleethnological, paleoethnological,** *adj.* —**paleethnologist, paleoethno-logist,** *n.*

paleoethnography the ethnography of the prehistoric races of man.

philanthropism 1. an affection for mankind, especially as manifested in the devotion of work or wealth to persons or socially useful purposes.
2. activity revealing this affection. Also called **philanthropy.** —**philanthropist,** *n.* —**philanthropic, philanthropical,** *adj.*

sociology 1. the science or study of the origin, development, organization, and functioning of human society.
2. the science of fundamental laws of social behavior, relations, institutions, etc. —**sociologist,** *n.* —**sociological,** *adj.*

sociometry the measurement of attitudes of social acceptance or rejection among members of a social grouping. —**sociometrist,** *n.* —**sociometric,** *adj.*

256. MANUSCRIPTS
See also 53. BOOKS; 249. LITERATURE; 428. WRITING.

bibliotics the art or science of analyzing handwriting, especially that of manuscripts, with the purpose of establishing their authorship or authenticity. —**bibliotist,** *n.* —**bibliotic,** *adj.*

codicology the study of early manuscripts. —**codicologist,** *n.* —**codicologic, codicological,** *adj.*

diplomatics the critical study of original historical documents, as registers, treaties, and charters, especially from medieval periods.

holograph a manuscript or other document written completely in the hand of the person above whose name it appears. —**holograph, holographic,** *adj.*

illumination 1. the art of decorating manuscripts with illustrations, as in the capitals, tracery, etc.
2. the decoration itself.

palimpsest a parchment from which earlier writing has been partially or completely removed by scraping so that it may be used again. —**palimpses-tic,** *adj.*

papyrology the study of papyrus manuscripts. —**papyrologist,** *n.* —**papyro-logical,** *adj.*

scriptorium a room in a monastery for the writing or copying of manuscripts.

scrivenery the art and practice of the scrivener or copyist. —**scrivener,** *n.*

257. MAPS
See also 178. GEOGRAPHY; 352. REPRESENTATION; 399. TRAVEL.

aerocartography the process of mapmaking by means of aerial survey.

cartography the production of maps, including construction of projections, design, compilation, drafting, and reproduction. Also **chartography, chartology.** —**cartographer,** *n.* —**cartographic,** *adj.*

chorography 1. a description, map, or chart of a particular region or area. 2. the art of preparing such descriptions or maps. —**chorographer,** *n.* —**chorographic,** *adj.*

loxodrome a rhumb line or curve on the surface of a sphere intersecting all meridians at the same angle; hence, the course of a ship or aircraft following a constant compass direction. —**loxodromic,** *adj.*

photogrammetry the use of photography for surveying or map-making.

phototopography surveying or map-making by means of photography. —**phototopographic, phototopographical,** *adj.*

planisphere a map showing half or more of the sphere of the heavens, indicating which part is visible at what hour from a given location. —**planispheric, planispherical,** *adj.*

topography 1. the detailed mapping or description of the features of a relatively small area, district, or locality. 2. the relief features or surface configuration of an area. —**topographer,** *n.* —**topographic,** *adj.*

258. MARRIAGE
See also 348. RELATIONSHIP; 418. WIFE.

adelphogamy the form of marriage in which brothers have a common wife or wives. —**adelphogamic,** *adj.*

bigamy the state or practice of being married to more than one wife or one husband at a time. —**bigamist,** *n.* —**bigamous,** *adj.*

celibacy the state of being single or unmarried, especially in the case of one bound by vows not to marry. —**celibate,** *n., adj.*

celibatist an advocate of celibacy.

cicisbeism the practice of a married woman having an escort or cavalier, called a *cicisbeo,* in attendance.

deuterogamy digamism. —**deuterogamist,** *n.* —**deuterogamous,** *adj.*

digamism, digamy a second legal marriage after the termination of a first marriage by death or divorce. Also called **deuterogamy.** —**digamist,** *n.* —**digamous,** *adj.*

endogamy the custom of marrying only within one's tribe or similar social unit. —**endogamic, endogamous,** *adj.*

epithalamium, epithalamy a song or poem composed and performed in honor of a bride or groom.

exogamy the practice of marrying only outside one's tribe or similar social unit. —exogamic, exogamous, *adj.*

gamomania 1. *Obsolete.* a form of mania characterized by strange and extravagant proposals of marriage.
2. an excessive longing for the married state.

gamophobia an abnormal fear of marriage.

mariticide the killing of a husband. —mariticidal, *adj.*

matrimony the act or state of marriage; married life. —matrimonial, *adj.*

misogamy a hatred of marriage. —misogamist, *n.* —misogamic, *adj.*

monandry the custom of marriage to only one man at a time. —monandrous, *adj.*

monogamy the custom of marriage to one wife or one husband at a time. —monogamous, *adj.*

morganatic designating or pertaining to a marriage between a man of high social standing and a woman of lower station in which the marriage contract stipulates that neither she nor their offspring will have claim to his rank or property.

neogamist a person recently married; a newlywed.

nubility the condition of being marriageable, especially in reference to a woman's age or physical development. —nubile, *adj.*

pantagamy a form of marriage in which every woman in a community is married to every man and every man is married to every woman. —pantagamic, *adj.*

paranymph the best man or maid of honor at a wedding.

polyandry the practice of having two or more husbands at a time. —polyandrous, *adj.*

polygamy the practice or state of being married to more than one person at a time. —polygamous, *adj.*

polygyny the practice of having two or more wives at a time. —polygynous, polygynious, *adj.*

prothalamion, prothalamium a nuptial or wedding song or verse.

trigamy the condition of having three spouses, especially in the criminal sense of having them simultaneously. —trigamous, *adj.*

259. MARS
See also 25. ASTRONOMY; 100. COSMOLOGY; 318. PLANETS.

areography *Astronomy.* a topographical description of the planet Mars.

areology *Astronomy.* the observation and study of the planet Mars. —areologist, *n.* —areologic, areological, *adj.*

260. MARY

See also 69. CATHOLICISM; 79. CHRIST; 80. CHRISTIANITY; 183. GOD and GODS; 349. RELIGION; 359. SAINTS; 392. THEOLOGY.

hyperdulia the veneration offered by Roman Catholics to the Virgin Mary as the most exalted of human beings.

Jovinianist an adherent of Jovinian, a 4th-century monk who opposed asceticism and denied the virginity of Mary.

Mariolatry an excessive and proscribed veneration of the Virgin Mary. —Mariolater, *n.* —Mariolatrous, *adj.*

Mariology 1. the body of belief and doctrine concerning the Virgin Mary. 2. the study of the Virgin Mary. —Mariologist, *n.*

261. MATERIALS, PROPERTIES OF

degradability the state or quality of being susceptible to breakdown or decomposition. —degradable, *adj.*

elasticity *Physics.* the property of a substance that makes it possible to change its length, volume, or shape in direct response to a force and to recover its original form upon the removal of a force. —elastic, *adj.*

frangibility the condition of being very easily broken.

friability the condition of being easily crumbled or pulverized.

infrangibility the state or condition of being unbreakable or indivisible. —infrangible, *adj.*

lubricity the state or condition of having smooth surface, as to facilitate movement against another surface with a minimum of friction. —lubricious, *adj.*

malleability the property of a substance that makes it capable of being extended or shaped by hammering or by pressure from rollers. —malleable, *adj.*

plasticity the property of a substance that makes it capable of being molded, given shape, or being made to assume a desired form. —plastic, *adj.*

rigidity the property of a substance that renders it inflexible, stiff, or nonpliable. —rigid, *adj.*

sabulosity the quality or condition of being sandy or gritty. —sabulous, *adj.*

serosity the quality or condition of being watery or thin, as a liquid. —serous, *adj.*

viscosity the quality or condition of being able to adhere to things. —viscous, *adj.*

vitreosity a state or quality resembling that of glass, as in hardness, brittleness, transparency, glossiness, etc. —vitreous, *adj.*

262. MATHEMATICS
See also 250. LOGIC; 295. NUMBERS.

algebra the branch of mathematics that treats the representation and manipulation of relationships among numbers, values, vectors, etc. —algebraic, *adj.*

algorism 1. the Arabic system of numbering.
2. the method of computation with the Arabic figures 1 through 9, plus the zero; arithmetic.
3. the rule for solving a specific kind of arithmetic problem, as finding an average; algorithm. —algorist, *n.* —algorismic, *adj.*

algorithm any methodology for solving a certain kind of problem.

analogism the construction of a proportion.

biometrics, biometry. 1. the calculation of the probable extent of human lifespans.
2. the application to biology of mathematical and statistical theory and methods. —biometric, biometrical, *adj.*

calculus a branch of mathematics that treats the measurement of changing quantities, determining rates of change (differential calculus) and quantities under changing conditions (integral calculus).

geodesy the branch of applied mathematics that studies the measurement and shape and area of large tracts, the exact position of geographical points, and the curvature, shape, and dimensions of the earth. Also called geodetics. —geodesist, *n.* —geodetic, geodetical, *adj.*

geometry the branch of mathematics that treats the measurement, relationship, and properties of points, lines, angles, and figures in space. —geometer, geometrician, *n.* —geometric, geometrical, *adj.*

isoperimetry the study of figures that have perimeters of equal length. —isoperimetrical, isoperimetral, *adj.*

logarithmomancy a form of divination involving logarithms.

logistic *Rare.* the art or science of calculation or arithmetic.

mathematics the systematic study of magnitude, quantitites, and their relationships as expressed symbolically in the form of numerals and forms. —mathematician, *n.* —mathematic, mathematical, *adj.*

metamathematics the logical analysis of the fundamental concepts of mathematics, as function, number, etc. —metamathematician, *n.* —metamathematical, *adj.*

orthogonality the state or quality of being right-angled or perpendicular. —orthogonal, *adj.*

parallelism the quality of being parallel.

philomathy 1. *Rare.* a love of learning.
2. a love of mathematics. —philomath, *n.* —philomathic, philomathical, philomathean, *adj.*

planimetry the geometry and measurement of plane surfaces. —planimeter, *n.* —planimetric, planimetrical, *adj.*

polynomialism a mathematical expression having the quality of two or more terms.

porism *Rare.* a kind of geometrical proposition of ancient Greek mathematics arising during the investigation of some other proposition either as a corollary or as a condition that will render a certain problem indeterminate. —porismatic, *adj.*

Pythagoreanism, Pythagorism the doctrines and theories of Pythagoras, ancient Greek philosopher and mathematician, and the Pythagoreans, especially number relationships in music theory, acoustics, astronomy, and geometry (the Pythagorean theorem for right triangles), a belief in metempsychosis, and mysticism based on numbers. —Pythagorean, *n., adj.* —Pythagorist, *n.*

quadratics the branch of algebra that deals with equations containing variables of the second power, i.e. squared, but no higher.

spheroidicity the state of having a roughly spherical shape. Also called spheroidism, spheroidity.

statistology *Rare.* a treatise on statistics.

theorematist a person who discovers or formulates a mathematical theorem. —theorematic, *adj.*

topology a branch of mathematics that studies the properties of geometrical forms that remain invariant under certain transformations, as bending or stretching. —topologist, *n.* —topologic, topological, *adj.*

trigonometry the branch of mathematics that treats the measurement of and relationships between the sides and angles of plane triangles and the solid figures derived from them. —trigonometric, trigonometrical, *adj.*

263. MATTER
See also 261. MATERIALS, PROPERTIES OF; 316. PHYSICS.

allomorphism variant crystalline structure in a chemical compound. —allomorphic, *adj.*

allotropism, allotropy the quality of certain substances to exist in more than one form, with different properties in each form. —allotropic, allotropical, *adj.*

hylozoism *Philosophy.* the doctrine that all matter has life. —hylozoist, *n.* —hylozoistic, *adj.*

materialism 1. the philosophical theory that regards matter and its phenomena as the only reality and explains all occurrences, including the mental, as due to material agencies.
2. attention to or emphasis on material objects, needs, and considerations, with a disinterest in or rejection of intellectual and spiritual values. —materialist, *n.* —materialistic, *adj.*

monism *Metaphysics.* any of various theories holding that there is only one basic substance or principle that is the ground of reality. —monist, *n.* —monistic, monistical, *adj.*

rheology *Chemistry and Geology.* the study of the flow and deformation of colloids, especially pastes. —rheologist, *n.* —rheologic, rheological, *adj.*

somatology *Obsolete.* the branch of physics that studies the properties of matter. Also called somatics.

264. MEASUREMENT
See also 226. INSTRUMENTS.

acetimetry the measurement of the relative amount of acetic acid in a given subtance. —acetimetrical, *adj.*

acidimetry *Chemistry.* the determination of the amount of free acid in a liquid. —acidimeter, *n.* —acidimetrical, *adj.*

algometry measurement of pain by means of an algometer.

atmidometry the measurement of evaporation in the air. —atmidometer, *n.*

autometry 1. the measurement of oneself.
2. the measurement of a part of a figure as a fraction of the total figure's height. —autometric, *adj.*

baculometry the measurement of distance or lines by means of a stave or staff.

chorometry the science of land surveying.

chronoscopy accurate measurement of short intervals of time by means of a chronoscope. —chronoscopic, *adj.*

cosmometry the science of measuring the universe.

cryometry the measurement of extremely low temperatures, by means of a cryometer.

cyclometry the measurement of circles.

dosimetry the measurement by a dosimeter of the dosage of radiation a person has received. See also 130. DRUGS. —dosimetrist, *n.* —dosimetric, dosimetrical, *adj.*

erythrocytometry measurement of the red blood cells in the blood, by use of an erythrocytometer.

eudiometry the science of measuring and analyzing gases by means of a eudiometer.

fluorometry the measurement of fluorescence, or visible radiation, by means of a fluorometer. —fluorometric, *adj.*

galvanometry the measurement of the strength of electric currents, by means of a galvanometer. —galvanometric, galvanometrical, *adj.*

gasometry the measurement of the amounts of the gases in a mixture. —gasometer, *n.* —gasometric, gasometrical, *adj.*

goniometry the practice or theory of measuring angles, especially by means of a goniometer.

halometry the measurement of the dimensions and angles of the planes of salt crystals. —halometer, *n.*

heliometry the practice of measuring the angular distance between stars by means of a heliometer. —heliometric, heliometrical, *adj.*

horometry the art or science of measuring time. —horometrical, *adj.*

hypsometry the measurement of altitude and heights, especially with reference to sea level. —hypsometric, hypsometrical, *adj.*

indigometry the practice and art of determining the strength and coloring power of an indigo solution.

isometry equality of measure. —isometric, isometrical, *adj.*

konimetry the measurement of impurities in the air by means of a konimeter. —konimetric, *adj.*

kymography, cymography 1. the measuring and recording of variations in fluid pressure, as blood pressure.
2. the measuring and recording of the angular oscillations of an aircraft in flight, with respect to an axis or axes fixed in space. —kymograph, *n.* —kymographic, *adj.*

megameter *Rare.* an instrument for measuring large objects. See also 178. GEOGRAPHY.

mensuration 1. the act, process, or science of measurement.
2. the branch of geometry dealing with measurement of length, area, or volume. —mensurate, mensurational, *adj.*

metrology the study and science of measures and weights. —metrologist, *n.* —metrological, *adj.*

osmometry the measurement of osmotic pressure, or the force a dissolved substance exerts on a semipermeable membrane through which it cannot pass when separated by it from a pure solvent. —osmometric, *adj.*

osteometry the measurement of bones.

oxidimetry the determination or estimation of the quantity of oxide formed on a substance. —oxidimetric, *adj*.

pantometry *Obsolete*. the realm of geometrical measurements, taken as a whole. —pantometer, *n*. —pantometric, pantometrical, *adj*.

piezometry the measurement of pressure or compressibility, as with a piezometer. —piezometric, *adj*.

plastometry the measurement of the plasticity of materials, as with a plastometer. —plastometric, *adj*.

pulmometry the measurement of the capacity of the lungs. —pulmometer, *n*.

pyrometry the measurement of temperatures greater than 1500 degrees Celsius. —pyrometer, *n*. —pyrometric, pyrometrical, *adj*.

radiometry the measurement of radiant energy by means of a radiometer. —radiometric, *adj*.

rheometry the measurement of electric current, usually with a galvanometer. —rheometric, *adj*.

stadia a means of surveying in which distances are measured by reading intervals on a graduated rod intercepted by two parallel cross hairs in the telescope of a surveying instrument. —stadia, *adj*.

stereometry 1. the process of determining the volume and dimensions of a solid.
2. the process of determining the specific gravity of a liquid. —stereometric, *adj*.

tachymetry the measurement of distance, height, elevation, etc., with a tachymeter.

telemetry the science or use of the telemeter; long-distance measurement.

turbidimetry the measurement of the turbidity of water or other fluids, as with a turbidimeter. —turbidimetric, *adj*.

urinometry measurement of the specific gravity of urine, by means of an urinometer.

volumenometry the measurement of the volume of a solid body by means of a volumenometer.

volumetry the measurement of the volume of solids, gases, or liquids; volumetric analysis. —volumetric, volumetrical, *adj*.

zoometry the measurement and comparison of the sizes of animals and their parts. —zoometric, *adj*.

265. MEDIA
See also 237. LANGUAGE STYLE; 343. RADIO.

feuilletonism 1. the practice among European newspapers of allowing space, usually at the bottom of a page or pages, for fiction, criticism, columnists, etc.
2. the practice of writing critical or familiar essays for the feuilleton pages. —**feuilletonist**, *n.*

journalese language typical of journalists and newspapers or magazines, characterized by use of neologism and unusual syntax. Also called **newspaperese**.

journalism 1. the occupation of reporting, writing, editing, photographing, or broadcasting news.
2. the occupation of running a news organization as a business.
3. the press, printed publications, and their employees.
4. an academic program preparing students in reporting, writing, and editing for periodicals and newspapers. —**journalist**, *n.* —**journalistic**, *adj.*

kinescope 1. a type of cathode-ray tube used in the reception of television images.
2. a recording of a television program on motion-picture film.

kinetophone an apparatus for projecting sound and pictures by a combination of a phonograph and a kinetoscope.

kinetoscope an early apparatus for producing a moving picture. See also 226. INSTRUMENTS. Cf. **kinetophone.**

newspaperese journalese.

periodicalist a person who publishes or writes for a periodical.

photojournalism a form of journalism in which photographs play a more important part than written copy. —**photojournalist**, *n.*

propagandism 1. the action, practice, or art of propagating doctrines, as in the Society for the Propagation of Christian Knowledge.
2. the deliberate spreading of information or ideas to promote or injure a cause, nation, etc. —**propagandist**, *n.* —**propagandistic**, *adj.*

reportage 1. the act or process of reporting news.
2. an account of a current or historical event, not appearing in conventional news media, written in a journalistic style.

sensationalism the act of shocking or intent to shock, especially through the media; the practice of using startling but superficial effects, in art, literature, etc., to gain attention. See also 248. LITERARY STYLE; 312. PHILOSOPHOPHY. —**sensationalist**, *n.*

266. MEDICAL SPECIALTIES
See also 14. ANATOMY; 122. DISEASE and ILLNESS; 130. DRUGS;
197. HEALTH; 350. REMEDIES; 388. SURGERY.

adenography the science of the description of glands. —adenographic, *adj.*

adenology the branch of medicine concerned with the study of the glands.
—adenological, *adj.* —adenologist, *n.*

aeromedicine the medical specialty concerned with the health of those
engaged in flying within the earth's atmosphere.

allergist a physician who specializes in the treatment of allergies.

allergology the branch of medicine dealing with the study of allergies.
—allergologist, *n.*

anaplasty *Obsolete.* any restorative or plastic surgery.

anatomy the study and description of the body. —anatomist, *n.* —anatomic,
adj.

anesthesiology, anaesthesiology the branch of medical science that studies
anesthesia and anesthetics. —anesthesiologist, anaesthesiologist, anesthetist,
anaesthetist, *n.*

arthrography the branch of anatomy dealing with the description of the
joints.

arthrology the study and treatment of the joints.

audiology 1. the branch of medical science that studies hearing, especially
impaired hearing.
2. the treatment of persons with impaired hearing. —audiologist, *n.*

autophony a form of auscultation in which the practitioner learns the condition of the patient's chest from the way in which his own voice is modified
as he speaks against the chest. See also 111. DEAFNESS.

bacterioscopy the study or examination of bacteria using a microscope.
—bacterioscopist, *n.*

biopsy the removal of a fragment of living tissue from the body for medical
study. —bioptic, *adj.*

bioscopy the process of examining a body to find out if it is alive.

cardiology the study, diagnosis, and treatment of diseases of the heart and
blood vessels. —cardiologist, *n.* —cardiological, *adj.*

choledology a medical treatise on bile.

chondrology the branch of medical science that studies cartilages.

dentistry the science and profession that treats the diseases and malformations of the teeth, gums, and mouth. —dentist, *n.*

dermatologist a physician who specializes in the diagnosis and treatment of
diseases of the skin and integument.

desmopathology the study of diseases that affect the ligaments or tendons.

diagnostics the branch of medical science that deals with diagnosis.

electrophysiology the branch of physiology that concerns itself with the electrical phenomena of living organisms. —electrophysiological, *adj.*

electrotherapeutics the treatment of disease by electrical shock and other techniques using electricity. Also called **electrotherapy.** —electrotherapeutic, electrotherapeutical, *adj.*

electrotherapy electrotherapeutics. —electrotherapist, *n.*

emetology the study of agents that cause vomiting. —emetic, *n.*, *adj.*

emmenology that branch of medicine that deals with menstruation and its related disorders. —emmenologist, *n.*

endocrinology the branch of medical science concerned with endocrine glands and their secretions. —endocrinologist, *n.* —endocrinologic, endocrinological, *adj.*

endodontist a dentist who specializes in the diagnosis and treatment of diseases and injuries of the pulp and periapical tissues of the teeth.

enterology the study of the intestines. —enterologic, enterological, *adj.* —enterologist, *n.*

epidemiology 1. the study of the relationships of the various factors determining the frequency and distribution of diseases in a human community. 2. the field of medicine that attempts to determine the exact causes of localized outbreaks of disease. —epidemiologist, *n.* —epidemiologic, epidemiological, *adj.*

exodontist a dentist who specializes in the extraction of teeth.

Galenism the medical system of Galen, a blend of humoralism and Pythagorean number lore. —galenic, *adj.*

gastroenterologist a physician, usually an internist, who specializes in diseases of the stomach, intestine and associated organs.

gastrology the study of stomach functions and disorders. —gastrologist, gastrologer, *n.* —gastrological, *adj.*

geriatrician a physician who specializes in the care of the elderly.

geriatrics 1. the science dealing with the diseases, debilities, and care of aged persons. 2. the study of the physical process and problems of aging; gerontology. —geriatric, *adj.* —geriatrist, geriatrician, geriatry, *n.*

gerodontics a dental specialty concerned with the care and treatment of the dental problems of the aged. —gerodontist, *n.*

gynecologist a physician who specializes in the care, diagnosis, and treatment of disorders of the female reproductive system.

helcology the branch of medical science that studies ulcers. —**helcologist**, *n.*

heparology the branch of medical science that studies the liver. —**heparologist**, *n.*

hepatology the study and treatment of the liver. —**hepatologist**, *n.* —**hepatological**, *adj.*

herniology *Pathology.* 1. the study and treatment of hernias.
2. a work on hernias. —**herniologist**, *n.* —**herniologic, herniological**, *adj.*

heterology 1. an abnormality in tissue structure, arrangement, or manner of formation.
2. the study of abnormalities in tissue structure or organization. —**heterologous**, *adj.*

hysterology scientific study of the uterus.

iamatology the branch of medicine that deals with remedies.

iatrology 1. the science of medicine or healing.
2. *Rare.* a treatise on medicine and physicians.

immunogenetics 1. the branch of immunology that studies immunity in relation to genetic formation.
2. the study of genetic relationships between animals by comparing immunological reactions. —**immunogenetic**, *adj.*

immunology the branch of biomedical science that studies immunity from disease and the production of such immunity. —**immunologist**, *n.* —**immunologic, immunological**, *adj.*

industrialist a physician who specializes in industrial medical problems.

internist a physician who specializes in the diagnosis and nonsurgical treatment of disease.

ischidrosis suppression of the process of perspiration.

kinesiatrics the branch of medicine that concerns itself with muscular exercise as a cure for disease. Also called **kinesipathy**.

laryngology the study and treatment of the larynx. —**laryngologist**, *n.* —**laryngological**, *adj.*

leprology the brand of medical science that studies leprosy and its treatment. —**leprologist**, *n.*

lingism *Rare.* a gymnastic treatment for disease, named after a Swedish physician, Peter H. Ling.

lymphography a description of the origin and function of the lymphatic system.

merology the study and treatment of body fluids and elementary tissues.

naprapathy a healing system based on the theory that disease or illness is caused by strained ligaments and other problems of connective tissue and can be treated by massage. —**naprapath**, *n.*

neonatology the art and science of diagnosis and treatment of the newborn. —**neonatologist**, *n.*

nephrology the branch of medical science that studies the kidneys. —**nephrologist**, *n.*

neurologist a physician who specializes in the diagnosis and treatment of diseases of the nerves and nervous system.

neuromechanism the structure and arrangement of the nervous system in relation to function.

neuropath a physician who specializes in diseases or disorders of the nerves. Also **neuropathist.**

neuropathology the branch of medicine that studies and treats the morphological and other features of nervous system disease. —**neuropathologist**, *n.* —**neuropathologic, neuropathological**, *adj.*

obstetrics the branch of medicine that specializes in care of women before, during and after childbirth. —**obstetrician**, *n.* —**obstetric, obstetrical**, *adj.*

oncology 1. the study of tumors.
2. the totality of medical knowledge concerning tumors. —**oncologist**, *n.* —**oncologic**, *adj.*

ophthalmology the medical specialty that studies and treats diseases of the eye. —**ophthalmologist**, *n.* —**ophthalmological**, *adj.*

opotherapy the treatment of illness and disease with extracts made from certain glands of animals, as the thyroid or adrenal glands. Also called **organotherapy.**

organicism 1. the theory that all symptoms are due to organic disease.
2. the theory that each of the organs of the body has its own special constitution. —**organicist**, *n.* —**organicistic**, *adj.*

organotherapy opotherapy.

orthodontics the branch of dentistry that specializes in treatment of malformed teeth and oral problems. —**orthodontist**, *n.* —**orthodontic**, *adj.*

orthopathy the treatment of illness or disease without the use of drugs.

orthopedics the branch of surgery that is specially concerned with the preservation and restoration of function of the skeletal system, its articulations, and associated structures. —**orthopedist**, *n.* —**orthopedic**, *adj.*

orthopraxy, orthopraxis the use of mechanical apparatus or devices to correct bodily deformities.

orthopsychiatry the branch of psychiatry that deals with incipient disorders of mind and conduct, especially in childhood and youth. —**orthopsychiatrist,** *n.* —**orthopsychiatric, orthopsychiatrical,** *adj.*

osteology 1. the scientific study of bones and their diseases.
2. the totality of medical knowledge concerning the bones of the skeletal system. Also called **skeletology.** —**osteologist,** *n.* —**osteologic, osteological,** *adj.*

osteopathy a medical specialty that emphasizes manipulation of the skeleton to treat illnesses. —**osteopath,** *n.* —**osteopathic,** *adj.*

otolaryngology the medical practice dealing with the ear, nose, and throat; otology and laryngology combined for medical study or practice. —**otolaryngologist,** *n.* —**otolaryngological,** *adj.*

otology the medical specialty that studies and treats diseases of the ear. —**otologist,** *n.* —**otological,** *adj.*

otorhinolaryngology otolaryngology. —**otorhinolaryngologist,** *n.* —**otorhinolaryngologic, otorhinolaryngological,** *adj.*

pathognomy the study of the signs that reveal certain physical conditions. —**pathognomonic,** *adj.*

pathology the branch of medicine that specializes in the study of disease. —**pathologist,** *n.*

pediatrics the branch of medicine that specializes in the care of infants, children and adolescents. —**pediatrician,** *n.* —**pediatric,** *adj.*

pedodontics the branch of dentistry that specializes in the care of children's teeth. —**pedodontist,** *n.* —**pedodontic,** *adj.*

pharmacomania a mania for medicines.

pharyngology *Physiology.* the study and treament of the pharynx. —**pharyngologist,** *n.* —**pharyngological,** *adj.*

phonocardiography stethography, def. 2.

physiatrics the medical use of natural, nonmanufactured agents. —**physiatrical,** *adj.*

physiatrist a physician who specializes in the use of physical therapy for treatment or rehabilitation following disease, trauma, or surgery.

physiology 1. the branch of medical science that studies the functions of living organisms or their parts.
2. the organic processes or functions of an organism or any of its parts. —**physiologist,** *n.* —**physiologic, physiological,** *adj.*

pneodynamics the study of the forces involved in respiration.

pneumatography a procedure for tracing the movements of the chest in respiration, obtained with a pneumatograph. —**pneumatogram,** *n.*

posology 1. the science of medicinal dosage.
2. a system of dosage. —posologic, posological, *adj*.

proctology the branch of medicine concerned with the disorders of the rectum and anus. —proctologist, *n*. —proctologic, proctological, *adj*.

prosthetics the branch of surgery dealing with the replacement of missing limbs or organs with artificial substitutes. —prosthetic, *adj*.

psychiatry the branch of medicine that is concerned with the study, treatment, and prevention of mental illness, using both medical and psychological therapies. —psychiatrist, *n*. —psychiatric, *adj*.

psychopathology 1. the branch of medicine that studies the causes and nature of mental disease.
2. the pathology of mental disease. —psychopathologist, *n*. —psychopathologic, psychopathological, *adj*.

psychopharmacology the study of drugs that effect emotional and mental states. —psychopharmacologic, psychopharmacological, *adj*.

psychosomatics the branch of medical science that studies the relation between psychical and emotional states and physical symptoms. —psychosomaticist, *n*. —psychosomatic, *adj*.

radiology the medical specialty involving the use of radiation for diagnosis and therapy. —radiologist, *n*. —radiologic, radiological, *adj*.

radiotherapy the treatment of diseases, especially malignant cancer, with radium or other radioactive substances. Also called radium therapy.

radiothermy a form of therapy using heat from a short-wave radio or diathermy apparatus.

roentgenology, röntgenology the science and use of x rays, especially in the diagnosis and treatment of illness and disease. —roentgenologist, röntgenologist, *n*.

roentgenotherapy, röntgenotherapy treatment of disease and illness by means of x rays.

sarcology *Archaic*. the anatomy of the soft parts of the body. Cf. osteology.

serology 1. the science of the preparation and use of serums.
2. the study of serums. —serologist, *n*. —serological, *adj*.

serotherapy treatment of illness or disease by means of serum obtained from inoculated animals.

spirometry the measurement of the breathing capacity of the lungs. —spirometer, *n*.

stethography 1. the use of a recording instrument to register movements of the chest.
2. the use of an instrument to record sounds made by the action of the heart. Also called phonocardiography. —stethographic, *adj*.

stomatology the branch of medicine concerned with the diagnosis and treatment of diseases of the mouth. —stomatologist, *n.* —stomatologic, stomatological, *adj.*

syndesmology the anatomy of the ligaments of the body; the science or study of ligaments.

tenography the scientific description of the tendons. —tenographic, tenographical, *adj.*

tenology the study and treatment of the tendons.

thereology the art of healing. —thereologist, *n.*

toxicology the scientific study of poisons, their detection and actions, and the treatment of the conditions they cause. —toxicologist, *n.* —toxicologic, toxicological, *adj.*

traumatology the science of wounds and their treatment. —traumatologist, *n.*

urethroscopy the use of the urethroscope to examine the urethra.

urinology urology, def. 2.

urinometry measurement of the specific gravity of urine, by means of an urinometer.

urinoscopy, uroscopy examination of the urine for diagnostic purposes. —urinoscopic, uroscopic, *adj.*

urology 1. a treatise on urine.
2. the branch of medicine that studies diseases of the kidneys, of the urinary tract, etc. Also called urinology.
3. *Obsolete.* the study of the composition and production of urine. —urologist, *n.* —urologic, urological, *adj.*

venereology the study of the diseases that are communicated by sexual intercourse. —venereologist, *n.* —venereological, *adj.*

virology the branch of medical science that studies viruses and the diseases they cause. —virologist, *n.* —virological, *adj.*

267. MEDITATION
See also 59. BUDDHISM; 285. MYSTICISM.

omphaloskepsis a form of religious meditation practiced by Eastern mystics who stare fixedly at their own navels to induce a mystical trance. Also called omphalism.

thanatopsis a survey of or meditation upon death.

TM the abbreviation for *transcendental meditation,* a form of contemplation in which the mind, released by the repetition of a mantra, becomes calm and creative.

268. MELANCHOLY
See also 28. ATTITUDES; 279. MOODS.

lypemania an abnormal tendency toward deep melancholy.

melancholia a condition of abnormal gloom or depression, often of an intensity to become a form of insanity. —melancholiac, *n., adj.* —melancholic, *n., adj.*

melancholy 1. black bile, one of the four bodily humors, formerly believed to be the cause of gloom, ill temper, and depression.
2. melancholia.
3. a pensive, contemplative mood.
4. *Obsolete.* ill temper. —melancholiac, *n., adj.* —melancholic, *n., adj.*

tristimania melancholia.

269. MEMORY

amnesia a loss or lack of memory. —amnesiac, *n.* —amnesic, *adj.*

anamnesis 1. a reminiscence.
2. (*cap.*) the section of Christian liturgies rehearsing the sacrifice of Christ and ending "Do this in remembrance of me." —anamnestic, *adj.*

cryptomnesia the occurrence in consciousness of images not recognized as produced by the memory and its storage of events and scenes. —cryptomnesic, *adj.*

déjà vu *Psychology.* the illusion of having previously experienced something actually being encountered for the first time.

memoria technica any mnemonic device or aide-memoire, especially a technical device.

mnemonics the process or technique of improving, assisting, or developing the memory. Also called **mnemotechnics.** —mnemonic, *adj.*

panmnesia the belief that every mental impression remains in the memory.

paramnesia *Psychiatry.* a distortion of memory in which fact and fancy are confused.

270. METALS

docimasy, docimacy the branch of metallurgy involved in the assaying of ores or metals. See also 190. GREECE and GREEKS.

metallography the study of metals and their structures and properties by the use of microscopy and x rays.

metallotherapy treatment of disease and illness with metals, particularly with the salt forms of metals.

metallurgy the science of preparing metals for use by separating them from their ores and refining them, as by smelting. —metallurgist, *n.* —metallurgic, metallurgical, *adj.*

radiometallography the study of metals and their structures by the use of x rays.

siderotechny *Rare.* the metallurgy of iron and steel.

271. METEORITES
See also 25. ASTRONOMY.

aerolithology the science of aerolites, whether meteoric stones or meteorites. Also called **aerolitics.**

astrolithology the study of meteorites. Also called **meteoritics.**

meteorist a specialist in the study of meteorites.

meteoritics astrolithology.

meteorophobia an abnormal fear of meteorites or meteors.

272. MILK
See also 76. CHEESE; 168. FOOD and NUTRITION.

galactopoietic any substance that stimulates the production and flow of milk. —galactopoietic, *adj.*

lactometer an instrument for measuring the richness of milk from its specific gravity. Also called **galactometer.**

lactoscope an instrument for measuring the opacity of milk so that its cream content can be determined.

273. MIRACLES
See also 79. CHRIST; 151. FAITH; 252. MAGIC; 349. RELIGION; 359. SAINTS.

thaumatology the study or lore of miracles.

thaumaturgy the working of wonders or miracles; magic. —thaumaturgist, thaumaturge, thaumaturgus, *n.* —thaumaturgic, thaumaturgical, *adj.*

274. MISSILES
See also 416. WEAPONRY.

ballistics 1. the science or study of the motion of projectiles.
2. the art or science of designing projectiles for maximum flight performance. —ballistician, *n.* —ballistic, *adj.*

ballistophobia an abnormal fear of missiles.

275. MOB
See also 105. CROWDS.

mobbism the behavior of a mob. —mobbish, *adj.* —mobbishly, *adv.*

mobolatry a reverence for and veneration of the mob.

ochlocracy a rule or government by a mob. —ochlocrat, *n.* —ochlocratic, ochlocratical, *adj.*

ochlophobia an abnormal fear of crowds or mobs. —ochlophobe, *n*. —ochlophobic, *adj*.

276. MONEY
See also 131. DUES and PAYMENT; 137. ECONOMICS; 160. FINANCE; 325. POVERTY; 398. TRADE.

agiotage the business of buying and selling the currencies of various countries by taking advantage of differences in rates of exchange. —agio, *n*.

anatocism the act of lending with interest.

aphnology *Rare*. the science of wealth.

arbitrage the business of buying and selling securities, currencies, and commodities on an international scale so as to take advantage of differences in rates of exchange and prices. —arbitrager, arbitrageur, *n*.

bimetallism the use of two metals jointly as a monetary standard with fixed values in relation to one another. —bimetallist, *n*. —bimetallistic, *adj*.

bullionism the doctrine that paper money should at all times be convertible into bullion. —bullionist, *n*.

cambism, cambistry the theory and practice of money exchange as an item of commerce, especially in its international features. —cambist, *n*.

chrematist a person whose chief goal in life is the gaining of wealth. —chrematistic, *adj*.

chrematistics 1. the study of wealth.
2. any theory of wealth as measured in money. —chrematistic, *adj*.

chrematomania a mania for money.

chrematophobia an abnormal fear or dislike of money.

cresomania a mania for great wealth.

gombeenism *Irish*. the lending of money at usurious interest. —gombeen, gombeenman, *n*.

mammonism the greedy pursuit of riches.

metallism a doctrine advocating the use of metal money instead of paper. —metallist, metalist, *n*.

monetarism an economic theory maintaining that stability and growth in the economy are dependent on a steady growth rate in the supply of money. —monetarist, *n*., *adj*.

moneyocracy government or domination of society by the rich.

monometallism 1. the use of only one metal, usually gold or silver, as a monetary standard.
2. the use of only one metal for coinage. —monometallist, *n*.

nabobism the lifestyle of a nabob, i.e., of one possessing considerable wealth.

plutolatry an excessive devotion to wealth.

plutology *Economics.* the scientific study or theory of wealth.

plutomania 1. an abnormal craving for wealth.
2. a mania characterized by delusions of wealth.

polymetallism the use of a number of different metals in coinage.

squandermania a mania for spending money.

symmetalism a system of coinage based on a unit of two or more metals in combination, each of a specified weight. —symmetallic, *adj.*

277. MONKS and NUNS
See also 81. CHURCH; 349. RELIGION.

anchoritism the practice of retiring to a solitary place for a life of religious seclusion. —anchorite, anchoret, *n.* —anchoritic, anchoretic, *adj.*

Benedictinism 1. the rule for monastic life developed by St. Benedict, used by several religious orders.
2. membership in an order of monks founded in Monte Cassino by St. Benedict about A.D. 530. —Benedictine, *n.*, *adj.*

cenobitism, coenobitism the action of or motivation for becoming a member of a religious order living in a monastery or convent. —cenobite, *n.* —cenobitic, *adj.*

Cistercianism the rule of an order of monks and nuns founded in 1098 in Citeaux, France. —Cistercian, *n.*, *adj.*

monachism the religious and work activities of a monk; monasticism. —monachist, monachal, *adj.*

monasticism a regularized program of religious observance, asceticism, and work followed in a monastery; monachism. —monastic, *n.*, *adj.*

monkery 1. *Often Contemptuous.* the customs, practices, etc., of monks.
2. a group or community of monks.
3. a monastery.

Redemptionist a Trinitarian.

Redemptorist a member of the Congregation of the Most Holy Redeemer, a Catholic order devoted to the education of the poor.

tonsure 1. the act or process of cutting the hair, especially as a religious rite or custom.
2. the shaved part of the head, usually the crown, of a member of a religious order. —tonsorial, *adj.*

Trappist a member of a Roman Catholic monastic order, a branch of the Cistercians, observing an austere, reformed rule, including a vow of silence. —Trappist, *adj.*

Trinitarian a member of the monastic order founded in the late 12th century to redeem captive Christians from the Moors, or Muslims. Also called **Redemptionist**.

Urbanist a member of an order of Franciscan nuns. See also 323. POPE.

278. MONSTERS
See also 286. MYTHOLOGY.

dysmorphophobia an abnormal dread of deformity, usually in others.

monstrosity 1. the state or quality of being monstrous.
2. a monster or monsterlike thing or person. —monstrous, *adj*.

prodigiosity 1. the state, quality, or phenomenon of being immense, wondrous, or extraordinary.
2. a prodigious thing, person, or event.

teratism a love of monsters or marvels. Also called teratosis.

teratoid *Biology*. resembling a monster.

teratology 1. the writing or collecting of fantasies containing monsters and prodigies.
2. *Biology*. the scientific study of monstrosities or abnormal formations in plants or animals. —teratologist, *n*. —teratological, *adj*.

teratophobia an abnormal fear of monsters or of giving birth to a monster.

teratosis teratism.

279. MOODS
See also 28. ATTITUDES; 41. BEHAVIOR; 120. DISCONTENT;
195. HAPPINESS; 208. HOMESICKNESS; 213. HUMOR; 268. MELANCHOLY.

cyclothymia a temperament characterized by cyclic alterations of mood between elation and depression. —cyclothyme, *n*. —cyclothymic, *adj*.

dysphoria a state or mood of dissatisfaction, restlessness, or anxiety. —dysphoric, *adj*.

euphoria a state or mood of well being, whether natural or induced. —euphoric, *adj*.

morbidity the state or quality of being excessively gloomy. —morbid, *adj*.

mordancy the quality or state of being sarcastic or caustic. —mordant, *adj*.

morosity the quality or state of being excessively sullen or gloomy. —morose, *adj*.

plerophory a state or quality of full confidence or absolute certainty.

280. MOON
See also 25. ASTRONOMY; 318. PLANETS; 387. SUN.

selenography the branch of astronomy that deals with the charting of the moon's surface. —selenographer, selenographist, *n.* —selenographic, selenographical, *adj.*

selenolatry the worship of the moon.

selenology the branch of astronomy that studies the physical characteristics of the moon. —selenologist, *n.* —selenological, *adj.*

selenomancy a form of divination involving observation of the moon.

281. MOTHER
See also 77. CHILDREN; 153. FATHER; 307. PARENTS; 327. PREGNANCY.

matriarchy a system of social order wherein final authority is vested in the mother or eldest female and in which descent is reckoned in the female line. —matriarchal, *adj.*

matricentric tending to move toward or centering upon the mother.

matricide 1. the killing of one's mother.
2. one who has killed his mother. —matricidal, *adj.*

matriliny tracing of descent through the mother's side of a family. —matrilinear, *adj.*

momism an excessive attachment and devotion of children to their mothers, resulting in a child's dependence and failure to achieve emotional emancipation.

282. MOTION
See also 399. TRAVEL.

apheliotropism the tendency of some plants to grow in a direction away from the sun.

apogeotropism the tendency of some plants to grow away from the earth and the pull of gravity. —apogeotropic, *adj.*

bradykinesia, bradykinesis slowness of movement. —bradykinetic, *adj.*

chemotaxis the property of some plants and animals of moving toward or away from certain chemicals.

chemotropism growth or motion in response to a chemical stimulus. —chemotropic, *adj.*

diatropism the capacity or tendency of some plants to adopt a position transverse to the line of force of an external stimulus. —diatropic, *adj.*

dromophobia kinetophobia.

galvanotropism growth or movement of an organism in response to an electric current. —galvanotropic, *adj.*

geotaxis the movement of an organism in response to the force of gravity.

kinematics the study of the motion of bodies considered independently of external forces. Also called phoronomy. —kinematic, *adj.*

kinesomania a mania for movement.

kinetics the branch of physics that studies the motion of masses in relation to the forces acting on them.

kinetophobia an abnormal fear or dislike of motion. Also called dromophobia.

phoronomy kinematics.

photokinesis movement of bodies, organisms, etc., in response to the stimulus of light. —photokinetic, *adj.*

phototaxis, phototaxy the movement of an organism away from or toward a source of light. —phototactic, *adj.*

phototropism motion in a particular direction under the stimulus of light, as exhibited by certain plants, organisms, etc. —phototropic, *adj.*

rheotaxis the tendency of certain living things to move in response to the mechanical stimulus of a current of water.

stereotaxis orientation or movement of an organism in response to the stimulus of a solid object. Cf. stereotropism. —stereotactic, *adj.*

stereotropism growth or movement determined by contact with a solid. Also called thigmotropism. Cf. stereotaxis. —stereotropic, *adj.*

tachophobia an abnormal fear of speed.

thigmotropism stereotropism. —thigmotropic, *adj.*

trochilics *Rare.* the science of rotary motion. —trochilic, *adj.*

trophotropism the movement of cells in relation to food or nutritive matter. —trophotropic, *adj.*

tropism the tendency of a plant, animal, or part to move or turn in response to an external stimulus, as sunlight or temperature. —tropistic, *adj.*

283. MOUNTAINS
See also 178. GEOGRAPHY; 202. HEIGHTS; 411. VOLCANOES.

acrophilia a love of high mountains and of heights. —acrophile, *n.*

alpinism the climbing of the Alps or any equally high mountain ranges. —alpinist, *n.*

orogenesis the process of the formation of mountains. Also called orogeny. —orogenic, *adj.*

orography, oreography *Physical Geography.* the study of mountains and mountain systems. —orographic, oreographic, oreographical, orographical, *adj.*

orology, oreology the scientific study of mountains. —orologist, oreologist, *n.* —orological, oreological, *adj.*

orometry the measurement of mountains. —**orometric,** *adj.*

orophilous *Botany.* referring to orophytes, a class of plants growing on mountains below the timberline.

284. MUSIC
See also 23. ART; 310. PERFORMING; 314. PHONOGRAPH RECORDS; 378. SONGS and SINGING; 380. SOUND; 403. TUNING.

agogics the theory that accent within a musical phrase can also be expressed by modifying the duration of certain notes rather than only by modifying dynamic stress. —**agogic,** *adj.*

atonalism 1. the composition of music without a definite key; dodecaphony. 2. the music so written. Also **atonality.** —**atonalist,** *n.* —**atonal, atonalistic,** *adj.*

choralism 1. the techniques of choral singing. 2. the composition of music for chorus illustrative of a cognizance of choral techniques and the possibilities and limitations of choral singing. —**choralistic,** *adj.*

chromaticism the use of the chromatic scale or chromatic halftones in musical compositions. Cf. **diatonicism.**

citharist, kitharist a performer on an ancient Greek form of lyre called a cithara.

contrapuntist 1. a composer of music employing counterpoint figures, as fugues. 2. a performer of music employing counterpoint figures. Also **contrapuntalist.**

diatonicism the use of the diatonic scale of five whole tones and two halftones in the composition of music. Also **diatonism.** Cf. **chromaticism.**

dodecaphony, dodecaphonism the composition of music employing the twelve-tone scale. Also called **dodecatonality, atonality.** —**dodecaphonist,** *n.* —**dodecaphonic,** *adj.*

doxology a short hymn expressing praise to God. —**doxological,** *adj.*

ethnomusicology 1. the study of the music of a particular region or people from the viewpoint of its social or cultural implications. 2. the comparative study of the music of more than one such region or people. —**ethnomusicologist,** *n.*

fuguism 1. the composition of fugues. 2. the performance of fugues. —**fuguist,** *n.*

gambist a performer on the viola da gamba.

Gregorianist *Obsolete.* a person versed in Gregorian chant. Also called **Gregorian.**

harmonist a person skilled in the principles of harmony. See also 249. LITERATURE.

homophony 1. music in which one voice carries the melody, sometimes with a chord accompaniment.
2. *Obsolete.* unison. Also called **monody, monophony.** —**homophonous,** *adj.*

hymnody 1. the singing of hymns; hymnology.
2. the composition of hymns.
3. a study of hymns and their composers.
4. the preparation of expository material and bibliographies concerning hymns; hymnography. —**hymnodist,** *n.*

kitharist citharist.

lyrism the act or art of playing the lyre. —**lyrist,** *n.*

melodics the branch of music theory that deals with melody.

melodist a person who composes or sings melodies.

melodramaticism the writing of romantic, sensational stage plays interspersed with songs and orchestral music. —**melodramatist,** *n.* —**melodramatic,** *adj.*

melomania an abnormal liking for music and melody. —**melomaniac,** *n., adj.* —**melomane,** *n.*

metronome an instrument for marking time in music, producing regular ticking sounds at a variety of settings. —**metronomic, metronomical,** *adj.*

minstrelsy 1. the art of minstrels.
2. their occupation.
3. a group of minstrels.
4. a collection of their music and songs.

monophony 1. music composed of a single melody with no accompaniment or harmony. Cf. **homophony, polyphony.**
2. monody. —**monophonic,** *adj.*

musicography the science of musical notation.

musicology the scholarly and scientific study of music, as in historical research, theory of composition, etc. —**musicologist,** *n.* —**musicological,** *adj.*

musicomania a mania for music.

musicophile a music lover.

musicophobia an intense dislike of music.

nickelodeon a juke-box, record-player, or player piano operated by the insertion of a nickel or other coin. See also 159. FILMS.

ophicleidist a performer on the ophicleide, an instrument, developed from the wooden serpent in the brass section of the orchestra.

pandiatonicism 1. the composition of music using all seven notes of the diatonic scale in a manner free from classical harmonic restrictions.
2. the music written in this style. —pandiatonic, *adj.*

pianism the technique of playing the piano. —pianist, *n.* —pianistic, *adj.*

pianologue a humorous performance at the piano, sometimes with a verbal accompaniment by the performer.

polyphonism polyphony.

polyphony, polyphonism the combination of a number of separate but harmonizing melodies, as in a fugue. Cf. homophony. —polyphonic, polyphonous, *adj.*

polytonalism the practice of using combinations of notes from two or more keys in writing musical compositions. Also polytonality. —polytonalist, *n.* —polytonal, *adj.*

psalmody 1. the art, practice, or act of singing psalms in worship services.
2. a collection of psalms. —psalmodist, *n.* —psalmodial, psalmodic, psalmodical, *adj.*

tetralogy any series of four related works, literary, dramatic, operatic, etc.

threnody, threnode a song, musical composition, or literary work created to honor or commemorate the dead; a funeral song. —threnodist, *n.* —threnodic, *adj.*

tonalist a composer who pays special attention to the tonal qualities of music. See also 23. ART.

verismo, verism the artistic use of commonplace, everyday, and contemporary material in opera, especially some 20th-century Italian and French works, as *Louise.* —verist, *n., adj.* —veristic, *adj.*

Wagnerism 1. the musical theory and practice of Richard Wagner, characterized by coordination of all musical and dramatic components, use of the leitmotif, and departure from the conventions of earlier Italian opera.
2. influence or imitation of Wagner's style. —Wagnerian, *n., adj.*

285. MYSTICISM
See also 267. MEDITATION; 349. RELIGION.

Boehmenism, Behmenism the mystical teachings of Jakob Boehme (1575–1624), an influence on George Fox and Quakerism. —Boehmenist, Boehmist, Boehmenite, *n.*

Bourigianism the mystical theories of Antoinette Bourignon (1616–80), popular in the Netherlands and in Scotland.

Gnosticism the beliefs and practices of pre-Christian and early Christian sects, condemned by the church, especially the conviction that matter is evil and that knowledge is more important than faith, and the practice of esoteric mysticism. —Gnostic, *n., adj.*

Hermeticism 1. the occult concepts, ideas, or philosophy set forth in the writings of the hermeticists of the late Middle Ages and the early Renaissance.
2. adherence to, belief in, or propagation of these concepts and ideas.
3. *Literature.* a symbolic and arcane style similar to that of the hermeticists, especially in the poetry of certain French symbolist poets. —**hermeticist, hermetist,** *n.* —**hermetic, hermetical,** *adj.*

metagnosticism the doctrine that knowledge of the Absolute is within human reach, but through a higher religious consciousness rather than by logical processes. See also 183. GOD AND GODS. —**metagnostic,** *adj.*

mystagogics, mystagogy 1. the principles, doctrines, and practices of mysticism.
2. the interpretation of mysteries, as the Eleusinian. —**mystagogue,** *n.* —**mystagogic, mystagogical,** *adj.*

mystagogue a teacher of mystical doctrines.

omphalopsychism the practice of staring at one's navel to induce a mystical trance. Also called **omphaloskepsis.** —**omphalopsychite,** *n.*

pleroma the Gnostic concept of the spiritual world, representing the fullness of the Divine Being and the eons emanating therefrom.

theosophy, theosophism 1. any of various forms of philosophical or religious thought claiming a mystical insight into the divine nature and natural phenomena.
2. (*cap.*) the system of belief and practice of the Theosophical Society. —**theosophist,** *n.* —**theosophical,** *adj.*

286. MYTHOLOGY
See also 183. GOD and GODS.

centauromachy battle between centaurs or between centaurs and men.

cornucopia 1. *Greek Mythology.* a horn of plenty, from the horn of the goat Amalthaea that dispensed an endless supply of food, drink, and other riches.
2. any copious or abundant supply or source. —**cornucopian,** *adj.*

dryad a wood nymph.

euhemerism the belief that the mythological gods were merely legendary kings and heroes deified. —**euhemerist,** *n.* —**euhemeristic,** *adj.*

hamadryad a dryad that is the spirit of a particular tree.

limniad, limoniad *Rare.* a water nymph or naiad.

mythicism the attribution of supernatural events to mythological causes.

mythicist 1. a student of myths.
2. an interpreter of myths.

mythoclast an opponent of myths. —**mythoclastic,** *adj.*

mythogenesis 1. the establishment and development of myths.
2. the tendency to create myths or to give mythical status to a person or event. Also called **mythogeny.** —**mythogenetic,** *adj.*

mythography 1. the collecting of myths.
2. the recording of myths in writing.
3. a critical collection of myths. —**mythographer, mythographist,** *n.*

mythologem a recurrent pattern, event, or theme in myths, as an explanation of the change of seasons; folklore motifs.

mythologer a narrator of myths and legends.

mythology 1. a body of stories relating the traditional origins and causes of the world, natural forces and phenomena, and cultural developments, as that of a particular people or relating to a particular person.
2. a collection of myths.
3. the science of myths. —**mythologist,** *n.* —**mythological,** *adj.*

mythopoesis the creation of myths. —**mythopoeist,** *n.* —**mythopoeic,** *adj.*

mythos, mythus 1. myth.
2. mythology.
3. the interrelationship of value structures and historical experiences of a people, usually given expression through the arts.

naiad a nymph or spirit of rivers and streams.

Oceanid any of the daughters of Oceanus and Tethys; a sea nymph.

theomythology a mixture of theology and mythology. —**theomythologer,** *n.*

undine according to Paracelsus, a water nymph or spirit, female in form and lacking a soul until married to a mortal and mother of his child.

vampirism 1. the state or condition of being a vampire.
2. the actions or habits of vampires.
3. belief in the existence of vampires. —**vampiric,** *adj.*

N

287. NAKEDNESS

Adamitism the practice of going naked for God; the beliefs of some ascetic sects in ritual nakedness. Cf. gymnosophy. —Adamite, *n.* —Adamitic, *adj.*

gymnomania a mania for nakedness.

gymnopedia, gymnopaedia a religious choral dance performed at ancient Greek festivals by naked youths. —gymnopedic, gymnopaedic, *adj.*

gymnophobia an abnormal fear of nudity.

gymnosophy the tenets of an ancient Hindu ascetic whose members wore little or no clothing. See also **Adamitism**. —gymnosophist, *n.* —gymnosophical, *adj.*

naturism a cult of nudity for reasons of health. —naturist, *n.* —naturistic, *adj.*

nudism the practice of going nude. —nudist, *n., adj.*

nudomania a mania for nudity.

288. NAMES

acronym a word formed from the initial letters or syllables taken from a group of words that form the name of a company, product, process, etc. —acronymic, acronymous, *adj.*

agnomen *Ancient Rome.* an additional name, usually given in honor of some signal achievement; hence, a nickname. —agnominal, *adj.*

allonymy a name of one person used by another, such as a writer using the name of someone other than himself for concealment of identity or other purpose. Cf. **pseudonym**. —allonymous, *adj.*

anthroponymy a branch of onomastics that studies personal names. —anthroponymist, *n.*

antonomasia 1. the use of an epithet or appellative for an individual's name, as *his excellency.*
2. the use of a proper name to express a general idea or to designate others sharing a particular characteristic, as *a Rockefeller.* —antonomastic, *adj.*

biosystematics biosystematy. —biosystematic, biosystematical, *adj.*

biosystematy the science of the classification of living things. Also **biosystematics.** —**biosystematic, biosystematical,** *adj.*

caconymic pertaining to a bad or objectionable name.

cognomen 1. *Ancient Rome.* the third and usually last name in Roman personal names, as *Caesar* of *Gaius Julius Caesar.*
2. a surname or family name.
3. a nickname. —**cognominal,** *adj.*

cryptonym a secret name.

eponym 1. the name of a real or legendary person that has been applied to a thing, institution, etc., as *atlas.*
2. the name of a person that is used to describe a time or period, as the *Augustan Age.* —**eponymic, eponymous,** *adj.*

eponymism the derivation of names for tribes, nations, or places, from that of a person, whether real or imaginary. Also **eponymy.** —**eponymous, eponymic,** *adj.*

eponymist a real or legendary person whose name has been used as an eponym.

euonym a name that is apt or fitting.

filionymic *Rare.* a name derived from that of a son.

hypocorism 1. the creation or use of pet names, as *Dick* for *Richard.*
2. a pet name.
3. baby talk. —**hypocoristic,** *adj.*

matronymic metronymic.

metonymy a rhetorical or stylistic device in which one thing is named or referred to by the name of another, related thing; for example, the use of *White House* in referring to the presidential administration. —**metonym,** *n.* —**metonymous, metonymic, metonymical,** *adj.*

metronymic, matronymic a name derived from a mother or a female ancestor. Cf. **patronymic.**

nomancy onomancy.

nomenclature 1. a system of names used in the classification of an art or science or other field or subject.
2. a naming system peculiar to a social group. See also 53. BOOKS; 83. CLASSIFICATION; 236.LANGUAGE; 290. NATURE.

onomancy, onomomancy a form of divination involving the letters of a name. Also called **nomancy.**

onomasticon a dictionary of proper names. —**onomastic,** *adj.*

onomastics onomatology. —**onomastician,** *n.* —**onomastic,** *adj.*

onomatology the science or study of the origin and forms of proper names. Also called **onomastics**. —**onomatologist**, *n.* —**onomatological**, *adj.*

onomatomania a preoccupation with words or names.

onomatophobia an abnormal fear of a certain name or word.

onym *Biology.* a technical name, as one that forms part of a system of nomenclature or classification.

onymy the application of onyms; classification or systematic nomenclature.

organonymy the nomenclature of organs. —**organonymal**, **organonymic**, *adj.*

paedonymic a name derived from one's child.

patronomatology *Rare.* the tracing of the origins of personal names.

patronymic a name derived from a father or paternal ancestor. Cf. **metronymic**.

poecilonymy the simultaneous use of several names or synonyms for one thing.

polyonymy the use of various names for one thing. —**polyonymous**, *adj.*

pseudonym a nom de plume or fictitious name, especially one used by an author to conceal his identity. Cf. **allonymy**. —**pseudonymous**, *adj.*

sobriquet, soubriquet a nickname.

tautonym a botanical or zoological name in which two terms are combined, the generic name and the specific, with both being the same. (a practice no longer approved by the International Code of Botanical Nomenclature.)

toponym 1. a place name.
2. a personal name derived from a place name.

toponymy 1. the study of the place names of a district.
2. *Anatomy.* the nomenclature of the regions of the body. —**toponymic**, **toponymical**, *adj.*

trinomialism the use of three terms or names in the classification of a species, genus, variety, etc. —**trinomial**, *n., adj.*

trionym a trinomial or name composed of three terms.

typocosmy *Rare.* a universal system of nomenclature or classification.

289. NATIONALISM
See also 10. ALLEGIANCE.

Anglo-Saxonism a belief in the innate superiority of the "Anglo-Saxon race."

chauvinism a zealous and belligerent patriotism. —**chauvinist**, *n.* —**chauvinistic**, *adj.*

civism 1. the attitudes and behavior of a good citizen.
2. *Obsolete.* devotion to the cause of the French Revolution.

ethnomania a fanaticism favoring ethnic or racial autonomy. —**ethnomaniac,** *n., adj.*

Gaelicism the characteristic of being Gaelic.

jingoism extreme or eccentric national loyalty that is hostile to the interests of any other nation. —**jingo, jingoist,** *n.* —**jingoistic,** *adj.*

Junkerism the militaristic, authoritarian spirit or character of the East Prussian aristocracy. —**Junker,** *n., adj.*

matriotism devotion to one's mother country.

nationalism 1. the spirit or aspirations of a country.
2. a devotion to the interests of one's own country.
3. a desire for national advancement.
4. the policy of asserting the interest of one's own nation, as separate from the interest of another nation and the common interest of all nations. —**nationalist,** *n., adj.* —**nationalistic,** *adj.*

nativism the custom or policy of favoring native-born citizens over immigrants, as in the awarding of government jobs. See also 312. PHILOSOPHY. —**nativist,** *n.* —**nativistic,** *adj.*

overpatriotism excessive patriotism.

Pan-Teutonism the idea that all Teutonic peoples should be joined in a union. —**Pan-Teutonist,** *n.* —**Pan-Teutonic,** *adj.*

patriotism a devoted love, support, and defense of one's country; national loyalty. —**patriot,** *n.* —**patriotic,** *adj.*

superpatriotism excessive patriotism. —**superpatriot,** *n.* —**superpatriotic,** *adj.*

ultranationalism excessive or extreme nationalism. —**ultranationalist,** *n.* —**ultranationalistic,** *adj.*

290. NATURE
See also 133. EARTH; 142. ENVIRONMENT.

aetiology etiology.

ambrology the study of the sources and formation of amber. —**ambrologic, ambrological,** *adj.*

anthropopsychism the assignment of a humanlike soul to nature. —**anthropopsychic,** *adj.*

azoology the study of inanimate nature.

chemism the quality of chemical activities, properties, or relationships.

conservationist a person who advocates the conservation of the natural resources of a country or region. —**conservational,** *adj.*

etiology, aetiology the science of the causes of natural phenomena. —**etiologic, aetiologic, etiological, aetiological,** *adj.*

physiolatry the worship of nature. —physiolater, *n*. —physiolatrous, *adj*.

physiosophy the body of wisdom about nature.

physis 1. the principle or concept of growth and change in nature.
2. nature considered as the source of growth and change.
3. something that grows or develops.

physitheism 1. the assignment of a physical form to a god.
2. the deification and worship of natural phenomena; physiolatry.

physiurgic produced by natural rather than divine or human forces.

thaumatography a dissertation on the wonders of nature. —thaumatographic, *adj*.

291. NERVES
See also 14. ANATOMY; 51. BODY, HUMAN; 56. BRAIN.

cataplexy a temporary paralytic or hypnotic state, often brought on by strong emotion. —cataplectic, *adj*.

electrotonus the state or condition of a nerve when an electric current is passing through it. —electrotonic, *adj*.

neuralgia a sharp and paroxysmal pain along the course of a nerve. —neuralgic, *adj*.

neurasthenia 1. *Medicine*. a nervous debility and exhaustion, as from overwork or prolonged nervous strain.
2. popularly, a nervous breakdown. —neurasthenic, *adj*.

neurism *Rare*. the theory that all the body's activity is controlled by nervous fluid.

neuritis 1. an inflammation in a nerve.
2. a continuous pain in a nerve, associated with paralysis, loss of reflexes, and sensory disturbances. —neuritic, *adj*.

neuroanatomy *Medicine*. the branch of anatomy that studies the anatomy of the nervous system. —neuroanatomical, *adj*.

neurography the branch of neurology concerned with description of the nerves and nervous system. —neurographic, neurographical, *adj*.

neurology the branch of medical science that studies the nerves and the nervous system, especially the diseases that affect them. —neurologist, *n*. —neurological, *adj*.

neuromimesis *Medicine*. a psychosomatic disease. —neuromimetic, *adj*.

neuropathology the pathology of the nervous system. —neuropathologist, *n*. —neuropathologic, neuropathological, *adj*.

neuropathy any disease or disorder of the nerves. —neuropathist, *n*. —neuropathic, *adj*.

neuropsychiatry the branch of medicine dealing with diseases affecting the mind and the nervous system. —**neuropsychiatrist,** *n.* —**neuropsychiatric,** *adj.*

neurosis a functional disorder of the nervous system. See also 334. PSYCHOLOGY. —**neurotic,** *n., adj.*

neurotomy the cutting of a nerve, as to relieve neuralgia. —**neurotomist,** *n.*

polyneuritis neuritis that affects several or many nerves.

prosopalgia neuralgia affecting the face.

pseudesthesia, pseudaesthesia *Pathology.* false or ghost sensations, such as those which seem to come from a missing limb. —**pseudesthetic, pseudaesthetic,** *adj.*

rhizotomy the surgical cutting of the nerve roots of the spine, usually the sensory or posterior roots, to relieve pain or eliminate paralysis.

292. NIGHT
See also 110. DARKNESS.

achluphobia an abnormal fear of darkness. Also called **scotophobia.**

noctimania an abnormal love of the night.

noctivagation the act of walking or wandering at night. —**noctivagant, noctivagous,** *adj.*

nyctalopia night-blindness.

sciophobia an abnormal fear of shadows.

scotophobia achluphobia.

293. NOSE
See also 14. ANATOMY; 51. BODY, HUMAN; 149. FACIAL FEATURES.

epistaxis bleeding from the nose; nosebleed.

nasology a scientific study of the nose. —**nasologist,** *n.* —**nasological,** *adj.*

nasoscope an electrically lighted instrument for examining the nasal cavities. —**nasoscopic,** *adj.*

noseology the analysis of character and intelligence by studying the physical characteristics of the nose. —**noseological,** *adj.*

rhinitis irritation of the nose, especially of the mucous membrane lining it.

rhinology the branch of medical science that studies the nose and its diseases. —**rhinologist,** *n.* —**rhinologic, rhinological,** *adj.*

294. NOVELTY
See also 150. FADS.

cainophobia an abnormal fear of novelty. Also called **cainotophobia.**

esoterica a collection of items of a special, rare, novel, or unusual quality.

esotericism 1. the holding of secret doctrines; the practice of limiting knowledge to a small group.
2. an interest in items of a special, rare, novel, or unusual quality. Also **esoterism.** —**esoterist,** *n.*

griffinism 1. the condition of being a griffin, or new arrival from Britain, in India.
2. behavior characteristic of a griffin.

kainomania a mania for novelty.

misoneism a hatred of novelty. Also called **neophobia.**

neolatry *Rare.* the worship of novelty. —**neolater,** *n.*

neophilism philoneism.

neophobia misoneism.

neoterist an innovator, expecially a coiner of new words.

philoneism an excessive love of novelty. Also called **neophilism.**

295. NUMBERS
See also 262. MATHEMATICS.

abacist a skilled user of the abacus.

acalculia *Psychiatry.* an inability to work with figures; a mental block concerning calculation.

arithmancy a form of divination involving numbers. Also called **arithmomancy.**

arithmomania 1. an obsession with numbers.
2. a compulsion to count things.

hebdomadism a belief that the number seven is sacred, as in ancient Babylon.

numerology a system of occultism based upon numbers. —**numerologist,** *n.* —**numerological,** *adj.*

O

296. OBSCENITY

aischrolatreia 1. the cult of the obscene.
2. the worship of filth.

aischrology the vocabulary of obscenity; linguistic filthiness.

comstockery the act or policy of censorship or expurgation on moral grounds, after Anthony Comstock (1844–1915), campaigner against vice.

coprolalia the habitual use of foul language.

coprolalomania a mania for foul speech.

coprology 1. the introduction of obscenity into art and literature.
2. obscene literature.
3. the study of obscene literature.
4. scatology.

coprophilia a love of obscenity.

pornographomania an abnormal interest in pornography.

pornography any literature, film, or pictures that are judged obscene or indecent, especially because of sexual explicitness. —**pornographer,** *n.* —**pornographic,** *adj.*

rhyparography the painting of sordid and obscene subjects. —**rhyparographer,** *n.* —**rhyparographic,** *adj.*

scatology the study of or preoccupation with excrement or obscenity. Also called **coprology.** —**scatologic, scatological,** *adj.*

297. OCCUPATIONS

See also 369. SKILL and CRAFT; 426. WORK.

amanuensis *Formal.* 1. a secretary.
2. a scribe or copyist.

cameist 1. a maker of cameos.
2. a collector of or authority on cameos.

Chekist a member of the Russian secret police (1917–1922) called *Cheka.*

factotum a general assistant, engaged to do all varieties of work.

métier an occupation, vocation or trade, especially in the sense of the work a person is best suited for.

millinery the art and trade of designing and making women's hats. —**milliner,** *n.*

modiste, modist a maker and seller of fashionable gowns and millinery for women.

mosaicist a mosaic maker or dealer in mosaics. Also **mosaist.**

myropolist *Obsolete.* a dealer in perfume or unguents.

oecist, oekist a colonizer.

ombudsman an individual charged with the duty of investigating and redressing the sources of complaints lodged by private citizens against businesses, institutions, and officials.

vitrailist a maker or designer of stained glass.

298. ODORS

anosmia *Medicine.* the absence of the sense of smell; olfactory anesthesia. Also called **anosphrasia.** —**anosmic,** *adj.*

halitosis bad breath; an unpleasant odor emanating from the mouth.

mephitis a rank or foul smell, especially one rising from the earth, as from a swamp. —**mephitic, mephitical,** *adj.*

myropolist *Obsolete.* a dealer in perfume or unguents.

olfactology the branch of medical science that studies the sense of smell. —**olfactologist,** *n.*

olfactophobia osmophobia.

osmatism the ability to perceive odors. —**osmatic,** *adj.*

osmidrosis an abnormal condition in which the sweat has a very strong odor.

osmonosology *Medicine.* the study of the sense of smell, especially its disorders. —**osmonologist,** *n.*

osmophobia an abnormal fear of odors.

osphresiology *Medicine.* the sum of information concerning odors and olfaction. Also called **osmology.**

osphresiophilia an inordinate love of smells.

osphresiophobia an abnormal dislike of odors.

oxyosphresia heightened acuteness of the sense of smell.

parosmia *Medicine.* a disorder of the sense of smell. Also called **parosphresia, parosphresis.**

299. OLD AGE
See also 3. AGE; 18. ANTIQUITY; 171. FOSSILS.

anecdotage old age, when a person may be prone to regale others with anecdotes about his past. [A humorous blend of *anecdote* and *dotage*.]

anility the condition of behaving like an old woman, used especially of men. Cf. senility.

caducity decrepit old age; senility.

gerascophobia the fear of growing old.

geratology the study of the decline of life, as in old age.   —geratologic, geratological, geratologous, *adj.*

geriatrics 1. the science dealing with the diseases, debilities, and care of aged persons.
2. the study of the physical process and problems of aging; gerontology. —geriatric, *adj.* —geriatrist, geriatrician, geriatry, *n.*

gerocomy gerontology.

gerodontics a dental specialty concerned with the care and treatment of the dental problems of the aged. —gerodontist, *n.*

geromorphism the condition of appearing older than one is.

gerontology the branch of science that studies aging and the special problems of the aged. Also called gerocomy. —gerontologist, *n.* —gerontological, *adj.*

nonagenarianism the state of being in one's nineties. —nonagenarian, *n., adj.* —nonagenary, *adj.*

nostology *Medicine, Obsolete.* the study of senility.

octogenarianism the state of being in one's eighties. —octogenarian, *n., adj.* —octogenary, *adj.*

opsimathy *Rare.* 1. a late education.
2. the process of acquiring education late in life.

senicide the killing off of the old men in a tribe. —senicidal, *adj.*

senility 1. the state or quality of being old, especially, being afflicted with the infirmity of body and mind that sometimes comes with old age.
2. *Informal.* a condition of weakness of mind and body, usually associated with advanced age, characterized by the inability to remember simple, recent events, general confusion and bewilderment, and increasing debility. Cf. anility. —senile, *adj.*

septuagenarianism the state of being in one's seventies. —septuagenarian *n., adj.* —septuagenary, *adj.*

300. OPINION
See also 216. IDEAS.

heterodoxy 1. the state of being at variance with established doctrines or beliefs.
2. a heterodox view or belief.

opinionist a person fond of his own opinions and of making them known.

301. ORDER and DISORDER
See also 83. CLASSIFICATION.

agenda things to be done or a list of those things, as a list of the matters to be discussed at a meeting.

anarchy extreme disorder. See also 185. GOVERNMENT.

ataxia, ataxy lack of order; irregularity. See also 122. DISEASE and ILLNESS.

bedlamism chaos, disorder. See also 224. INSANITY.

methodology 1. the science of method or orderly arrangement and classification.
2. any system created to impose order. See also 250. LOGIC. —**methodological,** *adj.*

Pandemonium 1. the abode of all demons; Hell.
2. (*l.c.*) any scene of wild confusion or disorder.

302. ORGANISMS
See also 16. ANIMALS; 32. BACTERIA; 44. BIOLOGY; 319. PLANTS;
430. ZOOLOGY.

anabolism *Biology, Physiology.* the synthesis in living organisms of more complex substances from simpler ones. Cf. **catabolism.** —**anabolic,** *adj.*

antibiosis a relationship or association between two or more organisms that is harmful to one of them. Cf. **symbiosis.**

biosynthesis the formation of chemical compounds by living organisms, either by synthesis or degradation. —**biosynthetic,** *adj.*

biotypology the science or study of biotypes, or organisms sharing the same hereditary characteristics. —**biotypologic, biotypological,** *adj.*

catabolism, katabolism *Biology, Physiology.* the destructive processes of chemical change in living organisms, characterized by the breaking down of complex substances into simpler ones, with a release of energy. Cf. **anabolism.** —**catabolic,** *adj.*

histology 1. the branch of biology that studies tissues of organisms.
2. the structure, especially the microscopic structure, of organic tissues. Also **histiology.** —**histologist,** *n.* —**histologic, histological,** *adj.*

katabolism catabolism. —**katabolic,** *adj.*

microorganism any one of a large variety of microscopic or ultramicroscopic organisms, as bacteria, viruses, etc.

monogenesis the theory that all organisms are descended from one original organism. —monogenetic, *adj.*

organism any living thing or anything that resembles a living thing in complexity of structure or function.

phenology, phaenology the study of the effects of climate on animal and plant life. —phenologist, phaenologist, *n.* —phenologic, phaenologic, phenological, phaenological, *adj.*

symbiosis a relationship or association between two or more organisms that is harmful to none of them. —symbiotic, *adj.*

xenogenesis 1. abiogenesis; spontaneous generation.
2. metagenesis, or alternation of generations.
3. production of an offspring entirely different from either of the parents. Also xenogeny. —xenogenic, —xenogenetic, *adj.*

xenogeny xenogenesis.

zygomorphism the state or quality of being bilaterally symmetrical, as certain organisms. —zygomorphic, zygomorphous, *adj.*

303. ORGANIZED LABOR

Boulwarism a form of labor-management negotiation in which management opens with a generous offer that is subject to little or no bargaining.

laborite a member of a political party or other group allied with the interests of labor.

Luddism the beliefs of bands of early 19th-century English workmen that attempted to prevent the use of labor-saving machinery by destroying it. Also Ludditism. —Luddite, *n.*

unionism the practices and policies of a labor union. —unionist, *n., adj.*

Whitleyism a system of permanent voluntary boards in English industries in which both management and workers settle matters of wages, hours, etc.

304. ORIGINS

aetiology etiology. —aetiological, *adj.*

anthropogeny the study of human origins. —anthropogenic, anthropogenetic *adj.*

archology the science of origins.

autochthonism, autochthony the state of being aboriginal or native to a particular area. —autochthonous, *adj.*

etiology the study of the causes for and origin of any phenomena. Also spelled aetiology. —etiological, *adj.*

isogenesis, isogeny the state or process of deriving from the same source or origins, as different parts deriving from the same embryo tissues. —isogenic, isogenetic, *adj*.

monogenism the theory that the entire human race is descended from a single ancestral pair. Also monogenesis, monogeny. —monogenist, *n*. —monogenistic, *adj*.

305. ORNAMENTATION
See also 23. ART.

decalcomania 1. the technique of transferring pictures and other designs onto glass, wood, china etc., using specially prepared paper pieces.
2. the picture so created. Also called **decal**.

decoupage, découpage 1. the art or technique of cutting out pictures or designs from paper or other material and applying them to a surface.
2. the work produced.

engrailment the ornamenting of the edge of a coin with grooves or other indentations or reliefs as a deterrent to clipping.

festoonery 1. decoration with festoons, strings of flowers, ribbons, etc., looped in curves between two points
2. festoons collectively.

fimbriation 1. the process of decorating with a fringe.
2. such decoration.

illumination 1. the process of decorating manuscripts with illustrations, as in the capitals, tracery, etc.
2. the decoration itself.

intarsia a form or method of decoration, dating from the Renaissance, consisting of inlaid, mosaiclike patterns, especially of wood.

marquetry a form of decoration, often used in furniture-making, composed of inlays of wood veneers of different colors.

ornamentist, ornamentalist 1. an artist who specializes in ornamentation.
2. a person whose work is considered to be ornament rather than art.

parquetry mosaic work in wood, a form of marquetry, used mostly for floors and wainscoting.

reticulation arrangement in the form of a network, as for decoration. —reticulate, *adj*.

tessellation decoration composed of multi-colored, small tiles, as found in a mosaic.

tracery ornamental work, composed of fine, interlaced ribbing or the like, used in windows, screens, etc.

vermiculation ornamentation resembling worm-holes or worm-tracks, as is found in mosaic pavements and rusticated masonry. See also 282. MOTION; 427. WORMS.

P

306. PAIN
See also 122. DISEASE and ILLNESS; 223. INJURY; 350. REMEDIES.

algogenic producing pain.

algolagnia a deriving of sexual pleasure from inflicting or enduring pain. Cf. masochism, sadism. —algolagnist, *n.* —algolagnic, *adj.*

algometry measurement of pain by means of an algometer, an instrument for determining sensitivity to pain produced by pressure. —algometric, algometrical, *adj.*

algophilia a love of pain.

algophobia an extreme fear of pain. Cf. odynophobia.

audialgesia otalgia.

brachialgia pain in the nerves of the upper arm.

cardialgia, cardialgy a burning or other painful feeling in the stomach or esophagus; heartburn.

cephalalgia *Medicine.* 1. a pain in the head.
2. a headache. Also called **cephalgia, cephalodynia.**

coxalgia, coxalgy pain in the hip joint.

dermatalgia neuralgia of the skin.

dolorifuge anything that drives away pain.

gastralgia pain in the stomach or abdominal region.

hemicrania 1. *Medicine.* a pain or aching on one side of the head.
2. migraine.

hypalgesia hypalgia.

hypalgia a decreased sensibility to pain. Also **hypalgesia.**

hyperalgesia an unusually high sensitivity to pain. —hyperalgesic, *adj.*

hysterodynia pain in the uterus.

415

masochism 1. *Psychiatry.* a condition in which sexual gratification is achieved through suffering physical pain and humiliation, especially inflicted on oneself.
2. any gratification gained from pain or deprivation inflicted or imposed on oneself. Cf. sadism. —**masochist,** *n.* —**masochistic,** *adj.*

odontalgia *Medicine.* a pain in a tooth. —**odontalgic,** *adj.*

odynophobia an abnormal fear of pain.

otalgia *Medicine.* an earache. —**otalgic,** *adj.*

photalgia pain in the eyes caused by light.

proctalgia pain in the rectum.

prosopalgia neuralgia affecting the face.

psychalgia mental or psychic pain.

rachialgia pain affecting the spine. —**rachialgic,** *adj.*

sadism 1. *Psychiatry.* a sexual gratification gained through causing physical pain or humiliation.
2. any enjoyment in being cruel. Cf. masochism. —**sadist,** *n.* —**sadistic,** *adj.*

sadomasochism *Psychiatry.* a condition of disturbed and destructive personality marked by the presence of both sadistic and masochistic traits. —**sadomasochist,** *n.* —**sadomasochistic,** *adj.*

stoicism an indifference to pleasure or pain. —**stoic,** *n., adj.* —**stoical,** *adj.*

synalgia pain in one part of the body resulting from hurt or injury in another part; referred pain.

uteralgia pain in the womb or uterus.

zoosadism sadism directed toward animals. —**zoosadist,** *n.* —**zoosadistic,** *adj.*

307. PARENTS
See also 15. ANCESTORS; 77. CHILDREN; 153. FATHER; 204. HEREDITY; 281. MOTHER.

compaternity the spiritual relationship between godparents, or between them and the actual parents of a child.

filiation 1. the fact or condition of being a son or daughter.
2. the relation of child to parent, especially father.

matricide 1. the killing of one's mother.
2. a person who has killed his mother. —**matricidal,** *adj.*

parentalism 1. the behavior of a parent.
2. the assumption by a nonparent of superior authority over a child; paternalism.

parentation *Archaic.* the performance of funeral rituals for one's parents.

parenticide the crime of parricide.

parricide 1. the act of killing one's parent or other close relative.
2. a person who has killed his parent. —parricidal, *adj.*

patricide 1. the killing of one's father.
2. a person who has killed his father. —patricidal, *adj.*

308. PAST
See also 18. ANTIQUITY; 174. FUTURE; 207. HISTORY; 269. MEMORY; 304. ORIGINS.

aboriginality the condition of being first in a place and of having a relatively simple nature. —aboriginal, *n., adj.*

antediluvianism adherence to or fondness for ancient things or customs. —antediluvian, *n., adj.*

antiquarianism interest in the culture of antiquity, especially that of classical Greece and Rome. —antiquary, antiquarian, *n.* —antiquarian, *adj.*

archaeolatry devotion to archaism. —archaeolater, *n.* —archaeolatrous, *adj.*

archaism an inclination toward old-fashioned things, speech, etc. Also archaicism. —archaist, *n.* —archaic, *adj.*

chronographer a person who records time or the events that have occurred in time.

chronography *Obsolete.* the recording or study of past events.

medievalism strong fondness or admiration for the culture, mores, etc., of the Middle Ages. —medievalist, *n.* —medievalistic, *adj.*

palaetiology paletiology.

paleology, palaeology the study of antiquities. —paleologist, palaeologist, *n.* —paleologic, palaeologic, paleological, palaeological, *adj.*

paleopathology, palaeopathology *Medicine.* the study of diseases from former times as found in fossils and mummified remains.

paletiology, palaetiology an explanation of events of the past through the laws of causation. —paletiologist, palaetiologist, *n.* —paletiological, palaetiological, *adj.*

papyrology the study of papyrus manuscripts. —papyrologist, *n.* —papyrological, *adj.*

philarchaist *Obsolete.* one devoted to the archaic. —philarchaic, *adj.*

309. PERCEPTION
See also 9. ALERTNESS; 198. HEARING; 397. TOUCH;
405. UNDERSTANDING.

Berkeleianism, Berkeleyanism the system of philosophical idealism developed by George Berkeley (1685?–1753), especially his tenet that the physical world does not have an independent reality but exists as a perception of the divine mind and the finite mind of man. Also **Berkeleyism.** —**Berkeleian, Berkeleyan,** *n.*, *adj.*

chromesthesia *Medicine.* the association of imaginary sensations of color with actual perceptions of hearing, taste, or smell. Also called **photism, color hearing.** Cf. **synesthesia.**

coenesthesia, coenesthesis, cenesthesia, cenesthesis the combination of organic sensations that comprise an individual's awareness of bodily existence. —**coenesthetic, cenesthetic,** *adj.*

dysesthesia an impaired condition of any of the senses.

kinesthesia *Medicine.* the sense by which movement, weight, position, etc. are perceived. —**kinesthetic,** *adj.*

oxygeusia extreme acuteness or sensitivity of the sense of taste.

oxyopia, oxyopy an extremely heightened acuteness of the eyesight, resulting from increased sensibility of the retina.

oxyosphresia heightened acuteness of the sense of smell.

panesthesia, panaesthesia the total or collective experience of all sensations or all the senses. —**panesthetic, panaesthetic,** *adj.*

paresthesia, paraesthesia any abnormal physical sensation, as itching, a tickling feeling, etc. —**paresthetic, paraesthetic,** *adj.*

phantasm a vision or other perception of something that has no physical or objective reality, as a ghost or other supernatural apparition. Also **phantasma.** See also 218. IMAGES; 312. PHILOSOPHY.

phonism a sound or a sensation of hearing produced by stimulus of another sense, as taste, smell, etc.

photism chromesthesia.

sensorium the sensory apparatus of the body as a whole; the seat of physical sensation, imagined to be in the gray matter of the brain.

synesthesia, synaesthesia *Medicine.* a secondary sensation accompanying an actual perception, as the perceiving of sound as a color or the sensation of being touched in a place at some distance from the actual place of touching. Cf. **chromesthesia.** —**synesthetic, synaesthetic,** *adj.*

telesthesia, telaesthesia a form of extrasensory perception, working over a distance and enabling the so gifted observer to perceive events, objects, etc., far away. —telesthetic, telaesthetic, *adj.*

310. PERFORMING
See also 2. ACROBATICS; 127. DRAMA; 159. FILMS; 284. MUSIC; 378. SONGS and SINGING; 395. TIGHTROPE WALKING.

Barnumism showmanship or any activity taking advantage of people's credulity or desire for sensational entertainment, as practiced by P. T. Barnum (1810–91).

callithumpian a participant in a noisy mock serenade, as a charivari.

charivari a mock serenade accompanied by much noise and revelry, often played as a joke on newly married couples.

ecdysiast a strip tease dancer.

equilibrist one who performs feats that require an unusual sense of balance, as a tightrope walker.

escapism the art or technique of escaping from chains, locked trunks, etc., as a form of entertainment. —escapist, *n., adj.*

funambulism the art or skill of tightrope walking. —funambulist, *n.*

harlequinade a performance involving Harlequin or other characters of the *Commedia dell'Arte*; hence, buffoonery or clownish behavior. Also called harlequinery.

illusionist a conjurer or magician who creates illusions, as by sleight of hand.

jugglery the art of the juggler.

legerdemain skill in or practice of feats of dexterity that create a magical illusion. —legerdemainist, *n.*

mimicry the art or practice of copying or imitating closely, especially by a person for the purpose of entertainment. See also 44. BIOLOGY. —mimic, mimical, *adj.*

monology 1. the art of performing monologues.
2. *Obsolete.* a monologue.

mummery 1. a performance by mummers, performers wearing masks or fantastic disguises.
2. any showy but empty performance.

pantomime the art of mute acting. —pantomimist, *n.*

pianologue a humorous performance at the piano, sometimes with a verbal accompaniment by the performer.

prestidigitation the art of legerdemain; sleight of hand. —prestidigitator, *n.* —prestidigitatorial, prestidigitatory, *adj.*

puppetry the art of making and handling puppets.

recitationist a person who recites poetry or other literary excerpts for enter-tainment.

shadowgraph an image formed by a shadow cast upon a lighted surface, as one formed by the hands for entertainment. —shadowgraphist, *n.*

311. -PHILE, -PHILIA, -PHILY
See also 41. BEHAVIOR; 91. COLLECTIONS and COLLECTING; 251. LOVE; 254. MANIAS; 313. PHOBIAS; 334. PSYCHOLOGY.

aileurophilia, ailurophilia an abnormal fondness for cats.

Anglophile a person with a fondness for England and things English.

audiophile a person especially interested in high-fidelity sound equipment and recordings on tape or disks.

audiophilia 1. the state or condition of an audiophile.
2. the state of one who listens to high-fidelity equipment solely for the qual-ity of reproduction. —audiophilic, *adj.*

bibliophile a lover of books.—bibliophilism, bibliophily, *n.*

carcinophilia an affinity for cancerous tissue, a property of certain chemical agents.

cinephilia avid moviegoing. —cinephile, *n., adj.*

claustrophilia an abnormal desire to be closed in, to shut all windows and doors. —claustrophile, *n.* —claustrophilic, *adj.*

demophilia a great fondness for crowds.

discophily, diskophily the zealous study and collection of phonograph rec-ords. Also called phonophily. —discophile, diskophile, *n.*

Francophile a person with a fondness for France and things French.

galeophilia aileurophilia.

Germanophile a person who is especially attracted to or interested in Ger-many, its people, culture, etc.

gramophile *British.* a lover and collector of phonograph records.

hydrophily an affinity for water, a property of certain materials. —hydro-philic, hydrophilous, *adj.*

iconophilist a person who collects pictures, as prints, engravings, lithographs, etc.

laparotomaphilia the abnormal desire to undergo abdominal surgery for sim-ulated reasons.

musicophile a music lover.

mysophilia an abnormal attraction to filth.

necrophilia, necrophily, necrophilism an abnormal attraction, especially erotic, to corpses. —necrophile, *n.*, *adj.* —necrophiliac, *n.*, *adj.*

nemophily a fondness or liking for forests, woods, or woodland scenery. —nemophilist, *n.* —nemophilous, *adj.*

nosophilia an abnormal desire to be ill. Also called pathophilia.

nyctophilia an abnormal preference for the night over the day.

pathophilia nosophilia.

phonophily discophily.

pyrophilia a love of fire

Russophilism great fondness for or interest in Russia, its people, customs, language, art, etc. —Russophile, *n.*, *adj.*

Slavophilism enthusiasm for or admiration of things Slavic, its literature, language, culture, customs, etc. —Slavophil, Slavophile, *n.*, *adj.*

taphophilia an abnormal love for funerals, graves, and cemeteries.

toxophily the art or sport of archery. —toxophilite, *n.*

zoophilism, zoophily love of animals. —zoophilist, *n.* —zoophilous, *adj.*

312. PHILOSOPHY
See also 21. ARGUMENTATION; 100. COSMOLOGY; 104. CRITICISM; 145. ETHICS; 216.IDEAS; 233. KNOWLEDGE; 250. LOGIC; 392. THEOLOGY; 393. THINKING; 402. TRUTH and ERROR; 405. UNDERSTANDING; 407. VALUES; 422. WISDOM.

accidentalism the philosophic doctrine that claims that events can or do occur without cause. —accidentalist, *n.*

actualism the doctrine that all reality is animate, in motion, or in process. —actualist, *n.* —actualistic, *adj.*

aesthetics, esthetics a branch of philosophy dealing with beauty and the beautiful. —aesthete, aesthetic, *n.*, *adj.* —aesthetical, *adj.*

analogism reasoning deductively, from a generalization to particular events.

architectonics the science of the systemization of knowledge. See also 20. ARCHITECTURE; 23. ART.

aretaics the study of virtue.

Aristotelianism the philosophy of Aristotle, especially an emphasis upon formal deductive logic, upon the concept that reality is a combination of form and matter, and upon investigation of the concrete and particular. —Aristotelian, *n.*, *adj.*

atomism the theory that minute, discrete, finite, and indivisible elements are the ultimate constituents of all matter. Also called atomic theory. —atomist, *n.* —atomistic, atomistical, *adj.*

Averroism, Averrhoism   the philosophy of Averroës, chiefly Aristotelianism tinged with Neoplatonism, asserting the unity of an active and divine intellect common to all while denying personal immortality. —Averroist, Averrhoist, *n*. —Averroistic, Averrhoistic, *adj*.

Benthamism   the philosophical theory of Jeremy Bentham that the morality of actions is estimated and determined by their utility and that pleasure and pain are both the ultimate standard of right and wrong and the fundamental motives influencing human actions and wishes. —Benthamite, *n*. —Benthamic, *adj*.

Bergsonism   the philosophy of Henri Bergson, emphasizing time or duration as the central fact of experience and asserting the existence of the *élan vital* as an original life force governing all organic processes in a way that can be explained only by intuition, not by scientific analysis. —Bergsonian, *n*., *adj*.

Berkeleianism   the philosophy and beliefs of George Berkeley denying the existence of the real world. —Berkeleian, *n*., *adj*.

Cartesianism   the philosophy of René Descartes and his followers, especially its emphasis on logical analysis, its mechanistic interpretation of physical nature, and its dualistic distinction between thought (mind) and extension (matter). —Cartesian, *n*., *adj*.

causationism   the principles and practices of universal causation.

commonsense realism   naive realism.

Comtism   positivism, def. 1.

conceptualism   the doctrine that universals exist only in the mind. Cf. idealism. —conceptualist, *n*. —conceptualistic, *adj*.

consciencism   the personal philosophy of Kwame Nkrumah (1909–72), president of Ghana (1960–66), devised and named by him.

cosmology   the branch of philosophy that studies the origin, evolution, and structure of the universe, especially such characteristics as space, time, causality, and freedom. —cosmologist, *n*. —cosmologic, cosmological, *adj*.

Cynicism   a Greek philosophy of the 4th century B.C. advocating the doctrines that virtue is the only good, that the essence of virtue is self-control and individual freedom, and that surrender to any external influence is beneath the dignity of man. —Cynic, *n*. —Cynical, *adj*.

Cyrenaicism   the principles of the school of the philosopher Aristippus of Cyrene. —Cyrenaic, *n*. —Cyrenean, Cyrenian, *adj*.

descendentalism   the doctrines of a school of philosophy emphasizing empiricism and positivism. Cf. transcendentalism. —descendentalist, *n*. —descendental, descendentalistic, *adj*.

determinism 1. the doctrine that all facts and events result from the operation of natural laws.
2. the doctrine that all events, including human choices and decisions, are necessarily determined by motives, which are regarded as external forces acting on the will. Also called **predeterminism**. Cf. **fatalism**. —**determinist**, *n.* —**deterministic**, *adj.*

doxography the compiling of extracts from ancient Greek philosophers, with editorial commentary. —**doxographer**, *n.* —**doxographical**, *adj.*

dualism 1. any theory in any field of philosophical investigation that reduces the variety of its subject matter to two irreducible principles, as good/evil or natural/supernatural.
2. *Metaphysics.* any system that reduces the whole universe to two principles, as the Platonic Ideas and Matter. Cf. **monism, pluralism**. —**dualist**, *n.* —**dualistic**, *adj.*

dynamism any of various theories or philosophical systems that seek to explain natural phenomena by the action and interaction of forces, as mechanism or Leibnizianism. Cf. **vitalism**. —**dynamist**, *n.* —**dynamistic**, *adj.*

dysteleology a doctrine denying the existence of a final cause or purpose in life or nature. Cf. **teleology**. —**dysteleologist**, *n.* —**dysteleological**, *adj.*

eclecticism 1. the use or advocacy of a method involving the selection of doctrines from various systems and their combination into a unified system of ideas.
2. such a system. —**eclectic**, *n., adj.*

Eleaticism a school of philosophy founded by Parmenides and its doctrines, especially those contributed by Zeno (of Elea), asserting the unreality of motion or change. —**Eleatic**, *adj.*

emanationism a theory of the origin of the world by a series of emanations from the Godhead. Also called **emanatism**. —**emanationist**, *n.* —**emanational**, *adj.*

empiricism 1. the doctrine that all ideas and categories are derived from sense experience and that knowledge cannot extend beyond experience, including observation, experiment, and induction.
2. an empirical method or practice. —**empiricist**, *n.* —**empirical**, *adj.*

entelechy *Vitalism.* a vital agent or force directing growth and life. Cf. **teleology**. —**entelechial**, *adj.*

Epicureanism the philosophical system of Epicurus, holding that the natural world is a series of fortuitous combinations of atoms, and that the highest good is freedom from disturbance and pain. Also **Epicurism**. —**Epicurean**, *n., adj.*

epiphenomenalism the doctrine that consciousness is a mere accessory and accompaniment of physiological processes and is powerless to affect these processes. —epiphenomenalist, *n.* —epiphenomenal, *adj.*

epistemology the branch of philosophy that studies the origin, nature, methods, validity, and limits of human knowledge. —epistemologist, *n.* —epistemic, epistemological, *adj.*

essentialism 1. a philosophical theory asserting that metaphysical essences are real and intuitively accessible.
2. a philosophical theory giving priority to the inward nature, true substance, or constitution of something over its existence. Cf. existentialism. —essentialist, *n.* —essentialistic, *adj.*

esthetics aesthetics.

ethical nihilism the belief that there are no bases for establishing a moral or ethical philosophy. Cf. nihilism.

ethical relativism the belief that morality is relative to the society where it exists and that its criticism and evaluation are irrelevant. Cf. relativism.

ethics the branch of philosophy that considers the good, moral principles, and right action. —ethicist, *n.* —ethical, *adj.*

etiology, aetiology the science of causation. —etiologic, aetiologic, etiological, aetiological, *adj.*

existentialism 1. the doctrine that man forms his essence in the course of the life resulting from his personal choices.
2. an emphasis upon man's creating his own nature as well as the importance of personal freedom, decision, and commitment. Also called philosophical existentialism. Cf. essentialism. —existentialist, *n., adj.*

experientialism the philosophical theory that states that experience is the source of all knowledge. —experientialist, *n.* —experiential, *adj.*

fatalism the doctrine that all things are subject to fate or inevitable predestination and that man is ultimately unable to prevent inevitabilities. Cf. determinism. —fatalist, *n.* —fatalistic, *adj.*

Fichteanism theories and beliefs of J. G. Fichte, German philosopher and social thinker, a precursor of socialism. —Fichtean, *n., adj.*

Gnosticism the doctrines of any of various dualistic sects among the Jews and the early Christians who claimed possession of superior spiritual knowledge, explained the creation of the world in an emanational manner, and condemned matter as evil. —Gnostic, *n., adj.*

gradualism a theory maintaining that two seemingly conflicting notions are not radically opposed, but are part of a gradually altering continuity. —gradualist, *n., adj.* —gradualistic, *adj.*

Haeckelism theories and doctrines of Ernst Haeckel, German biologist and philosopher, especially the notion "ontogeny recapitulates phylogeny." —Haeckelian, *adj.*

Hegelian dialectic an interpretive method, originally used to relate specific entities or events to the absolute idea, in which an assertable proposition (*thesis*) is necessarily opposed by its apparent contradiction (*antithesis*), and both reconciled on a higher level of truth by a third proposition (*synthesis*). Also called **Hegelian triad.**

Hegelianism the philosophy of Georg Wilhelm Friedrich Hegel and his followers, characterized by the use of a special dialectic as an analytical and interpretive method. See also **Hegelian dialectic.** —Hegelian, *n., adj.*

Hermeticism, hermeticism 1. the ideas or beliefs set forth in the writings of Hermes Trismegistus.
2. adherence to these ideas and beliefs.

Hobbism the philosophical beliefs of Thomas Hobbes, who maintained that an individual has the right to self-preservation and the pursuit of happiness. —Hobbist, *n.* —Hobbesian, *adj.*

holism the theory that whole entities, as fundamental components of reality, have an existence other than as the mere sum of their parts. Cf. **organicism.** —holist, *n.* —holistic, *adj.*

humanitarianism 1. *Ethics.* the doctrine that man's obligations are concerned wholly with the welfare of the human race.
2. *Theology.* the doctrine that man may achieve perfection without divine assistance. —humanitarian, *n., adj.*

hylicism, hylism 1. the materialist theories of the early Ionic philosophers. —hylicist, *n.*
2. the doctrines concerning the lowest of three Gnostic orders of mankind, the material or fleshly, unsavable as sons of the devil. Cf. **pneumatism, psychism.**
3. the theory that regards matter as the principle of evil, as in dualistic theology or philosophy. —hylic, *adj.*

hylomorphism the theory derived from Aristotle that every physical object is composed of two principles, an unchanging prime matter and a form deprived of actuality with every substantial change of the object. —hylomorphist, *n.* —hylomorphic, *adj.*

hypostasis the essential substance or underlying nature or principle of a thing. —hypostatic, hypostatical, *adj.*

hypothesis 1. a principle or proposition that is assumed for the sake of argument or that is taken for granted to proceed to the proof of the point in question.
2. a system or theory created to account for something that is not understood. —hypothesist, hypothetist, *n.* —hypothetic, hypothetical, *adj.*

idealism any system or theory that maintains that the real is of the nature of thought or that the object of external perception consists of ideas. Cf. realism. —idealist, *n.* —idealistic, *adj.*

illusionism a theory or doctrine that the material world is wholly or nearly wholly an illusion. —illusionist, *n.* —illusionistic, *adj.*

immaterialism the belief that material things have no objective existence but exist only as mental perceptions. —immaterialist, *n.* —immaterial, *adj.*

indifferentism a view that admits no real difference between true and false in religion or philosophy; a form of agnosticism. See also 28. ATTITUDES. —indifferentist, *n.*

instrumentalism a pragmatic philosophy holding that it is the function of thought to be a means to the control of environment, and that the value and truthfulness of ideas is determined by their usefulness in human experience or progress. —instrumentalist, *n., adj.*

irrationalism 1. a theory that nonrational forces govern the universe.
2. any attitude or set of beliefs having a nonrational basis, as nihilism. —irrationalist, *n., adj.* —irrationalistic, *adj.*

Kantianism the philosophy of Emmanuel Kant, asserting that the nature of the mind renders it unable to know reality immediately, that the mind interprets data presented to it as phenomena in space and time, and that the reason, in order to find a meaningful basis for experience or in order for ethical conduct to exist, may postulate things unknowable to it, as the existence of a soul. —Kantist, *n.* —Kantian, *adj.*

laxism the view of a school of Roman Catholic casuists who maintained that any chance of liberty, however slight, should be followed. —laxist, *n.*

Leibnizianism, Leibnitzianism the philosophy of Gottfied Wilhelm von Leibniz and his followers, especially monadism and the theory of preestablished harmony, the theory that this is the best of all possible worlds because God has chosen it (satirized by Voltaire in *Candide*), and proposals for a scientific language and a method of symbolic computation. —Leibnizian, Leibnitzian, *n., adj.*

libertarianism 1. one who advocates liberty, especially with regard to thought or conduct.
2. the philosophical doctrine of free will. Cf. necessitarianism, determinism, fatalism. —libertarian, *n., adj.*

logical positivism positivism, def. 2.

logicism a philosophical system that places strong emphasis on logic.

materialism the theory that regards matter and its various guises as constituting the universe, and all phenomena, including those of the mind, as caused by material agencies. —materialist, *n., adj.* —materialistic, *adj.*

mechanism 1. the theory that everything in the universe is produced by matter in process, capable of explanation by the laws of chemistry and physics. 2. the theory that a natural process is machinelike or is explainable in terms of Newtonian mechanics. —**mechanist,** *n.* —**mechanistic,** *adj.*

meliorism the doctrine that the world tends to become better of itself, or that it may improve more rapidly by proper human assistance. Cf. **optimism, pessimism.** —**meliorist,** *n.* —**melioristic,** *adj.*

mentalism the doctrine that objects of knowledge have no existence except in the mind of the perceiver, as in Berkeleianism. —**mentalist,** *n.* —**mentalistic,** *adj.*

mesology the study of ways of attaining happiness.

metaethics a branch of philosophy concerned with the foundations of ethics and especially with the definition of ethical terms and the nature of moral discourse.

metagnosticism the doctrine that knowledge of the Absolute is within human reach, but through a higher religious consciousness rather than by logical processes. —**metagnostic,** *adj.*

metaphysics a branch of philosophy concerned with being, first principles, and often including aspects of cosmology and epistemology. —**metaphysician,** *n.* —**metaphysical,** *adj.*

metempiricism a concept believed to be beyond but related to empirically gained data. Also **metempirics.**

miserabilism the philosophy of pessimism.

Mohism the doctrines of Mo-Tze, Chinese sage of the 5th century B.C., who advocated government by an absolute monarch and universal love. —**Mohist,** *n., adj.*

monadism 1. the Leibnizian doctrine of monads as unextended, indivisible, and indestructible entities that are the ultimate constituent of the universe and a microcosm of it. Also called **monadology.** 2. the doctrine of Giordano Bruno concerning monads as basic and irreducible metaphysical units that are psychically and spatially individuated. —**monadistic,** *adj.*

monism 1. *Metaphysics.* a theory that only one basic substance or principle exists as the ground of reality. Cf. **dualism, pluralism.** 2. *Metaphysics.* a theory that reality consists of a single element. Cf. **pluralism.** 3. *Epistemology.* a theory that the object and the sense datum of cognition are identical. —**monist,** *n.* —**monistic, monistical,** *adj.*

mortalism the philosophic doctrine that claims that the soul is mortal. —**mortalist,** *n.*

naive realism the theory that the world is perceived exactly as it is. Also called natural realism, commonsense realism. Cf. idealism, realism.

nativism the belief that the human brain is capable of spontaneous or innate ideas. See also 169. FOREIGNERS. —nativist, *n.* —nativistic, *adj.*

natural realism naive realism.

necessitarianism the doctrine of the determinism of the will by antecedent causes, as opposed to that of the freedom of the will. Also called necessarianism. Cf. determinism, fatalism, libertarianism. —necessitarian, *n., adj.*

negativism any system of thought opposed to positivism; doctrines based upon doubt and skepticism. —negativist, *n., adj.* —negativistic, *adj.*

Neoplatonism, Neo-Platonism a philosophical system originated in Alexandria in the 3rd century A.D., founded on Platonic doctrine, Aristotelianism, and Oriental mysticism, with later influences from Christianity. —Neoplatonist, *n.* —Neoplatonic, *adj.*

neo-Thomism the neo-scholastic philosophy closely related to the teachings of Thomas Aquinas. —neo-Thomist, *n.*

Nietzscheism the philosophy of Nietzsche, especially its emphasis on the will to power as the chief motivating force of both the individual and society. Also called Nietzscheanism. —Nietzschean, *n., adj.*

nihilism the belief that existence is not real and that there can be no objective basis of truth, a form of extreme skepticism. Cf. ethical nihilism. —nihilist, *n., adj.*

nominalism *Medieval Philosophy.* the doctrine that abstract words or universals do not represent objectively existing entities, and that universals are only names applied to individual physical particulars that alone exist objectively. —nominalist, *n., adj.* —nominalistic, *adj.*

noumenalism any of several philosophical concepts regarding the noumenon. —noumenalist, *n., adj.*

noumenon *Kantianism.* 1. that which can be the object only of a purely intellectual, nonsensuous intuition, the thing-in-itself (*Ding an Sich*). 2. an unknowable object (as God), the existence of which is not capable of proof. —noumenal, *adj.*

objectivism 1. any of various philosophical theories stressing the external or objective elements of cognition. 2. *Ethics.* any theory asserting that the moral good is objective and not influenced by human feelings. —objectivist, *n., adj.*

occasionalism the Cartesian philosophic doctrine that holds that mind and matter are incapable of affecting each other and that their reciprocal action must be owing to the intervention of God. —occasionalist, *n.* —occasionalistic, *adj.*

oligarchism adherence to oligarchy as a principle. —oligarchist, *n*.

ontology philosophical inquiry into the nature of being itself, a branch of metaphysics. —ontologist, *n*. —ontologic, ontological, ontologistic, *adj*.

operationism the idea that the concepts used in nonanalytical scientific statements must be definable in relation to identifiable operations. —operationist, *n*. —operationistic, *adj*.

optimism 1. the belief that good is ultimately triumphant over the evil in the world.
2. the Leibnizian doctrine that this is the best of all possible worlds.
3. the belief that goodness pervades reality. Cf. meliorism, pessimism. —optimist, *n*. —optimistic, *adj*.

organicism the theory that vital activities stem not from any single part of an organism but from its autonomous composition. Cf. holism, mechanism, vitalism. —organicist, *n*. —organicistic, *adj*.

organon a method or means for communicating knowledge or for philosophical inquiry.

Origenism the doctrines developed or ascribed to the 3rd-century Christian theologian Origen, especially an attempt to develop a Christian philosophy combining Platonism and the Scriptures. —Origenist, *n*. —Origenistic, *adj*.

pamphysicism the doctrine that material nature is the source of all phenomena. —pamphysicism, *adj*.

panaesthetism the theory that all matter has some consciousness.

paneogism solipsism.

panlogism 1. the doctrine that the universe is a realization or act of the Logos.
2. the Hegelian doctrine that logos or reason informs the absolute or absolute reality. —panlogist, *n*. —panlogical, panlogistic, panlogistical, *adj*.

panpsychism the doctrine that each object in the universe has a mind or an unconscious psyche and that all physical occurrences involve the mental. —panpsychist, *n*. —panpsychistic, *adj*.

panthelism the philosophical theory of Arthur Schopenhauer, who maintained that the ultimate reality of the universe is will.

parallelism the theory that mind and matter accompany each other but are not causally related.

pathematology the doctrine of the effects on the mind of pleasure and pain.

Peripateticism 1. the philosophy of Aristotle, who taught while walking.
2. the followers of Aristotle and his school of philosophy. —Peripatetic, *n*., *adj*.

pessimism 1. the doctrine that all things naturally tend to evil.
2. the doctrine that this is the worst of all possible worlds. Cf. **Leibnizianism.**
3. the doctrine that the evil and pain in the world outweigh goodness and happiness, and that the world is basically evil. Cf. **meliorism, optimism.** —pessimist, *n.* —pessimistic, *adj.*

phantasm the mental image or representation of a real person or thing. See also 182. GHOSTS; 309. PERCEPTION.

phenomenalism the doctrine that phenomena are the only objects of knowledge or the only form of reality. —phenomenalist, *n.* —phenomenalistic, *adj.*

phenomenology 1. the study of phenomena.
2. the philosophical system of Edmund Husserl and his followers, especially the careful description of phenomena in all areas of experience. —phenomenologist, *n.* —phenomenologic, phenomenological, *adj.*

philosophism a spurious philosophic argument. —philosophist, *n., adj.*

physicalism a doctrine, related to logical positivism, that all meaningful statements, with the exception of necessary statements of logic and mathematics, must relate either directly or indirectly to observable properties of the temporal. —physicalist, *n., adj.*

Platonism the philosophy of Plato and his followers, especially the doctrine that physical objects are imperfect and impermanent representations of unchanging ideas, and that knowledge is the mental apprehension of these ideas or universals. —Platonist, *n., adj.* —Platonistic, *adj.*

pluralism 1. a theory positing more than one principle or basic substance as the ground of reality. Cf. **dualism, monism.**
2. a theory that reality consists, not of an organic whole, but of two or more independent material or spiritual entities. —pluralist, *n.* —pluralistic, *adj.*

pneumatism the doctrines concerning the highest of three Gnostic orders of mankind, those who have received spiritual gifts and are therefore by nature capable of salvation. Cf. **hylicism, psychism.**

positivism 1. a philosophical system developed by Auguste Comte, concerned with positive facts and phenomena, the first verified by the methods of the empirical sciences, the second explainable by scientific laws. Also called **Comtism.**
2. a contemporary philosophical movement stressing the task of philosophy as criticizing and analyzing science, and rejecting all transcendental metaphysics. Also called **logical positivism.** —positivist, *n.* —positivistic, *adj.*

pragmatism a philosophical system stressing practical consequences and values as standards by which the validity of concepts are to be determined. —pragmatist, *n., adj.* —pragmatistic, *adj.*

pragmatistism the pragmatist philosophy of C. S. Peirce, especially his work in logic and problems in language. —pragmaticist, *n.*

predeterminism determinism.

probabilism the doctrine, introduced by the Skeptics and influential in the sciences and social sciences in modified form, that certainty is impossible and that probability suffices to govern belief and action. —probabilist, *n.* —probabilistic, *adj.*

prudentialism a doctrine of philosophy that is prudential.

psilosopher *Rare.* a false, sham, or foolish philosopher.

psychism the doctrines concerning the second of three Gnostic orders of mankind, those endowed with souls and free wills, savable through the right use of the latter. Cf. hylicism, pneumatism.

purposivism any of various theories of nature or of animal and human behavior based upon teleological doctrines. —purposivist, *n.*

Pyrrhonism 1. the Skeptic doctrines of Pyrrho and his followers, especially the assertion that, since all perceptions tend to be faulty, the wise man will consider the external circumstances of life to be unimportant and thus preserve tranquility.
2. extreme or absolute skepticism. Cf. Skepticism. —Pyrrhonist, *n.* —Pyrrhonian, Pyrrhonic, *n., adj.*

quiddity the essential nature or quality of something that makes it different and distinct from other things and establishes its identity. —quidditative, *adj.*

quintessence *Ancient and Medieval Philosophy.* the fifth essence, of which the heavenly bodies were thought to be made, distinguished from the four elements of fire, air, water, and earth; hence, the most pure essence or most perfect embodiment of a thing or being. —quintessential, *adj.*

quodlibet a nice or fine point, as in argument; a subtlety. —quodlibetal, *adj.*

quodlibetarian a person who likes to talk about or dispute fine points or quodlibets.

Ramism the doctrines of Pierre de la Ramée (Ramus), who opposed scholasticism and the dialectics of Aristotle. —Ramist, *n., adj.*

rationalism 1. the doctrine that knowledge is gained only through the reason, a faculty independent of experience.
2. the doctrine that all knowledge is expressible in self-evident propositions or their consequences. —rationalist, *n.* —rationalistic, *adj.*

realism 1. the doctrine that universals have a real objective existence. Cf. idealism.
2. the doctrine that objects of sense perception have an existence independent of the act of perception. —realist, *n.*

relationism 1. a doctrine asserting the existence of relations as entities. 2. a theory maintaining the conditioning of any ideological perspective or system by its sociocultural context. —relationist, *n*.

relativism any theory maintaining that criteria of judgment vary with individuals and their environments; relationism. Cf. ethical relativism. —relativist, *n*. —relativistic, *adj*.

restrictionism the philosophy that advocates restriction and restraint, as in trade dealings. —restrictionist, *n*., *adj*.

rigorism tutiorism.

Rosminianism the philosophy of Antonio Rosmini-Serbati, 19th-century Italian philosopher and ecclesiastic, who taught that the idea of true being is inborn and that through it true knowledge is made potential. —Rosminian, *n*., *adj*.

Schellingism the philosophy of idealism, as set forth by F. W. J. von Schelling.

schematism the representation in outline of a particular systematic arrangement or of a particular concept. —schematist, *n*.

scholarch a head of a school, especially the head of one of the ancient Athenian schools of philosophy.

Scholasticism the doctrines of the schoolmen; the system of theological and philosophical instruction of the Middle Ages, based chiefly upon the authority of the church fathers and on Aristotle and his commentators. —Scholastic, *n*., *adj*.

Scotism the philosophy of John Duns Scotus, medieval Scholastic, especially his proposal that philosophy and theology be made separate disciplines. —Scotist, *n*. —Scotistic, Scotistical, *adj*.

sensationalism 1. the doctrine that all ideas are derived from and essentially reducible to sense perceptions. Also called sensuism. 2. *Ethics*. the doctrine that the good is to be judged only by or through the gratification of the senses. Also called sensualism. See also 145. ETHICS; 248. LITERARY STYLE; 265. MEDIA. —sensationalist, *n*. —sensationalistic, *adj*.

sensualism sensationalism, def. 2.

sensuism sensationalism, def. 1.

singularism any philosophy that derives the universe from one principle.

Skepticism, Scepticism the doctrines or opinions of philosophical Skeptics, especially the doctrine that a true knowledge of things is impossible or that all knowledge is uncertain. Cf. Pyrrhonism. —Skeptic, Sceptic, *n*.

Socraticism, Socratism some aspect of Socrates' philosophy.

solipsism the theory that only the self exists or can be proved to exist. Also called panegoism. —solipsist, *n*. —solipsistic, *adj*.

sophistry 1. the teachings and ways of teaching of the ancient Greek sophists. 2. subtle, superficially plausible, but actually specious or fallacious reasoning, as was sometimes used by the sophists.

speciosity the state or quality of appearing to be greater or more than is to be found on a close examination, as an argument that has the appearance of merit but does not stand up to a close look. —specious, *adj.*

Spinozism the philosophy of Baruch Spinoza, who maintained that only thought and extension are capable of being apprehended by the human mind. —Spinozist, *n.* —Spinozistic, *adj.*

Stoicism the school of philosophy founded by Zeno (of Citium), who asserted that men should be free from passion, unmoved by joy or grief, and submit without complaint to unavoidable necessity. —Stoic, *n., adj.*

subjectivism 1. *Epistemology.* the doctrine that all knowledge is limited to experiences by the self and that all transcendent knowledge is impossible. 2. *Ethics.* the theory that certain states of feeling or thought are the highest good. 3. *Ethics.* the doctrine that the good and the right can be distinguished only by individual feeling. —subjectivist, *n.* —subjectivistic, *adj.*

syncretism the attempted reconciliation of different or opposing principles, practices, or parties, as in philosophy or religion. —syncretic, syncretical, syncretistic, syncretistical, *adj.*

synthesis the process of deductive reasoning, as from cause to effect, from the simple elements to the complex whole, etc. See also 230. JOINING. —synthesist, *n.* —synthetic, synthetical *adj.*

syntheticism the principles or practice of synthesis or synthetic methods or techniques.

synthetist a person who practices or believes in synthetic methods or principles.

teleology 1. the doctrine that final causes (purposes) exist. 2. the study of the evidences of design or purpose in nature. 3. such a design or purpose. 4. the belief that purpose and design are a part of or apparent in nature. 5. *Vitalism.* the doctrine that phenomena are guided by both mechanical forces and goals of self-realization. Cf. entelechy. —teleologist, *n.* —teleologic, teleological, *adj.*

temporalism the philosophical doctrine that emphasizes the ultimate reality of time instead of the reduction of time to a manifestation of the eternal. —temporalist, *n.* —temporalistic, *adj.*

terminism the belief that God has set a term for the probation of individuals during which time they are offered grace. —terminist, *n.*

Thomism the theological and philosophical doctrines of St. Thomas Aquinas and his followers. —**Thomist**, *n*. —**Thomistic**, *adj*.

transcendentalism 1. any philosophy based upon the doctrine that the principles of reality are to be discovered only through the analysis of the processes of thought, as Kantianism.
2. a philosophy emphasizing the intuitive and spiritual above the empirical, as the philosophy of Emerson. Cf. **descendentalism**. —**transcendentalist**, *n*. —**transcendentalistic**, *adj*.

tutiorism *Casuistry*. a position in the probabilistic controversy of the 16th and 17th centuries maintaining that, in the absence of moral certitude, only the most rigorous of any probable courses of ethical action should be taken. Also called **rigorism**. —**tutiorist**, *n*.

utilitarianism the philosophical tenets set forth by John Stuart Mill based on the principle of "the greatest good for the greatest number" and holding that the criterion of virtue lies in its utility. —**utilitarian**, *n*., *adj*.

vitalism 1. the doctrine that phenomena are only partly controlled by mechanical forces and are in some measure self-determining. Cf. **mechanism, organicism**.
2. the doctrine that ascribes the functions of a living organism to a vital principle (as *élan vital*) distinct from physical or chemical forces. Cf. **dynamism**. —**vitalist**, *n*., *adj*. —**vitalistic**, *adj*.

voluntarism any theory that regards the will rather than the intellect as the fundamental agency or principle in human activities and experience, as Nietzscheism. —**voluntarist**, *n*. —**voluntaristic**, *adj*.

313. PHOBIAS

See also 28. ATTITUDES; 41. BEHAVIOR; 156. FEAR; 254. MANIAS;
311. -PHILE, -PHILIA, -PHILY; 334. PSYCHOLOGY.

N.B.: noun forms end in **-phobe** and adjective forms end in **-phobic**, unless otherwise noted.

acarophobia a fear of skin infestation by mites or ticks.

achluophobia scotophobia.

acidophobia an inability to accommodate to acid soils, as certain plants.

acousticophobia an abnormal fear of noise.

acrophobia an abnormal fear of heights. Also called **altophobia, batophobia, hypsophobia**.

aelurophobia ailurophobia.

aerophobia an abnormal fear or dislike of drafts. Cf. **ancraophobia, anemophobia**.

agoraphobia an abnormal fear of being in crowded, public places, like markets. Cf. **demophobia**.

agyrophobia an abnormal fear of crossing streets. Also **dromophobia**.

aichmophobia an abnormal fear of pointed objects.

ailurophobia, aelurophobia, elurophobia an abnormal fear of cats. Also called **gatophobia, felinophobia**.

albuminurophobia a fear of albumin in one's urine as a sign of kidney disease.

algophobia an extreme fear of pain. Cf. **odynophobia**.

altophobia acrophobia.

amathophobia an abnormal fear of dust.

amaxophobia an abnormal fear of being or riding in vehicles.

ancraophobia an abnormal fear of wind. Cf. **aerophobia, anemophobia**.

androphobia 1. an abnormal fear of men.
2. a hatred of males. Cf. **gynephobia**.

anemophobia an abnormal fear of drafts or winds. Cf. **aerophobia, ancraophobia**.

anginophobia an abnormal fear of quinsy or other forms of sore throat.

Anglophobia a hatred or fear of England and things English.

anthophobia an abnormal fear of flowers.

anthropophobia an abnormal fear of people, especially in groups.

antlophobia an abnormal fear of floods.

apeirophobia an abnormal fear of infinity.

aphephobia an abnormal fear of touching or being touched. Also called **haphephobia, haptephobia, thixophobia**.

apiphobia, apiophobia an intense fear of bees. Also called **melissophobia**.

arachnephobia an abnormal fear of spiders.

asthenophobia an abnormal fear of weakness.

astraphobia, astrapophobia an abnormal fear of lightning. Cf. **brontophobia, keraunophobia**.

astrophobia siderophobia.

ataxiophobia, ataxophobia an abnormal fear of disorder.

atelophobia an abnormal fear of imperfection.

atephobia an abnormal fear of ruin.

aulophobia an abnormal fear of flutes.

aurophobia an abnormal dislike of gold.

automysophobia an abnormal fear or dislike of being dirty. Cf. **misophobia**.

autophobia, autophoby an abnormal fear of being by oneself. Also called eremiophobia, eremophobia, monophobia.

bacillophobia an abnormal fear of germs. Also called bacteriophobia.

ballistophobia an abnormal fear of missiles.

barophobia an abnormal fear of gravity.

basophobia, basiphobia in plants, an inability to accommodate to alkaline soils.

bathmophobia an abnormal dislike or fear of walking.

bathophobia 1. an abnormal fear of depth.
2. an intense dislike of bathing.

batophobia 1. acrophobia.
2. an abnormal fear of passing high buildings.

batrachophobia an abnormal fear of frogs and toads.

belonephobia an abnormal fear of pins and needles.

bibliophobia an abnormal dislike for books.

blennophobia an abnormal fear or dislike of slime. Also called myxophobia.

bogyphobia a dread of demons and goblins.

bromidrosiphobia an abnormal fear of having an unpleasant body odor.

brontophobia an abnormal fear of thunder and thunderstorms. Also called tonitrophobia. Cf. astraphobia, keraunophobia.

cainophobia an abnormal fear or dislike of novelty. Also called cainotophobia, neophobia.

carcinomophobia, carcinomatophobia, carcinophobia an abnormal fear of cancer. Also called cancerophobia.

cardiophobia an abnormal fear of heart disease.

cathisophobia an abnormal fear or dislike of sitting down.

catoptrophobia an abnormal fear of mirrors.

Celtophobia an intense dislike of Celts.

cenophobia, kenophobia an abnormal fear of a void or of open spaces.

ceraunophobia keraunophobia.

chaetophobia an abnormal fear of hair.

cheimaphobia, cheimatophobia an abnormal fear or dislike of cold. Cf. cryophobia, psychrophobia.

cherophobia an abnormal fear of gaiety.

chinophobia an abnormal fear or dislike of snow.

cholerophobia an intense fear of cholera.

chrematophobia an intense fear or dislike of wealth.

chrometophobia an abnormal fear or dislike of money.

chromophobia an abnormal fear of colors.

chronophobia an abnormal discomfort concerning time.

cibophobia an abnormal fear of food. Also called sitophobia, sitiophobia. Cf. phagophobia.

claustrophobia an abnormal fear of enclosed spaces. Also called cleistophobia.

cleptophobia kleptophobia.

clinophobia an abnormal fear or dislike of going to bed.

coitophobia an abnormal fear of sexual intercourse. Also called genophobia. Cf. erotophobia.

cometophobia an abnormal fear of comets.

computerphobia intense fear or dislike for computers and things associated with them.

coprophobia an abnormal fear of excrement.

cremnophobia an abnormal fear of precipices.

cryophobia an abnormal fear of ice or frost. Cf. cheimaphobia.

crystallophobia an abnormal fear of glass. Also called hyalophobia.

cymophobia an abnormal fear of waves.

cynophobia 1. an intense dread of dogs.
2. kynophobia.

cypridophobia an abnormal fear of venereal disease. Also called venereophobia.

deipnophobia an abnormal fear or dislike of dining and dinner conversation.

demonophobia an abnormal fear of spirits.

demophobia an intense dislike of crowds. Cf. agoraphobia.

dermatophobia an abnormal fear of skin disease. Also called dermatosiophobia, dermatopathophobia.

dextrophobia an abnormal fear of objects on the right side of the body. Cf. levophobia.

diabetophobia an intense fear of diabetes.

dikephobia an abnormal fear or dislike of justice.

dinophobia an abnormal fear of whirlpools.

diplopiaphobia an abnormal fear of double vision.

domatophobia an abnormal fear of being in a house.

doraphobia an abnormal fear or dislike of fur.

dromophobia 1. agyrophobia.
2. kinetophobia.

dysmorphophobia an abnormal dread of deformity, usually in others. Also called dysmorphomania.

ecclesiophobia an abnormal fear or dislike of church.

ecophobia, oecophobia, oikophobia an abnormal fear of or aversion to home surroundings.

eisoptrophobia an abnormal fear of mirrors.

eleutherophobia an abnormal fear of freedom.

elurophobia ailurophobia.

emetophobia an abnormal fear of vomiting.

enetophobia an abnormal fear of needles.

entomophobia an abnormal fear of insects.

eosophobia an abnormal fear of the dawn.

eremiophobia, eremophobia autophobia.

ergasiophobia an abnormal fear or dislike of work.

ergophobia a hatred of work.

erotophobia an abnormal fear of sexual feelings and their physical expression. Also called miserotica. Cf. coitophobia.

erythrophobia 1. an abnormal fear of the color red.
2. an abnormal fear of blushing.

eurotophobia an abnormal fear of female genitals.

febriphobia an abnormal fear of fever.

felinophobia ailurophobia.

Francophobia, Gallophobia a hatred of France or things French.

galeophobia an abnormal fear of sharks.

Gallophobia Francophobia.

gamophobia an abnormal fear or dislike of marriage.

gatophobia ailurophobia.

genophobia coitophobia.

gephyrophobia an abnormal fear of crossing a bridge.

gerascophobia an abnormal fear of growing old.

Germanophobia a hatred of Germany, or things German. Also called Teutophobia, Teutonophobia.

geumophobia an abnormal fear of tastes or flavors. Cf. olfactophobia.

glossophobia an abnormal fear of speaking in public or of trying to speak.

graphophobia a dislike of writing.

gringophobia in Spain or Latin America, an intense dislike of white strangers.

gymnophobia an abnormal fear of nudity. Also called **nudophobia**.

gynephobia, gynophobia an abnormal fear or hatred of women. Cf. **androphobia, parthenophobia**.

hadephobia an abnormal fear of hell. Also called **stygiophobia**.

haemaphobia hemophobia.

hagiophobia an intense dislike for saints and the holy.

hamartophobia an abnormal fear of error or sin.

haphephobia, haphophobia, haptephobia, haptophobia aphephobia. Also called **thixophobia**.

harpaxophobia an abnormal fear of robbers. Cf. **kleptophobia**.

hedonophobia an abnormal fear of pleasure.

heliophobia 1. an abnormal sensitivity to the effects of sunlight.
2. an abnormal fear of sunlight.

helminthophobia an abnormal fear of being infested with worms. Cf. **scoleciphobia**.

hemaphobia, haemaphobia, hemophobia an abnormal fear of the sight of blood. Also called **hematophobia**.

herpetophobia an abnormal fear of reptiles. Cf. **ophidiophobia**.

hierophobia an abnormal fear or dislike of sacred objects.

hippophobia an abnormal fear of horses.

hodophobia an abnormal fear or dislike of travel.

homichlophobia an abnormal fear of fog.

homilophobia a hatred for sermons.

homophobia fear of or apprehension about homosexuality. Cf. **uranophobia**.

hyalophobia crystallophobia.

hydrophobia 1. an abnormal fear of water.
2. the occurrence in humans of rabies. Also called **lyssa**.

hydrophobophobia an abnormal fear of rabies. Also called **lyssophobia**. Cf. **kynophobia**.

hygrophobia an abnormal fear of liquids in any form, especially wine and water.

hylephobia an intense dislike for wood or woods.

hypengyophobia an abnormal fear of responsibility. Cf. **paralipophobia**.

hypnophobia an abnormal fear of sleep.

hypsophobia, hypsiphobia acrophobia.

iatrophobia an abnormal fear of going to the doctor.

ichthyophobia an abnormal fear of fish.

iophobia an abnormal fear of poisons. Cf. toxiphobia.

isopterophobia an abnormal fear of termites.

Judophobism, Judophobia a hatred of Jews and of Jewish culture. Also called Judaeophobia.

kakorrhaphiophobia an abnormal fear of failure or defeat.

katagelophobia an abnormal fear or dislike of ridicule.

keraunophobia, ceraunophobia an abnormal fear of thunder and lightning. Cf. astraphobia, brontophobia.

kinetophobia an abnormal fear or dislike of motion. Also called dromophobia.

kleptophobia, cleptophobia an abnormal fear of thieves or of loss through thievery. Cf. harpaxophobia.

kopophobia an abnormal fear of mental or physical examination.

kynophobia, cynophobia an abnormal fear of pseudorabies. Cf. hydrophobophobia.

laliophobia, lalophobia an abnormal fear of talking.

lepraphobia an abnormal fear of leprosy.

levophobia an abnormal fear of objects on the left side of the body. Cf. dextrophobia.

limnophobia an abnormal fear of lakes.

linonophobia an abnormal fear of string.

logophobia an abnormal fear or dislike of words.

lyssophobia 1. an abnormal fear of becoming insane. 2. hydrophobophobia.

maieusiophobia tocophobia.

maniaphobia an abnormal fear of madness.

mastigophobia rhabdophobia.

mechanophobia an abnormal aversion to or fear of machinery.

melissophobia apiphobia.

meningitophobia an abnormal fear of meningitis.

merinthophobia an abnormal fear of being bound.

metallophobia an abnormal fear of metals.

meteorophobia an abnormal fear of meteors or meteorites.

misophobia, musophobia, mysophobia an abnormal fear of dirt, especially of being contaminated by dirt. Cf. automysophobia, rhypophobia.

molysomophobia an abnormal fear of infection.

monopathophobia an abnormal fear of sickness in a specified part of the body.

monophobia autophobia.

motorphobia an abnormal fear or dislike of motor vehicles.

musicophobia an intense dislike of music.

musophobia 1. an abnormal fear of mice.
2. misophobia.

mysophobia misophobia.

mythophobia an abnormal fear of making false statements.

myxophobia blennophobia.

necrophobia 1. Also called **thanatophobia**. an abnormal fear of death.
2. an abnormal fear of corpses.

negrophobia a strong dislike or fear of Negroes.

neophobia cainophobia.

nephophobia an abnormal fear of clouds.

noctiphobia an abnormal fear of the night. Cf. **nyctophobia**.

nosophobia an abnormal fear of contracting disease.

nudophobia, nudiphobia gymnophobia.

nyctophobia an abnormal fear of darkness or night. Cf. **noctiphobia**.

ochlophobia an abnormal fear of crowds.

ochophobia an abnormal fear of vehicles.

odontophobia an abnormal fear of teeth, especially those of animals.

odynophobia an abnormal fear of pain. Cf. **algophobia**.

oenophobia, oinophobia a dislike of or hatred for wine.

olfactophobia an abnormal fear or dislike of smells. Also called **osmophobia, osphresiophobia**. Cf. **geumophobia**.

ombrophobia an abnormal fear of rain.

ommatophobia an abnormal fear of eyes.

onomatophobia an abnormal fear of a certain name.

ophidiophobia an abnormal fear of snakes. Also called **ophiophobia**. Cf. **herpetophobia**.

ornithophobia an abnormal fear of birds.

osmophobia olfactophobia.

osphresiophobia olfactophobia.

ouranophobia uranophobia.

paedophobia pedophobia.

panophobia 1. a nonspecific fear; a state of general anxiety.
2. an abnormal fear of everything. Also panphobia, pantaphobia, pantophobia.

papaphobia an intense fear or dislike of the pope or the papacy.

paralipophobia an abnormal fear of neglect of some duty. Cf. hypengyophobia.

paraphobia an abnormal fear of sexual perversion.

parasitophobia an abnormal fear of parasites.

parthenophobia an extreme aversion to young girls. Cf. gynephobia.

pathophobia an abnormal fear of disease.

peccatiphobia, peccatophobia an abnormal fear of sinning.

pediculophobia an abnormal fear of lice. Also called phthiriophobia.

pedophobia, paedophobia an abnormal fear or dislike of dolls.

pellagraphobia an abnormal fear of catching pellagra.

peniaphobia an abnormal fear of poverty.

phagophobia an abnormal fear of eating. Cf. cibophobia.

pharmacophobia an abnormal fear of drugs.

phasmophobia an abnormal fear of ghosts. Cf. pneumatophobia, spectrophobia.

phengophobia an abnormal fear of daylight.

philosophobia an abnormal fear or dislike of philosophy or philosophers.

phobophobia an abnormal fear of fear itself.

phonophobia an abnormal fear or dislike of noise.

photalgiophobia an abnormal fear of photalgia, pain in the eyes caused by light.

photophobia 1. an abnormal fear of light.
2. a painful sensitivity to light, especially visually. Also called photodysphoria.
3. a tendency to thrive in reduced light, as exhibited by certain plants.

phronemophobia an abnormal fear of thinking.

phthiriophobia pediculophobia.

phthisiophobia an abnormal fear of tuberculosis. Also called tuberculophobia.

pneumatophobia an abnormal fear of incorporeal beings. Cf. phasmophobia, spectrophobia.

pnigophobia an abnormal fear of choking.

pogonophobia an abnormal fear or dislike of beards.

poinephobia an abnormal fear of punishment.

politicophobia a dislike or fear of politicians.

polyphobia an abnormal fear of many things. Cf. panophobia, def. 2.

ponophobia an abnormal fear of fatigue, especially through overworking.

potamophobia a morbid fear of rivers.

proctophobia *Medicine.* a mental apprehension in patients with a rectal disease.

proteinphobia a strong aversion to protein foods.

psychophobia an abnormal fear of the mind.

psychrophobia an abnormal fear of the cold. Cf. cheimaphobia.

pteronophobia an abnormal fear of feathers.

pyrexiophobia an abnormal fear of fever. Cf. thermophobia.

pyrophobia an abnormal fear of fire.

rhabdophobia 1. an abnormal fear of being beaten.
2. an abnormal fear of magic.

rhypophobia an abnormal fear of filth. Cf. misophobia.

Russophobism, Russophobia an excessive fear or dislike of Russians and things Russian.

Satanophobia an excessive fear of Satan.

scabiophobia an abnormal fear of scabies.

scatophobia 1. coprophobia.
2. an abnormal dread of using obscene language.

sciophobia an abnormal fear of shadows.

scoleciphobia an abnormal fear of worms. Also called vermiphobia. Cf. helminthophobia.

scopophobia an abnormal fear of being looked at. Also scoptophobia.

scotophobia an abnormal fear of the dark. Also called achluophobia.

selaphobia an abnormal fear or dislike of flashes of light.

siderodromophobia an abnormal fear or dislike of railroads or of traveling on trains.

siderophobia an abnormal fear of the stars. Also called astrophobia.

sitophobia, sitiophobia. cibophobia.

Slavophobia fear or hatred of things Slavic, especially of their real or imagined political influence.

spectrophobia an abnormal fear of specters or phantoms. Cf. phasmophobia, pneumatophobia.

stasibasiphobia 1. an abnormal conviction that one cannot stand or walk.
2. an abnormal fear of attempting to do either.

stygiophobia hadephobia.

symmetrophobia an abnormal fear or dislike of symmetry.

syphiliphobia, syphilophobia an abnormal fear of becoming infected with syphilis. Cf. **cypridophobia.**

tabophobia an abnormal fear of a wasting sickness.

tachophobia an abnormal fear of speed.

taphephobia, taphiphobia, taphophobia an abnormal fear of being buried alive.

tapinophobia an abnormal fear of small things.

taurophobia an abnormal fear of bulls.

teleophobia a dislike and rejection of teleology.

telephonophobia an abnormal fear of using the telephone.

teratophobia an abnormal fear of monsters or of giving birth to a monster.

Teutophobia, Teutonophobia Germanophobia.

thaasophobia an abnormal fear or dislike of being idle.

thalassophobia an abnormal fear of the sea.

thanatophobia necrophobia, def. 1.

theatrophobia an abnormal fear of theaters.

theophobia an abnormal fear of God.

thermophobia an abnormal fear or dislike of heat. Cf. **pyrexiophobia.**

thixophobia aphephobia.

tocophobia, tokophobia an abnormal fear of childbirth. Also called **maieusiophobia.**

tomophobia an abnormal fear of surgical operations.

tonitrophobia, tonitruphobia brontophobia.

topophobia *Rare.* an abnormal fear of certain places.

toxiphobia, toxicophobia an abnormal fear of being poisoned. Cf. **iophobia.**

traumatophobia an excessive or disabling fear of war or physical injury.

tremophobia an abnormal fear of trembling.

trichinophobia an abnormal fear of trichinosis. Also called **trichophobia, trichopathophobia.**

tridecaphobia triskaidekaphobia.

triskaidekaphobia an abnormal fear of the number *13.* Also called **tridecaphobia.**

trypanophobia vaccinophobia.

tuberculophobia phthisiophobia.

tyrannophobia an intense fear or hatred of tyrants.

uranophobia 1. an abnormal fear of homosexuals and homosexuality. Also **homophobia**.
2. an abnormal fear of the heavens. Also called **ouranophobia**.

urophobia an abnormal fear of passing urine.

vaccinophobia an abnormal fear of vaccines and vaccination. Also called **trypanophobia**.

venereophobia cypridophobia.

vermiphobia scoleciphobia.

xenophobia an abnormal fear or hatred of foreigners and strange things.

xerophobia an abnormal fear of dryness and dry places, like deserts.

zelophobia an abnormal fear of jealousy.

zoophobia an abnormal fear or dislike of animals.

314. PHONOGRAPH RECORDS

audiophile a person especially interested in high-fidelity sound equipment and recordings on tape or disks.

audiophilia 1. the state or condition of an audiophile.
2. the state of one who listens to high-fidelity equipment solely for the quality of reproduction. —**audiophilic**, *adj*.

discography, diskography 1. a list of musical recordings, usually with commentary, often concerning one composer, performer, or performing group.
2. the analysis, history, or classification of musical recordings.
3. the methods of such analysis or classification. —**discographer, diskographer**, *n*. —**discographical, diskographical**, *adj*.

discophily, diskophily the zealous study and collection of phonograph records. Also called **phonophily**. —**discophile, diskophile**, *n*.

gramophile *British*. a lover and collector of phonograph records.

gramophone *British*. phonograph.

graphophone an instrument for reproducing sound from records; a phonograph; a gramophone.

nickelodeon a juke-box, record-player, or player piano operated by the insertion of a nickel or other coin. See also 159. FILMS.

phonophily discophily.

315. PHOTOGRAPHY
See also 23. ART; 159. FILMS.

actinography 1. the measurement of the intensity of radiation with a recording actinometer, usually by the photochemical effect.
2. the calculation of suitable exposure times in photography through the use of a recording actinometer. —**actinographic,** *adj.*

astrophotography a form of photography used to record astronomical phenomena.

autoradiograph radioautograph.

autotype 1. a photographic process in which pictures are produced in one color or shades of one color by the use of a carbon pigment. Also called **autotypy.**
2. the picture so created.

chromophotography the art of making colored photographs.

cinematics the art or principles of making motion pictures. —**cinematic,** *adj.*

cinematography the art or technique of motion-picture photography. —**cinematographer, cinematographist,** *n.* —**cinematographic,** *adj.*

collotype 1. a photographic plate made with a gelatin film, capable of highly detailed reproductions.
2. the process of making such a plate.
3. the picture made with such a plate.

cyanotype a blueprint.

daguerreotype an obsolete form of photography in which images were produced on chemically treated plates of metal or glass. —**daguerreotypic, daguerreotypical,** *adj.* —**daguerreotypist,** *n.*

densitometer an optical device for measuring the density of a photographic negative.

electrography an apparatus for electrically transmitting pictures. —**electrograph,** *n.* —**electrographic,** *adj.*

ferrotype 1. an early photographic process in which a positive image was taken directly on a thin plate of sensitized iron or tin.
2. the picture produced by this method. Also called **stannotype, tintype.**

gastrophotography a form of photography for examining the interior of the stomach by introducing a small camera into it.

heliochromy the art or process of producing natural color photographic prints; color photography. —**heliochrome,** *n.* —**heliochromic,** *adj.*

heliotypography the practice of making phototypes.

heliotypy the process of making pictures by printing directly from gelatin film that has been exposed under a negative and fixed with chrome alum.

holography a technique for producing a three-dimensional photographic representation, recorded on film by a reflected laser beam of a subject illuminated by part of the same laser beam.

megalethoscope an optical device similar to a stereoscope in which a photograph is greatly magnified and the effect of perspective is deepened.

mutoscope an instrument for recording and reproducing the illusion of motion by means of a series of photographs.

nephograph an instrument for photographing clouds.

panchromatism the quality or condition of being sensitive to all colors, as certain types of photographic film. —panchromatic, *adj*.

photobibliography the use of photography as an aid to book description.

photobiography a biography related mostly or entirely through photographs.

photochromy the process or production of color photographs; color photography. Cf. heliochromy.

photochronograph 1. a camera for recording motion by a series of photographs taken at brief intervals.
2. the photograph so produced.
3. a camera that records the exact time of the event it is photographing by exposing a moving sensitized plate to the tracing of a thin beam of light synchronized with the event.

photodrama a photoplay or dramatic narrative illustrated with or related through photographs.

photoglyphy photogravure or the process of engraving by means of photography. —photoglyphic, *adj*.

photogrammetry the use of photography for surveying or map-making. Cf. phototopography.

photogravure 1. a form of photoengraving in which the photograph is reproduced on an intaglio surface and then transferred to paper.
2. the photograph produced by this process.

photojournalism a form of journalism in which photographs play a more important part than written copy. —photojournalist, *n*.

photolithography the process of making lithographs produced by photoengraving. Cf. photogravure. —photolithographer, *n*. —photolithographic, *adj*.

photomicrography the process of taking photographs through a microscope. Also called photomicroscopy. —photomicrograph, *n*.

phototopography surveying or map-making by means of photography. Cf. photogrammetry. —phototopographic, phototopographical, *adj*.

phototypy the art or technique of making photographic plates. —phototypic, *adj*.

platinotype 1. a photographic process in which a platinum salt is used in place of the more usual silver salts to produce a more permanent print. 2. a photographic print so made.

radioautograph a photograph produced on film by the radioactive rays from the object being photographed. Also called **autoradiograph.** —**radioautographic,** *adj.* —**radioautography,** *n.*

radiography the technique of producing images on photographic film by the action of x rays or other radioactive materials. Also called **scotography.** —**radiograph,** *n.*

radiophotography the process or technique of transmitting and receiving photographs by radio.

reprography a collective term for all kinds of processes used for the facsimile reproduction of documents or books.

roentgenography, röntgenography x-ray photography.

scotography radiography. See also 342. RADIATION. —**scotograph,** *n.*

sensitometer a device for determining the sensitivity of film. —**sensitometry,** *n.* —**sensitometric,** *adj.*

spectrography the technique of using a spectrograph, an optical device for breaking light down into a spectrum and recording the results photographically. —**spectrographic,** *adj.*

spectroheliogram a photograph of the sun made using monochromatic light.

stannotype ferrotype.

telephotography 1. the art or process of photographing distant objects by using a telephoto lens or a telescope with a camera. 2. electrography. —**telephotographic,** *adj.*

teliconograph an apparatus combining a telescope and the camera lucida, used for producing images of distant objects on a screen.

time lapse photography the motion-picture photography of a slow and continuous process, as the sprouting of a seed, especially by exposing one frame at a time at regular intervals.

tintype ferrotype.

tomography x-ray photography of a thin cross section of tissue.

vectography a stereoscopic process involving two superimposed images polarized at 90° to each other and viewed through polarizing glasses for a three-dimensional effect. —**vectograph,** *n.* —**vectographic,** *adj.*

woodburytype 1. an early photographic process in which a relief image on gelatin is used to produce an intaglio impression on a lead or other soft metal plate from which prints are then made in a press. 2. the picture produced by this process.

316. PHYSICS

See also 25. ASTRONOMY; 100. COSMOLOGY; 189. GRAVITY; 342. RADIATION.

anisotropy the state or quality of having different properties along different axes. See also 54. BOTANY. —**anisotropic,** *adj.*

astaticism the condition of constant, uninterrupted variability of direction or position. —**astatic,** *adj.*

atomology the theory of atoms.

biophysics the branch of physics that deals with living things. —**biophysicist,** *n.* —**biophysical,** *adj.*

ceraunics the study of heat and electricity.

crystallography the science that stuc ies crystallization and the forms and structures of crystals. —**crystallographe.**. *n.* —**crystallographic, crystallographical,** *adj.*

diamagnetism a property of certain materials of being repelled by both poles of a magnet, thus taking a position at right angles to the magnet's lines of influence.

dynamometry the measurement of energy used in doing work. —**dynamometer,** *n.* —**dynamometric, dynamometrical,** *adj.*

electrotropism orientation in relation to a current of electricity. —**electrotropic,** *adj.*

energetics the branch of physics that studies energy and its transformation. —**energeticist,** *n.* —**energeticistic,** *adj.*

energism a doctrine that asserts that certain phenomena can be explained in terms of energy. —**energist,** *n.*

faradism the application of alternating electrical current for therapeutic purposes. —**faradic,** *adj.*

focimetry the determination of focal length. —**focimetric,** *adj.*

Franklinism static electricity. Also called **Franklinic electricity.**

galvanism a direct electrical current, especially one produced by chemical action. —**galvanic,** *adj.*

galvanology a work on the production of electric current by chemical means. —**galvanologist,** *n.* —**galvanological,** *adj.*

galvanometry the measurement of the strength of electric currents, by means of a galvanometer. —**galvanometric, galvanometrical,** *adj.*

geophysics the physics of the earth, including oceanography, volcanology, seismology, etc. —**geophysicist,** *n.* —**geophysical,** *adj.*

gyrostatics the study of the behavior of rotating solid bodies. —**gyrostatic,** *adj.* —**gyrostatically,** *adv.*

halology *Chemistry*. the study of salts. Also called halotechny.

homeomorphism the similarity of the crystalline forms of substances that have different chemical compositions. —homeomorphous, *adj.*

hydraulics 1. the science concerned with the laws governing water and other liquids in motion and their engineering applications.
2. applied or practical hydrodynamics.

hydrodynamics the study of forces that act on or are produced by liquids. Also called hydromechanics. —hydrodynamic, hydrodynamical, *adj.*

hydrokinetics the branch of hydrodynamics dealing with the laws of gases or liquids in motion. —hydrokinetic, *adj.*

hydromechanics hydrodynamics. —hygrometric, hygrometrical, *adj.*

hydrostatics the study of the equilibrium and pressure of liquids. —hydrostatician, *n.* —hydrostatic, hydrostatical, *adj.*

hygrometry the branch of physics concerned with the measurement of moisture in the air. —hygrometric, hygrometrical, *adj.*

isomorphism close similarity between the forms of different crystals. See also 44. BIOLOGY. —isomorph, *n.* —isomorphic, *adj.*

kinematics the branch of mechanics that deals with motion without reference to force or mass. —kinematic, kinematical, *adj.*

magnetology the study of magnets and magnetism.

monosymmetry the state exhibited by a crystal, having three unequal axes with one oblique intersection; the state of being monoclinic. See also 44. BIOLOGY. —monosymmetric, monosymmetrical, *adj.*

optotechnics the technology of optical instruments and apparatus.

oscillography the study of the wave-forms of changing currents, voltages, or any other quantity that can be translated into electricity, as light or sound waves. —oscillographic, *adj.*

osmometry the measurement of osmotic pressure, or the force a dissolved substance exerts on a semipermeable membrane through which it cannot pass when separated by it from a pure solvent. —osmometric, *adj.*

physicism the doctrine that explains the universe in physical terms.

physics the science that studies matter and energy in terms of motion and force. —physicist, *n.* —physical, *adj.*

pleochroism a property of some crystals of showing variation in color when viewed in transmitted light or from different directions. Also called pleochromatism, polychroism, polychromatism. —pleochroic, pleochromatic, *adj.*

plenism the theory that nature contains no vacuums. Cf. vacuism. —plenist, *n.*

pleochromatism, polychroism, polychromatism pleochroism.

pyrology the study of fire and heat, especially with regard to chemical analysis.

radiometry the measurement of radiant energy by means of a radiometer, an instrument composed of vanes which rotate at speeds proportionate to the intensity of the energy source. —radiometric, *adj.*

radiophony the transformation of radiant energy into sound.

spectrobolometry measurement of the distribution of energy in a spectrum by means of a spectrobolometer, an instrument combining a bolometer and a spectroscope. —spectrobolometric, *adj.*

statics the branch of mechanics or physics that deals with matter and forces in equilibrium. —statical, *adj.*

sympalmograph an apparatus for illustrating in graphic form the composition of two simple harmonic motions at right angles.

telemechanics the science of operating or controlling mechanisms by remote control, especially by radio.

thermionics the science or study of the emission of electrons from substances at high temperatures. —thermionic, *adj.*

thermostatics the science or study of the equilibrium of heat.

tribology the science and technology of friction, lubrication, and wear.

trichroism a property, peculiar to certain crystals, of transmitting light of three different colors when viewed from three different directions. Also called trichromatism. —trichroic, *adj.*

trichromatism 1. the condition of having, using, or combining three colors. 2. trichroism. —trichromatic, *adj.*

trochilics *Rare.* the science of rotary motion. —trochilic, *adj.*

vacuism the theory that nature permits vacuums. Cf. plenism. —vacuist, *n.*

voltaism electricity generated by chemical means, as in a cell or battery; galvanism.

317. PLACES
See also 82. CITIES; 212. HOUSES; 381. SPACES.

anachorism the incorrect assignment of an event to a location; an error in geography.

anomalism the condition or state of being unusual or out of place. —anomaly, *n.*

nostopathy *Rare.* an abnormal fear of returning to familiar places.

penetralia the innermost parts or deepest recesses of a place, thing, etc.

sanctum sanctorum 1. the holy of holies; a place of great holiness. 2. a most private place.

topophobia *Rare.* an abnormal fear of certain places. —**topophobe,** *n.*

ubeity the condition or quality of being in a place or being located or situated; whereness or ubication.

ubication 1. *Obsolete.* location or situation.
2. the state or quality of being located or situated; ubeity or whereness.

318. PLANETS
    See also 24. ASTROLOGY; 25. ASTRONOMY; 100. COSMOLOGY;
    133. EARTH; 259. MARS; 280. MOON.

aphelion the point in the orbit of a heavenly body where it is farthest from the sun. See also **perihelion.**

apocynthion apolune.

apogee the farthest point in an orbit from the body being orbited.

apolune the farthest point from the moon in a lunar orbit, as that of a spacecraft. Also called **apocynthion.**

areography the study of the physical features of the planet Mars.

celidography *Archaic.* a description of the surface markings of the sun or a planet. —**celidographer,** *n.*

exobiology the branch of biology that studies life beyond the earth's atmosphere, as on other planets. —**exobiologist,** *n.*

meridian the highest point a planet or other orbiting heavenly body reaches in its orbit. —**meridian, meridional,** *adj.*

occultation the process of one heavenly body disappearing behind another as viewed by an observer.

pericynthion perilune.

perigee the closest point in an orbit to the body being orbited.

perihelion the point in the orbit of a heavenly body where it is nearest the sun. Also called **perihelium.** See also **aphelion.**

perihelium perihelion.

perilune the closest point to the moon in a lunar orbit, as that of a spacecraft. Also called **pericynthion.**

planetarium 1. a representation of the planetary system, particularly one in which the movements of the planets are simulated by projectors.
2. a room or building housing such an apparatus.

planetoid *Astronomy.* any of thousands of small celestial bodies that revolve about the sun in orbits chiefly between those of Mars and Jupiter ranging in diameter from one mile to 480 miles. Also called **asteroids, minor planets.** —**planetoidal,** *adj.*

zenography the study and description of Jupiter. —zenographical, *adj*.

319. PLANTS

See also 5. AGRICULTURE; 54. BOTANY; 167. FLOWERS; 188. GRASSES; 241. LEAVES; 302. ORGANISMS; 401. TREES.

acidophobia an inability to accommodate to acid soils. Cf. basophobia. —acidophobic, *adj*.

amensalism a parasitic relationship between plants that has a destructive effect on one and no effect on the other.

apheliotropism the tendency of some plants to grow in a direction away from the sun.

apogeotropism the tendency of some plants to grow away from the earth and the pull of gravity. —apogeotropic, *adj*.

aquapontics the cultivation of plants in nutrient solutions, usually for commercial purposes. Cf. hydroponics. —aquapontic, *adj*.

aquiculture hydroponics. —aquicultural, *adj*.

auxography the measurement of the swelling and shrinking of parts of plants. —auxographic, *adj*.

basophobia, basiphobia an inability to accommodate to alkaline soils. Cf. acidophobia. —basophobic, basiphobic, *adj*.

biodynamics the study of the physiological processes of plants and animals. —biodynamic, biodynamical, *adj*.

biostatics the study of the relation between structure and function in plants and animals. —biostatical, *adj*.

biota the animal or plant life of a particular region.

botanomancy a form of divination involving the examination of plants.

caricography the description of plants belonging to the genus *Carex*.

caricology the study of sedges. —caricologist, *n*.

cecidiology, cecidology *Biology*. the study of galls produced on trees and plants by fungi, insects, or mites. —cecidiologist, cecidologist, *n*.

chlorosis 1. a diseased condition of plants in which green parts lose their color or turn yellowish.
2. the process by which floral parts of a plant turn into leaves. Also chloranthy. See also 122. DISEASE and ILLNESS.

citriculture the cultivation of citrus fruits, as lemons, oranges, etc. —citriculturist, *n*.

crescography a technique for making apparent to the eye the successive stages of plant growth. —crescographic, *adj*.

cumaphytism the procedures involved in adapting plants for growth under surf conditions. —cumaphytic, *adj*.

dendrophilia the apparent preference of some plants, as orchids, to grow in or near trees. —**dendrophilous,** *adj.*

desmidiology the study of microscopic single-celled algae. —**desmidiologist,** *n.*

diatropism the capacity or tendency of some plants to adopt a position transverse to the line of force of an external stimulus. —**diatropic,** *adj.*

dichogamy the condition, in some flowering plants, in which the pistils and stamens mature at different times, thus preventing self-pollination. —**dichogamous,** *adj.*

ecesis the transplanting of a plant to a new environment.

epiphytism a form of mutualism in which one plant lives on the surface of another, as moss on a tree. —**epiphyte,** *n.*

etiolation 1. the process of growing plants away from the light to make them white and crisp, especially in vegetable gardening.
2. the condition of the plants grown in this manner. See also 122. DISEASE and ILLNESS.

exostosis a knot growing on the stem or root of a plant. See also 52. BONES.

florimania a mania for plants and flowers.

fungicide a substance that kills fungi or retards the growth of spores.

halophytism the ability of certain plants to grow normally in soils having a high mineral salt content. —**halophyte,** *n.* —**halophytic,** *adj.*

heliophilia an attraction or adaptation to sunlight, as the sunflower. —**heliophile,** *n.* —**heliophilic, heliophilous,** *adj.*

heliotaxis a tendency of certain plants to move in response to sunlight.

heliotropism the tendency in some plant species to turn or grow toward sunlight. —**heliotrope,** *n.* —**heliotropic,** *adj.*

herbalist a person who collects or deals in herbs, especially for medicinal purposes. See also 54. BOTANY.

herbarist *Obsolete.* a herbalist.

herbicide a substance for destroying plants, especially weeds or other unwanted species; a weed-killer. —**herbicidal,** *adj.*

heterosis abnormal development, especially increased size, in plants or animals, usually as a result of cross-breeding.

hydrophily ombrophily.

hydrophytism the ability of certain plants to grow naturally in water or in highly moist soils. —**hydrophyte,** *n.* —**hydrophytic,** *adj.*

hydroponics the science of growing plants in specially prepared solutions instead of in soil. Cf. **aquapontics.** —**hydroponic,** *adj.*

hypertrophy excessive growth of one part of a plant to the disadvantage or detriment of the plant as a whole. See also 51. BODY, HUMAN; 368. SIZE. —**hypertrophic, hypertrophical, hypertrophous,** *adj.*

hyponasty an increase in growth in a lower part of a plant causing it to bend upward. —**hyponastic,** *adj.*

mangonism *Obsolete.* any procedure for raising plants under other than natural conditions of growth.

mesophytism the ability of certain plants to grow naturally in moderate but constant moisture. —**mesophyte,** *n.* —**mesophytic,** *adj.*

mycolatry the worship of fungi, especially mushrooms.

olericulture the branch of horticulture that specializes in the cultivation of edible plants. —**olericultural,** *adj.*

ombrophily the capacity of some plants to thrive in the midst of copious rain. Also called hydrophily. —**ombrophilic, ombrophilous,** *adj.*

parasitism a relationship between plants in which one gains sustenance from the other. See also 16. ANIMALS; 44. BIOLOGY.

perigyny the state of having the pistils, stamens, petals, etc., arranged around a cuplike receptacle. —**perigynous,** *adj.*

pesticide any chemical substance used for killing pests, as insects, weeds, etc.

philobotanist *Rare.* a lover of plants.

photodynamics the science or study of light in relation to the movement of plants. —**photodynamic, photodynamical,** *adj.*

photonasty the tendency in certain plant species to respond to light by developing sufficient cellular force or growth on one side of an axis to change the form or position of the axis, as in the opening and closing of the flowers of four-o'clocks. Cf. thermonasty. —**photonastic,** *adj.*

photoperiodism the study of the relative amounts of light and darkness in a 24-hour period required to best effect the growth, reproduction, and flowering of plant species or the growth and reproduction of animals. Also photoperiodicity. Cf. thermoperiodism. —**photoperiodic, photoperiodical,** *adj.*

photophilia, photophily the necessity, in some plant species, for exposure to strong light. —**photophile, photophilic, photophilous,** *adj.*

photosynthesis the synthesis of complex organic substances from carbon dioxide, water, and inorganic salts, with sunlight as the energy source and a catalyst such as chlorophyll. —**photosynthetic,** *adj.*

phototropism motion in response to light, either toward it or away from it, as manifested by certain plants. —**phototropic,** *adj.*

phytogenesis, phytogeny the origin and evolution of plants. —**phytogenetic, phytogenetical, phytogenic,** *adj.*

phytoserology the identification, classification, and study of plant viruses. —phytoserologist, *n.* —phytoserologic, phytoserological, *adj.*

plagiotropism the tendency of some plants to diverge from the vertical in their growth. —plagiotropic, *adj.*

rheotropism the tendency of some plants to respond to a current of water by growing with it (*positive rheotaxis*) or against it (*negative rheotaxis*).

saprophytism the ability of certain plants to live in dead or decaying organic matter. —saprophyte, *n.* —saprophytic, *n., adj.*

sclerosis the hardening of the cell wall of a plant, as by the formation of wood. See also 51. BODY, HUMAN. —sclerotic, *adj.*

stirpiculture selective breeding to develop strains with particular characteristics. —stirpicultural, *adj.*

sycomancy the art of divination by inspection of figs or fig leaves.

thermonasty the tendency in certain plant species to respond to temperature changes by developing a sufficient cellular force or growth on one side of an axis to change the form or position of the axis, as in the closing or folding of rhododendron leaves in cold air. Cf. photonasty. —thermonastic, *adj.*

thermoperiodism the study of the relative day and night temperatures required, in a 24-hour period, to achieve the best growth, reproduction, or flowering of plant species or the growth and reproduction of animals. Also thermoperiodicity. Cf. photoperiodism. —thermoperiodic, thermoperiodical, *adj.*

thermotropism the tendency in some plant species to turn toward or away from a source of heat. —thermotropic, thermotropical, *adj.*

xenogamy cross-fertilization in plants or flowers.

xerophilia, xerophily the ability of some plants to survive in dosert or salt marsh areas by storing fresh water internally. —xerophilic, xerophilous, *adj.*

xerophytism the natural adaptation of plants living under desert or marsh conditions to store water internally. —xerophyte, *n.* —xerophytic, *adj.*

320. PLEASURE
See also 195. HAPPINESS; 347. RECREATION.

amenomania a mania for pleasing delusions.

epicurism, epicureanism 1. the cultivation of a refined taste, as in food, art, music, etc.; connoisseurship.
2. a devotion or adaptation to luxurious tastes, especially in drinking and eating, or to indulgence in sensual pleasures. —epicure, *n.* —epicurean, *n., adj.*

excursionism the characteristics of a pleasure trip. —excursionist, *n.* —excursional, *adj.*

hedonics hedonology.

hedonism 1. *Ethics.* the doctrine that pleasure or happiness is the highest good. See also epicurism.
2. a devotion to pleasure as a way of life. —hedonist, *n.* —hedonistic, *adj.*

hedonology *Rare.* the study of human pleasure. Also called **hedonics.**

hedonomania a mania for pleasure.

pleasurist *Rare.* a person devoted to worldly pleasure; hedonist or sybarite.

stoicism a form of conduct conforming to the precepts of the Stoics, especially as characterized by indifference to pain and pleasure. —stoic, *n., adj.* —stoical, *adj.*

sybaritism devotion to sensual pleasures. —sybarite, *n.* —sybaritic, *adj.*

321. POISON
See also 112. DEATH; 130. DRUGS; 232. KILLING.

alexipharmac, alexipharmic a remedy for or antidote against poison or infection. —alexipharmic, *adj.*

atropism poisoning caused by atropine or belladonna.

barbiturism a condition of chronic poisoning caused by excessive use of barbiturates.

botulism a disease of the nervous system caused by botulin developments in spoiled foods eaten by animals and man; a variety of bacterial food poisoning.

cantharidism a toxic condition caused by the misuse of the counterirritant and diuretic cantharides.

enriositatis drunkenness or intoxication from alcohol, especially as an habitual state.

enterotoxemia a condition in which the blood contains toxin from the intestines.

ergotism a condition caused by eating rye or some other grain infected with ergot fungus or by an overdose of an ergot medicinal agent.

iophobia an abnormal fear of poisons. Cf. **toxiphobia.**

mephitism mephitic or carbon dioxide poisoning. —mephitic, mephitical, *adj.*

mithridatism the production of immunity against the action of a poison by consuming it regularly in gradually larger doses.

mycetism any of a variety of toxic conditions produced by poisonous mushrooms. Also **mycetismus.**

phosphorism chronic phosphorus poisoning.

plumbism an acute toxic condition caused by the absorption of lead into the body by skin contact, ingestion, or inhalation; lead poisoning. Also called **saturnism.**

plutonism a poisoning caused by exposure to radioactive plutonium.

ptyalism excessive salivation, usually associated with chronic mercury poisoning.

rodenticide a substance that kills rodents.

salicylism a toxic condition produced by excessive intake of salicylic acid, marked by vomiting and ringing in the ears.

salmonellosis an illness caused by food tainted with certain species of salmonella bacteria.

sapremia, sapraemia blood poisoning caused by putrefactive microorganisms in the bloodstream.

saturnism plumbism.

septicemia, septicaemia blood poisoning caused by pathogenic microorganisms and their toxic products in the bloodstream. —**septicemic, septicaemic,** *adj.*

stibialism poisoning from antimony.

strychnism a toxic condition caused by excessive use of strychnine.

tabacism addiction to tobacco; poisoning from excessive use of tobacco. Also called **tabagism, tobaccoism.**

thebaism *Archaic.* a toxic condition produced by thebaine, a derivative of opium.

toxicology the branch of medical science that studies the effects, antidotes, detection, etc., of poisons. —**toxicologist,** *n.* —**toxicologic, toxicological,** *adj.*

toxiphobia an abnormal fear of poisoning. Also called **toxicophobia.** Cf. iophobia. —**toxiphobe, toxiphobiac,** *n.*

tyrotoxism poisoning caused by microbes in stale cheese or milk.

urotoxy, urotoxia 1. the toxicity or toxic content of urine.
2. the unit used in measuring the toxicity of urine, a quantity sufficient to kill an animal weighing one kilogram. —**urotoxic,** *adj.*

322. POLITICS
See also 185. GOVERNMENT.

activism the attitude of taking an active part in events, especially in a social context. —**activist,** *n.*

agrarianism the doctrine of an equal division of landed property and the advancement of agricultural groups. Also called **agrarian reform.** —**agrarian,** *adj.*

analytical stasiology an attempt, through the construction of conceptual frameworks, to develop a science of political parties.

anticivism opposition to doctrines on citizenship, especially those promulgated in France during the French Revolution. —**anticivic,** *adj.*

anti-Jacobinism opposition to the Jacobins, one of the revolutionary parties of the French revolution; by extension, the term denotes opposition to the French Revolution and any of its supporters. —**anti-Jacobin,** *n.*

antimilitarism the quality of being opposed to the establishment or maintenance of a governmental military force. —**antimilitarist,** *n.* —**antimilitaristic,** *adj.*

antiterrorism the techniques, policies, and training of special police who deal with terrorists, especially those who take hostages. —**antiterrorist,** *adj.*

anythingarianism the holding of no particular belief, creed, or political position. Cf. **nothingarianism.** —**anythingarian,** *n.*

Arabism a devotion to Arab interests, custom, culture, ideals, and political goals.

Arnoldist a follower of Arnold of Brescia, 12th-century Italian political reformer, especially his attacks upon clerical riches and corruption and upon the temporal power of the pope.

autonomy independent self-rule free from outside influence.

Babouvism a social and political doctrine advocating egalitarianism and communism. —**Babouvist,** *n.*

bipartisanism the state of being composed of members of two parties or of two parties cooperating, as in government. —**bipartisan,** *adj.*

Boloism the practice, during war, of promoting propaganda and defeatist activities favoring an enemy country.

Bonapartism 1. support of the actions and doctrines of Napoleon Bonaparte. 2. the desire for a leader to emulate Napoleon Bonaparte. —**Bonapartist,** *n.*

boodleism *U.S. Slang.* the practice of bribery or illicit payments, especially to or from a politician. Also **boodling.** —**boodler,** *n.*

bossism *U.S.* a control by bosses, especially political bosses.

Bourbonism 1. an adherence to the ideas and system of government developed by the Bourbons. 2. an extreme conservatism, especially in politics. —**Bourbonist,** *n.* —**Bourbonian, Bourbonic,** *adj.*

brinkmanship, brinksmanship the technique or practice in foreign policy of manipulating a dangerous situation to the limits of tolerance or safety in order to secure advantage, especially by creating diplomatic crises.

Caesarism the characteristics shown by a dictatorship or imperial authority. —**Caesarist,** *n.*

capitalism a theory or system in which property and investment in business are owned and controlled by individuals directly or through ownership of shares in companies. Cf. communism. —capitalist, *n.*, *adj.* —capitalistic, *adj.*

Carlism adherence to Don Carlos of Spain and to his successors. —Carlist, *n.*

Castroism the doctrines and policies of Fidel Castro, communist premier of Cuba.

centrism adherence to a middle-of-the-road position, neither left nor right, as in politics. —centrist, *adj.*, *n.*

Chartism the principles of a movement or party of English political reformers, chiefly workingmen, from 1838 to 1848, advocating better working and social conditions for laborers in its People's Charter (1838). —Chartist, *n.*

civicism the doctrine that all citizens have the same rights and obligations.

civilist *Obsolete.* a person who studies politics.

clubbism a system of political clubs, especially the clubs of the French Revolution. —clubbist, *n.* —clubbish, *adj.*

Cobdenism the political doctrines of Richard Cobden, who believed in peace and the withdrawal from European competition for balance of power.

collectivism the socialist principle of control by the state of all means of productive or economic activity. —collectivist, *n.*, *adj.* —collectivistic, *adj.*

communalism 1. a theory or system of organization in which the major political and social units are self-governing communes, and the nation is merely a federation of such groups.
2. the principles or practices of communal ownership. Cf. communism, socialism. —communalist, *n.* —communalistic, *adj.*

communism a theory or system in which all property is owned by all of the people equally, with its administration vested by them in the state or in the community. Cf. capitalism. —communist, *n.*, *adj.* —communistic, *adj.*

conservatism 1. the disposition to retain what is established and to practice a policy of gradualism rather than abrupt change. Cf. radicalism.
2. the principles and practices of political conservatives, especially of the British Conservative party. —conservative, *n.*, *adj.*

constitutionalism 1. the principles of the form of government defined by a constitution.
2. an adherence to these principles.
3. constitutional rule or authority. —constitutionalist, *n.*

continentalism 1. an attitude or policy of favoritism or partiality to a continent.
2. a policy advocating a restriction of political or economic relations to the countries of one continent. —continentalist, *n.*

corruptionist a person who practices or advocates corruption, especially in politics or public life.

cronyism favoritism, especially in the giving of political appointments.

culottism the habits and principles of nonrevolutionaries, of the bourgeoisie. Cf. sansculottism. —culottic, *adj.*

czarism 1. an autocratic government.
2. dictatorship. Also spelled tzarism, tsarism. —czarist, *n.*, *adj.*

Decembrist one of those who conspired to overthrow Russian Czar Nicholas I in December, 1825. Also Dekebrist.

Dekebrist Decembrist.

demagogism, demagoguism, demagogy the art and practice of gaining power and popularity by arousing the emotions, passions, and prejudices of the people. Also demagoguery.

democratism a doctrine of or belief in social equality or the right of all people to participate equally in politics.

denominationalism 1. the policy of being sectarian in spirit, especially in carrying out religious policy.
2. the tendency to separate or cause to separate into sects or denominations. —denominationalist, *n.*, *adj.*

departmentalism advocacy of the division of something, such as an educational institution, into departments. —departmentalization, *n.*

diversionism the actions used by a saboteur against his own government and military forces. —diversionist, *n.* —diversionary, *adj.*

dynamitism the activity of terrorists who use dynamite to blow up public places.

egalitarianism a social and political philosophy asserting the equality of all men, especially in their access to the rights and privileges of their society. Also equalitarianism. —egalitarian, *n.*, *adj.*

equalitarianism egalitarianism.

etatism a form of state socialism.

expansionism a policy of expansion, as of territory or currency. —expansionist, *n.*, *adj.* —expansionistic, *adj.*

factionalism, factionism the state or quality of being partisan or self-interested. —factional, *adj.* —factionalist, *n.*

Falangism the doctrines and practices of the Spanish fascist party. —Falangist, *n.*, *adj.*

Fayettism the beliefs and activities of the followers of the Marquis de Lafayette.

Fenianism the principles and practices of an Irish revolutionary organization founded in New York in 1858, especially its emphasis on the establishment of an independent Irish republic. —**Fenian,** *n.,* *adj.*

Feuillant (in France) a member of a club of constitutional monarchists, named after their meeting place at Notre Dame des Feuillants.

Free Soilism the principles of the Free Soil party (1846–56), which opposed the extension of slavery into any new territories of the United States. —**Free Soiler,** *n.*

fusionism the quality of having a coalition between certain political parties. —**fusionist,** *n.*

Gandhism, Gandhiism the principles of Mohandas K. Gandhi, Indian political and spiritual leader, especially his advocacy of passive resistance and noncooperation to achieve social and political reforms. —**Gandhist, Gandhiist,** *n.* —**Gandhian,** *adj.*

Gaullism 1. the principles and policies of Charles de Gaulle during World War II in support of the Free French and opposed to the Vichy regime.
2. the political principles, chiefly conservative and nationalistic, of de Gaulle as French president, 1959–69. —**Gaullist,** *n.,* *adj.*

geopolitics 1. the study or application of the effect of political or economic geography on the political structure, programs, or philosophy of a state.
2. a policy or policies based on such factors.
3. the complex of geographical and political factors affecting or determining the nature of a state or region.
4. the study of the relationship between geography and politics, applied especially to the study of the doctrines and actions of Nazi Germany in the context of world domination. —**geopolitician,** *n.* —**geopolitical,** *adj.*

Ghibellinism the principles of the imperial and aristocratic party of medieval Italy, especially their support of the German emperors. Cf. **Guelphism.** —**Ghibelline,** *n.,* *adj.*

Girondism a form of mild republicanism in France, 1791–1793, led by natives of the Gironde. —**Girondist,** *n.,* *adj.*

gradualism the principle or policy of achieving a goal, as political or economic, by gradual steps rather than by sudden and drastic innovation. Cf. **conservatism, radicalism.** —**gradualist,** *n.,* *adj.* —**gradualistic,** *adj.*

Guelphism, Guelfism the principles and practices of the papal and popular party in medieval Italy. Cf. **Ghibellinism.** —**Guelphic, Guelfic,** *adj.*

Guesdism the principles of Marxian socialism as interpreted by the French socialist, editor, and writer Jules Guesde. —**Guesdist,** *n.,* *adj.*

Hamiltonianism the political theories, doctrines, or policies of Alexander Hamilton, especially federalism, strong central government, and protective tariffs. —**Hamiltonian,** *n.,* *adj.*

heteronomy the condition of being under the rule or domination of another.

ideology the body of doctrine, myth, symbol, etc., with reference to some political or cultural plan, as that of communism, along with the procedures for putting it into operation. —ideologist, idealogue, *n.* —ideologic, ideological, *adj.*

illiberalism opposition to liberalism.

institutionalism 1. the system of institutions or organized societies devoted to public, political, or charitable, or similar purposes.
2. a strong attachment to established institutions, as political systems or religions. —institutionalist, *n.*

insurgentism the state of being an insurgent or rebel; the activities of insurgents or rebels.

internationalism 1. the belief in cooperation between nations for the common good.
2. advocacy of this concept. —internationalist, *n.*, *adj.*

interpolity *Rare.* the holding of mutual citizenship.

interventionism the doctrine supporting intervention, especially in international affairs and the politics of other countries. —interventionist, *n.*, *adj.*

irredentism 1. a national policy advocating the acquisition of some region in another country by reason of common linguistic, cultural, historical, ethnic, or racial ties.
2. (*cap.*) the policies of a 19th-century Italian party that sought to annex parts of certain neighboring regions with chiefly Italian populations. —irredentist, *n.*, *adj.*

isolationism the policy or doctrine directed toward the isolation of a country from the affairs of other nations by a deliberate abstention from political, military, and economic agreements. —isolationist, *n.*

isonomy the possession of equal political and legal rights by all citizens of a state.

isopolity the granting of equal or reciprocal political rights by different countries to each other's citizens. —isopolite, *n.* —isopolitical, *adj.*

Jacobinism the practices of the Jacobins, a political group advocating equalitarian democracy during the French Revolution. —Jacobin, *n.* —Jacobinic, *adj.*

Jeffersonianism the political theories, doctrines, or policies of Thomas Jefferson, especially rigid interpretation of the U.S. Constitution, belief in an agrarian economy, states' rights, and in the political acumen of the ordinary citizen. —Jeffersonian, *adj.*

jusquaboutism, jusquaboutisme a policy of self-sacrificing and determined radicalism. —jusquaboutist, *n.*, *adj.*

kaiserism the autocratic political system and policies of a German kaiser.

Khomeinism the religious and political doctrines of the Ayatollah Ruhollah Khomeini (1900?–), who founded the Islamic Republic in Iran in 1979.

Know-Nothingism doctrines of the American Party (1853–1856), the main goal of which was to bar foreign-born citizens from participating in government. —know-nothing, n.

leftism a radical or liberal position or doctrine, especially in politics. —leftist, n., adj.

liberalism 1. a political or social philosophy advocating the freedom of the individual, parliamentary legislatures, governmental assurances of civil liberties and individual rights, and nonviolent modification of institutions to permit continued individual and social progress.
2. the principles and practice of a liberal political party. —liberalist, n., adj. —liberalistic, adj.

liberationism the principles of the liberationists, an English society opposed to a state or established church and favoring disestablishment. —liberationist, n.

lobbyism the practice of influencing legislators to favor special interests. —lobbyist, n.

Locofocoism the doctrines of the Locofocos, a radical faction of the New York City Democrats, organized in 1835 to oppose the conservatives in the party. —Locofoco, n., adj.

Loyalism 1. a dedication to the British cause during the American revolution; Toryism.
2. an adherence to the cause of the republic during the Spanish Civil War. —Loyalist, n., adj.

Machiavellianism 1. the principles of government set forth in *The Prince* by Machiavelli, in which political expediency is exalted above morality and the use of craft and deceit to maintain authority or to effectuate policy is recommended. Also Machiavellism.
2. activity characterized by subtle cunning, duplicity, or bad faith. —Machiavellian, n., adj.

Malanism the principles and attitudes of Daniel F. Malan, prime minister of the Union of South Africa (1948–54), whose policies of apartheid and Afrikander supremacy were first made law during his term of office.

McCarthyism 1. *U.S.* the practice of making accusations of disloyalty, especially of pro-Communist activity, often unsupported or based on doubtful evidence.
2. any attempt to restrict political criticism or individual dissent by claiming it to be unpatriotic or pro-Communist.

Medism an attitude of sympathy towards the Medes (Persians), held by some Greeks in the 6th and 5th centuries B.C.

militarism 1. the principle of maintaining a large military establishment.
2. the policy of regarding military efficiency as the supreme ideal of the state, and the subordinating of all other ideals to those of the military. Also militaryism. —militarist, *n.* —militaristic, *adj.*

moderantism the principle or policy of moderation, especially in politics and international relations. —moderantist, *n.*

mugwumpism 1. the practice of independence, especially in politics.
2. an inability to make up one's mind, especially in politics; neutrality on controversial issues. Also mugwumpery. —mugwump, *n.* —mugwumpian, mugwumpish, *adj.*

multitudinism a doctrine that lays stress on the importance of the multitude instead of the individual. —multitudinist, *n., adj.* —multitudinal, *adj.*

Nazism, Naziism the principles and practices of the National Socialist Workers' party under Adolf Hitler from 1933 to 1945. —Nazi, *n., adj.*

negrophilism the advancement and advocacy of equal rights for Negroes. —negrophilist, *n.* —negrophile, *adj.*

neocolonialism domination of a small or weak country by a large or strong one without the assumption of direct government. —neocolonialist, *n.*, —neocolonial, *adj.*

neoconservatism a new movement in conservatism, usually seen as a move further to the right of the position currently occupied by conservatives in politics or in attitudes. —neoconservative, *n., adj.*

neoliberalism a movement that modifies classical liberalism in light of 20th-century conditions.

neutralism the practice or policy of remaining neutral in foreign affairs. —neutralist, *n.*

noninterventionism the doctrine that governments should not interfere in the politics of other countries. —noninterventionist, *n., adj.*

nonpartisanism the practice or policy of nonsupport for established or regular political parties. Also nonpartisanship. —nonpartisan, *n., adj.*

nothingarianism the holding of no belief, creed, or political position. Cf. anythingarianism. —nothingarian, *n.*

Pan-Africanism the doctrine or advocacy of alliance or cooperation among all African states. —Pan-Africanist, *n., adj.*

Pan-Americanism the idea of a single state including all of North and South America.

Pan-Arabism the doctrine or advocacy of alliance or cooperation among all Arab states. —Pan-Arabist, *n., adj.*

Pan-Germanism a 19th-century political movement whose aim was the unification of all Germans.

partisanism an action or spirit of partiality for a specific political party. Also **partisanship.** —**partisan,** *n.*, *adj.*

partyism 1. the system of political parties.
2. a strong adherence to a party. —**partyist,** *n.*

passivism 1. the state or quality of being passive.
2. the doctrine or advocacy of a passive policy, as passive resistance. —**passivist,** *n.*

physiocratism the principles and doctrines of political economists following the ideas of François Quesnay in holding that an inherent natural order adequately controlled society and advocating a laissez-faire economy based on land as the best system to prevent interference with natural laws. —**physiocrat,** *n.* —**physiocratic,** *adj.*

Pittism the policies of William Pitt the Younger, chief minister under King George III of England and sympathizer with the colonies during the American Revolution. —**Pittite,** *n.*

pluralism 1. *Ecclesiastic.* the holding of two or more church offices by a single person.
2. the state or condition of a common civilization in which various ethnic, racial, or religious groups are free to participate in and develop their common cultures.
3. a policy or principle supporting such cultural plurality. —**pluralist,** *n.* —**pluralistic,** *adj.*

politicomania a mania for politics.

politology the study of politics; political science. Also **politicology.** —**politologist,** *n.* —**politological,** *adj.*

polycentrism the existence of a number of basic guiding principles in the political system of a Communist government.

popular sovereignty 1. the doctrine that sovereign power is vested in the people and that those chosen by election to govern or to represent must conform to the will of the people.
2. *U.S. History.* a doctrine, held chiefly before 1865 by antiabolitionists, that new territories should be free of federal interference in domestic matters, especially concerning slavery.

populism 1. the principles and doctrines of any political party asserting that it represents the rank and file of the people.
2. (*cap.*) the principles and doctrines of a late 19th-century American party, especially its support of agrarian interests and a silver coinage. —**populist,** *n.*, *adj.* —**populistic,** *adj.*

pornocracy domination of government by prostitutes, especially in reference to the Roman government in the first half of the 10th century.

progressivism 1. Also called **progressionism, progressism.** the principles and practices of those advocating progress, change, or reform, especially in political matters.
2. (*cap.*) the doctrines and beliefs of the Progressive party in America. —**progressivist,** *n.*

proletarianism the practices, attitudes, social status, or political condition of an unpropertied class dependent for support on daily or casual labor. —**proletarian,** *n.*, *adj.*

proportionalism the principle of electing officials by proportionality. —**proportionalist,** *n.*, *adj.*

psephology the study of elections. —**psephologist,** *n.* —**psephological,** *adj.*

quislingism the traitorous rejection of one's native country followed by the acceptance of a position of authority in the government of an occupying power. —**quisling,** *n.*

radicalism 1. the holding or following of principles advocating drastic political, economic, or social reforms. Cf. **conservatism, gradualism.**
2. the principles or practices of radicals. —**radical,** *n.*, *adj.*

realpolitik realism in politics, especially policies or actions based on considerations of power rather than ideals.

Rebeccaism the beliefs of rioters in South Wales in 1843–44, who were led by a man dressed as a woman and called Rebecca. —**Rebeccaite,** *n.*

reformism the doctrine or movement of reform whether it be social, moral, or of any other type. —**reformist,** *n.* —**reformistic,** *adj.*

retrogradism adherence to reactionary politics. —**retrogradist,** *n.*, *adj.*

royalism the support or advocacy of a royal government. —**royalist,** *n.*, *adj.* —**royalistic,** *adj.*

sansculottism any extreme republican or revolutionary principles. Cf. culottism. —**sansculottist,** *n.* —**sansculotic, sansculotish,** *adj.*

secessionism the doctrines and practices of the secessionists. —**secessionist,** *n.*, *adj.* —**secessional,** *adj.*

separatism an advocacy of separation, especially ecclesiastical or political separation, as the secession of U.S. states before the Civil War. —**separatist,** *n.*, *adj.*

Sinarquism a secret Mexican counterrevolutionary movement, advocating the return to Christian social standards and opposing communism, labor unions, conscription, and Pan-Americanism. —**Sinarquist,** *n.*

Slavophobia fear or hatred of things Slavic, especially of real or imagined political influence. —**Slavophobe,** *n.* —**Slavophobic,** *adj.*

socialism 1. a theory or system of social organization advocating placing the ownership and control of capital, land, and means of production in the community as a whole. Cf. **utopian socialism**.
2. the procedures and practices based upon this theory.
3. *Marxist theory.* the first stage in the transition from capitalism to communism, marked by imperfect realizations of collectivist principles. —**socialist,** *n., adj.* —**socialistic,** *adj.*

Spartacist 1. a member of a German socialist party founded in 1918.
2. an extreme socialist. [Allusion to Spartacus, leader of a slave revolt against Rome, 73–71 B.C.]

stalwartism the principles and actions characteristic of one who is a strong partisan of a cause. —**stalwart,** *n.*

stand pattism extreme conservatism.

suffragettism militant advocacy of suffrage for women. Cf. **suffragism**.

suffragism any advocacy of the granting or extension of the suffrage to those now denied it, especially to women. —**suffragist,** *n.*

syndicalism 1. an economic system in which workers own and manage an industry.
2. a revolutionary form or development of trade unionism, originating in France, aiming at possession and control of the means of production and distribution and the establishment of a corporate society governed by trade unions and workers' cooperatives. —**syndicalist,** *n.* —**syndicalistic,** *adj.*

Tammanism, Tammanyism 1. the activities and principles of Tammany Hall, a powerful New York City Democratic political society of the 1800s, founded as a benevolent organization, which later deteriorated into a force for political patronage and corruption.
2. activities or beliefs similar to those of Tammany Hall. —**Tammanyite,** *n., adj.*

territorialism 1. the principle of the political predominance of the landed classes; landlordism.
2. the theory of church policy vesting supreme ecclesiastical authority in a civil government, as in 16th-century Germany. Also called **territorial system**. —**territorialist,** *n.*

terrorism 1. a method of government or of resisting government involving domination or coercion by various forms of intimidation, as bombing or kidnapping.
2. the state of fear and terror so produced. —**terrorist,** *n., adj.* —**terroristic,** *adj.*

Toryism 1. a support of the British cause during the American Revolution.
2. an advocacy of conservative principles opposed to reform and radicalism.
3. the actions of dispossessed Irishmen in the 17th century who were

declared outlaws and noted for their outrages and cruelty.
4. the principles of a conservative British party in power until 1832. —Tory, *n.*, *adj.*, —Toryish, *adj.*

two-partyism the condition in a nation of having two political parties with equal voting strength and little opposition from other parties.

tzarism, tsarism czarism.

ultraconservatism extreme conservatism, especially in politics. —ultraconservative, *n.*, *adj.*

ultraism 1. the principles of those who advocate extreme points of view or actions, as radicalism.
2. extremist activities. —ultraist, *n.*, *adj.* —ultraistic, *adj.*

un-Americanism the state or condition of being out of sympathy with or against an ideal of American behavior, attitudes, beliefs, etc. —un-American, *n.*, *adj.*

utopian socialism an economic theory based on the premise that voluntary surrender by capital of the means of production would bring about the end of poverty and unemployment. Cf. socialism.

Watergatism 1. any underhanded, illegal, unethical, or dishonest political practice or action.
2. behavior attempting to conceal such practices or action.

Whiggarchy *Rare.* government or rule by Whigs.

Whiteboyism the doctrines and activities of the Irish Whiteboys, a secret agrarian society formed in 1761 to fight high rents [from the white shirts worn by the members at night for identification]. —Whiteboy, *n.*

323. POPE
See also 69. CATHOLICISM; 80. CHRISTIANITY; 81. CHURCH; 349. RELIGION; 392. THEOLOGY.

chirograph, cheirograph an apostolic letter written by and signed by the pope.

encyclical, encyclic a letter from the Pope to the Roman Catholic clergy on matters of doctrine or other concerns of the Church, often meant to be read from the pulpit.

papolatry excessive veneration or worship of the pope. —papolatrous, *adj.*

pontificality 1. the papacy.
2. the state and government of the Vatican or the Pope.

popery *Derogatory & Offensive.* Roman Catholicism.

Urbanist a supporter of Pope Urban VI in the conflict of 1378 when an opposing faction established Clement VII as Pope. See also 277. MONKS and NUNS.

324. POTTERY
See also 369. SKILL and CRAFT.

ceramics, keramics 1. the art and technology of making objects of clay and other materials treated by firing.
2. articles of earthenware, porcelain, etc. —ceramist, keramist, ceramicist, keramicist, *n.*

ceramography an historical or descriptive work on pottery.

325. POVERTY

beggarism 1. *Rare.* the state of beggarhood.
2. behavior characteristic of a beggar.

pauperism the state or condition of utter poverty. Also called **pauperage.**

peniaphobia an abnormal fear of poverty.

penury extreme poverty or destitution. —penurious, *adj.*

Poplarism *British.* 1. a policy in local governments of providing relief for the poor, often excessive in amount.
2. any similar policy of government spending that leads to higher taxes. —Poplarist, *n.*

ptochocracy a form of rule by beggars or the poor.

ptochology the scientific study of pauperism, unemployment, etc.

slumism the development and growth of slums or substandard dwelling conditions in urban areas.

326. PRAISE
See also 210. HONORS and REGALIA.

dyslogy a written or spoken passage conveying disapproval or censure. Cf. eulogy. —dyslogist, *n.* —dyslogistic, dyslogistical, *adj.*

encomium formal praise; an elaborate or ceremonial panegyric or eulogy. —encomiast, *n.* —encomiastic, *adj.*

eulogy a written or spoken passage conveying approval, praise, and laudation, often of someone who has just died. Cf. dyslogy —eulogistic, eulogistical, *adj.* —eulogist, *n.*

panegyric 1. a formal speech of praise.
2. any form of enthusiastic praise. —panegyric, panegyrical, *adj.* —panegyrist, *n.*

327. PREGNANCY
See also 1. ABORTION; 46. BIRTH; 77. CHILDREN; 281. MOTHER; 307. PARENTS; 364. SEX.

cyesiology *Obsolete.* the part of medical science that studies pregnancy.

cyesis *Medicine.* the condition of pregnancy.

eccyesis a pregnancy that takes place outside the uterus.

embryography the scientific description of the fetus. —embryographic, *adj.*

fetology, foetology the branch of medicine that studies fetuses. —fetologist, foetologist, *n.*

gravidity the state or condition of pregnancy. —gravidness, *n.* —gravid, *adj.*

obstetrics the medical specialty that deals with pregnancy and childbirth. —obstetrician, *n.* —obstetric, obstetrical, *adj.*

pregnancy the state, condition, or quality of being with child. —pregnant, *adj.*

328. PRINTING
See also 53. BOOKS; 98. COPYING.

algraphy an offset process that uses an aluminum plate instead of a lithographic stone. Also called aluminography. —algraphic, *adj.*

autography the process in lithography of transferring writings and drawings to a stone surface. —autographic, *adj.* —autographically, *adv.*

chromolithography a printing process by which colored lithographs are produced by a series of stone or zinc plates, each of which carries different portions of the picture to be printed, inked in different colors.

chromoxylography printing in colors from a series of wooden blocks.

electrotypy the process of preparing a facsimile printing surface, involving the depositing of a thin copper or nickel shell by electrolytic action in a mold of the original and backing it with a lead alloy. —electrotyper, electrotypist, *n.* —electrotypic, *adj.*

glyphography a process for making letterpress plates by engraving a waxed copper plate, dusting with zinc, and preparing an electrotype. —glyphographer, *n.* —glyphographic, *adj.*

graphotype a device for embossing letters on thin sheets of metal.

imprimatur permission, particularly that given by the Roman Catholic Church, to publish or print; hence, any sanction or approval.

italicism the use of italics in printing text to indicate foreign words, abbreviations, emphasis, titles, etc.

lithography 1. the art or process of producing an image on a flat, specially prepared stone, treating the items to be printed with a greasy substance to which ink adheres, and of taking impressions from this on paper.
2. a similar process in which the stone is replaced by a zinc or aluminum plate, often provided with a photosensitive surface for reproducing an image photographically. —lithographer, *n.* —lithographic, *adj.*

lithotypy a printing process in which types are impressed in a soft matrix, the resulting hollow spaces being filled with a heated mixture that later solidifies and can be used for printing. —**lithotypic,** *adj.*

metallography an offset printing process, similar to lithography, using metal plates instead of stone.

offset lithography a printing method in which the image on a plate is offset onto a rubber blanket from which it is transferred onto the surface to be printed.

oleography the production of chromolithographs printed in oil colors on canvas or cloth as well as on paper. —**oleographic,** *adj.*

optotype type used in the testing of eyesight.

papyrography a process by which a line drawing or writing on paper is transferred to a zinc plate, which is then used for printing. —**papyrograph,** *n.* —**papyrographic,** *adj.*

photoxylography the process of producing a raised impression on wood from a photograph and using the block thus produced for printing.

polyautography *Obsolete.* lithography.

thermography a technique for imitating an engraved appearance, as on business cards, by dusting areas already printed with a powder attracted only to the inks and using heat to fuse the ink and powder. —**thermographer,** *n.* —**thermographic,** *adj.*

typography 1. the design, theory, and art of creating characters for printing.
2. the design and selection of printed matter.
3. the craft or business of composing type. —**typographic, typographical,** *adj.*

typothetae printers, especially master printers, usually found in the names of associations of printers.

xylography the art of engraving on wood or of printing from such engravings. —**xylographer,** *n.* —**xylographic, xylographical,** *adj.*

329. PROCESSES
    See also 158. **FERMENTATION.**

decoction 1. the process of boiling a substance in water to extract its essence.
2. the essence so produced.

decortication the process of stripping off or removing the cortex or outer layer.

deliquescence 1. the process of melting away or becoming moist from absorbing moisture from the air.
2. the liquid substance so formed. Cf. **efflorescence.** —**deliquescent,** *adj.*

deracination the process of pulling up by the roots; eradication.

despumation the process of removing scum or despumating; figuratively, clarification.

desquamation the peeling off of the skin in scales.

dimidiation the process of dividing in half; the state of being halved.

edulcoration the process of sweetening or removing the acid or other impurities from a substance.

effloresence 1. the process of drying out from evaporation.
2. the substance so formed. Cf. deliquescence. See also 414. WATER. —efflorescent, *adj*.

elution removal of soluble matter from a substance to be refined by washing it in water.

elutriation the process of elutriating, or purification by washing and straining.

emuscation *Rare*. the process of removing moss.

endosmosis (in osmosis) the more rapid spread of the less dense fluid through the membrane to join with the more dense. Cf. exosmosis. —endosmotic, *adj*.

enucleation 1. the process of extraction, as removing the kernel from a nut.
2. a process of clarification. Cf. exacination. —enucleator, *n*.

evanescence 1. the process of vanishing or fading away.
2. the condition of being transitory.

exacination *Rare*. the process of removing a kernel, as from a nut. Cf. enucleation.

excoriation the process of removing the skin or outer layer; flaying. See also 370. SKIN.

exosmosis (in osmosis) the slower spread of the more dense fluid through the membrane to merge with the less dense. Cf. endosmosis. —exosmotic, *adj*.

extirpation 1. the process of extirpating or destroying totally, as by tearing up the roots.
2. the condition of being totally destroyed.

fulmination the explosion that occurs when certain chemicals are detonated.

induration 1. the process of hardening or being hardened.
2. a hardened mass. —indurative, *adj*.

inspissation the process of rendering a liquid thicker by evaporation. —inspissant, *n*. —inspissate, *adj*.

instauration *Obsolete*. the restoration of something to its former condition; renewal or repair. —instaurator, *n*.

labefaction, labefactation the process of coming apart, especially falling into ruin or decay.

lactescence the process of becoming milky or the state of being milky. See also 272. MILK. —lactescent, *adj.*

lapidification the process of turning to stone. Also called **petrifaction, petrification.**

levigation 1. the process of grinding to a fine powder.
2. the process of mixing thoroughly or grinding to a smooth paste. —levigate, *adj.*

levitation the process of rising or being raised in the air.

lixiviation the process of leaching alkaline salts from ashes by pouring water on them. —lixivial, —lixivious, *adj.*

lyophilization a process for preserving substances such as blood or serum by freeze-drying in a high vacuum.

maceration the act or process of softening or separating by soaking or steeping.

mordancy, mordacity the property of acting as a fixative in dyeing. —mordant, *n., adj.*

osmosis the process by which fluids pass through a semipermeable membrane into a solution of lower concentration to equalize the concentration on both sides of the membrane. —osmotic, *adj.*

perscrutation a thorough search; a diligent and detailed inquiry.

petrification, petrifaction lapidification.

putrescence 1. the state or process of rotting or putrefying.
2. rotting or putrefying matter. —putrescent, *adj.*

quassation *Rare.* the act or process of shaking or being shaken.

recrudescence the process of renewal or rebirth. —recrudescent, *adj.*

regenesis the act or process of renewal or rebirth.

scintillation the process of giving of sparks or flashes, used of wit or humor and of the twinkling of the stars.

scorification the process of reducing to slag, scoria, or dross, as in the refining of metals.

330. PRONUNCIATION
See also 236. LANGUAGE; 382. SPEECH.

cacoepy the habit of unacceptable or bad pronunciation.

cacology 1. a defectively produced speech.
2. socially unacceptable enunciation.
3. nonconformist pronunciation.

etacism the pronunciation of Greek *eta* like the *e* in *be*. —etacist, *n.*

hyper-urbanism an overcorrected pronunciation or usage that attempts to mask guttural or provincial speech.

nasalism a tendency toward nasality in pronouncing words. Also **nasality.**

orthoepy the study of correct pronunciation. —**orthoepist,** *n.* —**orthoepic, orthoepical, orthoepistic,** *adj.*

331. PROPERTY and OWNERSHIP
See also 235. LAND.

abstraction the taking of another's property for one's own use.

amortization, amortizement the transfer or sale of property in mortmain.

burgage *British, Obsolete.* a form of land tenure under which land was held in return for payment of a fixed sum of money in rent or for rendering of service. Also called **socage.**

devisal the act of devising or bequeathing real property (as contrasted with personal property). Cf. **devise.**

devise 1. the bequeathing of real property by will.
2. the clause in a will devising real property.

disseizin, disseisin the process of wrongfully or unlawfully dispossessing a person of his rightful real property; deprivation of seizin.

dotation that which is endowed; an endowment.

enfeoffment 1. the act of investing with an estate held in fee.
2. the deed that enfeoffs.
3. the possession of a fief or estate held in fee.

entailment 1. the process of limiting an inheritance to a specific sequence of heirs, usually applied to large estates.
2. the estate entailed.

escheatment reversion of ownership of property, especially real property, to the crown in the absence of persons legally qualified to inherit. Also called **escheat.** —**escheatable,** *adj.*

expropriation the process of taking over property, especially real property, of another by any process, lawful or not.

feoff fief.

feoffment the granting of land to be held in fief.

feud fief.

fief *Feudal System.* heritable land in return for service as a vassal. The right to hold. Also called **feoff, feud.**

foreclosure the process by which mortgaged property enters into the possession of the mortgagee without right of redemption by the mortgagor, usually for reason of delinquency in mortgage payments.

freehold 1. ownership of property with the right to pass it on through inheritance.
2. the property held in this way. Cf. **leasehold.** —**freeholder,** *n.*

gavelkind *British. Obsolete.* 1. the equal division of the land of an intestate deceased among his sons.
2. a tenant's right to dispose of his land by feoffment at age fifteen.
3. land not escheating in the event the tenant was convicted as a felon.

heirship the state or condition of an heir; the right to inherit property; heirdom.

impoundage, impoundment the process of taking into legal custody, especially property. —**impounder,** *n.*

infeudation *Feudalism.* 1. the process of granting an estate in fee; enfeoffment.
2. the granting of tithes to laymen.

leasehold 1. the holding of property by lease.
2. the property held in this way. Cf. **freehold.**

lessee a person or entity to whom a lease is given; a person or entity that leases property as a tenant.

lessor a person or entity that grants a lease to another; a person or entity that leases property as a landlord.

mortgage 1. the giving of property, usually real property, as security to a creditor for payment of a debt.
2. the deed pledging the security.

mortgagee the person to whom property is mortgaged; the creditor in a mortgage transaction.

mortgagor a person who mortgages property or gives the property as security; the borrower in a mortgage transaction.

mortmain transfer or ownership of real property in perpetuity, as transfer to or ownership by a corporate body like a school, college, or church.

nonage formerly, a ninth part of a parishioner's movable property, which was claimed upon his death by the clergy in England. See also 239. LAW.

ownership 1. the state or quality of being an owner.
2. the state of owning.
3. right of possession or proprietorship.

parcenary coheirship, or the joint and undivided holding of inherited land by two or more coheirs.

parcener a coheir or joint heir; a person who holds property jointly by inheritance.

peculium *Roman Law.* property that might be held by a son, wife, or slave.

revaluation the assigning of a new, usually higher value, as to money, real estate, etc.

seizin, seisin 1. possession of a freehold estate.
2. the estate so possessed.

serjeanty, sergeanty (in medieval England) a form of land tenure in which a tenant holding land from the king owed services only to him.

severalty the ownership or holding of property by separate and individual right. See also 363. SEPARATION.

socage burgage

socager, socman a tenant by socage.

squatterism 1. the state or practice of being a squatter, or one who settles on government land, thereby establishing ownership.
2. the state or practice of settling in vacant or abandoned property, either for shelter or in an attempt to establish ownership. —squatter, *n.*

superfeudation, superinfeudation creation of a feudal estate out of or upon another feudal estate.

usucaption *Roman Law.* right to or ownership of property on the basis of possession of it for a prescribed period of time. —usucapient, *n.*

usufruct the right to enjoy benefits or profits from something, as real property, while not being the owner of it. —usufructuary, *n., adj.*

vassalage 1. the condition of land tenure of a vassal.
2. the fief or lands held.

villeinage the type of tenure under which a villein held his land. Also called villanage.

332. PROTESTANTISM
See also 80. CHRISTIANITY; 151. FAITH; 349. RELIGION;
392. THEOLOGY.

adiaphorism a tolerance of conduct or beliefs not specifically forbidden in the Scriptures. Cf. Flacianism, Philippism. —adiaphorist, *n.* —adiaphoristic, *adj.*

Adventism the principles and practices of certain Christian denominations that maintain that the Second Advent of Christ is imminent. Also called Second Adventist. —Adventist, *n., adj.*

Amyraldism the doctrines and practices of a liberal form of Calvinism established in France in the 17th century, especially its doctrines of universal atonement and salvation for all.

Anglicanism the adherence to the tenets and faith of the Anglican church.

Arminianism the doctrines and teaching of Jacobus Arminius, 17th-century Dutch theologian, who opposed the Calvinist doctrine of absolute predestination and maintained the possibility of universal salvation. Cf. **Calvinism.** —**Arminian,** *n.*, *adj.*

Brownism the views and doctrines of Robert Browne, the first formulator of the principles of Congregationalism. —**Brownist,** *n.* —**Brownistic,** *adj.*

Buchmanism 1. the principles of the international movement called **Moral Re-Armament** or the **Oxford Group.**
2. the belief in or adherence to these principles. —**Buchmanite,** *n.*, *adj.*

Calixtine an Utraquist. See **Utraquism.**

Calvinism 1. the doctrines of John Calvin or his followers, especially emphasis upon predestination and limited atonement, the sovereignty of God, the authority of the Scriptures and the irresistibility of grace.
2. adherence to these doctrines. Also called **Genevanism.** Cf. **Arminianism.** —**Calvinist,** *n.*, *adj.* —**Calvinistic, Calvinistical,** *adj.*

Christadelphianism the doctrines of a premillennial sect founded in the U.S. in the mid-19th-century, especially its denial of Trinitarianism and its acceptance of Unitarian and Adventist doctrines. —**Christadelphian,** *n.*, *adj.*

cirplanology the history and study of Methodist circuit plans.

commination the list of divine threats against sinners, read in the Anglican Church on Ash Wednesday. See also 96. CONFLICT.

Congregationalism 1. the doctrine and governmental practices of Congregational churches.
2. a form of church government in which each congregation is autonomous. —**Congregationalist,** *n.*, *adj.*

consociationism the theory or practice of associations or confederations of religious societies, usually for purposes of fellowship. —**consociational,** *adj.*

Darbyism the doctrines and practices of the Plymouth Brethren. —**Darbyite,** *n.*

denominationalism 1. the policy or spirit of denominations or sects.
2. the tendency to divide into denominations or sects. —**denominationalist,** *n.*

dissenterism nonconformism, def. 2.

ecumenism the doctrines and practices of the ecumenical movement, especially among Protestant groups since the 1800s, aimed at developing worldwide Christian unity and church union. Also **ecumenicalism, ecumenicism.**

Episcopalianism 1. the Protestant Episcopal Church of the Anglican communion.
2. adherence to the policy and practice of the Episcopal Church. —**Episcopalian,** *n.*, *adj.* —**Episcopal,** *adj.*

episcopalism a theory of church polity asserting that supreme ecclesiastical authority belongs to all bishops collectively and not to an individual except by delegation.

Flacianism the Lutheran doctrines and treatises of Matthias Flacius Illyricus, especially his attacks upon Melanchthon and others for distorting Luther's teachings and emphasizing adiaphorism. Cf. **Philippism**. —**Flacian**, *n.*

Freechurchism the principles of the Free Church, which split off from the Presbyterian Church in 1843. —**Freechurchman**, *n.*

fundamentalism 1. a conservative movement in 20th-century American Protestantism in reaction to modernism, asserting especially the inerrancy of the Scriptures as a historical record and as a guide to faith and morals, and emphasizing, as matters of true faith, belief in the virgin birth, the sacrifice and death of Christ upon the cross, physical resurrection, and the Second Coming. 2. an adherence to the doctrines and practices of this movement. —**fundamentalist**, *n., adj.*

Genevanism Calvinism.

Harmonist a member of a Protestant sect from Württemberg, Germany that settled in Harmony, Pennsylvania, in 1803, and believed in common ownership of property.

Hopkinsianism the doctrines of Dr. Samuel Hopkins, similar to those of Calvin except that Hopkins rejected the concept of original sin. —**Hopkinsonian**, *n., adj.*

Huguenotism the doctrines and practices of the Calvinistic communion in France in the 16th and 17th centuries. —**Huguenot**, *n.* —**Huguenotic**, *adj.*

Hussitism the doctrines of a reformist and nationalistic movement initiated by John Huss in Bohemia about 1402, especially its reflection of Wycliffite emphases upon clerical purity, communion in both bread and wine for the laity, and the supreme authority of the Scriptures. Also **Hussism**. —**Hussite**, *n., adj.*

Irvingite a member of the religious group founded by Edward Irving, a Scots minister who advocated strict observance of ritualistic practices.

Koreshanity the doctrines and beliefs of an American communal religious society founded in 1886, especially its goal of reforming both church and state and their mutual relationship to God. —**Koreshan**, *adj.*

Labadist an adherent of Jean de Labadie, a French mystic.

Laudianism the policies and practices of William Laud, Archbishop of Canterbury and opponent of Puritanism, especially his assertion that the Church of England preserves more fully than the Roman communion the orthodoxy of the early Christian church, his support of the divine right of kings and bishops, and his influence upon an architecture blending Gothic and Renaissance motifs. —**Laudian**, *n.*, *adj.*

liberalism a movement in modern Protestantism that emphasizes freedom from tradition and authority, the adjustment of religious beliefs to scientific conceptions, and the spiritual and ethical content of Christianity. —**liberalist**, *n.*, *adj.* —**liberalistic**, *adj.*

Lollardism 1. the religious teachings of John Wycliffe, 14th-century English theologian, religious reformer, and Bible translator.
2. adherence to these teachings, especially in England and Scotland in the 14th and 15th centuries. Also called **Lollardry, Lollardy, Wycliffism.** —**Lollard**, *n.*, *adj.*

Lutheranism 1. the religious doctrines and church polity of Martin Luther, 16th-century German theologian, author, and leader of the Protestant Reformation.
2. adherence to these doctrines or membership in the Lutheran Church. —**Lutheran**, *n.*, *adj.*

Methodism 1. the religious teachings and church polity of John Wesley, 18th-century English theologian and evangelist, or those of his followers.
2. the doctrines, polity, beliefs, and rituals of the Methodist Church, founded by Wesley, especially its emphasis on personal and social morality. Also called **Wesleyanism.** —**Methodist**, *n.*, *adj.*

Mormonism 1. the doctrines and polity of the Church of Jesus Christ of Latter-day Saints, founded in the U.S. in 1830 by Joseph Smith, especially its adoption of the *Book of Mormon* as an adjunct to the Bible.
2. adherence to these doctrines or membership in the Mormon Church. Also **Mormondom.** —**Mormon**, *n.*, *adj.*

neoorthodoxy a modern theological movement within the Protestant church, reaffirming some of the doctrines of the Reformation in reaction against recent liberal theology and practice. —**neoorthodox**, *adj.*

nonconformism 1. the state or practice of nonadherence to an established church or its doctrine, discipline, or polity.
2. (*cap.*) the condition of a Protestant in England who is not a member of the Church of England; dissenterism. —**nonconformist**, *n.*, *adj.*

nonjurorism 1. the practice of refusing to take a required oath, as of allegiance.
2. (*cap.*) the action of Church of England clergymen who refused, in 1689, to swear allegiance to William and Mary. —**nonjuror**, *n.*

Orangeism the principles of the Orangemen, members of a secret 17th-century Irish society that defended the reigning British monarch and supported the Anglican church.

Pajonism a theological doctrine proposed by the 17th-century French theologian Claude Pajon, especially its emphasis upon the indirect rather than direct influence of the Holy Spirit upon an individual.

parsonarchy the domination of a social group, especially a small rural community, by the parson.

Pentecostalism the beliefs and practices of certain Christian groups, often fundamentalist, that emphasize the activity of the Holy Spirit, stress a strict morality, and seek emotional spiritual experiences in worship rituals. —Pentecostal, *n.*, *adj.*

Philippism *Rare.* the doctrines of Philip Melanchthon, 16th-century German Protestant reformer, especially his rebuttals to the allegations of the Flacians that his attitude toward certain teachings of Martin Luther was adiaphoristic. —Philippist, *n.* —Philippistic, *adj.*

Pietism 1. a movement, begun in the 17th-century German Lutheran Church, exalting the practice of personal piety over religious orthodoxy and ritual.
2. the principles and practices of the Pietists. Also called **Spenerism**. —Pietist, *n.* —Pietistic, Pietistical, *adj.*

Presbyterianism 1. the doctrines, polity, and practices of Presbyterian churches, especially a Calvinist theology and a representative system of church government.
2. a system of church government in which ministers and congregationally elected elders participate in a graded series of legislative bodies and administrative courts. —Presbyterian, *n.*, *adj.*

Primitive Methodism the practices of the Primitive Methodist Church whose doctrines emphasize Wesleyanism and greater congregational participation in its government. —Primitive Methodist, *n.*

Puritanism 1. the principles and practices of a movement within 16th-century Anglicanism, demanding reforms in doctrine, polity, and worship, and greater strictness in religious discipline, chiefly in terms of Calvinist principles.
2. a political party developed from the religious movement in the 17th century that successfully gained control of England through revolution and briefly attempted to put Puritan principles to work on all levels of English life and government.
3. *U.S. History.* the principles and practices of the Congregationalist members of the religious movement who, having migrated to America in 1620, attempted to set up a theocratic state in which clergy had authority over both religious and civil life. —Puritan, *n.*, *adj.*

Puseyism Tractarianism, after Rev. E. B. Pusey, English clergyman. —Puseyite, *n.* —Puseyistic, Puseyistical *adj.*

Quakerism the principles and beliefs of the Society of Friends, a creedless sect founded in England about 1650 by George Fox, especially its emphasis upon the Inward Light of each believer, its rejection of oaths, and its opposition to all wars. Also **Quakerdom, Quakery.** (Terms made from *quake* are never used to or between members of the Society, who prefer *Friend* or *thee.*) —Quaker, *n.*, *adj.*

Reformation the 16th-century religious movement in Europe that resulted in the formation of Protestantism. —**Reformational,** *adj.*

restorationism the belief in a temporary future punishment and a final restoration of all sinners to the favor of God. Also called **restitutionism.** —**restorationist,** *n.*

reunionism advocacy of the reunion of the Anglican and Catholic churches. —reunionist, *n.* —reunionistic, *adj.*

revivalism that form of religious activity that manifests itself in evangelistic services for the purpose of effecting a religious awakening. —revivalist, *n.* —revivalistic, *adj.*

Russellites the former name of the sect called Jehovah's Witnesses.

salvationism 1. any religious teachings in which are emphasized doctrines concerning the saving of the soul.
2. the doctrines of the saving of the soul.
3. evangelism, especially that calling for individuals to make open and public conversions. —salvationist, *n.* —salvational, *adj.*

Second Adventist Adventism.

sectarianism the spirit or tendencies of sectarians, especially adherence or excessive devotion to a particular sect, especially in religion. —sectarian, *n.*, *adj.*

Shakerism the principles, beliefs, and practices of a millennial sect called the United Society of Believers in Christ's Second Coming, originating in England in the Shaking Quakers sect and brought to the U.S. in 1774 by Mother Ann Lee, especially an emphasis on communal and celibate living, on the dual nature of Christ as male and female, on their dances and songs as part of worship, and their honest, functional craftsmanship. —Shaker, *n.*, *adj.*

Spenerism Pietism, after Philipp Jakob Spener, German theologian.

Stundism the doctrines and practices of a Russian Protestant denomination founded about 1860, especially their emphasis upon evangelism, piety, and communal Bible study and prayer. —Stundist, *n.*

Swedenborgianism, Swedenborgism the doctrines, beliefs, and practices of the Church of the New Jerusalem, founded by the followers of Emmanuel Swedenborg in the late 18th century, especially its assertion that Christ is God Himself and not the Son of God, and its reliance upon accounts of mystical appearances of Christ to Swedenborg. —**Swedenborgian,** *n., adj.*

syncretism the attempted reconciliation or union of different or opposing principles, practices, parties, or denominations, as in the late 19th- and 20th-century discussions between Anglo-Catholics and Roman authorities. —**syncretic, syncretical, syncretistic, syncretistical,** *adj.*

Tractarianism the religious opinions and principles of the Oxford movement within Anglicanism, especially in its *Tracts for the Times*, a series of ninety treatises published between 1833 and 1841. Also called **Puseyism.** —**Tractarian,** *n., adj.*

Ubiquitism the doctrine that the body of Christ is present everywhere, held by some Lutherans and others. —**Ubiquitarian, Ubiquarian, Ubiquitary, Ubiquist, Ubiquitist,** *n., adj.*

Unitarianism the beliefs, principles, and practices of the Unitarian denomination, especially its doctrine that God is one being, and its emphasis upon autonomous congregational government. —**Unitarian,** *n., adj.*

Universalism 1. the theological doctrine that all men will finally be saved or brought back to holiness and God.
2. the doctrines and practices of the Universalist denomination. —**Universalist,** *n., adj.* —**Universalistic,** *adj.*

Utraquism the doctrines and practices of the Calixtins, a Hussite group demanding communion in both wafer and wine. —**Utraquist,** *n.* —**Utraquistic,** *adj.*

Wesleyanism, Wesleyism Methodism. —**Wesleyan,** *n., adj.*

Whitefieldism the principles, teachings, practices, and techniques of George Whitefield, English Methodist revivalist, who, after a request from Wesley that he visit America, made seven visits after 1738 and gained a reputation as an eloquent and fiery preacher, becoming a model for future American revivalists.

Wycliffism Lollardism.

333. PROVERBS
See also 422. WISDOM.

adage a maxim, axiom, proverb, or old saying.

analect 1. a fragment or extract from literature.
2. a collection of teachings, as the *Analects of Confucius*.

aphorism a terse saying embodying a general truth, as "Time flies." —**aphorist,** *n.* —**aphorismic, aphorismical, aphoristic,** *adj.*

apothegmatist, apophthegmatist a creator of short, pithy instructive sayings; aphorist. —**apothegmatic, apophthegmatic, apothegmatical, apophthegmatical,** *adj.* —**apothegm, apophthegm,** *n.*

bromide a trite saying; a platitude.

epigram a pithy statement, often containing a paradox. —**epigrammatist,** *n.*

gnomonology 1. a collection or anthology of gnomes, or aphorisms.
2. aphoristic writing.

logia maxims or sayings attributed to a religious leader. See also 79. CHRIST.

maxim a short, pithy statement that serves as a motto. —**maximist,** *n.*

paroemia a rhetorical proverb. —**paroemiac,** *adj.*

paroemiography, paremiography 1. the writing of proverbs.
2. the collecting of proverbs. —**paroemiographer,** *n.*

paroemiology, paremiology the study of proverbs. —**paroemiologist, paremiologist,** *n.*

proverbiology 1. proverbs taken as a group.
2. proverbs taken as a field of study. —**proverbiologist,** *n.* —**proverbiological,** *adj.*

smartism an aphorism or witty saying.

334. PSYCHOLOGY
See also 28. ATTITUDES; 41. BEHAVIOR; 129. DREAMS; 224. INSANITY; 254. MANIAS; 279. MOODS; 311. PHILE., -PHILIA, -PHILY; 313. PHOBIAS.

alienism the study or treatment of mental diseases, especially in their relation to legal problems. —**alienist,** *n.*

ambitendency the simultaneous presence in one person of positive and negative feelings towards a person, object, etc.; coexistence of mixed feelings.

automorphism the projection of one's own characteristics onto another person. —**automorphic,** *adj.*

behaviorism the theory or doctrine that observed behavior provides the only valid data of psychology. —**behaviorist,** *n., adj.* —**behavioristic,** *adj.*

bisexualism, bisexuality the state of being sexually responsive or attracted to members of both sexes. See also 51. BODY, HUMAN. —**bisexual,** *adj.*

configurationism *Gestalt Psychology.* the basic precept that psychological phenomena are the result of gestalts functioning separately or in relation to one another, as contrasted with individual elements, such as reflexes or sensations. —**configurationist,** *n.,* —**configurational, configurative,** *adj.*

corybantism *Medicine.* a frenzied, sleepless delirium accompanied by wild and frightening hallucinations. Also **corybantiasm.**

Couéism a method of self-help stressing autosuggestion, introduced into America by the French psychotherapist Emile Coué c. 1920 and featuring the slogan "Every day in every way I am getting better and better."

cryptesthesia, cryptaesthesia the innate ability to be clairvoyant, as in parapsychological experiments. —cryptesthetic, *adj.*

dereism a mode of thinking directed away from reality and toward fantasy without cognizance of ordinary rules of logic. —dereistic, *adj.*

dyspathy a condition characterized by a lack of sympathy or passion. —dyspathic, *adj.*

dysthymia extreme anxiety and depression accompanied by obsession. —dysthymic, *adj.*

eidology the study of mental imagery.

Freudianism theory and practice of Sigmund Freud, especially in the area of neuroses, their causes and treatment. —Freudian, *n.*, *adj.*

hypersensitivity extreme or abnormal sensitivity, as to criticism. —hypersensitive, *adj.*

hypnogenesis the process of producing a hypnotic condition or state of hypnosis. —hypnogenetic, *adj.*

hypnotherapy the treatment of disease and illness by hypnosis. —hypnotherapist, *n.*

hypnotism 1. the science dealing with the induction of hypnosis, especially for therapeutic purposes.
2. the act of inducing hypnosis; hypnotizing.
3. hypnosis. —hypnotist, *n.* —hypnotistic, *adj.*

hyponoia, hyponea a state of dulled mental activity or decrease in the function of thought. Also called hypopsychosis.

hypopsychosis hyponoia.

hysteria a condition of extreme excitement characterized by emotional disturbance, sensory and motor derangement and sometimes the simulation of organic disorders. —hysteric, *n.* —hysteric, hysterical, *adj.*

hysterogeny 1. the process of inducing hysteria.
2. the onset of hysteria. —hysterogenic, *adj.*

infantilism the condition of one who is not a child acting abnormally childlike. —infantility, *n.* —infantilistic, *adj.*

introspectionism the belief that psychology must be derived from introspective data. —introspectionist, *n.* —introspective, *adj.*

logotherapy psychotherapy that tries to find for the patient the aim and meaning of his own life as a human being and does not stress the medical aspect of mental health.

metapsychology 1. a speculation dealing systematically with concepts extending beyond the present limits of psychology as an empirical science.
2. a conception in psychoanalytic theory of mental processes involving causal relations, structural placement, and functional value. —**metapsychological,** *adj.*

neolalia the speech of a psychotic containing new combinations of words unknown to a hearer. See also 382. SPEECH.

neurosis any of a large variety of mental or psychic disorders, exhibiting a range of mental or physical symptoms, as anxiety, phobias, compulsions, and tics. —**neurotic,** *n., adj.*

neuroticism a neurotic condition; psychoneurosis.

orthosis the process of correcting bodily or mental distortion. —**orthotic,** *adj.*

pansexualism 1. the pervasion of all conduct and experience with sexual emotions.
2. the theory that regards all desire and interest as derived from sex instinct. Also **pansexuality.** —**pansexualist,** *n.*

paralogia, paralogy a reasoning disorder characterized by inappropriate responses to questions and illusional or delusional speech. —**paralogical,** *adj.*

parapraxis the process whereby a person fails to complete his intention, as by the mislaying of objects, thought to be the result of a conflict between unconscious and conscious intention.

parapsychology the branch of psychology that studies psychic phenomena, as telepathy, clairvoyance, extrasensory perception, and the like. —**parapsychological,** *adj.*

phrenography the branch of psychology concerned with description and comparison. —**phrenographic,** *adj.*

psychalgia mental or psychic pain.

psychoanalysis the method developed by Freud and others for treating neuroses and some other disorders of the mind. —**psychoanalyst,** *n.* —**psychoanalytic, psychoanalytical,** *adj.*

psychobiology the study of the relations or interrelations between body and mind, especially as exhibited in the nervous system. —**psychobiologist,** *n.* —**psychobiologic, psychobiological,** *adj.*

psychodiagnostics 1. the science or art of making a personality evaluation.
2. the diagnosis of a mental disorder. —**psychodiagnostician,** *n.* —**psychodiagnostic,** *adj.*

psychodynamics the systematic study of personality in terms of past and present experiences in relation to motivation. —**psychodynamic,** *adj.*

psychogony a theory of the development of the mind. —**psychogonic, psychogonical,** *adj.*

psycholepsy an attack of mental inertia and hopelessness following a period of elation, especially in sufferers from neurosis. —psycholeptic, *adj.*

psychologism the theory that emphasizes psychological conceptions in other fields outside of psychology, as philosophy and history.

psychology the science that studies the mind and mental processes, feelings, and desires. —psychologist, *n.* —psychologic, psychological, *adj.*

psychometrics, psychometry the measurement of mental traits, abilities, and processes. —psychometrist, *n.* —psychometric, *adj.*

psychometry 1. the alleged ability to divine the characteristics of an object or a person connected with it by touching the object.
2. the determination of the duration and intensity of processes of the mind. —psychometer, *n.* —psychometric, psychometrical, *adj.*

psychopathology *Medicine.* the science of the diseases of the mind. —psychopathologist, psychopathist, *n.* —psychopathologic, psychopathological, *adj.*

psychopathy a mental disorder. —psychopath, *n.* —psychopathic, *adj.*

psychopharmacology the study of drugs that effect emotional and mental states. —psychopharmacologic, psychopharmacological, *adj.*

psychophobia an abnormal fear of the mind.

psychophysics the branch of psychology that studies the relationships between physical stimuli and resulting sensations and mental states. —psychophysicist, *n.* —psychophysic, psychophysical, *adj.*

psychostatics 1. the study of the circumstances under which mental processes occur.
2. the theory that conscious states are made up of elements capable of separating and joining without loss of essential identity. —psychostatic, psychostatical, *adj.*

psychotherapy the science or method of treating psychological abnormalities and disorders by psychological techniques, especially by psychoanalysis, group therapy, or consultation. —psychotherapist, *n.* —psychotherapeutic, *adj.*

puerilism a mental condition marked by childish or infantile behavior. —puerility, *n.*

reactology the scientific study of psychological reactions. —reactologist, *n.* —reactological, *adj.*

reflexology the study of behavior and its interpretation according to a concept that regards behavior as a combination of simple and complex reflexes. —reflexologist, *n.* —reflexological, *adj.*

schizothymia a mild form of schizophrenia, characterized by withdrawal, inversion, etc. —schizothyme, *n.* —schizothymic, *adj.*

tachyphrenia abnormally rapid mental activity.

telepathy a communication between minds by some nontechnological means other than sensory perception. —**telepathist,** *n.* —**telepathic,** *adj.*

transsexualism, transsexuality the psychological phenomenon of a person identifying with the opposite sex, sometimes to the extent of undergoing surgery for change of sex. —**transsexual,** *n., adj.*

traumatism 1. any abnormal condition, either pathological or psychological, caused by wound or injury, either physical or psychological.
2. the trauma, wound, or injury itself. —**traumatic,** *adj.*

zoanthropy a form of insanity or mental disorder in which the sufferer imagines that he is an animal. —**zoanthropic,** *adj.*

zoopsia a form of hallucination in which the sufferer imagines he sees animals. Also called **zooscopy.**

335. PUNISHMENT
See also 34. BANISHMENT; 103. CRIME.

amercement, amerciament 1. punishment or penalty applied at the discretion of a court or other authority, as contrasted with a penalty predetermined by statute.
2. the imposing of such a penalty. —**amercer,** *n.*

caneology *Humorous.* advocacy of the use of a cane in corporal punishment.

elinguation *Obsolete.* the process of removing the tongue.

eviration *Obsolete.* the act of castrating.

excecation *Obsolete.* the process of blinding.

fustigation beating with a stick or club.

mastigophobia an abnormal fear of being beaten. Also called **rhabdophobia.**

poinephobia an abnormal fear of punishment.

336. PUNNING

adnomination *Obsolete.* the act of wordplay; punning. Also called **agnomination, annomination.**

equivocality, equivocacy the state or quality of being ambiguous in meaning or capable of double interpretation. —**equivocal,** *adj.*

equivoque, equivoke 1. an equivocal term or ambiguous expression.
2. a play upon words; pun.

paronomasia 1. *Rhetoric.* the use of a word in different senses or the use of words similar in sound for effect, as humor or ambiguity; punning.
2. a pun. —**paronomastic,** *adj.*

punnology the study of puns and punning. —**punnologist,** *n.*

337. PUZZLES
See also 176. GAMES.

enigmatography the art or skill of composing enigmas. —enigmatographer, *n.*
enigmatology the analysis of enigmas.
logology the pursuit of word puzzles or puzzling words. —logologist, *n.*

Q

338. QUESTIONING

catechesis a method of oral instruction involving question and answer techniques. —catechist, *n.*

catechetics that part of theological training that deals with the imparting of religious knowledge through catechesis and printed catechisms. —catechetic, catechetical, *adj.*

querist a person who makes inquiries or asks questions.

quizzism the act or practice of quizzing or questioning.

339. QUIETUDE
See also 267. MEDITATION.

eremiomania a mania for stillness.

kathisomania a mania for sitting.

quiescence, quiescency the state or quality of being in repose or at rest. —quiescent, *adj.*

quietude a state or quality of being calm, quiet, silent, or in repose.

R

340. RABIES
See also 122. DISEASE and ILLNESS.

hydrophobia rabies in human beings. Also called lyssa.

lyssophobia an abnormal fear of rabies. See also hydrophobophobia.

341. RACE
See also 17. ANTHROPOLOGY; 121. DISCRIMINATION; 204. HEREDITY.

albocracy rule by Caucasians, especially Europeans.

anthroposociology the sociological study of race using anthropological methods. —anthroposociological, *adj.*

apartheid the policy of strict racial segregation and political and economic discrimination against non-whites practiced in the Republic of South Africa.

Aryanism 1. a doctrine propagandized by Nazism asserting that the so-called Aryan peoples were superior to all others in the practice of government and the development of civilization.
2. a belief in this doctrine and acceptance of its social and ethical implications, especially with regard to the treatment of so-called inferior races. —Aryanist, *n.*

bigotry obtuse or narrow-minded intolerance, especially of other races or religions. —bigot, *n.*, —bigoted, *adj.*

biracialism the principle or practice of combining or representing two separate races, as white and Negro, on governing boards, committees, etc. —biracialist, biracial, *adj.*

cacogenics *Biology.* the study of the operation of factors that cause degeneration in offspring, especially as applied to factors unique to separate races. Also called dysgenics. —cacogenic, *adj.*

creolism the state of being a creole.

endemism the quality of belonging to a particular race, region, or country. —endemicity, *n.*

ethnocracy a government controlled by a particular race or national group. —ethnocratic, *adj.*

ethnogeography the study of the geographical distribution of racial groups and the relationship between them and their environments. —ethnogeographer, *n.* —ethnogeographic, *adj.*

ethnopsychology the psychology of races and peoples. —ethnopsychological, *adj.*

eugenism the blend of factors and influences most suitable for the improvement of the inherited characteristics of a breed or race, especially the human race. —eugenic, *adj.*

euthenics the art or science of improving a race or breed, especially the human race, by control of external influences, as environment. See also 219. IMPROVEMENT.

genocide 1. the deliberate and systematic extermination of a racial or national group.
2. an actor in this process. —genocidal, *adj.*

gentilism the state or quality of being non-Jewish, and especially a heathen or pagan.

Gobinism the theory or doctrine that the white race in general and the Germanic race in particular are superior to all other peoples.

integrationism the combination of educational and other public facilities, previously segregated by race, into unified systems shared by all races. —integrationist, *n.*, *adj.*

interracialism the principles, beliefs, and attitudes influencing actions aimed at improving relations among differing races. —interracial, *adj.*

Jensenism the belief that blacks are mentally inferior to whites, based on results of intelligence tests that failed to account for such differences as test questions slanted in favor of whites, lack of cultural and educational opportunities among blacks, etc. —Jensenist, *n.*, *adj.*

Melanochroism the condition of belonging to the Caucasian race and having dark hair and a light complexion. —Melanochroic, *adj.* —Melanochroid, *adj.*, *n.*

miscegenation 1. the interbreeding of members of different races.
2. cohabitation or marriage between a man and woman of different races, especially, in the U.S., between a Negro and a white person.
3. the mixing or mixture of races by interbreeding.

monogenesis monogenism. See also 302. ORGANISMS.

monogenism the belief that all human races descended from a common ancestral type. Also monogenesis, monogeny. —monogenist, *n.* —monogenistic, *adj.*

nigritude the condition of being black; blackness.

polygenism the theory that all human races descended from two or more ancestral types. —polygenist, *n.* —polygenistic, *adj.*

racialism the belief in or practice of the doctrine of racism. —racialist, *n.* —racialistic, *adj.*

racism a belief that human races have distinctive characteristics that determine their respective cultures, usually involving the idea that one's race is superior and has the right to control others. —racist, *adj.*

segregationism the views and policies of those who would separate or maintain as separate rights, public facilities, etc., on the basis of race. See also apartheid.

supremacist a person who advocates supremacy of a particular group, especially a racial group.

Xanthochroism the condition of belonging to the Caucasian race and having fair skin and blond hair. —Xanthochroi, Xanthocroid, *n.* —Xanthochroic, Xanthocroid, *adj.*

342. RADIATION
See also 316. PHYSICS.

actinotherapy radiotherapy.

bolograph the record produced by a bolometer.

bolometer a device used in bolometry.

bolometry the measurement of minute amounts of radiant energy, especially infrared spectra. —bolometrist, *n.* —bolometric, *adj.*

curiescopy radioscopy.

diathermancy the capacity to transmit infrared radiation. —diathermanous, *adj.*

dosimeter a device, carried or worn by people working near radiation for measuring the amount of radiation to which they are exposed.

dosimetry the measurement by a dosimeter of the dosage of radiation a person might have received. See also 130. DRUGS. —dosimetrist, *n.* —dosimetric, dosimetrical *adj.*

fluorometer an instrument for measuring the emission of radiation in the form of visible light and identifying the substance that is its source. —fluorometric, *adj.*

fluorometry the measurement of fluorescence, or visible radiation, by means of a fluorometer. —fluorometric, *adj.*

fluoroscopy an examination by means of a screen coated with a fluorescent substance responsive to radiation from x rays. —fluoroscopic, *adj.*

metallography the study of metals and their structures and properties by the use of microscopy and x rays.

pyelography the science or technique of making x-ray photographs of the kidneys, renal pelves, and ureters, using injection of opaque solutions or radiopaque dyes. —pyelographic, *adj*.

radiesthesia the sensitivity of some humans to radiation of various kinds, as in water divining or nonmedical diagnosis. —radiesthetic, *adj*.

radioactivity the state, property, or process of being radioactive.

radiography the production of photographic images on film using radiation from other radioactive substances instead of light. Also called x-ray scotography, shadowgraphy. —radiograph, radiographer, *n*. —radiographic, radiographical, *adj*.

radiology 1. the science that studies x rays or radiation from radioactive substances, esp. for medical purposes.
2. the examination or photographing of parts of the body with such rays.
3. the interpretation of the resulting photographs. —radiologist, *n*. —radiologic, radiological, *adj*.

radiometallography the study of metals and their structures by the use of x rays.

radioscopy the study or observation of the inner structure of opaque materials by means of x rays or other radioactive substances. Also called curiescopy.

radiosensibility sensitivity to the effects of radiation, as of parts of the body. Also called radiosensitivity.

radiosensitivity radiosensibility. —radiosensitive, *adj*.

radiotechnology the science and technology of applying radiation and x rays to industrial use. See also 343. RADIO.

radiotherapy a method of treating diseases with x rays or the radiation from other radioactive substances. Also called actinotherapy. —radiotherapist, *n*. —radiotherapeutic, *adj*.

roentgenism, röntgenism 1. the treatment of disease with x rays or roentgen rays.
2. the effect of misuse or overexposure to these rays.

roentgenogram, röntgenogram an x-ray photograph.

roentgenography, röntgenography x-ray photography.

scotograph a radiograph.

shadowgraphy radiography.

tomography x-ray photography of a selected plane of the body by a method that eliminates the outline of structures in other planes. —tomographic, *adj*.

xeroradiography a process of recording x-ray images by electrostatic means. —xeroradiographic, *adj*.

x-ray scotography radiography.

343. RADIO
See also 265. MEDIA.

phototelegraphy the transmission of pictures, print, etc., by means of radio or telegraphy. —**phototelegraphic**, *adj.*

radiophony radiotelephony. —**radiophonic**, *adj.*

radiotechnology the science and technology of radio engineering. —**radiotechnologic, radiotechnological**, *adj.* See also 342. RADIATION.

radiotelegraphy 1. the transmitting and receiving of messages by radiotelegraph.
2. the science and technology of the radiotelegraph. —**radiotelegraphic**, *adj.*

radiotelephony verbal communication at a distance by radio, using telephones. Also called **radiophony**. —**radiotelephonic**, *adj.*

telemechanics the science of operating or controlling mechanisms by remote control, especially by radio.

344. RAILROADS
See also 399. TRAVEL; 408. VEHICLES.

ferroequinology a mock classical term for enthusiasm about railroads. —**ferroequinologist**, *n.*

metrograph a device for recording the speed of locomotives and the time, place, and length of all their stops.

siderodromophobia an abnormal fear of railroads or of traveling on trains.

sideromania an obsession with railroad travel.

345. RAIN
See also 27. ATMOSPHERE; 85. CLIMATE; 87. CLOUDS; 246. LIGHTNING; 375. SNOW; 394. THUNDER; 414. WATER; 417. WEATHER.

hyetography the study of the geographical distribution of rainfall by annual totals. —**hyetographic, hyetographical**, *adj.*

hyetology *Rare.* the branch of meteorology that studies rainfall. —**hyetologist**, *n.* —**hyetological**, *adj.*

ombrology the branch of meteorology that studies rain. —**ombrological**, *n.*

ombrophobia an abnormal fear of rain.

pluviography the branch of meteorology that automatically measures rainfall and snowfall. —**pluviographic, pluviographical**, *adj.*

pluviometry the branch of meteorology concerned with the measurement of rainfall. —**pluviometric, pluviometrical**, *adj.*

pluvioscope an instrument for measuring rainfall; a rain gauge.

pluviosity raininess. —**pluvious**, *adj.*

udometry the measurement of rainfall with any of various types of rain gauges. —udometric, *adj*.

udomograph a self-registering rain gauge.

346. READING
See also 29. AUTHORS; 53. BOOKS; 248. LITERARY STYLE; 249. LITERATURE; 409. VERSE.

alexia dyslexia.

dyslexia an impairment of the ability to read because of a brain defect. Also called alexia. —dyslexic, *adj*.

strephosymbolia *Medicine.* 1. a disorder of perception causing objects to seem as if reversed in a mirror.
2. a reading difficulty characterized by confusion between similar but oppositely oriented letters (*b–d*, etc.) and a tendency to reverse direction in reading. —strephosymbolic, *adj*.

347. RECREATION
See also 26. ATHLETICS; 176. GAMES; 320. PLEASURE; 337. PUZZLES; 399. TRAVEL.

aestivation estivation.

estivation, aestivation *Obsolete.* summering; the taking of a summer holiday.

tourism 1. the activity of traveling for pleasure, to see sights, for recreation, etc.
2. the business founded upon this activity. —tourist, *n.*, *adj*.

348. RELATIONSHIP
See also 77. CHILDREN; 153. FATHER; 281. MOTHER; 307. PARENTS; 418. WIFE.

affinity the condition of close relationship. Cf. consanguinity. See also 258. MARRIAGE.

agnate a relation through descent on the male side. Cf. cognate. —agnate, agnatic, *adj*.

agnation relationship through male descent. Cf. cognation.

amity friendship or harmony between individuals or groups. Also called comity.

cognate a relation through descent on the female side. Cf. agnate. —cognate, —cognatic, *adj*.

cognation relationship through female descent. Cf. agnation. —cognate, *adj*.

comity amity.

congener a thing or person of the same kind as another.

consanguinity blood relationship. Cf. affinity.

cousinry cousins collectively or as a group or class.

enation the maternal relationship.

epigone an heir, descendant, or successor, frequently an inferior successor.

filiation 1. the fact or condition of being a son or daughter.
2. the relation of child to parent, especially father.

kinship family relationship or other close tie or relationship.

lineage line of descent from an ancestor or ancestors; family or ancestry.

matriliny descent through the female line, as in ancestry, inheritance, etc.
—matrilineal, matrilinear, adj.

patriliny relationship or descent through the male line, as in ancestry, inheritance, etc. —patrilineal, patrilinear, adj.

synomosy Ancient Greece. fellowship or brotherhood bound by solemn oath.

349. RELIGION
See also 43. BIBLE; 59. BUDDHISM; 69. CATHOLICISM;
80. CHRISTIANITY; 81. CHURCH; 135. EASTERN ORTHODOXY;
151. FAITH; 205. HERESY; 206. HINDUISM; 227. ISLAM; 231. JUDAISM;
260. MARY; 273. MIRACLES; 332. PROTESTANTISM; 358. SACREDNESS;
359. SAINTS; 384. SPIRITS and SPIRITUALISM; 392. THEOLOGY.

abbacy 1. the property or jurisdiction of an abbot.
2. the time during which a person serves as an abbot.

Adamitism the practice of going naked for God; the beliefs of some ascetic sects in ritual nakedness. See also 287. NAKEDNESS —Adamite, n. —Adamitic, adj.

anagoge, anagogy 1. Obsolete. a spiritual or mental elevation.
2. a mystical interpretation of a text (usually the Bible.) —anagogic, adj. —anagogically, adv.

anagogics the study of hidden meanings, usually in Bible passages.

angelology 1. Theology. the doctrine or theory concerning angels.
2. the beliefs concerning angels.

angelophany the appearance to men, in visible form, of angels.

antidisestablishmentarianism the principles of those who oppose the withdrawal of the recognition or support of the state from an established church, usually used in referring to the Anglican church in the 19th century in England.

apocalypticism Theology. 1. any doctrine concerning the end of the temporal world, especially one based on the Revelations of St. John the Divine.
2. the millennial doctrine of the Second Advent and the reign of Jesus Christ on earth. —apocalyptic, apocalyptical, adj.

apologia a formal apology, especially on behalf of some belief or doctrine.

apostasy relinquishing of a religious belief. —**apostate,** *n.*, *adj.*

apostolicity being of or contemporary with the Apostles in character.

babyolatry the worship of children.

Baha'ism the doctrines and practices of a sect growing out of Babism and reflecting some attitudes of the Islamic Shi'a sect, but with an emphasis on tolerance and the essential worth of all religions. —**Baha'i,** *n.*, *adj.* —**Baha'-ist,** *n.*, *adj.*

bigotry obtuse or narrow-minded intolerance, especially of other races or religions. —**bigot,** *n.* —**bigoted,** *adj.*

Bönism a pre-Buddhist religion of Tibet, involving worship of nature spirits and the practice of sacrifice, magic, and divination. It was influential on the Tibetan form of Buddhism.

Caodaism, Caodism the doctrines of an Indochinese religion, especially an amalgamation of features from Buddhism, Taoism, Confucianism, Christianity, and spiritualism. —**Caodaist,** *n.*

churchism belief in a church or religious system.

coeternity the state of eternal coexistence; eternal coexistence with another eternal entity. —**coeternal,** *adj.*

convertism the practice of converting people to a religion. —**convertist,** *n.*

cosmolatry the worship of the world.

crypto-Calvinism a term used in 16th-century Germany for secret sympathies toward Calvinists, held by professed Lutherans. —**crypto-Calvinist,** *n.*

devotionalism the quality or state of a person markedly characterized by religious devotion. —**devotionalist,** *n.*

Druidism the doctrines and practices of an order of Celtic priests in ancient Britain, Gaul, and Ireland. —**Druid,** *n.*, *adj.* —**Druidic, Druidical,** *adj.*

dualism *Theology.* 1. the doctrine of two independent divine beings or eternal principles, one good and the other evil.
2. the belief that man embodies two parts, as body or soul. —**dualist,** *n.* —**dualistic,** *adj.*

ecthesis the use of a thesis to state a belief, as the *Ecthesis of Heraclius,* forbidding discussion of the duality of Christ's will.

entheomania a mania for religion.

epiphany the appearance to man, in visible form, of a god or other supernatural being.

establishmentarianism official recognition of a church as a national institution, especially the Church of England. Cf. **antidisestablishmentarianism.**

exomologesis *Obsolete.* a complete, usually public, confession.

exotericism religious doctrines or practices that are easily understood by the general public. —exoteric, *n.*, *adj.*

familism the beliefs of the familists, members of an antinomian sect of 16th- and 17th-century Europe. —familist, *n.* —familistic, *adj.*

fanaticism the character, spirit, or conduct of a person with an extreme and uncritical enthusiasm or zeal, as in religion or politics. —fanatic, *n.*

flagellation whipping or flogging as a religious practice for the mortification of the flesh. —flagellant, *n.*, *adj.* —flagellator, *n.*

gentilism the state or quality of being non-Jewish, and especially a heathen or pagan. —gentile, *n.*, *adj.*

heathenism 1. a belief or practice of heathens.
2. pagan worship; idolatry.
3. irreligion.
4. barbaric morals or behavior. —heathen, *n.*, *adj.* —heathenistic, *adj.*

herolatry the worship of heroes.

hieraticism the principles, attitudes, and practices of priests as a group, both Christian and non-Christian. —hieratic, *adj.*

hieromania a mania for priests.

hierurgy 1. the performance of holy works.
2. the holy work itself.

High Churchism the principles that distinguish the Anglican church from the Calvinist and Protestant Nonconformist churches, especially deference to the authority and claims of the Episcopate and the priesthood and belief in the saving grace of the sacraments. —High Churchist, High Churchite, *n.*

homiletics the art of sacred speaking; preaching. —homiletic, homiletical *adj.*

Hsüan Chiao Taoism, def. 2.

Hypsistarianism the religion of a fourth-century Asiatic sect whose beliefs were composed of Christian, Jewish, and pagan elements.

idolism the belief in or worship of idols. —idolatry, idolist, *n.* —idolatrous, *adj.*

indifferentism a view that admits no real difference between true and false in religion or philosophy; a form of agnosticism. —indifferentist, *n.* See also 28. ATTITUDES.

inspirationism adherence to a theory or doctrine of divine influence, inspiration, or revelation, especially concerning the Scriptures.

Izedism the beliefs of the Izedis, a Mesopotamian sect said to worship the devil. —Izedi, Yezdi, Yezidi, *n.*

Jainism a dualistic, ascetic religion founded in the 6th century B.C. by a Hindu reformer as a revolt against the caste system and the vague world spirit of Hinduism. —Jain, *n.*, *adj.* —Jainist, *n.*

Jansenism a Christian sect founded by Cornelius Jansen, 17th-century Dutch religious reformer. See also 205. HERESY.

Jehovism the relation between Jehovah and his people and church.

Josephinism the policies and measures concerning religion introduced by Emperor Joseph II of Austria (1741–90). Also **Josephism.**

kerystics the study of homiletics. —kerystic, *adj.*

latitudinarianism tolerance or broadmindedness, especially in matters of religion; the liberal interpretation of beliefs or doctrines. —latitudinarian, *n.*, *adj.*

legalism *Theology.* 1. the doctrine that salvation is gained through good works.
2. the judging of conduct in terms of strict adherence to precise laws. —legalist, *n.* —legalistic, *adj.*

liturgics the study of public church ritual. —liturgist, *n.*

liturgiology the system of church rituals and their symbolism. —liturgiologist, *n.*

Low Churchism the principle that the Church of England is really little different from the Protestant Nonconformist churches in England and thus that the authority of the Episcopate and the priesthood, as well as the sacraments, are of comparatively minor importance. —Low Churchman, *n.*

mactation the killing of something for the purpose of sacrifice.

manaism 1. the doctrine of a generalized, supernatural force or power, which may be concentrated in objects or persons.
2. belief in mana. —manaistic, *adj.*

martyrdom 1. the condition of being a martyr.
2. the death or type of suffering of a particular martyr.
3. any arduous suffering or torment.

martyrologe *Obsolete.* a list, register or book of martyrs.

Mazdaism the worship of Ahura Mazda in Zoroastrianism as the source of all light and good. —Mazdaist, *n.*

Millerism the preachings of the American William Miller (1782–1849), founder of the Adventist church, who believed that the end of the world and the return of Christ would occur in 1843. —Millerite, *n.*

myalism a West Indian Negro cult, probably of West African origin, that believes in the Obeah.

mysticism 1. the doctrine that an immediate spiritual intuition of truth or an intimate spiritual union of the soul with God can be achieved through contemplation and spiritual exercises.
2. the beliefs, ideas, or practices of mystics.

neopaganism the revival of paganism. —neopagan, *adj.* —neopaganist, *n.*, *adj.*

nullifidian a person who has no religion; a religious skeptic.

nullifidianism 1. the state or position of being without religious faith or belief.
2. advocacy of such a state or position. —nullifidian, *n.*, *adj.*

occultism a belief that certain secret, mysterious, or supernatural agencies exist and that human beings may communicate with them or have their assistance. —occultist, *n.*, *adj.*

ontologism *Philosophy.* the doctrine that the human intellect has as its proper object the knowledge of God, that this knowledge is immediate and intuitive, and that all other knowledge must be built on this base. —ontologist, *n.* —ontologistic, *adj.*

Ophism the doctrines and beliefs of certain Gnostic sects that worshiped serpents as the symbol of the hidden divine wisdom and as having benefited Adam and Eve by encouraging them to eat the fruit of the tree of knowledge. Also **Ophitism.** —Ophite, *n.* —Ophitic, *adj.*

Orphism the religion of the Orphic mysteries, a cult of Dionysus (Bacchus) ascribed to Orpheus as its founder, especially its rites of initiation and doctrines of original sin, salvation, and purification through reincarnations. Also **Orphicism.** —Orphic, *n.*, *adj.*

orthodoxy the condition, quality, or practice of conforming, especially in religious belief. —orthodox, *adj.*

paganism 1. a hedonistic spirit or attitude in moral or religious matters.
2. the beliefs and practices of pagans, especially polytheists.
3. the state of being a pagan. —paganist, *n.*, *adj.* —paganistic, *adj.*

pantheism 1. the belief that identifies God with the universe.
2. the belief that God is the only reality, transcending all, and that the universe and everything in it are mere manifestations of Him. —pantheist, *n.*, *adj.* —pantheistic, *adj.*

patrolatry the worship of the Church Fathers.

piosity ostentatious piety; sanctimoniousness.

pneumatology the doctrine or theory of spiritual beings. —pneumatologist, *n.* —pneumatologic, pneumatological, *adj.*

polemics the study of the history of ecclesiastical disputes.

priestism a derogatory term for the practices and beliefs of priests or the priesthood.

prophetism 1. the behavior of a prophet or prophets.
2. the philosophical system of the Hebrew prophets.

Rastafarianism the religious beliefs of a West Indian sect who worship the late Emperor of Ethiopia, Haile Selassie (given name: Ras Tafari), and who believe that black people are the chosen of God, and that their promised land is Africa. Their use of marijuana in rituals was widely publicized.

recusance recusancy. —recusant, *adj.*

recusancy resistance to authority or refusal to conform, especially in religious matters, used of English Catholics who refuse to attend the services of the Church of England. Also called **recusance.** —recusant, *n., adj.*

regeneracy the act or quality of being renewed, reformed, or reborn, especially in a spiritual rebirth. —regenerate, *adj.*

religionism the strict adherence and devotion to religion. —religionist, *n.* —religionary, *adj.*

reliquism the worship of relics.

reunionism advocacy of the reunion of the Anglican and Catholic churches. —reunionist, *n.* —reunionistic, *adj.*

revelationist a person who believes in divine revelation or revealed religion.

Rosicrucianism the principles, institutions, or practices of the Rosicrucian Order, especially claims to various forms of occult knowledge and power, and esoteric religious practices. —Rosicrucian, *n., adj.*

Sabianism, Sabaeanism, Sabeanism the religious system of the Sabians, a group, according to the Koran, entitled to Muslim religious toleration. They have been associated with the Mandeans, who claim direct descent from the followers of John the Baptist. See also 25. ASTRONOMY.

Samaritanism the religious doctrines of the Samaritans.

Satanophany the appearance of Satan on earth.

schism a division especially peculiar to a Christian church or a religious body. —schismatic, *n.* —schismatical, *adj.*

Scientology the doctrines and beliefs of a religious movement founded in the mid-20th century by L. Ron Hubbard, especially an emphasis upon man's immortal spirit, reincarnation, and an extrascientific method of psychotherapy (dianetics). —Scientologist, *n., adj.*

secularism 1. a view that religion and religious considerations should be ignored or excluded from social and political matters.
2. an ethical system asserting that moral judgments should be made without reference to religious doctrine, as reward or punishment in an afterlife. —secularist, *n., adj.* —secularistic, *adj.*

seraphicism the simulation of religious, "seraphic" ecstasy.

sermonist 1. a person who delivers sermons.
2. a person who adopts a preaching attitude.

sermonology 1. the act of delivering a sermon.
2. sermons taken collectively.

shamanism 1. the tenets of the primitive religion of northern Asia, especially a belief in powerful spirits who can be influenced only by shamans in their double capacity of priest and doctor.
2. any similar religion, as among American Indians. —shamanist, *n.* —shamanistic, *adj.*

Shintoism the doctrines and practices of Shinto, the native religion of Japan, especially its system of nature and ancestor worship. —Shinto, *n., adj.* —Shintoistic, *adj.*

simonism the practices of simony, especially the making of a profit out of sacred things. —simonist, *n.* —simoniac, *n., adj.* —simoniacal, *adj.*

Taoism 1. a philosophical system evolved by Lao-tzu and Chuang-tzu, especially its advocacy of a simple and natural life and of noninterference with the course of natural events in order to have a happy existence in harmony with the Tao.
2. a popular Chinese religion, purporting to be based on the principles of Lao-tzu, but actually an eclectic polytheism characterized by superstition, alchemy, divination, and magic. Also called Hsüan Chiao.

theocracy a system of government in which a deity is considered the civil ruler. Also called thearchy.

theology the study of God and His relationship to the universe. —theologist, *n.* —theological, *adj.*

theomania a religious ecstasy in which the devotee believes that he is the deity.

theomorphism the state or condition of being formed in the image or likeness of God. —theomorphic, *adj.*

theophany a manifestation or appearance of God or a god to man. —theophanic, theophanous, *adj.*

theophilanthropism the doctrines or tenets of a deistic society in post-Revolutionary Paris that hoped to replace the outlawed Christian religion with a new religion based on belief in God, the immortality of the soul, and personal virtue. —theophilanthropist, *n.* —theophilanthropic, *adj.*

Theosophism the belief that knowledge not accessible to empirical study can be gained through direct contact with the divine principle. —Theosophist, *n.* —Theosophic, Theosophical, *adj.*

theotherapy treatment of illness or disease by prayer and other religious exercises. —**theotherapist**, *n*.

Therapeutism the beliefs and practices of the Therapeutae, a Jewish mystical sect in Egypt during the 1st century A.D.

Turcism, Turkism *Obsolete*. the religion of the Turks, i.e., Islam.

Vaudism the principles of the Vaudois or Waldenses, who did not acknowledge the primacy of the Pope. —**Waldensian**, *adj*.

Wahhabism the religious system of the Wahhabi, a Muslim order founded by Muhammad Ibn-Abdul Wahhab.

whoredom *Bible*. the worship of idols instead of God; idolatry.

Zombism the Kongo and Kimbundu system of religion, characterized by worship of a snake deity during voodoo rites.

Zoroastrianism the doctrines and practices of a dualistic Iranian religion, especially the existence of a supreme deity, Ahura Mazda, and belief in a cosmic struggle between a spirit of good and light and a spirit of evil and darkness. Also called **Zoroastrism, Zarathustrism, Mazdaism**. —**Zoroastrian**, *n*., *adj*.

350. REMEDIES

See also 122. DISEASE and ILLNESS; 130. DRUGS; 266. MEDICAL SPECIALTIES.

acology *Archaic*. the science of therapeutic remedies.

acupuncture the oriental art of inserting fine needles into various parts of the body to treat certain types of disorders. —**acupuncturist**, *n*.

alexipharmic an antidotal substance used to expel or resist poison. —**alexipharmic, alexipharmac**, *adj*.

aliptic *Obsolete*. an ointment.

alleviative any substance that alleviates a condition of disease or illness.

allopathy the method of treating diseases by using agents that produce effects different from those of the disease. Cf. **homeopathy**. —**allopath, allopathist**, *n*. —**allopathic**, *adj*.

analeptic a restorative, invigorating medicine.

anodyne a pain-relieving medicine, as an opiate or narcotic.

antidotary *Obsolete*. a treatise on antidotes. Also called **pharmacopoeia**.

antidote a remedy to counteract a harmful substance in the body.

antiperiodic a remedy used to prevent the recurrence of certain periodic illnesses as fevers.

antiphlogistic a medicine for reducing inflammation or fever; a febrifuge; an antipyretic. —**antiphlogistic**, *adj*.

antipyretic antiphlogistic.

antipyrotic a medicine for treating burns.

antiseptic any substance that inhibits infection, as alcohol.

antivenin 1. an antidote for venom, as snake venom, formed by gradually increased injection of the venom into the bloodstream.
2. the serum containing this antidote.

assuasive any medicinal substance or preparation that soothes or alleviates. —assuasive, *adj.*

bactericide an agent that destroys bacteria.

balneotherapy the treatment of illness or disease by bathing.

bibliotherapy *Psychiatry.* the therapeutic use of books and magazines in the treatment of mental illness or shock. —bibliotherapist, *n.* —bibliotherapeutic, *adj.*

biotherapy the treatment of illness and disease with substances derived from living organisms, as vaccines and serums.

cathartic a purgative medicine.

catholicon a universal remedy or panacea.

cerate a thick ointment composed of fat, wax, and other ingredients, applied externally to cure various diseases.

chemotherapy *Med.* the treatment of disease by the use of chemicals that have a toxic effect on the microorganisms causing the disease or that selectively destroy tumor tissues. —chemotherapist, *n.* —chemotherapeutic, *adj.*

chiropractic 1. Also called **chiropraxis.** a therapeutic system based on the doctrine that disease is the result of interference with nerve function and that adjusting the segments of the spinal column will restore a normal condition.
2. a chiropractor. —chiropractor, *n.*

chiropraxis chiropractic.

chromotherapy treatment of illness by colored lights.

cryotherapy a method of treatment involving applications of cold. Also crymotherapy.

demulcent a medicine or other preparation that has a soothing or emollient influence on an inflamed area.

diathermy a method of treatment involving the production of heat in the body by electric currents. Also **diathermia.** —diathermic, *adj.*

electrotherapeutics the branch of medicine that treats illness with electricity. Also electrotherapy. —electrotherapeutic, electrotherapeutical, *adj.*

electrotherapy electrotherapeutics.

elixir 1. a tincture composed of a sweetened solution of alcohol to which has been added a small amount of the drug to be administered.
2. a panacea, cure-all, or universal remedy. See also 7. ALCHEMY.

emollient a medical preparation that has a soothing effect on surface tissues.

epulotic a medicinal preparation that assists in the healing of wounds.

errhine a medicine used to clear the nose or to promote sneezing.

expectorant any medicine that assists the coughing up of phlegm, mucus, etc., from the chest.

febrifuge anything for reducing or ending fever; an antiphlogistic; an antipyretic.

heliotherapy a method of treating illness by exposure to the rays of the sun.

homeopathy, homoeopathy the method of treating diseases by drugs that produce symptoms similar to those of the disease. —homeopathist, homoeopathist, homeopath, homoeopath, n. —homeopathic, homoeopathic, adj.

homeotherapy, homoeotherapy a method of therapy using an agent that is similar to but not identical with the causative agent of the disease. —homeotherapeutic, homoeotherapeutic, adj.

hypnotherapy the treatment of disease and illness by hypnosis.

iamatology the branch of medicine that deals with remedies.

iatralipsis a method of treatment involving anointing and rubbing. Also iatraliptics.

jugulation an attempt to cure a disease by applying very severe, often life-threatening, measures. See also 232. KILLING.

kinesiatrics the branch of medicine that concerns itself with muscular exercise as a cure for disease. Also kinesipathy.

leechcraft Archaic. the doctor's craft; the art or science of healing.

leechdom Humorous or Derogatory. the world or realm of doctors or medicine.

lenitive a medicinal preparation or application for soothing pain; a palliative. —lenitive, adj.

lingism Rare. a gymnastic treatment for disease, named after a Swedish physician, Peter H. Ling.

massotherapy the use of massage as a treatment for certain illnesses or diseases.

maturative a medicinal preparation applied to an inflamed area to stimulate the process of suppuration or maturation.

mechanotherapy the process of treating illness or disease by mechanical means, as by massage. Cf. massotherapy.

metallotherapy treatment of disease and illness with metals, particularly with the salt forms of metals.

naprapathy a healing system based on the theory that disease or illness is caused by strained ligaments and other problems of connective tissue and can be treated by massage. —**naprapath,** *n.*

naturopathism, naturopathy a method of treating disease using food, exercise, heat, etc. to assist the natural healing process. —**naturopath,** *n.* —**naturopathic,** *adj.*

opotherapy the treatment of illness and disease with extracts made from certain glands of animals, as the thyroid or adrenal glands. Also called **organotherapy.**

organotherapy opotherapy.

orthopathy the treatment of illness or disease without the use of drugs.

osteopathy a method of treating ailments on the premise that they result from the pressure of misplaced bones on nerves, and are curable by manipulation. —**osteopath,** *n.* —**osteopathic,** *adj.*

panacea a cure-all or universal remedy; an elixir. —**panacean,** *adj.*

Perkinism a former treatment for rheumatism, developed by Dr. Elisha Perkins, in which the ends of two rods made of different metals were applied to the affected parts. Also called **tractoration.**

pharmacology the science of drugs, their preparation, uses, effects, and dispensation. —**pharmacologist,** *n.* —**pharmacologic, pharmacological,** *adj.*

pharmacopoeia a complete listing of all drugs and information concerning them.

phototherapy, phototherapeutics the treatment of disease, especially diseases of the skin, with light rays. —**phototherapeutic,** *adj.*

physiotherapy the treatment of disease, bodily defects, or bodily weaknesses by physical remedies, as massage, special exercises, etc., rather than by drugs. —**physiotherapist,** *n.*

polychrest a drug that serves as a remedy for several diseases. —**polychrestic,** *adj.*

psychotherapy the science or method of treating psychological abnormalities or disorders by psychological techniques. See also 266. MEDICAL SPECIALTIES. —**psychotherapist,** *n.*

radiotherapy the treatment of diseases, especially malignant cancer, with radium or other radioactive substances. Also called **radium therapy.**

radiothermy a form of therapy using heat from a short-wave radio or diathermy apparatus.

reflexology the oriental art of treating certain disorders by stimulating special areas on the sole of the foot. —**reflexologist,** *n.*

roentgenology, röntgenology the use of x rays in the treatment of illness and disease. —roentgenologist, röntgenologist, *n.*

roentgenotherapy, röntgenotherapy treatment of disease and illness by means of x rays.

sanability *Rare.* the state or condition of being curable; susceptibility to remedy. —sanable, *adj.*

serology 1. the science of the preparation and use of serums.
2. the study of serums. —serologist, *n.* —serological, *adj.*

serotherapy treatment of illness or disease by means of serum obtained from inoculated animals.

siriasis *Obsolete.* a sun bath or exposure to the sun for curative purposes.

superscription *Pharmacy.* the part of a prescription with the Latin word *recipe*, usually represented by the symbol R_x.

taeniafuge, teniafuge a preparation or agent for expelling tapeworms from the body.

tetrapharmacon *Rare.* an ointment composed of wax, resin, lard, and pitch.

theotherapy treatment of illness or disease by prayer and other religious exercises. —theotherapist, *n.*

theriac, theriaca a compound of sixty-four drugs made into an electuary by pulverization and the addition of honey, formerly used as an antidote for poison. Also called **Venice treacle**. —theriac, theriacal, therial, *adj.*

tincture *Pharmacy.* a medicinal substance in soluble form, especially in a solution of alcohol.

transillumination a form of medical examination in which a strong light is cast through the body or a body part so that blockages, foreign objects, etc., can be seen. —transilluminator, *n.*

urtication the former practice of flogging a paralyzed limb or part with nettles, for the stimulating effect.

ustulation *Pharmacy.* the process of heating moist substances so that they can be pulverized.

variolation, variolization inoculation against smallpox.

vermicide a substance for killing worms, especially intestinal worms, in animals or humans. Cf. vermifuge.

vermifuge a drug for expelling worms from the intestinal tract. Cf. vermicide. —vermifuge, *adj.*

351. RENUNCIATION
abdication the formal act by a regent of resigning from his position.

abjuration the act of renouncing upon oath, such as an alien applying for citizenship renouncing allegiance to a former country of nationality.

expatriation the process of abandoning one's native land or of being exiled. —expatriate, *n.*, *adj.*, *v.*

recusance recusancy. —recusant, *adj.*

recusancy resistance to authority or refusal to conform, especially in religious matters, used of English Catholics who refuse to attend the services of the Church of England. Also **recusance.** —recusant, *n.*, *adj.*

tergiversation 1. the act or process of subterfuge or evasion.
2. the abandoning of a cause or belief; apostasy. —tergiversator, *n.*

352. REPRESENTATION
See also 23. ART; 128. DRAWING; 141. ENGRAVING; 218. IMAGES.

adumbration a sketchy representation of something.

airscape a view or pictorial representation of the earth from above, as from an aircraft.

allegory an art form, as a story, painting, or sculpture, in which the components have a symbolic, figurative meaning. —allegorist, allegorizer, *n.* —allegorical, *adj.*

anaglyphoscope a pair of lenses of different colors used in spectacles for viewing a specially processed two-dimensional picture, creating a three-dimensional effect.

anamorphism a distorted image of an object, as in anamorphic art. Also **anamorphosis.** —anamorphic, *adj.*

anamorphoscope a cylindrical mirror for correcting the distorted image created by anamorphism.

anamorphosis anamorphism.

anamorphosy *Obsolete.* anamorphosis.

astrolabe a stereographic projection of the earth, as a sphere, on the plane of one of the great circles. Also called **planisphere.**

burlesque an exaggerated representation; grotesque parody or satire.

caricature a distorted representation, usually pictorial, often used to parody people in public life. —caricaturist, *n.*

cartogram a simplified or abstracted form of diagrammatic representation of statistical data, usually on a map base or distorted map base.

charactery 1. a system of symbols used to represent ideas.
2. expression by means of such symbols.

cinematography the art or technique of using a motion-picture camera or prjector. —cinematograph, *n.*, *v.* —cinematographer, *n.* —cinematographic, *adj.*

cityscape a view or representation of a city, especially in a painting, photograph, etc.

cloudscape a view or representation of clouds, particularly a painting of clouds.

conspectus a summary, outline, or general view of a situation.

cosmorama a display of scenes of different parts of the world. —**cosmoramic,** *adj.*

cosmosphere a hollow glass globe, for depicting the position of the earth in relation to the fixed stars at a given time.

culturist a person who is well acquainted with culture, as literature, the arts, etc., and who advocates their worth to society.

cyclorama a circular panorama, usually of a landscape or battle, designed to be viewed from a central point. Also called **panorama.** —**cycloramic,** *adj.*

diorama 1. a miniature, three-dimensional scene, often depicting a historical event.
2. an apparatus designed for giving extra realism to paintings by transmitting light through them in various colors and intensities at different times.

epitome something representative as a fine example of the whole group of things to which it belongs. See also 53. BOOKS.

georama a large globe or sphere in which a spectator can stand and view a representation of the earth's surface.

histogram *Statistics.* a graph showing frequency distribution in which rectangles based on the horizontal axis are assigned widths that correspond to class intervals and heights that correspond to frequency.

hologram a three-dimensional representation in photographic form, recorded on film by a reflected laser beam of a subject illuminated by part of the same laser beam.

hypermyriorama an exhibit or cyclorama showing a great variety of scenes.

idiograph 1. a signature or mark characteristic of or peculiar to a particular person, organization, etc.
2. a logotype or trademark.

macrograph a drawing, photograph, or other image that represents an object or scene with little or no magnification.

malkin *British Dialect.* a scarecrow or any grotesque effigy. Also spelled **mawkin.**

myriorama a form of landscape picture, made of several sections that can be combined in various ways to make different scenes.

neorama a type of panorama which represents the interior of a large building in which the spectator appears to be standing as he views the scene displayed.

panorama cyclorama; hence, any unlimited view or comprehensive survey. —panoramic, panoramical, *adj.*

phantasmagoria a type of magic-lantern show in which rapidly moving images blend, change size, etc.; hence, any series of images that move and change rapidly, as a dream. —phantasmagorial, phantasmagoric, *adj.*

planisphere an astrolabe.

praxinoscope an instrument that represents the effect of moving images on a screen.

purism *In literature and art.* strict adherence to particular concepts, rules, or ideals of form, style, etc., either as formulated by the artist or as dictated by a school with which the artist is allied. See also 23. ART; 104. CRITICISM; 236. LANGUAGE. —purist, *n.*, *adj.*

riverscape a view or representation of a river, especially in a painting, photograph, etc.

schema an outline or diagrammatic representation. See also 128. DRAWING. —schematic, *adj.*

schematism the form, disposition, or outline of a thing or concept. —schematist, *n.*

seascape a view or representation of the sea or seashore, especially in a painting, photograph, etc.

skyscape a view or representation of the sky, especially in a painting, photograph, etc.

stereopticon a projector with two complete lanterns, so that one picture appears to be dissolving while the other is appearing. —stereoptician, *n.* —stereoptican, *adj.*

symbolism symbology, defs. 1 and 2.

symbology 1. the study and interpretation of symbols.
2. representation by means of symbols. Also symbolism.
3. any system of symbols. —symbologist, *n.* —symbological, *adj.*

tachyscope a type of kinescope that presents the effect of moving pictures by use of a rotating glass plate with images attached to it.

teliconograph an apparatus combining a telescope and the camera lucida, used for producing images of distant objects on a screen.

thaumatrope a card with a different design or picture on each side that appear to merge when the card is whirled around. —thaumatropical, *adj.*

townscape a view or representation of a town, especially in a painting, photograph, etc.

travesty imitation or parody for the purpose of ridicule; a grotesque or ludicrous representation.

waterscape 1. a view of a stretch or body of water, as a lake.
2. a drawing or painting of such a view.

353. REPTILES
See also 16. ANIMALS; 374. SNAKES; 430. ZOOLOGY.

herpetography the scientific description of reptiles. —**herpetographical,** *adj.*

herpetology *Zoology.* the study of reptiles and amphibians. —**herpetologist,** *n.* —**herpetologic, herpetological,** *adj.*

herpetophobia an abnormal fear of reptiles. Also called **ophidiophobia.**

ophidiomania an abnormal love of reptiles.

ophidiophobia herpetophobia.

354. RHETORIC and RHETORICAL DEVICES
See also 21. ARGUMENTATION; 236. LANGUAGE; 237. LANGUAGE STYLE; 249. LITERATURE; 250. LOGIC; 382. SPEECH.

acroama 1. a discourse that is not part of an argument.
2. lectures heard only by disciples of a school, and not intended to be written down.

acroasis a spoken disquisition; a monologue.

adnomination *Obsolete.* **1.** paronomasia.
2. alliteration. Also called **agnomination, annomination.**

aeolism a tendency to longwindedness. —**aeolistic,** *adj.*

alliteration the repetition of a sound, especially a consonant, for rhetorical or poetic effect. Also called **adnomination, agnomination, annomination.** —**alliterative,** *adj.*

allocution 1. a particular or special way of speaking.
2. a formal address or speech.

anacoenosis in debate, an appeal by the speaker to his opponents or to the audience for an opinion of the point.

anadiplosis a device in which an unimportant word or the beginning of a phrase in one sentence is repeated in the following sentence, often with a change or extension of the sense. Cf. **epanastrophe.**

anaphora the repetition of a word or words at the beginning of two or more successive verses or clauses, as the repetition of *Blessed* in the Beatitudes. Cf. **epanaphora, epiphora.** —**anaphoral,** *adj.*

anastrophe a rhetorical device in which the usual word order of a phrase or sentence is reversed.

annomination adnomination.

antanaclasis a rhetorical device in which the same word is repeated but with a different sense each time. See also 186. GRAMMAR.

antimetathesis the switching of the terms of an antithesis.

antiphrasis the use of a word in a sense opposite to its proper meaning. —**antiphrastic, antiphrastical,** *adj.*

antithetics the proposing of opposing doctrines or contrasts. —**antithetic, antithetical,** *adj.*

apophasis a spoken or written figure in which an assertion is made in the midst of a denial, as in Mark Antony's funeral speech for Caesar. Also called **paralipsis.** —**apophasic,** *adj.*

aposiopesis a sudden breaking off in the middle of a sentence as if unable or unwilling to proceed. —**aposiopetic,** *adj.*

apostrophe a variety of personification in which the dead, absent, or inanimate are addressed as if present. —**apostrophic,** *adj.*

apostrophism a manner of speech in which the speaker continually interrupts his train of thought and continuity of subject by interjecting subordinate ideas and comments. —**apostrophist,** *n.*

Asiaticism a manner of speech, writing, or architecture distinguished by excessive ornamentation or floridity. —**Asiatical,** *adj.*

assonance resemblance of sound, particularly vowel sounds, occurring in words of close proximity.

asteism polite and ingenious irony.

asyndeton a rhetorical device in which conjunctions or other connecting words are omitted, produced a staccato, emphatic effect. —**asyndetic,** *adj.*

battology futile repetition in speech or writing.

chiasmus a reversal in the order of words in two otherwise parallel phrases, as "flowers are lovely, love is flowerlike" (Coleridge). —**chiastic,** *adj.*

deipnosophism the art of dinner conversation. —**deipnosophist,** *n.*

diallage a figure of rhetoric in which arguments are considered from different viewpoints and then turned to make one point.

dicaeology *Obsolete.* an excuse or justification.

ecbasis a rhetorical device in which an orator deals with things in terms of events and their consequences.

ecphonema, ecphonesis a sudden, inflamed exclamation, used for emphasis or to capture the attention.

elocution 1. the art of public speaking.
2. the manner or quality of a person's speech.
3. *Rare.* the act of speech.
4. *Obsolete.* eloquence.

elocutionist 1. a person skilled at public speaking.
2. a teacher of elocution.

eloquence graceful, forceful, or persuasive speech. —**eloquent**, *adj*.

epanadiplosis a figure of speech in which an orator or writer ends a sentence with the same word with which it was begun. Cf. **anadiplosis**.

epanados 1. the repeating of a phrase or sentence in reverse order.
2. a return to the main topic or heading after a digression.

epanalepsis repetition of the same word or phrase after other words have intervened.

epanaphora a rhetorical device consisting of repetition of a word or phrase at the beginning of successive sentences. Cf. **anaphora**.

epanastrophe a device in which the end of one clause is made the beginning of the next. Cf. **anadiplosis**.

epanorthosis a rhetorical device in which something just said is repeated and stronger or more apt words are substituted.

epiphora the repetition of a word or words at the end of two or more successive clauses, phrases, or verses, as "I should do Brutus wrong and Cassius wrong." Also called **epistrophe**. Cf. **anaphora**.

erotesis a manner of phrasing a question that presupposes an answer that is either a strong affirmative or, more often, a strong negative.

exordium the beginning or introductory part of a book or other printed work, or of a discourse.

fustian a high-flown, bombastic style of writing or speaking. —**fustianist**, *n*.

gemmination the immediate repetition of a word, phrase, sentence, etc., for emphasis and rhetorical effect.

gongorism, Gongorism an elaborate, florid, intricate style of writing, after Góngora y Argote.

hendiadys a rhetorical device in which a complex idea is expressed by two substantives joined by a conjunction instead of by a substantive qualified by an adjective.

homiletics the art of sacred speaking; preaching. —**homiletic, homiletical**, *adj*.

homily a sermon or serious admonition. —**homilist, homilete**, *n*.

homoeoptoton a rhetorical device consisting of the repetition of the same case endings, inflections, etc., at the end of phrases.

homoeoteleuton a device of rhetoric in which like-sounding words, syllables, or phrases are used at the end of succeeding sentences or lines.

hypallage the deliberate movement for effect and emphasis of one of a group of nouns from a more natural position to one less natural, as Virgil's "the trumpet's Tuscan blare" for "the Tuscan trumpet's blare." —**hypallactic**, *adj*.

hyperbaton a rhetorical device in which the usual or expected word order is inverted.

hyperbole 1. an obvious and intentional exaggeration.
2. an extravagant statement or figure of speech not intended to be taken literally, as "She's as big as a house." Cf. litotes. —hyperbolic, *adj*.

hyperbolism 1. the use of hyperbole, or exaggeration.
2. a hyperbolic or exaggerated statement. —hyperbolist, *n*.

hypotyposis the use of colorful description or word-picturing.

hysteron proteron a figure of speech in which what logically should come last comes first, as "bred and born" and "thunder and lightning." Also called hysterology.

laconicism, laconism a tendency to use few words to express a great deal; conciseness. —laconic, *adj*.

lexiphanicism *Archaic*. 1. the use of excessively learned and bombastic terminology.
2. an instance of this language style. —lexiphanic, *adj*.

litotes an understatement, especially one in which an affirmative is expressed by the negative of the contrary, as in "it's not unpleasant."

macaronicism a style of language in which Latin words are mixed with vernacular words, some of which have Latin endings affixed to them, as *skato, slippere, falli, bumptum*. —macaronic, *adj*.

mataeology a discourse that is fruitless or in vain. —mataeologian, *n*. —mataeological, *adj*.

meiosis an expressive understatement, especially litotes. —meiotic, *adj*.

metabasis a transition from one subject to another. Also metabola, metabole. —metabatic, *adj*.

metalepsis a rhetorical device in which a word that is used figuratively is taken through a succession of its different meanings or two or more tropes are united in the use of a single word. —metaleptic, *adj*.

metonymy a rhetorical or stylistic device in which one thing is named or referred to by the name of another, related thing; for example, the use of *White House* for the presidential administration. —metonym, *n*. —metonymous, metonymic, metonymical, *adj*.

nice-nellyism, nice-Nellyism a euphemism. See also 28. ATTITUDES; 237. LANGUAGE STYLE.

oxymoron a rhetorical device or figure of speech in which contradictory or opposite words or concepts are combined for effect. —oxymoronic, *adj*.

palilogy, palillogy the immediate repetition of a word for emphasis, as "the living, the living, he shall praise thee" (Isaiah 38:19).

paromology, paromologia a concession made by a speaker to an opponent in order to strengthen his own position. —**paromologetic,** *adj.*

paronomasia the use of a word in different senses or the use of words similar in sound for effect, as humor or ambiguity; punning. Also called **adnomination, agnomination, annomination.**

pathopoeia a speech, figure of speech, or rhetorical device aimed to stimulate the passions.

periphrasis 1. a roundabout way of speaking or writing; circumlocution.
2. an expression in such fashion. See also 236. LANGUAGE. —**periphrastic,** *adj.*

personification the attribution of personality to an inanimate object or abstraction, as "the table tripped me."Also called **prosopopoeia.** —**personificative,** *adj.*

philippic an oration or declamation full of bitter and accusatory invective, named after the orations of Demosthenes attacking Philip of Macedon.

pleonasm 1. the use of unnecessary words to express an idea; redundancy.
2. an instance of this, as *true fact.*
3. a redundant word or expression. —**pleonastic,** *adj.*

procatalepsis the anticipating and answering of an opponent's possible objections. —**procataleptic,** *adj.*

prolegomenon a preliminary remark or introduction, as to a speech; the foreword to a book or treatise. —**prolegomenary, prolegomenous,** *adj.*

punning paronomasia.

rhetorician 1. a teacher of rhetoric.
2. one skilled in the art of rhetoric.
3. a speaker who overuses rhetorical devices, especially a bombastic or overelaborate orator.

sardonicism a style of speaking or writing characterized by bitter, contemptuous, or scornful derision.

sophist 1. *Ancient Greece.* a teacher of rhetoric, philosophy, etc.; hence, a learned person.
2. one who is given to the specious arguments often used by the sophists.

sophistry 1. the teachings and ways of teaching of the Greek sophists.
2. specious or fallacious reasoning, as was sometimes used by the sophists.

syllepsis the use of a word with the same syntactic relation to two adjacent words, in a literal sense with one and a metaphorical sense with the other, as in "the ships collided, and the sailors and many dreams were drowned." —**sylleptic,** *adj.*

synaloepha, synalepha the contraction of two adjacent vowels into one syllable, as by elision.

synchoresis the making of a concession that will leave one's opponent open to a sharp retort. —synchoretic, *adj.*

syncrisis a rhetorical device that emphasizes the comparison of opposites; contrast.

synecdoche the use of a part for a whole or a whole for a part, the special for the general or the general for the special, as in "a Rockefeller" for a rich man or "wheels" for transportation. —synecdochic, synecdochical, *adj.*

synecdochism the style of speaking that utilizes synecdoche.

thetics the setting forth of propositions or principles. —thetic, thetical, *adj.*

triticism a trite, commonplace or hackneyed saying, expression, etc.; a platitude.

tropist a person who explains the Scriptures in terms of tropes, or figures of speech.

tropology 1. the use of figurative language in writing.
2. a treatise on figures of speech or tropes. —tropologic, tropological, *adj.*

zeugma the use of a word grammatically related to two adjacent words, but inappropriate for one of them, as in "he loved both his wife and his wallet." —zeugmatic, *adj.*

355. RIGHT
See also 242. LEFT.

dextrality 1. the condition of having the right side distinct or different from the left.
2. right-handedness.

dextrogyration dextrorotation. —dextrogyric, *adj.*

dextrorotation movement or rotation to the right, or clockwise. Also called dextrogyration.

dextroversion the state or process of turning to the right.

356. RIVERS
See also 234. LAKES; 360. SEA; 414. WATER.

alluvion 1. the gradual depositing by a river of earth and other material on the banks.
2. also called alluvium. the material deposited.

fluviation 1. the formation of rivers.
2. a river system.

lutulence *Obsolete.* the state or condition of being muddy or turbid. —lutulent, *adj.*

nilometer an instrument used for measuring the increase in the level of the River Nile during its flood period, consisting of a water chamber containing a graduated pillar. Also niloscope.

potamology the study of rivers. —potamologist, *n*. —potamological, *adj*.

potamophobia a morbid fear of rivers.

riparian a dweller on the bank of a river. —riparian, *adj*.

357. RUSSIA
See also 94. COMMUNISM.

Decembrist one of those who conspired to overthrow Russian Czar Nicholas I in December, 1825. Also **Dekebrist**.

Kremlinology study of the policies, doctrines, programs, etc., of the government of the Soviet Union. —Kremlinologist, *n*.

Russianism something characteristic of or influenced by Russia, its people, customs, language, etc.

Russomania an obsession with Russia and things Russian.

Russophilism great fondness for or interest in Russia, its people, customs, language, art, etc. —Russophile, *n*., *adj*.

Russophobism Russophobia.

Slavicist one who specializes in the study of Slavic languages, literatures, or other aspects of Slavic culture. Also **Slavist**.

Slavophilism enthusiasm for or admiration of things Slavic, as Slavic literature, language, culture, customs, etc. —Slavophil, Slavophile, *n*., *adj*.

Slavophobia fear or hatred of things Slavic, especially of real or imagined Soviet political influence. —Slavophobe, *n*. —Slavophobic, *adj*.

Sovietism, sovietism 1. the soviet system of government and the principles and practices of such a government.
2. a policy, action, etc., typical of the Soviet Union. —Sovietist, sovietist, *n*., *adj*.

Sovietology study of the Soviet Union, especially its government, policies, etc. —Sovietologist, *n*.

S

358. SACREDNESS

See also 81. CHURCH; 183. GOD and GODS; 349. RELIGION; 359. SAINTS.

halidom *Archaic.* 1. the state or condition of being holy or sacred.
2. a holy or sacred place; a sanctuary.
3. a sacred object or relic.

hierogram sacred writing or a sacred character or symbol. —**hierogrammatist,** *n.*, —**hierogrammatic, hierogrammatical,** *adj.*

hierography *Rare.* sacred writing; hierograms and the art of writing them. —**hierographer,** *n.* —**hierographic, hierographical,** *adj.*

hierolatry the worship of saints and of relics and other sacred objects.

hierology 1. the learning or literature concerning sacred things.
2. hierological materials. —**hierologist,** *n.* —**hierologic, hierological,** *adj.*

hieromancy a form of divination involving sacrificial remains or sacred objects.

hierophobia an abnormal fear of sacred objects.

hierurgy 1. the performance of holy works.
2. the holy work itself.

sanctum sanctorum the holy of holies; a place of great holiness.

359. SAINTS

See also 80. CHRISTIANITY; 273. MIRACLES; 349. RELIGION; 358. SACREDNESS; 392. THEOLOGY.

Bollandist any of the editors of the *Acta Sanctorum*, a critical and official hagiology begun by the Jesuits in the 17th century.

dulia the devotion, veneration, or respect accorded saints.

hagiography the writing and critical study of the lives of the saints; hagiology. —**hagiographer,** *n.* —**hagiographic, hagiographical,** *adj.*

hagiolatry the veneration or worship of saints. —**hagiolater,** *n.* —**hagiolatrous,** *adj.*

hagiology 1. the branch of literature comprising the lives and legends of the saints.
2. a biography or narrative of the life of a saint or saints.
3. a collection of such biographies. —hagiologist, *n.* —hagiologic, hagiological, *adj.*

hagiophobia an intense dislike for the saints and the holy.

360. SEA
See also 234. LAKES; 356. RIVERS; 414. WATER.

bathyclinograph a device used for measuring vertical currents in deep ocean areas.

bathygraphy the scientific exploration of the sea with sonic instruments. —bathygraph, bathygram, *n.*

bathyscaphe a vessel for exploring the depths of the oceans.

benthos 1. the depths or bottom of the sea.
2. organic life that inhabits the bottom of the sea.

benthoscope an apparatus for surveying the depths or bottom of the sea.

cymophobia an abnormal fear of waves.

equinoctial a severe storm at sea, usually occurring near the equinox and mistakenly thought to be the result of the sun crossing the equatorial line.

haliography *Obsolete.* a work describing the sea.

mare clausum a body or stretch of navigable water which is under the jurisdiction of a particular nation. Cf. mare liberum.

mare liberum a body or stretch of navigable water to which all nations or countries have unrestricted access. Cf. mare clausum.

maremma a marshy region adjoining the seashore.

marigraphy *Rare.* the measurement of the rise and fall of tides. Also mareography. —marigraphic, *adj.*

oceanography the branch of physical geography that studies oceans and seas. —oceanographer, *n.* —oceanographic, oceanographical, *adj.*

oceanology oceanography.

seascape a view or representation of the sea, especially in a painting, photograph, etc.

thalassocracy the sovereignty of the seas. —thalassocrat, *n.*

thalassography 1. the branch of oceanography that studies smaller bodies of water, as sounds, gulfs, etc.
2. oceanography in general. —thalassographer, *n.* —thalassographic, thalassographical, *adj.*

thalassomania an abnormal love of the sea.

thalassophobia an abnormal fear of the sea.

361. SEALS
sigillography the study of seals. —sigillographer, *n*. —sigillographic, *adj*.

sphragistics the scientific study of seals and signet rings. —sphragistic, *adj*.

362. SELF
See also 334. PSYCHOLOGY.

autodidactics the process of teaching oneself. —autodidact, *n*.

autolatry the worship of oneself.

autology the study of oneself.

automania an excessive liking for solitude.

autophilia a kind of self-love; narcissism. —autophile, *n*. —autophilic, *adj*.

autophobia, autophoby an abnormal fear of being by oneself. Also called eremiophobia, eremophobia, monophobia.

autoplagiarism the act or process of plagiarizing one's own work.

biosophy a mode of life based on intuition and self-education in order to improve one's character. —biosophist, *n*.

egocentricity the state of being self-centered; greater concern about the self than others to an excessive degree. —egocentric, *n.*, *adj*.

egocentrism 1. the philosophy or attitude of considering oneself the center of the universe.
2. the state or quality of being self-centered. —egocentric, *n.*, *adj*.

egoism an extreme individualism; thought and behavior based upon the premise that one's individual self is the highest product, if not the totality, of existence. Cf. individualism. —egoist, *n*. —egoistic, *adj*.

egomania a psychologically abnormal egotism. —egomaniac, *n*.

egotheism a deification of self.

egotism the practice of thought, speech, and conduct expressing high self-regard or self-exaltation, usually without skepticism or humility. —egotist, *n*. —egotistical, *adj*.

eremiophobia, eremophobia autophobia.

eremitism 1. the state of being a hermit.
2. an attitude favoring solitude and seclusion. —eremite, *n*. —eremitic, *adj*.

extraversion, extroversion *Psychology*. 1. the act of directing one's interest outward or to things outside the self.
2. the state of having thoughts and activities satisfied by things outside the self. Cf. introversion. —extravert, *n*. —extraversive, extravertive, *adj*.

factionalism, factionism the state or quality of being partisan or self-interested. —factional, *adj*. —factionalist, *n*.

individualism the practice of independence in thought and action on the premise that the development and expression of an individual character and personality are of the utmost importance. Cf. egoism. —individualist, *n*. —individualistic, *adj*.

individuation the act or process of becoming an individual or distinct entity.

introversion *Psychology*. 1. the act of directing one's interest inward or toward the self.
2. the state of being interested chiefly in one's own inner thoughts, feelings, and processes. Cf. extraversion. —introvert, *n*. —introvertive, introversive, *adj*.

ipse-dixitism a dictatorial atmosphere brought about by a person's demands based solely on his having uttered them.

ipsism an individual identity; selfhood. Also ipseity.

monologue a theatrical performance or scene with a single actor who speaks alone.

monology 1. the habit of talking to oneself; soliloquizing.
2. *Obsolete* a monologue. —monologist, *n*. —monologic, monological, *adj*.

monophobia autophobia.

narcissism an excessive admiration of oneself. Also narcism. —narcissist, narcist, *n*. —narcissistic, narcistic, *adj*.

nosism *Archaic*. the use of *we* in speaking of oneself.

personalism the individual or personal characteristics of a person or object. —personalist, *n*. —personalistic, *adj*.

philauty *Obsolete*. self love; an excessive regard for oneself.

reclusion the state of living apart from society, like a hermit. —recluse, *n*. —reclusive, *adj*.

seclusionist a person who seeks solitude or removes himself from the society of others; a recluse.

selfism the obsessive concentration on one's self-interests. —selfist, *n*.

soliloquy 1. the act or custom of talking to oneself or talking when alone.
2. *Drama*. a speech in which a character reveals his thoughts to the audience but not to other characters in the play. —soliloquist, *n*.

suicide 1. the killing of oneself.
2. a person who has killed himself. —suicidal, *adj*.

vitativeness *Phrenology*. the organ serving as the seat of instincts of self-preservation.

363. SEPARATION

abalienation the act of estrangement or separation, as in marriage. Also alienation.

alienation abalienation.

severalty the state or condition of being separate. See also 331. PROPERTY and OWNERSHIP.

severance 1. the act or process of severing or separating.
2. the state or condition of being severed or separated, as in the ending of a relationship.

364. SEX

See also 209. HOMOSEXUALITY; 253. MALE; 424. WOMEN.

algolagnia the finding of sexual pleasure in suffering or inflicting physical pain; sadomasochism. —algolagnist, *n.* —algolagnic, *adj.*

amphierotism *Rare.* bisexualism. —amphierotic, *adj.*

anaphrodisia *Medicine.* the absence or loss of sexual desire. Also called sexual anesthesia.

andromania nymphomania.

aphrodisia an extreme state of sexual desire.

aphrodisiac a food or other substance that creates sexual desire. —aphrodisiac, *adj.*

aphrodisiomania a mania for sexual pleasure.

autoeroticism *Psychoanalysis.* the arousal and satisfaction of sexual desires within or by oneself, usually by masturbation. Also autoerotism. —autoerotic, *adj.*

bawdry 1. *Archaic.* the practice or occupation of being a bawd or procurer.
2. *Obsolete.* fornication or unlawful intercourse.

bestiality sexual relations between a person and an animal. See also 41. BEHAVIOR.

biomagnetism 1. animal magnetism, or the power that enables some people to induce a hypnotic state in others.
2. physical attraction between members of the sexes. —biomagnetic, *adj.*

bisexualism, bisexuality the state of being sexually responsive or attracted to members of both sexes. Also called amphierotism. See also 51. BODY, HUMAN. —bisexual, *adj.*

carnalism, carnality the practice of finding satisfaction in activities related to fleshly desires and appetites, especially the sexual. —carnal, *adj.*

coitophobia an abnormal fear of sexual intercourse. Also called genophobia.

coprophilia 1. the use of obscene or scatological language for sexual gratification.
2. a love of obscenity.
3. *Psychiatry.* an abnormal interest in feces, especially as a source of sexual excitement.

cryptorchidism the failure of one or both testes to descend normally. —**cryptorchid,** *n., adj.*

defloration the act of having sexual intercourse with a virgin; devirgination.

devirgination *Obsolete.* the deflowering of a virgin. Also called **defloration.**

edeomania an obsession with genitals.

eonism *Psychiatry.* the adoption, by a male, of feminine mannerisms, clothing, etc. Also called **transvestism, transvestitism.**

epicenism the state or quality of combining characteristics of both sexes. —**epicenity,** *n.* —**epicene,** *adj.*

eroticism 1. the erotic or sexual quality of something.
2. the use of sexually arousing or stimulating materials in literature, drama, art, etc.
3. the condition of being sexually stimulated.
4. a sexual drive or tendency.
5. an abnormally persistent sexual drive. Also **erotism.**

eroticomania an abnormal interest in erotica.

erotographomania an abnormal interest in erotic literature.

erotology the study of sex as a skill.

erotomania abnormal or uncontrollable sexual desire. —**erotomaniac,** *n., adj.*

erotophobia an abnormal fear of sexual feelings and their physical expression.

estrus, oestrus the condition of being in rut or sexual arousal, applied particularly to the female. Also called **estrum, oestrum.** —**estrous, oestrous,** *adj.*

eunuchism 1. the process or tradition of castrating males.
2. the state of being a eunuch.

fetishism, fetichism *Psychiatry.* the compulsive use of some object or part of the body as a sexual stimulus, as a shoe, underclothes, a lock of hair, etc. —**fetishist, fetichist,** *n.* —**fetishistic, fetichistic,** *adj.*

flagellation whipping or flogging, either as a religious practice for the mortification of the flesh, or as a sexual activity, for sado-masochistic pleasure. —**flagellant,** *n., adj.* —**flagellator,** *n.*

free-lovism the doctrine or practice of having sexual relations without marriage or any other commitment to an obligation.

frottage the act of rubbing against another person for sexual gratification. —**frotteur,** *n.*

genesiology the study of reproduction.

genophobia coitophobia.

gerontophilia a sexual attraction to the elderly. —gerontophile, *n.* —gerontophilic, *adj.*

gynecomania satyriasis.

harlotry the state or practice of being a harlot or prostitute.

hetaerism, hetairism 1. the practice of concubinage.
2. a social system characterized by its regarding women as common property. —hetaerist, hetairist, *n.* —hetaeristic, hetairistic, *adj.*

hysteromania nymphomania.

infibulation the act and practice of attaching a clasp, ring, or other device to the genital organs to prevent sexual intercourse. See also 68. CAPTIVITY.

ithyphallicism the worship of an erect phallus or the use of a representation of one in ritual. —ithyphallic, *adj.*

lechery immoderate indulgence of sexual desire; lewd and lustful behavior. —lecher, lecherer, *n.* —lecherous, *adj.*

libido *Psychoanalysis.* the force or psychic energy behind human action, especially the sexual urge. —libidinous, *adj.*

lubricity lewd or lecherous behavior or attitude; lasciviousness. —lubricious, *adj.*

mentulomania an obsession with the penis.

monoecism the condition of having both male and female sex organs in an individual. —monoecious, *adj.*

necrophilia a sexual attraction to the dead. —necrophile, *n.* —necrophilic, *adj.*

necrosadism the mutilation of a corpse in order to excite or satisfy sexual urges. —necrosadist, *n.*

nymphomania *Pathology.* an excessive sexual desire in a female. Also called andromania, hysteromania, oestromania, uteromania. Cf. satyriasis. —nymphomaniac, *n., adj.* —nymphomaniacal, *adj.*

oestromania nymphomania.

oestrus estrus.

onanism 1. the practice of preejaculatory withdrawal during intercourse.
2. masturbation. —onanist, *n.* —onanistic, *adj.*

orchidomania an obsession with testicles.

panderism 1. the practice of acting as a go-between in amorous intrigues.
2. the action of soliciting customers for a prostitute or of procuring women for sexual purposes. Also **panderage.**

paraphilia the practice of, indulgence in, or addiction to unusual sexual activities. —paraphilic, *adj.*

paraphobia an abnormal fear of sexual perversion.

partialism 1. an emphasis of sexual interest upon one part of the body.
2. a form of fetishism in which the sexual stimulus is a part of the body, as pictures of feet.

pornographomania an abnormal interest in pornography.

priapism 1. *Pathology.* a continuous erection of the penis, especially as the result of a disease.
2. a prurient action or display. —priapismic, *adj.*

proxenetism the practice of pimping by females. —proxenetist, *n.*

prurience, pruriency an inclination toward lewdness or lustfulness; lustful behavior. —prurient, *adj.*

salacity 1. lewdness of speech.
2. lustful or lecherous behavior. —salacious, *adj.*

satyriasis *Pathology.* an abnormal, uncontrollable sexual desire in men. Also called gynecomania, satyrism, satyromania. Cf. nymphomania. —satyr, *n.* —satyric, *adj.*

scopophilia *Psychiatry.* 1. Also called passive scopophilia. the deriving of sexual pleasure from viewing nude bodies, sexual acts, or erotic photographs; voyeurism.
2. Also called active scopophilia, scoptophilia. an abnormal desire to be seen, especially genitally; exhibitionism. —scopophiliac, *n.* —scopophilic, *adj.*

sexology the study of normal and abnormal sexual behavior. —sexologist, *n.* —sexological, *adj.*

sexual anesthesia anaphrodisia.

sexualism emphasis upon sex as being a prime concern in life.

transsexualism, transsexuality the psychological phenomenon of a person identifying with the opposite sex, sometimes to the extent of undergoing surgery for change of sex. —transsexual, *n., adj.*

transvestism eonism.

ustulation *Obsolete.* a burning sexual desire; a lustful passion.

uteromania nymphomania.

venery *Archaic.* sexual activity; the gratification of sexual impulses.

voyeurism the practice of gaining sexual gratification by looking at sexual acts, erotic pictures, etc. —voyeur, *n.* —voyeuristic, *adj.*

whoredom the act or practice of prostitution.

whoremongery 1. the practice of being a whoremaster, or whoremonger.
2. the actions or behavior of a whoremaster, or whoremonger.

zoophilia a desire for sexual activity with animals. —**zoophilist,** *n.* —**zoophilic, zoophilous,** *adj.*

365. SHARPNESS

aichmophobia an abnormal fear of pointed objects.

belonephobia an abnormal fear of pins and needles.

366. SHIPS
See also 399. TRAVEL; 408. VEHICLES.

barratry *Law.* an act of fraud by a master or crew at the expense of the owners of a ship or the owners of its cargo. Also spelled **barretry.** —**barratrous,**
adj.

bottomry the pledging of a ship as security for a loan; if the ship is lost the
debt is canceled.

cabotage the act of navigating or trading along a coast.

demurrage 1. the delay of a ship at mooring beyond the time stipulated for
unloading or other purposes.
2. the charge levied for such delay.

flotsam material floating on the sea, especially debris or goods from ship-
wrecks. Cf. jetsam.

jetsam, jetsom 1. part of a ship's cargo thrown overboard, as to lighten the
load in the event of danger.
2. such cargo when it is washed ashore.
3. anything which is discarded. Cf. flotsam.

lodemanage *Obsolete.* the skill or art of the pilot; pilotage.

lodesman *Obsolete.* a ship's pilot.

loxodrome a rhumb line or curve on the surface of a sphere intersecting all
meridians at the same angle; hence, the course of a ship or aircraft following a constant compass direction. —**loxodromic,** *adj.*

loxodromics, loxodromy the art, science, or practice of sailing obliquely
across lines of longitude at a constant bearing to them. —**loxodromic,** *adj.*

naumachia, naumachy 1. a mock sea fight, as in ancient Rome.
2. the place where such fights were conducted.

naupathia seasickness.

nauropometer *Rare.* an apparatus for measuring the inclination of a heeling
or listing ship.

nauscopy the art, sometimes pretended, of being able to sight ships or land at
great distances.

pallograph an instrument for recording the vibrations of a steamship. —**pallographic,** *adj.*

pharology the technique or practice of guiding ships by means of signal lights, as in lighthouses.

pilotage 1. the act of piloting.
2. the skill or expertise of a pilot. See also 131. DUES and PAYMENT.

plunderage 1. the embezzling of goods on board ship.
2. the goods embezzled.

pratique permission given to a ship to do business with a port once quarantine and other regulations have been complied with.

prisage 1. the former privilege of the English monarch to receive two tuns of wine from every ship importing twenty tuns or more.
2. Also called **butlerage**. a duty of two shillings on every tun imported by foreign merchants.
3. (in England) the Crown's share of merchandise seized lawfully as a prize at sea.

salvage 1. the recovery of a ship or its contents or cargo after damage or sinking.
2. the material recovered and the compensation to those who recover it.
3. the rescue and use of any found or discarded material.

spoliation the act of seizing neutral ships with government permission in time of war. See also 81. CHURCH; 391. THEFT.

367. SIN
See also 146. EVIL; 203. HELL; 205. HERESY; 349. RELIGION; 392. THEOLOGY.

hamartiology *Theology.* the study or science of the doctrine of sin.

hamartomania an obsession with sin.

hamartophobia an abnormal fear of error or sin.

peccancy 1. the state or condition of being sinful or in sin.
2. a sinful act. —**peccant,** *adj.*

peccatiphobia, peccatophobia an abnormal fear of sinning.

simony the sin or offense of selling or granting for personal advantage church appointments, benefices, preferments, etc. —**simonist,** *n.*

368. SIZE
See also 187. GRANDEUR.

acromegaly *Medicine.* a disease resulting from abnormal activity of the pituitary gland in which bones of the extremities are enlarged. —**acromegalic,** *adj.*

Brobdingnagian a person of enormous size, as from Brobdingnag in Swift's *Gulliver's Travels.* Cf. Lilliputian.

decrescence the process of decreasing in size. —**decrescent,** *adj.*

dwarfism *Medicine.* the condition of being dwarfed or a dwarf. Also called nanism.

exiguity smallness of size. —exiguous, *adj.*

gigantism *Medicine.* the condition of abnormally great development in size or stature of the whole body or any of its parts, most often caused by a pituitary disorder. Cf. nanism.

gigantology the study of giants.

heterosis abnormal development, especially increased size, in plants or animals, usually as a result of cross-breeding.

homunculus 1. a small man or midget.
2. formerly, the microcosmic human form believed to be present in spermatozoon.

hypertrophy excessive growth of tissue or of an organ, independent of and out of proportion to the rest of the body. Cf. hypoplasia. See also 319. PLANTS. —hypertrophic, hypertrophical, *adj.* —hypertrophous, *adj.*

hypoplasia a condition in which tissue or an organ of the body fails to grow to normal size. Cf. hypertrophy. —hypoplastic, *adj.*

increscence the process of increasing in size, or waxing, as the moon. —increscent, *adj.*

inordinacy the quality of being immoderate, disordered, or without restraint or proportion. —inordinate, *adj.*

Lilliputian a diminutive person, about the height of an ink bottle, as from Lilliput in Swift's *Gulliver's Travels.* Cf. **Brobdingnagian.**

macromania a mania for becoming larger.

macrosomatia the condition of having an abnormally large body. —macrosomatous, *adj.*

manikin, mannikin 1. a dwarf, pygmy, or man of small stature.
2. a model of the human body, as used for teaching purposes in art, anatomy, etc. Also spelled **mannequin.**

micrography the study, examination, or description of things that are so small they must be viewed through a microscope. —micrograph, *n.* —micrographic, *adj.*

micromania a mania for becoming smaller.

monumentalism the state of having large and grand characteristics. —monumentality, *n.*

nanism *Medicine.* the condition of dwarfishness. Cf. **gigantism.**

pygmyism 1. the condition of being a pygmy.
2. the behavior attributed to or characteristic of pygmies.

369. SKILL and CRAFT
See also 297. OCCUPATIONS; 426. WORK.

artifice 1. skill, ingenuity, or craftiness.
2. *Obsolete.* the command of a learned trade or skill.

enginery 1. skill or craft.
2. a contrivance that is skillfully made.

expertise 1. the knowledge or skill of an expert.
2. the condition of being an expert.

generalist a person who has knowledge, aptitude, or skill in a variety of areas, as contrasted with a specialist.

370. SKIN
See also 14. ANATOMY; 51. BODY, HUMAN; 95. COMPLEXION.

achromasia absence of pigmentation in the skin.

albinism *Medicine.* a congenital absence of pigment in the skin, hair, and eyes, ranging in scope from partial to total. Also **albinoism.** Cf. **melanism.** —albino, *n.* —albinotic, *adj.*

dermabrasion the surgical process of removing the outer layer of the skin, as for cosmetic purposes in the removal of acne scars, etc.

dermatalgia neuralgia of the skin.

dermatoglyphics 1. the patterns of ridges of skin on the fingers and palm and the bottoms of the feet.
2. the study dealing with these patterns. —dermatoglyphic, *adj.*

dermatographism *Medicine.* a condition in which lightly touching or scratching the skin causes raised, reddish marks. Also **dermatographia, dermographia, dermographism.** —dermatographic, *adj.*

dermatography *Anatomy.* a description of the skin. —dermatographic, *adj.*

dermatology the branch of medicine that studies the skin and its diseases. —dermatologist, *n.* —dermatological, *adj.*

dermatophobia an abnormal fear of skin disease. Also **dermatosiophobia, dermatopathophobia.**

dermatoplasty any form of plastic surgery of the skin, as skin grafts.

dermographism, dermographia dermatographism.

horripilation the raising of the hairs on the skin as a response to cold or fear; goose bumps or goose pimples.

melanism a darkening of the skin caused by an unusually high amount of pigmentation.

pachydermia abnormal thickening of the skin. Cf. **pachymenia.** —pachydermic, *adj.*

pachymenia thickening of the skin or of a membrane. Cf. **pachydermia.**
—pachymenic, *adj.*

phaneromania a mania for picking at growths.

phototherapy, phototherapeutics the treatment of disease, especially diseases
of the skin, with light rays. —phototherapeutic, *adj.*

rugosity the state or quality of being wrinkled, as the skin. —rugose, *adj.*

xanthochroid a person with light-colored hair and fair complexion. —xanthochroid, xanthochroous, *adj.*

371. SLAVERY
See also 68. CAPTIVITY.

abolitionism the movement for the abolition of slavery, especially Negro slavery in the U.S. —abolitionist, *n.*

helotism the condition or quality of being a helot; serfdom or slavery. Also
helotage, helotry.

indentureship 1. the state or period of being indentured or apprenticed;
apprenticeship.
2. the state or period of being a servant bound to service for a specified time
in return for passage to a colony.

servilism a doctrine that advocates slavery. —servility, *n.*

372. SLEEP
See also 129. DREAMS; 154. FATIGUE.

autohypnotism, autohypnosis 1. the process of hypnotizing oneself.
2. the resulting state.

Braidism the practice of hypnotism by Dr. James Braid, British physician, in
the mid 19th century.

clinomania an obsession with bed rest.

clinophobia an abnormal fear or dislike of going to bed.

consopition *Obsolete.* the act of lulling or rocking to sleep.

dormancy the state of being dormant or inert.

hypnobate a somnambulist, or sleepwalker.

hypnobatia somnambulism. —hypnobate, *n.*

hypnology the science dealing with the phenomena of sleep and hypnotism.
See also 215. HYPNOSIS. —hypnologist, *n.* —hypnologic, hypnological, *adj.*

hypnomania a mania for sleep.

hypnopedia, hypnopaedia the art or process of learning while asleep by
means of lessons recorded on disk or tapes.

hypnophobia an abnormal fear of sleep.

lunambulism   the condition of sleepwalking only in the moonlight. Cf.
somnambulism. —lunambulist, *n.* —lunambulistic, *adj.*

narcoanalysis narcotherapy.

narcohypnia *Medicine.* a numbness often felt upon waking from sleep.

narcolepsy *Pathology.* a condition characterized by frequent and uncontrollable lapses into deep sleep. —narcoleptic, *adj.* —narcolept, *n.*

narcotherapy *Psychiatry.* 1. a method of treating certain mental disorders by
inducing sleep through barbiturates.
2. a type of psychotherapy involving the use of hypnotic drugs. Also
narcoanalysis. —narcotherapist, *n.*

noctambulism somnambulism. Also noctambulation. —noctambulist, noctambule, *n.* —noctambulous, noctambulant, noctambulistic, *adj.*

somnambulism the condition of sleepwalking. Also called hypnobatia, noctambulism. —somnambulant, *n.*, *adj.* —somnambulist, *n.* —somnambulistic,
adj.

somniloquism 1. the tendency to talk in one's sleep. Also somniloquy.
2. the words spoken. —somniloquist, *n.* —somniloquous, *adj.*

somnipathy a state of sleep induced by hypnosis or mesmerism.

somnolence the condition of drowsiness or sleepiness. Also somnolency, somnolism. —somnolent, *adj.*

373. SMOKE
   See also 162. FIRE.

capnomancy a form of divination involving smoke.

empyromancy a form of divination involving fire and smoke.

fuliginosity 1. the state or condition of being sooty or smoky.
2. soot or smoke. —fuliginous, *adj.*

374. SNAKES
   See also 16. ANIMALS; 353. REPTILES.

ophidiophobia 1. an abnormal fear of snakes. Also ophiophobia.
2. herpetophobia.

ophiography a description of snakes. —ophiographic, *adj.*

ophiolatry the worship of snakes. —ophiolater, *n.*

ophiology the branch of herpetology that studies snakes. Also called snakeology, snakology. —ophiologist, *n.* —ophiologic, ophiological, *adj.*

ophiomancy a form of divination involving snakes.

snakeology, snakology ophiology.

375. SNOW
See also 27. ATMOSPHERE; 85. CLIMATE; 87. CLOUDS; 90. COLD; 345. RAIN; 417. WEATHER.

chionomania a mania for snow.

chionophobia an abnormal fear or dislike of snow.

376. SOCIETY
See also 93. COMMUNALISM; 185. GOVERNMENT; 322. POLITICS.

activism the attitude of taking an active part in events, especially in a social context. —activist, *n.*

anthropophobia an abnormal fear of people, especially in groups.

aristocracy 1. government by the best people.
2. an upper class based on quality, nobility, etc.

aristocraticism a dedication to aristocratic behavior.

aristocratism the attitudes and actions of aristocrats.

autocracy a society or nation ruled by a person with absolute authority. —autocrat, *n.* —autocratic, *adj.*

beerocracy *In England.* the aristocracy that gained its wealth and social position from the ownership of breweries.

chemocracy a Utopian society in which all foods and other material needs will be prepared by chemical processes. —chemocrat, *n.*

chrysocracy an upper class based on wealth. Also **chrysoaristocracy.**

civics the area of political science concerned with citizenship.

confraternity a brotherhood, especially a group of men bound by a common goal or interest.

cottonocracy that portion of the upper class whose wealth comes from the cotton trade. —cottonocrat, *n.*

democratism a doctrine of or belief in social equality or the right of all people to participate equally in politics.

do-goodism attitudes or actions of well-intentioned but sometimes ineffectual people, especially in the area of social reform.

ecology, oecology the branch of sociology that studies the environmental spacing and interdependence of people and their institutions. —ecologist, oecologist, *n.* —ecologic, oecologic, ecological, oecological, *adj.*

enculturation the process by which a person adapts to and assimilates the culture in which he lives.

exclusionism the doctrine or practice of excluding certain groups or individuals from enjoyment of certain rights or privileges. —exclusionist, *n.*

Fichteanism theories and beliefs of J. G. Fichte (1762–1814), German philosopher and social thinker, a precursor of socialism. —Fichtean, *n., adj.*

foolocracy government or domination of society by fools.

fractionalism the state of being nonhomogeneous or inharmonious. —fractionalization, n.

fraternity a fellowship or association of men, as for a benevolent or charitable purpose or at a college.

kakotopia a state in which the worst possible conditions exist in government, society, law. etc. See also 406. UTOPIA.

landocracy a ruling class that owes its power to its possession of land. —landocrat, n.

manorialism 1. the system of manorial social and political organization, as in the Middle Ages.
2. its principles and practices.
3. *Sometimes Pejorative.* any small, strong unit of local political and social organization.

matriarchate 1. a matriarchal form of government.
2. a family, tribe, or other social group ruled by a matriarch or matriarchs. —matriarchic, *adj.*

mediocracy government or dominance of society by the mediocre.

meritocracy a powerful class composed of people who have achieved position on the basis of their merit rather than by birth or privilege. —meritocrat, n.

moneyocracy government or domination of society by the rich.

oecology ecology.

oiligarchy *Facetious.* a wealthy and dominant force in society whose wealth and power is based on control of oil.

orthogenesis the sociological theory that all cultures or societies follow the same fixed course of determinate evolution. See also 147. EVOLUTION. —orthogenetic, *adj.*

pariahism the condition of being outcast from society. —pariahdom, n.

parsonarchy the domination of a social group, especially a small rural community, by the parson.

parvenuism 1. behavior or attitudes typical of one who has recently acquired wealth or social position.
2. the state or quality of being a parvenu or upstart. —parvenu, n., *adj.*

phratry 1. a subdivision of an ancient Greek tribe or phyle.
2. a clan or other unit of a primitive tribe.

reclusion the state of living apart from society, like a hermit. —recluse, n. —reclusive, *adj.*

seneschalship the rank, position or jurisdiction of a steward of a medieval prince or nobleman.

snobocracy *Facetious.* snobs as a class in society.

socialization the process of adapting to a social group; social intercourse or activity.

sociocracy collective government or government by society as a whole.

sociologism a theory asserted sociologistically. —sociologistic, *adj.*

sociology 1. the science or study of the origin, development, organization, and functioning of human society.
2. the science of the fundamental laws of social relations, institutions, etc. —sociologist, *n.* —sociologic, sociological, *adj.*

sociometry the measurement of social attitudes within a group by sampling expressions of social acceptance or rejection. —sociometrist, *n.* —sociometric, *adj.*

socionomy *Rare.* the study of the laws that govern the development of society.

sodality a fellowship, brotherhood, or other association of a benevolent nature, especially in the Roman Catholic Church. —sodalist, *n.*, *adj.*

solidarism *Sociology.* a theory that the possibility of founding a social organization upon a solidarity of interests is to be found in the natural interdependence of members of a society. —solidarist, *n.* —solidaristic, *adj.*

solidarity the feeling or expression of union in a group formed by a common interest.

sorority a fellowship or association of women, as for a benevolent or charitable purpose or at a college.

sorosis a woman's club or society, named after a club of that name, founded in 1869.

squirearchy *In Britain.* the squires or landed gentry as a class.

syssitia the practice or custom, as among the ancient Spartans and Cretans, of eating the main meal of the day together in public to strengthen social and political bonds.

telesia, telesis the harnessing of natural and social forces for a beneficial goal.

totemism 1. the practice of having a natural object or animate being, as a bird or animal, as the emblem of a family, clan, or group.
2. the practice of regarding such a totem as mystically related to the family, clan, or group and therefore not to be hunted.
3. a system of tribal organization according to totems. —totemic, *adj.*

welfarism the beliefs and policies associated with the welfare system.

377. SOIL
See also 5. AGRICULTURE; 119.DIRT; 179. GEOLOGY.

agrogeology the branch of geology concerned with the adaptability of land to agriculture, soil quality, etc.

agrology the branch of soil science dealing especially with crop production. —agrologist, *n.* —agrological, *adj.*

edaphology pedology.

geopony the science of cultivation; agriculture. —geoponist, *n.* —geoponic, geoponical, *adj.*

lithification the process by which loose mineral fragments or particles of sand are solidified into stone.

paleopedology, palaeopedology the branch of pedology that studies the soil conditions of past geologic ages. —paleopedologist, palaeopedologist, *n.* —paleopedologic, palaeopedologic, paleopedological, palaeopedological, *adj.*

pedology the branch of agriculture that studies soils; soil science. —pedologist, *n.* —pedologic, pedological, *adj.*

pinguidity the state or quality of being rich or fertile. —pinguid, *adj.*

378. SONGS and SINGING
See also 284. MUSIC; 403. TUNING.

antiphonal a collection of antiphons, hymns, or psalms sung in alternating parts.

balladism the writing or singing of ballads. —balladist, *n.*

choristry the singing of a choir.

hymnology 1. the composing of hymns.
2. the study of the origins, development, and use of hymns.
3. *Obsolete.* the performing of hymns.

madrigal 1. a part song for several voices making much use of contrapuntal imitation.
2. a lyric poem suitable for setting to music, usually with love as a theme.
—madrigalist, *n.*

melismatics the practice of composing phrases of several notes to be sung on one syllable of text, as in plainsong.

minstrelsy 1. the art of minstrels.
2. their occupation.
3. a group of minstrels.
4. a collection of their music and songs.

myriologue an improvised funeral song, composed for the dead and sung by women in modern Greece. —myriologist, *n.* —myriologic, myriological, *adj.*

379. SOUL

See also 182. GHOSTS; 349 RELIGION; 384. SPIRITS and SPIRITUALISM; 392. THEOLOGY.

creationism *Theology.* a doctrine that God creates a new soul for every human being born. Cf. metempsychosis. —creationist, *n.* —creationistic, *adj.*

infusionism the doctrine or belief that the soul enters the body by divine infusion at conception or birth.

metempsychosis 1. the passage of a soul from one body to another.
2. the rebirth of the soul at death in another body, either human or animal. Cf. creationism. —metempsychic, metempsychosic, metempsychosical, *adj.*

monopsychism the theory that all souls are actually a single unity. —monopsychic, monopsychical, *adj.*

nullibism the denial that the soul exists. —nullibist, *n.*

panpsychism *Philosophy.* the doctrine that each object in the universe has either a mind or an unconscious soul. —panpsychist, *n.* —panpsychistic, *adj.*

polypsychism the belief that one person may have many souls or modes of intelligence. —polypsychic, polypsychical, *adj.*

psychagogy the guiding of a soul, especially that of a person recently dead into the lower world. —psychagogue, *n.* —psychagogic, *adj.*

psychomachy *Obsolete.* a conflict or battle between the soul and the body.

psychorrhagy the manifestation of a person's soul to another, usually at some distance from the body. —psychorrhagic, *adj.*

theopsychism the belief that the soul has a divine nature.

traducianism *Theology.* the doctrine that a new human soul is generated from the souls of the parents at the moment of conception. —traducianist, *n.* —traducianistic, *adj.*

transmigrationism any of various theories of metempsychosis or reincarnation, as the Hindu doctrines of Karma.

380. SOUND

See also 198. HEARING; 236. LANGUAGE; 284. MUSIC; 330. PRONUNCIATION; 378. SONGS and SINGING; 382. SPEECH; 394. THUNDER.

acoustics 1. *Physics.* the study of sound and sound waves.
2. the qualities or characteristics of a space, as an auditorium, that determine the audibility and fidelity of sounds in it. —acoustician, *n.* —acoustic, *adj.*

anacamptics *Obsolete.* the study of the reflection of sounds. —anacamptic, *adj.*

assonance likeness or approximate similarity in sound.

bombilation *Rare.* a rumbling sound.

bombination *Rare.* a buzzing or humming sound.

cacophony 1. a harshness of sound.
2. discordant noise. —cacophonic, cacophonous, *adj*.

crepitation a crackling sound.

diacoustics *Rare.* the science of sounds refracted through various media.

echolocation the fixing of the position of an object by transmitting a signal and measuring the time required for it to bounce back, typically done by radar or sonar and by bats.

echometry the measurement of the duration of and intervals between sounds. —echometer, *n*.

euphony 1. an agreeableness in sounds; a pleasantness to the ear; harmoniousness.
2. *Phonetics.* a harmoniousness in speech sounds, especially in word choices emphasizing various patterns of consonants or vowels. —euphonic, euphonical, euphonious, *adj*.

harmonometer an instrument for measuring the relationships between sounds.

homonymy the state or quality of sounding identical, whether spelled identically or not, as *bear* and *bare*.

homophony the state or condition of a letter, word, or symbol having the same sound as another but a different meaning, regardless of sameness or difference in spelling, as *choir/quire*. —homophonic, homophonous, *adj*.

kaleidophon, kaleidophone an instrument for the visual representation of sound waves.

monotony dullness or uniformity, similar to that experienced from a repeated sound. —monotonous, *adj*.

onomatopoeia the state or condition of a word formed to imitate the sound of its intended meaning, as *rustle*. —onomatopoeic, onomatopoetic, onomatopoietic, onomatopoeial, *adj*.

oxyphonia, oxyphony an unusually sharp quality or pitch of sound or voice.

phonology 1. the study of speech sounds, from either or both the phonetic and phonemic viewpoints.
2. the phonetic and phonemic systems of a language. See also 247. LINGUISTICS. —phonologist, *n*. —phonological, *adj*.

phonomania an abnormal love of noise.

phonophobia an abnormal fear of noise.

plangency the condition or quality of producing a deep or loud sound. —plangent, *adj*.

psychoacoustics the study of the relationship between sounds and their perception by the listener, especially with regard to how the perception depends on the physical characteristics of the sound rather than on the mind of the listener. —psychoacoustician, *n.* —psychoacoustic, *adj.*

raucity the state or quality of sounding hoarse or harsh. —raucous, *adj.*

sibilancy, sibilance the state or quality of a hissing sound. —sibilant, *adj.*

stridulation 1. the producing of a shrill, grating noise by chafing a serrated part of the body against a hard part.
2. the noise so produced. —stridulator, *n.* —stridulant, stridulatory, *adj.*

susurration 1. the act or process of whispering.
2. a whispering sound or soft rustling. Also susurrus. —susurrant, susurrous, *adj.*

tautophony repetition of the same sound. —tautophonic, tautophonical, *adj.*

ultrasonics the science or study of ultrasonic vibrations, those belonging to a frequency above the audio range. —ultrasonic, *adj.*

ululation 1. the act of wailing or hooting.
2. the sound thus produced. —ululant, *adj.*

381. SPACES
See also 317. PLACES.

agoramania a mania for open spaces.

agoraphobia an abnormal fear of being in crowded, public places like markets.

cenophobia, kenophobia an abnormal fear of a void or of open spaces.

claustrophobia an abnormal fear of enclosed spaces. Also called cleistophobia.

nihility nothingness.

382. SPEECH
See also 236. LANGUAGE; 330. PRONUNCIATION; 354. RHETORIC and RHETORICAL DEVICES; 380. SOUND.

acyrology 1. an incorrectness in diction.
2. cacology. —acyrological, *adj.*

alogy, alogia *Medicine.* an inability to speak, especially as the result of a brain lesion.

aphasia *Pathology.* an impairment or loss of the faculty of understanding or using spoken or written language. —aphasiac, *n.* —aphasic, *n., adj.*

aphonia, aphony loss of the power of speech; dumbness. —aphonic, —aphonous, *adj.*

aphrasia loss or absence of the power of speech.

biloquism the ability to speak in two distinct voices. —biloquist, *n.*

cacology 1. a defectively produced speech.
   2. socially unacceptable enunciation.
   3. nonconformist pronunciation.

deafmutism the condition of lacking both hearing and speech. Also called surdomutism. —deafmute, *n.*

dyslogy, dyslogia *Pathology.* an inability to express ideas or reasoning in speech because of a mental disorder.

dysphasia an impaired state of the power of speech or of the ability to comprehend language, caused by injury to the brain.

dysphemia any neurotic disorder of speech; stammering.

dysphonia speech problems resulting from damage to or malformation of the speech organs.

echolalia the uncontrollable and immediate repetition of sounds and words heard from others. —echolalic, *adj.*

elocution 1. the art of public speaking.
   2. the manner or quality of a person's speech. —elocutionist, *n.*

galimatias confused or unintelligible speech; gibberish.

glossograph an instrument for recording the movements of the tongue during speech.

glossolalia an ecstatic, usually unintelligible speech uttered in the worship services of any of several sects stressing emotionality and religious fervor. Also called speaking in tongues. —glossolalist, *n.*

glossophobia an abnormal fear of speaking in public or of trying to speak.

gutturalism a throaty manner of speaking.

hyperphasia a condition in which control of the speech organs is lost, resulting in meaningless and deranged speech.

labialism a tendency to articulate sounds with the lips rounded.

lalomania an abnormal love of speech or talking.

lalopathology the branch of medical science that studies disorders of speech. —lalopathy, *n.* —lalopathic, *adj.*

lalophobia an abnormal fear of speaking.

logopedia, logopaedia *Pathology.* the science that studies speech defects and their treatment. Also logopedics, logopaedics. —logopedic, logopaedic, *adj.*

mogilalia a pathological speech problem, as stammering.

mutism *Psychiatry.* a conscious or unconscious refusal to make verbal responses to questions, present in some mental disorders.

neolalia any speech that contains new words unintelligible to a hearer. See also 334. PSYCHOLOGY.

obmutescence *Obsolete.* loss of speech or the act of keeping silence.

paralalia a speech defect or disorder in which sounds are distorted.

paralogia a disorder of the faculty of reasoning, characterized by disconnected and meaningless speech.

paraphasia aphasia characterized by the inability to find the correct words to express meaning.

paraphrasia garbled or incoherent speech, the result of aphasia.

pectoriloquism, pectoriloquy speaking from the chest, a phenomenon observed with a stethoscope and caused by the voice reverberating in the lung cavities as a result of disease. —**pectoriloquial, pectoriloquous,** *adj.*

psellism the condition of stuttering or stammering.

psittacism a mechanical, repetitive, and usually meaningless speech.

surdomutism deafmutism. —**surdomute,** *n.*

susurration 1. the act or process of whispering.
2. a whispering sound or soft rustling. Also **susurrus.** —**susurrant, susurrous,** *adj.*

tachyphrasia an abnormality of speech characterized by extreme volubility.

tautophony repetition of the same sound. —**tautophonic, tautophonical,** *adj.*

traulism a stammering and stuttering speech.

ventrilocution ventriloquism.

ventriloquism the art or practice of speaking so that the voice seems not to come from the speaker but from another source, as from a mechanical doll. Also called **ventriloquy, ventrilocution, gastriloquism.** —**ventriloquist,** *n.* —**ventriloquistic,** *adj.*

verbigeration meaningless repetition of words and phrases.

383. SPELLING
See also 236. LANGUAGE.

cacography the practice or defect of incorrect spelling. —**cacographer,** *n.* —**cacographic, cacographical,** *adj.*

glossic a phonetic spelling system in which for each sound the letter or digraph most commonly found representing that sound is used.

hetericism *Rare.* the study of nonphonetic spelling. —**hetericist,** *n.*

heterography 1. the practice of spelling in a way contrary to standard usage.
2. the use of the same letters or combinations of letters to represent different sounds, as in English *tough* and *dough.* —**heterographic, heterographical,** *adj.*

orthography 1. the art of writing words according to accepted usage; correct spelling.
2. that part of grammar that treats of letters and spelling.
3. a method of spelling. —orthographer, *n.* —orthographic, *adj.*

phonography any phonetic spelling, writing, or shorthand system. —phonographer, phonographist, *n.* —phonographic, phonographical, *adj.*

384. SPIRITS and SPIRITUALISM
See also 182. GHOSTS; 285. MYSTICISM; 379. SOUL.

clairvoyance the ability to see, in a trance, into the world beyond the perception of the normal senses, especially with the ability to predict future events. —clairvoyant, *n.*, *adj.*

fluidism the belief in the existence of an invisible "fluidic" body corresponding to one's physical body. —fluidist, *n.*

hyperphysics the study of supernatural phenomena. —hyperphysical, *adj.*

mediumism 1. the belief that another person can serve as an instrument through which another personality or supernatural agency can communicate.
2. the art or practice of such a spiritualistic medium. —mediumistic, *adj.*

metapsychosis interaction or communication between minds without the intervention of any known physical agency or other known medium.

pneumatology 1. *Theology.* the belief in intermediary spirits between men and God, as angels.
2. the doctrine or theory of spiritual beings. —pneumatologist, *n.*

psychography 1. the reception of written spirit messages through a medium; spirit writing.
2. the production of images of spirits on film without the use of a camera, believed to be caused by spiritualistic forces. —psychographic, *adj.*

psychomancy communication between souls or with the spirit world. —psychomantic, *adj.*

spiritism spiritualism.

spiritualism 1. the belief that the dead survive as spirits that can communicate with the living, especially through a medium, a person particularly susceptible to their influence.
2. the practices or phenomena associated with this belief. Also spiritism. —spiritualist, *n.* —spiritualistic, *adj.* —supranatural, supranaturalistic, *adj.*

telegnosis clairvoyance or other occult or supernatural knowledge.

typtology *Rare.* the theory that departed souls communicate with the living by tapping. —typtologist, *n.* —typtological, *adj.*

Zemeism the belief in Zemis, supernatural beings known to the West Indian Tainos.

385. STONES
See also 177. GEMS; 179. GEOLOGY.

dolmen a construction consisting of two or more upright stones with a third on top, regarded by archaeologists as an ancient tomb or monument.

eolith a stone tool, as one used in the early Stone Age. —eolithic, *adj.*

lapidification the process of turning to stone. Also called **petrifaction, petrification.**

lithoidolatry the worship of rocks and stones. —lithoidolater, *n.* —lithoidolatrous, *adj.*

lithomancy a form of divination involving rocks or stones.

macrolith a tool made of stone, usually about 12 inches long.

megalith a stone of great size, as found in the monuments and constructions of ancient, particularly prehistoric, peoples. —megalithic, *adj.*

menhir an upright, monumental stone, as a cromlech, standing by itself or in a group or circle with others.

monolith a single large block of stone used in architecture or sculpture. —monolithic, *adj.*

neolith a stone artifact from the Neolithic (Stone) Age.

otolith a stonelike concretion in the inner ear of some vertebrates, as the whale.

pessomancy a form of divination involving pebbles. Also called **psephology.**

petrification, petrifaction lapidification.

petroglyphy the study of drawings or carvings made on rocks by a member of a prehistoric or primitive people. Also called **petrography.** —petroglyph, *n.* —petroglyphic, *adj.*

sabulosity the quality or condition of being sandy or gritty, as a stone. —sabulous, *adj.*

386. STRENGTH and WEAKNESS
See also 154. FATIGUE.

analepsis, analepsy *Obsolete.* recovery of strength after an illness. See also 168. FOOD and NUTRITION.

armipotence *Rare.* strength in battle.

asthenia *Medicine.* any of several conditions characterized by lack or loss of strength and energy, as neurasthenia, myasthenia, or somasthenia. —asthenic, *adj.*

equipollence, equipollency equalness of force, validity, etc. —equipollent, *adj.* See also 250. LOGIC.

hypopotencia, hypopotency *Medicine.* a condition of diminished power, especially of diminished electrical activity of the cerebral cortex.

hyposthenia a condition of abnormal weakness or loss of strength. —**hyposthenic**, *adj.*

impotency 1. a condition of reduced or absent power; weakness.
2. a complete failure of sexual power, especially in the male. Also called impotence, impotentness. —**impotent**, *adj.*

invalescence *Obsolete.* a state of good health; strength.

invertebracy the state or quality of being invertebrate or without a backbone, as certain organisms, animals, etc.; hence, spinelessness; exhibiting a lack of strength of character. —**invertebrate**, *adj.*

lability the susceptibility to error or lapses of any kind, as a human failing. —**labile**, *adj.*

milksopism 1. the state or quality of being a weak and ineffectual person.
2. behavior or attitudes typical of a milksop.

myoatrophy atrophy or wasting away of the muscles.

omnipotence the state or quality of being infinite in power, authority, or might. —**omnipotent**, *adj.*

sthenia strength of body; vital force. —**sthenic**, *adj.*

tonicity the state or quality of having good muscular tone or tension. —**tonic**, *adj.*

387. SUN
See also 25. ASTRONOMY; 85. CLIMATE; 100. COSMOLOGY;
143. EQUATOR; 245. LIGHT; 318. PLANETS; 417. WEATHER.

celidography *Archaic.* a description of the surface markings on a planet or the spots on the sun.

coronagraphy the observation of the corona of the sun by use of a telescope modified to simulate an eclipse. —**coronagraphic**, *adj.*

heliodon an instrument used in astronomy to show the apparent movement of the sun.

heliography 1. the measurement of the duration and intensity of sunlight.
2. the system or process of signaling by reflecting the sun's rays in a mirror.
3. an early photographic process involving coated metal plates exposed to sunlight. —**heliographer**, *n.* —**heliographic, heliographical**, *adj.*

heliolatry the worship of the sun. —**heliolator**, *n.*

heliology *Archaic.* the science of the sun. —**heliologist**, *n.*

heliomania an abnormal love of the sun.

heliophobia 1. an abnormal fear of sunlight.
2. an avoidance of sunlight.

helioseismology the study of motions of the solar surface.

heliotherapy a method of treating illness by exposure to the rays of the sun.

pyrheliometer an instrument for measuring the intensity of the sun's radiation. —pyrheliometric, *adj.*

radiometer an instrument for measuring the intensity of radiant energy, composed of vanes which rotate at speeds proportionate to the intensity of the energy source. —radiometric, *adj.*

radiometry the measurement of radiant energy by means of a radiometer. —radiometric, *adj.*

radiophony the transformation of radiant energy into sound.

siriasis 1. sunstroke.
    2. *Obsolete.* a sun bath or exposure to the sun for curative purposes.

solarism 1. the explanation of myths by reference to the sun or the personification of the sun, as the hero as sun-figure.
    2. an overreliance on this method of interpretation. —solarist, *n.*

solarium a room designed and situated so as to receive the maximum amount of sunlight.

388. SURGERY
See also 266. MEDICAL SPECIALTIES.

ablation *Medicine.* removal of part of the body by surgery.

apocope excision or amputation.

cauterism *Obsolete.* cautery.

cautery the act of cauterization, or burning away of dead tissue.

centesis a surgical perforation or puncture.

chirurgery *Archaic.* surgery.

comminution the breaking of a bone into small pieces. See also 52. BONES.

craniotome a surgical instrument for opening a hole in the skull.

cryosurgery a surgical technique using freezing to destroy tissue.

dermatoplasty any form of plastic surgery of the skin, as skin grafts.

elytroplasty surgery of the vagina.

neoplasty repair or restoration of part of the body by plastic surgery.

osteoplasty the surgical practice of bone-grafting.

osteotome a serrated instrument for bone surgery.

osteotomy 1. the dissection or anatomy of bones.
    2. the cutting of bones as part of a surgical operation. —osteotomist, *n.*

prosthetics the branch of surgery dealing with the replacement of missing limbs or organs with artificial substitutes. —prosthetic, *adj.*

tomomania an obsession with surgery.

traumatonesis the process of suture.

vasectomy surgical excision of part of the vas deferens, the duct which carries sperm from the testes, performed as a form of male contraception.

zooplasty the process of surgically grafting tissue from a lower animal onto the human body. —**zooplastic,** *adj.*

389. SYMMETRY
See also 170. FORM.

asymmetry the quality or condition of lacking symmetry. —**asymmetrical, asymmetric,** *adj.*

bisymmetry *Botany.* the condition of having two planes of symmetry at right angles to one another. —**bisymmetric, bisymmetrical,** *adj.*

monosymmetry 1. the state exhibited by a crystal, having three unequal axes with one oblique intersection; the state of being monoclinic. See also 44. BIOLOGY.
2. *Biology.* the state of being zygomorphic, or bilaterally symmetric, or divisible into symmetrical halves by one plane only. See also zygomorphism. See also PHYSICS. —**monosymmetric, monosymmetrical,** *adj.*

symmetromania a mania for symmetry.

symmetrophobia an abnormal fear or dislike of symmetry.

T

390. TEETH
See also 14. ANATOMY; 51. BODY, HUMAN.

acrodontism the condition of having teeth without roots attached to the alveolar ridge of the jaws, as in certain animals. —acrodont, *adj.*

bruxism the habit of purposelessly grinding one's teeth, especially during sleep. Also called **bruxomania.**

cariosity the condition of being decayed or carious, especially with regard to teeth.

dedentition the shedding of teeth.

dentition the production or cutting of teeth; teething. Also called **odontogeny.**

dentology odontology.

endodontics, endodontia the branch of dentistry concerned with diseases of the dental pulp and removal of the dental pulp, the nerve and other tissue of the pulp cavity; root canal therapy. Also **endodontology.** —endodontist, *n.*

endodontology endodontics.

exodontia the branch of dentistry concerned with the extraction of teeth. —exodontist, *n.*

gomphiasis a condition of the teeth in which they become loose, especially the molars.

odontogeny dentition. —odontogenic, *adj.*

odontography a treatise describing or giving the history of teeth. —odontographic, *adj.*

odontology 1. the science that studies teeth and their surrounding tissues, especially the prevention and cure of their diseases.
2. dentistry. Also called **dentology.** —odontologist, *n.* —odontological, *adj.*

odontophobia an abnormal fear of teeth, especially of animal teeth.

orthodontics, orthodontia the branch of dentistry that studies the prevention and correction of irregular teeth. —orthodontist, *n.* —orthodontic, *adj.*

periodontics, periodontia the branch of dentistry that studies and treats disease of the bone, connecting tissue, and gum surrounding a tooth. —periodontist, *n.* —periodontic, *adj.*

prophylactodontics, prophylactodontia preventive dentistry. —prophylactodontist, *n.* —prophylactodontic, *adj.*

prosthodontia the branch of dentistry concerned with the replacement of missing teeth with dentures, bridges, etc. —prosthodontist, *n.*

ulatrophia, ulatrophy a shrinking or wasting away of the gums.

391. THEFT
See also 103. CRIME.

abaction the stealing of whole herds of cattle, as contrasted with a few head. —abactor, *n.*

asportation unlawful removal of goods from where they are deposited or stored.

banditry the practice of being a bandit.

bibliokleptomania 1. a kleptomania specializing in books.
2. the motivations of a biblioklept. —bibliokleptomaniac, *n.*

brigandism the practice of pillage, often destructive, usually practiced by a band of robbers. Also **brigandage.** —brigand, *n.* —brigandish, *adj.*

dacoity murder and robbery committed by dacoits, a class of criminals in India and Burma.

despoliation a despoiling; an act of robbery on a large scale; pillage.

direption *Obsolete.* pillage; the act of plundering.

embezzlement the misappropriation of funds that have been entrusted to one for care or management. Also called **peculation.** —embezzler, *n.*

excoriation *Obsolete.* the act of stripping of possessions wrongfully and by force; spoliation or robbery.

harpaxophobia an abnormal fear of robbers.

kleptomania, cleptomania *Psychology.* an irresistible impulse to steal, especially when the thief can afford to pay. —kleptomaniac, *n.*

kleptophobia, cleptophobia an abnormal fear of thieves or of loss through thievery.

ladronism 1. *SW. U.S.* an act of thievery.
2. *Scots Dialect.* blackguardism and roguery. —ladrone, ladron, *n.*

peculation embezzlement. —peculator, *n.*

pilferage 1. petty stealing or pilfering.
2. the articles stolen in pilfering.

pillage 1. the act of plundering or large scale robbery, usually accompanied by violence as in wartime.
2. plundered property; booty.

piracy the act of robbery on the high seas. See also 366. SHIPS. —**pirate**, *n.* —**piratic, piratical,** *adj.*

plagiarism 1. the verbatim copying or imitation of the language, ideas, or thoughts of another author and representing them as one's own original work.
2. the material so appropriated. Also **plagiary**. —**plagiarist**, *n.* —**plagiaristic**, *adj.*

predation the act or process of pillaging or plundering.

rapacity the state or quality of being excessively greedy or given to theft. —**rapacious**, *adj.*

rapine the act of pillage or plundering.

spoliation the process of robbing or plundering, especially in time of war and on a large scale. See also 81. CHURCH; 366. SHIPS.

thievery 1. the act or practice of stealing or thieving.
2. *Rare.* the property stolen.

392. THEOLOGY
See also 43. BIBLE; 59. BUDDHISM; 69. CATHOLICISM;
80. CHRISTIANITY; 135. EASTERN ORTHODOXY; 151. FAITH; 183. GOD
and GODS; 203. HELL; 205. HERESY; 227. ISLAM; 231. JUDAISM;
332. PROTESTANTISM; 349. RELIGION.

Albertist a student or supporter of the theological ideas of Albertus Magnus, 13th-century German Scholastic philosopher.

annihilationism the theological doctrine that states that the wicked have no afterlife. —**annihilationist**, *n.*

antilapsarianism the doctrine that denies the fall of man. —**antilapsarian**, *n.*

antinomianism the belief that Christians are freed from the moral law by the virtue of God's grace. —**antinomian**, *n., adj.*

apologetics the study of the methods and content of defenses or proofs of Christianity. —**apologetical**, *adj.*

Augustinianism 1. the doctrines and ideas of St. Augustine, 5th-century archbishop of Hippo, and the religious rule developed by him.
2. the support of his doctrines.
3. adherence to his religious rule. —**Augustinian**, *n., adj.*

chiliasm the belief that Christ will return to earth in visible form and establish a kingdom to last 1000 years, after which the world will come to an end. Also called **millenarianism**. —**chiliast**, *n.* —**chiliastic**, *adj.*

confessionalism an advocacy of the maintenance of a confession of faith as a prerequisite to membership in a religious group. —**confessionalian**, *n., adj.*

consubstantiation the doctrine that the substance of the body and blood of Christ coexist in and with the substance of the bread and wine of the Eucharist. Cf. **receptionism, transubstantiation, virtualism.**

Erastianism the doctrine stating that in ecclesiastical affairs the state rules over the church. —**Erastian,** *n., adj.*

eschatology any set of doctrines concerning final matters, as death, the judgment, afterlife, etc. —**eschatological,** *adj.* —**eschatologist,** *n.*

Hutchinsonianism 1. the theories of John Hutchinson, an 18th-century Yorkshireman, who disputed Newton's theory of gravitation and maintained that a system of natural science was to be found in the Old Testament.
2. the tenets of the followers of Mrs. Anne Hutchinson, an antinomian who lived in the early days of the Massachusetts Colony. —**Hutchinsonian,** *adj.*

hypostasis 1. the unique nature of the Godhead and hence the Holy Trinity.
2. any of the three parts of the Holy Trinity.
3. the personality of Christ separate from his dual nature, human and divine. —**hypostatic, hypostatical,** *adj.*

impanation the theological doctrine that the body and blood of Christ are present in the bread and wine after they are consecrated.

Jehovist 1. *Obsolete.* a person who believes that the vowel-marks on the word *Jehovah* in Hebrew represent the actual vowels of the word.
2. the name given to the author(s) of the parts of the Hexateuch in which the sacred name is written *Jehovah,* instead of *Elohim.* —**Jehovistic,** *adj.*

latria worship of the highest order that can be offered only to God.

Majorism the doctrines of Georg Major, a German theologian who believed that good works, being a necessary product of Christian faith, are necessary for salvation. —**Majorist,** *n., adj.*

millenarianism chiliasm.

neologism neology.

neology 1. the introduction of new, especially rationalistic, views or doctrines in theology.
2. such a view or doctrine. Also **neologism.** See also **236. LANGUAGE.** —**neologist,** *n.*

Neo-Scholasticism the 19th-century movement by Catholic scholars to reinstitute the doctrines of the Schoolmen in their teachings. —**Neo-Scholastic,** *adj.*

Occamism 1. the precepts and ideas of William of Occam, 14th-century English Scholastic.
2. support of his precepts. —**Occamist, Occamite,** *n.* —**Occamistic,** *adj.*

Origenism 1. the doctrines and precepts of Origen of Alexandria, 3rd-century Christian theologian and teacher.
2. adherence to his doctrines. —Origenist, *n*. —Origenian, Origenistic, *adj*.

pantheology 1. *Obsolete*. all that is contained in theology.
2. a comprehensive, synthetic theology that covers all gods and religious systems. —pantheologist, *n*. —pantheologic, pantheological, *adj*.

patrology 1. Also **patristics**. the branch of theology that studies the teachings of the early church fathers.
2. a collection of the writings of the early church fathers. —patrologist, *n*. —patrologic, patrological, *adj*.

ponerology a branch of theology that studies the doctrine of evil. See also 146. EVIL.

pre-Adamitism the belief that a race of men existed before Adam. —pre-Adamite, *n*. —pre-Adamitic, *adj*.

predestinarianism a belief in predestination. —predestinarian, *n*., *adj*.

predestination 1. the action of God in foreordaining from eternity whatever comes to pass.
2. the doctrine that God chooses those who are to come to salvatior.

premillennialism the belief that the second coming of Christ will usher in the millennium. —premillennialist, *n*. —premillennian, *adj*.

receptionism the doctrine that in the communion service the body and blood of Christ are received but the bread and wine remain unchanged. Cf. consubstantiation, transubstantiation, virtualism. —receptionist, *n*.

Scholasticism the doctrines of the schoolmen; the system of theological and philosophical instruction of the Middle Ages, based chiefly upon the authority of the church fathers and on Aristotle and his commentators. —Scholastic, *n*., *adj*.

semi-Arianism the belief of a sect that arose in the 4th century that the substances of the Father and Son were similar but nonetheless different. —semi-Arian, *n*., *adj*.

solifidianism the theological doctrine that faith insures salvation, irrespective of good works. —solifidian, *n*.

soteriology, soterialogy the doctrine concerning the means and possibility of salvation. —soteriological, soterialogical, *adj*.

stercoranism the belief that the bread and wine consecrated in the Eucharist are subject to natural processes, as decay. —stercorarian, stercoranist, *adj*.

tartarology a doctrine concerning hell and punishment in the afterlife.

theologaster *Rare*. a quack or spurious theologian; a charlatan of theology.

theologism 1. any theological speculation.
2. the assumption that other disciplines, as philosophy or science, are inferior to theology.

transubstantiation the doctrine that the consecrated elements of the communion only appear as bread and wine, for they have been converted into the whole substance of the body and blood of Christ. Cf. **consubstantiation, receptionism, virtualism.** —**transubstantiationalist,** *n.*

trichotomy division into three parts, especially the theological division of man's nature into the body, the soul, and the spirit. —**trichotomic, trichotomous,** *adj.*

virtualism the doctrine attributed to Calvin and other reformers that the bread and wine of the communion remain unchanged but are the vehicle through which the spiritual body and blood of Christ are received by the communicant. Cf. **consubstantiation, receptionism, transabstantiation.**

393. THINKING
See also 21. ARGUMENTATION; 216. IDEAS; 240. LEARNING;
250. LOGIC; 300. OPINION; 312. PHILOSOPHY; 338. QUESTIONING;
405. UNDERSTANDING.

analysis the process of separating a whole into its parts to discover their function, relationship, etc. See also 250. LOGIC; 334. PSYCHOLOGY.

asemia loss or absence of the capacity to express thoughts or ideas by written, spoken, or gesticulated means.

cogitation 1. the act of meditation or contemplation.
2. the faculty of thinking.
3. a thought; a design or plan. —**cogitator,** *n.* —**cogitative,** *adj.*

dianoetic relating to the operation of the mind through logical rather than intuitive thought processes; intellectual activity.

dianoia the capacity for, process of, or result of discursive thinking. —**dianoetic,** *adj.*

divagation the act of digressing; wandering off the subject.

eduction the process of deducing or inferring. —**eductive,** *adj.*

escapism 1. the state of having wandering and imaginative thoughts in order to escape from reality. —**escapist,** *n., adj.*
2. the practice of engaging in activities that enable one to avoid having to deal with reality, as the persistent attendance at science-fiction films, reading of fantasy literature, etc.

factualism 1. excessive concern for facts.
2. a theory or belief relying heavily on fact. —**factualist,** *n.* —**factualistic,** *adj.*

free association *Psychoanalysis*. the unhampered and uncensored expression of ideas, impressions, etc., passing through the mind of the patient, used to permit access to the processes of the unconscious.

hyponoia, hyponea a state of dulled mental activity or decrease in the function of thought. Also called **hypopsychosis.**

hypopsychosis hyponoia.

ideation the process of forming ideas. —**ideational,** *adj.*

illation the process of inferring or deducing; also, that which is inferred or deduced. —**illative,** *adj.*

imponderabilia things or matters beyond measure or comprehension.

indagation the process of searching or inquiring; an investigation, especially of an intellectual nature. —**indagator,** *n.* —**indagative,** *adj.*

insularism the state of being narrow-minded.

intellection 1. the exercise or use of the intellect.
2. a particular act or process of the intellect.

noesis 1. understanding solely through the intellect.
2. thinking. —**noetic,** *adj.*

nomology the science of the laws of the mind. —**nomologist,** *n.* —**nomological,** *adj.*

obfuscation the process of darkening or obscuring so as to hinder ready analysis.

Pelmanism a system of mental development exercises.

perpension *Obsolete*. consideration; careful thought over a matter.

philosphy 1. the rational inquiry into the principles and truths of being, nature, knowledge, conduct, etc.
2. an individual set or system of principles and beliefs. —**philosopher,** *n.* —**philosophic, philosophical,** *adj.*

phronemomania a mania for thinking.

phronemophobia an abnormal fear of thinking.

quandary a state of doubt or uncertainty, especially with regard to the choice of alternatives; a dilemma.

ratiocination the process of logical reasoning or rational thought. —**ratiocinative,** *adj.*

reification the conversion of an abstract concept into something concrete; a viewing of the abstract as concrete.

rumination the act of pondering or meditating. —**ruminator,** *n.* —**ruminative,** *adj.*

speculation 1. the contemplation or consideration of some subject.
   2. an instance of such activity.
   3. a conclusion or opinion reached by such activity.
   4. a conjecture or surmise; a guess. —speculator, n. —speculative, adj.

speculativism the excessive use of speculation.

synthesis the process of deductive reasoning, as from cause to effect, from the simple elements to the complex whole, etc. See also 230. JOINING. —synthesist, n. —synthetic, synthetical, adj.

syntheticism the principles or practice of synthesis or synthetic methods or techniques.

tachyphrenia abnormally rapid mental activity.

witcraft Rare. the art of reasoning; logic.

394. THUNDER
See also 27. ATMOSPHERE; 87. CLOUDS; 246. LIGHTNING; 345. RAIN; 417. WEATHER.

brontograph 1. an instrument for recording thunderstorms.
   2. the record thus produced. Also called brontometer.

brontology Rare. a treatise on thunder.

brontometer brontograph.

brontophobia an abnormal fear of thunder and thunderstorms. Also tonitrophobia.

ceraunomancy keraunomancy.

fulmination thundering; the sound of thunder.

keraunomancy, ceraunomancy a form of divination involving the interpretation of an omen communicated by thunder.

keraunoscopia, keraunoscopy a form of divination involving the observation of thunder.

tonitrophobia brontophobia.

395. TIGHTROPE WALKING
See also 2. ACROBATICS.

aerialist a person who performs aerial acrobatics, as a trapeze artist, tightrope walker, stunt flier, etc.

funambulism the art or skill of tightrope walking. —funambulist, n.

396. TIME

See also 18. ANTIQUITY; 174. FUTURE; 308. PAST.

anachronism 1. a person or a thing remaining or appearing after its own time period; archaism.
2. an error in chronology. Also called antichronism. —anachronistic, anachronistical, anachronous, *adj.*

asynchronism the absence of concurrent time. Cf. synchronism. —asynchronic, *adj.* —asynchrony, *n.*

chronology 1. the science of arranging time in fixed periods for the purpose of dating events accurately and arranging them in order of occurrence.
2. a reference book organized according to the dates of past events. —chronologer, chronologist, *n.* —chronological, *adj.*

chronometry 1. the art of measuring time accurately.
2. the measurement of time by periods or divisions. —chronometric, chronometrical, *adj.*

chronophobia an abnormal discomfort concerning time.

chronoscope an instrument for accurate measurement of very short periods of time, as the time of trajectory of missiles.

chronoscopy accurate measurement of short intervals of time by means of a chronoscope. —chronoscopic, *adj.*

clepsydra an instrument for measuring time by the controlled flow of water or mercury through a small opening.

coetaneity coevalneity. —coetaneous, *adj.*

coeternity the state of eternal coexistence; eternal coexistence with another eternal entity. —coeternal, *adj.*

coevalneity the state or quality of being alike in age or duration; contemporaneity. Also called coetaneity. —coeval, *adj.*

cunctation the practice or habit of delay or tardiness; procrastination. —cunctator, *n.* —cunctatious, cunctatory, *adj.*

dendrochronology the science of fixing dates in the past by the study of growth rings in trees. —dendrochronologist, *n.* —dendrochronological, *adj.*

diachronism, diachrony the comparative study of a development based on its history. —diachronic, diachronistic, diachronistical, *adj.*

diuturnity *Rare.* the quality of long duration in time; length of time. —diuturnal, *adj.*

geochronology the chronology of the earth as induced from geologic data. —geochronologist, *n.* —geochronologic, geochronological, *adj.*

glottochronology the study of two or more related but distinct languages in order to determine when they separated, by examining the lexicon they share and those parts of it that have been replaced. —**glottochronologist,** *n.* —**glottochronological,** *adj.*

gnomonics the art or science of constructing dials, as sundials, which show the time of day by the shadow of the gnomon, a pin or triangle raised above the surface of the dial.

gnomonology a treatise or other work on the subject of gnomics.

horologe any instrument or device for telling time, especially a sundial and early forms of the clock.

horologiography 1. the description of watches and clocks.
2. the art of making timepieces. —**horologiographer, horologiographian,** *n.* —**horologiographic,** *adj.*

horology the art or science of making timepieces or of measuring time. —**horologist,** *n.* —**horological,** *adj.*

horometer an instrument for measuring time.

horometry the art or science of measuring time. —**horometrical,** *adj.*

immediatism immediateness; the quality or condition of being immediate.

intempestivity *Obsolete.* the state or condition of being untimely. —**intempestive,** *adj.*

isochronism 1. the characteristic of having a uniform period of vibration.
2. the condition of occurring at the same time as another event. —**isochronic,** *adj.* —**isochrony,** *n.*

menology a calendar of months.

mensality the state or condition of occurring monthly.

metachronism a chronological error in which an event is assigned a date after its real one. Cf. **parachronism.** —**metachronic,** *adj.*

microchronometer an instrument for measuring extremely small time intervals. —**microchronometric,** *adj.*

obsolescence the process or condition of going out of date or being no longer in use. —**obsolescent,** *adj.*

parachronism the dating of an event as later than its actual occurrence. Cf. **prochronism.** —**parachronic,** *adj.*

phenology the study of natural phenomena that occur periodically, as migration or blossoming, and their relation to climate and changes of season. —**phenologist,** *n.* —**phenological,** *adj.*

photochronograph 1. a camera for recording motion by a series of photographs taken at brief intervals.
2. the photograph so produced.

3. a camera that records the exact time of the event it is photographing by exposing a moving sensitized plate to the tracing of a thin beam of light synchronized with the event.

prevenance, prevenience the act or state of preceding or coming before. —prevenient, *adj.*

prochronism the dating of an event as earlier than its actual occurrence. Cf. parachronism. —prochronic, *adj.*

quotiety the proportionate frequency at which an event takes place. See also 295. NUMBERS.

sempiternity the state or quality of being eternal, without beginning or end. —sempiternal, *adj.*

synchronism, synchrony a coincidence in time; simultaneity. Cf. asynchronism. —synchronistic, synchronistical, *adj.*

synchronology an arrangement of events by date, grouping together all those of the same date; a comparative chronology. —synchronological, *adj.*

transience, transiency the state or quality of passing with time or being ephemeral or fleeting. —transient, *adj.*

397. TOUCH
See also 309. PERCEPTION.

haptophobia, haphophobia an abnormal fear of touching or being touched. Also called thixophobia.

thigmotaxis involuntary response or reaction to the touch of outside objects or bodies, as in motile cells. —thigmotactic, *adj.*

thixophobia haptophobia.

398. TRADE
See also 131. DUES and PAYMENT; 137. ECONOMICS; 160. FINANCE; 331. PROPERTY and OWNERSHIP.

cabotage the act of navigating or trading along a coast.

chreotechnics *Rare.* useful arts, as agriculture, commerce, and manufacturing.

coemption *Obsolete.* the purchase of all of a given commodity in order to control its price. —coemptive, *adj.*

duopoly the market condition that exists when there are only two sellers. —duopolist, *n.* —duopolistic, *adj.*

duopsony the market condition that exists when there are only two buyers. —duopsonistic, *adj.*

emption 1. *Rare.* the act of purchasing.
2. *Obsolete.* the thing purchased. —emptional, *adj.*

emptor *Law*. a buyer.

merchantry 1. merchants collectively.
2. the business of commerce or trade.

monopolism the practices and system of a monopoly. —monopolist, *n*. —monopolistic, *adj*.

monopoly an exclusive control of a commodity or service in a particular market, or a control that makes possible the manipulation of prices. —monopolist, *n*. —monopolistic, *adj*.

monopsony the market condition that exists when only one buyer will purchase the products of a number of sellers. —monopsonist, *n*. —monopsonistic, *adj*.

multiopoly the condition of free enterprise, without restriction as to the number of sellers of a given product.

multiopsony a market condition where no restriction on the number of buyers exists. —multiopsonist, *n*. —multiopsonistic, *adj*.

oligopoly the market condition that exists when there are few sellers. —oligopolistic, *adj*.

oligopsony a market condition in which there are few buyers. —oligopsonist, *n*. —oligopsonistic, *adj*.

paternalism fatherlike control over subordinates or employees in business. —paternalist, *n*. —paternalistic, *adj*.

preferentialism the policy of giving preferential treatment in international trade. —preferentialist, *n*.

399. TRAVEL
See also 169. FOREIGNERS; 178. GEOGRAPHY; 257. MAPS;
344. RAILROADS; 347. RECREATION; 366. SHIPS; 408. VEHICLES;
412. WALKING.

dromomania a mania for travel.

ecdemiomania a mania for wandering.

gephyromania a mania for crossing bridges.

gephyrophobia an abnormal fear of crossing bridges.

hodomania an abnormal love of travel.

hodophobia an abnormal fear or dislike of travel.

itinerancy, itineracy 1. the act or state of traveling from place to place.
2. persons, collectively, whose occupation obliges them to travel constantly.
3. such an occupation. —itinerant, *n.*, *adj*.

naupathia seasickness.

oberration *Obsolete*. the act of wandering about.

peregrination travel from place to place, especially on foot and with the suggestion of a roundabout route.

pererration *Obsolete.* the act of wandering or rambling around and about.

tourism 1. the activitiy of traveling for pleasure, to see sights, for recreation etc.
2. the business founded upon this activity. —tourist, *n.*, *adj.*

waftage *Archaic.* the act of wafting or being wafted; travel or conveyance by wafting.

400. TREASON
See also 103. CRIME.

collaborationism an act of cooperating with an invader of one's country. —collaborationist, *n.*

perfidy 1. breach of trust, especially treachery or treason.
2. an act or instance of this. —perfidious, *adj.*

recreancy cowardice, treason, or disloyalty. —recreant, *n.*, *adj.*

401. TREES
See also 241. LEAVES; 319. PLANTS; 425. WOOD.

arboretum a place where trees are grown for scientific observation, for pleasure, or both.

arboriculture the cultivation of trees and shrubs for scientific, commercial, or other purposes. —arboriculturist, *n.*

citriculture the cultivation of citrus fruits, as lemons, oranges, etc. —citriculturist, *n.*

decortication the process of stripping off or removing the cortex or outer layer.

dendrochronology the study of annual rings in trees to determine their age, climatic and other conditions and changes that might have affected them, etc. —dendrochronologist, *n.* —dendrochronological, *adj.*

dendrography the science of tree description. —dendrographic, dendrographical, *adj.*

dendrolatry the veneration of trees. —dendrolatrous, *adj.*

dendrology the branch of botany that studies trees. —dendrologist, *n.* —dendrologic, dendrological, *adj.*

forestation 1. the planting of forests.
2. the state of being covered with trees, as of a tract of land.

interlucation *Obsolete.* the act or process of cutting away branches of trees to let light through.

nemophily a fondness or liking for forests, woods, or woodland scenery. —nemophilist, *n*. —nemophilous, *adj*.

pomiculture the cultivation of fruit and fruit trees.

reforestation the process of planting new trees in areas where they have been removed by cutting or destroyed by fire, disease, etc.

silviculture, sylviculture the cultivation of forest trees; forestry. —silviculturist, sylviculturist, *n*.

stumpage 1. standing timber, with special reference to its value in money.
2. the right to cut such timber and its value on another's land.

xyloma a tumor or woodlike substance on a tree or plant.

402. TRUTH and ERROR
See also 250. LOGIC.

alethiology the branch of logic dealing with truth and error. —alethiologist, *n*. —alethiological, *adj*.

errancy 1. the condition of being in error.
2. the tendency to be in error or the capacity for being in error; fallibility.

falsism anything that is patently false or untrue; a fallacy.

Plinyism an assertion of doubtful truth or accuracy, as with some statements in Pliny's *Natural History*.

theopneusty the force or process of divine inspiration; the power by which the Holy Spirit reveals truth to men. —theopneustic, theopneusted, *adj*.

truism a self-evident, obvious truth. —truistic, truistical, *adj*.

403. TUNING
See also 284. MUSIC.

tonology the science of tones or of speech intonations, proceeding historically and comparatively. —tonological, *adj*.

tonometer an instrument for determining the pitch of a tone, as a tuning fork or graduated set of tuning forks. —tonometric, *adj*.

tonometry the art or science of measuring tones, especially with a tonometer. —tonometrist, *n*. —tonometric, *adj*.

404. TURKEY

Kemalism 1. the political doctrines and achievements of Kemal Ataturk (1881–1938), Turkish general and statesman.
2. support of or adherence to Ataturk. —Kemalist, *n*., *adj*.

Turkomania an obsession with Turkey and things Turkish.

U

405. UNDERSTANDING

See also 233. KNOWLEDGE; 240. LEARNING; 309. PERCEPTION; 312. PHILOSOPHY; 393. THINKING.

dysphasia an impaired state of the power of speech or of the ability to comprehend language, caused by injury to the brain.

empathy the power of entering into another's personality and imaginatively experiencing his feelings. —empathic, *adj.*

epexegesis an additional explanation; the use of more words to clarify further. —epexegetic, epexegetical, *adj.*

noology the science of intuition and reason as phenomena of the mind. —noological, *adj.*

406. UTOPIA

See also 376. SOCIETY.

dystopia an imaginary place where the conditions and quality of life are unpleasant. The opposite of Utopia.

Icarianism the precepts and opinions of Etienne Cabet and his followers, who settled communistic utopias in the U.S. during the 19th cent., as Nauvoo, Illinois (1849). —Icarian, *n., adj.*

kakotopia a state in which the worst possible conditions exist in government, society, law, etc. Cf. Utopia.

Utopia 1. name of an imaginary island; subject and title of a book by Sir Thomas More, that had a perfect political and social system.
2. (*l.c.*) any ideal place or situation.

utopianism 1. the views and habits of mind of a visionary or idealist, sometimes beyond realization.
2. impracticable schemes of political and social reform. —utopian, utopianist, utopist, *n., adj.*

V

407. VALUES
See also 145. ETHICS; 312. PHILOSOPHY.

axiology *Philosophy.* the study of values, as those of aesthetics, ethics, or religion. —axiologist, *n.* —axiological, *adj.*

floccinaucinihilipilification the categorizing of something as valueless trivia.

timology the theory or doctrine of values.

408. VEHICLES
See also 344. RAILROADS; 366. SHIPS; 399. TRAVEL.

amaxomania a mania for being in vehicles.

amaxophobia an abnormal fear of being in or riding in vehicles.

autonumerology the study of unusual and distinctive licence plate numbers.

delation *Obsolete.* carriage; the act of conveying.

ochophobia an abnormal fear of vehicles.

omnibology the study of motor buses.

telpherage, telferage a system of transportation in which cars or gondolas, usually powered by electricity, are suspended below wire cables.

409. VERSE
See also 236. LANGUAGE; 249. LITERATURE.

acrosticism the art or skill of writing a poem in which the lines or stanzas begin with letters of the alphabet in regular order or one in which the first, middle, or final letters of the line spell a word or a phrase. —acrostic, *n.*, *adj.*

Alexandrine an iambic hexameter, or iambic verse with six feet.

anapest a foot of three syllables, the first two short or unstressed, the third long or stressed. —anapestic, *adj.*

antibacchius 1. (in quantitative meter) two long syllables followed by a short.
2. (in accented meter) two stressed syllables followed by an unstressed. Cf. bacchius. —antibacchic, *adj.*

562

antistrophe the second of two metrically related sections in a poem. Cf. strophe. See also 127. DRAMA. —antistrophic, antistrophal, *adj.*

arsis the accented part of a foot of verse.

bacchius 1. (in quantitative meter) a short syllable followed by two long.
2. (in accented meter) an unstressed syllable followed by two stressed. Cf. antibacchius. —bacchic, *adj.*

bardism 1. the art or skill of one who composes and recites epic or heroic poetry, often to his own musical accompaniment.
2. membership in an ancient Celtic order of poets.

canto one of the main (larger) divisions in a long poem.

catalexis incompleteness of a foot, wherever it appears in a verse. —catalectic, *adj.*

dactyl a foot of three syllables, the first long or accented, the following two short or unaccented. —dactylist, *n.* —dactylic, *adj.*

diastole (in Greek and Latin verse) the lengthening of a short syllable. Cf. systole. —diastolic, *adj.*

dipody a double foot; a pair of similar feet comprising a metrical unit. —dipodic, *adj.*

distich a couplet or pair of verses or lines, usually read as a unit.

ecthlipsis (in Latin prosody) the elision of the last syllable of a word ending in *m* when the following word begins with a vowel.

heptameter a verse having seven metrical feet. —heptametrical, *adj.*

heptapody a verse having seven metrical feet; a heptameter. —heptapodic, *adj.*

hexameter a verse having six metrical feet. —hexametrical, *adj.*

hexapody a verse having six metrical feet; a hexameter. —hexapodous, *adj.*

iamb a foot of two syllables, the first short or unstressed, the second long or stressed. —iambic, *adj.*

ictus the stress or accent that indicates the rhythm of a verse or piece of music. See also 284. MUSIC.

lettrism a technique of poetic composition originated by Isidore Isou, characterized by strai.ṛe or meaningless arrangements of letters.

logaoedic a poem or verse composed of dactyls and trochees or anapests and iambs, resulting in a proselike rhythm. —logaoedic, *adj.*

lyricism the practice of writing verse in song form rather than narrative form to embody the poet's thoughts and emotions. Also lyrism. —lyricist, *n.* —lyrical, *adj.*

lyrism lyricism. —lyrist, *n.*

madrigal a lyric poem suitable for setting to music, usually with love as a theme. —madrigalist, *n.*

metricism 1. any of various theories and techniques of metrical composition. 2. the study of metrics. —metricist, *n.*

metrics 1. the science of meter. —metricist, *n.* 2. the art of composing metrical verse. —metrician, metrist, *n.*

metromania an abnormal compulsion for writing verse.

monopody a verse consisting of one foot. —monopodic, *adj.*

octonary a stanza of eight lines; an octave. —octonary, *adj.*

orthometry 1. the laws of versification. 2. the art or practice of applying these laws.

pentameter a verse of five metrical feet.

pentapody a line of verse containing five feet.

poesy 1. *Archaic.* poetry. 2. *Obsolete.* a poem.

poetastery poor or mediocre poetry.

poeticism the qualities of bad poetry: trite subject matter, banal or archaic and poetical language, easy rhymes, jingling rhythms, sentimentality, etc.; the standards of a poetaster.

poetics 1. *Lit. Crit.* the nature and laws of poetry. 2. the study of prosody. 3. a treatise on poetry. 4. (*cap.*) a treatise or collection of lecture notes on aesthetics composed by Aristotle.

proceleusmatic a metrical foot of four short syllables. —proceleusmatic, *adj.*

prosody 1. the science or study of poetic meters and versification. 2. a particular or distinctive system of metrics and versification, as that of Dylan Thomas. —prosodist, *n.* —prosodic, prosodical, *adj.*

pyrrhic a metrical foot composed of two short or unaccented syllables. —pyrrhic, *adj.*

rhapsodism the professional recitation of epic poems. —rhapsodist, *n.*

rhapsodomancy a form of divination involving verses.

rhopalism 1. the art or skill of writing verse in which each successive word in a line is longer by one syllable than the preceding word or in which each line of verse is longer by a syllable or a metrical foot than the preceding line. 2. an instance of rhopalic form. —rhopalist, *n.* —rhopalic, *adj.*

rhymester a poetaster or poet of little worth; a mere versifier.

scansion the analysis of verse into its metrical or rhythmic components.

spondee a foot of two syllables, both long or stressed. —spondiac, *adj.*

stanza a section of a poem containing a number of verses.

stich a line of a poem; verse.

stichomancy a form of divination involving lines of poetry or passages from books.

strophe the first of two metrically related sections in a poem. Cf. **antistrophe.** See also 127. DRAMA.

synonymous parallelism a term describing a couplet in which the second line repeats the idea or content of the first line, but in different terms, as by using different images, symbols, etc.

systole the shortening of a syllable that is naturally long. Cf. **diastole.** —systolic, *adj.*

tetrameter 1. a verse of four feet.
2. *Classical Prosody.* a verse consisting of four dipodies in trochaic, iambic, or anapestic meter. —tetrameter, *adj.*

tetrapody a verse of other measure having four metrical feet.

triadism the composition of poetic triads. —triadist, *n.*

tribrach a foot composed of three short syllables. —tribrachic, *adj.*

trimeter a verse having three metrical units.

triplet 1. a stanza of three verses.
2. any set of three verses. See also 284. MUSIC; 295. NUMBERS.

tripody a verse or measure of three metrical feet.

tristich a poem, strophe, or stanza of three lines. —tristichic, *adj.*

trochee a foot of two syllables, the first long or stressed, the second short or unstressed. —trochaic, *adj.*

truncation the omission of one or more unaccented syllables at the beginning or end of a verse. —truncated, *adj.*

410. VICTORY
See also 96. CONFLICT.

debellation *Obsolete.* the process of conquering or defeating; achieving victory.

paeanism celebration of victory with songs and clamor.

411. VOLCANOES
See also 179. GEOLOGY; 283. MOUNTAINS.

volcanism the phenomena connected with volcanoes and volcanic activity. Also vulcanism. —volcanist, *n.*

volcanology *Geology.* the scientific study of volcanoes and volcanic phenomena. Also vulcanology. —volcanologist, *n.* —volcanologic, volcanological, *adj.*

W

412. WALKING

See also 157. FEET and LEGS; 282. MOTION; 399. TRAVEL.

ambulomancy the practice of fortune-telling by walking.

bathmophobia an abnormal fear of walking.

claudication a limp or limping movement.

gyromancy a type of divination involving walking in a circle.

noctivagation the act of walking or wandering at night. —**noctivagant, noctivagous,** *adj.*

oberration *Obsolete.* the act of wandering about.

peregrination travel from place to place, especially on foot and with the suggestion of a roundabout route.

pererration *Obsolete.* the act of wandering or rambling around and about.

stasibasiphobia 1. an abnormal conviction that one cannot stand or walk. 2. an abnormal fear of attempting to do either.

413. WAR

See also 96. CONFLICT; 232. KILLING; 416. WEAPONRY.

angary the right of a nation at war to destroy the property of a neutral, subject to indemnification.

antiterrorism the techniques, policies, and training of special police who deal with terrorists, especially those who take hostages. —**antiterrorist,** *adj.*

armistice a temporary cessation of hostilities, by agreement between the belligerents, prior to the negotiation or signing of a peace treaty.

bellicism the advocacy of war. Cf. pacifism. —**bellicist,** *n.*

belligerence the state of being hostile or at war. —**belligerent,** *n., adj.*

copperheadism any expression of sympathy for the Confederate cause in the American Civil War. —**copperhead,** *n.*

demilitarization the process of demilitarization or removal of military activity or control from an area.

demobilization the process of being demobilized or mustered out of the military.

566

disarmament the reduction in size of military forces, by treaty, following defeat, etc. Also *Obsolete,* disarmature.

disarmature *Obsolete.* disarmament.

doveism, dovism the advocacy of peace or a conciliatory national attitude, especially on the part of a public official. Cf. hawkism. —dove, *n.* —doveish, *adj.*

gigantomachy 1. a war between giants, as in mythology.
2. war between large contestants, as major powers.

guerrillaism the practice and philosophy of guerrilla warfare.

hawkism the advocacy of war or a belligerent national attitude, especially on the part of a public official. Cf. doveism. —hawk, *n.* —hawkish, *adj.*

hostility 1. a feeling or state of antagonism.
2. an expression or act of war. —hostile, *adj.*

insurgence insurgency.

insurgency, insurgence 1. the state or condition of being in revolt or insurrection.
2. an uprising. —insurgent, *n., adj.*

irenicism an advocacy of peace and conciliation. —irenicist, *n.*

logistics the branch of military science concerned with the movement and supply of troops. —logistician, *n.*

martialism 1. an inclination to belligerency; bellicosity.
2. the qualities of a military existence. —martialist, *n.*

militancy 1. the state or condition of being combative or disposed to fight.
2. the active championing of a cause or belief. —militant, *n., adj.*

militarization the process of preparing for war; mobilization of troops or of an area.

monomachy, monomachia single combat, or a duel. —monomachist, *n.*

naumachia, naumachy 1. a mock sea fight, as in ancient Rome.
2. the flooded arena where such fights were conducted.

navalism the maintaining of naval interests. —navalist, *n.*

neutrality the state or position of being impartial or not allied with or committed to either party or viewpoint in a conflict, especially a war or armed conflict. —neutral, *adj.*

pacifism 1. an opposition to war or violence of any kind.
2. the principle or policy of establishing and maintaining universal peace.
3. nonresistance to aggression. Cf. bellicism. —pacifist, *n.* —pacifistic, *adj.*

pillage 1. the act of plundering or large scale robbery, usually accompanied by violence as in wartime.
2. plundered property; booty.

poliorcetics the art of siegecraft. —**poliorcetic,** *adj.*

sabotage destruction of or damage to equipment, installations, etc., in an industrial context, as in a labor dispute, or in a military context, as in the action of partisan or resistance movements. —**saboteur,** *n.*

siegecraft the science or craft of laying or carrying out sieges.

soldiery soldiership or military science or craft.

spoliation the process of robbing or plundering, especially in time of war and on a large scale. See also 81. CHURCH; 366. SHIPS.

stratography the art of directing an army. —**stratographer,** *n.*

tactician a person skilled in the art of tactics, in a military or other sense.

tactics 1. the art or science of disposing or managing military forces to best advantage against the enemy.
2. a skill or resource management in other contexts.

Titanomachy battle between Titans, referring to the unsuccessful revolt of the family of Iapetus against Zeus.

trierarchy an ancient Athenian policy allowing private citizens, as part of their civic duty, to fit out triremes for the defense of the city.

warcraft the science, art, or craft of war.

414. WATER
See also 36. BATHING; 107. DAMPNESS; 234. LAKES; 345. RAIN; 356. RIVERS; 360. SEA; 375. SNOW.

antlophobia an abnormal fear of floods.

aquiculture hydroponics. —**aquicultural,** *adj.*

atmology the science dealing with the behavior of water vapor. —**atmologist,** *n.* —**atmologic, atmological,** *adj.*

balneotherapy the treatment of illness or disease by bathing.

bletonism the skill or talent of water divining.

dehydration 1. the process of dehydrating or removing the water from a substance.
2. the state of being dehydrated.

deliquescence the property of a substance to attract and absorb moisture, especially from the air. Cf. efflorescence. —**deliquescent,** *adj.*

dowsing a form of divination involving a rod or wand, especially the art of finding underground supplies of water, ores, etc. Also called rhabdomancy.

efflorescence the property of a substance to yield up water through evaporation. Cf. deliquescence. See also 329. PROCESSES. —**efflorescent,** *adj.*

fluviology the science of watercourses, especially rivers. —**fluviologist,** *n.*

hydragogy *Obsolete.* the moving of water by an artificial channel.

hydriatrics hydropathy.

hydrodipsomania an abnormal love of drinking water.

hydrography 1. the study, description, and mapping of oceans, lakes, and rivers, especially with reference to their use for navigational purposes.
2. those parts of the map, collectively, that represent surface waters. —hydrographer, *n.* —hydrographic, hydrographical, *adj.*

hydrology the science that studies the occurrence, circulation, distribution, and properties of the waters of the earth and its atmosphere. —hydrologist, *n.* —hydrologic, hydrological, *adj.*

hydromancy a form of divination involving observations of water or of other liquids.

hydromania an excessive love of water.

hydropathy the "water cure," first developed in Germany in 1825. Also called hydriatrics. —hydropathist, *n.* —hydropathic, *adj.*

hydrophily *Botany.* the capacity of a plant to be pollinated through the agency of water. —hydrophilous, *adj.*

hydrophobia an abnormal fear of water.

hydroscope a device for viewing things below the surface of a body of water.

hydrotherapy the treatment of disorders by the use of water externally, especially in the form of exercises in a pool, etc. —hydrotherapist, *n.* —hydrotherapeutic, *adj.*

hydrotropism growth or movement in response to water as a stimulus. —hydrotropic, *adj.*

hygrology the branch of physics that studies atmospheric humidity.

hygrophobia 1. hydrophobia
2. an abnormal fear of water.

lecanomancy a form of divination involving the examination of water in a basin.

lecanoscopy a form of self-hypnotism involving staring at water in a basin.

limnology the scientific study of bodies of fresh water, as lakes or rivers, with reference to their physical, geographical, and biological features. —limnologist, *n.* —limnologic, limnological, *adj.*

orohydrography the branch of hydrography that studies the drainage phenomena of mountains. —orohydrographic, *adj.*

rheotaxis the tendency of some plants to respond to a current of water by growing with it (*positive rheotaxis*) or against it (*negative rheotaxis*).

rheotropism the tendency of certain living things to move in response to the mechanical stimulus of a current of water.

sympesiometer, sympiezometer an instrument for measuring the pressure exerted by currents of water. See also 226. INSTRUMENTS.

turbidimeter an instrument for measuring the turbidity of water or other fluids. —turbidimetric, *adj.*

turbidimetry the measurement of the turbidity of water or other fluids, as with a turbidimeter. —turbidimetric, *adj.*

415. WAX

cerography 1. the art or process of writing or engraving on wax.
2. *Rare.* the art or process of making paintings with colors mixed with beeswax and fixed with heat; encaustic painting. —cerographist, *n.* —cerographic, cerographical, *adj.*

ceromancy a form of divination involving dropping melted wax into water.

ceroplastics the art of modeling with wax. —ceroplastic, *adj.*

416. WEAPONRY
See also 22. ARROWS; 274. MISSILES; 413. WAR.

aeroballistics the science of ballistics combined with or from the special viewpoint of aerodynamics, particularly with regard to rockets, guided missiles, etc. —aeroballistic, *adj.*

artillery 1. the science of the manufacture and use of large guns.
2. the guns themselves. —artillerist, artilleryman, *n.*

aspidomancy a form of divination involving examination of a shield.

ballistomania an extreme interest in bullets.

cannonry 1. cannon collectively.
2. cannon fire.

enginery engines or machines collectively, especially engines of war. See also 369. SKILL and CRAFT.

gunnery 1. the science of the design and manufacture of heavy artillery.
2. the skill or practice of using heavy artillery.

missilery, missilry 1. the science of the design, construction, and launching of guided missiles.
2. guided missiles collectively.

musketry the art or skill of using muskets.

riflery the art or practice of shooting with a rifle, especially at targets as a match of skill.

weaponry 1. the design and manufacture of weapons.
2. weapons collectively, especially a nation's storehouse of armaments.

417. WEATHER

See also 27. ATMOSPHERE; 85. CLIMATE; 87. CLOUDS; 246. LIGHTNING; 345. RAIN; 375. SNOW; 387. SUN; 394. THUNDER; 420. WIND.

aerographics the study of atmospheric conditions. Also **aerography.** —**aerographer,** *n.*

aerology 1. *Obsolete.* the branch of meteorology that observed the atmosphere by using balloons, airplanes, etc.
2. meteorology. —**aerologist,** *n.* —**aerologic, aerological,** *adj.*

aeromancy 1. the art or science of divination by means of the air or winds.
2. *Humorous* weather forecasting.

barograph a barometer which automatically records, on a rotating cylinder, any variation in atmospheric pressure; a self-recording aneroid.

barometrography the branch of science that deals with the barometer.

barometry the art or science of barometric observation.

chonophobia an abnormal fear or dislike of snow.

climatology the science that studies climate or climatic conditions. —**climatologist,** *n.* —**climatologic, climatological,** *adj.*

cryophobia an abnormal fear of ice or frost.

frontogenesis the meeting of two masses of air, each with a different meteorological composition, thus forming a front, sometimes resulting in rain, snow, etc.

frontolysis the process by which a meteorological front is destroyed, as by mixture or deflection of the frontal air.

homichlophobia an abnormal fear of fog.

hyetology *Rare.* the branch of meteorology that studies rainfall. —**hyetologist,** *n.* —**hyetological,** *adj.*

hyetophobia an abnormal dislike or fear of rain.

hytherograph a graph that shows the relationship between temperature and either humidity or precipitation.

irroration *Obsolete.* 1. the process of moistening with dew.
2. the condition of being bedewed.

meteorology the study of weather and its changes, especially with the aim of predicting it accurately. —**meteorologist,** *n.* —**meteorologic, meteorological,** *adj.*

microbarograph a barograph for recording small fluctuations of atmospheric pressure.

nephology the scientific study of clouds. —**nephologist,** *n.*

ombrology the branch of meteorology that studies rain. —**ombrological,** *n.*

pluviography the branch of meteorology that automatically measures rainfall and snowfall. —pluviographic, pluviographical, *adj.*

pluviometry the branch of meteorology concerned with the measurement of rainfall. —pluviometric, pluviometrical, *adj.*

pluvioscope an instrument for measuring rainfall; a rain gauge.

pluviosity raininess. —pluvious, *adj.*

telemeteorography the recording of meteorological conditions at a distance, as in the use of sensing devices at various points that transmit their data to a central office. —telemeteorographic, *n.*

udometry the measurement of rainfall with any of various types of rain gauges. —udometric, *adj.*

udomograph a self-registering rain gauge.

vacuometer an instrument used for comparing barometers at varying pressures against a standard barometer.

weatherology *Informal.* meteorology, especially weather forecasts for radio or television.

418. WIFE
See also 258. MARRIAGE.

uxoricide 1. the murder of a wife by a husband.
2. a husband who murders his wife. —uxoricidal, *adj.*

viduage *Obsolete.* the condition of widowhood. Also viduity. —vidual, *adj.*

419. WILL

heteronomy the condition of being under the moral control of something or someone external; inability to be self-willing. —heteronymous, *adj.*

velleity a very weak or slight impulse of the will; a mere fancy that does not lead to action.

420. WIND
See also 27. ATMOSPHERE; 417. WEATHER.

ancraophobia an abnormal fear of wind.

anemography *Rare.* the recording of the measurement of wind speed by an anemometer. —anemographic, *adj.*

anemology the science of the winds. —anemological, *adj.*

anemometer an instrument for indicating wind velocity.

anemometry the measurement of wind speed and direction, often by an anemometrograph. —anemometric, anemometrical, *adj.*

anemophilia wind-loving, said of plants that are fertilized only through the action of winds. —anemophile, *n.* —anemophilous, *adj.*

anemophobia an abnormal fear of drafts or winds. —anemophobe, *n.*

anemoscope an instrument for recording the direction of the wind.

bise, bize a cold, dry wind that blows from the north or northeast in south central Europe.

breeze a light wind, 4 to 27 knots on the Beaufort scale.

cyclone an atmospheric disturbance characterized by powerful winds spinning in the shape of a vertical cylinder or horizontal disk, accompanied by low pressure at the center. —cyclonic, *adj.*

cyclonology the study of cyclones. —cyclonologist, *n.*

foehn, föhn a warm, dry wind that blows down the side of a mountain, as on the north side of the Alps.

gale a strong wind, 28 to 55 knots on the Beaufort scale.

haboob a heavy dust- or sandstorm of N. Africa, Arabia, and India.

hurricane a extremely strong wind, usually accompanied by foul weather, more than 65 knots on the Beaufort scale.

levanter a strong east wind in the Mediterranean region.

mistral a cold, dry wind that blows from the north in the south of France and vicinity.

Santa Ana a hot, dry, dust-bearing wind that blows from inland desert regions in southern California.

sirocco 1. a hot, dry, dust-laden wind that blows on the northern Mediterranean coast from Africa.
2. a sultry southeast wind in the same regions.
3. a hot, oppressive wind of cyclonic origin, as in Kansas.

tornado a highly localized, violent windstorm occurring over land, usually in the U.S. Midwest, characterized by a vertical, funnel-shaped cloud.

twister whirlwind.

typhoon a cyclone or hurricane in the western Pacific Ocean.

whirlwind any wind that has a spinning motion and is confined to a small area in the shape of a vertical cylinder.

421. WINE
See also 8. ALCOHOL; 39. BEER; 158. FERMENTATION.

enomania a mania for wine. Also oenomania, oinomania.

hygrophobia an abnormal fear of liquids, especially water and wine.

oenology, enology, oinology the science of making wines. Also called viniculture. —oenologist, enologist, oinologist, *n.*

oenomancy, enomancy, oinomancy a form of divination involving observation of the colors and other features of wine.

oenomania, oinomania a mania for wine. Also **enomania.**

oenophily, enophily, oinophily the love of wine; connoisseurship concerning wines. —**oenophile, enophile, oinophile,** *n.*

oenophobia, enophobia, oinophobia a dislike of or hatred for wine. —**oenophobe, enophobe, oinophobe,** *n.*

vigneron a cultivator of grape vines; viticulturist.

vindemiation *Rare.* the process of gathering or harvesting grapes.

viniculture the cultivation of grapes for winemaking. Also called **viticulture.** —**viniculturist,** *n.* —**vinicultural,** *adj.*

viticulture 1. the science that studies grapes and their culture.
2. the cultivation of grapes and grapevines. Also called **viniculture.** —**viticulturist,** *n.* —**viticultural, viticulturist,** *adj.*

422. WISDOM
See also 216. IDEAS; 233. KNOWLEDGE; 240. LEARNING; 393. THINKING.

adage a maxim, axiom, proverb, or old saying.

analect a collection of teachings, as the *Analects of Confucius.*

gnosis a superior form of wisdom, as that of the Gnostics, supposed to have been acquired mystically. See also 285. MYSTICISM.

logia maxims or sayings attributed to a religious leader. See also 79. CHRIST; 349. RELIGION.

protasis *Rare.* a proposition or maxim. See also 127. DRAMA; 186. GRAMMAR.

sophomania an excessive respect for one's own wisdom.

423. WOLVES
See also 16. ANIMALS.

lycanthrope 1. a person suffering from lycanthropy.
2. a werewolf or alien spirit in the form of a bloodthirsty wolf.
3. a person reputed to be able to change himself or another person into a wolf.

lycanthropy 1. *Psychiatry.* Also called **lycomania.** a kind of insanity in which the patient believes himself to be a beast, especially a wolf.
2. the supposed or fabled assumption of the form of a wolf by a human being. —**lycanthropic,** *adj.*

lycomania lycanthropy.

424. WOMEN
See also 253. MALE; 255. MANKIND; 281. MOTHER; 327. PREGNANCY; 364. SEX; 418. WIFE.

bluestockingism 1. the state of being a pedantic or literal-minded woman.
2. behavior characteristic of such a woman. —bluestocking, *n.*, *adj.*

coverture *Law.* the status of a married woman.

emmenology that branch of medicine that deals with menstruation and its related disorders.

femicide 1. the murder of a woman.
2. the murderer of a woman. Also called gynecide, gynaecide. —femicidal, *adj.*

gunocracy gynecocracy.

gynarchy a form of government by a woman or women. Also called gynecocracy. —gynarchic, *adj.*

gynecocracy rule by women. Also called gunocracy, gyneocracy, gynaeocracy.

gynecolatry, gynaecolatry the worship of women. Also gyneolatry. —gynecolater, *n.*

gynecology, gynaecology the branch of medical science that studies the diseases of women, especially of the reproductive organs. —gynecologist, *n.* —gynecologic, gynecological, *adj.*

gynecopathy, gynaecopathy any illness that afflicts only women. —gynecopathic, gynaecopathic, *adj.*

gynephobia, gynophobia an abnormal fear or hatred of women. —gynephobe, *n.*

gyniatrics the medical field dealing with women's dieases.

hoydenism ill-bred, boisterous, or tomboyish behavior in a woman. —hoyden, *n.* —hoydenish, *adj.*

maenadism behavior characteristic of a maenad or bacchante; raging or wild behavior in a woman.

matriarchate 1. a matriarchal form of government.
2. a family, tribe, or other social group ruled by a matriarch or matriarchs. —matriarchic, *adj.*

matriarchy 1. a community in which the mother or oldest female is the supreme authority, and descent is traced through the female line.
2. government by females, with one as supreme. —matriarchist, *n.* —matriarchic, matriarchical, *adj.*

misogyny a hatred of women —misogynist, *n.*

nubility the condition of being marriageable, especially in reference to a woman's age or physical development. —nubile, *adj.*

parthenolatry the worship of virgins.

parthenology *Physiology.* the study of virginity.

philogyny a love of or liking for women. —**philogynist,** *n.* —**philogynous,** *adj.*

pudicity modesty, especially chastity or chastefulness.

sexism the practice of discriminating against women in job opportunities, salary levels and increases, and in other matters now generally considered to be equally the right of women. —**sexist,** *n., adj.*

sorority a fellowship or association of women, as for a benevolent or charitable purpose or at a college.

suffragettism militant advocacy of suffrage for women. See also 322. POLITICS.

425. WOOD
See also 319. PLANTS; 401. TREES.

hylephobia an intense dislike for wood.

hylomania a mania for wood.

joinery the skill, craft, or trade of a joiner or carpenter; woodworking. —**joiner,** *n.*

lignification the process of turning into wood or becoming woodlike.

marquetry a form of decoration, often used in furniture-making, composed of inlays of wood veneers of different colors.

parquetry mosaic work in wood, a form of marquetry, used mostly for floors and wainscoting.

poker painting xylopyrography.

turnery the process or craft of fashioning wood on a lathe.

xylology a branch of dendrology that studies the structure of wood.

xylomancy a form of divination involving small pieces of wood.

xylopyrography the art or technique of producing a picture or design on a piece of wood by burning it with a heated, pointed instrument. Also called **poker painting.**

426. WORK
See also 297. OCCUPATIONS; 303. ORGANIZED LABOR.

drudgery dull, laborious, or menial work. —**drudge,** *n.*

empleomania an obsession with public employment.

ergasiophobia an abnormal fear of work.

ergograph an instrument that records the amount of work done when a muscle contracts. —**ergographic,** *adj.*

ergology the study of the effect of work on mind and body. —**ergologist,** *n.*

ergomania a mania for work.

ergophile a person who loves to work.

ergophobia a hatred of work.

faineance, faineancy laziness; the state of being idle. —**fainéant**, *adj*.

flexitime a work practice under which workers are able, within certain limits, to choose their own hours of work.

lucubration 1. laborious work or study, especially when done late at night. 2. the work, as a book or treatise, produced or apparently produced this way. —**lucubrator**, *n*.

operosity 1. the state or quality of being industrious or busy. 2. the condition of being toilsome. —**operose**, *adj*.

sinecurism the policy or practice of maintaining an office or position that provides income without demanding any or much work or attendance. Also **sinecureship.** —**sinecure**, *n*.

Taylorism the methods of scientific factory management first introduced in the early 19th century by the American engineer Frederick W. Taylor, especially the differential piece-rate system.

thaasophobia an abnormal fear or dislike of being idle.

volunteerism the practice or advocacy of working as a volunteer, often with the hope of thereby gaining paid employment in the same field.

427. WORMS
See also 430. ZOOLOGY.

helminthology the branch of zoology that studies worms, especially parasitic worms. —**helminthologist**, *n*. —**helminthologic, helminthological**, *adj*.

helminthophobia an abnormal fear of being infested with worms.

scoleciphobia an abnormal fear of worms.

scolecology a study of worms.

sericulture the breeding and raising of silk worms for the production of silk. —**sericulturist**, *n*. —**sericultural**, *adj*.

taeniacide, teniacide an agent or preparation for killing tapeworms. —**taeniacidal, teniacidal**, *adj*.

vermeology *Rare*. helminthology. —**vermeologist**, *n*.

vermicide a substance for killing worms, especially intestinal worms, in animals or humans. Cf. **vermifuge.**

vermiculation motion similar to that of a worm. See also 282. MOTION; 305. ORNAMENTATION.

vermifuge a drug for expelling worms from the intestinal tract. Cf. **vermicide.** —**vermifuge**, *adj*.

vermination the state or process of being infested with worms or vermin.

vermiphobia an abnormal fear of worms.

428. WRITING
See also 12. ALPHABET; 29. AUTHORS; 53. BOOKS; 236. LANGUAGE; 249. LITERATURE; 256. MANUSCRIPTS; 346. READING; 383. SPELLING.

acrology 1. the use of a symbol to represent phonetically the initial sound (syllable or letter) of the name of an object, as A is the first sound of Greek *alpha.*
2. the use of the name of the object as the name of the symbol representing its initial sound, as A in Greek is called *alpha* "ox." Also called **acrophony.** —acrologic, *adj.*

autography the act of writing something by hand. —autographer, *n.* —autographic, *adj.* —autographically, *adv.*

bibliotics the art or science of analyzing handwriting, especially that of manuscripts with the purpose of establishing their authorship or authenticity. —bibliotist, *n.* —bibliotic, *adj.*

brachygraphy an abbreviated writing; shorthand. —brachygraphic, *adj.*

cacography 1. bad handwriting. Cf. calligraphy.
2. the possession of poor spelling skills. See also orthography. —cacographer, *n.* —cacographic, cacographical, *adj.*

calligraphy 1. the art of beautiful penmanship.
2. handwriting in general.
3. good handwriting skills. Cf. cacography.
4. a script of a high aesthetic value produced by brush, especially that of Chinese, Japanese, or Arabic origin. —calligrapher, calligraphist, *n.* —calligraphic, calligraphical, *adj.*

chirography, cheirography 1. the penmanship of a person, especially when used in an important document, as in an apostolic letter written and signed by the pope.
2. the art of beautiful penmanship; calligraphy. —chirograph, chirographer, *n.* —chirographic, chirographical, *adj.*

chrysography 1. the art of writing in inks containing gold or silver in suspension.
2. the gold writing produced in this way. —chrysographer, *n.*

cryptography 1. the science or study of secret writing, especially code and cipher systems.
2. the procedures and methods of making and using secret languages, as codes or ciphers. —cryptographer, cryptographist, *n.* —cryptographic, cryptographical, cryptographal, *adj.*

curiologics, curiology the representation of things or sounds by means of their pictures instead of by symbols or words, as in hieroglyphics or a rebus. —**curiologic, curiological,** *adj.*

engrossment 1. a document or other piece of writing in a large, bold hand. 2. a formal document, as a proclamation, suitably written in a calligraphic hand and often illuminated. —**engrosser,** *n.*

grammalogue *Shorthand.* a word that is represented by a single symbol or character.

graphanalysis the reading of character or personality from a person's handwriting. Cf. graphology. —**graphanalyst,** *n.*

graphemics *Linguistics.* the study of systems of writing and their relationship to the systems of the languages they represent. Also called **graphonomy.** —**graphemic,** *adj.*

graphiology the art or craft of writing or delineating. —**graphiologist,** *n.*

graphology the study of handwriting, especially as regarded as an expression of character. Cf. graphanalysis. —**graphologist,** *n.* —**graphologic, graphological,** *adj.*

graphomania an obsession with writing.

graphonomy graphology.

graphopathology *Psychology.* the study of handwriting as a symptom of mental or emotional disorder. —**graphopathologist,** *n.* —**graphopathological,** *adj.*

graphophobia a dislike for writing.

graphorrhea 1. writing in excessive amounts, sometimes incoherently. 2. extreme wordiness in writing.

graptomancy a form of divination involving the examination of a person's handwriting.

haplography the accidental omission in writing or copying of one or more adjacent and similar letters, syllables, words, or lines, as *tagme* for *tagmeme.*

hieroglyphology the study of hieroglyphic writing, or a system employing a conventionalized pictographic script, esp. that used by the ancient Egyptians. —**hieroglyphologist,** *n.*

hierogram sacred writing or a sacred character or symbol. —**hierogrammatist,** *n.* —**hierogrammatic, hierogrammatical,** *adj.*

hierography *Rare.* sacred writing; hierograms and the art of writing them. —**hierographer,** *n.* —**hierographic, hierographical,** *adj.*

homography the process of using a distinct character to represent each sound. —**homographic,** *adj.*

iconomaticism a form of writing regarded as midway between picture writing, as hieroglyphics, and phonetic writing in which the names of the symbols are not the names of the objects they depict but phonetic elements only. —**iconomatic,** *adj.*

ideography a form of writing in which a written symbol represents an object rather than a word or speech sound. —**ideographic, ideographical,** *adj.*

isography *Rare.* the imitation of another person's handwriting. —**isographic, isographical,** *adj.*

lipography the avoidance of a certain letter or syllable in a text. —**lipogram,** *n.*

literation the act or process of representing with letters.

logogram a sign or symbol used to represent a word, as $ for *dollar.* Also **logograph.** —**logographic,** *adj.*

logography a method of reporting spoken language in longhand, esp. one using several reporters taking down a few words in succession. —**logographer,** *n.* —**logographic,** *adj.*

macrography abnormally large handwriting, often the result of a nervous disorder in the writer.

micrograph an apparatus used for miniature writing or drawing. —**micrography,** *n.*

micrography the art or technique of writing with extremely small characters. —**micrographic,** *adj.*

mogigraphy *Pathology.* physical difficulty in writing. —**mogigraphic,** *adj.*

monogram two or more letters, as initials, formed into a design to be placed on clothing, notepaper, etc., or as a crest. See also 305. ORNAMENTATION. —**monogrammatic, monogrammatical,** *adj.*

mutacism mytacism.

mytacism excessive use of or fondness for, or incorrect use of the letter *m* and the sound it represents. Also **mutacism.**

neography *Rare.* a new or novel way of writing.

noctograph a writing frame designed for use by blind people.

nomancy a form of divination involving the examination of letters, possibly from a graphological standpoint. Also **onomancy.**

ogham, ogam 1. an alphabetical script originally used for inscriptions in the Irish language from the 5th to the 10th centuries.
2. any of the 20 characters of this script.
3. an inscription in this script. —**oghamist, ogamist,** *n.*

onomancy, onomomancy nomancy.

opisthography 1. the practice of writing on both sides of the object used as a surface, as papyrus or stone.
2. the writing done in this fashion. —opisthography, *n.*

paleography, palaeography 1. ancient forms of writing, as in inscriptions, documents, and manuscripts.
2. the study of ancient writings, including decipherment, translation, and determination of age and date. —paleographer, palaeographer, *n.* —paleographic, palaeographic, *adj.*

paraph a flourish or other embellishment made after a signature, either as idiosyncrasy or to protect against forgery.

penmanship 1. the art or skill of handwriting or writing with a pen.
2. a particular person's manner or characteristic style of handwriting.

phonogram a symbol or character, as in shorthand, that represents a word, syllable, or sound.

phonography 1. any system of phonetic shorthand, as that of Pitman.
2. phonetic spelling, writing, or shorthand. —phonographer, phonographist, *n.* —phonographic, *adj.*

phraseogram a character or symbol, as in shorthand, that represents a phrase. Cf. phraseograph.

phraseograph a phrase that can be represented by a phraseogram. Cf. phraseogram.

pictography the use of pictorial symbols to communicate; picture writing with symbols that may be either ideographic or phonetic in function. —pictograph, *n.* —pictographic, *adj.*

runecraft the knowledge of runes and their interpretation; skill or expertise with runes.

runology the study of runes and runic writing. —runologist, *n.* —runological, *adj.*

scotograph an instrument for writing when unable to see.

scribblement 1. illegible handwriting.
2. the work of an inferior or untalented author.

scribomania a mania for writing

scription *Rare.* handwriting, especially a particular style of handwriting such as that of a particular person or period.

scrivenery the art and practice of the scrivener or copyist. —scrivener, *n.*

sematography the use of symbols other than letters in writing. —sematographic, *adj.*

semeiography 1. a system of symbolic notation. Also semiography. —semeiographic, semeiographical, *adj.*

sphenography *Rare.* the art of writing and deciphering cuneiform characters. —sphenographer, sphenographist, *n.* —sphenographic, *adj.*

stelography 1. the practice of chiseling commemorative inscriptions in pillars, tablets, and stelae.
2. any inscription so done. —stelographic, *adj.*

stenography the art of writing in shorthand. —stenographer, stenographist, *n.* —stenographic, stenographical, *adj.*

stenotypy a phonographic shorthand in which alphabetic letters, produced by hand or a special machine, are used to represent words and phrases. —stenotypist, *n.* —stenotypic, *adj.*

stylography the art of drawing, writing, or engraving with a stylus or similar instrument. —stylographic, stylographical, *adj.*

syllabary 1. a table of syllables, as might be used for teaching a language.
2. a system of characters or symbols representing syllables instead of individual sounds. Also syllabarium.

syllabism 1. the use of characters in writing that represent syllables rather than individual sounds, as in the Cherokee syllabary.
2. a division of a word into syllables.

tachygraphy 1. the ancient Greek and Roman shorthand systems.
2. cursive writing. —tachygrapher, tachygraphist, *n.* —tachygraphic, tachygraphical, *adj.*

telautography the transmission of writing or drawing such that the movements of the receiving pen copy those of the transmitting pen or pencil, yielding a facsimile reproduction at the receiving end. —telautograph, *n.* —telautographic, *adj.*

uncial a form of large, rounded script found in Latin and Greek manuscripts from the 3rd or 4th century until the 10th century. —uncial, *adj.*

Z

429. ZINC

See also 270. METALS.

photozincography *Obsolete.* a type of photoengraving using a sensitized zinc plate.

sherardisology the coating of steel and iron with a thin cladding of zinc. —sherardize, *v.*

zincography 1. a lithographic or offset process using zinc plates.
2. a letter press printing process using engraved or photoengraved zinc plates. —zincographer, *n.* —zincographic, zincographical, *adj.*

430. ZOOLOGY

See also 16. ANIMALS; 44. BIOLOGY; 45. BIRDS; 61. BULLS and
BULLFIGHTING; 64. BUTTERFLIES; 70. CATS; 88. COCKS; 125. DOGS;
164. FISH; 211. HORSES; 225. INSECTS; 302. ORGANISMS; 353. REPTILES;
374. SNAKES; 423. WOLVES; 427. WORMS.

acarology a division of zoology that studies mites and ticks. —acarologist, *n.*

aestivation estivation.

amphibiology the branch of zoology that studies amphibians. —amphibiological, *adj.*

arachnology a branch of zoology that studies spiders and other arachnids. Also called **arachnidology, araneology.** —arachnologist, *n.*

carcinology the branch of zoology that studies crustaceans. —carcinologist, *n.*

cetology the study of whales. —cetologist, *n.*

coadunation the state or condition of being united by growth. —coadunate, *adj.*

coccidology the branch of zoology that studies scales, mealy bugs, and other members of the family *Coccidea.*

conchology the branch of zoology that studies the shells of mollusks. Also called **malacology.** —conchologist, *n.* —conchological, *adj.*

crustaceology the branch of zoology that studies crustaceans.

cynology the branch of zoology that studies the dog, especially its natural history.

echinology the branch of zoology that studies echinoderms.

entomology the study of insects. —entomologist, *n.* —entomologic, entomological, *adj.*

epimorphosis development of an organism or form of animal life in which body segmentation is complete before hatching. —epimorphic, *adj.*

estivation, aestivation the practice of certain animals of sleeping throughout the summer. Cf. hibernation.

gemmation reproduction by budding. See also 54. BOTANY.

hibernation the practice of certain animals of sleeping throughout the winter. Cf. estivation.

invertebracy the state or quality of being invertebrate or without a backbone, as certain organisms, animals, etc.; hence, spinelessness; exhibiting a lack of strength of character. —invertebrate, *adj.*

lepidopterology the branch of entomology that studies butterflies. —lepidopterologist, lepidopterist, *n.*

malacology conchology. —malacologist, *n.*

mammalogy the branch of zoology that studies mammals. —mammalogist, *n.*

metamorphosis a change or succession of changes in form during the life cycle of an animal, allowing it to adapt to different environmental conditions, as a caterpillar into a butterfly.

ornithology the branch of zoology that studies birds. —ornithologist, *n.*

paleomammalogy, palaeomammalogy the branch of zoology that studies the mammals of past geologic ages.

stirpiculture selective breeding to develop strains with particular characteristics. —stirpicultural, *adj.*

taxonomy a system of naming things, as plants or animals. —taxonomist, *n.* —taxonomic, *adj.*

vivipara *pl.* animals whose young are born live, as mammals. —viviparity, *n.* —viviparous, *adj.*

zoogeography 1. the study of the geographical distribution of animals. 2. the study of the causes, effects, and other relations involved in such distributions. —zoogeographer, *n.*

zoonomia zoonomy.

zoonomy, zoonomia the laws of animal life or the animal kingdom. —zoonomist, *n.* —zoonomic, *adj.*

zoopathology the study or science of the diseases of animals; animal pathology. Also zoopathy.

zoopathy zoopathology.

zoophysiology the physiology of animals, as distinct from that of humans.

zoophytology the branch of zoology concerned with the zoophytes. —zoophytological, *adj.*

zootaxy zoological classification; the scientific classification of animals.

Index

Index

This Index lists all headwords, variant forms of headwords, and run-on entries from the text. Headwords are shown in **boldface type**, with reference to the category (number and name, in SMALL CAPITALS) or categories under which they may be found. Variants are also shown in boldface, with reference to category and headword under which they appear. Run-on entries are shown in lightface type, with reference to category and headword where they are to be found.

A

abacist 295. NUMBERS.
abaction 391. THEFT.
abactor 391. THEFT, **abaction.**
abalienation 224. INSANITY;
　363. SEPARATION.
abbacy 349. RELIGION.
Abderian 238. LAUGHTER.
abdication 351. RENUNCIATION.
Abecedarian 35. BAPTISM.
abecedarian 12. ALPHABET.
abecedarium 12. ALPHABET.
abecedary 12. ALPHABET, **abecedarian.**
aberrance 41. BEHAVIOR.
aberrancy 41. BEHAVIOR, **aberrance.**
abetment 6. AID; 103. CRIME.
abettal 6. AID, **abetment;** 103. CRIME, **abetment.**
abetter 6. AID, **abetment;** 103. CRIME, **abetment.**
abettor 6. AID, **abetment;** 103. CRIME, **abetment.**
abiogenesis 44. BIOLOGY;
　204. HEREDITY; 244. LIFE.
abiogenetic 44. BIOLOGY, **abiogenesis;**
　244. LIFE, **abiogenesis.**
abiogenetically 44. BIOLOGY, **abiogenesis.**

abiology 220. INANIMATE OBJECTS.
abiosis 244. LIFE.
abiotic 244. LIFE, **abiosis.**
abiotical 244. LIFE, **abiosis.**
abjuration 10. ALLEGIANCE;
　351. RENUNCIATION.
ablation 388. SURGERY.
ablepsia 48. BLINDNESS.
ablepsy 48. BLINDNESS, **ablepsia.**
ableptical 48. BLINDNESS, **ablepsia.**
ablutomania 84. CLEANLINESS.
abnormalism 41. BEHAVIOR.
abnormalist 41. BEHAVIOR.
abolitionism 371. SLAVERY.
abolitionist 371. SLAVERY, **abolitionism.**
aboriginal 308. PAST, **aboriginality.**
aboriginality 308. PAST.
aborticide 1. ABORTION.
abortifacient 1. ABORTION.
abracadabra 252. MAGIC, **abracadabrism.**
abracadabrism 252. MAGIC.
abridgement 53. BOOKS, **abridgment.**
abridgment 53. BOOKS.
absentee 235. LAND, **absenteeism.**
absenteeism 235. LAND.
absinthial 8. ALCOHOL, **absinthism.**

absinthian 8. ALCOHOL, **absinthism.**
absinthism 8. ALCOHOL.
absolutism 185. GOVERNMENT.
absolutist 185. GOVERNMENT,
 absolutism.
absolutistic 185. GOVERNMENT,
 absolutism.
abstinence 8. ALCOHOL.
abstinent 8. ALCOHOL, **abstinence.**
Abstract Expressionism 23. ART.
abstraction 331. PROPERTY and
 OWNERSHIP.
abstractionism 23. ART.
abstractionist 23. ART, **abstractionism.**
Abstractism 23. ART.
academese 236. LANGUAGE;
 237. LANGUAGE STYLE.
academic 240. LEARNING,
 academicism; 240. LEARNING,
 academism.
academical 240. LEARNING,
 academism.
academicism 240. LEARNING.
academism 240. LEARNING;
 240. LEARNING, **academicism.**
academist 240. LEARNING,
 academicism; 240. LEARNING,
 academism.
acalculia 295. NUMBERS.
acariasis 222. INFESTATION.
acaricide 222. INFESTATION;
 232. KILLING.
acarologist 430. ZOOLOGY, **acarology.**
acarology 430. ZOOLOGY.
acarophobia 225. INSECTS;
 313. PHOBIAS.
acatalepsy 233. KNOWLEDGE.
acataleptic 233. KNOWLEDGE,
 acatalepsy.
accelerometer 31. AVIATION;
 226. INSTRUMENTS.
acceptance 160. FINANCE.
accidence 186. GRAMMAR.
accidentalism 312. PHILOSOPHY.
accidentalist 312. PHILOSOPHY,
 accidentalism.
accismus 243. LIES and LYING.
accubation 168. FOOD and NUTRITION.
Aceldama 232. KILLING.
acetimetrical 264. MEASUREMENT,
 acetimetry.

acetimetry 264. MEASUREMENT.
acetonaemia 122. DISEASE and ILLNESS,
 acetonemia.
acetonemia 122. DISEASE and ILLNESS.
Achephali 135. EASTERN ORTHODOXY.
Achephalist 135. EASTERN ORTHODOXY,
 Achephali.
achluophobia 313. PHOBIAS.
achluphobia 110. DARKNESS;
 292. NIGHT.
achromasia 95. COMPLEXION; 370. SKIN.
achromaticity 92. COLOR.
achromatism 92. COLOR,
 achromaticity.
achromatopsia 92. COLOR,
 achromatopsy; 148. EYES,
 achromatopsy.
achromatopsy 92. COLOR; 148. EYES.
achromatosis 122. DISEASE and ILLNESS.
acidimeter 264. MEASUREMENT,
 acidimetry.
acidimetrical 264. MEASUREMENT,
 acidimetry.
acidimetry 264. MEASUREMENT.
acid intoxication 49. BLOOD and BLOOD
 VESSELS, **acidosis;** 122. DISEASE and
 ILLNESS, **acidosis.**
acidophobia 313. PHOBIAS; 319. PLANTS.
acidophobic 319. PLANTS, **acidophobia.**
acidosis 49. BLOOD and BLOOD VESSELS;
 122. DISEASE and ILLNESS.
acidotic 49. BLOOD and BLOOD VESSELS,
 acidosis; 122. DISEASE and ILLNESS,
 acidosis.
Acmeism 248. LITERARY STYLE.
acmeist 248. LITERARY STYLE,
 Acmeism.
acology 350. REMEDIES.
acomia 33. BALDNESS.
acomous 33. BALDNESS, **acomia.**
acosmic 183. GOD and GODS, **acosmism.**
acosmism 183. GOD and GODS.
acosmist 183. GOD and GODS, **acosmism.**
acoumeter 198. HEARING, **acoumetry.**
acoumetric 198. HEARING, **acoumetry.**
acoumetry 198. HEARING.
acoustic 380. SOUND, **acoustics.**
acoustician 380. SOUND, **acoustics.**
acousticophobia 313. PHOBIAS.
acoustics 380. SOUND.

acritochromacy 92. COLOR,
    achromatopsy; 148. EYES,
    achromatopsy.
acroama 354. RHETORIC and
    RHETORICAL DEVICES.
acroasis 354. RHETORIC and RHETORICAL
    DEVICES.
acrobatics 2. ACROBATICS.
acrobatism 2. ACROBATICS.
acrocephalic 51. BODY, HUMAN,
    acrocephaly.
acrocephalous 51. BODY, HUMAN,
    acrocephaly.
acrocephaly 51. BODY, HUMAN.
acrodont 16. ANIMALS, acrodontism;
    390. TEETH, acrodontism.
acrodontism 16. ANIMALS; 390. TEETH.
acrographer 141. ENGRAVING,
    acrography.
acrographic 141. ENGRAVING,
    acrography.
acrographical 141. ENGRAVING,
    acrography.
acrography 23. ART; 141. ENGRAVING.
acrologic 428. WRITING, acrology.
acrology 428. WRITING.
acromania 224. INSANITY; 254. MANIAS.
acromegalic 51. BODY, HUMAN,
    acromegaly; 52. BONES, acromegaly;
    122. DISEASE and ILLNESS, acromegaly;
    368. SIZE, acromegaly.
acromegaly 51. BODY, HUMAN;
    52. BONES; 122. DISEASE and ILLNESS;
    368. SIZE.
acronym 288. NAMES.
acronymic 288. NAMES, acronym.
acronymous 288. NAMES, acronym.
acrophile 283. MOUNTAINS, acrophilia.
acrophilia 283. MOUNTAINS.
acrophobia 202. HEIGHTS; 313. PHOBIAS.
acrophony 428. WRITING, acrology.
acropolis 20. ARCHITECTURE.
acrostic 409. VERSE, acrosticism.
acrosticism 409. VERSE.
actinic 200. HEAT, actinism.
actinism 200. HEAT.
actinographic 315. PHOTOGRAPHY,
    actinography.
actinography 315. PHOTOGRAPHY.
actinologic 245. LIGHT, actinology.
actinological 245. LIGHT, actinology.

actinology 245. LIGHT.
actinometric 245. LIGHT, actinometry.
actinometrical 245. LIGHT,
    actinometry.
actinometrist 245. LIGHT, actinometry.
actinometry 245. LIGHT.
actinotherapy 342. RADIATION.
Action Painting 23. ART.
active scopophilia 364. SEX,
    scopophilia.
activism 322. POLITICS; 376. SOCIETY.
activist 322. POLITICS, activism;
    376. SOCIETY, activism.
actualism 312. PHILOSOPHY.
actualist 312. PHILOSOPHY, actualism.
actualistic 312. PHILOSOPHY, actualism.
actuary 160. FINANCE.
acupuncture 350. REMEDIES.
acupuncturist 350. REMEDIES,
    acupuncture.
acyanoblepsia 92. COLOR; 148. EYES.
acyrological 382. SPEECH, acyrology.
acyrology 382. SPEECH.
adactyly 161. FINGERS and TOES.
adage 333. PROVERBS; 422. WISDOM.
Adamite 287. NAKEDNESS, Adamitism;
    349. RELIGION, Adamitism.
Adamitic 287. NAKEDNESS, Adamitism;
    349. RELIGION, Adamitism.
Adamitism 287. NAKEDNESS;
    349. RELIGION.
addendum 53. BOOKS.
adelphogamic 258. MARRIAGE,
    adelphogamy.
adelphogamy 258. MARRIAGE.
ademonist 114. DEMONS.
adenocele 66. CANCER.
adenographic 266. MEDICAL
    SPECIALTIES, adenography.
adenography 266. MEDICAL
    SPECIALTIES.
adenological 266. MEDICAL
    SPECIALTIES, adenology.
adenologist 266. MEDICAL SPECIALTIES,
    adenology.
adenology 266. MEDICAL SPECIALTIES.
adenosarcoma 66. CANCER.
adevism 183. GOD and GODS.
adevist 183. GOD and GODS, adevism.
adiabolist 117. DEVIL.
adiaphorism 332. PROTESTANTISM.

adiaphorist 332. PROTESTANTISM,
adiaphorism.
adiaphoristic 332. PROTESTANTISM,
adiaphorism.
adiathermancy 200. HEAT.
adipose 51. BODY, HUMAN, adiposity.
adiposity 51. BODY, HUMAN.
adjutancy 6. AID.
adjuvant 130. DRUGS.
adnomination 336. PUNNING;
354. RHETORIC and RHETORICAL
DEVICES.
adonism 38. BEAUTY.
adoptianism 79. CHRIST, adoptionism.
adoptionism 79. CHRIST.
adoptionist 79. CHRIST, adoptionism.
adumbration 352. REPRESENTATION.
advection 27. ATMOSPHERE.
advective 27. ATMOSPHERE, advection.
Adventism 332. PROTESTANTISM.
Adventist 332. PROTESTANTISM,
Adventism.
adventurism 41. BEHAVIOR.
adventurist 41. BEHAVIOR,
adventurism.
adventuristic 41. BEHAVIOR,
adventurism.
adversaria 53. BOOKS.
adynamia 122. DISEASE and ILLNESS.
adynamic 122. DISEASE and ILLNESS,
adynamia.
adynamy 122. DISEASE and ILLNESS,
adynamia.
aelurophile 70. CATS, ailurophile.
aelurophobia 70. CATS, ailurophobia;
313. PHOBIAS; 313. PHOBIAS,
ailurophobia.
aeolism 237. LANGUAGE STYLE;
354. RHETORIC and RHETORICAL
DEVICES.
aeolistic 237. LANGUAGE STYLE,
aeolism; 354. RHETORIC and
RHETORICAL DEVICES, aeolism.
aerialist 31. AVIATION; 395. TIGHTROPE
WALKING.
aeroballistic 31. AVIATION,
aeroballistics; 416. WEAPONRY,
aeroballistics.
aeroballistics 31. AVIATION;
416. WEAPONRY.
aerobatics 31. AVIATION.

aerobic 26. ATHLETICS, aerobics.
aerobics 26. ATHLETICS.
aerocartography 31. AVIATION;
257. MAPS.
aerodonetic 31. AVIATION,
aerodonetics.
aerodonetics 31. AVIATION.
aerodrome 31. AVIATION.
aerodromics 31. AVIATION.
aerodynamic 27. ATMOSPHERE,
aerodynamics.
aerodynamical 27. ATMOSPHERE,
aerodynamics.
aerodynamics 27. ATMOSPHERE.
aeroembolism 31. AVIATION;
122. DISEASE and ILLNESS.
aerogeologic 179. GEOLOGY,
aerogeology.
aerogeological 179. GEOLOGY,
aerogeology.
aerogeologist 179. GEOLOGY,
aerogeology.
aerogeology 179. GEOLOGY.
aerographer 27. ATMOSPHERE,
aerographics; 417. WEATHER,
aerographics.
aerographic 27. ATMOSPHERE,
aerographics.
aerographical 27. ATMOSPHERE,
aerographics.
aerographics 27. ATMOSPHERE;
417. WEATHER.
aerography 27. ATMOSPHERE,
aerographics.
aerolithology 25. ASTRONOMY;
271. METEORITES.
aerolitics 25. ASTRONOMY.
aerologic 27. ATMOSPHERE, aerology;
417. WEATHER, aerology.
aerological 27. ATMOSPHERE, aerology;
417. WEATHER, aerology.
aerologist 27. ATMOSPHERE, aerology;
417. WEATHER, aerology.
aerology 27. ATMOSPHERE;
417. WEATHER.
aeromancy 27. ATMOSPHERE;
124. DIVINATION; 417. WEATHER.
aeromedicine 31. AVIATION;
266. MEDICAL SPECIALTIES.
aerometric 27. ATMOSPHERE,
aerometry.

aerometry 27. ATMOSPHERE.
aeronaut 31. AVIATION, aeronautics.
aeronautic 31. AVIATION, aeronautics.
aeronautical 31. AVIATION,
  aeronautics.
aeronautics 31. AVIATION;
  31. AVIATION, aeronautism.
aeronautism 31. AVIATION.
aeroneurosis 122. DISEASE and ILLNESS.
aeropause 27. ATMOSPHERE;
  31. AVIATION.
aerophagy 122. DISEASE and ILLNESS.
aerophilately 91. COLLECTIONS and
  COLLECTING.
aerophobe 27. ATMOSPHERE,
  aerophobia.
aerophobia 27. ATMOSPHERE;
  313. PHOBIAS.
aerophone 31. AVIATION;
  111. DEAFNESS.
aerophysicist 31. AVIATION,
  aerophysics.
aerophysics 31. AVIATION.
aeroplanist 31. AVIATION.
aeroscepsis 27. ATMOSPHERE,
  aeroscepsy; 225. INSECTS, aeroscepsy.
aeroscepsy 27. ATMOSPHERE;
  225. INSECTS.
aerosphere 27. ATMOSPHERE.
aerostatic 31. AVIATION, aerostatics.
aerostatical 31. AVIATION, aerostatics.
aerostatics 31. AVIATION.
aesthete 312. PHILOSOPHY, aesthetics.
aesthetic 38. BEAUTY, aesthetics;
  312. PHILOSOPHY, aesthetics.
aesthetical 38. BEAUTY, aesthetics;
  312. PHILOSOPHY, aesthetics.
aesthetician 38. BEAUTY.
aestheticism 23. ART; 38. BEAUTY.
aesthetics 38. BEAUTY; 312. PHILOSOPHY.
aestivation 167. FLOWERS, estivation;
  347. RECREATION; 347. RECREATION,
  estivation; 430. ZOOLOGY;
  430. ZOOLOGY, estivation.
aetiologic 290. NATURE, etiology;
  312. PHILOSOPHY, etiology.
aetiological 290. NATURE, etiology;
  304. ORIGINS, aetiology;
  312. PHILOSOPHY, etiology.

aetiology 122. DISEASE and ILLNESS;
  122. DISEASE and ILLNESS, etiology;
  290. NATURE; 290. NATURE, etiology;
  304. ORIGINS; 312. PHILOSOPHY,
  etiology.
affinity 348. RELATIONSHIP.
aficionado 61. BULLS and
  BULLFIGHTING.
agamogenesis 44. BIOLOGY.
agamogenetic 44. BIOLOGY,
  agamogenesis.
agathism 184. GOODNESS.
agathist 184. GOODNESS, agathism.
agathologic 184. GOODNESS,
  agathology.
agathological 184. GOODNESS,
  agathology.
agathology 184. GOODNESS.
ageism 3. AGE; 121. DISCRIMINATION.
agenda 301. ORDER and DISORDER.
ageusia 122. DISEASE and ILLNESS.
ageustia 122. DISEASE and ILLNESS,
  ageusia.
Aggada 231. JUDAISM, Haggada.
Aggadah 231. JUDAISM, Haggada.
agio 160. FINANCE; 276. MONEY,
  agiotage.
agiotage 160. FINANCE; 276. MONEY.
agism 3. AGE, ageism;
  121. DISCRIMINATION, ageism.
agmatology 52. BONES.
agnate 348. RELATIONSHIP.
agnatic 348. RELATIONSHIP, agnate.
agnation 348. RELATIONSHIP.
agnoeology 233. KNOWLEDGE,
  agnoiology.
Agnoete 205. HERESY, Agnoetism.
Agnoetism 205. HERESY.
agnoiology 233. KNOWLEDGE.
Agnoite 205. HERESY, Agnoetism.
agnomen 288. NAMES.
agnominal 288. NAMES, agnomen.
agnomination 354. RHETORIC and
  RHETORICAL DEVICES, adnomination;
  354. RHETORIC and RHETORICAL
  DEVICES, alliteration; 354. RHETORIC
  and RHETORICAL DEVICES,
  paronomasia.
agnostic 183. GOD and GODS,
  agnosticism.
agnosticism 183. GOD and GODS.

agogic 284. MUSIC, **agogics.**
agogics 284. MUSIC.
agonist 26. ATHLETICS.
agonistic 26. ATHLETICS, **agonist.**
agonistical 26. ATHLETICS, **agonist.**
agonistics 26. ATHLETICS.
agoramania 254. MANIAS; 381. SPACES.
agoraphobia 313. PHOBIAS; 381. SPACES.
agrammatism 186. GRAMMAR.
agrarian 322. POLITICS, **agrarianism.**
agrarianism 322. POLITICS.
agrarian reform 322. POLITICS,
  agrarianism.
agricultural 5. AGRICULTURE,
  agriculture.
agriculturalist 5. AGRICULTURE,
  agriculture.
agriculture 5. AGRICULTURE.
agriculturist 5. AGRICULTURE,
  agriculture.
agriological 255. MANKIND, **agriology.**
agriologist 255. MANKIND, **agriology.**
agriology 255. MANKIND.
agrobiologic 44. BIOLOGY, **agrobiology.**
agrobiological 44. BIOLOGY,
  agrobiology.
agrobiologist 44. BIOLOGY,
  agrobiology.
agrobiology 44. BIOLOGY.
agrogeologist 5. AGRICULTURE,
  agrogeology.
agrogeology 5. AGRICULTURE;
  179. GEOLOGY; 377. SOIL.
agrological 377. SOIL, **agrology.**
agrologist 377. SOIL, **agrology.**
agrology 377. SOIL.
agronomics 5. AGRICULTURE.
agronomist 5. AGRICULTURE,
  agronomy.
agronomy 5. AGRICULTURE.
agrostographer 188. GRASSES,
  agrostography.
agrostography 188. GRASSES.
agrostologic 54. BOTANY, **agrostology.**
agrostological 54. BOTANY, **agrostology.**
agrostologist 54. BOTANY, **agrostology;**
  188. GRASSES, **agrostology.**
agrostology 54. BOTANY; 188. GRASSES.
agyiomania 254. MANIAS.
agyrophobia 313. PHOBIAS.

aichmophobia 313. PHOBIAS;
  365. SHARPNESS.
aileurophilia 311. -PHILE, -PHILIA,
  -PHILY.
ailuromania 70. CATS; 254. MANIAS.
ailurophile 70. CATS.
ailurophilia 311. -PHILE, -PHILIA,
  -PHILY, **aileurophilia.**
ailurophobia 70. CATS; 313. PHOBIAS.
airdrome 31. AVIATION, **aerodrome.**
airscape 352. REPRESENTATION.
aischrolatreia 119. DIRT;
  296. OBSCENITY.
aischrology 296. OBSCENITY.
akosmism 183. GOD and GODS,
  acosmism.
alacritous 9. ALERTNESS, **alacrity.**
alacrity 9. ALERTNESS.
alarmism 41. BEHAVIOR.
alarmist 41. BEHAVIOR, **alarmism.**
albedo 25. ASTRONOMY; 245. LIGHT.
Albertist 392. THEOLOGY.
albescence 92. COLOR.
albescent 92. COLOR, **albescence.**
albication 92. COLOR.
Albigenses 205. HERESY,
  Albigensianism.
Albigensian 205. HERESY,
  Albigensianism.
Albigensianism 205. HERESY.
albinism 370. SKIN.
albino 370. SKIN, **albinism.**
albinoism 370. SKIN, **albinism.**
albinotic 370. SKIN, **albinism.**
albocracy 341. RACE.
albuminurophobia 313. PHOBIAS.
alcoholic 8. ALCOHOL, **alcoholism.**
alcoholism 8. ALCOHOL.
alcoholomania 8. ALCOHOL;
  130. DRUGS; 254. MANIAS.
alcoholphile 8. ALCOHOL,
  alcoholphilia.
alcoholphilia 8. ALCOHOL.
Alcoranist 227. ISLAM.
alectoromachy 88. COCKS.
alectoromancy 88. COCKS;
  124. DIVINATION.
alectryomachy 88. COCKS,
  alectoromachy.

alectryomancy 88. COCKS, **alectoromancy;** 124. DIVINATION, **alectoromancy.**
alethiological 402. TRUTH and ERROR, **alethiology.**
alethiologist 402. TRUTH and ERROR, **alethiology.**
alethiology 402. TRUTH and ERROR.
aleuromancy 124. DIVINATION.
aleuromantic 124. DIVINATION, **aleuromancy.**
Alexandrianism 190. GREECE and GREEKS; 249. LITERATURE.
Alexandrianist 190. GREECE and GREEKS, **Alexandrianism;** 249. LITERATURE, **Alexandrianism.**
Alexandrine 409. VERSE.
alexia 346. READING.
alexipharmac 321. POISON; 350. REMEDIES, **alexipharmic.**
alexipharmic 321. POISON, **alexipharmac;** 350. REMEDIES; 350. REMEDIES, **alexipharmic.**
algebra 262. MATHEMATICS.
algebraic 262. MATHEMATICS, **algebra.**
algid 90. COLD, **algidity.**
algidity 90. COLD.
algogenic 306. PAIN.
algolagnia 306. PAIN; 364. SEX.
algolagnic 306. PAIN, **algolagnia;** 364. SEX, **algolagnia.**
algolagnist 306. PAIN, **algolagnia;** 364. SEX, **algolagnia.**
algological 54. BOTANY, **algology.**
algologist 54. BOTANY, **algology.**
algology 54. BOTANY.
algometer 226. INSTRUMENTS.
algometric 226. INSTRUMENTS, **algometer;** 306. PAIN, **algometry.**
algometrical 226. INSTRUMENTS, **algometer;** 306. PAIN, **algometry.**
algometry 264. MEASUREMENT; 306. PAIN.
algophilia 306. PAIN.
algophobia 306. PAIN; 313. PHOBIAS.
algorism 262. MATHEMATICS.
algorismic 262. MATHEMATICS, **algorism.**
algorist 262. MATHEMATICS, **algorism.**
algorithm 262. MATHEMATICS.
algraphic 328. PRINTING, **algraphy.**

algraphy 328. PRINTING.
alienage 169. FOREIGNERS.
alienation 363. SEPARATION.
alienism 334. PSYCHOLOGY.
alienist 334. PSYCHOLOGY, **alienism.**
alimentology 168. FOOD and NUTRITION.
aliptic 350. REMEDIES.
alkalosis 122. DISEASE and ILLNESS.
allegorical 23. ART, **allegory;** 249. LITERATURE, **allegory;** 352. REPRESENTATION, **allegory.**
allegorist 23. ART, **allegory;** 249. LITERATURE, **allegory;** 352. REPRESENTATION, **allegory.**
allegorizer 23. ART, **allegory;** 249. LITERATURE, **allegory;** 352. REPRESENTATION, **allegory.**
allegory 23. ART; 249. LITERATURE; 352. REPRESENTATION.
allergist 266. MEDICAL SPECIALTIES.
allergologist 266. MEDICAL SPECIALTIES, **allergology.**
allergology 266. MEDICAL SPECIALTIES.
alleviative 350. REMEDIES.
alliteration 354. RHETORIC and RHETORICAL DEVICES.
alliterative 354. RHETORIC and RHETORICAL DEVICES, **alliteration.**
allocution 354. RHETORIC and RHETORICAL DEVICES.
allodialism 235. LAND, **alodialism.**
allodialist 235. LAND, **alodialism.**
allodiary 235. LAND, **alodialism.**
allograph 239. LAW.
allographic 239. LAW, **allograph.**
allomeric 170. FORM, **allomerism.**
allomerism 170. FORM.
allomorphic 263. MATTER, **allomorphism.**
allomorphism 263. MATTER.
allonymity 29. AUTHORS.
allonymous 29. AUTHORS, **allonymy;** 288. NAMES, **allonymy.**
allonymy 29. AUTHORS; 288. NAMES.
allopath 350. REMEDIES, **allopathy.**
allopathic 350. REMEDIES, **allopathy.**
allopathist 350. REMEDIES, **allopathy.**
allopathy 350. REMEDIES.
allotheism 183. GOD and GODS.
allotriophagy 168. FOOD and NUTRITION.

allotropic 263. MATTER, **allotropism.**
allotropical 263. MATTER, **allotropism.**
allotropism 263. MATTER.
allotropy 263. MATTER, **allotropism.**
alluvion 356. RIVERS.
almanagist 11. ALMANACS.
almner 6. AID, **almoner.**
almoner 6. AID.
almonership 6. AID, **almoner.**
alodialism 235. LAND.
alodialist 235. LAND, **alodialism.**
alodiary 235. LAND, **alodialism.**
alogia 382. SPEECH, **alogy.**
alogic 41. BEHAVIOR, **alogy.**
alogical 41. BEHAVIOR, **alogy.**
alogism 21. ARGUMENTATION.
alogy 41. BEHAVIOR; 382. SPEECH.
alomancy 124. DIVINATION.
alopecia 33. BALDNESS, **acomia;**
  193. HAIR.
alopecic 193. HAIR, **alopecia.**
alopecist 33. BALDNESS.
alphabetarian 12. ALPHABET.
alphabetics 12. ALPHABET.
alphabetism 12. ALPHABET.
alphabetologist 12. ALPHABET,
  alphabetology.
alphabetology 12. ALPHABET.
alphitomancy 124. DIVINATION.
alpinism 283. MOUNTAINS.
alpinist 283. MOUNTAINS, **alpinism.**
altimeter 226. INSTRUMENTS.
altimetrical 202. HEIGHTS, **altimetry.**
altimetry 202. HEIGHTS.
altophobia 202. HEIGHTS; 313. PHOBIAS.
altruism 28. ATTITUDES.
altruist 28. ATTITUDES, **altruism.**
altruistic 28. ATTITUDES, **altruism.**
aluminography 328. PRINTING,
  algraphy.
aluminosis 122. DISEASE and ILLNESS.
amanuensis 6. AID; 297. OCCUPATIONS.
amateur 28. ATTITUDES, **amateurism.**
amateurism 28. ATTITUDES.
amathophobia 313. PHOBIAS.
amaurosis 48. BLINDNESS.
amaurotic 48. BLINDNESS, **amaurosis.**
amaxomania 254. MANIAS;
  408. VEHICLES.
amaxophobia 313. PHOBIAS;
  408. VEHICLES.

amazonism 41. BEHAVIOR.
ambidexterity 194. HANDS,
  ambidextrianism.
ambidextrianism 194. HANDS.
ambidextrous 194. HANDS,
  ambidextrianism.
ambitendency 334. PSYCHOLOGY.
amblyopia 48. BLINDNESS.
amblyopic 48. BLINDNESS, **amblyopia.**
amblyopy 48. BLINDNESS, **amblyopia.**
ambrologic 290. NATURE, **ambrology.**
ambrological 290. NATURE, **ambrology.**
ambrology 290. NATURE.
ambulomancy 124. DIVINATION;
  412. WALKING.
amenomania 254. MANIAS;
  320. PLEASURE.
amensalism 16. ANIMALS; 44. BIOLOGY;
  319. PLANTS.
amentia 224. INSANITY.
amenty 224. INSANITY.
amercement 335. PUNISHMENT.
amercer 335. PUNISHMENT,
  amercement.
amerciament 335. PUNISHMENT,
  amercement.
Americamania 13. AMERICA;
  254. MANIAS.
Americanism 69. CATHOLICISM;
  236. LANGUAGE.
Ameslan 111. DEAFNESS.
amicicide 232. KILLING.
amity 348. RELATIONSHIP.
ammeter 226. INSTRUMENTS.
amnesia 269. MEMORY.
amnesiac 269. MEMORY, **amnesia.**
amnesic 269. MEMORY, **amnesia.**
amniomancy 46. BIRTH;
  124. DIVINATION.
amoral 145. ETHICS, **amoralism.**
amoralism 145. ETHICS.
amoralist 145. ETHICS, **amoralism.**
amorphic 170. FORM, **amorphism.**
amorphism 170. FORM.
amorphy 170. FORM, **amorphism.**
amortization 160. FINANCE;
  331. PROPERTY and OWNERSHIP.
amortizement 160. FINANCE,
  amortization; 331. PROPERTY and
  OWNERSHIP, **amortization.**

ampelographer 54. BOTANY,
ampelography.
ampelography 54. BOTANY.
amphibiological 430. ZOOLOGY,
amphibiology.
amphibiology 430. ZOOLOGY.
amphibological 186. GRAMMAR,
amphibology.
amphibology 186. GRAMMAR.
amphibolous 186. GRAMMAR,
amphibology.
amphierotic 364. SEX, amphierotism.
amphierotism 364. SEX.
amphilogy 21. ARGUMENTATION.
amygdalitis 122. DISEASE and ILLNESS.
Amyraldism 332. PROTESTANTISM.
ana 91. COLLECTIONS and COLLECTING.
Anabaptism 35. BAPTISM.
Anabaptist 35. BAPTISM, Anabaptism.
anabasis 122. DISEASE and ILLNESS.
anabiosis 244. LIFE.
anabiotic 244. LIFE, anabiosis.
anabolic 302. ORGANISMS, anabolism.
anabolism 74. CHANGE;
302. ORGANISMS.
anacamptic 380. SOUND, anacamptics.
anacamptics 380. SOUND.
anachorism 249. LITERATURE;
317. PLACES.
anachoristic 249. LITERATURE,
anachorism.
anachronism 249. LITERATURE;
396. TIME.
anachronistic 249. LITERATURE,
anachronism; 396. TIME,
anachronism.
anachronistical 396. TIME,
anachronism.
anachronous 396. TIME, anachronism.
anacoenosis 354. RHETORIC and
RHETORICAL DEVICES.
anacoluthia 186. GRAMMAR,
anacoluthon.
anacoluthic 186. GRAMMAR,
anacoluthon.
anacoluthon 186. GRAMMAR.
anadiplosis 354. RHETORIC and
RHETORICAL DEVICES.
anadromous 164. FISH.
anaemia 122. DISEASE and ILLNESS,
anemia.

anaemic 122. DISEASE and ILLNESS,
anemia.
anaesthesia 197. HEALTH, anesthesia.
anaesthesiologist 197. HEALTH,
anesthesia; 266. MEDICAL
SPECIALTIES, anesthesiology.
anaesthesiology 266. MEDICAL
SPECIALTIES, anesthesiology.
anaesthesis 197. HEALTH, anesthesia.
anaesthetic 197. HEALTH, anesthesia.
anaesthetist 197. HEALTH, anesthesia;
266. MEDICAL SPECIALTIES,
anesthesiology.
anaglyph 23. ART, anaglyphy.
anaglyphic 23. ART, anaglyphy.
anaglyphoscope 352. REPRESENTATION.
anaglyphy 23. ART.
anaglyptic 23. ART, anaglyphy.
anaglyptographic 23. ART,
anaglyptography; 128. DRAWING,
anaglyptography.
anaglyptography 23. ART;
128. DRAWING.
anagnorisis 127. DRAMA.
anagoge 349. RELIGION.
anagogic 349. RELIGION, anagoge.
anagogically 349. RELIGION, anagoge.
anagogics 349. RELIGION.
anagogy 349. RELIGION, anagoge.
anagram 176. GAMES.
anagrammatism 176. GAMES;
236. LANGUAGE.
anagraph 104. CRITICISM.
analect 333. PROVERBS; 422. WISDOM.
analemma 65. CALENDAR.
analemmatic 65. CALENDAR,
analemma.
analepsis 122. DISEASE and ILLNESS;
168. FOOD and NUTRITION;
386. STRENGTH and WEAKNESS.
analepsy 122. DISEASE and ILLNESS,
analepsis; 168. FOOD and NUTRITION,
analepsis; 386. STRENGTH and
WEAKNESS, analepsis.
analeptic 350. REMEDIES.
analgesia 197. HEALTH.
analgesic 197. HEALTH, analgesia.
analgesy 197. HEALTH, analgesia.
analgetic 197. HEALTH, analgesia.
analogic 4. AGREEMENT, analogy.
analogical 4. AGREEMENT, analogy.

analogism 197. HEALTH;
262. MATHEMATICS; 312. PHILOSOPHY.
analogous 21. ARGUMENTATION,
analogy.
analogy 4. AGREEMENT;
21. ARGUMENTATION.
analphabetic 12. ALPHABET.
analysis 393. THINKING.
analytical stasiology 322. POLITICS.
anamnesis 269. MEMORY.
anamnestic 269. MEMORY, anamnesis.
anamorphic 23. ART, anamorphism;
44. BIOLOGY, anamorphism;
54. BOTANY, anamorphosis;
170. FORM, anamorphism;
179. GEOLOGY, anamorphism;
352. REPRESENTATION, anamorphism.
anamorphism 23. ART; 44. BIOLOGY;
170. FORM; 179. GEOLOGY;
352. REPRESENTATION.
anamorphoscope 23. ART; 170. FORM;
352. REPRESENTATION.
anamorphosis 23. ART; 44. BIOLOGY,
anamorphism; 54. BOTANY;
170. FORM; 352. REPRESENTATION.
anamorphosy 23. ART; 44. BIOLOGY,
anamorphism; 170. FORM,
anamorphosis; 352. REPRESENTATION.
anamorphotic 179. GEOLOGY,
anamorphism.
anapest 409. VERSE.
anapestic 409. VERSE, anapest.
anaphora 354. RHETORIC and
RHETORICAL DEVICES.
anaphoral 354. RHETORIC and
RHETORICAL DEVICES, anaphora.
anaphrodisia 364. SEX.
anaphylactic 122. DISEASE and ILLNESS,
anaphylaxis.
anaphylaxis 122. DISEASE and ILLNESS.
anaplasty 266. MEDICAL SPECIALTIES.
anarchic 185. GOVERNMENT,
anarchism.
anarchism 185. GOVERNMENT.
anarchist 185. GOVERNMENT,
anarchism.
anarchy 185. GOVERNMENT; 301. ORDER
and DISORDER.
anastomosis 44. BIOLOGY.
anastomotic 44. BIOLOGY, anastomosis.

anastrophe 354. RHETORIC and
RHETORICAL DEVICES.
anathema 80. CHRISTIANITY,
anathematism.
anathematism 80. CHRISTIANITY.
anatocism 276. MONEY.
anatomic 266. MEDICAL SPECIALTIES,
anatomy.
anatomical 14. ANATOMY, anatomy;
51. BODY, HUMAN, anatomy.
anatomist 14. ANATOMY, anatomy;
51. BODY, HUMAN, anatomy;
266. MEDICAL SPECIALTIES, anatomy.
anatomy 14. ANATOMY; 51. BODY,
HUMAN; 266. MEDICAL SPECIALTIES.
anatripsology 197. HEALTH.
anaudia 111. DEAFNESS; 198. HEARING.
anchorage 131. DUES and PAYMENT.
anchoret 277. MONKS and NUNS,
anchoritism.
anchoretic 277. MONKS and NUNS,
anchoritism.
anchorite 277. MONKS and NUNS,
anchoritism.
anchoritic 277. MONKS and NUNS,
anchoritism.
anchoritism 277. MONKS and NUNS.
ancraophobia 313. PHOBIAS; 420. WIND.
androcracy 253. MALE.
androcratic 253. MALE, androcracy.
androgenesis 253. MALE.
androgenetic 253. MALE, androgenesis.
androgyneity 51. BODY, HUMAN,
androgynism.
androgynism 51. BODY, HUMAN.
androgynous 51. BODY, HUMAN,
androgynism.
androgyny 51. BODY, HUMAN,
androgynism.
androlepsy 169. FOREIGNERS.
andromania 253. MALE; 254. MANIAS;
364. SEX.
androphagous 67. CANNIBALISM,
androphagy.
androphagy 67. CANNIBALISM.
androphilia 253. MALE.
androphilic 253. MALE, androphilia.
androphobia 253. MALE; 313. PHOBIAS.
androphonomania 232. KILLING.
androtomy 14. ANATOMY.
anecdotage 299. OLD AGE.

anecdotalism 237. LANGUAGE STYLE.
anecdotalist 237. LANGUAGE STYLE,
  anecdotalism.
anemia 122. DISEASE and ILLNESS.
anemic 122. DISEASE and ILLNESS,
  anemia.
anemographic 420. WIND,
  anemography.
anemography 420. WIND.
anemological 420. WIND, anemology.
anemology 420. WIND.
anemometer 420. WIND.
anemometric 420. WIND, anemometry.
anemometrical 420. WIND,
  anemometry.
anemometry 420. WIND.
anemophile 420. WIND, anemophilia.
anemophilia 420. WIND.
anemophilous 420. WIND, anemophilia.
anemophobe 420. WIND, anemophobia.
anemophobia 313. PHOBIAS; 420. WIND.
anemoscope 226. INSTRUMENTS;
  420. WIND.
anemotrophy 122. DISEASE and ILLNESS.
anencephaly 204. HEREDITY.
anergy 122. DISEASE and ILLNESS.
anesis 122. DISEASE and ILLNESS.
anesthesia 197. HEALTH.
anesthesiologist 197. HEALTH,
  anesthesia; 266. MEDICAL
  SPECIALTIES, anesthesiology.
anesthesiology 266. MEDICAL
  SPECIALTIES.
anesthesis 197. HEALTH, anesthesia.
anesthetic 197. HEALTH, anesthesia.
anesthetist 266. MEDICAL SPECIALTIES,
  anesthesiology.
aneurism 49. BLOOD and BLOOD
  VESSELS.
aneurysm 49. BLOOD and BLOOD
  VESSELS, aneurism.
angary 239. LAW; 413. WAR.
angelocracy 185. GOVERNMENT.
angelology 349. RELIGION.
angelophany 349. RELIGION.
anginophobia 199. HEART;
  313. PHOBIAS.
angiographic 49. BLOOD and BLOOD
  VESSELS, angiography.
angiographical 49. BLOOD and BLOOD
  VESSELS, angiography.

angiography 49. BLOOD and BLOOD
  VESSELS.
angiology 49. BLOOD and BLOOD
  VESSELS.
angiopathology 49. BLOOD and BLOOD
  VESSELS.
Anglicanism 332. PROTESTANTISM.
Anglicism 140. ENGLISH.
Anglicist 140. ENGLISH.
Anglist 139. ENGLAND.
Anglo-Catholic 69. CATHOLICISM,
  Anglo-Catholicism.
Anglo-Catholicism 69. CATHOLICISM.
Anglomania 139. ENGLAND.
Anglophile 139. ENGLAND, Anglophilia;
  311. -PHILE, -PHILIA, -PHILY.
Anglophilia 139. ENGLAND.
Anglophobe 139. ENGLAND,
  Anglophobia.
Anglophobia 139. ENGLAND;
  313. PHOBIAS.
Anglo-Saxonism 236. LANGUAGE;
  289. NATIONALISM.
aniconic 183. GOD and GODS,
  aniconism.
aniconism 183. GOD and GODS.
anility 299. OLD AGE.
Animalia 16. ANIMALS.
animalism 255. MANKIND.
animalist 255. MANKIND, animalism.
animalistic 255. MANKIND, animalism.
animality 16. ANIMALS.
animatism 220. INANIMATE OBJECTS.
animatistic 220. INANIMATE OBJECTS,
  animatism.
animism 183. GOD and GODS.
animist 183. GOD and GODS, animism.
animistic 183. GOD and GODS, animism.
animosity 28. ATTITUDES.
aniseikonia 148. EYES.
aniseikonic 148. EYES, aniseikonia.
anisoconia 148. EYES, aniseikonia.
anisogamic 44. BIOLOGY, anisogamy.
anisogamous 44. BIOLOGY, anisogamy.
anisogamy 44. BIOLOGY.
anisometropia 148. EYES.
anisometropic 148. EYES,
  anisometropia.
anisotropic 54. BOTANY, anisotropy;
  316. PHYSICS, anisotropy.
anisotropy 54. BOTANY; 316. PHYSICS.

ankylophobia 51. BODY, HUMAN.
ankylosis 122. DISEASE and ILLNESS.
annalist 207. HISTORY.
annihilationism 392. THEOLOGY.
annihilationist 392. THEOLOGY,
annihilationism.
annomination 354. RHETORIC and
RHETORICAL DEVICES.
annuity 160. FINANCE.
anodyne 350. REMEDIES.
anomalism 317. PLACES.
anomaly 317. PLACES, anomalism.
anomia 239. LAW, anomie.
anomic 239. LAW, anomie.
anomie 239. LAW.
anomy 239. LAW, anomie.
anoöpsia 48. BLINDNESS, anopsy.
anopsia 48. BLINDNESS, anopsy.
anopsy 48. BLINDNESS.
anorectic 122. DISEASE and ILLNESS,
anorexia; anorexia nervosa.
anorexia 122. DISEASE and ILLNESS;
168. FOOD and NUTRITION.
anorexia nervosa 122. DISEASE and
ILLNESS.
anorexic 122. DISEASE and ILLNESS,
anorexia; 122. DISEASE and ILLNESS,
anorexia nervosa.
anosmia 298. ODORS.
anosmic 298. ODORS, anosmia.
anosphrasia 298. ODORS, anosmia.
anoxemia 49. BLOOD and BLOOD
VESSELS.
anoxia 122. DISEASE and ILLNESS.
antagonism 28. ATTITUDES.
antagonist 96. CONFLICT.
antagonistic 28. ATTITUDES,
antagonism.
antanaclasis 186. GRAMMAR;
354. RHETORIC and RHETORICAL
DEVICES.
antarchism 185. GOVERNMENT.
antarchist 185. GOVERNMENT,
antarchism.
antarchistic 185. GOVERNMENT,
antarchism.
antediluvian 18. ANTIQUITY;
18. ANTIQUITY, antediluvian;
308. PAST, antediluvianism.
antediluvianism 308. PAST.
anthesis 167. FLOWERS.

anthoecologic 142. ENVIRONMENT,
anthoecology.
anthoecological 142. ENVIRONMENT,
anthoecology.
anthoecology 142. ENVIRONMENT;
167. FLOWERS.
anthography 167. FLOWERS.
anthologist 91. COLLECTIONS and
COLLECTING, anthology;
249. LITERATURE, anthology.
anthology 80. CHRISTIANITY;
91. COLLECTIONS and COLLECTING;
249. LITERATURE.
anthomania 167. FLOWERS.
anthophagous 167. FLOWERS,
anthophagy.
anthophagy 167. FLOWERS.
anthophobia 167. FLOWERS;
313. PHOBIAS.
anthracomancy 124. DIVINATION.
anthracomantic 124. DIVINATION,
anthracomancy.
anthracosis 122. DISEASE and ILLNESS.
anthropogenetic 304. ORIGINS,
anthropogeny.
anthropogenic 304. ORIGINS,
anthropogeny.
anthropogeny 304. ORIGINS.
anthropogeography 178. GEOGRAPHY.
anthropoglot 16. ANIMALS; 45. BIRDS;
255. MANKIND.
anthropographer 255. MANKIND,
anthropography.
anthropographic 255. MANKIND,
anthropography.
anthropography 255. MANKIND.
anthropoid 16. ANIMALS; 16. ANIMALS,
anthropoid; 255. MANKIND;
255. MANKIND, anthropoid.
anthropoidal 16. ANIMALS, anthropoid;
255. MANKIND, anthropoid.
anthropolatry 183. GOD and GODS.
anthropological 255. MANKIND,
anthropology.
anthropologist 255. MANKIND,
anthropology.
anthropology 255. MANKIND.
anthropomancy 124. DIVINATION.
anthropomantic 124. DIVINATION,
anthropomancy.

anthropomantist 124. DIVINATION, anthropomancy.
anthropometric 14. ANATOMY, anthropometry.
anthropometrical 14. ANATOMY, anthropometry.
anthropometrist 14. ANATOMY, anthropometry.
anthropometry 14. ANATOMY.
anthropomorphic 183. GOD and GODS, anthropomorphism.
anthropomorphical 183. GOD and GODS, anthropomorphism.
anthropomorphism 183. GOD and GODS.
anthropomorphist 183. GOD and GODS, anthropomorphism.
anthropomorphistic 183. GOD and GODS, anthropomorphism.
anthroponomical 255. MANKIND, anthroponomy.
anthroponomics 255. MANKIND, anthroponomy.
anthroponomist 255. MANKIND, anthroponomy.
anthroponomy 255. MANKIND.
anthroponymist 288. NAMES, anthroponymy.
anthroponymy 288. NAMES.
anthropopathic 16. ANIMALS, anthropopathism; 183. GOD and GODS, anthropopathism.
anthropopathism 16. ANIMALS; 183. GOD and GODS.
anthropopathite 183. GOD and GODS, anthropopathism.
anthropopathy 16. ANIMALS, anthropopathism; 183. GOD and GODS, anthropopathism.
anthropophagism 67. CANNIBALISM; 168. FOOD and NUTRITION.
anthropophagous 67. CANNIBALISM, anthropophagism; 168. FOOD and NUTRITION, anthropophagism.
anthropophagy 67. CANNIBALISM, anthropophagism; 168. FOOD and NUTRITION, anthropophagism.
anthropophilic 255. MANKIND.
anthropophobia 255. MANKIND; 313. PHOBIAS; 376. SOCIETY.
anthropophuism 183. GOD and GODS.

anthropophuistic 183. GOD and GODS, anthropophuism.
anthropopsychic 290. NATURE, anthropopsychism.
anthropopsychism 290. NATURE.
anthroposcopy 14. ANATOMY.
anthroposociologic 142. ENVIRONMENT, anthroposociology.
anthroposociological 142. ENVIRONMENT, anthroposociology; 341. RACE, anthroposociology.
anthroposociology 142. ENVIRONMENT; 341. RACE.
anthroposophical 255. MANKIND, anthroposophy.
anthroposophist 255. MANKIND, anthroposophy.
anthroposophy 255. MANKIND.
anthropotheism 183. GOD and GODS.
anthropotomical 14. ANATOMY, anthropotomy.
anthropotomist 14. ANATOMY, anthropotomy.
anthropotomy 14. ANATOMY.
antialcoholic 8. ALCOHOL, antialcoholism.
antialcoholism 8. ALCOHOL.
antibacchic 409. VERSE, antibacchius.
antibacchius 409. VERSE.
antibiosis 302. ORGANISMS.
antichristianism 80. CHRISTIANITY.
antichristianity 80. CHRISTIANITY, antichristianism.
antichronism 396. TIME, anachronism.
anticivic 322. POLITICS, anticivism.
anticivism 322. POLITICS.
anticlericalism 69. CATHOLICISM.
anticlericalist 69. CATHOLICISM, anticlericalism.
antidisestablishmentarianism 349. RELIGION.
antidotary 130. DRUGS, pharmacopoeia; 350. REMEDIES.
antidote 350. REMEDIES.
anti-Gallic 28. ATTITUDES, anti-Gallicanism.
anti-Gallican 28. ATTITUDES, anti-Gallicanism.
anti-Gallicanism 28. ATTITUDES.
anti-Hitlerism 152. FASCISM.

anti-intellectual 233. KNOWLEDGE,
anti-intellectualism; 240. LEARNING,
anti-intellectualism.
anti-intellectualism 233. KNOWLEDGE;
240. LEARNING.
anti-Jacobin 322. POLITICS, anti-
Jacobinism.
anti-Jacobinism 322. POLITICS.
anti-Klanism 28. ATTITUDES.
antilapsarian 392. THEOLOGY,
antilapsarianism.
antilapsarianism 392. THEOLOGY.
antilogy 21. ARGUMENTATION.
antimetathesis 354. RHETORIC and
RHETORICAL DEVICES.
antimilitarism 322. POLITICS.
antimilitarist 322. POLITICS,
antimilitarism.
antimilitaristic 322. POLITICS,
antimilitarism.
antinomia 239. LAW.
antinomian 239. LAW, antinomia;
239. LAW, antinomianism;
392. THEOLOGY, antinomianism.
antinomianism 239. LAW;
392. THEOLOGY.
antinomic 239. LAW, antinomia.
antinomist 239. LAW, antinomianism.
antinomy 239. LAW, antinomia.
antipaedobaptism 35. BAPTISM,
antipedobaptism.
antipaedobaptist 35. BAPTISM,
antipedobaptism.
antipathist 96. CONFLICT.
antipathy 96. CONFLICT.
antipedobaptism 35. BAPTISM.
antipedobaptist 35. BAPTISM,
antipedobaptism.
antiperiodic 350. REMEDIES.
antiphlogistic 350. REMEDIES;
350. REMEDIES, antiphlogistic.
antiphonal 378. SONGS and SINGING.
antiphrasis 249. LITERATURE;
354. RHETORIC and RHETORICAL
DEVICES.
antiphrastic 249. LITERATURE,
antiphrasis; 354. RHETORIC and
RHETORICAL DEVICES, antiphrasis.
antiphrastical 354. RHETORIC and
RHETORICAL DEVICES, antiphrasis.
antipodean 143. EQUATOR, antipodes.

antipodes 143. EQUATOR.
antiptosis 186. GRAMMAR.
antiptotic 186. GRAMMAR, antiptosis.
antipyretic 122. DISEASE and ILLNESS;
350. REMEDIES.
antipyrotic 350. REMEDIES.
antiquarian 18. ANTIQUITY,
antiquarianism; 308. PAST,
antiquarianism.
antiquarianism 18. ANTIQUITY;
308. PAST.
antiquary 308. PAST, antiquarianism.
antiquation 3. AGE.
Antiscians 143. EQUATOR.
Antiscii 143. EQUATOR, Antiscians.
anti-Semite 231. JUDAISM, anti-
Semitism.
anti-Semitism 231. JUDAISM.
antisepsis 197. HEALTH.
antiseptic 197. HEALTH, antisepsis;
350. REMEDIES.
antistrophal 127. DRAMA, antistrophe;
409. VERSE, antistrophe.
antistrophe 127. DRAMA; 409. VERSE.
antistrophic 127. DRAMA, antistrophe;
409. VERSE, antistrophe.
antiterrorism 322. POLITICS; 413. WAR.
antiterrorist 322. POLITICS,
antiterrorism; 413. WAR,
antiterrorism.
antithetic 354. RHETORIC and
RHETORICAL DEVICES, antithetics.
antithetical 354. RHETORIC and
RHETORICAL DEVICES, antithetics.
antithetics 354. RHETORIC and
RHETORICAL DEVICES.
antivenin 350. REMEDIES.
antlophobia 313. PHOBIAS; 414. WATER.
antonomasia 288. NAMES.
antonomastic 288. NAMES,
antonomasia.
anythingarian 322. POLITICS,
anythingarianism.
anythingarianism 322. POLITICS.
apagoge 21. ARGUMENTATION.
apagogic 21. ARGUMENTATION,
apagoge.
apartheid 185. GOVERNMENT;
341. RACE.
apeirophobia 313. PHOBIAS.
aphanite 179. GEOLOGY, aphanitism.

aphanitism 179. GEOLOGY.
apharesis 236. LANGUAGE, **aphetism.**
aphasia 382. SPEECH.
aphasiac 382. SPEECH, **aphasia.**
aphasic 382. SPEECH, **aphasia.**
aphelion 25. ASTRONOMY; 318. PLANETS.
apheliotropism 282. MOTION;
319. PLANTS.
aphephobia 313. PHOBIAS.
aphesis 236. LANGUAGE, **aphetism.**
aphetic 236. LANGUAGE, **aphetism.**
aphetism 236. LANGUAGE.
aphnology 137. ECONOMICS;
276. MONEY.
aphonia 382. SPEECH.
aphonic 382. SPEECH, **aphonia.**
aphonous 382. SPEECH, **aphonia.**
aphony 382. SPEECH, **aphonia.**
aphorism 333. PROVERBS.
aphorismic 333. PROVERBS, **aphorism.**
aphorismical 333. PROVERBS, **aphorism.**
aphorist 333. PROVERBS, **aphorism.**
aphoristic 333. PROVERBS, **aphorism.**
aphrasia 382. SPEECH.
aphrodisia 364. SEX.
aphrodisiac 364. SEX; 364. SEX,
aphrodisiac.
aphrodisiomania 254. MANIAS; 364. SEX.
apiarian 40. BEES, **apiary.**
apiarist 40. BEES.
apiary 40. BEES.
apiculture 40. BEES.
apiculturist 40. BEES, **apiculture.**
apimania 40. BEES; 254. MANIAS.
apiologist 40. BEES, **apiology.**
apiology 40. BEES.
apiophobia 40. BEES, **apiphobia;**
313. PHOBIAS, **apiphobia.**
apiphobia 40. BEES; 313. PHOBIAS.
apnea 122. DISEASE and ILLNESS.
apneal 122. DISEASE and ILLNESS, **apnea.**
apneic 122. DISEASE and ILLNESS, **apnea.**
apnoea 122. DISEASE and ILLNESS,
apnea.
apnoeal 122. DISEASE and ILLNESS,
apnea.
apnoeic 122. DISEASE and ILLNESS,
apnea.
apocalyptic 349. RELIGION,
apocalypticism.

apocalyptical 349. RELIGION,
apocalypticism.
apocalypticism 349. RELIGION.
apocope 388. SURGERY.
apocrypha 43. BIBLE.
apocryphal 43. BIBLE, **apocrypha.**
apocynthion 318. PLANETS;
318. PLANETS, **apolune.**
apodosis 186. GRAMMAR.
apogee 318. PLANETS.
apogeotropic 282. MOTION,
apogeotropism; 319. PLANTS,
apogeotropism.
apogeotropism 282. MOTION;
319. PLANTS.
Apollinarian 205. HERESY,
Apollinarianism.
Apollinarianism 205. HERESY.
apologetical 80. CHRISTIANITY,
apologetics; 392. THEOLOGY,
apologetics.
apologetics 80. CHRISTIANITY;
392. THEOLOGY.
apologia 349. RELIGION.
apologist 21. ARGUMENTATION.
apolune 25. ASTRONOMY; 318. PLANETS.
apomixis 44. BIOLOGY.
aponeurology 14. ANATOMY.
apophasic 354. RHETORIC and
RHETORICAL DEVICES, **apophasis.**
apophasis 354. RHETORIC and
RHETORICAL DEVICES.
apophthegm 333. PROVERBS,
apothegmatist.
apophthegmatic 333. PROVERBS,
apothegmatist.
apophthegmatical 333. PROVERBS,
apothegmatist.
apophthegmatist 333. PROVERBS,
apothegmatist.
aposiopesis 354. RHETORIC and
RHETORICAL DEVICES.
aposiopetic 354. RHETORIC and
RHETORICAL DEVICES, **aposiopesis.**
apostasy 349. RELIGION.
apostate 349. RELIGION, **apostasy.**
a posteriori 250. LOGIC.
apostolic 80. CHRISTIANITY,
apostolicism.
apostolical 80. CHRISTIANITY,
apostolicism.

apostolicism 80. CHRISTIANITY.
apostolicity 349. RELIGION.
apostrophe 354. RHETORIC and
RHETORICAL DEVICES.
apostrophic 354. RHETORIC and
RHETORICAL DEVICES, apostrophe.
apostrophism 354. RHETORIC and
RHETORICAL DEVICES.
apostrophist 354. RHETORIC and
RHETORICAL DEVICES, apostrophism.
apotelesm 24. ASTROLOGY.
apotelesmatic 24. ASTROLOGY,
apotelesm.
apothecary 130. DRUGS.
apothegm 333. PROVERBS,
apothegmatist.
apothegmatic 333. PROVERBS,
apothegmatist.
apothegmatical 333. PROVERBS,
apothegmatist.
apothegmatist 333. PROVERBS.
apotheosis 183. GOD and GODS;
210. HONORS and REGALIA.
apotropaic 252. MAGIC, apotropaism.
apotropaism 252. MAGIC.
apriorism 250. LOGIC.
aptotic 236. LANGUAGE.
aquapontic 319. PLANTS, aquapontics.
aquapontics 319. PLANTS.
aquarellist 23. ART.
aquatics 26. ATHLETICS.
aquicultural 319. PLANTS, aquiculture;
414. WATER, aquiculture.
aquiculture 319. PLANTS; 414. WATER.
Arabism 322. POLITICS.
arachnephobia 313. PHOBIAS.
arachnidology 430. ZOOLOGY,
arachnology.
arachnologist 430. ZOOLOGY,
arachnology.
arachnology 430. ZOOLOGY.
Aramaism 236. LANGUAGE.
araneology 430. ZOOLOGY,
arachnology.
arbalest 22. ARROWS, arbalist.
arbalist 22. ARROWS.
arbiter 4. AGREEMENT.
arbitrage 276. MONEY.
arbitrager 276. MONEY, arbitrage.
arbitrageur 276. MONEY, arbitrage.
arbitratrix 4. AGREEMENT.

arbitress 4. AGREEMENT, arbitratrix.
arboretum 401. TREES.
arboriculture 401. TREES.
arboriculturist 401. TREES,
arboriculture.
Arcadian 41. BEHAVIOR, Arcadianism.
Arcadianism 41. BEHAVIOR.
arcana 233. KNOWLEDGE, arcanum.
arcanum 7. ALCHEMY;
233. KNOWLEDGE.
archaeogeologic 179. GEOLOGY,
archeogeology.
archaeogeological 179. GEOLOGY,
archeogeology.
archaeogeology 179. GEOLOGY,
archeogeology.
archaeographer 18. ANTIQUITY,
archaeography.
archaeographical 18. ANTIQUITY,
archaeography.
archaeography 18. ANTIQUITY.
archaeolater 308. PAST, archaeolatry.
archaeolatrous 308. PAST, archaeolatry.
archaeolatry 308. PAST.
archaeologic 18. ANTIQUITY,
archaeology.
archaeological 18. ANTIQUITY,
archaeology.
archaeologist 18. ANTIQUITY,
archaeology.
archaeology 18. ANTIQUITY.
archaic 308. PAST, archaism.
archaicism 15. ANCESTORS, archaism;
308. PAST, archaism.
archaism 15. ANCESTORS; 23. ART;
237. LANGUAGE STYLE; 308. PAST.
archaist 15. ANCESTORS, archaism;
308. PAST, archaism.
archaistic 15. ANCESTORS, archaism.
archeogeologic 179. GEOLOGY,
archeogeology.
archeogeological 179. GEOLOGY,
archeogeology.
archeogeology 179. GEOLOGY.
archeologic 18. ANTIQUITY,
archaeology.
archeological 18. ANTIQUITY,
archaeology.
archeologist 18. ANTIQUITY,
archaeology.

archeology 18. ANTIQUITY, archaeology.
architectonic 20. ARCHITECTURE, architectonics.
architectonical 20. ARCHITECTURE, architectonics.
architectonics 20. ARCHITECTURE; 23. ART; 312. PHILOSOPHY.
archology 185. GOVERNMENT; 304. ORIGINS.
archon 190. GREECE and GREEKS.
arcograph 128. DRAWING.
arctophilist 91. COLLECTIONS and COLLECTING.
arcubalist 22. ARROWS, arbalist.
areography 259. MARS; 318. PLANETS.
areologic 25. ASTRONOMY, areology; 259. MARS, areology.
areological 25. ASTRONOMY, areology; 259. MARS, areology.
areologist 25. ASTRONOMY, areology; 259. MARS, areology.
areology 25. ASTRONOMY; 259. MARS.
aretaics 312. PHILOSOPHY.
argyria 122. DISEASE and ILLNESS, argyrism.
argyrism 122. DISEASE and ILLNESS.
argyrothecology 91. COLLECTIONS and COLLECTING.
arhythmia 199. HEART, arrhythmia.
arhythmic 199. HEART, arrhythmia.
Arian 79. CHRIST, Arianism; 205. HERESY, Arianism.
Arianism 79. CHRIST; 205. HERESY.
Arianistic 79. CHRIST, Arianism.
Arianistical 79. CHRIST, Arianism.
aristocracy 376. SOCIETY.
aristocraticism 376. SOCIETY.
aristocratism 376. SOCIETY.
aristologist 118. DINING, aristology.
aristology 118. DINING.
Aristotelian 312. PHILOSOPHY, Aristotelianism.
Aristotelian criticism 104. CRITICISM.
Aristotelianism 312. PHILOSOPHY.
arithmancy 124. DIVINATION; 295. NUMBERS.
arithmocracy 185. GOVERNMENT.
arithmocratic 185. GOVERNMENT, arithmocracy.

arithmomancy 295. NUMBERS, arithmancy.
arithmomania 295. NUMBERS.
Arminian 332. PROTESTANTISM, Arminianism.
Arminianism 332. PROTESTANTISM.
armipotence 386. STRENGTH and WEAKNESS.
armistice 4. AGREEMENT; 413. WAR.
armomancy 124. DIVINATION.
Arnoldist 322. POLITICS.
arrhythmia 199. HEART.
arrhythmic 199. HEART, arrhythmia.
arrivism 41. BEHAVIOR.
arriviste 41. BEHAVIOR, arrivism.
arrythmia 199. HEART, arrhythmia.
arrythmic 199. HEART, arrhythmia.
arsis 409. VERSE.
arsonist 162. FIRE.
arteriographic 14. ANATOMY, arteriography.
arteriographical 14. ANATOMY, arteriography.
arteriography 14. ANATOMY.
arthritic 122. DISEASE and ILLNESS, arthritism.
arthritical 122. DISEASE and ILLNESS, arthritism.
arthritism 122. DISEASE and ILLNESS.
arthrography 266. MEDICAL SPECIALTIES.
arthrology 266. MEDICAL SPECIALTIES.
arthropathology 122. DISEASE and ILLNESS.
arthropod 157. FEET and LEGS; 157. FEET and LEGS, arthropod.
arthropodal 157. FEET and LEGS, arthropod.
arthropodan 157. FEET and LEGS, arthropod.
arthropodous 157. FEET and LEGS, arthropod.
artifice 369. SKILL and CRAFT.
artillerist 416. WEAPONRY, artillery.
artillery 416. WEAPONRY.
artilleryman 416. WEAPONRY, artillery.
artiodactyl 16. ANIMALS; 157. FEET and LEGS.
artiodactylous 16. ANIMALS, artiodactyl; 157. FEET and LEGS, artiodactyl.

artistry 23. ART.
aruspex 16. ANIMALS, **haruspicy.**
Aryanism 341. RACE.
Aryanist 341. RACE, **Aryanism.**
arythmia 199. HEART, **arrhythmia.**
arythmic 199. HEART, **arrhythmia.**
ascetic 41. BEHAVIOR, **asceticism.**
asceticism 41. BEHAVIOR.
asemia 393. THINKING.
asepsis 84. CLEANLINESS.
aseptic 84. CLEANLINESS, **asepsis.**
asepticism 122. DISEASE and ILLNESS.
Asiatical 20. ARCHITECTURE,
 Asiaticism; 237. LANGUAGE STYLE,
 Asiaticism; 354. RHETORIC and
 RHETORICAL DEVICES, **Asiaticism.**
Asiaticism 20. ARCHITECTURE;
 237. LANGUAGE STYLE; 354. RHETORIC
 and RHETORICAL DEVICES.
aspidomancy 124. DIVINATION;
 416. WEAPONRY.
asportation 391. THEFT.
asseveration 239. LAW.
asseverative 239. LAW, **asseveration.**
asseverator 239. LAW, **asseveration.**
Assideanism 231. JUDAISM.
assonance 354. RHETORIC and
 RHETORICAL DEVICES; 380. SOUND.
assuasive 350. REMEDIES;
 350. REMEDIES, **assuasive.**
Assyriological 18. ANTIQUITY,
 Assyriology.
Assyriologist 18. ANTIQUITY,
 Assyriology.
Assyriology 18. ANTIQUITY.
astatic 316. PHYSICS, **astaticism.**
astaticism 316. PHYSICS.
asteism 354. RHETORIC and RHETORICAL
 DEVICES.
asterism 25. ASTRONOMY.
asterismal 25. ASTRONOMY, **asterism.**
asteroids 318. PLANETS, **planetoid.**
asthenia 386. STRENGTH and WEAKNESS.
asthenic 386. STRENGTH and WEAKNESS,
 asthenia.
asthenophobia 313. PHOBIAS.
astigmatic 148. EYES, **astigmatism.**
astigmatism 148. EYES.
astragalomancy 124. DIVINATION.
astraphobia 246. LIGHTNING;
 313. PHOBIAS.

astrapophobia 246. LIGHTNING,
 astraphobia; 313. PHOBIAS,
 astraphobia.
astroalchemist 24. ASTROLOGY,
 astroalchemy.
astroalchemy 24. ASTROLOGY.
astroblastoma 66. CANCER.
astrocytoma 66. CANCER.
astrodiagnosis 24. ASTROLOGY.
astrogation 25. ASTRONOMY.
astrogator 25. ASTRONOMY,
 astrogation.
astrogeny 25. ASTRONOMY.
astrogeology 25. ASTRONOMY.
astrognosy 25. ASTRONOMY.
astrogony 25. ASTRONOMY, **astrogeny.**
astrographic 25. ASTRONOMY,
 astrography.
astrography 25. ASTRONOMY.
astrolabe 226. INSTRUMENTS;
 352. REPRESENTATION.
astrolater 25. ASTRONOMY, **astrolatry.**
astrolatry 25. ASTRONOMY.
astrolithology 271. METEORITES.
astrologer 24. ASTROLOGY, **astrology.**
astrological 24. ASTROLOGY, **astrology.**
astrologist 24. ASTROLOGY, **astrology.**
astrology 24. ASTROLOGY;
 124. DIVINATION.
astromancer 25. ASTRONOMY,
 astromancy.
astromancy 25. ASTRONOMY;
 124. DIVINATION.
astromantic 25. ASTRONOMY,
 astromancy.
astrometric 25. ASTRONOMY,
 astrometry.
astrometrical 25. ASTRONOMY,
 astrometry.
astrometry 25. ASTRONOMY.
astronaut 25. ASTRONOMY,
 astronautics.
astronautic 25. ASTRONOMY,
 astronautics.
astronautical 25. ASTRONOMY,
 astronautics.
astronautics 25. ASTRONOMY.
astronavigation 25. ASTRONOMY.
astronavigator 25. ASTRONOMY,
 astronavigation.

astronomer 25. ASTRONOMY,
astronomy.
astronomical 25. ASTRONOMY,
astronomy.
astronomy 25. ASTRONOMY.
astrophile 25. ASTRONOMY.
astrophilic 25. ASTRONOMY, **astrophile.**
astrophobia 313. PHOBIAS.
astrophotography 25. ASTRONOMY;
315. PHOTOGRAPHY.
astrophysicist 25. ASTRONOMY,
astrophysics.
astrophysics 25. ASTRONOMY.
astrosphere 44. BIOLOGY.
asymmetric 389. SYMMETRY,
asymmetry.
asymmetrical 389. SYMMETRY,
asymmetry.
asymmetry 389. SYMMETRY.
asynchronic 396. TIME, **asynchronism.**
asynchronism 396. TIME.
asynchrony 396. TIME, **asynchronism.**
asyndetic 354. RHETORIC and
RHETORICAL DEVICES, **asyndeton.**
asyndeton 354. RHETORIC and
RHETORICAL DEVICES.
ataractic 195. HAPPINESS, **ataraxia.**
ataraxia 195. HAPPINESS.
ataraxic 195. HAPPINESS, **ataraxia.**
atavism 15. ANCESTORS.
atavist 15. ANCESTORS, **atavism.**
atavistic 15. ANCESTORS, **atavism.**
ataxia 122. DISEASE and ILLNESS;
301. ORDER and DISORDER.
ataxiophobia 313. PHOBIAS.
ataxophobia 313. PHOBIAS,
ataxiophobia.
ataxy 122. DISEASE and ILLNESS, **ataxia;**
301. ORDER and DISORDER, **ataxia.**
atelophobia 313. PHOBIAS.
Atenism 183. GOD and GODS.
atephobia 313. PHOBIAS.
athanasia 244. LIFE.
Athanasian 79. CHRIST,
Athanasianism.
Athanasianism 79. CHRIST.
athedonia 195. HAPPINESS.
athedonic 195. HAPPINESS, **athedonia.**
atheism 183. GOD and GODS.
atheist 183. GOD and GODS, **atheism.**
atheistic 183. GOD and GODS, **atheism.**

athermancy 200. HEAT.
athletic 26. ATHLETICS, **athleticism.**
athleticism 26. ATHLETICS.
atmidometer 264. MEASUREMENT,
atmidometry.
atmidometry 264. MEASUREMENT.
atmologic 414. WATER, **atmology.**
atmological 414. WATER, **atmology.**
atmologist 414. WATER, **atmology.**
atmology 414. WATER.
atmolysis 27. ATMOSPHERE.
atmolyzer 27. ATMOSPHERE, **atmolysis.**
atmospherics 27. ATMOSPHERE;
159. FILMS.
atomic theory 312. PHILOSOPHY,
atomism.
atomism 312. PHILOSOPHY.
atomist 312. PHILOSOPHY, **atomism.**
atomistic 312. PHILOSOPHY, **atomism.**
atomistical 312. PHILOSOPHY, **atomism.**
atomology 316. PHYSICS.
atomy 52. BONES.
atonal 284. MUSIC, **atonalism.**
atonalism 284. MUSIC.
atonalist 284. MUSIC, **atonalism.**
atonalistic 284. MUSIC, **atonalism.**
atonality 284. MUSIC, **atonalism;**
284. MUSIC, **dodecaphony.**
atonic 51. BODY, HUMAN, **atonicity.**
atonicity 51. BODY, HUMAN.
atony 51. BODY, HUMAN, **atonicity.**
atrabilarian 41. BEHAVIOR.
atrabilious 41. BEHAVIOR, **atrabilarian.**
atrichia 33. BALDNESS.
atrophy 113. DECAYING.
atropism 321. POISON.
Atticism 190. GREECE and GREEKS;
213. HUMOR.
Atticist 190. GREECE and GREEKS,
Atticism; 213. HUMOR, **Atticism.**
attitudinarian 41. BEHAVIOR,
attitudinarianism.
attitudinarianism 41. BEHAVIOR.
attorneyism 41. BEHAVIOR.
audialgesia 132. EAR; 306. PAIN.
audiclave 198. HEARING.
audiologist 198. HEARING, **audiology;**
266. MEDICAL SPECIALTIES, **audiology.**
audiology 198. HEARING; 266. MEDICAL
SPECIALTIES.
audiometer 198. HEARING.

audiometric 198. HEARING,
audiometer; 198. HEARING,
audiometry.
audiometrical 198. HEARING,
audiometry.
audiometrician 198. HEARING,
audiometry.
audiometrist 198. HEARING,
audiometry.
audiometry 198. HEARING;
198. HEARING, audiometer.
audiophile 311. -PHILE, -PHILIA, -PHILY;
314. PHONOGRAPH RECORDS.
audiophilia 311. -PHILE, -PHILIA, -PHILY;
314. PHONOGRAPH RECORDS.
audiophilic 311. -PHILE, -PHILIA, -PHILY,
audiophilia; 314. PHONOGRAPH
RECORDS, audiophilia.
auditognosis 198. HEARING.
augur 124. DIVINATION, augury;
174. FUTURE, augury.
augurial 124. DIVINATION, augury;
174. FUTURE, augury.
augurous 124. DIVINATION, augury;
174. FUTURE, augury.
augury 124. DIVINATION; 174. FUTURE.
Augustinian 392. THEOLOGY,
Augustinianism.
Augustinianism 392. THEOLOGY.
aulic 236. LANGUAGE, aulicism.
aulicism 236. LANGUAGE.
aulophobia 313. PHOBIAS.
auriscope 132. EAR; 226. INSTRUMENTS.
auriscopy 132. EAR; 226. INSTRUMENTS,
auriscope.
aurophobia 313. PHOBIAS.
austromancy 124. DIVINATION.
autarch 185. GOVERNMENT, autarchy.
autarchic 185. GOVERNMENT, autarchy.
autarchical 185. GOVERNMENT,
autarchy.
autarchy 185. GOVERNMENT.
autarkic 137. ECONOMICS, autarky.
autarkical 137. ECONOMICS, autarky.
autarkist 137. ECONOMICS, autarky.
autarky 137. ECONOMICS.
autecologic 142. ENVIRONMENT,
autecology.
autecological 142. ENVIRONMENT,
autecology.

autecology 44. BIOLOGY;
142. ENVIRONMENT.
authoritarian 28. ATTITUDES,
authoritarianism.
authoritarianism 28. ATTITUDES.
autism 129. DREAMS.
autistic 129. DREAMS, autism.
autochthonism 304. ORIGINS.
autochthonous 304. ORIGINS,
autochthonism.
autochthony 304. ORIGINS,
autochthonism.
autocracy 185. GOVERNMENT;
376. SOCIETY.
autocrat 185. GOVERNMENT, autocracy;
376. SOCIETY, autocracy.
autocratic 185. GOVERNMENT,
autocracy; 376. SOCIETY, autocracy.
autodidact 240. LEARNING,
autodidactics; 362. SELF,
autodidactics.
autodidactics 240. LEARNING; 362. SELF.
autoerotic 364. SEX, autoeroticism.
autoeroticism 364. SEX.
autoerotism 364. SEX, autoeroticism.
autogenic 46. BIRTH, autogeny.
autogenous 46. BIRTH, autogeny.
autogenously 46. BIRTH, autogeny.
autogeny 46. BIRTH.
autogonic 46. BIRTH, autogeny.
autogonous 46. BIRTH, autogeny.
autogonously 46. BIRTH, autogeny.
autogony 46. BIRTH, autogeny.
autographer 428. WRITING,
autography.
autographic 328. PRINTING,
autography; 428. WRITING,
autography.
autographically 328. PRINTING,
autography; 428. WRITING,
autography.
autography 328. PRINTING;
428. WRITING.
autohypnosis 215. HYPNOSIS,
autohypnotism; 372. SLEEP,
autohypnotism.
autohypnotism 215. HYPNOSIS;
372. SLEEP.
autointoxication 49. BLOOD and BLOOD
VESSELS, acidosis; 122. DISEASE and
ILLNESS, acidosis.

autolatry 362. SELF.
autology 362. SELF.
automania 254. MANIAS; 362. SELF.
automatism 41. BEHAVIOR.
automatist 41. BEHAVIOR, automatism.
autometric 264. MEASUREMENT,
autometry.
autometry 264. MEASUREMENT.
automobilism 30. AUTOMATION.
automobilist 30. AUTOMATION,
automobilism.
automobility 30. AUTOMATION,
automobilism.
automorphic 334. PSYCHOLOGY,
automorphism.
automorphism 334. PSYCHOLOGY.
automysophobia 84. CLEANLINESS;
119. DIRT; 313. PHOBIAS.
autonomism 94. COMMUNISM.
autonomous 185. GOVERNMENT,
autonomy.
autonomy 173. FREEDOM;
185. GOVERNMENT; 322. POLITICS.
autonumerology 408. VEHICLES.
autophagia 168. FOOD and NUTRITION,
autophagy.
autophagous 168. FOOD and NUTRITION,
autophagy.
autophagy 168. FOOD and NUTRITION.
autophile 362. SELF, autophilia.
autophilia 362. SELF.
autophilic 362. SELF, autophilia.
autophobia 313. PHOBIAS; 362. SELF.
autophoby 41. BEHAVIOR; 313. PHOBIAS,
autophobia; 362. SELF, autophobia.
autophonomania 112. DEATH;
254. MANIAS.
autophony 111. DEAFNESS;
266. MEDICAL SPECIALTIES.
autoplagiarism 249. LITERATURE;
362. SELF.
autopsy 99. CORPSES.
autoradiograph 315. PHOTOGRAPHY.
autotelic 23. ART, autotelism.
autotelism 23. ART.
autothaumaturgist 243. LIES and LYING.
autotheism 28. ATTITUDES; 79. CHRIST.
autotheist 79. CHRIST, autotheism.
autotheistic 79. CHRIST, autotheism.
autotype 315. PHOTOGRAPHY.

auxanographic 44. BIOLOGY,
auxanography.
auxanography 44. BIOLOGY.
auxanology 191. GROWTH, auxology.
auxesis 44. BIOLOGY; 72. CELLS;
191. GROWTH.
auxetic 44. BIOLOGY, auxesis;
72. CELLS, auxesis; 191. GROWTH,
auxesis.
auxographic 319. PLANTS, auxography.
auxography 319. PLANTS.
auxology 191. GROWTH.
Averrhoism 312. PHILOSOPHY,
Averroism.
Averrhoist 312. PHILOSOPHY,
Averroism.
Averrhoistic 312. PHILOSOPHY,
Averroism.
Averroism 312. PHILOSOPHY.
Averroist 312. PHILOSOPHY, Averroism.
Averroistic 312. PHILOSOPHY,
Averroism.
avicide 45. BIRDS; 232. KILLING.
aviculture 45. BIRDS.
aviculturist 45. BIRDS, aviculture.
avigation 31. AVIATION.
avinosis 31. AVIATION.
avionics 31. AVIATION.
avitaminosis 122. DISEASE and ILLNESS.
avitaminotic 122. DISEASE and ILLNESS,
avitaminosis.
avowtry 239. LAW.
axinomancy 124. DIVINATION.
axinomantic 124. DIVINATION,
axinomancy.
axiological 145. ETHICS, axiology;
407. VALUES, axiology.
axiologist 145. ETHICS, axiology;
407. VALUES, axiology.
axiology 145. ETHICS; 407. VALUES.
Ayurveda 206. HINDUISM, Ayurvedism.
Ayurvedic 206. HINDUISM, Ayurvedism.
Ayurvedism 206. HINDUISM.
azoology 290. NATURE.
Azymite 80. CHRISTIANITY.

B

Baalism 183. GOD and GODS.
Baalistic 183. GOD and GODS, Baalism.
Baalite 183. GOD and GODS, Baalism.

Babbittism 28. ATTITUDES.
Babbittry 28. ATTITUDES, **Babbittism.**
Babiism 227. ISLAM, **Babism.**
Babism 227. ISLAM.
Babist 227. ISLAM, **Babism.**
babooism 41. BEHAVIOR, **babuism.**
Babouvism 322. POLITICS.
Babouvist 322. POLITICS, **Babouvism.**
babuism 41. BEHAVIOR.
babyolatry 349. RELIGION.
bacchanalian 8. ALCOHOL,
  bacchanalianism.
bacchanalianism 8. ALCOHOL.
bacchic 409. VERSE, **bacchius.**
bacchius 409. VERSE.
bachelorism 253. MALE.
bacillophobia 313. PHOBIAS.
bactericide 232. KILLING;
  350. REMEDIES.
bacteriologic 32. BACTERIA,
  bacteriology.
bacteriological 32. BACTERIA,
  bacteriology.
bacteriologist 32. BACTERIA,
  bacteriology.
bacteriology 32. BACTERIA.
bacteriophobia 313. PHOBIAS,
  bacillophobia.
bacterioscopist 266. MEDICAL
  SPECIALTIES, **bacterioscopy.**
bacterioscopy 266. MEDICAL
  SPECIALTIES.
bacteriostasis 197. HEALTH.
bacteriostat 197. HEALTH,
  bacteriostasis.
bacteriostatic 197. HEALTH,
  bacteriostasis.
baculometry 264. MEASUREMENT.
Baha'i 349. RELIGION, **Baha'ism.**
Baha'ism 349. RELIGION.
Baha'ist 349. RELIGION, **Baha'ism.**
Bakuninism 94. COMMUNISM.
balladism 378. SONGS and SINGING.
balladist 378. SONGS and SINGING,
  balladism.
ballistic 274. MISSILES, **ballistics.**
ballistic galvanometer
  226. INSTRUMENTS.
ballistician 274. MISSILES, **ballistics.**
ballistics 274. MISSILES.

ballistomania 254. MANIAS;
  416. WEAPONRY.
ballistophobia 274. MISSILES;
  313. PHOBIAS.
ballooning 31. AVIATION.
balloonry 31. AVIATION, **ballooning.**
balneography 36. BATHING.
balneologic 36. BATHING, **balneology.**
balneological 36. BATHING, **balneology.**
balneologist 36. BATHING, **balneology.**
balneology 36. BATHING.
balneotherapy 350. REMEDIES;
  414. WATER.
banditry 391. THEFT.
Bantingism 168. FOOD and NUTRITION.
baptisaphily 35. BAPTISM.
baragnosis 189. GRAVITY.
Barbara 250. LOGIC.
barbarian 237. LANGUAGE STYLE,
  barbarism.
barbarism 237. LANGUAGE STYLE.
barbiturism 130. DRUGS; 321. POISON.
bardism 409. VERSE.
Barmalip 250. LOGIC.
Barnumism 41. BEHAVIOR;
  310. PERFORMING.
Baroco 250. LOGIC.
barognosis 189. GRAVITY.
barograph 27. ATMOSPHERE;
  417. WEATHER.
barology 189. GRAVITY.
barometer 226. INSTRUMENTS.
barometrography 27. ATMOSPHERE;
  417. WEATHER.
barometry 27. ATMOSPHERE;
  417. WEATHER.
barophobia 189. GRAVITY; 313. PHOBIAS.
baroque 20. ARCHITECTURE; 23. ART.
barrator 239. LAW, **barratry.**
barratrous 239. LAW, **barratry;**
  366. SHIPS, **barratry.**
barratry 239. LAW; 366. SHIPS.
barretry 366. SHIPS, **barratry.**
Bascology 236. LANGUAGE.
bashawism 41. BEHAVIOR.
basiphobia 313. PHOBIAS, **basophobia;**
  319. PLANTS, **basophobia.**
basiphobic 319. PLANTS, **basophobia.**
basophile 72. CELLS.
basophilic 72. CELLS, **basophile.**
basophilous 72. CELLS, **basophile.**

basophobia 313. PHOBIAS; 319. PLANTS.
basophobic 319. PLANTS, **basophobia.**
bastardism 77. CHILDREN.
bastardy 77. CHILDREN, **bastardism.**
bathmism 191. GROWTH.
bathmophobia 313. PHOBIAS;
412. WALKING.
bathometer 115. DEPTH.
bathophobia 36. BATHING;
313. PHOBIAS.
bathyclinograph 115. DEPTH; 360. SEA.
bathygram 360. SEA, **bathygraphy.**
bathygraph 360. SEA, **bathygraphy.**
bathygraphy 360. SEA.
bathymeter 115. DEPTH, **bathometer.**
bathymetric 115. DEPTH, **bathymetry.**
bathymetrical 115. DEPTH,
bathymetry.
bathymetry 115. DEPTH.
bathyscape 115. DEPTH, **bathyscaphe.**
bathyscaph 115. DEPTH, **bathyscaphe.**
bathyscaphe 115. DEPTH; 360. SEA.
bathyseism 134. EARTHQUAKES.
bathysphere 115. DEPTH.
bathythermograph 115. DEPTH.
batologist 54. BOTANY, **batology.**
batology 54. BOTANY.
batophobia 60. BUILDINGS;
202. HEIGHTS; 313. PHOBIAS.
batrachophobia 313. PHOBIAS.
battery 239. LAW.
battology 237. LANGUAGE STYLE;
354. RHETORIC and RHETORICAL
DEVICES.
bawdry 364. SEX.
beadledom 62. BUREAUCRACY.
beatnikism 28. ATTITUDES;
41. BEHAVIOR.
beauish 28. ATTITUDES, **beauism.**
beauism 28. ATTITUDES.
bedlamism 224. INSANITY; 301. ORDER
and DISORDER.
bedlamite 224. INSANITY.
beerocracy 39. BEER; 376. SOCIETY.
beggarism 325. POVERTY.
behaviorism 334. PSYCHOLOGY.
behaviorist 334. PSYCHOLOGY,
behaviorism.
behavioristic 334. PSYCHOLOGY,
behaviorism.

Behmenism 285. MYSTICISM,
Boehmenism.
belles lettres 249. LITERATURE,
belletrism.
belles-lettrism 249. LITERATURE,
belletrism.
belletrism 249. LITERATURE.
belletrist 249. LITERATURE, **belletrism.**
belletristic 249. LITERATURE,
belletrism.
bellicism 413. WAR.
bellicist 413. WAR, **bellicism.**
bellicose 28. ATTITUDES, **bellicosity.**
bellicosity 28. ATTITUDES.
belligerence 413. WAR.
belligerent 413. WAR, **belligerence.**
belomancy 22. ARROWS;
124. DIVINATION.
belonephobia 313. PHOBIAS;
365. SHARPNESS.
Benedictine 277. MONKS and NUNS,
Benedictinism.
Benedictinism 277. MONKS and NUNS.
Benthamic 312. PHILOSOPHY,
Benthamism.
Benthamism 312. PHILOSOPHY.
Benthamite 312. PHILOSOPHY,
Benthamism.
benthos 115. DEPTH; 360. SEA.
benthoscope 115. DEPTH; 360. SEA.
Berengarian 205. HERESY,
Berengarianism.
Berengarianism 205. HERESY.
Bergsonian 312. PHILOSOPHY,
Bergsonism.
Bergsonism 312. PHILOSOPHY.
Berkeleian 309. PERCEPTION,
Berkeleianism; 312. PHILOSOPHY,
Berkeleianism.
Berkeleianism 309. PERCEPTION;
312. PHILOSOPHY.
Berkeleyan 309. PERCEPTION,
Berkeleianism.
Berkeleyanism 309. PERCEPTION,
Berkeleianism.
Berkeleyism 309. PERCEPTION,
Berkeleianism.
bestiality 41. BEHAVIOR; 364. SEX.
bestiarian 16. ANIMALS.
bestiarist 16. ANIMALS.

bestiary 16. ANIMALS; 91. COLLECTIONS
and COLLECTING; 249. LITERATURE.
bestsellerism 249. LITERATURE.
betacism 247. LINGUISTICS.
betacist 247. LINGUISTICS, betacism.
biarchy 185. GOVERNMENT.
bibacious 8. ALCOHOL, bibacity.
bibacity 8. ALCOHOL.
biblicism 43. BIBLE.
biblicist 43. BIBLE.
biblioclasm 43. BIBLE.
biblioclast 43. BIBLE, biblioclasm.
bibliogenesis 53. BOOKS.
bibliogenetic 53. BOOKS, bibliogenesis.
bibliognost 53. BOOKS.
bibliognostic 53. BOOKS, bibliognost.
bibliogony 53. BOOKS.
bibliographer 53. BOOKS, bibliography.
bibliographic 53. BOOKS, bibliography.
bibliographical 53. BOOKS,
bibliography.
bibliography 53. BOOKS.
biblioklept 53. BOOKS,
bibliokleptomania.
bibliokleptomania 53. BOOKS;
391. THEFT.
bibliokleptomaniac 391. THEFT,
bibliokleptomania.
bibliolater 43. BIBLE; 53. BOOKS.
bibliolatrist 43. BIBLE, bibliolater;
53. BOOKS, bibliolater.
bibliolatry 53. BOOKS.
bibliologist 53. BOOKS, bibliology.
bibliology 53. BOOKS.
bibliomancy 43. BIBLE; 53. BOOKS;
124. DIVINATION.
bibliomania 53. BOOKS; 254. MANIAS.
bibliomaniac 53. BOOKS, bibliomania.
bibliomaniacal 53. BOOKS,
bibliomania.
bibliopegic 53. BOOKS, bibliopegy.
bibliopegist 53. BOOKS, bibliopegy.
bibliopegy 53. BOOKS.
bibliophage 53. BOOKS.
bibliophagous 53. BOOKS, bibliophage.
bibliophagy 53. BOOKS, bibliophage.
bibliophile 311. -PHILE, -PHILIA, -PHILY.
bibliophile 53. BOOKS, bibliophilism.
bibliophilic 53. BOOKS, bibliophilism.
bibliophilism 53. BOOKS;
91. COLLECTIONS and COLLECTING.

bibliophilist 53. BOOKS, bibliophilism.
bibliophily 53. BOOKS, bibliophilism;
91. COLLECTIONS and COLLECTING,
bibliophilism.
bibliophobe 53. BOOKS.
bibliophobia 53. BOOKS; 313. PHOBIAS.
bibliopole 53. BOOKS, bibliopolism.
bibliopolic 53. BOOKS, bibliopolism.
bibliopolism 53. BOOKS.
bibliopolist 53. BOOKS, bibliopolism.
bibliopoly 53. BOOKS, bibliopolism.
bibliotaph 53. BOOKS, bibliotaphy.
bibliotaphic 53. BOOKS, bibliotaphy.
bibliotaphy 53. BOOKS.
bibliothecary 53. BOOKS.
bibliotherapeutic 53. BOOKS,
bibliotherapy; 350. REMEDIES,
bibliotherapy.
bibliotherapist 53. BOOKS,
bibliotherapy; 350. REMEDIES,
bibliotherapy.
bibliotherapy 53. BOOKS;
350. REMEDIES.
bibliotic 256. MANUSCRIPTS, bibliotics;
428. WRITING, bibliotics.
bibliotics 256. MANUSCRIPTS;
428. WRITING.
bibliotist 256. MANUSCRIPTS, bibliotics;
428. WRITING, bibliotics.
bibulosity 8. ALCOHOL.
bibulous 8. ALCOHOL, bibulosity.
bicameral 185. GOVERNMENT,
bicameralism.
bicameralism 185. GOVERNMENT.
bicameralist 185. GOVERNMENT,
bicameralism.
bigamist 103. CRIME, bigamy;
258. MARRIAGE, bigamy.
bigamous 103. CRIME, bigamy;
258. MARRIAGE, bigamy.
bigamy 103. CRIME; 258. MARRIAGE.
bigot 28. ATTITUDES, bigotry;
341. RACE, bigotry; 349. RELIGION,
bigotry.
bigoted 28. ATTITUDES, bigotry;
341. RACE, bigotry; 349. RELIGION,
bigotry.
bigotry 28. ATTITUDES; 341. RACE;
349. RELIGION.
bilateralism 137. ECONOMICS.

bilateralistic 137. ECONOMICS,
  bilateralism.
bilingual 236. LANGUAGE, bilingualism.
bilingualism 236. LANGUAGE.
bilinguality 236. LANGUAGE,
  bilingualism.
bilinguist 236. LANGUAGE,
  bilingualism.
biliteral 236. LANGUAGE, biliteralism.
biliteralism 236. LANGUAGE.
billingsgate 236. LANGUAGE.
biloquism 382. SPEECH.
biloquist 382. SPEECH, biloquism.
bimetallism 276. MONEY.
bimetallist 276. MONEY, bimetallism.
bimetallistic 276. MONEY, bimetallism.
binomial 83. CLASSIFICATION.
bioastronautics 31. AVIATION; 51. BODY,
  HUMAN.
biochemical 244. LIFE, biochemistry.
biochemist 244. LIFE, biochemistry.
biochemistry 244. LIFE.
bioclimatician 27. ATMOSPHERE,
  bioclimatology.
bioclimatological 27. ATMOSPHERE,
  bioclimatology.
bioclimatologist 27. ATMOSPHERE,
  bioclimatology.
bioclimatology 27. ATMOSPHERE.
biodegradability 44. BIOLOGY;
  113. DECAYING.
biodegradable 44. BIOLOGY,
  biodegradability; 113. DECAYING,
  biodegradability.
biodynamic 16. ANIMALS, biodynamics;
  319. PLANTS, biodynamics.
biodynamical 16. ANIMALS,
  biodynamics; 319. PLANTS,
  biodynamics.
biodynamics 16. ANIMALS; 319. PLANTS.
bioecologic 16. ANIMALS, bioecology.
bioecological 16. ANIMALS, bioecology.
bioecologist 16. ANIMALS, bioecology;
  142. ENVIRONMENT, bioecology.
bioecology 16. ANIMALS;
  142. ENVIRONMENT.
biofeedback 56. BRAIN.
biogenesis 44. BIOLOGY; 244. LIFE.
biogenetic 44. BIOLOGY, biogenesis;
  244. LIFE, biogenesis.
biogenetically 44. BIOLOGY, biogenesis.

biogenic 44. BIOLOGY, biogenesis;
  244. LIFE, biogenesis.
biogenically 44. BIOLOGY, biogenesis.
biogeny 44. BIOLOGY, biogenesis;
  244. LIFE, biogenesis.
biogeography 44. BIOLOGY.
bioinstrumentation 226. INSTRUMENTS.
biolinguist 247. LINGUISTICS,
  biolinguistics.
biolinguistics 247. LINGUISTICS.
biological 244. LIFE, biology.
biologism 44. BIOLOGY.
biologist 244. LIFE, biology.
biologistic 44. BIOLOGY, biologism.
biology 244. LIFE.
bioluminescence 44. BIOLOGY.
bioluminescent 44. BIOLOGY,
  bioluminescence.
biolysis 244. LIFE.
biolytic 244. LIFE, biolysis.
biomagnetic 215. HYPNOSIS,
  biomagnetism; 364. SEX,
  biomagnetism.
biomagnetism 215. HYPNOSIS; 364. SEX.
biometeorology 27. ATMOSPHERE,
  bioclimatology.
biometric 44. BIOLOGY, biometrics;
  244. LIFE, biometrics;
  262. MATHEMATICS, biometrics.
biometrical 44. BIOLOGY, biometrics;
  244. LIFE, biometrics;
  262. MATHEMATICS, biometrics.
biometrics 44. BIOLOGY; 244. LIFE;
  262. MATHEMATICS.
biometry 44. BIOLOGY, biometrics;
  244. LIFE, biometrics;
  262. MATHEMATICS, biometrics.
bionic 30. AUTOMATION, bionics;
  51. BODY, HUMAN, bionics.
bionics 30. AUTOMATION; 51. BODY,
  HUMAN.
bionomic 44. BIOLOGY, bionomics;
  142. ENVIRONMENT, bionomics.
bionomical 44. BIOLOGY, bionomics;
  142. ENVIRONMENT, bionomics.
bionomics 44. BIOLOGY;
  142. ENVIRONMENT.
bionomist 44. BIOLOGY, bionomics;
  142. ENVIRONMENT, bionomics.

bionomy 44. BIOLOGY, bionomics;
142. ENVIRONMENT, bionomics;
142. ENVIRONMENT, ecology.
biophagery 168. FOOD and NUTRITION,
biophagism.
biophagism 168. FOOD and NUTRITION.
biophagous 168. FOOD and NUTRITION,
biophagism.
biophysical 316. PHYSICS, biophysics.
biophysicist 316. PHYSICS, biophysics.
biophysics 316. PHYSICS.
biophysiologist 44. BIOLOGY,
biophysiology; 51. BODY, HUMAN,
biophysiology.
biophysiology 44. BIOLOGY; 51. BODY,
HUMAN.
biopsy 51. BODY, HUMAN; 266. MEDICAL
SPECIALTIES.
bioptic 51. BODY, HUMAN, biopsy;
266. MEDICAL SPECIALTIES, biopsy.
bioscience 44. BIOLOGY.
bioscope 159. FILMS.
bioscopy 266. MEDICAL SPECIALTIES.
biosophist 362. SELF, biosophy.
biosophy 362. SELF.
biosphere 44. BIOLOGY; 133. EARTH;
244. LIFE.
biostatical 16. ANIMALS, biostatics;
319. PLANTS, biostatics.
biostatics 16. ANIMALS; 319. PLANTS.
biosynthesis 44. BIOLOGY;
302. ORGANISMS.
biosynthetic 44. BIOLOGY, biosynthesis;
302. ORGANISMS, biosynthesis.
biosystematic 44. BIOLOGY,
biosystematy; 83. CLASSIFICATION,
biosystematics; 83. CLASSIFICATION,
biosystematy; 288. NAMES,
biosystematics; 288. NAMES,
biosystematy.
biosystematical 44. BIOLOGY,
biosystematy; 83. CLASSIFICATION,
biosystematics; 83. CLASSIFICATION,
biosystematy; 288. NAMES,
biosystematics; 288. NAMES,
biosystematy.
biosystematics 44. BIOLOGY;
44. BIOLOGY, biosystematy;
83. CLASSIFICATION; 288. NAMES.
biosystematy 44. BIOLOGY;
83. CLASSIFICATION; 288. NAMES.

biota 16. ANIMALS; 319. PLANTS.
biotechnologic 255. MANKIND,
biotechnology.
biotechnological 255. MANKIND,
biotechnology.
biotechnologist 255. MANKIND,
biotechnology.
biotechnology 142. ENVIRONMENT;
255. MANKIND.
biotherapy 350. REMEDIES.
biotypologic 44. BIOLOGY, biotypology;
204. HEREDITY, biotypology;
302. ORGANISMS, biotypology.
biotypological 44. BIOLOGY,
biotypology; 204. HEREDITY,
biotypology; 302. ORGANISMS,
biotypology.
biotypology 44. BIOLOGY;
204. HEREDITY; 302. ORGANISMS.
bipartisan 185. GOVERNMENT,
bipartisanism; 322. POLITICS,
bipartisanism.
bipartisanism 185. GOVERNMENT;
322. POLITICS.
biped 157. FEET and LEGS.
bipedal 157. FEET and LEGS, biped.
biracial 341. RACE, biracialism.
biracialism 341. RACE.
biracialist 341. RACE, biracialism.
birefringence 245. LIGHT.
birefringent 245. LIGHT, birefringence.
bise 420. WIND.
bisexual 51. BODY, HUMAN, bisexualism;
334. PSYCHOLOGY, bisexualism;
364. SEX, bisexualism.
bisexualism 51. BODY, HUMAN;
334. PSYCHOLOGY; 364. SEX.
bisexuality 51. BODY, HUMAN,
bisexualism; 334. PSYCHOLOGY,
bisexualism; 364. SEX, bisexualism.
bissextile 65. CALENDAR, bissextus.
bissextus 65. CALENDAR.
bisymmetric 54. BOTANY, bisymmetry;
389. SYMMETRY, bisymmetry.
bisymmetrical 54. BOTANY,
bisymmetry; 389. SYMMETRY,
bisymmetry.
bisymmetry 54. BOTANY;
389. SYMMETRY.
bitheism 183. GOD and GODS.
bitheist 183. GOD and GODS, bitheism.

bitheistic 183. GOD and GODS, **bitheism.**
bizarrerie 41. BEHAVIOR.
bize 420. WIND, **bise.**
blackguardery 41. BEHAVIOR,
  blackguardism.
blackguardism 41. BEHAVIOR.
blackguardly 41. BEHAVIOR,
  blackguardism.
blastocytoma 66. CANCER, **blastoma.**
blastogenesis 204. HEREDITY.
blastogenetic 204. HEREDITY,
  blastogenesis.
blastoma 66. CANCER.
blazonry 210. HONORS and REGALIA.
blennophobia 84. CLEANLINESS;
  313. PHOBIAS.
blennorheal 122. DISEASE and ILLNESS,
  blennorrhea.
blennorheic 122. DISEASE and ILLNESS,
  blennorrhea.
blennorhoeal 122. DISEASE and ILLNESS,
  blennorrhea.
blennorhoeic 122. DISEASE and ILLNESS,
  blennorrhea.
blennorrhea 122. DISEASE and ILLNESS.
blennorrhoea 122. DISEASE and ILLNESS,
  blennorrhea.
blepharism 148. EYES.
blepharitis 148. EYES.
blepharoptosis 148. EYES.
bletonism 414. WATER.
bluestocking 424. WOMEN,
  bluestockingism.
bluestockingism 240. LEARNING;
  424. WOMEN.
Bocardo 250. LOGIC.
Boehmenism 285. MYSTICISM.
Boehmenist 285. MYSTICISM,
  Boehmenism.
Boehmenite 285. MYSTICISM,
  Boehmenism.
Boehmist 285. MYSTICISM,
  Boehmenism.
bogeyism 114. DEMONS, **bogyism.**
bogyism 114. DEMONS.
bogyphobia 313. PHOBIAS.
bohemian 41. BEHAVIOR,
  bohemianism.
bohemianism 41. BEHAVIOR.
Bollandist 359. SAINTS.
bolograph 342. RADIATION.

Boloism 322. POLITICS.
bolometer 342. RADIATION.
bolometric 342. RADIATION, **bolometry.**
bolometrist 342. RADIATION,
  bolometry.
bolometry 342. RADIATION.
Bolshevik 94. COMMUNISM, **Bolshevism.**
Bolshevism 94. COMMUNISM.
Bolshevist 94. COMMUNISM,
  Bolshevism.
bombilation 380. SOUND.
bombination 380. SOUND.
Bonapartism 322. POLITICS.
Bonapartist 322. POLITICS,
  Bonapartism.
Bönism 349. RELIGION.
boobyish 41. BEHAVIOR, **boobyism.**
boobyism 41. BEHAVIOR.
boodleism 322. POLITICS.
boodler 322. POLITICS, **boodleism.**
boodling 322. POLITICS, **boodleism.**
bossism 322. POLITICS.
botanical 54. BOTANY, **botany.**
botanist 54. BOTANY, **botany.**
botanomancy 124. DIVINATION;
  319. PLANTS.
botany 54. BOTANY.
bottomry 366. SHIPS.
botulism 168. FOOD and NUTRITION;
  321. POISON.
boulimia 122. DISEASE and ILLNESS,
  bulimia; 168. FOOD and NUTRITION,
  bulimia.
boulimiac 122. DISEASE and ILLNESS,
  bulimia; 168. FOOD and NUTRITION,
  bulimia.
boulimic 122. DISEASE and ILLNESS,
  bulimia; 168. FOOD and NUTRITION,
  bulimia.
boulimorexia 122. DISEASE and ILLNESS,
  bulimorexia; 168. FOOD and
  NUTRITION, **bulimorexia.**
boulimorexic 122. DISEASE and ILLNESS,
  bulimorexia; 168. FOOD and
  NUTRITION, **bulimorexia.**
Boulwarism 303. ORGANIZED LABOR.
Bourbonian 322. POLITICS,
  Bourbonism.
Bourbonic 322. POLITICS, **Bourbonism.**
Bourbonism 322. POLITICS.
Bourbonist 322. POLITICS, **Bourbonism.**

Bourigianism 285. MYSTICISM.
bovine 217. IDIOCY, **bovinity.**
bovinity 217. IDIOCY.
bowdlerism 249. LITERATURE.
bowdlerization 249. LITERATURE,
bowdlerism.
bowdlerize 249. LITERATURE,
bowdlerism.
boycotter 137. ECONOMICS, **boycottism.**
boycottism 137. ECONOMICS.
brachialgia 306. PAIN.
brachiation 16. ANIMALS.
brachycephalic 196. HEAD,
brachycephalism.
brachycephalism 196. HEAD.
brachycephalous 196. HEAD,
brachycephalism.
brachycephaly 196. HEAD,
brachycephalism.
brachygraphic 428. WRITING,
brachygraphy.
brachygraphy 428. WRITING.
brachylogy 58. BREVITY.
bradykinesia 282. MOTION.
bradykinesis 282. MOTION,
bradykinesia.
bradykinetic 282. MOTION,
bradykinesia.
bradyseism 134. EARTHQUAKES.
bradyseismic 134. EARTHQUAKES,
bradyseism.
braggart 41. BEHAVIOR, **braggartism.**
braggartism 41. BEHAVIOR.
braggartist 41. BEHAVIOR, **braggartism.**
Brahmanism 206. HINDUISM.
Brahminism 206. HINDUISM,
Brahmanism.
Brahmoism 206. HINDUISM.
Braidism 372. SLEEP.
Bramantip 250. LOGIC, **Barmalip.**
brandophily 91. COLLECTIONS and
COLLECTING.
brassage 131. DUES and PAYMENT.
breathalyzer 8. ALCOHOL,
drunkometer; 226. INSTRUMENTS.
brecciation 179. GEOLOGY.
breeze 420. WIND.
breviary 53. BOOKS; 69. CATHOLICISM.
brigand 391. THEFT, **brigandism.**
brigandage 391. THEFT, **brigandism.**
brigandish 391. THEFT, **brigandism.**

brigandism 391. THEFT.
brinkmanship 322. POLITICS.
brinksmanship 322. POLITICS,
brinkmanship.
Briticism 140. ENGLISH; 236. LANGUAGE.
Britishism 140. ENGLISH, **Briticism;**
236. LANGUAGE, **Briticism.**
Brobdingnagian 368. SIZE.
brokerage 131. DUES and PAYMENT.
bromatology 168. FOOD and NUTRITION.
bromide 333. PROVERBS.
bromidism 122. DISEASE and ILLNESS,
bromism.
bromidrosiphobia 84. CLEANLINESS;
313. PHOBIAS.
brominism 122. DISEASE and ILLNESS,
bromism.
bromism 122. DISEASE and ILLNESS.
bromography 168. FOOD and
NUTRITION.
brontograph 394. THUNDER.
brontolite 179. GEOLOGY, **brontolith.**
brontolith 179. GEOLOGY.
brontology 394. THUNDER.
brontometer 394. THUNDER.
brontophobia 313. PHOBIAS;
394. THUNDER.
Brownism 332. PROTESTANTISM.
Brownist 332. PROTESTANTISM,
Brownism.
Brownistic 332. PROTESTANTISM,
Brownism.
Brutalism 20. ARCHITECTURE.
brutalitarian 41. BEHAVIOR,
brutalitarianism.
brutalitarianism 41. BEHAVIOR.
brutish 41. BEHAVIOR, **brutism.**
brutism 41. BEHAVIOR.
bruxism 390. TEETH.
bruxomania 390. TEETH, **bruxism.**
bryologist 54. BOTANY, **bryology.**
bryology 54. BOTANY.
Buchmanism 332. PROTESTANTISM.
Buchmanite 332. PROTESTANTISM,
Buchmanism.
bucolic 28. ATTITUDES, **bucolicism.**
bucolical 28. ATTITUDES, **bucolicism.**
bucolicism 28. ATTITUDES.
Buddhism 59. BUDDHISM.
Buddhist 59. BUDDHISM, **Buddhism.**
Buddhistic 59. BUDDHISM, **Buddhism.**

Buddhistical 59. BUDDHISM, **Buddhism.**
buffoon 213. HUMOR, **buffoonism.**
buffoonery 213. HUMOR, **buffoonism.**
buffoonish 213. HUMOR, **buffoonism.**
buffoonism 213. HUMOR.
bugologist 225. INSECTS, **bugology.**
bugology 225. INSECTS.
bulimia 122. DISEASE and ILLNESS; 168. FOOD and NUTRITION.
bulimiac 122. DISEASE and ILLNESS, **bulimia;** 168. FOOD and NUTRITION, **bulimia.**
bulimic 122. DISEASE and ILLNESS, **bulimia;** 168. FOOD and NUTRITION, **bulimia.**
bulimorexia 122. DISEASE and ILLNESS; 168. FOOD and NUTRITION.
bulimorexic 122. DISEASE and ILLNESS, **bulimorexia;** 168. FOOD and NUTRITION, **bulimorexia.**
bulldogger 61. BULLS and BULLFIGHTING, **bulldogging.**
bulldogging 61. BULLS and BULLFIGHTING.
bullionism 276. MONEY.
bullionist 276. MONEY, **bullionism.**
bullyism 41. BEHAVIOR.
bumbledom 62. BUREAUCRACY.
bumpologist 196. HEAD, **bumpology.**
bumpology 196. HEAD.
Bund 152. FASCISM, **Bundist.**
Bundist 152. FASCISM.
bungaloid 20. ARCHITECTURE.
bureaucracy 62. BUREAUCRACY.
bureaucratese 62. BUREAUCRACY; 237. LANGUAGE STYLE.
bureaucratic 62. BUREAUCRACY, **bureaucracy.**
burgage 235. LAND; 331. PROPERTY and OWNERSHIP.
burinist 141. ENGRAVING.
burlesque 352. REPRESENTATION.
bursary 160. FINANCE.
businessese 237. LANGUAGE STYLE.
Byronism 248. LITERARY STYLE.
Byzantinism 80. CHRISTIANITY.

C

cabalism 231. JUDAISM.
cabalist 231. JUDAISM, **cabalism.**

cabalistic 231. JUDAISM, **cabalism.**
cabotage 366. SHIPS; 398. TRADE.
cacesthesia 122. DISEASE and ILLNESS.
cachexia 197. HEALTH.
cachexy 197. HEALTH, **cachexia.**
cachinnation 238. LAUGHTER.
caciquism 185. GOVERNMENT.
caciquismo 185. GOVERNMENT, **caciquism.**
cacodemonia 114. DEMONS.
cacodemoniac 114. DEMONS, **cacodemonia.**
cacodemonic 114. DEMONS, **cacodemonia.**
cacodemonomania 114. DEMONS, **cacodemonia.**
cacoepy 330. PRONUNCIATION.
cacoethes 122. DISEASE and ILLNESS.
cacoethic 122. DISEASE and ILLNESS, **cacoethes.**
cacogenic 341. RACE, **cacogenics.**
cacogenics 341. RACE.
cacographer 383. SPELLING, **cacography;** 428. WRITING, **cacography.**
cacographic 383. SPELLING, **cacography;** 428. WRITING, **cacography.**
cacographical 383. SPELLING, **cacography;** 428. WRITING, **cacography.**
cacography 383. SPELLING; 428. WRITING.
cacology 330. PRONUNCIATION; 382. SPEECH.
caconymic 288. NAMES.
cacophonic 380. SOUND, **cacophony.**
cacophonous 380. SOUND, **cacophony.**
cacophony 380. SOUND.
cadastration 235. LAND.
caducity 113. DECAYING; 299. OLD AGE.
caducous 113. DECAYING, **caducity.**
Caesarism 322. POLITICS.
Caesarist 322. POLITICS, **Caesarism.**
cagophily 91. COLLECTIONS and COLLECTING.
Cahenslyism 69. CATHOLICISM.
Cainism 205. HERESY.
Cainite 205. HERESY, **Cainism.**
Cainitism 205. HERESY, **Cainism.**

cainophobia 74. CHANGE,
cainotophobia; 74. CHANGE,
misoneism; 294. NOVELTY;
313. PHOBIAS.
cainotophobia 74. CHANGE;
74. CHANGE, misoneism;
294. NOVELTY, cainophobia;
313. PHOBIAS, cainophobia.
calciphilia 122. DISEASE and ILLNESS.
calculus 262. MATHEMATICS.
caldarium 36. BATHING.
calendographer 65. CALENDAR.
calenture 122. DISEASE and ILLNESS.
caliology 45. BIRDS.
calisthenic 26. ATHLETICS, calisthenics.
calisthenical 26. ATHLETICS,
calisthenics.
calisthenics 26. ATHLETICS.
Calixtine 332. PROTESTANTISM.
callid 106. CUNNING, callidity.
callidity 106. CUNNING.
calligrapher 428. WRITING,
calligraphy.
calligraphic 428. WRITING, calligraphy.
calligraphical 428. WRITING,
calligraphy.
calligraphist 428. WRITING,
calligraphy.
calligraphy 428. WRITING.
callipygia 51. BODY, HUMAN.
callipygian 51. BODY, HUMAN,
callipygia.
callipygous 51. BODY, HUMAN,
callipygia.
callipygy 51. BODY, HUMAN, callipygia.
callithumpian 310. PERFORMING.
calorimeter 200. HEAT, calorimetry.
calorimetric 200. HEAT, calorimetry.
calorimetry 200. HEAT.
calorist 200. HEAT.
caloristic 200. HEAT, calorist.
Calvinism 332. PROTESTANTISM.
Calvinist 332. PROTESTANTISM,
Calvinism.
Calvinistic 332. PROTESTANTISM,
Calvinism.
Calvinistical 332. PROTESTANTISM,
Calvinism.
calvities 33. BALDNESS.
calvity 33. BALDNESS, calvities.
calvous 33. BALDNESS, calvities.

cambism 160. FINANCE; 276. MONEY.
cambist 160. FINANCE; 160. FINANCE,
cambism; 276. MONEY, cambism.
cambistry 160. FINANCE; 276. MONEY,
cambism.
cameist 297. OCCUPATIONS.
cameography 141. ENGRAVING;
177. GEMS.
cameralism 137. ECONOMICS.
cameralist 137. ECONOMICS;
137. ECONOMICS, cameralism.
cameralistic 137. ECONOMICS,
cameralism; 137. ECONOMICS,
cameralist.
Camestres 250. LOGIC.
campanarian 42. BELLS.
campanile 42. BELLS.
campanist 42. BELLS.
campanologer 42. BELLS,
campanology.
campanological 42. BELLS,
campanology.
campanologist 42. BELLS.
campanology.
campanology 42. BELLS.
Canadianism 236. LANGUAGE.
cancericidal 66. CANCER.
cancerophobia 66. CANCER;
313. PHOBIAS, carcinomophobia.
cancroid 66. CANCER.
caneology 335. PUNISHMENT.
cannabism 130. DRUGS.
cannibalic 166. FLESH, cannibalism.
cannibalism 166. FLESH.
cannibalistic 166. FLESH, cannibalism.
cannonry 416. WEAPONRY.
cantharidism 321. POISON.
canto 409. VERSE.
Caodaism 349. RELIGION.
Caodaist 349. RELIGION, Caodaism.
Caodism 349. RELIGION, Caodaism.
capitalism 137. ECONOMICS;
322. POLITICS.
capitalist 137. ECONOMICS, capitalism;
322. POLITICS, capitalism.
capitalistic 137. ECONOMICS,
capitalism; 322. POLITICS, capitalism.
capnomancy 124. DIVINATION;
373. SMOKE.
caprification 54. BOTANY.
caprificator 54. BOTANY, caprification.

carcinectomy 66. CANCER.
carcinogen 66. CANCER.
carcinogenic 66. CANCER, **carcinogen.**
carcinoid 66. CANCER.
carcinologic 16. ANIMALS, **carcinology.**
carcinological 16. ANIMALS,
  carcinology.
carcinologist 16. ANIMALS, **carcinology;**
  430. ZOOLOGY, **carcinology.**
carcinology 16. ANIMALS;
  430. ZOOLOGY.
carcinolysis 66. CANCER.
carcinoma 66. CANCER.
carcinomatophobia 66. CANCER,
  carcinomophobia; 313. PHOBIAS,
  carcinomophobia.
carcinomatosis 66. CANCER.
carcinomatous 66. CANCER, **carcinoma.**
carcinomophobia 66. CANCER;
  313. PHOBIAS.
carcinophilia 66. CANCER; 311. -PHILE,
  -PHILIA, -PHILY.
carcinophilic 66. CANCER,
  carcinophilia.
carcinophobia 66. CANCER,
  carcinomophobia; 313. PHOBIAS,
  carcinomophobia.
carcinosis 66. CANCER.
carcinostatic 66. CANCER.
cardialgia 199. HEART; 306. PAIN.
cardialgy 199. HEART, **cardialgia;**
  306. PAIN, **cardialgia.**
cardioangiology 199. HEART.
cardiocentesis 199. HEART.
cardiodynamics 199. HEART.
cardiodynia 199. HEART.
cardiogenesis 199. HEART.
cardiograph 199. HEART.
cardiographer 199. HEART,
  cardiograph.
cardiographic 199. HEART,
  cardiograph.
cardiography 199. HEART.
cardiokinetic 199. HEART.
cardiologic 199. HEART, **cardiology.**
cardiological 199. HEART, **cardiology;**
  266. MEDICAL SPECIALTIES,
  cardiology.
cardiologist 199. HEART, **cardiology;**
  266. MEDICAL SPECIALTIES,
  cardiology.

cardiology 199. HEART; 266. MEDICAL
  SPECIALTIES.
cardiomalacia 199. HEART.
cardiomegaly 199. HEART.
cardiomyopathy 199. HEART.
cardiopaludism 199. HEART.
cardiopath 199. HEART, **cardiopathy.**
cardiopathic 199. HEART, **cardiopathy.**
cardiopathy 199. HEART.
cardiophobia 199. HEART; 313. PHOBIAS.
cardiopuncture 199. HEART.
cardioversion 199. HEART.
carditis 199. HEART.
careerism 41. BEHAVIOR.
careerist 41. BEHAVIOR, **careerism.**
caricature 352. REPRESENTATION.
caricaturist 352. REPRESENTATION,
  caricature.
caricography 319. PLANTS.
caricologist 54. BOTANY; 319. PLANTS,
  caricology.
caricology 319. PLANTS.
cariosity 113. DECAYING; 390. TEETH.
Carlism 322. POLITICS.
Carlist 322. POLITICS, **Carlism.**
carnal 364. SEX, **carnalism.**
carnalism 364. SEX.
carnality 364. SEX, **carnalism.**
carnivore 16. ANIMALS.
carnivorous 16. ANIMALS, **carnivore.**
carnosity 51. BODY, HUMAN.
carpetbaggery 185. GOVERNMENT,
  carpetbaggism.
carpetbaggism 185. GOVERNMENT.
carphology 122. DISEASE and ILLNESS.
carpological 54. BOTANY, **carpology.**
carpologist 54. BOTANY, **carpology.**
carpology 54. BOTANY.
carriage 131. DUES and PAYMENT.
cartage 131. DUES and PAYMENT.
cartel 137. ECONOMICS, **cartelism.**
cartelism 137. ECONOMICS.
Cartesian 312. PHILOSOPHY,
  Cartesianism.
Cartesianism 312. PHILOSOPHY.
cartogram 352. REPRESENTATION.
cartographer 257. MAPS, **cartography.**
cartographic 257. MAPS, **cartography.**
cartography 257. MAPS.
cartomancy 124. DIVINATION.

cartophily 91. COLLECTIONS and COLLECTING.
cartulary 53. BOOKS, chartulary.
caseation 51. BODY, HUMAN; 76. CHEESE; 122. DISEASE and ILLNESS.
Castroism 94. COMMUNISM; 185. GOVERNMENT; 322. POLITICS.
casualism 73. CHANCE.
casualty 73. CHANCE.
casuist 145. ETHICS.
casuistic 145. ETHICS, casuist.
casuistry 145. ETHICS.
catabaptist 35. BAPTISM.
catabasis 122. DISEASE and ILLNESS.
catabatic 122. DISEASE and ILLNESS, catabasis.
catabolic 113. DECAYING, catabolism; 302. ORGANISMS, catabolism.
catabolism 74. CHANGE; 113. DECAYING; 302. ORGANISMS.
cataclasm 113. DECAYING.
cataclasmic 113. DECAYING, cataclasm.
cataclysm 134. EARTHQUAKES.
cataclysmal 134. EARTHQUAKES, cataclysm.
catacoustics 136. ECHOES.
catadioptric 245. LIGHT, catadioptrics.
catadioptrical 245. LIGHT, catadioptrics.
catadioptrics 245. LIGHT.
catadromous 164. FISH.
catalectic 409. VERSE, catalexis.
catalepsis 122. DISEASE and ILLNESS, catalepsy.
catalepsy 122. DISEASE and ILLNESS.
cataleptic 122. DISEASE and ILLNESS, catalepsy.
catalexis 409. VERSE.
catalysis 74. CHANGE; 113. DECAYING.
catalyst 74. CHANGE, catalysis.
cataphonics 136. ECHOES, catacoustics.
cataphoresis 130. DRUGS.
cataplasia 44. BIOLOGY; 113. DECAYING.
cataplasis 113. DECAYING.
cataplastic 44. BIOLOGY, cataplasia; 113. DECAYING, cataplasia.
cataplectic 291. NERVES, cataplexy.
cataplexy 291. NERVES.
catastasis 127. DRAMA.
catastrophism 179. GEOLOGY.

catastrophist 179. GEOLOGY, catastrophism.
catatonia 224. INSANITY.
catatonic 224. INSANITY, catatonia.
catechesis 338. QUESTIONING.
catechetic 338. QUESTIONING, catechetics.
catechetical 80. CHRISTIANITY, catechism; 338. QUESTIONING, catechetics.
catechetics 338. QUESTIONING.
catechism 80. CHRISTIANITY.
catechist 80. CHRISTIANITY, catechism; 338. QUESTIONING, catechesis.
catechumen 69. CATHOLICISM, catechumenism.
catechumenal 69. CATHOLICISM, catechumenism.
catechumenical 69. CATHOLICISM, catechumenism.
catechumenism 69. CATHOLICISM.
Cathar 205. HERESY, Catharism.
Cathari 205. HERESY, Catharism.
Catharism 205. HERESY.
Catharist 205. HERESY, Catharism.
Catharistic 205. HERESY, Catharism.
catharsis 127. DRAMA.
cathartic 350. REMEDIES.
cathisophobia 313. PHOBIAS.
Catholic 80. CHRISTIANITY, Catholicism.
Catholicism 80. CHRISTIANITY.
catholicon 350. REMEDIES.
catoptric 245. LIGHT, catoptrics.
catoptrical 245. LIGHT, catoptrics.
catoptrically 245. LIGHT, catoptrics.
catoptrics 245. LIGHT.
catoptromancy 124. DIVINATION.
catoptrophobia 313. PHOBIAS.
causationism 312. PHILOSOPHY.
caustic 237. LANGUAGE STYLE, causticism.
causticism 237. LANGUAGE STYLE.
causticity 237. LANGUAGE STYLE, causticism.
causticness 237. LANGUAGE STYLE, causticism.
cauterism 388. SURGERY.
cautery 388. SURGERY.
caveat 239. LAW.
caveatee 239. LAW, caveat.

caveator 239. LAW, **caveat.**
caving 71. CAVES.
cecidiologist 319. PLANTS, **cecidiology.**
cecidiology 319. PLANTS.
cecidologist 319. PLANTS, **cecidiology.**
cecidology 319. PLANTS, **cecidiology.**
cecity 48. BLINDNESS.
ceilometer 87. CLOUDS.
Celarent 250. LOGIC.
celestial navigation 25. ASTRONOMY.
celibacy 69. CATHOLICISM;
258. MARRIAGE.
celibate 69. CATHOLICISM, **celibacy;**
258. MARRIAGE, **celibacy.**
celibatist 258. MARRIAGE.
celidographer 318. PLANETS,
celidography.
celidography 318. PLANETS; 387. SUN.
celiothelioma 66. CANCER.
cellarage 131. DUES and PAYMENT.
celo-navigation 25. ASTRONOMY,
astronavigation; 25. ASTRONOMY,
celestial navigation.
Celticism 236. LANGUAGE.
Celtophobia 313. PHOBIAS.
cenesthesia 51. BODY, HUMAN,
coenesthesia; 309. PERCEPTION,
coenesthesia.
cenesthesis 51. BODY, HUMAN,
coenesthesia; 309. PERCEPTION,
coenesthesia.
cenesthetic 51. BODY, HUMAN,
coenesthesia; 309. PERCEPTION,
coenesthesia.
cenobite 277. MONKS and NUNS,
cenobitism.
cenobitic 277. MONKS and NUNS,
cenobitism.
cenobitism 277. MONKS and NUNS.
cenophobia 313. PHOBIAS; 381. SPACES.
centauromachy 286. MYTHOLOGY.
centesis 388. SURGERY.
cento 248. LITERARY STYLE, **centonism.**
centonical 248. LITERARY STYLE,
centonism.
centonism 248. LITERARY STYLE.
centonization 248. LITERARY STYLE,
centonism.
centralism 185. GOVERNMENT.
centralist 185. GOVERNMENT,
centralism.

centralistic 185. GOVERNMENT,
centralism.
centrism 28. ATTITUDES; 322. POLITICS.
centrist 28. ATTITUDES, **centrism;**
322. POLITICS, **centrism.**
cephalalgia 306. PAIN.
cephalgia 306. PAIN, **cephalalgia.**
cephalodynia 306. PAIN, **cephalalgia.**
cephalomancy 124. DIVINATION;
196. HEAD.
cephalometer 196. HEAD,
cephalometry.
cephalometric 196. HEAD,
cephalometry.
cephalometrical 196. HEAD,
cephalometry.
cephalometry 196. HEAD.
ceramicist 324. POTTERY, **ceramics.**
ceramics 324. POTTERY.
ceramist 324. POTTERY, **ceramics.**
ceramography 324. POTTERY.
cerate 350. REMEDIES.
ceraunics 316. PHYSICS.
ceraunograph 246. LIGHTNING,
ceraunography.
ceraunographic 246. LIGHTNING,
ceraunography.
ceraunography 246. LIGHTNING;
246. LIGHTNING, **keraunography.**
ceraunomancy 124. DIVINATION;
394. THUNDER; 394. THUNDER,
keraunomancy.
ceraunophobia 246. LIGHTNING;
246. LIGHTNING, **keraunophobia;**
313. PHOBIAS; 313. PHOBIAS,
keraunophobia.
ceraunoscopia 246. LIGHTNING;
246. LIGHTNING, **keraunoscopia.**
cerebrology 56. BRAIN.
cerebroma 66. CANCER.
cerement 63. BURIAL; 86. CLOTHING;
112. DEATH.
cerements 63. BURIAL, **cerement;**
86. CLOTHING, **cerement;** 112. DEATH,
cerement.
ceremonialism 41. BEHAVIOR.
ceremonialist 41. BEHAVIOR,
ceremonialism.
cerographic 415. WAX, **cerography.**
cerographical 415. WAX, **cerography.**
cerographist 415. WAX, **cerography.**

cerography 415. WAX.
ceromancy 124. DIVINATION; 415. WAX.
ceroplastic 415. WAX, ceroplastics.
ceroplastics 415. WAX.
Cesare 250. LOGIC.
cetological 44. BIOLOGY, cetology.
cetologist 44. BIOLOGY, cetology;
430. ZOOLOGY, cetology.
cetology 44. BIOLOGY; 430. ZOOLOGY.
chaetophobia 193. HAIR; 313. PHOBIAS.
chalcography 128. DRAWING.
chalcologue 57. BRASS.
chalcomancy 57. BRASS;
124. DIVINATION.
chalcotript 57. BRASS.
Chaldaic 236. LANGUAGE, Chaldaism.
Chaldaism 236. LANGUAGE.
chalicosis 122. DISEASE and ILLNESS.
change ringing 42. BELLS.
chaomancy 27. ATMOSPHERE;
124. DIVINATION.
characterologic 41. BEHAVIOR,
characterology.
characterological 41. BEHAVIOR,
characterology.
characterologist 41. BEHAVIOR,
characterology.
characterology 41. BEHAVIOR.
charactery 12. ALPHABET;
352. REPRESENTATION.
charcoalist 23. ART; 128. DRAWING.
charisticary 135. EASTERN ORTHODOXY.
charivari 310. PERFORMING.
charlatanic 41. BEHAVIOR,
charlatanism.
charlatanism 41. BEHAVIOR.
Chartism 322. POLITICS.
Chartist 322. POLITICS, Chartism.
chartography 257. MAPS, cartography.
chartology 257. MAPS, cartography.
chartulary 53. BOOKS.
Chasidism 231. JUDAISM, Hasidism.
chatoyancy 92. COLOR; 177. GEMS;
245. LIGHT.
chatoyant 92. COLOR, chatoyancy;
177. GEMS, chatoyancy; 245. LIGHT,
chatoyancy.
chauvinism 121. DISCRIMINATION;
289. NATIONALISM.

chauvinist 121. DISCRIMINATION,
chauvinism; 289. NATIONALISM,
chauvinism.
chauvinistic 289. NATIONALISM,
chauvinism.
cheimaphobia 90. COLD; 313. PHOBIAS.
cheimatophobia 90. COLD,
cheimaphobia; 313. PHOBIAS,
cheimaphobia.
cheirognomist 194. HANDS,
chirognomy.
cheirognomy 194. HANDS, chirognomy.
cheirograph 323. POPE, chirograph.
cheirography 428. WRITING,
chirography.
cheirology 194. HANDS, chirology.
cheiromancy 124. DIVINATION,
chiromancy; 194. HANDS,
chiromancy.
cheironomic 181. GESTURE, chironomy.
cheironomy 181. GESTURE, chironomy.
Chekist 297. OCCUPATIONS.
chemism 290. NATURE.
chemocracy 376. SOCIETY.
chemocrat 376. SOCIETY, chemocracy.
chemosurgery 66. CANCER.
chemotaxis 282. MOTION.
chemotherapeutic 350. REMEDIES,
chemotherapy.
chemotherapist 350. REMEDIES,
chemotherapy.
chemotherapy 66. CANCER;
350. REMEDIES.
chemotropic 44. BIOLOGY,
chemotropism; 191. GROWTH,
chemotropism; 282. MOTION,
chemotropism.
chemotropism 44. BIOLOGY;
191. GROWTH; 282. MOTION.
chemurgic 221. INDUSTRY, chemurgy.
chemurgical 221. INDUSTRY, chemurgy.
chemurgy 221. INDUSTRY.
cherologic 247. LINGUISTICS, cherology.
cherological 247. LINGUISTICS,
cherology.
cherologist 247. LINGUISTICS,
cherology.
cherology 247. LINGUISTICS.
cheromania 195. HAPPINESS;
254. MANIAS.

cherophobia 195. HAPPINESS;
313. PHOBIAS.
chiarooscuro 128. DRAWING,
chiaroscuro.
chiaroscurist 128. DRAWING,
chiaroscuro.
chiaroscuro 128. DRAWING.
chiasmatypic 44. BIOLOGY,
chiasmatypy.
chiasmatypy 44. BIOLOGY.
chiasmus 354. RHETORIC and
RHETORICAL DEVICES.
chiastic 354. RHETORIC and RHETORICAL
DEVICES, chiasmus.
chiliarchy 185. GOVERNMENT.
chiliasm 79. CHRIST; 138. END OF THE
WORLD; 392. THEOLOGY.
chiliast 79. CHRIST, chiliasm; 138. END
OF THE WORLD, chiliasm;
392. THEOLOGY, chiliasm.
chiliastic 79. CHRIST, chiliasm;
138. END OF THE WORLD, chiliasm;
392. THEOLOGY, chiliasm.
Chinamania 78. CHINA; 254. MANIAS.
chinoiserie 23. ART; 78. CHINA.
chinophobia 313. PHOBIAS.
chionablepsia 48. BLINDNESS.
chionomania 254. MANIAS; 375. SNOW.
chionophobia 375. SNOW.
chiragra 194. HANDS.
chirapsia 194. HANDS.
chirocosmetic 194. HANDS,
chirocosmetics.
chirocosmetics 194. HANDS.
chirognomist 194. HANDS, chirognomy.
chirognomy 194. HANDS.
chirograph 323. POPE; 428. WRITING,
chirography.
chirographer 428. WRITING,
chirography.
chirographic 428. WRITING,
chirography.
chirographical 428. WRITING,
chirography.
chirography 428. WRITING.
chirology 194. HANDS.
chiromancy 124. DIVINATION;
194. HANDS.
chironomic 181. GESTURE, chironomy.
chironomy 181. GESTURE.
chiroplasty 194. HANDS.

chiropodial 157. FEET and LEGS,
chiropody.
chiropodist 157. FEET and LEGS,
chiropody.
chiropody 157. FEET and LEGS.
chiropractic 350. REMEDIES.
chiropractor 350. REMEDIES,
chiropractic.
chiropraxis 350. REMEDIES.
chirothesia 194. HANDS.
chirotony 194. HANDS.
chirurgery 388. SURGERY.
chloralism 122. DISEASE and ILLNESS.
chloroformism 130. DRUGS.
chloroma 66. CANCER.
chlorosis 95. COMPLEXION; 122. DISEASE
and ILLNESS; 319. PLANTS.
choledology 266. MEDICAL SPECIALTIES.
cholerophobia 313. PHOBIAS.
chondrocarcinoma 66. CANCER.
chondrology 266. MEDICAL
SPECIALTIES.
chondrosarcoma 66. CANCER.
chonophobia 417. WEATHER.
choralism 284. MUSIC.
choralistic 284. MUSIC, choralism.
chordoma 66. CANCER.
chorea 122. DISEASE and ILLNESS.
choregraphy 108. DANCING,
choreography.
choreodrama 108. DANCING;
127. DRAMA.
choreographer 108. DANCING,
choreography.
choreographic 108. DANCING,
choreography.
choreography 108. DANCING.
choreomania 108. DANCING;
254. MANIAS.
chorioblastoma 66. CANCER.
choriocarcinoma 66. CANCER.
choristry 378. SONGS and SINGING.
chorizontist 104. CRITICISM.
chorographer 257. MAPS, chorography.
chorographic 257. MAPS, chorography.
chorography 257. MAPS.
chorologic 44. BIOLOGY, chorology.
chorological 44. BIOLOGY, chorology.
chorology 44. BIOLOGY.
choromania 122. DISEASE and ILLNESS.

chorometry 235. LAND;
264. MEASUREMENT.
chrematheism 183. GOD and GODS.
chrematist 276. MONEY.
chrematistic 276. MONEY, chrematist;
276. MONEY, chrematistics.
chrematistics 276. MONEY.
chrematomania 254. MANIAS;
276. MONEY.
chrematophobia 276. MONEY;
313. PHOBIAS.
chreotechnics 5. AGRICULTURE;
221. INDUSTRY; 398. TRADE.
chrestomathic 91. COLLECTIONS and
COLLECTING, chrestomathy;
233. KNOWLEDGE, chrestomathics.
chrestomathics 233. KNOWLEDGE.
chrestomathy 91. COLLECTIONS and
COLLECTING.
chrism 69. CATHOLICISM.
chrismation 135. EASTERN ORTHODOXY.
Christadelphian 332. PROTESTANTISM,
Christadelphianism.
Christadelphianism
332. PROTESTANTISM.
Christendom 80. CHRISTIANITY.
Christianism 80. CHRISTIANITY.
Christological 79. CHRIST, Christology.
Christology 79. CHRIST.
Christophany 79. CHRIST.
chromaticism 284. MUSIC.
chromatics 92. COLOR.
chromatism 54. BOTANY; 92. COLOR.
chromatocracy 185. GOVERNMENT.
chromatography 92. COLOR,
chromatology.
chromatology 92. COLOR.
chromatolysis 72. CELLS.
chromatophobia 32. BACTERIA.
chromatophobic 32. BACTERIA,
chromatophobia.
chromatoscope 25. ASTRONOMY,
chromatoscopy.
chromatoscopy 25. ASTRONOMY.
chromatrope 92. COLOR.
chromesthesia 309. PERCEPTION.
chrometophobia 313. PHOBIAS.
chromograph 98. COPYING.
chromolithography 328. PRINTING.
chromophobia 92. COLOR;
313. PHOBIAS.

chromophotography
315. PHOTOGRAPHY.
chromoptometer 92. COLOR;
226. INSTRUMENTS.
chromotherapy 350. REMEDIES.
chromotypography 92. COLOR.
chromotypy 92. COLOR,
chromotypography.
chromoxylography 328. PRINTING.
chronographer 308. PAST.
chronography 207. HISTORY; 308. PAST.
chronologer 396. TIME, chronology.
chronological 396. TIME, chronology.
chronologist 396. TIME, chronology.
chronology 396. TIME.
chronomancy 124. DIVINATION.
chronometer 226. INSTRUMENTS.
chronometric 226. INSTRUMENTS,
chronometer; 396. TIME,
chronometry.
chronometrical 226. INSTRUMENTS,
chronometer; 396. TIME,
chronometry.
chronometry 396. TIME.
chronophobia 313. PHOBIAS; 396. TIME.
chronoscope 226. INSTRUMENTS;
396. TIME.
chronoscopic 264. MEASUREMENT,
chronoscopy; 396. TIME,
chronoscopy.
chronoscopy 264. MEASUREMENT;
396. TIME.
chrysocracy 376. SOCIETY.
chrysographer 428. WRITING,
chrysography.
chrysography 428. WRITING.
chrysology 137. ECONOMICS.
chthonian 133. EARTH, chthonic.
chthonic 133. EARTH.
churchism 349. RELIGION.
cibophobia 168. FOOD and NUTRITION;
313. PHOBIAS.
cicerone 192. GUIDES and GUIDING.
Ciceronian 248. LITERARY STYLE,
Ciceronianism.
Ciceronianism 248. LITERARY STYLE.
Ciceronist 248. LITERARY STYLE,
Ciceronianism.
cicisbeism 258. MARRIAGE.
cigrinophily 91. COLLECTIONS and
COLLECTING.

Cilicism 236. LANGUAGE.
cinchonism 130. DRUGS.
cinchonology 130. DRUGS.
cinematic 315. PHOTOGRAPHY,
cinematics.
cinematics 159. FILMS;
315. PHOTOGRAPHY.
cinematograph 352. REPRESENTATION,
cinematography.
cinematographer 159. FILMS,
cinematography; 315. PHOTOGRAPHY,
cinematography;
352. REPRESENTATION,
cinematography.
cinematographic 159. FILMS,
cinematography; 315. PHOTOGRAPHY,
cinematography;
352. REPRESENTATION,
cinematography.
cinematographist 159. FILMS,
cinematography; 315. PHOTOGRAPHY,
cinematography.
cinematography 159. FILMS;
315. PHOTOGRAPHY;
352. REPRESENTATION.
cinemese 159. FILMS; 237. LANGUAGE
STYLE.
cinephile 159. FILMS, cinephilia; 311.
-PHILE, -PHILIA, -PHILY, cinephilia.
cinephilia 159. FILMS; 311. -PHILE,
-PHILIA, -PHILY.
cinerarium 112. DEATH.
cinerary 112. DEATH, cinerarium.
cinquecentism 23. ART; 228. ITALY;
249. LITERATURE.
cinquecentist 23. ART, cinquecentism;
228. ITALY, cinquecentism;
249. LITERATURE, cinquecentism.
circularism 21. ARGUMENTATION.
circularity 21. ARGUMENTATION,
circularism.
cirplanology 332. PROTESTANTISM.
cirrhosis 122. DISEASE and ILLNESS.
cirrhotic 122. DISEASE and ILLNESS,
cirrhosis.
Cistercian 277. MONKS and NUNS,
Cistercianism.
Cistercianism 277. MONKS and NUNS.
citharist 284. MUSIC.

citriculture 5. AGRICULTURE;
319. PLANTS; 401. TREES.
citriculturist 5. AGRICULTURE,
citriculture; 319. PLANTS, citriculture;
401. TREES, citriculture.
citycism 82. CITIES.
cityscape 352. REPRESENTATION.
civicism 322. POLITICS.
civics 376. SOCIETY.
civilist 239. LAW; 322. POLITICS.
civism 289. NATIONALISM.
clairvoyance 384. SPIRITS and
SPIRITUALISM.
clairvoyant 384. SPIRITS and
SPIRITUALISM, clairvoyance.
classicalism 248. LITERARY STYLE.
classicalist 248. LITERARY STYLE,
classicalism.
classicalize 248. LITERARY STYLE,
classicalism.
classicism 18. ANTIQUITY;
20. ARCHITECTURE; 23. ART;
248. LITERARY STYLE.
classicist 18. ANTIQUITY, classicism;
23. ART, classicism; 248. LITERARY
STYLE, classicism.
classicistic 23. ART, classicism.
classicize 248. LITERARY STYLE,
classicism.
claudication 51. BODY, HUMAN;
412. WALKING.
claustrophile 311. -PHILE,
-PHILIA, -PHILY, claustrophilia.
claustrophilia 311. -PHILE,
-PHILIA, -PHILY.
claustrophilic 311. -PHILE,
-PHILIA, -PHILY, claustrophilia.
claustrophobia 313. PHOBIAS;
381. SPACES.
cledonism 236. LANGUAGE.
cleidomancy 124. DIVINATION.
cleistogamous 167. FLOWERS,
cleistogamy.
cleistogamy 167. FLOWERS.
cleistophobia 313. PHOBIAS,
claustrophobia; 381. SPACES,
claustrophobia.
clepsydra 226. INSTRUMENTS; 396. TIME.
cleptomania 391. THEFT, kleptomania.

cleptophobia 313. PHOBIAS;
313. PHOBIAS, kleptophobia;
391. THEFT, kleptophobia.
clericalism 69. CATHOLICISM.
clericalist 69. CATHOLICISM,
clericalism.
clerisy 233. KNOWLEDGE;
240. LEARNING.
cleromancy 124. DIVINATION.
clidomancy 124. DIVINATION,
cleidomancy.
climatographer 85. CLIMATE,
climatography.
climatographical 85. CLIMATE,
climatography.
climatography 85. CLIMATE.
climatologic 85. CLIMATE, climatology;
417. WEATHER, climatology.
climatological 85. CLIMATE,
climatology; 417. WEATHER,
climatology.
climatologist 85. CLIMATE,
climatology; 417. WEATHER,
climatology.
climatology 85. CLIMATE;
417. WEATHER.
clinomania 254. MANIAS; 372. SLEEP.
clinometer 179. GEOLOGY, clinometry.
clinometric 179. GEOLOGY, clinometry.
clinometrical 179. GEOLOGY,
clinometry.
clinometry 179. GEOLOGY.
clinophobia 313. PHOBIAS; 372. SLEEP.
cliometrician 207. HISTORY,
cliometrics.
cliometrics 207. HISTORY.
clonic 51. BODY, HUMAN, clonism;
122. DISEASE and ILLNESS, clonism.
clonism 51. BODY, HUMAN; 122. DISEASE
and ILLNESS.
cloudscape 352. REPRESENTATION.
clubbish 322. POLITICS, clubbism.
clubbism 322. POLITICS.
clubbist 322. POLITICS, clubbism.
coadjuvancy 6. AID.
coadunate 430. ZOOLOGY,
coadunation.
coadunation 430. ZOOLOGY.
coarctation 68. CAPTIVITY.
Cobdenism 137. ECONOMICS;
322. POLITICS.

cocainism 130. DRUGS.
coccidology 430. ZOOLOGY.
codicologic 256. MANUSCRIPTS,
codicology.
codicological 256. MANUSCRIPTS,
codicology.
codicologist 256. MANUSCRIPTS,
codicology.
codicology 256. MANUSCRIPTS.
coemption 398. TRADE.
coemptive 398. TRADE, coemption.
coenesthesia 51. BODY, HUMAN;
309. PERCEPTION.
coenesthesis 51. BODY, HUMAN,
coenesthesia; 309. PERCEPTION,
coenesthesia.
coenesthetic 51. BODY, HUMAN,
coenesthesia; 309. PERCEPTION,
coenesthesia.
coenobitism 277. MONKS and NUNS,
cenobitism.
coetaneity 3. AGE; 396. TIME.
coetaneous 3. AGE, coetaneity;
396. TIME, coetaneity.
coeternal 349. RELIGION, coeternity;
396. TIME, coeternity.
coeternity 349. RELIGION; 396. TIME.
coeval 3. AGE, coevalneity; 396. TIME,
coevalneity.
coevalneity 3. AGE; 396. TIME.
cogitation 393. THINKING.
cogitative 393. THINKING, cogitation.
cogitator 393. THINKING, cogitation.
cognate 348. RELATIONSHIP;
348. RELATIONSHIP, cognation.
cognatic 348. RELATIONSHIP, cognate.
cognation 348. RELATIONSHIP.
cognomen 288. NAMES.
cognominal 288. NAMES, cognomen.
coitophobia 313. PHOBIAS; 364. SEX.
colatitude 178. GEOGRAPHY.
Colbertism 137. ECONOMICS.
coleopterist 225. INSECTS,
coleopterology.
coleopterological 225. INSECTS,
coleopterology.
coleopterology 225. INSECTS.
collaborationism 400. TREASON.
collaborationist 400. TREASON,
collaborationism.
collectanea 53. BOOKS.

collectivism 322. POLITICS.
collectivist 322. POLITICS, collectivism.
collectivistic 322. POLITICS,
collectivism.
collectivization 93. COMMUNALISM;
94. COMMUNISM.
collegese 237. LANGUAGE STYLE.
collegialism 81. CHURCH.
colloquial 236. LANGUAGE,
colloquialism.
colloquialism 236. LANGUAGE.
collotype 315. PHOTOGRAPHY.
collyrium 148. EYES.
colonialism 185. GOVERNMENT.
colonialist 185. GOVERNMENT,
colonialism.
colonialistic 185. GOVERNMENT,
colonialism.
colophon 53. BOOKS.
color hearing 309. PERCEPTION,
chromesthesia.
colorimeter 92. COLOR, colorimetry.
colorimetric 92. COLOR, colorimetry.
colorimetrical 92. COLOR, colorimetry.
colorimetry 92. COLOR.
colorist 23. ART.
columbarium 45. BIRDS, columbary;
63. BURIAL; 112. DEATH.
columbary 45. BIRDS.
columniation 20. ARCHITECTURE.
comedocarcinoma 66. CANCER.
cometophobia 313. PHOBIAS.
comity 4. AGREEMENT;
348. RELATIONSHIP.
commensal 44. BIOLOGY,
commensalism; 168. FOOD and
NUTRITION, commensalism.
commensalism 16. ANIMALS;
44. BIOLOGY; 168. FOOD and
NUTRITION.
commercialism 137. ECONOMICS.
commercialist 137. ECONOMICS,
commercialism.
commercialistic 137. ECONOMICS,
commercialism.
commination 96. CONFLICT;
332. PROTESTANTISM.
comminution 52. BONES; 388. SURGERY.
commonsense realism
312. PHILOSOPHY.
communalism 322. POLITICS.

communalist 322. POLITICS,
communalism.
communalistic 322. POLITICS,
communalism.
communalization 93. COMMUNALISM.
communism 94. COMMUNISM;
322. POLITICS.
communist 94. COMMUNISM,
communism; 322. POLITICS,
communism.
communistic 94. COMMUNISM,
communism; 322. POLITICS,
communism.
communitarian 93. COMMUNALISM,
communitarianism.
communitarianism 93. COMMUNALISM.
communization 94. COMMUNISM.
compaternity 307. PARENTS.
complaisance 28. ATTITUDES.
complaisant 28. ATTITUDES,
complaisance.
compotation 8. ALCOHOL.
compotator 8. ALCOHOL.
compurgation 239. LAW.
compurgator 239. LAW; 239. LAW,
compurgation.
compurgatory 239. LAW,
compurgation.
computerese 30. AUTOMATION;
237. LANGUAGE STYLE.
computerphobia 313. PHOBIAS.
comstockery 296. OBSCENITY.
Comtism 312. PHILOSOPHY.
conatus 16. ANIMALS.
conceptism 248. LITERARY STYLE.
conceptualism 312. PHILOSOPHY.
conceptualist 312. PHILOSOPHY,
conceptualism.
conceptualistic 312. PHILOSOPHY,
conceptualism.
concettism 237. LANGUAGE STYLE.
conchological 430. ZOOLOGY,
conchology.
conchologist 91. COLLECTIONS and
COLLECTING, conchology;
430. ZOOLOGY, conchology.
conchology 91. COLLECTIONS and
COLLECTING; 430. ZOOLOGY.
conciliation 4. AGREEMENT.
conciliationism 21. ARGUMENTATION.

conciliationist 21. ARGUMENTATION,
  conciliationism.
conciliator 4. AGREEMENT,
  conciliation.
conciliatory 21. ARGUMENTATION,
  conciliationism.
concinnity 248. LITERARY STYLE.
concinnous 248. LITERARY STYLE,
  concinnity.
conditional baptism 35. BAPTISM.
condominate 185. GOVERNMENT,
  condominium.
condominium 185. GOVERNMENT.
confessionalian 392. THEOLOGY,
  confessionalism.
confessionalism 392. THEOLOGY.
configurational 334. PSYCHOLOGY,
  configurationism.
configurationism 334. PSYCHOLOGY.
configurationist 334. PSYCHOLOGY,
  configurationism.
configurative 334. PSYCHOLOGY,
  configurationism.
conformism 28. ATTITUDES.
conformist 28. ATTITUDES,
  conformism.
confraternity 376. SOCIETY.
Confucianism 78. CHINA.
congener 348. RELATIONSHIP.
Congregationalism
  332. PROTESTANTISM.
Congregationalist 332. PROTESTANTISM,
  Congregationalism.
congruence 4. AGREEMENT.
congruent 4. AGREEMENT, congruence.
congruity 4. AGREEMENT, congruence.
coniology 27. ATMOSPHERE, koniology;
  142. ENVIRONMENT, koniology.
conjunctivitis 148. EYES.
connivance 6. AID.
connivancy 6. AID.
consanguinity 348. RELATIONSHIP.
consciencism 312. PHILOSOPHY.
conservational 290. NATURE,
  conservationist.
conservationist 290. NATURE.
conservatism 322. POLITICS.
conservative 322. POLITICS,
  conservatism.
conservatory 167. FLOWERS.
consilience 4. AGREEMENT; 73. CHANCE.

consociational 332. PROTESTANTISM,
  consociationism.
consociationism 332. PROTESTANTISM.
consonance 4. AGREEMENT.
consonancy 4. AGREEMENT,
  consonance.
consopition 372. SLEEP.
consortism 44. BIOLOGY.
conspectus 352. REPRESENTATION.
constitutionalism 322. POLITICS.
constitutionalist 322. POLITICS,
  constitutionalism.
constitutional monarchy
  185. GOVERNMENT.
constructionism 28. ATTITUDES.
constructionist 28. ATTITUDES,
  constructionism; 239. LAW.
constructivism 127. DRAMA;
  248. LITERARY STYLE.
constructivist 127. DRAMA,
  constructivism; 248. LITERARY STYLE,
  constructivism.
consubstantiation 392. THEOLOGY.
consuetude 41. BEHAVIOR.
consumerism 137. ECONOMICS.
contextualism 104. CRITICISM.
contextualist 104. CRITICISM,
  contextualism.
continentalism 322. POLITICS.
continentalist 322. POLITICS,
  continentalism.
contortionist 26. ATHLETICS.
contortionistic 26. ATHLETICS,
  contortionist.
contrabandism 103. CRIME.
contrabandist 103. CRIME,
  contrabandism.
contrapuntist 284. MUSIC.
controversialism 28. ATTITUDES.
controversialist 28. ATTITUDES,
  controversialism.
contumacy 96. CONFLICT.
conundrum 176. GAMES.
conurbation 82. CITIES.
convection 27. ATMOSPHERE.
conventionalism 28. ATTITUDES.
conventionalist 28. ATTITUDES,
  conventionalism.
conversationalism 236. LANGUAGE.
conversationism 236. LANGUAGE,
  conversationalism.

convertism 349. RELIGION.
convertist 349. RELIGION, convertism.
cooperage 39. BEER.
Copernicanism 25. ASTRONOMY.
copoclephile 91. COLLECTIONS and
  COLLECTING, copoclephily.
copoclephily 91. COLLECTIONS and
  COLLECTING.
copperhead 413. WAR, copperheadism.
copperheadism 413. WAR.
coprolalia 296. OBSCENITY.
coprolalomania 236. LANGUAGE;
  254. MANIAS; 296. OBSCENITY.
coprolite 179. GEOLOGY.
coprology 296. OBSCENITY.
coprophagia 168. FOOD and NUTRITION,
  coprophagy.
coprophagous 168. FOOD and
  NUTRITION, coprophagy.
coprophagy 168. FOOD and NUTRITION.
coprophilia 296. OBSCENITY; 364. SEX.
coprophobia 84. CLEANLINESS;
  313. PHOBIAS.
copyism 98. COPYING.
copyist 98. COPYING, copyism.
corkage 131. DUES and PAYMENT.
cornification 52. BONES.
cornucopia 286. MYTHOLOGY.
cornucopian 286. MYTHOLOGY,
  cornucopia.
coronagraphic 387. SUN, coronagraphy.
coronagraphy 387. SUN.
corruptionist 103. CRIME; 322. POLITICS.
corybantiasm 334. PSYCHOLOGY,
  corybantism.
corybantism 334. PSYCHOLOGY.
coryza 122. DISEASE and ILLNESS.
coscinomancy 124. DIVINATION.
coscinomantic 124. DIVINATION,
  coscinomancy.
coseism 134. EARTHQUAKES.
coseismic 134. EARTHQUAKES, coseism.
cosmetological 38. BEAUTY,
  cosmetology.
cosmetologist 38. BEAUTY,
  cosmetology.
cosmetology 38. BEAUTY.
cosmism 100. COSMOLOGY.
cosmist 100. COSMOLOGY, cosmism.
cosmocracy 185. GOVERNMENT.

cosmogonic 100. COSMOLOGY,
  cosmogony.
cosmogonist 100. COSMOLOGY,
  cosmogony.
cosmogony 100. COSMOLOGY.
cosmographer 100. COSMOLOGY,
  cosmography.
cosmographic 100. COSMOLOGY,
  cosmography.
cosmographical 100. COSMOLOGY,
  cosmography.
cosmography 100. COSMOLOGY.
cosmolabe 25. ASTRONOMY;
  226. INSTRUMENTS.
cosmolatry 349. RELIGION.
cosmologic 100. COSMOLOGY,
  cosmology; 312. PHILOSOPHY,
  cosmology.
cosmological 100. COSMOLOGY,
  cosmology; 312. PHILOSOPHY,
  cosmology.
cosmologist 100. COSMOLOGY,
  cosmology; 312. PHILOSOPHY,
  cosmology.
cosmology 100. COSMOLOGY;
  312. PHILOSOPHY.
cosmometry 264. MEASUREMENT.
cosmonaut 25. ASTRONOMY,
  cosmonautics.
cosmonautical 25. ASTRONOMY,
  cosmonautics.
cosmonautics 25. ASTRONOMY.
cosmopolis 82. CITIES.
cosmopolitan 28. ATTITUDES,
  cosmopolitanism; 82. CITIES,
  cosmopolis.
cosmopolitanism 28. ATTITUDES;
  94. COMMUNISM.
cosmopolite 82. CITIES, cosmopolis.
cosmorama 352. REPRESENTATION.
cosmoramic 352. REPRESENTATION,
  cosmorama.
cosmosphere 133. EARTH;
  352. REPRESENTATION.
cosmotheism 100. COSMOLOGY.
cosmotheist 100. COSMOLOGY,
  cosmotheism.
cosmozoism 100. COSMOLOGY.
cottonocracy 376. SOCIETY.
cottonocrat 376. SOCIETY,
  cottonocracy.

Couéism 219. IMPROVEMENT; 334. PSYCHOLOGY.
counteridea 216. IDEAS.
courier 192. GUIDES and GUIDING.
cousinry 348. RELATIONSHIP.
couture 86. CLOTHING.
couturier 86. CLOTHING, couture.
couturière 86. CLOTHING, couture.
coverture 239. LAW; 424. WOMEN.
coxalgia 306. PAIN.
coxalgy 306. PAIN, coxalgia.
coxcombry 41. BEHAVIOR.
craniographer 52. BONES, craniography.
craniographic 52. BONES, craniography.
craniographical 52. BONES, craniography.
craniography 52. BONES.
craniologic 196. HEAD, craniology.
craniological 196. HEAD, craniology.
craniologist 196. HEAD, craniology.
craniology 196. HEAD.
craniometric 196. HEAD, craniometry.
craniometrical 196. HEAD, craniometry.
craniometrist 196. HEAD, craniometry.
craniometry 196. HEAD.
cranioscopic 196. HEAD, cranioscopy.
cranioscopical 196. HEAD, cranioscopy.
cranioscopist 196. HEAD, cranioscopy.
cranioscopy 196. HEAD.
craniotome 388. SURGERY.
craniotomy 56. BRAIN; 196. HEAD.
crapulence 8. ALCOHOL, crapulency; 168. FOOD and NUTRITION, crapulency.
crapulency 8. ALCOHOL; 168. FOOD and NUTRITION.
creationism 100. COSMOLOGY; 379. SOUL.
creationist 100. COSMOLOGY, creationism; 379. SOUL, creationism.
creationistic 379. SOUL, creationism.
crematorium 112. DEATH.
crematory 112. DEATH, crematorium.
cremnomania 202. HEIGHTS; 254. MANIAS.
cremnophobia 202. HEIGHTS; 313. PHOBIAS.
creolism 341. RACE.
creophagism 166. FLESH.

creophagous 166. FLESH, creophagism.
creophagy 166. FLESH, creophagism.
crepitation 380. SOUND.
crescographic 319. PLANTS, crescography.
crescography 319. PLANTS.
cresomania 254. MANIAS; 276. MONEY.
cretinism 217. IDIOCY.
cretinoid 217. IDIOCY, cretinism.
cretinous 217. IDIOCY, cretinism.
criminal 239. LAW, criminalism.
criminalism 239. LAW.
criminality 239. LAW, criminalism.
criminologic 103. CRIME, criminology.
criminological 103. CRIME, criminology.
criminologist 103. CRIME, criminology.
criminology 103. CRIME.
crinosity 193. HAIR.
crinous 193. HAIR, crinosity.
crithomancy 124. DIVINATION.
crithomantic 124. DIVINATION, crithomancy.
critic 249. LITERATURE, criticism.
criticism 249. LITERATURE.
cronyism 322. POLITICS.
crotism 199. HEART.
crustaceological 44. BIOLOGY, crustaceology.
crustaceologist 44. BIOLOGY, crustaceology.
crustaceology 44. BIOLOGY; 430. ZOOLOGY.
crustalogy 179. GEOLOGY.
cryogenic 90. COLD, cryogenics.
cryogenics 90. COLD.
cryology 90. COLD.
cryometer 90. COLD; 226. INSTRUMENTS.
cryometric 90. COLD, cryometry.
cryometry 90. COLD; 264. MEASUREMENT.
cryophile 90. COLD, cryophilia.
cryophilia 90. COLD.
cryophilic 90. COLD, cryophilia.
cryophobia 90. COLD; 313. PHOBIAS; 417. WEATHER.
cryoscopy 90. COLD.
cryosurgery 90. COLD; 388. SURGERY.
cryotherapy 350. REMEDIES.
cryptaesthesia 334. PSYCHOLOGY, cryptesthesia.

cryptanalysis 89. CODE.
cryptanalyst 89. CODE, **cryptanalysis.**
cryptanalytic 89. CODE, **cryptanalysis.**
cryptanalytical 89. CODE,
    cryptanalysis.
cryptanalytics 89. CODE, **cryptanalysis.**
cryptesthesia 334. PSYCHOLOGY.
cryptesthetic 334. PSYCHOLOGY,
    cryptesthesia.
cryptobiosis 44. BIOLOGY.
cryptobiotic 44. BIOLOGY, **cryptobiosis.**
crypto-Calvinism 349. RELIGION.
crypto-Calvinist 349. RELIGION,
    crypto-Calvinism.
cryptoclimate 85. CLIMATE.
cryptogamist 54. BOTANY.
cryptogram 89. CODE.
cryptogrammic 89. CODE, **cryptogram.**
cryptographal 236. LANGUAGE,
    cryptography; 428. WRITING,
    cryptography.
cryptographer 89. CODE,
    cryptography; 236. LANGUAGE,
    cryptography; 428. WRITING,
    cryptography.
cryptographic 89. CODE,
    cryptography; 236. LANGUAGE,
    cryptography; 428. WRITING,
    cryptography.
cryptographical 236. LANGUAGE,
    cryptography; 428. WRITING,
    cryptography.
cryptographist 89. CODE,
    cryptography; 236. LANGUAGE,
    cryptography; 428. WRITING,
    cryptography.
cryptography 89. CODE;
    236. LANGUAGE; 428. WRITING.
cryptologist 236. LANGUAGE,
    cryptology.
cryptology 89. CODE, **cryptography**;
    236. LANGUAGE.
cryptomnesia 269. MEMORY.
cryptomnesic 269. MEMORY,
    cryptomnesia.
cryptonym 288. NAMES.
cryptorchid 364. SEX, **cryptorchidism.**
cryptorchidism 364. SEX.
crystal-gazing 124. DIVINATION,
    gastromancy.

crystallographer 316. PHYSICS,
    crystallography.
crystallographic 316. PHYSICS,
    crystallography.
crystallographical 316. PHYSICS,
    crystallography.
crystallography 316. PHYSICS.
crystallomancy 124. DIVINATION.
crystallophobia 313. PHOBIAS.
ctetologic 44. BIOLOGY, **ctetology.**
ctetological 44. BIOLOGY, **ctetology.**
ctetology 44. BIOLOGY.
cubebism 130. DRUGS.
Cubism 23. ART.
Cubist 23. ART, **Cubism.**
Cubistic 23. ART, **Cubism.**
cubomancy 124. DIVINATION.
cubomantic 124. DIVINATION,
    cubomancy.
culinarian 168. FOOD and NUTRITION.
culottic 322. POLITICS, **culottism.**
culottism 322. POLITICS.
culpability 239. LAW.
culpable 239. LAW, **culpability.**
culteranismo 248. LITERARY STYLE,
    Gongorism.
cultismo 248. LITERARY STYLE,
    Gongorism.
cultural anthropology
    17. ANTHROPOLOGY.
culturist 5. AGRICULTURE; 23. ART;
    191. GROWTH; 249. LITERATURE;
    352. REPRESENTATION.
culturology 17. ANTHROPOLOGY,
    cultural anthropology.
cumaphytic 319. PLANTS,
    cumaphytism.
cumaphytism 319. PLANTS.
cumyxaphily 91. COLLECTIONS and
    COLLECTING.
cunctation 396. TIME.
cunctatious 396. TIME, **cunctation.**
cunctator 396. TIME, **cunctation.**
cunctatory 396. TIME, **cunctation.**
Curialism 69. CATHOLICISM.
curiescopy 342. RADIATION.
curiologic 428. WRITING, **curiologics.**
curiological 428. WRITING, **curiologics.**
curiologics 428. WRITING.
curiology 428. WRITING, **curiologics.**

curiosa 91. COLLECTIONS and COLLECTING.

cuspidal 20. ARCHITECTURE, **cuspidation.**

cuspidate 20. ARCHITECTURE, **cuspidation.**

cuspidation 20. ARCHITECTURE.

cyanometer 92. COLOR, **cyanometry.**

cyanometric 92. COLOR, **cyanometry.**

cyanometry 92. COLOR.

cyanopathy 122. DISEASE and ILLNESS.

cyanosis 122. DISEASE and ILLNESS.

cyanotic 122. DISEASE and ILLNESS, **cyanosis.**

cyanotype 315. PHOTOGRAPHY.

cybernetic 30. AUTOMATION, **cybernetics;** 56. BRAIN, **cybernetics.**

cyberneticist 30. AUTOMATION, **cybernetics;** 56. BRAIN, **cybernetics.**

cybernetics 30. AUTOMATION; 56. BRAIN.

cycle of indiction 65. CALENDAR, **indiction.**

cyclic 207. HISTORY, **cyclicism.**

cyclicism 207. HISTORY.

cyclicity 207. HISTORY, **cyclicism.**

cyclograph 128. DRAWING.

cyclometer 226. INSTRUMENTS.

cyclometry 264. MEASUREMENT.

cyclone 420. WIND.

cyclonic 420. WIND, **cyclone.**

cyclonologist 420. WIND, **cyclonology.**

cyclonology 420. WIND.

cyclopaedia 53. BOOKS, **cyclopedia.**

cyclopaedic 53. BOOKS, **cyclopedia.**

cyclopaedist 53. BOOKS, **cyclopedia.**

cyclopedia 53. BOOKS.

cyclopedic 53. BOOKS, **cyclopedia.**

cyclopedist 53. BOOKS, **cyclopedia.**

cyclorama 352. REPRESENTATION.

cycloramic 352. REPRESENTATION, **cyclorama.**

cyclostylar 98. COPYING, **cyclostyle.**

cyclostyle 98. COPYING.

cyclothyme 279. MOODS, **cyclothymia.**

cyclothymia 279. MOODS.

cyclothymic 279. MOODS, **cyclothymia.**

cyesiology 327. PREGNANCY.

cyesis 327. PREGNANCY.

cymography 264. MEASUREMENT, **kymography.**

cymophobia 313. PHOBIAS; 360. SEA.

cynanthropy 125. DOGS.

cynegetic 214. HUNTING, **cynegetics.**

cynegetics 214. HUNTING.

Cynic 312. PHILOSOPHY, **Cynicism.**

cynic 28. ATTITUDES, **cynicism.**

Cynical 312. PHILOSOPHY, **Cynicism.**

cynical 28. ATTITUDES, **cynicism.**

Cynicism 312. PHILOSOPHY.

cynicism 28. ATTITUDES.

cynologist 125. DOGS.

cynology 125. DOGS; 430. ZOOLOGY.

cynomania 125. DOGS; 254. MANIAS.

cynophobia 125. DOGS; 313. PHOBIAS; 313. PHOBIAS, **kynophobia.**

cynorexia 168. FOOD and NUTRITION.

cynosure 192. GUIDES and GUIDING.

cypridophobia 122. DISEASE and ILLNESS; 313. PHOBIAS.

Cyrenaic 312. PHILOSOPHY, **Cyrenaicism.**

Cyrenaicism 312. PHILOSOPHY.

Cyrenean 312. PHILOSOPHY, **Cyrenaicism.**

Cyrenian 312. PHILOSOPHY, **Cyrenaicism.**

Cyrillian 205. HERESY, **Cyrillianism.**

Cyrillianism 205. HERESY.

cystoma 66. CANCER.

cytochemical 72. CELLS, **cytochemistry.**

cytochemistry 72. CELLS.

cytogenetic 44. BIOLOGY, **cytogenetics.**

cytogenetical 44. BIOLOGY, **cytogenetics.**

cytogeneticist 44. BIOLOGY, **cytogenetics.**

cytogenetics 44. BIOLOGY.

cytologic 44. BIOLOGY, **cytology;** 72. CELLS, **cytology.**

cytological 44. BIOLOGY, **cytology;** 72. CELLS, **cytology.**

cytologist 44. BIOLOGY, **cytology;** 72. CELLS, **cytology.**

cytology 44. BIOLOGY; 72. CELLS.

cytolysis 72. CELLS; 113. DECAYING.

cytolytic 72. CELLS, **cytolysis;** 113. DECAYING, **cytolysis.**

cytopathologic 122. DISEASE and ILLNESS, **cytopathology.**

cytopathological 122. DISEASE and ILLNESS, **cytopathology.**

cytopathologist 122. DISEASE and
ILLNESS, cytopathology.
cytopathology 122. DISEASE and
ILLNESS.
cytoplasm 72. CELLS; 204. HEREDITY.
cytoplasmic 72. CELLS, cytoplasm.
cytotaxonomy 83. CLASSIFICATION.
cytotechnologic 66. CANCER,
cytotechnology; 72. CELLS,
cytotechnology.
cytotechnologist 66. CANCER,
cytotechnology; 72. CELLS,
cytotechnology.
cytotechnology 66. CANCER; 72. CELLS.
czarism 322. POLITICS.
czarist 322. POLITICS, czarism.

D

dacoity 391. THEFT.
dactyl 161. FINGERS and TOES;
409. VERSE.
dactylic 409. VERSE, dactyl.
dactylioglyph 141. ENGRAVING.
dactylioglyphist 141. ENGRAVING,
dactylioglyph.
dactylioglyphy 141. ENGRAVING.
dactyliographer 141. ENGRAVING,
dactyliography; 161. FINGERS and
TOES, dactyliography.
dactyliographic 141. ENGRAVING,
dactyliography; 161. FINGERS and
TOES, dactyliography.
dactyliography 141. ENGRAVING;
161. FINGERS and TOES; 177. GEMS.
dactyliologic 161. FINGERS and TOES,
dactyliology.
dactyliologist 161. FINGERS and TOES,
dactyliology.
dactyliology 111. DEAFNESS,
dactylology; 161. FINGERS and TOES.
dactyliomancy 124. DIVINATION;
161. FINGERS and TOES.
dactylist 409. VERSE, dactyl.
dactylitis 161. FINGERS and TOES.
dactylogram 161. FINGERS and TOES,
dactylography.
dactylographer 161. FINGERS and TOES,
dactylography.
dactylographic 161. FINGERS and TOES,
dactylography.

dactylography 161. FINGERS and TOES.
dactylologic 181. GESTURE,
dactylology.
dactylological 181. GESTURE,
dactylology.
dactylology 111. DEAFNESS;
161. FINGERS and TOES; 181. GESTURE.
dactylomegalic 161. FINGERS and TOES,
dactylomegaly.
dactylomegaly 161. FINGERS and TOES.
dactylonomy 161. FINGERS and TOES.
dactyloscopic 161. FINGERS and TOES,
dactyloscopy.
dactyloscopist 161. FINGERS and TOES,
dactyloscopy.
dactyloscopy 161. FINGERS and TOES.
dactylotogist 181. GESTURE,
dactylology.
Dadaism 23. ART.
Dadaist 23. ART, Dadaism.
daguerreotype 315. PHOTOGRAPHY.
daguerreotypic 315. PHOTOGRAPHY,
daguerreotype.
daguerreotypical 315. PHOTOGRAPHY,
daguerreotype.
daguerreotypist 315. PHOTOGRAPHY,
daguerreotype.
Daltonism 92. COLOR; 148. EYES.
dandy 28. ATTITUDES, dandyism;
150. FADS, dandyism.
dandyism 28. ATTITUDES; 150. FADS.
Danicism 236. LANGUAGE.
Dantesque 109. DANTE.
Dantomania 254. MANIAS.
Dantophile 109. DANTE, Dantophily.
Dantophily 109. DANTE.
Darapti 250. LOGIC.
Darbyism 332. PROTESTANTISM.
Darbyite 332. PROTESTANTISM,
Darbyism.
daredevil 41. BEHAVIOR, daredevilism.
daredevilism 41. BEHAVIOR.
daredeviltry 41. BEHAVIOR,
daredevilism.
Darii 250. LOGIC.
Darwinian 147. EVOLUTION,
Darwinism.
Darwinism 147. EVOLUTION.
Datisi 250. LOGIC.
dauber 23. ART, daubery.
daubery 23. ART.

daubry 23. ART, **daubery.**
daubster 23. ART, **daubery.**
deafmute 111. DEAFNESS, **deafmutism;**
382. SPEECH, **deafmutism.**
deafmutism 111. DEAFNESS;
382. SPEECH.
debacchation 41. BEHAVIOR.
debellation 410. VICTORY.
debenture 160. FINANCE.
decadarchy 185. GOVERNMENT,
decarchy.
decal 305. ORNAMENTATION,
decalcomania.
decalcomania 305. ORNAMENTATION.
decarchy 185. GOVERNMENT.
decathlon 26. ATHLETICS.
Decembrist 322. POLITICS; 357. RUSSIA.
decoction 329. PROCESSES.
decollation 232. KILLING.
decollator 232. KILLING, **decollation.**
decorous 41. BEHAVIOR, **decorum.**
decortication 329. PROCESSES;
401. TREES.
decorum 41. BEHAVIOR.
decoupage 305. ORNAMENTATION.
decrescence 368. SIZE.
decrescent 368. SIZE, **decrescence.**
decretalist 69. CATHOLICISM, **decretist.**
decretist 69. CATHOLICISM.
decussation 170. FORM.
dedentition 390. TEETH.
defalcation 103. CRIME.
defeatism 28. ATTITUDES.
defeatist 28. ATTITUDES, **defeatism.**
defection 10. ALLEGIANCE.
defectionist 10. ALLEGIANCE,
defection.
defector 10. ALLEGIANCE, **defection.**
defenestration 232. KILLING.
definienda 250. LOGIC, **definiendum.**
definiendum 250. LOGIC.
defloration 364. SEX.
deglutition 50. BODILY FUNCTIONS.
degradability 113. DECAYING;
261. MATERIALS, PROPERTIES OF.
degradable 113. DECAYING,
degradability; 261. MATERIALS,
PROPERTIES OF, **degradability.**
dehydration 414. WATER.
deicidal 183. GOD and GODS, **deicide.**
deicide 183. GOD and GODS.

deipnophobia 118. DINING;
313. PHOBIAS.
deipnosophism 118. DINING;
354. RHETORIC and RHETORICAL
DEVICES.
deipnosophist 118. DINING,
deipnosophism; 354. RHETORIC and
RHETORICAL DEVICES,
deipnosophism.
deism 183. GOD and GODS.
deist 183. GOD and GODS, **deism.**
deistic 183. GOD and GODS, **deism.**
déjà vu 269. MEMORY.
dekarchy 185. GOVERNMENT, **decarchy.**
Dekebrist 322. POLITICS; 357. RUSSIA,
Decembrist.
delation 408. VEHICLES.
delectus 53. BOOKS.
delinquency 160. FINANCE; 239. LAW.
delinquent 239. LAW, **delinquency.**
deliquescence 329. PROCESSES;
414. WATER.
deliquescent 329. PROCESSES,
deliquescence; 414. WATER,
deliquescence.
delirium 224. INSANITY.
delitescence 122. DISEASE and ILLNESS.
delitescent 122. DISEASE and ILLNESS,
delitescence.
deltiology 91. COLLECTIONS and
COLLECTING.
demagogism 322. POLITICS.
demagoguery 322. POLITICS,
demagogism.
demagoguism 322. POLITICS,
demagogism.
demagogy 322. POLITICS, **demagogism.**
dementia 224. INSANITY.
dementia praecox 224. INSANITY.
demilitarization 413. WAR.
demiurge 183. GOD and GODS,
demiurgism.
demiurgic 183. GOD and GODS,
demiurgism.
demiurgism 183. GOD and GODS.
demobilization 413. WAR.
democracy 185. GOVERNMENT.
democrat 185. GOVERNMENT,
democracy.
democratic 185. GOVERNMENT,
democracy.

democratism 173. FREEDOM;
322. POLITICS; 376. SOCIETY.
demographer 255. MANKIND,
demography.
demographic 255. MANKIND,
demography.
demography 255. MANKIND.
demological 255. MANKIND, demology.
demology 255. MANKIND.
demomania 105. CROWDS; 254. MANIAS.
demoniac 114. DEMONS, demonianism.
demoniacism 114. DEMONS,
demonianism.
demonian 114. DEMONS, demonianism;
224. INSANITY, demonianism.
demonianism 114. DEMONS;
224. INSANITY.
demonism 114. DEMONS.
demonist 114. DEMONS, demonism.
demonocracy 114. DEMONS;
185. GOVERNMENT.
demonocratic 114. DEMONS,
demonocracy; 185. GOVERNMENT,
demonocracy.
demonographer 114. DEMONS,
demonography.
demonography 114. DEMONS.
demonolatry 114. DEMONS.
demonologic 114. DEMONS,
demonology.
demonological 114. DEMONS,
demonology.
demonologist 114. DEMONS,
demonology.
demonology 114. DEMONS.
demonomagy 114. DEMONS; 252. MAGIC.
demonomancy 114. DEMONS;
124. DIVINATION.
demonomania 224. INSANITY.
demonomist 114. DEMONS.
demonomy 114. DEMONS.
demonopathy 224. INSANITY,
demonomania.
demonophobia 114. DEMONS;
313. PHOBIAS.
demonurgist 114. DEMONS, demonurgy.
demonurgy 114. DEMONS.
demophil 105. CROWDS, demophilia.
demophile 105. CROWDS, demophilia.
demophilia 105. CROWDS; 311. -PHILE,
-PHILIA, -PHILY.

demophobia 105. CROWDS;
255. MANKIND; 313. PHOBIAS.
demotic 236. LANGUAGE.
demotist 236. LANGUAGE.
demulcent 350. REMEDIES.
demurrage 131. DUES and PAYMENT;
366. SHIPS.
dendranthropologic
17. ANTHROPOLOGY,
dendranthropology.
dendranthropological
17. ANTHROPOLOGY,
dendranthropology.
dendranthropology
17. ANTHROPOLOGY.
dendrochronological 396. TIME,
dendrochronology; 401. TREES,
dendrochronology.
dendrochronologist 396. TIME,
dendrochronology; 401. TREES,
dendrochronology.
dendrochronology 396. TIME;
401. TREES.
dendrographic 401. TREES,
dendrography.
dendrographical 401. TREES,
dendrography.
dendrography 401. TREES.
dendrolatrous 401. TREES, dendrolatry.
dendrolatry 401. TREES.
dendrologic 54. BOTANY, dendrology;
401. TREES, dendrology.
dendrological 54. BOTANY, dendrology;
401. TREES, dendrology.
dendrologist 54. BOTANY, dendrology;
401. TREES, dendrology.
dendrology 54. BOTANY; 401. TREES.
dendrophilia 319. PLANTS.
dendrophilous 319. PLANTS,
dendrophilia.
denigration 47. BLACKENING and
BLACKNESS.
denigrator 47. BLACKENING and
BLACKNESS, denigration.
denominationalism 322. POLITICS;
332. PROTESTANTISM.
denominationalist 322. POLITICS,
denominationalism;
332. PROTESTANTISM,
denominationalism.
denouement 127. DRAMA.

densimeter 226. INSTRUMENTS.
densitometer 315. PHOTOGRAPHY.
dentist 266. MEDICAL SPECIALTIES,
dentistry.
dentistry 266. MEDICAL SPECIALTIES.
dentition 390. TEETH.
dentology 390. TEETH.
deontological 145. ETHICS, **deontology.**
deontologist 145. ETHICS, **deontology.**
deontology 145. ETHICS.
deoxyribonucleic acid (DNA)
204. HEREDITY.
departmentalism 322. POLITICS.
departmentalization 322. POLITICS,
departmentalism.
depeculation 103. CRIME.
deracination 329. PROCESSES.
dereism 334. PSYCHOLOGY.
dereistic 334. PSYCHOLOGY, **dereism.**
derism 236. LANGUAGE.
deristic 236. LANGUAGE, **derism.**
dermabrasion 370. SKIN.
dermatalgia 306. PAIN; 370. SKIN.
dermatoglyphic 370. SKIN,
dermatoglyphics.
dermatoglyphics 370. SKIN.
dermatographia 370. SKIN,
dermatographism.
dermatographic 370. SKIN,
dermatographism; 370. SKIN,
dermatography.
dermatographism 370. SKIN.
dermatography 370. SKIN.
dermatological 370. SKIN, **dermatology.**
dermatologist 266. MEDICAL
SPECIALTIES; 370. SKIN, **dermatology.**
dermatology 370. SKIN.
dermatopathophobia 313. PHOBIAS,
dermatophobia; 370. SKIN,
dermatophobia.
dermatophobia 313. PHOBIAS; 370. SKIN.
dermatoplasty 370. SKIN; 388. SURGERY.
dermatosiophobia 313. PHOBIAS,
dermatophobia; 370. SKIN,
dermatophobia.
dermographia 370. SKIN,
dermatographism; 370. SKIN,
dermographism.
dermographism 370. SKIN.
descendental 312. PHILOSOPHY,
descendentalism.

descendentalism 312. PHILOSOPHY.
descendentalist 312. PHILOSOPHY,
descendentalism.
descendentalistic 312. PHILOSOPHY,
descendentalism.
descriptive linguistics 247. LINGUISTICS,
synchronic linguistics.
desiderata 53. BOOKS.
desmidiologist 319. PLANTS,
desmidiology.
desmidiology 319. PLANTS.
desmographic 14. ANATOMY,
desmography.
desmographical 14. ANATOMY,
desmography.
desmography 14. ANATOMY.
desmopathology 266. MEDICAL
SPECIALTIES.
despoliation 391. THEFT.
despot 185. GOVERNMENT, **despotism.**
despotic 185. GOVERNMENT, **despotism.**
despotism 185. GOVERNMENT.
despumation 329. PROCESSES.
desquamation 50. BODILY FUNCTIONS;
329. PROCESSES.
deteriorism 113. DECAYING.
determinacy 233. KNOWLEDGE.
determinism 312. PHILOSOPHY.
determinist 312. PHILOSOPHY,
determinism.
deterministic 312. PHILOSOPHY,
determinism.
deus ex machina 127. DRAMA.
deuteragonist 127. DRAMA.
deuteranope 92. COLOR, **deuteranopia;**
148. EYES, **deuteranopia.**
deuteranopia 92. COLOR; 148. EYES.
deuteranopic 92. COLOR,
deuteranopia; 148. EYES,
deuteranopia.
deuterogamist 258. MARRIAGE,
deuterogamy.
deuterogamous 258. MARRIAGE,
deuterogamy.
deuterogamy 258. MARRIAGE.
deuteropathy 51. BODY, HUMAN.
deviationalism 94. COMMUNISM,
deviationism.
deviationism 94. COMMUNISM.
deviationist 94. COMMUNISM,
deviationism.

devilish 114. DEMONS, **devilism.**
devilism 114. DEMONS.
devirgination 364. SEX.
devisal 331. PROPERTY and OWNERSHIP.
devise 331. PROPERTY and OWNERSHIP.
devotionalism 349. RELIGION.
devotionalist 349. RELIGION,
    devotionalism.
dextrality 355. RIGHT.
dextrogyration 355. RIGHT.
dextrogyric 355. RIGHT,
    dextrogyration.
dextrophobia 313. PHOBIAS.
dextrorotation 355. RIGHT.
dextroversion 355. RIGHT.
diabetophobia 313. PHOBIAS.
diabolepsy 224. INSANITY.
diabolism 117. DEVIL.
diabolist 117. DEVIL, **diabolism.**
diabology 117. DEVIL.
diabolology 117. DEVIL, **diabology.**
diachronic 247. LINGUISTICS,
    diachronism; 396. TIME,
    diachronism.
diachronism 247. LINGUISTICS;
    396. TIME.
diachronistic 396. TIME, **diachronism.**
diachronistical 396. TIME, **diachronism.**
diachrony 247. LINGUISTICS,
    diachronism; 396. TIME,
    diachronism.
diaconate 81. CHURCH.
diacoustics 380. SOUND.
diagnostics 266. MEDICAL SPECIALTIES.
diagraph 98. COPYING; 128. DRAWING.
diagraphic 128. DRAWING, **diagraphics.**
diagraphical 128. DRAWING,
    diagraphics.
diagraphics 128. DRAWING.
diakinesis 44. BIOLOGY.
diakinetic 44. BIOLOGY, **diakinesis.**
dialect 247. LINGUISTICS.
dialectal 247. LINGUISTICS, **dialect.**
dialect geography 247. LINGUISTICS.
dialectical materialism
    94. COMMUNISM.
dialectical materialist 94. COMMUNISM,
    dialectical materialism.
dialectician 247. LINGUISTICS,
    dialectology.
dialecticism 236. LANGUAGE.

dialectologic 247. LINGUISTICS,
    dialectology.
dialectological 247. LINGUISTICS,
    dialectology.
dialectologist 247. LINGUISTICS,
    dialectology.
dialectology 247. LINGUISTICS.
diallage 354. RHETORIC and
    RHETORICAL DEVICES.
dialogic 248. LITERARY STYLE,
    dialogism.
dialogism 248. LITERARY STYLE.
dialogist 248. LITERARY STYLE,
    dialogism.
dialogue 4. AGREEMENT.
dialoguism 248. LITERARY STYLE,
    dialogism.
dialysis 44. BIOLOGY.
dialytic 44. BIOLOGY, **dialysis.**
diamagnetism 316. PHYSICS.
dianoetic 393. THINKING;
    393. THINKING, **dianoia.**
dianoia 393. THINKING.
diapause 44. BIOLOGY.
diapedesis 49. BLOOD and BLOOD
    VESSELS.
diaphoresis 50. BODILY FUNCTIONS.
diaphoretic 50. BODILY FUNCTIONS,
    diaphoresis; 130. DRUGS, **sudorific.**
diaphysis 52. BONES.
diaphytical 52. BONES, **diaphysis.**
diarch 185. GOVERNMENT, **diarchy.**
diarchy 185. GOVERNMENT.
diarthrosis 51. BODY, HUMAN;
    52. BONES.
diaskeuasis 53. BOOKS.
diaskeuast 53. BOOKS, **diaskeuasis.**
Diaspora 231. JUDAISM.
diastalsis 50. BODILY FUNCTIONS.
diastole 199. HEART; 409. VERSE.
diastolic 199. HEART, **diastole;**
    409. VERSE, **diastole.**
diastrophe 133. EARTH, **diastrophism.**
diastrophic 133. EARTH, **diastrophism;**
    179. GEOLOGY, **diastrophism.**
diastrophism 133. EARTH;
    179. GEOLOGY.
diatesseron 130. DRUGS.
diathermancy 342. RADIATION.
diathermanous 342. RADIATION,
    diathermancy.

diathermia 350. REMEDIES, **diathermy.**
diathermic 350. REMEDIES, **diathermy.**
diathermy 350. REMEDIES.
diathesis 122. DISEASE and ILLNESS.
diathetic 122. DISEASE and ILLNESS,
 diathesis.
diatonicism 284. MUSIC.
diatonism 284. MUSIC, **diatonicism.**
diatropic 282. MOTION, **diatropism;**
 319. PLANTS, **diatropism.**
diatropism 282. MOTION; 319. PLANTS.
dicaeology 354. RHETORIC and
 RHETORICAL DEVICES.
dicealolgy 239. LAW.
dicephalic 196. HEAD, **dicephalism.**
dicephalism 196. HEAD.
dicephalous 196. HEAD, **dicephalism.**
dicephaly 196. HEAD, **dicephalism.**
dichogamous 167. FLOWERS,
 dichogamy; 319. PLANTS, **dichogamy.**
dichogamy 167. FLOWERS; 319. PLANTS.
dichotomist 83. CLASSIFICATION,
 dichotomy.
dichotomy 83. CLASSIFICATION.
dichroic 92. COLOR, **dichroism;**
 245. LIGHT, **dichroism.**
dichroism 92. COLOR; 245. LIGHT.
dichromatic 92. COLOR, **dichromatism.**
dichromation 148. EYES.
dichromatism 92. COLOR.
diclinism 167. FLOWERS.
diclonous 167. FLOWERS, **diclinism.**
dicrotic 199. HEART, **dicrotism.**
dicrotism 199. HEART.
dictatorial 185. GOVERNMENT,
 dictatorship.
dictatorship 185. GOVERNMENT.
didachist 80. CHRISTIANITY.
didact 28. ATTITUDES, **didacticism;**
 240. LEARNING, **didacticism.**
didactic 28. ATTITUDES, **didacticism;**
 240. LEARNING, **didacticism.**
didacticism 28. ATTITUDES;
 240. LEARNING.
didactics 240. LEARNING.
die-hard 28. ATTITUDES, **die-hardism;**
 41. BEHAVIOR, **die-hardism.**
die-hardism 28. ATTITUDES;
 41. BEHAVIOR.
digamism 258. MARRIAGE.
digamist 258. MARRIAGE, **digamism.**

digamous 258. MARRIAGE, **digamism.**
digamy 258. MARRIAGE, **digamism.**
digenesis 44. BIOLOGY.
digenetic 44. BIOLOGY, **digenesis.**
digitalism 122. DISEASE and ILLNESS.
digitigrade 44. BIOLOGY, **digitigradism.**
digitigradism 44. BIOLOGY.
diglot 236. LANGUAGE.
diglottic 236. LANGUAGE, **diglot.**
diglottism 236. LANGUAGE,
 bilingualism.
digoneutic 46. BIRTH, **digoneutism.**
digoneutism 46. BIRTH.
dikephobia 239. LAW; 313. PHOBIAS.
dilettante 41. BEHAVIOR, **dilettantism.**
dilettantish 41. BEHAVIOR,
 dilettantism.
dilettantism 41. BEHAVIOR.
diluvianism 179. GEOLOGY.
Dimaris 250. LOGIC.
Dimatis 250. LOGIC.
dimidiation 329. PROCESSES.
dinophobia 313. PHOBIAS.
dioptometer 148. EYES;
 226. INSTRUMENTS.
dioptric 245. LIGHT, **dioptrics.**
dioptrics 245. LIGHT.
diorama 352. REPRESENTATION.
diplegia 122. DISEASE and ILLNESS.
diplegic 122. DISEASE and ILLNESS,
 diplegia.
diplomatics 256. MANUSCRIPTS.
diplomatology 249. LITERATURE.
diplopiaphobia 313. PHOBIAS.
dipodic 409. VERSE, **dipody.**
dipody 409. VERSE.
dipsomania 8. ALCOHOL.
dipsomaniac 8. ALCOHOL, **dipsomania.**
dipsomaniacal 8. ALCOHOL,
 dipsomania.
dipsophobe 8. ALCOHOL, **dipsophobia.**
dipsophobia 8. ALCOHOL.
dipterology 225. INSECTS.
diptych 23. ART; 218. IMAGES.
direption 391. THEFT.
Disamis 250. LOGIC.
disarmament 413. WAR.
disarmature 413. WAR.
disceptation 21. ARGUMENTATION.
disceptator 21. ARGUMENTATION,
 disceptation.

discobolus 26. ATHLETICS.
discographer 314. PHONOGRAPH
RECORDS, discography.
discographical 314. PHONOGRAPH
RECORDS, discography.
discography 314. PHONOGRAPH
RECORDS.
discophile 311. -PHILE, -PHILIA, -PHILY,
discophily; 314. PHONOGRAPH
RECORDS, discophily.
discophily 91. COLLECTIONS and
COLLECTING; 311. -PHILE,
-PHILIA, -PHILY;
314. PHONOGRAPH RECORDS.
disherison 239. LAW.
disintermediation 137. ECONOMICS.
diskographer 314. PHONOGRAPH
RECORDS, discography.
diskographical 314. PHONOGRAPH
RECORDS, discography.
diskography 314. PHONOGRAPH
RECORDS, discography.
diskophile 311. -PHILE, -PHILIA, -PHILY,
discophily; 314. PHONOGRAPH
RECORDS, discophily.
diskophily 311. -PHILE, -PHILIA, -PHILY,
discophily; 314. PHONOGRAPH
RECORDS, discophily.
disputant 21. ARGUMENTATION,
disputation.
disputation 21. ARGUMENTATION.
disseisin 103. CRIME, disseizin;
331. PROPERTY and OWNERSHIP,
disseizin.
disseizin 103. CRIME; 331. PROPERTY and
OWNERSHIP.
dissentation 21. ARGUMENTATION.
dissenter 21. ARGUMENTATION,
dissentation.
dissenterism 332. PROTESTANTISM.
distich 409. VERSE.
disyllabic 236. LANGUAGE, disyllabism.
disyllabical 236. LANGUAGE,
disyllabism.
disyllabism 236. LANGUAGE.
disyllable 236. LANGUAGE, disyllabism.
ditheism 183. GOD and GODS.
ditheist 183. GOD and GODS, ditheism.
ditheistic 183. GOD and GODS, ditheism.
ditheistical 183. GOD and GODS,
ditheism.

dithyramb 190. GREECE and GREEKS.
dithyrambic 190. GREECE and GREEKS,
dithyramb.
dittology 43. BIBLE.
diuresis 50. BODILY FUNCTIONS.
diuretic 50. BODILY FUNCTIONS,
diuresis.
diuturnal 396. TIME, diuturnity.
diuturnity 396. TIME.
divagation 393. THINKING.
divarication 21. ARGUMENTATION.
diversionary 322. POLITICS,
diversionism.
diversionism 322. POLITICS.
diversionist 322. POLITICS,
diversionism.
divisionism 23. ART.
divisionist 23. ART, divisionism.
DNA 204. HEREDITY.
Docetae 205. HERESY, Docetism.
Docetic 79. CHRIST, Docetism.
Docetism 79. CHRIST; 205. HERESY.
docimacy 270. METALS, docimasy.
docimasy 190. GREECE and GREEKS;
270. METALS.
dockage 131. DUES and PAYMENT.
doctrinaire 21. ARGUMENTATION,
doctrinarianism.
doctrinairism 21. ARGUMENTATION,
doctrinarianism.
doctrinarianism 21. ARGUMENTATION.
doctrinism 240. LEARNING.
doctrinist 240. LEARNING, doctrinism.
dodecaphonic 284. MUSIC,
dodecaphony.
dodecaphonism 284. MUSIC,
dodecaphony.
dodecaphonist 284. MUSIC,
dodecaphony.
dodecaphony 284. MUSIC.
dodecatonality 284. MUSIC,
dodecaphony.
dogmatic 21. ARGUMENTATION,
dogmatism.
dogmatism 21. ARGUMENTATION.
dogmatist 21. ARGUMENTATION,
dogmatism.
do-goodism 184. GOODNESS;
376. SOCIETY.
dolicephalic 196. HEAD,
dolichocephalism.

dolichocephalism 196. HEAD.
dolicocephalous 196. HEAD,
   dolichocephalism.
dolicocephaly 196. HEAD,
   dolichocephalism.
dolmen 385. STONES.
dolorifuge 306. PAIN.
domatophobia 212. HOUSES;
   313. PHOBIAS.
Donatism 205. HERESY.
Donatist 205. HERESY, Donatism.
Donatistic 205. HERESY, Donatism.
donkeyish 41. BEHAVIOR, donkeyism.
donkeyism 41. BEHAVIOR.
do-nothingism 41. BEHAVIOR.
Doppelgänger 182. GHOSTS.
doramania 254. MANIAS.
doraphobe 16. ANIMALS, doraphobia.
doraphobia 16. ANIMALS; 313. PHOBIAS.
Dorism 236. LANGUAGE.
dormancy 372. SLEEP.
dosimeter 226. INSTRUMENTS;
   342. RADIATION.
dosimetric 130. DRUGS, dosimetry;
   264. MEASUREMENT, dosimetry;
   342. RADIATION, dosimetry.
dosimetrical 130. DRUGS, dosimetry;
   264. MEASUREMENT, dosimetry;
   342. RADIATION, dosimetry.
dosimetrist 130. DRUGS, dosimetry;
   264. MEASUREMENT, dosimetry;
   342. RADIATION, dosimetry.
dosimetry 130. DRUGS;
   264. MEASUREMENT; 342. RADIATION.
dosiology 130. DRUGS.
dosology 130. DRUGS, dosiology.
dotation 331. PROPERTY and OWNERSHIP.
doubleganger 182. GHOSTS,
   Doppelgänger.
doublure 53. BOOKS.
doulocracy 185. GOVERNMENT.
dove 413. WAR, doveism.
doveish 413. WAR, doveism.
doveism 413. WAR.
dovism 413. WAR, doveism.
dowdyish 41. BEHAVIOR, dowdyism.
dowdyism 41. BEHAVIOR.
Down's syndrome 122. DISEASE and
   ILLNESS.
dowsing 414. WATER.

doxographer 91. COLLECTIONS and
   COLLECTING, doxography;
   312. PHILOSOPHY, doxography.
doxographic 91. COLLECTIONS and
   COLLECTING, doxography.
doxographical 312. PHILOSOPHY,
   doxography.
doxography 91. COLLECTIONS and
   COLLECTING; 312. PHILOSOPHY.
doxological 284. MUSIC, doxology.
doxology 284. MUSIC.
Draconian 239. LAW, Draconianism.
Draconianism 239. LAW.
Draconic 239. LAW, Draconianism.
dramalogue 127. DRAMA.
dramaticism 41. BEHAVIOR.
dramaturge 127. DRAMA, dramaturgy.
dramaturgist 127. DRAMA, dramaturgy.
dramaturgy 127. DRAMA.
drapetomania 144. ESCAPE;
   254. MANIAS.
drayage 131. DUES and PAYMENT.
dressage 211. HORSES.
dromomania 254. MANIAS; 399. TRAVEL.
dromophobia 282. MOTION;
   313. PHOBIAS.
drudge 426. WORK, drudgery.
drudgery 426. WORK.
Druid 349. RELIGION, Druidism.
Druidic 349. RELIGION, Druidism.
Druidical 349. RELIGION, Druidism.
Druidism 349. RELIGION.
drunkometer 8. ALCOHOL;
   226. INSTRUMENTS.
dryad 286. MYTHOLOGY.
dualism 312. PHILOSOPHY;
   349. RELIGION.
dualist 312. PHILOSOPHY, dualism;
   349. RELIGION, dualism.
dualistic 312. PHILOSOPHY, dualism;
   349. RELIGION, dualism.
duarchy 185. GOVERNMENT.
duecentism 23. ART; 228. ITALY;
   249. LITERATURE.
duecentist 23. ART, duecentism;
   228. ITALY, duecentism;
   249. LITERATURE, duecentism.
duelist 96. CONFLICT.
duellist 96. CONFLICT, duelist.
dulia 69. CATHOLICISM; 359. SAINTS.

dulocracy 185. GOVERNMENT,
  doulocracy.
dummyism 235. LAND.
duodrama 127. DRAMA.
duologue 127. DRAMA.
duopolist 398. TRADE, duopoly.
duopolistic 398. TRADE, duopoly.
duopoly 398. TRADE.
duopsonistic 398. TRADE, duopsony.
duopsony 398. TRADE.
duumvirate 185. GOVERNMENT.
dwarfism 368. SIZE.
dyarch 185. GOVERNMENT, diarchy.
dyarchy 185. GOVERNMENT, diarchy.
dynamism 312. PHILOSOPHY.
dynamist 312. PHILOSOPHY, dynamism.
dynamistic 312. PHILOSOPHY,
  dynamism.
dynamitism 322. POLITICS.
dynamometer 316. PHYSICS,
  dynamometry.
dynamometric 316. PHYSICS,
  dynamometry.
dynamometrical 316. PHYSICS,
  dynamometry.
dynamometry 316. PHYSICS.
dynast 185. GOVERNMENT, dynasticism.
dynasticism 185. GOVERNMENT.
dynasty 185. GOVERNMENT,
  dynasticism.
Dyophysite 79. CHRIST, Dyophysitism.
Dyophysitic 79. CHRIST, Dyophysitism.
Dyophysitism 79. CHRIST.
Dyothelete 79. CHRIST, Dyothelitism.
Dyotheletism 79. CHRIST,
  Dyothelitism.
Dyothelite 79. CHRIST, Dyothelitism.
Dyothelitism 79. CHRIST.
dyschromatopsia 92. COLOR; 148. EYES.
dyscrasia 197. HEALTH.
dyscrasic 197. HEALTH, dyscrasia.
dyscratic 197. HEALTH, dyscrasia.
dysesthesia 309. PERCEPTION.
dysgenesis 204. HEREDITY.
dysgenetic 204. HEREDITY, dysgenesis.
dysgenics 341. RACE, cacogenics.
dysidrosis 122. DISEASE and ILLNESS.
dyslexia 346. READING.
dyslexic 346. READING, dyslexia.
dyslogia 382. SPEECH, dyslogy.
dyslogist 326. PRAISE, dyslogy.

dyslogistic 326. PRAISE, dyslogy.
dyslogistical 326. PRAISE, dyslogy.
dyslogy 326. PRAISE; 382. SPEECH.
dysmenorrhea 122. DISEASE and
  ILLNESS.
dysmerogenesis 44. BIOLOGY.
dysmerogenetic 44. BIOLOGY,
  dysmerogenesis.
dysmorphmania 313. PHOBIAS,
  dysmorphophobia.
dysmorphophobia 278. MONSTERS;
  313. PHOBIAS.
dyspathic 334. PSYCHOLOGY, dyspathy.
dyspathy 334. PSYCHOLOGY.
dyspepsia 122. DISEASE and ILLNESS.
dyspeptic 122. DISEASE and ILLNESS,
  dyspepsia.
dyspeptical 122. DISEASE and ILLNESS,
  dyspepsia.
dysphagia 122. DISEASE and ILLNESS.
dysphagic 122. DISEASE and ILLNESS,
  dysphagia.
dysphagy 122. DISEASE and ILLNESS,
  dysphagia.
dysphasia 382. SPEECH;
  405. UNDERSTANDING.
dysphemia 382. SPEECH.
dysphemism 236. LANGUAGE.
dysphonia 382. SPEECH.
dysphoria 279. MOODS.
dysphoric 279. MOODS, dysphoria.
dyspnea 122. DISEASE and ILLNESS.
dyspneic 122. DISEASE and ILLNESS,
  dyspnea.
dyspnoea 122. DISEASE and ILLNESS,
  dyspnea.
dyspnoeic 122. DISEASE and ILLNESS,
  dyspnea.
dysteleological 312. PHILOSOPHY,
  dysteleology.
dysteleologist 312. PHILOSOPHY,
  dysteleology.
dysteleology 312. PHILOSOPHY.
dysthymia 334. PSYCHOLOGY.
dysthymic 334. PSYCHOLOGY,
  dysthymia.
dystopia 406. UTOPIA.
dystrophia 122. DISEASE and ILLNESS,
  dystrophy; 168. FOOD and NUTRITION,
  dystrophy.

dystrophic 122. DISEASE and ILLNESS, dystrophy.
dystrophy 122. DISEASE and ILLNESS; 168. FOOD and NUTRITION.
dysuria 122. DISEASE and ILLNESS.

E

Early Federal Style 20. ARCHITECTURE, Federalism.
Early Republican 20. ARCHITECTURE, Federalism.
easement 235. LAND; 239. LAW.
Eastern Orthodox 80. CHRISTIANITY, Eastern Orthodoxy.
Eastern Orthodoxy 80. CHRISTIANITY.
Ebionism 205. HERESY.
Ebionite 205. HERESY, Ebionism.
Ebionitic 205. HERESY, Ebionism.
Ebionitism 205. HERESY, Ebionism.
ebriety 8. ALCOHOL.
ebriosity 8. ALCOHOL.
ecbasis 354. RHETORIC and RHETORICAL DEVICES.
ecchymosis 49. BLOOD and BLOOD VESSELS.
ecclesiarch 69. CATHOLICISM, ecclesiarchy; 81. CHURCH.
ecclesiarchy 69. CATHOLICISM.
ecclesiastic 81. CHURCH, ecclesiasticism.
ecclesiastical 81. CHURCH, ecclesiasticism.
ecclesiasticism 81. CHURCH.
ecclesioclasticism 81. CHURCH.
ecclesiographer 81. CHURCH, ecclesiography.
ecclesiographic 81. CHURCH, ecclesiography.
ecclesiographical 81. CHURCH, ecclesiography.
ecclesiography 81. CHURCH.
ecclesiolatry 81. CHURCH.
ecclesiologic 81. CHURCH, ecclesiology.
ecclesiological 81. CHURCH, ecclesiology.
ecclesiologist 81. CHURCH, ecclesiology.
ecclesiology 81. CHURCH.
ecclesiophobia 81. CHURCH; 313. PHOBIAS.
eccrinology 14. ANATOMY.

eccyesis 327. PREGNANCY.
ecdemiomania 254. MANIAS; 399. TRAVEL.
ecdysial 44. BIOLOGY, ecdysis.
ecdysiast 108. DANCING; 310. PERFORMING.
ecdysis 44. BIOLOGY.
ecesis 142. ENVIRONMENT; 319. PLANTS.
echinologist 16. ANIMALS, echinology.
echinology 16. ANIMALS; 430. ZOOLOGY.
echoic 247. LINGUISTICS, echoism.
echoism 247. LINGUISTICS.
echolalia 382. SPEECH.
echolalic 382. SPEECH, echolalia.
echolocation 123. DISTANCE; 380. SOUND.
echometer 380. SOUND, echometry.
echometry 380. SOUND.
eclampsia 122. DISEASE and ILLNESS, eclamptism.
eclamptism 122. DISEASE and ILLNESS.
eclectic 312. PHILOSOPHY, eclecticism.
eclecticism 20. ARCHITECTURE; 23. ART; 312. PHILOSOPHY.
eclecticist 23. ART, eclecticism.
ecocide 142. ENVIRONMENT.
ecologic 142. ENVIRONMENT, ecology; 376. SOCIETY, ecology.
ecological 44. BIOLOGY, ecology; 142. ENVIRONMENT, ecology; 376. SOCIETY, ecology.
ecologically 44. BIOLOGY, ecology.
ecologist 44. BIOLOGY, ecology; 142. ENVIRONMENT, ecology; 376. SOCIETY, ecology.
ecology 44. BIOLOGY; 142. ENVIRONMENT; 376. SOCIETY.
economese 137. ECONOMICS; 237. LANGUAGE STYLE.
econometrics 137. ECONOMICS.
economic 137. ECONOMICS, economics.
economical 137. ECONOMICS, economics.
economics 137. ECONOMICS.
economism 137. ECONOMICS.
economist 137. ECONOMICS, economics; 137. ECONOMICS, economism.
ecophobia 212. HOUSES; 313. PHOBIAS.
ecosystem 142. ENVIRONMENT.
ecotonal 142. ENVIRONMENT, ecotone.
ecotone 142. ENVIRONMENT.

ecotype 142. ENVIRONMENT.
ecotypic 142. ENVIRONMENT, **ecotype.**
ecphonema 354. RHETORIC and
RHETORICAL DEVICES.
ecphonesis 354. RHETORIC and
RHETORICAL DEVICES, **ecphonema.**
ectasia 122. DISEASE and ILLNESS.
ecthesis 349. RELIGION.
ecthlipsis 409. VERSE.
ectomorphic 51. BODY, HUMAN,
ectomorphy.
ectomorphy 51. BODY, HUMAN.
ectoplasm 72. CELLS.
ectoplasmic 72. CELLS, **ectoplasm.**
ectypal 98. COPYING, **ectype.**
ectype 98. COPYING.
ectypography 141. ENGRAVING.
ecumenicalism 332. PROTESTANTISM,
ecumenism.
ecumenicism 332. PRÓTESTANTISM,
ecumenism.
Ecumenicist 80. CHRISTIANITY,
Ecumenism.
Ecumenism 80. CHRISTIANITY.
ecumenism 332. PROTESTANTISM.
edaphology 377. SOIL.
edema 122. DISEASE and ILLNESS.
edematose 122. DISEASE and ILLNESS,
edema.
edematous 122. DISEASE and ILLNESS,
edema.
edeomania 254. MANIAS; 364. SEX.
educationalist 240. LEARNING,
educationist.
educationist 240. LEARNING.
eduction 393. THINKING.
eductive 393. THINKING, **eduction.**
edulcoration 329. PROCESSES.
efflorescence 167. FLOWERS;
414. WATER.
efflorescent 167. FLOWERS,
efflorescence; 329. PROCESSES,
effloresence; 414. WATER,
efflorescence.
effloresence 329. PROCESSES.
egalitarian 322. POLITICS,
egalitarianism.
egalitarianism 322. POLITICS.
egestion 50. BODILY FUNCTIONS.
egocentric 362. SELF, **egocentricity;**
362. SELF, **egocentrism.**

egocentricity 362. SELF.
egocentrism 362. SELF.
egoism 28. ATTITUDES; 362. SELF.
egoist 28. ATTITUDES, **egoism;**
362. SELF, **egoism.**
egoistic 28. ATTITUDES, **egoism;**
362. SELF, **egoism.**
egomania 362. SELF.
egomaniac 362. SELF, **egomania.**
egotheism 362. SELF.
egotism 28. ATTITUDES; 362. SELF.
egotist 28. ATTITUDES, **egotism;**
362. SELF, **egotism.**
egotistical 28. ATTITUDES, **egotism;**
362. SELF, **egotism.**
Egyptian Revivalism
20. ARCHITECTURE.
Egyptological 18. ANTIQUITY,
Egyptology.
Egyptologist 18. ANTIQUITY,
Egyptology.
Egyptology 18. ANTIQUITY.
eidolism 182. GHOSTS.
eidology 334. PSYCHOLOGY.
eidolon 182. GHOSTS.
Eight-Fold Path, The 59. BUDDHISM.
eisegesis 43. BIBLE.
eisoptrophobia 313. PHOBIAS.
elastic 261. MATERIALS, PROPERTIES OF,
elasticity.
elasticity 261. MATERIALS, PROPERTIES
OF.
Eleatic 312. PHILOSOPHY, **Eleaticism.**
Eleaticism 312. PHILOSOPHY.
election 80. CHRISTIANITY.
electrobiological 44. BIOLOGY,
electrobiology.
electrobiologist 44. BIOLOGY,
electrobiology.
electrobiology 44. BIOLOGY.
electrograph 315. PHOTOGRAPHY,
electrography.
electrographic 315. PHOTOGRAPHY,
electrography.
electrography 315. PHOTOGRAPHY.
electrologist 193. HAIR, **electrology.**
electrology 193. HAIR.
electrophysiological 266. MEDICAL
SPECIALTIES, **electrophysiology.**
electrophysiology 266. MEDICAL
SPECIALTIES.

electrotherapeutic 266. MEDICAL
SPECIALTIES, electrotherapeutics;
350. REMEDIES, electrotherapeutics.
electrotherapeutical 266. MEDICAL
SPECIALTIES, electrotherapeutics;
350. REMEDIES, electrotherapeutics.
electrotherapeutics 266. MEDICAL
SPECIALTIES; 350. REMEDIES.
electrotherapist 266. MEDICAL
SPECIALTIES, electrotherapy.
electrotherapy 266. MEDICAL
SPECIALTIES; 350. REMEDIES.
electrotonic 291. NERVES, electrotonus.
electrotonus 291. NERVES.
electrotropic 316. PHYSICS,
electrotropism.
electrotropism 316. PHYSICS.
electrotyper 328. PRINTING,
electrotypy.
electrotypic 328. PRINTING,
electrotypy.
electrotypist 328. PRINTING,
electrotypy.
electrotypy 328. PRINTING.
electuary 130. DRUGS.
eleemosynary 6. AID; 75. CHARITY.
elenchic 250. LOGIC, elenchus.
elenchus 250. LOGIC.
elenctic 250. LOGIC, elenchus.
eleutheromania 173. FREEDOM.
eleutherophobia 173. FREEDOM;
313. PHOBIAS.
elinguation 335. PUNISHMENT.
elitism 28. ATTITUDES;
185. GOVERNMENT.
elitist 185. GOVERNMENT, elitism.
elixir 7. ALCHEMY; 350. REMEDIES.
elixir of life 7. ALCHEMY, elixir.
elocution 354. RHETORIC and
RHETORICAL DEVICES; 382. SPEECH.
elocutionist 354. RHETORIC and
RHETORICAL DEVICES; 382. SPEECH,
elocution.
Elohist 43. BIBLE.
eloquence 354. RHETORIC and
RHETORICAL DEVICES.
eloquent 354. RHETORIC and
RHETORICAL DEVICES, eloquence.
elurophobia 70. CATS, ailurophobia;
313. PHOBIAS; 313. PHOBIAS,
ailurophobia.

eluscation 48. BLINDNESS.
elution 329. PROCESSES.
elutriation 84. CLEANLINESS;
329. PROCESSES.
elytroplasty 388. SURGERY.
emaceration 51. BODY, HUMAN.
emanational 312. PHILOSOPHY,
emanationism.
emanationism 312. PHILOSOPHY.
emanationist 312. PHILOSOPHY,
emanationism.
emanatism 312. PHILOSOPHY,
emanationism.
emargination 53. BOOKS.
embadometry 235. LAND.
embezzlement 391. THEFT.
embezzler 391. THEFT, embezzlement.
emblazonry 210. HONORS and REGALIA.
emblematist 210. HONORS and REGALIA.
emblematologist 210. HONORS and
REGALIA, emblematology.
emblematology 210. HONORS and
REGALIA.
emblements 5. AGRICULTURE.
embolic 65. CALENDAR, embolism.
embolism 49. BLOOD and BLOOD
VESSELS; 65. CALENDAR.
embolismic 65. CALENDAR, embolism.
embolismical 65. CALENDAR,
embolism.
embracery 103. CRIME.
embryogenetic 44. BIOLOGY,
embryogeny; 72. CELLS,
embryogeny; 191. GROWTH,
embryogeny.
embryogenic 44. BIOLOGY,
embryogeny; 72. CELLS,
embryogeny; 191. GROWTH,
embryogeny.
embryogeny 44. BIOLOGY; 72. CELLS;
191. GROWTH.
embryographic 327. PREGNANCY,
embryography.
embryography 327. PREGNANCY.
emesis 122. DISEASE and ILLNESS.
emetic 122. DISEASE and ILLNESS,
emesis; 266. MEDICAL SPECIALTIES,
emetology.
emetology 266. MEDICAL SPECIALTIES.
emetophobia 313. PHOBIAS.

emmeniopathy 122. DISEASE and ILLNESS.

emmenologist 266. MEDICAL SPECIALTIES, emmenology.

emmenology 266. MEDICAL SPECIALTIES; 424. WOMEN.

emmetropia 148. EYES.

emmetropic 148. EYES, emmetropia.

emmetropy 148. EYES, emmetropia.

emollient 350. REMEDIES.

emotionalism 28. ATTITUDES.

emotionalist 28. ATTITUDES, emotionalism.

emotionalistic 28. ATTITUDES, emotionalism.

empathic 405. UNDERSTANDING, empathy.

empathy 405. UNDERSTANDING.

empiric 233. KNOWLEDGE, empiricism.

empirical 233. KNOWLEDGE, empiricism; 312. PHILOSOPHY, empiricism.

empiricism 233. KNOWLEDGE; 312. PHILOSOPHY.

empiricist 233. KNOWLEDGE, empiricism; 312. PHILOSOPHY, empiricism.

empiriocritical 104. CRITICISM, empirio-criticism.

empirio-criticism 104. CRITICISM.

empirism 233. KNOWLEDGE, empiricism.

empleomania 62. BUREAUCRACY; 254. MANIAS; 426. WORK.

emption 398. TRADE.

emptional 398. TRADE, emption.

emptor 398. TRADE.

empyema 122. DISEASE and ILLNESS.

empyromancy 124. DIVINATION; 373. SMOKE.

empyrosis 162. FIRE.

emuscation 329. PROCESSES.

enatation 144. ESCAPE.

enation 348. RELATIONSHIP.

encephalitis 56. BRAIN.

enchiridion 53. BOOKS.

encomiast 326. PRAISE, encomium.

encomiastic 326. PRAISE, encomium.

encomium 326. PRAISE.

Encratism 80. CHRISTIANITY; 205. HERESY.

Encratist 205. HERESY, Encratism.

Encratite 80. CHRISTIANITY, Encratism.

enculturation 376. SOCIETY.

encyclic 69. CATHOLICISM, encyclical; 323. POPE, encyclical.

encyclical 69. CATHOLICISM; 323. POPE.

encyclopaedia 53. BOOKS, encyclopedia.

encyclopaedic 53. BOOKS, encyclopedia.

encyclopaedical 53. BOOKS, encyclopedia.

encyclopaedist 53. BOOKS, encyclopedia.

encyclopedia 53. BOOKS.

encyclopedic 53. BOOKS, encyclopedia.

encyclopedical 53. BOOKS, encyclopedia.

encyclopedism 233. KNOWLEDGE.

encyclopedist 53. BOOKS, encyclopedia; 233. KNOWLEDGE, encyclopedism.

endarchy 185. GOVERNMENT.

endemicity 341. RACE, endemism.

endemism 341. RACE.

endocarditis 199. HEART.

endocrinologic 266. MEDICAL SPECIALTIES, endocrinology.

endocrinological 266. MEDICAL SPECIALTIES, endocrinology.

endocrinologist 266. MEDICAL SPECIALTIES, endocrinology.

endocrinology 266. MEDICAL SPECIALTIES.

endodontia 390. TEETH, endodontics.

endodontics 390. TEETH.

endodontist 266. MEDICAL SPECIALTIES; 390. TEETH, endodontics.

endodontology 390. TEETH.

endogamic 258. MARRIAGE, endogamy.

endogamous 258. MARRIAGE, endogamy.

endogamy 258. MARRIAGE.

endogenesis 44. BIOLOGY.

endogenicity 44. BIOLOGY, endogenesis; 191. GROWTH, endogeny.

endogenous 44. BIOLOGY, endogenesis; 191. GROWTH, endogeny.

endogeny 44. BIOLOGY, endogenesis; 191. GROWTH.

endomorphic 51. BODY, HUMAN,
endomorphy.
endomorphy 51. BODY, HUMAN.
endoplasm 72. CELLS.
endoplasmic 72. CELLS, endoplasm.
endosmosis 329. PROCESSES.
endosmotic 329. PROCESSES,
endosmosis.
endysial 44. BIOLOGY, endysis.
endysis 44. BIOLOGY.
energeticist 316. PHYSICS, energetics.
energeticistic 316. PHYSICS, energetics.
energetics 316. PHYSICS.
energism 316. PHYSICS.
energist 316. PHYSICS, energism.
energumen 114. DEMONS; 150. FADS.
enetophobia 313. PHOBIAS.
enfeoffment 331. PROPERTY and
OWNERSHIP.
enginery 369. SKILL and CRAFT;
416. WEAPONRY.
Englishism 140. ENGLISH, Anglicism.
Englishry 139. ENGLAND.
engrailment 305. ORNAMENTATION.
engrosser 428. WRITING, engrossment.
engrossment 428. WRITING.
enigmatographer 337. PUZZLES,
enigmatography.
enigmatography 337. PUZZLES.
enigmatology 337. PUZZLES.
enologist 421. WINE, oenology.
enology 421. WINE, oenology.
enomancy 421. WINE, oenomancy.
enomania 254. MANIAS; 421. WINE.
enophile 421. WINE, oenophily.
enophily 421. WINE, oenophily.
enophobe 421. WINE, oenophobia.
enophobia 421. WINE, oenophobia.
enoptromancy 124. DIVINATION.
enriositatis 49. BLOOD and BLOOD
VESSELS; 321. POISON.
entailment 331. PROPERTY and
OWNERSHIP.
entasis 20. ARCHITECTURE.
entelechial 312. PHILOSOPHY,
entelechy.
entelechy 312. PHILOSOPHY.
enterologic 266. MEDICAL SPECIALTIES,
enterology.
enterological 266. MEDICAL
SPECIALTIES, enterology.

enterologist 266. MEDICAL SPECIALTIES,
enterology.
enterology 266. MEDICAL SPECIALTIES.
enterotoxemia 49. BLOOD and BLOOD
VESSELS; 321. POISON.
entheomania 254. MANIAS;
349. RELIGION.
entomologic 225. INSECTS, entomology;
430. ZOOLOGY, entomology.
entomological 225. INSECTS,
entomology; 430. ZOOLOGY,
entomology.
entomologist 225. INSECTS,
entomology; 430. ZOOLOGY,
entomology.
entomology 225. INSECTS;
430. ZOOLOGY.
entomomania 225. INSECTS;
254. MANIAS.
entomophobia 225. INSECTS;
313. PHOBIAS.
entrepreneurship 160. FINANCE.
enucleation 329. PROCESSES.
enucleator 329. PROCESSES,
enucleation.
environmentalism 142. ENVIRONMENT.
environmentalist 142. ENVIRONMENT,
environmentalism.
enzymologic 44. BIOLOGY,
enzymology.
enzymological 44. BIOLOGY,
enzymology.
enzymologist 44. BIOLOGY,
enzymology; 158. FERMENTATION,
enzymology.
enzymology 44. BIOLOGY;
158. FERMENTATION.
eolith 385. STONES.
eolithic 385. STONES, eolith.
eonism 364. SEX.
eosophobia 313. PHOBIAS.
epagogic 21. ARGUMENTATION,
epagogue.
epagogue 21. ARGUMENTATION.
epanadiplosis 354. RHETORIC and
RHETORICAL DEVICES.
epanados 354. RHETORIC and
RHETORICAL DEVICES.
epanalepsis 354. RHETORIC and
RHETORICAL DEVICES.

epanaphora 354. RHETORIC and
RHETORICAL DEVICES.
epanastrophe 354. RHETORIC and
RHETORICAL DEVICES.
epanody 167. FLOWERS.
epanorthosis 354. RHETORIC and
RHETORICAL DEVICES.
eparchy 135. EASTERN ORTHODOXY;
190. GREECE and GREEKS.
epeirogenesis 133. EARTH, epeirogeny;
179. GEOLOGY, epeirogeny.
epeirogenetic 133. EARTH, epeirogeny;
179. GEOLOGY, epeirogeny.
epeirogenic 133. EARTH, epeirogeny;
179. GEOLOGY, epeirogeny.
epeirogeny 133. EARTH; 179. GEOLOGY.
epexegesis 405. UNDERSTANDING.
epexegetic 405. UNDERSTANDING,
epexegesis.
epexegetical 405. UNDERSTANDING,
epexegesis.
ephemeris 11. ALMANACS.
ephemeron 225. INSECTS.
epibolic 191. GROWTH, epiboly.
epiboly 191. GROWTH.
epicene 44. BIOLOGY, epicenism;
51. BODY, HUMAN, epicenism;
364. SEX, epicenism.
epicenism 44. BIOLOGY; 51. BODY,
HUMAN; 364. SEX.
epicenity 44. BIOLOGY, epicenism;
51. BODY, HUMAN, epicenism;
364. SEX, epicenism.
epicenter 134. EARTHQUAKES.
epicheirema 250. LOGIC.
epicrisis 104. CRITICISM.
epicure 320. PLEASURE, epicurism.
Epicurean 312. PHILOSOPHY,
Epicureanism.
epicurean 168. FOOD and NUTRITION,
epicureanism; 320. PLEASURE,
epicurism.
Epicureanism 312. PHILOSOPHY.
epicureanism 168. FOOD and NUTRITION;
320. PLEASURE, epicurism.
Epicurism 312. PHILOSOPHY,
Epicureanism.
epicurism 320. PLEASURE.
epidemic 122. DISEASE and ILLNESS.
epidemical 122. DISEASE and ILLNESS,
epidemic.

epidemicity 122. DISEASE and ILLNESS,
epidemic.
epidemiographer 122. DISEASE and
ILLNESS, epidemiography.
epidemiographic 122. DISEASE and
ILLNESS, epidemiography.
epidemiographical 122. DISEASE and
ILLNESS, epidemiography.
epidemiographist 122. DISEASE and
ILLNESS, epidemiography.
epidemiography 122. DISEASE and
ILLNESS.
epidemiologic 266. MEDICAL
SPECIALTIES, epidemiology.
epidemiological 266. MEDICAL
SPECIALTIES, epidemiology.
epidemiologist 266. MEDICAL
SPECIALTIES, epidemiology.
epidemiology 266. MEDICAL
SPECIALTIES.
epigenesis 44. BIOLOGY; 46. BIRTH;
72. CELLS; 122. DISEASE and ILLNESS;
179. GEOLOGY.
epigenesist 44. BIOLOGY; 46. BIRTH,
epigenesis.
epigenetic 44. BIOLOGY, epigenesis;
46. BIRTH, epigenesis; 72. CELLS,
epigenesis; 122. DISEASE and ILLNESS,
epigenesis; 179. GEOLOGY, epigenesis.
epigone 348. RELATIONSHIP.
epigram 236. LANGUAGE;
333. PROVERBS.
epigrammatic 237. LANGUAGE STYLE,
epigrammatism.
epigrammatism 237. LANGUAGE STYLE.
epigrammatist 237. LANGUAGE STYLE,
epigrammatism; 333. PROVERBS,
epigram.
epigrapher 18. ANTIQUITY, epigraphy.
epigraphic 18. ANTIQUITY, epigraphy.
epigraphical 18. ANTIQUITY,
epigraphy.
epigraphist 18. ANTIQUITY, epigraphy.
epigraphy 18. ANTIQUITY.
epilepsy 122. DISEASE and ILLNESS.
epileptic 122. DISEASE and ILLNESS,
epilepsy.
epilogistic 127. DRAMA, epilogue.
epilogue 127. DRAMA.
epimorphic 46. BIRTH, epimorphosis;
430. ZOOLOGY, epimorphosis.

epimorphosis 46. BIRTH; 430. ZOOLOGY.
epiphany 349. RELIGION.
epiphenomenal 312. PHILOSOPHY,
  epiphenomenalism.
epiphenomenalism 312. PHILOSOPHY.
epiphenomenalist 312. PHILOSOPHY,
  epiphenomenalism.
epiphora 354. RHETORIC and
  RHETORICAL DEVICES.
epiphyte 319. PLANTS, epiphytism.
epiphytism 319. PLANTS.
epiphytologist 54. BOTANY,
  epiphytology.
epiphytology 54. BOTANY.
Episcopal 332. PROTESTANTISM,
  Episcopalianism.
Episcopalian 332. PROTESTANTISM,
  Episcopalianism.
Episcopalianism 332. PROTESTANTISM.
episcopalism 332. PROTESTANTISM.
epistaxis 49. BLOOD and BLOOD VESSELS;
  293. NOSE.
epistemic 233. KNOWLEDGE,
  epistemology; 312. PHILOSOPHY,
  epistemology.
epistemological 233. KNOWLEDGE,
  epistemology; 312. PHILOSOPHY,
  epistemology.
epistemologist 233. KNOWLEDGE,
  epistemology; 312. PHILOSOPHY,
  epistemology.
epistemology 233. KNOWLEDGE;
  312. PHILOSOPHY.
epistemophilia 233. KNOWLEDGE.
epistemophiliac 233. KNOWLEDGE,
  epistemophilia.
epistolographic 249. LITERATURE,
  epistolography.
epistolography 249. LITERATURE.
epistrophe 354. RHETORIC and
  RHETORICAL DEVICES, epiphora.
episyllogism 21. ARGUMENTATION.
epitaph 112. DEATH.
epitaphial 112. DEATH, epitaph.
epitaphian 112. DEATH, epitaph.
epitaphic 112. DEATH, epitaph.
epitasis 122. DISEASE and ILLNESS;
  127. DRAMA.
epithalamium 258. MARRIAGE.
epithalamy 258. MARRIAGE,
  epithalamium.

epithelioma 122. DISEASE and ILLNESS.
epitheliomatous 122. DISEASE and
  ILLNESS, epithelioma.
epithesis 236. LANGUAGE.
epitome 352. REPRESENTATION.
epizoism 16. ANIMALS.
epizootic 16. ANIMALS.
epizootiologic 16. ANIMALS,
  epizootiology.
epizootiological 16. ANIMALS,
  epizootiology.
epizootiology 16. ANIMALS.
epizootology 16. ANIMALS,
  epizootiology.
epizooty 16. ANIMALS, epizootic.
eponym 288. NAMES.
eponymic 288. NAMES, eponym;
  288. NAMES, eponymism.
eponymism 288. NAMES.
eponymist 288. NAMES.
eponymous 288. NAMES, eponym;
  288. NAMES, eponymism.
eponymy 288. NAMES, eponymism.
epulosis 197. HEALTH.
epulotic 197. HEALTH, epulosis;
  350. REMEDIES.
equalitarianism 322. POLITICS.
equanimity 28. ATTITUDES.
equanimous 28. ATTITUDES,
  equanimity.
equestrian 211. HORSES, equestrianism.
equestrianism 211. HORSES.
equestrienne 211. HORSES,
  equestrianism.
equilibrist 2. ACROBATICS;
  310. PERFORMING.
equinoctial 360. SEA.
equipollence 4. AGREEMENT;
  250. LOGIC; 386. STRENGTH and
  WEAKNESS.
equipollency 4. AGREEMENT,
  equipollence; 250. LOGIC,
  equipollence; 386. STRENGTH and
  WEAKNESS, equipollence.
equipollent 4. AGREEMENT,
  equipollence; 386. STRENGTH and
  WEAKNESS, equipollence.
equitation 211. HORSES.
equivocacy 236. LANGUAGE,
  equivocality; 336. PUNNING,
  equivocality.

equivocal 236. LANGUAGE,
　equivocality; 336. PUNNING,
　equivocality.
equivocality 236. LANGUAGE;
　336. PUNNING.
equivoke 336. PUNNING, equivoque.
equivoque 336. PUNNING.
Erastian 392. THEOLOGY, Erastianism.
Erastianism 392. THEOLOGY.
eremiomania 254. MANIAS;
　339. QUIETUDE.
eremiophobia 313. PHOBIAS; 362. SELF.
eremite 28. ATTITUDES, eremitism;
　116. DESERTS; 362. SELF, eremitism.
eremitic 28. ATTITUDES, eremitism;
　116. DESERTS, eremite; 362. SELF,
　eremitism.
eremitism 28. ATTITUDES; 362. SELF.
eremology 116. DESERTS.
eremophobia 313. PHOBIAS,
　eremiophobia; 362. SELF,
　autophobia; 362. SELF,
　eremiophobia.
erethism 122. DISEASE and ILLNESS.
erethistic 122. DISEASE and ILLNESS,
　erethism.
erethitic 122. DISEASE and ILLNESS,
　erethism.
ergasiomania 254. MANIAS.
ergasiophobia 313. PHOBIAS; 426. WORK.
ergatocracy 185. GOVERNMENT.
ergograph 426. WORK.
ergographic 426. WORK, ergograph.
ergoism 41. BEHAVIOR.
ergologist 426. WORK, ergology.
ergology 426. WORK.
ergomania 254. MANIAS; 426. WORK.
ergonomic 142. ENVIRONMENT,
　ergonomics; 255. MANKIND,
　ergonomics.
ergonomics 142. ENVIRONMENT;
　255. MANKIND.
ergophile 426. WORK.
ergophobia 313. PHOBIAS; 426. WORK.
ergotism 21. ARGUMENTATION;
　321. POISON.
ergotize 21. ARGUMENTATION,
　ergotism.
eristic 21. ARGUMENTATION.
eristical 21. ARGUMENTATION, eristic.

erotesis 354. RHETORIC and RHETORICAL
　DEVICES.
eroticism 364. SEX.
eroticomania 254. MANIAS; 364. SEX.
erotism 364. SEX, eroticism.
erotographomania 249. LITERATURE;
　254. MANIAS; 364. SEX.
erotology 364. SEX.
erotomania 254. MANIAS; 364. SEX.
erotomaniac 364. SEX, erotomania.
erotophobia 313. PHOBIAS; 364. SEX.
errancy 402. TRUTH and ERROR.
erraticism 41. BEHAVIOR.
errhine 350. REMEDIES.
errinophily 91. COLLECTIONS and
　COLLECTING.
eructation 50. BODILY FUNCTIONS.
erysipelas 122. DISEASE and ILLNESS.
erythema 122. DISEASE and ILLNESS.
erythematous 122. DISEASE and ILLNESS,
　erythema.
erythrism 95. COMPLEXION.
erythrismal 95. COMPLEXION,
　erythrism.
erythristic 95. COMPLEXION, erythrism.
erythrocytometer 49. BLOOD and BLOOD
　VESSELS; 226. INSTRUMENTS.
erythrocytometry 49. BLOOD and BLOOD
　VESSELS; 264. MEASUREMENT.
erythroleukemia 66. CANCER.
erythromania 95. COMPLEXION;
　254. MANIAS.
erythromelalgia 122. DISEASE and
　ILLNESS.
erythromelalgic 122. DISEASE and
　ILLNESS, erythromelalgia.
erythrophobia 92. COLOR;
　313. PHOBIAS.
erythrosis 122. DISEASE and ILLNESS.
escapism 144. ESCAPE;
　310. PERFORMING; 393. THINKING.
escapist 144. ESCAPE, escapism;
　310. PERFORMING, escapism;
　393. THINKING, escapism.
eschatological 138. END OF THE WORLD,
　eschatology; 392. THEOLOGY,
　eschatology.
eschatologist 138. END OF THE WORLD,
　eschatology; 392. THEOLOGY,
　eschatology.

eschatology 138. END OF THE WORLD;
392. THEOLOGY.
escheatable 331. PROPERTY and
OWNERSHIP, escheatment.
escheatment 331. PROPERTY and
OWNERSHIP.
esoterica 91. COLLECTIONS and
COLLECTING; 294. NOVELTY.
esotericism 294. NOVELTY.
esoterism 294. NOVELTY, esotericism.
esoterist 294. NOVELTY, esotericism.
esotropia 148. EYES.
essayism 249. LITERATURE.
essayist 249. LITERATURE, essayism.
essentialism 312. PHILOSOPHY.
essentialist 312. PHILOSOPHY,
essentialism.
essentialistic 312. PHILOSOPHY,
essentialism.
establishmentarianism 349. RELIGION.
esthetician 38. BEAUTY, aesthetician.
estheticism 38. BEAUTY, aestheticism.
esthetics 38. BEAUTY, aesthetics;
312. PHILOSOPHY; 312. PHILOSOPHY,
aesthetics.
esthetology 23. ART.
estivation 167. FLOWERS;
347. RECREATION; 430. ZOOLOGY.
estrous 16. ANIMALS, estrus; 364. SEX,
estrus.
estrum 16. ANIMALS, estrus; 364. SEX,
estrus.
estrus 16. ANIMALS; 364. SEX.
etacism 190. GREECE and GREEKS;
330. PRONUNCIATION.
etacist 330. PRONUNCIATION, etacism.
etatism 322. POLITICS.
etheromania 130. DRUGS; 254. MANIAS.
ethical 312. PHILOSOPHY, ethics.
ethical nihilism 312. PHILOSOPHY.
ethical relativism 312. PHILOSOPHY.
ethicism 28. ATTITUDES.
ethicist 312. PHILOSOPHY, ethics.
ethics 312. PHILOSOPHY.
ethnarch 185. GOVERNMENT,
ethnarchy.
ethnarchy 185. GOVERNMENT.
ethnic 80. CHRISTIANITY, ethnicism.
ethnical 80. CHRISTIANITY, ethnicism.
ethnicism 80. CHRISTIANITY.

ethnobotanic 54. BOTANY,
ethnobotany.
ethnobotanical 54. BOTANY,
ethnobotany.
ethnobotanist 54. BOTANY,
ethnobotany.
ethnobotany 54. BOTANY.
ethnocentric 17. ANTHROPOLOGY,
ethnocentricity; 17. ANTHROPOLOGY,
ethnocentrism.
ethnocentricity 17. ANTHROPOLOGY.
ethnocentrism 17. ANTHROPOLOGY.
ethnocracy 341. RACE.
ethnocratic 341. RACE, ethnocracy.
ethnodicy 17. ANTHROPOLOGY.
ethnogenic 17. ANTHROPOLOGY,
ethnogeny.
ethnogenist 17. ANTHROPOLOGY,
ethnogeny.
ethnogeny 17. ANTHROPOLOGY.
ethnogeographer 341. RACE,
ethnogeography.
ethnogeographic 341. RACE,
ethnogeography.
ethnogeography 341. RACE.
ethnographer 17. ANTHROPOLOGY,
ethnography; 17. ANTHROPOLOGY,
ethography; 255. MANKIND,
ethnography.
ethnographic 17. ANTHROPOLOGY,
ethnography; 17. ANTHROPOLOGY,
ethography; 255. MANKIND,
ethnography.
ethnographical 17. ANTHROPOLOGY,
ethnography; 17. ANTHROPOLOGY,
ethography; 255. MANKIND,
ethnography.
ethnography 17. ANTHROPOLOGY;
255. MANKIND.
ethnologic 17. ANTHROPOLOGY,
ethnology.
ethnological 17. ANTHROPOLOGY,
ethnology.
ethnologist 17. ANTHROPOLOGY,
ethnology.
ethnology 17. ANTHROPOLOGY.
ethnomania 289. NATIONALISM.
ethnomaniac 289. NATIONALISM,
ethnomania.
ethnomusicologist 284. MUSIC,
ethnomusicology.

ethnomusicology 284. MUSIC.
ethnopsychological 341. RACE,
ethnopsychology.
ethnopsychology 341. RACE.
ethography 17. ANTHROPOLOGY.
ethologic 255. MANKIND, ethology.
ethological 16. ANIMALS, ethology;
255. MANKIND, ethology.
ethologist 16. ANIMALS, ethology.
ethology 16. ANIMALS; 255. MANKIND.
etiolation 95. COMPLEXION;
122. DISEASE and ILLNESS; 319. PLANTS.
etiologic 122. DISEASE and ILLNESS,
etiology; 290. NATURE, etiology;
312. PHILOSOPHY, etiology.
etiological 122. DISEASE and ILLNESS,
etiology; 290. NATURE, etiology;
304. ORIGINS, etiology;
312. PHILOSOPHY, etiology.
etiologist 122. DISEASE and ILLNESS,
etiology.
etiology 122. DISEASE and ILLNESS;
290. NATURE; 304. ORIGINS;
312. PHILOSOPHY.
Etruscologist 18. ANTIQUITY,
Etruscology.
Etruscology 18. ANTIQUITY.
etymologic 236. LANGUAGE, etymology.
etymological 236. LANGUAGE,
etymology; 247. LINGUISTICS,
etymology.
etymologicon 53. BOOKS;
236. LANGUAGE.
etymologist 236. LANGUAGE,
etymology; 247. LINGUISTICS,
etymology.
etymology 236. LANGUAGE;
247. LINGUISTICS.
Euchologion 135. EASTERN
ORTHODOXY.
euchology 135. EASTERN ORTHODOXY.
eucrasia 197. HEALTH.
eucrasic 197. HEALTH, eucrasia.
eucratic 197. HEALTH, eucrasia.
eudaemonics 145. ETHICS,
eudemonism; 195. HAPPINESS,
eudemonics.
eudaemonism 145. ETHICS,
eudemonism; 195. HAPPINESS,
eudemonism.

eudaemonist 145. ETHICS,
eudemonism; 195. HAPPINESS,
eudemonism.
eudemonia 195. HAPPINESS,
eudemonics.
eudemonic 195. HAPPINESS,
eudemonics.
eudemonical 195. HAPPINESS,
eudemonics.
eudemonics 145. ETHICS, eudemonism;
195. HAPPINESS.
eudemonism 145. ETHICS;
195. HAPPINESS.
eudemonist 145. ETHICS, eudemonism;
195. HAPPINESS, eudemonism.
eudiometer 27. ATMOSPHERE;
226. INSTRUMENTS.
eudiometry 264. MEASUREMENT.
Eudoxian 205. HERESY.
euectic 197. HEALTH, evectics.
euectics 197. HEALTH, evectics.
eugenic 219. IMPROVEMENT, eugenics;
341. RACE, eugenism.
eugenicist 219. IMPROVEMENT,
eugenics.
eugenics 219. IMPROVEMENT.
eugenism 341. RACE.
euhemerism 183. GOD and GODS;
286. MYTHOLOGY.
euhemerist 183. GOD and GODS,
euhemerism; 286. MYTHOLOGY,
euhemerism.
euhemeristic 183. GOD and GODS,
euhemerism; 286. MYTHOLOGY,
euhemerism.
eulogism 248. LITERARY STYLE.
eulogist 326. PRAISE, eulogy.
eulogistic 248. LITERARY STYLE,
eulogism; 326. PRAISE, eulogy.
eulogistical 326. PRAISE, eulogy.
eulogization 248. LITERARY STYLE,
eulogism.
eulogy 326. PRAISE.
eumerogenesis 44. BIOLOGY.
eumerogenetic 44. BIOLOGY,
eumerogenesis.
eunuchism 364. SEX.
euonym 288. NAMES.
eupepsia 197. HEALTH.
eupepsy 197. HEALTH, eupepsia.
eupeptic 197. HEALTH, eupepsia.

euphemious 236. LANGUAGE,
euphemism.
euphemism 236. LANGUAGE.
euphemist 236. LANGUAGE,
euphemism.
euphemistic 236. LANGUAGE,
euphemism.
euphemistical 236. LANGUAGE,
euphemism.
euphonic 380. SOUND, euphony.
euphonical 380. SOUND, euphony.
euphonious 380. SOUND, euphony.
euphony 380. SOUND.
euphoria 195. HAPPINESS; 279. MOODS.
euphoric 195. HAPPINESS, euphoria;
279. MOODS, euphoria.
euphory 195. HAPPINESS, euphoria.
Euphuism 248. LITERARY STYLE.
euphuist 248. LITERARY STYLE,
Euphuism.
euphuistic 248. LITERARY STYLE,
Euphuism.
eurhythmic 199. HEART, eurhythmy.
eurhythmy 20. ARCHITECTURE;
199. HEART.
Eurocommunism 94. COMMUNISM.
Europeanism 236. LANGUAGE.
eurotophobia 313. PHOBIAS.
euthanasia 112. DEATH; 232. KILLING.
euthanasic 232. KILLING, euthanasia.
euthenics 142. ENVIRONMENT;
219. IMPROVEMENT; 341. RACE.
euthenist 142. ENVIRONMENT,
euthenics; 219. IMPROVEMENT,
euthenics.
Eutychian 79. CHRIST, Eutychianism.
Eutychianism 79. CHRIST.
evanescence 329. PROCESSES.
evangelical 80. CHRISTIANITY,
evangelism.
evangelicalism 80. CHRISTIANITY,
evangelism.
evangelism 80. CHRISTIANITY.
evangelistic 80. CHRISTIANITY,
evangelism.
evectic 197. HEALTH, evectics.
evectics 197. HEALTH.
eviration 335. PUNISHMENT.
evolutionism 147. EVOLUTION.
evolutionist 147. EVOLUTION,
evolutionism.

exacination 329. PROCESSES.
exanthematologic 122. DISEASE and
ILLNESS, exanthematology.
exanthematological 122. DISEASE and
ILLNESS, exanthematology.
exanthematology 122. DISEASE and
ILLNESS.
exarch 135. EASTERN ORTHODOXY.
exarchal 135. EASTERN ORTHODOXY,
exarch.
exececation 48. BLINDNESS;
335. PUNISHMENT.
exclusionism 376. SOCIETY.
exclusionist 376. SOCIETY, exclusionism.
excoriation 329. PROCESSES; 391. THEFT.
excrescence 51. BODY, HUMAN.
excrescent 51. BODY, HUMAN,
excrescence.
excretion 50. BODILY FUNCTIONS.
excursional 320. PLEASURE,
excursionism.
excursionism 320. PLEASURE.
excursionist 320. PLEASURE,
excursionism.
exegesis 43. BIBLE; 104. CRITICISM.
exegete 43. BIBLE, exegetics.
exegetic 104. CRITICISM, exegesis.
exegetical 104. CRITICISM, exegesis.
exegetics 43. BIBLE.
exegetist 43. BIBLE.
exegist 43. BIBLE, exegetist.
exequy 63. BURIAL.
exhibitionism 41. BEHAVIOR.
exhibitionist 41. BEHAVIOR,
exhibitionism.
exhibitionistic 41. BEHAVIOR,
exhibitionism.
exiguity 368. SIZE.
exiguous 368. SIZE, exiguity.
existentialism 312. PHILOSOPHY.
existentialist 312. PHILOSOPHY,
existentialism.
exobiologist 318. PLANETS, exobiology.
exobiology 318. PLANETS.
exode 127. DRAMA.
exodontia 390. TEETH.
exodontist 266. MEDICAL SPECIALTIES;
390. TEETH, exodontia.
exogamic 258. MARRIAGE, exogamy.
exogamous 258. MARRIAGE, exogamy.
exogamy 258. MARRIAGE.

exomologesis 349. RELIGION.
exorcism 114. DEMONS.
exorcismal 114. DEMONS, exorcism.
exorcisory 114. DEMONS, exorcism.
exorcist 114. DEMONS, exorcism.
exorcistic 114. DEMONS, exorcism.
exorcistical 114. DEMONS, exorcism.
exordium 53. BOOKS; 354. RHETORIC and
   RHETORICAL DEVICES.
exosmosis 329. PROCESSES.
exosmotic 329. PROCESSES, exosmosis.
exosphere 27. ATMOSPHERE.
exostosis 52. BONES; 319. PLANTS.
exoteric 349. RELIGION, exotericism.
exotericism 349. RELIGION.
exotic 23. ART, exoticism.
exotical 23. ART, exoticism.
exoticism 23. ART.
exoticist 23. ART, exoticism.
expansionism 322. POLITICS.
expansionist 322. POLITICS,
   expansionism.
expansionistic 322. POLITICS,
   expansionism.
expatriate 34. BANISHMENT,
   expatriation; 351. RENUNCIATION,
   expatriation.
expatriation 34. BANISHMENT;
   351. RENUNCIATION.
expectorant 350. REMEDIES.
experiential 312. PHILOSOPHY,
   experientialism.
experientialism 312. PHILOSOPHY.
experientialist 312. PHILOSOPHY,
   experientialism.
experimentalism 233. KNOWLEDGE.
experimentalist 233. KNOWLEDGE,
   experimentalism.
expertise 369. SKILL and CRAFT.
expertism 233. KNOWLEDGE.
expressage 131. DUES and PAYMENT.
Expressionism 23. ART.
Expressionist 23. ART, Expressionism.
Expressionistic 23. ART, Expressionism.
expropriation 331. PROPERTY and
   OWNERSHIP.
extensometer 226. INSTRUMENTS.
externalism 28. ATTITUDES.
externalist 28. ATTITUDES, externalism.
extirpation 329. PROCESSES.

extispex 16. ANIMALS, extispicy;
   124. DIVINATION, extispicy.
extispicious 16. ANIMALS, extispicy;
   124. DIVINATION, extispicy.
extispicy 16. ANIMALS; 124. DIVINATION.
extortioner 103. CRIME, extortionist.
extortionist 103. CRIME.
extrascripturalism 69. CATHOLICISM.
extraversion 362. SELF.
extraversive 362. SELF, extraversion.
extravert 362. SELF, extraversion.
extravertive 362. SELF, extraversion.
extremism 28. ATTITUDES.
extremist 28. ATTITUDES, extremism.
extroversion 362. SELF, extraversion.

F

Fabian 137. ECONOMICS, Fabianism.
Fabianism 137. ECONOMICS.
fabism 122. DISEASE and ILLNESS.
fabulist 243. LIES and LYING.
facetiae 213. HUMOR.
facetious 213. HUMOR, facetiae.
factional 322. POLITICS, factionalism;
   362. SELF, factionalism.
factionalism 185. GOVERNMENT,
   factionism; 322. POLITICS; 362. SELF.
factionalist 322. POLITICS,
   factionalism; 362. SELF, factionalism.
factionary 185. GOVERNMENT,
   factionism.
factionism 185. GOVERNMENT;
   322. POLITICS, factionalism; 362. SELF,
   factionalism.
factionist 185. GOVERNMENT,
   factionism.
factotum 297. OCCUPATIONS.
factualism 233. KNOWLEDGE;
   393. THINKING.
factualist 233. KNOWLEDGE,
   factualism; 393. THINKING,
   factualism.
factualistic 233. KNOWLEDGE,
   factualism; 393. THINKING,
   factualism.
faddish 150. FADS, faddism.
faddishness 150. FADS, faddism.
faddism 150. FADS.
faddist 150. FADS, faddism.
fainéance 41. BEHAVIOR; 426. WORK.

faineancy 41. BEHAVIOR, fainéance;
426. WORK, faineance.
fainéant 41. BEHAVIOR, fainéance;
426. WORK, faineance.
fairyism 41. BEHAVIOR.
falalery 86. CLOTHING.
Falangism 152. FASCISM; 322. POLITICS.
Falangist 152. FASCISM, Falangism;
322. POLITICS, Falangism.
falconry 45. BIRDS; 214. HUNTING.
fallal 86. CLOTHING, falalery.
fallalery 86. CLOTHING, falalery.
fallowist 5. AGRICULTURE.
falsism 243. LIES and LYING; 402. TRUTH
and ERROR.
familism 349. RELIGION.
familist 349. RELIGION, familism.
familistic 349. RELIGION, familism.
fanatic 28. ATTITUDES, fanaticism;
349. RELIGION, fanaticism.
fanatical 28. ATTITUDES, fanaticism.
fanaticism 28. ATTITUDES;
349. RELIGION.
fanfaron 41. BEHAVIOR, fanfaronade.
fanfaronade 41. BEHAVIOR.
fantastic 23. ART, fantasticism.
fantasticality 23. ART, fantasticism.
fantasticalness 23. ART, fantasticism.
fantasticism 23. ART.
faradic 316. PHYSICS, faradism.
faradism 316. PHYSICS.
fascicle 53. BOOKS.
fascism 152. FASCISM;
185. GOVERNMENT.
fascist 152. FASCISM, fascism;
185. GOVERNMENT, fascism.
fascistic 152. FASCISM, fascism;
185. GOVERNMENT, fascism.
fatalism 28. ATTITUDES;
312. PHILOSOPHY.
fatalist 28. ATTITUDES, fatalism;
312. PHILOSOPHY, fatalism.
fatalistic 28. ATTITUDES, fatalism;
312. PHILOSOPHY, fatalism.
fatiloquence 174. FUTURE.
fauna 16. ANIMALS.
faunal 16. ANIMALS, fauna.
faunist 16. ANIMALS.
faunology 16. ANIMALS.
faustian 28. ATTITUDES, faustianism;
41. BEHAVIOR, faustianism.

faustianism 28. ATTITUDES;
41. BEHAVIOR.
Fauve 23. ART, Fauvism.
Fauvism 23. ART.
Fauvist 23. ART, Fauvism.
favism 122. DISEASE and ILLNESS,
fabism.
favoritism 155. FAVORITISM.
Fayettism 322. POLITICS.
fealty 10. ALLEGIANCE.
febrifacient 122. DISEASE and ILLNESS.
febrifuge 122. DISEASE and ILLNESS;
350. REMEDIES.
febriphobia 313. PHOBIAS.
feculence 119. DIRT.
feculency 119. DIRT, feculence.
feculent 119. DIRT, feculence.
federalese 62. BUREAUCRACY;
185. GOVERNMENT; 237. LANGUAGE
STYLE.
Federalism 20. ARCHITECTURE.
federalism 185. GOVERNMENT.
federalist 185. GOVERNMENT,
federalism.
federalistic 185. GOVERNMENT,
federalism.
Felapton 250. LOGIC.
felinophile 70. CATS.
felinophobia 70. CATS, ailurophobia;
313. PHOBIAS.
felo-de-se 232. KILLING.
femicidal 424. WOMEN, femicide.
femicide 424. WOMEN.
feminism 28. ATTITUDES.
feminist 28. ATTITUDES, feminism.
feministic 28. ATTITUDES, feminism.
Fenian 322. POLITICS, Fenianism.
Fenianism 322. POLITICS.
feoff 331. PROPERTY and OWNERSHIP.
feoffment 331. PROPERTY and
OWNERSHIP.
Ferio 250. LOGIC.
Feriso 250. LOGIC.
Ferison 250. LOGIC.
fermentologist 8. ALCOHOL,
fermentology.
fermentology 8. ALCOHOL.
ferroequinologist 344. RAILROADS,
ferroequinology.
ferroequinology 344. RAILROADS.
ferrotype 315. PHOTOGRAPHY.

Fesapo 250. LOGIC.
festilogy 81. CHURCH.
Festino 250. LOGIC.
festoonery 305. ORNAMENTATION.
fetation 46. BIRTH.
fetichism 364. SEX, **fetishism.**
fetichist 364. SEX, **fetishism.**
fetichistic 364. SEX, **fetishism.**
feticidal 1. ABORTION, **feticide.**
feticide 1. ABORTION.
fetishism 364. SEX.
fetishist 364. SEX, **fetishism.**
fetishistic 364. SEX, **fetishism.**
fetologist 327. PREGNANCY, **fetology.**
fetology 327. PREGNANCY.
feud 331. PROPERTY and OWNERSHIP.
feudal 185. GOVERNMENT, **feudalism;**
    235. LAND, **feudalism.**
feudalism 185. GOVERNMENT;
    235. LAND.
feudalistic 185. GOVERNMENT,
    feudalism; 235. LAND, **feudalism.**
feudality 185. GOVERNMENT,
    feudalism; 235. LAND, **feudalism.**
feudist 96. CONFLICT; 239. LAW.
Feuillant 322. POLITICS.
feuilletonism 265. MEDIA.
feuilletonist 265. MEDIA, **feuilletonism.**
fibrillation 199. HEART.
Fichtean 94. COMMUNISM,
    Fichteanism; 312. PHILOSOPHY,
    Fichteanism; 376. SOCIETY,
    Fichteanism.
Fichteanism 94. COMMUNISM;
    312. PHILOSOPHY; 376. SOCIETY.
fideism 151. FAITH.
fideist 151. FAITH, **fideism.**
fideistic 151. FAITH, **fideism.**
fiducial 239. LAW, **fiduciary.**
fiduciary 160. FINANCE; 239. LAW;
    239. LAW, **fiduciary.**
fief 331. PROPERTY and OWNERSHIP.
fiefdom 235. LAND.
fiendism 41. BEHAVIOR.
filiation 307. PARENTS;
    348. RELATIONSHIP.
filicidal 77. CHILDREN, **filicide.**
filicide 77. CHILDREN.
filicologist 54. BOTANY, **filicology.**
filicology 54. BOTANY.
filionymic 288. NAMES.

fimbriation 305. ORNAMENTATION.
finalism 28. ATTITUDES.
finalist 28. ATTITUDES, **finalism.**
finical 28. ATTITUDES, **finicalness.**
finicalism 28. ATTITUDES.
finicality 28. ATTITUDES, **finicalness.**
finicalness 28. ATTITUDES.
finicism 28. ATTITUDES.
Flacian 332. PROTESTANTISM,
    Flacianism.
Flacianism 332. PROTESTANTISM.
flagellant 80. CHRISTIANITY,
    flagellantism; 349. RELIGION,
    flagellation; 364. SEX, **flagellation.**
flagellantism 80. CHRISTIANITY.
flagellation 349. RELIGION; 364. SEX.
flagellator 349. RELIGION, **flagellation;**
    364. SEX, **flagellation.**
Fletcherism 168. FOOD and NUTRITION.
fletcherism 168. FOOD and NUTRITION,
    Fletcherism.
Fletcherite 168. FOOD and NUTRITION,
    Fletcherism.
Fletcherize 168. FOOD and NUTRITION,
    Fletcherism.
flexitime 426. WORK.
floccilation 122. DISEASE and ILLNESS.
floccinaucinihilipilification
    407. VALUES.
florescence 167. FLOWERS.
florescent 167. FLOWERS, **florescence.**
floretum 167. FLOWERS.
floribunda 167. FLOWERS.
floricultural 167. FLOWERS,
    floriculture.
floriculture 167. FLOWERS.
floriculturist 167. FLOWERS,
    floriculture.
florid 92. COLOR, **floridity;**
    95. COMPLEXION, **floridity;**
    248. LITERARY STYLE, **floridity.**
floridity 92. COLOR; 95. COMPLEXION;
    248. LITERARY STYLE.
florilegium 91. COLLECTIONS and
    COLLECTING; 249. LITERATURE.
florimania 167. FLOWERS; 254. MANIAS;
    319. PLANTS.
flotsam 366. SHIPS.
fluidism 122. DISEASE and ILLNESS;
    384. SPIRITS and SPIRITUALISM.

fluidist 122. DISEASE and ILLNESS, fluidism; 384. SPIRITS and SPIRITUALISM, fluidism.
flunkey 41. BEHAVIOR, flunkyism.
flunkeyism 41. BEHAVIOR, flunkyism.
flunky 41. BEHAVIOR, flunkyism.
flunkyism 41. BEHAVIOR.
fluorometer 226. INSTRUMENTS; 342. RADIATION.
fluorometric 226. INSTRUMENTS, fluorometer; 264. MEASUREMENT, fluorometry; 342. RADIATION, fluorometer; 342. RADIATION, fluorometry.
fluorometry 264. MEASUREMENT; 342. RADIATION.
fluoroscope 226. INSTRUMENTS.
fluoroscopic 342. RADIATION, fluoroscopy.
fluoroscopy 342. RADIATION.
fluvialist 179. GEOLOGY.
fluviation 356. RIVERS.
fluviologist 414. WATER, fluviology.
fluviology 414. WATER.
fluxmeter 226. INSTRUMENTS.
focimetric 316. PHYSICS, focimetry.
focimetry 316. PHYSICS.
foehn 420. WIND.
foetation 46. BIRTH, fetation.
foeticidal 1. ABORTION, feticide.
foeticide 1. ABORTION, feticide.
foetologist 327. PREGNANCY, fetology.
foetology 327. PREGNANCY, fetology.
fogeyish 28. ATTITUDES, fogyism.
fogeyism 28. ATTITUDES, fogyism.
fogyish 28. ATTITUDES, fogyism.
fogyism 28. ATTITUDES.
Fohism 59. BUDDHISM; 78. CHINA.
Fohist 59. BUDDHISM, Fohism; 78. CHINA, Fohism.
föhn 420. WIND, foehn.
Foism 59. BUDDHISM, Fohism; 78. CHINA, Fohism.
foliation 53. BOOKS.
folk etymology 247. LINGUISTICS.
folklore 255. MANKIND.
folklorist 255. MANKIND, folklore.
foolocracy 185. GOVERNMENT; 376. SOCIETY.
Fordism 137. ECONOMICS.

foreclosure 331. PROPERTY and OWNERSHIP.
foreignism 236. LANGUAGE.
forensic 21. ARGUMENTATION, forensics.
forensics 21. ARGUMENTATION.
forestation 401. TREES.
formal criticism 104. CRITICISM.
formalism 104. CRITICISM.
formalist 104. CRITICISM, formalism.
formalistic 104. CRITICISM, formalism.
formicarium 19. ANTS, formicary.
formicary 19. ANTS.
formication 19. ANTS; 51. BODY, HUMAN.
formularism 41. BEHAVIOR.
formularistic 41. BEHAVIOR, formularism.
formulary 53. BOOKS; 130. DRUGS.
formulism 28. ATTITUDES.
formulist 28. ATTITUDES, formulism.
formulistic 28. ATTITUDES, formulism.
fortuist 73. CHANCE, fortuitism.
fortuitism 73. CHANCE.
fortuitous 73. CHANCE, fortuity.
fortuitousness 73. CHANCE, fortuity.
fortuity 73. CHANCE.
fossilism 28. ATTITUDES; 41. BEHAVIOR; 171. FOSSILS.
fossilist 171. FOSSILS, fossilism.
Fourierism 93. COMMUNALISM.
Fourierist 93. COMMUNALISM, Fourierism.
Fourierite 93. COMMUNALISM, Fourierism.
fractionalism 376. SOCIETY.
fractionalization 376. SOCIETY, fractionalism.
frambesia 122. DISEASE and ILLNESS.
framboesia 122. DISEASE and ILLNESS, frambesia.
franchise 173. FREEDOM.
Francomania 172. FRANCE; 254. MANIAS.
Francophile 172. FRANCE; 311. -PHILE, -PHILIA, -PHILY.
Francophobia 172. FRANCE; 313. PHOBIAS.
frangibility 261. MATERIALS, PROPERTIES OF.
Franglais 236. LANGUAGE.

Franklinic electricity 316. PHYSICS, Franklinism.
Franklinism 316. PHYSICS.
fraternalism 41. BEHAVIOR.
fraternalist 41. BEHAVIOR, fraternalism.
fraternalistic 41. BEHAVIOR, fraternalism.
fraternity 376. SOCIETY.
fratricidal 232. KILLING, fratricide.
fratricide 232. KILLING.
free association 393. THINKING.
Freechurchism 332. PROTESTANTISM.
Freechurchman 332. PROTESTANTISM, Freechurchism.
freehold 331. PROPERTY and OWNERSHIP.
freeholder 331. PROPERTY and OWNERSHIP, freehold.
free-lovism 251. LOVE; 364. SEX.
Free Soiler 322. POLITICS, Free Soilism.
Free Soilism 322. POLITICS.
freightage 131. DUES and PAYMENT.
Frenchism 172. FRANCE; 236. LANGUAGE.
Fresison 250. LOGIC.
Freudian 104. CRITICISM, Freudianism; 334. PSYCHOLOGY, Freudianism.
Freudianism 104. CRITICISM; 334. PSYCHOLOGY.
friability 261. MATERIALS, PROPERTIES OF.
Froebelian 240. LEARNING, Froebelist.
Froebelist 240. LEARNING.
fromology 76. CHEESE.
frondescence 241. LEAVES.
frondescent 241. LEAVES, frondescence.
frontogenesis 417. WEATHER.
frontolysis 417. WEATHER.
frottage 364. SEX.
frotteur 364. SEX, frottage.
fruitarian 168. FOOD and NUTRITION, fruitarianism.
fruitarianism 168. FOOD and NUTRITION.
fugacious 113. DECAYING, fugacity.
fugacity 113. DECAYING.
fugitation 103. CRIME; 144. ESCAPE.
fuguism 284. MUSIC.
fuguist 284. MUSIC, fuguism.
fuliginosity 110. DARKNESS; 119. DIRT; 373. SMOKE.

fuliginous 110. DARKNESS, fuliginosity; 119. DIRT, fuliginosity; 373. SMOKE, fuliginosity.
fulmination 329. PROCESSES; 394. THUNDER.
funambulism 2. ACROBATICS; 310. PERFORMING; 395. TIGHTROPE WALKING.
funambulist 2. ACROBATICS, funambulism; 310. PERFORMING, funambulism; 395. TIGHTROPE WALKING, funambulism.
functionalism 20. ARCHITECTURE.
functionalist 20. ARCHITECTURE, functionalism.
functionarism 41. BEHAVIOR.
functionary 41. BEHAVIOR, functionarism.
fundamentalism 43. BIBLE; 332. PROTESTANTISM.
fundamentalist 43. BIBLE, fundamentalism; 332. PROTESTANTISM, fundamentalism.
fungicide 232. KILLING; 319. PLANTS.
fungological 54. BOTANY, fungology.
fungologist 54. BOTANY, fungology.
fungology 54. BOTANY.
fusionism 322. POLITICS.
fusionist 322. POLITICS, fusionism.
fustian 237. LANGUAGE STYLE; 354. RHETORIC and RHETORICAL DEVICES.
fustianist 237. LANGUAGE STYLE, fustian; 354. RHETORIC and RHETORICAL DEVICES, fustian.
fustigation 335. PUNISHMENT.
futilitarian 28. ATTITUDES, futilitarianism.
futilitarianism 28. ATTITUDES.
Futurism 23. ART.
futurism 174. FUTURE.
Futurist 23. ART, Futurism.
futurist 174. FUTURE, futurism.
Futuristic 23. ART, Futurism.
futuristic 174. FUTURE, futurism.
futurition 174. FUTURE.
futurology 174. FUTURE.

G

Gaelicism 289. NATIONALISM.
galactometer 226. INSTRUMENTS;
272. MILK, lactometer.
galactopoietic 130. DRUGS; 130. DRUGS,
galactopoietic; 272. MILK; 272. MILK,
galactopoietic.
galactosis 44. BIOLOGY; 50. BODILY
FUNCTIONS.
gale 420. WIND.
galenic 266. MEDICAL SPECIALTIES,
Galenism.
Galenism 266. MEDICAL SPECIALTIES.
galeophilia 70. CATS; 311. -PHILE,
-PHILIA, -PHILY.
galeophobia 313. PHOBIAS.
galimatias 382. SPEECH.
Gallican 69. CATHOLICISM,
Gallicanism.
Gallicanism 69. CATHOLICISM.
Gallicism 236. LANGUAGE.
Gallomania 172. FRANCE.
Gallophil 172. FRANCE.
Gallophile 172. FRANCE, Gallophil.
Gallophobia 172. FRANCE;
313. PHOBIAS; 313. PHOBIAS,
Francophobia.
galvanic 316. PHYSICS, galvanism.
galvanism 316. PHYSICS.
galvanograph 141. ENGRAVING,
galvanography.
galvanographic 141. ENGRAVING,
galvanography.
galvanography 141. ENGRAVING.
galvanological 316. PHYSICS,
galvanology.
galvanologist 316. PHYSICS,
galvanology.
galvanology 316. PHYSICS.
galvanometer 226. INSTRUMENTS.
galvanometric 226. INSTRUMENTS,
galvanometer; 264. MEASUREMENT,
galvanometry; 316. PHYSICS,
galvanometry.
galvanometrical 226. INSTRUMENTS,
galvanometer; 264. MEASUREMENT,
galvanometry; 316. PHYSICS,
galvanometry.

galvanometry 264. MEASUREMENT;
316. PHYSICS.
galvanoscope 226. INSTRUMENTS.
galvanothermy 200. HEAT.
galvanotropic 44. BIOLOGY,
galvanotropism; 191. GROWTH,
galvanotropism; 282. MOTION,
galvanotropism.
galvanotropism 44. BIOLOGY;
191. GROWTH; 282. MOTION.
gambist 284. MUSIC.
gamesmanship 176. GAMES.
gammacism 247. LINGUISTICS.
gammacismus 247. LINGUISTICS,
gammacism.
gamogenesis 44. BIOLOGY.
gamogenetic 44. BIOLOGY,
gamogenesis.
gamomania 254. MANIAS;
258. MARRIAGE.
gamophobia 258. MARRIAGE;
313. PHOBIAS.
Gandhian 322. POLITICS, Gandhism.
Gandhiism 322. POLITICS, Gandhism.
Gandhiist 322. POLITICS, Gandhism.
Gandhism 322. POLITICS.
Gandhist 322. POLITICS, Gandhism.
gangdom 103. CRIME.
gangster 41. BEHAVIOR, gangsterism.
gangsterism 41. BEHAVIOR.
gargoylism 14. ANATOMY; 52. BONES;
122. DISEASE and ILLNESS.
garmenture 86. CLOTHING.
gasconade 41. BEHAVIOR, gasconism.
gasconism 41. BEHAVIOR.
gasometer 264. MEASUREMENT,
gasometry.
gasometric 264. MEASUREMENT,
gasometry.
gasometrical 264. MEASUREMENT,
gasometry.
gasometry 264. MEASUREMENT.
gastralgia 306. PAIN.
gastricism 122. DISEASE and ILLNESS.
gastriloquism 382. SPEECH,
ventriloquism.
gastroenterologist 266. MEDICAL
SPECIALTIES.
gastrologer 266. MEDICAL SPECIALTIES,
gastrology.

gastrological 266. MEDICAL
SPECIALTIES, **gastrology**.
gastrologist 266. MEDICAL SPECIALTIES,
gastrology.
gastrology 266. MEDICAL SPECIALTIES.
gastromancy 124. DIVINATION.
gastromantic 124. DIVINATION,
gastromancy.
gastronome 168. FOOD and NUTRITION,
gastronomy.
gastronomic 168. FOOD and NUTRITION,
gastronomy.
gastronomist 168. FOOD and NUTRITION,
gastronomy.
gastronomy 168. FOOD and NUTRITION.
gastrophotography 315. PHOTOGRAPHY.
gatophobia 70. CATS; 313. PHOBIAS.
gaudery 86. CLOTHING.
Gaullism 322. POLITICS.
Gaullist 322. POLITICS, **Gaullism**.
gavage 168. FOOD and NUTRITION.
gavelkind 331. PROPERTY and
OWNERSHIP.
gazetteer 178. GEOGRAPHY.
gelastic 41. BEHAVIOR.
gelid 90. COLD, **gelidity**.
gelidity 90. COLD.
geloscopy 124. DIVINATION;
238. LAUGHTER.
gelotoscopy 124. DIVINATION,
geloscopy; 238. LAUGHTER,
geloscopy.
Gelup-Ka 59. BUDDHISM.
Gemaric 231. JUDAISM, **Gemarist**.
Gemarist 231. JUDAISM.
gemmary 177. GEMS.
gemmation 430. ZOOLOGY.
gemmination 354. RHETORIC and
RHETORICAL DEVICES.
gemmological 177. GEMS, **gemmology**.
gemmologist 177. GEMS, **gemmology**.
gemmology 177. GEMS.
gemology 177. GEMS, **gemmology**.
geneagenesis 204. HEREDITY.
geneagenetic 204. HEREDITY,
geneagenesis.
genealogic 207. HISTORY, **genealogy**.
genealogical 207. HISTORY, **genealogy**.
genealogist 207. HISTORY, **genealogy**.
genealogy 207. HISTORY.

genecologic 142. ENVIRONMENT,
genecology.
genecological 142. ENVIRONMENT,
genecology.
genecologist 142. ENVIRONMENT,
genecology.
genecology 142. ENVIRONMENT.
generalist 369. SKILL and CRAFT.
genesiology 364. SEX.
genethliac 24. ASTROLOGY.
genethliacism 24. ASTROLOGY.
genethliacs 24. ASTROLOGY;
124. DIVINATION, **genethlialogy**.
genethlialogic 24. ASTROLOGY,
genethlialogy.
genethlialogical 24. ASTROLOGY,
genethlialogy.
genethlialogy 24. ASTROLOGY;
124. DIVINATION.
genetic 44. BIOLOGY, **genetics**;
204. HEREDITY, **genetics**.
geneticist 44. BIOLOGY, **genetics**;
204. HEREDITY, **genetics**.
genetics 44. BIOLOGY; 204. HEREDITY.
Genevanism 332. PROTESTANTISM.
geniture 46. BIRTH.
genocidal 232. KILLING, **genocide**;
341. RACE, **genocide**.
genocide 232. KILLING; 341. RACE.
genophobia 313. PHOBIAS; 364. SEX.
genre criticism 104. CRITICISM.
genteelism 236. LANGUAGE;
248. LITERARY STYLE.
gentile 231. JUDAISM, **gentilism**;
349. RELIGION, **gentilism**.
gentilism 231. JUDAISM; 341. RACE;
349. RELIGION.
genuflection 10. ALLEGIANCE.
genuflexion 10. ALLEGIANCE,
genuflection.
geocentric 100. COSMOLOGY,
geocentricism.
geocentricism 100. COSMOLOGY.
geochronologic 133. EARTH,
geochronology; 396. TIME,
geochronology.
geochronological 133. EARTH,
geochronology; 396. TIME,
geochronology.

geochronologist 133. EARTH,
geochronology; 396. TIME,
geochronology.
geochronology 133. EARTH; 396. TIME.
geodesist 262. MATHEMATICS, geodesy.
geodesy 262. MATHEMATICS.
geodetic 262. MATHEMATICS, geodesy.
geodetical 262. MATHEMATICS, geodesy.
geodetics 262. MATHEMATICS, geodesy.
geodynamic 133. EARTH, geodynamics.
geodynamics 133. EARTH.
geognosist 179. GEOLOGY, geognosy.
geognost 179. GEOLOGY, geognosy.
geognostic 179. GEOLOGY, geognosy.
geognosy 179. GEOLOGY.
geogonic 133. EARTH, geogony.
geogony 133. EARTH.
geographer 178. GEOGRAPHY,
geography.
geographic 178. GEOGRAPHY,
geography.
geographical 178. GEOGRAPHY,
geography.
geography 178. GEOGRAPHY.
geolatry 133. EARTH.
geolinguist 247. LINGUISTICS,
geolinguistics.
geolinguistic 247. LINGUISTICS,
geolinguistics.
geolinguistics 247. LINGUISTICS.
geologic 133. EARTH, geology.
geological 133. EARTH, geology.
geologist 133. EARTH, geology.
geology 133. EARTH.
geomalic 133. EARTH, geomalism.
geomalism 133. EARTH.
geomancer 124. DIVINATION,
geomancy; 133. EARTH, geomancy.
geomancy 124. DIVINATION;
133. EARTH.
geometer 262. MATHEMATICS,
geometry.
geometric 262. MATHEMATICS,
geometry.
geometrical 262. MATHEMATICS,
geometry.
geometrician 262. MATHEMATICS,
geometry.
geometry 262. MATHEMATICS.

geomorphologic 133. EARTH,
geomorphology; 170. FORM,
geomorphology; 178. GEOGRAPHY,
geomorphology.
geomorphological 133. EARTH,
geomorphology; 170. FORM,
geomorphology; 178. GEOGRAPHY,
geomorphology.
geomorphologist 133. EARTH,
geomorphology; 170. FORM,
geomorphology; 178. GEOGRAPHY,
geomorphology.
geomorphology 133. EARTH; 170. FORM;
178. GEOGRAPHY.
geophagia 133. EARTH, geophagism.
geophagism 133. EARTH.
geophagist 133. EARTH, geophagism.
geophagous 133. EARTH, geophagism.
geophagy 133. EARTH, geophagism.
geophysical 316. PHYSICS, geophysics.
geophysicist 316. PHYSICS, geophysics.
geophysics 316. PHYSICS.
geopolitical 178. GEOGRAPHY,
geopolitics; 322. POLITICS,
geopolitics.
geopolitician 178. GEOGRAPHY,
geopolitics; 322. POLITICS,
geopolitics.
geopolitics 178. GEOGRAPHY;
180. GERMANY; 322. POLITICS.
geoponic 377. SOIL, geopony.
geoponical 377. SOIL, geopony.
geoponist 377. SOIL, geopony.
geopony 377. SOIL.
georama 133. EARTH;
352. REPRESENTATION.
Georgianism 20. ARCHITECTURE.
geotaxis 189. GRAVITY; 282. MOTION.
geotectology 179. GEOLOGY.
geotectonic 179. GEOLOGY,
geotectology.
geotectonics 179. GEOLOGY,
geotectology.
geothermometry 179. GEOLOGY;
200. HEAT.
geotropic 189. GRAVITY, geotropism.
geotropism 189. GRAVITY.
gephyromania 254. MANIAS;
399. TRAVEL.
gephyrophobia 313. PHOBIAS;
399. TRAVEL.

gerascophobia 299. OLD AGE;
313. PHOBIAS.
geratologic 113. DECAYING, geratology;
299. OLD AGE, geratology.
geratological 299. OLD AGE, geratology.
geratologous 113. DECAYING,
geratology; 299. OLD AGE,
geratology.
geratology 113. DECAYING; 299. OLD
AGE.
geriatric 266. MEDICAL SPECIALTIES,
geriatrics; 299. OLD AGE, geriatrics.
geriatrician 266. MEDICAL SPECIALTIES;
266. MEDICAL SPECIALTIES, geriatrics;
299. OLD AGE, geriatrics.
geriatrics 266. MEDICAL SPECIALTIES;
299. OLD AGE.
geriatrist 266. MEDICAL SPECIALTIES,
geriatrics; 299. OLD AGE, geriatrics.
geriatry 266. MEDICAL SPECIALTIES,
geriatrics; 299. OLD AGE, geriatrics.
Germanicism 236. LANGUAGE,
Germanism.
Germanism 180. GERMANY;
236. LANGUAGE.
Germanomania 180. GERMANY;
254. MANIAS.
Germanophile 180. GERMANY;
311. -PHILE, -PHILIA, -PHILY.
Germanophobia 180. GERMANY;
313. PHOBIAS.
germicidal 197. HEALTH, germicide;
232. KILLING, germicide.
germicide 197. HEALTH; 232. KILLING.
gerocomy 299. OLD AGE.
gerodontics 266. MEDICAL SPECIALTIES;
299. OLD AGE.
gerodontist 266. MEDICAL SPECIALTIES,
gerodontics; 299. OLD AGE,
gerodontics.
geromorphism 299. OLD AGE.
gerontocracy 185. GOVERNMENT.
gerontological 299. OLD AGE,
gerontology.
gerontologist 299. OLD AGE,
gerontology.
gerontology 299. OLD AGE.
gerontophile 364. SEX, gerontophilia.
gerontophilia 364. SEX.
gerontophilic 364. SEX, gerontophilia.
gestation 46. BIRTH.

geumophobia 313. PHOBIAS.
Ghazism 227. ISLAM.
Ghibelline 322. POLITICS,
Ghibellinism.
Ghibellinism 322. POLITICS.
gibbosity 170. FORM.
gibbous 170. FORM, gibbosity.
giganticide 232. KILLING.
gigantism 368. SIZE.
gigantology 368. SIZE.
gigantomachy 413. WAR.
gigmanism 28. ATTITUDES.
gipsy 41. BEHAVIOR, gypsyism.
gipsyish 41. BEHAVIOR, gypsyism.
gipsyism 41. BEHAVIOR, gypsyism.
gipsyologist 169. FOREIGNERS,
gypsyologist.
Girondism 172. FRANCE; 322. POLITICS.
Girondist 172. FRANCE, Girondism;
322. POLITICS, Girondism.
girouettism 28. ATTITUDES.
glaciological 179. GEOLOGY,
glaciology.
glaciologist 179. GEOLOGY, glaciology.
glaciology 179. GEOLOGY.
glaucescence 92. COLOR.
glaucescent 92. COLOR, glaucescence.
glaucoma 48. BLINDNESS; 148. EYES.
glaucomatous 48. BLINDNESS,
glaucoma; 148. EYES, glaucoma.
glioma 66. CANCER.
glossematic 247. LINGUISTICS,
glossematics.
glossematics 247. LINGUISTICS.
glossic 383. SPELLING.
glossitic 122. DISEASE and ILLNESS,
glossitis.
glossitis 122. DISEASE and ILLNESS.
glossograph 226. INSTRUMENTS;
382. SPEECH.
glossographer 249. LITERATURE,
glossography.
glossography 249. LITERATURE.
glossolalia 382. SPEECH.
glossolalist 382. SPEECH, glossolalia.
glossologist 247. LINGUISTICS.
glossology 247. LINGUISTICS.
glossophobia 313. PHOBIAS; 382. SPEECH.
glottochronological 247. LINGUISTICS,
glottochronology; 396. TIME,
glottochronology.

glottochronologist 247. LINGUISTICS,
glottochronology; 396. TIME,
glottochronology.,
glottochronology 247. LINGUISTICS;
396. TIME.
glottogonic 236. LANGUAGE,
glottogony.
glottogony 236. LANGUAGE.
glottology 247. LINGUISTICS.
glycophilia 122. DISEASE and ILLNESS.
glycosuria 122. DISEASE and ILLNESS.
glycosuric 122. DISEASE and ILLNESS,
glycosuria.
glyphographer 328. PRINTING,
glyphography.
glyphographic 328. PRINTING,
glyphography.
glyphography 328. PRINTING.
glyptic 177. GEMS.
glyptograph 141. ENGRAVING;
177. GEMS.
glyptographer 177. GEMS,
glyptography.
glyptographic 177. GEMS,
glyptography.
glyptography 177. GEMS.
glyptology 141. ENGRAVING; 177. GEMS.
glyptotheca 23. ART.
gnathic 149. FACIAL FEATURES,
gnathism.
gnathism 149. FACIAL FEATURES.
gnathonic 41. BEHAVIOR, gnathonism.
gnathonism 41. BEHAVIOR.
gnomonics 396. TIME.
gnomonology 333. PROVERBS; 396. TIME.
gnoseological 233. KNOWLEDGE,
gnosiology.
gnoseology 233. KNOWLEDGE,
gnosiology.
gnosiological 233. KNOWLEDGE,
gnosiology.
gnosiology 233. KNOWLEDGE.
gnosis 422. WISDOM.
Gnostic 205. HERESY, Gnosticism;
285. MYSTICISM, Gnosticism;
312. PHILOSOPHY, Gnosticism.
Gnosticism 205. HERESY;
285. MYSTICISM; 312. PHILOSOPHY.
gnostology 233. KNOWLEDGE,
gnosiology.
gnotobiotics 44. BIOLOGY.

Gobinism 341. RACE.
gombeen 276. MONEY, gombeenism.
gombeenism 276. MONEY.
gombeenman 276. MONEY,
gombeenism.
gomphiasis 390. TEETH.
gomphosis 52. BONES.
Gongoresque 248. LITERARY STYLE,
Gongorism.
Gongorism 248. LITERARY STYLE.
gongorism 354. RHETORIC and
RHETORICAL DEVICES.
Gongoristic 248. LITERARY STYLE,
Gongorism.
goniometer 226. INSTRUMENTS.
goniometry 264. MEASUREMENT.
gormand 41. BEHAVIOR, gourmandism.
gormandism 41. BEHAVIOR,
gourmandism.
Gothic 20. ARCHITECTURE, Gothicism.
gothic 248. LITERARY STYLE, gothicism.
Gothicism 20. ARCHITECTURE; 23. ART.
gothicism 248. LITERARY STYLE.
Gothicist 23. ART, Gothicism.
gothicist 248. LITERARY STYLE,
gothicism.
Gothic Revivalism 20. ARCHITECTURE.
gourmand 41. BEHAVIOR,
gourmandism.
gourmandism 28. ATTITUDES,
gourmetism; 41. BEHAVIOR.
gourmetism 28. ATTITUDES.
governmentalism 185. GOVERNMENT.
governmentalist 185. GOVERNMENT,
governmentalism.
gradualism 312. PHILOSOPHY;
322. POLITICS.
gradualist 312. PHILOSOPHY,
gradualism; 322. POLITICS,
gradualism.
gradualistic 312. PHILOSOPHY,
gradualism; 322. POLITICS,
gradualism.
Graecism 190. GREECE and GREEKS,
Grecism.
Graecomania 190. GREECE and GREEKS,
Grecomania.
graminologic 54. BOTANY,
graminology.
graminological 54. BOTANY,
graminology.

graminologist 54. BOTANY, graminology.
graminology 54. BOTANY; 188. GRASSES.
grammalogue 428. WRITING.
grammar 186. GRAMMAR; 247. LINGUISTICS.
grammarian 186. GRAMMAR, grammar; 247. LINGUISTICS, grammar.
grammarianism 186. GRAMMAR.
grammatic 247. LINGUISTICS, grammar.
grammatical 186. GRAMMAR, grammar; 247. LINGUISTICS, grammar.
grammaticism 186. GRAMMAR.
grammatism 186. GRAMMAR.
grammatist 186. GRAMMAR, grammatism.
grammatolatry 236. LANGUAGE.
gramophile 311. -PHILE, -PHILIA, PHILY; 314. PHONOGRAPH RECORDS.
gramophone 226. INSTRUMENTS; 314. PHONOGRAPH RECORDS.
grandeeism 41. BEHAVIOR.
granger 5. AGRICULTURE, grangerism.
grangerism 5. AGRICULTURE; 53. BOOKS.
grangerize 53. BOOKS, grangerism.
graphanalysis 428. WRITING.
graphanalyst 428. WRITING, graphanalysis.
graphemic 247. LINGUISTICS, graphemics; 428. WRITING, graphemics.
graphemics 12. ALPHABET; 247. LINGUISTICS; 428. WRITING.
graphiologist 128. DRAWING, graphiology; 428. WRITING, graphiology.
graphiology 128. DRAWING; 428. WRITING.
graphologic 428. WRITING, graphology.
graphological 428. WRITING, graphology.
graphologist 428. WRITING, graphology.
graphology 124. DIVINATION; 428. WRITING.
graphomania 254. MANIAS; 428. WRITING.
graphonomy 247. LINGUISTICS, graphemics; 428. WRITING.

graphopathological 428. WRITING, graphopathology.
graphopathologist 428. WRITING, graphopathology.
graphopathology 428. WRITING.
graphophobia 313. PHOBIAS; 428. WRITING.
graphophone 226. INSTRUMENTS; 314. PHONOGRAPH RECORDS.
graphorrhea 428. WRITING.
graphoscope 226. INSTRUMENTS.
graphotype 328. PRINTING.
graptomancy 124. DIVINATION; 428. WRITING.
gravamen 120. DISCONTENT.
graver 141. ENGRAVING, burinist.
gravid 46. BIRTH, gravidity; 327. PREGNANCY, gravidity.
gravidity 46. BIRTH; 327. PREGNANCY.
gravidness 327. PREGNANCY, gravidity.
Grecism 190. GREECE and GREEKS.
Grecomania 190. GREECE and GREEKS; 254. MANIAS.
Greek Revivalism 20. ARCHITECTURE.
greensickness 95. COMPLEXION.
Gregorian 284. MUSIC, Gregorianist.
Gregorianist 284. MUSIC.
griffinism 294. NOVELTY.
grimalkin 70. CATS.
gringophobia 313. PHOBIAS.
gromatic 235. LAND, gromatics.
gromatics 235. LAND.
Grundyism 28. ATTITUDES.
Grundyist 28. ATTITUDES, Grundyism.
Grundyite 28. ATTITUDES, Grundyism.
Guelfic 322. POLITICS, Guelphism.
Guelfism 322. POLITICS, Guelphism.
Guelphic 322. POLITICS, Guelphism.
Guelphism 322. POLITICS.
guerrillaism 413. WAR.
Guesdism 322. POLITICS.
Guesdist 322. POLITICS, Guesdism.
Guevarism 94. COMMUNISM.
Guevarist 94. COMMUNISM, Guevarism.
gunnery 416. WEAPONRY.
gunocracy 424. WOMEN.
gustation 50. BODILY FUNCTIONS.
gutturalism 382. SPEECH.
gymnasiast 26. ATHLETICS; 240. LEARNING.
Gymnasium 240. LEARNING.

gymnast 26. ATHLETICS.
gymnastic 26. ATHLETICS, **gymnastics.**
gymnastics 26. ATHLETICS.
gymnomania 254. MANIAS;
287. NAKEDNESS.
gymnopaedia 287. NAKEDNESS,
gymnopedia.
gymnopaedic 287. NAKEDNESS,
gymnopedia.
gymnopedia 287. NAKEDNESS.
gymnopedic 287. NAKEDNESS,
gymnopedia.
gymnophobia 287. NAKEDNESS;
313. PHOBIAS.
gymnosophical 287. NAKEDNESS,
gymnosophy.
gymnosophist 287. NAKEDNESS,
gymnosophy.
gymnosophy 287. NAKEDNESS.
gynaecide 424. WOMEN, **femicide.**
gynaecolatry 424. WOMEN,
gynecolatry.
gynaecology 424. WOMEN, **gynecology.**
gynaecopathic 424. WOMEN,
gynecopathy.
gynaecopathy 424. WOMEN,
gynecopathy.
gynaeocracy 424. WOMEN, **gynecocracy.**
gynandrism 51. BODY, HUMAN.
gynandroid 51. BODY, HUMAN,
gynandrism; 51. BODY, HUMAN,
gynandry.
gynandromorph 225. INSECTS,
gynandromorphism.
gynandromorphism 225. INSECTS.
gynandromorphous 225. INSECTS,
gynandromorphism.
gynandry 51. BODY, HUMAN,
gynandrism.
gynarchic 424. WOMEN, **gynarchy.**
gynarchy 424. WOMEN.
gynecide 424. WOMEN, **femicide.**
gynecocracy 424. WOMEN.
gynecolater 424. WOMEN, **gynecolatry.**
gynecolatry 424. WOMEN.
gynecologic 424. WOMEN, **gynecology.**
gynecological 424. WOMEN,
gynecology.
gynecologist 266. MEDICAL
SPECIALTIES; 424. WOMEN,
gynecology.

gynecology 424. WOMEN.
gynecomania 254. MANIAS; 364. SEX.
gynecomastia 51. BODY, HUMAN,
gynecomastism.
gynecomastism 51. BODY, HUMAN.
gynecomasty 51. BODY, HUMAN,
gynecomastism.
gynecopathic 424. WOMEN,
gynecopathy.
gynecopathy 424. WOMEN.
gyneocracy 424. WOMEN, **gynecocracy.**
gyneolatry 424. WOMEN, **gynecolatry.**
gynephobe 424. WOMEN, **gynephobia.**
gynephobia 313. PHOBIAS; 424. WOMEN.
gyniatrics 424. WOMEN.
gynophobia 313. PHOBIAS, **gynephobia;**
424. WOMEN, **gynephobia.**
gypsologist 169. FOREIGNERS,
gypsyologist.
gypsy 41. BEHAVIOR, **gypsyism.**
gypsyish 41. BEHAVIOR, **gypsyism.**
gypsyism 41. BEHAVIOR.
gypsyologist 169. FOREIGNERS.
gyromancy 124. DIVINATION;
412. WALKING.
gyrostatic 316. PHYSICS, **gyrostatics.**
gyrostatically 316. PHYSICS, **gyrostatics.**
gyrostatics 316. PHYSICS.

H

habiliments 86. CLOTHING.
haboob 420. WIND.
hadephobia 203. HELL; 313. PHOBIAS.
Haeckelian 44. BIOLOGY, **Haeckelism;**
312. PHILOSOPHY, **Haeckelism.**
Haeckelism 44. BIOLOGY;
312. PHILOSOPHY.
haemaphobia 49. BLOOD and BLOOD
VESSELS, **hemaphobia;** 313. PHOBIAS;
313. PHOBIAS, **hemaphobia.**
haematidrosis 49. BLOOD and BLOOD
VESSELS, **hematidrosis.**
haematocrit 49. BLOOD and BLOOD
VESSELS, **hematocrit.**
haematologic 49. BLOOD and BLOOD
VESSELS, **hematology.**
haematological 49. BLOOD and BLOOD
VESSELS, **hematology.**
haematologist 49. BLOOD and BLOOD
VESSELS, **hematology.**

haematology 49. BLOOD and BLOOD VESSELS, hematology.
haematomancy 49. BLOOD and BLOOD VESSELS, hematomancy; 124. DIVINATION, hematomancy.
haematopathology 49. BLOOD and BLOOD VESSELS, hemopathology.
haematophobia 49. BLOOD and BLOOD VESSELS, hematophobia.
haematopoiesis 49. BLOOD and BLOOD VESSELS, hematopoiesis.
haematopoietic 49. BLOOD and BLOOD VESSELS, hematopoiesis.
haematosis 49. BLOOD and BLOOD VESSELS, hematosis.
haemolysis 49. BLOOD and BLOOD VESSELS, hemolysis.
haemolytic 49. BLOOD and BLOOD VESSELS, hemolysis.
haemopathology 49. BLOOD and BLOOD VESSELS, hemopathology.
haemophile 32. BACTERIA, hemophile.
haemophilia 49. BLOOD and BLOOD VESSELS, hemophilia; 122. DISEASE and ILLNESS, hemophilia.
haemophiliac 49. BLOOD and BLOOD VESSELS, hemophilia; 122. DISEASE and ILLNESS, hemophilia.
haemostasia 49. BLOOD and BLOOD VESSELS, hemostasis.
haemostasis 49. BLOOD and BLOOD VESSELS, hemostasis.
haemostatic 49. BLOOD and BLOOD VESSELS, hemostatic.
Haggada 231. JUDAISM.
Haggadah 231. JUDAISM, Haggada.
haggadic 231. JUDAISM, Haggada.
haggadical 231. JUDAISM, Haggada.
Haggadist 231. JUDAISM.
hagiarchy 185. GOVERNMENT.
hagiocracy 185. GOVERNMENT.
hagiographer 359. SAINTS, hagiography.
hagiographic 359. SAINTS, hagiography.
hagiographical 359. SAINTS, hagiography.
hagiography 359. SAINTS.
hagiolater 359. SAINTS, hagiolatry.
hagiolatrous 359. SAINTS, hagiolatry.
hagiolatry 359. SAINTS.

hagiologic 359. SAINTS, hagiology.
hagiological 359. SAINTS, hagiology.
hagiologist 359. SAINTS, hagiology.
hagiology 359. SAINTS.
hagiophobia 313. PHOBIAS; 359. SAINTS.
Halachah 231. JUDAISM, Halaka.
Halachist 231. JUDAISM, Halaka.
Halaka 231. JUDAISM.
Halakah 231. JUDAISM, Halaka.
Halakic 231. JUDAISM, Halaka.
Halakist 231. JUDAISM, Halaka.
halidom 358. SACREDNESS.
halieutic 164. FISH, halieutics.
halieutics 164. FISH.
haliography 360. SEA.
halitosis 298. ODORS.
hallage 131. DUES and PAYMENT.
hallucinogen 130. DRUGS.
hallucinogenic 130. DRUGS, hallucinogen.
hallucinosis 224. INSANITY.
halology 316. PHYSICS.
halomancy 124. DIVINATION.
halometer 264. MEASUREMENT, halometry.
halometry 264. MEASUREMENT.
halophyte 319. PLANTS, halophytism.
halophytic 319. PLANTS, halophytism.
halophytism 319. PLANTS.
halotechny 316. PHYSICS, halology.
hamadryad 286. MYTHOLOGY.
hamartiology 367. SIN.
hamartomania 254. MANIAS; 367. SIN.
hamartophobia 313. PHOBIAS; 367. SIN.
Hamiltonian 322. POLITICS, Hamiltonianism.
Hamiltonianism 322. POLITICS.
haphephobia 313. PHOBIAS.
haphophobia 313. PHOBIAS, haphephobia; 397. TOUCH, haptophobia.
haplography 428. WRITING.
haptephobia 313. PHOBIAS, haphephobia.
haptophobia 313. PHOBIAS, haphephobia; 397. TOUCH.
hariolation 124. DIVINATION; 174. FUTURE.
harlequinade 41. BEHAVIOR; 310. PERFORMING.

harlequinery 41. BEHAVIOR,
harlequinade; 310. PERFORMING,
harlequinade.
harlotry 364. SEX.
Harmonist 93. COMMUNALISM, Rappist;
332. PROTESTANTISM.
harmonist 249. LITERATURE;
284. MUSIC.
Harmonite 93. COMMUNALISM,
Rappist.
harmonometer 380. SOUND.
harpaxophobia 313. PHOBIAS;
391. THEFT.
haruspex 16. ANIMALS, haruspicy;
124. DIVINATION, haruspicy.
haruspical 16. ANIMALS, haruspicy;
124. DIVINATION, haruspicy.
haruspication 16. ANIMALS;
124. DIVINATION, haruspicy.
haruspicy 16. ANIMALS;
124. DIVINATION.
Hasidic 231. JUDAISM, Hasidism.
Hasidim 231. JUDAISM, Hasidism.
Hasidism 231. JUDAISM.
haulage 131. DUES and PAYMENT.
hawk 413. WAR, hawkism.
hawkish 413. WAR, hawkism.
hawkism 413. WAR.
heathen 349. RELIGION, heathenism.
heathenism 349. RELIGION.
heathenistic 349. RELIGION,
heathenism.
hebdomadism 295. NUMBERS.
hebephrenia 224. INSANITY.
hebetude 154. FATIGUE.
hebetudinous 154. FATIGUE, hebetude.
Hebraic 236. LANGUAGE, Hebraism.
Hebraica 91. COLLECTIONS and
COLLECTING.
Hebraicism 236. LANGUAGE, Hebraism.
Hebraism 231. JUDAISM;
236. LANGUAGE.
Hebraist 231. JUDAISM, Hebraism;
236. LANGUAGE, Hebraism.
Hebraistic 231. JUDAISM, Hebraism;
236. LANGUAGE, Hebraism.
Hebraistical 231. JUDAISM, Hebraism.
hecatomb 232. KILLING.
hecatonarchy 185. GOVERNMENT.
Heckerism 69. CATHOLICISM.
hectograph 98. COPYING.

hectographic 98. COPYING,
hectography.
hectography 98. COPYING.
hedonics 320. PLEASURE.
hedonism 320. PLEASURE.
hedonist 320. PLEASURE, hedonism.
hedonistic 320. PLEASURE, hedonism.
hedonology 320. PLEASURE.
hedonomania 254. MANIAS;
320. PLEASURE.
hedonophobia 313. PHOBIAS.
Hegelian 312. PHILOSOPHY,
Hegelianism.
Hegelian dialectic 312. PHILOSOPHY.
Hegelianism 312. PHILOSOPHY.
Hegelian triad 312. PHILOSOPHY,
Hegelain dialectic.
hegira 144. ESCAPE.
hegumen 135. EASTERN ORTHODOXY.
heirship 331. PROPERTY and OWNERSHIP.
hektograph 98. COPYING, hectograph.
hektographic 98. COPYING,
hectography.
hektography 98. COPYING,
hectography.
helcologist 266. MEDICAL SPECIALTIES,
helcology.
helcology 266. MEDICAL SPECIALTIES.
heliocentric 100. COSMOLOGY,
heliocentricism.
heliocentricism 100. COSMOLOGY.
heliochrome 315. PHOTOGRAPHY,
heliochromy.
heliochromic 315. PHOTOGRAPHY,
heliochromy.
heliochromy 315. PHOTOGRAPHY.
heliodon 25. ASTRONOMY; 387. SUN.
heliographer 387. SUN, heliography.
heliographic 387. SUN, heliography.
heliographical 387. SUN, heliography.
heliography 387. SUN.
heliolator 387. SUN, heliolatry.
heliolatry 387. SUN.
heliologist 387. SUN, heliology.
heliology 387. SUN.
heliomania 254. MANIAS; 387. SUN.
heliometer 25. ASTRONOMY;
226. INSTRUMENTS.
heliometric 25. ASTRONOMY,
heliometry; 264. MEASUREMENT,
heliometry.

heliometrical 25. ASTRONOMY,
heliometry; 264. MEASUREMENT,
heliometry.
heliometry 25. ASTRONOMY;
264. MEASUREMENT.
heliophile 319. PLANTS, heliophilia.
heliophilia 319. PLANTS.
heliophilic 319. PLANTS, heliophilia.
heliophilous 319. PLANTS, heliophilia.
heliophobia 313. PHOBIAS; 387. SUN.
helioseismology 387. SUN.
heliotaxis 319. PLANTS.
heliotherapy 350. REMEDIES; 387. SUN.
heliotrope 319. PLANTS, heliotropism.
heliotropic 319. PLANTS, heliotropism.
heliotropism 319. PLANTS.
heliotypography 315. PHOTOGRAPHY.
heliotypy 315. PHOTOGRAPHY.
Hellenism 18. ANTIQUITY; 23. ART;
190. GREECE and GREEKS.
Hellenist 18. ANTIQUITY, Hellenism;
190. GREECE and GREEKS; 190. GREECE
and GREEKS, Hellenism.
helminthologic 427. WORMS,
helminthology.
helminthological 427. WORMS,
helminthology.
helminthologist 427. WORMS,
helminthology.
helminthology 16. ANIMALS;
427. WORMS.
helminthophobia 313. PHOBIAS;
427. WORMS.
helotism 371. SLAVERY.
hemadynamometry 49. BLOOD and
BLOOD VESSELS.
hemapathology 49. BLOOD and BLOOD
VESSELS, hemopathology.
hemaphobia 49. BLOOD and BLOOD
VESSELS; 313. PHOBIAS.
hematidrosis 49. BLOOD and BLOOD
VESSELS.
hematocrit 49. BLOOD and BLOOD
VESSELS.
hematologic 49. BLOOD and BLOOD
VESSELS, hematology.
hematological 49. BLOOD and BLOOD
VESSELS, hematology.
hematologist 49. BLOOD and BLOOD
VESSELS, hematology.

hematology 49. BLOOD and BLOOD
VESSELS.
hematomancy 49. BLOOD and BLOOD
VESSELS; 124. DIVINATION.
hematophobia 49. BLOOD and BLOOD
VESSELS; 313. PHOBIAS, hemaphobia.
hematopoiesis 49. BLOOD and BLOOD
VESSELS.
hematopoietic 49. BLOOD and BLOOD
VESSELS, hematopoiesis.
hematosis 49. BLOOD and BLOOD
VESSELS.
hemautograph 49. BLOOD and BLOOD
VESSELS, hemautography.
hemautographic 49. BLOOD and BLOOD
VESSELS, hemautography.
hemautography 49. BLOOD and BLOOD
VESSELS.
hemeralopia 48. BLINDNESS; 148. EYES.
hemeralopic 48. BLINDNESS,
hemeralopia.
hemerobaptism 35. BAPTISM.
hemerobaptist 35. BAPTISM,
hemerobaptism.
hemicrania 306. PAIN.
hemiplegia 122. DISEASE and ILLNESS.
hemiplegic 122. DISEASE and ILLNESS,
hemiplegia.
hemipterology 225. INSECTS.
hemitery 170. FORM.
hemolysis 49. BLOOD and BLOOD
VESSELS.
hemolytic 49. BLOOD and BLOOD
VESSELS, hemolysis.
hemopathology 49. BLOOD and BLOOD
VESSELS.
hemophile 32. BACTERIA.
hemophilia 49. BLOOD and BLOOD
VESSELS; 122. DISEASE and ILLNESS.
hemophiliac 49. BLOOD and BLOOD
VESSELS, hemophilia; 122. DISEASE and
ILLNESS, hemophilia.
hemophilic 32. BACTERIA, hemophile.
hemophobia 49. BLOOD and BLOOD
VESSELS, hemaphobia; 313. PHOBIAS,
hemaphobia.
hemostasia 49. BLOOD and BLOOD
VESSELS, hemostasis.
hemostasis 49. BLOOD and BLOOD
VESSELS.

hemostatic 49. BLOOD and BLOOD
VESSELS; 49. BLOOD and BLOOD
VESSELS, hemostatic.
hendiadys 354. RHETORIC and
RHETORICAL DEVICES.
henotheism 183. GOD and GODS.
henotheist 183. GOD and GODS,
henotheism.
heortological 65. CALENDAR,
heortology.
heortology 65. CALENDAR.
heparologist 266. MEDICAL
SPECIALTIES, heparology.
heparology 266. MEDICAL SPECIALTIES.
hepatitis 122. DISEASE and ILLNESS.
hepatographic 14. ANATOMY,
hepatography.
hepatographical 14. ANATOMY,
hepatography.
hepatography 14. ANATOMY.
hepatological 266. MEDICAL
SPECIALTIES, hepatology.
hepatologist 266. MEDICAL SPECIALTIES,
hepatology.
hepatology 266. MEDICAL SPECIALTIES.
hepatoma 66. CANCER.
heprographic 14. ANATOMY,
heprography.
heprographical 14. ANATOMY,
heprography.
heprography 14. ANATOMY.
heptameter 409. VERSE.
heptametrical 409. VERSE, heptameter.
heptapodic 409. VERSE, heptapody.
heptapody 409. VERSE.
heptarch 139. ENGLAND, heptarchy;
185. GOVERNMENT, heptarchy.
heptarchal 139. ENGLAND, heptarchy;
185. GOVERNMENT, heptarchy.
heptarchic 139. ENGLAND, heptarchy;
185. GOVERNMENT, heptarchy.
heptarchical 139. ENGLAND, heptarchy;
185. GOVERNMENT, heptarchy.
heptarchist 185. GOVERNMENT,
heptarchy.
heptarchy 139. ENGLAND;
185. GOVERNMENT.
heptathlon 26. ATHLETICS.
herald 210. HONORS and REGALIA,
heraldry.

heraldic 210. HONORS and REGALIA,
heraldry.
heraldry 210. HONORS and REGALIA.
herbalism 91. COLLECTIONS and
COLLECTING.
herbalist 54. BOTANY; 91. COLLECTIONS
and COLLECTING, herbalism;
319. PLANTS.
herbarian 54. BOTANY.
herbarism 54. BOTANY.
herbarist 54. BOTANY, herbarian;
319. PLANTS.
herbarium 54. BOTANY.
herbicidal 319. PLANTS, herbicide.
herbicide 232. KILLING; 319. PLANTS.
herbivore 16. ANIMALS.
herbivorous 16. ANIMALS, herbivore.
hereditist 204. HEREDITY.
heresiarch 205. HERESY.
heresimach 205. HERESY.
heresiography 205. HERESY.
heresiologist 205. HERESY, heresiology.
heresiology 205. HERESY.
heresy 205. HERESY.
heretic 205. HERESY, heresy.
heretical 205. HERESY, heresy.
heretocidal 205. HERESY, heretocide.
heretocide 205. HERESY.
hermaphrodite 51. BODY, HUMAN,
hermaphroditism.
hermaphroditic 51. BODY, HUMAN,
hermaphroditism.
hermaphroditism 51. BODY, HUMAN.
hermeneut 43. BIBLE, hermeneutics.
hermeneutics 43. BIBLE.
hermeneutist 43. BIBLE, hermeneutics.
hermetic 7. ALCHEMY, Hermeticism;
7. ALCHEMY, hermetics;
248. LITERARY STYLE, Hermeticism;
285. MYSTICISM, Hermeticism.
hermetical 7. ALCHEMY, Hermeticism;
7. ALCHEMY, hermetics;
248. LITERARY STYLE, Hermeticism;
285. MYSTICISM, Hermeticism.
Hermeticism 7. ALCHEMY;
248. LITERARY STYLE; 285. MYSTICISM;
312. PHILOSOPHY.
hermeticist 7. ALCHEMY, Hermeticism;
248. LITERARY STYLE, Hermeticism;
285. MYSTICISM, Hermeticism.
hermetics 7. ALCHEMY.

hermetist 7. ALCHEMY, **Hermeticism;**
7. ALCHEMY, **hermetics;**
248. LITERARY STYLE, **Hermeticism;**
285. MYSTICISM, **Hermeticism.**
hermitic 41. BEHAVIOR, **hermitism.**
hermitical 41. BEHAVIOR, **hermitism.**
hermitism 41. BEHAVIOR.
hermitry 41. BEHAVIOR, **hermitism.**
hermitship 41. BEHAVIOR, **hermitism.**
herniologic 266. MEDICAL SPECIALTIES,
herniology.
herniological 266. MEDICAL
SPECIALTIES, **herniology.**
herniologist 266. MEDICAL SPECIALTIES,
herniology.
herniology 266. MEDICAL SPECIALTIES.
heroic 101. COURAGE, **heroism.**
heroism 101. COURAGE.
herolatry 349. RELIGION.
heronry 45. BIRDS.
heroogony 183. GOD and GODS.
heroological 207. HISTORY, **heroology.**
heroologist 207. HISTORY, **heroology.**
heroology 207. HISTORY.
herotheism 183. GOD and GODS.
herpetographical 122. DISEASE and
ILLNESS, **herpetography;**
353. REPTILES, **herpetography.**
herpetography 122. DISEASE and
ILLNESS; 353. REPTILES.
herpetologic 353. REPTILES,
herpetology.
herpetological 353. REPTILES,
herpetology.
herpetologist 353. REPTILES,
herpetology.
herpetology 353. REPTILES.
herpetophobia 313. PHOBIAS;
353. REPTILES.
Hesychasm 135. EASTERN ORTHODOXY.
hesychast 135. EASTERN ORTHODOXY,
Hesychasm.
hesychastic 135. EASTERN ORTHODOXY,
Hesychasm.
hetaera 190. GREECE and GREEKS.
hetaerism 364. SEX.
hetaerist 364. SEX, **hetaerism.**
hetaeristic 364. SEX, **hetaerism.**
hetairism 364. SEX, **hetaerism.**
hetairist 364. SEX, **hetaerism.**
hetairistic 364. SEX, **hetaerism.**

hetericism 383. SPELLING.
hetericist 383. SPELLING, **hetericism.**
heterodoxy 300. OPINION.
heterogamete 44. BIOLOGY.
heterogamous 44. BIOLOGY,
heterogamy.
heterogamy 44. BIOLOGY.
heterogenesis 44. BIOLOGY.
heterogenetic 44. BIOLOGY,
heterogenesis.
heterographic 383. SPELLING,
heterography.
heterographical 383. SPELLING,
heterography.
heterography 383. SPELLING.
heterologous 266. MEDICAL
SPECIALTIES, **heterology.**
heterology 266. MEDICAL SPECIALTIES.
heterolysis 44. BIOLOGY.
heterolytic 44. BIOLOGY, **heterolysis.**
heteromorphic 170. FORM,
heteromorphism; 225. INSECTS,
heteromorphism.
heteromorphism 170. FORM;
225. INSECTS.
heteromorphy 170. FORM,
heteromorphism.
heteronomous 185. GOVERNMENT,
heteronomy.
heteronomy 185. GOVERNMENT;
322. POLITICS; 419. WILL.
heteronym 236. LANGUAGE,
heteronymy.
heteronymous 236. LANGUAGE,
heteronymy; 419. WILL, **heteronomy.**
heteronymy 236. LANGUAGE.
heteroousian 79. CHRIST,
heteroousianism.
heteroousianism 79. CHRIST.
heterophemism 236. LANGUAGE.
heterophemy 236. LANGUAGE,
heterophemism.
heterosis 16. ANIMALS; 319. PLANTS;
368. SIZE.
heterotopia 44. BIOLOGY, **heterotopy;**
56. BRAIN, **heterotopy.**
heterotopism 44. BIOLOGY;
44. BIOLOGY, **heterotopy;** 56. BRAIN,
heterotopy.
heterotopous 44. BIOLOGY, **heterotopy;**
56. BRAIN, **heterotopy.**

heterotopy 44. BIOLOGY; 56. BRAIN.
heterousianism 79. CHRIST,
heteroousianism.
heuristic 21. ARGUMENTATION,
heuristics.
heuristics 21. ARGUMENTATION.
hexameter 409. VERSE.
hexametrical 409. VERSE, hexameter.
hexapodous 409. VERSE, hexapody.
hexapody 409. VERSE.
hexarchy 185. GOVERNMENT.
hexicological 44. BIOLOGY, hexiology.
hexicology 44. BIOLOGY, hexiology.
hexiological 44. BIOLOGY, hexiology.
hexiology 44. BIOLOGY.
hiation 149. FACIAL FEATURES.
hibernation 430. ZOOLOGY.
Hibernian 236. LANGUAGE,
Hibernianism.
Hibernianism 236. LANGUAGE.
Hibernicism 236. LANGUAGE,
Hibernianism.
hidalgoism 28. ATTITUDES.
hidrotic 130. DRUGS, sudorific.
hierarchial 185. GOVERNMENT,
hierarchism.
hierarchism 185. GOVERNMENT.
hierarchization 185. GOVERNMENT,
hierarchism.
hieratic 349. RELIGION, hieraticism.
hieraticism 349. RELIGION.
hierocracy 69. CATHOLICISM.
hieroglyphologist 428. WRITING,
hieroglyphology.
hieroglyphology 428. WRITING.
hierogram 358. SACREDNESS;
428. WRITING.
hierogrammatic 358. SACREDNESS,
hierogram; 428. WRITING, hierogram.
hierogrammatical 358. SACREDNESS,
hierogram; 428. WRITING, hierogram.
hierogrammatist 358. SACREDNESS,
hierogram; 428. WRITING, hierogram.
hierographer 358. SACREDNESS,
hierography; 428. WRITING,
hierography.
hierographic 358. SACREDNESS,
hierography; 428. WRITING,
hierography.

hierographical 358. SACREDNESS,
hierography; 428. WRITING,
hierography.
hierography 358. SACREDNESS;
428. WRITING.
hierolatry 358. SACREDNESS.
hierologic 358. SACREDNESS, hierology.
hierological 358. SACREDNESS,
hierology.
hierologist 358. SACREDNESS, hierology.
hierology 358. SACREDNESS.
hieromancy 124. DIVINATION;
358. SACREDNESS.
hieromania 81. CHURCH; 254. MANIAS;
349. RELIGION.
hierophobia 313. PHOBIAS;
358. SACREDNESS.
hieroscopy 124. DIVINATION,
hieromancy.
hierurgy 349. RELIGION;
358. SACREDNESS.
High Churchism 349. RELIGION.
High Churchist 349. RELIGION, High
Churchism.
High Churchite 349. RELIGION, High
Churchism.
Higher Criticism 43. BIBLE.
Hildebrandic 69. CATHOLICISM,
Hildebrandism.
Hildebrandine 69. CATHOLICISM,
Hildebrandism.
Hildebrandism 69. CATHOLICISM.
himation 190. GREECE and GREEKS.
Hinayana 59. BUDDHISM, Hinayanism.
Hinayanism 59. BUDDHISM.
hippiatric 211. HORSES, hippiatrics.
hippiatrics 211. HORSES.
hippiatrist 211. HORSES, hippiatrics.
hippiatry 211. HORSES, hippiatrics.
hippodrome 211. HORSES.
hippology 211. HORSES.
hippomancy 124. DIVINATION;
211. HORSES.
hippomania 211. HORSES; 254. MANIAS.
hippopathology 211. HORSES.
hippophagism 168. FOOD and
NUTRITION.
hippophagous 168. FOOD and
NUTRITION, hippophagism.
hippophagy 168. FOOD and NUTRITION,
hippophagism.

hippophile 211. HORSES.
hippophobia 211. HORSES; 313. PHOBIAS.
hirsute 193. HAIR, hirsutism.
hirsutism 193. HAIR.
Hispanicism 236. LANGUAGE.
hispid 193. HAIR, hispidity.
hispidity 193. HAIR.
histiology 302. ORGANISMS, histology.
histogenesis 44. BIOLOGY; 191. GROWTH.
histogenetic 44. BIOLOGY, histogenesis;
  191. GROWTH, histogenesis.
histogenic 44. BIOLOGY, histogenesis;
  191. GROWTH, histogenesis.
histogeny 44. BIOLOGY, histogenesis;
  191. GROWTH, histogenesis.
histogram 352. REPRESENTATION.
histographer 44. BIOLOGY,
  histography.
histographic 44. BIOLOGY, histography.
histographical 44. BIOLOGY,
  histography.
histography 44. BIOLOGY.
histologic 302. ORGANISMS, histology.
histological 14. ANATOMY, histology;
  302. ORGANISMS, histology.
histologist 14. ANATOMY, histology;
  302. ORGANISMS, histology.
histology 14. ANATOMY;
  302. ORGANISMS.
histolysis 44. BIOLOGY; 113. DECAYING.
histolytic 44. BIOLOGY, histolysis;
  113. DECAYING, histolysis.
historical linguistics 247. LINGUISTICS,
  diachronism.
historicism 207. HISTORY.
historicist 207. HISTORY, historicism.
historiographer 207. HISTORY,
  historiography.
historiographic 207. HISTORY,
  historiography.
historiographical 207. HISTORY,
  historiography.
historiography 207. HISTORY.
historiology 207. HISTORY.
historism 207. HISTORY.
histriconism 41. BEHAVIOR.
histrionic 41. BEHAVIOR, histrionicism.
histrionicism 41. BEHAVIOR.
histrionics 41. BEHAVIOR, histrionicism;
  127. DRAMA.
histrionism 127. DRAMA, histrionics.

Hitlerism 152. FASCISM.
Hitlerite 152. FASCISM, Hitlerism.
Hobbesian 312. PHILOSOPHY, Hobbism.
Hobbism 312. PHILOSOPHY.
Hobbist 312. PHILOSOPHY, Hobbism.
hoboism 41. BEHAVIOR.
hodomania 254. MANIAS; 399. TRAVEL.
hodometer 123. DISTANCE.
hodophobia 313. PHOBIAS; 399. TRAVEL.
holidayism 41. BEHAVIOR.
holism 312. PHILOSOPHY.
holist 312. PHILOSOPHY, holism.
holistic 312. PHILOSOPHY, holism.
holobaptism 35. BAPTISM.
holobaptist 35. BAPTISM, holobaptism.
holocaust 232. KILLING.
hologram 218. IMAGES;
  352. REPRESENTATION.
holograph 218. IMAGES, hologram;
  256. MANUSCRIPTS; 256. MANUSCRIPTS,
  holograph.
holographic 256. MANUSCRIPTS,
  holograph.
holography 218. IMAGES, hologram;
  315. PHOTOGRAPHY.
holophrase 236. LANGUAGE,
  holophrasis.
holophrasis 236. LANGUAGE.
holophrasm 236. LANGUAGE,
  holophrasis.
holophrastic 236. LANGUAGE,
  holophrasis.
homeomorphism 316. PHYSICS.
homeomorphous 316. PHYSICS,
  homeomorphism.
homeopath 350. REMEDIES,
  homeopathy.
homeopathic 350. REMEDIES,
  homeopathy.
homeopathist 350. REMEDIES,
  homeopathy.
homeopathy 350. REMEDIES.
homeotherapeutic 350. REMEDIES,
  homeotherapy.
homeotherapy 350. REMEDIES.
homeothermal 49. BLOOD and BLOOD
  VESSELS, homoiothermy.
Homerology 190. GREECE and GREEKS.
homichlophobia 313. PHOBIAS;
  417. WEATHER.
homicidal 232. KILLING, homicide.

homicide 232. KILLING.
homicidomania 232. KILLING; 254. MANIAS.
homilete 354. RHETORIC and RHETORICAL DEVICES, homily.
homiletic 349. RELIGION, homiletics; 354. RHETORIC and RHETORICAL DEVICES, homiletics.
homiletical 349. RELIGION, homiletics; 354. RHETORIC and RHETORICAL DEVICES, homiletics.
homiletics 349. RELIGION; 354. RHETORIC and RHETORICAL DEVICES.
homilist 354. RHETORIC and RHETORICAL DEVICES, homily.
homilophobia 313. PHOBIAS.
homily 354. RHETORIC and RHETORICAL DEVICES.
hominid 255. MANKIND; 255. MANKIND, hominid.
homiothermal 49. BLOOD and BLOOD VESSELS, homoiothermy.
homodynamy 44. BIOLOGY.
homoeanism 79. CHRIST, homoiousianism.
homoeopath 350. REMEDIES, homeopathy.
homoeopathic 350. REMEDIES, homeopathy.
homoeopathist 350. REMEDIES, homeopathy.
homoeopathy 350. REMEDIES, homeopathy.
homoeoptoton 354. RHETORIC and RHETORICAL DEVICES.
homoeoteleuton 354. RHETORIC and RHETORICAL DEVICES.
homoeotherapeutic 350. REMEDIES, homeotherapy.
homoeotherapy 350. REMEDIES, homeotherapy.
homoerotic 209. HOMOSEXUALITY, homoeroticism.
homoeroticism 209. HOMOSEXUALITY.
homoerotism 209. HOMOSEXUALITY, homoeroticism.
homogenesis 44. BIOLOGY; 204. HEREDITY.

homogenetic 44. BIOLOGY, homogenesis; 204. HEREDITY, homogenesis.
homogonous 167. FLOWERS, homogony.
homogony 167. FLOWERS.
homographic 428. WRITING, homography.
homography 428. WRITING.
homoiothermal 49. BLOOD and BLOOD VESSELS, homoiothermy.
homoiothermic 49. BLOOD and BLOOD VESSELS, homoiothermy.
homoiothermism 49. BLOOD and BLOOD VESSELS, homoiothermy.
homoiothermous 49. BLOOD and BLOOD VESSELS, homoiothermy.
homoiothermy 49. BLOOD and BLOOD VESSELS.
homoiousian 79. CHRIST, homoiousianism.
homoiousianism 79. CHRIST.
homologoumena 91. COLLECTIONS and COLLECTING, homologumena.
homologous 44. BIOLOGY, homology.
homologumena 91. COLLECTIONS and COLLECTING.
homology 44. BIOLOGY.
homonym 236. LANGUAGE, homonymy.
homonymous 236. LANGUAGE, homonymy.
homonymy 236. LANGUAGE; 380. SOUND.
homoousian 79. CHRIST, homoousianism.
homoousianism 79. CHRIST.
homophobia 209. HOMOSEXUALITY; 313. PHOBIAS.
homophonic 380. SOUND, homophony.
homophonous 284. MUSIC, homophony; 380. SOUND, homophony.
homophony 284. MUSIC; 380. SOUND.
homotaxic 179. GEOLOGY, homotaxis.
homotaxis 179. GEOLOGY.
homotaxy 179. GEOLOGY, homotaxis.
homunculus 255. MANKIND; 368. SIZE.
honorarium 131. DUES and PAYMENT.
hooliganism 41. BEHAVIOR.
Hopkinsianism 332. PROTESTANTISM.
Hopkinsonian 332. PROTESTANTISM, Hopkinsianism.

horologe 396. TIME.
horological 396. TIME, **horology.**
horologiographer 396. TIME,
   horologiography.
horologiographian 396. TIME,
   horologiography.
horologiographic 396. TIME,
   horologiography.
horologiography 396. TIME.
horologist 396. TIME, **horology.**
horology 396. TIME.
horometer 226. INSTRUMENTS;
   396. TIME.
horometrical 264. MEASUREMENT,
   horometry; 396. TIME, **horometry.**
horometry 264. MEASUREMENT;
   396. TIME.
horoscoper 24. ASTROLOGY, **horoscopy;**
   124. DIVINATION, **horoscopy.**
horoscopist 24. ASTROLOGY, **horoscopy;**
   124. DIVINATION, **horoscopy.**
horoscopy 24. ASTROLOGY;
   124. DIVINATION.
horripilation 90. COLD; 156. FEAR;
   370. SKIN.
horsey 41. BEHAVIOR, **horsyism.**
horseyism 41. BEHAVIOR, **horsyism.**
horsily 41. BEHAVIOR, **horsyism.**
horsy 41. BEHAVIOR, **horsyism.**
horsyism 41. BEHAVIOR.
horticultural 5. AGRICULTURE,
   horticulture.
horticulture 5. AGRICULTURE.
horticulturist 5. AGRICULTURE,
   horticulture.
hospitalism 122. DISEASE and ILLNESS.
hostelaphily 91. COLLECTIONS and
   COLLECTING.
hostile 413. WAR, **hostility.**
hostility 413. WAR.
Hottentotism 41. BEHAVIOR.
hoyden 41. BEHAVIOR, **hoydenism;**
   424. WOMEN, **hoydenism.**
hoydenish 41. BEHAVIOR, **hoydenism;**
   424. WOMEN, **hoydenism.**
hoydenism 41. BEHAVIOR; 424. WOMEN.
Hsüan Chiao 349. RELIGION.
Huguenot 332. PROTESTANTISM,
   Huguenotism.
Huguenotic 332. PROTESTANTISM,
   Huguenotism.

Huguenotism 332. PROTESTANTISM.
humanism 255. MANKIND.
humanist 255. MANKIND, **humanism.**
humanistic 255. MANKIND, **humanism.**
humanitarian 312. PHILOSOPHY,
   humanitarianism.
humanitarianism 312. PHILOSOPHY.
humanoid 255. MANKIND;
   255. MANKIND, **humanoid.**
humbug 41. BEHAVIOR, **humbuggery.**
humbugger 41. BEHAVIOR,
   humbuggery.
humbuggery 41. BEHAVIOR.
humoral 41. BEHAVIOR, **humoralism.**
humoralism 41. BEHAVIOR.
humoural 41. BEHAVIOR, **humoralism.**
humouralism 41. BEHAVIOR,
   humoralism.
hurricane 420. WIND.
husbandry 5. AGRICULTURE.
Hussism 332. PROTESTANTISM,
   Hussitism.
Hussite 332. PROTESTANTISM,
   Hussitism.
Hussitism 332. PROTESTANTISM.
Hutchinsonian 43. BIBLE,
   Hutchinsonianism; 189. GRAVITY,
   Hutchinsonianism; 392. THEOLOGY,
   Hutchinsonianism.
Hutchinsonianism 43. BIBLE;
   189. GRAVITY; 392. THEOLOGY.
Hutterites 93. COMMUNALISM;
   93. COMMUNALISM, **Hutterian
   Brethren.**
hyalophobia 313. PHOBIAS.
hybrid 247. LINGUISTICS, **hybridism.**
hybridism 17. ANTHROPOLOGY;
   236. LANGUAGE; 247. LINGUISTICS.
hybridity 17. ANTHROPOLOGY,
   hybridism.
hydragogy 414. WATER.
hydraulics 316. PHYSICS.
hydriatrics 414. WATER.
hydriotaphia 63. BURIAL.
hydrodipsomania 254. MANIAS;
   414. WATER.
hydrodynamic 316. PHYSICS,
   hydrodynamics.
hydrodynamical 316. PHYSICS,
   hydrodynamics.
hydrodynamics 316. PHYSICS.

hydrogeological 179. GEOLOGY,
hydrogeology.
hydrogeology 179. GEOLOGY.
hydrographer 414. WATER,
hydrography.
hydrographic 414. WATER,
hydrography.
hydrographical 414. WATER,
hydrography.
hydrography 414. WATER.
hydrokinetic 316. PHYSICS,
hydrokinetics.
hydrokinetics 316. PHYSICS.
hydrologic 414. WATER, hydrology.
hydrological 414. WATER, hydrology.
hydrologist 414. WATER, hydrology.
hydrology 414. WATER.
hydromancy 124. DIVINATION;
414. WATER.
hydromania 254. MANIAS; 414. WATER.
hydromechanics 316. PHYSICS;
316. PHYSICS, hydrodynamics.
hydrometer 226. INSTRUMENTS.
hydropathic 414. WATER, hydropathy.
hydropathist 414. WATER, hydropathy.
hydropathy 414. WATER.
hydrophilic 311. -PHILE, -PHILIA, -PHILY,
hydrophily.
hydrophilous 311. -PHILE, -PHILIA,
-PHILY, hydrophily; 414. WATER,
hydrophily.
hydrophily 311. -PHILE, -PHILIA, -PHILY;
319. PLANTS; 414. WATER.
hydrophobia 313. PHOBIAS; 340. RABIES;
414. WATER.
hydrophobophobia 313. PHOBIAS.
hydrophyte 319. PLANTS,
hydrophytism.
hydrophytic 319. PLANTS,
hydrophytism.
hydrophytism 319. PLANTS.
hydroponic 319. PLANTS, hydroponics.
hydroponics 319. PLANTS.
hydroscope 414. WATER.
hydrostatic 316. PHYSICS, hydrostatics.
hydrostatical 316. PHYSICS,
hydrostatics.
hydrostatician 316. PHYSICS,
hydrostatics.
hydrostatics 316. PHYSICS.

hydrotherapeutic 36. BATHING,
hydrotherapy; 414. WATER,
hydrotherapy.
hydrotherapeutical 36. BATHING,
hydrotherapy.
hydrotherapeutics 36. BATHING,
hydrotherapy.
hydrotherapist 36. BATHING,
hydrotherapy; 414. WATER,
hydrotherapy.
hydrotherapy 36. BATHING;
414. WATER.
hydrotropic 414. WATER,
hydrotropism.
hydrotropism 414. WATER.
hyetographic 85. CLIMATE,
hyetography; 345. RAIN,
hyetography.
hyetographical 85. CLIMATE,
hyetography; 345. RAIN,
hyetography.
hyetography 85. CLIMATE; 345. RAIN.
hyetological 345. RAIN, hyetology;
417. WEATHER, hyetology.
hyetologist 345. RAIN, hyetology;
417. WEATHER, hyetology.
hyetology 345. RAIN; 417. WEATHER.
hyetophobia 417. WEATHER.
hygeist 197. HEALTH.
hygiantics 197. HEALTH, hygiastics.
hygiastics 197. HEALTH.
hygieist 197. HEALTH, hygeist.
hygienic 197. HEALTH, hygienics.
hygienics 197. HEALTH.
hygienist 197. HEALTH, hygienics.
hygieology 197. HEALTH.
hygiology 197. HEALTH, hygieology.
hygrology 414. WATER.
hygrometer 226. INSTRUMENTS.
hygrometric 316. PHYSICS,
hydromechanics; 316. PHYSICS,
hygrometry.
hygrometrical 316. PHYSICS,
hydromechanics; 316. PHYSICS,
hygrometry.
hygrometry 316. PHYSICS.
hygrophobia 107. DAMPNESS;
313. PHOBIAS; 414. WATER; 421. WINE.
hylephobia 313. PHOBIAS; 425. WOOD.
hylic 312. PHILOSOPHY, hylicism.
hylicism 312. PHILOSOPHY.

hylicist 312. PHILOSOPHY, hylicism.
hylism 312. PHILOSOPHY, hylicism.
hylomania 254. MANIAS; 425. WOOD.
hylomorphic 312. PHILOSOPHY,
　hylomorphism.
hylomorphism 312. PHILOSOPHY.
hylomorphist 312. PHILOSOPHY,
　hylomorphism.
hylotheism 183. GOD and GODS.
hylotheist 183. GOD and GODS,
　hylotheism.
hylozoism 263. MATTER.
hylozoist 263. MATTER, hylozoism.
hylozoistic 263. MATTER, hylozoism.
hymenopterology 225. INSECTS.
hymnodist 284. MUSIC, hymnody.
hymnody 284. MUSIC.
hymnology 378. SONGS and SINGING.
hypalgesia 306. PAIN.
hypalgia 306. PAIN.
hypallactic 354. RHETORIC and
　RHETORICAL DEVICES, hypallage.
hypallage 354. RHETORIC and
　RHETORICAL DEVICES.
hypengyophobia 313. PHOBIAS.
hyperactive 77. CHILDREN,
　hyperactivity.
hyperactivity 77. CHILDREN.
hyperaemia 49. BLOOD and BLOOD
　VESSELS, hyperemia.
hyperaemic 49. BLOOD and BLOOD
　VESSELS, hyperemia.
hyperaesthesia 122. DISEASE and
　ILLNESS, hyperesthesia.
hyperaesthetic 122. DISEASE and
　ILLNESS, hyperesthesia.
hyperalgesia 306. PAIN.
hyperalgesic 306. PAIN, hyperalgesia.
hyperbaton 354. RHETORIC and
　RHETORICAL DEVICES.
hyperbole 354. RHETORIC and
　RHETORICAL DEVICES.
hyperbolic 354. RHETORIC and
　RHETORICAL DEVICES, hyperbole.
hyperbolism 354. RHETORIC and
　RHETORICAL DEVICES.
hyperbolist 354. RHETORIC and
　RHETORICAL DEVICES, hyperbolism.
hyperchromatic 92. COLOR,
　hyperchromatism.
hyperchromatism 92. COLOR.

hypercritic 104. CRITICISM,
　hypercriticism.
hypercritical 104. CRITICISM,
　hypercriticism.
hypercriticism 104. CRITICISM.
hyperdulia 260. MARY.
hyperdynamia 122. DISEASE and
　ILLNESS.
hyperemia 49. BLOOD and BLOOD
　VESSELS.
hyperemic 49. BLOOD and BLOOD
　VESSELS, hyperemia.
hyperesthesia 122. DISEASE and ILLNESS.
hyperesthetic 122. DISEASE and ILLNESS,
　hyperesthesia.
hyperglycemia 122. DISEASE and
　ILLNESS.
hyperglycemic 122. DISEASE and
　ILLNESS, hyperglycemia.
hyperkinesia 51. BODY, HUMAN;
　122. DISEASE and ILLNESS.
hyperkinesis 51. BODY, HUMAN,
　hyperkinesia; 122. DISEASE and
　ILLNESS, hyperkinesia.
hyperkinetic 51. BODY, HUMAN,
　hyperkinesia; 122. DISEASE and
　ILLNESS, hyperkinesia.
hypermania 224. INSANITY; 254. MANIAS.
hypermetamorphosis 225. INSECTS.
hypermetropia 148. EYES.
hypermetropic 148. EYES,
　hypermetropia.
hypermyriorama
　352. REPRESENTATION.
hyperopia 148. EYES.
hyperopic 148. EYES, hyperopia.
hyperorexia 168. FOOD and NUTRITION.
hyperphasia 382. SPEECH.
hyperphysical 384. SPIRITS and
　SPIRITUALISM, hyperphysics.
hyperphysics 384. SPIRITS and
　SPIRITUALISM.
hyperpituitarism 122. DISEASE and
　ILLNESS.
hyperpituitary 122. DISEASE and
　ILLNESS, hyperpituitarism.
hyperpnea 122. DISEASE and ILLNESS.
hyperpyretic 122. DISEASE and ILLNESS,
　hyperpyrexia.
hyperpyrexia 122. DISEASE and ILLNESS.

hypersensitive 28. ATTITUDES,
hypersensitivity; 334. PSYCHOLOGY,
hypersensitivity.
hypersensitivity 28. ATTITUDES;
334. PSYCHOLOGY.
hyperthermia 122. DISEASE and ILLNESS.
hyperthermy 122. DISEASE and ILLNESS,
hyperthermia.
hyperthyroid 122. DISEASE and ILLNESS,
hyperthyroidism.
hyperthyroidism 122. DISEASE and
ILLNESS.
hypertrichosis 193. HAIR.
hypertrophic 51. BODY, HUMAN,
hypertrophy; 319. PLANTS,
hypertrophy; 368. SIZE, hypertrophy.
hypertrophical 51. BODY, HUMAN,
hypertrophy; 319. PLANTS,
hypertrophy; 368. SIZE, hypertrophy.
hypertrophous 51. BODY, HUMAN,
hypertrophy; 319. PLANTS,
hypertrophy; 368. SIZE, hypertrophy.
hypertrophy 51. BODY, HUMAN;
319. PLANTS; 368. SIZE.
hyper-urbanism 330. PRONUNCIATION.
hyphenism 41. BEHAVIOR.
hypnoanalysis 215. HYPNOSIS.
hypnoanalytic 215. HYPNOSIS,
hypnoanalysis.
hypnoanalytical 215. HYPNOSIS,
hypnoanalysis.
hypnobate 372. SLEEP; 372. SLEEP,
hypnobatia.
hypnobatia 372. SLEEP.
hypnogenesis 215. HYPNOSIS;
334. PSYCHOLOGY.
hypnogenetic 215. HYPNOSIS,
hypnogenesis; 334. PSYCHOLOGY,
hypnogenesis.
hypnologic 372. SLEEP, hypnology.
hypnological 372. SLEEP, hypnology.
hypnologist 372. SLEEP, hypnology.
hypnology 372. SLEEP.
hypnomania 254. MANIAS; 372. SLEEP.
hypnopaedia 372. SLEEP, hypnopedia.
hypnopedia 372. SLEEP.
hypnophobia 313. PHOBIAS; 372. SLEEP.
hypnotherapeutic 215. HYPNOSIS,
hypnotherapy.
hypnotherapist 334. PSYCHOLOGY,
hypnotherapy.

hypnotherapy 215. HYPNOSIS;
334. PSYCHOLOGY; 350. REMEDIES.
hypnotism 215. HYPNOSIS;
334. PSYCHOLOGY.
hypnotist 215. HYPNOSIS, hypnotism;
334. PSYCHOLOGY, hypnotism.
hypnotistic 334. PSYCHOLOGY,
hypnotism.
hypochondria 197. HEALTH,
hypochondriacism.
hypochondriac 197. HEALTH,
hypochondriacism.
hypochondriacal 197. HEALTH,
hypochondriacism.
hypochondriacism 122. DISEASE and
ILLNESS, nosomania; 197. HEALTH.
hypochondriasis 197. HEALTH,
hypochondriacism.
hypocorism 288. NAMES.
hypocoristic 288. NAMES, hypocorism.
hypocrisy 243. LIES and LYING.
hypocrite 243. LIES and LYING,
hypocrisy.
hypocritic 243. LIES and LYING,
hypocrisy.
hypocritical 243. LIES and LYING,
hypocrisy.
hypoglycemia 122. DISEASE and ILLNESS.
hypoglycemic 122. DISEASE and ILLNESS,
hypoglycemia.
hypomania 254. MANIAS.
hyponastic 319. PLANTS, hyponasty.
hyponasty 319. PLANTS.
hyponea 334. PSYCHOLOGY, hyponoia;
393. THINKING, hyponoia.
hyponoia 334. PSYCHOLOGY;
393. THINKING.
hypopituitarism 122. DISEASE and
ILLNESS.
hypopituitary 122. DISEASE and ILLNESS,
hypopituitarism.
hypoplasia 51. BODY, HUMAN; 368. SIZE.
hypoplastic 51. BODY, HUMAN,
hypoplasia; 368. SIZE, hypoplasia.
hypopotencia 386. STRENGTH and
WEAKNESS.
hypopotency 386. STRENGTH and
WEAKNESS, hypopotencia.
hypopsychosis 334. PSYCHOLOGY;
393. THINKING.

hypostasis 49. BLOOD and BLOOD
VESSELS; 312. PHILOSOPHY;
392. THEOLOGY.
hypostatic 49. BLOOD and BLOOD
VESSELS, hypostasis; 312. PHILOSOPHY,
hypostasis; 392. THEOLOGY,
hypostasis.
hypostatical 49. BLOOD and BLOOD
VESSELS, hypostasis; 312. PHILOSOPHY,
hypostasis; 392. THEOLOGY,
hypostasis.
hyposthenia 386. STRENGTH and
WEAKNESS.
hyposthenic 386. STRENGTH and
WEAKNESS, hyposthenia.
hypotactic 186. GRAMMAR, hypotaxis.
hypotaxis 186. GRAMMAR.
hypothecary 160. FINANCE,
hypothecation.
hypothecation 160. FINANCE.
hypothecator 160. FINANCE,
hypothecation.
hypothermal 51. BODY, HUMAN,
hypothermia.
hypothermia 51. BODY, HUMAN;
122. DISEASE and ILLNESS.
hypothermy 122. DISEASE and ILLNESS,
hypothermia.
hypothesis 21. ARGUMENTATION;
312. PHILOSOPHY.
hypothesist 21. ARGUMENTATION,
hypothesis; 312. PHILOSOPHY,
hypothesis.
hypothetic 21. ARGUMENTATION,
hypothesis; 312. PHILOSOPHY,
hypothesis.
hypothetical 21. ARGUMENTATION,
hypothesis; 312. PHILOSOPHY,
hypothesis.
hypothetist 21. ARGUMENTATION,
hypothesis; 312. PHILOSOPHY,
hypothesis.
hypothyroid 122. DISEASE and ILLNESS,
hypothyroidism.
hypothyroidism 122. DISEASE and
ILLNESS.
hypotyposis 354. RHETORIC and
RHETORICAL DEVICES.
hypsicephalic 196. HEAD, hypsicephaly.
hypsicephaly 196. HEAD.

hypsiphobia 202. HEIGHTS;
313. PHOBIAS, hypsophobia.
Hypsistarianism 349. RELIGION.
hypsographic 178. GEOGRAPHY,
hypsography; 202. HEIGHTS,
hypsography.
hypsographical 178. GEOGRAPHY,
hypsography; 202. HEIGHTS,
hypsography.
hypsography 178. GEOGRAPHY;
202. HEIGHTS.
hypsometer 202. HEIGHTS;
226. INSTRUMENTS.
hypsometric 202. HEIGHTS,
hypsometry; 264. MEASUREMENT,
hypsometry.
hypsometrical 202. HEIGHTS,
hypsometry; 264. MEASUREMENT,
hypsometry.
hypsometry 202. HEIGHTS;
264. MEASUREMENT.
hypsophobia 313. PHOBIAS.
hysteria 334. PSYCHOLOGY.
hysteric 334. PSYCHOLOGY, hysteria.
hysterical 334. PSYCHOLOGY, hysteria.
hysterocatalepsy 122. DISEASE and
ILLNESS.
hysterodynia 306. PAIN.
hysteroepilepsy 122. DISEASE and
ILLNESS.
hysteroepileptic 122. DISEASE and
ILLNESS, hysteroepilepsy.
hysterogenic 334. PSYCHOLOGY,
hysterogeny.
hysterogeny 334. PSYCHOLOGY.
hysterology 46. BIRTH; 266. MEDICAL
SPECIALTIES.
hysteromania 254. MANIAS; 364. SEX.
hysteron proteron 354. RHETORIC and
RHETORICAL DEVICES.
hysteropathy 122. DISEASE and ILLNESS.
hystricism 122. DISEASE and ILLNESS.
hytherograph 417. WEATHER.

I

iamatology 266. MEDICAL
SPECIALTIES; 350. REMEDIES.
iamb 409. VERSE.
iambic 409. VERSE, iamb.

iatralipsis 350. REMEDIES.
iatrochemist 7. ALCHEMY,
iatrochemistry.
iatrochemistry 7. ALCHEMY.
iatrology 266. MEDICAL SPECIALTIES.
iatrophobia 313. PHOBIAS.
Ibsenism 248. LITERARY STYLE.
Icarian 406. UTOPIA, Icarianism.
Icarianism 406. UTOPIA.
ichneumonology 225. INSECTS.
ichnographic 128. DRAWING,
ichnography.
ichnographical 128. DRAWING,
ichnography.
ichnography 128. DRAWING.
ichnolithology 171. FOSSILS, ichnology.
ichnological 171. FOSSILS, ichnology.
ichnology 171. FOSSILS.
ichnomancy 124. DIVINATION.
ichnomantic 124. DIVINATION,
ichnomancy.
ichor 51. BODY, HUMAN.
ichorous 51. BODY, HUMAN, ichor.
ichthyism 164. FISH.
ichthyismus 164. FISH, ichthyism.
ichthyolatry 164. FISH.
ichthyological 164. FISH, ichthyology.
ichthyologist 164. FISH, ichthyology.
ichthyology 164. FISH.
ichthyomancy 124. DIVINATION;
164. FISH.
ichthyomania 164. FISH; 254. MANIAS.
ichthyophagist 164. FISH,
ichthyophagy.
ichthyophagous 164. FISH,
ichthyophagy.
ichthyophagy 164. FISH.
ichthyophobia 164. FISH; 313. PHOBIAS.
ichthyosis 164. FISH.
ichthyotic 164. FISH, ichthyosis.
ichthyotomic 164. FISH, ichthyotomy.
ichthyotomist 164. FISH, ichthyotomy.
ichthyotomy 164. FISH.
iconism 218. IMAGES.
iconoclasm 218. IMAGES.
iconoclast 135. EASTERN ORTHODOXY,
iconoclasticism; 218. IMAGES,
iconoclasm.
iconoclastic 135. EASTERN ORTHODOXY,
iconoclasticism; 218. IMAGES,
iconoclasm.

iconoclasticism 135. EASTERN
ORTHODOXY.
iconodule 218. IMAGES.
iconodulist 218. IMAGES, iconodule.
iconography 23. ART, iconology.
iconolater 218. IMAGES, iconolatry.
iconolatry 218. IMAGES.
iconological 23. ART, iconology;
218. IMAGES, iconology.
iconologist 23. ART, iconology;
218. IMAGES, iconology.
iconology 23. ART; 218. IMAGES.
iconomachy 218. IMAGES.
iconomania 218. IMAGES; 254. MANIAS.
iconomatic 428. WRITING,
iconomaticism.
iconomaticism 428. WRITING.
iconophilist 91. COLLECTIONS and
COLLECTING; 311. -PHILE,
-PHILIA, -PHILY.
icterus 95. COMPLEXION.
ictus 51. BODY, HUMAN; 409. VERSE.
idealism 312. PHILOSOPHY.
idealist 312. PHILOSOPHY, idealism.
idealistic 312. PHILOSOPHY, idealism.
idealogue 322. POLITICS, ideology.
ideation 393. THINKING.
ideational 393. THINKING, ideation.
ideographic 428. WRITING, ideography.
ideographical 428. WRITING,
ideography.
ideography 428. WRITING.
ideologic 322. POLITICS, ideology.
ideological 216. IDEAS, ideology;
322. POLITICS, ideology.
ideologist 216. IDEAS, ideology;
322. POLITICS, ideology.
ideology 216. IDEAS; 322. POLITICS.
idiocrasy 41. BEHAVIOR.
idiograph 352. REPRESENTATION.
idiolect 247. LINGUISTICS.
idiomatology 236. LANGUAGE.
idiomorphic 170. FORM, idiomorphism.
idiomorphism 170. FORM.
idiopathic 122. DISEASE and ILLNESS,
idiopathy.
idiopathy 122. DISEASE and ILLNESS.
idiosyncrasy 41. BEHAVIOR.
idiosyncratic 41. BEHAVIOR,
idiosyncrasy.

idiosyncratical 41. BEHAVIOR, idiosyncrasy.
idiotic 217. IDIOCY, idiotism.
idiotism 217. IDIOCY.
Ido 236. LANGUAGE, Idoism.
Idoism 236. LANGUAGE.
Idoist 236. LANGUAGE, Idoism.
Idoistic 236. LANGUAGE, Idoism.
idolatrous 349. RELIGION, idolism.
idolatry 218. IMAGES, iconolatry; 349. RELIGION, idolism.
idolism 349. RELIGION.
idolist 349. RELIGION, idolism.
idoloclast 135. EASTERN ORTHODOXY.
idolomancy 124. DIVINATION.
idolomania 205. HERESY; 254. MANIAS.
ikebana 167. FLOWERS.
illation 393. THINKING.
illative 393. THINKING, illation.
illeism 236. LANGUAGE.
illeist 236. LANGUAGE, illeism.
illiberalism 322. POLITICS.
Illuminati 233. KNOWLEDGE, Illuminism.
illuminati 233. KNOWLEDGE, Illuminism.
illumination 256. MANUSCRIPTS; 305. ORNAMENTATION.
Illuminism 233. KNOWLEDGE.
Illuminist 233. KNOWLEDGE, Illuminism.
illuminist 233. KNOWLEDGE, Illuminism.
illusionism 312. PHILOSOPHY.
illusionist 252. MAGIC; 310. PERFORMING; 312. PHILOSOPHY, illusionism.
illusionistic 312. PHILOSOPHY, illusionism.
imaginational 28. ATTITUDES, imaginationalism.
imaginationalism 28. ATTITUDES.
Imagism 249. LITERATURE.
Imagist 249. LITERATURE, Imagism.
Imagistic 249. LITERATURE, Imagism.
Imamite 227. ISLAM.
immaculacy 84. CLEANLINESS.
immaculate 84. CLEANLINESS, immaculacy.
immaterial 312. PHILOSOPHY, immaterialism.

immaterialism 312. PHILOSOPHY.
immaterialist 312. PHILOSOPHY, immaterialism.
immediatism 396. TIME.
immersionism 35. BAPTISM, holobaptism.
immolation 232. KILLING.
immolator 232. KILLING, immolation.
immunogenetic 266. MEDICAL SPECIALTIES, immunogenetics.
immunogenetics 266. MEDICAL SPECIALTIES.
immunologic 266. MEDICAL SPECIALTIES, immunology.
immunological 266. MEDICAL SPECIALTIES, immunology.
immunologist 266. MEDICAL SPECIALTIES, immunology.
immunology 266. MEDICAL SPECIALTIES.
impanation 79. CHRIST; 392. THEOLOGY.
impenitence 80. CHRISTIANITY.
impenitency 80. CHRISTIANITY, impenitence.
impenitent 80. CHRISTIANITY, impenitence.
imponderabilia 393. THINKING.
impossibilism 28. ATTITUDES.
impotence 386. STRENGTH and WEAKNESS, impotency.
impotency 386. STRENGTH and WEAKNESS.
impotent 386. STRENGTH and WEAKNESS, impotency.
impotentness 386. STRENGTH and WEAKNESS, impotency.
impoundage 331. PROPERTY and OWNERSHIP.
impounder 331. PROPERTY and OWNERSHIP, impoundage.
impoundment 331. PROPERTY and OWNERSHIP, impoundage.
Impressionism 23. ART.
Impressionist 23. ART, Impressionism.
Impressionistic 23. ART, Impressionism.
imprimatur 69. CATHOLICISM; 328. PRINTING.
impudicity 28. ATTITUDES; 41. BEHAVIOR.

inamorata 251. LOVE.
inamorato 251. LOVE.
incendiarism 162. FIRE.
incendiary 162. FIRE, **incendiarism.**
inclinometer 133. EARTH.
inconsequentia 233. KNOWLEDGE.
incorporealism 170. FORM.
incorporeity 170. FORM,
  incorporealism.
increscence 368. SIZE.
increscent 368. SIZE, **increscence.**
incubi 114. DEMONS, **incubus.**
incubus 114. DEMONS.
incunabula 53. BOOKS, **incunabulum.**
incunabular 53. BOOKS, **incunabulum.**
incunabulist 53. BOOKS, **incunabulum.**
incunabulum 53. BOOKS.
indagation 393. THINKING.
indagative 393. THINKING, **indagation.**
indagator 393. THINKING, **indagation.**
indecorum 41. BEHAVIOR.
indentureship 4. AGREEMENT;
  371. SLAVERY.
indeterminism 28. ATTITUDES.
indeterminist 28. ATTITUDES,
  indeterminism.
indeterministic 28. ATTITUDES,
  indeterminism.
Indianism 41. BEHAVIOR.
Indianist 41. BEHAVIOR, **Indianism.**
indiction 65. CALENDAR.
indictional 65. CALENDAR, **indiction.**
indifferentism 28. ATTITUDES;
  312. PHILOSOPHY; 349. RELIGION.
indifferentist 28. ATTITUDES,
  indifferentism; 312. PHILOSOPHY,
  indifferentism; 349. RELIGION,
  indifferentism.
indigometer 92. COLOR;
  226. INSTRUMENTS.
indigometry 92. COLOR;
  264. MEASUREMENT.
individualism 28. ATTITUDES;
  362. SELF.
individualist 28. ATTITUDES,
  individualism; 362. SELF,
  individualism.
individualistic 28. ATTITUDES,
  individualism; 362. SELF,
  individualism.
individuation 362. SELF.

induration 329. PROCESSES.
indurative 329. PROCESSES, **induration.**
industrialism 137. ECONOMICS.
industrialist 137. ECONOMICS,
  industrialism; 266. MEDICAL
  SPECIALTIES.
inebriety 8. ALCOHOL.
infallibilism 69. CATHOLICISM.
infanticidal 232. KILLING, **infanticide.**
infanticide 232. KILLING.
infantilism 334. PSYCHOLOGY.
infantilistic 334. PSYCHOLOGY,
  infantilism.
infantility 334. PSYCHOLOGY,
  infantilism.
infarction 199. HEART.
infeudation 331. PROPERTY and
  OWNERSHIP.
infibulation 68. CAPTIVITY; 364. SEX.
inflationism 137. ECONOMICS.
inflationist 137. ECONOMICS,
  inflationism.
infralapsarian 80. CHRISTIANITY,
  infralapsarianism.
infralapsarianism 80. CHRISTIANITY.
infrangibility 261. MATERIALS,
  PROPERTIES OF.
infrangible 261. MATERIALS,
  PROPERTIES OF, **infrangibility.**
infusionism 379. SOUL.
ingrammatically 186. GRAMMAR,
  ingrammaticism.
ingrammaticism 186. GRAMMAR.
inordinacy 368. SIZE.
inordinate 368. SIZE, **inordinacy.**
inquiline 16. ANIMALS; 16. ANIMALS,
  inquiline.
inscience 233. KNOWLEDGE.
inscient 233. KNOWLEDGE, **inscience.**
insecticidal 225. INSECTS, **insecticide;**
  232. KILLING, **insecticide.**
insecticide 225. INSECTS; 232. KILLING.
insectology 225. INSECTS.
insobriety 8. ALCOHOL.
insouciance 28. ATTITUDES.
insouciant 28. ATTITUDES, **insouciance.**
inspirationism 43. BIBLE;
  349. RELIGION.
inspirationist 43. BIBLE, **inspirationism.**
inspirative 43. BIBLE, **inspirationism.**
inspissant 329. PROCESSES, **inspissation.**

inspissate 329. PROCESSES, **inspissation.**
inspissation 329. PROCESSES.
instauration 329. PROCESSES.
instaurator 329. PROCESSES,
  instauration.
institutionalism 322. POLITICS.
institutionalist 322. POLITICS,
  institutionalism.
instrumentalism 216. IDEAS;
  312. PHILOSOPHY.
instrumentalist 216. IDEAS,
  instrumentalism; 312. PHILOSOPHY,
  instrumentalism.
instrumentation 226. INSTRUMENTS.
insularism 393. THINKING.
insurgence 413. WAR; 413. WAR,
  insurgency.
insurgency 413. WAR.
insurgent 413. WAR, **insurgency.**
insurgentism 96. CONFLICT;
  322. POLITICS.
insurrectionary 41. BEHAVIOR,
  insurrectionism.
insurrectionism 41. BEHAVIOR.
insurrectionist 41. BEHAVIOR,
  insurrectionism.
intarsia 305. ORNAMENTATION.
integrationism 341. RACE.
integrationist 341. RACE,
  integrationism.
intellection 216. IDEAS; 393. THINKING.
intellectualism 233. KNOWLEDGE.
intellectualistic 233. KNOWLEDGE,
  intellectualism.
intempestive 396. TIME, **intempestivity.**
intempestivity 396. TIME.
intercalary 65. CALENDAR.
intercalation 65. CALENDAR,
  intercalary.
intercalative 65. CALENDAR,
  intercalary.
intercolumniation 20. ARCHITECTURE.
interferometer 226. INSTRUMENTS.
interferometry 226. INSTRUMENTS,
  interferometer.
Interlingua 236. LANGUAGE.
interlucation 401. TREES.
interlunar 25. ASTRONOMY,
  interlunation.
interlunation 25. ASTRONOMY.
Internationalism 20. ARCHITECTURE.

internationalism 322. POLITICS.
internationalist 322. POLITICS,
  internationalism.
International Style 20. ARCHITECTURE,
  Internationalism.
internist 266. MEDICAL SPECIALTIES.
interpolity 322. POLITICS.
interracial 341. RACE, **interracialism.**
interracialism 341. RACE.
interventionism 322. POLITICS.
interventionist 322. POLITICS,
  interventionism.
introspectionism 334. PSYCHOLOGY.
introspectionist 334. PSYCHOLOGY,
  introspectionism.
introspective 334. PSYCHOLOGY,
  introspectionism.
introsusception 50. BODILY FUNCTIONS.
introversion 362. SELF.
introversive 362. SELF, **introversion.**
introvert 362. SELF, **introversion.**
introvertive 362. SELF, **introversion.**
intuitionalism 233. KNOWLEDGE.
intuitionalist 233. KNOWLEDGE,
  intuitionalism.
intuitionism 233. KNOWLEDGE,
  intuitionalism.
intuitionist 233. KNOWLEDGE,
  intuitionalism.
intuitivism 233. KNOWLEDGE,
  intuitionalism.
intussusception 50. BODILY FUNCTIONS.
intussusceptive 50. BODILY FUNCTIONS,
  intussusception.
invalescence 197. HEALTH;
  386. STRENGTH and WEAKNESS.
invalidism 122. DISEASE and ILLNESS.
invertebracy 102. COWARDICE;
  386. STRENGTH and WEAKNESS;
  430. ZOOLOGY.
invertebrate 386. STRENGTH and
  WEAKNESS, **invertebracy;**
  430. ZOOLOGY, **invertebracy.**
invultuation 146. EVIL.
iodism 122. DISEASE and ILLNESS.
Ionicism 190. GREECE and GREEKS.
Ionism 190. GREECE and GREEKS,
  Ionicism.
ionosphere 27. ATMOSPHERE.
iophobia 313. PHOBIAS; 321. POISON.
iotacism 236. LANGUAGE.

iotacist 236. LANGUAGE, iotacism.
ipse-dixitism 362. SELF.
ipseity 362. SELF, ipsism.
ipsism 362. SELF.
irascibility 41. BEHAVIOR.
irascible 41. BEHAVIOR, irascibility.
irascibleness 41. BEHAVIOR, irascibility.
irenicism 413. WAR.
irenicist 413. WAR, irenicism.
Iricism 236. LANGUAGE.
iridescence 92. COLOR; 245. LIGHT.
iridescent 92. COLOR, iridescence;
   245. LIGHT, iridescence.
iridotomy 148. EYES.
irisation 92. COLOR.
iriscope 92. COLOR; 245. LIGHT.
Irishism 236. LANGUAGE.
irrationalism 312. PHILOSOPHY.
irrationalist 312. PHILOSOPHY,
   irrationalism.
irrationalistic 312. PHILOSOPHY,
   irrationalism.
irredentism 322. POLITICS.
irredentist 322. POLITICS, irredentism.
irroration 417. WEATHER.
Irvingite 332. PROTESTANTISM.
isagogic 43. BIBLE, isagogics.
isagogics 43. BIBLE.
ischialgia 122. DISEASE and ILLNESS.
ischidrosis 266. MEDICAL SPECIALTIES.
Isiac 183. GOD and GODS.
Islam 227. ISLAM.
Islamism 227. ISLAM, Islam.
Islamist 227. ISLAM, Islam.
Islamitic 227. ISLAM, Islam.
islandologist 178. GEOGRAPHY,
   islandology.
islandology 178. GEOGRAPHY.
isocephalic 196. HEAD, isocephalism.
isocephalism 196. HEAD.
isocephalous 196. HEAD, isocephalism.
isocephaly 196. HEAD, isocephalism.
isochronic 396. TIME, isochronism.
isochronism 396. TIME.
isochrony 396. TIME, isochronism.
isocracy 185. GOVERNMENT.
isocrat 185. GOVERNMENT, isocracy.
isocratic 185. GOVERNMENT, isocracy.
isogamete 44. BIOLOGY.
isogamous 44. BIOLOGY, isogamy.
isogamy 44. BIOLOGY.

isogenesis 44. BIOLOGY; 304. ORIGINS.
isogenetic 304. ORIGINS, isogenesis.
isogenic 304. ORIGINS, isogenesis.
isogeny 44. BIOLOGY, isogenesis;
   304. ORIGINS, isogenesis.
isogonic 44. BIOLOGY, isogonism.
isogonism 44. BIOLOGY.
isographic 428. WRITING, isography.
isographical 428. WRITING, isography.
isography 428. WRITING.
isolationism 322. POLITICS.
isolationist 322. POLITICS, isolationism.
isometric 26. ATHLETICS, isometrics;
   264. MEASUREMENT, isometry.
isometrical 264. MEASUREMENT,
   isometry.
isometric projection 128. DRAWING.
isometrics 26. ATHLETICS.
isometropia 148. EYES.
isometry 264. MEASUREMENT.
isomorph 44. BIOLOGY, isomorphism;
   316. PHYSICS, isomorphism.
isomorphic 44. BIOLOGY, isomorphism;
   316. PHYSICS, isomorphism.
isomorphism 44. BIOLOGY; 316. PHYSICS.
isonomy 322. POLITICS.
isopathy 122. DISEASE and ILLNESS.
isoperimetral 262. MATHEMATICS,
   isoperimetry.
isoperimetrical 262. MATHEMATICS,
   isoperimetry.
isoperimetry 262. MATHEMATICS.
isopolite 322. POLITICS, isopolity.
isopolitical 322. POLITICS, isopolity.
isopolity 322. POLITICS.
isopsephic 236. LANGUAGE,
   isopsephism.
isopsephism 236. LANGUAGE.
isopterophobia 313. PHOBIAS.
isostasy 179. GEOLOGY.
isostatic 179. GEOLOGY, isostasy.
isotely 190. GREECE and GREEKS.
isotonic 26. ATHLETICS, isotonics.
isotonics 26. ATHLETICS.
isthmian 17. ANTHROPOLOGY.
Italianism 236. LANGUAGE.
Italicism 236. LANGUAGE.
italicism 328. PRINTING.
Italomania 228. ITALY; 254. MANIAS.
ithyphallic 364. SEX, ithyphallicism.
ithyphallicism 364. SEX.

itineracy 399. TRAVEL, **itinerancy.**
itinerancy 399. TRAVEL.
itinerant 399. TRAVEL, **itinerancy.**
Izedi 117. DEVIL, **Izedism;**
349. RELIGION, **Izedism.**
Izedism 117. DEVIL; 349. RELIGION.

J

Jacobin 322. POLITICS, **Jacobinism.**
Jacobinic 322. POLITICS, **Jacobinism.**
Jacobinism 322. POLITICS.
jacquerie 96. CONFLICT.
jactation 51. BODY, HUMAN, **jactitation.**
jactitation 51. BODY, HUMAN.
Jain 349. RELIGION, **Jainism.**
Jainism 349. RELIGION.
Jainist 349. RELIGION, **Jainism.**
Jansenism 205. HERESY; 349. RELIGION.
Jansenist 205. HERESY, **Jansenism.**
Japanism 229. JAPAN.
Japonism 23. ART; 229. JAPAN;
236. LANGUAGE.
Japonisme 23. ART, **Japonism;**
229. JAPAN, **Japonism.**
jargonist 236. LANGUAGE.
jaundice 95. COMPLEXION.
Jeffersonian 322. POLITICS,
Jeffersonianism.
Jeffersonianism 322. POLITICS.
Jehovism 349. RELIGION.
Jehovist 392. THEOLOGY.
Jehovistic 392. THEOLOGY, **Jehovist.**
Jensenism 341. RACE.
Jensenist 341. RACE, **Jensenism.**
jerrybuilder 60. BUILDINGS, **jerryism.**
jerrybuilding 60. BUILDING, **jerryism.**
jerrybuilt 60. BUILDINGS, **jerryism.**
jerryism 60. BUILDINGS.
Jesuitic 69. CATHOLICISM, **Jesuitism.**
jesuitic 106. CUNNING, **jesuitism.**
Jesuitical 69. CATHOLICISM, **Jesuitism.**
jesuitical 106. CUNNING, **jesuitism.**
Jesuitism 69. CATHOLICISM.
jesuitism 106. CUNNING.
Jesuitocracy 185. GOVERNMENT.
Jesuitry 69. CATHOLICISM, **Jesuitism.**
jetsam 366. SHIPS.
jetsom 366. SHIPS, **jetsam.**
Jewry 231. JUDAISM.
jiggery-pokery 106. CUNNING.

jingo 289. NATIONALISM, **jingoism.**
jingoism 289. NATIONALISM.
jingoist 289. NATIONALISM, **jingoism.**
jingoistic 289. NATIONALISM, **jingoism.**
jocose 213. HUMOR, **jocosity.**
jocosity 213. HUMOR.
jocund 28. ATTITUDES, **jocundity;**
195. HAPPINESS, **jocundity;**
238. LAUGHTER, **jocundity.**
jocundity 28. ATTITUDES;
195. HAPPINESS; 238. LAUGHTER.
Johnsonese 248. LITERARY STYLE.
Johnsonian 41. BEHAVIOR,
Johnsonianism.
Johnsonianism 41. BEHAVIOR.
joiner 425. WOOD, **joinery.**
joinery 425. WOOD.
joint stockism 137. ECONOMICS.
Josephinism 349. RELIGION.
journalese 237. LANGUAGE STYLE;
265. MEDIA.
journalism 265. MEDIA.
journalist 265. MEDIA, **journalism.**
journalistic 265. MEDIA, **journalism.**
jovialist 28. ATTITUDES; 195. HAPPINESS.
joviality 195. HAPPINESS.
jovilabe 226. INSTRUMENTS.
Jovinianist 205. HERESY; 260. MARY.
jucundity 195. HAPPINESS.
Judaeophobia 231. JUDAISM,
Judophobism; 313. PHOBIAS,
Judophobism.
Judaic 231. JUDAISM, **Judaism.**
Judaica 91. COLLECTIONS and
COLLECTING.
Judaism 231. JUDAISM.
Judaist 231. JUDAISM, **Judaism.**
Judaistic 231. JUDAISM, **Judaism.**
Judophobia 231. JUDAISM,
Judophobism; 313. PHOBIAS,
Judophobism.
Judophobism 231. JUDAISM;
313. PHOBIAS.
jugglery 310. PERFORMING.
jugulation 232. KILLING;
350. REMEDIES.
jujuism 252. MAGIC.
jujuist 252. MAGIC, **jujuism.**
Julianism 79. CHRIST.
Julianist 79. CHRIST, **Julianism.**

Jungian criticism 104. CRITICISM.
juniority 3. AGE.
Junker 289. NATIONALISM, **Junkerism.**
Junkerism 289. NATIONALISM.
jurisprudence 239. LAW.
jurisprudent 239. LAW, **jurisprudence.**
jusquaboutism 322. POLITICS.
jusquaboutisme 322. POLITICS,
jusquaboutism.
jusquaboutist 322. POLITICS,
jusquaboutism.
justicialism 185. GOVERNMENT.
Justinian code 239. LAW, **Justinianist.**
Justinianist 239. LAW.
juvenile 41. BEHAVIOR, **juvenilism.**
juvenilia 248. LITERARY STYLE.
juvenilism 41. BEHAVIOR.
juvenility 41. BEHAVIOR, **juvenilism.**

K

Kaaba 227. ISLAM, **Kaabism.**
Kaabism 227. ISLAM.
kainomania 254. MANIAS; 294. NOVELTY.
kaiserism 322. POLITICS.
kakistocracy 185. GOVERNMENT.
kakorrhaphiophobia 313. PHOBIAS.
kakotopia 185. GOVERNMENT;
376. SOCIETY; 406. UTOPIA.
kaleidophon 226. INSTRUMENTS;
380. SOUND.
kaleidophone 226. INSTRUMENTS,
kaleidophon; 380. SOUND,
kaleidophon.
kaleidoscope 226. INSTRUMENTS.
kaleidoscopic 226. INSTRUMENTS,
kaleidoscope.
Kantian 312. PHILOSOPHY, **Kantianism.**
Kantianism 312. PHILOSOPHY.
Kantist 312. PHILOSOPHY, **Kantianism.**
Karaism 231. JUDAISM.
Karaite 231. JUDAISM, **Karaism.**
Karmathian 227. ISLAM.
karyologic 44. BIOLOGY, **karyology;**
72. CELLS, **karyology.**
karyological 44. BIOLOGY, **karyology;**
72. CELLS, **karyology.**
karyologist 44. BIOLOGY, **karyology.**
karyology 44. BIOLOGY; 72. CELLS.
karyoplasm 72. CELLS.
karyoplasmatic 72. CELLS, **karyoplasm.**

karyoplasmic 72. CELLS, **karyoplasm.**
karyotype 72. CELLS.
karyotypic 72. CELLS, **karyotype.**
karyotypical 72. CELLS, **karyotype.**
katabolic 302. ORGANISMS, **katabolism.**
katabolism 302. ORGANISMS;
302. ORGANISMS, **catabolism.**
katagelophobia 238. LAUGHTER;
313. PHOBIAS.
katamorphic 179. GEOLOGY,
katamorphism.
katamorphism 179. GEOLOGY.
kathisomania 254. MANIAS;
339. QUIETUDE.
Kemalism 404. TURKEY.
Kemalist 404. TURKEY, **Kemalism.**
kenophobia 313. PHOBIAS, **cenophobia;**
381. SPACES, **cenophobia.**
kenosis 79. CHRIST, **kenoticism.**
kenotic 79. CHRIST, **kenoticism.**
kenoticism 79. CHRIST.
kenoticist 79. CHRIST, **kenoticism.**
Kenticism 236. LANGUAGE.
keramicist 324. POTTERY, **ceramics.**
keramics 324. POTTERY, **ceramics.**
keramist 324. POTTERY, **ceramics.**
keratitis 148. EYES.
keratoplasty 148. EYES.
keratotomy 148. EYES.
keraunograph 246. LIGHTNING,
keraunography.
keraunographic 246. LIGHTNING,
keraunography.
keraunography 246. LIGHTNING.
keraunomancy 394. THUNDER.
keraunophobia 246. LIGHTNING;
313. PHOBIAS.
keraunoscopia 246. LIGHTNING;
394. THUNDER.
κeraunoscopy 246. LIGHTNING,
keraunoscopia; 394. THUNDER,
keraunoscopia.
kerugma 80. CHRISTIANITY, **kerygma.**
kerygma 80. CHRISTIANITY.
kerygmatic 80. CHRISTIANITY,
kerygma.
kerystic 349. RELIGION, **kerystics.**
kerystics 349. RELIGION.
Keynesian 137. ECONOMICS,
Keynesianism.
Keynesianism 137. ECONOMICS.

Khomeinism 322. POLITICS.
kibbutz 93. COMMUNALISM.
kibbutzim 93. COMMUNALISM, kibbutz.
kinematic 282. MOTION, kinematics;
   316. PHYSICS, kinematics.
kinematical 316. PHYSICS, kinematics.
kinematics 282. MOTION; 316. PHYSICS.
kinematograph 159. FILMS.
kinemics 181. GESTURE.
kinescope 265. MEDIA.
kinesiatrics 266. MEDICAL SPECIALTIES;
   350. REMEDIES.
kinesic 181. GESTURE, kinesics.
kinesics 181. GESTURE.
kinesiologic 51. BODY, HUMAN,
   kinesiology.
kinesiological 51. BODY, HUMAN,
   kinesiology.
kinesiology 51. BODY, HUMAN.
kinesipathy 266. MEDICAL SPECIALTIES,
   kinesiatrics; 350. REMEDIES,
   kinesiatrics.
kinesomania 254. MANIAS; 282. MOTION.
kinestherapy 51. BODY, HUMAN,
   kinesiology.
kinesthesia 309. PERCEPTION.
kinesthetic 309. PERCEPTION,
   kinesthesia.
kinetics 282. MOTION.
kinetogenesis 44. BIOLOGY.
kinetogenetic 44. BIOLOGY,
   kinetogenesis.
kinetograph 159. FILMS,
   kinematograph.
kinetophobia 282. MOTION;
   313. PHOBIAS.
kinetophone 265. MEDIA.
kinetoscope 226. INSTRUMENTS;
   265. MEDIA.
kinship 348. RELATIONSHIP.
Kiplingesque 248. LITERARY STYLE,
   Kiplingism.
Kiplingism 248. LITERARY STYLE.
kitharist 284. MUSIC; 284. MUSIC,
   citharist.
kitling 70. CATS.
Klanism 28. ATTITUDES.
kleptomania 391. THEFT.
kleptomaniac 391. THEFT,
   kleptomania.
kleptophobia 313. PHOBIAS; 391. THEFT.

knacker 60. BUILDINGS.
knave 103. CRIME, knavery.
knavery 103. CRIME.
knavish 103. CRIME, knavery.
Kneippism 36. BATHING.
know-nothing 322. POLITICS, Know-
   Nothingism.
Know-Nothingism 322. POLITICS.
konimeter 27. ATMOSPHERE;
   142. ENVIRONMENT;
   226. INSTRUMENTS.
konimetric 27. ATMOSPHERE,
   konimeter; 27. ATMOSPHERE,
   konimetry; 142. ENVIRONMENT,
   konimeter; 142. ENVIRONMENT,
   konimetry; 226. INSTRUMENTS,
   konimeter; 264. MEASUREMENT,
   konimetry.
konimetry 27. ATMOSPHERE;
   142. ENVIRONMENT;
   264. MEASUREMENT.
koniology 27. ATMOSPHERE;
   142. ENVIRONMENT.
kopophobia 154. FATIGUE;
   313. PHOBIAS.
Koreshan 332. PROTESTANTISM,
   Koreshanity.
Koreshanity 332. PROTESTANTISM.
Kremlinologist 94. COMMUNISM,
   Kremlinology; 357. RUSSIA,
   Kremlinology.
Kremlinology 94. COMMUNISM;
   357. RUSSIA.
Krishnaism 206. HINDUISM.
kritarchy 185. GOVERNMENT.
ktenology 112. DEATH.
Ku Kluxery 28. ATTITUDES, Klanism.
Ku Kluxism 28. ATTITUDES, Klanism.
kvutzah 93. COMMUNALISM, kibbutz.
kymograph 264. MEASUREMENT,
   kymography.
kymographic 264. MEASUREMENT,
   kymography.
kymography 264. MEASUREMENT.
kynophobia 313. PHOBIAS.
kyphosis 51. BODY, HUMAN.
kyphotic 51. BODY, HUMAN, kyphosis.

L

Labadist 332. PROTESTANTISM.
labdacism 247. LINGUISTICS,
 lambdacism.
labefactation 113. DECAYING,
 labefaction; 329. PROCESSES,
 labefaction.
labefaction 113. DECAYING;
 329. PROCESSES.
labeorphile 39. BEER, **labeorphily;**
 91. COLLECTIONS and COLLECTING,
 labeorphily.
labeorphilist 91. COLLECTIONS and
 COLLECTING, **labeorphily.**
labeorphily 39. BEER; 91. COLLECTIONS
 and COLLECTING.
labialism 382. SPEECH.
labile 386. STRENGTH and WEAKNESS,
 lability.
lability 386. STRENGTH and WEAKNESS.
laborite 303. ORGANIZED LABOR.
lachrimatory 148. EYES, **lacrymatory.**
lachrymation 50. BODILY FUNCTIONS.
laclabphily 76. CHEESE;
 91. COLLECTIONS and COLLECTING.
laconic 58. BREVITY, **laconism;**
 237. LANGUAGE STYLE, **laconicism;**
 354. RHETORIC and RHETORICAL
 DEVICES, **laconicism.**
laconical 58. BREVITY, **laconism.**
laconicism 58. BREVITY, **laconism;**
 237. LANGUAGE STYLE; 354. RHETORIC
 and RHETORICAL DEVICES.
laconism 58. BREVITY; 237. LANGUAGE
 STYLE, **laconicism;** 354. RHETORIC and
 RHETORICAL DEVICES, **laconicism.**
lacrimation 50. BODILY FUNCTIONS,
 lachrymation.
lacrymatory 148. EYES.
lactation 50. BODILY FUNCTIONS.
lactescence 329. PROCESSES.
lactescent 329. PROCESSES, **lactescence.**
lactometer 226. INSTRUMENTS;
 272. MILK.
lactoscope 226. INSTRUMENTS;
 272. MILK.
lacustrian 17. ANTHROPOLOGY.
lacustrine 234. LAKES.
ladron 391. THEFT, **ladronism.**

ladrone 391. THEFT, **ladronism.**
ladronism 391. THEFT.
lagophthalmia 148. EYES.
lagophthalmic 148. EYES,
 lagophthalmia.
lagophthalmus 148. EYES,
 lagophthalmia.
laicism 69. CATHOLICISM.
laissez-faireism 137. ECONOMICS.
laissez-faireist 137. ECONOMICS, **laissez-
 faireism.**
laity 69. CATHOLICISM, **laicism.**
laliophobia 313. PHOBIAS.
lallation 247. LINGUISTICS.
lalomania 254. MANIAS; 382. SPEECH.
lalopathic 382. SPEECH, **lalopathology.**
lalopathology 382. SPEECH.
lalopathy 382. SPEECH, **lalopathology.**
lalophobia 313. PHOBIAS, **laliophobia;**
 382. SPEECH.
Lamaism 59. BUDDHISM.
Lamaist 59. BUDDHISM, **Lamaism.**
Lamaistic 59. BUDDHISM, **Lamaism.**
Lamanism 59. BUDDHISM.
Lamanist 59. BUDDHISM, **Lamanism.**
Lamarckian 147. EVOLUTION,
 Lamarckism.
Lamarckism 147. EVOLUTION.
Lamaze technique 46. BIRTH.
lambdacism 247. LINGUISTICS.
lampadedromy 26. ATHLETICS;
 190. GREECE and GREEKS.
lampadephore 26. ATHLETICS,
 lampadist; 190. GREECE and GREEKS,
 lampadist.
lampadephoria 26. ATHLETICS,
 lampadedromy; 190. GREECE and
 GREEKS, **lampadedromy.**
lampadist 26. ATHLETICS; 190. GREECE
 and GREEKS.
lampadomancy 124. DIVINATION.
lampadophoros 26. ATHLETICS,
 lampadist; 190. GREECE and GREEKS,
 lampadist.
lampadrome 26. ATHLETICS,
 lampadedromy; 190. GREECE and
 GREEKS, **lampadedromy.**
landlordism 41. BEHAVIOR.
landlordly 41. BEHAVIOR, **landlordism.**
landocracy 376. SOCIETY.
landocrat 376. SOCIETY, **landocracy.**

landscapist 23. ART.
Laodiceanism 28. ATTITUDES.
laparotomaphilia 311. -PHILE,
-PHILIA, -PHILY.
lapidarian 177. GEMS, lapidary.
lapidarist 177. GEMS, lapidary.
lapidary 177. GEMS.
lapidation 223. INJURY; 232. KILLING.
lapidification 329. PROCESSES;
385. STONES.
lapidist 177. GEMS.
lapillus 179. GEOLOGY.
larkinism 41. BEHAVIOR.
larrikin 41. BEHAVIOR, larrikinism.
larrikinism 41. BEHAVIOR.
laryngitic 122. DISEASE and ILLNESS,
laryngitis.
laryngitis 122. DISEASE and ILLNESS.
laryngographic 14. ANATOMY,
laryngography.
laryngographical 14. ANATOMY,
laryngography.
laryngography 14. ANATOMY.
laryngological 266. MEDICAL
SPECIALTIES, laryngology.
laryngologist 266. MEDICAL
SPECIALTIES, laryngology.
laryngology 266. MEDICAL SPECIALTIES.
laryngoscope 226. INSTRUMENTS.
laryngoscopic 226. INSTRUMENTS,
laryngoscope.
laryngoscopist 226. INSTRUMENTS,
laryngoscope.
Latinism 236. LANGUAGE.
Latinity 236. LANGUAGE.
Latinize 236. LANGUAGE, Latinism.
latitudinarian 28. ATTITUDES,
latitudinarianism; 349. RELIGION,
latitudinarianism.
latitudinarianism 28. ATTITUDES;
349. RELIGION.
latria 80. CHRISTIANITY;
392. THEOLOGY.
laudanum 130. DRUGS.
Laudian 332. PROTESTANTISM,
Laudianism.
Laudianism 332. PROTESTANTISM.
laureate 210. HONORS and REGALIA.
laxism 312. PHILOSOPHY.
laxist 312. PHILOSOPHY, laxism.

leasehold 331. PROPERTY and
OWNERSHIP.
lecanomancy 124. DIVINATION;
414. WATER.
lecanoscopy 414. WATER.
lecher 364. SEX, lechery.
lecherer 364. SEX, lechery.
lecherous 364. SEX, lechery.
lechery 364. SEX.
lection 43. BIBLE.
lectionary 43. BIBLE; 81. CHURCH.
leechcraft 350. REMEDIES.
leechdom 350. REMEDIES.
leftism 322. POLITICS.
leftist 322. POLITICS, leftism.
legalese 237. LANGUAGE STYLE;
239. LAW.
legalism 239. LAW; 349. RELIGION.
legalist 349. RELIGION, legalism.
legalistic 239. LAW, legalism;
349. RELIGION, legalism.
legenda 91. COLLECTIONS and
COLLECTING.
legendary 91. COLLECTIONS and
COLLECTING.
legerdemain 252. MAGIC;
310. PERFORMING.
legerdemainist 252. MAGIC,
legerdemain; 310. PERFORMING,
legerdemain.
legist 239. LAW.
legitimism 185. GOVERNMENT,
legitimist.
legitimist 185. GOVERNMENT.
Leibnitzian 312. PHILOSOPHY,
Leibnizianism.
Leibnitzianism 312. PHILOSOPHY,
Leibnizianism.
Leibnizian 312. PHILOSOPHY,
Leibnizianism.
Leibnizianism 312. PHILOSOPHY.
Leiotrichan 17. ANTHROPOLOGY,
Leiotrichi; 193. HAIR, Leiotrichi.
Leiotrichi 17. ANTHROPOLOGY;
193. HAIR.
lemures 15. ANCESTORS.
lenient 28. ATTITUDES, lenity.
Leninism 94. COMMUNISM.
Leninist 94. COMMUNISM, Leninism.
Leninite 94. COMMUNISM, Leninism.

lenitive 350. REMEDIES; 350. REMEDIES, lenitive.
lenity 28. ATTITUDES.
leontiasis 122. DISEASE and ILLNESS.
Lepidoptera 64. BUTTERFLIES.
lepidopteral 64. BUTTERFLIES, *Lepidoptera.*
lepidopterist 64. BUTTERFLIES, lepidopterology; 430. ZOOLOGY, lepidopterology.
lepidopterologist 430. ZOOLOGY, lepidopterology.
lepidopterology 64. BUTTERFLIES; 430. ZOOLOGY.
lepidopterous 64. BUTTERFLIES, *Lepidoptera.*
lepraphobia 313. PHOBIAS.
leprologist 266. MEDICAL SPECIALTIES, leprology.
leprology 266. MEDICAL SPECIALTIES.
leptosomatic 51. BODY, HUMAN, leptosomy.
leptosome 51. BODY, HUMAN, leptosomy.
leptosomic 51. BODY, HUMAN, leptosomy.
leptosomy 51. BODY, HUMAN.
lesbian 209. HOMOSEXUALITY, lesbianism.
lesbianism 209. HOMOSEXUALITY.
lessee 331. PROPERTY and OWNERSHIP.
lessor 331. PROPERTY and OWNERSHIP.
lethomania 130. DRUGS; 254. MANIAS.
lettrism 409. VERSE.
leucippotomy 211. HORSES.
leucoderma 122. DISEASE and ILLNESS, leucodermia.
leucodermia 122. DISEASE and ILLNESS.
leucorrhea 122. DISEASE and ILLNESS.
leucoscope 148. EYES; 226. INSTRUMENTS.
leucosis 148. EYES.
leukemia 66. CANCER.
leukemic 66. CANCER, leukemia.
leukemoid 66. CANCER, leukemia.
leukocythemia 66. CANCER.
levanter 420. WIND.
levigate 329. PROCESSES, levigation.
levigation 329. PROCESSES.
levirate 231. JUDAISM; 231. JUDAISM, levirate.

leviratical 231. JUDAISM, levirate.
levitation 329. PROCESSES.
levity 28. ATTITUDES; 189. GRAVITY.
levoduction 242. LEFT.
levogyration 242. LEFT, sinistrogyration.
levophobia 313. PHOBIAS.
levorotation 242. LEFT; 245. LIGHT.
levorotatory 242. LEFT, levorotation; 245. LIGHT, levorotation.
levoversion 242. LEFT.
lexicographer 236. LANGUAGE, lexicography; 247. LINGUISTICS, lexicography.
lexicographic 236. LANGUAGE, lexicography; 247. LINGUISTICS, lexicography.
lexicographical 236. LANGUAGE, lexicography; 247. LINGUISTICS, lexicography.
lexicography 236. LANGUAGE; 247. LINGUISTICS.
lexicologic 247. LINGUISTICS, lexicology.
lexicological 247. LINGUISTICS, lexicology.
lexicologist 247. LINGUISTICS, lexicology.
lexicology 247. LINGUISTICS.
lexicostatistic 247. LINGUISTICS, lexicostatistics.
lexicostatistical 247. LINGUISTICS, lexicostatistics.
lexicostatistics 247. LINGUISTICS.
lexigraphic 247. LINGUISTICS, lexigraphy.
lexigraphy 247. LINGUISTICS.
lexiphanic 237. LANGUᴀɢᴇ ᴓᵼ ʏLE, lexiphanicism; 354. RHETORIC and RHETORICAL DEVICES, lexiphanicism.
lexiphanicism 237. LANGUAGE STYLE; 354. RHETORIC and RHETORICAL DEVICES.
libation 8. ALCOHOL.
liberalism 322. POLITICS; 332. PROTESTANTISM.
liberalist 322. POLITICS, liberalism; 332. PROTESTANTISM, liberalism.
liberalistic 322. POLITICS, liberalism; 332. PROTESTANTISM, liberalism.
liberationism 322. POLITICS.

liberationist 322. POLITICS, liberationism.
libertarian 173. FREEDOM, libertarianism; 312. PHILOSOPHY, libertarianism.
libertarianism 173. FREEDOM; 312. PHILOSOPHY.
liberticidal 173. FREEDOM, liberticide.
liberticide 173. FREEDOM.
libertinage 41. BEHAVIOR, libertinism.
libertine 41. BEHAVIOR, libertinism.
libertinism 41. BEHAVIOR.
libidinous 364. SEX, libido.
libido 364. SEX.
lichenologic 54. BOTANY, lichenology.
lichenological 54. BOTANY, lichenology.
lichenologist 54. BOTANY, lichenology.
lichenology 54. BOTANY.
lienteric 122. DISEASE and ILLNESS, lientery.
lientery 122. DISEASE and ILLNESS.
lighterage 131. DUES and PAYMENT.
lignification 425. WOOD.
Liguorian 69. CATHOLICISM, Liguorist.
Liguorist 69. CATHOLICISM.
Lilliputian 368. SIZE.
limner 53. BOOKS.
limniad 286. MYTHOLOGY.
limnologic 414. WATER, limnology.
limnological 414. WATER, limnology.
limnologist 179. GEOLOGY, limnology; 414. WATER, limnology.
limnology 179. GEOLOGY; 414. WATER.
limnophobia 234. LAKES; 313. PHOBIAS.
limoniad 286. MYTHOLOGY, limniad.
Lincolniana 91. COLLECTIONS and COLLECTING.
lineage 348. RELATIONSHIP.
lineament 149. FACIAL FEATURES.
lineamental 149. FACIAL FEATURES, lineament.
lingism 266. MEDICAL SPECIALTIES; 350. REMEDIES.
linguist 236. LANGUAGE.
linguistician 236. LANGUAGE, linguist.
linguistic typology 247. LINGUISTICS.
Linnaean 54. BOTANY, Linneanism.
Linnean 54. BOTANY, Linneanism.
Linneanism 54. BOTANY.
linonophobia 313. PHOBIAS.

lionism 41. BEHAVIOR; 122. DISEASE and ILLNESS.
lionize 41. BEHAVIOR, lionism.
lipogram 428. WRITING, lipography.
lipography 428. WRITING.
lipoma 122. DISEASE and ILLNESS.
lipoma sarcomatode 66. CANCER, liposarcoma.
lipomatous 122. DISEASE and ILLNESS, lipoma.
liposarcoma 66. CANCER.
lipothymia 122. DISEASE and ILLNESS.
lipothymic 122. DISEASE and ILLNESS, lipothymia.
lipothymous 122. DISEASE and ILLNESS, lipothymia.
lipothymy 122. DISEASE and ILLNESS, lipothymia.
lipotype 16. ANIMALS.
lipotypic 16. ANIMALS, lipotype.
lippitude 148. EYES.
lipsanographer 18. ANTIQUITY, lipsanography.
lipsanography 18. ANTIQUITY.
literalism 12. ALPHABET; 43. BIBLE.
literalist 12. ALPHABET, literalism; 43. BIBLE, literalism.
literaryism 237. LANGUAGE STYLE.
literati 240. LEARNING.
literation 428. WRITING.
literator 240. LEARNING.
lithiasis 122. DISEASE and ILLNESS.
lithification 179. GEOLOGY; 377. SOIL.
lithogenesy 133. EARTH; 179. GEOLOGY.
lithoglyph 141. ENGRAVING; 177. GEMS.
lithoglypher 141. ENGRAVING; 177. GEMS.
lithoglyphic 141. ENGRAVING, lithoglyph; 177. GEMS, lithoglyph.
lithoglyptic 141. ENGRAVING, lithoglyph; 141. ENGRAVING, lithoglyptics; 177. GEMS, lithoglyph; 177. GEMS, lithoglyptics.
lithoglyptics 141. ENGRAVING; 177. GEMS.
lithographer 328. PRINTING, lithography.
lithographic 328. PRINTING, lithography.
lithography 328. PRINTING.

lithoidolater 385. STONES,
lithoidolatry.
lithoidolatrous 385. STONES,
lithoidolatry.
lithoidolatry 385. STONES.
lithoidology 179. GEOLOGY.
lithologic 179. GEOLOGY, lithology.
lithological 179. GEOLOGY, lithology.
lithology 179. GEOLOGY.
lithomancy 124. DIVINATION;
385. STONES.
lithophanic 245. LIGHT, lithophany.
lithophany 245. LIGHT.
lithosphere 133. EARTH.
lithotome 179. GEOLOGY.
lithotypic 328. PRINTING, lithotypy.
lithotypy 328. PRINTING.
litigiomania 239. LAW.
litigious 41. BEHAVIOR, litigiousness.
litigiousness 41. BEHAVIOR.
litotes 354. RHETORIC and RHETORICAL
DEVICES.
liturgics 349. RELIGION.
liturgiologist 349. RELIGION,
liturgiology.
liturgiology 349. RELIGION.
liturgist 349. RELIGION, liturgics.
lixivial 329. PROCESSES, lixiviation.
lixiviation 329. PROCESSES.
lixivious 329. PROCESSES, lixiviation.
lobbyism 322. POLITICS.
lobbyist 322. POLITICS, lobbyism.
lobotomy 56. BRAIN.
localism 236. LANGUAGE.
localist 236. LANGUAGE, localism.
localistic 236. LANGUAGE, localism.
Locofoco 322. POLITICS, Locofocoism.
Locofocoism 322. POLITICS.
locoism 16. ANIMALS.
lodemanage 366. SHIPS.
lodesman 366. SHIPS.
logaoedic 409. VERSE.
logarithmomancy 124. DIVINATION;
262. MATHEMATICS.
logia 79. CHRIST; 333. PROVERBS;
422. WISDOM.
logical positivism 312. PHILOSOPHY.
logicaster 21. ARGUMENTATION.
logicism 312. PHILOSOPHY.
logistic 262. MATHEMATICS.
logistician 413. WAR, logistics.

logistics 413. WAR.
logocracy 236. LANGUAGE.
logodaedalus 236. LANGUAGE,
logodaedaly.
logodaedaly 236. LANGUAGE.
logogram 428. WRITING.
logographer 428. WRITING, logography.
logographic 428. WRITING, logogram;
428. WRITING, logography.
logography 428. WRITING.
logolatrous 236. LANGUAGE, logolatry.
logolatry 236. LANGUAGE.
logologist 337. PUZZLES, logology.
logology 337. PUZZLES.
logomach 236. LANGUAGE, logomachy.
logomacher 236. LANGUAGE,
logomachy.
logomachic 236. LANGUAGE,
logomachy.
logomachical 236. LANGUAGE,
logomachy.
logomachist 236. LANGUAGE,
logomachy.
logomachy 236. LANGUAGE.
logomancy 124. DIVINATION;
236. LANGUAGE.
logomania 236. LANGUAGE;
254. MANIAS.
logopaedia 382. SPEECH, logopedia.
logopaedic 382. SPEECH, logopedia.
logopaedics 382. SPEECH, logopedia.
logopedia 382. SPEECH.
logopedic 382. SPEECH, logopedia.
logopedics 382. SPEECH, logopedia.
logophile 236. LANGUAGE.
logophobia 236. LANGUAGE;
313. PHOBIAS.
logorrhea 236. LANGUAGE.
logorrheic 236. LANGUAGE, logorrhea.
logotherapy 334. PSYCHOLOGY.
loimographer 122. DISEASE and ILLNESS,
loimography.
loimographic 122. DISEASE and ILLNESS,
loimography.
loimographical 122. DISEASE and
ILLNESS, loimography.
loimography 122. DISEASE and ILLNESS.
loimology 122. DISEASE and ILLNESS.
Lollard 332. PROTESTANTISM,
Lollardism.
Lollardism 332. PROTESTANTISM.

Lollardry 332. PROTESTANTISM,
Lollardism.
Lollardy 332. PROTESTANTISM,
Lollardism.
Londonish 41. BEHAVIOR, **Londonism.**
Londonism 41. BEHAVIOR.
lordosis 51. BODY, HUMAN; 52. BONES.
lordotic 51. BODY, HUMAN, lordosis;
52. BONES, lordosis.
Low Churchism 349. RELIGION.
Low Churchman 349. RELIGION, Low
Churchism.
Lower Criticism 43. BIBLE.
loxodrome 178. GEOGRAPHY; 257. MAPS;
366. SHIPS.
loxodromic 178. GEOGRAPHY,
loxodrome; 257. MAPS, loxodrome;
366. SHIPS, loxodrome; 366. SHIPS,
loxodromics.
loxodromics 366. SHIPS.
loxodromy 366. SHIPS, loxodromics.
Loyalism 322. POLITICS.
Loyalist 322. POLITICS, Loyalism.
lubricious 73. CHANCE, lubricity;
261. MATERIALS, PROPERTIES OF,
lubricity; 364. SEX, lubricity.
lubricity 73. CHANCE; 261. MATERIALS,
PROPERTIES OF; 364. SEX.
lucid 237. LANGUAGE STYLE, lucidity.
lucidity 237. LANGUAGE STYLE.
lucidness 237. LANGUAGE STYLE,
lucidity.
lucubrate 240. LEARNING, lucubration.
lucubration 240. LEARNING; 426. WORK.
lucubrator 240. LEARNING,
lucubration; 426. WORK, lucubration.
Luddism 303. ORGANIZED LABOR.
Luddite 303. ORGANIZED LABOR,
Luddism.
Ludditism 303. ORGANIZED LABOR,
Luddism.
luetic 122. DISEASE and ILLNESS,
luetism.
luetism 122. DISEASE and ILLNESS.
luminarism 23. ART.
luminarist 23. ART, luminarism.
luminism 23. ART.
luminist 23. ART, luminism.
lunacy 224. INSANITY.
lunambulism 372. SLEEP.
lunambulist 372. SLEEP, lunambulism.

lunambulistic 372. SLEEP,
lunambulism.
lunatic 224. INSANITY, lunacy.
lunation 65. CALENDAR.
luster 65. CALENDAR, lustrum.
lustre 65. CALENDAR, lustrum.
lustrum 65. CALENDAR.
Lutheran 332. PROTESTANTISM,
Lutheranism.
Lutheranism 332. PROTESTANTISM.
lutulence 356. RIVERS.
lutulent 356. RIVERS, lutulence.
luxation 52. BONES.
lycanthrope 423. WOLVES.
lycanthropic 423. WOLVES,
lycanthropy.
lycanthropy 423. WOLVES.
lychnomancy 124. DIVINATION.
lycomania 254. MANIAS; 423. WOLVES.
lymphography 266. MEDICAL
SPECIALTIES.
lymphoma 66. CANCER.
lyophilization 90. COLD;
329. PROCESSES.
lypemania 224. INSANITY; 254. MANIAS;
268. MELANCHOLY.
lyrical 409. VERSE, lyricism.
lyricism 409. VERSE.
lyricist 409. VERSE, lyricism.
lyrism 284. MUSIC; 409. VERSE.
lyrist 284. MUSIC, lyrism; 409. VERSE,
lyrism.
Lysenkoism 44. BIOLOGY.
lysis 72. CELLS; 113. DECAYING;
197. HEALTH.
lyssa 313. PHOBIAS, hydrophobia;
340. RABIES, hydrophobia.
lyssophobia 224. INSANITY;
313. PHOBIAS; 340. RABIES.
lyterian 197. HEALTH, lysis.
lytic 72. CELLS, lysis; 197. HEALTH,
lysis.

M

macarism 195. HAPPINESS.
macarize 195. HAPPINESS, macarism.
macaroni 41. BEHAVIOR, macaronism.
macaronic 237. LANGUAGE STYLE,
macaronicism; 354. RHETORIC and
RHETORICAL DEVICES, macaronicism.

macaronicism 237. LANGUAGE STYLE;
354. RHETORIC and RHETORICAL
DEVICES.
macaronism 41. BEHAVIOR.
maccaroni 41. BEHAVIOR, macaronism.
maccaronism 41. BEHAVIOR,
macaronism.
Macedonian 205. HERESY,
Macedonianism.
Macedonianism 205. HERESY.
maceration 329. PROCESSES.
Machiavellian 322. POLITICS,
Machiavellianism.
Machiavellianism 322. POLITICS.
Machiavellism 322. POLITICS,
Machiavellianism.
macrobiosis 44. BIOLOGY,
macrobiotics.
macrobiotics 44. BIOLOGY.
macrobiotist 44. BIOLOGY,
macrobiotics.
macrocephalic 196. HEAD,
macrocephalism.
macrocephalism 196. HEAD.
macrocephalous 196. HEAD,
macrocephalism.
macrocephaly 196. HEAD,
macrocephalism.
macroeconomic 137. ECONOMICS,
macroeconomics.
macroeconomics 137. ECONOMICS.
macroeconomist 137. ECONOMICS,
macroeconomics.
macrograph 352. REPRESENTATION.
macrography 148. EYES; 428. WRITING.
macrolith 385. STONES.
macrology 237. LANGUAGE STYLE.
macromania 254. MANIAS; 368. SIZE.
macropicide 232. KILLING.
macroseism 134. EARTHQUAKES.
macroseismic 134. EARTHQUAKES,
macroseism.
macrosomatia 51. BODY, HUMAN;
368. SIZE.
macrosomatous 51. BODY, HUMAN,
macrosomatia; 368. SIZE,
macrosomatia.
mactation 232. KILLING; 349. RELIGION.
maculacy 119. DIRT.
maculate 119. DIRT, maculacy.
maculation 119. DIRT, maculacy.

madarosis 193. HAIR.
madisterium 193. HAIR;
226. INSTRUMENTS.
madrigal 378. SONGS and SINGING;
409. VERSE.
madrigalist 378. SONGS and SINGING,
madrigal; 409. VERSE, madrigal.
maenadic 41. BEHAVIOR, maenadism.
maenadism 41. BEHAVIOR; 424. WOMEN.
Magianism 24. ASTROLOGY.
magirics 168. FOOD and NUTRITION.
magirist 168. FOOD and NUTRITION,
magirics.
magirology 168. FOOD and NUTRITION,
magirics.
magma 130. DRUGS.
magmatic 130. DRUGS, magma.
magnetology 316. PHYSICS.
Mahayana 59. BUDDHISM,
Mahayanism.
Mahayanism 59. BUDDHISM.
Mahdism 227. ISLAM.
Mahdist 227. ISLAM, Mahdism.
maidism 28. ATTITUDES; 41. BEHAVIOR.
maieusiophobia 46. BIRTH;
313. PHOBIAS.
maieutic 233. KNOWLEDGE, maieutics.
maieutics 233. KNOWLEDGE.
Majorism 392. THEOLOGY.
Majorist 392. THEOLOGY, Majorism.
malacologist 44. BIOLOGY, malacology;
430. ZOOLOGY, malacology.
malacology 44. BIOLOGY;
430. ZOOLOGY.
Malanism 322. POLITICS.
malapropism 236. LANGUAGE.
malariologist 122. DISEASE and ILLNESS,
malariology.
malariology 122. DISEASE and ILLNESS.
malfeasance 103. CRIME.
malfeasant 103. CRIME, malfeasance.
malignant neuroma 66. CANCER,
neurosarcoma.
malism 28. ATTITUDES; 146. EVIL.
malkin 70. CATS; 352. REPRESENTATION.
malleability 261. MATERIALS,
PROPERTIES OF.
malleable 261. MATERIALS, PROPERTIES
OF, malleability.
Malthusian 137. ECONOMICS,
Malthusianism.

Malthusianism 137. ECONOMICS.
malversation 103. CRIME.
mammalogist 430. ZOOLOGY,
mammalogy.
mammalogy 430. ZOOLOGY.
Mammonism 183. GOD and GODS.
mammonism 276. MONEY.
Mammonist 183. GOD and GODS,
Mammonism.
Mammonite 183. GOD and GODS,
Mammonism.
manaism 349. RELIGION.
manaistic 349. RELIGION, manaism.
Manchesterism 137. ECONOMICS.
Manchesterist 137. ECONOMICS,
Manchesterism.
mancinism 194. HANDS.
manducation 50. BODILY FUNCTIONS.
manducatory 50. BODILY FUNCTIONS,
manducation.
manège 211. HORSES.
mangonism 319. PLANTS.
mania 150. FADS; 254. MANIAS.
maniac 254. MANIAS, mania.
maniacal 254. MANIAS, mania.
maniaphobia 224. INSANITY;
313. PHOBIAS.
Manichaeism 205. HERESY.
Manichean 205. HERESY, Manichaeism.
Manicheanism 205. HERESY,
Manichaeism.
Manicheism 205. HERESY,
Manichaeism.
Manicheistic 205. HERESY,
Manichaeism.
manikin 368. SIZE.
mannequin 368. SIZE, manikin.
Mannerism 23. ART.
mannerism 23. ART; 41. BEHAVIOR.
Mannerist 23. ART, mannerism.
mannerist 23. ART, mannerism;
41. BEHAVIOR, mannerism.
manneristic 23. ART, Mannerism;
41. BEHAVIOR, mannerism.
mannikin 368. SIZE, manikin.
manometer 49. BLOOD and BLOOD
VESSELS; 226. INSTRUMENTS.
manometric 49. BLOOD and BLOOD
VESSELS, manometer;
226. INSTRUMENTS, manometer.
manorialism 185. GOVERNMENT;
376. SOCIETY.

mansuetude 28. ATTITUDES.
mantic 124. DIVINATION, manticism.
mantichora 16. ANIMALS,
manticore.
manticism 124. DIVINATION.
manticore 16. ANIMALS.
mantle rock 179. GEOLOGY, regolith.
mantologist 124. DIVINATION,
mantology.
mantology 124. DIVINATION.
manualism 111. DEAFNESS.
manualist 111. DEAFNESS, manualism.
manumission 173. FREEDOM.
Maoism 78. CHINA; 94. COMMUNISM.
Maoist 78. CHINA, Maoism;
94. COMMUNISM, Maoism.
marasmic 51. BODY, HUMAN,
marasmus; 122. DISEASE and ILLNESS,
marasmus.
marasmus 51. BODY, HUMAN;
122. DISEASE and ILLNESS.
Marcionism 80. CHRISTIANITY.
Marcionite 80. CHRISTIANITY,
Marcionism.
mare clausum 360. SEA.
mare liberum 360. SEA.
maremma 360. SEA.
mareography 360. SEA, marigraphy.
margaritomancy 124. DIVINATION.
marginalia 53. BOOKS.
Marianism 69. CATHOLICISM.
marigraphic 360. SEA, marigraphy.
marigraphy 360. SEA.
Marinism 248. LITERARY STYLE.
Marinist 248. LITERARY STYLE,
Marinism.
Mariolater 69. CATHOLICISM,
Mariolatry; 260. MARY, Mariolatry.
Mariolatrous 69. CATHOLICISM,
Mariolatry; 260. MARY, Mariolatry.
Mariolatry 69. CATHOLICISM;
260. MARY.
Mariologist 260. MARY, Mariology.
Mariology 260. MARY.
mariticidal 232. KILLING, mariticide;
258. MARRIAGE, mariticide.
mariticide 232. KILLING;
258. MARRIAGE.
Marlovian 248. LITERARY STYLE,
Marlowism.

Marlowesque 248. LITERARY STYLE,
Marlowism.
Marlowish 248. LITERARY STYLE,
Marlowism.
Marlowism 248. LITERARY STYLE.
Maronism 69. CATHOLICISM.
Maronite 69. CATHOLICISM, Maronism.
marquetry 305. ORNAMENTATION;
425. WOOD.
marranism 69. CATHOLICISM.
marrano 69. CATHOLICISM, marranism.
marranoism 69. CATHOLICISM,
marranism.
martialism 413. WAR.
martialist 413. WAR, martialism.
martinet 41. BEHAVIOR, martinetism.
martinetish 41. BEHAVIOR,
martinetism.
martinetism 41. BEHAVIOR.
martyrdom 349. RELIGION.
martyrologe 349. RELIGION.
martyrologic 69. CATHOLICISM,
martyrology.
martyrological 69. CATHOLICISM,
martyrology.
martyrologist 69. CATHOLICISM,
martyrology.
martyrology 69. CATHOLICISM.
Marxian 94. COMMUNISM, Marxism.
Marxism 94. COMMUNISM.
Marxist 94. COMMUNISM, Marxism.
Maryolatry 69. CATHOLICISM,
Mariolatry.
Maryology 69. CATHOLICISM,
Mariolatry.
masculinism 28. ATTITUDES.
masochism 306. PAIN.
masochist 306. PAIN, masochism.
masochistic 306. PAIN, masochism.
Masorete 231. JUDAISM.
Masoretic 231. JUDAISM, Masorete.
Masoretical 231. JUDAISM, Masorete.
Masorite 231. JUDAISM, Masorete.
massotherapy 350. REMEDIES.
mastigophobia 313. PHOBIAS;
335. PUNISHMENT.
mataeologian 354. RHETORIC and
RHETORICAL DEVICES, mataeology.
mataeological 354. RHETORIC and
RHETORICAL DEVICES, mataeology.

mataeology 354. RHETORIC and
RHETORICAL DEVICES.
materialism 263. MATTER;
312. PHILOSOPHY.
materialist 263. MATTER, materialism;
312. PHILOSOPHY, materialism.
materialistic 263. MATTER,
materialism; 312. PHILOSOPHY,
materialism.
mathematic 262. MATHEMATICS,
mathematics.
mathematical 262. MATHEMATICS,
mathematics.
mathematician 262. MATHEMATICS,
mathematics.
mathematics 262. MATHEMATICS.
matriarch 185. GOVERNMENT,
matriarchy.
matriarchal 185. GOVERNMENT,
matriarchy; 281. MOTHER,
matriarchy.
matriarchate 185. GOVERNMENT;
376. SOCIETY; 424. WOMEN.
matriarchic 185. GOVERNMENT,
matriarchate; 376. SOCIETY,
matriarchate; 424. WOMEN,
matriarchate; 424. WOMEN,
matriarchy.
matriarchical 424. WOMEN,
matriarchy.
matriarchist 424. WOMEN, matriarchy.
matriarchy 185. GOVERNMENT;
281. MOTHER; 424. WOMEN.
matricentric 281. MOTHER.
matricidal 232. KILLING, matricide;
281. MOTHER, matricide;
307. PARENTS, matricide.
matricide 232. KILLING; 281. MOTHER;
307. PARENTS.
matrilineal 15. ANCESTORS, matriliny;
348. RELATIONSHIP, matriliny.
matrilinear 15. ANCESTORS, matriliny;
281. MOTHER, matriliny;
348. RELATIONSHIP, matriliny.
matriliny 15. ANCESTORS; 281. MOTHER;
348. RELATIONSHIP.
matrilocal 17. ANTHROPOLOGY,
matrilocality.
matrilocality 17. ANTHROPOLOGY.
matrimonial 258. MARRIAGE,
matrimony.

matrimony 258. MARRIAGE.
matriotism 289. NATIONALISM.
matronymic 288. NAMES; 288. NAMES, metronymic.
maturation 122. DISEASE and ILLNESS.
maturative 122. DISEASE and ILLNESS, maturation; 350. REMEDIES.
maudlin 41. BEHAVIOR, **maudlinism**.
maudlinism 41. BEHAVIOR.
mawkin 70. CATS, **malkin**.
maxim 333. PROVERBS.
maximist 333. PROVERBS, **maxim**.
mayhem 103. CRIME.
Mazdaism 183. GOD and GODS; 349. RELIGION.
Mazdaist 183. GOD and GODS, **Mazdaism**; 349. RELIGION, **Mazdaism**.
McCarthyism 322. POLITICS.
meadophile 39. BEER, **meadophily**.
meadophily 39. BEER.
mechanism 244. LIFE; 312. PHILOSOPHY.
mechanist 244. LIFE, **mechanism**; 312. PHILOSOPHY, **mechanism**.
mechanistic 244. LIFE, **mechanism**; 312. PHILOSOPHY, **mechanism**.
mechanographic 98. COPYING, **mechanography**.
mechanographist 98. COPYING, **mechanography**.
mechanography 98. COPYING.
mechanomorphic 183. GOD and GODS, **mechanomorphism**.
mechanomorphism 183. GOD and GODS.
mechanophobia 313. PHOBIAS.
mechanotherapy 350. REMEDIES.
meconism 130. DRUGS.
meconology 130. DRUGS.
meconophagism 130. DRUGS, **meconism**.
medalist 141. ENGRAVING; 210. HONORS and REGALIA.
medievalism 308. PAST.
medievalist 207. HISTORY; 308. PAST, **medievalism**.
medievalistic 308. PAST, **medievalism**.
mediocracy 185. GOVERNMENT; 376. SOCIETY.
Medism 236. LANGUAGE; 322. POLITICS.

mediumism 384. SPIRITS and SPIRITUALISM.
mediumistic 384. SPIRITS and SPIRITUALISM, **mediumism**.
medulloblastoma 66. CANCER.
megalethoscope 315. PHOTOGRAPHY.
megalith 385. STONES.
megalithic 385. STONES, **megalith**.
megalomania 187. GRANDEUR; 224. INSANITY.
megalomaniac 187. GRANDEUR, **megalomania**; 224. INSANITY, **megalomania**.
megalomaniacal 187. GRANDEUR, **megalomania**; 224. INSANITY, **megalomania**.
megalopolis 82. CITIES.
megalopolitan 82. CITIES, **megalopolitanism**.
megalopolitanism 82. CITIES.
megalopsia 148. EYES.
megalopsychy 28. ATTITUDES.
megameter 178. GEOGRAPHY; 226. INSTRUMENTS; 264. MEASUREMENT.
Megarianism 21. ARGUMENTATION.
megaseism 134. EARTHQUAKES.
megaseismic 134. EARTHQUAKES, **megaseism**.
meiosis 354. RHETORIC and RHETORICAL DEVICES.
meiotic 354. RHETORIC and RHETORICAL DEVICES, **meiosis**.
Mekhitarist 236. LANGUAGE; 249. LITERATURE.
melanaemia 49. BLOOD and BLOOD VESSELS, **melanemia**.
melancholia 224. INSANITY; 268. MELANCHOLY.
melancholiac 224. INSANITY, **melancholia**; 268. MELANCHOLY, **melancholy**.
melancholian 224. INSANITY.
melancholic 224. INSANITY, **melancholia**; 268. MELANCHOLY, **melancholia**; 268. MELANCHOLY, **melancholy**.
melancholy 268. MELANCHOLY.
melanemia 49. BLOOD and BLOOD VESSELS.

melanism 47. BLACKENING and
BLACKNESS; 95. COMPLEXION;
370. SKIN.
Melanochroic 341. RACE,
Melanochroism.
Melanochroid 341. RACE,
Melanochroism.
Melanochroism 341. RACE.
melanoma 66. CANCER.
melanopathia 122. DISEASE and ILLNESS.
melanopathy 122. DISEASE and ILLNESS,
melanopathia.
melanoscope 92. COLOR;
226. INSTRUMENTS.
melanosis 47. BLACKENING and
BLACKNESS.
melanosity 47. BLACKENING and
BLACKNESS; 148. EYES; 193. HAIR.
melanotic 47. BLACKENING and
BLACKNESS, melanosis.
melanuria 122. DISEASE and ILLNESS.
melanuric 122. DISEASE and ILLNESS,
melanuria.
meliorism 219. IMPROVEMENT;
312. PHILOSOPHY.
meliorist 219. IMPROVEMENT,
meliorism; 312. PHILOSOPHY,
meliorism.
melioristic 219. IMPROVEMENT,
meliorism; 312. PHILOSOPHY,
meliorism.
melismatics 378. SONGS and SINGING.
melissophobia 40. BEES, apiphobia;
313. PHOBIAS.
melittologist 40. BEES, melittology.
melittology 40. BEES.
melodics 284. MUSIC.
melodist 284. MUSIC.
melodrama 127. DRAMA.
melodramatic 127. DRAMA,
melodrama; 249. LITERATURE,
melodramaticism; 284. MUSIC,
melodramaticism.
melodramaticism 249. LITERATURE;
284. MUSIC.
melodramatics 41. BEHAVIOR.
melodramatist 249. LITERATURE,
melodramaticism; 284. MUSIC,
melodramaticism.
melomane 284. MUSIC, melomania.
melomania 284. MUSIC.

melomaniac 284. MUSIC, melomania.
memoirism 249. LITERATURE.
memoirist 249. LITERATURE,
memoirism.
memorabilia 91. COLLECTIONS and
COLLECTING.
memoranda 91. COLLECTIONS and
COLLECTING.
memoria technica 269. MEMORY.
mendacious 243. LIES and LYING,
mendacity.
mendacity 243. LIES and LYING.
Mendelian 44. BIOLOGY,
Mendelianism; 204. HEREDITY,
Mendelism.
Mendelianism 44. BIOLOGY.
Mendelism 204. HEREDITY.
menhir 385. STONES.
meningitophobia 313. PHOBIAS.
Menologion 65. CALENDAR, menology.
menology 65. CALENDAR; 396. TIME.
mensality 396. TIME.
Menshevik 94. COMMUNISM,
Menshevism.
Menshevism 94. COMMUNISM.
mensurate 264. MEASUREMENT,
mensuration.
mensuration 264. MEASUREMENT.
mensurational 264. MEASUREMENT,
mensuration.
mentalism 233. KNOWLEDGE;
312. PHILOSOPHY.
mentalist 233. KNOWLEDGE,
mentalism; 312. PHILOSOPHY,
mentalism.
mentalistic 233. KNOWLEDGE,
mentalism; 312. PHILOSOPHY,
mentalism.
menticide 56. BRAIN.
mentulomania 254. MANIAS; 364. SEX.
mephitic 298. ODORS, mephitis;
321. POISON, mephitism.
mephitical 298. ODORS, mephitis;
321. POISON, mephitism.
mephitis 298. ODORS.
mephitism 321. POISON.
mercantilism 137. ECONOMICS.
mercantilist 137. ECONOMICS,
mercantilism.
mercantilistic 137. ECONOMICS,
mercantilism.

merchantry 398. TRADE.
mercurial 28. ATTITUDES, mercuriality;
41. BEHAVIOR, mercuriality.
mercurialism 122. DISEASE and ILLNESS.
mercuriality 28. ATTITUDES;
41. BEHAVIOR.
mercy killing 112. DEATH, euthanasia.
meridian 25. ASTRONOMY;
178. GEOGRAPHY;
318. PLANETS.
meridional 25. ASTRONOMY, meridian;
178. GEOGRAPHY, meridian;
318. PLANETS, meridian.
merinthophobia 313. PHOBIAS.
merisis 44. BIOLOGY; 72. CELLS;
191. GROWTH.
meristic 44. BIOLOGY, merisis.
meritocracy 376. SOCIETY.
meritocrat 376. SOCIETY, meritocracy.
merogenesis 44. BIOLOGY.
merogenetic 44. BIOLOGY, merogenesis.
merology 266. MEDICAL SPECIALTIES.
merycism 122. DISEASE and ILLNESS.
mescalism 122. DISEASE and ILLNESS.
Mesmerism 215. HYPNOSIS.
mesmerist 215. HYPNOSIS, Mesmerism.
mesmerization 215. HYPNOSIS,
Mesmerism.
mesmerizer 215. HYPNOSIS, Mesmerism.
mesmeromania 215. HYPNOSIS;
254. MANIAS.
mesognathic 149. FACIAL FEATURES,
mesognathism.
mesognathism 149. FACIAL FEATURES.
mesognathous 149. FACIAL FEATURES,
mesognathism.
mesology 312. PHILOSOPHY.
mesomorphic 51. BODY, HUMAN,
mesomorphy.
mesomorphy 51. BODY, HUMAN.
mesophyte 319. PLANTS, mesophytism.
mesophytic 319. PLANTS, mesophytism.
mesophytism 319. PLANTS.
mesothelioma 66. CANCER.
Messianic 231. JUDAISM, Messianism.
Messianism 231. JUDAISM.
metabasis 122. DISEASE and ILLNESS;
354. RHETORIC and RHETORICAL
DEVICES.

metabatic 122. DISEASE and ILLNESS,
metabasis; 354. RHETORIC and
RHETORICAL DEVICES, metabasis.
metabola 122. DISEASE and ILLNESS,
metabasis; 354. RHETORIC and
RHETORICAL DEVICES, metabasis.
metabole 122. DISEASE AND ILLNESS,
metabasis; 354. RHETORIC and
RHETORICAL DEVICES, metabasis.
metabolism 74. CHANGE.
metabolize 74. CHANGE, metabolism.
metachromatism 92. COLOR.
metachronic 396. TIME, metachronism.
metachronism 396. TIME.
metaethics 145. ETHICS;
312. PHILOSOPHY.
metagalactic 25. ASTRONOMY,
metagalaxy.
metagalaxy 25. ASTRONOMY.
metage 131. DUES and PAYMENT.
metagenesis 44. BIOLOGY.
metagenetic 44. BIOLOGY, metagenesis.
metagenic 44. BIOLOGY, metagenesis.
metagnostic 285. MYSTICISM,
metagnosticism; 312. PHILOSOPHY,
metagnosticism.
metagnosticism 285. MYSTICISM;
312. PHILOSOPHY.
metagrammatism 176. GAMES;
236. LANGUAGE.
metagraphic 12. ALPHABET,
metagraphy.
metagraphy 12. ALPHABET.
metalepsis 354. RHETORIC and
RHETORICAL DEVICES.
metaleptic 354. RHETORIC and
RHETORICAL DEVICES, metalepsis.
metalinguist 247. LINGUISTICS,
metalinguistics.
metalinguistic 247. LINGUISTICS,
metalinguistics.
metalinguistical 247. LINGUISTICS,
metalinguistics.
metalinguistics 247. LINGUISTICS.
metalist 276. MONEY, metallism.
metallism 276. MONEY.
metallist 276. MONEY, metallism.
metallography 270. METALS;
328. PRINTING; 342. RADIATION.
metallophobia 313. PHOBIAS.

metallotherapy 270. METALS;
350. REMEDIES.
metallurgic 270. METALS, metallurgy.
metallurgical 270. METALS, metallurgy.
metallurgist 270. METALS, metallurgy.
metallurgy 270. METALS.
metalogic 250. LOGIC.
metalogical 250. LOGIC, metalogic.
metamathematical 262. MATHEMATICS,
metamathematics.
metamathematician
262. MATHEMATICS,
metamathematics.
metamathematics 262. MATHEMATICS.
metamorphic 74. CHANGE,
metamorphism; 74. CHANGE,
metamorphosis; 179. GEOLOGY,
metamorphism; 252. MAGIC,
metamorphosis.
metamorphism 74. CHANGE;
179. GEOLOGY.
metamorphosis 74. CHANGE;
252. MAGIC; 430. ZOOLOGY.
metamorphous 74. CHANGE,
metamorphosis; 252. MAGIC,
metamorphosis.
metaphrase 236. LANGUAGE,
metaphrasis.
metaphrasis 236. LANGUAGE.
metaphrast 236. LANGUAGE,
metaphrasis.
metaphrastic 236. LANGUAGE,
metaphrasis.
metaphrastical 236. LANGUAGE,
metaphrasis.
metaphysical 312. PHILOSOPHY,
metaphysics.
metaphysician 312. PHILOSOPHY,
metaphysics.
metaphysics 312. PHILOSOPHY.
metaphysis 74. CHANGE.
metapsychological 334. PSYCHOLOGY,
metapsychology.
metapsychology 334. PSYCHOLOGY.
metapsychosis 384. SPIRITS and
SPIRITUALISM.
metasomatism 179. GEOLOGY.
metasomatosis 179. GEOLOGY,
metasomatism.
metastasis 66. CANCER.
metastasize 66. CANCER, metastasis.

metastatic 66. CANCER, metastasis.
metempiricism 312. PHILOSOPHY.
metempirics 312. PHILOSOPHY,
metempiricism.
metempsychic 379. SOUL,
metempsychosis.
metempsychosic 379. SOUL,
metempsychosis.
metempsychosical 379. SOUL,
metempsychosis.
metempsychosis 379. SOUL.
metemptosis 65. CALENDAR.
meteorism 122. DISEASE and ILLNESS.
meteorist 271. METEORITES.
meteoritics 271. METEORITES.
meteorologic 85. CLIMATE,
meteorology; 417. WEATHER,
meteorology.
meteorological 85. CLIMATE,
meteorology; 417. WEATHER,
meteorology.
meteorologist 85. CLIMATE,
meteorology; 417. WEATHER,
meteorology.
meteorology 85. CLIMATE;
417. WEATHER.
meteoromancy 124. DIVINATION.
meteorophobia 271. METEORITES;
313. PHOBIAS.
meterage 131. DUES and PAYMENT.
Methodism 332. PROTESTANTISM.
Methodist 332. PROTESTANTISM,
Methodism.
methodological 83. CLASSIFICATION,
methodology; 250. LOGIC,
methodology; 301. ORDER and
DISORDER, methodology.
methodology 83. CLASSIFICATION;
250. LOGIC; 301. ORDER and DISORDER.
metic 190. GREECE and GREEKS.
métier 297. OCCUPATIONS.
metonym 288. NAMES, metonymy;
354. RHETORIC and RHETORICAL
DEVICES, metonymy.
metonymic 288. NAMES, metonymy;
354. RHETORIC and RHETORICAL
DEVICES, metonymy.
metonymical 288. NAMES, metonymy;
354. RHETORIC and RHETORICAL
DEVICES, metonymy.

metonymous 288. NAMES, metonymy;
354. RHETORIC and RHETORICAL
DEVICES, metonymy.
metonymy 288. NAMES; 354. RHETORIC
and RHETORICAL DEVICES.
metopomancy 124. DIVINATION;
149. FACIAL FEATURES.
metopomantic 149. FACIAL FEATURES,
metopomancy.
metoposcopic 149. FACIAL FEATURES,
metoposcopy.
metoposcopical 149. FACIAL FEATURES,
metoposcopy.
metoposcopist 149. FACIAL FEATURES,
metoposcopy.
metoposcopy 149. FACIAL FEATURES.
metrician 409. VERSE, metrics.
metricism 409. VERSE.
metricist 409. VERSE, metricism;
409. VERSE, metrics.
metrics 409. VERSE.
metrist 409. VERSE, metrics.
metrograph 226. INSTRUMENTS;
344. RAILROADS.
metrological 264. MEASUREMENT,
metrology.
metrologist 264. MEASUREMENT,
metrology.
metrology 264. MEASUREMENT.
metromania 409. VERSE.
metronome 226. INSTRUMENTS;
284. MUSIC.
metronomic 226. INSTRUMENTS,
metronome; 284. MUSIC, metronome.
metronomical 226. INSTRUMENTS,
metronome; 284. MUSIC, metronome.
metronymic 288. NAMES.
metropolitan 135. EASTERN
ORTHODOXY.
miasmology 27. ATMOSPHERE;
142. ENVIRONMENT.
Micawberish 249. LITERATURE,
Micawberism.
Micawberism 249. LITERATURE.
Michurinism 44. BIOLOGY.
Michurinist 44. BIOLOGY,
Michurinism.
Michurinite 44. BIOLOGY,
Michurinism.
microbarograph 27. ATMOSPHERE;
417. WEATHER.

microbicide 232. KILLING.
microbiologist 32. BACTERIA,
microbiology.
microbiology 32. BACTERIA.
microbiophobia 32. BACTERIA,
microphobia.
microcephalic 51. BODY, HUMAN,
microcephalism.
microcephalism 51. BODY, HUMAN.
microcephalous 51. BODY, HUMAN,
microcephalism.
microchronometer 396. TIME.
microchronometric 396. TIME,
microchronometer.
microclimatologic 85. CLIMATE,
microclimatology.
microclimatological 85. CLIMATE,
microclimatology.
microclimatologist 85. CLIMATE,
microclimatology.
microclimatology 85. CLIMATE.
microcosmography 255. MANKIND.
microeconomic 137. ECONOMICS,
microeconomics.
microeconomics 137. ECONOMICS.
microeconomist 137. ECONOMICS,
microeconomics.
micrograph 128. DRAWING; 368. SIZE,
micrography; 428. WRITING.
micrographic 368. SIZE, micrography;
428. WRITING, micrography.
micrography 128. DRAWING,
micrograph; 368. SIZE; 428. WRITING;
428. WRITING, micrograph.
microlith 179. GEOLOGY.
microlithic 179. GEOLOGY, microlith.
micrologic 83. CLASSIFICATION,
micrology.
micrological 83. CLASSIFICATION,
micrology.
micrologist 83. CLASSIFICATION,
micrology.
micrology 83. CLASSIFICATION.
micromania 254. MANIAS; 368. SIZE.
microorganism 302. ORGANISMS.
microphobia 32. BACTERIA.
microphobic 32. BACTERIA,
microphobia.
microscopical anatomy 14. ANATOMY.
microseism 134. EARTHQUAKES.

microseismic 134. EARTHQUAKES,
microseism.
microtomic 44. BIOLOGY, microtomy.
microtomist 44. BIOLOGY, microtomy.
microtomy 44. BIOLOGY.
micturate 50. BODILY FUNCTIONS,
micturition.
micturition 50. BODILY FUNCTIONS.
midwifery 46. BIRTH.
militancy 28. ATTITUDES; 413. WAR.
militant 28. ATTITUDES, militancy;
413. WAR, militancy.
militaria 91. COLLECTIONS and
COLLECTING.
militarism 322. POLITICS.
militarist 322. POLITICS, militarism.
militaristic 322. POLITICS, militarism.
militarization 413. WAR.
milksopism 41. BEHAVIOR;
386. STRENGTH and WEAKNESS.
millenarian 79. CHRIST,
millenarianism.
millenarianism 79. CHRIST; 138. END OF
THE WORLD; 392. THEOLOGY.
millenarist 79. CHRIST, millenarianism.
millennialism 79. CHRIST.
millennialist 79. CHRIST,
millennialism.
Millerism 138. END OF THE WORLD;
349. RELIGION.
Millerite 138. END OF THE WORLD,
Millerism; 349. RELIGION, Millerism.
milliner 86. CLOTHING, millinery;
297. OCCUPATIONS, millinery.
millinery 86. CLOTHING;
297. OCCUPATIONS.
mimesis 104. CRITICISM.
mimetic 104. CRITICISM, mimesis.
mimic 44. BIOLOGY, mimicry;
310. PERFORMING, mimicry.
mimical 44. BIOLOGY, mimicry;
310. PERFORMING, mimicry.
mimicism 41. BEHAVIOR.
mimicry 44. BIOLOGY;
310. PERFORMING.
mineralogic 179. GEOLOGY,
mineralogy.
mineralogical 179. GEOLOGY,
mineralogy.
mineralogist 179. GEOLOGY,
mineralogy.

mineralogy 179. GEOLOGY.
miniaturist 23. ART.
minor planets 318. PLANETS, planetoid.
minstrelsy 284. MUSIC; 378. SONGS and
SINGING.
miosis 148. EYES.
miotic 148. EYES, miosis.
misandria 28. ATTITUDES, misandry;
253. MALE, misandry.
misandry 28. ATTITUDES; 253. MALE.
misanthrope 28. ATTITUDES,
misanthropy; 255. MANKIND,
misanthropism.
misanthropic 28. ATTITUDES,
misanthropy; 255. MANKIND,
misanthropism.
misanthropism 255. MANKIND.
misanthropist 28. ATTITUDES,
misanthropy.
misanthropy 28. ATTITUDES;
255. MANKIND, misanthropism.
miscegenation 341. RACE.
miscellanea 53. BOOKS.
miscellaneous 53. BOOKS, miscellanea;
91. COLLECTIONS and COLLECTING,
miscellany.
miscellany 53. BOOKS, miscellanea;
91. COLLECTIONS and COLLECTING.
miscreancy 103. CRIME.
miscreant 103. CRIME, miscreancy.
miserabilism 312. PHILOSOPHY.
miserotica 313. PHOBIAS, errotophobia.
misfeasance 103. CRIME.
misfeasor 103. CRIME, misfeasance.
misocainea 216. IDEAS.
misogamic 258. MARRIAGE, misogamy.
misogamist 258. MARRIAGE, misogamy.
misogamy 258. MARRIAGE.
misogynism 28. ATTITUDES.
misogynist 424. WOMEN, misogyny.
misogyny 28. ATTITUDES, misogynism;
424. WOMEN.
misologist 21. ARGUMENTATION,
misology; 233. KNOWLEDGE,
misology.
misology 21. ARGUMENTATION;
233. KNOWLEDGE.
misoneism 74. CHANGE; 294. NOVELTY.
misopaedia 77. CHILDREN, misopedia.
misopaedist 77. CHILDREN, misopedia.
misopaterism 153. FATHER.

misopaterist 153. FATHER,
misopaterism.
misopedia 77. CHILDREN.
misopedist 77. CHILDREN, misopedia.
misophobia 119. DIRT; 313. PHOBIAS.
misosophist 28. ATTITUDES, misosophy.
misosophy 28. ATTITUDES.
misotheism 183. GOD and GODS.
misprision 103. CRIME.
missilery 416. WEAPONRY.
missilry 416. WEAPONRY, missilery.
mistral 420. WIND.
Mithraic 183. GOD and GODS,
Mithraism.
Mithraism 183. GOD and GODS.
Mithraist 183. GOD and GODS,
Mithraism.
mithridatism 321. POISON.
miticidal 222. INFESTATION, miticide;
232. KILLING, miticide.
miticide 222. INFESTATION;
232. KILLING.
mitosis 44. BIOLOGY; 72. CELLS.
mitotic 44. BIOLOGY, mitosis;
72. CELLS, mitosis.
mixologist 8. ALCOHOL, mixology.
mixology 8. ALCOHOL.
mnemonic 269. MEMORY, mnemonics.
mnemonics 269. MEMORY.
mnemotechnics 269. MEMORY,
mnemonics.
mobbish 275. MOB, mobbism.
mobbishly 275. MOB, mobbism.
mobbism 275. MOB.
mobocracy 105. CROWDS;
185. GOVERNMENT.
mobocrat 105. CROWDS, mobocracy;
185. GOVERNMENT.
mobocratic 105. CROWDS, mobocracy;
185. GOVERNMENT, mobocracy.
mobolatry 275. MOB.
modalism 205. HERESY.
modalist 205. HERESY, modalism.
modalistic 205. HERESY, modalism.
Modalistic Monarchianism
205. HERESY.
moderantism 322. POLITICS.
moderantist 322. POLITICS,
moderantism.
modernism 23. ART.
modernist 23. ART, modernism.

modernistic 23. ART, modernism.
modist 297. OCCUPATIONS, modiste.
modiste 297. OCCUPATIONS.
mogigraphic 428. WRITING,
mogigraphy.
mogigraphy 428. WRITING.
mogilalia 382. SPEECH.
Mohammedan 227. ISLAM,
Muhammadanism.
Mohammedanism 227. ISLAM,
Muhammadanism.
Mohism 78. CHINA; 312. PHILOSOPHY.
Mohist 78. CHINA, Mohism;
312. PHILOSOPHY, Mohism.
Molinism 69. CATHOLICISM.
Molinist 69. CATHOLICISM, Molinism.
molybdomancy 124. DIVINATION.
molysomophobia 122. DISEASE and
ILLNESS; 313. PHOBIAS.
momiology 18. ANTIQUITY.
momism 281. MOTHER.
monachal 277. MONKS and NUNS,
monachism.
monachism 277. MONKS and NUNS.
monachist 277. MONKS and NUNS,
monachism.
monad 72. CELLS.
monadal 72. CELLS, monad.
monadic 72. CELLS, monad.
monadical 72. CELLS, monad.
monadism 312. PHILOSOPHY.
monadistic 312. PHILOSOPHY,
monadism.
monandrous 258. MARRIAGE,
monandry.
monandry 258. MARRIAGE.
monarchian 80. CHRISTIANITY,
monarchianism.
monarchianism 80. CHRISTIANITY.
monarchic 185. GOVERNMENT,
monarchy.
monarchical 185. GOVERNMENT,
monarchism; 185. GOVERNMENT,
monarchy.
monarchism 185. GOVERNMENT.
monarchist 185. GOVERNMENT,
monarchism.
monarchy 185. GOVERNMENT.
monastic 80. CHRISTIANITY,
monasticism; 277. MONKS and NUNS,
monasticism.

monastical 80. CHRISTIANITY,
monasticism.
monasticism 80. CHRISTIANITY;
277. MONKS and NUNS.
monergism 205. HERESY.
monergist 205. HERESY, monergism.
monergistic 205. HERESY, monergism.
monetarism 137. ECONOMICS;
276. MONEY.
monetarist 137. ECONOMICS,
monetarism; 276. MONEY,
monetarism.
moneyocracy 185. GOVERNMENT;
276. MONEY; 376. SOCIETY.
mongolic 122. DISEASE and ILLNESS,
mongolism.
mongolism 122. DISEASE and ILLNESS.
mongrelism 125. DOGS.
mongrelization 125. DOGS,
mongrelism.
mongrely 125. DOGS, mongrelism.
monism 207. HISTORY;
233. KNOWLEDGE; 263. MATTER;
312. PHILOSOPHY.
monist 207. HISTORY, monism;
263. MATTER, monism;
312. PHILOSOPHY, monism.
monistic 207. HISTORY, monism;
263. MATTER, monism;
312. PHILOSOPHY, monism.
monistical 263. MATTER, monism;
312. PHILOSOPHY, monism.
monkery 277. MONKS and NUNS.
monoblepsia 148. EYES.
monoblepsis 148. EYES, monoblepsia.
monochromatic 92. COLOR,
monochromatism.
monochromation 148. EYES.
monochromatism 92. COLOR.
monochromist 23. ART.
monocracy 185. GOVERNMENT.
monocrotic 199. HEART, monocrotism.
monocrotism 199. HEART.
monocultural 5. AGRICULTURE,
monoculture.
monoculture 5. AGRICULTURE.
monodactylic 161. FINGERS and TOES,
monodactyly.
monodactylous 161. FINGERS and TOES,
monodactyly.
monodactyly 161. FINGERS and TOES.

monodiabolism 117. DEVIL.
monodrama 127. DRAMA.
monodramatic 127. DRAMA,
monodrama.
monody 284. MUSIC, homophony.
monoecious 364. SEX, monoecism.
monoecism 364. SEX.
monogamous 258. MARRIAGE,
monogamy.
monogamy 258. MARRIAGE.
monogenesis 44. BIOLOGY;
255. MANKIND, monogenism;
302. ORGANISMS; 304. ORIGINS,
monogenism; 341. RACE.
monogenetic 44. BIOLOGY,
monogenesis; 302. ORGANISMS,
monogenesis.
monogenism 255. MANKIND;
304. ORIGINS; 341. RACE.
monogenist 255. MANKIND,
monogenism; 304. ORIGINS,
monogenism; 341. RACE,
monogenism.
monogenistic 255. MANKIND,
monogenism; 304. ORIGINS,
monogenism; 341. RACE,
monogenism.
monogeny 255. MANKIND,
monogenism; 304. ORIGINS,
monogenism.
monoglot 236. LANGUAGE.
monogram 128. DRAWING;
428. WRITING.
monogrammatic 428. WRITING,
monogram.
monogrammatical 428. WRITING,
monogram.
monograph 53. BOOKS.
monographer 53. BOOKS, monograph.
monographic 53. BOOKS, monograph.
monographical 53. BOOKS,
monograph.
monography 53. BOOKS, monograph;
128. DRAWING, monogram.
monoideism 215. HYPNOSIS.
monolatry 183. GOD and GODS.
monolith 23. ART; 385. STONES.
monolithic 23. ART, monolith;
385. STONES, monolith.
monologic 362. SELF, monology.
monological 362. SELF, monology.

monologist 362. SELF, **monology.**
monologue 362. SELF.
monology 310. PERFORMING; 362. SELF.
monomachia 96. CONFLICT,
   monomachy; 413. WAR, **monomachy.**
monomachist 96. CONFLICT,
   monomachy; 413. WAR, **monomachy.**
monomachy 96. CONFLICT; 413. WAR.
monomania 254. MANIAS.
monometallism 276. MONEY.
monometallist 276. MONEY,
   monometallism.
monopathophobia 313. PHOBIAS.
monopathy 122. DISEASE and ILLNESS.
monophagism 168. FOOD and
   NUTRITION.
monophagous 168. FOOD and
   NUTRITION, **monophagism.**
monophagy 168. FOOD and NUTRITION,
   monophagism.
monophobia 313. PHOBIAS; 362. SELF;
   362. SELF, **autophobia.**
monophonic 284. MUSIC, **monophony.**
monophony 284. MUSIC; 284. MUSIC,
   homophony.
Monophysite 79. CHRIST,
   Monophysitism.
Monophysitic 79. CHRIST,
   Monophysitism.
Monophysitical 79. CHRIST,
   Monophysitism.
Monophysitism 79. CHRIST.
monopodic 409. VERSE, **monopody.**
monopody 409. VERSE.
monopolism 398. TRADE.
monopolist 398. TRADE, **monopolism;**
   398. TRADE, **monopoly.**
monopolistic 398. TRADE, **monopolism;**
   398. TRADE, **monopoly.**
monopoly 398. TRADE.
monopsonist 398. TRADE, **monopsony.**
monopsonistic 398. TRADE,
   monopsony.
monopsony 398. TRADE.
monopsychic 379. SOUL,
   monopsychism.
monopsychical 379. SOUL,
   monopsychism.
monopsychism 379. SOUL.
monopus 157. FEET and LEGS.

monosyllabic 236. LANGUAGE,
   monosyllabism.
monosyllabism 236. LANGUAGE.
monosyllable 236. LANGUAGE,
   monosyllabism.
monosymmetric 44. BIOLOGY,
   monosymmetry; 316. PHYSICS,
   monosymmetry; 389. SYMMETRY,
   monosymmetry.
monosymmetrical 44. BIOLOGY,
   monosymmetry; 316. PHYSICS,
   monosymmetry; 389. SYMMETRY,
   monosymmetry.
monosymmetry 44. BIOLOGY;
   316. PHYSICS; 389. SYMMETRY.
monotheism 183. GOD and GODS.
monotheist 183. GOD and GODS,
   monotheism.
Monothelete 79. CHRIST,
   Monothelitism.
Monotheletic 79. CHRIST,
   Monothelitism.
Monotheletism 79. CHRIST,
   Monothelitism.
Monothelism 79. CHRIST,
   Monothelitism.
Monothelite 79. CHRIST,
   Monothelitism.
Monothelitic 79. CHRIST,
   Monothelitism.
Monothelitism 79. CHRIST.
monotonous 380. SOUND, **monotony.**
monotony 380. SOUND.
monstrosity 278. MONSTERS.
monstrous 278. MONSTERS, **monstrosity.**
Montanism 205. HERESY.
Montanist 205. HERESY, **Montanism.**
monumentalism 368. SIZE.
monumentality 368. SIZE,
   monumentalism.
moralism 145. ETHICS.
moralist 145. ETHICS, **moralism.**
moralistic 145. ETHICS, **moralism.**
morbid 28. ATTITUDES, **morbidity;**
   279. MOODS, **morbidity.**
morbidity 28. ATTITUDES; 279. MOODS.
mordacity 92. COLOR, **mordancy;**
   213. HUMOR, **mordancy;**
   329. PROCESSES, **mordancy.**

mordancy 28. ATTITUDES; 92. COLOR;
213. HUMOR; 279. MOODS;
329. PROCESSES.
mordant 28. ATTITUDES, mordancy;
92. COLOR, mordancy; 213. HUMOR,
mordancy; 279. MOODS, mordancy;
329. PROCESSES, mordancy.
Moresque 23. ART; 23. ART, Moresque.
morganatic 258. MARRIAGE.
moribund 112. DEATH, moribundity.
moribundity 112. DEATH.
Mormon 332. PROTESTANTISM,
Mormonism.
Mormonism 332. PROTESTANTISM.
morologist 236. LANGUAGE, morology.
morology 236. LANGUAGE.
moromancy 124. DIVINATION.
moronic 217. IDIOCY, moronism.
moronism 217. IDIOCY.
morose 28. ATTITUDES, morosity;
279. MOODS, morosity.
morosity 28. ATTITUDES; 279. MOODS.
morphemicist 247. LINGUISTICS,
morphemics.
morphemics 247. LINGUISTICS.
morphinism 130. DRUGS.
morphinist 130. DRUGS, morphinism.
morphinmania 130. DRUGS,
morphiomania.
morphiomania 130. DRUGS.
morphogenesis 170. FORM.
morphogenetic 170. FORM,
morphogenesis.
morphogeny 170. FORM,
morphogenesis.
morphographer 170. FORM,
morphography.
morphographic 170. FORM,
morphography.
morphography 170. FORM.
morphologic 16. ANIMALS,
morphology; 44. BIOLOGY,
morphology; 170. FORM,
morphology.
morphological 16. ANIMALS,
morphology; 44. BIOLOGY,
morphology; 170. FORM,
morphology; 247. LINGUISTICS,
morphology.

morphologist 16. ANIMALS,
morphology; 44. BIOLOGY,
morphology; 170. FORM,
morphology; 247. LINGUISTICS,
morphology.
morphology 16. ANIMALS; 44. BIOLOGY;
170. FORM; 247. LINGUISTICS.
morphometrical 170. FORM,
morphometry.
morphometry 170. FORM.
morphonomic 170. FORM,
morphonomy.
morphonomy 170. FORM.
morphophonemic 247. LINGUISTICS,
morphophonemics.
morphophonemicist 247. LINGUISTICS,
morphophonemics.
morphophonemics 247. LINGUISTICS.
morphophyly 170. FORM.
mortalism 312. PHILOSOPHY.
mortalist 312. PHILOSOPHY, mortalism.
mortgage 160. FINANCE; 331. PROPERTY
and OWNERSHIP.
mortgagee 331. PROPERTY and
OWNERSHIP.
mortgagor 331. PROPERTY and
OWNERSHIP.
mortmain 331. PROPERTY and
OWNERSHIP.
Mosaic 231. JUDAISM, Mosaism.
mosaicist 297. OCCUPATIONS.
Mosaicity 231. JUDAISM.
Mosaism 231. JUDAISM.
Mosaist 231. JUDAISM, Mosaism.
mosaist 297. OCCUPATIONS, mosaicist.
motorphobia 313. PHOBIAS.
mouchard 103. CRIME, mouchardism.
mouchardism 103. CRIME.
mountebankery 41. BEHAVIOR,
mountebankism; 243. LIES and LYING,
mountebankism.
mountebankism 41. BEHAVIOR;
243. LIES and LYING.
muckerism 41. BEHAVIOR.
mugwump 322. POLITICS,
mugwumpism.
mugwumpery 322. POLITICS,
mugwumpism.
mugwumpian 322. POLITICS,
mugwumpism.

mugwumpish 322. POLITICS, mugwumpism.
mugwumpism 322. POLITICS.
Muhammadan 227. ISLAM, Muhammadanism.
Muhammadanism 227. ISLAM.
multilateralism 137. ECONOMICS.
multiopoly 398. TRADE.
multiopsonist 398. TRADE, multiopsony.
multiopsonistic 398. TRADE, multiopsony.
multiopsony 398. TRADE.
multiparity 46. BIRTH.
multiparous 46. BIRTH, multiparity.
multitudinal 322. POLITICS, multitudinism.
multitudinism 322. POLITICS.
multitudinist 322. POLITICS, multitudinism.
mummery 310. PERFORMING.
mumps 122. DISEASE and ILLNESS, parotitis.
munichism 28. ATTITUDES.
municipalism 185. GOVERNMENT.
municipalist 185. GOVERNMENT, municipalism.
munificence 28. ATTITUDES.
munificent 28. ATTITUDES, munificence.
muscologist 54. BOTANY, muscology.
muscology 54. BOTANY.
museographer 83. CLASSIFICATION, museography.
museographist 83. CLASSIFICATION, museography.
museography 83. CLASSIFICATION.
museologist 91. COLLECTIONS and COLLECTING, museology.
museology 91. COLLECTIONS and COLLECTING.
musicography 284. MUSIC.
musicological 284. MUSIC, musicology.
musicologist 284. MUSIC, musicology.
musicology 284. MUSIC.
musicomania 254. MANIAS; 284. MUSIC.
musicophile 284. MUSIC; 311. -PHILE, -PHILIA, -PHILY.
musicophobia 284. MUSIC; 313. PHOBIAS.
musketry 416. WEAPONRY.
musomania 16. ANIMALS; 254. MANIAS.

musophobia 16. ANIMALS; 119. DIRT, misophobia; 313. PHOBIAS; 313. PHOBIAS, misophobia.
mutacism 236. LANGUAGE; 428. WRITING.
mutism 382. SPEECH.
mutoscope 226. INSTRUMENTS; 315. PHOTOGRAPHY.
mutualism 41. BEHAVIOR; 44. BIOLOGY.
mutualist 41. BEHAVIOR, mutualism.
myalism 349. RELIGION.
mycetism 321. POISON.
mycetismus 321. POISON, mycetism.
mycolatry 319. PLANTS.
mycologic 54. BOTANY, mycology.
mycological 54. BOTANY, mycology.
mycologist 54. BOTANY, mycology.
mycology 54. BOTANY.
mydriasis 148. EYES.
mydriatic 148. EYES, mydriasis.
myiasis 122. DISEASE and ILLNESS.
myoatrophy 51. BODY, HUMAN; 113. DECAYING; 386. STRENGTH and WEAKNESS.
myocarditis 199. HEART.
myographic 14. ANATOMY, myography.
myography 14. ANATOMY.
myologic 14. ANATOMY, myology.
myology 14. ANATOMY.
myomancy 124. DIVINATION.
myopia 148. EYES.
myopic 148. EYES, myopia.
myosis 148. EYES; 148. EYES, miosis.
myotic 148. EYES, miosis; 148. EYES, myosis.
myotonia 51. BODY, HUMAN.
myotonic 51. BODY, HUMAN, myotonia.
myriarch 190. GREECE and GREEKS.
myriarchy 185. GOVERNMENT.
myriologic 112. DEATH, myriologue; 378. SONGS and SINGING, myriologue.
myriological 112. DEATH, myriologue; 378. SONGS and SINGING, myriologue.
myriologist 112. DEATH, myriologue; 378. SONGS and SINGING, myriologue.
myriologue 112. DEATH; 378. SONGS and SINGING.
myriorama 352. REPRESENTATION.
myrioscope 226. INSTRUMENTS.
myriotheism 183. GOD and GODS.
myrmecologic 19. ANTS, myrmecology.

myrmecological 19. ANTS,
myrmecology.
myrmecologist 19. ANTS,
myrmecology.
myrmecology 19. ANTS; 225. INSECTS.
myrmecophile 19. ANTS,
myrmecophilism.
myrmecophilism 19. ANTS.
myrmecophilous 19. ANTS,
myrmecophilism.
myrmecophily 19. ANTS,
myrmecophilism.
myrmecophobia 19. ANTS.
myrmecophobic 19. ANTS,
myrmecophobia.
myrmidon 10. ALLEGIANCE.
myrmidonian 10. ALLEGIANCE,
myrmidon.
myropolist 297. OCCUPATIONS;
298. ODORS.
mysophilia 119. DIRT; 311. -PHILE,
-PHILIA, -PHILY.
mysophobia 84. CLEANLINESS;
119. DIRT, misophobia; 313. PHOBIAS;
313. PHOBIAS, misophobia.
mystagogic 285. MYSTICISM,
mystagogics.
mystagogical 285. MYSTICISM,
mystagogics.
mystagogics 285. MYSTICISM.
mystagogue 285. MYSTICISM;
285. MYSTICISM, mystagogics.
mystagogy 285. MYSTICISM,
mystagogics.
mysticism 349. RELIGION.
mytacism 236. LANGUAGE;
428. WRITING.
mythic criticism 104. CRITICISM.
mythicism 286. MYTHOLOGY.
mythicist 286. MYTHOLOGY.
mythoclast 286. MYTHOLOGY.
mythoclastic 286. MYTHOLOGY,
mythoclast.
mythogenesis 286. MYTHOLOGY.
mythogenetic 286. MYTHOLOGY,
mythogenesis.
mythogeny 286. MYTHOLOGY,
mythogenesis.
mythographer 286. MYTHOLOGY,
mythography.

mythographist 286. MYTHOLOGY,
mythography.
mythography 286. MYTHOLOGY.
mythologem 286. MYTHOLOGY.
mythologer 286. MYTHOLOGY.
mythological 286. MYTHOLOGY,
mythology.
mythologist 286. MYTHOLOGY,
mythology.
mythology 286. MYTHOLOGY.
mythomania 243. LIES and LYING.
mythophobia 243. LIES and LYING;
313. PHOBIAS.
mythopoeic 286. MYTHOLOGY,
mythopoesis.
mythopoeist 286. MYTHOLOGY,
mythopoesis.
mythopoesis 286. MYTHOLOGY.
mythos 286. MYTHOLOGY.
mythus 286. MYTHOLOGY, mythos.
myxedema 122. DISEASE and ILLNESS.
myxedematous 122. DISEASE and
ILLNESS, myxedema.
myxedoematous 122. DISEASE and
ILLNESS, myxedema.
myxochondroma 122. DISEASE and
ILLNESS.
myxochondromatous 122. DISEASE and
ILLNESS, myxochondroma.
myxodermia 122. DISEASE and ILLNESS.
myxoedema 122. DISEASE and ILLNESS,
myxedema.
myxolipoma 122. DISEASE and ILLNESS.
myxoma 122. DISEASE and ILLNESS.
myxomatosis 122. DISEASE and ILLNESS.
myxomatous 122. DISEASE and ILLNESS,
myxoma.
myxophobia 84. CLEANLINESS;
313. PHOBIAS.

N

nabobism 276. MONEY.
naiad 286. MYTHOLOGY.
naive realism 312. PHILOSOPHY.
namby-pamby 28. ATTITUDES, namby-
pambyism; 41. BEHAVIOR, namby-
pambyism.
namby-pambyism 28. ATTITUDES;
41. BEHAVIOR.
nanism 368. SIZE.

naological 60. BUILDINGS, **naology.**
naology 60. BUILDINGS.
napery 118. DINING.
Napoleonic 185. GOVERNMENT,
Napoleonism.
Napoleonism 185. GOVERNMENT.
Napoleonist 185. GOVERNMENT,
Napoleonism.
naprapath 266. MEDICAL SPECIALTIES,
naprapathy; 350. REMEDIES,
naprapathy.
naprapathy 266. MEDICAL SPECIALTIES;
350. REMEDIES.
narcism 362. SELF, **narcissism.**
narcissism 362. SELF.
narcissist 362. SELF, **narcissism.**
narcissistic 362. SELF, **narcissism.**
narcist 362. SELF, **narcissism.**
narcistic 362. SELF, **narcissism.**
narcoanalysis 372. SLEEP.
narcohypnia 372. SLEEP.
narcohypnosis 130. DRUGS;
215. HYPNOSIS.
narcolepsy 122. DISEASE and ILLNESS;
372. SLEEP.
narcolept 372. SLEEP, **narcolepsy.**
narcoleptic 122. DISEASE and ILLNESS,
narcolepsy; 372. SLEEP, **narcolepsy.**
narcoma 130. DRUGS, **narcosis.**
narcomania 130. DRUGS.
narcosis 130. DRUGS.
narcosynthesis 130. DRUGS;
224. INSANITY.
narcotherapist 372. SLEEP,
narcotherapy.
narcotherapy 372. SLEEP.
narcoticism 130. DRUGS.
narcotism 130. DRUGS, **narcoticism.**
nasalism 247. LINGUISTICS;
330. PRONUNCIATION.
nasality 247. LINGUISTICS, **nasalism;**
330. PRONUNCIATION, **nasalism.**
nasological 293. NOSE, **nasology.**
nasologist 293. NOSE, **nasology.**
nasology 293. NOSE.
nasoscope 293. NOSE.
nasoscopic 293. NOSE, **nasoscope.**
natation 26. ATHLETICS.
natator 26. ATHLETICS.
natatorial 26. ATHLETICS, **natation.**
natatorium 26. ATHLETICS.
natatory 26. ATHLETICS, **natation.**

nationalism 289. NATIONALISM.
nationalist 289. NATIONALISM,
nationalism.
nationalistic 289. NATIONALISM,
nationalism.
nationalization 137. ECONOMICS.
nativism 169. FOREIGNERS;
289. NATIONALISM; 312. PHILOSOPHY.
nativist 169. FOREIGNERS, **nativism;**
289. NATIONALISM, **nativism;**
312. PHILOSOPHY, **nativism.**
nativistic 169. FOREIGNERS, **nativism;**
289. NATIONALISM, **nativism;**
312. PHILOSOPHY, **nativism.**
nativity 24. ASTROLOGY; 46. BIRTH.
Naturalism 23. ART.
Naturalist 23. ART, **Naturalism.**
Naturalistic 23. ART, **Naturalism.**
naturalistic humanism 255. MANKIND,
humanism.
naturalization 169. FOREIGNERS.
natural realism 312. PHILOSOPHY.
naturism 287. NAKEDNESS.
naturist 287. NAKEDNESS, **naturism.**
naturistic 287. NAKEDNESS, **naturism.**
naturopath 350. REMEDIES,
naturopathism.
naturopathic 350. REMEDIES,
naturopathism.
naturopathism 350. REMEDIES.
naturopathy 350. REMEDIES,
naturopathism.
naumachia 366. SHIPS; 413. WAR.
naumachy 366. SHIPS, **naumachia;**
413. WAR, **naumachia.**
naupathia 366. SHIPS; 399. TRAVEL.
nauropometer 226. INSTRUMENTS;
366. SHIPS.
nauscopy 123. DISTANCE; 148. EYES;
366. SHIPS.
navalism 413. WAR.
navalist 413. WAR, **navalism.**
Nazi 152. FASCISM, **Nazism;**
322. POLITICS, **Nazism.**
Naziism 322. POLITICS, **Nazism.**
Nazism 152. FASCISM; 322. POLITICS.
nealogic 16. ANIMALS, **nealogy.**
nealogy 16. ANIMALS.
neanderthal 28. ATTITUDES,
neanderthalism.
neanderthalism 28. ATTITUDES.

necessitarian 312. PHILOSOPHY,
necessitarianism.
necessitarianism 312. PHILOSOPHY.
necrolatry 112. DEATH.
necrologist 112. DEATH, necrology.
necrology 112. DEATH.
necromancer 112. DEATH, necromancy;
124. DIVINATION, necromancy.
necromancy 112. DEATH;
124. DIVINATION.
necromania 99. CORPSES; 112. DEATH;
254. MANIAS.
necromaniac 99. CORPSES, necromania.
necromant 112. DEATH, necromancy;
124. DIVINATION, necromancy.
necromantic 112. DEATH, necromancy;
124. DIVINATION, necromancy.
necromimesis 112. DEATH.
necrophage 99. CORPSES, necrophagy.
necrophagous 99. CORPSES,
necrophagy.
necrophagy 99. CORPSES.
necrophile 99. CORPSES, necrophilia;
112. DEATH, necrophilia; 311. -PHILE,
-PHILIA, -PHILY, necrophilia;
364. SEX, necrophilia.
necrophilia 99. CORPSES; 112. DEATH;
311. -PHILE, -PHILIA, -PHILY; 364. SEX.
necrophiliac 99. CORPSES, necrophilia;
311. -PHILE, -PHILIA, -PHILY,
necrophilia.
necrophilic 364. SEX, necrophilia.
necrophilism 99. CORPSES, necrophilia;
112. DEATH, necrophilia; 311. -PHILE,
-PHILIA, -PHILY, necrophilia.
necrophily 99. CORPSES, necrophilia;
311. -PHILE, -PHILIA, -PHILY,
necrophilia.
necrophobe 99. CORPSES, necrophobia.
necrophobia 99. CORPSES; 112. DEATH;
313. PHOBIAS.
necrophobic 99. CORPSES,
necrophobia.
necropolis 63. BURIAL.
necropsy 99. CORPSES.
necrosadism 364. SEX.
necrosadist 364. SEX, necrosadism.
necrosis 51. BODY, HUMAN; 112. DEATH;
113. DECAYING.

necrotic 51. BODY, HUMAN, necrosis;
112. DEATH, necrosis; 113. DECAYING,
necrosis.
necrotomic 99. CORPSES, necrotomy.
necrotomist 99. CORPSES, necrotomy.
necrotomy 99. CORPSES.
negativism 28. ATTITUDES;
312. PHILOSOPHY.
negativist 28. ATTITUDES, negativism;
312. PHILOSOPHY, negativism.
negativistic 28. ATTITUDES, negativism;
312. PHILOSOPHY, negativism.
negotiant 4. AGREEMENT, negotiation.
negotiation 4. AGREEMENT.
negotiator 4. AGREEMENT, negotiation.
negotriatrix 4. AGREEMENT,
negotiation.
Negroism 41. BEHAVIOR.
negrophile 322. POLITICS,
negrophilism.
negrophilism 322. POLITICS.
negrophilist 322. POLITICS,
negrophilism.
negrophobia 313. PHOBIAS.
nemophilist 311. -PHILE, -PHILIA,
-PHILY, nemophily; 401. TREES,
nemophily.
nemophilous 311. -PHILE, -PHILIA,
-PHILY, nemophily; 401. TREES,
nemophily.
nemophily 311. -PHILE, -PHILIA, -PHILY;
401. TREES.
Neo-Classic 23. ART, Neo-Classicism.
Neo-Classical 23. ART, Neo-Classicism.
Neo-Classicism 23. ART.
Neo-Classicist 23. ART, Neo-Classicism.
neocolonial 322. POLITICS,
neocolonialism.
neocolonialism 322. POLITICS.
neocolonialist 322. POLITICS,
neocolonialism.
neoconservatism 28. ATTITUDES;
322. POLITICS.
neoconservative 28. ATTITUDES,
neoconservatism; 322. POLITICS,
neoconservatism.
neocracy 185. GOVERNMENT.
Neo-Darwinian 147. EVOLUTION, Neo-
Darwinism.
Neo-Darwinism 147. EVOLUTION.

Neo-Darwinist 147. EVOLUTION, Neo-
Darwinism.
Neo-Expressionism 20. ARCHITECTURE.
Neo-Facist 152. FASCISM, Neo-Fascism.
Neo-Fascism 152. FASCISM.
neogamist 258. MARRIAGE.
neography 428. WRITING.
Neo-Hellenism 23. ART.
Neo-Hellenist 23. ART, Neo-Hellenism.
Neo-Hellenistic 23. ART, Neo-
Hellenism.
Neo-Impressionism 23. ART.
neolalia 334. PSYCHOLOGY; 382. SPEECH.
Neo-Lamarckian 147. EVOLUTION,
Neo-Lamarckism.
Neo-Lamarckism 147. EVOLUTION.
neolater 294. NOVELTY, neolatry.
neolatry 294. NOVELTY.
neoliberalism 322. POLITICS.
neolith 385. STONES.
neologian 236. LANGUAGE, neologism.
neologism 236. LANGUAGE;
392. THEOLOGY.
neologist 236. LANGUAGE, neologism;
392. THEOLOGY, neology.
neologistic 236. LANGUAGE, neologism.
neologistical 236. LANGUAGE,
neologism.
neology 236. LANGUAGE, neologism;
392. THEOLOGY.
Neo-Malthusian 137. ECONOMICS, Neo-
Malthusianism.
Neo-Malthusianism 137. ECONOMICS.
neomenia 65. CALENDAR.
neonatologist 266. MEDICAL
SPECIALTIES, neonatology.
neonatology 266. MEDICAL
SPECIALTIES.
neontologic 44. BIOLOGY, neontology.
neontological 44. BIOLOGY,
neontology.
neontologist 44. BIOLOGY, neontology.
neontology 44. BIOLOGY.
neoorthodox 332. PROTESTANTISM,
neoorthodoxy.
neoorthodoxy 332. PROTESTANTISM.
neopagan 349. RELIGION,
neopaganism.
neopaganism 349. RELIGION.
neopaganist 349. RELIGION,
neopaganism.

neophilism 294. NOVELTY.
neophobia 74. CHANGE; 294. NOVELTY;
313. PHOBIAS.
neophrasis 236. LANGUAGE.
neophrastic 236. LANGUAGE,
neophrasis.
neophyte 97. CONVERT, neophytism.
neophytic 97. CONVERT, neophytism.
neophytism 97. CONVERT.
neoplasia 51. BODY, HUMAN;
66. CANCER; 191. GROWTH.
neoplasm 51. BODY, HUMAN;
66. CANCER; 191. GROWTH.
neoplastic 51. BODY, HUMAN, neoplasia;
51. BODY, HUMAN, neoplasm;
66. CANCER, neoplasia; 66. CANCER,
neoplasm; 191. GROWTH, neoplasia;
191. GROWTH, neoplasm.
Neo-Plasticism 23. ART.
neoplasty 388. SURGERY.
Neoplatonic 312. PHILOSOPHY,
Neoplatonism.
Neoplatonism 312. PHILOSOPHY.
Neoplatonist 312. PHILOSOPHY,
Neoplatonism.
neorama 352. REPRESENTATION.
Neo-Scholastic 392. THEOLOGY, Neo-
Scholasticism.
Neo-Scholasticism 392. THEOLOGY.
neossology 45. BIRDS.
neotenous 225. INSECTS, neoteny.
neoteny 225. INSECTS.
neoteric 216. IDEAS.
neoterism 236. LANGUAGE.
neoterist 236. LANGUAGE, neoterism;
294. NOVELTY.
neo-Thomism 312. PHILOSOPHY.
neo-Thomist 312. PHILOSOPHY, neo-
Thomism.
nephalism 8. ALCOHOL.
nephalist 8. ALCOHOL, nephalism.
nephalistic 8. ALCOHOL, nephalism.
nephelognosy 87. CLOUDS;
124. DIVINATION.
nepheloscope 87. CLOUDS.
nephogram 87. CLOUDS.
nephograph 87. CLOUDS;
315. PHOTOGRAPHY.
nephologic 87. CLOUDS, nephology.
nephological 87. CLOUDS, nephology.

nephologist 87. CLOUDS, nephology; 417. WEATHER, nephology.
nephology 87. CLOUDS; 417. WEATHER.
nephophobia 87. CLOUDS; 313. PHOBIAS.
nephritic 122. DISEASE and ILLNESS, nephritis.
nephritical 122. DISEASE and ILLNESS, nephritis.
nephritis 122. DISEASE and ILLNESS.
nephrologist 266. MEDICAL SPECIALTIES, nephrology.
nephrology 266. MEDICAL SPECIALTIES.
nepotic 155. FAVORITISM, nepotism.
nepotism 155. FAVORITISM.
nepotist 155. FAVORITISM, nepotism.
Neptunian 183. GOD and GODS, Neptunianism.
Neptunianism 183. GOD and GODS.
neptunism 179. GEOLOGY.
neptunist 179. GEOLOGY, neptunism.
nerterology 112. DEATH.
Nestorian 79. CHRIST, Nestorianism.
Nestorianism 79. CHRIST.
neuralgia 291. NERVES.
neuralgic 291. NERVES, neuralgia.
neurasthenia 291. NERVES.
neurasthenic 291. NERVES, neurasthenia.
neurinoma 66. CANCER.
neurism 291. NERVES.
neuritic 291. NERVES, neuritis.
neuritis 291. NERVES.
neuroanatomical 291. NERVES, neuroanatomy.
neuroanatomy 291. NERVES.
neuroblastoma 66. CANCER.
neurographic 291. NERVES, neurography.
neurographical 291. NERVES, neurography.
neurography 291. NERVES.
neurological 291. NERVES, neurology.
neurologist 266. MEDICAL SPECIALTIES; 291. NERVES, neurology.
neurology 291. NERVES.
neuromechanism 266. MEDICAL SPECIALTIES.
neuromimesis 291. NERVES.
neuromimetic 291. NERVES, neuromimesis.
neuropath 266. MEDICAL SPECIALTIES.

neuropathic 291. NERVES, neuropathy.
neuropathist 266. MEDICAL SPECIALTIES, neuropath; 291. NERVES, neuropathy.
neuropathologic 266. MEDICAL SPECIALTIES, neuropathology; 291. NERVES, neuropathology.
neuropathological 266. MEDICAL SPECIALTIES, neuropathology; 291. NERVES, neuropathology.
neuropathologist 266. MEDICAL SPECIALTIES, neuropathology; 291. NERVES, neuropathology.
neuropathology 266. MEDICAL SPECIALTIES; 291. NERVES.
neuropathy 291. NERVES.
neuropsychiatric 291. NERVES, neuropsychiatry.
neuropsychiatrist 291. NERVES, neuropsychiatry.
neuropsychiatry 291. NERVES.
neuropterology 225. INSECTS.
neurosarcoma 66. CANCER.
neurosis 291. NERVES; 334. PSYCHOLOGY.
neurotic 291. NERVES, neurosis; 334. PSYCHOLOGY, neurosis.
neuroticism 334. PSYCHOLOGY.
neurotomist 291. NERVES, neurotomy.
neurotomy 291. NERVES.
neutral 96. CONFLICT, neutrality; 413. WAR, neutrality.
neutralism 322. POLITICS.
neutralist 322. POLITICS, neutralism.
neutrality 96. CONFLICT; 413. WAR.
neutrophile 72. CELLS.
neutrophilous 72. CELLS, neutrophile.
New Critic 104. CRITICISM, New Criticism.
New Criticism 104. CRITICISM.
New Formalism 20. ARCHITECTURE.
new humanism 104. CRITICISM.
new humanist 104. CRITICISM, new humanism.
New Realism 23. ART.
newspaperese 237. LANGUAGE STYLE; 265. MEDIA; 265. MEDIA, journalese.
New Yorkerism 236. LANGUAGE.
nice-nelly 28. ATTITUDES, nice-nellyism.

nice-nellyism 28. ATTITUDES;
236. LANGUAGE; 354. RHETORIC and
RHETORICAL DEVICES.
nickelodeon 159. FILMS; 284. MUSIC;
314. PHONOGRAPH RECORDS.
nicotinism 122. DISEASE and ILLNESS.
nictation 148. EYES, nictitation.
nictitation 148. EYES.
nidification 45. BIRDS.
nidologist 45. BIRDS, nidology.
nidology 45. BIRDS.
Nietzschean 312. PHILOSOPHY,
Nietzscheism.
Nietzscheanism 312. PHILOSOPHY,
Nietzscheism.
Nietzscheism 312. PHILOSOPHY.
nigrescence 47. BLACKENING and
BLACKNESS.
nigrescent 47. BLACKENING and
BLACKNESS, nigrescence.
nigritude 47. BLACKENING and
BLACKNESS; 341. RACE.
nigromancien 112. DEATH,
necromancy; 124. DIVINATION,
necromancy.
nigromancy 112. DEATH, necromancy;
124. DIVINATION, necromancy.
Nihilism 185. GOVERNMENT.
nihilism 28. ATTITUDES;
312. PHILOSOPHY.
nihilist 28. ATTITUDES, nihilism;
185. GOVERNMENT, Nihilism;
312. PHILOSOPHY, nihilism.
nihilistic 28. ATTITUDES, nihilism;
185. GOVERNMENT, Nihilism.
nihility 381. SPACES.
Nilometer 226. INSTRUMENTS.
nilometer 356. RIVERS.
Niloscope 226. INSTRUMENTS,
Nilometer.
niloscope 356. RIVERS, nilometer.
ninnyish 41. BEHAVIOR, ninnyism.
ninnyism 41. BEHAVIOR.
noctambulant 372. SLEEP,
noctambulism.
noctambulation 372. SLEEP,
noctambulism.
noctambule 372. SLEEP, noctambulism.
noctambulism 372. SLEEP.
noctambulist 372. SLEEP,
noctambulism.

noctambulistic 372. SLEEP,
noctambulism.
noctambulous 372. SLEEP,
noctambulism.
noctiluca 110. DARKNESS; 245. LIGHT.
noctilucence 87. CLOUDS.
noctilucent 87. CLOUDS, noctilucence.
noctilucine 110. DARKNESS, noctiluca;
245. LIGHT, noctiluca.
noctimania 110. DARKNESS;
254. MANIAS; 292. NIGHT.
noctiphobia 313. PHOBIAS.
noctivagant 292. NIGHT, noctivagation;
412. WALKING, noctivagation.
noctivagation 292. NIGHT;
412. WALKING.
noctivagous 292. NIGHT, noctivagation;
412. WALKING, noctivagation.
noctograph 48. BLINDNESS;
226. INSTRUMENTS; 428. WRITING.
nocturne 23. ART.
noesis 393. THINKING.
noetic 21. ARGUMENTATION, noetics;
393. THINKING, noesis.
noetics 21. ARGUMENTATION.
nomadic 41. BEHAVIOR, nomadism.
nomadism 41. BEHAVIOR.
nomancy 124. DIVINATION; 288. NAMES;
428. WRITING.
nomarchy 185. GOVERNMENT.
nome 185. GOVERNMENT, nomarchy.
nomenclator 53. BOOKS;
83. CLASSIFICATION.
nomenclature 53. BOOKS, nomenclator;
83. CLASSIFICATION; 288. NAMES.
nominalism 312. PHILOSOPHY.
nominalist 312. PHILOSOPHY,
nominalism.
nominalistic 312. PHILOSOPHY,
nominalism.
nomism 239. LAW.
nomocracy 239. LAW.
nomographer 239. LAW, nomography.
nomographic 239. LAW, nomography.
nomography 239. LAW.
nomological 239. LAW, nomology;
393. THINKING, nomology.
nomologist 239. LAW, nomology;
393. THINKING, nomology.
nomology 239. LAW; 393. THINKING.

nonage 81. CHURCH; 239. LAW; 331. PROPERTY and OWNERSHIP.

nonagenarian 299. OLD AGE, nonagenarianism.

nonagenarianism 299. OLD AGE.

nonagenary 299. OLD AGE, nonagenarianism.

nonconformism 28. ATTITUDES; 332. PROTESTANTISM.

nonconformist 28. ATTITUDES, nonconformism; 332. PROTESTANTISM, nonconformism.

nonconformity 28. ATTITUDES, nonconformism.

noninterventionism 185. GOVERNMENT; 322. POLITICS.

noninterventionist 185. GOVERNMENT, noninterventionism; 322. POLITICS, noninterventionism.

nonjuror 332. PROTESTANTISM, nonjurorism.

nonjurorism 332. PROTESTANTISM.

nonpartisan 322. POLITICS, nonpartisanism.

nonpartisanism 322. POLITICS.

nonpartisanship 322. POLITICS, nonpartisanism.

noological 405. UNDERSTANDING, noology.

noology 405. UNDERSTANDING.

Norbertine 69. CATHOLICISM.

norlandism 236. LANGUAGE.

Normanic 172. FRANCE, Normanism.

Normanism 172. FRANCE.

Normanist 172. FRANCE, Normanism.

noseological 293. NOSE, noseology.

noseology 293. NOSE.

nosism 362. SELF.

nosographer 122. DISEASE and ILLNESS, nosography.

nosographic 122. DISEASE and ILLNESS, nosography.

nosographical 122. DISEASE and ILLNESS, nosography.

nosography 122. DISEASE and ILLNESS.

nosologic 122. DISEASE and ILLNESS, nosology.

nosological 122. DISEASE and ILLNESS, nosology.

nosologist 122. DISEASE and ILLNESS, nosology.

nosology 122. DISEASE and ILLNESS.

nosomania 122. DISEASE and ILLNESS; 197. HEALTH, hypochondriacism; 254. MANIAS.

nosonomy 122. DISEASE and ILLNESS.

nosophilia 122. DISEASE and ILLNESS; 311. -PHILE, -PHILIA, -PHILY.

nosophobia 122. DISEASE and ILLNESS; 313. PHOBIAS.

nostology 299. OLD AGE.

nostomania 208. HOMESICKNESS.

nostopathy 317. PLACES.

notaphily 91. COLLECTIONS and COLLECTING.

nothingarian 322. POLITICS, nothingarianism.

nothingarianism 322. POLITICS.

noumenal 312. PHILOSOPHY, noumenon.

noumenalism 183. GOD and GODS; 312. PHILOSOPHY.

noumenalist 183. GOD and GODS, noumenalism; 312. PHILOSOPHY, noumenalism.

noumenon 312. PHILOSOPHY.

Novationism 69. CATHOLICISM.

Novationist 69. CATHOLICISM, Novationism.

nubilation 87. CLOUDS.

nubile 258. MARRIAGE, nubility; 424. WOMEN, nubility.

nubility 258. MARRIAGE; 424. WOMEN.

nudiphobia 313. PHOBIAS, nudophobia.

nudism 41. BEHAVIOR; 287. NAKEDNESS.

nudist 41. BEHAVIOR, nudism; 287. NAKEDNESS, nudism.

nuditarian 23. ART.

nudomania 254. MANIAS; 287. NAKEDNESS.

nudophobia 313. PHOBIAS.

nugae 213. HUMOR.

nullibism 379. SOUL.

nullibist 379. SOUL, nullibism.

nullifidian 349. RELIGION; 349. RELIGION, nullifidianism.

nullifidianism 349. RELIGION.

nullipara 46. BIRTH, nulliparity.

nulliparity 46. BIRTH.

nulliparous 46. BIRTH, nulliparity.

numerological 295. NUMBERS,
numerology.
numerologist 295. NUMBERS,
numerology.
numerology 124. DIVINATION;
295. NUMBERS.
numismatics 91. COLLECTIONS and
COLLECTING.
numismatist 91. COLLECTIONS and
COLLECTING, numismatics.
numismatographer 91. COLLECTIONS
and COLLECTING, numismatography.
numismatographic 91. COLLECTIONS
and COLLECTING, numismatography.
numismatography 91. COLLECTIONS
and COLLECTING.
nutation 25. ASTRONOMY; 133. EARTH.
nutational 25. ASTRONOMY, nutation;
133. EARTH, nutation.
nyctalopia 48. BLINDNESS; 148. EYES;
292. NIGHT.
nyctalopic 48. BLINDNESS, nyctalopia.
nyctophilia 311. -PHILE, -PHILIA, -PHILY.
nyctophobia 110. DARKNESS;
313. PHOBIAS.
nympholepsy 114. DEMONS.
nympholeptic 114. DEMONS,
nympholepsy.
nymphomania 254. MANIAS; 364. SEX.
nymphomaniac 364. SEX,
nymphomania.
nymphomaniacal 364. SEX,
nymphomania.
nystagmic 148. EYES, nystagmus.
nystagmus 148. EYES.

O

obduracy 28. ATTITUDES.
obdurate 28. ATTITUDES, obduracy.
obeahism 252. MAGIC.
obeisance 10. ALLEGIANCE.
obeisant 10. ALLEGIANCE, obeisance.
oberration 399. TRAVEL; 412. WALKING.
obfuscation 393. THINKING.
obi 252. MAGIC, obeahism.
obism 252. MAGIC, obeahism.
objectivism 28. ATTITUDES;
312. PHILOSOPHY.
objectivist 312. PHILOSOPHY,
objectivism.

objectivity 28. ATTITUDES, objectivism.
oblate 69. CATHOLICISM.
oblation 80. CHRISTIANITY.
obliquitous 25. ASTRONOMY, obliquity;
133. EARTH, obliquity.
obliquity 25. ASTRONOMY; 133. EARTH.
obliquity of the ecliptic
25. ASTRONOMY, obliquity;
133. EARTH, obliquity.
obmutescence 382. SPEECH.
obscurant 21. ARGUMENTATION,
obscurantism.
obscurantic 21. ARGUMENTATION,
obscurantism.
obscuranticism 21. ARGUMENTATION,
obscurantism.
obscurantism 21. ARGUMENTATION.
obscurantist 21. ARGUMENTATION,
obscurantism.
obsequence 28. ATTITUDES.
obsequent 28. ATTITUDES, obsequence.
obsequies 63. BURIAL.
obsequy 63. BURIAL, obsequies.
obsolescence 396. TIME.
obsolescent 396. TIME, obsolescence.
obsoletism 236. LANGUAGE.
obstetric 46. BIRTH, obstetrics;
266. MEDICAL SPECIALTIES, obstetrics;
327. PREGNANCY, obstetrics.
obstetrical 46. BIRTH, obstetrics;
266. MEDICAL SPECIALTIES, obstetrics;
327. PREGNANCY, obstetrics.
obstetrician 46. BIRTH, obstetrics;
266. MEDICAL SPECIALTIES, obstetrics;
327. PREGNANCY, obstetrics.
obstetrics 46. BIRTH; 266. MEDICAL
SPECIALTIES; 327. PREGNANCY.
obstructionism 21. ARGUMENTATION.
obstructionist 21. ARGUMENTATION,
obstructionism.
obstructionistic 21. ARGUMENTATION,
obstructionism.
obumbration 110. DARKNESS.
Occamism 392. THEOLOGY.
Occamist 392. THEOLOGY, Occamism.
Occamistic 392. THEOLOGY,
Occamism.
Occamite 392. THEOLOGY, Occamism.
occasionalism 312. PHILOSOPHY.
occasionalist 312. PHILOSOPHY,
occasionalism.

occasionalistic 312. PHILOSOPHY,
occasionalism.
Occidentalism 41. BEHAVIOR.
Occidentalist 41. BEHAVIOR,
Occidentalism.
occision 232. KILLING.
occultation 25. ASTRONOMY;
318. PLANETS.
occultism 349. RELIGION.
occultist 349. RELIGION, occultism.
Oceanid 286. MYTHOLOGY.
oceanographer 360. SEA,
oceanography.
oceanographic 360. SEA, oceanography.
oceanographical 360. SEA,
oceanography.
oceanography 360. SEA.
oceanology 360. SEA.
ochlocracy 275. MOB.
ochlocrat 275. MOB, ochlocracy.
ochlocratic 275. MOB, ochlocracy.
ochlocratical 275. MOB, ochlocracy.
ochlomania 105. CROWDS; 254. MANIAS.
ochlophobe 275. MOB, ochlophobia.
ochlophobia 105. CROWDS; 275. MOB;
313. PHOBIAS.
ochlophobic 275. MOB, ochlophobia.
ochophobia 313. PHOBIAS;
408. VEHICLES.
octogenarian 299. OLD AGE,
octogenarianism.
octogenarianism 299. OLD AGE.
octogenary 299. OLD AGE,
octogenarianism.
octogild 223. INJURY.
octonary 409. VERSE; 409. VERSE,
octonary.
oculist 148. EYES.
odious 28. ATTITUDES, odium.
odium 28. ATTITUDES.
odograph 123. DISTANCE.
odometer 123. DISTANCE;
226. INSTRUMENTS.
odontalgia 306. PAIN.
odontalgic 306. PAIN, odontalgia.
odontogenic 390. TEETH, odontogeny.
odontogeny 390. TEETH.
odontographic 390. TEETH,
odontography.
odontography 390. TEETH.
odontological 390. TEETH, odontology.

odontologist 390. TEETH, odontology.
odontology 390. TEETH.
odontophobia 313. PHOBIAS;
390. TEETH.
odylic 215. HYPNOSIS, odylism.
odylism 215. HYPNOSIS.
odynophobia 306. PAIN; 313. PHOBIAS.
oecist 297. OCCUPATIONS.
oecologic 142. ENVIRONMENT, ecology;
376. SOCIETY, ecology.
oecological 44. BIOLOGY, ecology;
142. ENVIRONMENT, ecology;
376. SOCIETY, ecology.
oecologically 44. BIOLOGY, ecology.
oecologist 44. BIOLOGY, ecology;
142. ENVIRONMENT, ecology;
376. SOCIETY, ecology.
oecology 44. BIOLOGY, ecology;
142. ENVIRONMENT, ecology;
376. SOCIETY; 376. SOCIETY, ecology.
oecophobia 212. HOUSES, ecophobia;
313. PHOBIAS, ecophobia.
Oecumenism 80. CHRISTIANITY;
80. CHRISTIANITY, Ecumenism.
oekist 297. OCCUPATIONS, oecist.
oenologist 421. WINE, oenology.
oenology 421. WINE.
oenomancy 124. DIVINATION;
421. WINE.
oenomania 421. WINE.
oenophile 421. WINE, oenophily.
oenophily 421. WINE.
oenophobe 421. WINE, oenophobia.
oenophobia 313. PHOBIAS; 421. WINE.
oestromania 254. MANIAS; 364. SEX.
oestrous 16. ANIMALS, estrus; 364. SEX,
estrus.
oestrum 16. ANIMALS, estrus; 364. SEX,
estrus.
oestrus 16. ANIMALS; 16. ANIMALS,
estrus; 364. SEX; 364. SEX, estrus.
officialdom 62. BUREAUCRACY.
officialese 62. BUREAUCRACY;
237. LANGUAGE STYLE.
officialism 62. BUREAUCRACY.
offset lithography 328. PRINTING.
ogam 428. WRITING, ogham.
ogamist 428. WRITING, ogham.
ogham 428. WRITING.
oghamist 428. WRITING, ogham.
ogreish 41. BEHAVIOR, ogreism.

ogreism 41. BEHAVIOR.
ohmmeter 226. INSTRUMENTS.
oikomania 208. HOMESICKNESS;
    254. MANIAS.
oikophobia 212. HOUSES, ecophobia;
    313. PHOBIAS, ecophobia.
oiligarchy 376. SOCIETY.
oinologist 421. WINE, oenology.
oinology 421. WINE, oenology.
oinomancy 124. DIVINATION,
    oenomancy; 421. WINE, oenomancy.
oinomania 254. MANIAS; 421. WINE,
    oenomania.
oinophile 421. WINE, oenophily.
oinophily 421. WINE, oenophily.
oinophobe 421. WINE, oenophobia.
oinophobia 313. PHOBIAS, oenophobia;
    421. WINE, oenophobia.
oleographic 328. PRINTING, oleography.
oleography 328. PRINTING.
olericultural 319. PLANTS, olericulture.
olericulture 319. PLANTS.
olfaction 50. BODILY FUNCTIONS.
olfactive 50. BODILY FUNCTIONS,
    olfaction.
olfactologist 298. ODORS, olfactology.
olfactology 298. ODORS.
olfactophobia 298. ODORS;
    313. PHOBIAS.
olfactory 50. BODILY FUNCTIONS,
    olfaction.
oligarch 185. GOVERNMENT, oligarchy.
oligarchic 185. GOVERNMENT,
    oligarchy.
oligarchical 185. GOVERNMENT,
    oligarchy.
oligarchism 312. PHILOSOPHY.
oligarchist 312. PHILOSOPHY,
    oligarchism.
oligarchy 185. GOVERNMENT.
oligidria 122. DISEASE and ILLNESS.
oligomania 254. MANIAS.
oligopolistic 398. TRADE, oligopoly.
oligopoly 398. TRADE.
oligopsonist 398. TRADE, oligopsony.
oligopsonistic 398. TRADE, oligopsony.
oligopsony 398. TRADE.
oligotrophic 142. ENVIRONMENT,
    oligotrophy.
oligotrophy 142. ENVIRONMENT.

ombrological 345. RAIN, ombrology;
    417. WEATHER, ombrology.
ombrology 345. RAIN; 417. WEATHER.
ombrophilic 319. PLANTS, ombrophily.
ombrophilous 319. PLANTS,
    ombrophily.
ombrophily 319. PLANTS.
ombrophobia 313. PHOBIAS; 345. RAIN.
ombudsman 297. OCCUPATIONS.
ommatophobia 148. EYES; 313. PHOBIAS.
omnibology 408. VEHICLES.
omniform 170. FORM, omniformity.
omniformity 170. FORM.
omnipotence 386. STRENGTH and
    WEAKNESS.
omnipotent 386. STRENGTH and
    WEAKNESS, omnipotence.
omniscience 233. KNOWLEDGE.
omniscient 233. KNOWLEDGE,
    omniscience.
omniscious 233. KNOWLEDGE,
    omniscience.
omnium-gatherum 91. COLLECTIONS
    and COLLECTING.
omophagia 166. FLESH.
omophagic 166. FLESH, omophagia.
omoplatoscopy 124. DIVINATION.
omphalism 267. MEDITATION,
    omphaloskepsis.
omphalomancy 46. BIRTH;
    124. DIVINATION.
omphalopsychism 285. MYSTICISM.
omphalopsychite 285. MYSTICISM,
    omphalopsychism.
omphaloskepsis 267. MEDITATION;
    285. MYSTICISM, omphalopsychism.
omphalotomy 46. BIRTH.
onanism 364. SEX.
onanist 364. SEX, onanism.
onanistic 364. SEX, onanism.
oncogenesis 66. CANCER.
oncogenic 66. CANCER, oncogenesis.
oncologic 266. MEDICAL SPECIALTIES,
    oncology.
oncologist 266. MEDICAL SPECIALTIES,
    oncology.
oncology 66. CANCER; 266. MEDICAL
    SPECIALTIES.
ondogram 226. INSTRUMENTS,
    ondograph.
ondograph 226. INSTRUMENTS.

ondometer 226. INSTRUMENTS.
Oneida Perfectionists
93. COMMUNALISM.
oneirocritic 129. DREAMS,
oneirocriticism.
oneirocritical 129. DREAMS,
oneirocriticism.
oneirocriticism 129. DREAMS.
oneirodynia 129. DREAMS.
oneirology 129. DREAMS.
oneiromancer 124. DIVINATION,
oneiromancy; 129. DREAMS,
oneiromancy.
oneiromancy 124. DIVINATION;
129. DREAMS.
oneiroscopy 129. DREAMS, **oneirology.**
oneupmanship 106. CUNNING;
176. GAMES.
oniomania 254. MANIAS.
onomancy 124. DIVINATION;
288. NAMES; 428. WRITING.
onomasiologic 247. LINGUISTICS,
onomasiology.
onomasiological 247. LINGUISTICS,
onomasiology.
onomasiologist 247. LINGUISTICS,
onomasiology.
onomasiology 247. LINGUISTICS.
onomastic 247. LINGUISTICS,
onomastics; 288. NAMES,
onomasticon; 288. NAMES,
onomastics.
onomastician 247. LINGUISTICS,
onomastics; 288. NAMES, **onomastics.**
onomasticon 288. NAMES.
onomastics 247. LINGUISTICS;
288. NAMES.
onomatological 288. NAMES,
onomatology.
onomatologist 288. NAMES,
onomatology.
onomatology 288. NAMES.
onomatomania 288. NAMES.
onomatophobia 288. NAMES;
313. PHOBIAS.
onomatopoeia 380. SOUND.
onomatopoeial 380. SOUND,
onomatopoeia.
onomatopoeic 380. SOUND,
onomatopoeia.
onomatopoetic 380. SOUND,
onomatopoeia.
onomatopoietic 380. SOUND,
onomatopoeia.
onomomancy 124. DIVINATION,
onomancy; 288. NAMES, **onomancy;**
428. WRITING, **onomancy.**
ontogenesis 44. BIOLOGY; 244. LIFE.
ontogenetic 44. BIOLOGY, **ontogenesis;**
244. LIFE, **ontogenesis.**
ontogenetical 44. BIOLOGY,
ontogenesis; 244. LIFE, **ontogenesis.**
ontogenic 44. BIOLOGY, **ontogeny;**
244. LIFE, **ontogeny.**
ontogeny 44. BIOLOGY; 244. LIFE.
ontologic 312. PHILOSOPHY, **ontology.**
ontological 312. PHILOSOPHY, **ontology.**
ontologism 349. RELIGION.
ontologist 312. PHILOSOPHY, **ontology;**
349. RELIGION, **ontologism.**
ontologistic 312. PHILOSOPHY, **ontology;**
349. RELIGION, **ontologism.**
ontology 312. PHILOSOPHY.
onychia 161. FINGERS and TOES.
onychomancy 124. DIVINATION;
161. FINGERS and TOES.
onychomantic 161. FINGERS and TOES,
onychomancy.
onychophagia 161. FINGERS and TOES.
onychophagy 161. FINGERS and TOES,
onychophagia.
onychoptosis 161. FINGERS and TOES.
onychosis 161. FINGERS and TOES.
onym 83. CLASSIFICATION; 288. NAMES.
onymy 83. CLASSIFICATION; 288. NAMES.
oogamous 44. BIOLOGY, **oogamy.**
oogamy 44. BIOLOGY.
oogenesis 44. BIOLOGY.
oogenetic 44. BIOLOGY, **oogenesis.**
oograph 45. BIRDS.
oologic 45. BIRDS, **oology.**
oological 45. BIRDS, **oology.**
oologist 45. BIRDS, **oology.**
oology 45. BIRDS.
oomancy 124. DIVINATION.
oometer 45. BIRDS; 226. INSTRUMENTS.
ooscopy 44. BIOLOGY; 45. BIRDS.
opalescence 92. COLOR.
opalescent 92. COLOR, **opalescence.**
operationism 312. PHILOSOPHY.

operationist 312. PHILOSOPHY,
   operationism.
operationistic 312. PHILOSOPHY,
   operationism.
operose 426. WORK, operosity.
operosity 426. WORK.
ophicleidist 284. MUSIC.
ophidiomania 254. MANIAS;
   353. REPTILES.
ophidiophobia 313. PHOBIAS;
   353. REPTILES; 374. SNAKES.
ophiographic 374. SNAKES,
   ophiography.
ophiography 374. SNAKES.
ophiolater 374. SNAKES, ophiolatry.
ophiolatry 374. SNAKES.
ophiologic 374. SNAKES, ophiology.
ophiological 374. SNAKES, ophiology.
ophiologist 374. SNAKES, ophiology.
ophiology 374. SNAKES.
ophiomancy 124. DIVINATION;
   374. SNAKES.
ophiophobia 313. PHOBIAS,
   ophidiophobia; 374. SNAKES,
   ophidiophobia.
Ophism 349. RELIGION.
Ophite 349. RELIGION, Ophism.
Ophitic 349. RELIGION, Ophism.
Ophitism 349. RELIGION, Ophism.
ophthalmologic 148. EYES,
   ophthalmology.
ophthalmological 148. EYES,
   ophthalmology; 266. MEDICAL
   SPECIALTIES, ophthalmology.
ophthalmologist 148. EYES,
   ophthalmology; 266. MEDICAL
   SPECIALTIES, ophthalmology.
ophthalmology 148. EYES; 266. MEDICAL
   SPECIALTIES.
opinionist 300. OPINION.
opiomania 130. DRUGS.
opiophagism 130. DRUGS.
opiophagy 130. DRUGS, opiophagism.
opisthognathic 149. FACIAL FEATURES,
   opisthognathism.
opisthognathism 149. FACIAL
   FEATURES.
opisthognathous 149. FACIAL FEATURES,
   opisthognathism.
opisthography 428. WRITING;
   428. WRITING, opisthography.

opiumism 130. DRUGS.
opotherapy 266. MEDICAL SPECIALTIES;
   350. REMEDIES.
opponency 96. CONFLICT.
opportunism 41. BEHAVIOR.
opportunist 41. BEHAVIOR,
   opportunism.
opportunistic 41. BEHAVIOR,
   opportunism.
oppugnancy 96. CONFLICT.
oppugnant 96. CONFLICT,
   oppugnancy.
opsimathy 240. LEARNING; 299. OLD
   AGE.
opsomania 168. FOOD and NUTRITION;
   254. MANIAS.
optic 245. LIGHT, optics.
optical 245. LIGHT, optics.
optician 148. EYES.
optics 245. LIGHT.
optimism 312. PHILOSOPHY.
optimist 312. PHILOSOPHY, optimism.
optimistic 312. PHILOSOPHY, optimism.
optogram 148. EYES.
optography 148. EYES.
optology 148. EYES.
optometrical 148. EYES, optometry.
optometrist 148. EYES, optometry.
optometry 148. EYES.
optophone 48. BLINDNESS.
optotechnics 226. INSTRUMENTS;
   316. PHYSICS.
optotype 148. EYES; 328. PRINTING.
oracularity 174. FUTURE.
oralism 111. DEAFNESS.
oralist 111. DEAFNESS, oralism.
Orangeism 332. PROTESTANTISM.
orchardist 5. AGRICULTURE.
orchesis 108. DANCING, orchesography.
orchesography 108. DANCING.
orchestics 108. DANCING,
   orchesography.
orchidologist 54. BOTANY, orchidology.
orchidology 54. BOTANY.
orchidomania 254. MANIAS; 364. SEX.
oreographic 283. MOUNTAINS,
   orography.
oreographical 283. MOUNTAINS,
   orography.
oreography 283. MOUNTAINS,
   orography.

oreological 283. MOUNTAINS, orology.
oreologist 283. MOUNTAINS, orology.
oreology 283. MOUNTAINS, orology.
organicism 266. MEDICAL SPECIALTIES;
312. PHILOSOPHY.
organicist 266. MEDICAL SPECIALTIES,
organicism; 312. PHILOSOPHY,
organicism.
organicistic 266. MEDICAL SPECIALTIES,
organicism; 312. PHILOSOPHY,
organicism.
organism 16. ANIMALS; 302. ORGANISMS.
organogenesis 44. BIOLOGY.
organogenetic 44. BIOLOGY,
organogenesis.
organogenic 44. BIOLOGY,
organogenesis.
organogeny 44. BIOLOGY,
organogenesis.
organographic 14. ANATOMY,
organography; 16. ANIMALS,
organography; 44. BIOLOGY,
organography.
organographical 14. ANATOMY,
organography; 16. ANIMALS,
organography; 44. BIOLOGY,
organography.
organographist 14. ANATOMY,
organography; 16. ANIMALS,
organography; 44. BIOLOGY,
organography.
organography 14. ANATOMY;
16. ANIMALS; 44. BIOLOGY.
organologic 16. ANIMALS, organology;
44. BIOLOGY, organology.
organological 16. ANIMALS,
organology; 44. BIOLOGY,
organology.
organologist 16. ANIMALS, organology;
44. BIOLOGY, organology.
organology 16. ANIMALS; 44. BIOLOGY.
organon 233. KNOWLEDGE;
312. PHILOSOPHY.
organonomic 44. BIOLOGY,
organonomy.
organonomy 44. BIOLOGY.
organonymal 44. BIOLOGY,
organonymy; 83. CLASSIFICATION,
organonymy; 288. NAMES,
organonymy.

organonymic 44. BIOLOGY,
organonymy; 83. CLASSIFICATION,
organonymy; 288. NAMES,
organonymy.
organonymy 44. BIOLOGY;
83. CLASSIFICATION; 288. NAMES.
organotherapy 266. MEDICAL
SPECIALTIES; 350. REMEDIES.
orgiast 8. ALCOHOL, orgy.
orgiastic 8. ALCOHOL, orgy.
orgy 8. ALCOHOL.
Orientalism 41. BEHAVIOR.
Orientalist 41. BEHAVIOR, Orientalism;
207. HISTORY.
Orientality 41. BEHAVIOR, Orientalism.
origami 23. ART.
origamist 23. ART, origami.
Origenian 392. THEOLOGY, Origenism.
Origenism 312. PHILOSOPHY;
392. THEOLOGY.
Origenist 312. PHILOSOPHY, Origenism;
392. THEOLOGY, Origenism.
Origenistic 312. PHILOSOPHY,
Origenism; 392. THEOLOGY,
Origenism.
orismologic 236. LANGUAGE,
orismology.
orismological 236. LANGUAGE,
orismology.
orismology 236. LANGUAGE.
ornamentalism 23. ART.
ornamentalist 23. ART, ornamentist;
305. ORNAMENTATION, ornamentist.
ornamentist 23. ART;
305. ORNAMENTATION.
ornithologic 45. BIRDS, ornithology.
ornithological 45. BIRDS, ornithology.
ornithologist 45. BIRDS, ornithology;
430. ZOOLOGY, ornithology.
ornithology 45. BIRDS; 430. ZOOLOGY.
ornithomancy 45. BIRDS;
124. DIVINATION.
ornithomania 45. BIRDS; 254. MANIAS.
ornithophobia 45. BIRDS; 313. PHOBIAS.
ornithopter 31. AVIATION.
ornithoscopy 45. BIRDS, ornithomancy;
124. DIVINATION, ornithomancy.
ornithosis 45. BIRDS.
ornithotomical 45. BIRDS, ornithotomy.
ornithotomist 45. BIRDS, ornithotomy.
ornithotomy 45. BIRDS.

orogenesis 283. MOUNTAINS.
orogenetic 179. GEOLOGY, orogeny.
orogenic 179. GEOLOGY, orogeny;
283. MOUNTAINS, orogenesis.
orogeny 179. GEOLOGY;
283. MOUNTAINS, orogenesis.
orographic 178. GEOGRAPHY,
orography; 283. MOUNTAINS,
orography.
orographical 178. GEOGRAPHY,
orography; 283. MOUNTAINS,
orography.
orography 178. GEOGRAPHY;
283. MOUNTAINS.
orohydrographic 414. WATER,
orohydrography.
orohydrography 414. WATER.
orological 283. MOUNTAINS, orology.
orologist 283. MOUNTAINS, orology.
orology 283. MOUNTAINS.
orometric 283. MOUNTAINS, orometry.
orometry 283. MOUNTAINS.
orophilous 283. MOUNTAINS.
orphanotrophy 6. AID.
Orphic 349. RELIGION, Orphism.
Orphicism 349. RELIGION, Orphism.
Orphism 23. ART; 349. RELIGION.
Orphist 23. ART, Orphism.
orthocephalic 196. HEAD,
orthocephalism.
orthocephalism 196. HEAD.
orthocephalous 196. HEAD,
orthocephalism.
orthocephaly 196. HEAD,
orthocephalism.
orthodontia 390. TEETH, orthodontics.
orthodontic 266. MEDICAL SPECIALTIES,
orthodontics; 390. TEETH,
orthodontics.
orthodontics 266. MEDICAL
SPECIALTIES; 390. TEETH.
orthodontist 266. MEDICAL
SPECIALTIES, orthodontics;
390. TEETH, orthodontics.
orthodox 349. RELIGION, orthodoxy.
orthodoxy 349. RELIGION.
orthoepic 330. PRONUNCIATION,
orthoepy.
orthoepical 330. PRONUNCIATION,
orthoepy.

orthoepist 330. PRONUNCIATION,
orthoepy.
orthoepistic 330. PRONUNCIATION,
orthoepy.
orthoepy 330. PRONUNCIATION.
orthogamous 44. BIOLOGY, orthogamy.
orthogamy 44. BIOLOGY.
orthogenesis 44. BIOLOGY;
147. EVOLUTION; 376. SOCIETY.
orthogenetic 44. BIOLOGY,
orthogenesis; 147. EVOLUTION,
orthogenesis; 376. SOCIETY,
orthogenesis.
orthognathic 149. FACIAL FEATURES,
orthognathism.
orthognathism 149. FACIAL FEATURES.
orthognathous 149. FACIAL FEATURES,
orthognathism.
orthogonal 170. FORM, orthogonality;
262. MATHEMATICS, orthogonality.
orthogonality 170. FORM;
262. MATHEMATICS.
orthographer 383. SPELLING,
orthography.
orthographic 383. SPELLING,
orthography.
orthographic projection 128. DRAWING.
orthography 383. SPELLING.
orthologer 236. LANGUAGE, orthology.
orthologian 236. LANGUAGE, orthology.
orthological 236. LANGUAGE,
orthology.
orthology 236. LANGUAGE.
orthometry 409. VERSE.
orthopathy 266. MEDICAL SPECIALTIES;
350. REMEDIES.
orthopedic 266. MEDICAL SPECIALTIES,
orthopedics.
orthopedics 266. MEDICAL SPECIALTIES.
orthopedist 266. MEDICAL SPECIALTIES,
orthopedics.
orthopnea 122. DISEASE and ILLNESS.
orthopneic 122. DISEASE and ILLNESS,
orthopnea.
orthopny 122. DISEASE and ILLNESS,
orthopnea.
orthopraxis 51. BODY, HUMAN,
orthopraxy; 266. MEDICAL
SPECIALTIES, orthopraxy.
orthopraxy 51. BODY, HUMAN;
266. MEDICAL SPECIALTIES.

orthopsychiatric 266. MEDICAL
SPECIALTIES, orthopsychiatry.
orthopsychiatrical 266. MEDICAL
SPECIALTIES, orthopsychiatry.
orthopsychiatrist 266. MEDICAL
SPECIALTIES, orthopsychiatry.
orthopsychiatry 266. MEDICAL
SPECIALTIES.
orthopter 31. AVIATION, ornithopter.
orthopterology 225. INSECTS.
orthoptic 148. EYES, orthoptics.
orthoptics 148. EYES.
orthoptist 148. EYES, orthoptics.
orthosis 51. BODY, HUMAN;
224. INSANITY; 334. PSYCHOLOGY.
orthotic 51. BODY, HUMAN, orthosis;
334. PSYCHOLOGY, orthosis.
oryctognosy 179. GEOLOGY, oryctology.
oryctology 179. GEOLOGY.
oscillographic 316. PHYSICS,
oscillography.
oscillography 316. PHYSICS.
oscitation 50. BODILY FUNCTIONS.
osmatic 298. ODORS, osmatism.
osmatism 298. ODORS.
osmidrosis 51. BODY, HUMAN;
298. ODORS.
osmology 298. ODORS, osphresiology.
osmometer 226. INSTRUMENTS.
osmometric 226. INSTRUMENTS,
osmometer; 264. MEASUREMENT,
osmometry; 316. PHYSICS,
osmometry.
osmometry 264. MEASUREMENT;
316. PHYSICS.
osmonologist 298. ODORS,
osmonosology.
osmonosology 298. ODORS.
osmophobia 298. ODORS; 313. PHOBIAS.
osmosis 72. CELLS; 329. PROCESSES.
osmotic 72. CELLS, osmosis;
329. PROCESSES, osmosis.
osphresiology 298. ODORS.
osphresiophilia 298. ODORS.
osphresiophobia 298. ODORS;
313. PHOBIAS.
Ossianic 248. LITERARY STYLE,
Ossianism.
Ossianism 248. LITERARY STYLE.
ossuarium 52. BONES; 112. DEATH.

ossuary 52. BONES, ossuarium;
112. DEATH, ossuarium.
osteoclasis 50. BODILY FUNCTIONS;
52. BONES.
osteoclastoma 66. CANCER.
osteogenic sarcoma 66. CANCER,
osteosarcoma.
osteographer 52. BONES, osteography.
osteographic 52. BONES, osteography.
osteographical 52. BONES, osteography.
osteography 52. BONES.
osteologer 52. BONES, osteology.
osteologic 14. ANATOMY, osteology;
52. BONES, osteology; 266. MEDICAL
SPECIALTIES, osteology.
osteological 14. ANATOMY, osteology;
52. BONES, osteology; 266. MEDICAL
SPECIALTIES, osteology.
osteologist 14. ANATOMY, osteology;
52. BONES, osteology; 266. MEDICAL
SPECIALTIES, osteology.
osteology 14. ANATOMY; 52. BONES;
266. MEDICAL SPECIALTIES.
osteomalacia 52. BONES.
osteomancy 52. BONES;
124. DIVINATION.
osteomantic 52. BONES, osteomancy;
124. DIVINATION, osteomancy.
osteomanty 52. BONES, osteomancy;
124. DIVINATION, osteomancy.
osteometry 52. BONES;
264. MEASUREMENT.
osteopath 52. BONES, osteopathy;
266. MEDICAL SPECIALTIES,
osteopathy; 350. REMEDIES,
osteopathy.
osteopathic 52. BONES, osteopathy;
266. MEDICAL SPECIALTIES,
osteopathy; 350. REMEDIES,
osteopathy.
osteopathist 52. BONES, osteopathy.
osteopathologic 52. BONES,
osteopathology.
osteopathological 52. BONES,
osteopathology.
osteopathologist 52. BONES,
osteopathology.
osteopathology 52. BONES.
osteopathy 52. BONES; 266. MEDICAL
SPECIALTIES; 350. REMEDIES.
osteophone 111. DEAFNESS.

osteoplasty 52. BONES; 388. SURGERY.
osteoporosis 51. BODY, HUMAN;
52. BONES.
osteosarcoma 66. CANCER.
osteotome 388. SURGERY.
osteotomist 52. BONES, osteotomy;
388. SURGERY, osteotomy.
osteotomy 52. BONES; 388. SURGERY.
ostiary 69. CATHOLICISM.
ostosis 52. BONES.
ostracism 34. BANISHMENT.
otalgia 132. EAR; 306. PAIN.
otalgic 306. PAIN, otalgia.
otiatric 132. EAR, otiatrics.
otiatrics 132. EAR.
otiatry 132. EAR, otiatrics.
oticodinia 132. EAR.
oticodinosis 132. EAR, oticodinia.
otitic 132. EAR, otitis.
otitis 132. EAR.
otocleisis 198. HEARING.
otography 132. EAR.
otolaryngological 266. MEDICAL
SPECIALTIES, otolaryngology.
otolaryngologist 266. MEDICAL
SPECIALTIES, otolaryngology.
otolaryngology 266. MEDICAL
SPECIALTIES.
otolith 385. STONES.
otologic 132. EAR, otology.
otological 132. EAR, otology;
266. MEDICAL SPECIALTIES, otology.
otologist 132. EAR, otology;
266. MEDICAL SPECIALTIES, otology.
otology 132. EAR; 266. MEDICAL
SPECIALTIES.
otomyasthenia 198. HEARING.
otomyasthenic 198. HEARING,
otomyasthenia.
otopathy 132. EAR.
otophone 198. HEARING.
otoplasty 132. EAR.
otopyorrhea 132. EAR.
otorhinolaryngologic 266. MEDICAL
SPECIALTIES, otorhinolaryngology.
otorhinolaryngological 266. MEDICAL
SPECIALTIES, otorhinolaryngology.
otorhinolaryngologist 266. MEDICAL
SPECIALTIES, otorhinolaryngology.
otorhinolaryngology 266. MEDICAL
SPECIALTIES.

otorrhea 132. EAR.
otoscopic 132. EAR, otoscopy.
otoscopy 132. EAR.
otosis 198. HEARING.
oubliette 68. CAPTIVITY.
ouranophobia 201. HEAVEN,
uranophobia; 313. PHOBIAS.
overoptimism 28. ATTITUDES.
overoptimist 28. ATTITUDES,
overoptimism.
overoptimistic 28. ATTITUDES,
overoptimism.
overpatriotism 289. NATIONALISM.
ovipara 16. ANIMALS.
oviparism 46. BIRTH.
oviparity 16. ANIMALS, ovipara;
46. BIRTH, oviparism.
oviparous 16. ANIMALS, ovipara;
46. BIRTH, oviparism.
ovism 44. BIOLOGY.
ovological 44. BIOLOGY, ovology.
ovologist 44. BIOLOGY, ovology.
ovology 44. BIOLOGY.
ovovivipara 16. ANIMALS.
ovoviviparism 46. BIRTH.
ovoviviparity 46. BIRTH,
ovoviviparism.
ovoviviparous 46. BIRTH,
ovoviviparism.
Owenism 93. COMMUNALISM;
137. ECONOMICS.
Owenite 93. COMMUNALISM, Owenism;
137. ECONOMICS, Owenism.
ownership 331. PROPERTY and
OWNERSHIP.
oxidimetric 264. MEASUREMENT,
oxidimetry.
oxidimetry 264. MEASUREMENT.
oxycephalic 51. BODY, HUMAN,
oxycephaly.
oxycephalous 51. BODY, HUMAN,
oxycephaly.
oxycephaly 51. BODY, HUMAN.
oxyesthesia 122. DISEASE and ILLNESS.
oxygeusia 51. BODY, HUMAN;
309. PERCEPTION.
oxymoron 354. RHETORIC and
RHETORICAL DEVICES.
oxymoronic 354. RHETORIC and
RHETORICAL DEVICES, oxymoron.
oxyopia 148. EYES; 309. PERCEPTION.

oxyopy 148. EYES, oxyopia;
309. PERCEPTION, oxyopia.
oxyosphresia 298. ODORS;
309. PERCEPTION.
oxyphonia 380. SOUND.
oxyphony 380. SOUND, oxyphonia.
oxytocic 46. BIRTH; 46. BIRTH, oxytocic.
ozonometer 27. ATMOSPHERE,
ozonometry.
ozonometric 27. ATMOSPHERE,
ozonometry.
ozonometry 27. ATMOSPHERE.

P

pacation 96. CONFLICT.
pachyaemia 49. BLOOD and BLOOD
VESSELS, pachyemia.
pachydermia 370. SKIN.
pachydermic 370. SKIN, pachydermia.
pachyemia 49. BLOOD and BLOOD
VESSELS.
pachymenia 370. SKIN.
pachymenic 370. SKIN, pachymenia.
pachymeter 226. INSTRUMENTS.
pachyotia 132. EAR.
pacifism 413. WAR.
pacifist 413. WAR, pacifism.
pacifistic 413. WAR, pacifism.
paeanism 410. VICTORY.
paedagogic 240. LEARNING, pedagogics.
paedagogical 240. LEARNING,
pedagogics.
paedagogics 77. CHILDREN,
pedagogics.
paedagogue 77. CHILDREN, pedagogics;
240. LEARNING, pedagogics.
paedagogy 240. LEARNING, pedagogy.
paederast 77. CHILDREN, pederasty.
paederasty 77. CHILDREN, pederasty.
paedeutics 240. LEARNING, paideutics.
paediatrician 77. CHILDREN,
pediatrics.
paediatrics 77. CHILDREN, pediatrics.
paedobaptism 35. BAPTISM,
pedobaptism.
paedobaptist 35. BAPTISM,
pedobaptism.
paedogogics 240. LEARNING,
pedagogics.
paedonymic 288. NAMES.

paedophobia 126. DOLLS, pedophobia;
313. PHOBIAS, pedophobia.
paganism 349. RELIGION.
paganist 349. RELIGION, paganism.
paganistic 349. RELIGION, paganism.
pagination 53. BOOKS.
paideutics 240. LEARNING.
Pajonism 332. PROTFSTANTISM.
palaeichthyological 171. FOSSILS,
paleichthyology.
palaeichthyologist 171. FOSSILS,
paleichthyology.
palaeichthyology 171. FOSSILS,
paleichthyology.
palaeobiologic 171. FOSSILS,
paleobiology.
palaeobiological 171. FOSSILS,
paleobiology.
palaeobiologist 171. FOSSILS,
paleobiology.
palaeobiology 171. FOSSILS,
paleobiology.
palaeobotanic 171. FOSSILS,
paleobotany.
palaeobotanical 171. FOSSILS,
paleobotany.
palaeobotanist 171. FOSSILS,
paleobotany.
palaeobotany 171. FOSSILS,
paleobotany.
palaeoecologic 142. ENVIRONMENT,
paleoecology.
palaeoecological 142. ENVIRONMENT,
paleoecology.
palaeoecology 142. ENVIRONMENT,
paleoecology.
palaeogeographer 178. GEOGRAPHY,
paleogeography.
palaeogeographic 178. GEOGRAPHY,
paleogeography.
palaeogeographical 178. GEOGRAPHY,
paleogeography.
palaeogeography 178. GEOGRAPHY,
paleogeography.
palaeographer 18. ANTIQUITY,
paleography; 249. LITERATURE,
paleography; 428. WRITING,
paleography.

palaeographic 18. ANTIQUITY,
paleography; 249. LITERATURE,
paleography; 428. WRITING,
paleography.
palaeography 18. ANTIQUITY,
paleography; 249. LITERATURE,
paleography; 428. WRITING,
paleography.
palaeoichthyological 171. FOSSILS,
paleichthyology.
palaeoichthyologist 171. FOSSILS,
paleichthyology.
palaeoichthyology 171. FOSSILS,
paleichthyology.
palaeologic 308. PAST, paleology.
palaeological 308. PAST, paleology.
palaeologist 308. PAST, paleology.
palaeology 308. PAST, paleology.
palaeomammalogy 430. ZOOLOGY,
paleomammalogy.
palaeontologic 171. FOSSILS,
paleontology.
palaeontological 171. FOSSILS,
paleontology.
palaeontologist 171. FOSSILS,
paleontology.
palaeontology 171. FOSSILS,
paleontology.
palaeopaedologic 179. GEOLOGY,
paleopedology.
palaeopaedological 179. GEOLOGY,
paleopedology.
palaeopaedologist 179. GEOLOGY,
paleopedology.
palaeopaedology 179. GEOLOGY,
paleopedology.
palaeopathology 308. PAST,
paleopathology.
palaeopedologic 377. SOIL,
paleopedology.
palaeopedological 377. SOIL,
paleopedology.
palaeopedologist 377. SOIL,
paleopedology.
palaeopedology 377. SOIL,
paleopedology.
palaeornithologic 171. FOSSILS,
paleornithology.
palaeornithological 171. FOSSILS,
paleornithology.

palaeornithology 171. FOSSILS,
paleornithology.
palaeozoologic 171. FOSSILS,
paleozoology.
palaeozoological 171. FOSSILS,
paleozoology.
palaeozoology 171. FOSSILS,
paleozoology.
palaestra 26. ATHLETICS.
palaestric 26. ATHLETICS, palaestra.
palaetiological 308. PAST, paletiology.
palaetiologist 308. PAST, paletiology.
palaetiology 308. PAST; 308. PAST,
paletiology.
Palamitism 135. EASTERN ORTHODOXY.
palatinate 185. GOVERNMENT.
palatoplegia 122. DISEASE and ILLNESS.
paleethnologic 255. MANKIND,
paleethnology.
paleethnological 255. MANKIND,
paleethnology.
paleethnologist 255. MANKIND,
paleethnology.
paleethnology 255. MANKIND.
paleichthyological 171. FOSSILS,
paleichthyology.
paleichthyologist 171. FOSSILS,
paleichthyology.
paleichthyology 171. FOSSILS.
paleobiologic 171. FOSSILS,
paleobiology.
paleobiological 171. FOSSILS,
paleobiology.
paleobiologist 171. FOSSILS,
paleobiology.
paleobiology 171. FOSSILS.
paleobotanic 171. FOSSILS,
paleobotany.
paleobotanical 171. FOSSILS,
paleobotany.
paleobotanist 171. FOSSILS,
paleobotany.
paleobotany 171. FOSSILS.
paleoecologic 142. ENVIRONMENT,
paleoecology.
paleoecological 142. ENVIRONMENT,
paleoecology.
paleoecology 142. ENVIRONMENT.
paleoethnography 255. MANKIND.
paleoethnological 255. MANKIND,
paleethnology.

paleoethnologist 255. MANKIND,
paleethnology.
paleoethnology 255. MANKIND,
paleethnology.
paleogeographer 178. GEOGRAPHY,
paleogeography.
paleogeographic 178. GEOGRAPHY,
paleogeography.
paleogeographical 178. GEOGRAPHY,
paleogeography.
paleogeography 178. GEOGRAPHY.
paleographer 18. ANTIQUITY,
paleography; 249. LITERATURE,
paleography; 428. WRITING,
paleography.
paleographic 18. ANTIQUITY,
paleography; 249. LITERATURE,
paleography; 428. WRITING,
paleography.
paleography 18. ANTIQUITY;
249. LITERATURE; 428. WRITING.
paleoichthyological 171. FOSSILS,
paleichthyology.
paleoichthyologist 171. FOSSILS,
paleichthyology.
paleoichthyology 171. FOSSILS,
paleichthyology.
paleologic 308. PAST, paleology.
paleological 308. PAST, paleology.
paleologist 308. PAST, paleology.
paleology 308. PAST.
paleomammalogy 430. ZOOLOGY.
paleontologic 171. FOSSILS,
paleontology.
paleontological 171. FOSSILS,
paleontology.
paleontologist 171. FOSSILS,
paleontology.
paleontology 171. FOSSILS.
paleopathology 308. PAST.
paleopedologic 179. GEOLOGY,
paleopedology; 377. SOIL,
paleopedology.
paleopedological 179. GEOLOGY,
paleopedology; 377. SOIL,
paleopedology.
paleopedologist 179. GEOLOGY,
paleopedology; 377. SOIL,
paleopedology.
paleopedology 179. GEOLOGY;
377. SOIL.

paleornithologic 171. FOSSILS,
paleornithology.
paleornithological 171. FOSSILS,
paleornithology.
paleornithology 171. FOSSILS.
paleozoologic 171. FOSSILS,
paleozoology.
paleozoological 171. FOSSILS,
paleozoology.
paleozoology 171. FOSSILS.
palestra 26. ATHLETICS, palaestra.
palestric 26. ATHLETICS, palaestra.
paletiological 308. PAST, paletiology.
paletiologist 308. PAST, paletiology.
paletiology 308. PAST.
palillogy 354. RHETORIC and
RHETORICAL DEVICES, palilogy.
palilogy 354. RHETORIC and
RHETORICAL DEVICES.
palimpsest 53. BOOKS;
256. MANUSCRIPTS.
palimpsestic 53. BOOKS, palimpsest;
256. MANUSCRIPTS, palimpsest.
palingenesia 46. BIRTH, palingenesis;
170. FORM, palingenesis.
palingenesian 35. BAPTISM,
palingenesis.
palingenesis 35. BAPTISM; 46. BIRTH;
170. FORM.
palingenesist 35. BAPTISM, palingenesis.
palingenesy 46. BIRTH, palingenesis;
170. FORM, palingenesis.
palingenetic 46. BIRTH, palingenesis;
170. FORM, palingenesis.
Palladianism 20. ARCHITECTURE.
pallid 92. COLOR, pallidity.
pallidity 92. COLOR.
pallograph 366. SHIPS.
pallographic 366. SHIPS, pallograph.
palmist 194. HANDS, palmistry.
palmistry 124. DIVINATION; 194. HANDS.
palpitation 199. HEART.
paludism 122. DISEASE and ILLNESS.
palynology 44. BIOLOGY.
pamphysicism 312. PHILOSOPHY;
312. PHILOSOPHY, pamphysicism.
panacea 350. REMEDIES.
panacean 350. REMEDIES, panacea.
panaesthesia 309. PERCEPTION,
panesthesia.

panaesthetic 309. PERCEPTION, panesthesia.
panaesthetism 312. PHILOSOPHY.
Pan-Africanism 322. POLITICS.
Pan-Africanist 322. POLITICS, Pan-Africanism.
Pan-Americanism 322. POLITICS.
Pan-Arabism 322. POLITICS.
Pan-Arabist 322. POLITICS, Pan-Arabism.
panarchy 185. GOVERNMENT.
panaris 161. FINGERS and TOES, paronychia.
Pan-Buddhism 59. BUDDHISM.
Pan-Buddhist 59. BUDDHISM, Pan-Buddhism.
panchromatic 92. COLOR, panchromatism; 315. PHOTOGRAPHY, panchromatism.
panchromatism 92. COLOR; 315. PHOTOGRAPHY.
pancosmic 100. COSMOLOGY, pancosmism.
pancosmism 100. COSMOLOGY.
pancratiast 26. ATHLETICS; 55. BOXING.
pancratiastic 26. ATHLETICS, pancratiast; 55. BOXING, pancratiast.
pandect 239. LAW.
pandectist 239. LAW.
pandects 239. LAW, pandect.
pandemia 122. DISEASE and ILLNESS.
pandemic 122. DISEASE and ILLNESS, pandemia.
pandemonism 114. DEMONS.
Pandemonium 114. DEMONS; 301. ORDER and DISORDER.
pandemy 122. DISEASE and ILLNESS, pandemia.
panderage 364. SEX, panderism.
panderism 364. SEX.
pandiatonic 284. MUSIC, pandiatonicism.
pandiatonicism 284. MUSIC.
pandiculation 50. BODILY FUNCTIONS.
panegyric 326. PRAISE; 326. PRAISE, panegyric.
panegyrical 326. PRAISE, panegyric.
panegyrist 326. PRAISE, panegyric.
panentheism 183. GOD and GODS.
panentheist 183. GOD and GODS, panentheism.

paneogism 312. PHILOSOPHY.
panesthesia 309. PERCEPTION.
panesthetic 309. PERCEPTION, panesthesia.
pangenesis 147. EVOLUTION; 204. HEREDITY.
pangenetic 147. EVOLUTION, pangenesis; 204. HEREDITY, pangenesis.
Pan-Germanism 322. POLITICS.
pangermism 122. DISEASE and ILLNESS.
Panhellenic 190. GREECE and GREEKS, Panhellinism.
Panhellenism 190. GREECE and GREEKS.
Panhellenist 190. GREECE and GREEKS, Panhellinism.
Pan-Islamic 227. ISLAM, Pan-Islamism.
Pan-Islamism 227. ISLAM.
Pan-Islamist 227. ISLAM, Pan-Islamism.
panjandrum 62. BUREAUCRACY.
panlogical 312. PHILOSOPHY, panlogism.
panlogism 312. PHILOSOPHY.
panlogist 312. PHILOSOPHY, panlogism.
panlogistic 312. PHILOSOPHY, panlogism.
panlogistical 312. PHILOSOPHY, panlogism.
panmnesia 269. MEMORY.
panophobe 156. FEAR, panophobia.
panophobia 156. FEAR; 313. PHOBIAS.
panophobic 156. FEAR, panophobia.
panorama 352. REPRESENTATION.
panoramic 352. REPRESENTATION, panorama.
panoramical 352. REPRESENTATION, panorama.
panphobia 313. PHOBIAS, panophobia.
panpsychism 312. PHILOSOPHY; 379. SOUL.
panpsychist 312. PHILOSOPHY, panpsychism; 379. SOUL, panpsychism.
panpsychistic 312. PHILOSOPHY, panpsychism; 379. SOUL, panpsychism.
Pansatanism 100. COSMOLOGY; 117. DEVIL.
pansexualism 334. PSYCHOLOGY.
pansexualist 334. PSYCHOLOGY, pansexualism.

pansexuality 334. PSYCHOLOGY,
pansexualism.
pansophic 233. KNOWLEDGE,
pansophy.
pansophism 233. KNOWLEDGE.
pansophist 233. KNOWLEDGE,
pansophism.
pansophistical 233. KNOWLEDGE,
pansophism.
pansophy 233. KNOWLEDGE.
pantagamic 258. MARRIAGE,
pantagamy.
pantagamy 258. MARRIAGE.
Pantagruelian 213. HUMOR,
Pantagruelism.
Pantagruelism 213. HUMOR.
pantaphobia 313. PHOBIAS,
panophobia.
pantaraxia 9. ALERTNESS.
Pan-Teutonic 289. NATIONALISM, Pan-
Teutonism.
Pan-Teutonism 289. NATIONALISM.
Pan-Teutonist 289. NATIONALISM, Pan-
Teutonism.
pantheism 183. GOD and GODS;
349. RELIGION.
pantheist 183. GOD and GODS,
pantheism; 349. RELIGION,
pantheism.
pantheistic 349. RELIGION, pantheism.
panthelism 312. PHILOSOPHY.
pantheologic 392. THEOLOGY,
pantheology.
pantheological 392. THEOLOGY,
pantheology.
pantheologist 392. THEOLOGY,
pantheology.
pantheology 392. THEOLOGY.
pantisocracy 185. GOVERNMENT.
pantisocratic 185. GOVERNMENT,
pantisocracy.
pantisocratical 185. GOVERNMENT,
pantisocracy.
pantisocratist 185. GOVERNMENT,
pantisocracy.
pantoglot 236. LANGUAGE,
pantoglottism.
pantoglottism 236. LANGUAGE.
pantograph 98. COPYING.
pantographic 98. COPYING,
pantograph.

pantologic 233. KNOWLEDGE,
pantology.
pantological 233. KNOWLEDGE,
pantology.
pantologist 233. KNOWLEDGE,
pantology.
pantology 233. KNOWLEDGE.
pantometer 264. MEASUREMENT,
pantometry.
pantometric 264. MEASUREMENT,
pantometry.
pantometrical 264. MEASUREMENT,
pantometry.
pantometry 264. MEASUREMENT.
pantomime 310. PERFORMING.
pantomimist 310. PERFORMING,
pantomime.
pantophagist 168. FOOD and NUTRITION,
pantophagy.
pantophagous 168. FOOD and
NUTRITION, pantophagy.
pantophagy 168. FOOD and NUTRITION.
pantophobia 313. PHOBIAS, panophobia.
papalism 69. CATHOLICISM.
papalist 69. CATHOLICISM, papalism.
papaphobia 313. PHOBIAS.
papism 69. CATHOLICISM.
papist 69. CATHOLICISM, papism.
papistic 69. CATHOLICISM, papism.
papistical 69. CATHOLICISM, papism.
papistry 69. CATHOLICISM, papism.
papolatrous 323. POPE, papolatry.
papolatry 323. POPE.
papyrocracy 185. GOVERNMENT.
papyrograph 328. PRINTING,
papyrography.
papyrographic 328. PRINTING,
papyrography.
papyrography 328. PRINTING.
papyrological 256. MANUSCRIPTS,
papyrology; 308. PAST, papyrology.
papyrologist 18. ANTIQUITY,
papyrology; 256. MANUSCRIPTS,
papyrology; 308. PAST, papyrology.
papyrology 18. ANTIQUITY;
256. MANUSCRIPTS; 308. PAST.
parabaptism 35. BAPTISM.
parabaptist 35. BAPTISM, parabaptism.
parabiosis 44. BIOLOGY; 230. JOINING.
parabiotic 44. BIOLOGY, parabiosis;
230. JOINING, parabiosis.
parachronic 396. TIME, parachronism.

parachronism 396. TIME.
Paraclete 80. CHRISTIANITY.
paracousia 111. DEAFNESS, **paracusis;**
198. HEARING, **paracusis.**
paracusis 111. DEAFNESS; 198. HEARING.
paradigm 186. GRAMMAR.
paradigmatic 186. GRAMMAR,
paradigm.
paradigmatical 186. GRAMMAR,
paradigm.
paradoxer 21. ARGUMENTATION,
paradoxology.
paradoxology 21. ARGUMENTATION.
paraesthesia 51. BODY, HUMAN,
paresthesia; 309. PERCEPTION,
paresthesia.
paraesthetic 51. BODY, HUMAN,
paresthesia; 309. PERCEPTION,
paresthesia.
paragoge 236. LANGUAGE.
paragogic 236. LANGUAGE, **paragoge.**
paragogical 236. LANGUAGE, **paragoge.**
paragraphia 122. DISEASE and ILLNESS.
paragraphic 122. DISEASE and ILLNESS,
paragraphia.
paragraphically 237. LANGUAGE STYLE,
paragraphism.
paragraphism 237. LANGUAGE STYLE.
paragraphist 237. LANGUAGE STYLE,
paragraphism.
paralalia 382. SPEECH.
paralellometer 226. INSTRUMENTS.
paralipomena 53. BOOKS.
paralipophobia 313. PHOBIAS.
paralipsis 354. RHETORIC and
RHETORICAL DEVICES, **apophasis.**
parallelism 262. MATHEMATICS;
312. PHILOSOPHY.
paralogia 21. ARGUMENTATION,
paralogism; 334. PSYCHOLOGY;
382. SPEECH.
paralogical 334. PSYCHOLOGY,
paralogia.
paralogism 21. ARGUMENTATION.
paralogist 21. ARGUMENTATION,
paralogism.
paralogistic 21. ARGUMENTATION,
paralogism.
paralogy 21. ARGUMENTATION,
paralogism; 334. PSYCHOLOGY,
paralogia.

paralysis 51. BODY, HUMAN;
122. DISEASE and ILLNESS.
paralytic 51. BODY, HUMAN, **paralysis;**
122. DISEASE and ILLNESS, **paralysis.**
paralytical 122. DISEASE and ILLNESS,
paralysis.
paramania 120. DISCONTENT;
254. MANIAS.
paramnesia 269. MEMORY.
paranoia 187. GRANDEUR;
224. INSANITY.
paranoiac 187. GRANDEUR, **paranoia;**
224. INSANITY, **paranoia.**
paranoid 187. GRANDEUR, **paranoia;**
224. INSANITY, **paranoia.**
paranoidism 224. INSANITY.
paranymph 258. MARRIAGE.
paraph 428. WRITING.
paraphasia 382. SPEECH.
paraphilia 364. SEX.
paraphilic 364. SEX, **paraphilia.**
paraphobia 313. PHOBIAS; 364. SEX.
paraphrase 236. LANGUAGE,
paraphrasis.
paraphrasia 382. SPEECH.
paraphrasis 236. LANGUAGE.
paraphrastic 236. LANGUAGE,
paraphrasis.
paraphrastical 236. LANGUAGE,
paraphrasis.
parapraxis 334. PSYCHOLOGY.
parapsychological 334. PSYCHOLOGY,
parapsychology.
parapsychology 334. PSYCHOLOGY.
paraselene 25. ASTRONOMY.
parasitic 44. BIOLOGY, **parasitism.**
parasitical 44. BIOLOGY, **parasitism.**
parasitism 16. ANIMALS; 44. BIOLOGY;
319. PLANTS.
parasitologist 44. BIOLOGY,
parasitology.
parasitology 44. BIOLOGY.
parasitophobia 313. PHOBIAS.
parasynthesis 236. LANGUAGE.
parasynthetic 236. LANGUAGE,
parasynthesis.
paratactic 186. GRAMMAR, **parataxis.**
parataxis 186. GRAMMAR.
parathesis 135. EASTERN ORTHODOXY.
parathetic 135. EASTERN ORTHODOXY,
parathesis.

parcenary 331. PROPERTY and
OWNERSHIP.
parcener 331. PROPERTY and
OWNERSHIP.
paremiography 333. PROVERBS,
paroemiography.
paremiologist 333. PROVERBS,
paroemiology.
paremiology 333. PROVERBS,
paroemiology.
parentalism 307. PARENTS.
parentation 307. PARENTS.
parenticide 307. PARENTS.
paresis 51. BODY, HUMAN; 122. DISEASE
and ILLNESS.
paresthesia 51. BODY, HUMAN;
309. PERCEPTION.
paresthetic 51. BODY, HUMAN,
paresthesia; 309. PERCEPTION,
paresthesia.
paretic 51. BODY, HUMAN, paresis;
122. DISEASE and ILLNESS, paresis.
parhidrosis 50. BODILY FUNCTIONS.
parhomologous 44. BIOLOGY,
parhomology.
parhomology 44. BIOLOGY.
pariahdom 376. SOCIETY, pariahism.
pariahism 376. SOCIETY.
pari-mutuel 175. GAMBLING.
parisological 236. LANGUAGE,
parisology.
parisology 236. LANGUAGE.
parity 46. BIRTH.
Parkinsonism 122. DISEASE and ILLNESS.
parliamentarian 185. GOVERNMENT,
parliamentarianism.
parliamentarianism 185. GOVERNMENT.
parmacopedic 130. DRUGS,
pharmacopedics.
Parnassian 249. LITERATURE,
Parnassianism.
Parnassianism 249. LITERATURE.
parochialism 28. ATTITUDES.
parochialist 28. ATTITUDES,
parochialism.
paroemia 333. PROVERBS.
paroemiac 333. PROVERBS, paroemia.
paroemiographer 333. PROVERBS,
paroemiography.
paroemiography 333. PROVERBS.

paroemiologic 236. LANGUAGE,
paroemiology.
paroemiological 236. LANGUAGE,
paroemiology.
paroemiologist 236. LANGUAGE,
paroemiology; 333. PROVERBS,
paroemiology.
paroemiology 236. LANGUAGE;
333. PROVERBS.
paromologetic 354. RHETORIC and
RHETORICAL DEVICES, paromology.
paromologia 354. RHETORIC and
RHETORICAL DEVICES, paromology.
paromology 354. RHETORIC and
RHETORICAL DEVICES.
paronomasia 336. PUNNING;
354. RHETORIC and RHETORICAL
DEVICES.
paronomastic 336. PUNNING,
paronomasia.
paronychia 161. FINGERS and TOES.
paronym 247. LINGUISTICS, paronymy.
paronymy 247. LINGUISTICS.
parosmia 298. ODORS.
parosphresia 298. ODORS, parosmia.
parosphresis 298. ODORS, parosmia.
parotitic 122. DISEASE and ILLNESS,
parotitis.
parotitis 122. DISEASE and ILLNESS.
Parousia 80. CHRISTIANITY.
parousiamania 254. MANIAS.
parquetry 305. ORNAMENTATION;
425. WOOD.
parrhesia 237. LANGUAGE STYLE.
parricidal 232. KILLING, parricidism;
307. PARENTS, parricide.
parricide 307. PARENTS.
parricidism 232. KILLING.
parrotism 41. BEHAVIOR.
parrotry 41. BEHAVIOR, parrotism.
Parseeism 183. GOD and GODS, Parsiism.
Parsi 183. GOD and GODS, Parsiism.
Parsiism 183. GOD and GODS.
parsonarchy 332. PROTESTANTISM;
376. SOCIETY.
parthenogenesis 44. BIOLOGY; 244. LIFE.
parthenogenetic 44. BIOLOGY,
parthenogenesis; 244. LIFE,
parthenogenesis.
parthenogenic 44. BIOLOGY,
parthenogenesis.

parthenolatry 424. WOMEN.
parthenology 424. WOMEN.
parthenophobia 313. PHOBIAS.
parthogeny 44. BIOLOGY,
parthenogenesis.
partialism 364. SEX.
particularism 41. BEHAVIOR.
particularist 41. BEHAVIOR,
particularism.
particularistic 41. BEHAVIOR,
particularism.
partisan 155. FAVORITISM, partisanism;
322. POLITICS, partisanism.
partisanism 155. FAVORITISM;
322. POLITICS.
parturiency 46. BIRTH.
parturient 46. BIRTH, parturiency;
46. BIRTH, parturition.
parturition 46. BIRTH.
partyism 322. POLITICS.
partyist 322. POLITICS, partyism.
parvanimity 28. ATTITUDES.
parvenu 41. BEHAVIOR, parvenuism;
376. SOCIETY, parvenuism.
parvenuism 41. BEHAVIOR;
376. SOCIETY.
pasigraphic 236. LANGUAGE,
pasigraphy.
pasigraphy 236. LANGUAGE.
pasimology 181. GESTURE.
passive scopophilia 364. SEX,
scopophilia.
passivism 28. ATTITUDES; 322. POLITICS.
passivist 28. ATTITUDES, passivism;
322. POLITICS, passivism.
pastelist 23. ART; 128. DRAWING.
pastellist 23. ART, pastelist;
128. DRAWING, pastelist.
pastoral 5. AGRICULTURE, pastoralism;
137. ECONOMICS, pastoralism.
pastoralism 5. AGRICULTURE;
137. ECONOMICS; 248. LITERARY STYLE.
pastoralist 5. AGRICULTURE,
pastoralism; 137. ECONOMICS,
pastoralism; 248. LITERARY STYLE,
pastoralism.
pasturage 5. AGRICULTURE;
137. ECONOMICS, pastoralism.
Patarene 205. HERESY, Patarinism.
Pataria 205. HERESY, Patarinism.
Patarine 205. HERESY, Patarinism.

Patarinism 205. HERESY.
paternalism 185. GOVERNMENT;
398. TRADE.
paternalist 185. GOVERNMENT,
paternalism; 398. TRADE,
paternalism.
paternalistic 185. GOVERNMENT,
paternalism; 398. TRADE,
paternalism.
pathematology 312. PHILOSOPHY.
pathogenic 122. DISEASE and ILLNESS,
pathogenicity.
pathogenicity 122. DISEASE and ILLNESS.
pathognomonic 149. FACIAL FEATURES,
pathognomy; 181. GESTURE,
pathognomy; 266. MEDICAL
SPECIALTIES, pathognomy.
pathognomy 149. FACIAL FEATURES;
181. GESTURE; 266. MEDICAL
SPECIALTIES.
pathologic 122. DISEASE and ILLNESS,
pathology.
pathological 122. DISEASE and ILLNESS,
pathology.
pathologist 122. DISEASE and ILLNESS,
pathology; 266. MEDICAL
SPECIALTIES, pathology.
pathology 122. DISEASE and ILLNESS;
266. MEDICAL SPECIALTIES.
pathomania 224. INSANITY; 254. MANIAS.
pathophilia 122. DISEASE and ILLNESS;
311. -PHILE, -PHILIA, -PHILY.
pathophobia 122. DISEASE and ILLNESS;
313. PHOBIAS.
pathopoeia 354. RHETORIC and
RHETORICAL DEVICES.
patriarch 135. EASTERN ORTHODOXY;
185. GOVERNMENT, patriarchy.
patriarchic 153. FATHER, patriarchy;
253. MALE, patriarchy.
patriarchical 153. FATHER, patriarchy;
253. MALE, patriarchy.
patriarchism 185. GOVERNMENT.
patriarchist 153. FATHER, patriarchy;
185. GOVERNMENT, patriarchism;
253. MALE, patriarchy.
patriarchy 153. FATHER;
185. GOVERNMENT; 253. MALE.
patricentric 153. FATHER.
patricianism 41. BEHAVIOR.
patriciate 41. BEHAVIOR, patricianism.

patricidal 232. KILLING, patricide;
307. PARENTS, patricide.
patricide 232. KILLING; 307. PARENTS.
patrilineal 15. ANCESTORS, patriliny;
348. RELATIONSHIP, patriliny.
patrilinear 15. ANCESTORS, patriliny;
348. RELATIONSHIP, patriliny.
patriliny 15. ANCESTORS;
348. RELATIONSHIP.
patrilocal 17. ANTHROPOLOGY,
patrilocality.
patrilocality 17. ANTHROPOLOGY.
patriot 289. NATIONALISM, patriotism.
patriotic 289. NATIONALISM, patriotism.
patriotism 289. NATIONALISM.
Patripassian 79. CHRIST,
Patripassianism; 205. HERESY,
Patripassianism.
Patripassianism 79. CHRIST;
205. HERESY.
Patripassianist 79. CHRIST,
Patripassianism.
patristics 392. THEOLOGY, patrology.
patrolatry 349. RELIGION.
patrologic 392. THEOLOGY, patrology.
patrological 392. THEOLOGY,
patrology.
patrologist 392. THEOLOGY, patrology.
patrology 392. THEOLOGY.
patronomatology 288. NAMES.
patronymic 288. NAMES.
pauciloquent 58. BREVITY, pauciloquy.
pauciloquy 58. BREVITY.
Paulian 79. CHRIST, Paulianism.
Paulianism 79. CHRIST.
Paulianist 79. CHRIST, Paulianism.
Paulinian 80. CHRISTIANITY, Paulinism.
Paulinism 80. CHRISTIANITY.
Paulist 80. CHRISTIANITY, Paulinism.
pauperage 325. POVERTY, pauperism.
pauperism 325. POVERTY.
paysagist 23. ART.
peccancy 367. SIN.
peccant 367. SIN, peccancy.
peccatiphobia 313. PHOBIAS; 367. SIN.
peccatophobia 313. PHOBIAS,
peccatiphobia; 367. SIN,
peccatiphobia.

Pecksniffery 249. LITERATURE,
Pecksniffianism.
Pecksniffian 249. LITERATURE,
Pecksniffianism.
Pecksniffianism 249. LITERATURE.
pectoriloquial 51. BODY, HUMAN,
pectoriloquism; 382. SPEECH,
pectoriloquism.
pectoriloquism 51. BODY, HUMAN;
382. SPEECH.
pectoriloquous 51. BODY, HUMAN,
pectoriloquism; 382. SPEECH,
pectoriloquism.
pectoriloquy 51. BODY, HUMAN,
pectoriloquism; 382. SPEECH,
pectoriloquism.
peculation 103. CRIME; 391. THEFT.
peculator 391. THEFT, peculation.
peculium 331. PROPERTY and
OWNERSHIP.
pedage 131. DUES and PAYMENT.
pedagese 237. LANGUAGE STYLE.
pedagog 77. CHILDREN, pedagogics;
240. LEARNING, pedagogics.
pedagogic 240. LEARNING, pedagogics.
pedagogical 240. LEARNING,
pedagogics.
pedagogics 77. CHILDREN;
240. LEARNING.
pedagogism 240. LEARNING.
pedagogue 77. CHILDREN, pedagogics;
240. LEARNING, pedagogics.
pedagogy 77. CHILDREN, pedagogics;
240. LEARNING.
pedant 240. LEARNING, pedanticism.
pedantic 240. LEARNING, pedanticism.
pedanticism 240. LEARNING.
pedantocracy 185. GOVERNMENT;
240. LEARNING.
pedantry 240. LEARNING.
pederast 77. CHILDREN, pederasty.
pederasty 77. CHILDREN.
pedestrian 237. LANGUAGE STYLE,
pedestrianism.
pedestrianism 237. LANGUAGE STYLE.
pediatric 266. MEDICAL SPECIALTIES,
pediatrics.
pediatrician 77. CHILDREN, pediatrics;
266. MEDICAL SPECIALTIES, pediatrics.
pediatrics 77. CHILDREN; 266. MEDICAL
SPECIALTIES.

pediculophobia 225. INSECTS;
313. PHOBIAS.
pediculosis 225. INSECTS.
pediculous 225. INSECTS, pediculosis.
pedicure 157. FEET and LEGS.
pedicurist 157. FEET and LEGS,
pedicure.
pedobaptism 35. BAPTISM.
pedobaptist 35. BAPTISM, pedobaptism.
pedodontia 77. CHILDREN,
pedodontics.
pedodontic 266. MEDICAL SPECIALTIES,
pedodontics.
pedodontics 77. CHILDREN;
266. MEDICAL SPECIALTIES.
pedodontist 77. CHILDREN,
pedodontics; 266. MEDICAL
SPECIALTIES, pedodontics.
pedologic 377. SOIL, pedology.
pedological 77. CHILDREN, pedology;
377. SOIL, pedology.
pedologist 77. CHILDREN, pedology;
377. SOIL, pedology.
pedology 77. CHILDREN; 377. SOIL.
pedomancy 124. DIVINATION.
pedometer 123. DISTANCE;
226. INSTRUMENTS.
pedophilia 77. CHILDREN.
pedophiliac 77. CHILDREN, pedophilia.
pedophilic 77. CHILDREN, pedophilia.
pedophobia 77. CHILDREN; 126. DOLLS;
313. PHOBIAS.
pedophobiac 77. CHILDREN,
pedophobia.
peerage 53. BOOKS.
pegomancy 124. DIVINATION.
pegomantic 124. DIVINATION,
pegomancy.
pejoration 113. DECAYING.
pejoratism 236. LANGUAGE.
peladophobia 33. BALDNESS.
Pelagian 205. HERESY, Pelagianism.
Pelagianism 205. HERESY.
pellagraphobia 313. PHOBIAS.
pellucid 237. LANGUAGE STYLE,
pellucidity.
pellucidity 237. LANGUAGE STYLE.
pellucidness 237. LANGUAGE STYLE,
pellucidity.
Pelmanism 393. THINKING.
peloria 167. FLOWERS.

pelorian 167. FLOWERS, peloria.
peloric 167. FLOWERS, peloria.
pelycologic 14. ANATOMY, pelycology.
pelycological 14. ANATOMY,
pelycology.
pelycology 14. ANATOMY.
pendactylate 194. HANDS,
pendactylism.
pendactylic 194. HANDS, pendactylism.
pendactylism 194. HANDS.
pendactylous 194. HANDS,
pendactylism.
penetralia 317. PLACES.
penetrometer 226. INSTRUMENTS.
peniaphobia 313. PHOBIAS;
325. POVERTY.
penisterophily 45. BIRDS.
penitence 80. CHRISTIANITY;
103. CRIME.
penitency 80. CHRISTIANITY, penitence;
103. CRIME, penitence.
penitent 80. CHRISTIANITY, penitence;
103. CRIME, penitence.
penmanship 428. WRITING.
penologist 103. CRIME, penology.
penology 103. CRIME.
pensionary 6. AID.
pentadactylate 157. FEET and LEGS,
pentadactylism.
pentadactylic 157. FEET and LEGS,
pentadactylism.
pentadactylism 157. FEET and LEGS;
161. FINGERS and TOES.
pentadactylous 157. FEET and LEGS,
pentadactylism; 161. FINGERS and
TOES, pentadactylism.
pentaglot 236. LANGUAGE;
236. LANGUAGE, pentaglot.
Pentagonese 237. LANGUAGE STYLE.
pentameter 409. VERSE.
pentapody 409. VERSE.
pentathlon 26. ATHLETICS.
Pentecostal 332. PROTESTANTISM,
Pentecostalism.
Pentecostalism 332. PROTESTANTISM.
penurious 325. POVERTY, penury.
penury 325. POVERTY.
perastadic 31. AVIATION, perastadics.
perastadics 31. AVIATION.
perceptionism 233. KNOWLEDGE.

perceptionist 233. KNOWLEDGE,
perceptionism.
peregrination 399. TRAVEL;
412. WALKING.
peregrine 169. FOREIGNERS,
peregrinism.
peregrinism 169. FOREIGNERS.
pererration 399. TRAVEL;
412. WALKING.
perfectibilism 28. ATTITUDES.
perfectibilist 28. ATTITUDES,
perfectibilism.
perfectionism 28. ATTITUDES.
perfectionist 28. ATTITUDES,
perfectionism.
perfectionistic 28. ATTITUDES,
perfectionism.
perfidious 400. TREASON, perfidy.
perfidy 400. TREASON.
pericarditis 199. HEART.
pericynthion 318. PLANETS.
perigee 318. PLANETS.
perigenesis 204. HEREDITY.
perigenetic 204. HEREDITY, perigenesis.
perigraph 128. DRAWING.
perigynous 167. FLOWERS, perigyny;
319. PLANTS, perigyny.
perigyny 167. FLOWERS; 319. PLANTS.
perihelion 25. ASTRONOMY;
318. PLANETS.
perihelium 25. ASTRONOMY;
318. PLANETS.
perilune 25. ASTRONOMY; 318. PLANETS.
perimorphic 179. GEOLOGY,
perimorphism.
perimorphism 179. GEOLOGY.
perimorphous 179. GEOLOGY,
perimorphism.
periodicalist 265. MEDIA.
periodontia 390. TEETH, periodontics.
periodontic 390. TEETH, periodontics.
periodontics 390. TEETH.
periodontist 390. TEETH, periodontics.
Peripatetic 312. PHILOSOPHY,
Peripateticism.
Peripateticism 312. PHILOSOPHY.
peripeteia 127. DRAMA.
peripetia 127. DRAMA, peripeteia.
peripety 127. DRAMA, peripeteia.

periphrasis 186. GRAMMAR,
periphrastic; 236. LANGUAGE;
354. RHETORIC and RHETORICAL
DEVICES.
periphrastic 186. GRAMMAR;
236. LANGUAGE, periphrasis;
354. RHETORIC and RHETORICAL
DEVICES, periphrasis.
perissodactylate 157. FEET and LEGS,
perissodactylism; 194. HANDS,
perissodactylism.
perissodactylic 157. FEET and LEGS,
perissodactylism; 194. HANDS,
perissodactylism.
perissodactylism 157. FEET and LEGS;
194. HANDS.
perissodactylous 157. FEET and LEGS,
perissodactylism; 194. HANDS,
perissodactylism.
perissology 236. LANGUAGE.
peristalsis 50. BODILY FUNCTIONS.
peristaltic 50. BODILY FUNCTIONS,
peristalsis.
perjurer 243. LIES and LYING, perjury.
perjurious 243. LIES and LYING, perjury.
perjury 243. LIES and LYING.
perk 131. DUES and PAYMENT,
perquisite.
Perkinism 350. REMEDIES.
Peronism 185. GOVERNMENT.
perpension 393. THINKING.
perquisite 131. DUES and PAYMENT.
perscrutation 329. PROCESSES.
personalism 362. SELF.
personalist 362. SELF, personalism.
personalistic 362. SELF, personalism.
personification 354. RHETORIC and
RHETORICAL DEVICES.
personificative 354. RHETORIC and
RHETORICAL DEVICES,
personification.
pertussal 122. DISEASE and ILLNESS,
pertussis.
pertussis 122. DISEASE and ILLNESS.
pessimism 28. ATTITUDES;
312. PHILOSOPHY.
pessimist 28. ATTITUDES, pessimism;
312. PHILOSOPHY, pessimism.
pessimistic 28. ATTITUDES, pessimism;
312. PHILOSOPHY, pessimism.

pessomancy 124. DIVINATION;
385. STONES.
pesticide 225. INSECTS; 232. KILLING;
319. PLANTS.
petalism 34. BANISHMENT.
Petrarchan 248. LITERARY STYLE,
Petrarchism.
Petrarchism 248. LITERARY STYLE.
Petrarchist 248. LITERARY STYLE,
Petrarchism.
petrifaction 329. PROCESSES,
petrification; 385. STONES,
petrification.
petrification 329. PROCESSES;
385. STONES.
Petrinism 69. CATHOLICISM.
Petrinist 69. CATHOLICISM, **Petrinism.**
petrogensis 179. GEOLOGY.
petrogeny 179. GEOLOGY, **petrogensis.**
petroglyph 385. STONES, **petroglyphy.**
petroglyphic 385. STONES, **petroglyphy.**
petroglyphy 385. STONES.
petrographer 179. GEOLOGY,
petrography.
petrographic 179. GEOLOGY,
petrography.
petrographical 179. GEOLOGY,
petrography.
petrography 179. GEOLOGY;
385. STONES, **petroglyphy.**
petrologic 179. GEOLOGY, **petrology.**
petrological 179. GEOLOGY, **petrology.**
petrologist 179. GEOLOGY, **petrology.**
petrology 179. GEOLOGY.
pettifogger 239. LAW.
pettifoggery 239. LAW, **pettifogger.**
petulance 28. ATTITUDES.
petulancy 28. ATTITUDES, **petulance.**
petulant 28. ATTITUDES, **petulance.**
phaeism 47. BLACKENING and
BLACKNESS.
phaenologic 302. ORGANISMS,
phenology.
phaenological 302. ORGANISMS,
phenology.
phaenologist 302. ORGANISMS,
phenology.
phaenology 302. ORGANISMS,
phenology.
phagocyte 49. BLOOD and BLOOD
VESSELS.

phagocytic 49. BLOOD and BLOOD
VESSELS, **phagocyte.**
phagocytosis 49. BLOOD and BLOOD
VESSELS; 72. CELLS.
phagology 168. FOOD and NUTRITION.
phagomania 168. FOOD and NUTRITION;
254. MANIAS.
phagophobia 168. FOOD and NUTRITION;
313. PHOBIAS.
phalacrosis 33. BALDNESS.
phalansterianism 93. COMMUNALISM.
phalanx 105. CROWDS.
phallicism 183. GOD and GODS.
phallicist 183. GOD and GODS,
phallicism.
phallist 183. GOD and GODS, **phallicism.**
phaneromania 254. MANIAS; 370. SKIN.
phantascope 148. EYES,
phantasmascope; 226. INSTRUMENTS,
phantasmascope.
Phantasiast 79. CHRIST; 205. HERESY.
phantasm 182. GHOSTS; 218. IMAGES;
309. PERCEPTION; 312. PHILOSOPHY.
phantasma 182. GHOSTS, **phantasm.**
phantasmagoria 129. DREAMS;
218. IMAGES; 352. REPRESENTATION.
phantasmagorial 129. DREAMS,
phantasmagoria; 218. IMAGES,
phantasmagoria;
352. REPRESENTATION,
phantasmagoria.
phantasmagoric 129. DREAMS,
phantasmagoria; 218. IMAGES,
phantasmagoria;
352. REPRESENTATION,
phantasmagoria.
phantasmascope 148. EYES;
226. INSTRUMENTS.
phantasmatography 25. ASTRONOMY.
phantasmology 182. GHOSTS.
Pharisaic 231. JUDAISM, **Phariseeism.**
pharisaic 231. JUDAISM, **Phariseeism.**
Pharisaism 231. JUDAISM, **Phariseeism.**
Pharisee 231. JUDAISM, **Phariseeism.**
pharisee 231. JUDAISM, **Phariseeism.**
Phariseeism 231. JUDAISM.
pharmaceutics 130. DRUGS.
pharmacist 130. DRUGS, **pharmacy.**
pharmacodynamic 130. DRUGS,
pharmacodynamics.

pharmacodynamical 130. DRUGS,
pharmacodynamics.
pharmacodynamics 130. DRUGS.
pharmacognosia 130. DRUGS,
pharmacognosy.
pharmacognosis 130. DRUGS,
pharmacognosy.
pharmacognosist 130. DRUGS,
pharmacognosy.
pharmacognostic 130. DRUGS,
pharmacognosy.
pharmacognostics 130. DRUGS,
pharmacognosy.
pharmacognosy 130. DRUGS.
pharmacography 130. DRUGS.
pharmacologia 130. DRUGS,
pharmacology.
pharmacologic 130. DRUGS,
pharmacology; 350. REMEDIES,
pharmacology.
pharmacological 130. DRUGS,
pharmacology; 350. REMEDIES,
pharmacology.
pharmacologist 130. DRUGS,
pharmacology; 350. REMEDIES,
pharmacology.
pharmacology 130. DRUGS;
350. REMEDIES.
pharmacomania 122. DISEASE and
ILLNESS; 254. MANIAS; 266. MEDICAL
SPECIALTIES.
pharmacopedia 130. DRUGS,
pharmacopedics.
pharmacopedics 130. DRUGS.
pharmacophobia 130. DRUGS;
313. PHOBIAS.
pharmacopoeia 130. DRUGS;
350. REMEDIES.
pharmacopolist 130. DRUGS.
pharmacy 130. DRUGS.
pharology 192. GUIDES and GUIDING;
245. LIGHT; 366. SHIPS.
pharyngism 122. DISEASE and ILLNESS.
pharyngographic 14. ANATOMY,
pharyngography.
pharyngographical 14. ANATOMY,
pharyngography.
pharyngography 14. ANATOMY.
pharyngological 266. MEDICAL
SPECIALTIES, pharyngology.

pharyngologist 266. MEDICAL
SPECIALTIES, pharyngology.
pharyngology 266. MEDICAL
SPECIALTIES.
phasmophobia 182. GHOSTS;
313. PHOBIAS.
phelloplastics 23. ART.
phengophobia 245. LIGHT;
313. PHOBIAS.
phenologic 85. CLIMATE, phenology;
302. ORGANISMS, phenology.
phenological 85. CLIMATE, phenology;
302. ORGANISMS, phenology;
396. TIME, phenology.
phenologist 85. CLIMATE, phenology;
302. ORGANISMS, phenology;
396. TIME, phenology.
phenology 85. CLIMATE;
302. ORGANISMS; 396. TIME.
phenomenalism 312. PHILOSOPHY.
phenomenalist 312. PHILOSOPHY,
phenomenalism.
phenomenalistic 312. PHILOSOPHY,
phenomenalism.
phenomenologic 312. PHILOSOPHY,
phenomenology.
phenomenological 312. PHILOSOPHY,
phenomenology.
phenomenologist 312. PHILOSOPHY,
phenomenology.
phenomenology 312. PHILOSOPHY.
philanthropic 28. ATTITUDES,
philanthropy; 75. CHARITY,
philanthropy; 255. MANKIND,
philanthropism.
philanthropical 255. MANKIND,
philanthropism.
philanthropism 255. MANKIND.
philanthropist 28. ATTITUDES,
philanthropy; 255. MANKIND,
philanthropism.
philanthropy 28. ATTITUDES;
75. CHARITY; 255. MANKIND,
philanthropism.
philarchaic 308. PAST, philarchaist.
philarchaist 308. PAST.
philatelist 91. COLLECTIONS and
COLLECTING, philately.
philately 91. COLLECTIONS and
COLLECTING.
philauty 251. LOVE; 362. SELF.

Philhellenic 190. GREECE and GREEKS, **Philhellenism.**
Philhellenism 190. GREECE and GREEKS.
Philhellenist 190. GREECE and GREEKS, **Philhellenism.**
philippic 354. RHETORIC and RHETORICAL DEVICES.
Philippism 332. PROTESTANTISM.
Philippist 332. PROTESTANTISM, **Philippism.**
Philippistic 332. PROTESTANTISM, **Philippism.**
philistine 28. ATTITUDES, **philistinism.**
philistinism 28. ATTITUDES.
phillumenist 91. COLLECTIONS and COLLECTING, **phillumeny.**
phillumeny 91. COLLECTIONS and COLLECTING.
philobiblist 53. BOOKS.
philobotanist 319. PLANTS.
philocalist 38. BEAUTY.
philocaly 38. BEAUTY, **philocalist.**
philocubist 175. GAMBLING.
philocynic 125. DOGS, **philocynism.**
philocynical 125. DOGS, **philocynism.**
philocynism 125. DOGS.
philocyny 125. DOGS, **philocynism.**
philofelist 70. CATS.
philogalist 70. CATS.
philogynist 424. WOMEN, **philogyny.**
philogynous 424. WOMEN, **philogyny.**
philogyny 424. WOMEN.
philologer 236. LANGUAGE, **logophile;** 247. LINGUISTICS, **philology.**
philologic 247. LINGUISTICS, **philology.**
philological 247. LINGUISTICS, **philology.**
philologist 247. LINGUISTICS, **philology.**
philologue 236. LANGUAGE, **logophile.**
philology 247. LINGUISTICS.
philomath 262. MATHEMATICS, **philomathy.**
philomathean 262. MATHEMATICS, **philomathy.**
philomathic 262. MATHEMATICS, **philomathy.**
philomathical 262. MATHEMATICS, **philomathy.**
philomathy 262. MATHEMATICS.
philometry 91. COLLECTIONS and COLLECTING.

philoneism 294. NOVELTY.
Philonian 231. JUDAISM, **Philonism.**
Philonic 231. JUDAISM, **Philonism.**
Philonism 231. JUDAISM.
Philonist 233. KNOWLEDGE, **philonoist.**
philonoist 233. KNOWLEDGE.
philopater 28. ATTITUDES.
philopatridomania 208. HOMESICKNESS; 254. MANIAS.
philopolemic 21. ARGUMENTATION.
philopolemist 21. ARGUMENTATION, **philopolemic.**
philosopher 393. THINKING, **philosphy.**
philosopher's stone 7. ALCHEMY, **elixir.**
philosophic 393. THINKING, **philosphy.**
philosophical 393. THINKING, **philosphy.**
philosophical existentialism 312. PHILOSOPHY, **existentialism.**
philosophical humanism 255. MANKIND, **humanism.**
philosophism 312. PHILOSOPHY.
philosophist 312. PHILOSOPHY, **philosophism.**
philosophobia 313. PHOBIAS.
philosphy 393. THINKING.
philostorgy 251. LOVE.
philotheism 183. GOD and GODS.
philotheist 183. GOD and GODS, **philotheism.**
philotheistic 183. GOD and GODS, **philotheism.**
phlebographical 49. BLOOD and BLOOD VESSELS, **phlebography.**
phlebography 49. BLOOD and BLOOD VESSELS.
phlebological 49. BLOOD and BLOOD VESSELS, **phlebology.**
phlebology 49. BLOOD and BLOOD VESSELS.
phlebotomic 49. BLOOD and BLOOD VESSELS, **phlebotomy.**
phlebotomical 49. BLOOD and BLOOD VESSELS, **phlebotomy.**
phlebotomist 49. BLOOD and BLOOD VESSELS, **phlebotomy.**
phlebotomize 49. BLOOD and BLOOD VESSELS, **phlebotomy.**
phlebotomy 49. BLOOD and BLOOD VESSELS.
phlogistic 162. FIRE, **phlogiston.**

phlogiston 162. FIRE.
phobophobia 156. FEAR; 313. PHOBIAS.
phocomelia 51. BODY, HUMAN.
phocomely 51. BODY, HUMAN,
  phocomelia.
phonautographic 111. DEAFNESS,
  phonautography.
phonautography 111. DEAFNESS.
phonematics 247. LINGUISTICS.
phonemicist 247. LINGUISTICS,
  phonemics.
phonemics 247. LINGUISTICS.
phonetic 247. LINGUISTICS, phonetics.
phonetical 247. LINGUISTICS, phonetics.
phonetician 247. LINGUISTICS,
  phonetics.
phonetics 247. LINGUISTICS.
phonism 198. HEARING;
  309. PERCEPTION.
phonocamptics 136. ECHOES.
phonocardiography 266. MEDICAL
  SPECIALTIES; 266. MEDICAL
  SPECIALTIES, stethography.
phonogram 428. WRITING.
phonographer 383. SPELLING,
  phonography; 428. WRITING,
  phonography.
phonographic 383. SPELLING,
  phonography; 428. WRITING,
  phonography.
phonographical 383. SPELLING,
  phonography.
phonographist 383. SPELLING,
  phonography; 428. WRITING,
  phonography.
phonography 383. SPELLING;
  428. WRITING.
phonological 247. LINGUISTICS,
  phonology; 380. SOUND, phonology.
phonologist 247. LINGUISTICS,
  phonology; 380. SOUND, phonology.
phonology 247. LINGUISTICS;
  380. SOUND.
phonomania 254. MANIAS; 380. SOUND.
phonophile 91. COLLECTIONS and
  COLLECTING, phonophily.
phonophily 91. COLLECTIONS and
  COLLECTING; 311. -PHILE,
  -PHILIA, -PHILY;
  314. PHONOGRAPH RECORDS.
phonophobia 313. PHOBIAS; 380. SOUND.

phorologist 122. DISEASE and ILLNESS,
  phorology.
phorology 122. DISEASE and ILLNESS.
phoronomy 282. MOTION.
phosphorism 321. POISON.
photalgia 148. EYES; 245. LIGHT;
  306. PAIN.
photalgiophobia 313. PHOBIAS.
photangiophobia 148. EYES; 245. LIGHT.
photics 245. LIGHT.
Photinianism 205. HERESY.
photism 309. PERCEPTION.
photobibliography 53. BOOKS;
  315. PHOTOGRAPHY.
photobiography 315. PHOTOGRAPHY.
photochromy 315. PHOTOGRAPHY.
photochronograph 315. PHOTOGRAPHY;
  396. TIME.
photodrama 127. DRAMA;
  315. PHOTOGRAPHY.
photodrome 226. INSTRUMENTS;
  245. LIGHT.
photodynamic 245. LIGHT,
  photodynamics; 319. PLANTS,
  photodynamics.
photodynamical 245. LIGHT,
  photodynamics; 319. PLANTS,
  photodynamics.
photodynamics 245. LIGHT;
  319. PLANTS.
photodysphoria 245. LIGHT,
  photophobia; 313. PHOBIAS,
  photophobia.
photoglyphic 141. ENGRAVING,
  photoglyphy; 315. PHOTOGRAPHY,
  photoglyphy.
photoglyphy 141. ENGRAVING;
  315. PHOTOGRAPHY.
photogrammetry 235. LAND; 257. MAPS;
  315. PHOTOGRAPHY.
photographer 245. LIGHT,
  photography.
photographic 245. LIGHT,
  photography.
photographical 245. LIGHT,
  photography.
photography 245. LIGHT.
photogravure 141. ENGRAVING;
  315. PHOTOGRAPHY.
photojournalism 265. MEDIA;
  315. PHOTOGRAPHY.

photojournalist 265. MEDIA,
photojournalism; 315. PHOTOGRAPHY,
photojournalism.
photokinesis 245. LIGHT; 282. MOTION.
photokinetic 245. LIGHT, photokinesis;
282. MOTION, photokinesis.
photolithographer 141. ENGRAVING,
photolithography;
315. PHOTOGRAPHY,
photolithography.
photolithographic 141. ENGRAVING,
photolithography;
315. PHOTOGRAPHY,
photolithography.
photolithography 141. ENGRAVING;
315. PHOTOGRAPHY.
photology 245. LIGHT.
photolysis 113. DECAYING; 245. LIGHT.
photolytic 113. DECAYING, photolysis;
245. LIGHT, photolysis.
photomania 245. LIGHT; 254. MANIAS.
photometer 226. INSTRUMENTS.
photometric 245. LIGHT, photometry.
photometrician 245. LIGHT,
photometry.
photometrist 245. LIGHT, photometry.
photometry 245. LIGHT.
photomicrograph 315. PHOTOGRAPHY,
photomicrography.
photomicrography 315. PHOTOGRAPHY.
photomicroscopy 315. PHOTOGRAPHY,
photomicrography.
photonastic 319. PLANTS, photonasty.
photonasty 319. PLANTS.
photopathic 245. LIGHT, photopathy.
photopathy 245. LIGHT.
photoperiod 44. BIOLOGY,
photoperiodism.
photoperiodic 44. BIOLOGY,
photoperiodism; 319. PLANTS,
photoperiodism.
photoperiodical 319. PLANTS,
photoperiodism.
photoperiodicity 44. BIOLOGY,
photoperiodism; 319. PLANTS,
photoperiodism.
photoperiodism 44. BIOLOGY;
319. PLANTS.
photophile 319. PLANTS, photophilia.
photophilia 319. PLANTS.

photophilic 245. LIGHT, photophily;
319. PLANTS, photophilia.
photophilous 319. PLANTS, photophilia.
photophily 245. LIGHT; 319. PLANTS,
photophilia.
photophobia 245. LIGHT; 313. PHOBIAS.
photopia 110. DARKNESS, scotopia;
148. EYES.
photopic 148. EYES, photopia.
photoreconnaisance 31. AVIATION.
photosynthesis 44. BIOLOGY;
245. LIGHT; 319. PLANTS.
photosynthetic 44. BIOLOGY,
photosynthesis; 245. LIGHT,
photosynthesis; 319. PLANTS,
photosynthesis.
phototactic 245. LIGHT, phototaxis;
282. MOTION, phototaxis.
phototaxis 245. LIGHT; 282. MOTION.
phototaxy 245. LIGHT, phototaxis;
282. MOTION, phototaxis.
phototelegraphic 98. COPYING,
phototelegraphy; 343. RADIO,
phototelegraphy.
phototelegraphy 98. COPYING;
343. RADIO.
phototherapeutic 245. LIGHT,
phototherapy; 350. REMEDIES,
phototherapy; 370. SKIN,
phototherapy.
phototherapeutics 245. LIGHT,
phototherapy; 350. REMEDIES,
phototherapy; 370. SKIN,
phototherapy.
phototherapy 245. LIGHT;
350. REMEDIES; 370. SKIN.
phototopographic 235. LAND,
phototopography; 257. MAPS,
phototopography;
315. PHOTOGRAPHY,
phototopography.
phototopographical 235. LAND,
phototopography; 257. MAPS,
phototopography;
315. PHOTOGRAPHY,
phototopography.
phototopography 235. LAND; 257. MAPS;
315. PHOTOGRAPHY.

phototropic 44. BIOLOGY,
phototropism; 167. FLOWERS,
phototropism; 245. LIGHT,
phototropism; 282. MOTION,
phototropism.
phototropism 44. BIOLOGY; 245. LIGHT;
282. MOTION; 319. PLANTS.
phototypic 315. PHOTOGRAPHY,
phototypy.
phototypy 315. PHOTOGRAPHY.
photoxylography 328. PRINTING.
photozincography 429. ZINC.
phraseogram 428. WRITING.
phraseograph 428. WRITING.
phraseologic 236. LANGUAGE,
phraseology.
phraseological 236. LANGUAGE,
phraseology.
phraseologist 236. LANGUAGE,
phraseology.
phraseology 236. LANGUAGE.
phratry 17. ANTHROPOLOGY;
190. GREECE and GREEKS;
376. SOCIETY.
phrenographic 334. PSYCHOLOGY,
phrenography.
phrenography 334. PSYCHOLOGY.
phrenologic 196. HEAD, phrenology.
phrenological 196. HEAD, phrenology.
phrenologist 196. HEAD, phrenology.
phrenology 196. HEAD.
phrenomagnetism 56. BRAIN.
phronemomania 254. MANIAS;
393. THINKING.
phronemophobia 313. PHOBIAS;
393. THINKING.
phthiriophobia 225. INSECTS;
313. PHOBIAS.
phthisic 122. DISEASE and ILLNESS,
phthisis.
phthisical 122. DISEASE and ILLNESS,
phthisis.
phthisiology 122. DISEASE and ILLNESS.
phthisiomania 122. DISEASE and
ILLNESS; 254. MANIAS.
phthisiophobia 313. PHOBIAS.
phthisis 122. DISEASE and ILLNESS.
phycographic 54. BOTANY,
phycography.
phycography 54. BOTANY.
phycologist 54. BOTANY, phycology.

phycology 54. BOTANY.
phyllody 167. FLOWERS; 241. LEAVES.
phyllomancy 124. DIVINATION;
241. LEAVES.
phyllomania 241. LEAVES.
phyllomorphosis 241. LEAVES.
phyllomorphy 167. FLOWERS,
phyllody; 241. LEAVES.
phyllotactic 241. LEAVES, phyllotaxy.
phyllotaxis 241. LEAVES, phyllotaxy.
phyllotaxy 241. LEAVES.
phylogenetic 147. EVOLUTION,
phylogeny.
phylogenist 147. EVOLUTION,
phylogeny.
phylogeny 147. EVOLUTION.
phylon 16. ANIMALS.
phylum 16. ANIMALS; 54. BOTANY;
83. CLASSIFICATION.
physiatrical 266. MEDICAL SPECIALTIES,
physiatrics.
physiatrics 266. MEDICAL SPECIALTIES.
physiatrist 266. MEDICAL SPECIALTIES.
physical 316. PHYSICS, physics.
physical anthropology
17. ANTHROPOLOGY; 51. BODY,
HUMAN, somatology.
physicalism 312. PHILOSOPHY.
physicalist 312. PHILOSOPHY,
physicalism.
physicism 316. PHYSICS.
physicist 316. PHYSICS, physics.
physics 316. PHYSICS.
physiocrat 322. POLITICS,
physiocratism.
physiocratic 322. POLITICS,
physiocratism.
physiocratism 322. POLITICS.
physiogenesis 44. BIOLOGY,
physiogeny.
physiogenetic 44. BIOLOGY,
physiogeny.
physiogenic 44. BIOLOGY, physiogeny;
122. DISEASE and ILLNESS.
physiogeny 44. BIOLOGY.
physiognomic 149. FACIAL FEATURES,
physiognomy.
physiognomical 149. FACIAL FEATURES,
physiognomy.
physiognomics 149. FACIAL FEATURES,
physiognomy.

physiognomist 149. FACIAL FEATURES, physiognomy.
physiognomy 149. FACIAL FEATURES.
physiographer 83. CLASSIFICATION, physiography; 178. GEOGRAPHY, physiography.
physiographic 83. CLASSIFICATION, physiography; 178. GEOGRAPHY, physiography.
physiographical 83. CLASSIFICATION, physiography; 178. GEOGRAPHY, physiography.
physiography 83. CLASSIFICATION; 178. GEOGRAPHY.
physiolater 290. NATURE, physiolatry.
physiolatrous 290. NATURE, physiolatry.
physiolatry 290. NATURE.
physiologic 244. LIFE, physiology; 266. MEDICAL SPECIALTIES, physiology.
physiological 244. LIFE, physiology; 266. MEDICAL SPECIALTIES, physiology.
physiologist 244. LIFE, physiology; 266. MEDICAL SPECIALTIES, physiology.
physiology 244. LIFE; 266. MEDICAL SPECIALTIES.
physiosophy 290. NATURE.
physiotherapist 350. REMEDIES, physiotherapy.
physiotherapy 350. REMEDIES.
physis 74. CHANGE; 191. GROWTH; 290. NATURE.
physitheism 183. GOD and GODS; 290. NATURE.
physiurgic 290. NATURE.
phytobiological 44. BIOLOGY, phytobiology.
phytobiologist 44. BIOLOGY, phytobiology.
phytobiology 44. BIOLOGY.
phytogenesis 54. BOTANY; 319. PLANTS.
phytogenetic 54. BOTANY, phytogenesis; 319. PLANTS, phytogenesis.
phytogenetical 54. BOTANY, phytogenesis; 319. PLANTS, phytogenesis.
phytogenic 319. PLANTS, phytogenesis.

phytogeny 319. PLANTS, phytogenesis.
phytogeographer 54. BOTANY, phytogeography.
phytogeographic 54. BOTANY, phytogeography.
phytogeographical 54. BOTANY, phytogeography.
phytogeography 54. BOTANY.
phytographer 54. BOTANY, phytography.
phytographic 54. BOTANY, phytography.
phytographical 54. BOTANY, phytography.
phytographist 54. BOTANY, phytography.
phytography 54. BOTANY.
phytolithology 171. FOSSILS.
phytology 54. BOTANY.
phytoserologic 319. PLANTS, phytoserology.
phytoserological 319. PLANTS, phytoserology.
phytoserologist 319. PLANTS, phytoserology.
phytoserology 319. PLANTS.
phytosociologic 54. BOTANY, phytosociology.
phytosociological 54. BOTANY, phytosociology.
phytosociologist 54. BOTANY, phytosociology.
phytosociology 54. BOTANY.
pianism 284. MUSIC.
pianist 284. MUSIC, pianism.
pianistic 284. MUSIC, pianism.
pianologue 213. HUMOR; 284. MUSIC; 310. PERFORMING.
picador 61. BULLS and BULLFIGHTING.
piccage 131. DUES and PAYMENT.
pictograph 428. WRITING, pictography.
pictographic 428. WRITING, pictography.
pictography 428. WRITING.
Pietism 332. PROTESTANTISM.
Pietist 332. PROTESTANTISM, Pietism.
Pietistic 332. PROTESTANTISM, Pietism.
Pietistical 332. PROTESTANTISM, Pietism.
piezometer 226. INSTRUMENTS.

piezometric 226. INSTRUMENTS,
   piezometer; 264. MEASUREMENT,
   piezometry.
piezometry 264. MEASUREMENT.
piggery 16. ANIMALS.
pilferage 391. THEFT.
pillage 391. THEFT; 413. WAR.
pilose 193. HAIR, pilosism.
pilosism 193. HAIR.
pilosity 193. HAIR, pilosism.
pilotage 131. DUES and PAYMENT;
   366. SHIPS.
pilpulist 21. ARGUMENTATION.
pilpulistic 21. ARGUMENTATION,
   pilpulist.
pinacotheca 23. ART.
pinguid 51. BODY, HUMAN, pinguidity;
   377. SOIL, pinguidity.
pinguidity 51. BODY, HUMAN; 377. SOIL.
piosity 349. RELIGION.
piracy 391. THEFT.
pirate 391. THEFT, piracy.
piratic 391. THEFT, piracy.
piratical 391. THEFT, piracy.
piscary 164. FISH.
piscatology 164. FISH.
piscatorialist 164. FISH, piscatorian.
piscatorian 164. FISH.
piscicultural 164. FISH, pisciculture.
pisciculture 164. FISH.
pisciculturist 164. FISH, pisciculture.
pistic 151. FAITH.
pistology 151. FAITH.
Pittism 322. POLITICS.
Pittite 322. POLITICS, Pittism.
plagiarism 391. THEFT.
plagiarist 391. THEFT, plagiarism.
plagiaristic 391. THEFT, plagiarism.
plagiary 391. THEFT, plagiarism.
plagiocephalic 196. HEAD,
   plagiocephalism.
plagiocephalism 196. HEAD.
plagiocephalous 196. HEAD,
   plagiocephalism.
plagiocephaly 196. HEAD,
   plagiocephalism.
plagiotropic 191. GROWTH,
   plagiotropism; 319. PLANTS,
   plagiotropism.
plagiotropism 191. GROWTH;
   319. PLANTS.

planation 133. EARTH.
planetarium 25. ASTRONOMY;
   318. PLANETS.
planetoid 318. PLANETS.
planetoidal 318. PLANETS, planetoid.
planetologic 25. ASTRONOMY,
   planetology.
planetological 25. ASTRONOMY,
   planetology.
planetologist 25. ASTRONOMY,
   planetology.
planetology 25. ASTRONOMY.
planganologist 91. COLLECTIONS and
   COLLECTING, planganology;
   126. DOLLS.
planganology 91. COLLECTIONS and
   COLLECTING.
plangency 380. SOUND.
plangent 380. SOUND, plangency.
planimeter 262. MATHEMATICS,
   planimetry.
planimetric 262. MATHEMATICS,
   planimetry.
planimetrical 262. MATHEMATICS,
   planimetry.
planimetry 262. MATHEMATICS.
planisphere 25. ASTRONOMY; 257. MAPS;
   352. REPRESENTATION.
planispheric 25. ASTRONOMY,
   planisphere; 257. MAPS, planisphere.
planispherical 25. ASTRONOMY,
   planisphere; 257. MAPS, planisphere.
planktology 164. FISH.
planktonology 164. FISH, planktology.
planographic 128. DRAWING,
   planography.
planographical 128. DRAWING,
   planography.
planographist 128. DRAWING,
   planography.
planography 128. DRAWING.
planometer 226. INSTRUMENTS.
plastic 261. MATERIALS, PROPERTIES OF,
   plasticity.
plasticism 23. ART.
plasticity 261. MATERIALS, PROPERTIES
   OF.
plastometer 226. INSTRUMENTS.
plastometric 226. INSTRUMENTS,
   plastometer; 264. MEASUREMENT,
   plastometry.

plastometry 264. MEASUREMENT.
platinotype 315. PHOTOGRAPHY.
platitudinarian 236. LANGUAGE,
platitudinarianism.
platitudinarianism 236. LANGUAGE.
Platonic criticism 104. CRITICISM.
Platonism 312. PHILOSOPHY.
Platonist 312. PHILOSOPHY, Platonism.
Platonistic 312. PHILOSOPHY,
Platonism.
pleasurist 320. PLEASURE.
plebeian 41. BEHAVIOR, plebeianism.
plebeianism 41. BEHAVIOR.
plein-air 23. ART, plein-airism.
plein-airism 23. ART.
plenism 316. PHYSICS.
plenist 316. PHYSICS, plenism.
pleochroic 316. PHYSICS, pleochroism.
pleochroism 316. PHYSICS.
pleochromatic 316. PHYSICS,
pleochroism.
pleochromatism 316. PHYSICS.
pleomorphic 44. BIOLOGY,
pleomorphism.
pleomorphism 44. BIOLOGY.
pleomorphous 44. BIOLOGY,
pleomorphism.
pleomorphy 44. BIOLOGY,
pleomorphism.
pleonasm 236. LANGUAGE;
354. RHETORIC and RHETORICAL
DEVICES.
pleonastic 236. LANGUAGE, pleonasm;
354. RHETORIC and RHETORICAL
DEVICES, pleonasm.
pleroma 285. MYSTICISM.
plerophory 28. ATTITUDES;
233. KNOWLEDGE; 279. MOODS.
Plinyism 402. TRUTH and ERROR.
plousiocracy 185. GOVERNMENT,
plutocracy.
plumbism 321. POISON.
plunderage 366. SHIPS.
pluralism 312. PHILOSOPHY;
322. POLITICS.
pluralist 312. PHILOSOPHY, pluralism;
322. POLITICS, pluralism.
pluralistic 312. PHILOSOPHY, pluralism;
322. POLITICS, pluralism.
plutocracy 185. GOVERNMENT.

plutocrat 185. GOVERNMENT,
plutocracy.
plutolatry 276. MONEY.
plutology 137. ECONOMICS; 276. MONEY.
plutomania 276. MONEY.
plutonism 179. GEOLOGY; 321. POISON.
plutonist 179. GEOLOGY, plutonism.
plutonomy 137. ECONOMICS, plutology.
pluviographic 345. RAIN, pluviography;
417. WEATHER, pluviography.
pluviographical 345. RAIN,
pluviography; 417. WEATHER,
pluviography.
pluviography 345. RAIN; 417. WEATHER.
pluviometric 345. RAIN, pluviometry;
417. WEATHER, pluviometry.
pluviometrical 345. RAIN, pluviometry;
417. WEATHER, pluviometry.
pluviometry 345. RAIN; 417. WEATHER.
pluvioscope 345. RAIN; 417. WEATHER.
pluviosity 345. RAIN; 417. WEATHER.
pluvious 345. RAIN, pluviosity;
417. WEATHER, pluviosity.
pneodynamics 266. MEDICAL
SPECIALTIES.
pneuma 80. CHRISTIANITY.
pneumatics 27. ATMOSPHERE;
27. ATMOSPHERE, pneumodynamics.
pneumatism 312. PHILOSOPHY.
pneumatogram 266. MEDICAL
SPECIALTIES, pneumatography.
pneumatograph 226. INSTRUMENTS.
pneumatography 266. MEDICAL
SPECIALTIES.
pneumatologic 80. CHRISTIANITY,
pneumatology; 349. RELIGION,
pneumatology.
pneumatological 80. CHRISTIANITY,
pneumatology; 349. RELIGION,
pneumatology.
pneumatologist 80. CHRISTIANITY,
pneumatology; 349. RELIGION,
pneumatology; 384. SPIRITS and
SPIRITUALISM, pneumatology.
pneumatology 80. CHRISTIANITY;
349. RELIGION; 384. SPIRITS and
SPIRITUALISM.
pneumatolysis 179. GEOLOGY.
pneumatolytic 179. GEOLOGY,
pneumatolysis.
pneumatophobia 313. PHOBIAS.

pneumoconiosis 122. DISEASE and
ILLNESS.
pneumograph 14. ANATOMY,
pneumography.
pneumographic 14. ANATOMY,
pneumography.
pneumographical 14. ANATOMY,
pneumography.
pneumography 14. ANATOMY.
pneumological 51. BODY, HUMAN,
pneumology.
pneumology 51. BODY, HUMAN.
pneumonoultramicroscopicsilicovolcanoconiosis 122. DISEASE and
ILLNESS.
pneumonoultramicroscopicsilicovolcanokoniosis 122. DISEASE and
ILLNESS, pneumonoultramicroscopicsilicovolcanoconiosis.
pnigalion 129. DREAMS.
pnigophobia 313. PHOBIAS.
pococurante 41. BEHAVIOR,
pococurantism.
pococurantism 28. ATTITUDES;
41. BEHAVIOR.
pococurantist 41. BEHAVIOR,
pococurantism.
podagra 157. FEET and LEGS.
podagral 157. FEET and LEGS, podagra.
podagric 157. FEET and LEGS, podagra.
podagrical 157. FEET and LEGS,
podagra.
podagrous 157. FEET and LEGS,
podagra.
podiatric 157. FEET and LEGS, podiatry.
podiatrist 157. FEET and LEGS, podiatry.
podiatry 157. FEET and LEGS.
podology 157. FEET and LEGS.
podomancy 124. DIVINATION.
poecilonymy 288. NAMES.
poesy 409. VERSE.
poetasterism 248. LITERARY STYLE.
poetastery 409. VERSE.
poeticism 409. VERSE.
poetics 409. VERSE.
pogoniasis 37. BEARDS.
pogonologist 37. BEARDS, pogonology.
pogonology 37. BEARDS.
pogonophile 37. BEARDS.

pogonophobia 37. BEARDS;
313. PHOBIAS.
pogonotomy 37. BEARDS.
pogonotrophy 37. BEARDS.
poikilothermal 49. BLOOD and BLOOD
VESSELS, poikilothermy.
poikilothermic 49. BLOOD and BLOOD
VESSELS, poikilothermy.
poikilothermism 49. BLOOD and BLOOD
VESSELS, poikilothermy.
poikilothermous 49. BLOOD and BLOOD
VESSELS, poikilothermy.
poikilothermy 49. BLOOD and BLOOD
VESSELS.
poinephobia 313. PHOBIAS;
335. PUNISHMENT.
Pointillism 23. ART.
Pointillist 23. ART, Pointillism.
Pointillistic 23. ART, Pointillism.
poker painting 128. DRAWING,
xylopyrography; 425. WOOD.
polarimetry 245. LIGHT.
polemic 21. ARGUMENTATION,
polemics.
polemical 21. ARGUMENTATION,
polemicist.
polemically 21. ARGUMENTATION,
polemics.
polemicist 21. ARGUMENTATION.
polemics 21. ARGUMENTATION;
349. RELIGION.
polemist 21. ARGUMENTATION,
polemicist.
poliorcetic 413. WAR, poliorcetics.
poliorcetics 413. WAR.
politicology 322. POLITICS, politology.
politicomania 254. MANIAS;
322. POLITICS.
politicophobia 313. PHOBIAS.
politological 322. POLITICS, politology.
politologist 322. POLITICS, politology.
politology 322. POLITICS.
pollinosis 122. DISEASE and ILLNESS.
Pollyannaism 28. ATTITUDES.
Polonist 236. LANGUAGE.
poltroon 102. COWARDICE,
poltroonery.
poltroonery 41. BEHAVIOR,
poltroonism; 102. COWARDICE.

poltroonish 41. BEHAVIOR,
poltroonism; 102. COWARDICE,
poltroonery.
poltroonism 41. BEHAVIOR.
polyandrous 258. MARRIAGE,
polyandry.
polyandry 258. MARRIAGE.
polyarchical 185. GOVERNMENT,
polyarchy.
polyarchist 185. GOVERNMENT,
polyarchy.
polyarchy 185. GOVERNMENT.
polyautography 328. PRINTING.
polycentrism 94. COMMUNISM;
322. POLITICS.
polycentrist 94. COMMUNISM,
polycentrism.
polychrest 350. REMEDIES.
polychrestic 350. REMEDIES, polychrest.
polychroism 316. PHYSICS,
pleochromatism.
polychromatic 23. ART, polychromy;
92. COLOR, polychromatism.
polychromatism 92. COLOR;
316. PHYSICS, pleochromatism.
polychromatist 23. ART, polychromy.
polychromic 23. ART, polychromy;
92. COLOR, polychromatism.
polychromy 23. ART.
polydactylism 157. FEET and LEGS;
161. FINGERS and TOES; 194. HANDS.
polydactylous 157. FEET and LEGS,
polydactylism; 161. FINGERS and TOES,
polydactylism; 194. HANDS,
polydactylism.
polydaemonism 114. DEMONS,
polydemonism.
polydaemonistic 114. DEMONS,
polydemonism.
polydemonism 114. DEMONS.
polydemonistic 114. DEMONS,
polydemonism.
polydiabolism 117. DEVIL.
polydipsia 8. ALCOHOL.
polyeidism 191. GROWTH.
polygamist 103. CRIME, polygamy.
polygamous 103. CRIME, polygamy;
258. MARRIAGE, polygamy.
polygamy 103. CRIME; 258. MARRIAGE.
polygenesis 44. BIOLOGY.
polygenetic 44. BIOLOGY, polygenesis.

polygenic 44. BIOLOGY, polygenesis.
polygenism 44. BIOLOGY, polygenesis;
341. RACE.
polygenist 341. RACE, polygenism.
polygenistic 341. RACE, polygenism.
polyglot 53. BOOKS; 236. LANGUAGE,
polyglottism.
polyglottic 53. BOOKS, polyglot;
236. LANGUAGE, polyglot.
polyglottism 236. LANGUAGE.
polyglottous 53. BOOKS, polyglot;
236. LANGUAGE, polyglot.
polygraph 243. LIES and LYING.
polygrapher 98. COPYING, polygraphy;
243. LIES and LYING, polygraph.
polygraphic 98. COPYING, polygraphy;
243. LIES and LYING, polygraph.
polygraphist 98. COPYING, polygraphy;
243. LIES and LYING, polygraph.
polygraphy 98. COPYING.
polygynious 258. MARRIAGE, polygyny.
polygynous 258. MARRIAGE, polygyny.
polygyny 258. MARRIAGE.
polyhistor 233. KNOWLEDGE.
polyhistoric 233. KNOWLEDGE,
polyhistor.
polylemma 250. LOGIC.
polymastic 51. BODY, HUMAN,
polymastism.
polymastism 51. BODY, HUMAN.
polymath 233. KNOWLEDGE,
polymathy.
polymathy 233. KNOWLEDGE.
polymetallism 276. MONEY.
polymorphism 44. BIOLOGY,
pleomorphism; 225. INSECTS.
polymorphous 225. INSECTS,
polymorphism.
polyneuritis 291. NERVES.
polynological 44. BIOLOGY,
palynology.
polynologist 44. BIOLOGY, palynology.
polynomialism 262. MATHEMATICS.
polyology 236. LANGUAGE.
polyonymous 288. NAMES, polyonymy.
polyonymy 288. NAMES.
polyopia 148. EYES.
polyopsia 148. EYES, polyopia.
polyopsy 148. EYES, polyopia.
polyopy 148. EYES, polyopia.

polyphagia 44. BIOLOGY; 122. DISEASE and ILLNESS; 168. FOOD and NUTRITION.
polyphagian 168. FOOD and NUTRITION, polyphagia.
polyphagic 44. BIOLOGY, polyphagia; 168. FOOD and NUTRITION, polyphagia.
polyphagist 44. BIOLOGY, polyphagia.
polyphagous 168. FOOD and NUTRITION, polyphagia.
polyphagy 44. BIOLOGY, polyphagia; 122. DISEASE and ILLNESS, polyphagia; 168. FOOD and NUTRITION, polyphagia.
polyphobia 156. FEAR; 313. PHOBIAS.
polyphonic 284. MUSIC, polyphony.
polyphonism 284. MUSIC; 284. MUSIC, polyphony.
polyphonous 284. MUSIC, polyphony.
polyphony 284. MUSIC.
polypragmacy 41. BEHAVIOR, polypragmatism.
polypragmatic 41. BEHAVIOR, polypragmatism.
polypragmatism 41. BEHAVIOR.
polypragmatist 41. BEHAVIOR, polypragmatism.
polypragmaty 41. BEHAVIOR, polypragmatism.
polypsychic 379. SOUL, polypsychism.
polypsychical 379. SOUL, polypsychism.
polypsychism 379. SOUL.
polyptych 23. ART.
polysemy 236. LANGUAGE.
polysyllabic 236. LANGUAGE, polysyllabism.
polysyllabical 236. LANGUAGE, polysyllabism.
polysyllabism 236. LANGUAGE.
polysyllable 236. LANGUAGE, polysyllabism.
polysyllogism 21. ARGUMENTATION.
polytechnic 240. LEARNING.
polytheism 183. GOD and GODS.
polytheist 183. GOD and GODS, polytheism.
polytonal 284. MUSIC, polytonalism.
polytonalism 284. MUSIC.
polytonalist 284. MUSIC, polytonalism.
polytonality 284. MUSIC, polytonalism.
polyuria 50. BODILY FUNCTIONS.

polyuric 50. BODILY FUNCTIONS, polyuria.
polyzoic 44. BIOLOGY, polyzoism.
polyzoism 44. BIOLOGY.
pomiculture 5. AGRICULTURE; 319. PLANTS; 401. TREES.
pomiculturist 319. PLANTS, pomiculture.
pomologist 54. BOTANY, pomology.
pomology 54. BOTANY.
ponerology 146. EVIL; 392. THEOLOGY.
ponophobia 154. FATIGUE; 313. PHOBIAS.
pontificality 323. POPE.
Pop Art 23. ART.
popeism 69. CATHOLICISM.
popery 69. CATHOLICISM, popeism; 323. POPE.
Poplarism 325. POVERTY.
Poplarist 325. POVERTY, Poplarism.
popular sovereignty 322. POLITICS.
populism 322. POLITICS.
populist 322. POLITICS, populism.
populistic 322. POLITICS, populism.
poriomania 122. DISEASE and ILLNESS.
porism 262. MATHEMATICS.
porismatic 262. MATHEMATICS, porism.
pornerast 41. BEHAVIOR.
pornocracy 322. POLITICS.
pornographer 296. OBSCENITY, pornography.
pornographic 296. OBSCENITY, pornography.
pornographomania 249. LITERATURE; 254. MANIAS; 296. OBSCENITY; 364. SEX.
pornography 296. OBSCENITY.
portiforium 69. CATHOLICISM.
portmantologism 236. LANGUAGE.
portraitist 23. ART.
portraiture 23. ART.
positivism 312. PHILOSOPHY.
positivist 312. PHILOSOPHY, positivism.
positivistic 312. PHILOSOPHY, positivism.
posologic 266. MEDICAL SPECIALTIES, posology.
posological 266. MEDICAL SPECIALTIES, posology.
posology 266. MEDICAL SPECIALTIES.
postclassical 237. LANGUAGE STYLE, postclassicism.

postclassicism 237. LANGUAGE STYLE.
post-diluvian 18. ANTIQUITY;
  18. ANTIQUITY, post-diluvian.
Post-Impressionism 23. ART.
Post-Impressionist 23. ART, Post-
  Impressionism.
postremogeniture 77. CHILDREN;
  239. LAW.
postulator 69. CATHOLICISM.
potamological 356. RIVERS,
  potamology.
potamologist 356. RIVERS, potamology.
potamology 356. RIVERS.
potamophobia 313. PHOBIAS;
  356. RIVERS.
potation 8. ALCOHOL..
potomania 8. ALCOHOL; 130. DRUGS;
  254. MANIAS.
potvalency 101. COURAGE, potvaliancy.
potvaliancy 101. COURAGE.
potvaliant 101. COURAGE, potvaliancy.
potvalor 101. COURAGE, potvaliancy.
poultry 45. BIRDS.
poundage 131. DUES and PAYMENT.
powwow 252. MAGIC, powwowism.
powwowism 252. MAGIC.
practical criticism 104. CRITICISM.
pragmaticist 312. PHILOSOPHY,
  pragmatistism.
pragmatism 312. PHILOSOPHY.
pragmatist 312. PHILOSOPHY,
  pragmatism.
pragmatistic 312. PHILOSOPHY,
  pragmatism.
pragmatistism 312. PHILOSOPHY.
pratique 366. SHIPS.
praxeological 41. BEHAVIOR,
  praxeology.
praxeology 41. BEHAVIOR.
praxinoscope 159. FILMS;
  226. INSTRUMENTS;
  352. REPRESENTATION.
praxiology 41. BEHAVIOR, praxeology.
pre-Adamite 392. THEOLOGY, pre-
  Adamitism.
pre-Adamitic 392. THEOLOGY, pre-
  Adamitism.
pre-Adamitism 392. THEOLOGY.
precentor 81. CHURCH.
preciosity 41. BEHAVIOR;
  236. LANGUAGE.

precipitancy 41. BEHAVIOR.
precipitant 41. BEHAVIOR,
  precipitancy.
precisionism 28. ATTITUDES.
precisionist 28. ATTITUDES,
  precisionism.
precisionistic 28. ATTITUDES,
  precisionism.
predacean 16. ANIMALS.
predaceous 16. ANIMALS, predacean.
predacious 16. ANIMALS, predacean.
predation 16. ANIMALS; 391. THEFT.
predatory 16. ANIMALS, predation.
predestinarian 392. THEOLOGY,
  predestinarianism.
predestinarianism 392. THEOLOGY.
predestination 392. THEOLOGY.
predeterminism 312. PHILOSOPHY.
preferentialism 398. TRADE.
preferentialist 398. TRADE,
  preferentialism.
preformation 44. BIOLOGY.
preformationism 44. BIOLOGY.
preformationist 44. BIOLOGY,
  preformationism.
prefrontal lobotomy 56. BRAIN,
  lobotomy.
pregnancy 327. PREGNANCY.
pregnant 327. PREGNANCY, pregnancy.
premillennialism 392. THEOLOGY.
premillennialist 392. THEOLOGY,
  premillennialism.
premillennian 392. THEOLOGY,
  premillennialism.
Premonstrant 69. CATHOLICISM.
Premonstratensian 69. CATHOLICISM,
  Premonstrant.
prepotency 204. HEREDITY.
prepotent 204. HEREDITY, prepotency.
Pre-Raphaelite 23. ART, Pre-
  Raphaelitism.
Pre-Raphaelitism 23. ART.
presbyopia 148. EYES, presbytism.
Presbyterian 332. PROTESTANTISM,
  Presbyterianism.
Presbyterianism 332. PROTESTANTISM.
presbytia 148. EYES, presbytism.
presbytic 148. EYES, presbytism.
presbytism 148. EYES.
prescriptivism 236. LANGUAGE.

presentationalist 233. KNOWLEDGE,
  presentationism.
presentationism 233. KNOWLEDGE.
presentationist 233. KNOWLEDGE,
  presentationism.
preservationist 142. ENVIRONMENT.
prestidigitation 194. HANDS;
  252. MAGIC; 310. PERFORMING.
prestidigitator 194. HANDS,
  prestidigitation; 252. MAGIC,
  prestidigitation; 310. PERFORMING,
  prestidigitation.
prestidigitatorial 194. HANDS,
  prestidigitation; 252. MAGIC,
  prestidigitation; 310. PERFORMING,
  prestidigitation.
prestidigitatory 194. HANDS,
  prestidigitation; 252. MAGIC,
  prestidigitation; 310. PERFORMING,
  prestidigitation.
prestigiation 194. HANDS,
  prestidigitation.
preterism 80. CHRISTIANITY.
preterist 80. CHRISTIANITY, preterism.
preternatural 252. MAGIC,
  preternaturalism.
preternaturalism 252. MAGIC.
Pretorianism 185. GOVERNMENT.
prettyism 23. ART.
prevenance 396. TIME.
prevenience 396. TIME, prevenance.
prevenient 396. TIME, prevenance.
priapism 364. SEX.
priapismic 364. SEX, priapism.
priestism 349. RELIGION.
prigger 41. BEHAVIOR, priggism.
priggish 41. BEHAVIOR, priggism.
priggism 41. BEHAVIOR.
primigravida 46. BIRTH.
primipara 46. BIRTH.
primiparity 46. BIRTH, primipara.
primiparous 46. BIRTH, primipara.
Primitive Methodism
  332. PROTESTANTISM.
Primitive Methodist
  332. PROTESTANTISM, Primitive
  Methodism.
primitivism 23. ART.
primitivist 23. ART, primitivism.
primitivistic 23. ART, primitivism.
primogeniture 77. CHILDREN; 239. LAW.

primordialism 147. EVOLUTION.
prisage 366. SHIPS.
Priscillianism 205. HERESY.
Priscillianist 205. HERESY,
  Priscillianism.
privatization 137. ECONOMICS.
probabilism 312. PHILOSOPHY.
probabilist 312. PHILOSOPHY,
  probabilism.
probabilistic 312. PHILOSOPHY,
  probabilism.
procatalepsis 354. RHETORIC and
  RHETORICAL DEVICES.
procataleptic 354. RHETORIC and
  RHETORICAL DEVICES, procatalepsis.
proceleusmatic 409. VERSE; 409. VERSE,
  proceleusmatic.
prochronic 396. TIME, prochronism.
prochronism 396. TIME.
proctalgia 306. PAIN.
proctologic 266. MEDICAL SPECIALTIES,
  proctology.
proctological 266. MEDICAL
  SPECIALTIES, proctology.
proctologist 266. MEDICAL SPECIALTIES,
  proctology.
proctology 266. MEDICAL SPECIALTIES.
proctophobia 313. PHOBIAS.
prodigiosity 278. MONSTERS.
prodromata 122. DISEASE and ILLNESS.
prodromatic 122. DISEASE and ILLNESS,
  prodromata.
prodrome 122. DISEASE and ILLNESS,
  prodromata.
proem 53. BOOKS.
proemium 53. BOOKS, proem.
proemptosis 65. CALENDAR.
professional 28. ATTITUDES,
  professionalism.
professionalism 28. ATTITUDES.
professorial 240. LEARNING,
  professorialism.
professorialism 240. LEARNING.
profligacy 41. BEHAVIOR.
profligate 41. BEHAVIOR, profligacy.
prognathic 149. FACIAl FEATURES,
  prognathism.
prognathism 149. FACIAL FEATURES.
prognathous 149. FACIAL FEATURES,
  prognathism.
prognostication 174. FUTURE.

prognosticative 174. FUTURE,
   prognostication.
prognosticator 174. FUTURE,
   prognostication.
progressivism 322. POLITICS.
progressivist 322. POLITICS,
   progressivism.
Prohibition 8. ALCOHOL,
   prohibitionism.
prohibitionism 8. ALCOHOL.
prohibitionist 8. ALCOHOL,
   prohibitionism.
prolegomenary 53. BOOKS,
   prolegomenon; 354. RHETORIC and
   RHETORICAL DEVICES,
   prolegomenon.
prolegomenon 53. BOOKS;
   354. RHETORIC and RHETORICAL
   DEVICES.
prolegomenous 53. BOOKS,
   prolegomenon; 354. RHETORIC and
   RHETORICAL DEVICES,
   prolegomenon.
prolepsis 21. ARGUMENTATION;
   174. FUTURE.
proleptic 21. ARGUMENTATION,
   prolepsis; 174. FUTURE, prolepsis.
proletarian 322. POLITICS,
   proletarianism.
proletarianism 322. POLITICS.
prolicidal 77. CHILDREN, prolicide.
prolicide 77. CHILDREN.
prolix 236. LANGUAGE, prolixity.
prolixity 236. LANGUAGE.
promorphological 170. FORM,
   promorphology.
promorphologist 170. FORM,
   promorphology.
promorphology 170. FORM.
propaedeutic 240. LEARNING,
   propaedeutics.
propaedeutical 240. LEARNING,
   propaedeutics.
propaedeutics 240. LEARNING.
propagandism 265. MEDIA.
propagandist 265. MEDIA,
   propagandism.
propagandistic 265. MEDIA,
   propagandism.
propheticism 236. LANGUAGE.
prophetism 349. RELIGION.

prophylactic 197. HEALTH,
   prophylaxis.
prophylactodontia 390. TEETH,
   prophylactodontics.
prophylactodontic 390. TEETH,
   prophylactodontics.
prophylactodontics 390. TEETH.
prophylactodontist 390. TEETH,
   prophylactodontics.
prophylaxis 197. HEALTH.
proportionalism 322. POLITICS.
proportionalist 322. POLITICS,
   proportionalism.
propositus 15. ANCESTORS.
prosaic 248. LITERARY STYLE,
   prosaicism.
prosaical 248. LITERARY STYLE,
   prosaicism.
prosaicism 248. LITERARY STYLE.
prosaism 248. LITERARY STYLE,
   prosaicism.
prosaist 248. LITERARY STYLE,
   prosaicism.
prosector 14. ANATOMY.
prosectorial 14. ANATOMY, prosector.
proselyte 97. CONVERT, proselytism.
proselyter 97. CONVERT, proselytism.
proselytism 97. CONVERT.
proselytist 97. CONVERT, proselytism.
proselytistic 97. CONVERT, proselytism.
proselytize 97. CONVERT, proselytism.
prosencephalic 56. BRAIN,
   prosencephalon.
prosencephalon 56. BRAIN.
prosodic 409. VERSE, prosody.
prosodical 409. VERSE, prosody.
prosodist 409. VERSE, prosody.
prosody 409. VERSE.
prosopalgia 149. FACIAL FEATURES;
   291. NERVES; 306. PAIN.
prosopographer 207. HISTORY,
   prosopography.
prosopography 149. FACIAL FEATURES;
   207. HISTORY.
prosthetic 266. MEDICAL SPECIALTIES,
   prosthetics; 388. SURGERY,
   prosthetics.
prosthetics 266. MEDICAL SPECIALTIES;
   388. SURGERY.
prosthodontia 390. TEETH.

prosthodontist 390. TEETH,
  prosthodontia.
prosyllogism 250. LOGIC.
protagonism 41. BEHAVIOR.
protagonist 41. BEHAVIOR,
  protagonism; 127. DRAMA.
protanope 92. COLOR, protanopia;
  148. EYES, protanopia.
protanopia 92. COLOR; 148. EYES.
protanopic 92. COLOR, protanopia;
  148. EYES, protanopia.
protasis 127. DRAMA; 186. GRAMMAR;
  422. WISDOM.
protatic 127. DRAMA, protasis;
  186. GRAMMAR, protasis.
protectionism 137. ECONOMICS.
protectionist 137. ECONOMICS,
  protectionism.
proteinphobia 168. FOOD and
  NUTRITION; 313. PHOBIAS.
proteolysis 50. BODILY FUNCTIONS.
proteolytic 50. BODILY FUNCTIONS,
  proteolysis.
protervity 28. ATTITUDES;
  41. BEHAVIOR.
Protestant 80. CHRISTIANITY,
  Protestantism.
Protestantism 80. CHRISTIANITY.
prothalamion 258. MARRIAGE.
prothalamium 258. MARRIAGE,
  prothalamion.
protohistorical 207. HISTORY,
  protohistory.
protohistory 207. HISTORY.
protopepsia 50. BODILY FUNCTIONS.
protozoological 44. BIOLOGY,
  protozoology.
protozoologist 44. BIOLOGY,
  protozoology.
protozoology 44. BIOLOGY.
proverbialism 236. LANGUAGE.
proverbialist 236. LANGUAGE,
  proverbialism.
proverbiological 333. PROVERBS,
  proverbiology.
proverbiologist 333. PROVERBS,
  proverbiology.
proverbiology 333. PROVERBS.
provincialism 236. LANGUAGE.
proxenetism 364. SEX.
proxenetist 364. SEX, proxenetism.

prudentialism 312. PHILOSOPHY.
prurience 364. SEX.
pruriency 364. SEX, prurience.
prurient 364. SEX, prurience.
Prussian 185. GOVERNMENT,
  Prussianism.
Prussianism 185. GOVERNMENT.
psalmodial 284. MUSIC, psalmody.
psalmodic 284. MUSIC, psalmody.
psalmodical 284. MUSIC, psalmody.
psalmodist 284. MUSIC, psalmody.
psalmody 284. MUSIC.
psellism 382. SPEECH.
psephism 190. GREECE and GREEKS.
psephological 322. POLITICS,
  psephology.
psephologist 322. POLITICS,
  psephology.
psephology 124. DIVINATION;
  322. POLITICS; 385. STONES,
  pessomancy.
psephomancy 124. DIVINATION.
pseudaesthesia 291. NERVES,
  pseudesthesia.
pseudaesthetic 291. NERVES,
  pseudesthesia.
pseudandrous 29. AUTHORS,
  pseudandry.
pseudandry 29. AUTHORS.
pseudepigrapha 43. BIBLE.
pseudepigraphic 43. BIBLE,
  pseudepigrapha.
pseudepigraphical 43. BIBLE,
  pseudepigrapha.
pseudepigraphous 43. BIBLE,
  pseudepigrapha.
pseudesthesia 291. NERVES.
pseudesthetic 291. NERVES,
  pseudesthesia.
pseudism 243. LIES and LYING.
pseudo-classic 23. ART, pseudo-
  classicism.
pseudo-classical 23. ART, pseudo-
  classicism.
pseudo-classicism 23. ART.
pseudogynous 29. AUTHORS,
  pseudogyny.
pseudogyny 29. AUTHORS.
pseudolatry 183. GOD and GODS.
pseudologer 243. LIES and LYING,
  pseudology.

pseudological 243. LIES and LYING,
  pseudology.
pseudologist 243. LIES and LYING,
  pseudology.
pseudology 243. LIES and LYING.
pseudomancy 124. DIVINATION;
  243. LIES and LYING.
pseudomania 243. LIES and LYING.
pseudonym 29. AUTHORS; 288. NAMES.
pseudonymity 29. AUTHORS.
pseudonymous 29. AUTHORS,
  pseudonym; 288. NAMES, pseudonym.
pseudosyllogism 21. ARGUMENTATION.
psilanthropic 79. CHRIST,
  psilanthropism.
psilanthropism 79. CHRIST.
psilanthropist 79. CHRIST,
  psilanthropism.
psilology 236. LANGUAGE.
psilosis 193. HAIR.
psilosopher 312. PHILOSOPHY.
psittacism 382. SPEECH.
psittacosis 45. BIRDS.
psittacotic 45. BIRDS, psittacosis.
psychagogic 379. SOUL, psychagogy.
psychagogics 41. BEHAVIOR.
psychagogue 41. BEHAVIOR,
  psychagogics; 379. SOUL, psychagogy.
psychagogy 41. BEHAVIOR,
  psychagogics; 379. SOUL.
psychalgia 306. PAIN; 334. PSYCHOLOGY.
psycheism 215. HYPNOSIS.
psychiatric 266. MEDICAL SPECIALTIES,
  psychiatry.
psychiatrist 266. MEDICAL SPECIALTIES,
  psychiatry.
psychiatry 266. MEDICAL SPECIALTIES.
psychism 312. PHILOSOPHY.
psychoacoustic 380. SOUND,
  psychoacoustics.
psychoacoustician 380. SOUND,
  psychoacoustics.
psychoacoustics 380. SOUND.
psychoanalysis 334. PSYCHOLOGY.
psychoanalyst 334. PSYCHOLOGY,
  psychoanalysis.
psychoanalytic 334. PSYCHOLOGY,
  psychoanalysis.
psychoanalytical 334. PSYCHOLOGY,
  psychoanalysis.

psychoanalytical criticism
  104. CRITICISM.
psychobabble 236. LANGUAGE.
psychobiologic 44. BIOLOGY,
  psychobiology; 334. PSYCHOLOGY,
  psychobiology.
psychobiological 44. BIOLOGY,
  psychobiology; 334. PSYCHOLOGY,
  psychobiology.
psychobiologist 44. BIOLOGY,
  psychobiology; 334. PSYCHOLOGY,
  psychobiology.
psychobiology 44. BIOLOGY;
  334. PSYCHOLOGY.
psychodiagnostic 334. PSYCHOLOGY,
  psychodiagnostics.
psychodiagnostician 334. PSYCHOLOGY,
  psychodiagnostics.
psychodiagnostics 334. PSYCHOLOGY.
psychodynamic 334. PSYCHOLOGY,
  psychodynamics.
psychodynamics 334. PSYCHOLOGY.
psychogenesis 122. DISEASE and ILLNESS.
psychogenetic 122. DISEASE and ILLNESS,
  psychogenesis.
psychogenic 122. DISEASE and ILLNESS,
  psychogenesis; 122. DISEASE and
  ILLNESS, psychogenicity.
psychogenicity 122. DISEASE and
  ILLNESS.
psychogonic 334. PSYCHOLOGY,
  psychogony.
psychogonical 334. PSYCHOLOGY,
  psychogony.
psychogony 334. PSYCHOLOGY.
psychographic 384. SPIRITS and
  SPIRITUALISM, psychography.
psychography 384. SPIRITS and
  SPIRITUALISM.
psychokinesis 56. BRAIN.
psychokinetic 56. BRAIN, psychokinesis.
psycholepsy 334. PSYCHOLOGY.
psycholeptic 334. PSYCHOLOGY,
  psycholepsy.
psycholinguist 247. LINGUISTICS,
  psycholinguistics.
psycholinguistic 247. LINGUISTICS,
  psycholinguistics.
psycholinguistics 247. LINGUISTICS.
psychologic 334. PSYCHOLOGY,
  psychology.

psychological 334. PSYCHOLOGY,
psychology.
psychologism 334. PSYCHOLOGY.
psychologist 334. PSYCHOLOGY,
psychology.
psychology 334. PSYCHOLOGY.
psychomachy 379. SOUL.
psychomancy 124. DIVINATION;
384. SPIRITS and SPIRITUALISM.
psychomantic 384. SPIRITS and
SPIRITUALISM, psychomancy.
psychometer 334. PSYCHOLOGY,
psychometry.
psychometric 334. PSYCHOLOGY,
psychometrics; 334. PSYCHOLOGY,
psychometry.
psychometrical 334. PSYCHOLOGY,
psychometry.
psychometrics 334. PSYCHOLOGY.
psychometrist 334. PSYCHOLOGY,
psychometrics.
psychometry 334. PSYCHOLOGY;
334. PSYCHOLOGY, psychometrics.
psychopannychian 80. CHRISTIANITY,
psychopannychism.
psychopannychism 80. CHRISTIANITY.
psychopannychist 80. CHRISTIANITY,
psychopannychism.
psychopannychistic 80. CHRISTIANITY,
psychopannychism.
psychopath 334. PSYCHOLOGY,
psychopathy.
psychopathic 122. DISEASE and ILLNESS,
psychopathy; 334. PSYCHOLOGY,
psychopathy.
psychopathist 334. PSYCHOLOGY,
psychopathology.
psychopathologic 266. MEDICAL
SPECIALTIES, psychopathology;
334. PSYCHOLOGY, psychopathology.
psychopathological 266. MEDICAL
SPECIALTIES, psychopathology;
334. PSYCHOLOGY, psychopathology.
psychopathologist 266. MEDICAL
SPECIALTIES, psychopathology;
334. PSYCHOLOGY, psychopathology.
psychopathology 266. MEDICAL
SPECIALTIES; 334. PSYCHOLOGY.
psychopathy 122. DISEASE and ILLNESS;
334. PSYCHOLOGY.

psychopharmacologic 266. MEDICAL
SPECIALTIES, psychopharmacology;
334. PSYCHOLOGY,
psychopharmacology.
psychopharmacological 266. MEDICAL
SPECIALTIES, psychopharmacology;
334. PSYCHOLOGY,
psychopharmacology.
psychopharmacology 266. MEDICAL
SPECIALTIES; 334. PSYCHOLOGY.
psychophobia 313. PHOBIAS;
334. PSYCHOLOGY.
psychophysic 334. PSYCHOLOGY,
psychophysics.
psychophysical 334. PSYCHOLOGY,
psychophysics.
psychophysicist 334. PSYCHOLOGY,
psychophysics.
psychophysics 334. PSYCHOLOGY.
psychoprophylactic 46. BIRTH,
psychoprophylaxis.
psychoprophylaxis 46. BIRTH.
psychorrhagic 379. SOUL,
psychorrhagy.
psychorrhagy 379. SOUL.
psychosis 224. INSANITY.
psychosomatic 266. MEDICAL
SPECIALTIES, psychosomatics.
psychosomaticist 266. MEDICAL
SPECIALTIES, psychosomatics.
psychosomatics 266. MEDICAL
SPECIALTIES.
psychostatic 334. PSYCHOLOGY,
psychostatics.
psychostatical 334. PSYCHOLOGY,
psychostatics.
psychostatics 334. PSYCHOLOGY.
psychosurgeon 56. BRAIN,
psychosurgery.
psychosurgery 56. BRAIN.
psychotheism 183. GOD and GODS.
psychotherapeutic 334. PSYCHOLOGY,
psychotherapy.
psychotherapist 334. PSYCHOLOGY,
psychotherapy; 350. REMEDIES,
psychotherapy.
psychotherapy 334. PSYCHOLOGY;
350. REMEDIES.
psychotic 224. INSANITY, psychosis.
psychroesthesia 51. BODY, HUMAN;
90. COLD.

psychrometric 107. DAMPNESS, psychrometry.
psychrometrical 107. DAMPNESS, psychrometry.
psychrometry 107. DAMPNESS.
psychrophobia 90. COLD; 313. PHOBIAS.
pteridography 54. BOTANY.
pteridologist 54. BOTANY, pteridology.
pteridology 54. BOTANY.
pteronophobia 45. BIRDS; 313. PHOBIAS.
pterylography 45. BIRDS, pterylology.
pterylology 45. BIRDS.
ptochocracy 185. GOVERNMENT; 325. POVERTY.
ptochology 325. POVERTY.
Ptolemaism 25. ASTRONOMY.
Ptolemaist 25. ASTRONOMY.
ptyalism 321. POISON.
publicist 239. LAW.
pudency 28. ATTITUDES.
pudicity 28. ATTITUDES; 424. WOMEN.
puerilism 334. PSYCHOLOGY.
puerility 334. PSYCHOLOGY, puerilism.
puerperal 46. BIRTH, puerperium.
puerperium 46. BIRTH.
pugilism 55. BOXING.
pugilist 55. BOXING.
pugilistic 55. BOXING, pugilism.
pulchritude 38. BEAUTY.
pulchritudinous 38. BEAUTY, pulchritude.
pulmometer 264. MEASUREMENT, pulmometry.
pulmometry 264. MEASUREMENT.
pulsimeter 51. BODY, HUMAN; 226. INSTRUMENTS.
pulsometer 51. BODY, HUMAN, pulsimeter; 226. INSTRUMENTS, pulsimeter.
punning 354. RHETORIC and RHETORICAL DEVICES.
punnologist 336. PUNNING, punnology.
punnology 336. PUNNING.
puppetry 310. PERFORMING.
puppyism 41. BEHAVIOR..
purism 23. ART; 104. CRITICISM; 236. LANGUAGE; 249. LITERATURE; 352. REPRESENTATION.

purist 23. ART, purism; 104. CRITICISM, purism; 236. LANGUAGE, purism; 249. LITERATURE, purism; 352. REPRESENTATION, purism.
Puritan 332. PROTESTANTISM, Puritanism.
Puritanism 332. PROTESTANTISM.
purposivism 312. PHILOSOPHY.
purposivist 312. PHILOSOPHY, purposivism.
purulence 50. BODILY FUNCTIONS.
purulency 50. BODILY FUNCTIONS, purulence.
purulent 50. BODILY FUNCTIONS, purulence.
Puseyism 332. PROTESTANTISM.
Puseyistic 332. PROTESTANTISM, Puseyism.
Puseyistical 332. PROTESTANTISM, Puseyism.
Puseyite 332. PROTESTANTISM, Puseyism.
pusillanimity 102. COWARDICE.
pusillanimous 102. COWARDICE, pusillanimity.
putrescence 113. DECAYING; 329. PROCESSES.
putrescent 113. DECAYING, putrescence; 329. PROCESSES, putrescence.
putschism 152. FASCISM.
putschist 152. FASCISM, putschism.
pycnometer 226. INSTRUMENTS.
pyelographic 342. RADIATION, pyelography.
pyelography 342. RADIATION.
pygmyism 368. SIZE.
pyretographer 122. DISEASE and ILLNESS, pyretography.
pyretographic 122. DISEASE and ILLNESS, pyretography.
pyretography 122. DISEASE and ILLNESS.
pyretology 122. DISEASE and ILLNESS.
pyrexiophobia 313. PHOBIAS.
pyrheliometer 226. INSTRUMENTS; 387. SUN.
pyrheliometric 226. INSTRUMENTS, pyrheliometer; 387. SUN, pyrheliometer.
pyritology 179. GEOLOGY.
pyrochromatography 171. FOSSILS.
pyrogenesis 200. HEAT.

pyrogenetic 200. HEAT, **pyrogenesis.**
pyrogenic 162. FIRE, **pyrogenous.**
pyrogenous 162. FIRE.
pyrograph 162. FIRE, **pyrography.**
pyrographer 23. ART, **pyrography;**
 162. FIRE, **pyrography.**
pyrographic 23. ART, **pyrography;**
 162. FIRE, **pyrography.**
pyrography 23. ART; 162. FIRE.
pyrogravure 23. ART, **pyrography.**
pyrolater 162. FIRE.
pyrolator 162. FIRE, **pyrolater.**
pyrolatry 162. FIRE.
pyrolitic 200. HEAT, **pyrolysis.**
pyrology 316. PHYSICS.
pyrolysis 200. HEAT.
pyromancy 124. DIVINATION; 162. FIRE.
pyromania 162. FIRE.
pyrometer 226. INSTRUMENTS;
 264. MEASUREMENT, **pyrometry.**
pyrometric 226. INSTRUMENTS,
 pyrometer; 264. MEASUREMENT,
 pyrometry.
pyrometrical 264. MEASUREMENT,
 pyrometry.
pyrometry 226. INSTRUMENTS,
 pyrometer; 264. MEASUREMENT.
pyrophilia 162. FIRE; 311. -PHILE,
 -PHILIA, -PHILY.
pyrophobia 162. FIRE; 313. PHOBIAS.
pyrophotometer 200. HEAT;
 226. INSTRUMENTS.
pyrosis 50. BODILY FUNCTIONS;
 122. DISEASE and ILLNESS.
pyrotechnic 163. FIREWORKS,
 pyrotechnics.
pyrotechnical 163. FIREWORKS,
 pyrotechnics.
pyrotechnician 163. FIREWORKS.
pyrotechnics 163. FIREWORKS.
pyrotechnist 163. FIREWORKS,
 pyrotechnician.
pyrotechny 163. FIREWORKS,
 pyrotechnics.
pyrrhic 409. VERSE; 409. VERSE,
 pyrrhic.
Pyrrhonian 312. PHILOSOPHY,
 Pyrrhonism.
Pyrrhonic 312. PHILOSOPHY,
 Pyrrhonism.
Pyrrhonism 312. PHILOSOPHY.

Pyrrhonist 312. PHILOSOPHY,
 Pyrrhonism.
Pythagorean 262. MATHEMATICS,
 Pythagoreanism.
Pythagoreanism 262. MATHEMATICS.
Pythagorism 262. MATHEMATICS,
 Pythagoreanism.
Pythagorist 262. MATHEMATICS,
 Pythagoreanism.
pythonism 124. DIVINATION.

Q

quack 243. LIES and LYING, **quackery.**
quackery 243. LIES and LYING.
quackism 243. LIES and LYING.
quadragenarian 3. AGE,
 quadragenarianism.
quadragenarianism 3. AGE.
quadragenary 3. AGE,
 quadragenarianism.
Quadragesima 80. CHRISTIANITY.
Quadragesimal 80. CHRISTIANITY,
 Quadragesima.
quadragesimal 80. CHRISTIANITY,
 Quadragesima.
quadrant 226. INSTRUMENTS.
quadrantal 226. INSTRUMENTS,
 quadrant.
quadrat 16. ANIMALS.
quadratics 262. MATHEMATICS.
quadrivium 233. KNOWLEDGE;
 240. LEARNING.
quadrumane 194. HANDS.
quadrumanous 194. HANDS,
 quadrumane.
Quaker 332. PROTESTANTISM,
 Quakerism.
Quakerdom 332. PROTESTANTISM,
 Quakerism.
Quakerism 332. PROTESTANTISM.
Quakery 332. PROTESTANTISM,
 Quakerism.
quandary 393. THINKING.
quarterage 131. DUES and PAYMENT.
quassation 329. PROCESSES.
quattrocentism 23. ART; 228. ITALY;
 248. LITERARY STYLE.
quattrocentist 23. ART, **quattrocentism;**
 228. ITALY, **quattrocentism;**
 248. LITERARY STYLE, **quattrocentism.**

querist 338. QUESTIONING.
quidditative 312. PHILOSOPHY,
   quiddity.
quiddity 312. PHILOSOPHY.
quiescence 339. QUIETUDE.
quiescency 339. QUIETUDE, quiescence.
quiescent 339. QUIETUDE, quiescence.
quietism 205. HERESY.
quietist 205. HERESY, quietism.
quietude 339. QUIETUDE.
quinarian 83. CLASSIFICATION;
   83. CLASSIFICATION, quinarian.
quinary 83. CLASSIFICATION,
   quinarian.
quininism 130. DRUGS.
quinism 130. DRUGS, quininism.
quinology 130. DRUGS, cinchonology.
quinquagenarian 3. AGE,
   quinquagenarianism.
quinquagenarianism 3. AGE.
quinquagenary 3. AGE,
   quinquagenarianism.
Quinquagesima 80. CHRISTIANITY.
Quinquagesimal 80. CHRISTIANITY,
   Quinquagesima.
quinquegesimal 80. CHRISTIANITY,
   Quinquagesima.
quinquennalia 26. ATHLETICS.
quintessence 312. PHILOSOPHY.
quintessential 312. PHILOSOPHY,
   quintessence.
Quirinal 185. GOVERNMENT; 228. ITALY.
quisling 322. POLITICS, quislingism.
quislingism 322. POLITICS.
quixotic 41. BEHAVIOR, quixotism.
quixotical 41. BEHAVIOR, quixotism.
quixotism 41. BEHAVIOR.
quizzism 338. QUESTIONING.
quodlibet 21. ARGUMENTATION;
   312. PHILOSOPHY.
quodlibetal 21. ARGUMENTATION,
   quodlibet; 312. PHILOSOPHY,
   quodlibet.
quodlibetarian 21. ARGUMENTATION;
   312. PHILOSOPHY.
quotiety 396. TIME.

R

rabbinic 231. JUDAISM, rabbinism.
rabbinical 231. JUDAISM, rabbinism.

rabbinism 231. JUDAISM.
rabbitry 16. ANIMALS.
Rabelaisian 213. HUMOR; 213. HUMOR,
   Rabelaisian.
Rabelaisianism 213. HUMOR,
   Rabelaism.
Rabelaism 213. HUMOR.
rabulism 41. BEHAVIOR.
rabulistic 41. BEHAVIOR, rabulism.
rabulous 41. BEHAVIOR, rabulism.
rachialgia 306. PAIN.
rachialgic 306. PAIN, rachialgia.
racialism 341. RACE.
racialist 341. RACE, racialism.
racialistic 341. RACE, racialism.
racism 28. ATTITUDES;
   121. DISCRIMINATION; 341. RACE.
racist 28. ATTITUDES, racism;
   341. RACE, racism.
Racovianism 205. HERESY.
radar 31. AVIATION.
radical 322. POLITICS, radicalism.
radicalism 322. POLITICS.
radiesthesia 342. RADIATION.
radiesthetic 342. RADIATION,
   radiesthesia.
radioactivity 342. RADIATION.
radioastronomy 25. ASTRONOMY.
radioautograph 315. PHOTOGRAPHY.
radioautographic 315. PHOTOGRAPHY,
   radioautograph.
radioautography 315. PHOTOGRAPHY,
   radioautograph.
radiogenetics 204. HEREDITY.
radiogenic 204. HEREDITY,
   radiogenetics.
radiograph 315. PHOTOGRAPHY,
   radiography; 342. RADIATION,
   radiography.
radiographer 342. RADIATION,
   radiography.
radiographic 342. RADIATION,
   radiography.
radiographical 342. RADIATION,
   radiography.
radiography 315. PHOTOGRAPHY;
   342. RADIATION.
radiologic 266. MEDICAL SPECIALTIES,
   radiology; 342. RADIATION, radiology.
radiological 266. MEDICAL SPECIALTIES,
   radiology; 342. RADIATION, radiology.

radiologist 266. MEDICAL SPECIALTIES,
radiology; 342. RADIATION, radiology.
radiology 266. MEDICAL SPECIALTIES;
342. RADIATION.
radiometallography 270. METALS;
342. RADIATION.
radiometer 226. INSTRUMENTS; 387. SUN.
radiometric 226. INSTRUMENTS,
radiometer; 264. MEASUREMENT,
radiometry; 316. PHYSICS,
radiometry; 387. SUN, radiometer;
387. SUN, radiometry.
radiometry 264. MEASUREMENT;
316. PHYSICS; 387. SUN.
radiophonic 343. RADIO, radiophony.
radiophony 316. PHYSICS; 343. RADIO;
387. SUN.
radiophotography 315. PHOTOGRAPHY.
radioscopy 342. RADIATION.
radiosensibility 51. BODY, HUMAN;
342. RADIATION.
radiosensible 51. BODY, HUMAN,
radiosensibility.
radiosensitive 342. RADIATION,
radiosensitivity.
radiosensitivity 51. BODY, HUMAN,
radiosensibility; 342. RADIATION.
radiotechnologic 343. RADIO,
radiotechnology.
radiotechnological 343. RADIO,
radiotechnology.
radiotechnology 221. INDUSTRY;
342. RADIATION; 343. RADIO.
radiotelegraphic 343. RADIO,
radiotelegraphy.
radiotelegraphy 343. RADIO.
radiotelephonic 343. RADIO,
radiotelephony.
radiotelephony 343. RADIO.
radiotherapeutic 342. RADIATION,
radiotherapy.
radiotherapist 342. RADIATION,
radiotherapy.
radiotherapy 266. MEDICAL
SPECIALTIES; 342. RADIATION;
350. REMEDIES.
radiothermy 266. MEDICAL
SPECIALTIES; 350. REMEDIES.
radium therapy 266. MEDICAL
SPECIALTIES, radiotherapy;
350. REMEDIES, radiotherapy.

Ramaism 206. HINDUISM.
Ramaite 206. HINDUISM, Ramaism.
Ramism 312. PHILOSOPHY.
Ramist 312. PHILOSOPHY, Ramism.
rapacious 391. THEFT, rapacity.
rapacity 391. THEFT.
rapine 391. THEFT.
Rappist 93. COMMUNALISM.
Rappite 93. COMMUNALISM, Rappist.
Rastafarianism 349. RELIGION.
ratiocination 393. THINKING.
ratiocinative 393. THINKING,
ratiocination.
rationalism 312. PHILOSOPHY.
rationalist 312. PHILOSOPHY,
rationalism.
rationalistic 312. PHILOSOPHY,
rationalism.
raucity 380. SOUND.
raucous 380. SOUND, raucity.
reactionism 41. BEHAVIOR.
reactionist 41. BEHAVIOR, reactionism.
reactological 334. PSYCHOLOGY,
reactology.
reactologist 334. PSYCHOLOGY,
reactology.
reactology 334. PSYCHOLOGY.
Reaganomics 137. ECONOMICS.
realia 240. LEARNING.
Realism 23. ART.
realism 312. PHILOSOPHY.
Realist 23. ART, Realism.
realist 312. PHILOSOPHY, realism.
realpolitik 322. POLITICS.
Rebeccaism 322. POLITICS.
Rebeccaite 322. POLITICS, Rebeccaism.
rebeldom 96. CONFLICT.
receptionism 392. THEOLOGY.
receptionist 392. THEOLOGY,
receptionism.
Rechabite 8. ALCOHOL.
recidivism 103. CRIME.
recidivist 103. CRIME, recidivism.
recidivistic 103. CRIME, recidivism.
recidivous 103. CRIME, recidivism.
recitationist 310. PERFORMING.
recluse 362. SELF, reclusion;
376. SOCIETY, reclusion.
reclusion 362. SELF; 376. SOCIETY.
reclusive 362. SELF, reclusion;
376. SOCIETY, reclusion.

recombinant DNA 204. HEREDITY.
recreancy 102. COWARDICE;
400. TREASON.
recreant 102. COWARDICE, recreancy;
400. TREASON, recreancy.
recrudescence 46. BIRTH; 122. DISEASE
and ILLNESS; 329. PROCESSES.
recrudescent 46. BIRTH, recrudescence;
122. DISEASE and ILLNESS,
recrudescence; 329. PROCESSES,
recrudescence.
recusance 69. CATHOLICISM, recusancy;
349. RELIGION; 351. RENUNCIATION.
recusancy 69. CATHOLICISM;
349. RELIGION; 351. RENUNCIATION.
recusant 69. CATHOLICISM, recusancy;
349. RELIGION, recusance;
349. RELIGION, recusancy;
351. RENUNCIATION, recusance;
351. RENUNCIATION, recusancy.
redaction 53. BOOKS.
redactor 53. BOOKS, redaction.
redactorial 53. BOOKS, redaction.
redargution 21. ARGUMENTATION.
redargutory 21. ARGUMENTATION,
redargution.
Redemptionist 277. MONKS and NUNS.
Redemptorist 277. MONKS and NUNS.
red-tapeism 62. BUREAUCRACY.
red-tapery 62. BUREAUCRACY, red-
tapeism.
red-tapism 62. BUREAUCRACY, red-
tapeism.
red-tapist 62. BUREAUCRACY, red-
tapeism.
referee 21. ARGUMENTATION.
reflexological 334. PSYCHOLOGY,
reflexology.
reflexologist 334. PSYCHOLOGY,
reflexology; 350. REMEDIES,
reflexology.
reflexology 334. PSYCHOLOGY;
350. REMEDIES.
reforestation 401. TREES.
Reformation 332. PROTESTANTISM.
Reformational 332. PROTESTANTISM,
Reformation.
reformism 322. POLITICS.
reformist 322. POLITICS, reformism.
reformistic 322. POLITICS, reformism.
regalism 185. GOVERNMENT.

regeneracy 46. BIRTH; 349. RELIGION.
regenerate 46. BIRTH, regeneracy;
349. RELIGION, regeneracy.
regenesis 46. BIRTH; 329. PROCESSES.
regicidal 232. KILLING, regicidism.
regicide 232. KILLING, regicidism.
regicidism 232. KILLING.
regionalism 249. LITERATURE.
regionalist 249. LITERATURE,
regionalism.
regionalistic 249. LITERATURE,
regionalism.
regolith 179. GEOLOGY.
reification 393. THINKING.
relationism 312. PHILOSOPHY.
relationist 312. PHILOSOPHY,
relationism.
relativism 312. PHILOSOPHY.
relativist 312. PHILOSOPHY, relativism.
relativistic 312. PHILOSOPHY,
relativism.
relict 16. ANIMALS.
religionary 349. RELIGION, religionism.
religionism 349. RELIGION.
religionist 349. RELIGION, religionism.
reliquism 349. RELIGION.
Renaissance Revivalism
20. ARCHITECTURE.
reparteeist 213. HUMOR.
reportage 265. MEDIA.
reporterism 41. BEHAVIOR.
representationalism 23. ART.
reprography 98. COPYING;
315. PHOTOGRAPHY.
republicanism 185. GOVERNMENT.
resistentialism 220. INANIMATE
OBJECTS.
restitutionism 332. PROTESTANTISM,
restorationism.
restorationism 332. PROTESTANTISM.
restorationist 332. PROTESTANTISM,
restorationism.
restrictionism 312. PHILOSOPHY.
restrictionist 312. PHILOSOPHY,
restrictionism.
resurrectionism 99. CORPSES.
resurrection man 99. CORPSES,
resurrectionism.
retainer 131. DUES and PAYMENT.
reticulate 305. ORNAMENTATION,
reticulation.

reticulation 305. ORNAMENTATION.
retinoblastoma 66. CANCER.
retinoscopist 148. EYES, **retinoscopy.**
retinoscopy 148. EYES.
retrogradism 322. POLITICS.
retrogradist 322. POLITICS,
retrogradism.
reunionism 41. BEHAVIOR;
69. CATHOLICISM;
332. PROTESTANTISM; 349. RELIGION.
reunionist 41. BEHAVIOR, **reunionism;**
69. CATHOLICISM, **reunionism;**
332. PROTESTANTISM, **reunionism;**
349. RELIGION, **reunionism.**
reunionistic 69. CATHOLICISM,
reunionism; 332. PROTESTANTISM,
reunionism; 349. RELIGION,
reunionism.
revaluation 331. PROPERTY and
OWNERSHIP.
revanche 185. GOVERNMENT,
revanchism.
revanchism 185. GOVERNMENT.
revanchist 185. GOVERNMENT,
revanchism.
revelationist 349. RELIGION.
reverist 129. DREAMS.
revisionary 239. LAW, **revisionism.**
revisionism 94. COMMUNISM;
207. HISTORY; 239. LAW.
revisionist 94. COMMUNISM,
revisionism; 207. HISTORY,
revisionism; 239. LAW, **revisionism.**
revivalism 332. PROTESTANTISM.
revivalist 332. PROTESTANTISM,
revivalism.
revivalistic 332. PROTESTANTISM,
revivalism.
revolutional 41. BEHAVIOR,
revolutionism.
revolutionary 41. BEHAVIOR,
revolutionism.
revolutionism 41. BEHAVIOR.
revolutionist 41. BEHAVIOR,
revolutionism.
Rexist 152. FASCISM.
rhabdomancy 124. DIVINATION;
414. WATER, **dowsing.**
rhabdophobia 313. PHOBIAS;
335. PUNISHMENT, **mastigophobia.**
rhapsodism 409. VERSE.

rhapsodist 409. VERSE, **rhapsodism.**
rhapsodomancy 124. DIVINATION;
409. VERSE.
rheologic 263. MATTER, **rheology.**
rheological 263. MATTER, **rheology.**
rheologist 263. MATTER, **rheology.**
rheology 263. MATTER.
rheometric 264. MEASUREMENT,
rheometry.
rheometry 264. MEASUREMENT.
rheotaxis 282. MOTION; 414. WATER.
rheotropism 319. PLANTS; 414. WATER.
rhetorician 354. RHETORIC and
RHETORICAL DEVICES.
rheumatic 122. DISEASE and ILLNESS,
rheumatism.
rheumatism 122. DISEASE and ILLNESS.
rheumatologist 122. DISEASE and
ILLNESS, **rheumatology.**
rheumatology 122. DISEASE and ILLNESS.
rhigosis 51. BODY, HUMAN; 90. COLD.
rhinitis 293. NOSE.
rhinologic 293. NOSE, **rhinology.**
rhinological 293. NOSE, **rhinology.**
rhinologist 293. NOSE, **rhinology.**
rhinology 293. NOSE.
rhizotomy 291. NERVES.
rhopalic 409. VERSE, **rhopalism.**
rhopalism 409. VERSE.
rhopalist 409. VERSE, **rhopalism.**
rhotacism 247. LINGUISTICS.
rhotacistic 247. LINGUISTICS,
rhotacism.
rhotacize 247. LINGUISTICS, **rhotacism.**
rhymester 409. VERSE.
rhyparographer 296. OBSCENITY,
rhyparography.
rhyparographic 296. OBSCENITY,
rhyparography.
rhyparography 23. ART, **rhypography;**
296. OBSCENITY.
rhypography 23. ART.
rhypophobia 119. DIRT; 313. PHOBIAS.
ribald 213. HUMOR, **ribaldry;**
236. LANGUAGE, **ribaldry.**
ribaldry 213. HUMOR; 236. LANGUAGE.
Ribandism 69. CATHOLICISM,
Ribbonism.
Ribandist 69. CATHOLICISM,
Ribbonism.
Ribbonism 69. CATHOLICISM.

Ribbonist 69. CATHOLICISM, Ribbonism.
ribonucleic acid (RNA) 204. HEREDITY.
Ricardian 137. ECONOMICS; 137. ECONOMICS, Ricardian.
rictus 51. BODY, HUMAN.
riflery 416. WEAPONRY.
rigid 261. MATERIALS, PROPERTIES OF, rigidity.
rigidity 261. MATERIALS, PROPERTIES OF.
rigorism 312. PHILOSOPHY.
riparian 356. RIVERS; 356. RIVERS, riparian.
risibility 238. LAUGHTER.
ritualism 28. ATTITUDES.
ritualist 28. ATTITUDES, ritualism.
ritualistic 28. ATTITUDES, ritualism.
riverscape 352. REPRESENTATION.
RNA 204. HEREDITY.
robotics 30. AUTOMATION; 221. INDUSTRY.
robotism 30. AUTOMATION.
robotistic 30. AUTOMATION, robotism.
rocketry 31. AVIATION.
rococo 23. ART; 23. ART, rococo.
rodenticide 232. KILLING; 321. POISON.
roentgenism 342. RADIATION.
roentgenogram 342. RADIATION.
roentgenography 315. PHOTOGRAPHY; 342. RADIATION.
roentgenologist 266. MEDICAL SPECIALTIES, roentgenology; 350. REMEDIES, roentgenology.
roentgenology 266. MEDICAL SPECIALTIES; 350. REMEDIES.
roentgenotherapy 266. MEDICAL SPECIALTIES; 350. REMEDIES.
Romaic 236. LANGUAGE.
romanism 18. ANTIQUITY; 69. CATHOLICISM.
romanist 69. CATHOLICISM, romanism.
romanistic 69. CATHOLICISM, romanism.
Romanticism 23. ART.
Romanticist 23. ART, Romanticism.
Ronsardism 248. LITERARY STYLE.
röntgenism 342. RADIATION, roentgenism.
röntgenogram 342. RADIATION, roentgenogram.

röntgenography 315. PHOTOGRAPHY, roentgenography; 342. RADIATION, roentgenography.
röntgenologist 266. MEDICAL SPECIALTIES, roentgenology; 350. REMEDIES, roentgenology.
röntgenology 266. MEDICAL SPECIALTIES, roentgenology; 350. REMEDIES, roentgenology.
röntgenotherapy 266. MEDICAL SPECIALTIES, roentgenotherapy; 350. REMEDIES, roentgenotherapy.
rookery 16. ANIMALS; 45. BIRDS.
ropery 103. CRIME.
rosarium 167. FLOWERS.
Rosicrucian 349. RELIGION, Rosicrucianism.
Rosicrucianism 349. RELIGION.
Rosminian 312. PHILOSOPHY, Rosminianism.
Rosminianism 312. PHILOSOPHY.
rotund 51. BODY, HUMAN, rotundity.
rotundity 51. BODY, HUMAN.
routinism 41. BEHAVIOR.
routinist 41. BEHAVIOR, routinism.
rowdy 41. BEHAVIOR, rowdyism.
rowdyism 41. BEHAVIOR.
royalism 322. POLITICS.
royalist 322. POLITICS, royalism.
royalistic 322. POLITICS, royalism.
rubescence 92. COLOR; 95. COMPLEXION.
rubescent 92. COLOR, rubescence; 95. COMPLEXION, rubescence.
rubicund 95. COMPLEXION, rubicundity.
rubicundity 95. COMPLEXION.
rubric 53. BOOKS; 53. BOOKS, rubric.
rubricator 53. BOOKS, rubric.
rubrician 28. ATTITUDES, rubricism.
rubricism 28. ATTITUDES.
rufescence 92. COLOR.
rufescent 92. COLOR, rufescence.
ruffian 41. BEHAVIOR, ruffianism.
ruffianism 41. BEHAVIOR.
rugose 370. SKIN, rugosity.
rugosity 370. SKIN.
rumination 393. THINKING.
ruminative 393. THINKING, rumination.
ruminator 393. THINKING, rumination.
runecraft 428. WRITING.

runological 428. WRITING, **runology.**
runologist 428. WRITING, **runology.**
runology 428. WRITING.
ruralism 28. ATTITUDES.
ruralist 28. ATTITUDES, **ruralism.**
Russellites 332. PROTESTANTISM.
Russianism 23. ART; 236. LANGUAGE; 357. RUSSIA.
Russomania 254. MANIAS; 357. RUSSIA.
Russophile 311. -PHILE, -PHILIA, -PHILY, **Russophilism;** 357. RUSSIA, **Russophilism.**
Russophilism 311. -PHILE, -PHILIA, -PHILY; 357. RUSSIA.
Russophobia 313. PHOBIAS, **Russophobism.**
Russophobism 313. PHOBIAS; 357. RUSSIA.
rustic 236. LANGUAGE, **rusticism.**
rusticism 236. LANGUAGE.
rusticity 236. LANGUAGE, **rusticism.**

S

Sabaean 185. GOVERNMENT, **Sabaeanism.**
Sabaeanism 25. ASTRONOMY, **Sabianism;** 185. GOVERNMENT; 349. RELIGION, **Sabianism.**
Sabaism 25. ASTRONOMY.
Sabbatarian 231. JUDAISM, **Sabbatarianism.**
sabbatarian 80. CHRISTIANITY, **sabbatarianism.**
Sabbatarianism 231. JUDAISM.
sabbatarianism 80. CHRISTIANITY.
Sabeanism 25. ASTRONOMY, **Sabianism;** 349. RELIGION, **Sabianism.**
Sabellian 205. HERESY, **Sabellianism.**
Sabellianism 205. HERESY.
Sabianism 25. ASTRONOMY; 349. RELIGION.
sabotage 413. WAR.
saboteur 413. WAR, **sabotage.**
sabulosity 261. MATERIALS, PROPERTIES OF; 385. STONES.
sabulous 261. MATERIALS, PROPERTIES OF, **sabulosity;** 385. STONES, **sabulosity.**
sacerdotal 69. CATHOLICISM, **sacerdotalism.**

sacerdotalism 69. CATHOLICISM.
sacramentalism 80. CHRISTIANITY.
sacramentalist 80. CHRISTIANITY, **sacramentalism.**
sacrist 81. CHURCH.
sacristan 81. CHURCH, **sacrist.**
Sadducean 231. JUDAISM, **Sadduceeism.**
Sadducee 231. JUDAISM, **Sadduceeism.**
Sadduceeism 231. JUDAISM.
Sadducism 231. JUDAISM, **Sadduceeism.**
sadism 306. PAIN.
sadist 306. PAIN, **sadism.**
sadistic 306. PAIN, **sadism.**
sadomasochism 306. PAIN.
sadomasochist 306. PAIN, **sadomasochism.**
sadomasochistic 306. PAIN, **sadomasochism.**
sagittary 22. ARROWS.
sagittate 22. ARROWS.
Saint-Simonism 137. ECONOMICS.
Saint-Simonist 137. ECONOMICS, **Saint-Simonism.**
Saivism 206. HINDUISM, **Sivaism.**
Saktism 206. HINDUISM, **Shaktism.**
salacious 364. SEX, **salacity.**
salacity 364. SEX.
salicylism 321. POISON.
salmonellosis 321. POISON.
salvage 131. DUES and PAYMENT; 366. SHIPS.
salvational 332. PROTESTANTISM, **salvationism.**
salvationism 332. PROTESTANTISM.
salvationist 332. PROTESTANTISM, **salvationism.**
Samaritanism 349. RELIGION.
sanability 197. HEALTH; 350. REMEDIES.
sanable 197. HEALTH, **sanability;** 350. REMEDIES, **sanability.**
sanctum sanctorum 317. PLACES; 358. SACREDNESS.
sanguine 28. ATTITUDES, **sanguinity.**
sanguinity 28. ATTITUDES.
sanies 122. DISEASE and ILLNESS.
sanious 122. DISEASE and ILLNESS, **sanies.**
sanscullotic 322. POLITICS, **sanscullotism.**
sanscullotish 322. POLITICS, **sanscullotism.**

sanscullotism 322. POLITICS.
sanscullotist 322. POLITICS,
sanscullotism.
Santa Ana 420. WIND.
Sanusi 227. ISLAM, Senusism.
Sanusism 227. ISLAM, Senusism.
Sanusiya 227. ISLAM, Senusism.
Sapphism 209. HOMOSEXUALITY,
lesbianism.
sapraemia 49. BLOOD and BLOOD
VESSELS, sapremia; 321. POISON,
sapremia.
sapremia 49. BLOOD and BLOOD
VESSELS; 321. POISON.
saprophyte 319. PLANTS, saprophytism.
saprophytic 319. PLANTS,
saprophytism.
saprophytism 319. PLANTS.
sarcology 266. MEDICAL SPECIALTIES.
sarcoma 66. CANCER; 122. DISEASE and
ILLNESS.
sarcomatoid 122. DISEASE and ILLNESS,
sarcoma.
sarcomatosis 122. DISEASE and ILLNESS.
sarcomatous 122. DISEASE and ILLNESS,
sarcoma.
sarcophagous 166. FLESH, sarcophagy;
168. FOOD and NUTRITION,
sarcophagy.
sarcophagy 166. FLESH; 168. FOOD and
NUTRITION.
sardonicism 237. LANGUAGE STYLE;
354. RHETORIC and RHETORICAL
DEVICES.
Satanism 41. BEHAVIOR; 117. DEVIL.
Satanist 41. BEHAVIOR, Satanism;
117. DEVIL, Satanism.
Satanophany 117. DEVIL;
349. RELIGION.
Satanophobia 313. PHOBIAS.
sati 206. HINDUISM, sutteeism.
satirist 213. HUMOR.
satrapy 185. GOVERNMENT.
saturnism 321. POISON.
satyr 364. SEX, satyriasis.
satyriasis 364. SEX.
satyric 364. SEX, satyriasis.
satyrism 364. SEX, satyriasis.
satyromania 254. MANIAS; 364. SEX,
satyriasis.
savagedom 41. BEHAVIOR, savagism.

savagism 41. BEHAVIOR.
savant 233. KNOWLEDGE;
240. LEARNING.
Saxonism 236. LANGUAGE.
scabiophobia 313. PHOBIAS.
scansion 409. VERSE.
scaphism 232. KILLING.
scapulomancy 52. BONES;
124. DIVINATION.
scapulomantic 52. BONES,
scapulomancy; 124. DIVINATION,
scapulomancy.
scatologic 296. OBSCENITY, scatology.
scatological 296. OBSCENITY, scatology.
scatology 171. FOSSILS; 296. OBSCENITY.
scatomancy 124. DIVINATION.
scatophobia 313. PHOBIAS.
scenarist 159. FILMS.
scenographer 128. DRAWING,
scenography.
scenographic 128. DRAWING,
scenography.
scenographical 128. DRAWING,
scenography.
scenography 128. DRAWING.
Sceptic 312. PHILOSOPHY, Skepticism.
Scepticism 312. PHILOSOPHY,
Skepticism.
scepticism 28. ATTITUDES, skepticism.
Schellingism 312. PHILOSOPHY.
schema 352. REPRESENTATION.
schematic 352. REPRESENTATION,
schema.
schematism 25. ASTRONOMY; 170. FORM;
250. LOGIC; 312. PHILOSOPHY;
352. REPRESENTATION.
schematist 170. FORM, schematism;
216. IDEAS; 312. PHILOSOPHY,
schematism; 352. REPRESENTATION,
schematism.
schematomancy 51. BODY, HUMAN;
124. DIVINATION.
schism 349. RELIGION.
schismatic 349. RELIGION, schism.
schismatical 349. RELIGION, schism.
schizophrenia 224. INSANITY.
schizophrenic 224. INSANITY,
schizophrenia.
schizothyme 224. INSANITY,
schizothymia; 334. PSYCHOLOGY,
schizothymia.

schizothymia 224. INSANITY;
334. PSYCHOLOGY.
schizothymic 224. INSANITY,
schizothymia; 334. PSYCHOLOGY,
schizothymia.
schizotrichia 193. HAIR.
scholarch 240. LEARNING;
312. PHILOSOPHY.
Scholastic 312. PHILOSOPHY,
Scholasticism; 392. THEOLOGY,
Scholasticism.
Scholasticism 312. PHILOSOPHY;
392. THEOLOGY.
scholiast 53. BOOKS, scholium;
249. LITERATURE.
scholiastic 249. LITERATURE, scholiast.
scholium 53. BOOKS.
scholy 53. BOOKS, scholium.
schoolboyish 41. BEHAVIOR,
schoolboyism.
schoolboyism 41. BEHAVIOR.
Schwendenerism 54. BOTANY.
sciamachy 96. CONFLICT; 218. IMAGES.
sciatica 122. DISEASE and ILLNESS.
scientific humanism 255. MANKIND,
humanism.
scientism 28. ATTITUDES.
scientistic 28. ATTITUDES, scientism.
Scientologist 349. RELIGION,
Scientology.
Scientology 349. RELIGION.
scintillation 329. PROCESSES.
sciolism 233. KNOWLEDGE.
sciolist 233. KNOWLEDGE, sciolism.
sciolistic 233. KNOWLEDGE, sciolism.
sciolous 233. KNOWLEDGE, sciolism.
sciomachy 96. CONFLICT, sciamachy;
218. IMAGES, sciamachy.
sciomancy 124. DIVINATION;
182. GHOSTS.
sciomantic 124. DIVINATION,
sciomancy; 182. GHOSTS, sciomancy.
sciophobia 110. DARKNESS; 292. NIGHT;
313. PHOBIAS.
sciosophist 233. KNOWLEDGE,
sciosophy.
sciosophy 233. KNOWLEDGE.
sciotheism 182. GHOSTS.
sclerosis 51. BODY, HUMAN; 122. DISEASE
and ILLNESS; 319. PLANTS.

sclerotic 51. BODY, HUMAN, sclerosis;
122. DISEASE and ILLNESS, sclerosis;
319. PLANTS, sclerosis.
scoleciphobia 313. PHOBIAS;
427. WORMS.
scolecology 427. WORMS.
scoliosis 51. BODY, HUMAN.
scoliotic 51. BODY, HUMAN, scoliosis.
scopophilia 364. SEX.
scopophiliac 364. SEX, scopophilia.
scopophilic 364. SEX, scopophilia.
scopophobia 313. PHOBIAS.
scoptophilia 364. SEX, scopophilia.
scoptophobia 313. PHOBIAS,
scopophobia.
scorbutic 122. DISEASE and ILLNESS,
scorbuticism.
scorbuticism 122. DISEASE and ILLNESS.
scorification 329. PROCESSES.
Scoticism 236. LANGUAGE, Scotticism.
Scotism 312. PHILOSOPHY.
Scotist 312. PHILOSOPHY, Scotism.
Scotistic 312. PHILOSOPHY, Scotism.
Scotistical 312. PHILOSOPHY, Scotism.
scotograph 48. BLINDNESS;
315. PHOTOGRAPHY, scotography;
342. RADIATION; 428. WRITING.
scotography 315. PHOTOGRAPHY.
scotoma 48. BLINDNESS.
scotomy 48. BLINDNESS, scotoma.
scotophobia 110. DARKNESS; 292. NIGHT;
313. PHOBIAS.
scotopia 110. DARKNESS; 148. EYES.
scotopic 110. DARKNESS, scotopia;
148. EYES, scotopia.
Scotticism 236. LANGUAGE.
Scottishism 236. LANGUAGE, Scotticism.
scoundrelism 41. BEHAVIOR.
scoundrelly 41. BEHAVIOR,
scoundrelism.
scribblement 428. WRITING.
scribism 231. JUDAISM.
scribomania 254. MANIAS; 428. WRITING.
scription 428. WRITING.
scriptorium 256. MANUSCRIPTS.
Scripturalism 43. BIBLE.
scrivener 256. MANUSCRIPTS,
scrivenery; 428. WRITING, scrivenery.
scrivenery 256. MANUSCRIPTS;
428. WRITING.
scutage 131. DUES and PAYMENT.

scyphomancy 124. DIVINATION.
seascape 352. REPRESENTATION;
360. SEA.
secernent 50. BODILY FUNCTIONS,
secernment.
secernment 50. BODILY FUNCTIONS.
secessional 322. POLITICS, secessionism.
secessionism 322. POLITICS.
secessionist 322. POLITICS, secessionism.
seclusionist 41. BEHAVIOR; 362. SELF.
Second Advent 80. CHRISTIANITY,
Parousia.
Second Adventist 332. PROTESTANTISM.
Second Coming 80. CHRISTIANITY,
Parousia.
sectarian 332. PROTESTANTISM,
sectarianism.
sectarianism 332. PROTESTANTISM.
sectionalism 185. GOVERNMENT.
sectionalist 185. GOVERNMENT,
sectionalism.
secularism 349. RELIGION.
secularist 349. RELIGION, secularism.
secularistic 349. RELIGION, secularism.
secundigravida 46. BIRTH.
segregationism 341. RACE.
seisin 331. PROPERTY and OWNERSHIP,
seizin.
seism 134. EARTHQUAKES, seismism.
seismic 134. EARTHQUAKES, seismism.
seismicity 134. EARTHQUAKES.
seismism 134. EARTHQUAKES.
seismogram 134. EARTHQUAKES.
seismograph 134. EARTHQUAKES;
226. INSTRUMENTS.
seismographer 134. EARTHQUAKES,
seismograph.
seismographic 134. EARTHQUAKES,
seismograph.
seismographical 134. EARTHQUAKES,
seismograph.
seismography 134. EARTHQUAKES.
seismologic 134. EARTHQUAKES,
seismology.
seismological 134. EARTHQUAKES,
seismology.
seismologist 134. EARTHQUAKES,
seismology.
seismology 134. EARTHQUAKES.
seismometer 134. EARTHQUAKES.

seismometric 134. EARTHQUAKES,
seismometer.
seismometry 134. EARTHQUAKES,
seismometer.
seizin 331. PROPERTY and OWNERSHIP.
selaphobia 245. LIGHT; 313. PHOBIAS.
selenographer 25. ASTRONOMY,
selenography; 280. MOON,
selenography.
selenographic 25. ASTRONOMY,
selenography; 280. MOON,
selenography.
selenographical 25. ASTRONOMY,
selenography; 280. MOON,
selenography.
selenographist 25. ASTRONOMY,
selenography; 280. MOON,
selenography.
selenography 25. ASTRONOMY;
280. MOON.
selenolatry 280. MOON.
selenologic 25. ASTRONOMY, selenology.
selenological 25. ASTRONOMY,
selenology; 280. MOON, selenology.
selenologist 25. ASTRONOMY,
selenology; 280. MOON, selenology.
selenology 25. ASTRONOMY; 280. MOON.
selenomancy 124. DIVINATION;
280. MOON.
self-critical 104. CRITICISM, self-
criticism.
self-criticism 104. CRITICISM.
selfism 362. SELF.
selfist 362. SELF, selfism.
semantic 236. LANGUAGE, semantics;
247. LINGUISTICS, semantics.
semantician 236. LANGUAGE,
semantics.
semanticist 236. LANGUAGE, semantics;
247. LINGUISTICS, semantics.
semantics 236. LANGUAGE;
247. LINGUISTICS.
semaphore 165. FLAGS.
semaphoric 165. FLAGS, semaphore.
semaphorical 165. FLAGS, semaphore.
semaphorist 165. FLAGS, semaphore.
semasiology 247. LINGUISTICS.
sematographic 428. WRITING,
sematography.
sematography 428. WRITING.

sematology 233. KNOWLEDGE;
247. LINGUISTICS, **semasiology**.
semeiographer 122. DISEASE and
ILLNESS, **semeiography**.
semeiographic 122. DISEASE and
ILLNESS, **semeiography**;
428. WRITING, **semeiography**.
semeiographical 122. DISEASE and
ILLNESS, **semeiography**;
428. WRITING, **semeiography**.
semeiography 122. DISEASE and ILLNESS;
428. WRITING.
semeiologic 247. LINGUISTICS,
semeiology.
semeiological 247. LINGUISTICS,
semeiology.
semeiologist 247. LINGUISTICS,
semeiology.
semeiology 122. DISEASE and ILLNESS;
247. LINGUISTICS.
semi-Arian 392. THEOLOGY, **semi-Arianism**.
semi-Arianism 392. THEOLOGY.
semiography 428. WRITING,
semeiography.
semiologic 247. LINGUISTICS,
semeiology.
semiological 247. LINGUISTICS,
semeiology.
semiologist 247. LINGUISTICS,
semeiology.
semiology 247. LINGUISTICS,
semeiology.
semiotic 233. KNOWLEDGE, **semiotics**;
247. LINGUISTICS, **semiotics**.
semiotician 247. LINGUISTICS,
semiotics.
semioticist 247. LINGUISTICS, **semiotics**.
semiotics 233. KNOWLEDGE;
247. LINGUISTICS.
Semi-Pelagianism 205. HERESY.
Semiticism 236. LANGUAGE.
Semiticist 231. JUDAISM, **Semitics**;
236. LANGUAGE, **Semitics**.
Semitics 231. JUDAISM; 236. LANGUAGE.
Semitism 231. JUDAISM.
Semitist 231. JUDAISM, **Semitics**;
236. LANGUAGE, **Semitics**.
semology 247. LINGUISTICS,
semeiology.
sempiternal 396. TIME, **sempiternity**.

sempiternity 396. TIME.
seneschalship 376. SOCIETY.
senicidal 299. OLD AGE, **senicide**.
senicide 299. OLD AGE.
senile 299. OLD AGE, **senility**.
senility 299. OLD AGE.
sensationalism 23. ART; 145. ETHICS;
237. LANGUAGE STYLE; 248. LITERARY
STYLE; 265. MEDIA; 312. PHILOSOPHY.
sensationalist 23. ART, **sensationalism**;
145. ETHICS, **sensationalism**;
248. LITERARY STYLE, **sensationalism**;
265. MEDIA, **sensationalism**;
312. PHILOSOPHY, **sensationalism**.
sensationalistic 248. LITERARY STYLE,
sensationalism; 312. PHILOSOPHY,
sensationalism.
sensitometer 315. PHOTOGRAPHY.
sensitometric 315. PHOTOGRAPHY,
sensitometer.
sensitometry 315. PHOTOGRAPHY,
sensitometer.
sensorial 41. BEHAVIOR, **sensorialism**.
sensorialism 41. BEHAVIOR.
sensorium 56. BRAIN; 309. PERCEPTION.
sensualism 145. ETHICS;
312. PHILOSOPHY.
sensuism 312. PHILOSOPHY.
sentimentalism 248. LITERARY STYLE.
sentimentalist 248. LITERARY STYLE,
sentimentalism.
Senusi 227. ISLAM, **Senusism**.
Senusism 227. ISLAM.
Senusiya 227. ISLAM, **Senusism**.
separatism 322. POLITICS.
separatist 322. POLITICS, **separatism**.
sepelition 63. BURIAL.
Sepher Torah 231. JUDAISM.
sepsis 49. BLOOD and BLOOD VESSELS.
septic 49. BLOOD and BLOOD VESSELS,
sepsis.
septicaemia 49. BLOOD and BLOOD
VESSELS, **septicemia**; 321. POISON,
septicemia.
septicaemic 49. BLOOD and BLOOD
VESSELS, **septicemia**; 321. POISON,
septicemia.
septicemia 49. BLOOD and BLOOD
VESSELS; 321. POISON.

septicemic 49. BLOOD and BLOOD VESSELS, **septicemia;** 321. POISON, **septicemia.**

septuagenarian 299. OLD AGE, **septuagenarianism.**

septuagenarianism 299. OLD AGE.

septuagenary 299. OLD AGE, **septuagenarianism.**

seraphicism 349. RELIGION.

seraphism 41. BEHAVIOR.

serendipitous 73. CHANCE, **serendipity.**

serendipity 73. CHANCE.

serfdom 185. GOVERNMENT, **serfism.**

serfism 185. GOVERNMENT.

sergeanty 331. PROPERTY and OWNERSHIP, **serjeanty.**

sericultural 427. WORMS, **sericulture.**

sericulture 427. WORMS.

sericulturist 427. WORMS, **sericulture.**

serigrapher 23. ART, **serigraphy.**

serigraphy 23. ART.

serjeanty 331. PROPERTY and OWNERSHIP.

sermonist 41. BEHAVIOR; 349. RELIGION.

sermonology 349. RELIGION.

serological 266. MEDICAL SPECIALTIES, **serology;** 350. REMEDIES, **serology.**

serologist 266. MEDICAL SPECIALTIES, **serology;** 350. REMEDIES, **serology.**

serology 266. MEDICAL SPECIALTIES; 350. REMEDIES.

serosity 261. MATERIALS, PROPERTIES OF.

serotherapy 266. MEDICAL SPECIALTIES; 350. REMEDIES.

serous 261. MATERIALS, PROPERTIES OF, **serosity.**

servilism 371. SLAVERY.

servility 371. SLAVERY, **servilism.**

servo 30. AUTOMATION, **servomechanism.**

servomechanical 30. AUTOMATION, **servomechanism.**

servomechanism 30. AUTOMATION.

sesquipedal 236. LANGUAGE, **sesquipedalianism.**

sesquipedalian 236. LANGUAGE, **sesquipedalianism.**

sesquipedalianism 236. LANGUAGE.

sesquipedalism 236. LANGUAGE, **sesquipedalianism.**

sesquipedality 236. LANGUAGE, **sesquipedalianism.**

Sethian 183. GOD and GODS, **Sethite.**

Sethite 183. GOD and GODS.

severalty 331. PROPERTY and OWNERSHIP; 363. SEPARATION.

severance 363. SEPARATION.

sexagenarian 3. AGE, **sexagenarianism.**

sexagenarianism 3. AGE.

sexagenary 3. AGE, **sexagenarianism.**

sexdigitism 194. HANDS.

sexdigitist 157. FEET and LEGS; 161. FINGERS and TOES; 194. HANDS.

sexism 28. ATTITUDES; 121. DISCRIMINATION; 424. WOMEN.

sexist 424. WOMEN, **sexism.**

sexological 364. SEX, **sexology.**

sexologist 364. SEX, **sexology.**

sexology 364. SEX.

sextant 226. INSTRUMENTS.

sexual anesthesia 364. SEX.

sexualism 364. SEX.

shadowgraph 310. PERFORMING.

shadowgraphist 310. PERFORMING, **shadowgraph.**

shadowgraphy 342. RADIATION.

Shaker 332. PROTESTANTISM, **Shakerism.**

Shakerism 332. PROTESTANTISM.

Shakespearian 248. LITERARY STYLE, **Shakespearianism.**

Shakespearianism 248. LITERARY STYLE.

Shakta 206. HINDUISM, **Shaktism.**

Shakti 206. HINDUISM, **Shaktism.**

Shaktism 206. HINDUISM.

shamanism 349. RELIGION.

shamanist 349. RELIGION, **shamanism.**

shamanistic 349. RELIGION, **shamanism.**

Shandyism 41. BEHAVIOR.

Shavian 248. LITERARY STYLE, **Shavianism.**

Shavianism 248. LITERARY STYLE.

sherardisology 429. ZINC.

sherardize 429. ZINC, **sherardisology.**

Shiism 227. ISLAM.

Shiite 227. ISLAM, **Shiism.**

Shinto 349. RELIGION, **Shintoism.**

Shintoism 349. RELIGION.

Shintoistic 349. RELIGION, **Shintoism.**

Shivaism 206. HINDUISM, Sivaism.
siagonologic 52. BONES, siagonology.
siagonological 52. BONES, siagonology.
siagonology 52. BONES.
sialagogic 50. BODILY FUNCTIONS,
sialagogue.
sialagogue 50. BODILY FUNCTIONS.
sialism 122. DISEASE and ILLNESS.
sialismus 122. DISEASE and ILLNESS,
sialism.
sialorrhea 50. BODILY FUNCTIONS.
sialorrhoea 50. BODILY FUNCTIONS,
sialorrhea.
sibilance 380. SOUND, sibilancy.
sibilancy 380. SOUND.
sibilant 380. SOUND, sibilancy.
sibyl 124. DIVINATION.
sibylic 124. DIVINATION, sibyl.
sibyllic 124. DIVINATION, sibyl.
sibylline 124. DIVINATION, sibyl.
sibyllist 124. DIVINATION.
siderodromophobia 313. PHOBIAS;
344. RAILROADS.
siderograph 141. ENGRAVING,
siderography.
siderographic 141. ENGRAVING,
siderography.
siderographical 141. ENGRAVING,
siderography.
siderographist 141. ENGRAVING,
siderography.
siderography 141. ENGRAVING.
sideromancer 25. ASTRONOMY,
sideromancy.
sideromancy 25. ASTRONOMY;
124. DIVINATION.
sideromania 254. MANIAS;
344. RAILROADS.
sideromantic 25. ASTRONOMY,
sideromancy.
siderophobia 25. ASTRONOMY;
313. PHOBIAS.
siderosis 122. DISEASE and ILLNESS.
siderotechny 270. METALS.
siegecraft 413. WAR.
sigillographer 361. SEALS,
sigillography.
sigillographic 361. SEALS, sigillography.
sigillography 177. GEMS; 361. SEALS.
sigmatism 247. LINGUISTICS.
signalment 103. CRIME.

Sikh 206. HINDUISM, Sikhism.
Sikhism 206. HINDUISM.
silicosis 122. DISEASE and ILLNESS.
sillographer 249. LITERATURE,
sillography.
sillography 249. LITERATURE.
silviculture 401. TREES.
silviculturist 401. TREES, silviculture.
similarity 4. AGREEMENT.
simoniac 69. CATHOLICISM, simonism;
81. CHURCH, simonism;
349. RELIGION, simonism.
simoniacal 349. RELIGION, simonism.
simonism 69. CATHOLICISM;
81. CHURCH; 349. RELIGION.
simonist 69. CATHOLICISM, simonism;
81. CHURCH, simonism;
349. RELIGION, simonism; 367. SIN,
simony.
simony 69. CATHOLICISM, simonism;
81. CHURCH, simonism; 367. SIN.
simplism 21. ARGUMENTATION.
simplistic 21. ARGUMENTATION,
simplism.
simulacrum 218. IMAGES.
sinapism 122. DISEASE and ILLNESS.
Sinarquism 322. POLITICS.
Sinarquist 322. POLITICS, Sinarquism.
sindology 63. BURIAL.
sindonologist 79. CHRIST, sindonology.
sindonology 79. CHRIST.
sinecure 426. WORK, sinecurism.
sinecurism 426. WORK.
singularism 312. PHILOSOPHY.
Sinicism 78. CHINA.
sinistral 194. HANDS, sinistrality;
242. LEFT, sinistrality.
sinistrality 194. HANDS; 242. LEFT.
sinistration 242. LEFT, sinistrality.
sinistrogyration 242. LEFT.
sinistrogyric 242. LEFT,
sinistrogyration.
Sinological 78. CHINA, Sinology.
Sinologist 78. CHINA, Sinology.
Sinologue 78. CHINA, Sinology.
Sinology 78. CHINA.
Sinonism 243. LIES and LYING.
siriasis 350. REMEDIES; 387. SUN.
sirocco 420. WIND.
sitiophobia 168. FOOD and NUTRITION,
sitophobia; 313. PHOBIAS, sitophobia.

sitomania 168. FOOD and NUTRITION;
254. MANIAS.
sitophobia 168. FOOD and NUTRITION;
313. PHOBIAS.
Sivaism 206. HINDUISM.
Sivaite 206. HINDUISM, Sivaism.
skeletology 52. BONES; 266. MEDICAL
SPECIALTIES, osteology.
Skeptic 312. PHILOSOPHY, Skepticism.
skeptic 28. ATTITUDES, skepticism.
skeptical 28. ATTITUDES, skepticism.
Skepticism 312. PHILOSOPHY.
skepticism 28. ATTITUDES.
skiagram 128. DRAWING, skiagraphy.
skiagrapher 128. DRAWING, skiagraphy.
skiagraphy 128. DRAWING.
skiascopy 148. EYES, retinoscopy.
skulduggery 103. CRIME.
skyscape 352. REPRESENTATION.
slangism 236. LANGUAGE.
Slavicism 236. LANGUAGE.
Slavicist 236. LANGUAGE; 357. RUSSIA.
Slavist 236. LANGUAGE, Slavicist;
357. RUSSIA, Slavicist.
Slavophil 311. -PHILE, -PHILIA, -PHILY,
Slavophilism; 357. RUSSIA,
Slavophilism.
Slavophile 311. -PHILE, -PHILIA, -PHILY,
Slavophilism; 357. RUSSIA,
Slavophilism.
Slavophilism 311. -PHILE, -PHILIA,
-PHILY; 357. RUSSIA.
Slavophobe 322. POLITICS,
Slavophobia; 357. RUSSIA,
Slavophobia.
Slavophobia 313. PHOBIAS;
322. POLITICS; 357. RUSSIA.
Slavophobic 322. POLITICS,
Slavophobia; 357. RUSSIA,
Slavophobia.
slumism 82. CITIES; 325. POVERTY.
smartism 333. PROVERBS.
snakeology 374. SNAKES.
snakology 374. SNAKES, snakeology.
snob 28. ATTITUDES, snobbism.
snobbery 28. ATTITUDES, snobbism.
snobbish 28. ATTITUDES, snobbism.
snobbism 28. ATTITUDES.
snobby 28. ATTITUDES, snobbism.
snobocracy 376. SOCIETY.
snooperscope 226. INSTRUMENTS.

sobriquet 288. NAMES.
socage 235. LAND; 331. PROPERTY and
OWNERSHIP.
socager 331. PROPERTY and OWNERSHIP.
social anthropology
17. ANTHROPOLOGY.
socialism 185. GOVERNMENT;
322. POLITICS.
socialist 322. POLITICS, socialism.
socialistic 322. POLITICS, socialism.
socialist realism 23. ART;
94. COMMUNISM.
socialization 94. COMMUNISM;
376. SOCIETY.
societyese 237. LANGUAGE STYLE.
Socinian 205. HERESY, Socinianism.
Socinianism 205. HERESY.
sociocracy 185. GOVERNMENT;
376. SOCIETY.
sociologese 237. LANGUAGE STYLE.
sociologic 376. SOCIETY, sociology.
sociological 255. MANKIND, sociology;
376. SOCIETY, sociology.
sociologism 376. SOCIETY.
sociologist 255. MANKIND, sociology;
376. SOCIETY, sociology.
sociologistic 376. SOCIETY, sociologism.
sociology 255. MANKIND; 376. SOCIETY.
sociometric 255. MANKIND, sociometry;
376. SOCIETY, sociometry.
sociometrist 255. MANKIND, sociometry;
376. SOCIETY, sociometry.
sociometry 255. MANKIND; 376. SOCIETY.
socionomy 376. SOCIETY.
socman 331. PROPERTY and OWNERSHIP,
socager.
Socraticism 312. PHILOSOPHY.
Socratism 312. PHILOSOPHY,
Socraticism.
sodalist 69. CATHOLICISM, sodality;
376. SOCIETY, sodality.
sodality 69. CATHOLICISM;
376. SOCIETY.
solarism 387. SUN.
solarist 387. SUN, solarism.
solarium 387. SUN.
solatium 131. DUES and PAYMENT.
soldiery 413. WAR.
solecism 186. GRAMMAR.
solecist 186. GRAMMAR, solecism.
solecistic 186. GRAMMAR, solecism.

solecistical 186. GRAMMAR, solecism.
solidarism 376. SOCIETY.
solidarist 376. SOCIETY, solidarism.
solidaristic 376. SOCIETY, solidarism.
solidarity 376. SOCIETY.
solidism 122. DISEASE and ILLNESS.
solidist 122. DISEASE and ILLNESS,
   solidism.
solidistic 122. DISEASE and ILLNESS,
   solidism.
solifidian 392. THEOLOGY,
   solifidianism.
solifidianism 392. THEOLOGY.
soliloquist 127. DRAMA, soliloquy;
   362. SELF, soliloquy.
soliloquy 127. DRAMA; 362. SELF.
solipsism 312. PHILOSOPHY.
solipsist 312. PHILOSOPHY, solipsism.
solipsistic 312. PHILOSOPHY, solipsism.
somatics 51. BODY, HUMAN,
   somatology; 263. MATTER,
   somatology.
somatism 122. DISEASE and ILLNESS.
somatist 122. DISEASE and ILLNESS,
   somatism.
somatogenic 122. DISEASE and ILLNESS.
somatologic 51. BODY, HUMAN,
   somatology.
somatological 51. BODY, HUMAN,
   somatology.
somatology 17. ANTHROPOLOGY;
   51. BODY, HUMAN; 263. MATTER.
somatotype 51. BODY, HUMAN.
somnambulant 372. SLEEP,
   somnambulism.
somnambulism 372. SLEEP.
somnambulist 372. SLEEP,
   somnambulism.
somnambulistic 372. SLEEP,
   somnambulism.
somniloquism 372. SLEEP.
somniloquist 372. SLEEP,
   somniloquism.
somniloquous 372. SLEEP,
   somniloquism.
somniloquy 372. SLEEP, somniloquism.
somnipathist 215. HYPNOSIS,
   somnipathy.
somnipathy 215. HYPNOSIS; 372. SLEEP.
somnolence 372. SLEEP.
somnolency 372. SLEEP, somnolence.

somnolent 372. SLEEP, somnolence.
somnolism 372. SLEEP, somnolence.
sonometer 198. HEARING.
sonometric 198. HEARING, sonometer.
sonometry 198. HEARING, sonometer.
Sophianism 135. EASTERN ORTHODOXY.
Sophianist 135. EASTERN ORTHODOXY,
   Sophianism.
Sophiology 135. EASTERN ORTHODOXY,
   Sophianism.
sophiology 216. IDEAS.
sophism 21. ARGUMENTATION.
sophist 21. ARGUMENTATION;
   240. LEARNING; 354. RHETORIC and
   RHETORICAL DEVICES.
sophister 21. ARGUMENTATION,
   sophism.
sophistic 21. ARGUMENTATION,
   sophism; 240. LEARNING, sophist.
sophistical 240. LEARNING, sophist.
sophistry 21. ARGUMENTATION;
   240. LEARNING; 312. PHILOSOPHY;
   354. RHETORIC and RHETORICAL
   DEVICES.
sophomania 254. MANIAS; 422. WISDOM.
Sorbonist 240. LEARNING.
sorcerer 252. MAGIC, sorcery.
sorcerous 252. MAGIC, sorcery.
sorcery 252. MAGIC.
sorites 250. LOGIC.
soritic 250. LOGIC, sorites.
soritical 250. LOGIC, sorites.
sororicidal 232. KILLING, sororicide.
sororicide 232. KILLING.
sorority 376. SOCIETY; 424. WOMEN.
sorosis 376. SOCIETY.
sortilege 124. DIVINATION; 252. MAGIC.
sortition 175. GAMBLING.
soterialogical 392. THEOLOGY,
   soteriology.
soterialogy 392. THEOLOGY,
   soteriology.
soteriologic 79. CHRIST, soteriology.
soteriological 79. CHRIST, soteriology;
   197. HEALTH, soteriology;
   392. THEOLOGY, soteriology.
soteriology 79. CHRIST; 197. HEALTH;
   392. THEOLOGY.
soubriquet 288. NAMES, sobriquet.
Sovietism 185. GOVERNMENT;
   357. RUSSIA.

sovietism 185. GOVERNMENT,
Sovietism; 357. RUSSIA, Sovietism.
Sovietist 185. GOVERNMENT, Sovietism;
357. RUSSIA, Sovietism.
sovietist 185. GOVERNMENT, Sovietism;
357. RUSSIA, Sovietism.
Sovietologist 357. RUSSIA, Sovietology.
Sovietology 357. RUSSIA.
spagyrist 7. ALCHEMY.
Spartacist 322. POLITICS.
spartan 28. ATTITUDES, spartanism.
spartanism 28. ATTITUDES.
spasmatomancy 122. DISEASE and
ILLNESS; 124. DIVINATION.
spasmodic 41. BEHAVIOR, spasmodism.
spasmodical 41. BEHAVIOR,
spasmodism.
spasmodism 41. BEHAVIOR.
spasmodist 41. BEHAVIOR, spasmodism.
spasmophile 122. DISEASE and ILLNESS,
spasmophilia.
spasmophilia 122. DISEASE and ILLNESS.
spatalamancy 124. DIVINATION,
spatilomancy.
spatilomancy 124. DIVINATION.
spatulamancy 52. BONES;
124. DIVINATION.
spatulamantic 52. BONES,
spatulamancy; 124. DIVINATION,
spatulamancy.
specialism 233. KNOWLEDGE.
specialist 233. KNOWLEDGE, specialism.
specialistic 233. KNOWLEDGE,
specialism.
speciation 44. BIOLOGY.
speciosity 218. IMAGES;
312. PHILOSOPHY.
specious 218. IMAGES, speciosity;
312. PHILOSOPHY, speciosity.
spectacularism 28. ATTITUDES.
spectrobolometer 226. INSTRUMENTS.
spectrobolometric 226. INSTRUMENTS,
spectrobolometer; 316. PHYSICS,
spectrobolometry.
spectrobolometry 316. PHYSICS.
spectrogram 92. COLOR; 245. LIGHT.
spectrograph 92. COLOR; 245. LIGHT.
spectrographic 92. COLOR,
spectrograph; 245. LIGHT,
spectrograph; 315. PHOTOGRAPHY,
spectrography.

spectrography 92. COLOR; 245. LIGHT;
315. PHOTOGRAPHY.
spectroheliogram 315. PHOTOGRAPHY.
spectrological 182. GHOSTS,
spectrology.
spectrology 182. GHOSTS.
spectrophobia 182. GHOSTS;
313. PHOBIAS.
spectroscope 226. INSTRUMENTS.
spectroscopy 226. INSTRUMENTS,
spectroscope.
speculation 393. THINKING.
speculative 393. THINKING, speculation.
speculativism 393. THINKING.
speculator 393. THINKING, speculation.
speedometer 226. INSTRUMENTS.
spelaeological 71. CAVES, speleology.
spelaeologist 71. CAVES, speleology.
spelaeology 71. CAVES, speleology.
speleological 71. CAVES, speleology.
speleologist 71. CAVES, speleology.
speleology 71. CAVES.
spelunk 71. CAVES, spelunker.
spelunker 71. CAVES.
Spencerian 100. COSMOLOGY,
Spencerianism.
Spencerianism 100. COSMOLOGY.
Spenerism 332. PROTESTANTISM.
spermicidal 46. BIRTH, spermicide;
232. KILLING, spermicide.
spermicide 46. BIRTH; 232. KILLING.
spermism 44. BIOLOGY.
spermist 44. BIOLOGY, spermism.
sphagnologist 54. BOTANY,
sphagnology.
sphagnology 54. BOTANY.
sphenographer 428. WRITING,
sphenography.
sphenographic 428. WRITING,
sphenography.
sphenographist 428. WRITING,
sphenography.
sphenography 428. WRITING.
sphericist 133. EARTH.
spheroidicity 262. MATHEMATICS.
spheroidism 262. MATHEMATICS,
spheroidicity.
spheroidity 262. MATHEMATICS,
spheroidicity.
sphragistic 361. SEALS, sphragistics.
sphragistics 361. SEALS.

sphygmograph 49. BLOOD and BLOOD VESSELS, sphygmography; 226. INSTRUMENTS.
sphygmographic 49. BLOOD and BLOOD VESSELS, sphygmography.
sphygmographical 49. BLOOD and BLOOD VESSELS, sphygmography.
sphygmography 49. BLOOD and BLOOD VESSELS.
sphygmology 49. BLOOD and BLOOD VESSELS.
sphygmomanometer 49. BLOOD and BLOOD VESSELS; 226. INSTRUMENTS.
Spinozism 312. PHILOSOPHY.
Spinozist 312. PHILOSOPHY, Spinozism.
Spinozistic 312. PHILOSOPHY, Spinozism.
spiritism 384. SPIRITS and SPIRITUALISM.
spiritualism 384. SPIRITS and SPIRITUALISM.
spiritualist 384. SPIRITS and SPIRITUALISM, spiritualism.
spiritualistic 384. SPIRITS and SPIRITUALISM, spiritualism.
spirometer 266. MEDICAL SPECIALTIES, spirometry.
spirometry 266. MEDICAL SPECIALTIES.
splanchnology 14. ANATOMY.
spodomancy 124. DIVINATION.
spodomantic 124. DIVINATION, spodomancy.
spoliation 81. CHURCH; 366. SHIPS; 391. THEFT; 413. WAR.
spondee 409. VERSE.
spondiac 409. VERSE, spondee.
spongologist 44. BIOLOGY, spongology.
spongology 44. BIOLOGY.
spontaneous generation 204. HEREDITY, abiogenesis; 244. LIFE.
spookology 182. GHOSTS.
Spoonerism 236. LANGUAGE.
spoonerize 236. LANGUAGE, Spoonerism.
sporogenesis 44. BIOLOGY.
sporogenetic 44. BIOLOGY, sporogenesis.
sporogenous 44. BIOLOGY, sporogenesis.
squandermania 254. MANIAS; 276. MONEY.

squatter 239. LAW, squatterism; 331. PROPERTY and OWNERSHIP, squatterism.
squatterism 239. LAW; 331. PROPERTY and OWNERSHIP.
squirearchy 139. ENGLAND; 376. SOCIETY.
stadia 235. LAND; 264. MEASUREMENT.
stadiometer 226. INSTRUMENTS.
stagecraft 127. DRAMA.
stagese 237. LANGUAGE STYLE.
Stakhanovism 94. COMMUNISM.
Stakhanovite 94. COMMUNISM, Stakhanovism.
Stalinism 94. COMMUNISM.
Stalinist 94. COMMUNISM, Stalinism.
Stalinistic 94. COMMUNISM, Stalinism.
stalwart 322. POLITICS, stalwartism.
stalwartism 322. POLITICS.
staminody 167. FLOWERS.
standpattism 28. ATTITUDES; 322. POLITICS.
stannotype 315. PHOTOGRAPHY.
stanza 409. VERSE.
stasibasiphobia 313. PHOBIAS; 412. WALKING.
stasis 50. BODILY FUNCTIONS.
stateism 185. GOVERNMENT, statism.
statical 316. PHYSICS, statics.
statics 316. PHYSICS.
statism 185. GOVERNMENT.
statist 185. GOVERNMENT, statism.
statistology 262. MATHEMATICS.
statuary 23. ART.
steatopygia 51. BODY, HUMAN.
steatopygic 51. BODY, HUMAN, steatopygia.
steatopygy 51. BODY, HUMAN, steatopygia.
steganographer 236. LANGUAGE, steganography.
steganography 236. LANGUAGE.
stelographic 428. WRITING, stelography.
stelography 428. WRITING.
stenographer 428. WRITING, stenography.
stenographic 428. WRITING, stenography.
stenographical 428. WRITING, stenography.

stenographist 428. WRITING,
  stenography.
stenography 428. WRITING.
stenotypic 428. WRITING, stenotypy.
stenotypist 428. WRITING, stenotypy.
stenotypy 428. WRITING.
stercoranism 392. THEOLOGY.
stercoranist 392. THEOLOGY,
  stercoranism.
stercorarian 392. THEOLOGY,
  stercoranism.
stereochromatic 23. ART,
  stereochromy.
stereochromic 23. ART, stereochromy.
stereochromy 23. ART.
stereographer 128. DRAWING,
  stereography.
stereographic 128. DRAWING,
  stereography.
stereographical 128. DRAWING,
  stereography.
stereography 128. DRAWING.
stereometric 264. MEASUREMENT,
  stereometry.
stereometry 264. MEASUREMENT.
stereoptican 352. REPRESENTATION,
  stereopticon.
stereoptician 352. REPRESENTATION,
  stereopticon.
stereopticon 352. REPRESENTATION.
stereotactic 44. BIOLOGY, stereotaxis;
  191. GROWTH, stereotaxis;
  282. MOTION, stereotaxis.
stereotaxis 44. BIOLOGY; 191. GROWTH;
  282. MOTION.
stereotropic 44. BIOLOGY,
  stereotropism; 191. GROWTH,
  stereotropism; 282. MOTION,
  stereotropism.
stereotropism 44. BIOLOGY;
  191. GROWTH; 282. MOTION.
sternomancy 124. DIVINATION.
sternutation 50. BODILY FUNCTIONS.
sternutative 50. BODILY FUNCTIONS,
  sternutation.
sternutatory 50. BODILY FUNCTIONS,
  sternutation.
stethographic 266. MEDICAL
  SPECIALTIES, stethography.
stethography 266. MEDICAL
  SPECIALTIES.

sthenia 386. STRENGTH and WEAKNESS.
sthenic 386. STRENGTH and WEAKNESS,
  sthenia.
stibialism 321. POISON.
stich 409. VERSE.
stichomancy 124. DIVINATION;
  409. VERSE.
stichometric 237. LANGUAGE STYLE,
  stichometry.
stichometrical 237. LANGUAGE STYLE,
  stichometry.
stichometry 237. LANGUAGE STYLE.
stichomythia 127. DRAMA.
stichomythic 127. DRAMA,
  stichomythia.
stigmata 69. CATHOLICISM, stigmatism.
stigmatic 69. CATHOLICISM,
  stigmatism.
stigmatism 69. CATHOLICISM.
stignomancy 124. DIVINATION.
stirpicultural 16. ANIMALS,
  stirpiculture; 44. BIOLOGY,
  stirpiculture; 54. BOTANY,
  stirpiculture; 319. PLANTS,
  stirpiculture; 430. ZOOLOGY,
  stirpiculture.
stirpiculture 16. ANIMALS; 44. BIOLOGY;
  54. BOTANY; 319. PLANTS;
  430. ZOOLOGY.
Stoic 312. PHILOSOPHY, Stoicism.
stoic 306. PAIN, stoicism; 320. PLEASURE,
  stoicism.
stoical 306. PAIN, stoicism;
  320. PLEASURE, stoicism.
Stoicism 312. PHILOSOPHY.
stoicism 306. PAIN; 320. PLEASURE.
stomatologic 266. MEDICAL
  SPECIALTIES, stomatology.
stomatological 266. MEDICAL
  SPECIALTIES, stomatology.
stomatologist 266. MEDICAL
  SPECIALTIES, stomatology.
stomatology 266. MEDICAL SPECIALTIES.
storiologist 249. LITERATURE,
  storiology.
storiology 249. LITERATURE.
strabism 148. EYES.
strabismal 148. EYES, strabism.
strabismic 148. EYES, strabism.
strabismus 148. EYES, strabism.

stratigrapher 179. GEOLOGY,
   stratigraphy.
stratigraphic 179. GEOLOGY,
   stratigraphy.
stratigraphical 179. GEOLOGY,
   stratigraphy.
stratigraphy 179. GEOLOGY.
stratocracy 185. GOVERNMENT.
stratographer 413. WAR, stratography.
stratography 413. WAR.
stratosphere 27. ATMOSPHERE.
strephosymbolia 346. READING.
strephosymbolic 346. READING,
   strephosymbolia.
stridulant 225. INSECTS, stridulation;
   380. SOUND, stridulation.
stridulation 225. INSECTS; 380. SOUND.
stridulator 225. INSECTS, stridulation;
   380. SOUND, stridulation.
stridulatory 225. INSECTS, stridulation;
   380. SOUND, stridulation.
strophe 127. DRAMA; 409. VERSE.
strophic 127. DRAMA, strophe.
structuralism 20. ARCHITECTURE;
   247. LINGUISTICS.
structuralist 247. LINGUISTICS,
   structuralism.
structural linguistics 247. LINGUISTICS,
   structuralism.
Struldbrugism 249. LITERATURE.
strychnism 321. POISON.
stultiloquence 217. IDIOCY.
stumpage 401. TREES.
Stundism 332. PROTESTANTISM.
Stundist 332. PROTESTANTISM,
   Stundism.
stygiophobia 203. HELL; 313. PHOBIAS.
stylistics 23. ART; 248. LITERARY STYLE.
stylographic 128. DRAWING,
   stylography; 141. ENGRAVING,
   stylography; 428. WRITING,
   stylography.
stylographical 128. DRAWING,
   stylography; 141. ENGRAVING,
   stylography; 428. WRITING,
   stylography.
stylography 128. DRAWING;
   141. ENGRAVING; 428. WRITING.
styptic 49. BLOOD and BLOOD VESSELS,
   stypticity.

stypticity 49. BLOOD and BLOOD
   VESSELS.
subjectivism 28. ATTITUDES;
   312. PHILOSOPHY.
subjectivist 312. PHILOSOPHY,
   subjectivism.
subjectivistic 312. PHILOSOPHY,
   subjectivism.
subjectivity 28. ATTITUDES,
   subjectivism.
submania 224. INSANITY; 254. MANIAS.
subordinationism 80. CHRISTIANITY.
subordinationist 80. CHRISTIANITY,
   subordinationism.
suburbanism 28. ATTITUDES; 82. CITIES.
suburbanist 82. CITIES, suburbanism.
succuba 114. DEMONS, succubus.
succubae 114. DEMONS, succubus.
succubi 114. DEMONS, succubus.
succubus 114. DEMONS.
sudarium 84. CLEANLINESS.
sudatorium 84. CLEANLINESS.
sudorific 130. DRUGS; 130. DRUGS,
   sudorific.
suffragettism 322. POLITICS;
   424. WOMEN.
suffragism 322. POLITICS.
suffragist 322. POLITICS, suffragism.
Sufi 227. ISLAM, Sufiism.
Sufiism 227. ISLAM.
Sufism 227. ISLAM, Sufiism.
suicidal 232. KILLING, suicide;
   362. SELF, suicide.
suicide 232. KILLING; 362. SELF.
Sumerologist 236. LANGUAGE,
   Sumerology.
Sumerology 236. LANGUAGE.
Sundayism 41. BEHAVIOR.
Sunnism 227. ISLAM.
Sunnite 227. ISLAM, Sunnism.
superfetation 44. BIOLOGY; 46. BIRTH.
superfeudation 331. PROPERTY and
   OWNERSHIP.
superinfeudation 331. PROPERTY and
   OWNERSHIP, superfeudation.
supermanism 41. BEHAVIOR.
supermanly 41. BEHAVIOR,
   supermanism.

supernatural 182. GHOSTS,
supernaturalism; 183. GOD and GODS,
supernaturalism; 252. MAGIC,
supernaturalism.
supernaturalism 182. GHOSTS; 183. GOD
and GODS; 252. MAGIC.
supernaturalist 182. GHOSTS,
supernaturalism; 183. GOD and GODS,
supernaturalism; 252. MAGIC,
supernaturalism.
supernaturalistic 182. GHOSTS,
supernaturalism; 183. GOD and GODS,
supernaturalism; 252. MAGIC,
supernaturalism.
superpatriot 289. NATIONALISM,
superpatriotism.
superpatriotic 289. NATIONALISM,
superpatriotism.
superpatriotism 289. NATIONALISM.
Superrealism 23. ART, Surrealism.
superscription 350. REMEDIES.
supersonic 31. AVIATION.
suppuration 122. DISEASE and ILLNESS.
supralapsarian 80. CHRISTIANITY,
supralapsarianism.
supralapsarianism 80. CHRISTIANITY.
supranatural 182. GHOSTS,
supranaturalism; 183. GOD and GODS,
supranaturalism; 252. MAGIC,
supranaturalism; 384. SPIRITS and
SPIRITUALISM, spiritualism.
supranaturalism 182. GHOSTS; 183. GOD
and GODS; 252. MAGIC.
supranaturalist 182. GHOSTS,
supranaturalism; 183. GOD and GODS,
supranaturalism; 252. MAGIC,
supranaturalism.
supranaturalistic 182. GHOSTS,
supranaturalism; 183. GOD and GODS,
supranaturalism; 252. MAGIC,
supranaturalism; 384. SPIRITS and
SPIRITUALISM, spiritualism.
supremacist 341. RACE.
surdism 111. DEAFNESS.
surdomute 111. DEAFNESS,
surdomutism; 382. SPEECH,
surdomutism.
surdomutism 111. DEAFNESS;
382. SPEECH.
Surrealism 23. ART.
Surrealist 23. ART, Surrealism.

Surrealistic 23. ART, Surrealism.
susurrant 380. SOUND, susurration;
382. SPEECH, susurration.
susurration 380. SOUND; 382. SPEECH.
susurrous 380. SOUND, susurration;
382. SPEECH, susurration.
susurrus 380. SOUND, susurration;
382. SPEECH, susurration.
suttee 206. HINDUISM, sutteeism;
232. KILLING.
sutteeism 206. HINDUISM.
Swedenborgian 332. PROTESTANTISM,
Swedenborgianism.
Swedenborgianism
332. PROTESTANTISM.
Swedenborgism 332. PROTESTANTISM,
Swedenborgianism.
sybarite 41. BEHAVIOR, sybaritism;
320. PLEASURE, sybaritism.
sybaritic 41. BEHAVIOR, sybaritism;
320. PLEASURE, sybaritism.
sybaritism 41. BEHAVIOR;
320. PLEASURE.
sybotism 16. ANIMALS.
sycomancy 124. DIVINATION;
319. PLANTS.
sycophancy 41. BEHAVIOR,
sychophantism.
sycophant 41. BEHAVIOR,
sycophantism.
sycophantic 41. BEHAVIOR,
sycophantism.
sycophantism 41. BEHAVIOR.
syllabarium 236. LANGUAGE;
428. WRITING, syllabary.
syllabary 236. LANGUAGE;
428. WRITING.
syllabism 428. WRITING.
syllepsis 186. GRAMMAR; 354. RHETORIC
and RHETORICAL DEVICES.
sylleptic 186. GRAMMAR, syllepsis;
354. RHETORIC and RHETORICAL
DEVICES, syllepsis.
sylleptical 186. GRAMMAR, syllepsis.
syllogism 21. ARGUMENTATION;
250. LOGIC.
syllogistic 21. ARGUMENTATION,
syllogism.
sylviculture 401. TREES, silviculture.
sylviculturist 401. TREES, silviculture.
symbiosis 44. BIOLOGY; 302. ORGANISMS.

symbiotic 44. BIOLOGY, symbiosis;
302. ORGANISMS, symbiosis.
symbolaeographer 239. LAW,
symbolaeography.
symbolaeography 239. LAW.
Symbolism 249. LITERATURE.
symbolism 218. IMAGES;
352. REPRESENTATION.
Symbolist 249. LITERATURE,
Symbolism.
symbological 218. IMAGES, symbology;
352. REPRESENTATION, symbology.
symbologist 218. IMAGES, symbology;
352. REPRESENTATION, symbology.
symbology 218. IMAGES;
352. REPRESENTATION.
symmetalism 276. MONEY.
symmetallic 276. MONEY, symmetalism.
symmetromania 254. MANIAS;
389. SYMMETRY.
symmetrophobia 313. PHOBIAS;
389. SYMMETRY.
sympalmograph 226. INSTRUMENTS;
316. PHYSICS.
sympathism 41. BEHAVIOR.
symphyogenesis 54. BOTANY.
symphyogenetic 54. BOTANY,
symphyogenesis.
symphyseal 52. BONES, symphysis.
symphysial 52. BONES, symphysis.
symphysis 52. BONES.
symphystic 52. BONES, symphysis.
symphytic 44. BIOLOGY, symphytism.
symphytism 44. BIOLOGY; 230. JOINING.
sympiesometer 27. ATMOSPHERE;
226. INSTRUMENTS; 414. WATER.
sympiezometer 27. ATMOSPHERE,
sympiesometer; 226. INSTRUMENTS,
sympiesometer; 414. WATER,
sympiesometer.
symposiarch 168. FOOD and NUTRITION;
190. GREECE and GREEKS;
240. LEARNING.
symposiast 240. LEARNING.
symposion 240. LEARNING, symposium.
symposium 240. LEARNING.
symptomatologic 122. DISEASE and
ILLNESS, symptomatology.
symptomatological 122. DISEASE and
ILLNESS, symptomatology.

symptomatology 122. DISEASE and
ILLNESS.
symptosis 113. DECAYING; 122. DISEASE
and ILLNESS.
synaesthesia 309. PERCEPTION,
synesthesia.
synaesthetic 309. PERCEPTION,
synesthesia.
synalepha 354. RHETORIC and
RHETORICAL DEVICES, synaloepha.
synalgia 306. PAIN.
synaloepha 354. RHETORIC and
RHETORICAL DEVICES.
synanthous 167. FLOWERS, synanthy.
synanthy 167. FLOWERS.
synartesis 230. JOINING.
synastry 24. ASTROLOGY.
synaxarist 135. EASTERN ORTHODOXY.
syncategorematic 236. LANGUAGE;
236. LANGUAGE, syncategorematic.
synchoresis 354. RHETORIC and
RHETORICAL DEVICES.
synchoretic 354. RHETORIC and
RHETORICAL DEVICES, synchoresis.
synchronic linguistics 247. LINGUISTICS.
synchronism 23. ART; 396. TIME.
synchronist 23. ART, synchronism.
synchronistic 23. ART, synchronism;
396. TIME, synchronism.
synchronistical 396. TIME,
synchronism.
synchronological 396. TIME,
synchronology.
synchronology 396. TIME.
synchrony 396. TIME, synchronism.
syncretic 312. PHILOSOPHY, syncretism;
332. PROTESTANTISM, syncretism.
syncretical 312. PHILOSOPHY,
syncretism; 332. PROTESTANTISM,
syncretism.
syncretism 312. PHILOSOPHY;
332. PROTESTANTISM.
syncretistic 312. PHILOSOPHY,
syncretism; 332. PROTESTANTISM,
syncretism.
syncretistical 312. PHILOSOPHY,
syncretism; 332. PROTESTANTISM,
syncretism.
syncrisis 354. RHETORIC and
RHETORICAL DEVICES.
syndactylic 194. HANDS, syndactylism.

syndactylism 194. HANDS.
syndactyly 194. HANDS, syndactylism.
syndesmography 14. ANATOMY.
syndesmology 14. ANATOMY;
266. MEDICAL SPECIALTIES.
syndicalism 94. COMMUNISM;
322. POLITICS.
syndicalist 94. COMMUNISM,
syndicalism; 322. POLITICS,
syndicalism.
syndicalistic 94. COMMUNISM,
syndicalism; 322. POLITICS,
syndicalism.
synecdoche 354. RHETORIC and
RHETORICAL DEVICES.
synecdochic 354. RHETORIC and
RHETORICAL DEVICES, synecdoche.
synecdochical 354. RHETORIC and
RHETORICAL DEVICES, synecdoche.
synecdochism 17. ANTHROPOLOGY;
252. MAGIC; 354. RHETORIC and
RHETORICAL DEVICES.
synechia 148. EYES.
synecologic 142. ENVIRONMENT,
synecology.
synecological 142. ENVIRONMENT,
synecology.
synecology 44. BIOLOGY;
142. ENVIRONMENT.
synectics 56. BRAIN.
synergism 130. DRUGS; 205. HERESY.
synergist 205. HERESY, synergism.
synergistic 130. DRUGS, synergism;
205. HERESY, synergism.
synergy 130. DRUGS, synergism.
synesis 186. GRAMMAR.
synesthesia 309. PERCEPTION.
synesthetic 309. PERCEPTION,
synesthesia.
syngenesis 46. BIRTH.
syngenetic 46. BIRTH, syngenesis.
synnecrosis 44. BIOLOGY.
synodal 69. CATHOLICISM, synodist.
synodical 69. CATHOLICISM, synodist.
synodist 69. CATHOLICISM.
synoecious 82. CITIES, synoecism.
synoecism 82. CITIES.
synoecy 82. CITIES, synoecism.
synomosy 190. GREECE and GREEKS;
348. RELATIONSHIP.
synonymous parallelism 409. VERSE.

synoptic 43. BIBLE, synoptist.
synoptist 43. BIBLE.
synousiast 80. CHRISTIANITY, synusiast.
syntactic 186. GRAMMAR, syntax;
247. LINGUISTICS, syntax.
syntactical 186. GRAMMAR, syntax;
247. LINGUISTICS, syntax.
syntax 186. GRAMMAR; 247. LINGUISTICS.
syntectic 51. BODY, HUMAN, syntexis;
113. DECAYING, syntexis; 122. DISEASE
and ILLNESS, syntexis.
syntectical 51. BODY, HUMAN, syntexis;
113. DECAYING, syntexis; 122. DISEASE
and ILLNESS, syntexis.
synteresis 145. ETHICS; 197. HEALTH.
syntexis 51. BODY, HUMAN;
113. DECAYING; 122. DISEASE and
ILLNESS.
synthesis 230. JOINING;
312. PHILOSOPHY; 393. THINKING.
synthesist 230. JOINING, synthesis;
312. PHILOSOPHY, synthesis;
393. THINKING, synthesis.
synthetic 230. JOINING, synthesis;
312. PHILOSOPHY, synthesis;
393. THINKING, synthesis.
synthetical 230. JOINING, synthesis;
312. PHILOSOPHY, synthesis;
393. THINKING, synthesis.
syntheticism 230. JOINING; 250. LOGIC;
312. PHILOSOPHY; 393. THINKING.
synthetist 230. JOINING;
312. PHILOSOPHY.
syntomia 58. BREVITY, syntomy.
syntomy 58. BREVITY.
syntrierarch 190. GREECE and GREEKS,
syntrierarchy.
syntrierarchy 190. GREECE and GREEKS.
syntropic 14. ANATOMY, syntropy.
syntropy 14. ANATOMY.
syntypic 83. CLASSIFICATION,
syntypicism.
syntypicism 83. CLASSIFICATION.
synusiast 80. CHRISTIANITY.
syphiliphobia 313. PHOBIAS.
syphilophobia 313. PHOBIAS,
syphiliphobia.
Syriacism 236. LANGUAGE.
syssarcosis 14. ANATOMY; 52. BONES.

syssitia 168. FOOD and NUTRITION; 190. GREECE and GREEKS; 376. SOCIETY.
systasis 230. JOINING.
systematician 83. CLASSIFICATION, systematics.
systematics 83. CLASSIFICATION.
systematism 83. CLASSIFICATION.
systematist 83. CLASSIFICATION, systematics.
systematology 83. CLASSIFICATION.
systole 199. HEART; 409. VERSE.
systolic 199. HEART, systole; 409. VERSE, systole.

T

tabaccoism 321. POISON, tabacism.
tabacism 122. DISEASE and ILLNESS; 130. DRUGS; 321. POISON.
tabacosis 122. DISEASE and ILLNESS.
tabagism 122. DISEASE and ILLNESS, nicotinism; 122. DISEASE and ILLNESS, tabacism; 122. DISEASE and ILLNESS, tobaccoism; 130. DRUGS, tabacism; 321. POISON, tabacism.
tabes 51. BODY, HUMAN.
tabescence 51. BODY, HUMAN; 113. DECAYING; 122. DISEASE and ILLNESS.
tabescent 51. BODY, HUMAN, tabescence; 113. DECAYING, tabescence; 122. DISEASE and ILLNESS, tabescence.
tabetic 51. BODY, HUMAN, tabes.
tabitude 51. BODY, HUMAN; 113. DECAYING; 122. DISEASE and ILLNESS.
tabophobia 313. PHOBIAS.
Tachism 23. ART.
Tachisme 23. ART, Tachism.
Tachist 23. ART, Tachism.
Tachiste 23. ART, Tachism.
tachistoscope 226. INSTRUMENTS.
tachometer 226. INSTRUMENTS.
tachophobia 282. MOTION; 313. PHOBIAS.
tachycardia 199. HEART.
tachygrapher 428. WRITING, tachygraphy.

tachygraphic 428. WRITING, tachygraphy.
tachygraphical 428. WRITING, tachygraphy.
tachygraphist 428. WRITING, tachygraphy.
tachygraphy 428. WRITING.
tachymeter 123. DISTANCE; 202. HEIGHTS; 226. INSTRUMENTS.
tachymetry 123. DISTANCE; 202. HEIGHTS; 264. MEASUREMENT.
tachyphrasia 382. SPEECH.
tachyphrenia 334. PSYCHOLOGY; 393. THINKING.
tachypnea 122. DISEASE and ILLNESS.
tachypnoea 122. DISEASE and ILLNESS, tachypnea.
tachyscope 159. FILMS; 226. INSTRUMENTS; 352. REPRESENTATION.
tactician 413. WAR.
tactics 413. WAR.
taeniacidal 222. INFESTATION, taeniacide; 232. KILLING, taeniacide; 427. WORMS, taeniacide.
taeniacide 222. INFESTATION; 232. KILLING; 427. WORMS.
taeniafuge 350. REMEDIES.
taeniasis 222. INFESTATION.
tagmemic 247. LINGUISTICS, tagmemics.
tagmemics 247. LINGUISTICS.
taliped 157. FEET and LEGS, talipes.
talipes 157. FEET and LEGS.
talismanist 227. ISLAM.
tallage 131. DUES and PAYMENT.
Talmudic 231. JUDAISM, Talmudism.
Talmudism 231. JUDAISM.
Talmudist 231. JUDAISM, Talmudism.
Tammanism 322. POLITICS.
Tammanyism 322. POLITICS, Tammanism.
Tammanyite 322. POLITICS, Tammanism.
tanist 185. GOVERNMENT, tanistry.
tanistry 185. GOVERNMENT.
tantalism 41. BEHAVIOR.
Tantrayana 59. BUDDHISM.
Tantrayanic 59. BUDDHISM, Tantrayana.
Tantric 206. HINDUISM, Tantrism.

Tantrism 206. HINDUISM.
Tantrist 206. HINDUISM, **Tantrism.**
Taoism 349. RELIGION.
taphephilia 112. DEATH, **taphophilia.**
taphephobia 63. BURIAL; 313. PHOBIAS.
taphiphobia 63. BURIAL, **taphephobia;**
   313. PHOBIAS, **taphephobia.**
taphophilia 63. BURIAL; 112. DEATH;
   311. -PHILE, -PHILIA, -PHILY.
taphophobia 63. BURIAL, **taphephobia;**
   313. PHOBIAS, **taphephobia.**
tapinophobia 313. PHOBIAS.
tarantism 122. DISEASE and ILLNESS.
Targumic 43. BIBLE, **Targumist.**
Targumist 43. BIBLE.
Targumistic 43. BIBLE, **Targumist.**
tartarology 392. THEOLOGY.
tartuffery 41. BEHAVIOR, **tartuffism.**
tartuffism 41. BEHAVIOR.
tauricide 61. BULLS and BULLFIGHTING.
taurobolium 61. BULLS and
   BULLFIGHTING.
tauroboly 61. BULLS and BULLFIGHTING;
   taurobolium.
taurokathapsia 61. BULLS and
   BULLFIGHTING.
tauromachian 61. BULLS and
   BULLFIGHTING, **tauromachy.**
tauromachic 61. BULLS and
   BULLFIGHTING, **tauromachy.**
tauromachy 61. BULLS and
   BULLFIGHTING.
tauromaquia 61. BULLS and
   BULLFIGHTING, **tauromachy.**
taurophobia 61. BULLS and
   BULLFIGHTING; 313. PHOBIAS.
Taurus 61. BULLS and BULLFIGHTING.
tautological 236. LANGUAGE, **tautology.**
tautologism 236. LANGUAGE.
tautologist 236. LANGUAGE, **tautology.**
tautologous 236. LANGUAGE, **tautology.**
tautology 236. LANGUAGE.
tautonym 54. BOTANY;
   83. CLASSIFICATION; 288. NAMES.
tautonymic 83. CLASSIFICATION,
   tautonym.
tautonymous 83. CLASSIFICATION,
   tautonym.
tautophonic 380. SOUND, **tautophony;**
   382. SPEECH, **tautophony.**

tautophonical 380. SOUND, **tautophony;**
   382. SPEECH, **tautophony.**
tautophony 380. SOUND; 382. SPEECH.
taxiarch 190. GREECE and GREEKS.
taxidermist 16. ANIMALS, **taxidermy.**
taxidermy 16. ANIMALS.
taxology 83. CLASSIFICATION,
   taxonomy.
taxonomic 83. CLASSIFICATION,
   taxonomy; 430. ZOOLOGY, **taxonomy.**
taxonomical 83. CLASSIFICATION,
   taxonomy.
taxonomist 83. CLASSIFICATION,
   taxonomy; 430. ZOOLOGY, **taxonomy.**
taxonomy 83. CLASSIFICATION;
   430. ZOOLOGY.
Taylorism 426. WORK.
teaism 130. DRUGS.
technocracy 185. GOVERNMENT.
technocrat 185. GOVERNMENT,
   technocracy.
technocratic 185. GOVERNMENT,
   technocracy.
technography 233. KNOWLEDGE;
   240. LEARNING.
technological 216. IDEAS, **technology.**
technologist 216. IDEAS, **technology.**
technology 216. IDEAS.
tecnology 77. CHILDREN.
tectological 170. FORM, **tectology.**
tectology 170. FORM.
tectonic 20. ARCHITECTURE, **tectonics;**
   179. GEOLOGY, **tectonics.**
tectonics 20. ARCHITECTURE;
   179. GEOLOGY.
tectonist 20. ARCHITECTURE, **tectonics.**
teetotaler 8. ALCOHOL, **teetotalism.**
teetotalism 8. ALCOHOL.
tegestologist 91. COLLECTIONS and
   COLLECTING, **tegestology.**
tegestology 91. COLLECTIONS and
   COLLECTING.
tegetologist 39. BEER, **tegetology.**
tegetology 39. BEER.
telaesthesia 309. PERCEPTION,
   telesthesia.
telaesthetic 309. PERCEPTION,
   telesthesia.
telangiectasis 95. COMPLEXION.
telangiectic 95. COMPLEXION,
   telangiectasis.

telautograph 428. WRITING,
telautography.
telautographic 428. WRITING,
telautography.
telautography 428. WRITING.
telegnosis 124. DIVINATION;
174. FUTURE; 233. KNOWLEDGE;
384. SPIRITS and SPIRITUALISM.
telegonic 204. HEREDITY, telegony.
telegony 204. HEREDITY.
telegraphese 58. BREVITY;
237. LANGUAGE STYLE.
telekinesis 189. GRAVITY.
telekinetic 189. GRAVITY, telekinesis.
telelograph 165. FLAGS.
telemechanics 316. PHYSICS; 343. RADIO.
telemeteorographic 417. WEATHER,
telemeteorography.
telemeteorography 417. WEATHER.
telemeter 123. DISTANCE;
226. INSTRUMENTS.
telemetry 123. DISTANCE;
264. MEASUREMENT.
telencephalic 56. BRAIN, telencephalon.
telencephalon 56. BRAIN.
teleologic 312. PHILOSOPHY, teleology.
teleological 312. PHILOSOPHY,
teleology.
teleologism 100. COSMOLOGY.
teleologist 100. COSMOLOGY,
teleologism; 312. PHILOSOPHY,
teleology.
teleology 100. COSMOLOGY,
teleologism; 312. PHILOSOPHY.
teleophobia 313. PHOBIAS.
telepathic 334. PSYCHOLOGY, telepathy.
telepathist 334. PSYCHOLOGY,
telepathy.
telepathy 334. PSYCHOLOGY.
telepheme 123. DISTANCE.
telephonophobia 313. PHOBIAS.
telephotographic 315. PHOTOGRAPHY,
telephotography.
telephotography 315. PHOTOGRAPHY.
teleportation 189. GRAVITY, telekinesis.
telergy 56. BRAIN.
teleseism 134. EARTHQUAKES.
teleseismic 134. EARTHQUAKES,
teleseism.
telesia 219. IMPROVEMENT;
376. SOCIETY.

telesis 219. IMPROVEMENT, telesia;
376. SOCIETY, telesia.
telesthesia 309. PERCEPTION.
telesthetic 309. PERCEPTION,
telesthesia.
telferage 408. VEHICLES, telpherage.
teliconograph 218. IMAGES;
315. PHOTOGRAPHY;
352. REPRESENTATION.
tellurian 133. EARTH, tellurist.
tellurist 133. EARTH.
telmatology 178. GEOGRAPHY.
telpherage 408. VEHICLES.
temporalism 312. PHILOSOPHY.
temporalist 312. PHILOSOPHY,
temporalism.
temporalistic 312. PHILOSOPHY,
temporalism.
teniacidal 222. INFESTATION,
taeniacide; 232. KILLING, taeniacide;
427. WORMS, taeniacide.
teniacide 222. INFESTATION, taeniacide;
232. KILLING, taeniacide; 427. WORMS,
taeniacide.
teniafuge 350. REMEDIES, taeniafuge.
teniasis 222. INFESTATION, taeniasis.
tenographic 266. MEDICAL SPECIALTIES,
tenography.
tenographical 266. MEDICAL
SPECIALTIES, tenography.
tenography 266. MEDICAL SPECIALTIES.
tenology 266. MEDICAL SPECIALTIES.
tephramancy 124. DIVINATION;
162. FIRE.
tephromancy 124. DIVINATION,
tephramancy; 162. FIRE,
tephramancy.
tepid 200. HEAT, tepidity.
tepidity 200. HEAT.
teratism 278. MONSTERS.
teratoid 278. MONSTERS.
teratologic 44. BIOLOGY, teratology.
teratological 44. BIOLOGY, teratology;
191. GROWTH, teratology;
249. LITERATURE, teratology;
278. MONSTERS, teratology.
teratologist 44. BIOLOGY, teratology;
191. GROWTH, teratology;
249. LITERATURE, teratology;
278. MONSTERS, teratology.

teratology 44. BIOLOGY; 191. GROWTH; 249. LITERATURE; 278. MONSTERS.
teratophobia 278. MONSTERS; 313. PHOBIAS.
teratosis 278. MONSTERS.
tergiversation 106. CUNNING; 205. HERESY; 351. RENUNCIATION.
tergiversator 106. CUNNING, tergiversation; 205. HERESY, tergiversation; 351. RENUNCIATION, tergiversation.
terminism 312. PHILOSOPHY.
terminist 312. PHILOSOPHY, terminism.
terminologic 83. CLASSIFICATION, terminology; 236. LANGUAGE, terminology.
terminological 83. CLASSIFICATION, terminology; 236. LANGUAGE, terminology.
terminology 83. CLASSIFICATION; 236. LANGUAGE.
terrarium 16. ANIMALS.
territorialism 322. POLITICS.
territorialist 322. POLITICS, territorialism.
terrorism 322. POLITICS.
terrorist 322. POLITICS, terrorism.
terroristic 322. POLITICS, terrorism.
Tertullianism 205. HERESY.
Tertullianist 205. HERESY, Tertullianism.
tessellation 305. ORNAMENTATION.
testaceological 44. BIOLOGY, testaceology.
testaceology 44. BIOLOGY.
tetralogical 249. LITERATURE, tetralogy.
tetralogist 249. LITERATURE, tetralogy.
tetralogy 127. DRAMA; 249. LITERATURE; 284. MUSIC.
tetrameter 409. VERSE; 409. VERSE, tetrameter.
tetramorph 170. FORM, tetramorphism.
tetramorphic 170. FORM, tetramorphism.
tetramorphism 170. FORM.
tetrapharmacon 350. REMEDIES.
tetrapody 409. VERSE.
tetrarch 185. GOVERNMENT, tetrarchy.
tetrarchate 185. GOVERNMENT, tetrarchy.

tetrarchic 185. GOVERNMENT, tetrarchy.
tetrarchical 185. GOVERNMENT, tetrarchy.
tetrarchy 185. GOVERNMENT.
Teutonic 236. LANGUAGE, Teutonicism.
Teutonicism 180. GERMANY; 236. LANGUAGE.
Teutonism 236. LANGUAGE, Germanism.
Teutonomania 180. GERMANY; 254. MANIAS.
Teutonophobia 313. PHOBIAS, Teutophobia.
Teutophobia 313. PHOBIAS.
textual critic 104. CRITICISM, textual criticism.
textual criticism 104. CRITICISM.
textualism 43. BIBLE.
textualist 43. BIBLE, textualism.
textuary 43. BIBLE; 43. BIBLE, textualism.
thaasophobia 313. PHOBIAS; 426. WORK.
thalassocracy 360. SEA.
thalassocrat 360. SEA, thalassocracy.
thalassographer 360. SEA, thalassography.
thalassographic 360. SEA, thalassography.
thalassographical 360. SEA, thalassography.
thalassography 360. SEA.
thalassomania 254. MANIAS; 360. SEA.
thalassophobia 313. PHOBIAS; 360. SEA.
thanatism 112. DEATH, thanatology.
thanatoid 112. DEATH.
thanatological 112. DEATH, thanatology.
thanatology 112. DEATH.
thanatomania 112. DEATH; 254. MANIAS.
thanatophobia 99. CORPSES; 112. DEATH; 313. PHOBIAS.
thanatopsis 112. DEATH; 267. MEDITATION.
thaumatographic 290. NATURE, thaumatography.
thaumatography 290. NATURE.
thaumatology 273. MIRACLES.
thaumatrope 352. REPRESENTATION.
thaumatropical 352. REPRESENTATION, thaumatrope.

thaumaturge 273. MIRACLES,
thaumaturgy.
thaumaturgic 252. MAGIC,
thaumaturgism; 273. MIRACLES,
thaumaturgy.
thaumaturgical 273. MIRACLES,
thaumaturgy.
thaumaturgism 252. MAGIC.
thaumaturgist 252. MAGIC,
thaumaturgism; 273. MIRACLES,
thaumaturgy.
thaumaturgus 273. MIRACLES,
thaumaturgy.
thaumaturgy 252. MAGIC,
thaumaturgism; 273. MIRACLES.
theanthropic 79. CHRIST,
theanthropism.
theanthropism 79. CHRIST; 183. GOD and
GODS.
theanthropist 79. CHRIST,
theanthropism; 183. GOD and GODS,
theanthropism.
theanthroposophy 183. GOD and GODS,
theanthropism.
thearchic 185. GOVERNMENT, thearchy.
thearchy 185. GOVERNMENT;
349. RELIGION, theocracy.
theatrical 127. DRAMA, theatrics.
theatricalism 41. BEHAVIOR.
theatrics 127. DRAMA.
theatrocracy 190. GREECE and GREEKS.
theatromania 127. DRAMA; 254. MANIAS.
theatrophobia 313. PHOBIAS.
thebaism 321. POISON.
theism 183. GOD and GODS.
theocentric 183. GOD and GODS,
theocentrism.
theocentricity 183. GOD and GODS,
theocentrism.
theocentrism 183. GOD and GODS.
theocracy 185. GOVERNMENT;
349. RELIGION.
theocrasia 183. GOD and GODS,
theocrasy.
theocrasy 183. GOD and GODS.
theocrat 185. GOVERNMENT, theocracy.
theocratic 185. GOVERNMENT,
theocracy.
theodicean 183. GOD and GODS,
theodicy; 184. GOODNESS, theodicy.

theodicy 183. GOD and GODS;
184. GOODNESS.
theodolite 226. INSTRUMENTS;
235. LAND.
theodolitic 226. INSTRUMENTS,
theodolite; 235. LAND, theodolite.
theogonist 183. GOD and GODS,
theogony.
theogony 183. GOD and GODS.
theolepsy 183. GOD and GODS.
theoleptic 183. GOD and GODS,
theolepsy.
theologaster 392. THEOLOGY.
theological 183. GOD and GODS,
theology; 349. RELIGION, theology.
theologism 392. THEOLOGY.
theologist 183. GOD and GODS, theology;
349. RELIGION, theology.
theology 183. GOD and GODS;
349. RELIGION.
theomachist 183. GOD and GODS.
theomachy 183. GOD and GODS,
theomachist.
theomancy 124. DIVINATION; 183. GOD
and GODS.
theomania 183. GOD and GODS;
349. RELIGION.
theomorphic 349. RELIGION,
theomorphism.
theomorphism 349. RELIGION.
theomythologer 286. MYTHOLOGY,
theomythology.
theomythology 286. MYTHOLOGY.
Theopaschite 205. HERESY,
Theopaschitism.
Theopaschitism 205. HERESY.
theopathetic 183. GOD and GODS,
theopathy.
theopathic 183. GOD and GODS,
theopathy.
theopathy 183. GOD and GODS.
theophagite 183. GOD and GODS,
theophagy.
theophagous 183. GOD and GODS,
theophagy.
theophagy 183. GOD and GODS.
theophanic 349. RELIGION, theophany.
theophanous 349. RELIGION,
theophany.
theophany 349. RELIGION.

theophilanthropic 349. RELIGION,
theophilanthropism.
theophilanthropism 349. RELIGION.
theophilanthropist 349. RELIGION,
theophilanthropism.
theophobia 183. GOD and GODS;
313. PHOBIAS.
theopneusted 80. CHRISTIANITY,
theopneusty; 402. TRUTH and ERROR,
theopneusty.
theopneustic 80. CHRISTIANITY,
theopneusty; 402. TRUTH and ERROR,
theopneusty.
theopneusty 80. CHRISTIANITY;
402. TRUTH and ERROR.
theopsychism 379. SOUL.
theorematic 262. MATHEMATICS,
theorematist.
theorematist 262. MATHEMATICS.
theoretical criticism 104. CRITICISM.
theoretics 216. IDEAS.
theorist 216. IDEAS; 240. LEARNING.
Theosophic 349. RELIGION,
Theosophism.
Theosophical 349. RELIGION,
Theosophism.
theosophical 285. MYSTICISM,
theosophy.
Theosophism 349. RELIGION.
theosophism 285. MYSTICISM,
theosophy.
Theosophist 349. RELIGION,
Theosophism.
theosophist 285. MYSTICISM, theosophy.
theosophy 285. MYSTICISM.
theotechnic 249. LITERATURE,
theotechny.
theotechny 249. LITERATURE.
theotherapist 349. RELIGION,
theotherapy; 350. REMEDIES,
theotherapy.
theotherapy 349. RELIGION;
350. REMEDIES.
Therapeutism 349. RELIGION.
thereologist 266. MEDICAL SPECIALTIES,
thereology.
thereology 266. MEDICAL SPECIALTIES.
theriac 130. DRUGS; 130. DRUGS,
theriac; 350. REMEDIES;
350. REMEDIES, theriac.

theriaca 130. DRUGS, theriac;
350. REMEDIES, theriac.
theriacal 130. DRUGS, theriac;
350. REMEDIES, theriac.
therial 130. DRUGS, theriac;
350. REMEDIES, theriac.
therianthropism 16. ANIMALS,
theriomorphism.
theriolatry 16. ANIMALS,
theriomorphism.
theriomancy 16. ANIMALS;
124. DIVINATION.
theriomorphic 16. ANIMALS,
theriomorphism.
theriomorphism 16. ANIMALS.
theriomorphous 16. ANIMALS,
theriomorphism.
thermatology 200. HEAT.
thermionic 200. HEAT, thermionics;
316. PHYSICS, thermionics.
thermionics 200. HEAT; 316. PHYSICS.
thermochemical 200. HEAT,
thermochemistry.
thermochemist 200. HEAT,
thermochemistry.
thermochemistry 200. HEAT.
thermodynamic 200. HEAT,
thermodynamics.
thermodynamical 200. HEAT,
thermodynamics.
thermodynamicist 200. HEAT,
thermodynamics.
thermodynamics 200. HEAT.
thermogenesis 200. HEAT.
thermogenic 200. HEAT, thermogenesis.
thermogenous 200. HEAT,
thermogenesis.
thermogeny 200. HEAT, thermogenesis.
thermogeographical 178. GEOGRAPHY,
thermogeography.
thermogeography 178. GEOGRAPHY.
thermographer 200. HEAT,
thermography; 328. PRINTING,
thermography.
thermographic 200. HEAT,
thermography; 328. PRINTING,
thermography.
thermography 200. HEAT;
328. PRINTING.
thermokinematic 200. HEAT,
thermokinematics.

thermokinematics 200. HEAT.
thermology 200. HEAT.
thermoluminescence 200. HEAT.
thermoluminescent 200. HEAT,
thermoluminescence.
thermolysis 200. HEAT.
thermolytic 200. HEAT, thermolysis.
thermometer 226. INSTRUMENTS.
thermometric 200. HEAT,
thermometry.
thermometry 200. HEAT.
thermonastic 319. PLANTS,
thermonasty.
thermonasty 319. PLANTS.
thermoperiod 44. BIOLOGY,
thermoperiodism.
thermoperiodic 44. BIOLOGY,
thermoperiodism; 319. PLANTS,
thermoperiodism.
thermoperiodical 319. PLANTS,
thermoperiodism.
thermoperiodicity 44. BIOLOGY,
thermoperiodism.
thermoperiodism 44. BIOLOGY;
319. PLANTS.
thermophobia 200. HEAT; 313. PHOBIAS.
thermoscope 200. HEAT.
thermoscopic 200. HEAT, thermoscope.
thermostatics 200. HEAT; 316. PHYSICS.
thermotactic 200. HEAT, thermotaxis.
thermotaxic 200. HEAT, thermotaxis.
thermotaxis 200. HEAT.
thermotherapy 200. HEAT.
thermotics 200. HEAT.
thermotropic 319. PLANTS,
thermotropism.
thermotropical 319. PLANTS,
thermotropism.
thermotropism 319. PLANTS.
therologic 44. BIOLOGY, therology.
therological 44. BIOLOGY, therology.
therologist 44. BIOLOGY, therology.
therology 44. BIOLOGY.
thetic 354. RHETORIC and RHETORICAL
DEVICES, thetics.
thetical 354. RHETORIC and RHETORICAL
DEVICES, thetics.
thetics 354. RHETORIC and RHETORICAL
DEVICES.
theurgic 183. GOD and GODS, theurgy;
252. MAGIC, theurgist.

theurgical 183. GOD and GODS, theurgy;
252. MAGIC, theurgist.
theurgist 183. GOD and GODS, theurgy;
252. MAGIC.
theurgy 183. GOD and GODS; 252. MAGIC,
theurgist.
thievery 391. THEFT.
thigmotactic 44. BIOLOGY, thigmotaxis;
397. TOUCH, thigmotaxis.
thigmotaxis 44. BIOLOGY; 397. TOUCH.
thigmotropic 44. BIOLOGY,
thigmotropism; 191. GROWTH,
thigmotropism; 282. MOTION,
thigmotropism.
thigmotropism 44. BIOLOGY;
191. GROWTH; 282. MOTION.
thixophobia 313. PHOBIAS; 397. TOUCH.
Thomism 312. PHILOSOPHY.
Thomist 312. PHILOSOPHY, Thomism.
Thomistic 312. PHILOSOPHY, Thomism.
thoracopagus 46. BIRTH.
thremmatology 16. ANIMALS.
threnode 284. MUSIC, threnody.
threnodic 284. MUSIC, threnody.
threnodist 284. MUSIC, threnody.
threnody 284. MUSIC.
thrombophilia 122. DISEASE and
ILLNESS.
thug 206. HINDUISM, thuggeeism.
thuggee 206. HINDUISM, thuggeeism.
thuggeeism 206. HINDUISM.
thuggery 206. HINDUISM, thuggeeism.
thyroidism 122. DISEASE and ILLNESS.
tidology 189. GRAVITY.
tidyism 41. BEHAVIOR.
tillage 5. AGRICULTURE.
timbrology 91. COLLECTIONS and
COLLECTING.
timbromania 91. COLLECTIONS and
COLLECTING; 254. MANIAS.
time lapse photography
315. PHOTOGRAPHY.
timocracy 185. GOVERNMENT.
timocratic 185. GOVERNMENT,
timocracy.
timocratical 185. GOVERNMENT,
timocracy.
timology 407. VALUES.
Timonism 41. BEHAVIOR.

tincture 130. DRUGS; 350. REMEDIES.
tinnitus 132. EAR.
tintinnabular 42. BELLS, **tintinnabulation.**
tintinnabulation 42. BELLS.
tintype 315. PHOTOGRAPHY.
titanic 183. GOD and GODS, **titanism.**
titanism 183. GOD and GODS.
Titanomachy 413. WAR.
titlist 26. ATHLETICS.
Titoism 94. COMMUNISM.
Titoist 94. COMMUNISM, **Titoism.**
TM 267. MEDITATION.
toady 41. BEHAVIOR, **toadyism.**
toadyish 41. BEHAVIOR, **toadyism.**
toadyism 41. BEHAVIOR.
tobaccoism 122. DISEASE and ILLNESS; 130. DRUGS, **tabacism.**
tocological 46. BIRTH, **tocology.**
tocologist 46. BIRTH, **tocology.**
tocology 46. BIRTH.
tocophobia 46. BIRTH; 313. PHOBIAS.
toggery 86. CLOTHING.
tokenism 28. ATTITUDES; 41. BEHAVIOR.
tokological 46. BIRTH, **tocology.**
tokologist 46. BIRTH, **tocology.**
tokology 46. BIRTH, **tocology.**
tokophobia 46. BIRTH, **tocophobia**; 313. PHOBIAS, **tocophobia.**
Tolstoyism 248. LITERARY STYLE.
Tolstoyist 248. LITERARY STYLE, **Tolstoyism.**
tomboyish 41. BEHAVIOR, **tomboyism.**
tomboyism 41. BEHAVIOR.
tomographic 342. RADIATION, **tomography.**
tomography 315. PHOTOGRAPHY; 342. RADIATION.
tomomania 122. DISEASE and ILLNESS; 254. MANIAS; 388. SURGERY.
tomophobia 122. DISEASE and ILLNESS; 313. PHOBIAS.
tonalist 23. ART; 284. MUSIC.
tonetic 247. LINGUISTICS, **tonetics.**
tonetician 247. LINGUISTICS, **tonetics.**
tonetics 247. LINGUISTICS.
tonic 51. BODY, HUMAN, **tonicity**; 197. HEALTH, **tonicity**; 386. STRENGTH and WEAKNESS, **tonicity.**
tonicity 51. BODY, HUMAN; 197. HEALTH; 386. STRENGTH and WEAKNESS.

tonitrophobia 313. PHOBIAS; 394. THUNDER.
tonitruphobia 313. PHOBIAS, **tonitrophobia.**
tonological 403. TUNING, **tonology.**
tonology 403. TUNING.
tonometer 403. TUNING.
tonometric 403. TUNING, **tonometer**; 403. TUNING, **tonometry.**
tonometrist 403. TUNING, **tonometry.**
tonometry 403. TUNING.
tonsorial 193. HAIR, **tonsure**; 277. MONKS and NUNS, **tonsure.**
tonsure 193. HAIR; 277. MONKS and NUNS.
tontine 160. FINANCE; 160. FINANCE, **tontine.**
toparchy 185. GOVERNMENT.
topectomy 56. BRAIN.
topographer 257. MAPS, **topography.**
topographic 178. GEOGRAPHY, **topography**; 257. MAPS, **topography.**
topographical 178. GEOGRAPHY, **topography.**
topography 178. GEOGRAPHY; 257. MAPS.
topologic 178. GEOGRAPHY, **topology**; 262. MATHEMATICS, **topology.**
topological 178. GEOGRAPHY, **topology**; 262. MATHEMATICS, **topology.**
topologist 178. GEOGRAPHY, **topology**; 262. MATHEMATICS, **topology.**
topology 178. GEOGRAPHY; 262. MATHEMATICS.
toponym 288. NAMES.
toponymic 288. NAMES, **toponymy.**
toponymical 288. NAMES, **toponymy.**
toponymy 288. NAMES.
topophobe 317. PLACES, **topophobia.**
topophobia 313. PHOBIAS; 317. PLACES.
Torah 231. JUDAISM.
toreumatology 23. ART.
toreutic 23. ART, **toreutics.**
toreutics 23. ART.
tornado 420. WIND.
torticollis 51. BODY, HUMAN.
Tory 322. POLITICS, **Toryism.**
Toryish 322. POLITICS, **Toryism.**
Toryism 322. POLITICS.
tosaphist 231. JUDAISM.
tosaphoth 231. JUDAISM.

total abstinence 8. ALCOHOL,
  teetotalism.
totalitarian 185. GOVERNMENT,
  totalitarianism.
totalitarianism 185. GOVERNMENT.
totalizator 175. GAMBLING.
totalizer 175. GAMBLING, totalizator.
totemic 376. SOCIETY, totemism.
totemism 376. SOCIETY.
totipalmate 45. BIRDS, totipalmation.
totipalmation 45. BIRDS.
tourism 347. RECREATION; 399. TRAVEL.
tourist 347. RECREATION, tourism;
  399. TRAVEL, tourism.
townscape 352. REPRESENTATION.
toxaemia 49. BLOOD and BLOOD
  VESSELS, toxemia.
toxaemic 49. BLOOD and BLOOD
  VESSELS, toxemia.
toxemia 49. BLOOD and BLOOD VESSELS.
toxemic 49. BLOOD and BLOOD VESSELS,
  toxemia.
toxicologic 266. MEDICAL SPECIALTIES,
  toxicology; 321. POISON, toxicology.
toxicological 266. MEDICAL
  SPECIALTIES, toxicology; 321. POISON,
  toxicology.
toxicologist 266. MEDICAL SPECIALTIES,
  toxicology; 321. POISON, toxicology.
toxicology 266. MEDICAL SPECIALTIES;
  321. POISON.
toxicomania 130. DRUGS.
toxicophobia 313. PHOBIAS, toxiphobia;
  321. POISON, toxiphobia.
toxiphobe 321. POISON, toxiphobia.
toxiphobia 313. PHOBIAS; 321. POISON.
toxiphobiac 321. POISON, toxiphobia.
toxophilite 311. -PHILE, -PHILIA, -PHILY,
  toxophily.
toxophily 311. -PHILE, -PHILIA, -PHILY.
tracery 305. ORNAMENTATION.
trachoma 148. EYES.
trachomatous 148. EYES, trachoma.
Tractarian 332. PROTESTANTISM,
  Tractarianism.
Tractarianism 332. PROTESTANTISM.
tractoration 350. REMEDIES, Perkinism.
traditionalism 28. ATTITUDES;
  69. CATHOLICISM.

traditionalist 28. ATTITUDES,
  traditionalism; 69. CATHOLICISM,
  traditionalism.
traditionalistic 69. CATHOLICISM,
  traditionalism.
traditionism 28. ATTITUDES,
  traditionalism.
traducianism 379. SOUL.
traducianist 379. SOUL, traducianism.
traducianistic 379. SOUL, traducianism.
tramontane 169. FOREIGNERS;
  169. FOREIGNERS, tramontane.
trampoline 26. ATHLETICS,
  trampolinist.
trampoliner 26. ATHLETICS,
  trampolinist.
trampolinist 26. ATHLETICS.
transatlanticism 236. LANGUAGE.
transcalency 200. HEAT.
transcalent 200. HEAT, transcalency.
transcendentalism 312. PHILOSOPHY.
transcendentalist 312. PHILOSOPHY,
  transcendentalism.
transcendentalistic 312. PHILOSOPHY,
  transcendentalism.
transformationalist 247. LINGUISTICS.
transformism 147. EVOLUTION.
transformist 147. EVOLUTION,
  transformism.
transhumance 5. AGRICULTURE.
transhumant 5. AGRICULTURE,
  transhumance.
transience 396. TIME.
transiency 396. TIME, transience.
transient 396. TIME, transience.
transillumination 350. REMEDIES.
transilluminator 350. REMEDIES,
  transillumination.
transliteration 12. ALPHABET.
transmigrationism 379. SOUL.
transmogrification 74. CHANGE.
transmutation 7. ALCHEMY;
  74. CHANGE.
transmutationist 7. ALCHEMY;
  7. ALCHEMY, transmutation;
  74. CHANGE, transmutation.
transmutative 7. ALCHEMY,
  transmutation; 74. CHANGE,
  transmutation.

transsexual 334. PSYCHOLOGY,
transsexualism; 364. SEX,
transsexualism.
transsexualism 334. PSYCHOLOGY;
364. SEX.
transsexuality 334. PSYCHOLOGY,
transsexualism; 364. SEX,
transsexualism.
transubstantiation 392. THEOLOGY.
transubstantiationalist 392. THEOLOGY,
transubstantiation.
transudation 50. BODILY FUNCTIONS.
transudatory 50. BODILY FUNCTIONS,
transudation.
transvestism 364. SEX.
transvestitism 364. SEX, eonism.
Trappist 69. CATHOLICISM; 277. MONKS
and NUNS.
traulism 382. SPEECH.
traumatic 223. INJURY, traumatism;
334. PSYCHOLOGY, traumatism.
traumatism 223. INJURY;
334. PSYCHOLOGY.
traumatologist 266. MEDICAL
SPECIALTIES, traumatology.
traumatology 266. MEDICAL
SPECIALTIES.
traumatonesis 388. SURGERY.
traumatophilia 122. DISEASE and
ILLNESS.
traumatophobia 313. PHOBIAS.
travesty 352. REPRESENTATION.
tremophobia 313. PHOBIAS.
trenchancy 21. ARGUMENTATION.
trenchant 21. ARGUMENTATION,
trenchancy.
triadism 409. VERSE.
triadist 409. VERSE, triadism.
trial by wager of law 239. LAW,
compurgation.
triarchy 185. GOVERNMENT.
triathlon 26. ATHLETICS.
tribade 209. HOMOSEXUALITY,
tribadism.
tribadic 209. HOMOSEXUALITY,
tribadism.
tribadism 209. HOMOSEXUALITY.
tribady 209. HOMOSEXUALITY,
tribadism.
tribalism 185. GOVERNMENT.
tribology 316. PHYSICS.

triboluminescence 245. LIGHT.
triboluminescent 245. LIGHT,
triboluminescence.
tribrach 409. VERSE.
tribrachic 409. VERSE, tribrach.
trichiasis 148. EYES; 193. HAIR.
trichinophobia 313. PHOBIAS.
trichinosis 168. FOOD and NUTRITION.
trichinous 168. FOOD and NUTRITION,
trichinosis.
trichoanesthesia 193. HAIR.
trichobezoar 193. HAIR.
trichoclasia 193. HAIR.
trichologia 193. HAIR, trichotillomania.
trichologist 193. HAIR, trichology.
trichology 193. HAIR.
trichoma 193. HAIR.
trichomania 193. HAIR; 254. MANIAS.
trichomycosis 193. HAIR.
trichopathic 193. HAIR, trichopathy.
trichopathophobia 313. PHOBIAS,
trichinophobia.
trichopathy 193. HAIR.
trichophagy 193. HAIR.
trichophobia 313. PHOBIAS,
trichinophobia.
trichorrhexomania 193. HAIR;
254. MANIAS.
trichoschisticism 21. ARGUMENTATION.
trichosis 193. HAIR.
trichotillomania 193. HAIR.
trichotomic 83. CLASSIFICATION,
trichotomy; 392. THEOLOGY,
trichotomy.
trichotomous 392. THEOLOGY,
trichotomy.
trichotomy 83. CLASSIFICATION;
392. THEOLOGY.
trichroic 92. COLOR, trichroism;
316. PHYSICS, trichroism.
trichroism 92. COLOR; 316. PHYSICS.
trichromatic 92. COLOR,
trichromatism; 316. PHYSICS,
trichromatism.
trichromatism 92. COLOR; 316. PHYSICS.
trichtomous 83. CLASSIFICATION,
trichotomy.
tricrotic 51. BODY, HUMAN, tricrotism;
199. HEART, tricrotism.
tricrotism 51. BODY, HUMAN;
199. HEART.

tridecaphobia 313. PHOBIAS.
trierarchy 413. WAR.
trieteric 183. GOD and GODS.
trieterical 183. GOD and GODS, trieteric.
trigamous 103. CRIME, trigamy;
258. MARRIAGE, trigamy.
trigamy 103. CRIME; 258. MARRIAGE.
trigonometric 262. MATHEMATICS,
trigonometry.
trigonometrical 262. MATHEMATICS,
trigonometry.
trigonometry 262. MATHEMATICS.
trilogical 249. LITERATURE, trilogy.
trilogist 249. LITERATURE, trilogy.
trilogy 249. LITERATURE.
trimeter 409. VERSE.
trimorphic 170. FORM, trimorphism.
trimorphism 170. FORM.
trimorphous 170. FORM, trimorphism.
Trinitarian 277. MONKS and NUNS.
trinitarian 79. CHRIST, trinitarianism.
trinitarianism 79. CHRIST.
trinomial 83. CLASSIFICATION,
trinomialism; 288. NAMES,
trinomialism.
trinomialism 83. CLASSIFICATION;
288. NAMES.
trionym 83. CLASSIFICATION;
288. NAMES.
tripersonal 183. GOD and GODS,
tripersonality.
tripersonality 183. GOD and GODS.
triplet 409. VERSE.
tripody 409. VERSE.
triptych 218. IMAGES.
tripudiary 108. DANCING, tripudiation.
tripudiation 108. DANCING.
triskaidekaphobia 313. PHOBIAS.
tristich 409. VERSE.
tristichic 409. VERSE, tristich.
tristimania 254. MANIAS;
268. MELANCHOLY.
tritanope 92. COLOR, tritanopia;
148. EYES, tritanopia.
tritanopia 92. COLOR; 148. EYES.
tritanopic 92. COLOR, tritanopia;
148. EYES, tritanopia.
tritheism 80. CHRISTIANITY; 183. GOD
and GODS.
tritheist 80. CHRISTIANITY, tritheism;
183. GOD and GODS, tritheism.

tritheistic 80. CHRISTIANITY, tritheism.
tritheistical 80. CHRISTIANITY,
tritheism.
triticism 236. LANGUAGE;
354. RHETORIC and RHETORICAL
DEVICES.
triumvirate 185. GOVERNMENT,
triarchy.
trivia 233. KNOWLEDGE.
trivial 28. ATTITUDES, trivialism;
233. KNOWLEDGE, trivia.
trivialism 28. ATTITUDES.
triviality 28. ATTITUDES, trivialism.
trivium 233. KNOWLEDGE;
240. LEARNING.
trochaic 409. VERSE, trochee.
trochee 409. VERSE.
trochilic 282. MOTION, trochilics;
316. PHYSICS, trochilics.
trochilics 282. MOTION; 316. PHYSICS.
troglodyte 28. ATTITUDES,
troglodytism.
troglodytic 28. ATTITUDES,
troglodytism.
troglodytism 28. ATTITUDES.
tromomania 8. ALCOHOL; 130. DRUGS,
potomania; 254. MANIAS.
tromometer 134. EARTHQUAKES.
trophic 168. FOOD and NUTRITION,
trophism.
trophism 168. FOOD and NUTRITION.
trophology 168. FOOD and NUTRITION.
trophoplasm 72. CELLS; 168. FOOD and
NUTRITION.
trophoplasmatic 72. CELLS,
trophoplasm; 168. FOOD and
NUTRITION, trophoplasm.
trophoplasmic 72. CELLS,
trophoplasm; 168. FOOD and
NUTRITION, trophoplasm.
trophotropic 72. CELLS,
trophotropism; 282. MOTION,
trophotropism.
trophotropism 72. CELLS; 282. MOTION.
tropism 282. MOTION.
tropist 43. BIBLE; 354. RHETORIC and
RHETORICAL DEVICES.
tropistic 282. MOTION, tropism.
tropologic 354. RHETORIC and
RHETORICAL DEVICES, tropology.

tropological 43. BIBLE, **tropology;**
354. RHETORIC and RHETORICAL
DEVICES, **tropology.**
tropology 43. BIBLE; 354. RHETORIC and
RHETORICAL DEVICES.
tropopause 27. ATMOSPHERE.
troposphere 27. ATMOSPHERE.
Trotskyism 94. COMMUNISM.
Trotskyite 94. COMMUNISM,
Trotskyism.
truism 402. TRUTH and ERROR.
truistic 402. TRUTH and ERROR, **truism.**
truistical 402. TRUTH and ERROR,
truism.
truncated 409. VERSE, **truncation.**
truncation 409. VERSE.
trypanophobia 122. DISEASE and
ILLNESS; 197. HEALTH; 313. PHOBIAS.
tsarism 322. POLITICS, **tzarism.**
tsiology 168. FOOD and NUTRITION.
tuberculophobia 313. PHOBIAS.
tuchungism 185. GOVERNMENT.
tuism 236. LANGUAGE.
tulipomania 167. FLOWERS.
tulipomaniac 167. FLOWERS,
tulipomania.
turbidimeter 226. INSTRUMENTS;
414. WATER.
turbidimetric 226. INSTRUMENTS,
turbidimeter; 264. MEASUREMENT,
turbidimetry; 414. WATER,
turbidimeter; 414. WATER,
turbidimetry.
turbidimetry 264. MEASUREMENT;
414. WATER.
Turcism 41. BEHAVIOR; 349. RELIGION.
turgescence 51. BODY, HUMAN.
turgescency 51. BODY, HUMAN,
turgescence.
turgescent 51. BODY, HUMAN,
turgescence.
Turkism 41. BEHAVIOR, **Turcism;**
349. RELIGION, **Turcism.**
Turkomania 254. MANIAS; 404. TURKEY.
turnery 425. WOOD.
tutiorism 312. PHILOSOPHY.
tutiorist 312. PHILOSOPHY, **tutiorism.**
twister 420. WIND.
two-partyism 322. POLITICS.
tychism 147. EVOLUTION.
tympanism 122. DISEASE and ILLNESS.

tympanites 122. DISEASE and ILLNESS,
meteorism.
tympanitic 122. DISEASE and ILLNESS,
tympanism.
typhlology 48. BLINDNESS.
typhlophile 48. BLINDNESS.
typhlosis 48. BLINDNESS.
typhlotic 48. BLINDNESS, **typhlosis.**
typhomania 122. DISEASE and ILLNESS.
typhoon 420. WIND.
typocosmy 83. CLASSIFICATION;
288. NAMES.
typographic 328. PRINTING,
typography.
typographical 328. PRINTING,
typography.
typography 328. PRINTING.
typological 43. BIBLE, **typology.**
typologist 43. BIBLE, **typology.**
typology 43. BIBLE.
typomania 29. AUTHORS; 254. MANIAS.
typothetae 328. PRINTING.
typtological 384. SPIRITS and
SPIRITUALISM, **typtology.**
typtologist 384. SPIRITS and
SPIRITUALISM, **typtology.**
typtology 384. SPIRITS and SPIRITUALISM.
tyrannicidal 232. KILLING, **tyrannicide.**
tyrannicide 232. KILLING.
tyrannophobia 313. PHOBIAS.
tyrology 240. LEARNING.
tyromancy 76. CHEESE;
124. DIVINATION.
tyrosemiophily 76. CHEESE;
91. COLLECTIONS an l COLLECTING.
tyrotoxism 321. POISON.
tzarism 322. POLITICS.

U

ubbenite 35. BAPTISM.
ubeity 317. PLACES.
ubication 317. PLACES.
Ubiquarian 332. PROTESTANTISM,
Ubiquitism.
Ubiquist 332. PROTESTANTISM,
Ubiquitism.
Ubiquitarian 332. PROTESTANTISM,
Ubiquitism.
Ubiquitary 332. PROTESTANTISM,
Ubiquitism.

ubiquitary 183. GOD and GODS.
Ubiquitism 332. PROTESTANTISM.
Ubiquitist 332. PROTESTANTISM,
  Ubiquitism.
udometric 345. RAIN, udometry;
  417. WEATHER, udometry.
udometry 345. RAIN; 417. WEATHER.
udomograph 226. INSTRUMENTS;
  345. RAIN; 417. WEATHER.
ulatrophia 390. TEETH.
ulatrophy 390. TEETH, ulatrophia.
ulocarcinoma 66. CANCER.
Ulotrichi 17. ANTHROPOLOGY;
  193. HAIR.
Ulotrichous 17. ANTHROPOLOGY,
  Ulotrichi.
ulotrichous 193. HAIR, Ulotrichi.
ultimogeniture 77. CHILDREN;
  239. LAW.
ultraconservatism 322. POLITICS.
ultraconservative 322. POLITICS,
  ultraconservatism.
ultracrepidarian 41. BEHAVIOR,
  ultracrepidarianism.
ultracrepidarianism 41. BEHAVIOR.
ultraism 28. ATTITUDES; 322. POLITICS.
ultraist 28. ATTITUDES, ultraism;
  322. POLITICS, ultraism.
ultraistic 28. ATTITUDES, ultraism;
  322. POLITICS, ultraism.
ultramodernism 23. ART.
ultramodernist 23. ART,
  ultramodernism.
ultramodernistic 23. ART,
  ultramodernism.
ultramontane 69. CATHOLICISM,
  ultramontanism.
ultramontanism 69. CATHOLICISM.
ultramontanist 69. CATHOLICISM,
  ultramontanism.
ultramontanistic 69. CATHOLICISM,
  ultramontanism.
ultranationalism 289. NATIONALISM.
ultranationalist 289. NATIONALISM,
  ultranationalism.
ultranationalistic 289. NATIONALISM,
  ultranationalism.
ultrasonic 380. SOUND, ultrasonics.
ultrasonics 380. SOUND.
ultrastructural 44. BIOLOGY,
  ultrastructure.

ultrastructure 44. BIOLOGY.
ululant 380. SOUND, ululation.
ululation 380. SOUND.
un-American 13. AMERICA,
  un-Americanism; 28. ATTITUDES,
  un-Americanism; 169. FOREIGNERS,
  un-Americanism; 322. POLITICS,
  un-Americanism.
un-Americanism 13. AMERICA;
  28. ATTITUDES; 169. FOREIGNERS;
  322. POLITICS.
uncial 428. WRITING; 428. WRITING,
  uncial.
undine 286. MYTHOLOGY.
ungulate 16. ANIMALS.
Uniat 69. CATHOLICISM, Uniatism.
Uniate 69. CATHOLICISM, Uniatism.
Uniatism 69. CATHOLICISM.
unicameral 185. GOVERNMENT,
  unicameralism.
unicameralism 185. GOVERNMENT.
unicameralist 185. GOVERNMENT,
  unicameralism.
uniformitarian 147. EVOLUTION,
  uniformitarianism; 179. GEOLOGY,
  uniformitarianism.
uniformitarianism 147. EVOLUTION;
  179. GEOLOGY.
unigenesis 44. BIOLOGY; 244. LIFE.
unigenetic 44. BIOLOGY, unigenesis;
  244. LIFE, unigenesis.
unigeniture 77. CHILDREN.
unigravida 46. BIRTH.
unilateralism 185. GOVERNMENT.
unilateralist 185. GOVERNMENT,
  unilateralism.
unilaterality 185. GOVERNMENT,
  unilateralism.
unionism 303. ORGANIZED LABOR.
unionist 303. ORGANIZED LABOR,
  unionism.
Unitarian 332. PROTESTANTISM,
  Unitarianism.
unitarian 79. CHRIST, unitarianism.
Unitarianism 332. PROTESTANTISM.
unitarianism 79. CHRIST.
Universalism 332. PROTESTANTISM.
Universalist 332. PROTESTANTISM,
  Universalism.
Universalistic 332. PROTESTANTISM,
  Universalism.

universologist 100. COSMOLOGY, universology.
universology 100. COSMOLOGY.
univocacy 236. LANGUAGE.
univocal 236. LANGUAGE, univocacy.
uraemia 49. BLOOD and BLOOD VESSELS, uremia.
uraemic 49. BLOOD and BLOOD VESSELS, uremia.
uranianism 25. ASTRONOMY; 209. HOMOSEXUALITY.
uranism 209. HOMOSEXUALITY.
uranist 209. HOMOSEXUALITY, uranism.
uranographer 25. ASTRONOMY, uranography; 201. HEAVEN, uranography.
uranographic 25. ASTRONOMY, uranography; 201. HEAVEN, uranography.
uranographical 25. ASTRONOMY, uranography; 201. HEAVEN, uranography.
uranographist 25. ASTRONOMY, uranography; 201. HEAVEN, uranography.
uranography 25. ASTRONOMY; 201. HEAVEN.
uranology 25. ASTRONOMY; 201. HEAVEN.
uranometria 25. ASTRONOMY, uranometry.
uranometrical 25. ASTRONOMY, uranometry; 201. HEAVEN, uranometry.
uranometry 25. ASTRONOMY; 201. HEAVEN.
uranophobia 201. HEAVEN; 209. HOMOSEXUALITY; 313. PHOBIAS.
urbanism 28. ATTITUDES; 82. CITIES.
Urbanist 277. MONKS and NUNS; 323. POPE.
urbanist 82. CITIES, urbanism.
urbanistic 28. ATTITUDES, urbanism.
urbanologist 82. CITIES, urbanology.
urbanology 82. CITIES.
urbiculture 82. CITIES.
uredinologist 54. BOTANY, uredinology.
uredinology 54. BOTANY.
uremia 49. BLOOD and BLOOD VESSELS.
uremic 49. BLOOD and BLOOD VESSELS, uremia.

urethroscopy 266. MEDICAL SPECIALTIES.
uridrosis 122. DISEASE and ILLNESS.
urination 50. BODILY FUNCTIONS.
urinology 266. MEDICAL SPECIALTIES.
urinometer 226. INSTRUMENTS.
urinometry 264. MEASUREMENT; 266. MEDICAL SPECIALTIES.
urinoscopic 266. MEDICAL SPECIALTIES, urinoscopy.
urinoscopy 266. MEDICAL SPECIALTIES.
urning 209. HOMOSEXUALITY, urningism.
urningism 209. HOMOSEXUALITY.
urnism 209. HOMOSEXUALITY, urningism.
urologic 266. MEDICAL SPECIALTIES, urology.
urological 266. MEDICAL SPECIALTIES, urology.
urologist 266. MEDICAL SPECIALTIES, urology.
urology 266. MEDICAL SPECIALTIES.
uromancy 124. DIVINATION.
uromantic 124. DIVINATION, uromancy.
urophobia 313. PHOBIAS.
uroscopic 266. MEDICAL SPECIALTIES, urinoscopy.
uroscopy 266. MEDICAL SPECIALTIES, urinoscopy.
urotoxia 321. POISON, urotoxy.
urotoxic 321. POISON, urotoxy.
urotoxy 321. POISON.
urtication 350. REMEDIES.
ustorious 162. FIRE, ustulation.
ustulate 162. FIRE, ustulation.
ustulation 162. FIRE; 350. REMEDIES; 364. SEX.
usucapient 331. PROPERTY and OWNERSHIP, usucaption.
usucaption 331. PROPERTY and OWNERSHIP.
usufruct 331. PROPERTY and OWNERSHIP.
usufructuary 331. PROPERTY and OWNERSHIP, usufruct.
usurer 160. FINANCE, usury.
usurious 160. FINANCE, usury.
usury 160. FINANCE.
uteralgia 306. PAIN.
uterogestation 44. BIOLOGY; 46. BIRTH.

uteromania 364. SEX.
utilitarian 145. ETHICS, utilitarianism;
312. PHILOSOPHY, utilitarianism.
utilitarianism 145. ETHICS;
312. PHILOSOPHY.
Utopia 406. UTOPIA.
utopian 406. UTOPIA, utopianism.
utopianism 406. UTOPIA.
utopianist 406. UTOPIA, utopianism.
utopian socialism 322. POLITICS.
utopist 406. UTOPIA, utopianism.
Utraquism 332. PROTESTANTISM.
Utraquist 332. PROTESTANTISM,
Utraquism.
Utraquistic 332. PROTESTANTISM,
Utraquism.
uveitic 148. EYES, uveitis.
uveitis 148. EYES.
uxoricidal 232. KILLING, uxoricide;
418. WIFE, uxoricide.
uxoricide 232. KILLING; 418. WIFE.

V

vaccary 16. ANIMALS.
vaccinophobia 122. DISEASE and
ILLNESS; 197. HEALTH,
trypanophobia; 313. PHOBIAS.
vachery 16. ANIMALS, vaccary.
vacuism 316. PHYSICS.
vacuist 316. PHYSICS, vacuism.
vacuometer 27. ATMOSPHERE;
226. INSTRUMENTS; 417. WEATHER.
vagabond 41. BEHAVIOR, vagabondism.
vagabondage 41. BEHAVIOR,
vagabondism.
vagabondism 41. BEHAVIOR.
Vaishnava 206. HINDUISM,
Vaishnavism.
Vaishnavism 206. HINDUISM.
Vaishnavite 206. HINDUISM,
Vaishnavism.
Valentinian 205. HERESY,
Valentinianism.
Valentinianism 205. HERESY.
valet-de-place 192. GUIDES and
GUIDING.
valetudinarian 122. DISEASE and
ILLNESS, valetudinarianism;
197. HEALTH, valetudinarianism.

valetudinarianism 122. DISEASE and
ILLNESS; 197. HEALTH.
valgus 51. BODY, HUMAN; 52. BONES.
valiancy 101. COURAGE.
valience 101. COURAGE, valiancy.
valvulitis 199. HEART.
vampiric 286. MYTHOLOGY, vampirism.
vampirism 286. MYTHOLOGY.
vandal 41. BEHAVIOR, vandalism.
vandalish 41. BEHAVIOR, vandalism.
vandalism 41. BEHAVIOR.
vandalization 41. BEHAVIOR,
vandalism.
vanguardism 41. BEHAVIOR.
vanguardist 41. BEHAVIOR,
vanguardism.
vanillism 122. DISEASE and ILLNESS.
Varietyese 237. LANGUAGE STYLE.
variolation 350. REMEDIES.
variolization 350. REMEDIES,
variolation.
variorum 53. BOOKS.
vasectomy 46. BIRTH; 388. SURGERY.
vassalage 239. LAW; 331. PROPERTY and
OWNERSHIP.
vassalism 185. GOVERNMENT.
Vaticanism 69. CATHOLICISM.
Vaticanist 69. CATHOLICISM,
Vaticanism.
vaticidal 232. KILLING, vaticide.
vaticide 232. KILLING.
vaticination 174. FUTURE.
vaticinator 174. FUTURE, vaticination.
Vaudism 349. RELIGION.
vectograph 315. PHOTOGRAPHY,
vectography.
vectographic 315. PHOTOGRAPHY,
vectography.
vectography 315. PHOTOGRAPHY.
vecturist 91. COLLECTIONS and
COLLECTING.
Vedaic 206. HINDUISM, Vedaism.
Vedaism 206. HINDUISM.
Vedantic 206. HINDUISM, Vedantism.
Vedantism 206. HINDUISM.
Vedantist 206. HINDUISM, Vedantism.
Vedic 206. HINDUISM, Vedaism.
Vedism 206. HINDUISM, Vedaism.
vegetarian 168. FOOD and NUTRITION,
vegetarianism.

vegetarianism 168. FOOD and
NUTRITION.
velitation 96. CONFLICT.
velleity 419. WILL.
vellication 51. BODY, HUMAN.
velocimeter 226. INSTRUMENTS.
venatic 214. HUNTING, venation.
venatical 214. HUNTING, venation.
venation 214. HUNTING.
venational 214. HUNTING, venation.
venereological 266. MEDICAL
SPECIALTIES, venereology.
venereologist 266. MEDICAL
SPECIALTIES, venereology.
venereology 266. MEDICAL SPECIALTIES.
venereophobia 122. DISEASE and
ILLNESS; 313. PHOBIAS.
venery 214. HUNTING; 364. SEX.
venesection 49. BLOOD and BLOOD
VESSELS, phlebotomy.
Venice Treacle 130. DRUGS, theriac;
350. REMEDIES, theriac.
ventrilocution 382. SPEECH.
ventriloquism 382. SPEECH.
ventriloquist 382. SPEECH,
ventriloquism.
ventriloquistic 382. SPEECH,
ventriloquism.
ventriloquy 382. SPEECH,
ventriloquism.
ventripotence 51. BODY, HUMAN.
ventripotent 51. BODY, HUMAN,
ventripotence.
ventrosity 51. BODY, HUMAN.
verbalism 236. LANGUAGE.
verbiage 236. LANGUAGE.
verbicide 236. LANGUAGE.
verbigeration 236. LANGUAGE;
382. SPEECH.
verbomania 236. LANGUAGE.
verbose 236. LANGUAGE, verbosity.
verbosity 236. LANGUAGE.
verdancy 92. COLOR.
verdant 92. COLOR, verdancy.
Verism 23. ART.
verism 284. MUSIC, verismo.
verismo 284. MUSIC.
Verist 23. ART, Verism.
verist 284. MUSIC, verismo.
Veristic 23. ART, Verism.
veristic 284. MUSIC, verismo.

vermeologist 427. WORMS, vermeology.
vermeology 427. WORMS.
vermicide 350. REMEDIES; 427. WORMS.
vermiculation 305. ORNAMENTATION;
427. WORMS.
vermifuge 350. REMEDIES; 427. WORMS.
vermination 222. INFESTATION;
427. WORMS.
vermiphobia 313. PHOBIAS; 427. WORMS.
vernacular 236. LANGUAGE,
vernacularism.
vernacularism 236. LANGUAGE.
vespiary 225. INSECTS.
vestrydom 28. ATTITUDES, vestryism;
185. GOVERNMENT, vestryism.
vestryish 28. ATTITUDES, vestryism;
185. GOVERNMENT, vestryism.
vestryism 28. ATTITUDES;
185. GOVERNMENT.
vesuvian 162. FIRE.
vexillary 165. FLAGS.
vexillological 165. FLAGS, vexillology.
vexillologist 91. COLLECTIONS and
COLLECTING, vexillology; 165. FLAGS,
vexillology.
vexillology 91. COLLECTIONS and
COLLECTING; 165. FLAGS.
vexillum 165. FLAGS.
viameter 123. DISTANCE;
226. INSTRUMENTS.
viatic 80. CHRISTIANITY, viaticum;
112. DEATH, viaticum.
viatical 80. CHRISTIANITY, viaticum;
112. DEATH, viaticum.
viaticum 80. CHRISTIANITY; 112. DEATH.
viatometer 123. DISTANCE, viameter;
226. INSTRUMENTS.
vibroscope 226. INSTRUMENTS.
Victorianism 41. BEHAVIOR.
videophone 226. INSTRUMENTS.
viduage 418. WIFE.
vidual 418. WIFE, viduage.
viduity 418. WIFE, viduage.
vigneron 421. WINE.
Vikingism 41. BEHAVIOR.
villagism 236. LANGUAGE.
villeinage 331. PROPERTY and
OWNERSHIP.
villosity 193. HAIR.
villous 193. HAIR, villosity.
vindemiation 421. WINE.

vinicultural 421. WINE, viniculture.
viniculture 421. WINE.
viniculturist 421. WINE, viniculture.
viridescence 92. COLOR.
viridescent 92. COLOR, viridescence.
virilescence 16. ANIMALS; 45. BIRDS;
253. MALE.
virilescent 16. ANIMALS, virilescence;
45. BIRDS, virilescence; 253. MALE,
virilescence.
virilism 122. DISEASE and ILLNESS.
virility 122. DISEASE and ILLNESS,
virilism.
virological 266. MEDICAL SPECIALTIES,
virology.
virologist 266. MEDICAL SPECIALTIES,
virology.
virology 266. MEDICAL SPECIALTIES.
virtualism 392. THEOLOGY.
viscosity 261. MATERIALS, PROPERTIES
OF.
viscous 261. MATERIALS, PROPERTIES OF,
viscosity.
visible speech 111. DEAFNESS,
phonautography.
vitalism 244. LIFE; 312. PHILOSOPHY.
vitalist 244. LIFE, vitalism;
312. PHILOSOPHY, vitalism.
vitalistic 244. LIFE, vitalism;
312. PHILOSOPHY, vitalism.
vitascope 159. FILMS.
vitativeness 244. LIFE; 362. SELF.
viticultural 421. WINE, viticulture.
viticulture 421. WINE.
viticulturist 421. WINE, viticulture.
vitrailist 297. OCCUPATIONS.
vitreosity 261. MATERIALS, PROPERTIES
OF.
vitreous 261. MATERIALS, PROPERTIES
OF, vitreosity.
vivarium 16. ANIMALS.
vivary 16. ANIMALS.
vivipara 16. ANIMALS; 430. ZOOLOGY.
viviparism 46. BIRTH.
viviparity 16. ANIMALS, vivipara;
46. BIRTH, viviparism; 430. ZOOLOGY,
vivipara.
viviparous 16. ANIMALS, vivipara;
46. BIRTH, viviparism; 430. ZOOLOGY,
vivipara.
vocalic 247. LINGUISTICS, vocalism.

vocalism 247. LINGUISTICS.
Volapükist 236. LANGUAGE.
volcanism 411. VOLCANOES.
volcanist 411. VOLCANOES, volcanism.
volcanologic 411. VOLCANOES,
volcanology.
volcanological 411. VOLCANOES,
volcanology.
volcanologist 411. VOLCANOES,
volcanology.
volcanology 411. VOLCANOES.
volitation 31. AVIATION; 45. BIRDS.
Volsteadism 8. ALCOHOL.
voltagraphy 98. COPYING.
Voltairian 248. LITERARY STYLE,
Voltairianism.
Voltairianism 248. LITERARY STYLE.
Voltairism 248. LITERARY STYLE,
Voltairianism.
voltaism 316. PHYSICS.
voltammeter 226. INSTRUMENTS.
voltmeter 226. INSTRUMENTS.
volumenometer 226. INSTRUMENTS.
volumenometry 264. MEASUREMENT.
volumescope 226. INSTRUMENTS.
volumeter 226. INSTRUMENTS.
volumetric 226. INSTRUMENTS,
volumeter; 264. MEASUREMENT,
volumetry.
volumetrical 226. INSTRUMENTS,
volumeter; 264. MEASUREMENT,
volumetry.
volumetry 264. MEASUREMENT.
voluntarism 312. PHILOSOPHY.
voluntarist 312. PHILOSOPHY,
voluntarism.
voluntaristic 312. PHILOSOPHY,
voluntarism.
volunteerism 426. WORK.
vomition 50. BODILY FUNCTIONS.
vomiturition 50. BODILY FUNCTIONS.
voodooism 252. MAGIC.
voodooist 252. MAGIC, voodooism.
Vorticism 23. ART.
Vorticist 23. ART, Vorticism.
voudouism 252. MAGIC, voodooism.
voyeur 41. BEHAVIOR, voyeurism;
364. SEX, voyeurism.
voyeurism 41. BEHAVIOR; 364. SEX.
voyeuristic 41. BEHAVIOR, voyeurism;
364. SEX, voyeurism.

vulcanism 411. VOLCANOES, volcanism.
vulgarian 236. LANGUAGE, vulgarism.
vulgarism 236. LANGUAGE.
vulgarist 236. LANGUAGE, vulgarism.
vulpicide 16. ANIMALS.
vulpine 41. BEHAVIOR, vulpinism;
106. CUNNING, vulpinism.
vulpinism 41. BEHAVIOR; 106. CUNNING.
vulturism 28. ATTITUDES;
41. BEHAVIOR.
vulturous 28. ATTITUDES, vulturism;
41. BEHAVIOR, vulturism.

W

waftage 399. TRAVEL.
Wagnerian 284. MUSIC, Wagnerism.
Wagnerism 284. MUSIC.
Wahhabism 349. RELIGION.
Waldensian 349. RELIGION, Vaudism.
Wall Streetese 160. FINANCE;
237. LANGUAGE STYLE.
Waltonian 164. FISH.
warcraft 413. WAR.
wardage 131. DUES and PAYMENT.
ward penny 131. DUES and PAYMENT,
wardage.
warlockry 252. MAGIC.
Washingtonese 237. LANGUAGE STYLE.
Washingtonian 8. ALCOHOL.
water-colorist 23. ART.
Watergatism 322. POLITICS.
waterscape 352. REPRESENTATION.
weaponry 416. WEAPONRY.
weatherology 417. WEATHER.
wegotism 236. LANGUAGE.
Weismannian 204. HEREDITY,
Weismannism.
Weismannism 204. HEREDITY.
welfarism 376. SOCIETY.
weregild 131. DUES and PAYMENT.
werewolfism 41. BEHAVIOR.
wergild 131. DUES and PAYMENT,
weregild.
Wertherian 249. LITERATURE,
Wertherism.
Wertherism 249. LITERATURE.
Wesleyan 332. PROTESTANTISM,
Wesleyanism.
Wesleyanism 332. PROTESTANTISM.

Wesleyism 332. PROTESTANTISM,
Wesleyanism.
westernism 236. LANGUAGE.
wharfage 131. DUES and PAYMENT.
Whiggarchy 322. POLITICS.
whirlwind 420. WIND.
Whiteboy 322. POLITICS, Whiteboyism.
Whiteboyism 322. POLITICS.
Whitefieldism 332. PROTESTANTISM.
Whitefoot 103. CRIME, Whitefootism.
Whitefootism 103. CRIME.
whites, the 122. DISEASE and ILLNESS,
leucorrhea.
Whitleyism 303. ORGANIZED LABOR.
whoredom 218. IMAGES; 349. RELIGION;
364. SEX.
whoremongery 364. SEX.
witchery 252. MAGIC.
witcraft 393. THINKING.
witticism 236. LANGUAGE.
wizard 252. MAGIC, wizardry.
wizardry 252. MAGIC.
woodburytype 315. PHOTOGRAPHY.
wordsmanship 176. GAMES;
236. LANGUAGE.
Wycliffism 332. PROTESTANTISM.

X

Xanaduism 249. LITERATURE.
Xanaduist 249. LITERATURE,
Xanaduism.
xanthelasma 122. DISEASE and ILLNESS,
xanthoma.
Xanthochroi 341. RACE,
Xanthochroism.
Xanthochroic 341. RACE,
Xanthochroism.
xanthochroid 95. COMPLEXION;
193. HAIR; 370. SKIN.
Xanthochroism 341. RACE.
xanthochrous 95. COMPLEXION,
xanthochroid; 193. HAIR,
xanthochroid; 370. SKIN,
xanthochroid.
Xanthocroid 341. RACE,
Xanthochroism.
xanthocyanopsy 92. COLOR; 148. EYES.
xanthocyanopy 92. COLOR,
xanthocyanopsy; 148. EYES,
xanthocyanopsy.
xanthoma 122. DISEASE and ILLNESS.

Y

Yogin 206. HINDUISM, **Yogism.**
Yogism 206. HINDUISM.
yokelism 28. ATTITUDES; 41. BEHAVIOR.
Yorkshireism 236. LANGUAGE.

Z

zanyism 41. BEHAVIOR.
Zarathustrism 349. RELIGION,
   Zoroastrianism.
Zealotism 231. JUDAISM.
zealotism 41. BEHAVIOR.
zealotry 41. BEHAVIOR, **zealotism.**
zeism 168. FOOD and NUTRITION.
zeismus 168. FOOD and NUTRITION,
   zeism.
zelophobia 313. PHOBIAS.
zelotypia 41. BEHAVIOR.
zelotypic 41. BEHAVIOR, **zelotypia.**
Zemeism 384. SPIRITS and SPIRITUALISM.
Zemiism 183. GOD and GODS.
Zen 59. BUDDHISM, **Zen Buddhism.**
Zen Buddhism 59. BUDDHISM.
Zendaic 252. MAGIC, **Zendicism.**
Zendic 252. MAGIC, **Zendicism.**
Zendicism 252. MAGIC.
Zendik 252. MAGIC, **Zendicism.**
Zenic 59. BUDDHISM, **Zen Buddhism.**
Zenism 59. BUDDHISM, **Zen Buddhism.**
zenographical 318. PLANETS,
   zenography.
zenography 318. PLANETS.
zeugma 354. RHETORIC and RHETORICAL
   DEVICES.
zeugmatic 354. RHETORIC and
   RHETORICAL DEVICES, **zeugma.**
zincographer 141. ENGRAVING,
   zincography; 429. ZINC, **zincography.**
zincographic 141. ENGRAVING,
   zincography; 429. ZINC, **zincography.**
zincographical 141. ENGRAVING,
   zincography; 429. ZINC, **zincography.**
zincography 141. ENGRAVING;
   429. ZINC.
Zionism 231. JUDAISM.
Zionist 231. JUDAISM, **Zionism.**
Zionistic 231. JUDAISM, **Zionism.**
Zionite 93. COMMUNALISM;
   221. INDUSTRY; 231. JUDAISM, **Zionism.**

zoanthropic 16. ANIMALS, **zoanthropy;**
   224. INSANITY, **zoanthropy;**
   334. PSYCHOLOGY, **zoanthropy.**
zoanthropy 16. ANIMALS; 224. INSANITY;
   334. PSYCHOLOGY.
zoiatria 16. ANIMALS.
Zoili 104. CRITICISM, **Zoilism.**
Zoilism 104. CRITICISM.
Zoilus 104. CRITICISM, **Zoilism.**
zoism 244. LIFE.
zoist 244. LIFE, **zoism.**
zoistic 244. LIFE, **zoism.**
Zolaism 248. LITERARY STYLE.
Zolaist 248. LITERARY STYLE, **Zolaism.**
Zombism 349. RELIGION.
zomotherapy 168. FOOD and NUTRITION.
zonesthesia 51. BODY, HUMAN.
zoobiology 16. ANIMALS.
zoogamous 44. BIOLOGY, **zoogamy.**
zoogamy 44. BIOLOGY.
zoogenic 16. ANIMALS, **zoogony.**
zoogeny 16. ANIMALS, **zoogony.**
zoogeographer 16. ANIMALS,
   zoogeography; 430. ZOOLOGY,
   zoogeography.
zoogeographic 16. ANIMALS,
   zoogeography.
zoogeographical 16. ANIMALS,
   zoogeography.
zoogeography 16. ANIMALS;
   430. ZOOLOGY.
zoogonic 16. ANIMALS, **zoogony.**
zoogony 16. ANIMALS.
zoographer 16. ANIMALS, **zoography.**
zoographic 16. ANIMALS, **zoography.**
zoographical 16. ANIMALS, **zoography.**
zoography 16. ANIMALS.
zoolater 16. ANIMALS, **zoolatry.**
zoolatry 16. ANIMALS.
zoological 16. ANIMALS, **zoology.**
zoologist 16. ANIMALS, **zoology.**
zoology 16. ANIMALS.
zoomancy 16. ANIMALS;
   124. DIVINATION.
zoomania 16. ANIMALS; 254. MANIAS.
zoometric 264. MEASUREMENT,
   zoometry.
zoometry 16. ANIMALS;
   264. MEASUREMENT.
zoomorphic 16. ANIMALS,
   zoomorphism.

zoomorphism 16. ANIMALS; 183. GOD and GODS.
zoonomia 16. ANIMALS, zoonomy; 430. ZOOLOGY, zoonomy.
zoonomic 16. ANIMALS, zoonomy; 430. ZOOLOGY, zoonomy.
zoonomist 16. ANIMALS, zoonomy; 430. ZOOLOGY, zoonomy.
zoonomy 16. ANIMALS; 430. ZOOLOGY.
zoonosis 122. DISEASE and ILLNESS.
zoonotic 122. DISEASE and ILLNESS, zoonosis.
zoopathology 16. ANIMALS; 430. ZOOLOGY.
zoopathy 16. ANIMALS; 430. ZOOLOGY.
zooperal 16. ANIMALS, zoopery.
zoopery 16. ANIMALS.
zoophile 16. ANIMALS, zoophilia.
zoophilia 16. ANIMALS; 364. SEX.
zoophilic 364. SEX, zoophilia.
zoophilism 16. ANIMALS; 311. -PHILE, -PHILIA, -PHILY.
zoophilist 16. ANIMALS, zoophilism; 311. -PHILE, -PHILIA, -PHILY, zoophilism; 364. SEX, zoophilia.
zoophilous 16. ANIMALS, zoophilism; 311. -PHILE, -PHILIA, -PHILY, zoophilism; 364. SEX, zoophilia.
zoophily 16. ANIMALS, zoophilism; 311. -PHILE,-PHILIA,-PHILY, zoophilism.
zoophobe 16. ANIMALS, zoophobia.
zoophobia 16. ANIMALS; 313. PHOBIAS.
zoophysical 16. ANIMALS, zoophysics.
zoophysics 16. ANIMALS.
zoophysiology 16. ANIMALS; 430. ZOOLOGY.
zoophyte 16. ANIMALS.
zoophytic 16. ANIMALS, zoophyte.
zoophytical 16. ANIMALS, zoophyte.
zoophytoid 16. ANIMALS, zoophyte.
zoophytological 16. ANIMALS, zoophytology; 430. ZOOLOGY, zoophytology.
zoophytology 16. ANIMALS; 430. ZOOLOGY.
zooplastic 16. ANIMALS, zooplasty; 51. BODY, HUMAN, zooplasty; 388. SURGERY, zooplasty.
zooplasty 16. ANIMALS; 51. BODY, HUMAN; 388. SURGERY.
zoopraxiscope 159. FILMS.

zoopsia 16. ANIMALS; 224. INSANITY; 334. PSYCHOLOGY.
zoopsychology 16. ANIMALS.
zoosadism 306. PAIN.
zoosadist 306. PAIN, zoosadism.
zoosadistic 306. PAIN, zoosadism.
zooscopy 16. ANIMALS; 224. INSANITY; 334. PSYCHOLOGY, zoopsia.
zootaxy 16. ANIMALS; 83. CLASSIFICATION.
zootechnical 16. ANIMALS, zootechny.
zootechnician 16. ANIMALS, zootechny.
zootechnics 16. ANIMALS, zootechny.
zootechny 16. ANIMALS.
zootheism 16. ANIMALS.
zootheist 16. ANIMALS, zootheism.
zootomic 14. ANATOMY, zootomy; 16. ANIMALS, zootomy.
zootomical 14. ANATOMY, zootomy; 16. ANIMALS, zootomy.
zootomist 14. ANATOMY, zootomy; 16. ANIMALS, zootomy.
zootomy 14. ANATOMY; 16. ANIMALS.
Zoroastrian 349. RELIGION, Zoroastrianism.
Zoroastrianism 349. RELIGION.
Zoroastrism 349. RELIGION, Zoroastrianism.
Zwinglian 80. CHRISTIANITY, Zwinglianism.
Zwinglianism 80. CHRISTIANITY.
Zwinglianist 80. CHRISTIANITY, Zwinglianism.
zygomorphic 44. BIOLOGY, zygomorphism; 302. ORGANISMS, zygomorphism.
zygomorphism 44. BIOLOGY; 302. ORGANISMS.
zygomorphous 44. BIOLOGY, zygomorphism; 302. ORGANISMS, zygomorphism.
zygose 44. BIOLOGY, zygosis.
zygosis 44. BIOLOGY.
zymetology 158. FERMENTATION.
zymogenesis 44. BIOLOGY; 158. FERMENTATION.
zymogenic 44. BIOLOGY, zymogenesis; 158. FERMENTATION, zymogenesis.
zymogenous 44. BIOLOGY, zymogenesis; 158. FERMENTATION, zymogenesis.

zymologic 44. BIOLOGY, **zymology.**
zymologist 44. BIOLOGY, **zymology.**
zymology 44. BIOLOGY;
158. FERMENTATION.
zymolysis 158. FERMENTATION.
zymolytic 158. FERMENTATION,
zymolysis.
zymometer 158. FERMENTATION.

zymosis 122. DISEASE and ILLNESS;
158. FERMENTATION.
zymotechnic 158. FERMENTATION,
zymotechnics.
zymotechnics 158. FERMENTATION.
zymotic 122. DISEASE and ILLNESS,
zymosis; 158. FERMENTATION;
158. FERMENTATION, **zymosis.**